Criminology

Theories, Patterns, and Typologies

Sixth Edition

Criminology

Theories, Patterns, and Typologies

Sixth Edition

Larry J. Siegel

University of Massachusetts at Lowell

West/Wadsworth Publishing Company

I(T)P® An International Thomson Publishing Company

Belmont, CA Albany, NY Bonn Boston Cincinnati Detroit Johannesburg London Madrid
Melbourne Mexico City New York Paris Singapore Tokyo Toronto Washington

Criminal Justice Editor: Sabra Horne
Assistant Editor: Claire Masson
Editorial Assistant: Jeff Kellner
Marketing Manager: Mike Dew
Senior Project Coordinator: Debby Kramer
Print Buyer: Karen Hunt
Permissions Editor: Bob Kauser
Production: Del Mar Associates
Text and Cover Designer: Jeanne Calabrese
Copy Editor: Jackie Estrada
Illustrator: Gail Williams
Photo Research: Linda Rill
Cover Image: © Sandra Dionisi/SIS
Compositor/Separator: Digital Output
Printer: Von Hoffman Press

Printed in the United States of America
1 2 3 4 5 6 7 8 9 10

For more information, contact Wadsworth Publishing Company, 10 Davis Drive, Belmont, CA 94002, or electronically at
http://www.thomson.com/wadsworth.html

International Thomson Publishing Europe
Berkshire House 168-173
High Holborn
London, WC1V 7AA, England

International Thomson Editores
Campos Eliseos 385, Piso 7
Col. Polanco
11560 México D.F. México

Thomas Nelson Australia
102 Dodds Street
South Melbourne 3205
Victoria, Australia

International Thomson Publishing Asia
221 Henderson Road
#05-10 Henderson Building
Singapore 0315

Nelson Canada
1120 Birchmount Road
Scarborough, Ontario
Canada M1K 5G4

International Thomson Publishing Japan
Hirakawacho Kyowa Building, 3F
2-2-1 Hirakawacho
Chiyoda-ku, Tokyo 102, Japan

International Thomson Publishing GmbH
Königswinterer Strasse 418
53227 Bonn, Germany

International Thomson Publishing Southern Africa
Building 18, Constantia Park
240 Old Pretoria Road
Halfway House, 1685 South Africa

Library of Congress Cataloging-in-Publication Data

Siegel, Larry J.
    Criminology: theories, patterns, and typologies/Larry J. Siegel.—6th ed.
      p. cm.
    Originally published: Minneapolis/St. Paul: West, © 1995.
    Includes bibliographical references and index.
    ISBN 0-534-53649-2 (alk. paper)
    1. Criminology. 2. Crime—United States. I. Title.
  HV6025.S48 1997
  364—dc21   97-26781
                                                      CIP

This book is dedicated to my children, Julie, Andrew, Eric, and Rachel Siegel, and to my wife, Therese J. Libby.

Contents

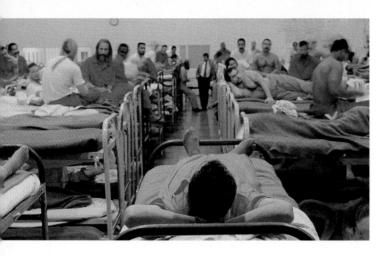

3 Crime Typologies 275

Chapter 14
Public Order Crimes:
Sex and Substance Abuse   375

Preface

events of the past few years remind us of the great impact that crime, law, and justice have had on the American public. The already famous, such as sports figure O. J. Simpson, actor Hugh Grant, and politician Jim Guy Tucker, governor of Arkansas, made headlines when they were accused or convicted of criminal acts. Some formerly unknown individuals, such as Timothy McVeigh, Susan Smith, Heidi Fleiss, and Theodore Kaczynski, became household names when they were involved in criminal acts that captured public attention. Lawyers who defended people accused of high-profile crimes, such as Simpson's attorney Johnnie Cochran, emerged as public figures whose opinions were sought on TV talk shows. The nation was horrified when Bill Cosby's son Ennis was killed in what appeared to be a random robbery; the Cosby case proved that no one, no matter how well known or affluent, is safe from crime.

The media seem incapable of ever losing interest in notorious killers, serial murderers, drug lords, and sex criminals. It is not surprising, then, that many Americans are more concerned about crime than almost any other social problem. Most people worry about becoming the victims of violent crime, having their houses broken into, or having their cars stolen. People alter their behavior to limit the risk of victimization and question whether legal punishment alone can control criminal offenders. They are shocked at graphic news accounts of drive-by shootings, police brutality, and prison riots. They are fascinated by books, movies, and TV shows about law firms, clients, fugitives, and stone-cold killers.

I, too, have had a lifelong interest in crime, law, and justice. Why do people behave the way they do? What causes one person to become violent and antisocial, while another channels his or her energy into work, school, and family? How can the behavior of the "good boy in the high-crime neighborhood"—the "at-risk" kid who successfully resists the temptation of the streets—be explained? Conversely, what accounts for the behavior of the multimillionaire who cheats on his or her taxes or engages in fraudulent schemes? The former has nothing yet is able to resist crime; the latter has everything and falls prey to its lure. Is behavior a function of personal characteristics? Upbringing and experience? Culture and environment? Or a combination of all these influences?

I have been able to channel this interest into a career as a teacher of criminology. My goal in writing this text is to help students generate the same interest in criminology that has sustained me during my 25 years in college teaching. What could be more important or fascinating than a field of study that deals with such wide-ranging topics as the motivation for mass murder, the association between media violence and interpersonal aggression, the family's influence on drug abuse, and the history of organized crime? Criminology is a dynamic field, changing constantly with the release of major research studies, Supreme Court rulings, and governmental policy. Its dynamism and diversity make it an important and engrossing area of study.

One reason that the study of criminology is so important is that debates continue over the nature and extent of crime and the causes and prevention of criminality. Some view criminals as society's victims who are forced to violate the law because of poverty and the lack of opportunity. Others view aggressive, antisocial behavior as a product of mental and physical abnormalities, present at birth or soon after, that are stable over the life course. Still another view is that crime is a function of the rational choice of greedy, selfish people who can only be deterred through the threat of harsh punishments. There is thus an ongoing debate over the nature and cause of crime.

Concern also continues about the treatment of known criminals: Should they be punished? Helped? Locked up? Given a second chance? Should crime control policy focus on punishment or rehabilitation? When an American boy, Michael Fay, was flogged in Singapore in 1994, some commentators openly praised that country's government for its tough stance on crime; a few even voiced the opinion that corporal punishment might work well in this country. Would you like to see a whipping post set up in your town?

Because interest in crime and justice is so great and so timely, this text is designed to review these ongoing issues and cover the field of criminology in an organized and comprehensive manner. It is meant as a broad overview of the field, designed to whet the reader's appetite and encourage further and more in-depth exploration.

Topic Areas

The text is divided into four main sections or topic areas.

Section 1 provides a framework for studying criminology. The first chapter defines the field and discusses its most basic concepts: the definition of crime, the component areas of criminology, the history of criminology, criminological research methods, and the ethical issues that confront the field. The second chapter covers the criminal law and its functions, processes, defenses, and reform. Chapter 3 covers the nature, extent, and patterns of crime. Chapter 4 is devoted to the concept of victimization, including the nature of victims, theories of victimization, and programs designed to help crime victims.

Section 2 contains six chapters that cover criminological theory: Why do people engage in criminal behavior? These views include theories of criminal choice (Chapter 5); biological and psychological views (Chapter 6); structural, cultural, and ecological theories (Chapter 7); social process theories that focus on socialization and include learning and control (Chapter 8); and theories of social conflict (Chapter 9). Chapter 10 covers attempts by criminologists to integrate various theories into a unified whole.

Section 3 is devoted to the major forms of criminal behavior. These four chapters cover violent crime, common theft offenses, white-collar and organized crimes, and public order crimes, including sex offenses and substance abuse.

The text has been carefully structured to cover relevant material in a comprehensive, balanced, and objective fashion.

Features

This edition is in full color, which helps make photos, charts, and figures come alive. The fold-out time line of criminological history has been retained, updated, and redesigned. Each chapter includes a chapter outline, a list of the key terms contained in the chapter, discussion questions designed to focus classroom interaction, and at least one boxed insert, or Close-Up. These boxes contain a detailed discussion or reading of an important and intriguing topic, issue, or program. For example, a Close-Up in Chapter 11 focuses on serial killing and mass murder, while the Close-Up in Chapter 14 covers child prostitution in the United States and Japan.

"Connections" boxes are now located in appropriate places throughout each chapter. These brief inserts link the material being currently discussed with relevant information located elsewhere in the text. Connections either expand on the subject matter or show how it can be applied to other areas or topics. For example, a Connections box in Chapter 2 alerts the reader to the link between the ancient legal practice of *lex talionis* ("an eye for an eye") and the modern "just desert" philosophy that aims to make punishment "fit the crime," discussed in Chapter 5.

The Internet is becoming an important academic research tool. Consequently, scattered throughout the text are "Internet Bookmarks" that guide the reader to webpages containing material that supplements the text. For example, in Chapter 4 an Internet Bookmark describes the UNCJIN—Countries of the World reference page that provides data on cross-national crime rates.

What's New in This Edition

This edition retains the same organizational features of the previous edition, with some notable differences. A few of the new topics and areas covered include the following:

Chapter 1, "Crime and Criminology," has been updated with new material on international crime rates and the growing problem of international crime. The time line tracing the history of criminological thought has been expanded.

Chapter 2, "The Criminal Law and Its Processes," contains material on new types of criminal laws, including stalking laws and community notification laws.

Chapter 3, "The Nature and Extent of Crime," covers crime trends and patterns. New material is presented on gun control as well as the findings of an important new study that followed chronic juvenile offenders into their adulthood.

Chapter 4, "Victims and Victimization," focuses on the nature and extent of victimization, theories of victimization, and the government's response to victimization. New material is included on repeat victimization and the link between victimization and antisocial behaviors.

Chapter 5, "Choice Theory," offers new material on the efforts to measure the interaction among opportunity, motivation, and crime, as well as a new section on the rationality of drug use.

Chapter 6, "Trait Theories," now includes a discussion of arousal theory as well as expanded sections on evolutionary theories of crime, including "cheater" theory. The discussion of IQ and crime is updated with reference to *The Bell Curve,* the controversial book by Richard Herrnstein and Charles Murray.

Chapter 7, "Social Structure Theories," now contains an analysis of William Julius Wilson's new book *When Work Disappears.*

Chapter 8, "Social Process Theories," shows how institutional involvement and belief can influence crime rates.

Chapter 9, "Social Conflict Theory," contains new material on radical feminist theory, left realism, peacemaking, and deconstructionism. There is a new Close-Up on restorative justice.

Chapter 10, "Integrated Theories," has been updated with Terrie Moffit's research on "adolescent limited" and "life course persistent" offenders as well as early- versus late-onset delinquency.

Chapter 11, "Violent Crime," offers new material on mass murder, hate crimes, spouse abuse, and the causes of violence. There is a new Close-Up on genocide as a form of political terrorism.

Chapter 12, "Property Crimes," contains sections on combating shoplifting and on the "occupation" of burglary.

Chapter 13, "White-Collar and Organized Crime," includes new sections on check kiting and Internet crime.

Chapter 14, "Public Order Crimes: Sex and Substance Abuse," has sections on sex offenders and their victims, child prostitution in Japan, and the monetary value of the sex-for-profit industry.

Ancillary Materials

A number of pedagogic supplements are provided by Wadsworth to help instructors use *Criminology* in their courses and to aid students in preparing for exams. These include:

- Instructor's Resource Manual by Mike Kaune
- Computerized Testing Items (ESA Software)
- Study Guide by Alex Alvarez
- Power Point Presentation software by Larry Bassi
- CNN video

Additional useful resources and materials include:

- Internet Investigator card (brochurelike card that features the most useful crime-related URLs)
- Guide to the Internet for Criminal Justice (small booklet with basic start-up instructions on how to use the Internet for CJ research)
- Wadsworth Criminal Justice Resource Center web site, which contains many crime-related links
- Blackenship/Vito, *Your Research: Data Analysis for Criminal Justice and Criminology*
- Harr/Hess, *Employment in Criminal Justice,* a monograph that provides information on finding employment, job interviewing techniques, and other criminal justice career information.

Alternative Versions

Once again, there are two versions of *Criminology.* Both have 14 identical chapters covering crime, law, criminological theory, and crime typologies. The larger version, titled simply *Criminology,* contains an additional 4 chapters covering the criminal justice system, while the other, titled *Criminology: Theories, Patterns, and Typologies,* omits these chapters. The 18-chapter book is designed for instructors who wish to cover criminal justice institutions and practices within a criminology course, while the 14-chapter version is aimed at programs in which material on criminal justice is taught in a separate course or where time constraints limit the amount of textual material that can be covered.

Perspective

We've made every effort to make the presentation of material interesting, balanced, and objective. No single political or theoretical position dominates the text; instead, it presents the many diverse views that are contained within criminology and that characterize its interdisciplinary nature. The text analyzes the most important scholarly works and scientific research reports, while also presenting topical information on recent cases and events, such as the military sexual assault scandal and the Heidi Fleiss prostitution ring. To enliven the presentation, boxed inserts focus on important criminological issues and topics, such as the female burglar and whether crime pays.

Acknowledgments

Many people helped make this book possible. Those who reviewed this edition and made suggestions that I attempted to follow to the best of my ability include: Alexander Alvarez, Northern Arizona University; Timothy Austin, Indiana University of Pennsylvania; Stephen G. Gibbons, Western Oregon State University; Casey Jordan, Western Connecticut State University; Hugh E. O'Rourke, SUNY/Westchester Community College; and Joanne Ziembo-Vogl, Grand Valley State University.

Others who helped with material or advice include Thomas Arvanites, Jim Ruiz, Kevin Thompson, Agnes Baro, John Martin, Mae Conley, Mary Dietz, Ed Wells, Patricia Atchison, Joseph Blake, Thomas Courtless, Julia Hall, Linda O'Daniel, Nikos Passas, Kip Schlegel, Joseph Vielbig, Daniel Georges-Abeyie, Bonnie Berry, James Black, Stephen Brodt, Edward Green, Dennis Hoffman, Alan Lincoln, Gerrold Hotaling, Joseph Jacoby, James McKenna, Paul Tracy, Kimberly Kempf-Leonard, Jack McDevitt, Henry Pontell, G. David Curry, Charles Vedder, Peter Cordella, Sam Walker, David Friedrichs, Chris Eskridge, William Wakefield, Frank Cullen, Marty Schwartz, Chuck Fenwick, Spencer Rathus, Bob Regoli, Marvin Zalman, James Fyfe, Lee Ellis, Lorne Yeudall, Darrell Steffensmeier, M. Douglas Anglin, Bob Langworthy, Jim Inciardi, Alphonse Sallett, Charles Faupel, Graeme Newman, Meda Chesney-Lind, Colin McCauley, Terrie Moffitt, Jamie Fox, Jack Levin, and John Laub. I'd also like to thank Jamie and Jack, as well as Scott Decker (and his colleagues Dietrich Smith, Allison Redfern Rooney, and Richard Wright), Ronald Clarke, Marcus Felson, Lee Ellis, Kathleen Heide, Travis Hirschi, Mike Gottfredson, and Diana Fishbein for taking the time to send me their photos for use in this book. I think it is important for students to be able to put an occasional face to the names they are reading about. Special thanks must also go to Kathleen Maguire, editor of the *Sourcebook of Criminal Justice;* the staff at the Hindelang Research Center in Albany, New York; Joyce Buchanan at the Institute for Social Research at the University of Michigan; and Kristina Rose and Janet Rosenbaum of the National Criminal Justice Reference Service.

The form and content of this edition were directed by my new editor, Sabra Horne. It has been a pleasure working with Sabra and my other new colleagues on the Wadsworth "team": editorial assistants Kate Barrett and Jeff Kellner, project coordinator Debby Kramer, production manager Nancy Sjoberg, copy editor Jackie Estrada, photo editor Linda Rill, and marketing manager Mike Dew. This is the first book I have written with my new Wadsworth colleagues, and these folks made me feel right at home. They must be given a lot of credit for putting together a beautiful design and going out of their way to be patient, kind, and sensitive.

Larry Siegel
Bedford, New Hampshire

Criminology

Theories, Patterns, and Typologies

Sixth Edition

gression (1968)

E.O. Wilson
Sociobiology (1975)

Mednick & Volavka
Biology and Crime (1980)

Ellis
*Evolutionary
Sociobiology* (1989)

Rowe
*The Limits of Family
Influence* (1995)

Christiansen
Gene-Crime Connection (1977)

strual Syndrome (1971)

Bandura
Aggression (1973)

Hirschi & Hindelang
*Intelligence and
Delinquency* (1977)

Henggeler
*Delinquency in
Adolescence* (1989)

**Cognitive
Theory**

Moffitt
Neuropsychology of Crime (1992)

(1964)

Murray & Herrnstein
The Bell Curve (1994)

ects

Martinson
What Works (1974)

Cohen & Felson
Routine Activities
(1979)

**Rational
Choice and
Deterrence
Theory**

Clarke
Situational Crime Prevention (1992)

J.Q. Wilson
Thinking About Crime (1975)

Katz
Seductions of Crime (1988)

Sanction (1968)

**Conflict
Theory**

Chambliss & Seidman
Law, Order & Power (1971)

Lea & Young
Left Realism (1984)

Hagan
Structural Criminology (1989)

**Restorative
Justice**

58)

Taylor, Walton, & Young
The New Criminology (1973)

Daly & Chesney-Lind
Feminist Theory (1988)

Quinney & Pepinsky
Criminology as Peacemaking (1991)

lin
d Opportunity (1960)

Blau & Blau
*The Cost of
Inequality*
(1982)

**Social
Ecology
Theory**

Wilson
*The Truly
Disadvantaged*
(1987)

Agnew
General Strain Theory (1992)

of Poverty (1966)

Messner & Rosenfeld
Crime and the American Dream (1994)

Schur
*Labeling
Deviant
Behavior*
(1972)

**Control
Theories**

Akers
Deviant Behavior
(1977)

Kaplan
General Theory of Deviance (1992)

Heimer & Matsueda
Differential Social Control (1994)

West & Farrington
Delinquent Way of Life
(1977)

Weis
*Social
Development
Theory*
(1981)

Wilson & Herrnstein
Crime and Human Nature (1985)

Gottfredson & Hirschi
General Theory of Crime (1990)

Thornberry
Interactional Theory (1987)

Sampson & Laub
Crime in the Making (1993)

	Watergate		Reagan Era	Fall of European Communism	Clinton Administration	
	1975		**1980**	**1991**	**1995**	**1997**

Classical Theory

ORIGIN   About 1764

FOUNDERS   Cesare Beccaria, Jeremy Bentham

MOST IMPORTANT WORKS
Beccaria, *On Crimes and Punishments* (1764); Bentham, *Moral Calculus* (1789)

CORE IDEAS   People choose to commit crime after weighing the benefits and costs of their actions. Crime can be deterred by certain, severe, and swift punishment.

MODERN OUTGROWTHS
Rational Choice Theory, Routine Activities Theory, General Deterrence Theory, Specific Deterrence, Incapacitation

Marxist/Cont

ORIGIN   Abo

FOUNDERS   Karl

MOST IMPORTANT
Mar
Bon;
Geo
Stru
Indu

CORE IDEAS   Crin
emp
and

MODERN OUTGRO
Con
New
Dec

The Granger Collection

Cesare Beccaria

The Granger Collection

Jeremy Bentham

Stock Montage, Inc.

Karl

cal Theories

lict Theory

it 1848

Marx, Willem Bonger, Ralf Dahrendorf, George Vold

WORKS

and Friedrich Engels, *The Communist Manifesto* (1848);
er, *Criminality and Economic Conditions* (1916);
ge Rusche and Otto Kircheimer, *Punishment and Social
ture* (1939); Dahrendorf, *Class and Class Conflict in
strial Society* (1959)

e is a function of class struggle. The capitalist system's
nasis on competition and wealth produces an economic
social environment in which crime is inevitable.

WTHS

lict Theory, Radical Theory, Critical Criminology, the
Criminology, Radical Feminist Theory, Left Realism,
instructionism, Peacemaking

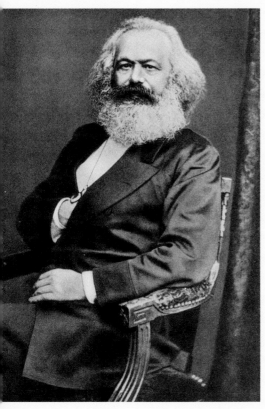

Marx

Biological Positivism

ORIGIN   About 1810

FOUNDERS   Franz Joseph Gall, Johann Spurzheim,
                Lombroso, Enrico Ferri, Raffaele Garo
                Charles Goring

MOST IMPORTANT WORKS
                Lombroso, *Criminal Man* (1863); Garo
                Ferri, *Criminal Sociology* (1884); Gorin
                (1913); William Sheldon, *Varieties of D*
                Eleanor Glueck and Sheldon Glueck, *U*
                Delinquency (1950)

CORE IDEAS   Some people have biological and ment
                them crime-prone. These traits are inhe
                birth. Mental and physical degeneracie
                crime.

MODERN OUTGROWTHS
                Biosocial Theory, Psychodynamic Theo
                Behavioral Theory, Evolutionary Theor

Stock Montage, Inc.

Cesare Lombroso

Theories

OSITIVISM

oso *l Man*	Garofalo *Criminology* (1885)	Dugdale *The Jukes* (1910)	Kretschmer *Physique and Character* (1921)	Hooton *American Criminal* (1939)	Montagu *Man and A*
	Ferri *Criminal Sociology* (1884)	Goring *The English Convict* (1913)		Sheldon *Somatotyping* (1940)	Dalton *The Preme*

sley *ogy of Mind* (1867)		Tarde **Theory of Imitation** *Penal Philosophy* (1912)	Freud **Psychoanalytic Theory** *General Introduction to Psychoanalysis* (1920)	Friedlander **Behavioral Theory** *Psychoanalytic Approach to Delinquency* (1947)	Eysenck *Crime and Personality*

Kant *Philosophy of Law* (1887)	Brockway *The American Reformatory* (1910)	Mabbott *Punishment* (1939)	Andenaes *General Preventive E of Punishment* (1966)
			Packer *The Limits of Crimin*

	Bonger *Criminality and Economic Conditions* (1916)	Rusche & Kircheimer **Marxist Theory** *Punishment and Social Structure* (1939)	Vold *Theoretical Criminology* (1
			Dahrendorf *Class and Class Conflict in Industrial Society* (1959)

SOCIOLOGICAL THEORY

Durkeim *Suicide* (1897)	Park, Burgess, & McKenzie *The City* (1925)	**The Chicago School** Merton *Social Structure and Anomie* (1938)	**Strain Theory** **Cultural Deviance Theory** Cloward & O *Delinquency a*
		Sellin *Culture, Confllict and Crime* (1938)	Lewis *The Cultur*

Sutherland **Learning Theories** *Principles of Criminology* (1939)	Lemert **Labeling Theories** *Social Pathology* (1951)	Hirschi *Causes of Delinquenc* (1969)

INTEGRATED THEORY

Glueck & Glueck *500 Criminal Careers* (1930)	Glueck & Glueck *Unraveling Juvenile Delinquen* (1950)

	Einstein's Special Theory of Relativity 1905	World War I	Depression	World War II	Cold War	Vietnam War
tionalism						
1875	**1900**		**1925**	**1940**	**1950**	**1969**

Time Line of Criminological

Current Terminology

BIOSOCIAL THEORIES

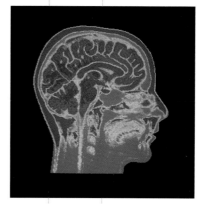

PSYCHOLOGICAL THEORIES

Musées Royaux Des Beaux-Arts, Art Resource, NY

© Mehan Kulyk/Science Photo Library–Photo Researchers, Inc.

BIOLOGICAL F

Phrenology   Lombr
Crimin
(1863)

Mauc
Patho

CHOICE THEORY

CLASSICAL THEORY

Beccaria
On Crimes and Punishment (1764)

Bentham
Moral Calculus (1789)

SOCIAL CONFLICT THEORY

© Todd Bigelow/Black Star

MARXIST THEORY

Marx
Communist Manifesto
(1848)

SOCIAL STRUCTURE THEORY

SOCIAL PROCESS THEORY

© Richard Hutchings/Photo Edit

INTEGRATED THEORY

Sumerian Culture	Pyramids Built	Roman Empire	Fall of Rome	Feudalism		Age of Science		Bach, Mozart, and Haydn Compose		Declaration of Independence	Industrial Age	Lodon Police Formed		Charles Darwin *Origin of Species* 1859	N
B.C. 3000	2000	1000 500	A.D. 500	1000	1500	1700		1725	1750	1775	1800	1825		1850	

Jesus of Nazareth

J. K. Lavater, Cesare
falo, Earnest Hooton,

falo, *Criminology* (1885);
, *The English Convict*
linquent Youth (1949);
Inraveling Juvenile

l traits that make
rited and present at
are the cause of

ry, Cognitive Theory,

Sociological Theory

ORIGIN   1897

FOUNDERS   Emile Durkheim, Robert Ezra Park, Ernest Burgess, Clifford Shaw, Walter Reckless, Frederic Thrasher

MOST IMPORTANT WORKS

Durkheim, *The Division of Labor in Society* (1893), and *Suicide: A Study in Sociology* (1897); Park, Burgess, and John McKenzie, *The City* (1925); Thrasher, *The Gang* (1926); Shaw, et al., *Delinquency Areas* (1925); Edwin Sutherland, *Criminology* (1924)

CORE IDEAS   A person's place in the social structure determines his or her behavior. Disorganized urban areas are the breeding ground of crime. A lack of legitimate opportunities produces criminal subcultures. Socialization within the family, within school, and the peer group controls behavior.

MODERN OUTGROWTHS

Social Ecology Theory, Strain Theory, Cultural Deviance Theory, Learning Theory, Social Control Theory

Corbis/Bettmann

Emile Durkheim

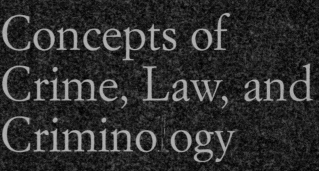

How is crime defined? How much crime is there, and what are the trends and patterns in the crime rate? How many people fall victim to crime, and who is likely to become a crime victim? How did our system of criminal law develop, and what are the basic elements of crimes? What is the science of criminology all about? These are some of the core issues that will be addressed in the first four chapters of this text. Chapter 1 introduces students to the field of criminology: its nature, area of study, methodologies, and historical development. Concern about crime and justice has been an important part of the human condition for more than 5,000 years, since the first criminal codes were set down in the Middle East. And while the scientific study of crime—criminology—is considered a modern science, it has existed for more than 200 years.

Concepts of Crime, Law, and Criminology

Chapter 2 introduces students to one of the key components of criminology—the development of criminal law. It discusses the social history of law, the purpose of law, and how law defines crime, and it briefly examines criminal defenses and the reform of the law. The final two chapters of this section review the various sources of crime data to derive a picture of crime in the United States. Chapter 3 focuses on the nature and extent of crime, while Chapter 4 is devoted to victims and victimization. Important, stable patterns in the rates of crime and victimization indicate that these are not random events. The way crime and victimization are organized and patterned profoundly influences how criminologists view the causes of crime.

Chapter 1
Crime and Criminology

On September 6, 1996 David Graham, a student at the Air Force Academy, and his fiancée, Diane Zamora, who was attending the U.S. Naval Academy, confessed to police that they had conspired to kill a young Texas girl: 16-year-old Adrienne Jones. Graham, obsessively in love with Zamora, told police he had acted out of shame and guilt over a brief sexual encounter he had had with Jones; killing her was the only way to make up for his infidelity:

> She [Zamora] had been betrayed, deceived and forgotten . . . Diane had always held her virginity as one of her highest virtues. When we agreed to be married, she finally let her guard down long enough for our teen-age hormones to kick in. When this precious relationship we had was damaged by my thoughtless actions, the only thing that could satisfy her womanly vengeance was the life of the one that has, for an instant, taken her place.[1]

The plan the two allegedly hatched was simple. Graham made a date with Jones and drove her to a deserted area; Zamora was hidden in the backseat of the car. When they arrived at the secluded spot, they attacked the unsuspecting Jones. After failing to break her neck, they bashed her head with weights and then shot her as she tried to run off into a field. Afterward, the couple exchanged vows of love, cleaned up their clothes, and drove home.

Police were stymied in the case until the morning of August 25, 1996 when Zamora was sitting around with two fellow students at the Naval Academy and told them that she and her boyfriend shared a secret that they "would take to their graves." "What did you do," they asked Zamora, "commit murder?" When she told the classmates that the pair had in fact killed someone, her friends called police, and a subsequent investigation revealed the tragic details.

This case, which made national headlines, helps illustrate why crime and criminal behavior are topics that have long fascinated people. Crime touches all segments of society. Both the poor and desperate and the affluent engage in criminal activity. Crime occurs across racial, class, and gender lines. It involves some acts that shock the conscience and others that may seem to be relatively harmless human foibles.

Criminal acts may be the work of strangers who prey on people they have never met. Or they can involve friends and family members in **intimate violence**.[2] Regardless of whether crime is shocking or pardonable, there is still little consensus about its cause or what can be done to prevent it. What might compel a couple like David Graham and Diane Zamora to commit such a crime? They came from suburban small-town communities with tree-shaded parks, ranch-style homes, and athletic fields. The couple had planned their wedding date for their graduation on August 13, 2000; they had been featured in the *Fort Worth Star-Telegraph* as a young couple with a bright, well-planned future.[3] Could such outrageous behavior be better understood

David Graham shares a happy moment with his fiancée Diane Zamora (left). The two military academy students confessed to police that they had conspired to kill Adrienne Jones (right), a 16-year-old Texas girl with whom Graham had a brief sexual encounter while still in high school. How can the violent behavior of two such "model" teenagers ever be explained? Is it possible to deter such senseless acts of violence through the threat of severe legal punishments, such as the death penalty?

People in the United States are justifiably concerned about crime; most people view it as a major social problem. Public opinion polls indicate that almost half of all Americans feel it is not safe to walk at night in their own neighborhood. There are grounds for this concern, considering that the United States is more crime-prone than other industrialized countries. According to the Sentencing Project, a private, nonprofit agency devoted to improving the justice system, the crime rate in the United States exceeds that of most other nations. The project has found that the United States leads the world in murder, rape, and robbery rates. The U.S. murder rate is 4 times Italy's, 9 times England's, and 11 times Japan's—even twice that of war-torn Northern Ireland. Violence directed against women is, comparatively, even more shocking: the rape rate in the United States is 8 times higher than in France, 15 times higher than in England, 20 times higher than in Portugal, 23 times higher than in Italy, 26 times higher than in Japan, and 46 times higher than in Greece. The robbery rate in the United States is 150 times that of Japan, 47 times that of Ireland, and over 100 times that of Greece. Put another way, if the United States had the same murder rate as England's, it would experience 2,500 homicides a year instead of 23,000; if it had Japan's robbery rate, 4,500 robberies would occur annually instead of the actual number of more than 600,000!

Considering these statistics, it is not surprising that the United States puts far more people in prison than other countries do. The percentage of the population sent to prison and jail in the United States exceeds that of such notoriously punitive countries as Singapore, Romania, and South Africa (Figure 1.A).

There are a number of explanations for the high U.S. crime rate. Among the suspected reasons are a large underclass; urban areas in which the poorest and wealthiest citizens reside in close proximity; racism and discrimination; the failure of an underfunded educational system;

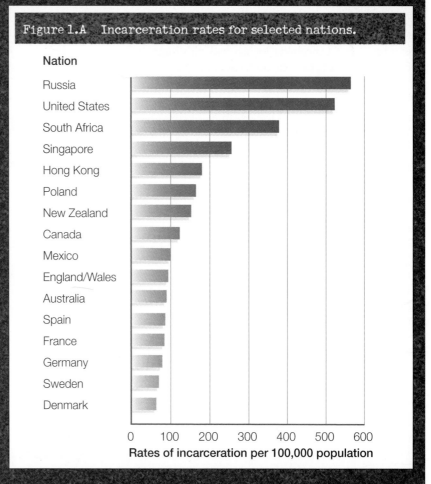

Figure 1.A   Incarceration rates for selected nations.

Nation

the troubled American family; easy access to handguns; and a culture that defines success in terms of material wealth. Each of these factors may explain the disproportionate amount of crime in the United States.

Of course, these findings must be interpreted with some caution. International crime rate differences may be a function of the way crime data are gathered and processed: U.S. crime data may be more (or less) accurate than the statistics collected in other developed nations. And, while the United States is still the "world leader" in violence, there is evidence of a disturbing upswing in violent crime abroad. For example, sharp increases have occurred in the murder rates in England, Germany, and Sweden. Racial assaults and hate crimes have increased

dramatically in Germany and England. And Russia and the former Soviet republics have seen the rise of large-scale organized crime gangs that commonly use violence and intimidation.

Fueling the rise in European violence has been a dramatic growth in the number of illegal guns smuggled in from the former Soviet republics. Unrestrictive immigration has brought newcomers who face cultural differences, lack of job prospects, and racism. Social and economic pressures, including unemployment and cutbacks in the social welfare system, add pressure.

There have also been reports of increased criminal activity in Asia. For example, juvenile delinquency in the island nation of Singapore is on the rise; the number of arrests of young people more than doubled between 1991 and 1995. The delinquency increase is ironic, considering that Singapore's draconian justice policies became notorious in 1993 when American teen Michael Fay was flogged after being convicted for vandalism.

Singapore is not alone among Asian nations experiencing an upsurge in crime. Authorities in Vietnam report a troubling increase in street crimes such as burglary and theft. Many crimes are drug related: there are an estimated 200,000 opium addicts in the country, and almost 50,000 acres of land are now being cultivated for growing the poppy from which heroin is produced. Although it is difficult to obtain accurate crime data from China, the world's largest nation seems to be going through a crackdown on criminal offending. In the first few months of 1996, Chinese courts sentenced more than 100,000 street criminals, including 1,000 given death sentences and many thousands more sentenced to life in prison.

During a single month (June 1996), 250 people were executed. The current wave of punishments is a response to a significant increase in street crimes, including robberies and drug trafficking.

Rising world crime rates may be tied in part to a rapid increase in the female crime rate. Countries such as Germany, France, Brazil, and India all report an increase in robberies and drug trafficking involving female offenders. In Italy, the 23-year-old daughter of a slain Mafia chieftain took over her father's criminal activities, a development that would have been unheard of only a few years ago. While some nations (such as Poland, the Philippines, and Argentina) have not experienced rising female crime rates, the trend is global, linked to the growing emancipation of women in developing countries. Although crime rates of other nations are still relatively low compared to that of the United States, these trends indicate that international crime rates may yet converge.

CRITICAL THINKING QUESTIONS
1. Will countries such as Japan experience growth in their crime rates as they become more economically dominant?
2. What factors do you think contribute to the high U.S. crime rate?

Sources: "With Women's Liberation Comes a Growing Involvement in Crime," *CJ International* 12 (1996): 19; "Crime Crackdown Continues as Statistics Increase," *CJ International* 12 (1996): 8; Sean Malinowski, "Battling an Emerging Crime Problem," *CJ International* 12 (1996): 3–4; "Singapore Says Delinquency Up," *Boston Globe* 17 February 1996, p. 4; James Lynch, "A Serious Crime Cross-National Comparison of the Length of Custodial Sentences for Serious Crimes," *Justice Quarterly* 10 (1993): 639–660; Gunther Kaiser, "Juvenile Delinquency in the Federal Republic of Germany," *International Journal of Comparative and Applied Criminal Justice* 16 (1992): 185–197; Marc Mauer, *Americans Behind Bars: The International Use of Incarceration* (Washington, D.C.: Sentencing Project, 1994); Elizabeth Neuffer, "Violent Crime Rise Fueling Fears in a Changing Europe," *Boston Globe*, 10 April 1994, p. 1.

if it had been committed by indigent teens who were the product of bad neighborhoods and dysfunctional homes? Could someone who was really "normal" ever commit such a horrible crime? Is it possible that if the couple were convicted and executed that this extreme punishment could deter others? Research indicates that habitually aggressive behavior is often learned in homes in which children are victimized and parents serve as aggressive role models; learned violence then persists into adulthood.[4] Is it possible to overcome a predisposition to violence through the fear of punishment?

Connections

Experts have suggested a variety of explanations for bizarre violent episodes such as the killing of Adrienne Jones. While some focus on cultural factors, others lay the blame on psychological abnormality. Psychologists link violent behavior to a number of psychological influences, including observational learning from violent TV shows, traumatic childhood experiences, mental illness, impaired cognitive processes, and a psychopathic personality structure. Chapter 11 reviews the most prominent of these prescriptions for violence.

Crime stories such as this one take their toll on the American public; about half of U.S. citizens say they're afraid to walk alone in their own neighborhood at night.[5] The public's fear may be justified because, as the Close-Up "Is the United States Crime-Prone?" indicates, the United States may be more crime-prone than most other nations—although the rest of the world seems to be catching up.

Concern about crime and the need to develop effective measures to control criminal behavior has spurred the development of the study of *criminology*. This academic discipline is devoted to the development of valid and reliable information about the causes of crime as well as crime patterns and trends. **Criminologists** use scientific methods to study the nature, extent, cause, and control of criminal behavior. Unlike media commentators, whose opinions about crime can be colored by personal experiences, biases, and values, criminologists bring objectivity and the scientific method to the study of crime and its consequences. Because of the threat of crime and the social problems it represents, the field of criminology has gained prominence as an academic area of study.

This chapter introduces criminology: how it is defined, its goals, and its history. It also addresses such questions as: How do criminologists define crime? How do they conduct research? What ethical issues face those wishing to conduct criminological research?

What Is Criminology?

Criminology is the scientific approach to the study of criminal behavior. In their classic definition, criminologists Edwin Sutherland and Donald Cressey state:

> Criminology is the body of knowledge regarding crime as a social phenomenon. It includes within its scope the processes of making laws, of breaking laws, and of reacting toward the breaking of laws. . . . The objective of criminology is the development of a body of general and verified principles and of other types of knowledge regarding this process of law, crime, and treatment.[6]

Sutherland and Cressey's definition includes the most important areas of interest to criminologists: the development of criminal law and its use to define crime, the cause of law violations, and the methods used to control criminal behavior. Also important is their use of the term *verified principles* to signify the use of the scientific method in criminology. Criminologists use objective research methods to pose research questions (hypotheses), gather data, create theories, and test the validity of theories. They use every method of established social science inquiry: analysis of existing records, experimental designs, surveys, historical analysis, and content analysis.

An essential part of criminology is the fact that it is an *interdisciplinary* science. Relatively few academic centers grant graduate degrees in criminology. Many criminologists have also been trained in other fields, most commonly sociology but also criminal justice, political science, psychology, economics, and the natural sciences. While for most of the 20th century, criminology's primary orientation has been sociological, today it can be viewed as an integrated approach to the study of criminal behavior. Although it combines elements from many other fields, the primary interest of criminologists is understanding the true nature of law, crime, and justice.

Criminology and Criminal Justice

In the late 1960s, interest in the so-called crime problem gave rise to the development of research projects, such as those conducted by the American Bar Foundation, aimed at understanding the way police, courts, and correctional agencies actually operated.[7] Eventually, academic programs devoted to studying the **criminal justice system** were opened.

Although the terms *criminology* and *criminal justice* may seem similar, and people often confuse the two, there are major differences between these fields of study. Criminology explains the etiology (origin), extent, and nature of crime in society, whereas criminal justice refers to the agencies of social control that handle criminal offenders.

Whereas criminologists are mainly concerned with identifying the nature, extent, and cause of crime, criminal justice scholars are engaged in describing, analyzing, and explaining the behavior of the agencies of justice—police departments, courts, and correctional facilities—and identifying effective methods of crime control.[8]

Because both fields are crime related, they do overlap. Criminologists must be aware of how the agencies of justice operate and how they influence crime and criminals. Criminal justice experts cannot begin to design programs of crime prevention or rehabilitation without understanding something of the nature of crime. It is common, therefore, for criminal justice programs to feature courses on criminology and for criminology courses to evaluate the agencies of justice. The tremendous interest in criminal justice has led to the creation of more than a thousand justice-related academic programs; not surprisingly, these programs are often staffed by criminologists. Thus, these two fields not only coexist but help each other grow and develop.

Criminology and Deviance

Criminology is also sometimes confused with the study of **deviant behavior.** However, significant distinctions can be made between these areas of scholarship. *Deviant behavior* is behavior that departs from social norms.[9] Included within the broad spectrum of deviant acts are behaviors that range from committing a violent crime to joining a nudist colony.

Crime and deviance are often confused, yet not all crimes are deviant or unusual acts, and not all deviant acts are illegal or criminal. For example, using recreational drugs, such as marijuana, may be illegal, but is it deviant? A significant percentage of American youth have used or are using drugs. Therefore, to argue that all crimes are behaviors that depart from the norms of society is probably erroneous. Conversely, many deviant acts are not criminal even though they may be shocking. For example, suppose a passerby observes a person drowning and makes no effort to save that victim. Although the general public would probably condemn the person's behavior as callous, immoral, and deviant, no legal action could be taken, since citizens are not required by law to effect rescues. In sum, many criminal acts, but not all, fall within the concept of deviance. Similarly, some deviant acts, but not all, are considered crimes.

Two issues that involve deviance are of particular interest to criminologists: (1) How do deviant behaviors become crimes? and (2) When should crimes be **legalized**—considered socially deviant behaviors immune to state sanction and legal punishment? The first issue involves the historical development of law. Many acts that are legally forbidden today were once considered merely unusual or deviant behavior. For example, the sale and possession of marijuana was legal in this country until 1937, when it was prohibited under federal law. To understand the nature and purpose of law, criminologists study the process by which

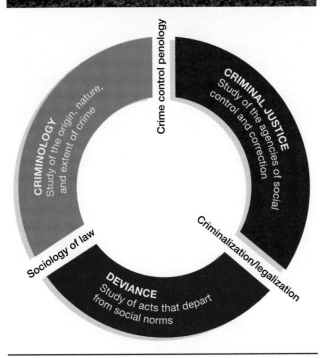

Figure 1.1 The relationship between criminology, criminal justice, and deviance.

Crime control penology

CRIMINOLOGY
Study of the origin, nature, and extent of crime

CRIMINAL JUSTICE
Study of the agencies of social control and correction

Sociology of law

Criminalization/legalization

DEVIANCE
Study of acts that depart from social norms

crimes are created from deviance. Marijuana use was banned because of an extensive lobbying effort by Harry Anslinger, head of the Federal Bureau of Narcotics, who used magazine articles, public appearances, and public testimony to sway public opinion against marijuana use.[10] In one famous article, which appeared in 1937, Anslinger told how "an entire family was murdered by a youthful [marijuana] addict in Florida . . . [who] with an axe had killed his father, mother, two brothers, and a sister."[11] As a result of these efforts, a deviant behavior—marijuana use—became a criminal behavior, and previously law-abiding citizens were now defined as criminal offenders.

Connections

It is interesting that some of the drugs considered highly dangerous today were once sold openly and considered medically beneficial. For example, the narcotic drug heroin, now considered extremely addicting and dangerous, was originally named in the mistaken belief that its painkilling properties would prove "heroic" to medical patients. The history of drug and alcohol abuse is discussed further in Chapter 13.

Criminologists also consider whether outlawed behaviors have evolved into social norms and, if so, whether they should either be legalized or have their penalties reduced (be **decrim-**

inalized). For example, debate continues over the legalization of abortion, recreational drugs, and assisted suicide.

There is also frequent discussion about where to draw the line between behavior that is merely considered deviant and unusual and behavior that is outlawed and criminal. For example, when does sexually oriented material cross the line from being merely suggestive to being pornographic? Can a "bright line" be drawn that separates sexually oriented materials into two groups, one that is legally acceptable and a second that is considered depraved or obscene? And, if such a line can be drawn, who gets to draw it? If an illegal act becomes a norm, should society reevaluate its criminal status and let it become merely an unusual or deviant act? Conversely, if scientists show that a normative act, such as smoking or drinking, poses a serious health hazard, should it be made illegal? Many recent efforts have been made to control morally questionable behavior and restrict the rights of citizens to freedom of their actions.

In sum, criminologists are concerned with the concept of deviance and its relationship to criminality. The shifting definition of deviant behavior is closely associated with our concepts of crime. The relationship between criminology, criminal justice, and deviance is illustrated in Figure 1.1.

A Brief History of Criminology

The scientific study of crime and criminality is a relatively recent development. Although written criminal codes have existed for thousands of years, they were for the most part restricted to defining crime and setting punishments. What motivated people to violate the law remained a matter of conjecture.

Connections

While the English common law is the immediate antecedent of the U.S. legal system, the influence of some of the earliest written codes, such as those of Hebrews and Babylonians, can still be detected. Chapter 2 traces the history of the law in some detail.

During the Middle Ages, superstition and fear of satanic possession dominated thinking. People who violated social norms or religious practices were believed to be witches or possessed by demons. The prescribed method for dealing with the possessed was burning at the stake, a practice that survived into the 17th century. For example, between 1575 and 1590 Nicholas Remy, head of the Inquisition in the French province of Lorraine, ordered 900 sorcerers and witches burned to death; a contemporary, Peter Binsfield, the bishop of the German city of Trier, ordered the deaths of 6,500 people. An estimated 100,000 people

During the Middle Ages, superstition and fear of satanic possession dominated thinking. People who violated social norms or religious practices were believed to be witches or possessed by demons. The prescribed method for dealing with the possessed was burning at the stake, a practice that survived into the 17th century. This painting, *The Trial of George Jacobs, August 5, 1692* by J. H. Matteson (1855), depicts the ordeal of Jacobs, a patriarch of Salem, Massachusetts. During the witch craze, he had ridiculed the trials, only to find himself being accused, tried, and executed.

were prosecuted throughout Europe for witchcraft during the 16th and 17th centuries.

It was also commonly believed that some families produced offspring who were unsound or unstable and that social misfits were inherently damaged by reason of their "inferior blood."[12] Even those who questioned demonic possession advocated extremely harsh penalties as a means of punishing criminals and setting an example for others. Both violent and property crimes were often punished with execution.

Classical Criminology

By the mid-18th century, social philosophers had begun to call for rethinking the prevailing concepts of law and justice. They argued for a more rational approach to punishment, stressing that the relationship between crimes and their punishment should be balanced and fair. This view was based on the prevailing philosophy of the time called **utilitarianism,** which emphasized that behavior must be useful, purposeful, and reasonable. Rather than

cruel public executions designed to frighten people into obedience or to punish those the law failed to deter, reformers called for a more moderate and just approach to penal sanctions. The most famous of these was Cesare Beccaria (1738–1794), whose writings described both a motive for committing crime and methods for its control.

Beccaria believed that people want to achieve pleasure and avoid pain. Crimes must therefore provide some pleasure to the criminal. It follows that to deter crime, one must administer pain in an appropriate amount to counterbalance the pleasure obtained from crime. Beccaria's famous theorem was that:

> In order for punishment not to be in every instance, an act of violence of one or many against a private citizen, it must be essentially public, prompt, necessary, the least possible in the given circumstances, proportionate to the crimes, and dictated by the laws.[13]

The writings of Beccaria and his followers form the core of what today is referred to as **classical criminology.** As originally conceived in the 18th century, classical criminology theory had several basic elements:

1. In every society, people have *free will* to choose criminal or lawful solutions to meet their needs or settle their problems.

2. Criminal solutions may be more attractive than lawful ones because they usually require less work for a greater payoff.

3. People's choice of criminal solutions may be controlled by their fear of punishment.

4. The more *severe, certain, and swift* the punishment, the better able it is to control criminal behavior.

The classical perspective influenced judicial philosophy during much of the late 18th and the 19th centuries. Prisons began to be used as a form of punishment, and sentences were geared proportionately to the seriousness of the crime. Capital punishment was still widely used but began to be employed for only the most serious crimes. The byword was "Let the punishment fit the crime."

During the 19th century, a new vision of the world challenged the validity of classical theory and presented an innovative way of looking at the causes of crime.

Nineteenth-Century Positivism

While the classical position held sway as a guide to crime, law, and justice for almost 100 years, during the late 19th century, a new movement began that would challenge its dominance. **Positivism** developed as the scientific method began to take hold in Europe. This movement was inspired by new discoveries in biology, astronomy, and chemistry. If the scientific method could be applied to the study of nature, why not use it to study human behavior? Auguste Comte (1798–1857), considered the founder of sociology, applied scientific methods to the study of society. According to Comte, societies pass through stages that can be grouped on the basis of how people try to understand the world in which they live. People in primitive societies consider inanimate objects as having life (for example, the sun is a god); in later social stages, people embrace a rational, scientific view of the world. Comte called this final stage the positive stage, and those who followed his writings became known as *positivists.*

As we understand it today, the positivist tradition has two main elements. The first is the belief that human behavior is a function of external forces that are beyond individual control. Some of these forces are social, such as the effect of wealth and class, while others are political and historical, such as war and famine. Other forces are more personal and psychological, such as an individual's brain structure and his or her biological makeup or mental ability. Each of these forces operates to influence human behavior.

The second aspect of positivism is its embracing of the scientific method to solve problems. Positivists rely on the strict use of empirical methods to test hypotheses. That is, they believe in the factual, firsthand observation and measurement of conditions and events. Positivists would agree that an abstract concept such as "intelligence" exists because it can be measured by an IQ test. However, they would challenge a concept such as the "soul" because it is a condition that cannot be verified by the scientific method. The positivist tradition was spurred on by Charles Darwin (1809–1882), whose work on the evolution of man encouraged a 19th-century "cult of science" that mandated that all human activity could be verified by scientific principles.

Positivist Criminology

If the scientific method could be used to explain all behavior, then it was to be expected that by the mid-19th century "scientific" methods were being applied to understanding criminality. The earliest of these scientific studies were biologically oriented. Physiognomists, such as J. K. Lavater (1741–1801), studied the facial features of criminals to determine whether the shape of ears, nose, and eyes and the distance between them were associated with antisocial behavior. Phrenologists, such as Franz Joseph Gall (1758–1828) and Johann Kaspar Spurzheim (1776–1832), studied the shape of the skull and bumps on the head to determine whether these physical attributes were linked to criminal behavior. Phrenologists believed that external cranial characteristics dictate which areas of the brain control physical activity. Though their primitive techniques and quasi-scientific methods have been thoroughly discredited, these efforts were an early attempt to use a scientific approach to studying crime.

By the early 19th century, abnormality in the human mind was being linked to criminal behavior patterns. Philippe Pinel (1745–1826), one of the founders of French psychiatry, claimed that some people behave abnormally even without being mentally ill. He coined the phrase *manie sans delire* to denote what eventually was referred to as a psychopathic personality. In 1812 an American, Benjamin Rush (1745–1813), described patients with an "innate preternatural moral depravity."[14] Another early criminological pioneer, English physician Henry Maudsley (1835–1918), believed that insanity and criminal behavior are strongly linked: "Crime is a sort of outlet in which their unsound tendencies are discharged; they would go mad if they were not criminals, and they do not go mad because they are criminals."[15] These early research efforts shifted attention to brain functioning and personality as the key to criminal behavior.

Cesare Lombroso and the Criminal Man

In Italy, Cesare Lombroso was studying the cadavers of executed criminals in an effort to scientifically determine whether law violators were physically different from people of conventional values and behavior. Lombroso (1835–1909), known as the "father of criminology," was a physician who served much of his career in the Italian army. That experience gave him ample opportunity to study the physical characteristics of soldiers convicted and executed for criminal offenses. Later, he studied inmates at institutes for the criminally insane at Pavia, Pesaro, and Reggio Emilia.[16]

Lombrosian theory can be outlined in a few simple statements.[17] First, Lombroso believed that serious offenders—those who engage in repeated assault- or theft-related activities—have inherited criminal traits. These "born criminals" have inherited physical problems that impel them into a life of crime. This view helped spur interest in a **criminal anthropology**.[18] Second, he held that born criminals suffer from **atavistic anomalies**—physically, they are throwbacks to more primitive times when people were savages. Thus, criminals supposedly have the enormous jaws and strong canine teeth common to carnivores and savages who devour raw flesh. In addition, Lombroso compared criminals' behavior to that of the mentally ill and those suffering from certain forms of epilepsy. He concluded that criminogenic traits can be acquired through indirect heredity: from a "degenerate family with frequent cases of insanity, deafness, syphilis, epilepsy, and alcoholism among its members." Direct heredity—being related to a family of criminals—is the second primary cause of crime.

Lombroso's version of criminal anthropology was brought to the United States via articles and textbooks that adopted his ideas. He attracted a circle of followers who expanded on his vision of biological determinism. His work was actually more popular in the United States than in Europe. By the turn of the century, American authors were discussing "the science of penology" and "the science of criminology."[19]

Connections

The theories of criminology that have their roots in Lombroso's biological determinism will be discussed in Chapter 6. Criminologists who today suggest that crime has a biological basis also believe the environmental conditions influence human behavior. Hence, the term *biosocial theory* has been coined to reflect the assumed link between physical and mental traits, the social environment, and behavior.

The Development of Sociological Criminology

At the same time that biological views were dominating criminology, another group of positivists were developing the field of sociology to scientifically study the major social changes that were then taking place in 19th-century society.

Sociology seemed an ideal perspective from which to study society. After thousands of years of stability, the world was undergoing a population explosion: The population, estimated at 600 million in 1700, had risen to 900 million by 1800. People were flocking to cities in ever-increasing numbers. Manchester, England, had 12,000 inhabitants in 1760 and 400,000 in 1850; during the same period, the population of Glasgow, Scotland, rose from 30,000 to 300,000. The development of such machinery as power looms had doomed cottage industries and given rise to a factory system in which large numbers of people toiled for extremely low wages. The spread of agricultural machines increased the food supply while reducing the need for a large rural workforce; the excess laborers further swelled the cities' populations. At the same time, political, religious, and social traditions continued to be challenged by the scientific method.

The foundations of sociological criminology can be traced to the works of L. A. J. (Adolphe) Quetelet (1796–1874) and Emile Durkheim (1858–1917).

L. A. J. QUETELET. Quetelet was a Belgian mathematician who began (along with a Frenchman, Andre-Michel Guerry) what is known as the *cartographic school* of criminology.[20] Quetelet, who made use of social statistics developed in France in the early 19th century (called the *Comptes generaux de l'administration de la justice*), was one of the first social scientists to use objective mathematical techniques to investigate the influence of social factors, such as season, climate, sex, and age, on the propensity to commit crime. Quetelet's most important finding was that social forces were significantly correlated with crime rates. In addition to finding a strong influence of age and sex on crime, Quetelet also uncovered evidence that season, climate, population composition, and poverty were also related to criminality. More specifically, he found that crime rates were greatest in the summer, in southern areas, among heterogeneous populations, and among the poor and uneducated and were influenced by drinking habits.[21] Quetelet was a pioneer of sociologically oriented criminology. He identified many of the relationships between crime and social phenomena that still serve as a basis for criminology today.

EMILE DURKHEIM. (David) Emile Durkheim (1858–1917) was one of the founders of sociology and a significant contributor to criminology.[22] His definition of crime as a normal and necessary social event has been more influential on modern criminology than any other.

According to Durkheim's vision of social positivism, crime is part of human nature because it has existed in every age, in both poverty and prosperity.[23] Crime is normal because it is virtually impossible to imagine a society in which criminal behavior is totally absent. Such a society would almost demand that all people be and act exactly alike. The inevitability of crime is linked to the differences (heterogeneity) within society. Because people are so different from one another and use such a variety of methods and forms of behavior to meet their needs, it is not surprising that some will resort to criminality. Even if "real" crimes were eliminated, human weaknesses and petty vices would be elevated to the status of crimes. As long as human differences exist, then, crime is inevitable and one of the fundamental conditions of social life.

Crime, argued Durkheim, can also be useful and on occasion even healthy for a society to experience. The existence of crime implies that a way is open for social change and that the social structure is not rigid or inflexible. Put another way, if crime did not exist, it would mean that everyone behaves the same way and agrees totally on what is right and wrong. Such universal conformity would stifle creativity and independent thinking. Durkheim offered the example of the Greek philosopher Socrates, who was considered a criminal and put to death for corrupting the morals of youth, simply because he questioned the social order. In addition, Durkheim argued that crime is beneficial because it calls attention to social ills. A rising crime rate can signal the need for social change and promote a variety of programs designed to relieve the human suffering that may have caused crime in the first place.

In *The Division of Labor in Society,* Durkheim described the consequences of the shift from a small, rural society, which he labeled "mechanical," to the more modern "organic" society with a large urban population, division of labor, and personal isolation. From this shift flowed **anomie,** or norm and role confusion, a powerful sociological concept that helps describe the chaos and disarray accompanying the loss of traditional values in modern society. Durkheim's research on suicide indicated that anomic societies maintain high suicide rates; by implication, anomie might cause other forms of deviance to develop.

The Chicago School and Beyond

The primacy of sociological positivism was secured by research begun in the early 20th century by Robert Ezra Park (1864–1944), Ernest W. Burgess (1886–1966), Louis Wirth (1897–1952), and their colleagues in the Sociology Department at the University of Chicago. Known as the **Chicago School,** these sociologists pioneered research on the social ecology of the city and inspired a generation of scholars to conclude that social forces operating in urban areas create criminal interactions; some neighborhoods become "natural areas" for crime.[24] These urban neighborhoods maintain such a high level of poverty that critical social institutions, such as the school and the family, break down. The resulting social disorganization reduces the ability of social institutions to control behavior, and the outcome is a high crime rate.

The Chicago School sociologists and their contemporaries focused on the functions of social institutions and how their breakdown influences behavior. They pioneered the ecological study of crime—crime as a function of where one lives.

During the 1930s, another group of sociologists, influenced by psychology, began to add a social-psychological component to criminological theory. They concluded that the individual's relationship to important social processes, such as education, family life, and peer relations, is the

Net Bookmark

The Chicago school linked criminal activity to gangs and youth groups. To find out more about gangs in America, visit the National Youth Gang Center. This site provides critical information about youth gangs and effective responses to them.
http://www.iir.com/nygc/nygc.htm

key to understanding human behavior. In any social milieu, children who grow up in a home racked by conflict, attend an inadequate school, and associate with deviant peers become exposed to pro-crime forces. One position was that people *learn* criminal attitudes from older, more experienced law violators; another view was that crime occurs when families fail to *control* adolescent misbehavior. Each of these views linked criminality to the failure of socialization.

By mid-century, most criminologists had embraced either the ecological or the socialization view of crime. However, these were not the only views of how social institutions influence human behavior. In Europe, the writings of another social thinker, Karl Marx (1818–1883), had pushed the understanding of social interaction in another direction and sowed the seeds for a new approach in criminology.[25]

Conflict Criminology

Oppressive labor conditions prevalent during the rise of industrial capitalism convinced Marx that the character of every civilization is determined by its mode of production—the way its people develop and produce material goods (materialism). The most important relationship in industrial culture is between the owners of the means of production—the capitalist **bourgeoisie**—and the people who do the actual labor—the **proletariat.** The economic system controls all facets of human life; consequently, people's lives revolve around the means of production. The exploitation of the working class, he believed, would eventually lead to class conflict and the end of the capitalist system.

While Marx did not attempt to develop a theory of crime and justice, his writings were applied to legal studies by a few social thinkers, including Ralf Dahrendorf, George Vold, and Willem Bonger.[26]

Though these writings laid the foundation for a Marxist criminology, decades passed before Marxist theory had an important impact on criminology. In the United States during the 1960s, social and political upheaval was fueled by the Vietnam war, the development of an antiestablishment counterculture movement, the civil rights movement, and the women's movement. Young sociologists who became interested in applying Marxist principles to the study of crime began to analyze the social conditions in the United States that promoted class conflict and crime. What emerged from this intellectual ferment was a Marxist-based radical criminology that indicted the economic system as producing the conditions that support a high crime rate. The radical tradition has played a significant role in criminology ever since.

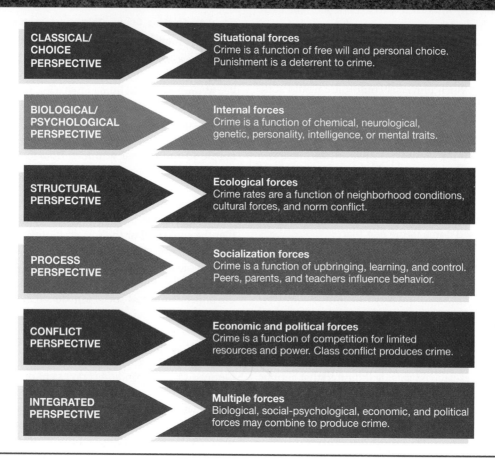

Figure 1.2 The major perspectives of criminology focus on individual (biological, psychological, and choice theories), social (structural and process theories), political and economic (conflict), and multiple (integrated) factors.

CLASSICAL/ CHOICE PERSPECTIVE
Situational forces
Crime is a function of free will and personal choice. Punishment is a deterrent to crime.

BIOLOGICAL/ PSYCHOLOGICAL PERSPECTIVE
Internal forces
Crime is a function of chemical, neurological, genetic, personality, intelligence, or mental traits.

STRUCTURAL PERSPECTIVE
Ecological forces
Crime rates are a function of neighborhood conditions, cultural forces, and norm conflict.

PROCESS PERSPECTIVE
Socialization forces
Crime is a function of upbringing, learning, and control. Peers, parents, and teachers influence behavior.

CONFLICT PERSPECTIVE
Economic and political forces
Crime is a function of competition for limited resources and power. Class conflict produces crime.

INTEGRATED PERSPECTIVE
Multiple forces
Biological, social-psychological, economic, and political forces may combine to produce crime.

Criminology Today

The various schools of criminology developed over a 200-year period. Although they have undergone great change and innovation, each continues to have an impact on the field. For example, classical theory has evolved into *rational choice* and *deterrence theories*. Choice theorists today argue that criminals are rational and use available information to decide whether crime is a worthwhile undertaking; deterrence theory holds that this choice is structured by the fear of punishment.

Criminal anthropology has also evolved considerably. While criminologists no longer believe that a single trait or inherited characteristic can explain crime, some are convinced that biological and mental traits interact with environmental factors to influence all human behavior, including criminality. Biological and psychological theorists study the association between criminal behavior and such traits as diet, hormonal makeup, personality, and intelligence.

Sociological theories, tracing back to Quetelet and Durkheim, maintain that individuals' lifestyles and living conditions directly control their criminal behavior. Those at the bottom of the social structure cannot achieve success and thus experience anomie, strain, failure, and frustration. This is referred to today as the structural perspective.

Some sociologists who have added a social-psychological dimension to their views of crime causation find that individuals' learning experiences and socialization directly control their behavior. In some cases, children learn to commit crime by interacting with and modeling their behavior after others they admire, while other criminal offenders are people whose life experiences have shattered their social bonds to society. This is called the social process perspective.

The writings of Marx and his followers continue to be influential. Today conflict criminologists still see social and political conflict as the root cause of crime. In their view, the inherently unfair economic structure of the United States and other advanced capitalist countries is the engine that drives the high crime rate.

Criminology, then, has had a rich history that still exerts an important influence on the thinking of its current practitioners. Each of the major perspectives is summarized in Figure 1.2.

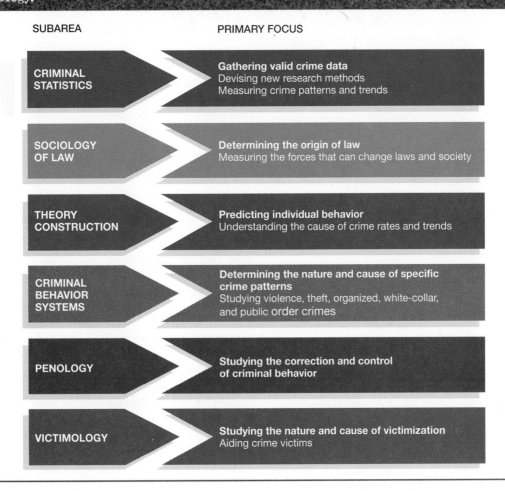

SUBAREA | PRIMARY FOCUS

CRIMINAL STATISTICS
Gathering valid crime data
Devising new research methods
Measuring crime patterns and trends

SOCIOLOGY OF LAW
Determining the origin of law
Measuring the forces that can change laws and society

THEORY CONSTRUCTION
Predicting individual behavior
Understanding the cause of crime rates and trends

CRIMINAL BEHAVIOR SYSTEMS
Determining the nature and cause of specific crime patterns
Studying violence, theft, organized, white-collar, and public order crimes

PENOLOGY
Studying the correction and control of criminal behavior

VICTIMOLOGY
Studying the nature and cause of victimization
Aiding crime victims

Connections

The modern versions of the various schools of criminological thought will be discussed in greater detail throughout the book. Choice theories, the modern offshoot of Beccaria, are reviewed in Chapter 5. Current biological and psychological theories are the topic of Chapter 6. Contemporary theories based on Durkheim's views as well as theories based on the writings of the Chicago School are contained in Chapter 7. The social process view will be discussed in Chapter 8, while Marxist views are covered in Chapter 9. Finally, efforts to integrate a variety of theoretical ideas into a single unified theory are discussed in Chapter 10.

inal behavior. As Marvin Wolfgang and Franco Ferracuti put it:

> A criminologist is one whose professional training, occupational role, and pecuniary reward are primarily concentrated on a scientific approach to, and study and analysis of, the phenomenon of crime and criminal behavior.[27]

Within the broader arena of criminology are several subareas that, taken together, make up the **criminological enterprise.** Criminologists may specialize in a subarea, in the same way that psychologists might specialize in a subfield of psychology, such as child development, perception, personality, psychopathology, or sexuality. Some of the more important criminological subareas are described in this section and summarized in Figure 1.3.

What Criminologists Do: the Criminological Enterprise

Regardless of their background or training, criminologists are primarily interested in studying crime and crim-

Criminal Statistics

The subarea of criminal statistics involves measuring the amount and trends of criminal activity. How much crime occurs annually? Who commits it? When and where does it occur? Which crimes are the most serious? Criminologists interested in criminal statistics try to create valid and reliable measurements of criminal behavior. For example, they create techniques to access the records of police and court agencies. They develop paper-and-pencil survey instruments and then use them with large samples of citizens to determine the percentage of people who actually commit crime and the number of law violators who escape detection by the justice system. They also develop techniques to identify the victims of crime to establish more accurate indicators of the "true" number of criminal acts—how many people are victims of crime and what percentage report crime to police. The study of criminal statistics is one of the most crucial aspects of the criminological enterprise because without valid and reliable data sources, efforts to conduct research on crime and create criminological theories would be futile.

Sociology of Law

The sociology of law is a subarea of criminology concerned with the role that social forces play in shaping criminal law and, concomitantly, the role of criminal law in shaping society. Criminologists study the history of legal thought in an effort to understand how criminal acts, such as theft, rape, and murder, evolved into their present form. Criminologists may also be asked to join in the debate when a new law is proposed to banish or control behavior. For example, across the United States a debate has been raging over the legality of art works, films, photographs, and even rock albums that some people find offensive and lewd and others consider harmless. What role should the law take in curbing the public's access to media and culture? Should society curb actions that some people consider immoral but by which no one is actually harmed? And how is harm defined: Is a child who reads a pornographic magazine "harmed"?

Criminologists also partake in updating the content of the criminal law. The law must be flexible to respond to changing times and conditions. Computer fraud, airplane hijacking, theft from automatic teller machines, and illegally tapping into TV cable lines are acts that obviously did not exist when the criminal law was originally formed. Sometimes, the law must respond to new versions of traditional or common acts. For example, Dr. Jack Kevorkian has made headlines for helping people kill themselves by using his "suicide machine." While some believe that Kevorkian's actions are criminal, immoral, and socially harmful, before he brought national media coverage to the issue there was no law banning second-party help in suicides. In response, Michigan passed legislation making it a felony to help anyone commit suicide.[28] Are Kevorkian's activities the product of a care and concern for human suffering, or a callous criminal act? At the time of this writing no jury has yet convicted Kevorkian, despite his acknowledged role in assisted suicides. Should a law be passed that a majority of the general public disapproves of—a condition that makes the law virtually unenforceable? Conversely, should the criminal law be restricted to only those acts that are unpopular with the general public?

Theory Construction

A question that has tormented criminologists from the first is, Why do people engage in criminal acts? Why, when they know their actions can bring harsh punishment and social disapproval, do they steal, rape, and murder? In short, why do people behave the way they do? Does crime have a social or an individual basis? Is it a psychological, biological, social, political, or economic phenomenon? Since criminologists bring their personal beliefs and backgrounds to bear when they study criminal behavior, there are diverse theories of crime causation. Some criminologists have a psychological orientation and view crime as a function of personality, development, social learning, or cognition. Others investigate the biological correlates of antisocial behavior and study the biochemical, genetic, and neurological linkages to crime. Sociologists look at the social forces producing criminal behavior, including neighborhood conditions, poverty, socialization and group interaction.

Understanding the true cause of crime remains a difficult problem. Criminologists are still unsure why, given similar conditions, one person elects criminal solutions to his or her problems while another conforms to accepted social rules of behavior. Further, understanding crime rates and trends has proven difficult: Why do rates rise and fall? Why are crime rates higher in some areas or regions than in others? Why are some groups more crime-prone than others?

Criminal Behavior Systems

The criminal behavior systems subarea of criminology involves research on specific criminal types and patterns: violent crime, theft crime, public order crime, and organized crime. Numerous attempts have been made to describe and understand particular crime types. For example, Marvin Wolfgang's famous study, *Patterns in Criminal Homicide,* is considered a landmark analysis of the nature of homicide and the relationship between victim and offender.[29] Edwin Sutherland's analysis of business-related offenses helped coin a new phrase—**white-collar crime**—to describe economic crime activities.

The study of criminal behavior also involves research on the links between different types of crime and criminals. This is known as *crime typology.* Unfortunately, typologies often disagree, so no standard exists within the field. Some typologies focus on the criminal, suggesting the existence of offender groups, such as professional criminals, psychotic criminals, occasional criminals, and so on. Others focus on the crimes, clustering them into such categories as property crimes, sex crimes, and so on.

Penology

The study of penology involves the correction and control of known criminal offenders. Penologists formulate strate-

Victimology has taken on greater importance as more criminologists focus their attention on the victim's role in the criminal event. For example, what effect does victim behavior have on the criminal process? Here Robert Giugliano, one of the victims of Colin Ferguson's shooting rampage on a New York commuter train in December 1993, addresses the media at the close of Ferguson's trial on February 17, 1995. Giugliano holds a picture of Marita Magoto, who was killed in the attack. At his right is Carolyn McCarthy, whose husband was killed and son wounded. Ferguson was sentenced to life in prison for killing 6 people and wounding 19 others. The plight of these victims prompted a public outcry, which sparked reinstatement of the death penalty in New York.

gies for crime control and then help implement these policies in "the real world." While the field of criminal justice overlaps this area, criminologists have continued their efforts to develop new crime-control programs and policies. Some criminologists view penology as involving rehabilitation and treatment. Their efforts are directed at providing behavior alternatives for would-be criminals and treatment for individuals convicted of law violations. This view portrays the criminal as someone society has failed; someone under social, psychological, or economic stress; someone who can be helped if society is willing to pay the price. Others argue that crime can be prevented only through a strict policy of social control. They advocate such strict penological measures as capital punishment and mandatory prison sentences. Future penological research efforts seem warranted, since most criminal offenders continue to commit crimes after their release from prison (recidivate).

Victimology

In two classics of criminology, one by Hans von Hentig and another by Stephen Schafer, the critical role of the victim in the criminal process was first identified. These authors were among the first to suggest that victim behavior is often a key determinant of crime, that a victim's actions may actually precipitate crime, and that the study of crime is not complete unless the victim's role is considered.[30]

Connections

In recent years, criminologists have devoted ever-increasing attention to the victim's role in the criminal process. It has been suggested that individuals' lifestyles and behavior may actually increase the risk that they will become crime victims. Some have suggested that living in a high-crime neighborhood increases risk, while others point their finger at the problems caused by associating with dangerous peers and companions. For a discussion of victimization risk, see Chapter 4.

The areas of particular interest in victimology include: using victim surveys to measure the nature and extent of criminal behavior, calculating the actual costs of crime to victims, creating probabilities of victimization risk, studying victim culpability or precipitation of crime, and designing services for the victims of crime. Victimology has taken on greater importance as more criminologists focus their attention on the victim's role in the criminal event.

How Do Criminologists View Crime?

Professional criminologists usually align themselves with one of several schools of thought or perspectives in their field. Each perspective maintains its own view of what constitutes criminal behavior and what causes people to engage in criminality. This diversity of thought is not unique to criminology; biologists, psychologists, sociologists, historians, economists, and natural scientists disagree among themselves about critical issues in their fields. It is not surprising that conflicting views exist within criminology, considering the multidisciplinary nature of the field. In fact, it is common for criminologists to disagree on the nature and definition of crime itself. A criminologist's choice of orientation or perspective depends in part on his or her definition of crime—the beliefs and research orientations of most criminologists are related to their conceptualization of crime. This section discusses the three most common concepts of crime used by criminologists.

The Consensus View of Crime

According to the consensus view, crimes are behaviors believed to be repugnant to all elements of society. The substantive criminal law, which sets out the definition of crimes and their punishments, reflects the values, beliefs, and opinions of society's mainstream. The term *consensus* is used because it implies that there is general agreement among a majority of citizens on what behaviors should be outlawed by the criminal law and henceforth viewed as crimes.

Several attempts have been made to create a concise, yet thorough and encompassing, consensus definition of crime. The eminent criminologists Edwin Sutherland and Donald Cressey have taken the popular stance of linking crime with the criminal law:

> Criminal behavior is behavior in violation of the criminal law . . . [I]t is not a crime unless it is prohibited by the criminal law [which] is defined conventionally as a body of specific rules regarding human conduct which have been promulgated by political authority, which apply uniformly to all members of the classes to which the rules refer, and which are enforced by punishment administered by the state.[31]

This approach to crime implies that its definition is a function of the beliefs, morality, and direction of the existing legal power structure. Note also Sutherland and Cressey's statement that the criminal law is applied "uniformly to all members of the classes to which the rules refer." This statement reveals the authors' faith in the concept of an ideal legal system that can deal adequately with all classes and types of people. While laws banning burglary and robbery are directed at controlling the neediest members of society, laws banning insider trading, embezzlement, and corporate price fixing are aimed at controlling the wealthiest. The reach of the criminal law is not restricted to any single element of society.

The consensus model of crime is probably accepted by a majority of practicing criminologists and is the one most often used in criminology texts. Nonetheless, a number of its premises have been disputed, especially the relationship of crime to morality. Let us now examine that issue in more depth.

The Conflict View of Crime

In opposition to the consensus view, the conflict view depicts society as a collection of diverse groups—owners, workers, professionals, students—who are in constant and continuing conflict. Groups able to assert their political power use the law and the criminal justice system to advance their economic and social position. Criminal laws, therefore, are viewed as acts created to protect the haves from the have-nots. Conflict criminologists often compare and contrast the harsh penalties exacted on the poor for their "street crimes" (burglary, robbery, and larceny) with the minor penalties the wealthy receive for their white-collar crimes (securities violations and other illegal business practices). While the poor go to prison for minor law violations, the wealthy are given lenient sentences for even the most serious breaches of law.

According to the conflict view, the definition of crime is controlled by wealth, power, and position and not by moral consensus or the fear of social disruption.[32] Crime, according to this definition, is a political concept designed to protect the power and position of the upper classes at the expense of the poor. Even crimes prohibiting violent acts, such as rape and murder, may have political undertones: Banning violent acts ensures domestic tranquillity and guarantees that the anger of the poor and disenfranchised classes will not be directed at their wealthy capitalist exploiters. The conflict view of crime then would include in a list of "real" crimes: violations of human rights due to racism, sexism, and imperialism; unsafe working conditions, inadequate child care, inadequate opportunities for employment and education, and substandard housing and medical care; crimes of economic and political domination; pollution of the environment; price fixing; police brutality; assassinations and war making; violations of human dignity (that is, the denial of physical needs and necessities) and impediments to self-determination; deprivation of adequate food; and blocked opportunities to participate in political decision making.[33] While this list might be criticized as containing vague and subjectively chosen acts, an advocate of the conflict view would counter that consensus law also contains crimes that reflect opinion and taste, such as obscenity, substance abuse, and gambling.

According to the interactionist view, crimes are outlawed behaviors because society defines them that way and not because they are inherently evil or immoral acts. Here federal agents seize a ship filled with illegal aliens being smuggled into the United States. Are these people criminals who are trying to force their way into our country or brave and courageous freedom lovers who simply want to share in the American dream? Should they be arrested or welcomed with open arms? Before you answer, think about the Pilgrims coming ashore in Plymouth, Massachusetts. What would have happened to them if the Native Americans had attempted to deport them forcibly? Should the pilgrims have been considered "illegals"?

Net Bookmark

The conflict school of crime links criminality to social malaise and inequality. Across the United States efforts are being made by both private and governmental agencies to correct some of these inequalities. For example, the At-Risk Institute supports a range of research and development activities designed to improve the education of students at risk of educational failure because of limited English proficiency, poverty, race, geographic location, or economic disadvantage.

http://www.ed.gov/offices/OERI/At-Risk/

The Interactionist View of Crime

The interactionist view of crime traces its antecedents to the symbolic interaction school of sociology, first popularized by George Herbert Mead, Charles Horton Cooley, and W. I. Thomas.[34] This position holds that (1) people act according to their own interpretations of reality, according to the meaning things have for them; (2) they learn the meaning of a thing from the way others react to it, either positively or negatively; and (3) they reevaluate and interpret their own behavior according to the meaning and symbols they have learned from others.

According to this perspective, the definition of crime reflects the preferences and opinions of people who hold social power in a particular legal jurisdiction and who use their influence to impose their definition of right and wrong on the rest of the population. Criminals are individuals whom society chooses to label as outcasts or deviants because they have violated social rules. In a classic statement, sociologist Howard Becker argued, "The deviant is one to whom that label has successfully been applied; deviant behavior is behavior people so label."[35] Crimes are outlawed behaviors because society defines them that way and not because they are inherently evil or immoral acts.

The interactionist view of crime is similar to the conflict perspective because they both suggest that behavior is outlawed when it offends people who maintain the social, economic, and political power necessary to have the law conform to their interests or needs. However, unlike the conflict view, the interactionist perspective does not attribute capitalist economic and political motives to the process of defining crime. Instead, interactionists see the criminal law as conforming to the beliefs of "moral crusaders" or **moral**

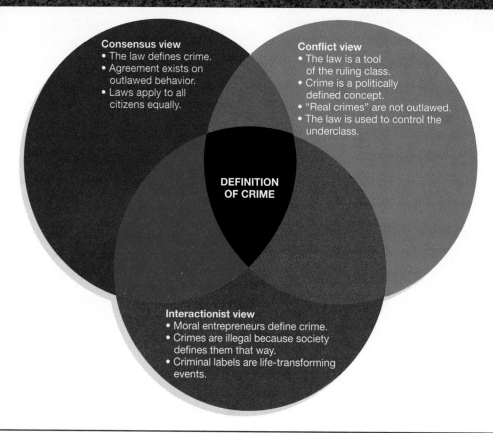

Consensus view
- The law defines crime.
- Agreement exists on outlawed behavior.
- Laws apply to all citizens equally.

Conflict view
- The law is a tool of the ruling class.
- Crime is a politically defined concept.
- "Real crimes" are not outlawed.
- The law is used to control the underclass.

DEFINITION OF CRIME

Interactionist view
- Moral entrepreneurs define crime.
- Crimes are illegal because society defines them that way.
- Criminal labels are life-transforming events.

entrepreneurs who use their influence to shape the legal process in the way they see fit.[36] Laws against pornography, prostitution, and drugs are believed to be motivated more by moral crusades than by capitalist sensibilities. Consequently, interactionists are concerned with shifting moral and legal standards. To the interactionist, crime has no meaning unless people react to it, labeling perpetrators as deviant and setting them on a course of sustained criminal activity. The one-time criminal, if not caught or labeled, can simply return to a "normal" way of life with little permanent damage—the college student who tries marijuana does not view himself, nor do others view him, as a criminal or a drug addict. Only when prohibited acts are recognized and sanctioned do they become important, life-transforming events.

Connections

Because of the damage it does, interactionists believe that society should intervene as little as possible in the lives of law violators lest they be labeled and stigmatized. Labeling theory, discussed in Chapter 8, is based on interactionist views and holds that the application of negative labels leads first to a damaged identity and then to a criminal career.

Defining Crime

The consensus view of crime dominated criminological thought until the late 1960s. Criminologists devoted themselves to learning why lawbreakers violated the rules of society. The criminal was viewed as an outlaw who, for one reason or another, flaunted the rules defining acceptable conduct and behavior. In the 1960s, the interactionist perspective gained prominence. The rapid change U.S. society was experiencing made traditional law and values questionable. Many criminologists were swept along in the social revolution of the 1960s and likewise embraced an ideology that suggested that crimes reflected rules imposed by a conservative majority on nonconforming members of society. At the same time, more radical scholars gravitated toward conflict explanations (see Figure 1.4).

Today, each position still has many followers. This is important because criminologists' personal definitions of crime dominate their thinking, research, and attitudes toward their profession. Because they view crime differently, criminologists have taken a variety of approaches in explaining its causes and suggesting methods for its control. Considering these differences, it is possible to take elements from each school of thought to formulate an integrated definition of crime:

Crime is a violation of societal rules of behavior as interpreted and expressed by a criminal legal code created by people holding social and political power. Individuals who violate these rules are subject to sanctions by state authority, social stigma, and loss of status.

This definition combines the consensus view's position that the criminal law defines crimes with the conflict perspective's emphasis on political power and control and the interactionist view's concepts of stigma. Thus, crime as defined here is a political, social, and economic function of modern life.

Doing Criminology

Criminologists have used a wide variety of research techniques to measure the nature and extent of criminal behavior. To understand and evaluate theories and patterns of criminal behavior, it is important to develop some knowledge of how these data are collected. It is also important to understand the methods used in criminology, as this understanding provides insight into how professional criminologists approach various problems and questions in their field.

Survey Research

A great deal of crime measurement is based on analysis of survey data. Surveys include interviewing or questioning a group of subjects about the research topics under consideration. This method is also referred to as **cross-sectional research,** since it involves the simultaneous measurement of subjects in a sample who come from different backgrounds and groups (that is, a cross-section of the community). Most surveys involve *sampling*—selecting for study a limited number of subjects who are representative of entire groups sharing similar characteristics, called *populations.* For example, a criminologist might interview a sample of 3,000 prison inmates drawn from the population of more than 1 million inmates in the United States; in this case, the sample represents the entire population of U.S. inmates. Or a sample of burglary incidents could be taken from Miami; here, the sample would represent the population of Miami burglaries. It is assumed that the characteristics of people or events in a carefully selected sample will be quite similar to those of the population at large.

Survey research can be designed to measure the attitudes, beliefs, values, personality traits, and behavior of participants. Self-report surveys ask participants to describe in detail their recent and lifetime criminal activity; victimization surveys seek information from people who have been victims of crime; attitude surveys may measure the attitudes, beliefs, and values of various groups, such as prostitutes, students, drug addicts, police officers, judges, or juvenile delinquents.

The cross-sectional survey is one of the most widely used methods of criminological study. It is an excellent and cost-effective technique for measuring the characteristics of large numbers of people. Because questions and methods are standardized for all subjects, uniformity is unaffected by the perceptions or biases of the person gathering the data. The statistical analysis of data from carefully drawn samples enables researchers to generalize their findings from small groups to large populations. Though surveys measure subjects at a single point in their life span, questions can elicit information on subjects' prior behavior as well as their future goals and aspirations.[37]

Net Bookmark

How is research conducted in criminology? Large-scale projects are often conducted by private agencies that provide resources and expertise. The Vera Institute of Justice is a private nonprofit organization dedicated to making government politics and practices more humane, fair, and efficient. Vera works with government and local communities to expand the practice of justice.

http://broadway.vera.org/index.html

Despite their utility, surveys are not without their problems. Since they typically involve a single measurement, they are of limited value in showing how subjects change over time. In addition, surveys have been criticized because they assume that subjects will be honest and forthright. Though efforts are usually made to ensure the validity of questionnaire items, it is difficult to guard against people who either deliberately lie and misrepresent information or are unsure of answers and give mistaken responses. Surveys of delinquents and criminals are especially suspect, as they rely on the willingness of a group of people not known for their candor about intimate and personal matters. Surveys are also limited when the area to be studied involves the way people interact with one another or involves other topics an individual may not be able to judge personally, such as how he or she is perceived by significant others. Despite these drawbacks, surveys continue to be an extremely popular method of gathering criminological data.

Longitudinal (Cohort) Research

Longitudinal (cohort) research involves the observation of a **cohort**—a group of people who share a like characteristic—over time. For example, researchers might select all girls born in Albany, New York, in 1970 and then follow their behavior patterns for 20 years. The research data might include their school experiences, arrests, and hospitalizations, and information about their family life (divorces, parental relations). The subjects might be given repeated intelligence and physical exams; their diets could be monitored. Data could be collected directly from the subjects or without their knowledge from schools, police, and other sources. If the research were carefully conducted, it might be possible to determine which life experiences, such as growing up in a broken home or failing at school, typically preceded the onset of crime and delinquency.

Since it is extremely difficult, expensive, and time-consuming to follow a cohort over time and since most of the sample do not become serious criminals, another approach is to take an intact cohort of known offenders and look back into their early life experiences by checking their educational, family, police, and hospital records; this format is known as a retrospective cohort study.[38]

To carry out cohort studies, criminologists frequently use records of social organizations, such as hospitals, schools, welfare departments, courts, police departments, and prisons. School records contain data on a student's academic performance, attendance, intelligence, disciplinary problems, and teacher ratings. Hospitals record incidents of drug use and suspicious wounds indicative of child abuse. Police files contain reports of criminal activity, arrest data, personal information on suspects, victim reports, and actions taken by police officers. Court records allow researchers to compare the personal characteristics of offenders with the outcomes of their court appearances—conviction rates and types of sentences. Prison records contain information on inmates' personal characteristics, adjustment problems, disciplinary records, rehabilitation efforts, and length of sentence served.

Connections

Some critical criminological research has been based on cohort studies. Some of the most important research has been conducted by University of Pennsylvania criminologist Marvin Wolfgang and his colleagues. Their findings have been instrumental in developing knowledge about the onset and development of a criminal career. Wolfgang's cohort research is discussed in Chapter 2.

Aggregate Data Research

Criminologists also make use of large databases gathered by government agencies and research foundations. U.S. Census Bureau data, Labor Department employment data, reports of state correctional departments, and so on have all been used by criminologists in their research. The most important of these sources is the Uniform Crime Report (UCR), compiled by the Federal Bureau of Investigation (FBI).[39] The UCR is an annual report that reflects the number of crimes reported by citizens to local police departments and the number of arrests made by police agencies in a given year. The UCR is probably the most important source of official crime statistics and will be discussed more completely in Chapter 3.

Aggregate data can be used to focus on the social forces that affect crime. For example, to study the relationship between crime and poverty, criminologists make use of data collected by the Census Bureau on income and the number of people on welfare and single-parent families in an urban area and then cross-reference this information with official crime statistics from the same locality. Aggregate data can tell us about the effect of overall social trends and patterns on the crime rate.

Experimental Research

To conduct experimental research, criminologists manipulate or intervene in the lives of their subjects to see the outcome or effect the intervention has. True experiments usually have three elements: (1) random selection of subjects; (2) a control or comparison group; and (3) an experimental condition. For example, experimental research might involve a sample of convicted felons who have been sentenced to prison. Some of the sample, chosen at random, would be asked to participate in a community-based treatment program. A follow-up could then determine whether those placed in the community program were less likely to recidivate (repeat their offenses) than those who served time in the correctional institution.

A quasi-experiment is undertaken when it is impossible to randomly select subjects or manipulate conditions. For example, researchers may want to measure the change in driving fatalities and drunk driving arrests brought about by a new state law creating mandatory jail sentences for persons convicted of driving while intoxicated (DWI). Since they cannot ask police to randomly arrest drunk drivers, they can compare the state's DWI arrest and fatality trends with those of nearby states that have more lenient DWI statutes. While not a true experiment, this approach would give an indication of the effectiveness of mandatory sentences, since the states are comparable except for their drunk driving legislation.

Another approach, referred to as a time-series design, would be to record statewide DWI arrest and fatality data for the months and years preceding and following passage of the mandatory jail statute. The effectiveness of mandatory jail terms as a deterrent to DWI would be supported if a drop in the arrest and fatality rates coincided with the bill's adoption.

Criminological experiments are relatively rare because they are difficult and expensive to conduct; they involve the manipulation of subjects' lives, which can cause ethical and legal roadblocks; and they require long follow-up periods to verify results. Nonetheless, they have been an important source of criminological data.

Observational and Interview Research

Sometimes criminologists focus their research on relatively few subjects, interviewing them in depth or observing them as they go about their activities. This research often obtains the kind of in-depth data absent in large-scale surveys. For example, a recent study by Claire Sterck-Elifson focused on the lives of middle-class female drug abusers.[40] The 34 interviews she conducted provide insight into a group whose behavior might not be captured in a large-scale survey. Sterck-Elifson found that these women were introduced to cocaine at first "just for fun": "I do drugs," one 34-year-old lawyer told her, "because I like the feeling. I would never let drugs take over my life."[41] Unfortunately, a number later lost control of their habit and suffered both emotional and financial stress.

Another common criminological method is the first-hand observation of criminals to gain insight into their motives and activities. This may involve going into the field and participating in group activities, such as was done in William Whyte's famous study of a Boston gang, *Street Corner Society*.[42] Other observers conduct field studies but remain in the background, observing but not being part of the ongoing activity.[43]

Still another type of observation involves bringing subjects into a structured laboratory setting and observing how they react to a predetermined condition or stimulus. This approach is common in studies testing the effect of observational learning on aggressive behavior, such as exposing subjects to violent films and then observing their subsequent behavioral changes.[44]

Criminology thus relies on many of the basic research methods common to other fields, including sociology, psychology, and political science. Multiple methods are needed to ensure that the goals of criminological inquiry can be achieved.

Ethical Issues in Criminology

A critical issue facing students of criminology is recognizing the field's political and social consequences. All too often, criminologists forget the social responsibility they bear as experts in the area of crime and justice. When acted on by government agencies, their pronouncements and opinions become the basis for sweeping social policy. The lives of millions of people can be influenced by criminological research data. We have witnessed many debates over gun control, capital punishment, and mandatory sentences. While some criminologists have successfully argued for social service, treatment, and rehabilitation programs to reduce the crime rate, others consider them a waste of time, suggesting instead that a massive prison construction program coupled with tough criminal sentences can bring the crime rate down. By holding themselves up to be experts on law-violating behavior, criminologists place themselves in a position of power; the potential consequences of their actions are enormous. Therefore, they must be aware of the ethics of their profession and prepared to defend their work in the light of public scrutiny. Major ethical issues include what is to be studied, who is to be studied, and how studies are to be conducted.

Under ideal circumstances, when criminologists choose a subject for study, they are guided by their own scholarly interests, pressing social needs, the availability of accurate data, and other, similar concerns. Nonetheless, in recent years a great influx of government and institutional funding has influenced the direction of criminological inquiry. Major sources of monetary support include the Justice Department's National Institute of Justice and the Office of Juvenile Justice and Delinquency Prevention. Both the National Science Foundation and the National Institute of Mental Health have been prominent sources of government funding. Private foundations, such as the Edna McConnell Clark Foundation, have also played an important role in supporting criminological research.

Though the availability of research money has spurred criminological inquiry, it has also influenced the directions research has taken. Since state and federal governments provide a significant percentage of available research funds, they may also dictate the areas that can be studied. In recent years, for example, the federal government has spent millions of dollars funding long-term cohort studies of criminal careers. Academic researchers are prompted to study criminal careers because that's the area where funding is available. Other areas of inquiry may be ignored because there are simply no funds to pay for or sponsor the research.

A potential conflict of interest may arise when the institution funding research is itself one of the principal subjects of the research project. For example, governments may be reluctant to fund research on fraud and abuse of power by government officials. They may also exert a not-so-subtle influence on the criminologists seeking research funding: If criminologists are too critical of the government's efforts to reduce or counteract crime, perhaps they will be barred from receiving further financial help. This situation is even more acute when we consider that criminologists typically work for universities or public agencies and are under pressure to bring in a steady flow of research funds or to maintain the continued viability of their agency. Even when criminologists maintain discretion of choice, the direction of their efforts may not be truly objective.

A second major ethical issue in criminology concerns who is to be the subject of inquiries and study. Too often, criminologists have focused their attention on the poor and minorities while ignoring the middle-class criminal, white-collar crime, organized crime, and government crime. Critics have charged that by "unmasking" the poor and desperate, criminologists have justified any harsh measures taken against them. For example, a few social scientists have suggested that criminals have lower intelligence quotients than the average citizen and that because minority group members have lower-than-average IQ scores, their crime rates are high.[45] This was the conclusion reached in *The Bell Curve*, a popular though highly controversial book written by Richard Herrnstein and Charles Murray.[46] Though such research is often methodologically unsound, it can focus attention on the criminality of one element of the community while ignoring others. Is it ethical for criminologists to publish highly tentative research findings and ignore the social harm they may cause?

Also, subjects are often misled about the purpose of the research. When white and African American youngsters are asked to participate in a survey of their behavior or take an IQ test, they are rarely told in advance that the data they provide may later be used to prove the existence of significant racial differences in their self-reported crime rates. Should subjects be told what the true purpose of a survey is? Would such disclosures make meaningful research impossible? How far should criminologists go when collecting data? Is it ever permissible to deceive subjects to collect data?

Summary

Criminology is the scientific approach to the study of criminal behavior and society's reaction to law violations and violators. It is essentially an interdisciplinary field; many of its practitioners were originally trained as sociologists, psychologists, economists, political scientists, historians, and natural scientists.

A number of fields are related to criminology. In the late 1960s, criminal justice programs were created to examine and improve the U.S. system of justice. Today, many criminologists work in criminal justice educational programs. Criminology and criminal justice are mutually dedicated to understanding the nature and control of criminal behavior. The study of deviant behavior also overlaps with criminology because many "deviant" acts, but not all, are violations of the criminal law.

Criminology has a rich history with roots in the utilitarian philosophy of Beccaria, the biological positivism of Lombroso, the social theory of Durkheim, and the political philosophy of Marx.

Included among the various subareas that make up the criminological enterprise are criminal statistics, the sociology of law, theory construction, criminal behavior systems, penology, and victimology.

In viewing crime, criminologists use one of three perspectives: the consensus view, the conflict view, or the interactionist view. The consensus view is that crime is illegal behavior defined by the existing criminal law, which reflects the values and morals of a majority of citizens. The conflict view is that crime is behavior created so that economically powerful individuals can retain their control over society. The interactionist view portrays criminal behavior as a relativistic, constantly changing concept that reflects society's current moral values. According to the interactionist view, criminal behavior is behavior so labeled by those in power; criminals are people society chooses to label as outsiders or deviants.

Criminologists use a variety of research methods. These include cross-sectional surveys, longitudinal cohort studies, experiments, and observations. In doing research, criminologists must be concerned about ethical standards because their findings can have a significant impact on individuals and groups.

Key Terms

intimate violence
criminologists
criminology
criminal justice system
deviant behavior
legalization
decriminalization
utilitarianism
classical criminology
positivism
criminal anthropology

atavistic anomalies
anomie
Chicago school
bourgeoisie
proletariat
criminological enterprise
white-collar crime
moral entrepreneurs
cross-sectional research
longitudinal research
cohort

Notes

1. Jerry Adler, "Young, in Love, in Jail," *Newsweek* 23 September 1996, p. 63; Sue Anne Pressley, "In Texas, Twisted Tale of Love, Murder," *Boston Globe* 15 September 1996, p. A8.

2. See, generally, Joel Milner, ed., "Special Issue: Physical Child Abuse," *Criminal Justice and Behavior* 18 (1991); Russell Dobash, R. Emerson Dobash, Margo Wilson, and Martin Daly, "The Myth of Sexual Symmetry in Marital Violence," *Social Problems* 39 (1992): 71–86; Martin Schwartz and Walter DeKeseredy, "The Return of the 'Battered Husband Syndrome': Typification of Women as Violent," *Crime, Law and Social Change* 4 (1993): 37–43.

3. Pressley, "In Texas, Twisted Tale of Love, Murder," p. A8.

4. For a thorough review, see Robin Malinosky-Rummell and David Hansen, "Long-Term Consequences of Childhood Physical Abuse," *Psychological Bulletin* 114 (1993): 68–79.

5. Roper Poll, in Kathleen Maguire, Ann Pastore, and Timothy Flanagan, *Sourcebook of Criminal Justice Statistics 1995* (Washington, D.C.: U.S. Government Printing Office, 1996), p. 153.

6. Edwin Sutherland and Donald Cressey, *Principles of Criminology,* 6th ed. (Philadelphia: J. B. Lippincott, 1960), p. 3.

7. For a review of the development of criminal justice as a field of study, see Frank Remington, "Development of Criminal Justice as an Academic Field," *Journal of Criminal Justice Education* 1 (1990): 9–20.

8. Marvin Zalman, *A Heuristic Model of Criminology and Criminal Justice* (Chicago: Joint Commission on Criminology Education and Standards, University of Illinois, Chicago Circle, 1981), pp. 9–11.

9. Charles McCaghy, *Deviant Behavior* (New York: Macmillan, 1976), pp. 2–3.

10. Edward Brecher, *Licit and Illicit Drugs* (Boston: Little, Brown, 1972), pp. 413–416.

11. Ibid., p. 414.

12. Eugen Weber, *A Modern History of Europe* (New York: W. W. Norton, 1971), p. 398.

13. Marvin Wolfgang, *Patterns in Criminal Homicide* (Philadelphia: University of Pennsylvania Press, 1958).

14. Described in David Lykken, "Psychopathy, Sociopathy, and Crime," *Society* 34 (1996): 29–38.

15. See Peter Scott, "Henry Maudsley," in *Pioneers in Criminology,* ed. Hermann Mannheim (Montclair, N.J.: Prentice-Hall, 1981).

16. Howard Becker, *Outsiders: Studies in the Sociology of Deviance* (New York: Free Press, 1963), p. 21.

17. Ibid., p. 9.

18. Nicole Hahn Rafter, "Criminal Anthropology in the United States," *Criminology* 30 (1992): 525–547.

19. Ibid., p. 535.

20. L. A. J. Quetelet, *A Treatise on Man and the Development of His Faculties* (Gainesville, Fla.: Scholars' Facsimiles and Reprints, 1969), pp. 82–96.

21. Ibid., p. 85.

22. See, generally, Robert Nisbet, *The Sociology of Emile Durkheim* (New York: Oxford University Press, 1974), p. 209.

23. Emile Durkheim, *Rules of the Sociological Method*, trans. S. A. Solvay and J. H. Mueller, ed. G. Catlin (New York: Free Press, 1966), pp. 65–73; Emile Durkheim, *De la Division de Travail Social: Étude sur L'organisation des Societies Superieures* (Paris: Felix Alcan, 1893); idem, *The Division of Labor in Society* (New York: Free Press, 1964); idem, *Suicide: A Study in Sociology* (Glencoe, Ill.: Free Press, 1951).

24. Robert Park and Ernest Burgess, *The City* (Chicago: University of Chicago Press, 1925).

25. Karl Marx and Friedrich Engels, *Capital: A Critique of Political Economy,* trans. E. Aveling (Chicago: Charles Kern, 1906); Karl Marx, *Selected Writings in Sociology and Social Philosophy,* trans. P. B. Bottomore (New York: McGraw-Hill, 1956). For a general discussion of Marxist thought, see Michael Lynch and W. Byron Groves, *A Primer in Radical Criminology* (New York: Harrow and Heston, 1986), pp. 6–26.

26. Willem Bonger, *Criminality and Economic Conditions* (1916, abridged ed., Bloomington: Indiana University Press, 1969); Ralf Dahrendorf, *Class and Class Conflict in Industrial Society* (Palo Alto, Calif.: Stanford University Press, 1959).

27. Marvin Wolfgang and Franco Ferracuti, *The Subculture of Violence* (London: Social Science Paperbacks, 1967), p. 20.

28. Associated Press, "Michigan Senate Acts to Outlaw Aiding Suicides," *Boston Globe,* 20 March 1994, p. 22.

29. Wolfgang, *Patterns in Criminal Homicide.*

30. Hans von Hentig, *The Criminal and His Victim* (New Haven, Conn.: Yale University Press, 1948); Stephen Schafer, *The Victim and His Criminal* (New York: Random House, 1968).

31. Sutherland and Cressey, *Criminology,* p. 8.

32. Eugene Doleschal and Nora Klapmuts, "Toward a New Criminology," *Crime and Delinquency* 5 (1973): 607.

33. Michael Lynch and W. Byron Groves, *A Primer in Radical Criminology* (Albany, N.Y.: Harrow and Heston, 1989), p. 32.

34. See Herbert Blumer, *Symbolic Interactionism* (Englewood Cliffs, N.J.: Prentice-Hall, 1969).

35. Becker, *Outsiders,* p. 9.

36. Ibid.

37. Michael Gottfredson and Travis Hirschi, "The Methodological Adequacy of Longitudinal Research on Crime," *Criminology* 25 (1987): 581–614.

38. See, generally, David Farrington, Lloyd Ohlin, and James Q. Wilson, *Understanding and Controlling Crime* (New York: Springer-Verlag, 1986), pp. 11–18.

39. Federal Bureau of Investigation, *Crime in the United States, 1995* (Washington, D.C.: U.S. Government Printing Office, 1996).

40. Claire Sterck-Elifson, "Just for Fun? Cocaine Use Among Middle-Class Women," *Journal of Drug Issues* 26 (1996): 63–76.

41. Ibid., p. 63.

42. William F. Whyte, *Street Corner Society* (Chicago: University of Chicago Press, 1955).

43. Herman Schwendinger and Julia Schwendinger, *Adolescent Subcultures and Delinquency* (New York: Praeger, 1985).

44. For a review of these studies, see L. Rowell Huesmann and Neil Malamuth, eds., "Media Violence and Antisocial Behavior," *Journal of Social Issues* 42 (1986): 31–53.

45. See, for example, Michael Hindelang and Travis Hirschi, "Intelligence and Delinquency: A Revisionist Review," *American Sociological Review* 42 (1977): 471–486.

46. Richard Herrnstein and Charles Murray, *The Bell Curve* (New York: Free Press, 1994).

Chapter 2
The Criminal Law and Its Processes

t he criminal law controls the definition and content of crime. Developed over many generations, it incorporates historical traditions, moral beliefs, and social values, as well as political and economic developments and conditions. The criminal law is a living concept, constantly evolving to keep pace with society. It governs the form and direction of almost all human interaction. Business practices, family life, education, property transfer, inheritance, and other common forms of social relations must conform to the rules set out by the legal code. Most important for our purposes, the law defines the behaviors that society labels as criminal. Consequently, it is important for students of criminology to have a basic understanding of the law and its relationship to crime and deviance. This chapter will review the nature and purpose of the law, chart its history, and discuss its elements.

Net Bookmark

Those of you who read this chapter may become interested in pursuing a legal career. The American Bar Association Criminal Justice Section CJS On-Line provides downloadable Association policy statements, as well as other reports and publications relevant to criminal justice practice and research.

http://www.abanet.org/crimjust/home.html

The Origins of Law

We know that crimes and criminal behavior were recognized in many early societies.[1] In preliterate societies, common custom and tradition (mores and folkways) were the equivalents of law. Each group had its own set of customs, which were created to deal with situations that arose in daily living. These customs would often be followed long after the reason for their origin was forgotten. Many customs had the force of law, and eventually some developed into formal or written law.

Early Legal Codes

The concept of crime was recognized in the earliest surviving legal codes. One of the first was developed in about 2000 B.C. by King Dungi of Sumer (an area that is part of present-day Iraq). Its content is known today because it was later adopted by Hammurabi (1792–1750 B.C.), the sixth king of Babylon, in his famous set of written laws today known as the Code of Hammurabi. Preserved on basalt rock columns, the code set out crimes and their correction. Punishment was based on physical retaliation, or lex talionis ("an eye for an eye"). The severity of punishment depended on class standing: for assault, slaves would be put to death; freemen might lose a limb.

Babylonian laws were strictly enforced by judges who were themselves controlled by advisers to the king. Such

Connections

While not exactly an "eye for an eye," efforts are now being made to make punishments fit the crime. See the sections on "just desert" in Chapter 5 for more on the view that crimes and punishment should be closely aligned.

crimes as burglary and theft were common in ancient Babylon, and officials had to take their duties seriously. Local officials were expected to apprehend criminals. If they failed in their duties, they had to personally replace lost property; if murderers were not caught, the responsible official paid a fine to the deceased's relatives.

Another of the ancient legal codes still surviving is the Mosaic Code of the Israelites (1200 B.C.). According to tradition, God entered into a covenant or contract with the tribes of Israel in which they agreed to obey his law, as presented to them by Moses, in return for God's special care and protection. The Mosaic Code is not only the foundation of Judeo-Christian moral teachings, but it also is a basis for the U.S. legal system: Prohibitions against murder, theft, perjury, and adultery precede by several thousand years the same laws found in the U.S. legal system.

Also surviving is the Roman law contained in the Twelve Tables (451 B.C.). The Twelve Tables were formulated by a special commission of ten men in response to pressure from the lower classes (plebeians). The plebeians believed that an unwritten code gave arbitrary and unlimited power to the wealthy classes (patricians) who served as magistrates. The original code was written on bronze plaques, which have been lost, but records of sections, which were memorized by every Roman male, survive. The remaining laws deal with debt, family relations, property, and other daily matters. A sample section of this code is set out in Table 2.1.

The Dark Ages

The early formal legal codes were lost during the Dark Ages, which lasted for hundreds of years after the fall of

Table 2.1 Table VIII of the Twelve Tables: Torts or Delicts

If any person has sung or composed against another person a song such as was causing slander or insult to another, he shall be clubbed to death. If a person has maimed another's limb, let there be retaliation in kind unless he makes agreement for settlement with him. Any person who destroys by burning any building or heap of corn deposited alongside a house shall be bound, scourged, and put to death by burning at the stake, provided that he has committed the said misdeed with malice aforethought; but if he shall have committed it by accident, that is, by negligence, it is ordained that he repair the damage, or, if he be too poor to be competent for such punishment, he shall receive a lighter chastisement.

Rome. During this period, superstition and fear of magic and satanic black arts dominated thinking.

Some attempts were made at regulating the definition and punishments of crime during the early feudal period. Those that still exist indicate that monetary payments were the main punishments for crimes. Some early German and Anglo-Saxon societies developed legal systems featuring compensation (**wergild**) for criminal violations. For example, under the legal code of the Salic Franks, killing a free-woman of childbearing age was punished by wergild in the amount of 24,000 denars; if the woman was past childbearing age, the wergild was reduced to 8,000 denars.

Guilt was determined by ordeals, such as having the accused place his or her hand in boiling water or hold a hot iron to see whether God would intervene and heal the wounds. It was also possible to challenge one's accuser to a duel, the outcome determining the legitimacy of the accusation (trial by combat). Guilt could be disputed with the aid of **oath-helpers**, groups of 12 to 25 people who would support the accused's innocence.

Despite such "reforms," up until the 18th century the systems of crime, punishment, law, and justice were chaotic. The law was controlled by the lords of the great manors, who tried cases according to local custom and rule. Although there was general agreement that such acts as theft, assault, treason, and blasphemy constituted crimes, the penalties on law violators were often arbitrary, discretionary, and cruel. Punishments included public flogging, branding, beheading, and burning. Peasants who violated the rule of their masters were violently put down. According to a 14th-century Norman chronicle, disobedient peasants or those who stole from their masters were treated harshly: Some had their teeth pulled out, others were impaled, had their eyes torn out, their hands cut off, their ankles charred; others were burned alive or plunged in boiling lead.[2] Even simple wanderers and vagabonds were viewed as dangerous and subject to these extreme penalties.

Origins of Common Law

Because the ancient legal codes had been lost during the Middle Ages, the concept of law and crime was chaotic, guided by superstition and local custom. Slowly, in England, a common law developed that helped standardize law and justice. The foundation of law in the United States is the English common law.

Before the Norman Conquest in 1066, the legal system among the Anglo-Saxons in England, like elsewhere in Europe, was decentralized. Each county (**shire**) was divided into units called **hundreds,** which were groups of 100 families. Each hundred was further divided into groups of ten called **tithings**. Each tithings were responsible for maintaining order among themselves and dealing with disturbances, fires, wild animals, and so on.

Petty cases were tried by courts of the hundred group, the **hundred-gemot.** More serious and important cases could be heard by an assemblage of local landholders, or the **shire-gemot,** or by the local nobleman, the **hali-gemot;** if the act concerned in any way spiritual matters, it could be judged by clergymen and church officials in courts known as holy-motes or ecclesiastics. Therefore, the law varied in substance from county to county, hundred to hundred, and tithing to tithing.

CRIME AND CUSTOM. Crimes during this period were viewed as personal wrongs, and compensation therefore was often paid to the victims. If payment was not made, the victims' families would attempt to forcibly collect damages or seek revenge. The result could be a blood feud between two families. The recognized crimes included treason, homicide, rape, property theft, assault (putting another in fear), and battery (wounding another). For treasonous acts, the punishment was death. Theft during the Anglo-Saxon era could result in slavery for the thieves and their families. If caught in the act of fleeing with the stolen goods, the thief could be killed.

For many other acts, including both theft and violence, compensation could be paid to the victim. For example, even a homicide could be settled by paying wergild to the deceased's family, unless the crime was carried out by poison or ambush—in which case, it was punished by death. Eventually, wergild was divided so that of the sum (*bot*) paid, part (*wer*) went to the king, and the remainder (*wite*) went to the victim or, in the case of death, the deceased's kin.

A scale of compensation existed for lesser injuries, such as the loss of an arm or an eye. Important persons, churchmen, and nuns received greater restitution than the general population, and they paid more if they were the criminal defendant (*wer* means "worth" and referred to what the person, and therefore the crime, was worth). The nobility began to see the value in the wer, and it became the predominant portion of the bot; it was the precursor of the modern-day criminal fine. To a great degree, criminal law was designed to provide an equitable solution to what was considered a private dispute.

THE NORMAN CONQUEST. After the Norman Conquest in 1066, William the Conqueror, the Norman leader, did not immediately change the substance of Anglo-Saxon law. At the outset of William's reign, justice was administered as it had been in previous centuries. The church courts handled acts that might be considered sin, and the local hundred or manor courts (referred to as **court-leet**) dealt with most secular violations. However, to secure control of the countryside and to ensure military supremacy over his newly won lands, William replaced the local tribunals with royal administrators who dealt with the most serious breaches of the peace.

Because the royal administrators could not constantly be present in each community, a system was developed in

Trial by fire was a common practice during the Middle Ages. Guilt was determined by ordeals, such as having the accused place his or her hand in boiling water or hold a hot iron to see if God would intervene and heal the wounds. This painting illustrates an account given by the 12th century historian Godfrey of Viterbo. A count in the court of Holy Roman Emperor Otto the III (890–1002) was accused and executed for adultery with the Empress. Otto forced her to undergo trial by fire. She is shown here holding a piece of red-hot metal that has been heated in the fire at her feet. When her hand is burned, the test "proves" her guilt. Her burning at the stake is shown at the top of the panel.

In early medieval Europe and England, disputed criminal charges were often decided by an ordeal. In a trial by fire, the accused individuals would have a hot iron placed in their hand, and if the wound did not heal properly, it was considered proof of their guilt. In a trial by combat, the defendant could challenge his accuser to a duel; the accuser had the option of finding an alternate to fight in his place.

Settling trials by ordeal fell out of favor when the Catholic Church, at the Fourth Lateran Council (1215), decreed that priests could no longer participate in trials by ordeal. Without the use of the ordeal in "disputed" criminal cases, courts both in England and in the rest of Europe were not sure how to proceed.

In England, the Church ban on ordeal meant that a new method of deciding criminal trials needed to be developed. To fill the gap, British justices adapted a method that had long been used to determine real estate taxes. Since the time of William the Conqueror, 12 knights in each district had been called before an "in-quest" of the king's justices to give local tax information. Instead of the slow determination of feudal taxes by judges, these "twelve free and lawful men of the neighbourhood" would view the land and testify as to who last had peaceful possession so that an accurate accounting could be made. Since they were available when the king's justices were present on circuit, the Writ of Novel Disseisin, first established in 1166 under Henry II, also required them to settle "claim jumping" disputes over land.

By 1219, the jury (from the Latin term *jurati*, to be sworn) called to decide land cases also began to hear criminal cases. At first, jurors were like witnesses, telling the judge what they knew about the case; these courts were known as assise or assize (from the Latin *assideo*, to sit together). By the 14th century, jurors had become the deciders of fact. Over the centuries, the English jury came to be seen as a check on the government. The great case that established the principle of jury independence, *Bushell's* case (1670), arose when a London jury acquitted William Penn, a leading Quaker and later the founder of Pennsylvania, of unlawful assembly in connection with his preaching in the street after a Quaker church was padlocked. The jurors were imprisoned by an angry royalist judge. They were freed when British Chief Judge Vaughn held that unless a jury were corrupt, they were free to reach a verdict based on the evidence, or else the jury would be nothing but a rubber stamp and useless.

CRITICAL THINKING QUESTIONS

1. Do you think that the common-law development of a jury trial is relevant in today's world?

2. Should a jury of one's peers be replaced by professionals who are schooled in the law?

Source: Marvin Zalman and Larry Siegel, *Criminal Procedure, Constitution and Society* (St. Paul: West Publishing, 1991).

---

which they traveled in a circuit throughout the land, holding court in each county several times a year. When court was in session, the royal administrator, or judge, would summon a number of citizens who would, on their oath, tell of the crimes and serious breaches of the peace that had occurred since the judge's last visit. The royal judge would then decide what to do in each case, using local custom and rules of conduct as his guide. If, for example, a local freeholder was convicted of theft, he might be executed if those before him had suffered that fate for a similar offense. However, if in previous cases the thief had been forced to make restitution to the victim, then *that* judgment would be rendered in the current case. This system, known as ***stare decisis*** (Latin for "to stand by decided cases"), was used by the early courts to determine the outcome of future cases; courts were bound to follow the law established in previously decided cases unless the law was overruled by a higher authority, such as the king or the pope.

The current English system of law came into existence during the reign of Henry II (1154–1189). Henry also used traveling judges, better known as circuit judges. These judges followed a specific route known as a circuit and heard cases that had previously been under the jurisdiction of local courts. Juries, which began to develop about this time, were groups of local landholders whom the judges called not only to decide the facts of cases but also to investigate the crimes, accuse suspected offenders, and even give testimony at trials (see the Close-Up "Origin of the Jury Trial"). Gradually, royal prosecutors came into being. These representatives of the Crown submitted evidence and brought witnesses to testify before the jury. But not until much later was the accused in a criminal action allowed to bring forth witnesses to rebut charges; and not until the 18th century were witnesses required to take oaths. Few formal procedures existed, and both the judge and the prosecutor felt free to intimidate witnesses and jurors when they considered it necessary. The development of these routine judicial processes heralded the beginnings of the common law.

The Common Law

As it is used today, the term **common law** refers to a law applied to all subjects of the land, without regard for geographic or social differences. As best they could, Henry's judges began to apply a national law instead of the law that held sway in local jurisdictions. This attempt was somewhat confused at first, from having to take into account both local custom and the Norman conquerors' feudal law. However, as new situations arose, judges took advantage of legal uncertainty by either inventing new solutions or borrowing from the laws of European countries. During formal and informal gatherings, the circuit judges shared these incidents, talked about unique cases, and discussed their decisions, thus developing an oral tradition of law. Later, as cases began to be written about, more concrete examples of common-law decisions began to emerge. Together, these cases and decisions filtered through the national court system and eventually produced a fixed body of legal rule and principles. Thus, common law is judge-made law, or case law. It is the law found in previously decided cases. Crimes such as murder, burglary, arson, and rape are common-law crimes—they were initially defined and created by judges.

Common Law and Statutory Law

The common law was and still is the law of the land in England. In most instances, the common law retained traditional Anglo-Saxon concepts. For example, the common law originally defined murder as the unlawful killing of another human being with malice aforethought.[3] By this definition, for offenders to be found guilty of murder, they must have (1) planned the crime and (2) intentionally killed the victim out of spite or hatred. However, this general definition proved inadequate to deal with the many situations in which one person took another's life. Over time, to bring the law closer to the realities of human behavior, English judges added other forms of murder: killing someone in the heat of passion, killing someone out of negligence, and killing someone in the course of committing another crime, such as during a robbery. Each form of murder was given a different title (manslaughter, felony murder, and so on) and provided with a different degree of punishment. Thus, the common law was a constantly evolving legal code.

> ### Connections
> Common-law practices still guide modern legal codes. For example, murder statutes still retain different degrees of seriousness based on the intent of the actor. Each degree is correlated with a level of punishment commensurate with its seriousness. The degrees of murder and other definitional issues are discussed in Chapter 11.

In some instances, the creation of a new common-law crime can be traced back to a particular case. For example, an unsuccessful attempt to commit an illegal act was not considered a crime under early common law. The modern doctrine that criminal attempt can be punished under law can be traced directly back to 1784 and the case of *Rex v. Scofield*. In that case, Scofield was charged with having put a lit candle and combustible material in a house he was renting, with the intention of burning it down; however, the house did not burn. Scofield defended himself by arguing that an attempt to commit a misdemeanor was not actually a misdemeanor. In rejecting this argument, the court stated: "The intent may make an act, innocent in itself, criminal; nor is the completion of an act, criminal in itself, necessary to constitute criminality."[4] After *Scofield*, attempt became a common-law crime, and today most U.S. jurisdictions have enacted some form of criminal attempt law (**inchoate crimes**).

When the situation required it, the English Parliament enacted legislation to supplement the judge-made common law. Violations of these laws are referred to as *statutory crimes*. For example, in 1723 the Waltham Black Act punished with death offenses against rural property, from the poaching of small game to arson, if the criminal was armed or disguised.[5] Moreover, the act eroded the rights of the accused; it allowed the death sentence to be carried out without a trial if the accused failed to surrender when ordered to do so. The underlying purpose of the act was Parliament's desire to control the behavior of peasants whose poverty forced them to poach on royal lands. In the Black Act, then, the British ruling class created a mechanism for protecting its property and position of social power. Statutory laws usually reflect existing social conditions. They deal with issues of morality, such as gambling, sexual activity, and drug-related offenses. For example, a whole series of statutory laws, such as those concerning embezzlement and fraud, were created to protect the well-being of British, and later U.S., business enterprise.[6]

Common Law in America

Before the American Revolution, the colonies, then under British rule, were subject to the law handed down by English judges. After the colonies acquired their independence, they adapted and changed the English law to fit their needs. In many states, legislatures standardized such common-law crimes as murder, burglary, arson, and rape by putting them into statutory form. In other states, comprehensive penal codes were passed, thus abolishing the common-law crimes. Today few states allow prosecution for common-law violations. Those that do, such as Michigan, allow prosecutions for acts that were crimes under the common law but for which no new statutes have been created.[7]

Conversion to statutory law allowed for the modification and modernizing of common-law principles. An example of this process can be found in the Massachusetts statute defining arson. The common-law definition of *arson* is "the malicious burning of the dwelling of another." Massachusetts has expanded this definition by passing legislation defining *arson* as "the willful and malicious setting fire to, or burning of, *any building or contents thereof even if they were burned by the owner.*"[8] (Emphasis added.)

As in England, whenever the common law proved inadequate to deal with changing social and moral issues, the states and Congress supplemented it with legislative statutes, creating new elements in the various state and federal legal codes. For example, early in the nation's history it was both legal and relatively easy to obtain narcotics, such as heroin, opium, and cocaine.[9] Their use became habits of the middle class. However, public and governmental concern arose over the use of narcotics by immigrants, such as the Chinese, who had come to the United States to build railroads and work in mines. Eventually, changes in public sentiment resulted in the 1914 passage of the Harrison Act, which outlawed trade in opium and its derivatives. Later, in 1937, pressure from federal law enforcement officials led to passage of the Marijuana Tax Act, which outlawed the sale or possession of that drug.

We can see in the case of marijuana how the statutory law is subject to change. When use of "pot" became widespread among the middle class in the 1960s, several states revised their laws and effectively decriminalized the possession of marijuana. The statutory law began to reflect the views of individual states' legislatures on the use of soft drugs by their citizens. In some states, marijuana possession is still punished by many years in prison; in others, by a small fine.

Common Law in Other Cultures

The British common-law tradition was imposed not only on the American colonies but also on its other overseas possessions, including its African colonies. In some instances, this has created a dual legal system divided between traditional tribal law and British common law. For example, Edna Erez and Bankole Thompson have described the conflict between traditional tribal and British common law in the African country of Sierra Leone.[10] According to Erez and Thompson, women in Sierra Leone are still considered the property of their fathers and later their husbands or heads of families. If a woman is raped, the case is usually brought to the customary courts, which handle complaints according to traditional tribal customs. If the accused is found to be guilty of sexual assault, referred to as "woman-damage," he will be forced to pay compensation to the victim's family. Because this is a property issue, consent of the victim is not important; the "damage" involves a trespass or misuse of "someone's property." The victim's story is usually accepted because the tribal custom is that a woman should confess a wrongful sexual act or else suffer divinely inspired ill fate and misfortune. After admitting guilt, the accused typically agrees to compensate either the husband or the victim's parents for the damage he caused. If the defendant refuses to admit guilt or pay damages, the case can be brought under the jurisdiction of the General Courts, which use British common law; the maximum penalty can be life in prison. Threat of complaint to the formal justice system is used as an incentive to settle the case according to tribal law and pay monetary penalties rather than face trial, conviction, and imprisonment. In Sierra Leone, British common law and the traditional tribal customs are often at cross-purposes. Yet the two systems can function together because each serves to maintain group norms.

Classification of Law

Law can be classified in a number of ways that can help us understand its nature and purpose. Three of the most important classifications are (1) crimes and torts, (2) felonies and misdemeanors, and (3) *mala in se* and *mala prohibitum.*

Crimes and Torts

Law can be divided into two broad categories: criminal law and civil law. Civil law is all law other than criminal law and includes such legal areas as property law (the law governing transfer and ownership of property) and contract law (the law of personal agreements). Of all areas of the civil law, **tort law** (the law of personal wrongs and damage) is most similar in intent and form to the criminal law.

A *tort* is a civil action in which an individual asks to be compensated for personal harm. The harm may be either physical or mental and includes such acts as trespass, assault and battery, invasion of privacy, libel (false and injurious writings), and slander (false and injurious statements). A tort can occur when someone is injured by the actions of another. As the O.J. Simpson civil trial illustrates, someone can be sued for damages even if he or she has been acquitted of a criminal act (the reason being that the standards of evidence for a finding are lower in civil cases).

A tort may also occur when a behavior is an indirect cause of injury—that is, when it sets off a chain of events that leads to injury or death. In 1990, for example, the families of two youths who had attempted suicide sued the heavy metal rock group Judas Priest and CBS Records because they claimed the group had put the subliminal message "Do it" in its albums to effect "mind control" over the band's fans. Though the group was vindicated, the judge ruled that its recordings were not protected by the First Amendment right to free speech if indeed they had carried privacy-invading mind-control messages.[11]

Because some torts are similar to some criminal acts, a person can possibly be held both criminally and civilly liable for one action. For example, if one man punches another, it is possible for the assailant not only to be charged by the state with assault and battery—and imprisoned if found guilty—but to be sued by the victim in a tort action of assault in which he could be required to pay monetary damages. In a 1993 Massachusetts case, Jennifer Hoult received an award of $500,000 from her father, David, after a federal court accepted her claim that he had raped her at least 3,000 times from the time she was a child of 4 until she reached age 16. The case is a milestone because the statute of limitations for bringing a tort action in a rape case was three years. However, in the *Hoult* case, the jury found that because the plaintiff had repressed her memory of the rapes, the statute of limitations did not start running until she had regained her memory through psychological therapy.[12]

Perhaps the most important similarity between criminal law and civil law is that they have a common purpose. Both attempt to control people's behavior by setting limits on what acts are permissible; both accomplish this through state-imposed sanctions.

Of course, there are also several differences between criminal law and civil law. First, the main purpose of criminal law is to give the state the power to protect the public from harm by punishing individuals whose actions threaten the social order. In tort law, the harm or injury is considered a private wrong, and the main concern is to compensate individuals for harm done to them by others.

In a criminal action, the state initiates the legal proceedings by bringing charges and prosecuting the violator. If it is determined that the criminal law has been broken, the state can impose punishment, such as imprisonment, probation (community supervision by the court), or a fine payable to the state. In a civil action, however, the injured person must initiate proceedings. In a successful action, the injured individual usually receives financial compensation for the harm done.

Another major difference is the burden of proof required to establish the defendant's liability. In criminal matters, the defendant's guilt must be proven beyond a reasonable doubt. This standard, while less than absolute certainty, means that the deciders of guilt, after considering the evidence presented to them, are entirely satisfied that the party is guilty as charged; if there is any doubt, they must find for the defendant. In a civil case, the defendant is required to pay damages if, by a *preponderance of the evidence,* the trier of fact finds that he or she committed the wrong. According to this doctrine, while both parties may share some blame, the defendant is at fault if he or she contributed more than 50% to the cause of the dispute. Establishing guilt by a preponderance of the evidence is easier than establishing it beyond a reasonable doubt.[13] Table 2.2 summarizes the differences and similarities between crimes and torts.

Felonies and Misdemeanors

In addition to being divided from civil law, criminal laws can be further classified as either felonies or misdemeanors. The distinction is based on seriousness: A **felony** (from the

term *felonia,* an act by which a vassal forfeited his fee) is a serious offense; a **misdemeanor** is a minor or petty crime. Such crimes as murder, rape, and burglary are felonies; such crimes as unarmed assault and battery, petty larceny, and disturbing the peace are misdemeanors. Most states distinguish between a felony and a misdemeanor on the basis of time sentenced and place of imprisonment. Under this model of classification, a felony is usually defined as a crime punishable by death or imprisonment for more than one year in a state prison; a misdemeanor is defined as a crime punished by less than a year in a local county jail or house of correction. Some common-law felonies and misdemeanors are defined in Table 2.3.

Mala in Se and Mala Prohibitum

It is also possible to classify crimes as *mala in se* or *mala prohibitum.* Some illegal acts, referred to as ***mala in se*** crimes, are rooted in the core values inherent in Western civilization. These "natural laws" are designed to control such behaviors as inflicting physical harm on others (assault, rape, murder), taking possessions that rightfully belong to another

Table 2.2 Comparison of Criminal and Tort Law	
SIMILARITIES	
Both criminal and tort law seek to control behavior.	
Both laws impose sanctions.	
Similar areas of legal action exist—for example, personal assault and control of white-collar offenses, such as environmental pollution.	
DIFFERENCES	
Criminal Law	**Tort Law**
Crime is a public offense.	Tort is a civil or private wrong.
The sanction associated with criminal law is incarceration or death.	The sanction associated with a tort is monetary damages.
The right of enforcement belongs to the state.	The individual brings the action.
The government ordinarily does not appeal.	Both parties can appeal.
Fines go to the state.	The individual receives compensation for harm done.
The standard of proof is "beyond a reasonable doubt."	Guilt is established by a preponderance of the evidence.

Table 2.3   Common-Law Crimes

CRIMES AGAINST THE PERSON	EXAMPLES
First-degree murder. Unlawful killing of another human being with malice aforethought and with premeditation and deliberation.	A woman buys some poison and pours it into a cup of coffee her husband is drinking, intending to kill him. The motive—to get the insurance benefits of the victim.
Voluntary manslaughter. Intentional killing committed under extenuating circumstances that migitate the killing, such as killing in the heat of passion after being provoked.	A husband coming home early from work finds his wife in bed with another man. The husband goes into a rage and shoots and kills both lovers with a gun he keeps by his bedside.
Battery. Unlawful touching of another with intent to cause injury.	A man seeing a stranger sitting in his favorite seat in the cafeteria goes up to that person and pushes him out of the seat.
Assault. Intentional placing of another in fear of receiving an immediate battery.	A student aims an unloaded gun at her professor who believes the gun is loaded. She says she is going to shoot.
Rape. Unlawful sexual intercourse with a female without her consent.	After a party, a man offers to drive a young female acquaintance home. He takes her to a wooded area and, despite her protests, forces her to have sexual relations with him.
Robbery. Wrongful taking and carrying away of personal property from a person by violence or intimidation.	A man armed with a loaded gun approaches another man on a deserted street and demands his wallet.

INCHOATE (INCOMPLETE) OFFENSES	EXAMPLES
Attempt. An intentional act for the purpose of committing a crime that is more than mere preparation or planning of the crime. The crime is not completed, however.	A person intending to kill another person places a bomb in the intended victim's car so that it will detonate when the ignition key is used. The bomb is discovered before the car is started. Attempted murder has been committed.
Conspiracy. Voluntary agreement between two or more persons to achieve an unlawful object or to achieve a lawful object using means forbidden by law.	A drug company sells larger-than-normal quantities of drugs to a doctor, knowing that the doctor is distributing the drugs illegally. The drug company is guilty of conspiracy.

CRIMES AGAINST PROPERTY	EXAMPLES
Burglary. Breaking and entering of a dwelling house of another in the nighttime with the intent to commit a felony.	Intending to steal some jewelry and silver, a young man breaks a window and enters another's house at 10 P.M.
Arson. Intentional burning of a dwelling house of another.	A secretary, angry that her boss did not give her a raise, goes to her boss's house and sets fire to it.
Larceny. Taking and carrying away the personal property of another with the intent to steal the property.	While a woman is shopping, she sees a diamond ring displayed at the jewelry counter. When no one is looking, the woman takes the ring and walks out of the store.

Source: Developed by Therese J. Libby, J.D.

(larceny, burglary, robbery), or harming another person's property (malicious damage, trespass) that have traditionally been considered a violation of the morals of Western civilization.

Another type of crime, sometimes called statutory crime or **mala prohibitum** crime, involves violations of laws that reflect current public opinion and social values. In essence, statutory crimes are acts that conflict with contemporary standards of morality. Crimes are periodically created to control behaviors that conflict with the functioning of society. *Mala prohibitum* offenses include drug use and possession of unlicensed handguns. While it is relatively easy to link *mala in se* crimes to an objective concept of morality, it is much more difficult to do so if the acts are *mala prohibitum.*

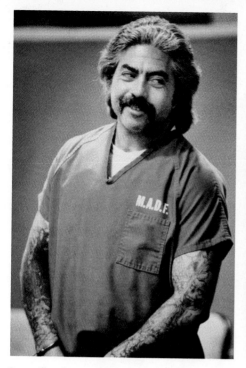

Some illegal acts, referred to as *mala in se* crimes, are rooted in the core values inherent in Western civilization. These "natural laws" are designed to control behaviors that have traditionally been considered a violation of the morals of Western civilization. There is little debate about the seriousness of these acts or their need for control. When Richard Allen Davis was convicted of the abduction and killing of 12-year-old Polly Klaas, the revulsion felt toward his behavior was universal and absolute. During a sentencing hearing, Polly's father Marc Klaas said, "Mr. Davis, when you get to where you're going, say hello to Hitler, to Dahmer, and to Bundy. Good riddance, and the sooner you get there the better we'll all be." Davis was sentenced to death on September 26, 1996.

Functions of the Criminal Law

The substantive criminal law today is a written code defining crimes and their punishments. In the United States, state and federal governments have developed their own unique criminal codes. Although all the codes have their differences, most use comparable terms, and the behaviors they are designed to control are often quite similar. Regardless of which culture or jurisdiction created them or when, criminal codes have several distinct functions. The most important of these include (1) providing social control, (2) discouraging revenge, (3) expressing public opinion and morality, (4) deterring criminal behavior, and (5) maintaining the social order.

Providing Social Control

The primary purpose of the criminal law is to control the behavior of people within its jurisdiction. The criminal law is a written statement of rules to which people must conform their behavior. Every society also maintains unwritten rules of conduct—ordinary customs and conventions referred to

as **folkways** and universally followed behavior called norms and morals, or **mores**. However, it is the criminal law that formally prohibits behaviors believed by those in political power to threaten societal well-being and that may challenge their own authority. For example, in U.S. society, the criminal law incorporates centuries-old prohibitions against the following behaviors harmful to others: taking the possessions of another person, physically harming another person, damaging another person's property, and cheating another person out of his or her possessions. Similarly, the law prevents actions that challenge the legitimacy of the government, such as planning its overthrow, collaborating with its enemies, and so on. Whereas violations of mores and folkways may be informally punished by any person, control of the criminal law is given to those in political power.

Discouraging Revenge

By delegating enforcement to others, the criminal law controls an individual's need to seek revenge or vengeance against those who have violated his or her rights. By punishing people who infringe on the rights, property, and freedom of others, the law shifts the burden of retribution

One of the goals of criminal law is to eliminate the need for personal revenge, turning the punishment of criminal offenses over to the state. In June of 1993 Lorena Bobbitt made national headlines when she cut off her husband John's penis with a knife after, she claimed, he sexually abused her. Should such acts of vengeance be severely punished? Can a person ever be justified in taking the "law into his or her own hands"?

from the individual to the state. As Oliver Wendell Holmes stated, this prevents "the greater evil of private retribution."[14] Although state retaliation may offend the sensibilities of many citizens, it is greatly preferable to a system in which people would have to seek justice for themselves.

Expressing Public Opinion and Morality

The criminal law also reflects constantly changing public opinions and moral values. *Mala in se* crimes, such as mur-

der and forcible rape, are almost universally prohibited, but the prohibition of legislatively created *mala prohibitum* crimes, such as traffic law and gambling violations, changes according to shifting social conditions and attitudes. The criminal law is used to codify these changes. For example, if a state government decides to legalize certain outlawed behaviors, such as gambling or marijuana possession, it will amend the state's criminal code. The criminal law then has the power to define the boundaries of moral and immoral behavior. Nonetheless, it has proven difficult to legally control public morality, because of the problems associated with (1) gauging the will of the majority, (2) respecting the rights of the minority, and (3) enforcing laws that many people consider trivial or self-serving.

The power of the law to express norms and values can be viewed in the development of the crime of **vagrancy** (the going about from place to place by a person who has no visible means of support and who, though able to work for his or her maintenance, refuses to do so). In a famous treatise, criminologist William Chambliss linked the historical development of the law of vagrancy to the prevailing economic interests of the ruling class. He argued that the original vagrancy laws were formulated in the 14th century after the bubonic plague had killed significant numbers of English peasants, threatening the labor-intensive feudal economy. The first vagrancy laws were aimed at preventing workers from leaving their estates to secure higher wages elsewhere. The laws punished migration and permissionless travel, thereby mooring peasants to their manors and aiding wealthy landowners.[15]

In an opposing view of the social conditions that influenced the creation of vagrancy laws, Jeffrey Adler argues that early English vagrancy laws were less concerned with maintaining capitalism than with controlling beggars and relieving the overburdened public relief and welfare systems.[16] Adler suggests that early American vagrancy laws provided town officials with a mechanism to repel the moral threat to the community posed by vagrants, "sabbath breakers," paupers, and the wandering poor; economic demands had little to do with the content of the law.

Deterring Criminal Behavior

The criminal law's social control function is realized through its ability to deter potential law violators. The threat of punishment associated with violating the law is designed to prevent crimes before they occur. During the Middle Ages, public executions were held to drive this point home. Today, the criminal law's impact is felt through news accounts of long prison sentences and an occasional execution.

The deterrent power of the criminal law is tied to the power it gives the state to sanction offenders. Whereas violations of folkways and mores are controlled informally, breaches of the criminal law are left to the jurisdiction of political agencies. Those violating mores and folkways can be subject to social disapproval, whereas criminal law violators alone are subject to physical coercion and punishment. Today, the most common punishments are fines, community supervision or probation, incarceration in jails or prison, and, in rare instances, execution.

Maintaining the Social Order

All legal systems are designed to support and maintain the boundaries of the social system they serve. In medieval England, the law protected the feudal system by defining an orderly system of property transfer and ownership. Laws in some socialist nations protect the primacy of the state by strictly curtailing profiteering and individual enterprise. Our own capitalist system is also supported and sustained by the criminal law. In a sense, the content of the criminal law is more of a reflection of the needs of those who control the existing economic and political system than a representation of some idealized moral code. In U.S. society, by meting out punishment to those who damage or steal property, the law promotes the activities needed to sustain an economy based on the accumulation of wealth. It would be impossible to conduct business through the use of contracts, promissory notes, credit, banking, and so on unless the law protected private capital. Maintaining a legal climate in which capitalism can thrive is an underlying goal of the criminal law.

Connections

The social control function of the criminal law assumes that the threat of punishment will deter crime. This assumption is actually the subject of significant debate: If the criminal law can deter crime, then how come there is so much crime today? For the answer, see the discussion of general deterrence in Chapter 5.

Net Bookmark

The criminal law interest in maintaining the social order may sometimes infringe on the rights of the minority in order to favor or support the majority. Making sure there is an "even playing field" is the American Civil Liberties Union, whose attorneys are ready to bring action if laws trample on people's civil rights. Their home page can be reached at:

http://www.aclu.org/

The criminal law has not always protected commercial enterprise; if one merchant cheated another, it was considered a private matter. Then in 1473, in the *Carrier's* case, an English court ruled that a merchant who held and transported merchandise for another was guilty of theft if he kept the goods for his own purposes.[17] Before the *Carrier's* case, the law did not consider it a crime for people to keep something that was already in their possession. Breaking with legal precedent, the British court recognized that the new English mercantile trade system could not be sustained if property rights had to be individually enforced. To this day, the substantive criminal law prohibits such business-related acts as larceny, fraud, embezzlement, and commercial theft. Without the law to protect it, the free enterprise system could not exist.

The Legal Definition of a Crime

The media often tell us about people who admit at trial that they committed the act they are accused of but who are not found guilty of the crime. In most instances, this occurs because state or federal prosecutors have not proven that the defendant's behavior falls within the legal definition of a crime. To fulfill the legal definition, all elements of the crime must be proven. For example, in Massachusetts, the common-law crime of burglary in the first degree is defined as:

> Whoever breaks and enters a dwelling house in the nighttime, with intent to commit a felony, or whoever, after having entered with such intent, breaks into such dwelling house in the nighttime, any person being lawfully therein, and the offender being armed with a dangerous weapon at the time of such breaking or entry, or so arriving himself in such house or making an actual assault on a person lawfully therein, commits the crime of burglary.[18]

Note that burglary in the first degree has the following elements:

- It happens at night.
- It involves breaking or entering or both.
- It happens at a dwelling house.
- The accused is armed or arms himself or herself after entering the house or commits an actual assault on a person lawfully in the house.
- The accused intends to commit a felony.

For the state to prove that a crime occurred and that the defendant committed it, the prosecutor must show that the accused engaged in the guilty act, or ***actus reus,*** and had the ***mens rea,*** or intent to commit the act. The *actus reus* can be either an aggressive act, such as taking someone's money, burning a building, or shooting someone, or a failure to act when there is a legal duty to do so, such as a parent's neglecting to seek medical attention for a sick child. The *mens rea* (guilty mind) refers to an individual's state of mind at the time of the act or, more specifically, the person's intent to commit the crime. For most crimes, both the *actus reus* and the *mens rea* must be present for the act to be considered a crime. For example, if George decides to kill Bob and then takes a gun and shoots Bob, George can be convicted of the crime of murder, because both elements are present. George's shooting of Bob is the *actus reus;* his decision to kill Bob is the *mens rea.* However, if George only thinks about shooting Bob but does nothing about it, the element of *actus reus* is absent, and no crime has been committed. Thoughts of committing an act do not alone constitute a crime. Let us now look more closely at these issues.

Actus Reus

As mentioned, the *actus reus* is the criminal act itself. For an act to be considered illegal, the action must be volun-

tary. For example, one person shooting another could certainly be considered a voluntary act. However, if the shooting occurs while the person holding the gun is having an epileptic seizure or a heart attack or is sleepwalking, he or she will not be held criminally liable, because the act is not voluntary. But if the individual knows he or she has such a condition and does not take precautions to prevent the act from occurring, the person could be held responsible for the criminal act. For instance, if Tom had an epileptic seizure while he is hunting and his gun went off and killed Victor, Tom would not be held responsible for Victor's death. But if Tom knew of his condition and further knew that a seizure could occur at any time, he could be convicted of the crime because it was possible for him to foresee the danger of handling a gun, yet he did nothing about it. The central issue concerning voluntariness is whether the individual has control over his or her actions.

A second type of *actus reus* is the failure to act when there is a legal duty to do so. A legal duty arises in three common situations:

1. *Relationship of parties based on status.* Such relationships include parent and child and husband and wife. If a husband finds his wife unconscious because she took an overdose of sleeping pills, he has a duty to try to save her life by seeking medical aid. If he fails to do so and she dies, he can be held responsible for her death.

2. *Imposition by statute.* For example, some states have passed laws that require a person who observes an automobile accident to stop and help the other parties involved.

3. *Contractual relationship.* Such relationships include lifeguard and swimmer, doctor and patient, and babysitter and child. Because lifeguards have been hired to ensure the safety of swimmers, they have a legal duty to come to the aid of drowning persons. If a lifeguard knows a swimmer is in danger and does nothing about it and the swimmer drowns, the lifeguard is legally responsible for the swimmer's death.

The duty to act is a legal and not a moral one. The obligation arises from the relationship between the parties or from explicit legal requirements. For example, a private citizen who sees a person drowning is under no legal obligation to save that person. Although we may find it morally reprehensible, the private citizen could walk away and let the swimmer drown without facing legal sanctions.

In any discussion of the *actus reus* of a crime, it should be mentioned that in some circumstances, words are considered acts. In the crime of sedition, the words of disloyalty constitute the *actus reus.* Further, if a person falsely yells "Fire!" in a crowded theater and people are injured in the rush to exit, that person is held responsible for the injuries, because his or her word constitutes an illegal act.

Mens Rea

In most situations, for an act to constitute a crime it must be done with criminal intent—otherwise known as *mens rea*. *Intent* in the legal sense can mean carrying out an act intentionally, knowingly, and willingly. However, the definition also encompasses situations in which recklessness or negligence establishes the required criminal intent. Some crimes require specific intent, and others require general intent. The type of intent needed to establish criminal liability varies depending on how the crime is defined. Most crimes require a general intent, or an intent to commit the crime. Thus, when Ann picks Bill's pocket and takes his wallet, her intent is to steal. Specific intent, on the other hand, is an intent to accomplish a specific purpose as an element of the crime. It involves an intent in addition to the intent to commit the crime. For example, burglary is the breaking and entering of a dwelling house with the intent to commit a felony. The breaking and entering aspect requires a general intent; the intent to commit a felony is a specific intent. If Dan breaks into and enters Emily's house because he intends to steal Emily's diamonds, he is guilty of burglary. However, if Dan merely breaks into and enters Emily's house but has no intent to commit a crime once inside, he cannot be convicted of burglary because he lacked specific intent. He would be guilty of breaking and entering, however.

Criminal intent also exists if the results of an action, though originally unintended, are substantially certain to occur. For example, Kim, out for revenge against her former boyfriend John, poisons the punch bowl at John's party. Before John has a drink himself, several of his guests die as a result of drinking the punch. Kim could be said to have intentionally killed the guests even though that was not the original purpose of her action. The law would hold that Kim or any other person should be substantially certain that the others at the party would drink the punch and be poisoned along with John.

The concept of *mens rea* also encompasses the situation in which a person intends to commit a crime against one person but injures another party instead. For instance, if Sam, intending to kill Larry, shoots at Larry but misses and kills John, Sam is guilty of murdering John, even though he did not intend to do so. Under the doctrine of **transferred intent,** the original criminal intent is transferred to the unintended victim.

Mens rea is also found in situations in which harm has resulted because a person has acted negligently or recklessly. Negligence involves a person's acting unreasonably under the circumstances. Criminal negligence is often found in situations involving drunken driving. If a drunken driver speeding and zigzagging across lanes hits and kills another person, criminal negligence exists. In the case of drunken driving, the law maintains that a reasonable person would not drive a car when drunk and thus unable to control the vehicle. The intent that underlies the finding of criminal liability for an unintentional act is known as **constructive intent.**

Strict Liability

Both the *actus reus* and the *mens rea* must be present before a person can be convicted of a crime. However, several crimes defined by statute do not require *mens rea*. The actor is guilty simply by doing what the statute prohibits; mental intent does not enter the picture. These offenses are known as **strict-liability crimes,** or public welfare offenses. Health and safety regulations, traffic laws, and narcotic control laws are strict-liability statutes. For example, a person stopped for speeding is guilty of breaking the traffic laws regardless of whether he or she had intended to go over the speed limit or had done it by accident, out of carelessness, or for any other reason. The underlying purpose of these laws is to protect the public; therefore, intent is not required.[19]

> ### Connections
>
> Many white-collar crimes such as pollution of the environment are considered strict liability. A person who is detected dumping toxic wastes is guilty of crime; proving intent is usually not required. For an analysis of white-collar law enforcement, see Chapter 13.

Criminal Defenses

When people defend themselves against criminal charges, they must refute one or more of the elements of the crime of which they have been accused. A number of approaches can be taken to criminal defense. First, defendants may deny the *actus reus* by arguing that they were falsely accused and that the real culprit has yet to be identified. Defendants may also claim that while they did engage in the criminal act they are accused of, they lacked the *mens rea*, or mental intent needed to be found guilty of the crime. If a person whose mental state is impaired commits a criminal act, it is possible for the person to excuse his or her law-violating actions by claiming he or she lacked the capacity to form sufficient intent to be held criminally responsible for the actions. Ignorance, insanity, and intoxication are among the types of excuse defenses.

Another type of defense is that of justification. Here, the individual usually admits committing the criminal act but maintains that the act was justified and that he or she therefore should not be held criminally liable. Among the justification defenses are necessity, duress, self-defense, and entrapment.

Persons standing trial for criminal offenses may defend themselves by claiming either that their actions were justified under the circumstances or that their behavior can be excused by their lack of *mens rea*. If either the physical or mental elements of a crime cannot be proven, then the defendant cannot be convicted. We will now examine some of these defenses and justifications in greater detail.

Ignorance or Mistake

As a general rule, ignorance of the law is no excuse. However, courts have recognized that ignorance can be an excuse if the government fails to make enactment of a new law public or if the offender relied on an official statement of the law that was later deemed incorrect. Ignorance or mistake can be an excuse if it negates an element of a crime. For example, if Andrew purchases stolen merchandise from Eric but is unaware that the material was illegally obtained, he cannot be convicted of receiving stolen merchandise because he had no intent to do so. But if Rachel attempts to purchase marijuana from a drug dealer and mistakenly buys hashish, she can be convicted of a drug charge because she intended to purchase illegal goods; ignorance does not excuse evil intent.[20]

While ignorance or mistake does not excuse crime when there is evil intent, conflict occurs when the evil was purely of moral and not legal consequence. For example, some cases of statutory rape (sexual relations with minor females) have been defended on the grounds that the perpetrators were ignorant of their victim's true age. This defense has been allowed in states where sex between consenting adults is legal, under the rationale that if a reasonable mistake had not been made, no crime would have occurred. Nonetheless, if the mistake seems unreasonable (for example, if the victim was a preteen), the original charge will stand.[21]

Insanity

Insanity is a defense to criminal prosecution in which the defendant's state of mind negates his or her criminal responsibility. A successful insanity defense results in a verdict of "not guilty by reason of insanity." Insanity here is a legal category. As used in U.S. courts, it does not necessarily mean that persons using the defense are mentally ill or unbalanced, only that their state of mind at the time the crime was committed made it impossible for them to have the necessary intent to satisfy the legal definition of a crime. Thus, a person can be diagnosed as a psychopath or psychotic but still be judged legally sane. However, it is usually left to psychiatric testimony in court to prove a defendant legally sane.

A person found to be legally insane at the time of trial is placed in the custody of state mental health authorities until diagnosed as sane. Sometimes, a person who was sane when he or she committed a crime becomes insane soon afterward. In that instance, the person receives psychiatric care until capable of standing trial and is then tried on the criminal charge, since the person actually had *mens rea* at the time the crime was committed. On rare occasions, persons who were legally insane at the time they committed a crime become rational soon afterward. In that instance, the state can neither try them for the criminal offense nor have them committed to a mental health facility.

The test used to determine whether a person is legally insane varies among jurisdictions. U.S. courts generally use either the M'Naghten Rule or the substantial capacity test.

THE M'NAGHTEN RULE. In 1843 an English court established the M'Naghten Rule, also known as the right-wrong test. Daniel M'Naghten, believing Edward Drummond to be Sir Robert Peel, the prime minister of Great Britain, shot and killed Drummond (Peel's secretary). At his trial for murder, M'Naghten claimed that he could not be held responsible for the murder because his delusions had caused him to act. The jury agreed with M'Naghten and found him not guilty by reason of insanity.

Because of the importance of the people involved in the case, the verdict was not well received. The British House of Lords reviewed the decision and requested the court to clarify the law with respect to insane delusions. The court's response became known as the **M'Naghten Rule:**

> To establish a defense on the ground of insanity, it must be proved that at the time of the committing of the act the party accused was labouring under such a defect of reason from disease of the mind, as not to know the nature and quality of the act he was doing; or, if he did know, that he did not know he was doing what was wrong.[22]

Essentially, the M'Naghten Rule maintains that an individual is insane if he or she is unable to tell the difference between right and wrong because of some mental disability. The M'Naghten Rule is a widely used test for legal insanity in the United States. In about half the states, this rule is the legal test when an issue of insanity is presented. However, over the years, much criticism has arisen concerning M'Naghten. First, great confusion has surfaced over such wording as "disease of the mind" and "know the nature and quality of the act." These phrases have never been properly clarified. Second, critiques, mainly from the mental health profession, have pointed out that the rule is unrealistic and narrow in that it does not cover situations in which people know right from wrong but cannot control their actions.

Because of questions about M'Naghten, approximately 15 states have supplemented the rule with another test, known as the *irresistible impulse test.*[23] This test allows the defense of insanity to be used for situations in which defendants were unable to control their behavior because of a mental disease. Thus, the defendants do not have to prove that they did not know the difference between right and wrong, only that they could not control themselves at the time of the crime.

THE SUBSTANTIAL CAPACITY TEST.

The **substantial capacity test,** originally a section of the American Law Institute's Model Penal Code, states:

> A person is not responsible for criminal conduct if at the time of such conduct as a result of mental disease or defect he lacks substantial capacity either to appreciate the criminality [wrongfulness] of his conduct or to conform his conduct to the requirement of the law.[24]

The substantial capacity test is essentially a combination of the M'Naghten Rule and the irresistible impulse test. It is, however, broader in its interpretation of insanity, for it requires only a lack of substantial capacity instead of complete impairment, as in M'Naghten and the irresistible impulse test. This test also differs in that it uses the term *appreciate* instead of *know,* the term used in M'Naghten. About half the states now use variations of the substantial capacity test. The federal government's definition omits the term *substantial* (i.e., "lacks the capacity") and also leaves out the inability "to conform" aspect of the substantial capacity test.

THE INSANITY CONTROVERSY.

The insanity defense has been the source of debate and controversy. Many critics of this defense maintain that inquiry into a defendant's psychological makeup is inappropriate at the trial stage; they would prefer that the issue be raised at the sentencing stage, after guilt has been determined. Opponents also charge that criminal responsibility is separate from mental illness and that the two should not be equated. It is a serious mistake, they argue, to consider criminal responsibility as a trait or quality that can be detected by a psychiatric evaluation. Moreover, some criminals avoid punishment because they are erroneously judged by psychiatrists to be mentally ill. Conversely, some people who are found not guilty by reason of insanity because they suffer from a mild personality disturbance are incarcerated as mental patients far longer than they would have been imprisoned if they had been convicted of a criminal offense.

Advocates of the insanity defense say that it serves a unique purpose. Most successful insanity verdicts result in the defendant's being committed to a mental institution until he or she has recovered. The general assumption, according to two legal authorities, Wayne LaFave and Austin Scott, is that the insanity defense makes it possible to single out for special treatment certain persons who would otherwise be subjected to further penal sanctions following conviction. LaFave and Scott further point out that the "real function of the insanity defense is to authorize the state to hold those who must be found not to possess the guilty mind, even though the criminal law demands that no person be held criminally responsible if doubt is cast on any material element of the offense charged."[25]

The insanity plea was thrust into the spotlight when John Hinckley, Jr.'s unsuccessful attempt to kill President Ronald Reagan was captured by news cameras. Hinckley was found not guilty by reason of insanity. Public outcry against this seeming miscarriage of justice prompted some states to revise their insanity statutes. New Mexico, Georgia, Alaska, Delaware, Michigan, Illinois, and Indiana, among other states, have created the plea of guilty but insane, in which the defendant is required to serve the first part of his or her sentence in a hospital and, once "cured," to be then sent to prison. In 1984 the federal government revised its criminal code to restrict insanity as a defense solely to individuals who are unable to understand the nature and wrongfulness of their acts; a defendant's irresistible impulse will no longer be considered. The burden of proof has made an important shift from the prosecutor's need to prove sanity to the defendant's need to prove insanity.[26]

About 11 states have followed the federal government's lead and made significant changes in their insanity defenses, such as shifting the burden of proof from prosecution to defense; 3 states (Idaho, Montana, and Utah) no longer use evidence of mental illness as a defense in court, although psychological factors can influence sentencing. On March 28, 1994 the U.S. Supreme Court failed to overturn the Montana law (*Cowan v. Montana,* 93-1264), thereby giving the states the right to abolish the insanity defense if they so choose.

Although such backlash against the insanity plea is intended to close supposed legal loopholes allowing dangerous criminals to go free, the public's fear may be misplaced. It is estimated the insanity plea is used in fewer than 1% of all cases.[27] Moreover, evidence shows that relatively few insanity defense pleas are successful.

> ## Connections
>
> One reason there are so few successful insanity pleas is that there may be relatively few insane criminals. The association between mental illness and crimes seems to be tenuous at best. For a discussion of this issue, see the sections in Chapter 6 on mental illness and crime.

Even if the defense is successful, the offender must be placed in a secure psychiatric hospital or the psychiatric ward of a state prison. Since many defendants who successfully plead insanity are nonviolent offenders, it is certainly possible that their hospital stay will be longer than the prison term they would have received if they had been convicted of the crimes of which they were originally accused.[28] Despite efforts to ban its use, the insanity plea is probably here to stay. Most crimes require *mens rea,* and unless we are willing to forgo that standard of law, we will be forced to find not guilty those people whose mental state makes it impossible for them to rationally control their behavior.

On Dec. 30, 1994, John Salvi walked into two Planned Parenthood clinics in the Boston area and began shooting with a rifle, killing two receptionists and wounding five others. It was the worst anti-abortion violence in U.S. history. Salvi was tried and convicted of murder, despite the fact that his lawyers claimed he suffered from mental illness. Salvi later hung himself in prison. Should the concept of insanity be abolished if people such as Salvi and serial killer Jeffrey Dahmer (who ate his victims' bodies) are considered legally sane? If their behavior is "sane," what does it take to be considered "insane"?

Intoxication

Intoxication, which includes the taking of alcohol or drugs, is generally not considered a defense. However, there are two exceptions to this rule. First, an individual who becomes intoxicated by mistake, through force, or under duress can use involuntary intoxication as a defense. Second, voluntary intoxication is a defense when specific intent is needed and the person could not have formed the intent because of his or her intoxicated condition. For example, if a person breaks into and enters another's house but is so drunk that he or she cannot form the intent to commit a felony, the intoxication is a defense against burglary but not against the breaking and entering.

Duress

Duress is a defense to a crime when the defendant commits an illegal act because the defendant or a third person has been threatened by another with death or serious bodily harm if the act is not performed. For example, if Pete, holding a gun on Jerry, threatens to kill Jerry unless he breaks into and enters Bill's house, Jerry has a defense of duress for the crime of breaking and entering. This defense, however, does not cover the situation in which defendants commit a serious crime, such as murder, to save themselves or others. The reason for this exception is that the defense is based on the social policy that, when faced with two evils (harm to oneself or violating the criminal law), it is better to commit the lesser evil to avoid the threatened harm. In the situation of murder versus threatened harm, however, taking another's life is considered the greater of the two evils.

Necessity

The defense of necessity is applied in situations in which a person must break the law to avoid a greater evil caused by natural physical forces (storms, earthquakes, illness). This defense is available only when committing the crime is the lesser of two evils. For example, a person lacking a driver's license is justified in driving a car to escape a fire. However, as the famous English case *Regina v. Dudley and Stephens* indicates, necessity does not justify the intentional killing of another.[29] In that case, three sailors and a cabin boy had been shipwrecked and floating in the open seas in a lifeboat. After nine days without food and seven without water, two of the sailors, Dudley and Stephens, killed the cabin boy, and the three sailors ate his body and drank his blood. Four days later, the sailors were rescued. The court acknowledged that the cabin boy most likely would have died naturally because he was in the weakest condition, but nevertheless judged the killing unjustified.

Self-Defense

Self-defense involves a claim that the defendant's actions were a justified response to the provocative behavior of the victim. Self-defense can be used to protect one's person or one's property.

An individual is justified in using force against another to protect himself or herself. When that happens, the person claims to have acted in self-defense and is therefore not guilty of the harm done. If the defendant was justified in using force, self-defense excuses such crimes as murder, manslaughter, and assault and battery. The law, however, has set limits as to what is reasonable and necessary self-defense. First, defendants must have a reasonable belief that they are in danger of death or great harm and that it is necessary for them to use force to prevent harm to themselves. For example, if Mary threatens to kill Jan but it is obvious that Mary is unarmed, Jan is not justified in pulling her gun and shooting Mary. However, if Mary, after threatening Jan, reaches into her pocket as if to get a gun and Jan then pulls her gun and shoots Mary, Jan could claim self-defense, even if it is discovered that Mary was unarmed. In this situation, Jan had a reasonable belief that harm was imminent and that it was necessary to shoot first to avoid injury to herself.

Second, the amount of force used must be no greater than that necessary to prevent personal harm. For instance, if Steve punches Ben, Ben could not justifiably hit Steve with an iron rod. Ben could, however, punch Steve back if he believed Steve was going to continue punching. Another issue arises concerning self-defense in situations in which deadly force may be necessary: Does a person have a duty to avoid using deadly force against an attacker by retreating if possible? U.S. courts are split on this issue. The majority of states maintain that the person attacked does not have to retreat, even if he or she can do so safely. This position is based on the policy that a person should not be forced to act in a humiliating or cowardly manner. However, many states do require that a person try to retreat, if it is possible to do so safely, before using deadly force. Even in most of these jurisdictions, however, people are not required to retreat if attacked in their homes or offices. The rules concerning self-defense also apply to situations involving the defense of a third person. Thus, if a person reasonably believes that another is in danger of unlawful bodily harm from an assailant, the person may use the force necessary to prevent the danger.

Using force to defend one's property from trespass or theft is allowable if the force is reasonable. This means that the use of force should be a last resort after requests to stop interfering with the property or legal action have failed. Also, the use of deadly force is not considered reasonable when only protection of property is concerned. This is based on the social policy that human life is more important than property.

The self-defense concept received national publicity when, on December 22, 1984, Bernhard Goetz shot four would-be robbers on a subway train in New York. Despite some concern over the racial nature of the incident (Goetz is white and his assailants were African American), public support seemed overwhelmingly on the side of self-defense. The four youths admitted that they were on their way to steal money from video game machines and that they had demanded money from Goetz in a threatening manner. However, the prosecution charged that Goetz was only approached by two of the youths, who were panhandling, and that Goetz not only overreacted to the instant provocation but used an illegal handgun to shoot the youths. The most powerful evidence for the prosecution was the taped interviews Goetz made after he had surrendered to police in Concord, New Hampshire. He said on the videotape, "I wanted to kill those guys. I wanted to maim those guys. I wanted to make them suffer in every way I could." On the tape, Goetz claimed to have approached one of the boys he shot and, leaning over him, said, "You look all right, here's another." The tapes were used by the prosecutor to show Goetz as an obsessed, paranoid person who lived by his own rules.

In his defense, Goetz argued that his videotaped statements should be discounted as the unreliable perceptions of a traumatized crime victim. He also brought in psychological testimony that indicated that the extreme fear he felt may have caused his body to go on "automatic pilot." The prosecution's case was not helped when two of the boys were convicted for violent offenses, including the rape of a pregnant woman, before the trial began. Nor was it helped by the fact that the jury foreman had been the victim of a subway robbery in 1981. In the end, the case hinged on the judge's instructions to the jury that under New York law, the use of force is justified if the defendant had a reasonable belief that he or she was under the threat of deadly force himself or herself or that the defendant was to become the victim of a violent felony, such as robbery. The jury believed Goetz acted reasonably under the circumstances and acquitted him of all charges, except the relatively minor one of possessing an illegal handgun.[30]

Entrapment

Entrapment is another defense that excuses a defendant from criminal liability. The entrapment defense is raised when the defendant maintains that law enforcement officers induced him or her to commit a crime. The defendant would not have committed the crime had it not been for trickery, persuasion, or fraud on the officers' part. In other words, if law enforcement officers plan a crime, implant the criminal idea in a person's mind, and pressure that person into doing the act, the person may plead entrapment. This situation is different from that in which an officer simply provides an opportunity for the crime to be committed and the defendant is willing and ready to do the act. For example, if a plainclothes police officer poses as a potential customer and is approached by a prostitute, no entrapment has occurred. However, if the same officer approaches a woman and persuades her to commit an act of prostitution, the defense of entrapment is appropriate.

In an important decision, the U.S. Supreme Court in *Jacobson v. United States* ruled that it was entrapment when a Nebraska man was arrested who had ordered pornographic magazines from a company that was really a front for a government "sting" operation. Jacobson had previously ordered legal albeit sexually oriented material. Government agents had gotten his name from the mailing list of the bookstore that had mailed him the materials and sent him repeated offers to buy more. Because the law had changed, it was now illegal to receive the sexually oriented material through the mail. When he placed an order, he was arrested. After his conviction, Jacobson was able to prove that the government had repeatedly solicited him for 26 months before he placed the order. The Court ruled that the repeated solicitations amounted to entrapment. The fact that Jacobson was predisposed to view the material did not mean he was predisposed to break the law![31]

Changing the Criminal Law

In recent years, many states and the federal government have been examining their substantive criminal law. Since the law, in part, reflects public opinion regarding various forms of behavior, what was a crime 40 years ago may not be considered so today. In some states, crimes such as possession of marijuana have been *decriminalized*—given reduced penalties. Such crimes may be punishable by a fine instead of a prison sentence. Other former criminal offenses, such as vagrancy, have been *legalized*—all criminal penalties have been removed. And, in some jurisdictions, penalties have been toughened, especially for violent crimes, such as rape and spousal assault.

Net Bookmark

Interested in criminal law reform? The Counsel Connect site can aim you in the right direction. For example, you can read a summary of the Superfund Cleanup Acceleration Act of 1997, introduced by Senators Bob Smith (R-NH) and John Chafee (R-RI), as well as summaries of other important legislation.

http://www.counsel.com/lawlinks/

In some instances new criminal laws have been created to conform to emerging social issues. For example, assisted suicide became the subject of a national debate when Dr. Jack Kevorkian began practicing what he calls **obitiatry**, helping people take their lives.[32] To stop Kevorkian, Michigan passed a statutory ban on assisted suicide, reflecting what lawmakers believed to be prevailing public opinion.[33] Kevorkian's repeated acquittals shed doubt on the wisdom of the law and prompted the U.S. Supreme Court to consider during its 1997 term the issue of whether states can control physician-assisted suicide.

Assisted suicide is but one of many emerging social issues that have prompted change in the criminal law. More than 25 states have enacted **stalking** statutes, which prohibit and punish acts described typically as "the willful, malicious and repeated following and harassing of another person."[34] Although stalking laws were originally formulated to protect women terrorized by former husbands and boyfriends, the laws have often applied to people stalked by strangers or casual acquaintances.

Community notification laws are a response to public concern about sexual predators moving into neighborhoods. These are usually referred to as "Megan's law," a New Jersey law named after seven-year-old Megan Kanka of Hamilton Township, N.J., who was killed in 1994. Charged with the crime was a convicted sex offender who the Kankas were unaware lived across the street from them. The New Jersey law required notification of neighbors in the community. In 1996 the federal government passed legislation requiring that the general public be informed of the existence of convicted pedophiles in their midst, although officials would determine how much public warning is necessary, based on the danger posed by the offender. States would have to establish a warning system by September 1997 or they could lose some federal anti-crime funds.[35]

Similarly, new laws have been passed to keep the sexually dangerous under control. For example, California's "sexual predator" law allows authorities to keep some criminals in custody even after their sentences are served. The law, which took effect January 1, 1996, allows for the commitment of people who have been convicted of sexually violent crimes against two or more victims. After offenders have served their prison terms, civil juries may recommend commitment to a mental institution, which would be reviewed every two years. The law has already been upheld by appellate court judges in the state.[36]

The federal government has also revised the U.S. legal code to reflect changing social conditions. Recent federal crime legislation under the Clinton administration has included the Brady Handgun Control Law of 1993, requiring a five-business-day waiting period before an individual can buy a handgun.

The future direction of the criminal law in the United States remains unclear; both expansions and contractions can be expected. Certain actions will be adopted as criminal and given more attention, such as crimes by corporations and political corruption. Other offenses, such as recreational drug use, may be reduced in importance or removed entirely from the criminal law system. In addition, changing technology will require modification in the criminal law. For example, such technologies as automated teller machines and cellular phones have already spawned a new generation of criminal acts involving "theft" of access numbers and cards and software piracy. As the "information highway" is laid down, the nation's computer network advances, and biotechnology produces new substances, the criminal law will be forced to address threats to the public safety that are today unknown.

Connections

Chapter 13 contains sections on technological crimes, including the newly emerging area of computer crime. The criminal law must be constantly modified to include areas that only a few years earlier were unknown.

Summary

The substantive criminal law is a set of rules that specifies the behavior society has outlawed. The criminal law can be distinguished from the civil law on the basis that the former involves powers given to the state to enforce social rules, while the latter controls interactions between private citizens. The criminal law serves several important purposes: It represents public opinion and moral values, it enforces social controls, it deters criminal behavior and wrongdoing, it punishes transgressors, and it banishes private retribution. The criminal law used in U.S. jurisdictions traces its origin to the English common law. Common law was formulated during the Middle Ages when King Henry II's judges began to use precedents set in one case to guide actions in another; this system is called *stare decisis.*

In the U.S. legal system, common-law crimes have been codified by lawmakers into state and federal penal codes. Today, most crimes fall into the category of felony or misdemeanor. Felonies are serious crimes usually punished by a prison term, whereas misdemeanors are minor crimes that carry a fine or a light jail sentence. Common felonies include murder, rape, assault with a deadly weapon, and robbery; misdemeanors include larceny, simple assault, and possession of small amounts of drugs.

Every crime has specific elements. In most instances, these elements include the *actus reus* (guilty act), which is the actual physical part of the crime (for example, taking money or burning a building) and the *mens rea* (guilty mind), which refers to the state of mind of the individual who commits a crime—more specifically, the person's intent to do the act.

At trial, accused individuals can defend themselves by claiming to have lacked *mens rea* and, therefore, were not responsible for the criminal actions. One type of defense is excuse for mental reasons, such as insanity, intoxication, necessity, or duress. Another defense is justification by reason of self-defense or entrapment. Of all defenses, insanity is perhaps the most controversial. In most states, persons using an insanity defense claim that they did not know what they were doing when they committed a crime or that their mental state did not allow them to tell the difference between right and wrong (the M'Naghten Rule). Insanity defenses can also include the claims that the offender was motivated by an irresistible impulse or lacked the substantial capacity to conform his or her conduct to the criminal law. Regardless of the insanity defense used, critics charge that mental illness is separate from legal responsibility and that the two should not be equated. Supporters counter that the insanity defense allows mentally ill people to avoid penal sanctions.

The criminal law is undergoing constant reform. Some acts are being decriminalized—their penalties are being reduced—while laws are being revised to make penalties for some acts more severe. The law must confront social and technological change.

Key Terms

Code of Hammurabi	misdemeanor
lex talionis	*mala in se*
Mosaic Code	*mala prohibitum*
Twelve Tables	folkways
wergild	mores
oath-helpers	vagrancy
shire	*actus reus*
hundreds	*mens rea*
tithings	transferred intent
hundred-gemot	constructive intent
shire-gemot	strict-liability laws
hali-gemot	insanity
court-leet	M'Naghten Rule
stare decisis	substantial capacity test
common law	obitiatry
inchoate crimes	entrapment
tort law	stalking
felony	community notification laws

Notes

1. The historical material in the following sections was derived from a number of sources. The most important include Rene Wormser, *The Story of Law,* rev. ed. (New York: Simon & Schuster, 1962); Jackson Spielvogel, *Western Civilization* (St. Paul: West Publishing, 1991); Eugen Weber, *A Modern History of Europe* (New York: W. W. Norton, 1971); James Heath, *Eighteenth-Century Penal Theory* (New York: Oxford University Press, 1963); David Jones, *History of Criminology* (Westport, Conn.: Greenwood Press, 1986); Fred Inbau, James Thompson, and James Zagel, *Criminal Law and Its Administration* (Mineola, N.Y.: Foundation Press, 1974); Wayne LaFave and Austin Scott, *Criminal Law,* 2nd ed. (St. Paul: West Publishing, 1986); and Sanford Kadish and Monrad Paulsen, *Criminal Law and Its Processes* (Boston: Little, Brown, 1975).

2. Weber, *A Modern History of Europe,* p. 9.

3. Wayne LaFave and Austin Scott, *Handbook on Criminal Law* (St. Paul, Minn.: West Publishing, 1982), pp. 528–529.

4. Caldwell 397 (1784), cited in LaFave and Scott, *Handbook on Criminal Law,* p. 422.

5. 9 George I, C. 22, 1723, cited in Douglas Hay, "Crime and Justice in Eighteenth and Nineteenth Century England," in *Crime and Justice,* vol. 2, ed. Norval Norris and Michael Tonrey (Chicago: University of Chicago Press, 1980), p. 51.

6. Jerome Hall, *Theft, Law, and Society* (Indianapolis, Ind.: Bobbs-Merrill, 1952); Chapter 1 is generally considered the best source for the history of common-law theft crimes.

7. Marvin Zalman, John Strate, Denis Hunter, and James Sellars, "Michigan Assisted Suicide Three Ring Circus: The Intersection of Law and Politics," *Ohio Northern Law Review* 23 (1997): in press.

8. Mass. Gen. Laws Ann. (West 1982) ch. 266, pp. 1–2.

9. See, generally, Alfred Lindesmith, *The Addict and the Law* (New York: Vintage Books, 1965), Chapter 1.

10. Edna Erez and Bankole Thompson, "Rape in Sierra Leone: Conflict Between the Sexes and Conflict of Laws," *International Journal of Comparative and Applied Criminal Justice* 14 (1990): 201–210.

11. William Henry, "Did the Music Say 'Do It'?" *Time,* 30 July 1990, p. 65.

12. Mathew Brelis, "Man Must Pay $500,000 for Raping Daughter," *Boston Globe,* 2 July 1993, p. 1.

13. For example, see *Brinegar v. United States,* 388 U.S. 160 (1949); *Speiser v. Randall,* 357 U.S. 513 (1958); *In re Winship,* 397 U.S. 358 (1970).

14. Oliver Wendell Holmes, *The Common Law,* ed. Mark De Wolf (Boston: Little, Brown, 1881), p. 36.

15. William Chambliss, "A Sociological Analysis of the Law of Vagrancy," *Social Problems* 12 (1964): 67–77; idem, "On Trashing Marxist Criminology," *Criminology* 27 (1989): 231–239.

16. Jeffrey Adler, "A Historical Analysis of the Law of Vagrancy," *Criminology* 27 (1989): 209–230; Adler, "Vagging the Demons and Scoundrels: Vagrancy and the Growth of St. Louis, 1830–1861," *Journal of Urban History* 13 (1986): 3–30.

17. *Carrier's* case, Y.B. 13 Edw. 4, f. 9, pl. 5 (Star Chamber and Exchequer Chamber, 1473), discussed at length in Jerome Hall, *Theft, Law and Society* (Indianapolis: Bobbs-Merrill, 1952), Chapter 1.

18. Mass. Gen. Laws Ann. (West 1983) ch. 266, p. 14.

19. 320 U.S. 277 (1943).

20. LaFave and Scott, *Handbook on Criminal Law,* p. 356.

21. Ibid., p. 361.

22. 8 Eng. Rep. 718 (1843).

23. Kadish and Paulsen, *Criminal Law and Its Processes,* pp. 215–216.

24. Model Penal Code 401 (1952).

25. LaFave and Scott, *Handbook on Criminal Law,* p. 516.

26. Comprehensive Crime Control Act of 1984—Pub. L. No. 98-473, 403. 23.

27. Rita Simon and David Aaronson, *The Insanity Defense: A Critical Assessment of Law and Policy in the Post-Hinckley Era* (New York: Praeger, 1988).

28. Samuel Walker, *Sense and Nonsense About Crime* (Monterey, Calif.: Brooks/Cole, 1985), p. 120.

29. *Regina v. Dudley and Stephens,* 14 Q.B. 273 (1884).

30. John Kennedy, "Goetz Acquitted of Major Charges in Subway Shooting," *Boston Globe,* 17 June 1987, p. 1.

31. *Jacobson v. United States* 112 S.Ct. 1535, 118 L. Ed. 2d 174 (1992).

32. Zalman et al., "Michigan Assisted Suicide Three Ring Circus."

33. 1992 P.A. 270 as amended by 1993 P.A.3, M.C. L. ss. 752.1021 to 752. 1027.

34. National Institute of Justice, *Project to Develop a Model Anti-stalking Statute* (Washington, D.C.: National Institute of Justice, 1994).

35. "Clinton Signs Tougher Megan's Law," CNN News Service, 17 May, 1996.

36. Associated Press, "Judge Upholds State's Sexual Predator Law," Bakersfield *Californian,* 2 October 1996.

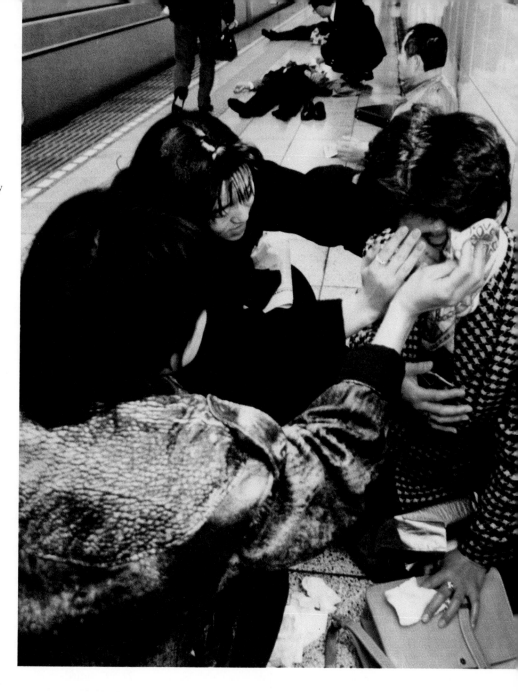

Chapter 3
The Nature
and Extent of Crime

how much crime is there? What are the patterns and trends in crime? Who commits crime? What is the nature of criminality? These are some of the most important questions in the study of criminology. Without such information, it would not be possible to formulate theories that explain the onset of crime or to devise social policies that facilitate its control or elimination.

In this chapter, data collected on criminal offenders are reviewed in some detail and then used to provide a summary of crime patterns and trends. The chapter addresses a number of questions: Are crime rates increasing? What factors influence crime rate trends? Where and when does crime take place? What are the social and individual patterns that affect the crime rate? What effect do social class, age, gender, and race have on the crime rate? Finally, the chapter reviews the concept of criminal careers and what available crime data can tell us about the onset, continuation, and termination of criminality.

Net Bookmark

Imagine, if you will, an organization in which the communication among police chiefs, police officers, crime analysts, detectives, security personnel, and other people interested in tracking and analyzing crime data in a scholarly manner could be networked together into an international association. To learn more about the International Association of Crime Analysts, log on to their web site at:

http://web2.airmail.net/iaca/join.html

The Uniform Crime Report

The Federal Bureau of Investigation's **Uniform Crime Report (UCR)** is the best-known and most widely cited source of aggregate criminal statistics.[1] The FBI receives and compiles records from over 16,000 police departments serving a majority of the U.S. population. Its major unit of analysis involves the **index crimes,** or **Part I crimes:** murder and nonnegligent manslaughter, forcible rape, robbery, aggravated assault, burglary, larceny, motor vehicle theft, and arson. Table 3.1 defines these crimes. The FBI tallies and annually publishes the number of reported offenses by city, county, standard metropolitan statistical area, and geographical divisions of the United States. In addition to these statistics, the UCR provides information on the number and characteristics (age, race, gender) of individuals who have been arrested for these and all other crimes, except traffic violations **(Part II crimes).**

Collecting the UCR

The methods used to compile the UCR are quite complex. Each month, law enforcement agencies report the number of index crimes known to them. A count of these crimes is

Net Bookmark

Auto theft makes up a significant portion of the UCR data. To learn more about why it occurs and what is being done to reduce its incidence, see the web page of the International Association of Auto Theft Investigators (IAATI).

http://www-personal.umich.edu/~gmbrown/IAATI/

taken from records of all complaints of crime these agencies received from victims, officers who discovered the infractions, or other sources.

Whenever complaints of crime are determined, through investigation, to be unfounded or false, they are eliminated from the actual count. The number of "actual offenses known" is reported to the FBI whether or not anyone is arrested for the crime, the stolen property is recovered, or prosecution is undertaken.

In addition, law enforcement agencies each month report the total crimes that were *cleared.* Crimes are cleared in two ways: (1) when at least one person is arrested, charged, and turned over to the court for prosecution, or (2) by exceptional means, when some element beyond police control precludes the physical arrest of an offender (for example, the offender leaves the country). Traditionally, about 20% of all reported index crimes are cleared by arrest.

Violent crimes are more likely to be solved than property crimes, probably because police devote more resources to these more serious acts, because witnesses (including the victim) are available to identify offenders, and because, in many instances, the victim and offender were previously acquainted.

Data on the number of clearances involving only the arrest of offenders under the age of 18, data on the value of property stolen and recovered in connection with Part I offenses, and detailed information pertaining to criminal homicide are also reported.

The UCR uses three methods to express crime data. First, the number of crimes reported to the police and arrests made are expressed as raw figures (for example, 21,597 murders occurred in 1995). In addition, the percentage changes in the amount of crime between years are computed (for example, murder decreased 7.4% between 1994 and 1995). Finally, crime rates per 100,000 people are computed. That is, when the UCR indicates that the murder rate was 8.2 in 1995, it means that about 8 people in every 100,000 were murdered between January 1 and December 31 of 1995. The equation used is:

$$\frac{\text{Number of reported crimes}}{\text{Total U.S. population}} \times 100{,}000 = \text{Rate per } 100{,}000$$

The Accuracy of the UCR

Despite its importance and wide use by criminologists, the accuracy of the UCR has been suspect. We'll address the

Table 3.1   Part I Index Crime Offenses

CRIME	DESCRIPTION
Criminal homicide	a. Murder and nonnegligent manslaughter: the willful (nonnegligent) killing of one human being by another. Deaths caused by negligence, attempts to kill, assaults to kill, suicides, accidental deaths, and justifiable homicides are excluded. Justifiable homicides are limited to: (1) the killing of a felon by a law enforcement officer in the line of duty; and (2) the killing of a felon, during the commission of a felony, by a private citizen. b. Manslaughter by negligence: the killing of another person through gross negligence. Traffic fatalities are excluded. While manslaughter by negligence is a Part I crime, it is not included in the Crime Index.
Forcible rape	The carnal knowledge of a female forcibly and against her will. Included are rapes by force and attempts or assaults to rape. Statutory offenses (no force used—victim under age of consent) are excluded.
Robbery	The taking or attempting to take anything of value from the care, custody, or control of a person or persons by force or threat of force or violence and/or by putting the victim in fear.
Aggravated assault	An unlawful attack by one person upon another for the purpose of inflicting severe or aggravated bodily injury. This type of assault usually is accompanied by the use of a weapon or by means likely to produce death or great bodily harm. Simple assaults are excluded.
Burglary/breaking or entering	The unlawful entry of a structure to commit a felony or a theft. Attempted forcible entry is included.
Larceny/theft (except motor vehicle theft)	The unlawful taking, carrying, leading, or riding away of property from the possession or constructive possession of another. Examples are thefts of bicycles or automobile accessories, shoplifting, pocket-picking, or the stealing of any property or article which is not taken by force and violence or by fraud. Attempted larcenies are included. Embezzlement, "con" games, forgery, worthless checks, etc., are excluded.
Motor vehicle theft	The theft or attempted theft of a motor vehicle. A motor vehicle is self-propelled and runs on the surface and not on rails. Specifically excluded from this category are motorboats, construction equipment, airplanes, and farming equipment.
Arson	Any willful or malicious burning or attempt to burn, with or without intent to defraud, a dwelling house, public building, motor vehicle or aircraft, personal property of another, etc.

Source: FBI, Uniform Crime Report, 1995, p. 373.

three main areas of concern: reporting practices, law enforcement practices, and methodological problems.

REPORTING PRACTICES. One major concern of criminologists is that many serious crimes are not reported by victims to police and therefore do not become part of the UCR. The reasons for not reporting vary. Some people do not have property insurance and therefore believe it is useless to report theft-related crimes. In other cases, the victim may fear reprisals from the offender's friends or family.

Surveys of crime victims indicate that fewer than 40% of all criminal incidents are reported to the police, chiefly because the victim believed the incident was "a private matter," that "nothing could be done," or that the "victimization was not important enough."[2] These findings indicate that the UCR data may significantly underrepresent the total number of annual criminal events.

LAW ENFORCEMENT PRACTICES. The way police departments record and report criminal and delinquent activity also affects the validity of UCR statistics. This effect was recognized more than 40 years ago, when between 1948 and 1952 the number of burglaries in New York City rose from 2,726 to 42,491, and larcenies increased from 7,713 to 70,949.[3] These increases were found to be related to the change from a precinct to a centralized reporting system for crime statistics.[4]

How law enforcement agencies interpret the definitions of index crimes may also affect reporting practices. Some departments may define crimes loosely—for example, reporting a trespass as a burglary or an assault on a women as an attempted rape—while others pay strict attention to FBI guidelines; these reporting practices may help explain interjurisdictional differences in crime.[5] Patrick Jackson found, for example, that arson may be seriously underreported because many fire departments do not report to the FBI, and those that do define as accidental or spontaneous many fires that are probably set by arsonists.[6]

Some local police departments make systematic errors in UCR reporting. Some count an arrest only after a formal booking procedure, although the UCR requires arrests to be counted if the suspect is released without a formal charge. One survey of arrests found an error rate of about 10% in every Part I offense category.[7]

Of a more serious nature are allegations that police officials may deliberately alter reported crimes to improve their department's public image. Police administrators interested in lowering the crime rate may falsify crime reports, such as by classifying a burglary as a nonreportable trespass.[8]

Ironically, boosting police efficiency and professionalism may actually help *increase* crime rates. Higher crime rates may occur as departments adopt more sophisticated computer-aided technology and hire better-educated and better-trained employees. One study by Robert O'Brien found that crime rates are significantly affected by the way law enforcement agencies process UCR data. As the number of nonsworn (civilian) police employees assigned to dispatching, record keeping, and criminal incident reporting increased in the United States, so, too, did national crime rates. What appears to be a rising crime rate may have been an artifact of improved police record-keeping ability.[9]

METHODOLOGICAL PROBLEMS. Methodological issues also raise questions about the UCR's validity. Among the most often cited are

1. No federal crimes are reported.

2. Reports are voluntary and vary in accuracy and completeness.

3. Not all police departments submit reports.

4. The FBI uses estimates in its total crime projections.

5. If multiple crimes are committed by an offender, only the most serious is recorded. Thus, if a narcotics addict rapes, robs, and murders a victim, only the murder is recorded as a crime. Consequently, many lesser crimes go unreported.

6. Each act is listed as a single offense for some crimes but not others. If a man robbed six people in a bar, the offense is listed as one robbery; but if he assaulted or murdered them, it would be listed as six assaults and/or six murders.

7. Incomplete acts are lumped together with completed ones.

8. Important differences exist between the FBI's definitions of certain crimes and those used in a number of states.[10]

Future of the Uniform Crime Report

What does the future hold for the UCR? The FBI is preparing to implement some important changes in the Uniform Crime Report. First, the definitions of many crimes will be revised. For example, rape will be defined in sexually neutral terms: *the carnal knowledge of a person, forcibly and/or against that person's will; or not forcibly or against the person's will where the victim is incapable of giving consent because of his or her temporary or permanent mental incapacity.*

An attempt will also be made to provide more detailed information on individual criminal incidents through the National Incident-Based Reporting System. Instead of submitting statements of the kinds of crimes that individual citizens have reported to the police and summary statements of resulting arrests, local police agencies will provide at least a brief account of each incident and arrest within 22 crime patterns, including incident, victim, and offender information. These expanded crime categories will include numerous additional crimes, such as blackmail, embezzlement, drug offenses, and bribery. This will permit a national database on the nature of crime, victims, and criminals to be developed.[11] Other information to be collected will include statistics gathered by federal law enforcement agencies, as well as data on hate or bias crimes. These changes were initiated in 1989, and the first reports reflecting them should be out in the near future. If it is implemented on schedule, this new UCR program may bring about greater uniformity in cross-jurisdictional reporting and improve the accuracy of official crime data.

Self-Report Surveys

The problems associated with official statistics have led many criminologists to seek alternative sources of information in assessing the true extent of crime patterns. In addition, official statistics do not say much about the personality, attitudes, and behavior of individual criminals. They also are of little value in charting the extent of substance abuse in the population, because relatively few abusers are arrested. Criminologists have therefore sought additional sources to supplement and expand official data.

One commonly used alternative to official statistics is the **self-report survey.** Self-report studies are designed to allow participants to reveal information about their violations of the law. The studies have many formats. For example, the criminologist can approach people who have been arrested by police, or even prison inmates, and interview them about their illegal activities. Subjects can also first be telephoned at home and then mailed a survey form. Most often, self-report surveys are administered to large groups through a mass distribution of questionnaires. The names of subjects can be requested, but more commonly, they remain anonymous. The basic assumption of self-report

Table 3.2 Self-Report Survey Questions

PLEASE INDICATE HOW OFTEN IN THE PAST 12 MONTHS YOU DID EACH ACT. (CHECK THE BEST ANSWER.)

	NEVER DID ACT	ONE TIME	2–5 TIMES	6–9 TIMES	10+ TIMES
Stole something worth less than $50	_____	_____	_____	_____	_____
Stole something worth more than $50	_____	_____	_____	_____	_____
Used cocaine	_____	_____	_____	_____	_____
Been in a fistfight	_____	_____	_____	_____	_____
Carried a weapon such as a gun or knife	_____	_____	_____	_____	_____
Fought someone using a weapon	_____	_____	_____	_____	_____

studies is that the anonymity of the respondents and the promise of confidentiality backed by the academic credentials of the survey administrator will encourage people to accurately describe their illegal activities. Self-reports are viewed as a mechanism to get at the "dark figures of crime," the figures missed by official statistics. Table 3.2 shows some typical self-report items.

The Focus of Self-Reports

Most self-report studies have focused on juvenile delinquency and youth crime, for two reasons.[12] First, the school setting makes it convenient to test thousands of subjects simultaneously, all of them with the means to respond to a research questionnaire at their disposal (pens, desks, time). Second, since attendance is universal, a school-based self-report survey is an estimate of the activities of a cross-section of the community.

Self-reports, though, are not restricted to youth crime and have been used to examine the offense histories of prison inmates, drug users, and other subsets of the population.

Self-reports make it possible to assess the number of people in the population who have committed illegal acts and the frequency of their law violations. They are particularly useful for assessing the extent of the national substance abuse problem, as most drug use goes undetected by police. And, because most self-report instruments also contain items measuring subjects' attitudes, values, personal characteristics, and behaviors, the data obtained from them can be used for various purposes, such as testing theories, measuring attitudes toward crime, and computing the association between crime and important social variables, such as family relations, educational attainment, and income.

Self-reports provide a broader picture of the distribution of criminality than official data because they do not depend on the offender being apprehended. They can be used to estimate the number of criminal offenders who are unknown to the police and who never figure in the official crime statistics, some of whom may even be serious or chronic offenders.[13] Since many criminologists believe that class, gender, and racial bias exists in the criminal justice system, self-reports allow evaluation of the distribution of criminal behavior across racial, class, and gender lines. Their use enables criminologists to determine whether the official arrest data are truly representative of the offender population or reflects bias, discrimination, and selective enforcement. For example, racial bias may be present if surveys indicate that blacks and whites report equal amounts of crime, but the official data indicate that minorities are *arrested* more often than whites. In sum, self-reports can provide a significant amount of information about offenders that cannot be found in the official statistics.

The Accuracy of Self-Reports

Though self-report data have had a profound effect on criminological inquiry, some important methodological issues have been raised about their accuracy. Critics of self-report studies suggest that it is unreasonable to expect people to candidly admit illegal acts. They have nothing to gain, and the ones taking the greatest risk are the ones with official records who may be engaging in the most criminality. On the other hand, some people may exaggerate their criminal acts, may forget some of them, or may be confused about what is being asked. Most surveys contain an overabundance of trivial offenses—skipping school, running away, using a false ID—often lumped together with serious crimes to form a "total crime index." Consequently, comparisons between groups can be highly misleading. Nor can we be certain how valid self-report studies are, because we have nothing reliable to measure them against. Correlation with official reports is expected to be low, because the inadequacies of those reports were largely responsible for the development of self-reports in the first place.

Various techniques have been used to verify self-report data.[14] The "known group" method compares incarcerated youths with "normal" groups to see whether the former report more delinquency. Another approach is to use peer informants who can verify the honesty of a subject's answers. Subjects may also be tested twice to see whether their answers remain stable. Sometimes questions are designed to reveal respondents who are lying on the survey; for example, an item might say: "I have never done anything wrong in my life." It is also possible to compare the answers youths give with their official police records. A typical approach is to ask youths if they have ever been arrested for or convicted of a delinquent act and then check their official records against their self-reported responses. A number of studies using this method have found a remarkable uniformity between self-reported answers and the official record.[15] In a classic study, John Clark and Larry Tifft used a polygraph to verify the responses given on a self-report survey; they reported that the "lie detector" results validated survey data.[16] In what is probably the most thorough analysis of self-report methodologies, Michael Hindelang, Travis Hirschi, and Joseph Weis closely reviewed the literature concerning the reliability and validity of self-reports and concluded that (a) the problems of accuracy in self-reports are "surmountable," (b) self-reports are more accurate than most criminologists believe, and (c) self-reports and official statistics are quite compatible.[17]

The "Missing Cases" Issue

Although these findings are encouraging, nagging questions still remain about the validity of self-reports. Even if 90% of a school population voluntarily participate in a self-report study, researchers can never know for sure whether the few who refuse to participate or are absent that day make up a significant portion of the school's population of persistent high-rate offenders.

Connections

Criminologists suspect that a few high-rate offenders are responsible for a disproportionate share of all serious crime. Results would be badly skewed if even a few of these chronic offenders were absent or refused to participate in a schoolwide self-report survey. For more on the chronic offenders, see the sections at the end of this chapter.

School surveys also miss incarcerated youth and dropouts, whose numbers may include some of the most serious offenders. Research by Terence Thornberry and his associates implies that the "missing cases" in self-reports may be more crime-prone than the general population.[18]

It is also possible that self-reports are weakest in the one area in which they are most heavily relied on: measuring substance abuse.[19] Thomas Gray and Eric Wish have found that drug users may significantly underreport the frequency of their substance abuse. Gray and Wish surveyed a group of juvenile detainees and also tested them with urinalysis. They found that *less than one-third* of the kids who tested positively for marijuana also reported using it, while only 15% of those testing positive for cocaine admitted to having used it during the prior month. While this research involves a sample of incarcerated youth who might be expected to underreport drug use, the findings undercut the validity of self-report surveys.[20] Wish and Christina Polsenberg conducted similar research with adult pretrial detainees in Washington, D.C. and again found that self-reports significantly undercounted drug abuse.[21]

So while self-reports are a widely used measure of criminal behavior, their accuracy in determining the behavior of two critical elements of the offending population, chronic offenders and persistent drug abusers, may be limited.

Connections

Self-report data are used as the standard measure of the nation's youth drug population. When reading the results of national drug use surveys in Chapter 14, keep in mind this research on the validity of self-report surveys. Are heavy crack cocaine users likely to accurately respond to a self-report survey?

Victim Surveys

A third source of crime data are surveys that ask the victims of crime about their encounters with criminals. Because many victims do not report their experiences to the police, victim surveys are considered a method of getting at the dark figures of crime.

The first national survey of 10,000 households was conducted in 1966 as part of the President's Commission on Law Enforcement and the Administration of Justice. The commission was a groundbreaking attempt that brought many of the nation's leading law enforcement and academic experts together to develop a picture of the crime problem in the United States and how the criminal justice system responds to criminal behavior. The national survey indicated that the number of criminal victimizations in the United States was far higher than previously believed, as many victims failed to report crime to the police, fearing retaliation or official indifference.

This early research encouraged development of the most widely used and most extensive victim survey to date, the **National Crime Victimization Survey (NCVS)**.[22]

The National Crime Victimization Survey

The National Crime Victimization Survey is conducted by the U.S. Bureau of the Census in cooperation with the Bureau of Justice Statistics of the U.S. Department of Justice. In the national surveys, samples of housing units are selected using a complex, multistage sampling technique.

The total annual sample size for the most recent national survey is about 56,000 households, containing about 120,000 individuals over 12 years of age. The total sample is interviewed twice a year about victimizations suffered in the preceding six months. The crimes they are asked about include personal and household larcenies, burglary, motor vehicle theft, assaults, robberies, and any other violent acts.

Households remain in the sample for about three years, and new homes rotate into the sample on an ongoing basis. The NCVS reports that the interview completion rate in the national sample is usually more than 90% of those selected to be interviewed in any given period. Considering the care with which the samples are drawn and the high completion rate, NCVS data are considered a relatively unbiased and valid estimate of all victimizations for the target crimes included in the survey.

Connections

Not only do victim surveys provide indications of criminal incidents, but they can also be used to describe the individuals who are most at risk to crime and where and when they are most likely to become victimized. Data from recent NCVS surveys are used in Chapter 4 to draw a portrait of the nature and extent of victimization in the United States.

Is the NCVS Valid?

Like the UCR and self-report surveys, the NCVS may suffer from some methodological problems, so its findings must be interpreted with caution. Among the potential problems are

- Overreporting due to victims' misinterpretation of events. For example, a lost wallet is reported as stolen, or an open door is viewed as a burglary attempt.
- Underreporting due to embarrassment of reporting crime to interviewers, fear of getting in trouble, or simply forgetting an incident.
- Inability to record the personal criminal activity of those interviewed, such as drug use or gambling; murder is also not included, for obvious reasons.
- Sampling errors which produce a group of respondents who are not representative of the nation as a whole.
- Inadequate question format which invalidates responses. Some groups such as adolescents may be particularly susceptible to error because of question format.[23]

In 1992 the NCVS was redesigned to improve its validity. One important change is that victims are now asked directly whether they have been raped or sexually assaulted. In the past, rape was indirectly surveyed with the question "Did anything else happen to you?"

Are Crime Statistics Sources Compatible?

Characteristic When Where

Are the various sources of criminal statistics compatible? Each has its own strengths and weaknesses. The FBI survey is carefully tallied and contains data on the number of murders and people arrested, information that the other data sources lack; yet it omits the many crimes that victims choose not to report to the police and is subject to the reporting caprices of individual police departments. The NCVS does contain unreported crime and important information on the personal characteristics of victims, but the data consist of estimates made from relatively limited samples of the total U.S. population, so that even narrow fluctuations in the rates of some crimes can have a major impact on findings; it also relies on personal recollections that may be inaccurate. The NCVS does not include data on important crime patterns, including murder and drug abuse. In their favor, self-report surveys can provide information on the personal characteristics of offenders—their attitudes, values, beliefs, and psychological profile—that is unavailable from any other source. Yet, at their core, self-reports rely on the honesty of criminal offenders and drug abusers, a population not generally known for accuracy and integrity.

Despite these differences, a number of prominent criminologists have concluded that the data sources are more compatible than was first believed possible. While their tallies of crimes are certainly not in synch, the **crime patterns and trends** they record are often quite similar.[24] For example, all three sources are in general agreement about the personal characteristics of serious criminals (such as age and gender) and where and when crime occurs (such as urban areas, nighttime, and summer months).

While this finding may be persuasive, some criminologists still question the compatibility between the data sources and imply that they measure separate concepts (for example, reported crimes, actual crimes, and victimization rates).[25] This ongoing academic debate punctuates the fact that interpreting crime data is often problematic. Because each source of crime data uses a different method to obtain results, differences will inevitably occur between them. These differences must be carefully considered when interpreting the data on the nature and trends in crime that follow.[26]

Official Crime Trends in the United States

Studies using official statistics have indicated that a gradual increase in the crime rate, especially in violent crime,

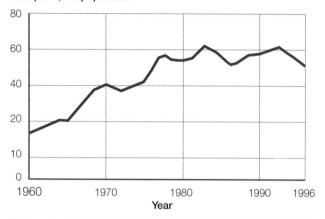

Figure 3.1 Crime rate trends, 1960–1996. The overall crime rate declined during the first half of the 1990s. Rates dropped about 15% between 1991 and 1996.

Rate per 1,000 population

Source: FBI, Uniform Crime Report, 1995 updated 1996.

occurred from 1830 to 1860. Following the Civil War, this rate increased significantly for about 15 years. Then, from 1880 to the time of World War I, with the possible exception of the years immediately preceding and following the war, the number of reported crimes decreased. After a period of readjustment, the overall crime rate steadily declined until the Depression (about 1930), whereupon another general increase, or crime wave, was recorded.[27] Crime rates increased gradually following the 1930s until the 1960s, when they grew much faster. The homicide rate, which had declined from the 1930s to the 1970s, began a period of sharp increase.

As Figure 3.1 indicates, the crime rate began to increase sharply in 1960 and continued to do so through the 1970s until 1981, when more than 13.4 million index crimes were reported—a rate of 5,950 per 100,000 people. After a decline in the mid-1980s to 11.1 million crimes, the number of crimes again increased to about 14 million 1991 and then began to decline. As Figure 3.1 shows, the crime rate has been in decline ever since. In 1996 about 13.4 million crimes were reported to police, down from 13.8 million in 1995. The decline is both unexpected and welcome. However, it remains to be seen whether crime rates will continue to stabilize or turn course and increase.

Self-Report Trends

In general, self-reports indicate that the number of people who break the law is far greater than the number projected by the official statistics. In fact, when truancy, alcohol consumption, petty theft, and recreational drug use are included in self-report scales, almost everyone tested is found to have violated some law.[28] Furthermore, self-reports dispute the notion that criminals and delinquents specialize in

one type of crime or another; offenders seem to engage in a "mixed bag" of crime and deviance.[29]

Self-report studies indicate that the most common offenses are truancy, alcohol abuse, use of a false ID, shoplifting or larceny under $50, fighting, marijuana use, and damage to the property of others. It is not unusual for self-reports to find combined substance abuse, theft, violence, and damage rates of more than 50% among suburban, rural, and urban high school youths. What is surprising is the consistency of these findings in samples taken from southern, eastern, midwestern, and western states.

When the results of recent self-report surveys are compared with various studies conducted over a 20-year period, a uniform pattern emerges. The use of drugs and alcohol increased markedly in the 1970s, leveled off in the 1980s, and then began to increase in the mid-1990s; theft, violence, and damage-related crimes seem more stable. Although a self-reported crime wave has not occurred, neither has there been any visible reduction in self-reported criminality.[30]

Table 3.3 contains data from a self-report study called *Monitoring the Future,* which is conducted on an annual basis by researchers at the University of Michigan Institute for Social Research (ISR). This national survey of over 2,500 high school seniors, one of the most important sources of self-report data, also finds a widespread yet stable pattern of youth crime since 1978.[31] The ISR survey does show that young people commit a great deal of crime. About 30% of

Table 3.3 Self-Reported Delinquent Activity during the Past 12 Months—High School Senior Class of 1995

	PERCENT ENGAGING IN OFFENSES	
CRIME CATEGORY	**At Least One Offense**	**Multiple Offenses**
Serious fight	8%	7%
Gang fight	10%	8%
Hurt someone badly	7%	6%
Used a weapon to steal	2%	2%
Stole less than $50	14%	17%
Stole more than $50	4%	6%
Shoplifted	12%	17%
Did breaking and entering	11%	13%
Committed arson	1.5%	1%
Damaged school property	6%	8%

Source: *Monitoring the Future, 1995* (Ann Arbor, Mich.: Institute for Social Research, 1996).

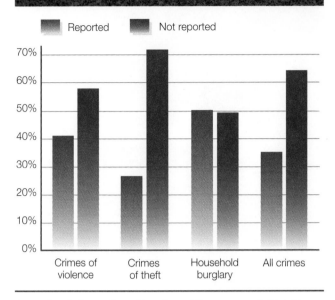

Figure 3.2 Percent of victimizations, by type of crime and whether or not reported to the police. Victim surveys indicate that fewer than half of all crimes are reported to police.

Source: Craig Perkins and Patsy Klaus, *Criminal Victimization in the United States 1994* (Washington, D.C.: Bureau of Justice Statistics, 1996).

high school seniors now report having stolen at least once in the previous 12 months, almost 20% said they had been involved in a "gang fight," and more than 10% had injured someone so badly that the victim had to see a doctor. About 30% admitted to shoplifting, and almost one quarter had engaged in breaking and entering. While the self-reported delinquency rate has been stable, the fact that at least one-third of all U.S. high school students had engaged in theft and at least 19% had committed a serious violent act during the past year shows that criminal activity is widespread and not restricted to a few "bad apples."

Victim Survey Trends

According to the most recently available NCVS data (1995), about 40 million crimes occur each year, including 10 million personal crimes (rape, robbery) and about 30 million property crimes.

There has been a stable but steady decrease in the total number of victimizations in the 1990s, a finding that reflects the official crime (UCR) data. For example, between 1993 and 1995 the number of victimizations declined by about 4 million, or almost 10%. The decline in the violent crimes measured by the NCVS has been even greater than that recorded by the UCR. Especially encouraging was the significant decline of 18% in reported rapes in a single year (1994–1995).

While the decline in NCVS rates mirrors recent UCR trends, it is quite apparent that the number of crimes accounted for by the NCVS is considerably larger than the

number of crimes reported to the FBI. For example, whereas the UCR recorded about 540,000 robberies in 1995, the NCVS estimates that about 1.1 million actually occurred. The reason for such discrepancies is that fewer than half the violent crimes, less than one-third the personal theft crimes (such as pocket picking), and fewer than half the household thefts are reported to police (see Figure 3.2). The reasons most often given by victims for not reporting crime include believing that "nothing can be done about it," that it was a "private matter," or that they did not want to "get involved." Victims seem to report to the police only crimes that involve considerable loss or injury. If we are to believe NCVS findings, the official statistics do not provide an accurate picture of the crime problem, as more than half of crimes go unreported to the police.

Explaining Crime Trends

What factors produce increases or decreases in the crime rate? How can the recent decline in the violence rate be explained? A number of critical factors have been used to explain crime rate trends. A few of the most important are discussed here.

AGE. Criminologists see changes in the age distribution of the population as having had the greatest influence on recent violent crime trends. As a general rule, the crime rate follows the proportion of young males in the population (see Figure 3.3). The postwar baby-boom generation reached their teenage years in the 1960s, just as the crime rate began a sharp increase. Since both the victims and perpetrators of crime tend to fall in the 18-to-25 age category, the rise in crime reflected the age structure of society. With the "graying" of society in the 1980s and a decline in the birth rate, it was not

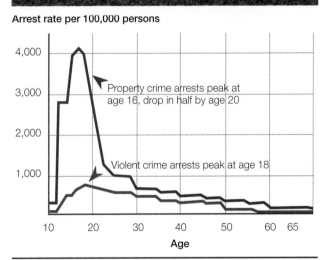

Figure 3.3 The relationship between age and serious crime arrests.

Arrest rate per 100,000 persons

Property crime arrests peak at age 16, drop in half by age 20

Violent crime arrests peak at age 18

Age

Source: FBI, Uniform Crime Report, 1995, pp. 218–219.

The availability of firearms may influence the crime rate, especially the proliferation of weapons in the hands of teens. It is still relatively easy to buy high powered weapons, and there is evidence that more guns than ever before are finding their way into the hands of young people. Sophisticated automatic weapons, some of which are laser-aimed, have become armament for juvenile gangs and criminal groups.

surprising that the overall crime rate stabilized between 1990 and 1995. Because the number of juveniles should be increasing over the next decade, some criminologists fear that this will signal a return to escalating crime rates.

Despite a recent dip in juvenile violence rates, this generation of teens seems more violent than earlier cohorts. Between 1970 and 1995, the rate of adolescents arrested for homicide *more than doubled,* while homicide arrest rates for adults actually *declined.*[32] It remains to be seen whether teenage crime rates will continue their upward progression; stabilization would substantially lower crime rates, as teens make up a significant proportion of offenders.

THE ECONOMY. There is still debate over the effects the economy has on crime rates. Some criminologists believe that a poor economy actually helps lower crime rates! Unemployed parents are at home to supervise children and guard their homes. And because there is less money to spend, a poor economy means that there are actually fewer valuables around worth stealing. It also seems unlikely that law-abiding, middle-aged workers will suddenly turn to a life of crime if they are laid off during an economic downturn.

However, it is possible that long-term periods of sustained economic weakness and unemployment may eventually affect crime rates. The long-term economic recession that occurred in the late 1980s may have produced a climate of hopelessness in the nation's largest cities, which saw increased violence rates between 1985 and 1990.

Teenage unemployment rates are especially high in urban areas that contain large at-risk populations.

SOCIAL MALAISE. As the level of social problems increases, so do crime rates. Increases in the number of single-parent families, in divorce and dropout rates, in non-recreational drug use, and in teen pregnancies may also influence crime rates. Cross-national research indicates that child homicide rates are greatest in those nations, including the United States, that have the highest rates of illegitimacy and teenage mothers.[33] As illegitimacy rates rise and social spending is cut, the rate of violent crime might trend upward. Social malaise may explain why some cities and regions have higher crime rates than others.

Connections

The link between the economy, social malaise, and the crime rate is important for criminological theory. If crime rates are higher in poor or distressed regions, there may be an association between poverty and crime. This is the assumption made by the social structure theorists, who are discussed in Chapter 7.

GUNS. The availability of firearms, especially the proliferation of weapons in the hands of teens, may influence the crime rate. There is evidence that more guns than ever

While crime rates are higher in the United States than in most other Western nations, violence abroad is not unknown. The most catastrophic incident occurred in the village of Dunblane, Scotland, at 3:10 p.m. on July 8, 1996, when heavily armed Horret Campbell walked onto the grounds of St. Lukes Infants School and began to methodically shoot children in this kindergarten class. Sixteen children and their teacher were killed. The Dunblane massacre prompted the passage of legislation to control handguns in Scotland and England, which failed to please some critics who felt there should be an outright ban on the possession of guns.

before are finding their way into the hands of young people. The number of juveniles arrested on weapons charges rose 75% between 1986 and 1995.[34] Joseph Sheley and James Wright conducted a comprehensive analysis of data acquired from 835 male inmates in six correctional facilities and 758 male students in ten inner-city high schools. More than half of high school students had friends who owned guns, and 42% routinely carried them around outside the home! Sheley and Wright also found a disturbing trend of gun ownership and use among the inmates (86%) and students (30%).[35] The Sheley and Wright survey suggests that in at least some areas of the United States juvenile gun possession is all too prevalent and may in part be responsible for increasing violence rates.

GANGS. Another factor in crime rates may be the explosive growth in teenage gangs. Surveys indicate that there are more than 500,000 gang members in the United States. There has been an upswing in gang violence. For example, Chicago, which had never experienced more than 88 gang homicides per year prior to 1990, had 240 in 1994 and almost as many in 1995.[36] One reason is that there is a clear connection between gang membership and firearm use. Gang members engage in a far higher level of firearm possession than other boys, and members participate in firearm-related activity much more often than nonmembers.

DRUGS. Increasing drug use may affect crime rates. According to Alfred Blumstein, groups and gangs involved in the urban drug trade recruit juveniles because they work cheaply, are immune from heavy criminal penalties, and are "daring and willing to take risks."[37] Arming themselves for protection, these drug-dealing kids present a menace that persuades neighborhood adolescents to arm themselves for protection. The result is an "arms race" that produces an increasing spiral of violence.

Some experts tie increases in the violent crime rate between 1980 and 1990 to the "crack cocaine" epidemic that swept the nation's largest cities and the drug-trafficking gangs that fought over "drug turf." These well-armed gangs did not hesitate to use violence to control territories, intimidate rivals, and increase "market share." Washington, D.C. provides a dramatic example of the drug-crime relationship: In 1985, 21% of the homicides there were reported as drug related; by 1988, 80% of the homicides were drug related.[38] With the waning of the crack epidemic (users are switching to heroin), violence seems to have subsided in New York City and other metropolitan areas where the crack epidemic was rampant.[39]

JUSTICE POLICY. Some law enforcement experts have suggested that reduction in crime rates may be attributed to aggressive police practices that target "quality of life"

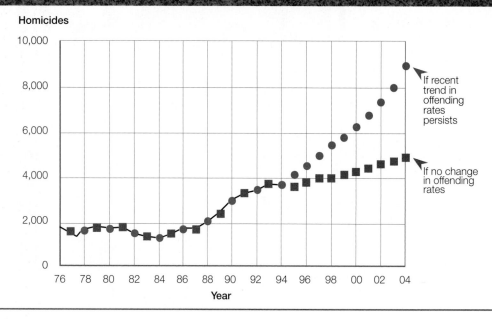

Source: James Alan Fox, *Trends in Juvenile Violence: A Report to the United States Attorney General on Current and Future Rates of Juvenile Offending* (Boston, Mass.: Northeastern University, 1996).

Connections

The drug-crime connection is a critical one for lawmakers. If drug use causes crime rates to increase, then the outright ban on drugs is warranted. If there is no drug-crime connection, efforts to legalize drug use might be justified. For sections on the drug-crime connection and the legalization issue, see Chapter 14.

crimes such as panhandling, graffiti, petty drug dealing, and loitering. By showing that even the smallest infractions will be dealt with seriously, aggressive police departments may be able to discourage potential criminals from committing even more serious crimes.

It is also possible that tough laws targeting drug dealing and repeat offenders with lengthy prison terms can have an effect on crime rates. The fear of punishment may inhibit some would-be criminals. Lengthy sentences also help boost the nation's prison population It is possible that placing a significant number of potentially high-rate offenders behind bars helps stabilize crime rates.

Connections

While there is still a great deal of debate over the impact that incarcerating criminals has on crime rates, most scholars dispute the idea that "locking 'em up" alone can bring crime rates down. New criminals are continually coming along to replace those behind bars. For more on this topic, see the sections in Chapter 6 on incapacitation.

What the Future Holds

It is always risky to speculate about the future of crime trends, since current conditions can change rapidly. But some criminologists have gone out on a limb to predict future patterns. Darrell Steffensmeier and Miles Harer suggest that violent crime will drop during the remainder of the 1990s as the baby boomers pass into middle and old age, while the property crime rate will at first decline, then level off and begin rising toward the end of the decade as the baby-boomlet kids born in the early 1980s begin to hit their "peak" crime years. After the year 2000, both property and violent crimes are predicted to increase.[40] Steffensmeier and Harer consider the age structure of society to be the single most powerful influence on the crime rate.

In a similar vein, criminologist James A. Fox predicts a significant increase in teen violence if current trends persist. In 1996 there were 39 million children in the United States under age 10, more than we have had for decades. Lacking stable families and adequate supervision, these kids will soon be entering their "prime crime" years. As a result, Fox predicts a wave of youth violence that will be even worse than that of the past ten years. If current trends persist, the number of juvenile homicides should grow from less than 4,000 today to about 9,000 in 2004 (see Figure 3.4).[41]

Of course, such predictions are based on population trends and can be thrown off by changes in the economy, justice policy, drug use, gun availability, gang membership, and other socio-cultural forces. Fox suggests that if social conditions worsen, teen homicide might increase even more. It is also possible that current national outrage over violent crime will help make violence so unpalatable that

Despite the fact that Japan is a large industrialized country whose population is jammed into overcrowded urban areas, its crime rate is extremely low compared to that of the United States. It is not surprising that the fear of crime is also relatively low in Japan, even though—like their American counterparts—the Japanese news media tend to focus a lot of attention on the few lurid and violent incidents that do occur. How can this difference be explained?

Cultural differences may play an important role in controlling crime in Japan. In the United States, individualism and self-gratification are emphasized, and success is defined in terms of material goods and possessions. To achieve an upper-class lifestyle, people are willing to engage in confrontations, increasing the likelihood of violence.

In Japan, honor is the most important personal trait. Japan's homogeneous society has a written history that spans 14 centuries. The Japanese are deeply loyal to historical traditions, which provide a sense of moral order. They belong to a network of social groups that provide a sense of place and of self, which creates a strong commitment to social norms. In contrast, America's melting pot society has not allowed the same sort of moral order or tradition to develop. The most important cultural norms in Japan are extraordinary patience when seeking change, a cooperative approach to decision making, extreme respect for seniority and age, and concern for society at the expense of the individual. Japanese

customs that subordinate personal feelings for the good of the group produce fewer violent confrontations than the U.S. stress on individualism.

Nowhere are obedience and respect more important in Japan than in relationships with family members and friends. Children owe parents total respect; younger siblings must obey older brothers and sisters; younger friends show reverence toward older acquaintances; and all show respect to the emperor. Bowing, a familiar Japanese custom, symbolizes this respect. The Japanese, then, are deterred from criminal behavior not only because of moral principles of right and wrong but also to avoid embarrassment to self, family, or acquaintances. John Braithwaite notes that this fear of shame is the key to the crime rate differences between the United States and Japan. While lawbreakers are shunned in the United States, in Japan shameful acts are confronted in an effort to reintegrate offenders into society.

Although Japanese crime rates are low, what crime there is tends to involve organized criminal gangs. Youth in the *bosozoku* (hot-rodder) and "yankee" gangs flaunt conventional dress and speech codes so important in Japan. Members embrace an overtly macho behavioral code, featuring violence, reckless driving, and drug use. They may "graduate" into *yakuza gangs*, the huge organized crime groups that are responsible for a significant portion of all crimes in Japan. *Yakuza* engage in drug trafficking, extortion, gambling, and other criminal conspiracies sim-

ilar to American organized crime activities. They are often hired by legitimate enterprises to "settle" labor disputes, close business deals, and collect debts. While membership in traditional organized crime families is on the wane in the United States, the number of *yakuza* members has increased sharply to an estimated 88,000, four times that of their American "colleagues." Interestingly, the *yakuza* demand the same sense of loyalty and respect given legitimate social institutions; honor in Japan has no bounds.

CRITICAL THINKING QUESTIONS

1. Considering all things, what aspects of Japanese society do you think are responsible for its low crime rate?
2. What can be done to bring the crime rate down in the United States?

Sources: Ted Westermann and James Burfeind, *Crime and Justice in Two Societies, Japan and the United States* (Pacific Grove, Calif.: Brooks/Cole, 1991); Joachim Kersten, "Street Youths, *Bosozoku*, and *Yakuza*: Subculture Formation and Social Reactions in Japan," *Crime and Delinquency* 39 (1993): 277–295; Koichiro Ito, "Research on the Fear of Crime: Perceptions and Realities of Crime in Japan," *Crime and Delinquency* 39 (1993): 392–395; Michael Vaughn and Nobuho Tomita, "A Longitudinal Analysis of Japanese Crime from 1926–1987: The Pre-War, War and Post-War Eras," *International Journal of Comparative and Applied Criminal Justice* 14 (1990): 145–160; John Braithwaite, *Crime, Shame and Reintegration* (Cambridge: Cambridge University Press, 1989).

local residents will be willing to take drastic actions to reduce crime, including cooperating with the police and pressuring neighborhood families to control their young. Research by Rosemary Gartner and Robert Nash Parker shows that murder rates in Japan and Scotland have been unaffected by population trends because in these nations violence is considered shameful and a disgrace.[42] Can changing moral values influence crime rates? The Close-Up "Crime and Shame: Crime Rates in the United States and Japan" takes a closer look at this question.

Net Bookmark

Comparing cross-national crime rates can be difficult because each country measures crime differently. International criminal justice crime data references can be found at the UNCJIN—Countries of the World reference page. This is an attempt to bring together information on as many countries as possible.

http://www.ifs.univie.ac.at/~uncjin/country.html

Crime Patterns

What do the various sources of criminological statistics tell us about crime in the United States? What is known about the nature of crime and criminals? What trends or patterns exist in the crime rate that can help us understand the causes of crime?

Criminologists look for stable patterns in the crime rate to gain insight into the nature of crime. If crime rates are consistently higher at certain times, in certain areas, and among certain groups, this knowledge might be used to explain the onset or cause of crime. For example, if criminal statistics show that crime rates are consistently higher in poor neighborhoods in large urban areas, then crime may be a function of poverty and neighborhood decline. If, in contrast, crime rates are spread evenly across the social structure, there would be little evidence that crime has an economic basis; crime might then be linked to socialization, personality, intelligence, or some other trait *unrelated* to class position or income. What, then, are the main traits and patterns in crime statistics?

The Ecology of Crime

There seem to be patterns in the crime rate that are linked to temporal and ecological factors. Some of the most important of these factors are the day, season, and climate; the temperature; population density; and geographical region.

DAY, SEASON, AND CLIMATE. Most reported crimes occur during the warm summer months of July and August. During the summer, teenagers, who usually have the highest crime levels, are out of school and have greater opportunity to commit crime. During warm weather, people spend more time outdoors, making themselves easier targets. Similarly, homes are left vacant more often during the summer, making them more vulnerable to property crimes. Two exceptions to this trend are murders and robberies, which occur most frequently in December and January (although rates are also high during the summer).

Crime rates may also be higher on the first day of a month than at any other time. Potential criminals believe that government welfare and social security checks arrive at this time and therefore increase such activities as breaking into mailboxes and accosting recipients on the streets. Also, people may have more disposable income at this time, and the availability of extra money may relate to behaviors associated with crime such as drinking, partying, gambling, and so on.[43]

TEMPERATURE. Although weather effects (that is, swings in temperature) may also influence violent crime rates, laboratory studies suggest that the association between temperature and crime resembles an inverted U-shaped curve: Crime rates increase with a rise in temperature and then begin to decline at some point (85° +) when it may simply be too hot for any physical exertion.[44] However, field studies indicate that the rates of some (such as domestic assault), but not all (such as rape) crimes continue to increase as temperatures rise.[45] Research has shown that a long stretch of highly uncomfortable weather is related to increased homicide rates, indicating that the stress of long-term exposure to extreme temperatures may prove sufficiently stressful to increase violence rates.[46] In their study of temperature effects on assault, Ellen Cohn and James Rotton found evidence that the effect was highly significant, especially during the morning and evening hours: A person is four times as likely to be assaulted at midnight when temperatures exceed 90° than when they are at 10° below zero![47]

POPULATION DENSITY. Areas with low per capita crime rates tend to be rural—large urban areas have by far the highest violence rates. These findings are also supported by victim data. Exceptions to this trend are low-population resort areas with large transient or seasonal populations, such as Atlantic City, New Jersey, and Nantucket, Massachusetts.

REGION. Definite differences are apparent in regional crime rates. For many years, southern states had significantly higher rates in almost all crime categories than were found in other regions of the country; these data convinced some criminologists that there was a *southern subculture of violence.* However, the western states now have the dubious distinction of having the highest crime and violence rates (see Figure 3.5).

Use of Firearms

There is little question that firearms play a major role in the commission of crime. According to the NCVS, firearms are involved in 20% of robberies, 10% of assaults, and 6% of rapes. In 1995 the UCR reported that 70% of all murders involved firearms; most of these weapons were handguns.

The relationship between crime and firearms is not surprising, considering the widespread availability and use of handguns.[48] The issue of gun control is discussed in the Close-Up on page 60.

Social Class and Crime

A still unresolved issue in the criminological literature is the relationship between social class and crime. Traditionally, crime has been thought of as a lower-class phenomenon. After all, people at the lowest rungs of the social structure have the greatest incentive to commit crimes. Those unable to obtain desired goods and services through conventional means may resort to theft and other illegal activities—such as the sale of narcotics—to obtain them; these activities are referred to as **instrumental crimes.** Those living in poverty areas are also believed to engage in disproportionate amounts of **expressive crimes,** such as rape and assault, as a means of expressing their rage, frustration, and anger

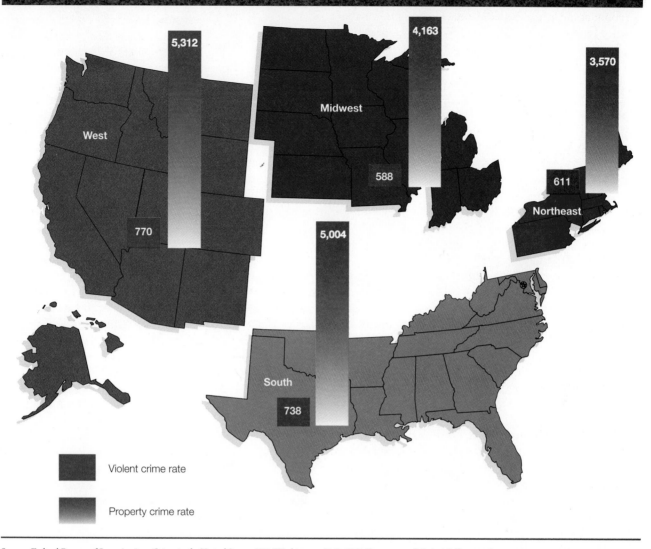

Figure 3.5 Regional violent and property crime rates (per 100,000 inhabitants). Note that the western states have the highest rates.

5,312

4,163

3,570

Midwest

588

West

611

Northeast

770

5,004

South

738

Violent crime rate

Property crime rate

Source: Federal Bureau of Investigation, *Crime in the United States, 1993* (Washington, D.C.: U.S. Government Printing Office, 1994), p. 9.

against society. Alcohol and drug abuse, common in poverty areas, helps fuel violent episodes.[49]

Official statistics indicate that crime rates in inner-city, high-poverty areas are generally higher than those in suburban or wealthier areas; for example, the highest homicide victimization levels are in deteriorated inner-city areas.[50] Studies using aggregate police statistics (arrest records) have consistently shown that crime rates in lower-class areas are higher than in wealthier neighborhoods. Another "official" indicator of a class-crime relationship can be obtained through surveys of prison inmates, which consistently show that prisoners were members of the lower class and unemployed or underemployed in the years before their incarceration.

An alternate explanation for these findings is that the relationship between official crime and social class is a function of law enforcement practices and not actual criminal behavior patterns. Police may devote more resources to poverty areas, and consequently, apprehension rates may be higher there. Similarly, police may be more likely to formally arrest and prosecute lower-class citizens than those in the middle and upper classes, which may account for the lower class's overrepresentation in the official statistics and the prison population.

CLASS AND SELF-REPORTS. Because of these factors, self-report data have been used extensively to test the class-crime relationship. If people in all social classes self-report similar crime patterns but only those in the lower class are formally arrested, that would explain the higher crime rates in lower-class neighborhoods. However, if

Considering the estimated more than 50 million illegal handguns in the United States today, it should come as no surprise that handguns are linked to many violent crimes, including 20% of all injury deaths (second to autos) and 60% of all homicides and suicides. Handguns are the cause of death for about two-thirds of all police killed in the line of duty. The association between guns and crime has spurred many Americans to advocate control of the sale of handguns and a ban on cheap "Saturday night specials." In contrast, most conservatives view gun control as a threat to personal liberty and call for severe punishment of criminals rather than control of handguns. What is more, they argue, the Second Amendment of the U.S. Constitution protects the "right to bear arms."

CONTROL METHODS

Efforts to control handguns have many sources. Each state and many local jurisdictions have laws banning or restricting sales or possession of guns. Others regulate dealers who sell guns. For example, the Federal Gun Control Act of 1968 prohibits dealers from selling guns to minors, ex-felons, and drug users. In addition, each dealer must keep detailed records of who purchases guns. Unfortunately, the resources available to enforce this law are meager.

Another method is to create a waiting period before a purchaser can obtain a handgun so that authorities can check the buyer's background. In 1993 Congress passed the *Brady Bill*, which requires a week-long waiting period (to do a background check) before a gun can be sold to an applicant. The bill was named after former Press Secretary James Brady, who was severely wounded in the attempted assassination of President Ronald Reagan by John Hinckley, Jr. Between March 1994 and June 1996, for all states together, there were almost 9 million applications to purchase firearms and an estimated 186,000 rejections. On average each month, an estimated 6,600 firearm purchases were prevented by background checks of potential gun buyers during the 28 months after the effective date of the Brady Handgun Violence Prevention Act. The checks revealed purchasers' ineligibility under federal or state laws to buy a handgun or other firearm. Over 70% of the rejected purchasers were convicted or indicted. The data do not indicate whether rejected purchasers later obtained a firearm through other means.

While this legislation has been a good step, the question remains as to whether such measures can actually control gun violence. A methodologically sophisticated analysis by David McDowall and his colleagues of jurisdictions that have already

increased waiting periods indicates that such measures have little effect on gun violence.

Another approach is to severely punish people caught with unregistered handguns. The most famous attempt to regulate handguns is the Massachusetts Bartley-Fox law, which provides a mandatory one-year prison term for possession of a handgun (outside the home) without a permit. A detailed analysis of violent crime in Boston in the years after the law's passage found that the use of handguns in robberies and murders did decline substantially (in robberies by 35% and in murders by 55% in a two-year period). However, these optimistic results must be tempered by two facts: Rates for similar crimes dropped significantly in comparable cities that did *not* have gun control laws, and the use of other weapons, such as knives, increased in Boston.

Some jurisdictions have attempted to reduce gun violence by adding an extra punishment, such as a mandatory prison sentence, for any crime involving a handgun. So far, evaluations of this method show mixed results. David McDowall, Colin Loftin, and Brian Wiersma found that mandatory sentencing laws for gun crimes significantly reduced homicide rates in six different jurisdictions; assault and robbery rates, however, were not affected by the gun crime laws.

---

lower-class people report greater criminal activity than their middle- and upper-class peers, it would indicate that the official statistics are an accurate representation of the crime problem.

Surprisingly, early self-report studies conducted in the 1950s, specifically those conducted by James Short and F. Ivan Nye, did not find a direct relationship between social class and youth crime.[51] They found that socioeconomic class was related to official processing by police, court, and correctional agencies but not to the actual commission of crimes. In other words, while lower- and middle-class youth self-reported equal amounts of crime, the lower-class youth had a greater chance of getting arrested, convicted, and incarcerated and becoming official delinquents. In addition, factors generally associated with lower-class membership, such as broken homes, were found to be related to institu-

tionalization but not to admissions of delinquency. Other studies of this period reached similar conclusions.[52]

For more than 20 years after the use of self-reports became widespread, a majority of self-report studies agreed that a class-crime relationship did not exist: If the poor possessed more extensive criminal records than the wealthy, it was because of differential law enforcement and not class-based behavior differences. In what is considered to be the definitive work on this subject, Charles Tittle, Wayne Villemez, and Douglas Smith reviewed 35 studies containing 363 separate estimates concerning the relationship between class and crime.[53] They concluded that little if any support exists for the contention that crime is primarily a lower-class phenomenon. Consequently, Tittle and his associates argued that official statistics probably reflect class bias in the processing of lower-class offenders. The Tittle review is usually cited by

Even when positive results from gun control laws have been found, gun advocates have tried to refute the findings. When Loftin and his associates showed that a handgun control law was an effective instrument for reducing the homicide rate in Washington, D.C., Gary Kleck, Chester Britt, and David Bordua reanalyzed the data and claimed that positive findings may be an artifact of faulty methodology. By adjusting the years in which comparisons were made, the Kleck research found that gun homicides actually *increased* rather than *decreased* in the Washington area after the passage of the gun control law. In a study evaluating the handgun laws of all 50 states, David Lester found scant evidence that strict handgun laws influenced homicide rates. So while there is some evidence that gun control laws can reduce violence rates, the issue is far from settled.

THE DIFFICULTY OF GUN CONTROL

Why is it difficult to show that gun control efforts have a significant effect on the level of violence? Most guns used in crime are obtained illegally. And even if legitimate gun stores were more strictly regulated, private citizens would not be inhibited from selling, bartering, or trading handguns. Unregulated gun fairs and auctions are common throughout the United States. So many guns are in use that

controlling their ownership or banning their manufacture would have a negligible impact for years to come. Sophisticated automatic weapons, some of which are laser-aimed, have become armament for juvenile gangs and criminal groups. Some police departments, feeling "outgunned," have switched from the traditional .38-caliber police special revolver to 9 mm pistols that have 15 rounds.

If handguns were banned or outlawed, they would become more valuable, and illegal importation of guns might increase, as it has for another controlled substance—narcotics. Increasing penalties for gun-related crimes has also met with limited success, since judges may be reluctant to alter their sentencing policies to accommodate legislators. Regulating dealers is difficult, and placing tighter controls on them would only encourage private sales and bartering. Many gun deals are made at gun shows, with few questions asked. Even if purchased by a legitimate gun enthusiast, these weapons can fall into the wrong hands as a result of burglaries and break-ins.

Despite the difficulty of effective control, some combination of oversight and penalty seems imperative, and efforts should be made to discover, if at all possible, whether handgun control could, indeed, reduce violent crime rates.

CRITICAL THINKING QUESTIONS
1. Should the sale and possession of handguns be banned?
2. What are some of the possible negative consequences of a strict handgun control law?

Sources: Don Manson, *Presale Firearm Checks* (Washington, D.C.: Bureau of Justice Statistics, 1997); Gary Kleck, "Guns and Violence: An Interpretive Review of the Field," *Social Pathology* 1 (1995): 12–45; David McDowall, Colin Loftin, and Brian Wiersma, "A Comparative Study of the Preventive Effects of Mandatory Sentencing Laws for Gun Crimes," *Journal of Criminal Law and Criminology* 83 (1992): 378–391; M. Dwayne Smith, "Possession and Carrying of Firearms Among a Sample of Inner-City High School Females," paper presented at the annual meeting of the American Society of Criminology, Phoenix, Arizona, November 1993; Colin Loftin, David McDowall, Brian Wiersma, and Talbert Cottey, "Effects of Restrictive Licensing of Handguns on Homicide and Suicide in the District of Columbia," *New England Journal of Medicine* 325 (1991): 1615–1620; Gary Kleck, Chester Britt, and David Bordua, "The Emperor Has No Clothes: Using Interrupted Time Series Designs to Evaluate Social Policy," paper presented at the annual meeting of the American Society of Criminology, Phoenix, Arizona, November 1993; Gary Kleck, "The Incidence of Gun Violence Among Young People," *Public Perspective* 4 (1993): 3–6; Samuel Walker, *Sense and Nonsense About Crime and Drugs* (Monterey, Calif.: Brooks/Cole, 1985); Glenn Pierce and William Bowers, "The Bartley-Fox Gun Law's Short-Term Impact on Crime," *Annals* 455 (1981): 120–137; Colin Loftin, Milton Heumann, and David McDowall, "Mandatory Sentencing and Firearms Violence: Evaluating an Alternative to Gun Control," *Law and Society Review* 17 (1983): 287–319; David Lester, *Gun Control* (Springfield, Ill.: Charles Thomas, 1984); James Wright, Peter Rossi, and Kathleen Daly, *Under the Gun: Weapons, Crime and Violence in America* (New York: Aldine, 1983).

criminologists as the strongest statement refuting the claim that the lower class is disproportionately criminal. In 1990, writing with Robert Meier, Tittle once again reviewed existing data (published between 1978 and 1990) on the class-crime relationship and again found little evidence that a consistent association could be found between class and crime.[54]

EVIDENCE FOR A CLASS-CRIME RELATIONSHIP.
While convincing, this research has sparked significant debate over the validity of studies assessing the class-crime relationship. Many self-report instruments include trivial offenses, such as using a false ID or drinking alcohol. Their inclusion may obscure the true class-crime relationship because affluent youth often engage in trivial offenses, such as petty larceny, drug use, and simple assault. Those who support a class-crime relationship suggest that if only serious felony offenses are considered, a significant association can be observed.[55] Those studies showing middle- and lower-class youths to be equally delinquent rely on measures weighted toward minor crimes (for example, using a false ID or skipping school); when serious crimes, such as burglary and assault, are used in the comparison, lower-class youths register as significantly more delinquent.[56]

THE CLASS-CRIME CONTROVERSY.
The relationship between class and crime is an important one for criminological theory. If crime is related to social class, it follows that economic and structural factors, such as poverty and neighborhood disorganization, are a significant cause of criminal behavior.

In 1993 Congress passed the *Brady Bill,* which requires a week-long waiting period (to do a background check) before a gun can be sold to an applicant. The bill was named after former Press Secretary James Brady shown here with President Clinton at the signing on November 30, 1993. Behind the President and Brady are Vice President Al Gore, Attorney General Janet Reno, Sarah Brady, and the Brady's children. Brady was severely wounded in the attempted assassination of President Ronald Reagan by John Hinckley. There is some question whether such measures can control violent crime, because jurisdictions that have already increased the waiting period have not experienced a downturn in gun violence.

Connections

If class and crime are unrelated, the causes of crime must be found in factors experienced by members of all social classes—psychological impairment, family conflict, peer pressure, school failure, and so on. Theories that view crime as a function of problems experienced by members of all social classes are reviewed in Chapter 8.

One reason that a true measure of the class-crime relationship has thus far eluded criminologists is that the methods used to measure "class" vary widely. So many different indicators are used that findings are ambiguous. For example, David Brownfield found that some widely used measures of social class, such as father's occupation and education, are only weakly related to self-reported crime, while others, such as unemployment or membership on the welfare roles, are much stronger correlates of criminality.[57]

It is also possible that the association between class and crime may be more complex than a simple linear relationship (the poorer you are, the more crime you commit). Age, race, and gender may all influence the connection between class and crime.[58] For example, Sally Simpson and Lori Elis found that indigent white females are more likely to be offenders than indigent African American females. They speculate that exclusion from paid labor creates resentment and criminality in those who expect better treatment than they are getting; white females have had their expectations raised by the women's movement and expect greater occupational opportunities than minority females, whose vision is tempered by the economic reality of joblessness in minority neighborhoods.[59] Considering these findings, it is not surprising that the true relationship between class and crime is difficult to determine: The effect may be obscured because its impact varies within and between groups.

Like so many other criminological controversies, the debate over the true relationship between class and crime will most likely persist. The weight of recent evidence seems to suggest that serious and official crime is more prevalent among the lower classes, while less-serious and self-reported crime is spread more evenly throughout the social structure.[60] Income inequality, poverty, and resource deprivation are all associated with the most serious violent crimes, including homicide and assault.[61] Nonetheless, while crime rates may be higher in lower-class areas, *poverty* alone cannot explain why a *particular* individual becomes a chronic violent criminal; if it *could,* the crime problem would be much worse than it is now.[62]

Age and Crime

There is general agreement that age is inversely related to criminality. Criminologists Travis Hirschi and Michael Gottfredson state, "Age is everywhere correlated with crime. Its effects on crime do not depend on other demographic correlates of crime."[63] Regardless of economic status, marital status, race, sex, and so on, younger people commit crime more often than their older peers; research indicates this relationship has remained stable across time periods ranging from 1935 to the present.[64]

Official statistics tell us that young people are arrested at a disproportionate rate to their numbers in the population; victim surveys generate similar findings for crimes in which the age of the assailant can be determined. While youths ages 13 to 17 make up about 6% of the total U.S. population, they account for about 30% of the index crime arrests and 18% of the arrests for all crimes. As a general rule, the peak age for property crime is believed to be 16; for violence, it's 18. In contrast, adults 45 and over, who make up 32% of the population, account for only 8% of the index crime arrests. The elderly are particularly resistant to the temptations of crime; they make up more than 12% of the population and less than 1% of the arrests. Elderly males 65 and over are predominantly arrested for alcohol-related matters (public drunkenness, drunk driving), and elderly females for larceny theft (shoplifting); the crime rate of both groups has remained stable for the past 20 years.[65]

It is also possible to derive some estimates of rates of offending by age for the violent personal crimes measured by the National Crime Victim Survey because victims had the opportunity to view their attackers and estimate their ages. Research shows that the estimated rates of offending for youths ages 18 to 20 is about three times greater than the estimated rate of adults 21 and over; youths ages 12 to 17 offended at a rate twice that of adults. For some specific crimes,

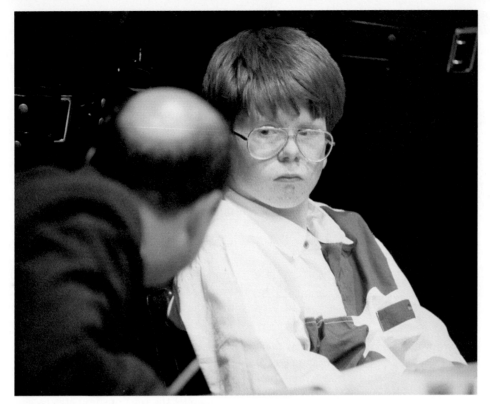

While youths aged 13 to 17, collectively, make up about 6% of the total U.S. population, they account for about 30% of the index crime arrests and 18% of the arrests for all crimes. There have been many shocking cases of very young children who commit violent crimes. Here Eric Smith, aged 14, is seen in court where in 1994 he was found guilty of murdering a preschooler. Smith's lawyer argued unsuccessfully that Smith suffers from a disorder that makes him prone to uncontrollable rage.

such as robbery and personal larceny, the youthful offending rate is perceived to be almost six times the adult rate.[66]

AGE AND CRIME I: AGE DOES NOT MATTER. The relationship between age and crime is of major theoretical importance because many existing criminological theories fail to adequately explain why the crime rate drops with age, which is referred to as **aging out,** or the **desistance phenomenon.** This theoretical failure has been the subject of considerable academic debate. One position, championed by respected criminologists Travis Hirschi and Michael Gottfredson, is that the relationship between age and crime is constant and that therefore the age variable is actually irrelevant to the study of crime. Because all people, regardless of their demographic characteristics (race, gender, class, family structure, domicile, work status, and so on), commit less crime as they age, it is not important to consider age as a factor in explaining crime.[67] Even hard-core chronic offenders commit less crime as they age.[68] Hirschi and Gottfredson find that differences in offending rates for groups (for example, between males and females or between the rich and poor) that exist at any point in their respective life cycles will be maintained throughout their lives. As Figure 3.6 illustrates, if 15-year-old boys are four times as likely to commit crime as 15-year-old girls, then 50-year-old men will be four times as likely to commit crime as 50-year-old women, although the actual number of crimes committed by both males and females will constantly be declining.

Connections

Hirschi and Gottfredson have used their views on the age-crime relationship as a basis for their *general theory of crime.* This important theory holds that the factors that produce crime change little after birth and that the association between crime and age is a constant. For more on their views see Chapter 10.

AGE AND CRIME II: AGE MATTERS. Those who oppose the Hirschi and Gottfredson view of the age-crime relationship suggest that personal factors, such as gender and race, and social factors, such as lifestyle, economic situation, and peer relations, have a significant impact on the age-crime relationship.[69] There are a number of reasons that criminal behavior is not constant. Evolving patterns or

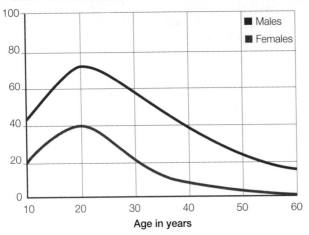

Figure 3.6 Gender and crime over the life span.

Percent committed crime

■ Males
■ Females

Age in years

In sum, some criminologists view the relationship between crime and age as constant, while others believe that it varies according to offense and offender. This difference has important implications for criminological research and theory. If age is a constant, then the criminality of any group can be accurately measured at any single point in time. If, on the other hand, the relationship between age and crime varies, it would be necessary to conduct longitudinal studies that follow criminals over their life cycle to fully understand how their age influences their offending patterns.[79] Crime would then be conceived of as a type of social event that takes on different meanings at different times in a person's life.[80]

Disagreements over this critical issue have produced some of the most spirited debates in the recent criminological literature.[81] Right now, efforts are being undertaken to examine this issue in the United States and in other nations (using cohorts drawn in Sweden and Britain). Early results from the Scandinavian study find many general similarities with U.S. research.[82] Clearly, more research is required on this important topic.

cycles of criminal behavior may be keyed to personal characteristics and lifestyle, including gender, race, and class.[70] For example, gender seems to influence the age-crime association: The male-to-female crime ratio difference appears to decline with age.[71] The female homicide rate peaks at age 20 and then continues at a *stable* but low rate throughout adulthood; in contrast, the male homicide rate is much higher but begins to drop after age 30.[72]

The likelihood of a long-term criminal career may be determined by the age at which offending commences.[73] People who get involved in criminality at a very early age (**early onset**) and who gain official records will be the ones most likely to become chronic offenders.[74] Research shows that preschoolers (under age 5) who are labeled as "troublesome" or "difficult" by parents are the ones most likely to become persistent offenders through their adolescence.[75] Their criminal behavior is resistant to the aging-out process.

Desistance may also be influenced by criminal specialization; crime types may peak at different ages and follow different trajectories. Crimes that provide significant economic gain, such as gambling, embezzlement, and fraud, are less likely to decline with maturity than are high-risk, low-profit offenses, such as assault.[76] People who are frequent cocaine and heroin users continue to commit criminal acts *10 years* or more past the age when nonaddicts have terminated their criminal activity.[77]

TWO CLASSES OF CRIMINALS? The population thus may contain different sets of criminal offenders, one or more groups whose criminality declines with age (as predicted by Hirschi and Gottfredson) and another whose criminal behavior remains constant through their maturity.[78] The age-crime pattern may also undergo change; it has been noted that a greater proportion of violent criminal behavior is concentrated among youthful offenders than it was 40 years ago (although the youth violence rate declined in 1995).

WHY DOES AGING OUT OCCUR? Despite the debate raging over the relationship between age and crime, there is little question that the overall crime rate declines with age. Why does this phenomenon take place? One view is that there is a direct relationship between aging and desistance. As they mature, troubled youths are able to develop a long-term life view and resist the need for immediate gratification.[83] Gordon Trasler found that kids view teenage crime as "fun." Youths view their petty but risky and exciting crimes as a social activity that provides adventure in an otherwise boring and unsympathetic world. As they grow older, Trasler finds, their life patterns are inconsistent with criminality; delinquents literally grow out of crime.[84]

James Q. Wilson and Richard Herrnstein argue that the aging-out process is a function of the natural history of the human life cycle.[85] Deviance in adolescence is fueled by the need for conventionally unobtainable money and sex and reinforced by close relationships with peers who defy conventional morality. At the same time, teenagers are becoming independent from parents and other adults who enforce conventional standards. They have a new sense of energy and strength and are involved with peers who are similarly vigorous and frustrated. Adulthood brings increasingly powerful ties to conventional society, not the least of which is the acquisition of a family. Adults also develop the ability to delay gratification and forgo the immediate gains that law violations bring; crime rates consequently decline with age.

> When you're a teenager, you're rowdy. Nowadays, you aren't rowdy. You know, you want to settle down because you can go to jail now. [When] you are a boy, you can be put into a detention home. But you can go to jail now. Jail ain't no place to go.[86]

Aging out of crime may also be influenced by the success or failure of interpersonal relationships. Children who are labeled antisocial by teachers, police, parents, and neighbors find they may have little choice but to remain committed to their criminal careers.[87] If, however, youngsters believe that they have little chance of achieving success, money, and happiness through crimes, they are more likely to desist.[88] As they mature, individuals may be influenced by their adult relationships. For example, people who maintain successful marriages are more likely to desist from antisocial behaviors than those whose marriages fail.[89]

Connections

The belief that life events influence behavior choices is at the core of life-course theories. They hold that as people and their social environment change, so do their criminal behavior patterns. Theories of the criminal life course are discussed in Chapter 10.

Although most people age out of crime, some may find a criminal career a reasonable alternative. Yet even people who actively remain in a criminal career will eventually slow down as they age. Crime is too dangerous, physically taxing, and unrewarding, and punishments are too harsh and long-lasting, to become a long-term way of life for most people. The uniformity of maturational changes in the crime rate suggests that it must be part of a biological "evolutionary process."[90] By middle age, even the most chronic offenders terminate criminal behavior.

Gender and Crime

The three major forms of criminal statistics generally agree on the finding that male crime rates are probably much higher than those for females; victims report that their assailant was a male in more than 80% of all violent personal crimes. The Uniform Crime Report arrest statistics indicate that the overall male-female arrest ratio is today about three male offenders to one female offender; for violent crimes, the ratio is closer to six males to one female.

Recent self-report data collected by the Institute for Social Research at the University of Michigan also show that males commit more serious crimes, such as robbery, assault, and burglary, than females. However, while the patterns in self-reports are parallel to those in official data, the ratios seem smaller. In other words, males self-report more criminal behavior than females, but not to the degree suggested by official data.

EXPLAINING GENDER DIFFERENCES: BIOSOCIAL DIFFERENCES. How can the gender differences in the crime rate be explained? Early criminologists pointed to the emotional, physical, and psychological differences between males and females. They maintained that because females were weaker and more passive, they were less likely to commit

crimes. The most widely cited evidence was contained in Cesare Lombroso's 1895 book, *The Female Offender*.[91] Lombroso argued that there was a small group of female criminals who lacked "typical" female traits of "piety, maternity, undeveloped intelligence, and weakness."[92] In physical appearance as well as in emotionality, delinquent females appeared closer to men than to other women. Lombroso's theory became known as the **masculinity hypothesis;** in essence, a few "masculine" females were responsible for the handful of crimes committed by women.

Another early view of female crime focused on the supposed dynamics of sexual relationships. Female criminals were viewed as either sexually controlling or sexually naive, either manipulating men for profit or being manipulated by them. The female's criminality was often masked, because criminal justice authorities were reluctant to take action against a woman.[93] Referred to as the **chivalry hypothesis,** this view holds that much of the criminality of females is hidden because of the generally protective and benevolent attitudes toward them in our culture.[94] In other words, police are less likely to arrest, juries less likely to convict, and judges less likely to incarcerate female offenders.

While these early writings are no longer taken seriously, some criminologists still consider trait differences as a key determinant of crime rate differences. For example, some criminologists link antisocial behavior to hormonal influences by arguing that male sex hormones (**androgens**) account for their more aggressive behavior and that gender-related hormonal differences can also explain the gender gap in in the crime rate.[95]

Connections

Gender differences in the crime rate may be a function of androgen levels because these hormones cause areas of the brain to become less sensitive to environmental stimuli, making males more likely to seek high levels of stimulation and to tolerate more pain in the process. Chapter 6's discussion of the biosocial causes of crime reviews this issue in greater detail.

EXPLAINING GENDER DIFFERENCES: SOCIALIZATION. By mid-century, it was common for criminologists to describe gender differences in the crime rate as a function of socialization. Textbooks explained the relatively low female crime rate by citing the fact that in contrast to boys, girls were supervised more closely and protected from competition.[96] The few female criminals were seen as troubled individuals, alienated at home, who pursued crime as a means of compensating for their disrupted personal lives.[97] The streets became a "second home" to girls whose physical and emotional adjustment was hampered by a strained home life, marked by such conditions as absent fathers, overly competitive mothers, and so on.

Some experts continue to explain gender-based crime differences as a function of socialization. Most girls, they argue, are socialized to be less aggressive than boys; they are supervised more closely by parents.[98] The majority of females learn to respond to provocation by feeling anxious and depressed, whereas boys are encouraged to retaliate with aggression.[99] While females get angry as often as males, many have been taught to blame themselves for harboring such negative feelings. Females are therefore much more likely than males to respond to anger with feelings of depression, anxiety, fear, and shame. While females are socialized to fear that their anger will harm valued relationships, males react with "moral outrage," looking to blame others for their discomfort.[100] Overall, women are much more likely to feel distressed than men, experiencing sadness, anxiety, and uneasiness.[101] The relatively few females who commit violent crimes report having home and family relationships that are more troubled than those experienced by male delinquents.[102]

EXPLAINING GENDER DIFFERENCES: FEMINIST VIEWS. In the 1970s, several influential works, most notably Freda Adler's *Sisters in Crime*[103] and Rita James Simon's *The Contemporary Woman and Crime,*[104] revolutionized the thinking on the cause of gender differences in the crime rate. Their research, which today is referred to as **liberal feminist theory,** focused attention on the social and economic role of women in society and its relationship to female crime rates. Both Adler and Simon believed that the traditionally lower crime rate for women could be explained by their "second-class" economic and social position. They further contended that as women's social roles changed and their lifestyles became more like those of males, the crime rates would converge.

Criminologists, responding to this research, began to refer to the "new female criminal." The rapid increase in the female crime rate during the 1960s and 1970s, especially in what had traditionally been male-oriented crimes (burglary, larceny), gave support to the convergence model presented by Adler and Simon. In addition, self-report studies seem to indicate that (a) the pattern of female criminality, if not its frequency, is quite similar to that of male criminality, and (b) the factors that predispose male criminals to crime have an equal impact on female criminals.[105] The contributions of Adler and Simon encouraged other criminologists to assess the association among economic issues, gender roles, and criminality.

IS CONVERGENCE POSSIBLE? Will the gender differences in the crime rate eventually dissolve? Are gender differences permanent and unchanging? Some criminologists, most notably Darrell Steffensmeier, find that gender-based crime rate differences remain significant and argue that the emancipation of women has had relatively little influence on female crime rates.[106] They dispute the idea that increases in the female arrest rate reflect economic or social changes brought about by the women's movement. For one

Connections

Critical criminologists view gender inequality as stemming from the unequal power of men and women in a capitalist society and the exploitation of females by fathers and husbands. Women are considered a "commodity" worth possessing, like land or money; female crime patterns can be explained by these exploitive power relationships. These views, referred to as Marxist or radical feminism, are considered more fully in Chapter 9.

thing, many female criminals come from the socioeconomic class least affected by the women's movement; their crimes seem more a function of economic inequality than women's rights. For another, the offense patterns of women are still quite different from those of men, who are still committing a disproportionate share of serious crimes, such as robbery, burglary, murder, and assault.[107] Steffensmeier and his associates have conducted research in the United States and abroad that fails to find an association between economic development and female crime rates.[108] That is, there is little evidence that nations undergoing economic development also experience increases in the female violence rate.[109]

Perhaps it is too soon for criminologists to write off "the new female criminal." After all, though male arrest rates are still considerably higher than female rates, the female rates seem to be increasing at a faster pace. For example, between 1986 and 1995, male arrests increased 12%, while female arrests increased 38%. And more recently, between 1991 and 1995, male arrests increased 2.6% while female arrests increased almost 14%. More important, the increase in the arrests of teenage girls during the 1991–1995 period was double the increase of teenage boys (16% versus 32% increase), a finding that suggests the younger generation of females are increasing their offending rates at a pace even greater than that of their older sisters.[110]

It is possible, as Roy Austin claims, that convergence has been delayed by a slower-than-expected change in gender roles; the women's movement has not yet achieved its full impact on social life.[111] One reason is that while expanding their economic role, women have not abandoned their conventional role of taking care of family and home; women today are being forced to cope with added financial and social burdens. If gender roles are truly equivalent, crime rates may eventually converge; these changes appear to now be taking place.

Race and Crime

Official crime data indicate that minority-group members are involved in a disproportionate share of criminal activity. The UCR tells us that although African Americans make up about 12% of the general population, they account for about 44% of Part I violent crime arrests and 33% of the property crime arrests, as well as a disproportionate number of Part II arrests (except for alcohol-related arrests, which primarily are of white offenders).

Because the UCR statistics represent arrest data, racial differences in the crime rate may be more of a reflection of police practices than a true picture of criminal participation. Consequently, criminologists have sought to verify the UCR findings through analysis of NCVS and self-report data.

The NCVS supplies racial data on crimes in which victims were able to observe their attackers: rape, assault, and robbery. Analysis of these data shows that although the results are somewhat consistent with the official crime statistics, the proportions are slightly less than reported in the UCR arrest statistics, especially for the crime of rape.[112] This could mean that police are more likely to arrest black suspects for that crime or that women attacked by black offenders are more likely to report the crime to police. Also, rape tends to be an intraracial crime, and black women are more likely to report rapes to police than white women are.

Another way to examine this issue is to compare the racial differences in self-reported data with those found in the official delinquency records. Charges of racial discrimination in the arrest process would be supported if the racial difference in self-report data is insignificant.

Early efforts by Leroy Gould in Seattle, Harwin Voss in Honolulu, and Ronald Akers in seven midwestern states found the relationship between race and self-reported delinquency to be virtually nonexistent.[113]

Two recent self-report studies that make use of large national samples of youth have also found little evidence of racial disparity in offending. The first, conducted by the Institute for Social Research at the University of Michigan, found that if anything, young blacks self-report less delinquent behavior and substance abuse than whites do.[114] The second, a nationwide study of youth by social scientists at the Behavioral Science Institute at Boulder, Colorado, found few interracial differences in crime rates, although black youths maintained a much greater chance of being arrested and taken into custody.[115]

These and other self-report studies seem to indicate that the delinquent behavior rates of black and white teenagers are generally similar and that differences in arrest statistics may indicate a differential selection policy by police.[116]

CAUSES OF RACIAL DISPARITY IN CRIME. Racial differences in the crime rate remain an extremely sensitive issue. Although there are still questions about the validity of UCR data, the fact remains that African Americans are arrested for a disproportionate amount of violent crime, such as robbery and murder. While it is possible that the UCR is merely a reflection of discriminatory justice practices, as self-report studies would have us believe, it is improbable that police discretion alone could account for these proportions: It is doubtful that police routinely ignore white killers, robbers, and rapists while arresting violent black offenders. Also, the NCVS indicates that a disproportionate number of violent crimes are committed by racial minorities (although the proportions are somewhat less than the racial differences in the arrest statistics).

Today, many criminologists concede that recorded differences in the black-white violent crime arrest rate cannot be explained away solely by racism or differential treatment within the criminal justice system.[117] To do so would be to ignore the social problems that exist in the nation's inner cities. How, then, can racial patterns be explained?

Most theories focus on economic deprivation, social disorganization, subcultural adaptations, and the legacy of racism and discrimination on personality and behavior.[118] The fact that U.S. culture influences African American crime rates is underscored by the fact that black violence rates are much lower in other nations—both those that are predominantly white, such as Canada, and those that are predominantly black, such as Nigeria.[119]

One approach has been to trace the black experience in the United States. Some criminologists view black crime as a function of socialization in a society where the black family was torn apart and black culture destroyed in such a way that recovery has proven impossible. James P. Comer argues that the early slave experiences left a wound that has been deepened by racism and lack of opportunity.[120] Children of the slave society were thrust into a system of forced dependency and negative self-feelings. Comer writes that it was a system that promoted powerful forces for identification with an aggressor (slave master and other whites) and ambivalence and antagonism toward one's self and group. After emancipation, blacks were shut out of the social and political mainstream. Frustrated and angry, they were isolated in segregated communities, turning within for support. Their entire American experience provided for negative self-images, anger, and rage. Comer states:

> In reaction to failure, the most vibrant and reactive often become disrupted and violent in and out of schools, both individually and in groups or gangs. Neighborhoods and communities of adequately functioning families are then overwhelmed by the reactive and most troubled individuals and families. Models of violence and other troublesome behavior for children abound in relatives, friends, and neighbors unsuccessful in previous generations.[121]

According to Comer, the intraracial nature of black violence is in reaction to an "inability to cope with the larger society or to identify with black and white leaders and institutional achievements. Frustration and anger is taken out on people most like self."[122]

Comer's view fits well with the criminological concept that a subculture of violence has developed in inner-city ghetto areas that condones the use of physical force as a solution for everyday encounters.[123]

In his influential book *Criminal Violence, Criminal Justice,* Charles Silberman also views the problem as a function of the black experience in this country—"an experience that differs from that of other ethnic groups." Silberman's provocative argument is that black citizens have learned to be violent because of their treatment in U.S. society. First, they were violently uprooted from their African homelands. Then their slavery was maintained by violence. After emancipation, their lower-class position was enforced by violent means, such as intimidation by the Ku Klux Klan. To strike back brought harsh retaliation by the white-controlled law. Moving to northern cities, blacks suffered two burdens unknown to other migrants: their color and their heritage of slavery. After all, the color black in U.S. culture connotes sinister, dirty, evil, or bad things, while white stands for goodness and purity (the good guys always wear white hats; social outcasts are blacklisted; brides wear white; witches wear black). Consequently, to survive and reach cultural and personal fulfillment, African Americans have developed their own set of norms, values, and traditions. In the 1960s, many blacks began to adopt the image, first developed in southern folklore and myth, of being "bad" in their personal lives. After 350 years of fearing whites, Silberman writes, black Americans "have discovered that the fear runs the other way, that whites are intimidated by their very presence; it would be hard to overestimate what an extraordinarily liberating force this discovery is. . . . 350 years of festering hatred has come spilling out."[124]

IS CONVERGENCE POSSIBLE?   Considering these overwhelming social problems, is it possible that racial differences in the crime rate will soon converge? One argument is that if economic conditions improve in the minority community, the differences in black and white crime rates will eventually disappear.[125] A trend toward residential integration, which has been underway since 1980, may also help reduce crime rate differentials.[126]

There are also data showing that improvement in the nation's overall economic condition and increased integration may *not* be enough to produce convergence. African Americans have been shut out of the economic mainstream even during periods of relative prosperity. Between the economic boom years of 1960 and 1988, white crime rates tended to *decrease.* Economic expansion had the opposite effect on African American crime rates; they actually *increased* during periods of national economic growth.[127] This seemingly inexplicable finding may be a result of a two-tiered African American culture, one desperately poor and the other relatively affluent. Both lower- and middle-class whites and middle-class African Americans are able to prosper during periods of economic growth. In contrast, lower-class African Americans, left out of the economic mainstream, experience a growing sense of frustration and failure. It should come as no surprise that an element of the population that is shut out of educational and economic opportunities enjoyed by the rest of society may be subject to the lure of illegitimate gain and criminality. Gary LaFree and his associates find that young African American males in the inner city believe they lack social and economic opportunity. While the economic data say they are doing better, news accounts of "protests, riots and acts of civil disobedience" tell them otherwise.[128]

Connections

The concept of *relative deprivation* refers to the fact that people compare their success to those they are in immediate contact with. Even if conditions improve, they may still feel like they are falling behind. A sense of relative deprivation, discussed in Chapter 7, may lead to criminal activity.

In sum, the weight of the evidence shows that while there is little difference in the self-reported crime rates of racial groups, African Americans are more likely to be arrested for serious violent crimes. The causes of black crime have been linked to poverty, racism, hopelessness, lack of opportunity, and urban problems experienced by all too many black citizens.

Criminal Careers

The crime data show that most offenders commit a single criminal act and upon arrest discontinue their antisocial activity. Others commit a few crimes of less serious nature. However, a small group of individuals account for a majority of all crimes committed. These persistent offenders are referred to as **career criminals,** or **chronic offenders.**

Delinquency in a Birth Cohort

The concept of the chronic or career offender is most closely associated with the research efforts of Marvin Wolfgang, Robert Figlio, and Thorsten Sellin.[129] In their landmark 1972 study, *Delinquency in a Birth Cohort,* Wolfgang, Figlio, and Sellin used official records to follow the criminal careers of a cohort of 9,945 boys born in Philadelphia in 1945 from the time of their birth until they reached 18 years of age in 1963. Official police records were used to identify delinquents. About one-third of the boys (3,475) had some police contact. The remaining two-thirds (6,470) had none. Each delinquent's actions were given a seriousness weight score for every delinquent act.[130] The weighting of delinquent acts allowed the researchers to differentiate, for example, between a simple assault requiring no medical attention for the victim and a serious assault in which the victim needed hospitalization.

The most well-known discovery of Wolfgang and his associates was the *chronic offender.* The cohort data indicated that 54% (1,862) of the sample's delinquent youths were repeat offenders, while the remaining 46% (1,613) were one-time offenders. However, the repeaters could be further categorized as nonchronic recidivists and chronic recidivists. The former consisted of 1,235 youths who had been arrested more than once but fewer than five times and who made up 35.6% of all delinquents. The latter were a group of 627 boys arrested five times or more, who accounted for 18% of the delinquents and 6% of the total sample of 9,945.

It was the chronic offenders (known today as "the chronic 6%") who were involved in the most dramatic amounts of delinquent behavior; they were responsible for 5,305 offenses, or 51.9% of all offenses. Even more striking was the involvement of chronic offenders in serious criminal acts. Of the entire sample, they committed 71% of the homicides, 73% of the rapes, 82% of the robberies, and 69% of the aggravated assaults.

Wolfgang and his associates found that arrest and court experience did little to deter the chronic offender. In fact, punishment was *inversely* related to chronic offending: The more stringent the sanctions chronic offenders received, the more likely they would be to engage in repeated criminal behavior.

Birth Cohort II

The subjects who made up Wolfgang's original birth cohort were born in 1945. How have behavior patterns changed in subsequent years? To answer this question, Wolfgang and his associates selected a new, larger birth cohort, born in Philadelphia in 1958, and followed them until their maturity.[131] The 1958 cohort was larger than the original, having more than 27,000 subjects, including 13,000 males and 14,000 females.

Although the proportion of delinquent youths was about the same as that in the 1945 cohort, those in the larger sample were involved in 20,089 delinquent arrests. Chronic offenders (five or more arrests as juveniles) made up 7.5% of the 1958 sample (compared with 6.3% in 1945) and 23% of all delinquent offenders (compared with 18% in 1945). Chronic female delinquency was relatively rare—only 1% of the females in the survey were chronic offenders.

Chronic male delinquents continued to commit more than their share of criminal behavior. They accounted for 61% of the total offenses and a disproportionate amount of the most serious crimes: 61% of the homicides, 76% of the rapes, 73% of the robberies, and 65% of the aggravated assaults. The chronic female offender was less likely to be involved in serious crimes.

It is interesting that the 1958 cohort, as a group, were involved in significantly more serious crimes than the 1945 group. For example, their violent offense rate (149 per 1,000 in the sample) was three times higher than the rate for the 1945 cohort (47 per 1,000 subjects).

In the 1945 cohort chronic offenders dominated the total crime rate and continued their law-violating careers as adults. The newer cohort study is showing that the chronic offender syndrome is being maintained in a group of subjects born 13 years later than the original cohort and, if anything, more violent than that first group. Finally, the efforts of the justice system seem to have little preventive effect on

the behavior of chronic offenders: The more often a person was arrested, the more likely he or she was to be arrested again. For males, 26% of the entire group had one violent-offense arrest; of that 26%, 34% went on to commit a second violent offense, while 43% of the three-time losers went on to a fourth arrest, and so on.

Chronic Offender Research

Wolfgang's pioneering effort to identify the chronic career offender has been replicated by a number of other important research studies. Lyle Shannon also used the cohort approach to investigate career delinquency patterns.[132] He studied three cohorts totaling 6,127 youths born in 1942, 1949, and 1955 in Racine, Wisconsin. Shannon also encountered the phenomenon of the chronic career offender who engages in a disproportionate amount of delinquent behavior and later becomes involved in adult criminality. He found that less than 25% of each cohort's male subjects had five or more nontraffic offenses but accounted for 77%–83% of all police contacts (by males) in their cohort. Similarly, from 8%–14% of the persons in each cohort were responsible for all the serious felony offenses. According to Shannon, if one wished to identify the persons responsible for about 75% of the felonies and most of the other crimes—then approximately 5% of each cohort— the persons with two or three felony contacts would be the target population. It is important to note that involvement of juveniles with the justice system did little to inhibit their adult criminality. Although most youths discontinued their criminal behavior after their teenage years, the few who continued were those who had become well known to the police when they were teenagers.

A number of other cohort studies have accumulated data supportive of the Wolfgang research. D. J. West and D. P. Farrington's ongoing study of youths born in London from 1951 to 1954 has also shown that a small number of recidivists continue their behavior as adults and that arrest and conviction have little influence on their behavior other than to amplify the probability of their law violations: Youths with multiple convictions as juveniles tend to have multiple convictions as adults.[133] The most important childhood risk factors associated with chronic offending include a history of troublesomeness, a personality that reveres daring behavior, a delinquent sibling, and a convicted parent. Farrington finds that the most chronic offenders could be identified by age 10 on the basis of personality and background features.[134]

Stability in Crime: From Delinquent to Criminal

Are persistent juvenile offenders likely to continue their criminal careers into adulthood? In an important study, a 10% sample of the original Pennsylvania cohort (974 subjects) were followed through their adulthood to age 30.[135] Seventy percent of the "persistent" adult offenders had also been chronic juvenile offenders; they had an 80% chance of becoming adult offenders and a 50% chance of being arrested four or more times as adults. In comparison, subjects with no juvenile arrests had only an 18% chance of being arrested as an adult. The chronic offenders also continued to engage in the most serious crimes. Although they accounted for only 15% of the follow-up sample, the former chronic delinquents were involved in 74% of all arrests and 82% of all serious crimes, such as homicide, rape, and robbery.

The stability of criminal careers was also detected by Paul Tracy and Kimberly Kempf-Leonard in their important follow-up study of all subjects in the 1958 cohort. By age 26, cohort II subjects were displaying the same behavior patterns as their older peers. Few delinquent offenders (about one-third) and even fewer nondelinquent offenders (10%) became adult criminals, a finding that supports desistance. Nonetheless, those delinquents with high rates of juvenile offending—who started their delinquent career early, committed a violent crime, and continued offending throughout adolescence—were the ones most likely to persist as adults. Tracy and Kempf-Leonard found that delinquents who began their offending career with serious (violent) offenses or who quickly increased the severity of their offending early in life were the ones who persisted into adulthood. Severity of offending, not frequency, had the greatest impact on later adult criminality.[136]

The cohort follow-ups clearly show that chronic juvenile offenders continue their law-violating careers as adults, a concept referred to as the **continuity of crime.** Kids who are found to be disruptive and antisocial as early as age 5 or 6 are the ones most likely to exhibit stable, long-term patterns of disruptive behavior through adolescence.[137] They have measurable behavior problems in such areas as learning and motor skills, cognitive abilities, family relations, and other areas of social, psychological, and physical functioning.[138] Youthful offenders who persist are more likely to abuse alcohol, get into trouble while in military service, become economically dependent, have lower aspirations, get divorced or separated, and have a weak employment record.[139]

Criminal Careers in Other Cultures

While developmental research has been ongoing in the United States, additional studies have been conducted in Europe to corroborate findings. The Stockholm cohort project (Project Metropolitan) contains 15,117 male and female subjects. Recent analysis of data from this project indicates that criminal career development in Sweden follows many of the same patterns found in U.S. cohorts.[140]

Similarly, David Farrington and J. David Hawkins used data from a sample of 411 males born in London to chart the life courses of delinquent offenders. Farrington and Hawkins found that the frequency of offending was predicted by early onset of antisocial behavior, associating with deviant peers, certain personality traits (such as a low level of anxiety), poor school achievement, and dysfunc-

tional family relations; this finding is not dissimilar from data gathered in the United States. Those delinquents who persisted into adulthood (ages 21 to 32) exhibited low IQs, substance abuse, chronic unemployment, and a low degree of commitment to school.[141] Further analysis of these data shows that the persistent offender group may be further subdivided into high- and low-rate offenders, with the former committing two or three times as many offenses as the latter.[142] Punishment does little to deter their behavior and, if anything, prompts escalation of their criminal activities.

In sum, research in both the United States and Europe shows that a small group of offenders are responsible for a great deal of all crime. These youths begin their offending career at an extremely young age and persist into their adulthood.

Implications of the Chronic Offender Concept

The findings of the cohort studies and the discovery of the chronic offender have revitalized criminological theory. If relatively few offenders become chronic, persistent criminals, it is possible that they possess some individual trait that is responsible for their criminality. Most people exposed to troublesome social conditions, such as poverty, do not become chronic offenders; thus, it is unlikely that social conditions alone can cause chronic offending. If not, what does?

Traditional theories of criminal behavior have failed to distinguish between chronic and occasional offenders. They have concentrated more on explaining why people begin to commit crime and paid scant attention to the reasons that people stop offending. The "discovery" of the chronic offender 25 years ago has forced criminologists to consider such issues as persistence and desistence in their explanations of crime; more recent theories account not only for the onset of criminality but also its termination. Why do most offenders "age out" of crime? Why do some persist into adulthood? Ongoing research efforts are now aimed at answering these critical questions.

The chronic offender concept has also raised questions about the treatment of known offenders: If we can identify chronic offenders, what should we do about them? How can chronic offenders be controlled if punishment actually escalates the frequency of their criminal activity? The chronic offender has thus become a central focus of crime control policy. Concern about repeat offenders has been translated into programs at various stages of the justice process. For example, police departments and district attorneys' offices around the nation have set up programs to focus their resources on capturing and prosecuting dangerous or repeat offenders.[143]

Even more important has been the effect of the chronic offender on sentencing policy. Around the country, legal jurisdictions are developing sentencing policies designed to incapacitate serious offenders for long periods of time with-

Studies in Europe show that persistent chronic offenders account for a significant portion of all criminal acts. Frequency of offenses has been associated with early onset of antisocial behavior, association with deviant peers, personality disorders, poor school achievement, dysfunctional family relations, low IQ, substance abuse, chronic unemployment, and a low degree of commitment to school. Could these neo-Nazi youth based in Berlin be influenced by the same personal characteristics that promote and sustain chronic criminal offending?

out hope of probation or parole. Among the policies spurred by the chronic offender concept is mandatory sentences for violent or drug-related crimes in more than 30 states, commonly known as a "three strikes and you're out" policy. Whether such policies can be effective in reducing crime rates or are merely "get tough" measures designed to placate conservative voters still remains to be seen.

Summary

There are three primary sources of crime statistics: the Uniform Crime Report based on police data accumulated by the FBI, self-reports of criminal behavior, and victim surveys. All three sources tell us that there is quite a bit of crime in the United States and that the amount of violent crime is increasing. Each data source has its strengths and weaknesses, and though quite different from one another, they actually agree on the nature of criminal behavior.

The data sources show some stable patterns in the crime rate. Ecological patterns show that some areas of the country are more crime-prone than others, that there are seasons and times for crime, and that these patterns are quite stable. There is also evidence of a gender and age gap in the crime rate: Men usually commit more crime than women; young people commit more crime than the elderly.

The crime data show that people commit less crime as they age, but the significance and cause of this pattern is still not completely understood.

Similarly, there appear to be racial and class patterns in the crime rate. However, it is still unclear whether these are true differences or a function of discriminatory law enforcement.

One of the most important findings from cohort research is the existence of the chronic offender, a repeat criminal responsible for a significant amount of all law violations. Chronic offenders begin their career early in life and, rather than aging out of crime, persist in their criminal behavior into adulthood. The discovery of the chronic offender has led to the study of developmental criminology—why people persist, desist, terminate, or escalate their deviant behavior.

Key Terms

Uniform Crime Report (UCR)	National Crime Victimization Survey (NCVS)
index crimes	
Part I crimes	crime patterns and trends
Part II crimes	instrumental crimes
self-report survey	expressive crimes

aging out
desistance phenomenon
early onset
masculinity hypothesis
chivalry hypothesis

androgens
liberal feminist theory
career criminals
chronic offenders
continuity of crime

Notes

1. Federal Bureau of Investigation, *Crime in the United States, 1995* (Washington, D.C.: U.S. Government Printing Office, 1996). Herein cited as FBI, *Uniform Crime Report* in footnotes and referred to in text as Uniform Crime Report, or UCR. Uniform Crime Report data are supplemented with preliminary data from the 1996 FBI crime survey.

2. Craig Perkins and Patsy Klaus, *Criminal Victimization, 1994* (Washington, D.C.: Bureau of Justice Statistics, 1996). Hereinafter cited as NCVS, 1994.

3. Paul Tappan, *Crime, Justice and Corrections* (New York: McGraw-Hill, 1960).

4. Daniel Bell, *The End of Ideology* (New York: Free Press, 1967), p. 152.

5. Duncan Chappell, Gilbert Geis, Stephen Schafer, and Larry Siegel, "Forcible Rape: A Comparative Study of Offenses Known to the Police in Boston and Los Angeles," in *Studies in the Sociology of Sex*, ed. James Henslin (New York: Appleton-Century-Crofts, 1971), pp. 169–193.

6. Patrick Jackson, "Assessing the Validity of Official Data on Arson," *Criminology* 26 (1988): 181–195.

7. Lawrence Sherman and Barry Glick, "The Quality of Arrest Statistics," *Police Foundation Reports* 2 (1984): 1–8.

8. David Seidman and Michael Couzens, "Getting the Crime Rate Down: Political Pressure and Crime Reporting," *Law and Society Review* 8 (1974): 457.

9. Robert O'Brien, "Police Productivity and Crime Rates: 1973–1992," *Criminology* 34 (1996): 183–207.

10. Leonard Savitz, "Official Statistics," in *Contemporary Criminology*, ed. Leonard Savitz and Norman Johnston (New York: Wiley, 1982), pp. 3–15.

11. Roger Hood and Richard Sparks, *Key Issues in Criminology* (New York: McGraw-Hill, 1970), p. 72.

12. A pioneering effort in self-report research is A. L. Porterfield, *Youth in Trouble* (Fort Worth, Tx.: Leo Potishman Foundation, 1946); for a review, see Robert Hardt and George Bodine, *Development of Self-Report Instruments in Delinquency Research: A Conference Report* (Syracuse, N.Y.: Syracuse University Youth Development Center, 1965). See also Fred Murphy, Mary Shirley, and Helen Witner, "The Incidence of Hidden Delinquency," *American Journal of Orthopsychology* 16 (1946): 686–696.

13. Franklyn Dunford and Delbert Elliott, "Identifying Career Criminals Using Self-Reported Data," *Journal of Research in Crime and Delinquency* 21 (1983): 57–86.

14. See, for example, Spencer Rathus and Larry Siegel, "Crime and Personality Revisited: Effects of MMPI Sets on Self-Report Studies," *Criminology* 18 (1980): 245–251; John Clark and Larry Tifft, "Polygraph and Interview Validation of Self-Reported Deviant Behavior," *American Sociological Review* 31 (1966): 516–523.

15. See, for example, Harwin Voss, "Ethnic Differences in Delinquency in Honolulu," *Journal of Criminal Law, Criminology and Police Science* 54 (1963): 322–327; Maynard Erickson and LaMar Empey, "Court Records, Undetected Delinquency and Decision Making," *Journal of Criminal Law, Criminology and Police Science* 54 (1963): 456–459; H. B. Gibson, Sylvia Morrison, and D. J. West, "The Confession of Known Offenses in Response to a Self-Reported Delinquency Schedule," *British Journal of Criminology* 10 (1970): 277–280; John Blackmore, "The Relationship Between Self-Reported Delinquency and Official Convictions Amongst Adolescent Boys," *British Journal of Criminology* 14 (1974): 172–176.

16. Clark and Tifft, "Polygraph and Interview Validation of Self-Reported Deviant Behavior."

17. Michael Hindelang, Travis Hirschi, and Joseph Weis, *Measuring Delinquency* (Beverly Hills: Sage, 1981).

18. Terence Thornberry, Beth Bjerregaard, and William Miles, "The Consequences of Respondent Attrition in Panel Studies: A Simulation Based on the Rochester Youth Development Study," *Journal of Quantitative Criminology* 9 (1993): 127–158.

19. Minu Mathur, Richard Dodder, and Harjit Sandhu, "Inmate Self-Report Data: A Study of Reliability," *Criminal Justice Review* 17 (1992): 258–267.

20. Thomas Gray and Eric Wish, *Maryland Youth at Risk: A Study of Drug Use in Juvenile Detainees* (College Park, Md.: Center for Substance Abuse Research, 1993).

21. Eric Wish and Christina Polsenberg, "Arrestee Urine Tests and Self-Reports of Drug Use: Which Is More Related to Rearrest?" (Paper presented at the annual meeting of the American Society of Criminology, Phoenix, Arizona, November 1993).

22. NCVS, 1992, p. 2.

23. L. Edward Wells and Joseph Rankin, "Juvenile Victimization: Convergent Validation of Alternative Measurements," *Journal of Research in Crime and Delinquency* 32 (1995): 287–307.

24. Alfred Blumstein, Jacqueline Cohen, and Richard Rosenfeld, "Trend and Deviation in Crime Rates: A Comparison of UCR and NCVS data for Burglary and Robbery," *Criminology* 29 (1991): 237–248. See also Hindelang, Hirschi, and Weis, *Measuring Delinquency*.

25. For a critique, see Scott Menard, "Residual Gains, Reliability, and the UCR-NCVS Relationship: A Comment on Blumstein, Cohen and Rosenfeld (1991)," *Criminology* 30 (1992): 105–115.

26. David McDowall and Colin Loftin, "Comparing the UCR and NCVS over Time," *Criminology* 30 (1992): 125–133.

27. Clarence Schrag, *Crime and Justice: American Style* (Washington, D.C.: U.S. Government Printing Office, 1971).

28. For example, the following studies have noted the great discrepancy between official statistics and self-report studies: Erickson and Empey, "Court Records"; Martin Gold, "Undetected Delinquent Behavior," *Journal of Research in Crime and Delinquency* 3 (1966): 27–46; James Short and F. Ivan Nye, "Extent of Undetected Delinquency, Tentative Conclusions," *Journal of Criminal Law, Criminology and Police Science* 49 (1958): 296–302; Michael Hindelang, "Causes of Delinquency: A Partial Replication and Extension," *Social Problems* 20 (1973): 471–487.

29. D. Wayne Osgood, Lloyd Johnston, Patrick O'Malley, and Jerald Bachman, "The Generality of Deviance in Late Adolescence and Early Adulthood," *American Sociological Review* 53 (1988): 81–93.

30. D. Wayne Osgood, Patrick O'Malley, Jerald Bachman, and Lloyd Johnston, "Time Trends and Age Trends in Arrests and Self-Reported Illegal Behavior," *Criminology* 27 (1989): 389–417.

31. Lloyd Johnston, Patrick O'Malley, and Jerald Bachman, *Monitoring the Future, 1990* (Ann Arbor, Mich.: Institute for Social Research, 1991); Timothy Flanagan and Kathleen Maguire, *Sourcebook of Criminal Justice Statistics, 1989* (Washington, D.C.: U.S. Government Printing Office, 1990), pp. 290–291.

32. Glenn Pierce and James Alan Fox, *Recent Trends in Violent Crime: A Closer Look* (Boston: National Crime Analysis Program, Northeastern University, 1992).

33. Rosemary Gartner, "Family Structure, Welfare Spending, and Child Homicide in Developed Democracies," *Journal of Marriage and the Family* 53 (1991): 231–240.

34. UCR, 1995, p. 212.

35. Joseph Sheley and James Wright, *In the Line of Fire: Youth, Guns, and Violence in Urban America* (New York: Aldine de Gruyter, 1995).

36. Carolyn Block, Michael Biritz, Ayad Paul Jacob, Irving Spergel, and Susan Grossman, "The Early Warning System for Street Gang Violence: A Community Approach to Gang Violence Reduction." Paper presented at the annual meeting of the American Society of Criminology, Chicago, Ill., November 1996.

37. Alfred Blumstein, "Violence by Young People: Why the Deadly Nexus," *National Institute of Justice Journal* 229 (1995): 2–9.

38. Steven Dillingham, *Violent Crime in the United States* (Washington, D.C.: Bureau of Justice Statistics, 1991), p. 17.

39. Bruce Johnson, Andrew Golub, and Jeffrey Fagan, "Careers in Crack, Drug Use, Drug Distribution, and Nondrug Criminality," *Crime and Delinquency* 41 (1995): 275–295.

40. Darrell Steffensmeier and Miles Harer, "Did Crime Rise or Fall During the Reagan Presidency? The Effects of an 'Aging' U.S. Population on the Nation's Crime Rate," *Journal of Research in Crime and Delinquency* 28 (1991): 330–339.

41. James A. Fox, *Trends in Juvenile Violence: A Report to the United States Attorney General on Current and Future Rates of Juvenile Offending* (Boston, Mass: Northeastern University, 1996).

42. Rosemary Gartner and Robert Nash Parker, "Cross-National Evidence on Homicide and the Age Structure of the Population," *Social Forces* 69 (1990): 351–371.

43. Ellen Cohn, "The Effect of Weather and Temporal Variations on Calls for Police Service," *American Journal of Police* 15 (1996): 23–43.

44. R. A. Baron, "Aggression as a Function of Ambient Temperature and Prior Anger Arousal," *Journal of Personality and Social Psychology* 21 (1972): 183–189.

45. Ellen Cohn, "The Prediction of Police Calls for Service: The Influence of Weather and Temporal Variables on Rape and Domestic Violence," *Journal of Environmental Psychology* 13 (1993): 71–83.

46. Derral Cheatwood, "The Effects of Weather on Homicide," *Journal of Quantitative Criminology* 11 (1995): 51–70.

47. Ellen Cohn and James Rotton, "Assault as a Function of Time and Temperature: A Moderator-Variable Times-Series Analysis." Paper presented at the annual meeting of the American Society of Criminology, Chicago, Ill., November 1996, p. 23.

48. Joseph Sheley and James Wright, *Gun Acquisition and Possession in Selected Juvenile Samples* (Washington, D.C.: National Institute of Justice, 1993).

49. Robert Nash Parker, "Bringing 'Booze' Back In: The Relationship Between Alcohol and Homicide," *Journal of Research in Crime and Delinquency* 32 (1995): 3–38.

50. Victoria Brewer and M. Dwayne Smith, "Gender Inequality and Rates of Female Homicide Victimization Across U.S. Cities," *Journal of Research in Crime and Delinquency* 32 (1995): 175–190.

51. Short and Nye, "Extent of Undetected Delinquency."

52. F. Ivan Nye, James Short, and Virgil Olsen, "Socio-economic Status and Delinquent Behavior," *American Journal of Sociology* 63 (1958): 381–389; Robert Dentler and Lawrence Monroe, "Social Correlates of Early Adolescent Theft," *American Sociological Review* 63 (1961): 733–743. See also Terence Thornberry and Margaret Farnworth, "Social Correlates of Criminal Involvement: Further Evidence of the Relationship Between Social Status and Criminal Behavior," *American Sociological Review* 47 (1982): 505–518.

53. Charles Tittle, Wayne Villemez, and Douglas Smith, "The Myth of Social Class and Criminality: An Empirical Assessment of the Empirical Evidence," *American Sociological Review* 43 (1978): 643–656.

54. Charles Tittle and Robert Meier, "Specifying the SES/Delinquency Relationship," *Criminology* 28 (1990): 271–301.

55. Delbert Elliott and Suzanne Ageton, "Reconciling Race and Class Differences in Self-Reported and Official Estimates of Delinquency," *American Sociological Review* 45 (1980): 95–110.

56. See also Delbert Elliott and David Huizinga, "Social Class and Delinquent Behavior in a National Youth Panel: 1976–1980," *Criminology* 21 (1983): 149–177. For a similar view, see John Braithwaite, "The Myth of Social Class and Criminality Reconsidered," *American Sociological Review* 46 (1981): 35–58, and Hindelang, Hirschi, and Weis, *Measuring Delinquency,* p. 196.

57. David Brownfield, "Social Class and Violent Behavior," *Criminology* 24 (1986): 421–439.

58. Douglas Smith and Laura Davidson, "Interfacing Indicators and Constructs in Criminological Research: A Note on the Comparability of Self-Report Violence Data for Race and Sex Groups," *Criminology* 24 (1986): 473–488.

59. Sally Simpson and Lori Elis, "Doing Gender: Sorting Out the Case and Crime Conundrum," *Criminology* 33 (1995): 47–81.

60. Judith Blau and Peter Blau, "The Cost of Inequality: Metropolitan Structure and Violent Crime," *American Sociological Review* 147 (1982): 114–129; Richard Block, "Community Environment and Violent Crime," *Criminology* 17 (1979): 46–57; Robert Sampson, "Structural Sources of Variation in Race-Age-Specific Rates of Offending Across Major U.S. Cities," *Criminology* 23 (1985): 647–673.

61. Chin-Chi Hsieh and M. D. Pugh, "Poverty, Income Inequality, and Violent Crime: A Meta-Analysis of Recent Aggregate Data Studies," *Criminal Justice Review* 18 (1993): 182–199.

62. Alan Lizotte, Terence Thornberry, Marvin Krohn, Deborah Chard-Wierschem, and David McDowall, "Neighborhood Context and Delinquency: A Longitudinal Analysis," in *Cross National Longitudinal Research on Human Development and Criminal Behavior,* ed., E. M. Weitekamp and H. J. Kerner (Stavernstr, Netherlands: Kluwer, 1994), pp. 217–227.

63. Travis Hirschi and Michael Gottfredson, "Age and Explanation of Crime," *American Journal of Sociology* 89 (1983): 552–584.

64. Darrell Steffensmeier and Cathy Streifel, "Age, Gender, and Crime Across Three Historical Periods: 1935, 1960 and 1985," *Social Forces* 69 (1991): 869–894.

65. For a comprehensive review of crime and the elderly, see Kyle Kercher, "Causes and Correlates of Crime Committed by the Elderly," in *Critical Issues in Aging Policy,* ed. E. Borgatta and R. Montgomery (Beverly Hills: Sage, 1987), pp. 254–306, and Darrell Steffensmeier, "The Invention of the 'New' Senior Citizen Criminal," *Research on Aging* 9 (1987): 281–311.

66. John Laub, David Clark, Leslie Siegel, and James Garofolo, *Trends in Juvenile Crime in the United States: 1973–1983* (Albany, N.Y.: Hindelang Research Center, 1987).

67. Hirschi and Gottfredson, "Age and the Explanation of Crime."

68. Michael Gottfredson and Travis Hirschi, "The True Value of Lambda Would Appear to Be Zero: An Essay on Career Criminals, Criminal Careers, Selective Incapacitation, Cohort Studies and Related Topics," *Criminology* 24 (1986): 213–234; further support for their position can be found in Lawrence Cohen and Kenneth Land, "Age Structure and Crime," *American Sociological Review* 52 (1987): 170–183.

69. Kyle Kercher, "Explaining the Relationship Between Age and Crime: The Biological Versus Sociological Model." Paper presented at the American Society of Criminology meeting, Montreal, Canada, November 1987.

70. Alfred Blumstein, Jacqueline Cohen, and David Farrington, "Criminal Career Research: Its Value for Criminology," *Criminology* 26 (1988): 1–37.

71. Sung Joon Jang and Marvin Krohn, "Developmental Patterns of Sex Differences in Delinquency Among African American Adolescents: A Test of the Sex-Invariance Hypothesis," *Journal of Quantitative Criminology* 11 (1995): 195–220.

72. Candace Kruttschnitt, "Violence by and Against Women: A Comparative and Cross-National Analysis," *Violence and Victims* 8 (1994): 1–28.

73. David Greenberg, "Age, Crime, and Social Explanation," *American Journal of Sociology* 91 (1985): 1–21.

74. Marvin Wolfgang, Robert Figlio, and Thorsten Sellin, *Delinquency in a Birth Cohort* (Chicago: University of Chicago Press, 1972); Lyle Shannon, *Assessing the Relationship of Adult Criminal Careers to Juvenile Careers: A Summary* (Washington, D.C.: U.S. Department of Justice, 1982); D. J. West and David P. Farrington, *The Delinquent Way of Life* (London: Hienemann, 1977); Donna Hamparian, Richard Schuster, Simon Dinitz, and John Conrad, *The Violent Few* (Lexington, Mass.: Lexington Books, 1978).

75. Rolf Loeber, Magda Stouthamer-Loeber, and Stephanie Green, "Age at Onset of Problem Behaviour in Boys and Later Disruptive and Delinquent Behaviours," *Criminal Behaviour and Mental Health* 1 (1991): 229–246.

76. Darrell Steffensmeier, Emilie Andersen Allan, Miles Harer, and Cathy Streifel, "Age and the Distribution of Crime: Variant or Invariant?" Paper presented at the American Society of Criminology meeting, Montreal, Canada, November 1987.

77. Hilary Saner, Robert MacCoun, and Peter Reuter, "On the Ubiquity of Drug Selling Among Youthful Offenders in Washington, DC., 1985–1991: Age, Period, or Cohort Effect?"*Journal of Quantitative Criminology* 11 (1995): 362–373.

78. Arnold Barnett, Alfred Blumstein, and David Farrington, "Probabilistic Models of Youthful Criminal Careers," *Criminology* 25 (1987): 83–107.

79. Peter Greenwood, "Differences in Criminal Behavior and Court Responses Among Juvenile and Young Adult Defendants," in *Crime and Justice, An Annual Review of Research,* ed. Michael Tonry and Norval Morris (Chicago: University of Chicago Press, 1986), pp. 151–189.

80. John Hagan and Alberto Palloni, "Crimes as Social Events in the Life Course: Reconceiving a Criminological Controversy," *Criminology* 26 (1988): 87–101.

81. Travis Hirschi and Michael Gottfredson, "Age and Crime, Logic and Scholarship: Comment on Greenberg," *American Journal of Sociology* 91 (1985): 22–27; idem, "All Wise After the Fact Learning Theory, Again: Reply to Baldwin," *American Journal of Sociology* 90 (1985): 1330–1333; John Baldwin, "Thrill and Adventure Seeking and the Age Distribution of Crime: Comment on Hirschi and Gottfredson," *American Journal of Sociology* 90 (1985): 1326–1329.

82. Per-Olof Wikstrom, "Age and Crime in a Stockholm Cohort," *Journal of Quantitative Criminology* 6 (1990): 61–82.

83. Edward Mulvey and John LaRosa, "Delinquency Cessation and Adolescent Development: Preliminary Data," *American Journal of Orthopsychiatry* 56 (1986): 212–224.

84. Gordon Trasler, "Cautions for a Biological Approach to Crime," in *The Causes of Crime, New Biological Approaches,* ed. Sarnoff Mednick, Terrie Moffitt, and Susan Stack (Cambridge: Cambridge University Press, 1987), pp. 7–25.

85. James Q. Wilson and Richard Herrnstein, *Crime and Human Nature* (New York: Simon & Schuster, 1985), pp. 126–147.

86. Ibid., p. 219.

87. Charles Tittle, "Two Empirical Regularities (Maybe) in Search of an Explanation: Commentary on the Age/Crime Debate," *Criminology* 26 (1988): 75–85.

88. Neal Shover and Carol Thompson, "Age, Differential Expectations and Crime Desistance," *Criminology* 30 (1992): 89–105.

89. Erich Labouvie, "Maturing Out of Substance Use: Selection and Self-Correction," *Journal of Drug Issues* 26 (1996): 457–474.

90. Walter Gove, "The Effect of Age and Gender on Deviant Behavior: A Biopsychosocial Perspective," in *Gender and the Life Course,* ed. A. Ross (Chicago: Aldine, 1985), p. 131.

91. Cesare Lombroso, *The Female Offender* (New York: Appleton Publishers, 1895/1920).

92. Ibid., p. 122.

93. Otto Pollack, *The Criminality of Women* (Philadelphia: University of Pennsylvania, 1950).

94. For a review of this issue, see Darrell Steffensmeier, "Assessing the Impact of the Women's Movement on Sex-Based Differences in the Handling of Adult Criminal Defendants," *Crime and Delinquency* 26 (1980): 344–357.

95. Alan Booth and D. Wayne Osgood, "The Influence of Testosterone on Deviance in Adulthood: Assessing and Explaining the Relationship," *Criminology* 31 (1993): 93–118.

96. Darrell Steffensmeier and Robert Clark, "Sociocultural Versus Biological/Sexist Explanations of Sex Differences in Crime: A Survey of American Criminology Textbooks, 1918–1965," *American Sociologist* 15 (1980): 246–255.

97. Gisela Konopka, *The Adolescent Girl in Conflict* (Englewood Cliffs, N.J.: Prentice-Hall, 1966); Clyde Vedder and Dora Somerville, *The Delinquent Girl* (Springfield, Ill.: Charles C Thomas, 1970).

98. Dennis Giever, "An Empirical Assessment of the Core Elements of Gottfredson and Hirschi's General Theory of Crime." Paper presented at the American Society of Criminology meeting, Boston, Mass., November 1995.

99. John Mirowsky and Catherine Ross, "Sex Differences in Distress: Real or Artifact?"*American Sociological Review* 60 (1995): 449–468.

100. For a review of this issue see Anne Campbell, *Men, Women and Aggression* (New York: Basic Books, 1993).

101. Mirowsky and Ross, "Sex Differences in Distress," pp. 460–465.

102. Robert Hoge, D. A. Andrews, and Alan Leschied, "Tests of Three Hypotheses Regarding the Predictors of Delinquency," *Journal of Abnormal Child Psychology* 22 (1994): 547–559.

103. Freda Adler, *Sisters in Crime* (New York: McGraw-Hill, 1975).

104. Rita James Simon, *The Contemporary Woman and Crime* (Washington, D.C.: U.S. Government Printing Office, 1975).

105. David Rowe, Alexander Vazsonyi, and Daniel Flannery, "Sex Differences in Crime: Do Mean and Within-Sex Variation Have Similar Causes?" *Journal of Research in Crime and Delinquency* 32 (1995): 84–100; Michael Hindelang, "Age, Sex, and the Versatility of Delinquency Involvements," *Social Forces* 14 (1971): 525–534; Martin Gold, *Delinquent Behavior in an American City* (Belmont, Calif.: Brooks/Cole, 1970); Gary Jensen and Raymond Eve, "Sex Differences in Delinquency: An Examination of Popular Sociological Explanations," *Criminology* 13 (1976): 427–448.

106. Darrel Steffensmeier and Renee Hoffman Steffensmeier, "Trends in Female Delinquency," *Criminology* 18 (1980): 62–85; see also idem, "Crime and the Contemporary Woman: An Analysis of Changing Levels of Female Property Crime, 1960–1975," *Social Forces* 57 (1978): 566–584; Joseph Weis, "Liberation and Crime: The Invention of the New Female Criminal," *Crime and Social Justice* 1 (1976): 17–27; Carol Smart, "The New Female Offender: Reality or Myth," *British Journal of Criminology* 19 (1979): 50–59; Steven Box and Chris Hale, "Liberation/Emancipation, Economic Marginalization or Less Chivalry," *Criminology* 22 (1984): 473–478.

107. Meda Chesney-Lind, "Female Offenders: Paternalism Reexamined," in *Women, the Courts and Equality,* ed. Laura Crites and Winifred Hepperle (Newberry Park, Calif.: Sage, 1987), pp. 114–139.

108. Darrell Steffensmeier, Emilie Allan, and Cathy Streifel, "Development and Female Crime: A Cross-National Test of Alternative Explanations," *Social Forces* 68 (1989): 262–283.

109. Kruttschnitt, "Violence by and Against Women."

110. UCR, 1995, p. 215.

111. Roy Austin, "Recent Trends in the Male and Female Crime Rate: The Convergence Controversy," *Journal of Criminal Justice* 21 (1993): 447–466.

112. NCVS, 1994.

113. Leroy Gould, "Who Defines Delinquency: A Comparison of Self-Report and Officially Reported Indices of Delinquency for Three Racial Groups," *Social Problems* 16 (1969): 325–336; Voss, "Ethnic Differentials in Delinquency in Honolulu"; Ronald Akers, Marvin Krohn, Marcia Radosevich, and Lonn Lanza-Kaduce, "Social Characteristics and Self-Reported Delinquency," *Sociology of Delinquency,* ed. Gary Jensen (Beverly Hills: Sage, 1981), pp. 48–62.

114. Institute for Social Research, *Monitoring the Future* (Ann Arbor, Mich.: ISR, 1992), pp. 102–104.

115. David Huizinga and Delbert Elliott, "Juvenile Offenders: Prevalence, Offender Incidence, and Arrest Rates by Race," *Crime and Delinquency* 33 (1987): 206–223. See also Dale Dannefer and Russell Schutt, "Race and Juvenile Justice Processing in Court and Police Agencies," *American Journal of Sociology* 87 (1982): 1113–1132.

116. Paul Tracy, "Race and Class Differences in Official and Self-Reported Delinquency," in *From Boy to Man, from Delinquency to Crime,* ed. Marvin Wolfgang, Terence Thornberry, and Robert Figlio (Chicago: University of Chicago Press, 1987), p. 120.

117. Daniel Georges-Abeyie, "Definitional Issues: Race, Ethnicity and Official Crime/Victimization Rates," in *The Criminal Justice System and Blacks,* ed. D. Georges-Abeyie (New York: Clark Boardman,

1984), p. 12; Robert Sampson, "Race and Criminal Violence: A Demographically Disaggregated Analysis of Urban Homicide," *Crime and Delinquency* 31 (1985): 47–82.

118. Barry Sample and Michael Philip, "Perspectives on Race and Crime in Research and Planning," in *The Criminal Justice System and Blacks,* pp. 21–36.

119. Kruttschnitt, "Violence by and Against Women," p. 4.

120. James P. Comer, "Black Violence and Public Policy," in *American Violence and Public Policy,* ed. Lynn Curtis (New Haven, Conn.: Yale University Press, 1985), pp. 63–86.

121. Ibid., p. 80.

122. Ibid., p. 81.

123. Marvin Wolfgang and Franco Ferracuti, *The Subculture of Violence* (London: Tavistock, 1967).

124. Charles Silberman, *Criminal Violence, Criminal Justice* (New York: Random House, 1979), pp. 153–165.

125. Roy Austin, "Progress Toward Racial Equality and Reduction of Black Criminal Violence," *Journal of Criminal Justice* 15 (1987): 437–459.

126. Reynolds Farley and William Frey, "Changes in the Segregation of Whites from Blacks During the 1980s: Small Steps Toward a More Integrated Society," *American Sociological Review* 59 (1994): 23–45.

127. Melvin Thomas, "Race, Class and Personal Income: An Empirical Test of the Declining Significance of Race Thesis, 1968–1988," *Social Problems* 40 (1993): 328–339.

128. Gary LaFree, Kriss Drass, and Patrick O'Day, "Race and Crime in Postwar America: Determinants of African-American and White Rates, 1957–1988," *Criminology* 30 (1992): 157–188.

129. Marvin Wolfgang, Robert Figlio, and Thorsten Sellin, *Delinquency in a Birth Cohort* (Chicago: University of Chicago Press, 1972).

130. See Thorsten Sellin and Marvin Wolfgang, *The Measurement of Delinquency* (New York: Wiley, 1964), p. 120.

131. Paul Tracy and Robert Figlio, "Chronic Recidivism in the 1950 Birth Cohort." Paper presented at the American Society of Criminology meeting, Toronto, October 1982; Marvin Wolfgang, "Delinquency in Two Birth Cohorts," in *Perspective Studies of Crime and Delinquency,* ed. Katherine Teilmann Van Dusen and Sarnoff Mednick (Boston: Kluwer-Nijhoff, 1983), pp. 7–17. The following sections rely heavily on these sources.

132. Lyle Shannon, *Criminal Career Opportunity* (New York: Human Sciences Press, 1988); idem, *Assessing the Relationship of Adult Criminal Careers to Juvenile Careers.*

133. D. J. West and David P. Farrington, *The Delinquent Way of Life* (London: Hienemann, 1977).

134. David Farrington and D. J. West, "Criminal, Penal and Life Histories of Chronic Offenders: Risk and Protective Factors and Early Identification," *Criminal Behavior and Mental Health* **in press** (1994).

135. See, generally, Wolfgang, Thornberry, and Figlio, eds. *From Boy to Man, from Delinquency to Crime.*

136. Paul Tracy and Kimberly Kempf-Leonard, *Continuity and Discontinuity in Criminal Careers* (New York: Plenum Press, 1996).

137. R. Tremblay, R. Loeber, C. Gagnon, P. Charlebois, S. Larivee, and M. LeBlanc, "Disruptive Boys with Stable and Unstable High Fighting Behavior Patterns During Junior Elementary School," *Journal of Abnormal Child Psychology* 19 (1991): 285–300.

138. Jennifer White, Terrie Moffitt, Felton Earls, Lee Robins, and Phil Silva, "How Early Can We Tell? Predictors of Childhood Conduct Disorder and Adolescent Delinquency," *Criminology* 28 (1990): 507–535.

139. John Laub and Robert Sampson, "Unemployment, Marital Discord, and Deviant Behavior: The Long-Term Correlates of Childhood Misbehavior." Paper presented at the annual meeting of the American Society of Criminology, Baltimore, November 1990; rev. version.

140. Wikstrom, "Age and Crime in a Stockholm Cohort."

141. David Farrington and J. David Hawkins, "Predicting Participation, Early Onset, and Later Persistence in Officially Recorded Offending," *Criminal Behavior and Mental Health* 1 (1991): 1–33.

142. Daniel Nagin, David Farrington, and Terrie Moffitt, "Life-Course Trajectories of Different Types of Offenders," *Criminology* 33 (1995): 111–139.

143. Susan Martin, "Policing Career Criminals: An Examination of an Innovative Crime Control Program," *Journal of Criminal Law and Criminology* 77 (1986): 1159–1182.

Chapter 4
Victims and Victimization

for many years, crime victims were not considered an important topic for criminological study. Victims were viewed as the passive receptors of a criminal's anger, greed, or frustration; they were people considered to be in the "wrong place at the wrong time." In the late 1960s, a number of pioneering studies found that, contrary to popular belief, the victim's function is an important one in the crime process. Victims can influence criminal behavior by playing an active role in the criminal incident, such as when an assault victim initially insults and provokes his eventual attacker. Research efforts have found that victims can also play an indirect role in the criminal incident, such as when a woman adopts a lifestyle that continually brings her into high-crime areas.

The discovery that the victim plays an important role in the crime process has prompted the scientific study of the victim, or **victimology**; those criminologists who focus their attention on the crime victim refer to themselves as **victimologists.** Victim studies have also taken on great importance because of concern for those injured in violent crimes or who suffer loss due to economic crimes. The National Crime Victimization Survey (NCVS) indicates that the number of victimizations in the United States approaches 40 million incidents annually.

Net Bookmark

The National Justice Information Center—part of the National Criminal Justice Reference Service (NCJRS)—provides information about various kinds of victimization, including child abuse, and addresses protection and other issues as well.

http://www.ncjrs.org/victhome.html

In this chapter, the focus is on victims and their relationship to the criminal process. First, using available victim data, we analyze the nature and extent of victimization. We then turn to a discussion of the relationship between victims and criminal offenders, and we summarize the various theories of victimization. Finally, we look at how society has responded to the needs of victims and at the special problems they still face.

Problems of Crime Victims: Loss

Being the target or a victim of rape, robbery, or assault is in itself a terrible burden and one that can have considerable long-term consequences.[1] Based on data regarding property taken during larcenies, burglaries, and other reported crimes, the FBI estimates that victims lose about $13 billion per year and that after the crime has been cleared they recover about $5 billion of their losses.[2]

Property losses are only a small part of the toll that crime takes on victims. Productivity losses due to injury,

CRIME	TANGIBLE COSTS	INTANGIBLE COSTS	TOTAL COSTS
Murder	$1,030,000	$1,910,000	$2,940,000
Rape/sexual assault	5,100	81,400	86,500
Robbery/attempt with injury	5,200	13,800	19,000
Assault or attempt	1,550	7,800	9,350
Burglary or attempt	1,100	300	1,400

Table 4.1   Costs per Victimization

Source: Ted Miller, Mark Cohen, and Brian Wiersema, *The Extent and Costs of Crime Victimization: A New Look* (Washington, D.C.: National Institute of Justice, 1996), p. 2.

medical costs, and the "value" that can be placed on pain and emotional trauma also take their toll. According to a recent study by Urban Institute researchers, whereas the total cost of victimization in terms of property and productivity loss and medical expenses is $105 billion, the total value of all crime-related costs—including long-term suffering, trauma, and risk of death—amounts to $450 billion annually, or about $1,800 per person.[3] This finding is based on an estimate of about 49 million criminal victimizations per year, a figure that includes crimes such as child abuse, drunk driving, and arson, which are not contained in the NCVS. Taking a civil law approach, which is used to assess costs in damage suits, the researchers assigned a "value" to each crime type based on tangible direct costs (property loss, medical bills, productivity loss) and indirect costs (long-term psychological pain and suffering).[4] Table 4.1 shows the amounts computed for various crime types.

Connections

In early common law, value was attached to the damages caused by criminal acts in an effort to extract wergild. Civil damages for assault and other violent crimes are the descendent of that practice. See Chapter 2 for more on wergild.

Problems of Crime Victims: Suffering

The problems associated with crime are not restricted to its costs. Victims are likely to suffer serious physical injury, often requiring medical treatment. And victims' suffering does not end when the attacker leaves the scene of the crime. They may suffer more "victimization" at the hands

The pain and suffering experienced by crime victims does not stop after the criminal act is over. Many go through a fundamental life change, viewing the world more suspiciously and less as a safe, controllable, and meaningful place. Victims are also more likely to suffer psychological stress for extended periods of time. In 1993 tennis great Monica Seles was stabbed in the back by a fan of her rival Steffi Graf. Seles found it difficult to get back on the tour after the incident and remains fearful of further attacks. Her stabbing shows that even the most famous celebrities are not immune from violent victimization.

of the justice system. While the crime is still fresh in their minds, victims may be subjected to insensitive questioning by police, including innuendos or suspicion that the victim was somehow at fault. Victims may also have difficulty learning what is going on in the case. In addition, their property is often kept for a long time as evidence and may never be returned, and their wages may be lost for time spent testifying in court.

Time may be wasted when victims appear in court only to have their case postponed or dismissed. Furthermore, they may find that authorities are indifferent to their fear of retaliation if they cooperate in the offender's prosecution, and they may be fearful of testifying in court and being embarrassed by defense attorneys.[5]

After the incident is over, the victim may suffer stress and anxiety, even when physical traumas and financial losses and the justice process have been forgotten. For example, girls who were sexually and physically abused as children are more suicidal as adults than are nonabused females.[6] Those who suffered the pains of abuse also have significantly higher levels of homelessness; a history of physical and sexual abuse is especially common among homeless women who also display symptoms of mental illness.[7] The long-term emotional trauma suffered by women in the aftermath of spousal assault is also well documented.[8] Spousal abuse victims suffer an extremely high prevalence of depression, posttraumatic stress disorder, anxiety disorder, and

obsessive-compulsive disorder.[9] Symptoms include nightmares, hyperarousal, and repression of the abuse.[10]

Women are not the only ones who suffer in the aftermath of violence; male victims of violent attacks also suffer postcrime stress disorders. Viewing themselves from a "male frame of reference," these victims express feelings of being "weak and helpless." Also, whereas female victims tend to internalize and place the blame for their victimization on themselves, males are more likely to externalize blame, expressing anger toward their attackers.[11]

In short, the pain and suffering experienced by crime victims does not stop after the criminal incident is over. Many go through a fundamental life change, viewing the world more suspiciously and less as a safe, controllable, and meaningful place. Those who do are more likely to suffer psychological stress for extended periods of time.[12]

Some victims may find that the physical wounds received during a criminal incident haunt them for the rest of their lives. There is a growing population of violent crime victims who are physically disabled due to the serious wounds sustained during episodes of random violence. A growing number suffer spinal cord injuries, resulting in paralysis. Many victims have no insurance, and treatment costs overload an already overburdened health care system. Of all spinal cord injuries, shooting accounted for 43% of the African Americans injured, 37% of Hispanics, and 7% of Caucasians.[13]

Problems of Crime Victims: Antisocial Behavior

In the 1996 film *Never Talk to Strangers,* a psychiatrist played by Rebecca DeMornay suspects that her new boyfriend (Antonio Banderas) is a killer. As the bodies begin to pile up, the audience begins to share her suspicions. In the film's surprise ending, we learn that DeMornay is the real killer. It seems her personality was irrevocably damaged when her father sexually abused her as a child and murdered her mother while she looked on.

Connections

It has become common for Hollywood to depict women as psychopathic serial killers (*Friday the 13th, Black Widow, The Crush*). Are women commonly serial killers? Most research shows that movies aside, women are rarely involved in multiple murders. Chapter 11 reviews serial murder in some detail.

There is growing evidence that the association between early victimization and later criminality is not merely the fictional subject of Hollywood films; people who are the victims of crime also seem more likely to commit crime themselves. For example, an analysis of juvenile court records from a Midwestern metropolitan area conducted by Tim Ireland and Cathy Spatz Widom found that child maltreatment was a significant predictor of future criminality. Having been abused or neglected increased the odds of being arrested as a juvenile and also of having at least one alcohol- or drug-related arrest in adulthood. The odds of adult arrest were 39% greater for maltreated than for nonabused adolescents.[14] Widom has referred to the phenomenon of child victims later becoming adult criminals as the **cycle of violence**.[15]

The cycle of violence hypothesis is supported by research showing that young males are more likely to engage in violent behavior if they were (a) the target of physical abuse and (b) exposed to interadult violence, especially if weapons were used.[16] The association between victimiza-

tion and future behavioral difficulties is not limited to males; research efforts have found that females exposed to family violence may be even more likely to manifest behavioral and adjustment problems as they mature.[17]

Victimization thus presents financial, physical, and emotional strains that are difficult to overcome.

The Nature of Victimization

The National Crime Victimization Survey is the leading source of information today about the nature and extent of victimization. It uses a highly sophisticated and complex sampling methodology to annually collect data from thousands of citizens. Statistical estimation techniques are then applied to the sample data to make estimates of victimization rates, trends, and patterns that occur in the entire U.S. population. In 1992 the NCVS was redesigned to provide more accurate and valid data; as a consequence, the number of reported victimizations increased significantly.

How many criminal victimizations are there today? At last count, an estimated 39.6 million criminal events occurred during 1995 (see Figure 4.1). Similar to the UCR data, the NCVS findings show that victimization incidents were stable or declining during the 1990–1995 period.

Some patterns in the victimization survey findings are stable and repetitive. These patterns are critical social facts because they indicate that victimization is not random but rather a function of personal and ecological factors. The stability of these patterns allows judgments to be made about the nature of victimization; policies can then be created that might eventually reduce the victimization rate. Who are victims? Where does victimization take place? What is the relationship between victims and criminals? Answers to these questions can come from the NCVS data. In the following sections, some of the most important patterns and trends in victimization are discussed.

The Social Ecology of Victimization

The NCVS data can tell us a lot about the ecology of victimization: where, when, and how it occurs. For instance, violent crimes are equally likely to take place during the daytime or evening hours, although the more serious forms of these crimes—rape and aggravated assault—typically take place after 6 P.M.; less serious forms of violence, unarmed robberies, and personal larcenies such as purse snatching are more likely to occur during the daytime.

The most likely site for every crime category is either an open, public area (such as a street, a park, or a field) or a commercial establishment such as a tavern; more than 10% of violent incidents usually take place on schoolgrounds. Only the crimes of rape and simple assault with injury are likely to occur in the home. Nonetheless, a significant number of rapes, robberies, and aggravated assaults occur in public places.

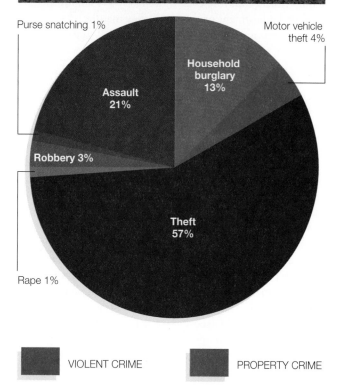

Figure 4.1   Percent distribution of victimization by type of crime, 1995.

Purse snatching 1%

Motor vehicle theft 4%

Household burglary 13%

Assault 21%

Robbery 3%

Theft 57%

Rape 1%

■ VIOLENT CRIME   ■ PROPERTY CRIME

Neighborhood characteristics influence the chances of victimization. Those living in the central city have significantly higher rates of theft and violence than suburbanites; people living in nonmetropolitan, rural areas have a victimization rate almost half that of city dwellers. The risk for murder victimization, for both men and women, is significantly higher in disorganized inner city areas where gangs flourish and drug trafficking is commonplace.[18]

The Victim's Household

Another way to look at the social ecology of victimization patterns is to examine the type of household or dwelling unit most likely to contain victims or to be victimized.[19] What factors are associated with households that contain crime victims? The NCVS tells us that larger, higher-income, African American, western, and urban areas are the most vulnerable to crime. In contrast, poor, rural white homes in the northeast are the least likely to contain crime victims or to be the target of theft offenses, such as burglary or larceny. People who own their own home are less vulnerable than renters.

NCVS data indicate that recent population movements and changes may be accounting for current patterns in household victimization patterns. American society has become extremely mobile, moving from urban areas to suburban and rural areas. In addition, family size has been re-

duced; more people than ever before are living in single-person homes (about 25% of households). It is possible that the decline in household victimization rates during the past 15 years can be explained by the fact that smaller households in less populated areas have a lower victimization risk.

Because of the high incidence of crime, Americans maintain a significant chance of becoming a victim sometime during their lifetime. The probability of the average 12-year-old being the victim of violent crime sometime in his or her life is about 83%; 25% of all U.S. citizens will experience violence three or more times. Even more startling is the fact that 99% of the U.S. population will experience personal theft at least once, and 87% will become a theft victim three or more times.

Victim Characteristics

A number of social and demographic characteristics distinguish victims from nonvictims. The most important of these factors are gender, age, social status, marital status, and race.

GENDER.   The NCVS provides information on the background characteristics of the victims of crime, including gender. Men are about twice as likely as women to be victims of robbery and twice as likely to be at risk for aggravated assault; they are also more likely to experience theft, but the difference is less pronounced. Although women are far more likely than men to be the victims of sexual assault (3.7 per 1,000), the NCVS estimates that .2 males are assaulted per 1,000 population; assuming a male population of 125 million, that means about 25,000 males are raped or sexually assaulted each year.

When men are the victims of violent crime, the perpetrator is usually a stranger. Women are much more likely to be attacked by a relative than men; about two-thirds of all attacks against women are committed by a husband, boyfriend, family member, or acquaintance.[20] In two-thirds of sexual assaults, the victim knows or is acquainted with her attacker.

AGE.   Young people face a much greater victimization risk than older persons. Victim risk diminishes rapidly after age 25. The elderly, who are thought of as being the helpless targets of predatory criminals, are actually much safer than their grandchildren. People over age 65, who make up 14% of the population, account for only 1% of violent victimizations. Teens ages 12 to 19, who also make up 14% of the population, account for 32% of violent victimizations.

The association between age and victimization may be bound up in the lifestyle shared by most young people. Adolescents often stay out late at night, go to public places, and hang out with other kids who have a high risk of criminal involvement. Most adolescents ages 12 to 19 are attacked by offenders in the same age category, while a great majority of adults are victimized by adult criminals. Teens face a high victimization risk because they spend a great deal of time in the most dangerous building in the community: the local schoolhouse!

A recent survey of state correctional inmates underscores the risks faced by young people. About 19% of all state inmates surveyed had committed a crime against a person under 18 years of age; 20% of violent criminals had committed crimes against children; about 7 of 10 offenders with child victims reported that they had been imprisoned for a rape or sexual assault.

Who victimizes children? Most are older white males with no prior criminal record. They are more likely to have themselves been physically or sexually abused as children than other inmates (although the majority had not suffered such abuse). Nearly a third of their victims had been their own children; only 1 in 7 reported that their victim had been a total stranger.[21]

In addition, the prison survey showed that a significant portion of inmates had victimized their own children. This finding is not surprising, as national surveys have shown that American homes can be dangerous places. One survey conducted by sociologists Richard Gelles and Murray Straus in 1979 found that in a given year between 1.4 and 1.9 million children in the United States are subject to physical abuse by their parents.[22] The survey showed that physical abuse was rarely a one-time act; the average number of assaults per year was 10.5, and the median was 4.5. In addition to parent-child abuse, Gelles and Straus found that 16% of the couples in their sample reported a violent act toward a spouse (husband or wife), and 50% of multi-child families reported attacks between siblings and 20% had incidents where children attacked parents. In another national survey conducted in 1985, Gelles and Straus found that the incidence of severe violence toward children may be on the decline.[23] Nonetheless, they still estimated that annually approximately 1.5 million children are subjected to severe violence.

The National Committee to Prevent Child Abuse (NCPCA) surveys social service agencies in all 50 states to determine the number and trends of reported child abuse cases.[24] The latest NCPCA survey indicates that more than 3 million cases were reported to police and social service agencies in 1995 (the last data available), an increase of more than 50% from 1985. More than 1 million of these cases were considered verifiable incidents of abuse. Of these, about 10% involved sexual abuse, and an estimated 1,215 deaths were attributed to abuse.[25]

It is uncertain whether this increase in reported abuse is a result of an increase in actual incidents or the result of greater public awareness of the problem, state efforts to encourage reporting, the proliferation of programs to prevent maltreatment, and expansion of the definition of abuse. Nonetheless, these data help explain in part why adolescents have a much greater victimization risk than adults.

able 4.2 Proper Victimization Rates				
	VICTIMIZATIONS PER 1,000 HOUSEHOLDS			
Characteristics	**Total**	**Burglary**	**Motor Vehicle Theft**	**Theft**
Race				
White	301.9	51.7	15.6	234.6
Black	341.3	70.8	26.6	243.8
Other	334.9	64.3	34.1	236.5
Ethnicity				
Hispanic	425.5	71.0	39.9	314.5
Non-Hispanic	298.0	53.1	15.6	229.3
Household Income				
Less than $7,500	295.8	78.6	13.9	203.2
$7,500–$14,999	296.6	65.4	15.2	216.0
$15,000–$24,999	307.0	60.5	16.3	230.2
$25,000–$34,999	307.1	50.9	20.0	236.3
$35,000–$49,999	325.8	51.6	17.0	257.2
$50,000–$74,999	356.3	39.6	20.7	296.0
$75,000 or more	356.6	40.9	17.7	297.9
Residence				
Urban	376.4	69.4	29.3	277.7
Suburban	296.5	46.5	15.6	234.3
Rural	246.4	49.6	6.9	189.8
Form of Tenure				
Home owned	272.2	45.5	14.5	212.2
Home rented	371.2	70.3	22.8	278.1

Source: Bruce Taylor, *Changes in Criminal Victimization, 1994–1995* (Washington, D.C.: Bureau of Justice Statistics, 1997).

While children are at great risk to victimization, there are also incidents in which violent youth victimize their own parents. This issue is the topic of the Close-Up "Parents Who Get Killed and the Children Who Kill Them."

SOCIAL STATUS. The poorest Americans might be expected to be the most likely victims of crime, since they live in areas that are crime-prone: inner-city, urban neighborhoods. The NCVS does in fact show that the least affluent (annual incomes of less than $7,500) are by far the most likely to be victims of violent crimes, and this association occurs across all gender, racial, and age groups (see Table 4.2). While the poor are almost twice as likely to become the victims of burglary, the wealthy are more likely to be the target of theft crimes, such as pocket picking and purse snatching. Perhaps the affluent, who sport more expensive attire and drive better cars, earn the attention of thieves looking for attractive targets.

Victim data suggest that thieves choose their targets carefully, selecting those who seem best able to provide them with a substantial haul. In contrast, the targets of violence, an expressive crime, are among the nation's poorest

The nation was fascinated in 1994 by the sensational case of Eric and Lyle Menendez, two wealthy California brothers who killed their parents. The boys claimed that they had acted in "self-defense" after years of physical and sexual abuse at their father's hands; both were convicted of murder after two widely followed trials. Their acts are referred to as **parricide,** or the killing of a close relative. Most often, this crime involves **patricide,** the killing of a father, or **matricide,** the killing of a mother.

University of South Florida criminologist Kathleen Heide has conducted extensive research on the nature and extent of family homicides. She has found that the killing of a parent is an almost daily event in the United States, averaging about 300 incidents per year. While such killings are typically committed by adults, about 15% of murdered mothers and 25% of fathers were killed by juvenile offspring. In addition, about 30% of murdered stepmothers and 34% of stepfathers were killed by adolescents. These numbers are quite startling when we consider that only 10% of all homicide arrests involve juveniles.

Heide found five conditions that foreshadow parricide. Children who will one day kill their parents are raised in a dysfunctional family of substance-abusing parents; they are severely abused verbally, physically, or sexually; violence in the family escalates throughout their life; the child becomes increasingly vulnerable to stressors in the home environment; and firearms are readily available.

Heide, a licensed psychotherapist, has found that parricide is typically committed by one of three types of offenders:

1. *The severely abused child.* An estimated 90% of parricide cases involve children who had been severely abused by parents. These kids were psychologically abused and then witnessed or suffered physical, sexual, and verbal abuse. Their parricide represented an act of desperation—the

only way out of a situation they could no longer endure. This type of crime made national headlines in 1983, when 16-year-old Richard Jahnke and his 17-year-old sister, Deborah, killed their father, an Internal Revenue Service agent, after years of sexual and physical abuse at his hands.

2. *The severely mentally ill child.* A few children who kill are suffering from severe psychosis. Their personalities are disorganized, perceptions distorted, and communication disjointed. They experience hallucinations and bizarre delusions. Heide tells of the case of Jonathan Cantero, who stabbed his mother 40 times and tried to cut off her left hand to "demonstrate his allegiance to Satan."

3. *The dangerously antisocial child.* Some parricidal youth have an antisocial or psychopathic personality. They kill their parents for purely selfish ends, such as obtaining an inheritance or getting money for drugs. Heide relates the case of Michelle White, 14, and her 17-year-old brother, John, Jr., who hired a neighbor to kill their father and then used his credit cards to buy $1,000 worth of videogames, television sets, and other merchandise; their father's corpse lay decaying in the kitchen as they cooked their meals.

Heide found that the typical parent or stepparent slain was a white, non-Hispanic male. The slayer, a son who was an adult at the time the crime occurred, used a handgun to kill the parent. Slayings involving multiple offenders and multiple victims were quite rare.

Mothers, more so than fathers, tended to be killed by older offspring. Perhaps the mother-child bond is stronger and more enduring, protecting the mother while the child is young. The strength of this bond may tie them together for a longer period of time, making violence more likely as the child becomes an

Kathleen Heide, author of *Why Kids Kill Parents: Child Abuse and Adolescent Homicide.*

adult. The number of stepparents being killed has trended upward, a pattern of concern considering the changing face of American families. Heide finds that public attitudes toward parricidal youth are changing from horror to sympathy now that there is recognition that most kids who kill are responding to life-threatening physical abuse.

CRITICAL THINKING QUESTIONS
1. Should abuse be considered a defense to parricide?
2. How would you handle the case of a 10-year-old who kills his father after an argument?

Sources: Kathleen Heide, *Why Kids Parents: Child Abuse and Adolescent Homicide* (Columbus, Ohio: Ohio State University Press, 1992); "Parents Who Get Killed and the Children Who Kill Them," *Journal of Interpersonal Violence* 8 (1993): 531–544; "Juvenile Involvement in Multiple Offender and Multiple Victim Parricides," *Journal of Police and Criminal Psychology* 9 (1993): 53–64; "Weapons Used by Juveniles and Adults to Kill Parents," *Behavioral Sciences and the Law* 11 (1993): 397–405; "Evidence of Child Maltreatment Among Adolescent Parricide Offenders," *International Journal of Offender Therapy and Comparative Criminology* 38 (1994): 151–162.

people. And while the wealthy face a higher rate of personal theft, the poorest are the most likely to be the victim of burglaries, probably because they live in close proximity to their attackers.

MARITAL STATUS. Marital status also influences victimization risk. The unmarried or never married are victimized more often than married people or widows and widowers. These relationships are probably influenced by age, gender, and lifestyle. Many of the young people who have the highest victim risk are actually too young to have been married. Younger unmarried people also go out in public more often and interact with high-risk peers, increasing their exposure to victimization. In contrast, widows, who are more likely to be older females, suffer much lower victimization rates because they interact with older people, are more likely to stay home at night, and avoid public places. These data are further evidence of the relationship between lifestyle and victimization risk.

RACE. One of the most important distinctions found in the NCVS data is the racial differences in the victim rate. African Americans experience violent crimes at a higher rate than other groups. The NCVS data show that African American citizens have strikingly higher rates of violent victimization than whites. While the risk of theft victimization was more similar for blacks and whites, African Americans were still more likely to be victimized.

Crimes committed against African Americans tended to be more serious than those committed against whites. For example, African Americans experience higher rates of aggravated assault, while whites are more often the victims of simple assault. The most striking difference between racial groups recorded by the NCVS is in the incidence of robberies: African Americans are about three times more likely to become robbery victims than whites.

Young African American males are also at great risk for homicide victimization. They face a murder risk 4–5 times greater than that of young African American females, 5–8 times that of young white males, and 16–22 times that of young white females. A longitudinal analysis conducted by the Centers for Disease Control indicates that the murder victimization rate of African American males is increasing at a much faster pace than that for other groups.[26]

Why do these discrepancies exist? One reason is that young black males tend to live in the nation's largest cities in areas beset by alcohol and drug abuse, poverty, racial discrimination, and violence. Forced to live in the nation's most dangerous areas, their lifestyle places them in the highest "at risk" population group.

Repeat Victimization

Does prior victimization enhance or reduce the chances of future victimization? It is possible that certain stable patterns of behavior encourage victimization and that a few people who maintain them become "chronic victims" who are constantly the target of predatory crimes. It is also possible that "once burnt, twice shy": People who have been victimized take precautions to limit their risk.

Most research efforts do in fact show that prior victimization is a strong predictor of future victimization: Individuals who have had prior victimization experiences have a significantly higher chance of future victimization than those who have remained nonvictims.[27] Research also shows that households that have experienced victimization in the past are the ones most likely to experience it again in the future.[28] Repeat victimizations are most likely to occur in areas with high crime rates, and they account for a significant portion of all criminal acts. For instance, one study found that during a four-year period 40% of all trauma patients in an urban medical center in Ohio were repeat victims.[29]

What factors predict chronic victimization? It is possible that some combination of personal and social factors encourages victimization risk. Most repeats occur soon after a previous crime has occurred, suggesting that such victims share some personal characteristic that makes them a magnet for predators.[30] For example, kids who are shy, physically weak, or socially isolated may be prone to being bullied in the schoolyard.[31] David Finkelhor and Nancy Asdigian identified three specific types of characteristics that increase the potential for victimization:

1. *Target vulnerability.* The victims' physical weakness or psychological distress renders them incapable of resisting or deterring crime and makes them easy targets.

2. *Target gratifiability.* Some victims have characteristics that increase their risk because they have some quality, possession, skill, or attribute that an offender wants to obtain, use, have access to, or manipulate. Having attractive possessions such as a leather coat may make one vulnerable to predatory crime.

3. *Target antagonism.* Some characteristics increase risk because they arouse anger, jealousy, or destructive impulses in the offender. Being gay or effeminate may bring on undeserved attacks in the street; being disobedient or stubborn may produce child abuse in the home.[32]

Social, personal, and experiential factors may also interact to enhance chronic victimization. For example, boys who are bullied at school because they are depressed, shy, and withdrawn may become even more introverted after being victimized, increasing their chances for future victimization events.[33]

Repeat victimization may also be a function of rational choice and offender decision making: Offenders "learn" the weaknesses of victims and use them over and over again. For example, when the abusive husband finds out that his battered wife will not call police, he repeatedly victimizes her; when police do not respond to reported hate

Though most violent crimes are committed by strangers, relatively few children are actually abducted and killed by strangers. When such a crime occurs, it sends a chill across the entire nation. In Missouri, friends help Rhonda Senter, the mother of 10-year-old murder victim Cassidy Senter, to the gravesite of her daughter. Cassidy was the victim of a serial killer, who in 1993 abducted, molested, and killed another young girl and attempted the abduction of another.

crimes, the perpetrators learn they have little to fear from the law.[34]

Victims and Their Criminals

The NCVS data can be used to tell us something about the characteristics of criminals who actually came in contact with the victim through such crimes as rape, assault, or robbery.

Although most violent crimes are committed by strangers, a surprising number of violent crime victims are either related to or acquainted with their attackers. In all, about 40% of all violent crimes are committed by people described at least as well known to the victim.

In the NCVS victims reported that a majority of crimes were committed by a single offender over age 20. About one-fourth of the victims indicated their assailant was under 30 years of age, a pattern that may reflect the criminal activities of youth gangs and groups in the United States.

Whites were the offenders in a majority of single-offender rapes and assault, but a majority of multiple-offender crimes involved black criminals. Matching UCR data, a majority of robberies were committed by individual or groups of African American offenders.

Crime tends to be intraracial: Blacks victimize blacks and whites victimize whites. However, most crimes by white offenders are committed against other whites, whereas only half of all crimes by African American offenders are against African American victims. These findings are supported by surveys of prison inmates: While 4.7% of white inmates report having attacked black victims, black inmates report that 43% of their victims were white.[35] The racial pattern recorded here reflects the nation's population makeup: Because the country's population is predominantly white, it stands to reason that, regardless of the offender's racial characteristics, the victims will also most likely be white. Nonetheless, most crimes do seem to involve people who share the same racial characteristics.

The NCVS also asks victims whether their assailants were under the influence of drugs or alcohol. Victims reported that substance abuse was involved in about one-third of violent crime incidents. If anything, these estimates may underestimate the association between substance abuse and crime. Surveys of prison inmates find that over half of violent inmates report having been under the influence of either drugs or alcohol at the time they committed the crime for which they were incarcerated.[36]

Theories of Victimization

For many years, criminological theory focused on the actions of the criminal offender, and the role of the victim was virtually ignored. Then a number of scholars noted that the victim is not a passive target in crime but someone whose behavior can influence his or her own fate. One of the first criminologists to discover that victims are an important part of the crime process was Hans Von Hentig. In the 1940s, his writings portrayed the crime victim as someone who "shapes and molds the criminal."[37] The criminal might have been a predator, but the victim may have helped the offender by becoming a willing prey. Another pioneering victimologist, Stephen Schafer, focused on the victim's responsibility in the "genesis of crime."[38] Schafer found that some victims may have provoked or encouraged the criminal. These early works helped focus attention on the role of the victim in the crime problem and led to further research efforts that have sharpened the image of the crime victim. Today, there are a number of theories that attempt to explain the causes of victimization. We address three of these theories here: victim precipitation, lifestyles, and routine activities.

Victim Precipitation Theory

Is it possible that people cause their own victimization? According to the **victim precipitation** view, some people may actually initiate the confrontation that eventually leads to their injury or death. Victim precipitation can be either active or passive.

Active precipitation occurs when victims act provocatively, use threats or "fighting words," or even attack first. This model of victim-precipitated crime was first popularized by Marvin Wolfgang in his 1958 study of criminal homicide. He defined the term *victim precipitation* as follows:

> "Victim-precipitated" is applied to those criminal homicides in which the victim is a direct, positive precipitator in the crime. The role of the victim is characterized by his having been the first in the homicide drama to use physical force against his subsequent slayer. The victim-precipitated cases are those in which the victim was the first to show and use a deadly weapon, to strike a blow in an altercation—in short, the first to commence the interplay or resort to physical violence.[39]

Examples of a victim-precipitated homicide include the death of an aggressor in a barroom brawl or a wife who kills her husband after he attacks and threatens to kill her. Wolfgang found that 150, or 26%, of the 588 homicides in his sample could be classified as victim-precipitated.[40]

ACTIVE PRECIPITATION AND RAPE. Nowhere is the concept of victim precipitation more controversial than in the crime of rape. In 1971 Menachim Amir suggested that female victims often contribute to their attacks through a relationship with the rapist.[41] While Amir's findings are controversial, courts have continued to return not guilty verdicts in rape cases if a victim's actions can in any way be construed as consenting to sexual intimacy. And date rapes, which may at first start out as romantic though nonintimate relationships and then deteriorate into rape, are rarely treated with the same degree of punitiveness as stranger rapes.[42] As law professor Susan Estrich claims in her book *Real Rape,*

The force standard continues to protect, as "seduction," conduct which should be considered criminal. It ensures broad male freedom to "seduce" women who feel themselves to be powerless, vulnerable, and afraid. It effectively guarantees men freedom to intimidate women and exploit their weakness and passivity, so long as they don't "fight" with them, and it makes clear that the responsibility should be placed squarely on the women.[43]

While this legal victimization is publicly condemned, there are still numerous instances of defendants being found not guilty because judges or juries believe that a sexual assault was victim-precipitated. In one nationally publicized 1989 case, a Florida defendant was acquitted after jury members concluded his victim "asked for it the way she was dressed." Steven Lord, the 26-year-old defendant, was freed after the jury was told his victim had been wearing a lace miniskirt with nothing on underneath and "was advertising for sex." The acquittal came despite the fact that other women testified that they had been raped by Lord.[44]

> ### Connections
> Efforts to disassociate the casualties of rape from the concept of victim precipitation have resulted in modification of rape laws, which are discussed further in Chapter 11.

PASSIVE PRECIPITATION. **Passive precipitation** occurs when the victim exhibits some personal characteristic that unknowingly threatens or encourages the attacker. The threat can occur because of personal conflict, such as when two people are in competition over a job, promotion, love interest, or some other scarce and coveted commodity. Although the victim may never have met his or her attacker or even knew of the attacker's existence, the attacker feels menaced and acts accordingly.[45]

In another scenario, the victim may belong to a group whose mere presence threatens the attacker's reputation, status, or economic well-being. For example, hate crime violence may be precipitated by immigrant group members arriving in the community to compete for jobs and housing, or women in the workforce may threaten insecure and emotionally unstable men and prompt sexual violence. Research indicates that passive precipitation is related to power; if the target group can establish themselves economically or gain political power in the community, their vulnerability will diminish. While still a potential threat, they are now too formidable a target to attack; they are no longer passive precipitators. For example, research conducted in Canada by Rosemary Gartner and Bill McCarthy showed that employed women were underrepresented as homicide victims, whereas unemployed women suffered higher homicide victimization rates.[46] By implication, economic power reduced victimization risk.

Whether active or passive, the concept of victim precipitation implies that in some but not all crimes, the victim's actions in some way cause the crime: It could not take place without action on the part of the victim.

Lifestyle Theories

Some criminologists believe that people may become crime victims because they have a **lifestyle** that increases their exposure to criminal offenders. Both NCVS and UCR data sources show that victimization risk is increased by such behaviors as staying single, associating with young men, going out in public places late at night, and living in an urban area. Conversely, one's chances of victimization can be reduced by staying home at night, moving to a rural area, staying out of public places, earning more money, and getting married. The important point is that crime is not a random occurrence but rather a function of the behavior and actions of its targets.

Criminality and victimization thus seem bound in an association in which the probability of crime is dependent on the activities of the potential victim.[47] Crime occurs because victims have a lifestyle that places them in jeopardy: A person's chances of being attacked are much greater in an unguarded New York City park at 2 A.M. than in a locked farmhouse in rural North Dakota.

The likelihood of victimization is greatest among groups with high-risk lifestyles. For example, teens may have the greatest risk of victimization because their lifestyle places them in an at risk location—the neighborhood high school. That's where the most criminal element of the population, teenage males, congregate; each year millions of crimes occur on schoolgrounds.[48]

An adolescent's lifestyle continues to place him or her at risk after leaving the schoolgrounds. Gary Jensen and David Brownfield found that kids who hang out with their friends and get involved in the "recreational pursuit of fun" face an elevated risk for victimization. For example, their friends may give them a false I.D. so they can go drinking; hanging out in bars places them at risk because many fights and assaults occur in places that serve liquor.[49]

Adolescents are not the only ones with high-risk lifestyles. A number of studies have found that the homeless population is extremely vulnerable to physical harm because they are constantly exposed to the criminal population in large urban areas.[50] Recent research by Kevin Fitzpatrick, Mark La Gory, and Ferris Ritchey found that the homeless not only had a considerably higher victimization risk than the general population but that homeless victims tended to be more vulnerable than the general homeless population: They had a history of mental hospitalization, depression, and physical problems, including fainting and blackout spells.[51]

THE EQUIVALENT GROUP HYPOTHESIS. The lifestyle view suggests that victims and criminals share similar characteristics because they are not actually separate groups and that in fact a criminal lifestyle exposes people to increased levels of victimization risk.

The **equivalent group hypothesis** is supported by research showing that crime victims also self-report significant amounts of criminal behavior. A number of studies have shown that adolescents who engage in delinquent behavior or join gangs also face the greatest risk of victimization. For example, Joan McDermott found that the young victims of school crime were likely to strike back at other students in order to regain lost possessions or recover their self-respect.[52] In another study, Simon Singer, using data from the Philadelphia cohort (see Chapter 3), found that the victims of violent assault were those most likely to become offenders themselves.[53] Similarly, Janet Lauritsen, John Laub, and Robert Sampson found a significant association between participation in self-reported delinquent behavior and personal victimization in such crimes as robbery and assault.[54] Gary Jensen and David Brownfield concluded that "for personal victimizations, those most likely to be the victims of crime are those who have been most involved in crime; and the similarity of victims and offenders reflects that association."[55]

The criminal-victim connection may exist because the conditions that create criminality also predispose people to victimization. Both share similar lifestyle and residence characteristics. Some former criminals may later become targets because they are perceived as vulnerable: Criminal offenders are unlikely to call the police, and if they do, who will believe them? Some victims may commit crime out of frustration; others may use violence as a means of revenge, self-defense, or social control. Some may have learned antisocial behavior as a consequence of their own victimization experiences, as in the case of abused children.[56] Research by Elise Lake shows that over 85% of female offenders had experienced physical and sexual violence both inside and outside the home, at the hands of parents, intimate partners, and strangers.[57]

THE PROXIMITY HYPOTHESIS. Lifestyle theory implies that some people willingly put themselves in jeopardy by choosing high-risk lifestyles.[58] It is also possible that some people become victims because they are forced to live in close physical proximity to criminals and are selected because they share similar backgrounds and circumstances.[59] For example, people who reside in socially disorganized "high crime areas" have the greatest risk of coming into contact with criminal offenders, irrespective of their own behavior or lifestyle. Thus, according to the **proximity hypothesis**, victims do not encourage crime; they are simply in the "wrong place at the wrong time."[60] Thus, there may be little reason for residents in lower-class areas to alter their lifestyle or take safety precautions, since personal behavior choices do not in fact influence the likelihood of victimization.[61]

In this view, the probability of victimization is more dependent on where one lives than how one lives. People who risk exposure to criminals because they live in close proximity to them are at much greater risk of victimization than people who reside in less risky areas but have attractive, unguarded homes.[62] Neighborhood crime levels are more important for determining the chances of victimization than individual characteristics. Even those people who exhibit high-risk traits, such as unmarried males, will increase their chances of victimization if they reside in a high-crime area.[63]

THE DEVIANT PLACE HYPOTHESIS. The proximity hypothesis suggests that there are "natural areas" for crime, places in which crime flourishes regardless of the precautions taken by their residents. Rodney Stark has described these areas as poor, densely populated, highly transient neighborhoods in which commercial and residential property exist side by side.[64] The commercial property provides criminals with easy access to targets for theft crimes, such as shoplifting and larceny. Successful people stay out of these stigmatized areas; they are homes for "demoralized kinds of people," who are easy targets for crime: the homeless, the addicted, the retarded, and the elderly poor.[65]

William Julius Wilson has described how people who can afford to leave dangerous areas do so and has noted that the ability to leave is related to race; "white flight" has become a familiar term in the United States.[66] As a result, crime rates influence the racial and social composition of an area. More-affluent people realize that criminal victimization can be avoided by moving to an area with greater law enforcement and lower crime rates. Because there are significant interracial income differences, white residents are better able to flee inner-city high-crime areas, leaving members of racial minorities behind to suffer high victimization rates.[67]

Which has the greatest influence on victimization risk, place of residence or lifestyle? Perhaps both. A recent study by Pamela Wilcox Rountree, Kenneth Land, and Terance Miethe of crime and victimization rates across Seattle neighborhoods indicates that both victim lifestyle and place of domicile interact to produce crime and victimization rates. People who live in more affluent areas and take safety precautions significantly lower their chances of becoming crime victims. Residents of poor areas have a much greater risk of becoming victims because they live in areas with many motivated offenders; to protect themselves, they have to "try harder" to be safe than the more affluent.[68]

The Rountree research shows that a victim's behavior and habitat are both linked to criminality: People who take chances, who live in high-risk neighborhoods, and who are law violators themselves share the greatest risk of victimization.[69] While victim behavior cannot, of course, explain the onset of criminality, it can influence the occasion of crime. Although criminal motivation may be acquired early in life, the decision to commit a particular crime may depend on the actions and reactions of potential victims.

Routine Activities Theory

An important attempt to formally describe the conditions that produce victim risk is contained in a series of papers by Lawrence Cohen and Marcus Felson. Their view is referred to as **routine activities** theory.[70]

Cohen and Felson assume that the motivation to commit crime is constant.[71] In every society, there will always be some people who are willing to break the law for gain, revenge, greed, or some other motive. Consequently, the volume and distribution of **predatory crime** (violent crimes against the person and crimes in which an offender attempts to steal an object directly) are closely related to the interaction of three variables that reflect the routine activities of the typical American lifestyle: the availability of **suitable targets** (such as homes containing easily salable goods); the absence of **capable guardians** (such as police, homeowners, neighbors, friends, and relatives); and the presence of **motivated offenders** (such as a large number of unemployed teenagers). The presence of these components increases the likelihood that a predatory crime will take place: Targets are more likely to be victimized if they are poorly guarded and are exposed to a large group of motivated offenders (see Figure 4.2).

Cohen and Felson have used the routine activities approach to explain the rise in the crime rate between 1960 and 1980. They note that the number of adult caretakers at home during the day (guardians) decreased because of increased female participation in the workforce; while mothers are at work and children are in daycare, homes are left unguarded. Similarly, with the growth of suburbia and the decline of the traditional neighborhood, the number of such familiar "guardians" as family, neighbors, and friends diminished. At the same time, the volume of easily transportable wealth increased, creating a greater number of available targets. In one study, Cohen and his associates linked burglary rates to the proliferation of a commodity easily stolen and disposed of: television sets.[72] Finally, with the baby-boom generation coming of age during the period of 1960 to 1980, there was an excess of motivated offenders, and the crime rate increased in predicted fashion.

ROUTINE ACTIVITIES AND LIFESTYLE. Routine activities theory is similar to the lifestyle approach because it shows how routine living arrangements can affect victim risk: People who live in unguarded areas are going to be at the mercy of motivated offenders. In an important book, Terance Miethe and Robert Meier argue that there is actually a great deal of congruence between the two theories, each relying on four basic concepts: (a) proximity to criminals; (b) time of exposure to criminals; (c) target attractiveness; and (d) guardianship.[73] For example, both routine activities theory and lifestyle theory would predict that (a) people who live in high crime areas (b) who go out late at night (c) carrying valuables such as an expensive watch (d) without friends or family to watch or help them increase their victimization risk.

The Close-Up on "Crime and Everyday Life" shows how these relationships can be influenced by cultural and structural change.

Figure 4.2 Routine activities theory posits the interaction of three factors.

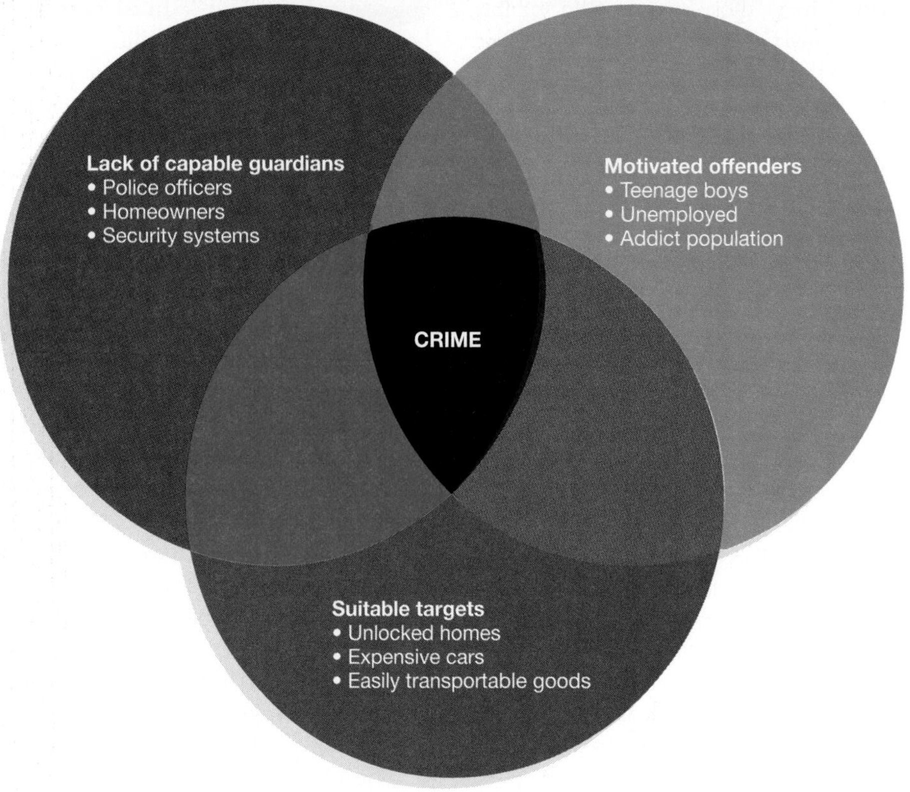

Lack of capable guardians
- Police officers
- Homeowners
- Security systems

Motivated offenders
- Teenage boys
- Unemployed
- Addict population

CRIME

Suitable targets
- Unlocked homes
- Expensive cars
- Easily transportable goods

TESTING ROUTINE ACTIVITIES THEORY. Numerous attempts have been made to substantiate the principles of routine activities theory.[74] For example, Cohen and Felson maintain that certain personal characteristics increase the likelihood that one's routine activities will place one at a greater risk for victimization. These characteristics include being a young minority-group member, having a low socioeconomic status, living in an urban area, and being a single parent. Supporting this view, Michael Maxfield found that victimization was most common in homes composed of a single parent and multiple children. Single parents may be less able to protect their families and themselves from the most common predatory criminals: other family members and former loved ones.[75]

Homes that are well guarded are the least likely to be burglarized.[76] Rape rates are high in areas where socioeconomic distress results in divorce, unemployment, and overcrowded living conditions—factors that reduce the number of guardians and increase the number of potential offenders.[77] The routine activities view also suggests that lifestyle plays an important role in victimization risk. Those who maintain a high-risk lifestyle by staying out late at night and having frequent activity outside the home also run increased chances of victimization.[78] Interestingly, when

Steven Messner and Kenneth Tardiff studied patterns of urban homicide, they found that lifestyles significantly influenced victimization: People who tended to stay at home were the ones most likely to be killed by family or friends.[79] James Lasley found that youth in Britain who stay out late at night and use excessive amounts of alcohol stand the greatest risk of becoming crime victims.[80]

Because of the uniformity of this supporting research, routine activities theory has become "the most popular theory of victimization."[81]

IS THE ROUTINE ACTIVITY APPROACH VALID? Not all criminologists support the routine activity model. In a recent review, Christopher Birkbeck and Gary LaFree argued that empirical tests of routine activity are often based on false and ambiguous assumptions.[82] For example, according to routine activities theory, the affluent should have a lower victimization risk than the poor because they have the means to purchase security. Yet affluence allows people to increase activity outside the home, and wealth makes a tempting target—factors that are also associated with greater risk. According to Birkbeck and LaFree, routine activities theory may explain why some people become victims, but it fails to explain whether others were

A core premise of routine activities theory is that all things being equal, the greater the *opportunity* to commit crime, the *higher* the crime and victimization rate.

This thesis is cogently presented in a new work by Marcus Felson titled *Crime and Everyday Life.* Using a routine activities perspective, Felson tries to show why American crime rates are so high and why U.S. citizens suffer such high rates of victimization.

According to Felson, crime in the United States grew as the country changed from a nation of small villages and towns to one of large urban environments. In a village not only could thieves be easily recognized, but the commodities they stole could be identified long after the crime occurred. Cities provided the critical population mass that allowed predatory criminals to hide and evade apprehension. After the crime, criminals could blend into the crowd and disperse their loot; the public transportation system provided a quick exit for escape.

The modern-day equivalent of the urban center is the shopping mall. Here strangers converge in large numbers and youths "hang out." The interior is filled with people, so drug deals can be concealed in the pedestrian flow. Stores have attractively displayed goods, encouraging shoplifting and employee pilferage. Substantial numbers of cars are parked in areas that make larceny and car theft virtually undetectable. Cars carrying away stolen merchandise have an undistinguished appearance; who notices people placing items in a car in a shopping mall lot? In addition, shoppers can be attacked in parking lots as they walk in isolation to and from their cars.

As American suburbs grew in importance, labor and family life began to be dispersed away from the household, decreasing guardianship. The microwave, freezer, and automatic dishwasher freed adolescents from common household chores. Rather than help prepare the family dinner and wash dishes afterward, adolescents had the freedom to meet with their peers and avoid parental controls. As car ownership increased, teens had greater access to transportation outside of parental control. Greater mobility makes it impossible for neighbors to know whether a teen belongs in an area or is an intruder planning to commit a crime. Schools have become larger and more complex in modern society, providing an ideal site for crime. The many hallways and corridors prevent teachers from knowing who belongs where; spacious schoolgrounds reduce teacher supervision.

Felson has found that these changes in the structure and function of society helped increase and sustain crime rates. The upshot is that rather than change people, crime prevention strategies must reduce the opportunity to commit crime.

Marcus Felson, author of *Crime and Everyday Life.*

CRITICAL THINKING QUESTIONS
1. What recent technological changes have influenced crime rates—video games? paging systems? fax machines?
2. Would increased family contact reduce adolescent crime rates, or would it increase the opportunity for child abuse?

Source: Marcus Felson, *Crime and Everyday Life: Insights and Implications for Society* (Thousand Oaks, Calif: Pine Forge Press, 1994).

---

first considered as potential targets and then discarded and if so, why that decision was made.[83]

Some empirical efforts have failed to find the relationships predicted by routine activities theory. For example, when James Massey and his associates examined data on property victimization in Atlanta, they found that the risk of property crime victimization was not dependent or affected by "guardianship." Their conclusion: "Support for routine activities is weak at best."[84]

It has also been suggested that routine activities theory overemphasizes the victim and overlooks offender differences. Why do offenders choose to commit crime? It is unlikely that all offenders perceive criminal opportunity or apprehension risk in a similar fashion. Leslie Kennedy and Stephen Baron suggest that peer group pressure and cultural norms exert pressure on potential offenders, guide their motivation, and influence their choices; routine activities theory, they conclude, neglects to account for the factors that shape criminal choice.[85]

Caring for the Victim

National victim surveys indicate that almost every American age 12 and over will at one point in their life become the victim of common-law crimes, such as larceny and burglary, and in the aftermath will suffer financial problems, mental stress, and physical hardship.[86] For example, Dean

A police officer helps an injured teen in Miami. Americans are becoming increasingly defensive about crime by stocking up on guns, buying security systems, joining street patrols, and demanding greater police protection. However, helping the victim to cope is the responsibility of all of society. Law enforcement agencies, courts, and correctional and human service systems have come to realize that due process and human rights exist both for the defendant and for the victim of criminal behavior.

Kilpatrick and his associates found that among 391 adult females in a southern city 75% had been victimized by crime at least once in their lives, including having been raped (25%) and sexually molested (18%). Disturbingly, 25% of the victims had developed posttraumatic stress syndrome, and their psychological symptoms had lasted for more than a decade after the crime occurred.[87] The long-term effect of sexual victimization can include years of problem avoidance, social withdrawal, and self-criticism.[88]

Net Bookmark

Helping victims cope is the responsibility of all of society. Law enforcement agencies, courts, and correctional and human service systems have come to realize that due process and human rights exist both for the defendant and for the victim of criminal behavior.

The Government's Response

Because of public concern over violent personal crime, President Ronald Reagan created a Task Force on Victims of Crime in 1982.[89] This group was to undertake an extensive study on crime victimization in the United States and determine how victims could be assisted. The task force found that crime victims had been transformed into a group of citizens burdened by a justice system that had been designed for their protection. Their participation both as victims and as witnesses was often overlooked, and concern for the defendant's rights was given greater emphasis. The task force suggested that a balance be achieved between recognition of the rights of the victim and provision for due process for the defendant. Its most significant recommendation was that the Sixth Amendment to the U.S. Constitution be augmented by a statement saying that "In every criminal prosecution, the victim shall have the right to be present and to be heard at all critical stages of the judicial proceedings."[90] Other recommendations included providing for the protection of witnesses and victims from intimidation, requiring restitution in criminal cases, developing guidelines for fair treatment of crime victims and witnesses, and expanding programs of victim compensation.[91] Consequently, the Justice Department provided research funds to create and expand victim-witness programs, which identify the needs of victims and witnesses involved in a criminal incident. In addition, the Omnibus Victim and Witness Protection Act required the use of victim impact statements at sentencing in federal criminal cases, greater protection for witnesses, more stringent bail laws, and the use of restitution in criminal cases. In 1984 the Comprehensive Crime Control Act and the Victims of Crime Act authorized federal funding for state victim compensation and assistance projects.[92] With these acts, the federal government began to take action to address the plight of victims and make their assistance an even greater concern of the public and the justice system.

As a result of these efforts, an estimated 2,000 victim-witness assistance programs have developed around the United States.[93] These programs are organized on a variety of governmental levels and serve a variety of clients. Following is a discussion of the most prominent forms of victim services in operation in the United States.[94]

Victim Compensation

One of the primary agendas of victim advocates has been to lobby for legislation creating crime **victim compensation** programs.[95] As a result of such legislation, the victim ordinarily receives compensation from the state to pay for damages associated with the crime. Rarely are two compensation schemes alike, however, and many state programs suffer from lack of adequate funding and proper organization within the criminal justice system. Today, victim compensation programs exist in 45 states as well as at the federal level. Compensation may be made for medical bills, loss of wages, loss of future earnings, and counseling. In the case of death, the victim's survivors can receive burial expenses and aid for loss of support.[96] Awards are typically in the $100 to $15,000 range, although Alaska provides aid up to $40,000. An important service of most victim programs is to familiarize clients with compensation options and help them apply for aid. On occasion, programs will provide emergency assistance to indigent victims until compensation is available. Emergency assistance may come in the form of food vouchers or replacement of prescription medicines.

Court Services

A common victim program service is to help victims deal with the criminal justice system. One approach is to prepare victims and witnesses by explaining court procedures: how to be a witness, how bail works, what to do if the defendant makes a threat. Lack of such knowledge can cause confusion, making some victims reluctant to testify in court proceedings. Many victim programs also provide transportation to and from court and counselors who remain in the courtroom during hearings to explain procedures and provide support. Court escorts are particularly important for elderly victims, the handicapped, victims of child abuse

and assault, and those who have been intimidated by friends or relatives of the defendant.

Public Education

More than half of all victim programs engage in public education programs that help familiarize the general public with their services and with other agencies that help crime victims. In some instances these are primary education programs that teach methods of dealing with conflict without resorting to violence. For example, school-based programs present information on spouse and dating abuse, followed by discussion of how to reduce violent incidents.[97] Some victim assistance projects seek to help victims learn about victim compensation services and related programs.

Sometimes the "educational" aspect of victim services can be more immediate and personal. Most programs will help employers understand the plight of their employee victims. Because victims may miss work or suffer postcrime emotional trauma, they may need to be absent from work for extended periods of time. If employers are unwilling to give them leave, victims may refuse to participate in the criminal justice process. Being an advocate with employers and explaining the needs of victims is a service provided by more than half of all victim programs.

Crisis Intervention

Most victim programs make referrals for services to help victims recover from their ordeal. It is common to refer clients to the local network of public and private social service agencies that can provide emergency and long-term assistance with transportation, medical care, shelter, food, and clothing. In addition, more than half of the victim programs provide **crisis intervention** to victims, many of whom are feeling isolated, vulnerable, and in need of immediate services. Some programs offer counseling at the service's office, while others do outreach in victims' homes, at the crime scene, or in a hospital. No crime requires more crisis intervention efforts than rape and sexual assault. After years of rape being ignored by the justice system, increased sensitivity to this crime and its victims has spurred the opening of crisis centers around the country. These centers typically feature 24-hour-a-day emergency phone lines and information on police, medical, and court procedures.

Some provide volunteers to assist the victim as her case is processed through the justice system. The growth of these services—which began with the Washington, D.C. Rape Crisis Center's phone line in 1972—has been so explosive that services are now available in more than 1,000 centers located in almost all major cities and college communities.[98]

Most rape crisis centers provide the following services to victims: (1) emergency assistance, including information, referral, and some support, usually over the telephone, and available 24 hours a day; (2) face-to-face crisis intervention, or accompaniment, usually provided in the hospital, police station, courts, or other public location, also available 24 hours a day; and (3) counseling, either one on one or in groups, in a varying number of sessions, often provided at the center, usually scheduled, and limited to business hours and evenings.[99]

While crisis intervention has become widespread, child care for victims is less common. According to the national survey of victim programs, about one-third are able to provide some form of child care, most often short term, while the victim is in consultation or in court.

Victim-Offender Reconciliation Programs (VORP)

Victim-offender reconciliation programs (VORPs) use mediators to facilitate face-to-face encounters between victims and their attackers. The aim, according to victim expert Andrew Karmen, is to engage in direct negotiations that lead to restitution agreements and possibly reconciliation between the two parties involved.[100] More than 120 reconciliation programs are currently in operation, and they handle an estimated 16,000 cases per year. While at first designed to handle routine misdemeanors such as petty theft and vandalism, it is now common for these programs to hammer out restitution agreements in more serious incidents, including residential burglary and even attempted murder.

Connections

Reconciliation programs are based on the concept of *restorative justice.* Restorative justice rejects punitive correctional measures and instead suggests that crimes of violence and theft should be viewed as interpersonal conflicts that need to be settled in the community through noncoercive means. The theoretical roots of the restorative justice concept can be found in Chapter 9's discussion of "peacemaking criminology."

Victims' Rights

In an important article, Frank Carrington suggested in 1981 that crime victims have legal rights that should assure them basic services from the government.[101] According to Carrington, just as the law guarantees that offenders have

the right to counsel and a fair trial, so society also has the obligation to ensure basic rights for law-abiding citizens. These rights range from adequate protection under the law from violent crimes to victim compensation and assistance from the criminal justice system. Among suggested changes that might enhance the relationship between the victim and the criminal justice system are

- Liberally using preventive detention (pretrial jailing without the right to bail) for dangerous criminals who are awaiting trial.
- Eliminating delays between the arrest and the initial hearing and between the hearing and the trial, which would limit the offender's opportunity to intimidate victims or witnesses.
- Eliminating plea bargaining or, if that proves impossible, allowing victims to participate in the plea negotiations.
- Controlling the defense attorney's cross-examination of victims.
- Allowing hearsay testimony of police at the preliminary hearing, instead of requiring the victim to appear.
- Abolishing the exclusionary rule, which allows the guilty to go free on technicalities.
- Allowing victims to participate in sentencing.
- Creating minimum sentences that convicted offenders must serve.
- Prohibiting murderers given life sentences from being freed on furlough or parole.
- Making criminals serve time on each crime they are convicted of and reducing the use of concurrent sentences, which allow them to simultaneously serve time for multiple crimes.
- Tightening the granting of parole and allowing victims to participate in parole hearings.
- Providing full restitution and compensation to victims in all crimes.

Some of these suggestions seem reasonable policy alternatives, while others, such as repudiating the exclusionary rule, may be impossible to achieve since they violate offenders' due process protections. However, about 14 states have actually incorporated similar language into their legal codes in a "Victim's Bill of Rights." Victims are now entitled to find out about the progress of their cases in 22 states, to be present at sentencing hearings in 37 states, and to attend parole hearings in 36 states.[102] In *Payne v. Tennessee,* the U.S. Supreme Court ruled that juries are permitted to consider the emotional impact of a victim's murder on surviving family members. *Payne* overruled the standing prohibition against victim statements in death penalty cases (presumably because criminals who killed familyless victims would have an advantage at sentencing) and may signal greater judicial sensitivity to the rights of victims.

Victim advocacy today is offered by an eclectic group of organizations, some independent, others government sponsored, and some self-help. Advocates can be especially helpful when victims need to interact with the agencies of

While the general public generally approves of the police, fear of crime and concern about community safety has prompted many people to become their own "police force" and take an active role in community protection and citizen crime-control groups. The more crime in an area, the greater the amount of fear and the more likely residents will engage in self-protective measures. Citizens groups have been demanding more police protection and banding together to form groups that attempt to control crime in their own neighborhoods.

justice. For example, they can lobby police departments to keep investigations open and request the return of recovered stolen property. They can demand from prosecutors and judges protection from harassment and reprisals, as making "no contact" a condition of bail. They can help victims make statements during sentencing hearings and probation and parole revocation procedures. Victim advocates can also interact with the news media, making sure that reporting is not inaccurate and that victim privacy is not violated. Andrew Karmen suggests that advocates be part of an independent agency similar to a legal aid society. If successful, topnotch advocates might one day open a private office, similar to attorneys, private investigators, or jury consultants.[103]

Self-Protection

Although the general public generally approves of the police, fear of crime and concern about community safety have prompted many people to become their own "police force" and take an active role in community protection and citizen crime control groups.[104] The more crime in an area, the greater the amount of fear and the more likely residents will engage in self-protective measures.[105] Research indicates that a significant number of crimes may not be re-

ported to police simply because victims prefer to take matters into their own hands.[106]

One way this self-protection trend has manifested is in the concept of **target hardening,** or making one's home and business crime-proof through locks, bars, alarms, and other devices.[107] A national victimization risk survey found that substantial numbers of people have taken specific steps to secure their homes or place of employment.[108] One-third of the households reported taking one or more crime-prevention measures, including having a burglar alarm (7%), participating in a neighborhood watch program (7%), or engraving valuables with an identification number (25%). Other commonly used crime-prevention techniques include installing a fence or barricade at the entrance of a home or business; an intercom or phone to gain access to the building, surveillance cameras, window bars, or warning signs; hiring a doorkeeper, guard, or receptionist in an apartment building; and obtaining dogs known for their ability to guard premises. Use of these measures is inversely proportional to perception of neighborhood safety: People who fear crime are more likely to use crime-prevention techniques.

Though the true relationship is still unclear, there is mounting evidence that people who engage in household protection are less likely to become victims of property crimes.[109] One study conducted in the Philadelphia area found that people who install burglar alarms are less likely to become the burglary victims than those who forgo similar preventive measures.[110]

Fighting Back

Some people take self-protection to its ultimate end and are prepared to fight back when they are attacked by criminals. How successful are victims when they fight back? Research indicates that victims who fight back often frustrate their attackers but also face increased odds of being physically harmed during the attack.[111] For example, Polly Marchbanks and her associates found that fighting back did in fact decrease the odds of a rape being completed but increased the victim's chances of injury.[112] Marchbanks speculates that while resistance may draw the attention of bystanders and make the rape physically difficult to complete, it can also cause offenders to escalate their violence. Similar results were obtained in a federal survey that found robbery victims who fought back were less likely to experience completed crimes than passive victims, but they were also more likely to be injured during the robbery. The victims who escaped both serious injury and property loss were the ones who used the most violent responses to crime, such as a weapon, or the least violent, such as reasoning with their attackers. Those who fought back with their fists or who tried to get help were the most likely to experience both injury and theft.[113]

Because unarmed victims are the most likely to be injured when they fight back, are those who use firearms much more successful? Gary Kleck found that armed victims are ready and willing to use their guns against offenders. Each year victims use guns for defensive purposes 2.5 million times, a number that is not surprising, considering that about one-third of U.S. households contain guns.[114] Kleck has estimated that armed victims kill 1,500 to 2,800 potential felons each year and wound between 8,700 and 16,000. Kleck's research shows, ironically, that by fighting back victims kill far more criminals than the estimated 250 to 1,000 killed annually by police.[115] Kleck has found that the risk of collateral injury is relatively rare and that potential victims should be encouraged to fight back.[116] According to Kleck, empirical research studies unanimously show that defensive gun use is associated with both lower rates of crime completion and lower rates of injury to the victim.[117]

While Kleck is a strong supporter of an "armed citizenry," other criminologists such as Gary Green speculate that firearm ownership brings with it a number of problems, including accidental deaths and the use of stolen guns in other crimes.[118]

Community Organization

Not everyone is capable of buying a handgun or semiautomatic weapon and doing battle with predatory criminals. Another approach has been for communities to organize on the neighborhood level against crime. Citizens have been working independently and in cooperation with local police agencies in neighborhood patrol and block watch programs. These programs organize local citizens in urban areas to patrol neighborhoods, watch for suspicious people, help secure the neighborhood, lobby for improvements (such as better lighting), report crime to police, put out community newsletters, conduct home security surveys, and serve as a source for crime information or tips.[119]

While such programs are welcome additions to police services, there is little evidence that they have an appreciable effect on the crime rate. There is also concern that their effectiveness is spottier in low-income, high-crime areas, which are in the most need of crime prevention assistance.[120] Block watches and neighborhood patrols seem more successful when they are part of general-purpose or multi-issue community groups, rather than when they focus directly on crime problems.[121]

In sum, community crime-prevention programs, target hardening, and self-defense measures are flourishing around the United States. They are a response to the fear of crime and the perceived shortcomings of police agencies to ensure community safety. Along with private security, they represent attempts to supplement municipal police agencies and expand the "war on crime" to become a personal, neighborhood, and community concern.

Summary

Criminologists now consider victims and victimization a major focus of study. More than 30 million U.S. citizens suffer from crime each year, and the social and economic costs of crime are in the billions of dollars. Like crime, victimization has stable patterns and trends. Violent crime victims tend to be young, poor, single males living in large cities. Crime takes place more often at night in open public places. Many victimizations occur in the home, and many victims are the target of relatives and loved ones. Sometimes parents are the victims of their children, a crime known as parricide.

There are a number of theories of victimization. One view, called victim precipitation, is that victims provoke criminals. Lifestyle theories suggest that victims put themselves in danger by engaging in high-risk activities, such as going out late at night, living in a high-crime area, and associating with high-risk peers. The routine activities theory maintains that a pool of motivated offenders exists and that they will take advantage of unguarded, suitable targets. The major theories of victimization are summarized in Table 4.3.

Numerous programs help victims by providing court services, economic compensation, public education, and crisis intervention. Some advocates have gone so far as to suggest that the U.S. Constitution be amended to include protection of victims' rights.

Rather than depend on the justice system, some victims have attempted to help themselves. In some instances, this

Table 4.3 Victim Theories

THEORY	MAJOR PREMISE	STRENGTHS
Victim precipitation	Victims trigger criminal acts by their provocative behavior. Active precipitation involves fighting words or gestures. Passive precipitation occurs when victims unknowingly threaten their attacker.	Explains multiple victimizations. If people precipitate crime, it follows that they will become repeat victims if their behavior persists over time.
Lifestyle	Victimization risk is increased when people have a high-risk lifestyle. Placing oneself at risk by going out to dangerous places results in increased victimization.	Explains victimization patterns in the social structure. Males, young people, and the poor have high victim rates because they have a higher risk lifestyle than females, the elderly, and the affluent.
Equivalent group hypothesis	Criminals and victims are one and the same. Both crime and victimization is part of a high-risk lifestyle.	Shows that the conditions that create criminality also produce high victimization risk. Victims may commit crime out of a need for revenge or frustration.
Routine activities	Crime rates can be explained by the availability of suitable targets, the absence of capable guardians, and the presence of motivated offenders.	Can explain crime rates and trends. Shows how victim behavior can influence criminal opportunity. Suggests that victim risk can be reduced by increasing guardianship and/or reducing target vulnerability.
Proximity hypothesis	People who live in deviant places are at high risk to crime. Victim behavior has little influence over the criminal act.	Places the focus of crime on deviant places. Shows why people with conventional lifestyles become crime victims.

self-help means community organization for self-protection. In other instances, victims have armed themselves and fought back against their attackers. There is evidence that fighting back reduces the number of completed crimes but is also related to victim injury.

Key Terms

victimology
victimologists
cycle of violence
parricide
patricide
matricide
victim precipitation
active precipitation
passive precipitation
lifestyle
equivalent group
  hypothesis

proximity hypothesis
routine activities
predatory crime
suitable targets
capable guardians
motivated offenders
victim compensation
crisis intervention
target hardening

Notes

1. Arthur Lurigio, "Are All Victims Alike? The Adverse, Generalized, and Differential Impact of Crime," *Crime and Delinquency* 33 (1987): 452–467.

2. FBI, *Crime in the United States,* 1995 (Washington, D.C.: U.S. Government Printing Office, 1996), p. 196. Hereinafter cited as FBI, Uniform Crime Report, 1995.

3. Ted Miller, Mark Cohen, and Brian Wiersema, *The Extent and Costs of Crime Victimization: A New Look* (Washington, D.C.: National Institute of Justice, 1996).

4. Ibid.

5. Peter Finn, *Victims* (Washington, D.C.: Bureau of Justice Statistics, 1988), p. 1.

6. Susan Leslie Bryant and Lillian Range, "Suicidality in College Women Who Were Sexually and Physically Abused and Physically Punished by Parents," *Violence and Victims* 10 (1995): 195–215.

7. Sally Davies-Netley, Michael Hurlburt, and Richard Hough, "Childhood Abuse as a Precursor to Homelessness for Homeless Women with Severe Mental Illness," *Violence and Victims* 11 (1996): 129–142.

8. See, generally, M. D. Pagelow, *Woman Battering: Victims and Their Experiences* (Beverly Hills, Calif.: Sage, 1981).

9. Walter Gleason, "Mental Disorders in Battered Women," *Violence and Victims* 8 (1993): 53–66.

10. Daniel Saunders, "Posttraumatic Stress Symptom Profiles of Battered Women: A Comparison of Survivors in Two Settings," *Violence and Victims* 9 (1994): 31–43.

11. Elizabeth Stanko and Kathy Hobdell, "Assault on Men, Masculinity and Male Victimization," *British Journal of Criminology* 33 (1993): 400–415.

12. Robert Davis, Bruce Taylor, and Arthur Lurigio, "Adjusting to Criminal Victimization: The Correlates of Postcrime Distress," *Violence and Victimization* 11 (1996): 21–34.

13. James Anderson, Terry Grandison, and Laronistine Dyson, "Victims of Random Violence and the Public Health Implication: A Health Care of Criminal Justice Issue," *Journal of Criminal Justice* 24 (1996): 379–393.

14. Timothy Ireland and Cathy Spatz Widom, *Childhood Victimization and Risk for Alcohol and Drug Arrests* (Washington, D.C.: National Institute of Justice, 1995).

15. Cathy Spatz Widom, *The Cycle of Violence* (Washington, D.C.: National Institute of Justice, 1992), p. 1.

16. Steve Spaccarelli, J. Douglas Coatsworth, and Blake Sperry Bowden, "Exposure to Serious Family Violence Among Incarcerated Boys: Its Association with Violent Offending and Potential Mediating Variables," *Violence and Victims* 10 (1995): 163–180.

17. Jerome Kolbo, "Risk and Resilience Among Children Exposed to Family Violence," *Violence and Victims* 11 (1996): 113–127.

18. M. Dwayne Smith and Victoria Brewer, "A Sex-Specific Analysis of Correlates of Homicide Victimization in United States Cities," *Violence and Victims* 7 (1992): 279–287.

19. Michael Rand, *Crime and the Nation's Households, 1992* (Washington, D.C.: Bureau of Justice Statistics, 1993).

20. Ronet Bachman, *Violence Against Women* (Washington, D.C.: Bureau of Justice Statistics, 1994).

21. Lawrence Greenfeld, *Child Victimizers: Violent Offenders and Their Victims* (Washington, D.C.: Bureau of Justice Statistics, 1996).

22. Murray Straus, Richard Gelles, and Suzanne Steinmentz, *Behind Closed Doors: Violence in the American Family* (Garden City, N.Y.: Anchor Books, 1980); Richard Gelles and Murray Straus, "Violence in the American Family," *Journal of Social Issues* 35 (1979): 15–39.

23. Richard Gelles and Murray Straus, *Is Violence Toward Children Increasing? A Comparison of 1975 and 1985 National Survey Rates* (Durham, N.H.: Family Violence Research Program, 1985).

24. Ching-Tung Lung and Deborah Daro, *Current Trends in Child Abuse Reporting and Fatalities: The Results of the 1995 Annual Fifty-State Survey* (Chicago: National Committee to Prevent Child Abuse, 1996).

25. Sexual abuse data are restricted to reporting from 25 states.

26. U.S. Centers for Disease Control, "Homicide Among Young Black Males—United States, 1978–1987," *Morbidity and Mortality Weekly Report* 39 (7 December 1990): 869–873.

27. Janet Lauritsen and Kenna Davis Quinet, "Repeat Victimizations Among Adolescents and Young Adults," *Journal of Quantitative Criminology* 11 (1995): 143–163.

28. Denise Osborn, Dan Ellingworth, Tim Hope, and Alan Trickett, "Are Repeatedly Victimized Households Different?" *Journal of Quantitative Criminology* 12 (1996): 223–245.

29. Terry Buss and Rashid Abdu, "Repeat Victims of Violence in an Urban Trauma Center," *Violence and Victims* 10 (1995): 183–187.

30. Graham Farrell, "Predicting and Preventing Revictimization," in *Crime and Justice: An Annual Review of Research,* vol. 20, ed. Michael Tonry and David Farrington (Chicago: University of Chicago Press, 1995), pp. 61–126.

31. Ibid., p 161.

32. David Finkelhor and Nancy Asdigian, "Risk Factors for Youth Victimization: Beyond a Lifestyles/Routine Activities Theory Approach," *Violence and Victimization* 11 (1996): 3–19.

33. Lauritsen and Quinet, "Repeat Victimizations," p. 161.

34. Graham Farrell, Coretta Phillips, and Ken Pease, "Like Taking Candy, Why Does Repeat Victimization Occur?" *British Journal of Criminology* 35 (1995): 384–399.

35. Christopher Innes and Lawrence Greenfeld, *Violent State Prisoners and Their Victims* (Washington, D.C.: Bureau of Justice Statistics, 1990), p. 4.

36. Ibid.

37. Hans Von Hentig, *The Criminal and His Victim: Studies in the Sociobiology of Crime* (New Haven, Conn.: Yale University Press, 1948), p. 384.

38. Stephen Schafer, *The Victim and His Criminal* (New York: Random House, 1968), p. 152.

39. Marvin Wolfgang, *Patterns of Criminal Homicide* (Philadelphia: University of Pennsylvania Press, 1958).

40. Ibid., p. 252.

41. Menachim Amir, *Patterns in Forcible Rape* (Chicago: University of Chicago Press, 1971).

42. Susan Estrich, *Real Rape* (Cambridge, Mass.: Harvard University Press, 1987).

43. Ibid., p. 69.

44. Associated Press, "Jury Stirs Furor by Citing Dress in Rape Acquittal," *Boston Globe,* 6 October 1989, p. 12.

45. Martin Daly and Margo Wilson, *Homicide* (New York: Aldine de Gruyter, 1988).

46. Rosemary Gartner and Bill McCarthy, "The Social Distribution of Femicide in Urban Canada, 1921–1988," *Law and Society Review* 25 (1991): 287–311.

47. Lawrence Cohen and Marcus Felson, "Social Change and Crime Rate Trends: A Routine Activities Approach," *American Sociological Review* 44 (1979): 588–608; L. Cohen, James Kleugel, and Kenneth Land, "Social Inequality and Predatory Criminal Victimization: An Exposition and Test of a Formal Theory," *American Sociological Review* 46 (1981): 505–524; Steven Messner and Kenneth Tardiff, "The Social Ecology of Urban Homicide: An Application of the Routine Activities Approach," *Criminology* 23 (1985): 241–267.

48. See, generally, Gary Gottfredson and Denise Gottfredson, *Victimization in Schools* (New York: Plenum Press, 1985).

49. Gary Jensen and David Brownfield, "Gender, Lifestyles, and Victimization: Beyond Routine Activity Theory," *Violence and Victims* 1 (1986): 85–99.

50. Less Whitbeck and Ronald Simons, "A Comparison of Adaptive Strategies and Patterns of Victimization Among Homeless Adolescents and Adults," *Violence and Victims* 8 (1993): 135–151.

51. Kevin Fitzpatrick, Mark La Gory, and Ferris Ritchey, "Criminal Victimization Among the Homeless," *Justice Quarterly* 10 (1993): 353–368.

52. Joan McDermott, "Crime in the School and in the Community: Offenders, Victims and Fearful Youth," *Crime and Delinquency* 29 (1983): 270–283.

53. Simon Singer, "Homogeneous Victim-Offender Populations: A Review and Some Research Implications," *Journal of Criminal Law and Criminology* 72 (1981): 779–799.

54. Janet Lauritsen, John Laub, and Robert Sampson, "Conventional and Delinquent Activities: Implications for the Prevention of Violent Victimization Among Adolescents," *Violence and Victims* 7 (1992): 91–102.

55. Gary Jensen and David Brownfield, "Gender, Lifestyles and Victimization: Beyond Routine Activities," *Violence and Victims* 1 (1986): 85–101.

56. Ross Vasta, "Physical Child Abuse: A Dual Component Analysis," *Developmental Review* 2 (1982): 128–135.

57. Elise Lake, "An Exploration of the Violent Victim Experiences of Female Offenders," *Violence and Victims* 8 (1993): 41–50.

58. Jeffrey Fagan, Elizabeth Piper, and Yu-Teh Cheng, "Contributions of Victimization to Delinquency in Inner Cities," *The Journal of Criminal Law and Criminology* 78 (1987): 586–613.

59. Ibid.

60. James Garofalo, "Reassessing the Lifestyle Model of Criminal Victimization," in *Positive Criminology,* ed. Michael Gottfredson and Travis Hirschi (Newbury Park, Calif.: Sage Publications, 1987), pp. 23–42.

61. Terance Miethe and David McDowall, "Contextual Effects in Models of Criminal Victimization," *Social Forces* 71 (1993): 741–759.

62. Terance Miethe and Robert Meier, "Opportunity, Choice, and Criminal Victimization: A Test of a Theoretical Model," *Journal of Research in Crime and Delinquency* 27 (1990): 243–266.

63. Robert Sampson and Janet Lauritsen, "Deviant Lifestyles, Proximity to Crime and the Offender-Deviant Link in Personal Violence," *Journal of Research in Crime and Delinquency* 27 (1990): 110–139.

64. Rodney Stark, "Deviant Places: A Theory of the Ecology of Crime," *Criminology* 25 (1987): 893–911.

65. Ibid., p. 902.

66. William Julius Wilson, *The Truly Disadvantaged* (Chicago: University of Chicago Press, 1987).

67. Allen Liska and Paul Bellair, "Violent-Crime Rates and Racial Composition: Convergence over Time," *American Journal of Sociology* 101 (1995): 578–610.

68. Pamela Wilcox Rountree, Kenneth Land, and Terance Miethe, "Macro-Micro Integration in the Study of Victimization: A Hierarchical Logistic Model Analysis Across Seattle Neighborhoods." Paper presented at the annual meeting of the American Society of Criminology, Phoenix, Arizona, November 1993.

69. Sampson and Lauritsen, "Deviant Lifestyles."

70. Lawrence Cohen and Marcus Felson, "Social Change and Crime Rate Trends: A Routine Activities Approach," *American Sociological Review* 44 (1979): 588–608.

71. For a review, see James LeBeau and Thomas Castellano, *The Routine Activities Approach: An Inventory and Critique* (Carbondale, Ill.: Center for the Studies of Crime, Delinquency and Corrections, Southern Illinois University—Carbondale, unpublished, 1987).

72. Lawrence Cohen, Marcus Felson, and Kenneth Land, "Property Crime Rates in the United States: A Macrodynamic Analysis, 1947–1977, with Ex-ante Forecasts for the Mid-1980s," *American Journal of Sociology* 86 (1980): 90–118.

73. Terance Miethe and Robert Meier, *Crime and Its Social Context: Toward an Integrated Theory of Offenders, Victims, and Situations* (Albany: State University of New York Press, 1994).

74. See Messner and Tardiff, "The Social Ecology of Urban Homicide"; Philip Cook, "The Demand and Supply of Criminal Opportunities," in *Crime and Justice,* vol. 7, ed. Michael Tonry and Norval Morris (Chicago: University of Chicago Press, 1986), pp. 1–28; Ronald Clarke and Derek Cornish, "Modeling Offender's Decisions: A Framework for Research and Policy," in *Crime and Justice,* vol. 6, ed. Michael Tonry and Norval Morris (Chicago: University of Chicago Press, 1985), pp. 147–187.

75. Michael Maxfield, "Household Composition, Routine Activity, and Victimization: A Comparative Analysis," *Journal of Quantitative Criminology* 3 (1987): 301–320.

76. James Lynch and David Cantor, "Ecological and Behavioral Influences on Property Victimization at Home: Implications for Opportunity Theory," *Journal of Research in Crime and Delinquency* 29 (1992): 335–362.

77. David Maume, "Inequality and Metropolitan Rape Rates: A Routine Activities Approach," *Justice Quarterly* 6 (1989): 513–527.

78. Terance Miethe, Mark Stafford, and Douglas Stone, "Lifestyle Changes and Risks of Criminal Victimization," *Journal of Quantitative Criminology* 6 (1990): 357–375.

79. Messner and Tardiff, "The Social Ecology of Urban Homicide."

80. James Lasley, "Drinking Routines, Lifestyles and Predatory Victimization: A Causal Analysis," *Justice Quarterly* 6 (1989): 529–542.

81. Christopher Birkbeck and Gary LaFree, "The Situational Analsysis of Crime and Deviance," *Annual Review of Sociology* 19 (1993): 113–137.

82. Ibid., pp. 127–128.

83. Ibid., p. 128.

84. James Massey, Marvin Krohn, and Lisa Bonati, "Property Crime and the Routine Activities of Individuals," *Journal of Research in Crime and Delinquency* 26 (1989): 378–400.

85. Leslie Kennedy and Stephen Baron, "Routine Activities and a Subculture of Violence: A Study of Violence on the Street," *Journal of Research in Crime and Delinquency* 30 (1993): 88–112.

86. Patricia Resnick, "Psychological Effects of Victimization: Implications for the Criminal Justice System," *Crime and Delinquency* 33 (1987): 468–478.

87. Dean Kilpatrick, Benjamin Saunders, Lois Veronen, Connie Best, and Judith Von, "Criminal Victimization: Lifetime Prevalence, Reporting to Police, and Psychological Impact," *Crime and Delinquency* 33 (1987): 479–489.

88. Mark Santello and Harold Leitenberg, "Sexual Aggression by an Acquaintance: Methods of Coping and Later Psychological Adjustment," *Violence and Victims* 8 (1993): 91–103.

89. U.S. Department of Justice, *Report of the President's Task Force on Victims of Crime* (Washington, D.C.: U.S. Government Printing Office, 1983).

90. Ibid., p. 115.

91. Ibid., pp. 2–10; and "Review on Victims—Witnesses of Crime," *Massachusetts Lawyers Weekly,* 25 April 1983, p. 26.

92. Robert Davis, *Crime Victims: Learning How to Help Them* (Washington, D.C.: National Institute of Justice, 1987).

93. Peter Finn and Beverly Lee, *Establishing a Victim-Witness Assistance Program* (Washington, D.C.: U.S. Government Printing Office, 1988).

94. This section leans heavily on Albert Roberts, "Delivery of Services to Crime Victims: A National Survey," *American Journal of Orthopsychiatry* 6 (1991): 128–137; see also idem., *Helping Crime Victims: Research, Policy and Practice* (Newbury Park, Calif.: Sage Publications, 1990).

95. Randall Schmidt, "Crime Victim Compensation Legislation: A Comparative Study," *Victimology* 5 (1980): 428–437.

96. See, generally, Andrew Karmen, *Crime Victims,* 3rd ed. (Belmont, Calif.: Wadsworth, 1996), pp. 294–334.

97. Pater Jaffe, Marlies Sudermann, Deborah Reitzel, and Steve Killip, "An Evaluation of a Secondary School Primary Prevention Program on Violence in Intimate Relationships," *Violence and Victims* 7 (1992): 129–145.

98. Vicki McNickel Rose, "Rape as a Social Problem: A By-Product of the Feminist Movement," *Social Problems* 25 (1977): 75–89.

99. Janet Gornick, Martha Burt, and Karen Pittman, "Structure and Activities of Rape Crisis Centers in the Early 1980s," *Crime and Delinquency* 31 (1985): 247–268.

100. Andrew Karmen, "Victim-Offender Reconciliation Programs: Pro and Con," *Perspectives of the American Probation and Parole Association* 20 (1996): 11–14.

101. See Frank Carrington, "Victim's Rights Litigation: A Wave of the Future," in *Perspectives on Crime Victims,* ed. Burt Galaway and Joe Hudson (St. Louis: Mosby, 1981).

102. Andrew Karmen, "Towards the Institutionalization of a New Kind of Justice Professional: The Victim Advocate," *The Justice Professional* 9 (1995): 2–15.

103. Ibid., pp. 9–10.

104. Karmen, *Crime Victims,* pp. 362–364.

105. Pamela Wilcox Rountree and Kenneth Land, "Burglary Victimization, Perceptions of Crime Risk, and Routine Activities: A Multilevel Analysis Across Seattle Neighborhoods and Census Tracts," *Journal of Research in Crime and Delinquency* 33 (1996): 1147–1180.

106. Leslie Kennedy, "Going It Alone: Unreported Crime and Individual Self-Help," *Journal of Criminal Justice* 16 (1988): 403–413.

107. Ronald Clarke, "Situational Crime Prevention: Its Theoretical Basis and Practical Scope," in *Annual Review of Criminal Justice Research,* ed. Michael Tonry and Norval Morris (Chicago: University of Chicago Press, 1983).

108. Catherine Whitaker, *Crime Prevention Measures* (Washington, D.C.: Bureau of Justice Statistics, 1986).

109. Rosenbaum, "Community Crime Protection, A Review and Synthesis of the Literature," *Justice Quarterly* 5 (1988): 323–395.

110. Andrew Buck, Simon Hakim, and George Rengert, "Burglar Alarms and the Choice Behavior of Burglars," *Journal of Criminal Justice* 21 (1993): 497–507; for an opposing view, see Lynch and Cantor, "Ecological and Behavioral Influences on Property Victimization at Home."

111. Alan Lizotte, "Determinants of Completing Rape and Assault," *Journal of Quantitative Criminology* 2 (1986): 213–217.

112. Polly Marchbanks, Kung-Jong Lui, and James Mercy, "Risk of Injury from Resisting Rape," *American Journal of Epidemiology* 132 (1990): 540–549.

113. Caroline Wolf Harlow, *Robbery Victims* (Washington, D.C.: Bureau of Justice Statistics, 1987).

114. Gary Kleck, "Guns and Violence: An Interpretive Review of the Field," *Social Pathology* 1 (1995): 12–45.

115. James Fyfe, "Police Use of Deadly Force: Research and Reform," *Justice Quarterly* 5 (1988): 157–176.

116. Gary Kleck, "Rape and Resistance," *Social Problems* 37 (1990): 149–162.

117. Personal communication with Gary Kleck, January 10, 1997; see also Kleck, "Guns and Violence: An Interpretive Review of the Field."

118. Gary Green, "Citizen Gun Ownership and Criminal Deterrence: Theory, Research and Policy," *Criminology* 25 (1987): 63–81.

119. James Garofalo and Maureen McLeod, *Improving the Use and Effectiveness of Neighborhood Watch Programs* (Washington, D.C.: National Institute of Justice, 1988).

120. Peter Finn, *Block Watches Help Crime Victims in Philadelphia* (Washington, D.C.: National Institute of Justice, 1986).

121. Ibid.

An important goal of the criminological enterprise is to create valid and accurate theories of crime causation. Social scientists have defined theory as sets of statements that explain why and how several concepts are related. For a set of statements to qualify as a theory, we must be able to deduce some conclusions from it that are subject to empirical verification; that is, theories must predict or prohibit certain observable events or conditions.*

Criminologists have sought to collect vital facts about crime and interpret them in a scientifically meaningful fashion. By developing empirically verifiable statements, or hypotheses, and organizing them into theories of crime causation, they hope to identify the causes of crime.

Since the late 19th century, criminological theory has pointed to various underlying causes of crime. The earliest theories generally attributed crime to a single underlying cause: atypical

Theories of
Crime Causation

body build, genetic abnormality, insanity, physical anomalies, and poverty. Later theories attributed crime causation to multiple factors: poverty, peer influence, school problems, and family dysfunction.

In this section, theories of crime causation are grouped into five chapters. Chapters 4 and 5 focus on theories based on individual traits. They hold that crime is either a free-will choice made by an individual, a function of personal psychological or biological abnormality, or both. Chapters 6 through 9 investigate theories based in sociology and political economy. These theories portray crime as a function of the structure, process, and conflicts of social living. Chapter 10 is devoted to theories that combine or integrate these various concepts into a cohesive, complex view of crime.

*Rodney Stark, *Sociology*, 2nd ed. (Belmont, Calif.: Wadsworth, 1987), p. 618.

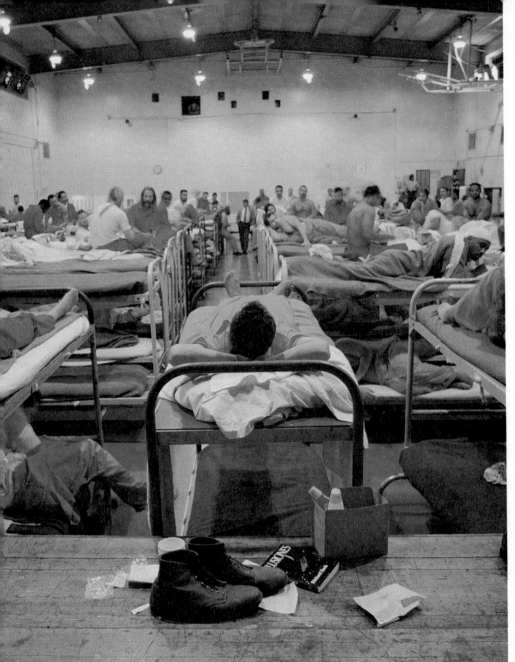

Chapter 5
Choice Theory

Crime data tell us that criminality is a young man's game: Most offenders are young males who desist from crime as they mature; the bulk of adult offending is committed by relatively few persistent offenders. Why do these youths commit criminal acts? Given that most young offenders age out or desist from crime, why do some continue to violate the law and risk apprehension, trial, and punishment well into adulthood?

To some criminologists, persistence is a function of *personal choice.* The decision to violate the law—commit a robbery, sell drugs, attack a rival, fill out a false tax return—is made for a variety of personal reasons, including greed, revenge, need, anger, lust, jealousy, thrill seeking, or vanity. The central issue is that the illegal act is a matter of individual decision making, a rational choice made after weighing the potential benefits and consequences of crime. The jealous suitor concludes that the risk of punishment is worth the satisfaction of "punching out" a rival; the greedy shopper considers the chance of apprehension by store detectives so small that she takes a "five-finger discount" on a new sweater; the drug dealer concludes that the huge profits he can earn from a single shipment of cocaine far outweigh the possible costs of apprehension. In the final analysis, people choose crime simply because it is rewarding, satisfying, easy, or fun.

This chapter will review the philosophical underpinnings of **choice theory,** which first appeared as **classical criminology.** Our discussion will then turn to more recent theoretical models that flow from the concept of choice and hold that because criminals are rational, their behavior can be controlled or deterred by the fear of punishment; desistence can then be explained by a growing and intense fear of punishment. These models include situational crime prevention, general deterrence theory, specific deterrence theory, and incapacitation. Finally, the chapter briefly reviews how choice theory has influenced policy making in the area of criminal justice.

The Development of Classical Theory

Theories of crime based on the rational decision making of motivated criminals can trace their roots to the classical school of criminology. As you may recall from Chapter 1, classical criminology was based on the works of Cesare Beccaria and other utilitarian philosophers. At its core was the concept that (a) people choose all behavior, including criminal behavior, (b) people's choices can be controlled by the fear of punishment, and (c) the more severe, certain, and swift the punishment, the greater its ability to control criminal behavior.[1]

In keeping with his utilitarian views, Beccaria called for fair and certain punishment to deter crime. Because people

are egotistical and self-centered, they must be goaded by the fear of punishment, which provides a tangible motive for them to obey the law and suppress the "despotic spirit" that resides in every person.[2]

Beccaria felt that, to be effective, punishments must be proportional to their crimes. Without proportionality, people will not be deterred from committing more serious offenses. For example, if both rape and murder were punished by death, a rapist would have little reason to refrain from killing his victim in order to eliminate the potential threat of the victim contacting the police and giving evidence in court.

Although some have questioned Beccaria's principles and motives, even his harshest critics recognize that he was one of the rare reformers to have an enduring influence on justice policy and a true criminological success story.[3] Beccaria's ideas and writings have inspired criminologists who believe that criminals choose to commit crime and that crime can be controlled by the judicious application of criminal punishments.

Beccaria's vision has had a powerful influence on events in the criminal justice system.[4] The belief that punishment should fit the crime and that people should be punished proportionately for what they did and not to satisfy the whim of a capricious judge or ruler was widely adopted throughout Europe and the United States. In Britain, philosopher Jeremy Bentham (1748–1833) helped popularize Beccaria's views in his writings on **utilitarianism.** According to this theory, actions are evaluated by their tendency to produce advantage, pleasure, and happiness and to avoid or prevent mischief, pain, evil, or unhappiness.[5] Bentham believed that the purpose of all law is to produce and support the total happiness of the community it serves. Since punishment is in itself harmful, its existence is justified only if it promises to prevent greater evil than it creates. Punishment, therefore, has four main objectives:

1. To prevent all criminal offenses

2. When it cannot prevent a crime, to convince the offender to commit a less serious one

3. To ensure that a criminal uses no more force than is necessary

4. To prevent crime as cheaply as possible[6]

The most stunning example of how the classical philosophy of Beccaria and Bentham was embraced in Europe occurred in 1789, when France's postrevolutionary Constituent Assembly adopted these ideas in the Declaration of the Rights of Man:

> the law has the right to prohibit only actions harmful to society. . . . The law shall inflict only such punishments as are strictly and clearly necessary . . . no person shall be punished except by virtue of a law enacted and promulgated previous to the crime and applicable to its terms.

Similarly, a prohibition against "cruel and unusual punishments" was incorporated into the Eighth Amendment to the U.S. Constitution.

The use of torture and severe punishments was largely abandoned in the 19th century. The practice of incarcerating criminals and structuring prison sentences to fit the severity of the crime was a reflection of classical criminology. Although the proportionality demanded by Beccaria was often ignored by the legal system, the general theme of gearing punishment to deter crime was widely accepted.

By the end of the 19th century, the popularity of the classical approach began to decline, after 100 years of dominance, and by the mid-20th century this perspective was neglected by mainstream criminologists. During this period, positivist criminologists focused on the internal and external factors—poverty, low IQ, poor education, inadequate home life—believed to be the true causes of criminality. Since these conditions could not be easily curbed, the concept of punishing people for behaviors beyond their control seemed both foolish and cruel. Although classical principles still controlled the way police, courts, and correctional agencies operated, most criminologists rejected classical criminology as an explanation of criminal behavior.

Choice Theory Emerges

Beginning in the mid-1970s, the classical approach began to enjoy a resurgence of popularity. The rehabilitation of known criminals, considered a cornerstone of positivist policy, came under attack. According to positivist criminology, if crime were caused by some social or psychological problem, such as poverty, crime rates could be reduced by providing good jobs and economic opportunities. A number of national surveys (the best known being Robert Martinson's "What Works?") failed to uncover examples of rehabilitation programs that prevented future criminal activity.[7] A well-publicized book, *Beyond Probation* by Charles Murray and Louis Cox, went so far as suggesting that punishment-oriented programs could suppress future criminality much more effectively than those that relied on rehabilitation and treatment efforts.[8]

A significant increase in the reported crime rate, as well as serious disturbances in the nation's prisons, frightened the general public. To many criminologists, reviving the classical concepts of social control and punishment made more sense than futilely trying to improve entrenched social conditions or rehabilitate criminals using ineffectual methodologies.[9]

Beginning in the late 1970s, a number of criminologists began producing books and monographs expounding the theme that criminals are rational actors who plan their crimes, fear punishment, and deserve to be penalized for their misdeeds. In a 1975 book that came to symbolize renewed interest in classical views, *Thinking About Crime,* political scientist James Q. Wilson debunked the positivist

view that crime is a function of external forces, such as poverty, that can be altered by government programs. Instead, he argued, efforts should be made to reduce criminal opportunity by deterring would-be offenders and incarcerating known criminals.[10]

Persons who are likely to commit crime, Wilson maintained, lack inhibition against misconduct, value the excitement and thrills of breaking the law, have a low stake in conformity, and are willing to take greater chances than the average person. If they can be convinced that their actions will bring severe punishment, only the totally irrational will be willing to engage in crime. While incapacitating criminals should not be the sole goal of the justice system, such a policy does have the advantage of restraining offenders and preventing their future criminality without having to figure out how to change their attitudes or nature, a goal that has proven difficult to accomplish. Wilson made this famous observation:

> Wicked people exist. Nothing avails except to set them apart from innocent people. And many people, neither wicked nor innocent, but watchful, dissembling, and calculating of their chances, ponder our reaction to wickedness as a clue to what they might profitably do.[11]

Here Wilson seems to be saying that unless we react forcefully to crime, those "sitting on the fence" will get a clear message: Crime pays. The accompanying Close-Up discusses whether in fact criminals can profit from crime.

Coinciding with the publication of Wilson's book was a conservative shift in U.S. public policy that resulted in the election of Ronald Reagan to the presidency in 1980. Political decision makers embraced ideas suggested by Wilson as a means of bringing the crime rate down. These views have helped shape criminal justice policy for the past two decades.

From these roots, a more contemporary version of classical theory evolved that is based on intelligent thought processes and criminal decision making; it is today referred to as the **rational choice** approach to crime causation.[12]

The Concepts of Rational Choice

According to the rational choice approach, law-violating behavior occurs when an offender decides to risk transgressing after considering both personal factors (such as need for money, revenge, thrills, and entertainment) and situational factors (how well a target is protected, the efficiency of the local police force). Before choosing to commit a crime, the reasoning criminal evaluates the risk of apprehension, the seriousness of expected punishment, the potential value of the criminal enterprise, and his or her immediate need for criminal gain.

The decision to commit a specific type of crime, then, is a matter of personal decision making based on weighing

close-up: *Does Crime Pay?*

Rational offenders might be induced to commit crime if they perceive that crime pays more than they could possibly earn from a legitimate job. Crime pays if, taking into account the probability of arrest and the cost of punishment, the benefits of employment are lower than the expected benefits of theft. Does crime, in fact, pay?

To answer this question, James Q. Wilson and Allan Abrahamse used a sample of incarcerated inmates to determine their perceived and actual "take" from crime. Wilson and Abrahamse divided the group into mid- and high-rate offenders in one of six crime categories: burglary, theft, swindling, auto theft, robbery and mixed offenses predominantly involving drug sales.

Using crime loss estimates derived from the NCVS survey, Wilson and Abrahamse found that mid-rate burglars on average earn about $2,368 per year from crime—far less than the $7,391 (after taxes) they could have earned in a legitimate job. High-rate burglars, who commit an average of 193 crimes per year, take home $5,711, roughly the same they would have earned from a job (the potential earnings of high-rate burglars are reduced because they spend more time behind bars). Even if free for the entire year, high-rate burglars would earn about the same as if they had held a job for the same period—a little less than $10,000.

Crime profits are reduced by the costs of a criminal career: legal fees, bail bonds, loss of family income, and the psychic cost of a prison sentence. Given these costs, most criminals actually earn little from crime. Would you, ask Wilson and Abrahamse, be willing to become a high-rate robber if you knew that you would be spending half your life in prison for an annual salary of under $15,000?

If crime pays so little, why are there so many criminals? There are a number of reasons criminals choose crime despite its relatively low payoff.

One reason is that criminals tend to overestimate the money they can earn from crime. Wilson and Abrahamse found that in some cases, criminals' estimates were more than 12 times higher than a realistic assessment of their earning potential. For example, burglars estimated that they could earn $2,674 per month from crime, while a more realistic figure is only $230!

Some criminals believe that they have no choice but to commit crime because legitimate work is unavailable. This may be a false assumption. About two-thirds of the inmates reported having been employed before they were imprisoned.

Rather than being excluded from the job market, criminals seem to be relatively unsuccessful participants within it; they are underemployed, not unemployed.

Criminals are realistic about their long-term careers, believing that eventually everyone is caught and punished. However, they are overly *optimistic* about getting away with each individual crime. They believe that the odds of getting caught for a particular crime are rather small, and being impulsive, they take the short-term view that each particular crime *is worth the risk;* they may eventually get caught, *but not this time.*

Crime could be deterred if would-be criminals understood the true costs of committing crime and the relatively small payoff of a criminal career, but that does not usually occur, nor is there an easy way to make it happen.

CRITICAL THINKING QUESTIONS

1. What crimes, if any, do pay?
2. How would you design an effective crime control policy, considering the misunderstanding criminals have about their own vocation?

Source: James Q. Wilson and Allan Abrahamse, "Does Crime Pay?" *Justice Quarterly* 9 (1992): 359–377.

---

the available information. Conversely, the decision to forgo crime may be based on the criminal's perception that the economic benefits are no longer there or that the risk of apprehension is too great. For example, studies of residential burglary indicate that criminals will forgo activity if they believe a neighborhood is well patrolled by police.[13] In fact, evidence exists that when police begin to concentrate patrols in a particular area of the city, crime rates tend to increase in adjacent areas that may be perceived by criminals as "safer" (referred to as **crime displacement**).[14]

Offense and Offender Specifications

Rational choice theorists view crime as both offense- and offender-specific.[15] **Offense-specific crime** refers to the fact that offenders will react selectively to the characteristics of particular offenses. The decision of whether to commit an individual burglary, for example, might involve evaluating the target's likely cash yield; the availability of resources, such as a getaway car; and the probability of capture by police.[16]

Offender-specific crime refers to the fact that criminals are not simply driven people who for one reason or another engage in random acts of antisocial behavior. Before deciding to partake in crime, they analyze whether they have the prerequisites for committing a criminal act, including their skills, motives, needs, and fears. Criminal acts might be ruled out if the potential offenders perceive that they can reach a desired personal goal through legitimate means or if they are too afraid of getting caught.[17]

Note the distinction made here between crime and criminality.[18] Crime is an event; criminality is a personal trait. Criminals do not commit crime all the time; even the most honest citizens may on occasion violate the law.

Some high-risk people lacking opportunity may never commit crime, whereas given enough provocation or opportunity, a low-risk, law-abiding person may commit crime. What, then, are the conditions that promote crime and criminality?

Structuring Criminality

A number of personal factors condition people to choose criminality. Perceptions of economic opportunity may influence offending choices: Offenders are more likely to desist from crime if they believe that (a) their future criminal earnings will be relatively low, and (b) attractive and legal income-generating opportunities are available.[19] In this sense, making a rational choice is a function of perception of conventional alternatives and opportunities.

Fluctuations in the perceptions of risk over the life course may also influence behavior choices. Neal Shover found that experienced criminals may turn from a life of crime when they develop a belief that the risks from crime are greater than its potential profit.[20] The veteran criminal has discovered the limitations of his or her powers and knows when to take a chance and when to be cautious. Thus, learning and experience may be important elements in the choice of crime.[21]

Personality and lifestyle also help structure criminal choices. According to sociologist Robert Agnew, those people who choose crime over conformity share a number of personal traits: (1) They perceive freedom of movement and lack of social constraints; (2) they have less self-control than other people and seem unaffected by fear of social control (that is, criminal punishment);[22] and (3) they are typically under stress or facing some serious personal problem or condition that forces them to choose risky behavior.[23]

Structuring Crime

The evidence indicates that the decision to commit crime, regardless of its substance, is structured by the choice of (a) where the crime occurs, (b) the characteristics of the target, and (c) the means (techniques) available for its completion.

CHOOSING THE PLACE OF CRIME. Criminals appear to choose the place of crime. Bruce Jacobs's interviews with 40 active street dealers of crack cocaine in a midwestern city showed that dealers carefully evaluated the desirability of their "sales area" before setting up shop.[24] Dealers considered the middle of a long block the best choice because they could see everything coming toward them from both directions; police raids could then be spotted ahead of time.[25] Another tactic was to entice buyers who seemed suspicious either into spaces between apartment buildings or into backlots to do drug deals. While the dealer may have lost the tactical edge of being on a public street, he gained a measure of protection because his confederates could watch over the operation and come to the rescue if the buyer tried to "pull something."[26]

CHOOSING TARGETS. Evidence of rational choice may also be found in the way criminals locate their targets. Victimization data indicate that high-income households ($25,000 or more annually) are the most likely targets of property crimes; in contrast, the wealthy are rarely the victims of violent crimes.[27] It is unlikely that these patterns could result from random events.

Studies of both professional and occasional criminals also yield evidence that choosing targets is a rational event. Burglars seem to make prudent choices when they check to make sure that no one is home before they enter a residence. Some call ahead, while others ring the doorbell, preparing to claim they had the wrong address if someone answers. Some check to find out which families have star high school athletes, since those that do are sure to be at the game, leaving their houses unguarded.[28] Others seek the unlocked door and avoid the one with a deadbolt; houses with dogs are usually considered off limits.[29]

Burglars indicate that they carefully choose their targets. Some avoid freestanding buildings because they can more easily be surrounded by police; others select targets that are known to do a primarily cash business, such as bars, supermarkets, and restaurants.[30] Burglars also report being sensitive to the activities of their victims. They note that homemakers often develop predictable behavior patterns, which helps them plan their crimes.[31] Burglars seem to prefer "working" between 9 A.M. and 11 A.M. and in mid-afternoon, when parents are either working or dropping off or picking up kids at school. Burglars avoid Saturdays because most families are at home; Sunday morning during church hours is considered a prime time for weekend burglaries.[32]

LEARNING CRIMINAL TECHNIQUES. Criminals report learning the techniques of crime that help them avoid detection. Bruce Jacobs reports that crack dealers learn how to "stash" crack cocaine in some undisclosed location so that they will not be forced to carry large amounts of product on their persons. Others master the trick of conversing while hiding five $20 rocks of cocaine in their mouths.[33]

Females drawn into drug dealing tell how they have learned the "trade" in a businesslike manner:

> He taught me how to "recon" [reconstitute] cocaine, cutting and repacking a brick from 91 proof to 50 proof, just like a business. He treats me like an equal partner, and many of the friends are business associates. I am a catalyst . . . I even get guys turned on to drugs.[34]

Note here the business terminology used. This coke dealer could be talking about taking a computer training course at a major corporation!

In sum, rational choice involves both the shaping of criminality and the structuring of crime. Personality, age, status, risk, and opportunity seem to influence the decision to become a criminal; place, target, and techniques help to structure crime.

Rational Choice and Routine Activities

Rational choice theory dovetails with routine activities theory.[35] As you may recall from Chapter 4, routine activities theory maintains that along with a supply of motivated offenders, the absence of capable guardians and the presence of suitable targets determine crime and victimization rate trends. Routine activities provides a *macro* view of crime, predicting how change in social and economic conditions influences the overall crime and victimization rates. In contrast, rational choice theory provides a *micro* view of why individual offenders decide to commit specific crimes. While not identical, these approaches agree that crime rates are a product of criminal opportunity: Increase the number of guardians, decrease the suitability of targets, or reduce the offender population, and crime rates should likewise decline; increase opportunity and reduce guardianship and crime rates should increase.

What are the connections between rational choice and routine activities?

SUITABLE TARGETS. Research indicates that criminal choice is influenced by the perception of target vulnerability. As they go about their daily activities, traveling to school or work, potential criminals may encounter targets of illegal opportunity: an empty carport, an open door, an unlocked car, a bike left on the street. Paul Cromwell and his associates found that corner homes, usually near traffic lights or stop signs, are the ones most likely to be burglarized: stop signs give criminals a legitimate reason to stop their cars and look for an attractive target.[36] Secluded homes, such as those at the end of a cul-de-sac, surrounded by wooded areas, make suitable targets.[37] Thieves also report being concerned about the convenience of their target. They are more apt to choose sites for burglaries and robberies that are familiar to them and that are located in easily accessible and open areas.[38]

Because criminals often go on foot or use public transportation, they are unlikely to travel long distances to commit crimes and are more likely to drift toward the center of a city than to move toward outlying areas.[39] Garland White found that "permeable neighborhoods," those with a greater than usual number of access streets from traffic arteries into the neighborhood, are the ones most likely to have high crime rates.[40] It is possible that criminals choose these neighborhoods for burglaries because they are familiar and well traveled, because they appear more open and vulnerable, and because they offer more potential escape routes.[41] Here, we can see the influence of a routine activity on criminal choice: The more suitable and accessible the target, the more likely that crime will occur.[42]

CAPABLE GUARDIANS. Routine activity also implies that the presence of **capable guardians** may deter crime. Criminals tend to shy away from victims who are perceived to be armed and potentially dangerous. In a series of interviews conducted with career property offenders, Kenneth Tunnell found that burglars will avoid targets if they feel there are police in the area or if "nosy neighbors" might be suspicious and cause trouble.[43] And evidence is accumulating that predatory criminals are aware of law enforcement capability: Communities that enjoy the reputation of employing aggressive "crime-fighting" cops are less likely to attract potential offenders than areas perceived as having passive law enforcers.[44]

Guardianship can also involve passive or mechanical devices, such as security fences or burglar alarms. Research indicates that physical security measures can improve guardianship and limit offender access to targets.[45]

MOTIVATED CRIMINALS. Routine activities theory predicts that crime rates correspond to the number of **motivated criminals** in the population (that is, teenage males, drug users, unemployed adults). Rational offenders may be less likely to commit crimes if they believe they can achieve personal goals through legitimate means; in short, job availability reduces crime. In contrast, criminal motivation increases when there is a need to accumulate wealth; a rising cost of living has been associated with increasing criminal motivation.[46]

If crime is rational, criminal motivation should be reduced if potential offenders perceive alternatives to crime; in contrast, the perception of blocked legitimate opportunities should increase criminal motivation.

> ## Connections
>
> Lack of conventional opportunity is a persistent theme in sociological theories of crime. The frustration caused by a perceived lack of opportunity explains the high crime rates in lower-class areas. Chapter 7 sections on strain and cultural deviance theories provide an alternative explanation of how lack of opportunity is associated with crime.

Tunnell's career criminals said they committed crimes because they considered legitimate opportunities unavailable to people with their limited education and background. As one offender told him:

> I tried to stay away from crime. . . . Nobody would hire me. I was an ex-con and I tried, I really tried to get gainful employment. There was nobody looking to hire me with my record. I went in as a juvenile and came out as an adult and didn't have any legitimate employment résumé to submit. Employment was impossible. So, I started robbing.[47]

Note how crime became the choice when legitimate alternatives were absent. In contrast, potential offenders who perceive legitimate alternatives, such as high-paying jobs, are less likely to choose crime.[48]

INTERACTIVE EFFECTS. According to the routine activities approach, motivation, opportunity, and targets are

Research indicates that criminal choice is influenced by the perception of target vulnerability. One form of crime prevention is to make targets less "vulnerable" by installing security measures. The bombing of the World Trade Center in New York City and the Murrah Federal Building in Oklahoma City has heightened awareness of the threat of terrorist bombings, and consequently crime prevention measures have been increased. Sights such as security guards inspecting packages are not uncommon. Here at a federal building in San Francisco, a security guard checks a worker's lunch bag before allowing her to enter.

interactive: The presence of any one factor encourages the others. Motivated criminals will not commit crime unless they have suitable targets available and the opportunity to attack them. Motivated offenders must also have the opportunity to commit crime; without opportunity, even the most driven will forgo criminality. The presence of guardians will deter even the most motivated offenders, rendering even the most attractive targets off-limits. Ronald Clarke shows the interrelationship between opportunity, routine activities, and environmental factors in Figure 5.1.

Figure 5.1 shows that criminal opportunities (suitable victims and targets) abound in urban environments where facilitators (guns, drugs) are readily found. Environmental factors such as physical layout and cultural style may either facilitate or restrict criminal opportunity. Motivated offenders living in these urban "hot spots" continually learn about criminal opportunities from peers, the media, and their own perceptions. This information may either escalate their criminal motivation or warn them of its danger.[49]

Efforts to measure the interaction between opportunity, motivation, and crime show that the relationship is in fact significant. For example, Mark Warr found that kids who are attached to their parents and spend their weekends at home report little in the way of criminal motivation; lack of opportunity may reduce motivation.[50] John Hagan's research indicates that kids whose family relationships are strained, distant, and unrewarding are more likely to become attached to deviant peers, which in turn helps increase criminal motivation.[51]

In an important study, D. Wayne Osgood and his associates examined a nationally drawn sample of 1,700 youths ages 18–26. They found that adolescents who spend a great deal of time socializing with peers in the absence of authority figures (riding around in cars, going to parties, going out at night for fun) are also the ones most likely to engage in deviant behaviors.[52] In the presence of "motivated peers," the lack of structure and guardianship leaves more opportunity for antisocial behaviors, including substance abuse, crime, and dangerous driving. Osgood found that participation in unstructured activities helps explain the association between crime rates and gender, age, and status: Teenage boys have the highest crime rates because they are the group most likely to engage in unsupervised socialization. Opportunity combined with lack of guardianship increases criminal motivation.

Figure 5.1 The opportunity structure for crime.

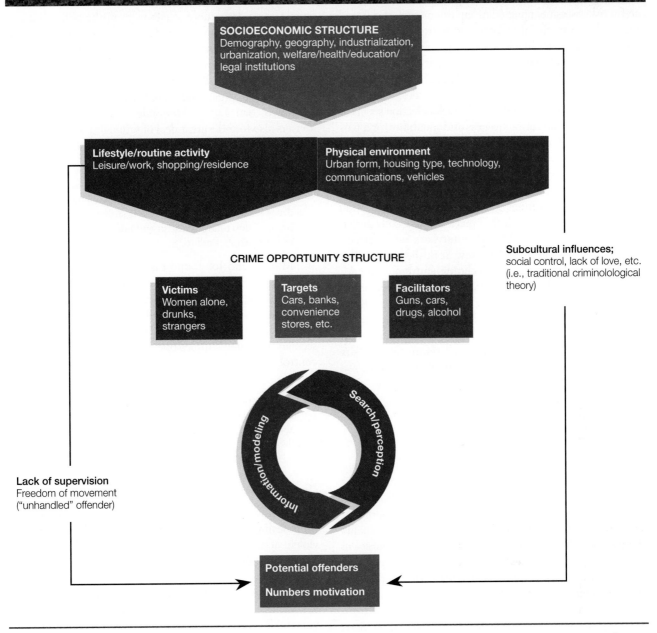

Source: Ronald Clarke, "Situational Crime Prevention" in *Building a Safer Society: Strategic Approaches to Crime Prevention,* vol. 19 of *Crime and Justice, A Review of Research,* ed. Michael Tonry and David Farrington (Chicago: University of Chicago Press, 1995), p. 103. Reprinted by permission.

Is Crime Rational?

Is crime rational? It is relatively easy to show that some crimes are the product of rational and objective thought, especially when they involve an ongoing criminal conspiracy centered on economic gain. When prominent bankers in the savings and loan industry were indicted for criminal fraud, their elaborate financial schemes not only showed signs of rationality but exhibited brilliant, though flawed, financial expertise.[53] The stock market manipulations of Wall Street insiders, such as Ivan Boesky and Michael Milken, and the drug dealings of organized crime bosses demonstrate a reasoned analysis of market conditions, interests, and risks.

Are Street Crimes Rational?

While it is not surprising that ongoing criminal conspiracies involving organized and white-collar crime exhibit rationality, what about common street crimes such as prostitution and petty theft? These would seem more likely to be random acts of criminal opportunity than well-thought-out, planned conspiracies. However, there is evidence that even these "unplanned" street crimes may also be the product of careful risk assessment, including environmental, social, and structural factors. Ronald Clarke and Patricia Harris found that auto thieves are highly selective in their choice of targets. If they want to strip cars for their parts, they are most likely to choose Volkswagens; if they want to sell the cars or keep them permanently, they choose Mercedes; for temporary use, Buicks are top ranked.[54] Vehicle selection seems to be based on the cars' attractiveness and suitability for a particular purpose: German automobiles are selected for stripping because they usually have high-quality audio equipment that has good value on the second-hand market; thus, target selection seems highly rational.

Studies of prostitutes suggest that even these often desperate women make clear choices in their daily activities. For example, Lisa Maher's interviews with "street-level sex workers" in Brooklyn, New York show that today prices for sexual services are declining and that competition is increasing. Increasing drug use has produced an influx of women new to the street willing to charge little to support their habits. Despite fierce competition, more-experienced street workers still resist sex practices that compromise their chances of survival, refuse to trade sex for drugs, and refuse to service clients they consider too dangerous or distasteful.[55] These activities show clear signs of rational choice.

Is Drug Use Rational?

Is it possible that drug users and dealers, a group not usually associated with clear thinking, make rational choices? Research does in fact show that from its onset, drug use is controlled by rational decision making. Users report that they begin taking drugs when they believe that the benefits of substance abuse outweigh its costs—that is, drugs will provide an enjoyable, exciting, thrilling experience. Their entry into substance abuse is facilitated by their perception that valued friends and family members endorse and encourage drug use and abuse substances themselves.[56]

In adulthood, heavy drug users and dealers show signs of rationality and cunning in their daily activity. Bruce Jacobs found that they used specific techniques to avoid apprehension by police. They play what they call the "peep game" before dealing drugs, scoping out the territory to make sure the turf is free from anything out of place that may be a potential threat, such as police officers or rival gang members.[57] One crack dealer told Jacobs:

> There was this red Pontiac sittin' on the corner one day with two white guys inside. They was just sittin' there for an hour, not doin' nothin'. Another day, diff'rent people be walkin' up and down the street you don't really recognize. You think they might be kin of someone but then you be askin' around and they [neighbors] ain't never seen them before neither. When ya' see strange things like that, you think somethin' be goin' on [and you don't deal].[58]

Drug dealers told Jacobs that they also give careful consideration to whether they should deal alone or in groups: large groups draw more attention from the police but can offer more protection. Drug-dealing gangs and groups can help divert the attention of police: If their drug dealing is noticed by detectives, a dealer can slyly walk away or dispose of evidence while confederates distract the cops.[59]

Patricia Morgan and Karen Ann Joe's three-city (San Francisco, San Diego, Honolulu) study of female drug abusers also found a great deal of rationality and careful decision making. One dealer who earns $50,000 per year told them:

> I stayed within my goals, basically... I don't go around doing stupid things. I don't walk around telling people I have drugs for sale, I don't have people sitting out in front of my house. I don't have traffic in and out of my house... I control the people I sell to.[60]

Morgan and Joe found that these female dealers consider drug distribution a positive experience that provides them with economic independence, self-esteem, increased ability to function, professional pride, and the ability to maintain control over their lives. These women often seemed more like yuppies opening a boutique than out-of-control addicts:

> I'm a good dealer. I don't cut my drugs, I have high-quality drugs insofar as it's possible to get high quality drugs. I want to be known as somebody who sells good drugs, but doesn't always have them, as opposed to someone who always has them and sometimes the drugs are good.[61]

Can Violence Be Rational?

While there is evidence that instrumental crimes, such as drug dealing and burglaries, are rational, is it possible that violent acts through which the offender gains little material benefit are the product of a reasoned decision-making process?

Evidence exists that even violent criminals are selective in their choice of suitable targets, picking people who are vulnerable and lack adequate defenses. For example, robbery offenders are likely to choose victims who are vulnerable and have low coercive power—victims who do not pose any threat.[62] In their interview survey of violent felons, James Wright and Peter Rossi found that violent offenders avoid victims who may be armed and dangerous. About three-fifths of all felons surveyed were more afraid of armed victims than of police, about 40% had avoided a victim because they believed the victim was armed, and almost one-third reported that they had been scared off, wounded, or captured by armed victims.[63] Even serial murderers, outwardly the most irrational of all offenders, tend to pick their targets with care. Most choose victims who are either defenseless or cannot count on police protection: prostitutes, gay men, hitchhikers, children, hospital patients, the elderly, the homeless. Rarely do serial killers tar-

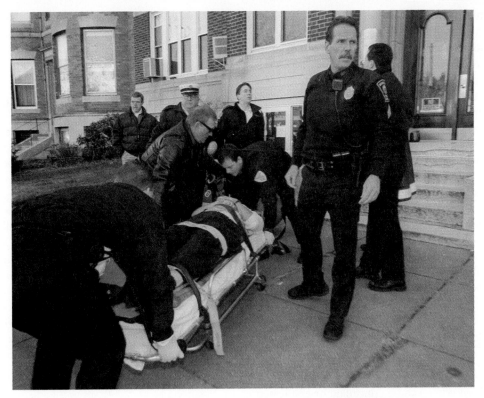

Police removing a victim injured in John Salvi's attack on a Boston Planned Parenthood clinic. While drug deals and white collar crimes seem rational, can violent crimes be explained as a matter of criminal choice? Evidence exists that even violent criminals are selective in their choice of suitable targets by picking people who are vulnerable and lack adequate defenses. Could greater security discourage even the most obsessed killers such as a John Salvi?

get weightlifters, martial arts experts, or any other potentially powerful group.[64]

A number of recent studies have found that even the most violent and lethal interactions seem to be motivated by rational thought and not unthinking rage. Scott Decker, using murder data from St. Louis, found that people most often killed acquaintances in disputes involving drug deals gone awry. Even in apparently senseless killings among strangers, the "real" motive was revenge for a prior dispute or disagreement among the parties involved (or their families).[65] Similarly, Richard Felson and Steven Messner found that many homicides were motivated by the offenders' desire to avoid retaliation from a victim they had assaulted or to avoid future prosecutions by getting rid of witnesses.[66] While some killings are the result of angry aggression, others seem to show signs of rational planning. So while violent acts appear to be irrational, they also involve calculation of risk and reward.

The Seductions of Crime

The focus of rational choice theory is on the opportunity to commit crime and on how criminal choices are structured by the social environment. There will always be people willing and able to bypass the law, given the proper conditions and opportunity. Some irrational or mentally disturbed people may commit crimes without thought to potential hazard, but it seems likely that immediate or situational variables determine and guide most criminal behavior: People commit crime when they view its outcome as beneficial.[67] For many, crime is attractive; it brings rewards, excitement, prestige and other desirable outcomes without lengthy work or effort. Whether it is violent or profit oriented, crime has an allure that some people cannot resist.

Sociologist Jack Katz argues that there are in fact immediate benefits to criminality, which he labels the **seductions of crime.**[68] These situational inducements directly precede the commission of a crime and draw offenders into law violations. Someone challenges their authority or moral position, and they vanquish their opponent with a beating; they want to maximize their pleasure by doing something exciting, so they break into and vandalize a school building.

According to Katz, choosing crime can help satisfy personal needs. For some people, shoplifting and vandalism are attractive because getting away with it is a thrilling demonstration of personal competence (Katz calls this "sneaky thrills"); monetary gain is not their primary motive. Even murder can have an emotional payoff. Killers behave like the avenging gods of mythology, choosing to have life-or-death control over their victims.

Katz finds that situational inducements created from emotional upheaval can also structure the decision to commit crime. When an individual is faced with humiliation, righteousness, arrogance, or ridicule, violent reactions seem a natural response. When someone is rebuked at a party because he or she is disturbing people, the person responds, "So, I'm acting like a fool, am I?" and goes on the attack. Public embarrassment leads to action: The person must "sacrifice" or injure the body of the victim to maintain his or her "honor."

A number of research studies have supported Katz's view that situational inducements play an important role in causing adolescent misbehavior.[69] For example, Bill McCarthy showed that people are most likely to be "seduced" if they fear neither the risk of apprehension nor its social consequences. People who either fear losing the respect of their peers or suffering legal punishments are the ones most likely to forgo the seductions of crime.[70]

Eliminating Crime

It follows that if crime is rational and people choose to commit crime, then crime can be controlled or eradicated by convincing potential offenders that the choice of crime is a poor one, that it will not bring them rewards but instead pain, hardship, and deprivation. Evidence exists that jurisdictions with relatively low incarceration rates also experience the highest crime rates.[71] Perhaps "street smart" offenders know which areas offer the least threat and plan their crimes accordingly. A number of potential strategies flow from this premise:

1. *Situational crime prevention* is aimed at convincing would-be criminals to avoid specific targets. It relies on the doctrine that crime can be avoided if motivated offenders are denied access to suitable targets. When people install security systems in their homes or hire security guards, they are broadcasting the message: Guardianship is great here; stay away—the potential reward is not worth the risk of apprehension.

2. *General deterrence strategies* are aimed at making potential criminals fear the consequences of crime. The threat of punishment is aimed at convincing rational criminals that crime does not pay.

3. *Specific deterrence* refers to punishing known criminals severely so that they will never be tempted to repeat their offenses. If choosing crime is rational, then painful punishments should reduce its future allure.

4. *Incapacitation strategies* attempt to reduce crime rates by denying motivated offenders the opportunity to commit crime. If, despite the threat of law and punishment, some people still find crime attractive, the only way to control their behavior is to take them out of society.

In the following sections, each of these crime reduction or control strategies based on the rationality of criminal behavior is discussed in some detail.

Situational Crime Prevention

Rational choice theory suggests that because criminal activity is offense-specific, crime prevention—or at least crime reduction—should be achieved through policies that convince potential criminals to desist from criminal activities, delay their actions, or avoid a particular target. Criminal acts will be avoided if (a) potential targets are carefully guarded, (b) the means to commit crime are controlled, and (c) potential offenders are carefully monitored. Desperate people may contemplate crime, but only the truly irrational will attack a well-defended, inaccessible target and risk strict punishments. Crime prevention, then, can be achieved by reducing the opportunities people have to commit particular crimes, a practice known as **situational crime prevention.**

Situational crime prevention was first popularized in the United States in the early 1970s by Oscar Newman, who coined the term **defensible space** to signify that crime can be prevented or displaced through the use of residential architectural designs that reduce criminal opportunity, such as well-lit housing projects that maximize surveillance.[72] In 1971 C. Ray Jeffery wrote *Crime Prevention Through Environmental Design,* which extended Newman's concepts and applied them to nonresidential areas, such as schools and factories.[73] According to this view, such mechanisms as security systems, deadbolt locks, high-intensity street lighting,

Ronald Clarke, author of *Situational Crime Prevention,* has written extensively on the strategies and tactics to reduce criminal incidents.

Table 5.1 Sixteen Techniques of Situational Prevention

INCREASING PERCEIVED EFFORT	INCREASING PERCEIVED RISKS	REDUCING ANTICIPATED REWARDS	INDUCING GUILT OR SHAME
1. *Target hardening* Slug rejector devices Steering locks Bandit screens	5. *Entry/exit screening* Automatic ticket gates Baggage screening Merchandise tags	9. *Target removal* Removable car radio Women's refuges Phone Card	13. *Rule setting* Harassment codes Customs declaration Hotel registrations
2. *Access control* Parking lot barriers Fenced yards Entry phones	6. *Formal surveillance* Burglar alarms Speed cameras Security guards	10. *Identifying property* Property marking Vehicle licensing Cattle branding	14. *Strengthening moral condemnation* "Shoplifting is stealing" Roadside speedometers "Bloody idiots drink and drive"
3. *Deflecting offenders* Bus stop placement Tavern location Street closures	7. *Surveillance by employees* Pay phone location Park attendants CCTV systems	11. *Reducing temptation* Gender-neutral phone lists Off-street parking	15. *Controlling disinhibitors* Drinking age laws Ignition interlock Server intervention
4. *Controlling facilitators* Credit card photo Caller-ID Gun controls	8. *Natural surveillance* Defensible space Street lighting Cab driver ID	12. *Denying benefits* Ink merchandise tags PIN for car radios Graffiti cleaning	16. *Facilitating compliance* Improved library checkout Public lavatories Trash bins

Source: Ronald Clark and Ross Homel, "A Revised Classification of Situational Crime Prevention Techniques," 1996 (in preparation).

and neighborhood watch patrols should be able to reduce criminal opportunity.[74] In 1992 Ronald Clarke published *Situational Crime Prevention,* which compiled the best-known strategies and tactics to reduce criminal incidents.[75]

Crime-Prevention Strategies

Criminologists have suggested a number of situational crime-prevention efforts that might reduce crime rates. One approach is not to target a specific crime but create an overall strategy or plan to reduce crime in general. For example, Marcus Felson suggests that such "total community" strategy might include some or all of the following elements:

- Uniform school release schedules so that there is no doubt when kids belong in school and when they are truant
- Truancy control efforts
- After-school activities to keep kids under adult supervision
- Organized weekend activities with adult supervision
- School lunch programs designed to keep kids in school and away from shopping areas
- No-cash policies in schools to reduce kids' opportunity to either be targets or engage in the consumption of drugs or alcohol
- Keep shopping areas and schools separate
- Construct housing to maximize guardianship and minimize illegal behavior
- Encourage neighborhood stability so that residents will be acquainted with one another

- Encourage privatization of parks and recreation facilities so that people will be responsible for their area's security[76]

Felson's suggestions are designed to reduce crime by limiting the access that members of a highly motivated offender group (high school kids) have to tempting targets. Notice that it is not designed to eliminate a specific crime but to reduce the overall crime rate.

Targeting Specific Crimes

Situational crime prevention can also involve developing tactics to reduce or eliminate a specific crime problem, such as shoplifting in an urban mall or street-level drug dealing. According to criminologists Ronald Clarke and Ross Homel, crime-prevention tactics in use today generally fall in one of four categories: (1) increasing the effort needed to commit the crime; (2) increasing the risks of committing the crime; (3) reducing the rewards for committing the crime; and (4) inducing guilt or shame for committing the crime. These basic techniques and some specific methods that can be used to achieve them are listed in Table 5.1.

Some of the tactics to increase the offender's effort include *target-hardening techniques,* such as putting unbreakable glass on storefronts, locking gates, and fencing yards. Technological advances can be used to make it more difficult to commit crimes, such as having an owner's photo on credit cards to reduce the use of stolen cards. The development of new products, such as placing steering locks on cars, can make it more difficult to commit crimes. Empirical evidence indicates that the use of steering locks has helped reduce car theft in the United States, Britain, and Germany.[77] In another such study, Barbara Morse and Delbert Elliott found that installing a locking device on cars that prevents inebriated drivers from starting the vehicle significantly reduced drunk-driving rates.[78]

It is also possible to *increase the risks* from committing crime by increasing the chances of apprehension. Improving surveillance lighting, creating neighborhood watch programs, controlling building entrances and exits, installing burglar alarms and security systems, and increasing the number of private security officers and police patrols all may help reduce crime rates. In her analysis of gasoline "drive-offs" from convenience stores, Nancy LaVigne found that removing signs from store windows, installing brighter lights, and instituting a pay-first policy can reduce the number of incidents of people filling their tanks and driving off without paying.[79]

Net Bookmark

Private security firms have been employed to provide situational crime prevention. One of the largest of these is the Wackenhut Co. You can learn more about their services by logging on to their home page at:

http://www.wackenhut.com/wcc/wccindex.html

Target reduction strategies are designed to reduce the value of crime to the potential criminal. These include making car radios removable so they can be kept at home at night, marking property so that it is more difficult to sell when stolen, and having gender-neutral phone listings to discourage obscene phone calls. Tracking systems, such as those made by the LOJACK Corporation, help police locate and return stolen vehicles.

Inducing guilt or shame might include such techniques as setting strict rules that embarrass offenders, such as publishing "John lists" in the newspaper to punish those arrested for soliciting prostitutes, or facilitating compliance by providing trash bins whose easy access might "shame" chronic litterers into using them. Ronald Clarke demonstrated that caller-ID in New Jersey resulted in significant reductions in the number of obscene phone calls. Caller-ID displays the telephone number of the party placing the call. The threat of exposure had a deterrent effect on the number of obscene calls reported to police.[80]

Crime Discouragers

The success of situational crime prevention may also rest on the behavior of people whose actions directly influence the prevention of crime; these are known as "crime discouragers." Discouragers can be grouped into three categories: *guardians,* who monitor targets (such as store security guards); *handlers,* who monitor potential offenders (such as parole officers and parents); and *managers,* who monitor places (such as homeowners and doormen). Marcus Felson notes that crime discouragers also have different levels of responsibility, ranging from highly personal involvement, such as the homeowner protecting her house and the parent controlling his children, to the most impersonal general involvement, such as a stranger who stops someone from shoplifting in the mall[81] (see Table 5.2).

Felson suggests that the concept of crime discouragement can be useful to plan situational crime-prevention tactics. More effective crime reduction may occur if (a) managers are given tools to better monitor places, (b) guardians are better equipped to protect targets, and (c) handlers are allowed to exert greater control over offenders. For example, a store clerk can have her discouragement role enhanced by giving her a mirror to watch merchandise and a button to summon supervisory help. A handler will become more effective if he is supplied with hidden cameras and eavesdropping devices. Managers given greater supervisory powers will help reduce crime by exerting better control over their charges.

Ramifications of Situational Prevention

Although situational crime prevention seems plausible, it can also produce unforeseen and unwanted consequences. Preventing crime from occurring in one locale does little to deter criminal motivation. People who desire the benefits of crime may choose alternative targets. Crime, then, is not prevented but deflected or displaced.[82] For example, beefed-up police patrols in one area may shift crimes to a more vulnerable neighborhood.[83] While crime displacement cannot be a solution to the general problem of crime, some evidence exists that deflection efforts can partially reduce the frequency of crime or produce less serious offense patterns.[84]

There is also the problem of **extinction:** Crime reduction programs may produce a short-term positive effect, but benefits dissipate as criminals adjust to new conditions. They learn to dismantle alarms or avoid patrols; they may become motivated to try new offenses they had previously avoided. For example, if every residence in a neighborhood is provided with a foolproof burglar alarm system, motivated offenders might then turn to armed robbery, a riskier and more violent crime.

While displacement and extinction may be a problem, Ronald Clarke and David Weisburd note a hidden benefit of situational crime prevention, **diffusion of benefits.**[85] Diffusion occurs when (a) efforts to prevent one crime cause the unintended prevention of another, and (b) crime control efforts in one locale reduce crime in other, nontarget areas.

Diffusion may be produced by two independent effects. Crime control efforts may deter criminals by causing them to fear apprehension. For example, video cameras set up in a mall to reduce shoplifting can also reduce property damage, because would-be vandals fear they are being caught on camera. One recent evaluation of a police program to crack down on drugs in targeted areas of Jersey

Table 5.2 Crime Discouragers

LEVEL OF RESPONSIBILITY	TYPES OF SUPERVISORS AND OBJECTS OF SUPERVISION		
	A. Guardians (monitoring suitable targets)	B. Handlers (monitoring likely offenders)	C. Managers (monitoring amenable places)
1. *Personal* (owners, family, friends)	Student keeps eye on own bookbag	Parent makes sure child gets home	Homeowner monitors area near home
2. *Assigned* (employees with specific assignment)	Store clerk monitors jewelry	Principal sends kids back to school	Doorman protects building
3. *Diffuse* (employees with general assignment)	Accountant notes shoplifting	School clerk discourages truancy	Hotel maid impairs trespasser
4. *General* (strangers, other citizens)	Bystander inhibits shoplifting	Stranger questions boys at mall	Customer observes parking structure

Source: Marcus Felson, "Those Who Discourage Crime," in John Eck and David Weisburd, *Crime and Place* (Monsey, NY: Criminal Justice Press, 1995), p. 59. Reprinted by permission.

City, New Jersey, also produced a reduction in public morals crimes.[86]

Another type of diffusion effect is called **discouragement.** By limiting one type of target, would-be lawbreakers may forgo other criminal activity because crime no longer pays. Lorraine Green found in her study of the effects of the SMART program (a drug enforcement program in Oakland, California that utilizes enforcement of municipal codes and nuisance abatement laws) that not only did drug dealing decrease in targeted areas but improvement was found in surrounding areas. She suggests that the program most likely discouraged buyers and sellers who saw familiar hangouts closed. The sign that drug dealing would not be tolerated probably decreased the total number of people involved in drug activity even though they did not operate in the targeted area.[87]

General Deterrence

According to the rational choice view, motivated, rational people will violate the law if left free and unrestricted. Rational offenders want the goods and services crime provides without having to work for them; they will commit crime if they do not fear apprehension and punishment. The concept of **general deterrence** holds that crime rates will be influenced and controlled by the threat of criminal punishment. If people fear apprehension and punishment, they will not risk breaking the law. An inverse relationship should thus exist between crime rates and the certainty, severity, and celerity (speed) of legal sanctions. If, for example, the punishment for a crime is increased and if the effectiveness and efficiency of the criminal justice system in enforcing the law prohibiting that act is improved, the number of people engaging in that act should decline.

The factors of certainty, severity, and celerity may also influence one another. For example, if a crime—say, robbery—is punished severely but few robbers are ever caught or punished, it is likely that the severity of punishment for robbery will not deter people from robbing. On the other hand, if the certainty of apprehension and conviction is increased by modern technology, more efficient police work, or some other factor, even minor punishments might deter the potential robber. Do these factors actually affect the decision to commit crime and consequently general crime rates?

Certainty of Punishment

According to deterrence theory, if the probability of arrest, conviction, and sanctioning increases, crime rates should decline. Rational offenders will soon realize that the increased likelihood of being punished outweighs any benefit they perceive from committing crimes.

A few research efforts do in fact show an inverse relationship between crime rates and the certainty of punishment.[88] In one often-cited study of arrest probability in Florida, Charles Tittle and Alan Rowe concluded that if police could make an arrest in at least 30% of all reported crimes, the crime rate would significantly decline.[89]

While these results seem to support the deterrent effect of certainty of punishment, the relationship between certainty and crime rates is far from settled. Most efforts have found little relationship between the likelihood of being arrested or imprisoned and corresponding crime rates.[90]

One reason for this ambivalent finding is that the certainty of punishment–crime association may be both crime- and group-specific. For example, research by Jiang Wu and Allen Liska found the effect to be race-specific: African American arrest probability influences African American

The concept of general deterrence holds that crime rates will be influenced and controlled by the threat of criminal punishment. If people fear apprehension and punishment, they will not risk breaking the law. This mock "tombstone" warning would-be hunters of the consequences of their actions is an attempt to reduce the incidence of poaching though a general deterrence strategy. Would you take a chance on illegal hunting after seeing this rather graphic warning?

offense rates alone, while white arrest probabilities affect white offending patterns. Wu and Liska conclude that in large cities the threat of arrest is communicated within neighborhoods and has an independent effect on residents of each racial grouping.[91]

Some research efforts have found a crime-specific deterrent effect. For example, Edwin Zedlewski's research shows that increased certainty of arrest helps lower the burglary rate, while larceny rates remain unaffected by law enforcement efforts.[92]

THE EFFECT OF POLICE ACTIONS. If the increased certainty of apprehension and punishment deters criminal behavior, it follows that increasing the number of police officers on the street should be able to bring the crime rate down. Moreover, if these police officers are active and aggressive crimefighters, would-be criminals should be con-

vinced that the risk of apprehension outweighs the benefits they can gain from crime.

There has been some debate as to whether the mere number of police officers on the street can bring the crime rate down. Some authors, such as David Bayley, have been skeptical that police presence is actually a crime deterrent.[93] Bayley's suspicions are justified by numerous studies that failed to show that increasing the number of police officers in a community can lower crime rates.[94]

While these results are discouraging, the lack of association between police presence and crime rates may be a result of the methodological difficulty in measuring a police-crime association. One problem is that at times when crime rates are high and increasing, communities begin to add police officers. The number of officers increases along with the crime rate, making it appear that adding police actually increases community crime rates!

A recent, more sophisticated study conducted by Thomas Marvell and Carlisle Moody solves some of these methodological problems. They found that adding police may actually reduce crime rates. They estimate that for every officer added, there would be 24 fewer crimes per year.[95] Marvell and Moody used aggregate state level data in their analysis, so it is difficult to conclude that adding police would be beneficial in every community. Nonetheless, their research seems to indicate that adding police officers may in the long run provide a general deterrent effect.

POLICE EXPERIMENTS. Some police departments have conducted experiments to determine whether increasing police activities or allocation of services can influence crime rates. Perhaps the most famous experiment to evaluate the general deterrent effect of police activity was conducted by the Kansas City, Missouri, police department.[96] To evaluate the effectiveness of police patrols, 15 independent police beats or districts were divided into three groups. The first retained a normal police patrol; the second (*proactive*) was supplied with two to three times the normal amount of patrol forces; and the third (*reactive*) eliminated its preventive patrol entirely, and police officers responded only when summoned by citizens to the scene of a crime. Surprisingly, data from the Kansas City study indicated that these variations in patrol techniques had little effect on the crime patterns in the 15 locales. The presence or absence of patrol forces did not seem to affect residential or business burglaries, auto thefts, larcenies involving auto accessories, robberies, vandalism, or other criminal behavior. Variations in police patrol techniques appeared to have little effect on citizens' attitudes toward the police, their satisfaction with police, or their fear of future criminal behavior.

Other police departments have instituted **crackdowns**—sudden changes in police activity designed to increase the communicated threat or actual certainty of punishment—to lower crime rates. For example, a police task force targets street-level narcotics dealers by using undercover agents and surveillance cameras in known

Table 5.3 Examples of Police Crackdowns

Police crackdowns can target specific neighborhoods or specific offenses, and their duration can range from a few weeks to several years. The following illustrate this range. Initial and residual deterrent effects varied, sometimes based on factors outside the scope of the crackdowns themselves.

Drug crackdown, Washington, D.C. A massive police presence—60 police officers per day and a parked police trailer—in the Hanover Place neighborhood open-air drug market provided an effective initial deterrent.

Lynn, Massachusetts, open-air heroin market. A four-year crackdown using 4 to 6 police officers led to 140 drug arrests in the first ten months and increased demand for drug treatment.

Operation Clean Sweep, Washington, D.C. The city allocated 100 to 200 officers—many on overtime—to 59 drug markets, making 60 arrests a day. Tactics included roadblocks, observation of open-air markets, "reverse-buy" sell-and-bust by undercover officers, and seizure of cars.

Repeat Call Address Policing (RECAP) Experiment, Minneapolis. A special unit of 5 police officers attempted to reduce calls for service from 125 residential addresses by increasing their presence with landlords and tenants. This short-term targeting of resources led to a 15% drop in calls from these addresses, compared to 125 control addresses.

Nashville, Tennessee, patrol experiment. A sharp increase in moving patrols at speeds under 20 miles per hour in four high-crime neighborhoods netted a measurable decrease in Type 1 index crime during two short crackdowns (11 days and 15 days).

Disorder crackdown in Washington, D.C. Massive publicity accompanied a crackdown on illegal parking and disorder that was attracting street crime to the Georgetown area of the city. Police raised their weekend manpower 30% and installed a trailer at a key intersection to book arrestees.

New York City subway crackdown. This massive crackdown involved increasing the number of police officers from 1,200 to 3,100, virtually guaranteeing an officer for every train and every station. Crime fell during the first two years of the crackdown but rose again during the following six years.

Cheshire, England, drunk-driving crackdowns. During two short-term crackdowns, one accompanied by continuing publicity, police increased breathalyzer tests up to sixfold between 10 P.M. and 2 A.M. Significant deterrent effects continued up to six months after the crackdowns ceased.

London prostitution crackdown. Stepped up arrests of prostitutes, pimps, and brothel keepers—combined with cautions of their customers—succeeded in reducing "curb crawling," with no displacement.

New Zealand drunk-driving crackdowns. Deterrent effects of two short-term crackdowns were felt even before they began, because of intensive publicity about the impending crackdowns and stepped up administration of breathalyzer tests.

Source: Lawrence Sherman, "Police Crackdowns," *NIJ Reports,* March/April 1990, p. 3.

drug-dealing locales. An analysis of 18 police crackdowns by Lawrence Sherman indicates that they may have an initial deterrent effect on controlling crime that suffers diffusion over time. Table 5.3 describes various police crackdowns.[97]

Severity of Punishment

The introduction or threat of severe punishments should also bring the crime rate down. Some studies have found that increasing sanction levels can in fact control common criminal behaviors. For example, Gary Green has shown that they have an effect for at least one crime: using an illegal, unauthorized descrambler to obtain pay cable television programs.[98] Green first determined how many people out of a sample of 3,500 in a western town were using a descrambler and avoiding payments to the local cable company. Threatening letters were sent to the 67 violators, conveying the general message that illegal theft of cable signals would be criminally prosecuted; the letter did not indicate that the subject's personal violation had been discovered. Green found that about two-thirds of the 67 violators reacted to the threat by desisting and trying to hide their

crime by removing the illegal device; a six-month follow-up showed that the intervention had a long-lasting effect.

While the Green research shows that the threat of strict punishment can deter crime, there is little consensus that draconian sanctions can alone reduce criminal activities. H. Laurence Ross's analysis of the deterrent effects of anti-drunk-driving laws on motor vehicular violations is an example of the limited utility of sanctioning severity. Ross found that when laws are toughened, there is a short-term deterrent effect. However, because the likelihood of getting caught is relatively low, the impact of deterrent measures on alcohol-impaired driving is negligible over the long term.[99] In a later study, Ross, along with Richard McCleary and Gary LaFree, evaluated the effect of a new law in Arizona that mandated jail sentences for drunk-driving convictions; time series analysis indicated that the new law had little deterrent effect.[100]

Research has also been devoted to the effect that firearm sentencing laws has on violent crime rate. These laws provide expanded and mandatory sentences for felonies committed with guns. Some research efforts claim that these laws can lower crime rates, while others question their deterrent effect.[101] A recent study of firearm control by Thomas Marvell and Carlisle Moody suggests that these controls may reduce crime in some states but that there is little evidence that they can reduce crime or increase the prison population on a national level.[102]

In sum, there is little evidence that increasing the punishments for specific crimes can alone deter their occurrence.

The Special Case of Capital Punishment

It stands to reason that if punishment severity can have a deterrent effect on crime, fear of the death penalty, the ultimate legal deterrent, should significantly reduce murder rates. Because no one denies its emotional impact, failure of the death penalty to deter violent crime jeopardizes the validity of the entire deterrence concept.

Various studies have tested the assumption that capital punishment deters violent crime. The research can be divided into three types: immediate impact studies, comparative research, and time series analysis.

IMMEDIATE IMPACT STUDIES. If capital punishment is a deterrent, the reasoning goes, it should have the greatest impact after a well-publicized execution has taken place. Robert Dann began testing this assumption in 1935 when he chose five highly publicized executions of convicted murderers in different years and determined the number of homicides in the 60 days before and after each execution.[103] He found that each 120-day period had approximately the same number of homicides, as well as the same number of days on which homicides occurred. Dann's study revealed that an average of 4.4 more homicides occurred during the 60 days following an execution than during those preceding it, suggesting that the overall impact of executions might actually *increase* the incidence of homicide.

That executions may actually increase the likelihood of murder was labeled by William Bowers and Glenn Pierce as the **brutalization effect.** They suggested that potential criminals model their behavior after state authorities: If the government can kill its enemies, so can they.[104] The brutalization effect was more recently encountered by John Cochran, Mitchell Chamlin, and Mark Seth when they studied the influence of a well-publicized execution in Oklahoma: After the execution, murders of strangers actually increased by one per month.[105]

The findings of some criminologists have indicated that in the short run executing criminals can bring the murder rate down. David Phillips studied the immediate effect of executions in Britain from 1858 to 1914 and found a temporary deterrent effect based on the publicity following the execution.[106] A more contemporary (1950 to 1980) evaluation of executions in the United States by Steven Stack concluded that capital punishment does indeed have an immediate impact and that 16 well-publicized executions may have saved 480 lives.[107]

In sum, a number of criminologists find that executions actually increase murder rates, while others argue that their immediate impact can lower murder rates.

COMPARATIVE RESEARCH. Another type of research compares the murder rates in jurisdictions that have abolished the death penalty with the rates of those that have the death penalty. Using this approach, Karl Schuessler analyzed 11 states' murder rates for the years 1930 to 1949 while considering their "execution risk" (the numbers of executions for murder per 1,000 homicides per year). His conclusion: Homicide rates and execution risks move independently of each other.[108] Two pioneering studies, one by Thorsten Sellin (1959) and the other by Walter Reckless (1969), also showed little difference in the murder rates of adjacent states, regardless of their use of the death penalty; capital punishment did not appear to influence the reported rate of homicide.[109]

More recent updates of research have also shown little reason to believe that executions deter homicide.[110] In one sophisticated study, Derral Cheatwood identified 293 pairs of counties in the United States and compared their murder rates while also considering whether they were located in a state having a death penalty statute, the number of people on death row, and the number of people executed since 1976. His conclusion: Having and using a death penalty has no deterrent effect on violent crime rates.[111]

The failure to show a deterrent effect of the death penalty is not limited to cross-state comparisons. Research by Dane Archer, Rosemary Gartner, and Marc Beittel in 14 nations around the world found little evidence that countries with a death penalty have lower violence rates than those without; homicide rates actually decline after capital punishment is abolished, a direct contradiction to its supposed deterrent effect.[112]

TIME SERIES ANALYSIS. The development of econometric statistical analysis has allowed researchers to accurately gauge whether the murder rate changes when death penalty statutes are created or eliminated. The most widely cited study is Isaac Ehrlich's 1975 work, which made use of national crime and execution data.[113] According to Ehrlich, the perception of execution risk is an important determinant of whether one individual will murder another. As a result of his analysis, Ehrlich concluded that each individual execution per year in the United States would save seven or eight people from being victims of murder.

Ehrlich's research has been widely cited by advocates of the death penalty as empirical proof of the deterrent effect of capital punishment. However, subsequent research that attempted to replicate Ehrlich's analysis showed that his approach was flawed and that capital punishment is no more effective as a deterrent than life imprisonment.[114]

In sum, studies that have attempted to show the deterrent effect of capital punishment on the murder rate indicate that the execution of convicted criminals has relatively little influence on behavior.[115] While it is still uncertain why the threat of capital punishment has failed as a deterrent, the cause may lie in the nature of homicide itself: Murder is often an expressive "crime of passion" involving people who know each other and who may be under the influence of drugs and alcohol; murder is also found to be a by-product of the criminal activity of people who suffer from the burdens of poverty and income inequality.[116] These factors may either prevent or inhibit rational evaluation of the long-term consequences of an immediate violent act.

The failure of the "ultimate deterrent" to deter the "ultimate crime" has been used by critics to question the validity of the general deterrence hypothesis that severe punishments will reduce crime rates. In general, there is little direct evidence that the severity of punishments alone can reduce or eliminate crime.

Perception and Deterrence

A core element of general deterrence theory is that people who believe that they are likely to be caught and severely punished will abstain from crime; thus, deterrence theory would be discredited if perceptions of future punishment have little or no effect on behavior.[117]

Research measuring the association between the perception of punishment and deterrence has at best been inconclusive. Some efforts have found that the greater the perceived risk of apprehension, the less likely criminals are willing to risk crime.[118] However, others have found little association between fear of future punishments and criminal activity.[119]

Where deterrence has been found, it is the certainty and not the severity of punishment that seems to influence people.[120] A cross-sectional survey by Steven Klepper and Daniel Nagin found that people who believe they will be caught and subjected to criminal prosecution are less likely to engage in tax evasion.[121] Scott Decker and his associates found that the perceived risk of getting caught influenced active burglars, while the threat of severe punishments had relatively little deterrent effect.[122] These research efforts suggest that perceived risk of apprehension rather than punishment severity can deter active criminal offenders.

One criticism of this **perceptual deterrence** research is that it usually involves samples of noncriminals, such as college students, and crimes of minor seriousness, such as smoking marijuana. Experienced offenders, who are more criminally motivated and less committed to moral values, may be less likely to be deterred by the perception that they will be punished in the future.[123]

There are indications that experienced offenders are in fact the ones least threatened by the idea of future punishment.[124] Research by Eleni Apospori, Geoffrey Alpert, and Raymond Paternoster found that prior sanctions actually lower the perception that crime is a risky undertaking; criminals with the greatest number of prior convictions have the lowest fear of legal sanctions.[125] Perhaps punishments were less fearsome than they had anticipated; only the most severe and draconian punishments seem to have any influence on experienced criminals.[126]

In sum, research measuring the perceptions of punishment seem in sync with studies using aggregate criminal justice data to determine deterrent effects. The certainty of punishment seems to have a greater influence on the choice of crime than the severity of punishment, and people who believe they are certain to be arrested and punished for a crime are less likely to break the law regardless of the severity of the punishment.[127] Nonetheless, there is little clear-cut evidence that either the perception or the reality of punishment can deter most crimes.

Informal Sanctions

Evidence is accumulating that the fear of **informal sanctions** may have a greater crime-reducing impact than the fear of formal legal punishments.

Informal sanctions occur when significant others, such as parents, peers, neighbors, and teachers, direct their disapproval, anger, and indignation toward an offender. If this happens, law violators run the risk of feeling shame, being embarrassed, and suffering a loss of respect.[128] Can the fear of public humiliation deter crime?

Research efforts have in fact established the influence of informal sanctions. In a national survey of almost 2,000 subjects, Charles Tittle found that perception of informal sanctions was a more effective determinant of deterrence than perception of formal sanctions.[129] Tittle concluded that social control seems to be rooted almost entirely in how people perceive negative reactions from interpersonal acquaintances (family, friends), while formal sanctions (arrest, prison) are irrelevant to the general public. Tittle found that legal sanctions do no more than supplement informal control processes by influencing a small segment of "criminally inclined" persons.[130]

Other studies have also found that people who are committed to conventional moral values and believe crime to be "sinful" are unlikely to violate the law.[131] Evidence from Britain shows that efforts to control drunk driving by shaming offenders produced a moral climate that helped reduce its incidence.[132] Perhaps the same moral effect can help reduce drug use in the United States.

Those fearful of being rejected by family and peers are also reluctant to engage in deviant behavior.[133] Two factors seem to stand out: personal shame over violating the law and the fear of public humiliation if the deviant behavior becomes public knowledge. In a series of studies, Harold Grasmick and Robert Bursik found that people who say that involvement in crime will cause them to feel ashamed are less likely to commit theft, fraud, and motor vehicular offenses than those people who report not feeling ashamed about crime.[134] People have been found to be more likely to respond to antilittering drives and anti-drunk-driving campaigns if the thought of being accused of littering or driving drunk makes them feel ashamed or embarrassed.[135] There is also evidence that women are much more likely to fear shame and embarrassment than men, a finding that may help explain gender differences in the crime rate.[136]

Other research efforts have also found that fear of shame and embarrassment can be a powerful deterrent to crime.[137] In one study, Kirk Williams and Richard Hawkins found that spouse abusers were more afraid of social costs (for example, loss of friends and family disapproval) than they were of legal punishments (such as going to jail). Williams and Hawkins found that the potential for self-stigma and personal humiliation was the greatest deterrent to crime.[138]

The effect of informal sanctions may vary according to the cohesiveness of community structure and type of crime. Informal sanctions may be most effective in highly unified areas where everyone knows one another and the crime cannot be hidden from public view. The threat of informal sanctions may also have the greatest influence on instrumental crimes, which involve planning, and not on impulsive or expressive criminal behaviors or those associated with substance abuse.[139]

This research seems to indicate that public education on the social cost of crime that stresses the risk of shame and humiliation may be a more effective crime-prevention tool than the creation and distribution of legal punishments; potential offenders may be deterred if they can be convinced that crime is sinful or immoral.[140]

General Deterrence in Review

Some experts, such as Ernest Van Den Haag, believe that the purpose of the law and justice system is to create a "threat system."[141] That is, the threat of legal punishment should, on the face of it, deter lawbreakers through fear. Who among us can claim that they never had an urge to commit crime but were deterred by fear of discovery and its consequences? Nonetheless, the relationship between crime rates and deterrent measures is far less than choice theorists might expect. Despite efforts to punish criminals and make them fear crime, there is little evidence that the fear of apprehension and punishment can reduce crime rates. How can this discrepancy be explained?

First, deterrence theory assumes a rational offender who weighs the costs and benefits of a criminal act before deciding on a course of action. There is reason to believe that in many instances, criminals are desperate people acting under the influence of drugs and alcohol or suffering from personality disorders. Surveys show a significant portion of all offenders, perhaps up to 80%, are substance abusers.[142] Chronic offender research indicates that a relatively small group of offenders commit a significant percentage of all serious crimes. Some psychologists believe that this select group suffer from an innate or inherited emotional state that renders them both (a) incapable of fearing punishment and (b) less likely to appreciate the consequences of crime.[143] It is likely that the threat of future punishment has little deterrent effect on these people.

Second, many offenders are members of what is referred to as the underclass—people cut off from society, lacking the education and skills they need to be in demand in the modern economy.[144] It may be unlikely that such desperate people will be deterred from crime by fear of punishment because, in reality, they perceive few other options for success.

Third, as Beccaria's famous equation tells us, the threat of punishment involves not only its severity but its certainty and speed. Our legal system is not very effective. Only 10% of all serious offenses result in apprehension (since half go unreported and police make arrests in about 20% of reported crimes). Police routinely do not arrest suspects in personal disputes, even when they lead to violence.[145] As apprehended offenders are processed through all the stages of the criminal justice system, the odds of their receiving serious punishment diminishes. Thus, some offenders may believe that they will not be severely punished for their acts and consequently have little regard for the law's deterrent power.

As you may recall, only offenders who suffer the most severe and draconian sanctions are likely to fear future legal punishments. Raymond Paternoster found that adolescents, a group responsible for a disproportionate amount of crime, may be well aware that the juvenile court "is generally lenient in the imposition of meaningful sanctions on even the most serious offenders."[146] Research by James Williams and Daniel Rodeheaver shows that even those accused of murder, the most serious of crimes, are often convicted of lesser offenses and spend relatively short amounts of time behind bars.[147] In making their "rational choice," offenders may be aware that the deterrent effect of the law is minimal.

Specific Deterrence

The general deterrence model focuses on future or potential criminals. In contrast, the theory of **specific** (also called special or particular) **deterrence** holds that criminal sanctions should be so powerful that known criminals will never repeat their criminal acts. For example, the drunk driver whose sentence is a large fine and a week in the county jail will, it is hoped, be convinced that the price to be paid for drinking and driving is too great to consider future violations; burglars who spend five years in a tough, maximum-security prison should find their enthusiasm for theft dampened.[148] In principle, punishment works if a connection can be established between the planned action and memories of its consequence. If these recollections are adequately intense, the action will be prevented or reduced in frequency.[149]

Does Specific Deterrence Deter Crime?

At first glance, specific deterrence does not seem to work, as a majority of known criminals are not deterred by their punishment. Chronic offender research indicates that a stay in a juvenile justice facility has little deterrent effect on the likelihood that a persistent delinquent will become an adult criminal.[150] It comes as no surprise, then, that most prison inmates had prior records of arrest and conviction before their current offense.[151] About two-thirds of all convicted felons are rearrested within three years of their release from prison, and those who have been punished in the past are the most likely to recidivate.[152] Research also shows that offenders sentenced to prison have no lower rates of recidivism than those receiving community sentences for similar crimes. For example, David Weisburd, Elin Waring and Ellen Chayet found that white-collar offenders who received a prison sentence were as likely to recidivate as a matched group of offenders who received an alternative sanction.[153]

Some research efforts have actually shown that rather than reducing the frequency of crime, punishment increases reoffending rates.[154] It is possible that (a) punishment brings defiance rather than deterrence or (b) the stigma of apprehension helps lock offenders into a criminal career instead of convincing them to avoid one.

Connections

Theoretically, experiencing punishment should deter future crime. However, punishment stigmatizes people and "spoils" their identity, a turn of events that may encourage antisocial behavior. The two factors may cancel each other out, helping to explain why punishment does not substantially reduce future criminality. The effects of stigma and negative labels are discussed further in Chapter 8.

There does exist some empirical research indicating that in a few instances, offenders who receive harsher punishments than their peers will be less likely to recidivate, or if they do commit crimes again, they will do so less frequently.[155] However, the consensus is that the association between crime and specific deterrent measures remains uncertain at best.

The Domestic Violence Studies

Efforts to reduce the incidence of spouse abuse and domestic violence through mandatory arrest policies showcase the specific deterrent effect of legal punishment. The groundbreaking research was conducted in Minneapolis, Minnesota, by Lawrence Sherman and Richard Berk.[156] Sherman and Berk examined the effect of police action on domestic dispute cases. They had police officers randomly assign treatments to the domestic assault cases they encountered on their beat. One approach was to give some sort of advice and mediation, another was to send the assailant from the home for a period of eight hours, and the third was to arrest the assailant. They found that where police took formal action (arrest), the chance of recidivism was substantially less than when they took less punitive measures, such as warning the offenders or ordering them out of the house for a cooling-off period. A six-month follow-up found that only 10% of the arrested group repeated their violent behavior, compared to 19% of the advised group and 24% of the sent-away group. Sherman and Berk concluded that a formal arrest, the most punitive alternative, was the most effective means of controlling domestic violence, regardless of what happened to the offender in court. This research finding was considered highly significant, because it was one of the few instances in which a specific deterrent effect could be identified.

While the findings of the Minneapolis experiment seemed to affirm the effectiveness of specific deterrence, efforts to replicate the experimental design in other locales, including Omaha, Milwaukee, Atlanta, Colorado Springs, Dade County (Florida), and Charlotte (North Carolina), have so far failed to duplicate the original findings.[157] In these locales, formal arrest was not a greater deterrent to spouse abuse than warning or advising the assailant; in fact in some cases, the frequency of domestic assaults increased after arrest.[158] There are also indications that police officers in the original Minneapolis experiment failed to assign cases in a random fashion, which altered the experimental findings.[159]

Despite these setbacks, it is still unsure whether the findings of the original Minneapolis experiment were invalid. An in-depth review of the replication studies concludes that the available information is still incomplete and inadequate for a definitive statement about the effect of arrest on spousal abuse.[160]

It may then be premature to dismiss the specific deterrent effect of arrest on spouse abuse. There are indications that specific deterrence policies can, under some circumstances, deter domestic abuse. One study showed that a period of short-term custody lasting about three hours may reduce recidivism; unfortunately, deterrent effects decayed over time.[161] Evidence also exists that one subset of offenders—those with a greater stake in conformity—are more deterrable than those with little social commitment; deterrence seems to work with those who have more to lose, such as a high-paying job.[162]

Police officers help a victim of domestic violence escape through a window in her Florida home. Efforts to reduce the incidence of spouse abuse and domestic violence through mandatory arrest policies showcase the specific deterrent effect of legal punishment. Early research efforts conducted by Larry Sherman and Richard Berk in Minneapolis found a specific deterrent effect. However, subsequent efforts failed to replicate the initial findings. While the replications yielded disappointing results, there are indications that specific deterrence policies can, under some circumstances, deter domestic abuse. For example, specific deterrence seems to work better with those who have more to lose, such as a high-paying job.

It is difficult to explain why the specific deterrent effect of arrest can be absent, decay over time, or only affect a subset of offenders (those married and employed).[163] It is possible that offenders who suffer arrest are initially fearful of punishment but eventually replace fear with anger and violent intent toward their mate when their case does not result in severe punishment. However, research on the effectiveness of prosecution of spousal abusers indicates that little specific deterrence occurs even when an abuse case is brought before the criminal court.[164]

Pain Versus Shame

If current efforts at specific deterrence are less than successful, should new approaches be attempted? In their two widely discussed works on specific deterrence, criminologists Graeme Newman and John Braithwaite take opposing approaches to reforming criminals.

Newman embraces traditional concepts of specific deterrence in his book *Just and Painful*.[165] However, he adds a new wrinkle in his provocative suggestion that society should return to the use of corporal punishment. He advocates the use of electric shocks to punish offenders because they are over with quickly, they have no lasting effect, and they can easily be adjusted to fit the severity of a crime.

According to Newman, corporal punishment could be used as an alternative sanction to fill the gap between the severe punishment of prison and the nonpunishment of probation. Electric shocks can be controlled and calibrated to fit the crime. For violent crimes in which the victim was terrified and humiliated and for which a local community does not wish to incarcerate, a violent corporal punishment should be considered, such as whipping. In these cases, humiliation of the offender is seen as justifiably deserved. In sum, Newman embraces specific deterrence strategies if they can be relatively inexpensive, immediate, and individualized and leave no lasting disabilities. His ideas received national attention in 1994 when a young American boy was flogged in Singapore after he pled guilty to vandalizing property. The Singapore incident produced a nationwide debate over the value of corporal punishment.

Braithwaite's *Crime, Shame and Reintegration* takes a radically different approach from Newman's.[166] Braithwaite notes that countries, such as Japan, in which conviction for crimes brings an inordinate amount of shame have extremely low crime rates. In Japan, prosecution of the criminal proceeds only when the normal process of public apology, compensation, and forgiveness by the victim breaks down.

Shame is a powerful tool of informal social control. Citizens in cultures in which crime is not shameful do not internalize an abhorrence for crime because when they are punished, they view themselves as merely "victims" of the justice system; their punishment comes at the hands of neutral strangers being paid to act. In contrast, shaming relies on the participation of victims.[167]

Braithwaite divides the concept of shame into two distinct types. The most common form of shaming typically involves **stigmatization.** This form of shaming is an ongoing process of degradation in which the offender is branded as an evil person and cast out of society. Shaming can occur at a school disciplinary hearing or a criminal court trial. Bestowing stigma and degradations may have a general deterrent effect: It makes people afraid of social rejection and public humiliation. As a specific deterrent, stigma is doomed to failure, since people who suffer humiliation at the hands of the justice system "reject their rejectors" by joining a deviant subculture of like-minded people who, collectively, resist social control.

Braithwaite argues that crime control can be better achieved through a policy of **reintegrative shaming.** Here, disapproval is extended to the offenders' evil deed, while they are cast as respected people who can be reaccepted by society. A critical element of reintegrative shaming occurs when the offenders begin to understand and recognize their wrongdoing and shame themselves. To be reintegrative, shaming must be brief and controlled and then followed by "ceremonies" of forgiveness, apology, and repentance.

To prevent crime, Braithwaite charges, society must encourage reintegrative shaming. For example, the women's movement can reduce domestic violence by mounting a crusade to shame spouse abusers.[168] In addition, an effort must be made to create pride in solving problems nonviolently, in caring for others, and in respecting the rights of women.

As you may recall, there is evidence that the fear of personal shame can have a general deterrent effect. It may also be applied to produce specific deterrence. Braithwaite and Stephen Mugford report on attempts to apply reintegrative shaming techniques with juvenile offenders in Australia. One program brings offenders together with victims (so that they can experience shame) and with close family members and peers (who help with reintegration).[169] Efforts like these can humanize a system of justice that today relies on repression and not forgiveness as the basis of specific deterrence.

Rethinking Deterrence

So far both specific and general deterrence strategies have not yielded the results predicted by choice theorists. While a few studies have shown expected effects, there is still little conclusive evidence that formal sanctions can convince would-be criminals to forgo their intended behavior or convince experienced offenders that "crime does not pay."

In an important paper, Mark Stafford and Mark Warr have called for the reconceptualization of both specific and general deterrence.[170] They argue that these concepts should not be considered independent but rather interactive: Most people have had experience with the direct effect of punishment (specific deterrence) and the indirect effect of the fear of punishment (general deterrence). In addition, they may have experienced punishment avoidance, either getting away with crime themselves or knowing about others who have escaped detection or have been punished (vicarious deterrence). The total deterrent effect includes a combination of personal and vicarious experiences with punishment and its aftermath.

The two effects may cancel each other out, explaining in part the ambiguity of deterrent effects: An experienced criminal may instinctively fear apprehension, but his experiences tells him that the law's "bark is worse than its bite." A person with criminal friends may find his or her fear of punishment diminished when the friends describe how easy it is to get away with crime. Empirical research shows that people are in fact influenced by both general and specific deterrent effects and that both work in concert to influence behavior.[171] Stafford and Warr's views may help criminologists better understand the forces that promote deterrence so that the concept can be studied in a more rational fashion.

Incapacitation Strategies

It stands to reason that if more criminals were sent to prison, the crime rate should go down. Because most people age out of crime, the duration of a criminal career is limited. Placing offenders behind bars during their "prime crime" years should lessen their lifetime opportunity to commit crime. The shorter the span of opportunity, the fewer the number of offenses they can commit over their life course; hence, crime is reduced.

Seems logical, but does it work? For the past 20 years, there has been significant growth in the number and percentage of the population held in prison and jails; today, more than 1.5 million Americans are incarcerated. Advocates of incapacitation suggest that this effort has been responsible for the overall stabilization and actual decline in crime rates in the 1990s. Others suggest that this association is illusory and that a stable crime rate is actually controlled by such factors as the size of the teenage population, the threat of tough new mandatory sentences, a healthy economy, the initiation of tougher gun laws, the end of the "crack epidemic," and the implementation of tough and aggressive policing strategies in large cities such as New York.[172]

It is also possible that what appears to be an incapacitation effect may actually reflect the effect of some other legal phenomenon and not the fact that so many criminals are locked up. If, for example, the crime rate drops as more and more people are sent to prison, it would appear that incapacitation works. However, crime rates may really be dropping because potential criminals now fear punishment and are being deterred from crime. What appears to be an incapacitation effect may actually be an effect of general deterrence.[173]

Can Incapacitation Reduce Crime?

Research on the direct benefits of incapacitation has not shown that increasing the number of people behind bars or the length of their stay can effectively reduce crime. A number of studies have set out to measure the precise effect of incarceration rates on crime rates, and the results have not supported a strict incarceration policy. In an often-cited study, David Greenberg used prison and FBI index crime data to estimate the effect of imprisonment on crime rates. He found that if the prison population were cut in half, the crime rate would most likely go up only 4%; if prisons were entirely eliminated, crime might increase 8%.[174] Looking at this relationship from another perspective, if the average prison sentence were increased 50%, the crime rate might be reduced only 4%. Greenberg concluded that prisons may be terribly unpleasant, psychologically destructive, and at times dangerous to life and limb, but there is no compelling evidence that imprisonment substantially increases (or decreases) the likelihood of criminal involvement.[175]

Isaac Ehrlich obtained similar results in a study of prison rates and incapacitation; he estimated that a 50% reduction in average time served would result in a 4.6% increase in property crime and a 2.5% increase in violent crime.[176] Lee Bowker found that an increase in incarceration rates may actually lead to an increase in crime rates.[177]

A few studies have found an inverse relationship between incarceration rates and crime rates. Reuel Shinnar and Shlomo Shinnar's research on incapacitation in New York led them to conclude that a policy of mandatory prison sentences of 5 years for violent crime and 3 for property offenses could reduce the reported crime rate by a factor of four or five.[178] Similarly, Stephan Van Dine, Simon Dinitz, and John Conrad estimated that a mandatory prison sentence of 5 years for any felony offense could reduce the murder, rape, robbery, and serious assault rates by 17%. A similar sentence limited to repeat felons would reduce the rate of these crimes by 6%.[179]

With these few exceptions, existing research indicates that the crime control effects of a strict incarceration policy are modest at best.[180]

The Logic of Incarceration

Why hasn't an incarceration strategy worked? There is little evidence that incapacitating criminals will deter them from future criminality and even more reason to believe that they may be more inclined to commit crimes upon release. As you may recall, prison has few specific deterrent effects: The more prior incarceration experiences inmates had, the more likely they were to recidivate (and return to prison) within 12 months of their release.[181] Whatever reason they had to commit crime before their incarceration, there is little to suggest that a prison sentence will reduce those criminogenic forces. The criminal label precludes their entry into many legitimate occupations and solidifies their attachment to criminal careers.

The economics of crime suggest that if money can be made from criminal activity, there will always be someone to take the place of the incarcerated offender. New criminals will be recruited and trained, offsetting any benefit accrued by incarceration. Incarcerating established offenders may open new opportunities for competitors who were suppressed by the more experienced criminals. For example, the incarceration of organized crime members helped open drug markets to new gangs; the flow of narcotics into the country increased after organized crime leaders were imprisoned.

Incarceration may not work because the majority of criminal offenses are committed by teens and very young adult offenders who are unlikely to be sent to prison for a single felony conviction. Incarcerated criminals, aging behind bars, are already past the age where they are "at risk" to commit crime. A strict incarceration policy may result in people being kept in prison beyond the time they are a threat to society while a new cohort of high-rate adolescents are on the street.

It is also expensive to maintain an incapacitation strategy. The prison system costs billions of dollars each year. Even if incarceration could reduce the crime rate, the costs would be enormous. At a time of deficits and fiscal austerity, would U.S. taxpayers be willing to spend billions more on new prison construction and annual maintenance fees?

Selective Incapacitation: Three Strikes and You're Out

A more efficient incapacitation model is suggested by the "discovery" of the chronic career criminal. If in fact a relatively small number of people account for a relatively large percentage of the nation's crime rates, then an effort to incapacitate these few troublemakers might have a significant payoff. In an often-cited work, Peter Greenwood of the Rand Corporation suggested that a policy of **selective incapacitation** could be an effective crime-reduction strategy.[182] In his study of over 2,000 inmates serving time for theft offenses in California, Michigan, and Texas, he found that the selective incapacitation of chronic offenders could reduce the rate of robbery offenses by 15% and the inmate population by 5%.

According to Greenwood's model, chronic offenders can be distinguished on the basis of their offending patterns and lifestyle (for example, their employment record and history of substance abuse). Once identified, high-risk offenders would be eligible for sentencing enhancements that would substantially increase the time they serve in prison.

Another concept receiving widespread attention is the "three strikes and you're out" policy of giving people convicted of three violent offenses a mandatory life term without parole. Many states already have habitual offender laws that provide long (or life) sentences for repeat offenders. Criminologist Marc Mauer argues that such strategies, though compelling, will not work, because (1) most "three-time losers" are at the verge of aging out of crime anyway, (2) current sentences for violent crimes are already severe, (3) an expanding prison population will drive up already high prison costs, (4) there would be racial disparity in sentencing, and (5) the police would be in danger because two-time offenders would violently resist a third arrest, knowing they face a life sentence.[183]

Policy Implications of Choice Theory

From the origins of classical theory to the development of modern rational choice views, the belief that criminals choose to commit crime has had an important influence on the relationship between law, punishment, and crime. When police patrol in well-marked cars, it is assumed that their presence will deter would-be criminals. When the harsh realities of prison life are portrayed in movies and TV shows, the lesson is not lost on potential criminals. Nowhere is the idea that the threat of punishment can control crime more evident than in the implementation of tough mandatory criminal sentences to control violent crime and drug trafficking.

Despite its questionable deterrent effect, the death penalty is also viewed as an effective means of restricting criminal choice; at the least, it ensures that convicted criminals never get the opportunity to kill again. Many observers are dismayed because people who are convicted of murder sometimes kill again when released on parole. One study of 52,000 incarcerated murderers found that 810 had been previously convicted of murder and had killed 821 people following their previous release from prison.[184] About 9% of all inmates on death row have had prior convictions for homicide; if they had been executed for their first offense, hundreds of people would be alive today.[185]

So while research on the core principles of choice theory and deterrence theories produces mixed results, there is little doubt that these models have had an important impact on crime-prevention strategies.

The concept of criminal choice has also prompted the creation of justice policies referred to as **just desert.** The just desert position has been most clearly spelled out by criminologist Andrew Von Hirsch in his book *Doing Justice.*[186]

Von Hirsch suggests the concept of desert as a theoretical model to guide justice policy.[187] Von Hirsch's views can be summarized in these three statements:

1. Those who violate others' rights deserve to be punished.

2. We should not deliberately add to human suffering; punishment makes those punished suffer.

3. However, punishment may prevent more misery than it inflicts; this conclusion reestablishes the need for desert-based punishment.[188]

This utilitarian view is the key to the desert approach: Punishment is needed to preserve the social equity disturbed by crime; nonetheless, the severity of the punishment should be commensurate with the seriousness of the crime.

Desert theory is also concerned with the rights of the accused. It alleges that the rights of the person being punished should not be unduly sacrificed for the good of others (as with deterrence). The offender should not be treated as more (or less) **blameworthy** than is warranted by the character of his or her offense. For example, Von Hirsch asks the following question: If two crimes, A and B, are equally serious, but if severe penalties are shown to have a deterrent effect only with respect to A, would it be fair to punish the person who has committed crime A more harshly simply to deter others from committing the crime? Conversely, imposing a light sentence for a serious crime would be unfair, because it would treat the offender as being less blameworthy than he or she is. In sum, the just desert model suggests that retribution justifies punishment because people deserve what they get for past deeds. Punishment based on deterrence or incapacitation is wrong because it involves an offender's future actions, which cannot accurately be predicted. Punishment should be the same for all people who commit the same crime. Criminal sentences based on individual needs or characteristics are inherently unfair, as all people are equally blameworthy for their misdeeds.

The influence of Von Hirsch's views can be seen in sentencing models that give the same punishments to all people who commit the same type of crime.

Summary

Choice theory assumes that criminals carefully choose whether to commit criminal acts. These theories are summarized in Table 5.4. However, people are influenced by their fear of the criminal penalties associated with being caught and convicted for law violations. The more severe, certain, and swift the punishment, the more likely it is to control crime. The choice approach is rooted in the classical criminology of 18th-century social philosophers Cesare Beccaria and Jeremy Bentham.

Table 5.4 Choice Theories

THEORY	MAJOR PREMISE	STRENGTHS
Rational choice	Law-violating behavior is an event that occurs after offenders weigh information on their personal needs and the situational factors involved in the difficulty and risk of committing a crime.	Explains why high-risk youth do not constantly engage in delinquency acts. Relates theory to delinquency control policy. It is not limited by class or other social variables.
Routine activities	Crime and delinquency is a function of the presence of motivated offenders, the availability of suitable targets, and the absence of capable guardians.	Can explain fluctuations in crime and delinquency rates. Shows how victim behavior influences criminal choice.
General deterrence	People will commit crime and delinquency if they perceive that the benefits outweigh the risks. Crime is a function of the severity, certainty, and speed of punishment.	Shows the relationship between crime and punishment. Suggests a real solution to crime.
Specific deterrence	If punishment is severe enough, criminals will not repeat their illegal acts.	Provides a strategy to reduce crime.
Incapacitation	Keeping known criminals out of circulation will reduce crime rates.	Recognizes the role opportunity plays in criminal behavior. Provides solution to chronic offending.

The growth of positivist criminology, which stressed external causes of crime and rehabilitation of known offenders, reduced the popularity of the classical approach in the 20th century. However, in the late 1970s the concept of criminal choice once again became an important perspective of criminologists. Today, choice theorists view crime as offense- and offender-specific. Research shows that offenders consider their targets carefully before deciding on a course of action. By implication, crime can be prevented or displaced by convincing potential criminals that the risks of violating the law exceed the benefits.

Deterrence theory holds that if criminals are indeed rational, an inverse relationship should exist between punishment and crime. However, a number of factors confound the relationship. For example, if people do not believe they will be caught, even harsh punishment may not deter crime. Deterrence theory has been criticized on the grounds that it wrongfully assumes that criminals make a rational choice before committing crimes, it ignores the intricacies of the criminal justice system, and it does not take into account the social and psychological factors that may influence criminality. Research designed to test the validity of the deterrence concept has not indicated that deterrent measures actually reduce the crime rate.

Specific deterrence theory holds that the crime rate can be reduced if known offenders are punished so severely that they never commit crimes again. There is little evidence that harsh punishments actually reduce the crime rate. Incapacitation theory maintains that if deterrence does not work, the best course of action is to incarcerate known offenders for long periods of time so that they lack criminal opportunity. Research efforts have not provided clear-cut proof that increasing the number of people in prison—and increasing prison sentences—will reduce crime rates.

Choice theory has been influential in shaping public policy. The criminal law is designed to deter potential criminals and fairly punish those who have been caught engaging in illegal acts. Some courts have changed sentencing policies to adapt to classical principles, and the U.S. correctional system seems geared toward incapacitation and special deterrence. The renewed use of the death penalty is testimony to the importance of classical theory.

Key Terms

classical criminology
choice theory
utilitarianism
rational choice
crime displacement
offense-specific crime
offender-specific crime
capable guardians
motivated criminals
seductions of crime
situational crime
 prevention
defensible space
extinction

diffusion of benefits
discouragement
general deterrence
crackdowns
brutalization effect
perceptual deterrence
informal sanctions
specific deterrence
stigmatization
reintegrative shaming
selective incapacitation
just desert
blameworthy

Notes

1. Francis Edward Devine, "Cesare Beccaria and the Theoretical Foundations of Modern Penal Jurisprudence," *New England Journal on Prison Law* 7 (1982): 8–21.

2. Ibid.

3. Graeme Newman and Pietro Marongiu, "Penological Reform and the Myth of Beccaria," *Criminology* 28 (1990): 325–346.

4. Bob Roshier, *Controlling Crime* (Chicago: Lyceum Books, 1989), p. 10.

5. Jeremy Bentham, *A Fragment on Government and an Introduction to the Principle of Morals and Legislation,* ed. Wilfred Harrison (Oxford: Basil Blackwell, 1967).

6. Ibid., p. xi.

7. Robert Martinson, "What Works?—Questions and Answers About Prison Reform," *Public Interest* 35 (1974): 22–54.

8. Charles Murray and Louis Cox, *Beyond Probation* (Beverly Hills, Calif.: Sage, 1979).

9. Ronald Bayer, "Crime, Punishment and the Decline of Liberal Optimism," *Crime and Delinquency* 27 (1981): 190.

10. James Q. Wilson, *Thinking About Crime,* rev. ed. (New York: Vintage Books, 1983), p. 260.

11. Ibid., p. 128.

12. See, generally, Derek Cornish and Ronald Clarke, eds. *The Reasoning Criminal: Rational Choice Perspectives on Offending* (New York: Springer Verlag, 1986); Philip Cook, "The Demand and Supply of Criminal Opportunities," in *Crime and Justice,* vol. 7, ed. Michael Tonry and Norval Morris (Chicago: University of Chicago Press, 1986), pp. 1–28; Ronald Clarke and Derek Cornish, "Modeling Offender's Decisions: A Framework for Research and Policy," in *Crime and Justice,* vol. 6, ed. Michael Tonry and Norval Morris (Chicago: University of Chicago Press, 1985), pp. 147–187; Morgan Reynolds, *Crime by Choice: An Economic Analysis* (Dallas: Fisher Institute, 1985).

13. George Rengert and John Wasilchick, *Suburban Burglary: A Time and Place for Everything* (Springfield, Ill.: Charles C Thomas, 1985).

14. John McIver, "Criminal Mobility: A Review of Empirical Studies," in *Crime Spillover,* ed. Simon Hakim and George Rengert (Beverly Hills, Calif.: Sage, 1981), pp. 110–121; Carol Kohfeld and John Sprague, "Demography, Police Behavior, and Deterrence," *Criminology* 28 (1990): 111–136.

15. Derek Cornish and Ronald Clarke, "Understanding Crime Displacement: An Application of Rational Choice Theory," *Criminology* 25 (1987): 933–947.

16. Lloyd Phillips and Harold Votey, "The Influence of Police Interventions and Alternative Income Sources on the Dynamic Process of Choosing Crime as a Career," *Journal of Quantitative Criminology* 3 (1987): 251–274.

17. Ibid.

18. Michael Gottfredson and Travis Hirschi, *A General Theory of Crime* (Stanford, Calif.: Stanford University Press, 1990).

19. Liliana Pezzin, "Earnings Prospects, Matching Effects, and the Decision to Terminate a Criminal Career," *Journal of Quantitative Criminology* 11 (1995): 29–50.

20. Neal Shover, *Aging Criminals* (Beverly Hills, Calif.: Sage, 1985).

21. Ronald Akers, "Rational Choice, Deterrence and Social Learning Theory in Criminology: The Path Not Taken," *Journal of Criminal Law and Criminology* 81 (1990): 653–676.

22. Robert Agnew, "Determinism, Indeterminism, and Crime: An Empirical Exploration," *Criminology* 33 (1995): 83–109.

23. Ibid., pp. 103–104.

24. Bruce Jacobs, "Crack Dealers' Apprehension Avoidance Techniques: A Case of Restrictive Deterrence," *Justice Quarterly* 13 (1996): 359–381.

25. Ibid., p. 367.

26. Ibid., p. 372.

27. Michael Rand, *Crime and the Nation's Households, 1989* (Washington, D.C.: Bureau of Justice Statistics, 1990), p. 4.

28. Paul Cromwell, James Olson, and D'Aunn Wester Avery, *Breaking and Entering: An Ethnographic Analysis of Burglary* (Newbury Park, Calif.: Sage, 1989).

29. Ibid., pp. 30–32.

30. John Gibbs and Peggy Shelly, "Life in the Fast Lane: A Retrospective View by Commercial Thieves," *Journal of Research in Crime and Delinquency* 19 (1982): 229–230.

31. George Rengert and John Wasilchick, *Space, Time and Crime: Ethnographic Insights into Residential Burglary* (Washington, D.C.: National Institute of Justice, 1989); see also idem, *Suburban Burglary.*

32. Cromwell, Olson, and Avery, *Breaking and Entering.*

33. Jacobs, "Dealers' Apprehension Avoidance Tactics," p. 369.

34. Leanne Fiftal Alarid, James Marquart, Velmer Burton, Francis Cullen, and Steven Cuvelier, "Women's Roles in Serious Offenses: A Study of Adult Felons," *Justice Quarterly* 13 (1996): 431–454.

35. Ronald Clarke and Marcus Felson, "Introduction: Criminology, Routine Activity and Rational Choice," in *Routine Activity and Rational Choice* (New Brunswick, N.J.: Transaction Publishers, 1993), pp. 1–14.

36. Cromwell, Olson, and Avery, *Breaking and Entering.*

37. Andrew Buck, Simon Hakim, and George Rengert, "Burglar Alarms and the Choice Behavior of Burglars: A Suburban Phenomenon," *Journal of Criminal Justice* 21 (1993): 497–507.

38. Ralph Taylor and Stephen Gottfredson, "Environmental Design, Crime, and Prevention: An Examination of Community Dynamics," in *Communities and Crime,* ed. Albert Reiss and Michael Tonry (Chicago: University of Chicago Press, 1986), pp. 387–416.

39. Michael Costanzo, William Halperin, and Nathan Gale, "Criminal Mobility and the Directional Component in Journeys to Crime," in *Metropolitan Crime Patterns,* ed. Robert Figlio, Simon Hakim, and George Rengert (Monsey, N.Y.: Criminal Justice Press, 1986), pp. 73–95.

40. Garland White, "Neighborhood Permeability and Burglary Rates," *Justice Quarterly* 7 (1990): 57–67.

41. Ibid., p. 65.

42. James Massey, Marvin Krohn, and Lisa Bonati, "Property Crime and the Routine Activities of Individuals," *Journal of Research in Crime and Delinquency* 26 (1989): 378–400; note, however, that the findings here generally disagree with routine activities theory.

43. Kenneth Tunnell, *Choosing Crime* (Chicago: Nelson-Hall, 1992), p. 105.

44. Robert Sampson and Jacqueline Cohen, "Deterrent Effects of the Police on Crime: A Replication and Theoretical Extension," *Law and Society Review* 22 (1988): 163–188.

45. Marcus Felson et al. "Preventing Crime at Newark Subway Stations," *Security Journal* 1 (1990): 137–140.

46. Simha Landau and Daniel Fridman, "The Seasonality of Violent Crime: The Case of Robbery and Homicide in Israel," *Journal of Research in Crime and Delinquency* 30 (1993): 163–191.

47. Tunnell, *Choosing Crime,* p. 67.

48. Angela Browne and Kirk Williams, "Exploring the Effect of Resource Availability and the Likelihood of Female-Perpetrated Homicides," *Law and Society Review* 23 (1989): 89–93.

49. Ronald Clarke, "Situational Crime Prevention," in *Building a Safer Society: Strategic Approaches to Crime Prevention,* vol. 19 of *Crime and Justice, A Review of Research,* ed. Michael Tonry and David Farrington (Chicago: University of Chicago Press, 1995): 91–151.

50. Mark Warr, "Parents, Peers, and Delinquency," *Social Forces* 72 (1993): 247–264.

51. John Hagan, "Destiny and Drift: Subcultural Preferences, Status Attainments, and the Risks and Rewards of Youth," *American Sociological Review* 56 (1991): 567–582.

52. D. Wayne Osgood, Janet Wilson, Patrick O'Malley, Jerald Bachman, and Lloyd Johnston, "Routine Activities and Individual Deviant Behavior," *American Sociological Review* 61 (1996): 635–655.

53. Associated Press, "Thrift Hearings Resume Today in Senate," *Boston Globe,* 2 January 1991, p. 10.

54. Ronald Clarke and Patricia Harris, "Auto Theft and Its Prevention," in *Crime and Justice: An Annual Edition,* ed. Michael Tonry and Norval Morris (Chicago: University of Chicago Press, 1992), pp. 1–54, at 20–21.

55. Lisa Maher, "Hidden in the Light: Occupational Norms Among Crack-Using Street-Level Sex Workers," *Journal of Drug Issues* 26 (1996): 143–173.

56. John Petraitis, Brian Flay, and Todd Miller, "Reviewing Theories of Adolescent Substance Use: Organizing Pieces in the Puzzle," *Psychological Bulletin* 117 (1995): 67–86.

57. Bruce Jacobs, "Crack Dealers' Apprehension Avoidance Techniques: A Case of Restrictive Deterrence," *Justice Quarterly* 13 (1996): 359–381.

58. Ibid., p. 367.

59. Ibid., p. 368.

60. Patricia Morgan and Karen Ann Joe, "Citizens and Outlaws: The Private Lives and Public Lifestyles of Women in the Illicit Drug Economy," *Journal of Drug Issues* 26 (1996): 125–142.

61. Ibid., p. 136.

62. Richard Felson and Steven Messner, "To Kill or Not to Kill? Lethal Outcomes in Injurious Attacks," *Criminology* 34 (1996): 519–545.

63. James Wright and Peter Rossi, *Armed and Considered Dangerous: A Survey of Felons and Their Firearms* (Hawthorne, N.Y.: Aldine, 1983), pp. 141–159.

64. Eric Hickey, *Serial Murderers and Their Victims* (Pacific Grove, Calif.: Brooks/Cole, 1991), p. 84.

65. Scott Decker, "Deviant Homicide: A New Look at the Role of Motives and Victim-Offender Relationships," *Journal of Research in Crime and Delinquency* 33 (1996): 427–449.

66. Felson and Messner, "To Kill or Not to Kill?"

67. Christopher Birkbeck and Gary LaFree, "The Situational Analysis of Crime and Deviance," *American Review of Sociology* 19 (1993): 113–137; Karen Heimer and Ross Matsueda, "Role-Taking, Role Commitment, and Delinquency: A Theory of Differential Social Control," *American Sociological Review* 59 (1994): 111–131.

68. Jack Katz, *Seductions of Crime* (New York: Basic Books, 1988).

69. Bill McCarthy and John Hagan, "Mean Streets: The Theoretical Significance of Situational Delinquency Among Homeless Youths," *American Journal of Sociology* 3 (1992): 597–627.

70. Bill McCarthy, "Not Just 'For the Thrill of It': An Instrumentalist Elaboration of Katz's Explanation of Sneaky Thrill Property Crime," *Criminology* 33 (1995): 519–539.

71. George Rengert, "Spatial Justice and Criminal Victimization," *Justice Quarterly* 6 (1989): 543–564.

72. Oscar Newman, *Defensible Space: Crime Prevention Through Urban Design* (New York: Macmillan, 1973).

73. C. Ray Jeffery, *Crime Prevention Through Environmental Design* (Beverly Hills, Calif.: Sage, 1971).

74. See also Pochara Theerathorn, "Architectural Style, Aesthetic Landscaping, Home Value, and Crime Prevention," *International Journal of Comparative and Applied Criminal Justice* 12 (1988): 269–277.

75. Ronald Clarke, *Situational Crime Prevention: Successful Case Studies* (Albany, N.Y.: Harrow and Heston, 1992).

76. Marcus Felson, "Routine Activities and Crime Prevention," in *Studies on Crime and Crime Prevention, Annual Review,* vol. 1, National Council for Crime Prevention (Stockholm: Scandinavian University Press, 1992), pp. 30–34.

77. Barry Webb, "Steering Column Locks and Motor Vehicle Theft: Evaluations for Three Countries," in *Crime Prevention Studies,* ed. Ronald Clarke (Monsey, N.Y.: Criminal Justice Press, 1994), pp. 71–89.

78. Barbara Morse and Delbert Elliott, "Effects of Ignition Interlock Devices on DUI Recidivism: Findings from a Longitudinal Study in Hamilton County, Ohio," *Crime and Delinquency* 38 (1992): 131–157.

79. Nancy LaVigne, "Gasoline Drive-Offs: Designing a Less Convenient Environment," in *Crime Prevention Studies,* vol. 2, ed. Ronald Clarke (Monsey, N.Y.: Criminal Justice Press, 1994), pp. 91–114.

80. Ronald Clark, "Deterring Obscene Phone Callers: The New Jersey Experience," *Situational Crime Prevention,* ed. Ronald Clark (Albany, N.Y.: Harrow and Heston, 1992), pp. 124–132.

81. Marcus Felson, "Those Who Discourage Crime" in *Crime and Place, Crime Prevention Studies,* vol. 4, ed. John Eck and David Weisburd (Monsey, N.Y.: Criminal Justice Press, 1995), pp. 53–66; John Eck, *Drug Markets and Drug Places: A Case-Control Study of the Spatial Structure of Illicit Drug Dealing.* Doctoral dissertation, University of Maryland, College Park, 1994.

82. Robert Barr and Ken Pease, "Crime Placement, Displacement, and Deflection," in *Crime and Justice, A Review of Research,* vol. 12, ed. Michael Tonry and Norval Morris (Chicago: University of Chicago Press, 1990), pp. 277–319.

83. Clarke, *Situational Crime Prevention,* p. 27.

84. Ibid., p. 35.

85. Ronald Clarke and David Weisburd, "Diffusion of Crime Control Benefits: Observations of the Reverse of Displacement," in *Crime Prevention Studies,* vol. 2, ed. Ronald Clarke (New York: Criminal Justice Press, 1994).

86. David Weisburd and Lorraine Green, "Policing Drug Hot Spots: The Jersey City Drug Market Analysis Experiment," *Justice Quarterly* 12 (1995): 711–734.

87. Lorraine Green, "Cleaning Up Drug Hot Spots in Oakland, California: The Displacement and Diffusion Effects," *Justice Quarterly* 12 (1995): 737–754.

88. R. Yeaman, *The Deterrent Effectiveness of Criminal Justice Sanction Strategies: Summary Report* (Washington, D.C.: U.S. Government Printing Office, 1972); see, generally, Jack Gibbs, "Crime Punishment and Deterrence," *Social Science Quarterly* 48 (1968): 515–530.

89. Charles Tittle and Alan Rowe, "Certainty of Arrest and Crime Rates: A Further Test of the Deterrence Hypothesis," *Social Forces* 52 (1974): 455–462.

90. Robert Bursik, Harold Grasmick, and Mitchell Chamlin, "The Effect of Longitudinal Arrest Patterns on the Development of Robbery Trends at the Neighborhood Level," *Criminology* 28 (1990): 431–450; Theodore Chiricos and Gordon Waldo, "Punishment and Crime: An Examination of Some Empirical Evidence," *Social Problems* 18 (1970): 200–217.

91. Jiang Wu and Allen Liska, "The Certainty of Punishment: A Reference Group Effect and Its Functional Form," *Criminology* 31 (1993): 447–464.

92. Edwin Zedlewski, "Deterrence Findings and Data Sources: A Comparison of the Uniform Crime Rates and the National Crime Surveys," *Journal of Research in Crime and Delinquency* 20 (1983): 262–276.

93. David Bayley, *Policing for the Future* (New York: Oxford, 1994).

94. For a review, see Thomas Marvell and Carlisle Moody, "Specification Problems, Police Levels, and Crime Rates," *Criminology* 34 (1996): 609–646.

95. Ibid., p. 632.

96. George Kelling, Tony Pate, Duane Dieckman, and Charles Brown, *The Kansas City Preventive Patrol Experiment: A Summary Report* (Washington, D.C.: Police Foundation, 1974).

97. Lawrence Sherman, "Police Crackdowns," *NIJ Reports,* March/April 1990, pp. 2–6.

98. Gary Green, "General Deterrence and Television Cable Crime: A Field Experiment in Social Crime," *Criminology* 23 (1986): 629–645.

99. H. Laurence Ross, "Implications of Drinking-and-Driving Law Studies for Deterrence Research," in *Critique and Explanation, Essays in Honor of Gwynne Nettler,* ed. Timothy Hartnagel and Robert

Silverman (New Brunswick, N.J.: Transaction Books, 1986), pp. 159–171.

100. H. Laurence Ross, Richard McCleary, and Gary LaFree, "Can Mandatory Jail Laws Deter Drunk Driving? The Arizona Case," *Journal of Criminal Law and Criminology* 81 (1990): 156–167.

101. For a review, see Jeffrey Roth, *Firearms and Violence* (Washington, D.C.: National Institute of Justice, 1994).

102. Thomas Marvell and Carlisle Moody, "The Impact of Enhanced Prison Terms for Felonies Committed with Guns," *Criminology* 33 (1995): 247–281.

103. Robert Dann, "The Deterrent Effect of Capital Punishment," *Friends Social Service Series* 29, 1935.

104. William Bowers and Glenn Pierce, "Deterrence or Brutalization: What Is the Effect of Executions?" *Crime and Delinquency* 26 (1980): 453–484.

105. John Cochran, Mitchell Chamlin, and Mark Seth, "Deterrence or Brutalization? An Impact Assessment of Oklahoma's Return to Capital Punishment," *Criminology* 32 (1994): 107–134.

106. David Phillips, "The Deterrent Effect of Capital Punishment," *American Journal of Sociology* 86 (1980): 139–148; Hans Zeisel, "A Comment on 'The Deterrent Effect of Capital Punishment' by Phillips," *American Journal of Sociology* 88 (1982): 167–169; see also Sam McFarland, "Is Capital Punishment a Short-Term Deterrent to Homicide? A Study of the Effects of Four Recent American Executions," *Journal of Criminal Law and Criminology* 74 (1984): 1014–1032.

107. Steven Stack, "Publicized Executions and Homicide, 1950–1980," *American Sociological Review* 52 (1987): 532–540; for a study challenging Stack's methods, see William Bailey and Ruth Peterson, "Murder and Capital Punishment: A Monthly Time-Series Analysis of Execution Publicity," *American Sociological Review* 54 (1989): 722–743.

108. Karl Schuessler, "The Deterrent Influence of the Death Penalty," *Annals of the Academy of Political and Social Sciences* 284 (1952): 54–62.

109. Thorsten Sellin, *The Death Penalty* (Philadelphia: American Law Institute, 1959); Walter Reckless, "Use of the Death Penalty," *Crime and Delinquency* 15 (1969): 43–51.

110. Richard Lempert, "The Effect of Executions on Homicides: A New Look in an Old Light," *Crime and Delinquency* 29 (1983): 88–115.

111. Derral Cheatwood, "Capital Punishment and the Deterrence of Violent Crime in Comparable Counties," *Criminal Justice Review* 18 (1993): 165–181.

112. Dane Archer, Rosemary Gartner, and Marc Beittel, "Homicide and the Death Penalty: A Cross-National Test of a Deterrence Hypothesis," *Journal of Criminal Law and Criminology* 74 (1983): 991–1014.

113. Isaac Ehrlich, "The Deterrent Effect on Capital Punishment: A Question of Life and Death," *American Economic Review* 65 (1975): 397–417.

114. James Fox and Michael Radelet, "Persistent Flaws in Econometric Studies of the Deterrent Effect of the Death Penalty," *Loyola of Los Angeles Law Review* 23 (1987): 29–44; William B. Bowers and Glenn Pierce, "The Illusion of Deterrence in Isaac Ehrlich's Research on Capital Punishment," *Yale Law Journal* 85 (1975): 187–208.

115. William Bailey, "Disaggregation in Deterrence and Death Penalty Research: The Case of Murder in Chicago," *Journal of Criminal Law and Criminology* 74 (1986): 827–859.

116. Steven Messner and Kenneth Tardiff, "Economic Inequality and Level of Homicide: An Analysis of Urban Neighborhoods," *Criminology* 24 (1986): 297–317.

117. Donald Green, "Past Behavior as a Measure of Actual Future Behavior: An Unresolved Issue in Perceptual Deterrence Research," *Journal of Criminal Law and Criminology* 80 (1989): 781–804.

118. Donna Bishop, "Deterrence: A Panel Analysis," *Justice Quarterly* 1 (1984): 311–328; Julie Horney and Ineke Haen Marshall, "Risk Perceptions Among Serious Offenders: The Role of Crime and Punishment," *Criminology* 30 (1992): 575–594.

119. Raymond Paternoster, "Decisions to Participate in and Desist from Four Types of Common Delinquency: Deterrence and the Rational Choice Perspective," *Law and Society Review* 23 (1989): 7–29; idem, "Examining Three-Wave Deterrence Models: A Question of Temporal Order and Specification," *Journal of Criminal Law and Criminology* 79 (1988): 135–163; Raymond Paternoster, Linda Saltzman, Gordon Waldo, and Theodore Chiricos, "Estimating Perceptual Stability and Deterrent Effects: The Role of Perceived Legal Punishment in the Inhibition of Criminal Involvement," *Journal of Criminal Law and Criminology* 74 (1983): 270–297; M. William Minor and Joseph Harry, "Deterrent and Experiential Effects in Perceptual Deterrence Research: A Replication and Extension," *Journal of Research in Crime and Delinquency* 19 (1982): 190–203; Lonn Lanza-Kaduce, "Perceptual Deterrence and Drinking and Driving Among College Students," *Criminology* 26 (1988): 321–341.

120. Harold Grasmick and Robert Bursik, "Conscience, Significant Others, and Rational Choice: Extending the Deterrence Model," *Law and Society Review* 24 (1990): 837–861.

121. Steven Klepper and Daniel Nagin, "The Deterrent Effect of Perceived Certainty and Severity of Punishment Revisited," *Criminology* 27 (1989): 721–746.

122. Scott Decker, Richard Wright, and Robert Logie, "Perceptual Deterrence Among Active Residential Burglars: A Research Note," *Criminology* 31 (1993): 135–147.

123. Irving Piliavin, Rosemary Gartner, Craig Thornton, and Ross Matsueda, "Crime, Deterrence, and Rational Choice," *American Sociological Review* 51 (1986): 101–119.

124. Eleni Apospori, Geoffrey Alpert, and Raymond Paternoster, "The Effect of Involvement with the Criminal Justice System: A Neglected Dimension of the Relationship Between Experience and Perceptions," *Justice Quarterly* 9 (1992): 379–392.

125. Ibid., p. 390.

126. Eleni Apospori and Geoffrey Alpert, "Research Note: The Role of Differential Experience with the Criminal Justice System in Changes in Perceptions of Severity of Legal Sanctions over Time," *Crime and Delinquency* 39 (1993): 184–194.

127. Harold Grasnick and George Bryjak, "The Deterrent Effect of Perceived Severity of Punishment," *Social Forces* 59 (1980): 471–491.

128. Harold Grasmick, Robert Bursik, and Karyl Kinsey, "Shame and Embarrassment as Deterrents to Noncompliance with the Law: The Case of an Anti-Littering Campaign." Paper presented at the annual meeting of the American Society of Criminology, Baltimore, November 1990, p. 3.

129. Charles Tittle, *Sanctions and Social Deviance* (New York: Praeger, 1980).

130. For an opposite view, see Steven Burkett and David Ward, "A Note on Perceptual Deterrence, Religiously Based Moral Condemnation, and Social Control," *Criminology* 31 (1993): 119–134.

131. Ibid.

132. John Snortum, "Drinking-Driving Compliance in Great Britain: The Role of Law as a 'Threat' and as a 'Moral Eye-Opener,'" *Journal of Criminal Justice* 18 (1990): 479–499.

133. Green, "Past Behavior as a Measure of Actual Future Behavior," p. 803; Matthew Silberman, "Toward a Theory of Criminal Deterrence," *American Sociological Review* 41 (1976): 442–461; Linda Anderson, Theodore Chiricos, and Gordon Waldo, "Formal and Informal Sanctions: A Comparison of Deterrent Effects," *Social Problems* 25 (1977): 103–114; see also Maynard Erickson and Jack Gibbs, "Objective and Perceptual Properties of Legal Punishment and Deterrence Doctrine," *Social Problems* 25 (1978): 253–264.

134. Grasmick and Bursik, "Conscience, Significant Others, and Rational Choices," p. 854.

135. Grasmick, Bursik, and Kinsey, "Shame and Embarrassment as Deterrents to Noncompliance with the Law"; Harold Grasmick, Robert Bursik, and Bruce Arneklev, "Reduction in Drunk Driving as a Response to Increased Threats of Shame, Embarrassment, and Legal Sanctions," *Criminology* 31 (1993): 41–69.

136. Harold Grasmick, Brenda Sims Blackwell, and Robert Bursik, "Changes in the Sex Patterning of Perceived Threats of Sanctions," *Law and Society Review* 27 (1993): 679–699.

137. Daniel Nagin and Raymond Paternoster, "Enduring Individual Differences and Rational Choice Theories of Crime," *Law and Society Review* 27 (1993): 467–485.

138. Kirk Williams and Richard Hawkins, "The Meaning of Arrest for Wife Assault," *Criminology* 27 (1989): 163–181.

139. Thomas Peete, Trudie Milner, and Michael Welch, "Levels of Social Integration in Group Contexts and the Effects of Informal Sanction Threat on Deviance," *Criminology* 32 (1994): 85–105.

140. Ronet Bachman, Raymond Paternoster, and Sally Ward, "The Rationality of Sexual Offending: Testing a Deterrence/Rational Choice Conception of Sexual Assault," *Law and Society Review* 26 (1992): 343–358.

141. Ernest Van Den Haag, "The Criminal Law as a Threat System," *Journal of Criminal Law and Criminology* 73 (1982): 709–785.

142. Thomas Feucht, *1995 Drug Use Forecasting* (Washington, D.C.: National Institute of Justice, 1996).

143. David Lykken, "Psychopathy, Sociopathy, and Crime," *Society* 34 (1996): 30–38.

144. Ken Auletta, *The Under Class* (New York: Random House, 1982).

145. David Klinger, "Policing Spousal Assault," *Journal of Research in Crime and Delinquency* 32 (1995): 308–324.

146. Paternoster, "Decisions to Participate in and Desist from Four Types of Common Delinquency."

147. James Williams and Daniel Rodeheaver, "Processing of Criminal Homicide Cases in a Large Southern City," *Sociology and Social Research* 75 (1991): 80–88.

148. Wilson, *Thinking About Crime.*

149. James Q. Wilson and Richard Herrnstein, *Crime and Human Nature* (New York: Simon & Schuster, 1985), p. 494.

150. Paul Tracy and Kimberly Kempf-Leonard, *Continuity and Discontinuity in Criminal Careers* (New York: Plenum Press, 1996).

151. Lawrence Greenfeld, *Examining Recidivism* (Washington, D.C.: U.S. Government Printing Office, 1985).

152. Allen Beck and Bernard Shipley, *Recidivism of Prisoners Released in 1983* (Washington, D.C.: Bureau of Justice Statistics, 1989).

153. David Weisburd, Elin Waring, and Ellen Chayet, "Specific Deterrence in a Sample of Offenders Convicted of White-Collar Crimes," *Criminology* 33 (1995): 587–607.

154. Raymond Paternoster and Alex Piquero, "Reconceptualizing Deterrence: An Empirical Test of Personal and Vicarious Experiences," *Journal of Research in Crime and Delinquency* 32 (1995): 201–228.

155. Charles Murray and Louis Cox, *Beyond Probation* (Beverly Hills, Calif.: Sage, 1979); Perry Shapiro and Harold Votey, "Deterrence and Subjective Probabilities of Arrest: Modeling Individual Decisions to Drink and Drive in Sweden," *Law and Society Review* 18 (1984): 111–149; Douglas Smith and Patrick Gartin, "Specifying Specific Deterrence: The Influence of Arrest on Future Criminal Activity," *American Sociological Review* 54 (1989): 94–105.

156. Lawrence Sherman and Richard Berk, "The Specific Deterrent Effects of Arrest for Domestic Assault," *American Sociological Review* 49 (1984): 261–272; see also Richard Berk and Phyllis J. Newman, "Does Arrest Really Deter Wife Battery? An Effort to Replicate the Findings of the Minneapolis Spouse Abuse Experiment," *American Sociological Review* 50 (1985): 253–262.

157. See, generally, Franklyn Dunford, "The Measurement of Recidivism in Cases of Spouse Assault," *Journal of Criminal Law and Criminology* 83 (1992): 120–136.

158. J. David Hirschel, Ira Hutchinson, and Charles Dean, "The Failure of Arrest to Deter Spouse Abuse," *Journal of Research in Crime and Delinquency* 29 (1992): 7–33; J. David Hirschel and Ira Hutchinson, "Female Spouse Abuse and the Police Response: The Charlotte, North Carolina Experiment," *Journal of Criminal Law and Criminology* 83 (1992): 73–119; David Huizinga and Delbert Elliott, "The Role of Arrest in Domestic Assault: The Omaha Experiment," *Criminology* 28 (1990): 183–206; David Hirschel, Ira Hutchinson, Charles Dean, Joseph Kelley, and Carolyn Pesackis, *Charlotte Spouse Abuse Replication Project: Final Report* (Washington, D.C.: National Institute of Justice, 1990).

159. Richard Berk, Gordon Smyth, and Lawrence Sherman, "When Random Assignment Fails: Some Lessons from the Minneapolis Spouse Abuse Experiment," *Journal of Quantitative Criminology* 4 (1989): 209–223.

160. Joel Garner, Jeffrey Fagan, and Christopher Maxwell, "Published Findings from the Spouse Assault Replication Program: A Critical Review," *Journal of Quantitative Criminology* 11 (1995): 2–28.

161. Lawrence Sherman, Janell Schmidt, Dennis Rogan, Patrick Gartin, Ellen Cohn, Dean Collins, and Anthony Bacich, "From Initial Deterrence to Long-Term Escalation: Short-Custody Arrest for Poverty Ghetto Domestic Violence," *Criminology* 29 (1991): 821–850.

162. Anthony Pate and Edwin Hamilton, "Formal and Informal Deterrents to Domestic Violence: The Dade County Spouse Assault Experiment," *American Sociological Review* 57 (1992): 691–697.

163. Richard Berk, Alec Campbell, Ruth Klap, and Bruce Western, "The Deterrent Effect of Arrest in Incidents of Domestic Violence: A Bayesian Analysis of Four Field Experiments," *American Sociological Review* 57 (1992): 698–708.

164. Jeffrey Fagan, "Cessation of Family Violence: Deterrence and Dissuasion," in *Family Violence,* ed. Lloyd Ohlin and Michael Tonry (Chicago: University of Chicago Press, 1989), pp. 377–426.

165. Graeme Newman, *Just and Painful* (New York: Macmillan, 1983), pp. 139–143.

166. John Braithwaite, *Crime, Shame and Reintegration* (Melbourne, Australia: Cambridge University Press, 1989).

167. Ibid., p. 81.

168. For more on this approach, see Jane Mugford and Stephen Mugford, "Shame and Reintegration in the Punishment and Deterrence of Spouse Assault." Paper presented at the annual meeting of the American Society of Criminology, San Francisco, 1991.

169. John Braithwaite and Stephen Mugford, "Conditions of Successful Reintegration Ceremonies: Dealing with Juvenile Offenders," *British Journal of Criminology,* in press.

170. Mark Stafford and Mark Warr, "A Reconceptualization of General and Specific Deterrence," *Journal of Research on Crime and Delinquency* 30 (1993): 123–135.

171. Paternoster and Alex Piquero, "Reconceptualizing Deterrence: An Empirical Test of Personal and Vicarious Experiences."

172. Andrew Karmen, "Why Is New York City's Murder Rate Dropping So Sharply?" John Jay College, New York City, preliminary draft, 1996.

173. See, generally, Raymond Paternoster, "Absolute and Restrictive Deterrence in a Panel of Youth: Explaining the Onset, Persistence/Desistance, and Frequency of Delinquent Offending," *Social Problems* 36 (1989): 289–307; idem, "The Deterrent Effect of Perceived Severity of Punishment: A Review of the Evidence and Issues," *Justice Quarterly* 42 (1987): 173–217.

174. David Greenberg, "The Incapacitive Effects of Imprisonment: Some Estimates," *Law and Society Review* 9 (1975): 541–580.

175. Ibid., p. 558.

176. Isaac Ehrlich, "Participation in Illegitimate Activities: An Economic Analysis," *Journal of Political Economy* 81 (1973): 521–567.

177. Lee Bowker, "Crime and the Use of Prisons in the United States: A Time Series Analysis," *Crime and Delinquency* 27 (1981): 206–212.

178. Reuel Shinnar and Shlomo Shinnar, "The Effects of the Criminal Justice System on the Control of Crime: A Quantitative Approach," *Law and Society Review* 9 (1975): 581–611.

179. Stephan Van Dine, Simon Dinitz, and John Conrad, *Restraining the Wicked: The Dangerous Offender Project* (Lexington, Mass.: Lexington Books, 1979).

180. For review of this issue, see James Austin and John Irwin, *Does Imprisonment Reduce Crime? A Critique of "Voodoo" Criminology* (San Francisco: National Council of Crime and Delinquency, 1993).

181. John Wallerstedt, *Returning to Prison,* Bureau of Justice Statistics Special Report (Washington, D.C.: U.S. Department of Justice, 1984).

182. Peter Greenwood, *Selective Incapacitation* (Santa Monica, Calif.: Rand Corporation, 1982).

183. Marc Mauer, Testimony before the U.S. Congress, House Judiciary Committee on "Three Strikes and You're Out," 1 March 1994.

184. Stephen Markman and Paul Cassell, "Protecting the Innocent: A Response to the Bedeau-Radelet Study," *Stanford Law Review* 41 (1988): 121–170 at 153.

185. James Stephan and Tracy Snell, *Capital Punishment, 1994* (Washington, D.C.: Bureau of Justice Statistics, 1996), p. 8.

186. Andrew Von Hirsch, *Doing Justice* (New York: Hill and Wang, 1976).

187. Ibid., pp. 15–16.

188. Ibid.

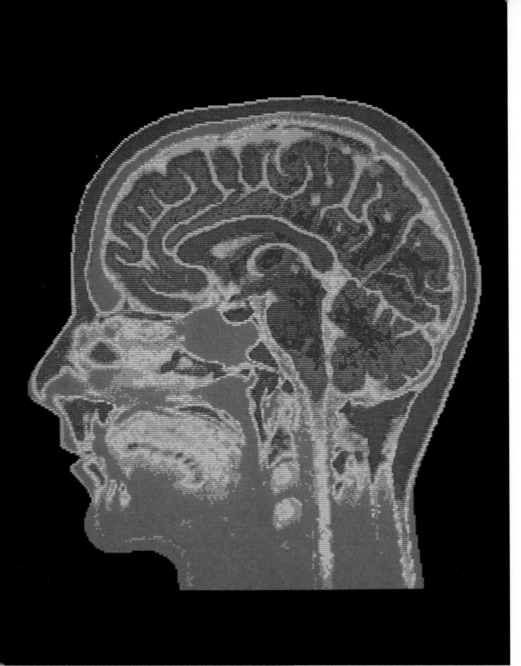

Chapter 6
Trait Theories

a generation of Americans have grown up on films and TV shows that portray violent criminals as mentally deranged and physically abnormal. Beginning with Alfred Hitchcock's film *Psycho,* producers have made millions depicting the ghoulish acts of people who at first seem normal and even friendly but turn out to be demented and dangerous. Lurking out there are crazed babysitters (*The Hand That Rocks the Cradle*), frenzied airline passengers (*Turbulence*), deranged roommates (*Single, White Female*), psychotic tenants (*Pacific Heights*), demented secretaries (*The Temp*), unhinged police officers (*Maniac Cop*), irrational fans (*The Fan, Misery*), abnormal girlfriends (*Fatal Attraction*) and boyfriends (*Fear*), unstable husbands (*Sleeping with the Enemy*) and wives (*Black Widow*), loony fathers (*The Stepfather*) and mothers (*Friday the 13th, Part 1*), maniacal children (*The Good Son*), and psychotic teenaged admirers (*The Crush*). And no one can be safe when even the psychologists and psychiatrists who should be treating these disturbed people turn out to be demonic murderers themselves (*Silence of the Lambs, Dressed to Kill, Never Talk to Strangers*). Is it any wonder that we respond to a particularly horrible crime by saying of the perpetrator, "That guy must be crazy" or "She is a monster!"

Connections

Some critics have called for the strict regulation of movies, videos, and TV shows, believing that viewing them is harmful to their mostly adolescent audience. Does watching all these aggressive, crazed people cause viewers to act violently themselves? For more on this issue, see the Close-Up on media violence later in this chapter.

The view that criminals bear physical or mental traits that makes them "different" and "abnormal" is not restricted to the moviegoing public. Since the 19th century, criminologists have suggested that biological and psychological traits may influence behavior. It is believed that some personal trait must separate the deviant members of society from the nondeviant. These personal differences explain why, when faced with the same life situations, one person commits crime and becomes a chronic offender, while another attends school, church, and neighborhood functions and obeys the laws of society. All people may be aware of and even fear the sanctioning power of the law, but some are unable to control their urges and passions. The variations on this view of crime causation are referred to as **trait theories.**

Trait theorists do not suggest that a single biological or psychological attribute is thought to adequately explain all criminality. Rather, as common sense would suggest, each offender is considered unique, physically and mentally; consequently, there must be a unique explanation for each person's behavior. Some may have inherited criminal tendencies; others are suffering from nervous system (neurological) problems; some may have a blood chemistry disorder that heightens their antisocial activity. Criminologists who focus on the individual thus see many explanations for crime because, in fact, there are many differences among criminal offenders.

Trait theorists are not overly concerned with legal definitions of crime; they do not try to explain why people violate particular statutory laws such as car theft or burglary. After all, these are artificial legal concepts based on arbitrary boundaries (for example, speeding is arbitrarily defined as exceeding 65 miles per hour). Instead, trait theorists focus on basic human behavior and drives—aggression, violence, and impulsivity—that are linked to antisocial behavior patterns. They also recognize that human traits alone do not produce criminality and that crime-producing interactions involve both personal traits—such as intelligence, personality, and chemical and genetic makeup—and environmental factors—such as family life, educational attainment, and neighborhood conditions. While some people may have a predisposition toward aggression, environmental stimuli can either suppress or trigger antisocial acts. Physical or mental traits are, therefore, but one part of a large pool of environmental, social, and personal factors that account for criminality.

Trait theories have gained prominence recently because of what is now known about chronic recidivism and the development of criminal careers. If only a small percentage of all offenders go on to become persistent repeaters, it is possible that what sets them apart from the criminal population is an abnormal biochemistry, brain structure, or genetic makeup.[1] Even if criminals do "choose crime," the fact that some repeatedly make that choice could well be linked to their physical and mental makeup.

This chapter reviews the two major divisions of trait theory: the biological and the psychological.

Biological Trait Theory

Development of Biological Theories

Cesare Lombroso's work on the "born criminal" was a direct offshoot of the application of the scientific method to the study of crime. His identification of primitive atavistic anomalies was based on what he believed to be sound empirical research using established scientific methods.

Connections

Biological explanations of criminal behavior first became popular during the middle part of the 19th century with the introduction of positivism—the use of the scientific method and empirical analysis to study behavior. Positivism was discussed in Chapter 1 in the context of the history of criminology.

Lombroso was not alone in the early development of biological theory. A contemporary of Lombroso's, Raffaele Garofalo (1852–1934) shared his belief that certain physical characteristics indicate a criminal nature. For example, Garofalo stated that among criminals, "a lower degree of sensibility to physical pain seems to be demonstrated by the readiness with which prisoners submit to the operation of tattooing."[2] Enrico Ferri (1856–1929), another student of Lombroso's, believed that a number of biological, social, and organic factors caused delinquency and crime.[3] Ferri added a social dimension to Lombroso's work and was a pioneer in the view that criminals should not be held personally or morally responsible for their actions, because forces outside their control cause criminality.

Advocates of the inheritance school traced the activities of several generations of families believed to have an especially large number of criminal members. The most famous of these studies involved the Jukes and the Kallikaks. Richard Dugdale's *The Jukes: A Study in Crime, Pauperism, Disease, and Heredity* (1875) and Arthur Estabrook's later work *The Jukes in 1915* traced the history of the Jukes, a family responsible for a disproportionate amount of crime.[4]

A later attempt at criminal anthropology, the body-build or **somatotype** school developed by William Sheldon, held that criminals manifest distinct physiques that make them susceptible to particular types of delinquent behavior. *Mesomorphs,* for example, have well-developed muscles and an athletic appearance. They are active, aggressive, sometimes violent, and the most likely to become criminals. *Endomorphs* have heavy builds and are known for lethargic behavior. *Ectomorphs* are tall, thin, and less social and more intellectual than the other types.[5]

The work of Lombroso and his contemporaries is regarded today as a historical curiosity, not scientific fact. Their research methodology has been discredited. They did not use control groups from the general population to compare results. Many of the traits they assumed to be inherited are not genetically determined. Many of the biological features they identified could be caused by deprivation in surroundings and diet. Even if most criminals shared certain biological traits, these traits might be products not of heredity but of some environmental condition, such as poor nutrition or health care. It is equally likely that only criminals who suffer from biological abnormality are caught and punished by the justice system. In his later writings, even Lombroso admitted that the born criminal was just one of many criminal types. Because of these deficiencies, the validity of individual-oriented explanations of criminality became questionable and for a time passed from the criminological mainstream.

SOCIOBIOLOGY. Biological explanations of crime fell out of favor in the early 20th century. During this period, criminologists became concerned about the sociological influences on crime, such as the neighborhood, peer group, family life, and social status. The work of biocriminologists was viewed as methodologically unsound and generally invalid by the sociologists who dominated the field and held views that have been referred to as **biophobia,** the belief that no serious consideration should be given to biological factors when attempting to understand human nature.[6]

But this situation changed. As Pierre van den Bergle put it in 1974:

> What seems no longer tenable at this juncture is any theory of human behavior which ignores biology and relies exclusively on socio-cultural learning. . . . Most social scientists have been wrong in their dogmatic rejection and blissful ignorance of the biological parameters of our behavior.[7]

In the early 1970s, spurred by the publication of *Sociobiology* by Edmund O. Wilson, the biological basis for crime once again emerged into the limelight.[8] **Sociobiology** differs from earlier theories of behavior in that it stresses that biological and genetic conditions affect the perception and learning of social behaviors, which in turn are linked to existing environmental structures. Sociobiologists view the gene as the ultimate unit of life that controls all human destiny. While the environment and experience do have an impact on behavior, most actions are controlled by a person's "biological machine." Most important, sociobiology holds that people are controlled by the innate need to have their genetic material survive and dominate others. Consequently, they do everything in their power to ensure their own survival and that of others who share their gene pool (relatives, fellow citizens, and so forth). Even when they come to the aid of others (reciprocal altruism), people are motivated by the belief that their actions will be reciprocated and that their gene survival capability will be enhanced.

Sociobiologists view biology, environment, and learning as mutually interdependent factors. Problems in one area can be altered by efforts in another. For example, people suffering from learning disorders can be given special tutoring to improve their reading skills. In this view then, people are biosocial organisms whose personalities and behaviors are influenced by physical as well as environmental conditions.

Although sociobiology has been criticized as methodologically unsound and socially dangerous, it has had a tremendous effect on reviving interest in finding a basis for crime and delinquency, because if biological (genetic) makeup controls human behavior, it follows that it should also be responsible for determining whether a person chooses law-violating or conventional behavior.

MODERN BIOLOGICAL THEORIES. The influence of sociobiology helped revive interest in the biological basis of crime. Rather than view the criminal as a person whose behavior is controlled by biological conditions determined at birth, modern biological trait theorists believe that physical, environmental, and social conditions work in concert to produce human behavior. They assume that environmental forces can either "trigger" antisocial behavior in people biologically predisposed to deviance, or conversely,

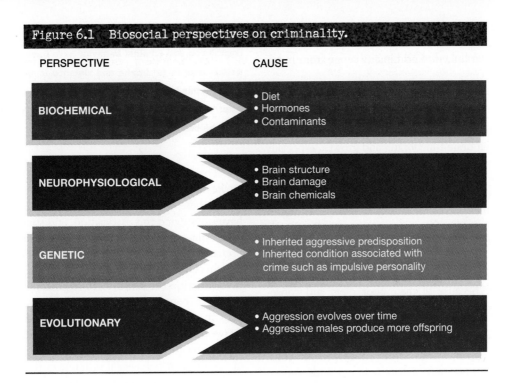

Figure 6.1 Biosocial perspectives on criminality.

PERSPECTIVE	CAUSE
BIOCHEMICAL	• Diet • Hormones • Contaminants
NEUROPHYSIOLOGICAL	• Brain structure • Brain damage • Brain chemicals
GENETIC	• Inherited aggressive predisposition • Inherited condition associated with crime such as impulsive personality
EVOLUTIONARY	• Aggression evolves over time • Aggressive males produce more offspring

if conditions are right, help mediate or offset the effects of biological predisposition.

Today criminologists interested in identifying a physical basis of antisocial behavior typically refer to themselves as trait theorists, biocriminologists, biosocial criminologists, or biologically oriented criminologists, and the terms are used here interchangeably.

Biological trait theory has several core principles.[9] First, it assumes that genetic makeup contributes significantly to human behavior. Not all humans are born with equal potential to learn and achieve (**equipotentiality**). Whereas sociologically oriented criminologists suggest, either explicitly or implicitly, that all people are born equal and that thereafter their behavior is controlled by social forces (parents, schools, neighborhoods, friends), biosocial theorists argue that no two people are alike (with rare exceptions, such as identical twins) and that the combination of human genetic traits and the environment produces individual behavior patterns.

Another critical focus of modern biological theory is the importance of brain functioning, mental processes, and learning. Social behavior, including criminal behavior, is learned. Each individual organism is believed to have a unique potential for learning. The physical and social environments interact to either limit or enhance an organism's capacity for learning. However, people learn through a process involving the brain and central nervous system, and learning is not controlled by social interactions but by biochemistry and cellular interaction. Learning can take place only when physical changes occur in the brain. There is a significant link, therefore, between behavior patterns and physical or chemical changes that occur in the brain and nervous system.[10]

Some, but not all, biosocial theorists also believe that learning is influenced by instinctual drives. Developed over

the course of human history, **instincts** are inherited, natural, and unlearned dispositions that activate specific behavior patterns designed to reach certain goals. For example, people are believed to have a drive to "possess and control" other people and things; thus, some theft offenses may be motivated by the instinctual need to possess goods and commodities. Rape and other sex crimes may be linked to the primitive instinctual drive males have to "possess and control" females.[11]

The following subsections examine some of the more important subbranches or schools of thought within biological criminology (see Figure 6.1 for an overview).[12] First we will review the biochemical factors believed to affect the learning of proper behavior patterns. Then we'll consider the relationship of brain function and crime, and we'll analyze current ideas about the association between genetic factors and crime. Finally, we will evaluate evolutionary views of crime causation.

Biochemical Conditions and Crime

Some trait theorists believe that biochemical conditions, including both those that are genetically predetermined and those acquired through diet and environment, control and influence antisocial behavior. This view of crime received national attention in 1979 when Dan White, the confessed killer of San Francisco Mayor George Moscone and city councilman Harvey Milk, claimed his behavior was precipitated by an addiction to sugar-laden junk foods.[13] White's successful "Twinkie defense" prompted a California jury to find him guilty of the lesser offense of diminished capacity manslaughter rather than first-degree murder. (White committed suicide after serving his prison sentence.) Some of the more important biochemical factors that have been linked to criminality range from nutrition to hormones.

NUTRITIONAL DEFICIENCIES. Biocriminologists maintain that minimum levels of vitamins and minerals are needed for normal brain functioning and growth, especially in the early years of life. If people with normal needs do not receive the appropriate nutrition, they will suffer from vitamin deficiency. If people have genetic conditions that cause greater-than-normal needs for certain vitamins and minerals, they are said to suffer from vitamin dependency. People with vitamin deficiency or dependency can manifest many physical, mental, and behavioral problems, including lower intelligence test scores.[14] Alcoholics often suffer from thiamine deficiency because of their poor diets and consequently are susceptible to the serious, often fatal Korsakoff's disease.[15]

Research conducted over the past decade shows that the dietary inadequacy of certain chemicals and minerals, including sodium, potassium, calcium, amino acids, monoamines, and peptides, can lead to depression, mania, cognitive problems, memory loss, and abnormal sexual activity.[16] Research studies examining the relationship between crime and vitamin deficiency and dependency have seemed to find a close link between antisocial behavior and insufficient quantities of some B vitamins (B_3 and B_6) and vitamin C. In addition, studies have purported to show that a major proportion of all schizophrenics and children with learning and behavior disorders are dependent on vitamins B_3 and B_6.[17]

SUGAR AND CRIME.   Another suspected nutritional influence on behavior is a diet especially high in carbohydrates and sugar.[18] For example, some recent research found that the way the brain processed glucose was related to scores on tests measuring reasoning power.[19] In addition, sugar intake levels have been associated with attention span deficiencies.[20]

Diets high in sugar and carbohydrates have also been linked to violence and aggression. Stephen Schoenthaler conducted an experiment with 276 incarcerated youths to determine whether a change in the amount of sugar in their diet would have a corresponding influence on their behavior within the institutional setting.[21] In the experiment, several dietary changes were made: Sweet drinks were replaced with fruit juices, table sugar was replaced with honey, breakfast cereals high in sugar were eliminated, molasses was substituted for sugar in cooking, and so on. Schoenthaler found that these changes produced a significant reduction in disciplinary actions within the institution; the number of assaults, thefts, fights, and incidents of disobedience within the institution declined about 45%. It is important to note that these results were consistent when such factors as age, previous offense record, and race of the offender were considered.

Net Bookmark

Aggression and criminal behavior have been linked to diet. The debate over sugar intake and violence is still ongoing. To read more on this topic log onto "Foods That Harm, Foods That Heal": http://foods.readersdigest.co.uk/extracts/pages/aggression.html

These are but a few of the research efforts linking sugar intake to emotional, cognitive, and behavioral performance.[22] While these results are impressive, a number of biologists have questioned this association, and some recent research efforts have failed to find a link between sugar consumption and violence.[23] In one important study, a group of researchers had 25 preschool children and 23 school-age children described as sensitive to sugar follow a different diet for three consecutive three-week periods. One diet was high in sucrose, the second substituted aspartame (Nutrasweet) as a sweetener, and the third relied on saccharin. Careful measurement of the subjects found little evidence of cognitive or behavioral differences that could be linked to diet. If anything, sugar seemed to have a calming effect on the children.[24]

In sum, while some research efforts allege a sugar-violence association, others suggest that many people who maintain diets high in sugar and carbohydrates are not violent or crime-prone and that in some cases sugar intake may actually reduce or curtail violent tendencies.[25]

HYPOGLYCEMIA.   **Hypoglycemia** is a condition that occurs when glucose (sugar) in the blood falls below levels necessary for normal and efficient brain functioning. The brain is sensitive to the lack of blood sugar because it is the only organ that obtains its energy solely from the combustion of carbohydrates. Thus, when the brain is deprived of blood sugar, it has no alternate food supply to call on, and its metabolism slows down, impairing its function. Symptoms of hypoglycemia include irritability, anxiety, depression, crying spells, headaches, and confusion.

Studies have linked hypoglycemia to outbursts of antisocial behavior and violence. As early as 1943, D. Hill and W. Sargent linked murder to hypoglycemia.[26] Several other studies have related assaults and fatal sexual offenses to hypoglycemic reactions.[27] Hypoglycemia has also been connected with a syndrome characterized by aggressive and assaultive behavior, glucose disturbance, and brain dysfunction. Studies of jail and prison inmate populations have found a higher than normal level of hypoglycemia,[28] and high levels of reactive hypoglycemia have been found in groups of habitually violent and impulsive offenders.[29]

HORMONAL INFLUENCES.   Criminologist James Q. Wilson, in his 1993 book *The Moral Sense,* concludes that hormones, enzymes, and neurotransmitters may be the key to understanding human behavior. These chemicals help explain gender differences in the crime rate. Males, Wilson writes, are biologically and naturally more aggressive than females, while women are more nurturing of the young and more important for survival of the species.[30] Hormone levels also help explain the aging-out process: Levels of the principal male steroid hormone decline during the life cycle, which may explain why violence rates diminish over time.[31]

A number of biosocial theorists are now evaluating the association between violent behavior episodes and hormone levels, and the findings suggest that abnormal levels of male sex hormones (**androgens**) do in fact produce aggressive behavior.[32] There is a growing body of evidence suggesting that hormonal changes are related to mood and behavior and, concomitantly, that adolescents experience more intense mood swings, anxiety, and restlessness than their elders.[33] An association between hormonal activity and antisocial behavior is suggested because rates of both factors peak in adolescence.

One area of concern has been **testosterone,** the most abundant androgen, which controls secondary sex characteristics, such as facial hair and voice timbre.[34] Research conducted on both human and animal subjects has found that prenatal exposure to unnaturally high levels of androgens permanently alters behavior. Girls who were unintentionally exposed to elevated amounts of androgens during their fetal development display an unusually high long-term tendency toward aggression; boys prenatally exposed to steroids that decrease androgen levels displayed decreased aggressiveness.[35] In contrast, samples of inmates indicate that testosterone levels are higher in men who committed violent crimes than in the other prisoners.[36]

How do hormone levels influence violent behaviors? Hormones cause areas of the brain to become less sensitive to environmental stimuli. Males, who possess high androgen levels, are more likely than females to need excess stimulation and to be willing to tolerate pain in their quest for thrills. Androgens are linked to brain seizures that, under stressful conditions, can result in emotional volatility. Androgens affect the brain structure itself, influencing the left hemisphere of the neocortex, the part of the brain that controls sympathetic feelings toward others.[37]

Some of the physical reactions produced by hormones that have been linked to violence include:

1. A lowering of average resting arousal under normal environmental conditions to a point that individuals are motivated to seek unusually high levels of environmental stimulation and are less sensitive to any harmful aftereffects resulting from this stimulation

2. A lowering of seizuring thresholds in and around the limbic system, increasing the likelihood that strong and impulsive emotional responses will be made to stressful environmental encounters

3. A rightward shift in neocortical functioning, resulting in an increased reliance on the brain hemisphere that is most closely integrated with the limbic system and is

least prone to reason in logical-linguistic forms or to respond to linguistic commands[38]

According to Lee Ellis and Phyllis Coontz, these effects promote violence and other serious crimes by causing people to seek greater levels of environmental stimulation and to tolerate more punishment, increasing impulsivity, emotional volatility, and antisocial emotions.[39]

Although some studies have been unable to demonstrate hormonal differences in samples of violent and nonviolent offenders, drugs that decrease testosterone levels are now being used to treat male sex offenders.[40] The female hormones estrogen and progesterone have been administered to sex offenders to decrease their sexual potency.[41] The long-term side effects of this treatment and their potential danger are still unknown.[42]

PREMENSTRUAL SYNDROME (PMS). Hormonal research has not been limited to male offenders. The suspicion has long existed that the onset of the menstrual cycle triggers excessive amounts of the female sex hormones, affecting antisocial, aggressive behavior. This condition is commonly referred to as **premenstrual syndrome (PMS).**[43] The link between PMS and delinquency was first popularized by Katharina Dalton, whose studies of English women indicated that females are more likely to commit suicide and be aggressive and otherwise antisocial just before or during menstruation.[44] While the Dalton research is often cited as evidence of the link between PMS and crime, methodological problems make it impossible to accept her findings at face value.

Debate continues over any link between PMS and aggression. Some doubters, such as criminologist Julie Horney, argue that the relationship is spurious; it is equally likely that the psychological and physical stress of aggression brings on menstruation and not vice versa.[45] In contrast, Diana Fishbein, a noted expert on biosocial theory,

Diana Fishbein, a noted expert on biosocial theory, has conducted research on the biochemical reactions that precede aggressive behavior.

concludes that an association does in fact exist between elevated levels of female aggression and menstruation. Research efforts, she argues, show that (1) a significant number of incarcerated females committed their crimes during the premenstrual phase, and (2) at least a small percentage of women appear vulnerable to cyclical hormonal changes that make them more prone to anxiety and hostility.[46] While the debate is ongoing, it is important to remember that the overwhelming majority of females who suffer anxiety and hostility prior to and during menstruation do not actually engage in violent criminal behavior, so any link between PMS and crime is tenuous at best.[47]

ALLERGIES. Allergies are defined as unusual or excessive reactions of the body to foreign substances.[48] For example, hay fever is an allergic reaction caused when pollen cells enter the body and are fought or neutralized by the body's natural defenses. The result of the battle is itching, red eyes and active sinuses.

Cerebral allergies cause an excessive reaction of the brain, whereas neuroallergies affect the nervous system. Cerebral allergies and neuroallergies are believed to cause the allergic person to produce enzymes that attack wholesome foods as if they were dangerous to the body.[49] They may also cause swelling of the brain and produce sensitivity in the central nervous system, conditions linked to mental, emotional, and behavioral problems. Research indicates a connection between these allergies and hyperemotionality, depression, aggressiveness, and violent behavior.[50]

Neuroallergy and cerebral allergy problems have also been linked to hyperactivity in children, which may portend antisocial behavior and the labeling of children as potential delinquents. The foods most commonly involved in producing such allergies are cow's milk, wheat, corn, chocolate, citrus, and eggs; however, about 300 other foods have been identified as allergens. The potential seriousness of the problem has been raised by studies linking the average consumption of one suspected cerebral allergen—corn—to cross-national homicide rates.[51]

ENVIRONMENTAL CONTAMINANTS. Dangerous quantities of copper, cadmium, mercury, and inorganic gases, such as chlorine and nitrogen dioxide, can now be found in the ecosystem. Research indicates that these environmental contaminants can influence behavior. At high levels, these substances can cause severe illness or death; at more moderate levels, they have been linked to emotional and behavioral disorders.[52] Some studies have linked the ingestion of food dyes and artificial colors and flavors to hostile, impulsive, and otherwise antisocial behavior in youths.[53] Lighting may be another important environmental influence on antisocial behavior. Research projects have suggested that radiation from artificial light sources, such as fluorescent tubes and television sets, may produce antisocial, aggressive behavior.[54]

A number of recent research studies have also linked lead ingestion to problem behaviors. Ingestion of lead may help explain why hyperactive children manifest conduct problems and antisocial behavior.[55] Deborah Denno investigated the behavior of more than 900 African American youth and found that lead poisoning was one of the most significant predictors of male delinquency and persistent adult criminality.[56] Herbert Needleman and his associates tracked 300 boys from ages 7 to 11 and found that those who had high lead concentrations in their bones were much more likely to report attention problems, delinquency, and aggressiveness.[57] High lead ingestion is also related to lower IQ scores, a factor linked to aggressive behavior.[58]

Neurophysiological Conditions and Crime

Some criminologists focus their attention on **neurophysiology,** or the study of brain activity.[59] They believe that neurological and physical abnormalities are acquired as early as the fetal or perinatal stage or through birth delivery trauma and then control behavior throughout the life span.[60]

The relationship between neurological dysfunction and crime first received a great deal of attention in 1968, when Charles Whitman, after killing his wife and his mother, barricaded himself in a tower at the University of Texas with a high-powered rifle and proceeded to kill 14 people and wound 24 others before he was killed by police. An autopsy revealed that Whitman suffered from a malignant infiltrating brain tumor. Whitman had previously experienced uncontrollable urges to kill and had gone to a psychiatrist seeking help for his problems. He kept careful notes documenting his feelings and his inability to control his homicidal urges, and he left instructions for his estate to be given to a mental health foundation so it could study mental problems such as his own.[61]

Since the Whitman case a great deal of attention has focused on the association between neurological impairment and crime. Studies conducted in the United States and in other nations have indicated that the relationship is significant between impairment in executive brain functions (abstract reasoning, problem-solving skills, motor behavior skills) and aggressive behavior.[62]

NEUROLOGICAL IMPAIRMENTS AND CRIME. There are numerous ways to measure neurological functioning, including memorization and visual awareness tests, short-term auditory memory tests, and verbal IQ tests. These tests have been found to distinguish criminal offenders from noncriminal control groups.[63]

Probably the most important measure of neurophysiological functioning is the **electroencephalograph (EEG).** An EEG records the electrical impulses given off by the brain.[64] It represents a signal composed of various rhythms and transient electrical discharges, commonly called brain waves, which can be recorded by electrodes placed on the scalp. The frequency is given in cycles per second, measured in hertz (Hz), and usually ranges from 0.5 to 30 Hz.

Measurements of the EEG reflect the activity of neurons located in the cerebral cortex. The rhythmic nature of this brain activity is determined by mechanisms that involve subcortical structures, primarily the thalamus.

In what is considered the most significant investigation of EEG abnormality and crime, a randomly selected group of 335 violent delinquents was divided into those who were habitually violent and those who had committed only a single violent act. While 65% of the habitually aggressive had abnormal EEG recordings, only 24% of the one-time offenders had recordings that deviated from the norm. When the records of individuals who had brain damage, were mentally retarded, or were epileptic were removed from the sample, the percentage of abnormality among boys who had committed a solitary violent crime was the same as that of the general population, about 12%. However, the habitually aggressive subjects showed a 57% abnormality.

Other research efforts have linked abnormal EEG recordings to antisocial behavior in children. Although about 5%–15% of the general population have abnormal EEG readings, about 50%–60% of adolescents with known behavior disorders display abnormal recordings.[65] Behaviors highly correlated with an abnormal EEG included poor impulse control, inadequate social adaptation, hostility, temper tantrums, and destructiveness.[66]

Studies of adults have associated slow and bilateral brain waves with hostile, hypercritical, irritable, nonconforming, and impulsive behavior.[67] Psychiatric patients with EEG abnormalities have been reported to be highly combative and to suffer episodes of rage. Studies of murderers have shown that a disproportionate number manifest abnormal EEG recordings.[68] EEG analysis, then, shows that measures of brain activity are significantly associated with antisocial behavior.[69]

MINIMAL BRAIN DYSFUNCTION. **Minimal brain dysfunction (MBD)** is related to an abnormality in cerebral structure. It has been defined as abruptly appearing maladaptive behavior that interrupts the lifestyle and life flow of an individual. In its most serious form, MBD has been linked to serious antisocial acts, an imbalance in the urge-control mechanisms of the brain, and chemical abnormality. The category of minimal brain dysfunction includes several abnormal behavior patterns, such as dyslexia, visual perception problems, hyperactivity, poor attention span, temper tantrums, and aggressiveness. One type of minimal brain dysfunction is manifested through episodic periods of explosive rage. This form of the disorder is considered an important cause of such behavior as spouse beating, child abuse, suicide, aggressiveness, and motiveless homicide. One perplexing feature of this syndrome is that people who are afflicted with it often maintain warm and pleasant personalities between episodes of violence.

Some studies measuring the presence of minimal brain dysfunction in offender populations have found that up to 60% exhibit brain dysfunction on psychological tests.[70] Criminals have been characterized as having dysfunction of

Table 6.1 Symptoms of Attention Deficit/Hyperactivity Disorder

Lack of Attention
Frequently fails to finish projects
Does not seem to pay attention
Does not sustain interest in play activities
Cannot sustain concentration on schoolwork or related tasks
Is easily distracted

Impulsivity
Frequently acts without thinking
Often "calls out" in class
Does not want to wait his or her turn in lines or games
Shifts from activity to activity
Cannot organize tasks or work
Requires constant supervision

Hyperactivity
Constantly runs around and climbs on things
Shows excessive motor activity while asleep
Cannot sit still; is constantly fidgeting
Does not remain in his or her seat in class
Is constantly on the go like a "motor"

Source: Adapted from American Psychiatric Association, *Diagnostic and Statistical Manual of Mental Disorders,* 4th ed. (Washington, D.C.: American Psychiatric Press, 1994).

the dominant hemisphere of the brain.[71] Researchers using brain wave data have predicted with 95% accuracy the recidivism of violent criminals.[72]

ATTENTION DEFICIT/HYPERACTIVITY DISORDER. Many parents have noticed that their children do not pay attention to them—they run around and do things in their own way. Sometimes this inattention is a function of age; in other instances, it is a symptom of **attention deficit/hyperactivity disorder (AD/HD),** in which a child shows a developmentally inappropriate lack of attention, impulsivity, and hyperactivity. The various symptoms of AD/HD are described in Table 6.1. About 3% of U.S. children, most often boys, are believed to suffer from this disorder, and it is the most common reason children are referred to mental health clinics. The condition has been associated with poor school performance, grade retention, placement in special needs classes, bullying, stubbornness, and lack of response to discipline.[73] Although the origins of AD/HD are still unknown, suspected causes include neurological damage, prenatal stress, and even food additives and chemical allergies; recent research has suggested a genetic link.[74]

A series of research studies now link AD/HD, minimal brain dysfunctions (such as poor motor function), hyperactivity, and below-average written and verbal cognitive ability to the onset and sustenance of a delinquent career. Research by Terrie Moffitt and Phil Silva suggests that youths who suffer both AD/HD and MBD and grow up in

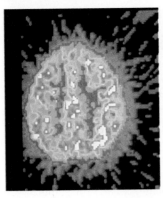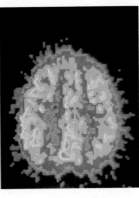

This scan compares a normal brain (left) and an AD/HD brain (right). The areas of orange and white demonstrate a higher rate of metabolism, while areas of blue and green represent an abnormally low metabolic rate. Why is AD/HD so prevalent in the U.S. today? Some experts believe that our immigrant forebears were risk takers who impulsively left their homelands for a life in the new world. They may have also brought with them a genetic predisposition for AD/HD.

a dysfunctional family are the ones most vulnerable to chronic and persistent delinquency.[75] Eugene Maguin and his associates have found that the relationship between chronic delinquency and attention disorders may be mediated by school failure: Kids who are poor readers are the most prone to antisocial behavior; many poor readers also have attention problems.[76]

This AD/HD-crime association is important because symptoms of AD/HD seem stable through adolescence into adulthood.[77] Early diagnosis and treatment of children suffering AD/HD may enhance their life chances. Today, the most typical treatment is doses of stimulants, such as Ritalin and Dexedrine, which ironically help control emotional and behavioral outbursts.

OTHER BRAIN DYSFUNCTIONS. Other brain dysfunctions have been related to violent crime. Persistent criminality has been linked to dysfunction in the frontal and temporal regions of the brain, since they are believed to play an important role in the regulation and inhibition of human behavior, including the formation of plans and intentions, and in the regulation of complex behaviors.[78] Brain lesions that occur at specific points of the neurological system, such as the auditory system, can have permanent effects on behavior.[79] Clinical evaluation of depressed and aggressive psychopathic subjects showed a significant number (more than 75%) had dysfunction of the temporal and frontal regions of the brain.[80]

TUMORS, INJURY, AND DISEASE. The presence of brain tumors has also been linked to a wide variety of psychological problems, including personality changes, hallucinations, and psychotic episodes.[81] There is evidence that people with tumors are prone to depression, irritability, temper outbursts, and even homicidal attacks (as in the Whitman case). Clinical case studies of patients suffering from brain tumors indicate that previously docile people may undergo behavior changes so great that they attempt to seriously harm their families and friends; when the tumor is removed, their behavior returns to normal.[82] In addition to brain tumors, head injuries caused by accidents, such as falls or auto crashes, have been linked to personality reversals marked by outbursts of antisocial and violent behavior.[83]

A variety of central nervous system diseases, including cerebral arteriosclerosis, epilepsy, senile dementia, Korsakoff's syndrome, and Huntington's chorea, have also been associated with memory deficiency, orientation loss, and affective (emotional) disturbances dominated by rage, anger, and increased irritability.[84]

BRAIN CHEMISTRY AND CRIME. Neurotransmitters are chemical compounds that influence or activate brain functions. Those studied in relation to aggression include androgens, dopamine, norepinephrine, serotonin, monoamine oxidase, and GABA.[85] Evidence exists that abnormal levels of these chemicals are associated with aggression. For example, several researchers have reported inverse correlations between serotonin concentrates in the blood and impulsive or suicidal behavior.[86] Recent studies of habitually violent Finnish criminals show that low serotonin (5-hydroxytryptamine; 5-HT) levels are associated with poor impulse control and hyperactivity. In addition, a relatively low concentration of 5-hydroxyindoleactic acid (5-HIAA) is predictive of increased irritability, sensation seeking, and impaired impulse control.[87]

Biocriminologist Lee Ellis has found that prenatal exposure of the brain to high levels of androgens can result in a brain structure that is less sensitive to environmental inputs. Affected individuals seek more intense and varied stimulation and are willing to tolerate more adverse consequences than individuals not so affected.[88] Such exposure also results in a rightward shift in (brain) hemispheric functioning and a concomitant diminution of cognitive and emotional tendencies. It should not be surprising then that left-handers are disproportionately represented in the criminal population, since the movement of each hand tends to be controlled by the hemisphere of the brain on the opposite side of the body.

In another analysis, Ellis found that individuals with a low supply of the enzyme monoamine oxidase (MAO) engage in behaviors linked with violence and property crime, including defiance of punishment, impulsivity, hyperactivity, poor academic performance, sensation seeking and risk taking, and recreational drug use. Abnormal levels of MAO may explain both individual and group differences in the crime rate. For example, Ellis finds that females have higher levels of MAO than males, a condition that may explain gender differences in the crime rate.[89]

Connections

Jack Katz has written on the seductions of crime. Perhaps some people may be "seduced" into crime because the experience produces the "natural high" they crave. Katz's work is discussed in Chapter 5.

Biocriminologist Lee Ellis has found that prenatal exposure of the brain to high levels of androgens can result in a brain structure that is less sensitive to environmental inputs. Ellis has also found that people with high arousal levels are more prone to violent and aggressive behaviors.

Because this linkage has been found, it is not uncommon for violence-prone people to be treated with antipsychotic drugs that help control levels of neurotransmitters; these treatments are sometimes referred to as "chemical restraints" or "chemical straightjackets."

The brain and neurological system can also produce natural or endogenous opiates, which are chemically similar to the narcotics opium and morphine. It has been suggested that the risk and thrills involved in crime cause the brain to produce increased amounts of these natural narcotics. The result is an elevated mood state, perceived as an exciting and rewarding experience that acts as a positive reinforcer to crime.[90] The brain then produces its own natural "high" as a reward for risk-taking behavior. While some people achieve this high by rock climbing and skydiving, others engage in crimes of violence.

AROUSAL THEORY. It has long been suspected that obtaining thrills is a motivator of crime. Adolescents may engage in such crimes as shoplifting and vandalism simply because they offer the attraction of "getting away with it"; delinquency is a thrilling demonstration of personal competence.[91] Is it possible that thrill seekers are people who have some form of abnormal brain functioning that directs their behavior?

According to **arousal theory,** for a variety of genetic and environmental reasons, some people's brains function differently in response to environmental stimuli. People seek to maintain a preferred or optimal level of arousal: Too much stimulation leaves them anxious and stressed out; too little makes them feel bored and weary. There is, however, variation in the way people's brains process sensory input. Some nearly always feel comfortable with little stimulation, while others require a high degree of environmental input to feel comfortable. The latter group become "sensation seekers" who seek out stimulating activities, which may include aggressive, violent behavior patterns.[92]

The factors that determine a person's optimal level of arousal are not fully determined. Suspected sources include brain chemistry (serotonin levels) and brain structure. For instance, some people have brains with many more nerve cells with receptor sites for neurotransmitters than others.

Genetics and Crime

Early biological theorists believed that criminality ran in families. Though research on deviant families, such as the Jukes and Kallikaks, is not taken seriously today, modern biosocial theorists are still interested in genetics. If some human behaviors are influenced by heredity, why not antisocial tendencies? Evidence exists that animals can be bred to have aggressive traits: Pit bulldogs, fighting bulls, and fighting cocks have been selectively mated to produce superior predators. Of course, no similar data are available for people, but a growing body of research is focusing on the genetic factors associated with human behavior.[93] There is evidence, for example, that some personality traits, including extraversion, openness, agreeableness, and conscientiousness, are genetically determined.[94] There are also data suggesting that human traits associated with criminality have a genetic basis.[95] Personality conditions linked to aggression—such as psychopathy, impulsivity, and neuroticism—and psychopathology, such as schizophrenia, may be heritable.[96]

This line of reasoning was cast in the spotlight when Richard Speck, the convicted killer of eight nurses in Chicago, was said to have inherited an abnormal XYY chromosomal structure (XY is the normal sex chromosome pattern in males). There was much public concern that all XYYs were potential killers and should be closely controlled. Civil libertarians expressed fear that all XYYs could be labeled dangerous and violent regardless of whether they had engaged in violent activities.[97] When it was disclosed that neither Speck nor most violent offenders actually had an extra Y chromosome, interest in the XYY theory dissipated.[98] However, the Speck case drew researchers' attention to looking for a genetic basis of criminal behavior

(Speck died in prison in 1996; after his death shocking videotapes were released showing him freely using drugs and engaging in sex with fellow inmates.)

Is it possible that the tendency for crime and aggression is inherited? Since the Speck case numerous researchers have carefully explored the heritability of criminal tendencies using a variety of techniques. The most commonly used approaches are twin studies and adoption studies.

TWIN STUDIES. If, in fact, inherited traits cause criminal behaviors, twins should be quite similar in their antisocial activities. However, since twins are usually brought up in the same household and are exposed to the same set of social conditions, determining whether their behavior was a result of biological, sociological, or psychological conditions would be difficult. Trait theorists have tried to overcome this dilemma by comparing identical, monozygotic (MZ) twins with fraternal, dizygotic (DZ) twins of the same sex.[99] MZ twins are genetically identical, while DZ twins have only half their genes in common. If heredity does determine criminal behavior, the MZ twins should be much more similar in their antisocial activities than the DZ twins.

The earliest studies conducted on the behavior of twins detected a significant relationship between the criminal activities of MZ twins and a much lower association between those of DZ twins. A review of relevant studies conducted between 1929 and 1961 found that 60% of MZ twins shared criminal behavior patterns (if one twin was criminal, so was the other), while only 30% of DZ twins were similarly related.[100] These findings may be viewed as powerful evidence for a genetic basis to criminality. More recent studies have supported these findings. Karl Christiansen studied 3,586 male twin pairs and found a 52% concordance for MZ pairs and a 22% concordance for DZ pairs. This result suggests that the MZ twins may share a genetic characteristic that increases the risk of their engaging in criminality.[101] Similarly, David Rowe and D. Wayne Osgood have analyzed the factors that influence self-reported delinquency in a sample of twin pairs and concluded that genetic influences actually have significant explanatory power.[102] Genetic effects have been found to be a significant predictor of problem behaviors in children as young as 3 years old.[103] A recent symposium on the genetics of criminal behavior uncovered significant associations between genetic makeup and criminality. While the behavior of some twin pairs seemed to be influenced by their environment, others displayed behavior disturbances that could only be explained by their genetic similarity.[104]

The controversy over the heritability of crime still rages. On the one hand, opponents suggest that available evidence provides little conclusive proof that crime is genetically predetermined. Not all research efforts have found that MZ twin pairs are more closely related in their criminal behavior than DZ or ordinary sibling pairs, and some that have found an association that it is at best modest.[105] On the other hand, one of the leading experts in this field, David Rowe, has recently reviewed the available research and concluded that individuals who share genes are alike in personality regardless of how they are reared; in contrast, he concluded, environment induces little or no personality resemblance in twin pairs.[106]

ADOPTION STUDIES. It seems logical that if the behavior of adopted children is more similar to that of their biological parents than to that of their adoptive parents, the idea of a genetic basis for criminality would be supported. If, on the other hand, adoptees are more similar to their adoptive parents than their biological parents, an environmental basis for crime would seem more valid.

Several studies indicate that some relationship may exist between biological parents' behavior and the behavior of their children, even when their contact has been infrequent.[107] In what is considered the most significant study in this area, Barry Hutchings and Sarnoff Mednick analyzed 1,145 male adoptees born in Copenhagen, Denmark, between 1927 and 1941; of these, 185 had criminal records.[108] After following up on 143 of the criminal adoptees and matching them with a control group of 143 noncriminal adoptees, Hutchings and Mednick found that the criminality of the biological father was a strong predictor of the child's criminal behavior. When both the biological and the adoptive fathers were criminal, the probability that the youth would engage in criminal behavior greatly expanded: 24.5% of the boys whose adoptive and biological fathers were criminals had been convicted of a criminal law violation; only 13.5% of those whose biological and adoptive fathers were not criminals had similar conviction records.[109]

A more recent analysis of Swedish adoptees also found that genetic factors were highly significant, accounting for 59% of the variation in their petty crime rates; boys who had criminal parents were significantly more likely to violate the law; environmental influences were signficantly less important, predicting about 19% of the variance in crime. Nonetheless, having a positive environment, such as being adopted into a more affluent home, helped inhibit genetic predisposition.[110]

EVALUATING GENETIC RESEARCH. The findings of the twin and adoption studies give some tentative support to a genetic basis for criminality. However, those who oppose the genes-crime relationship point to the inadequate research designs and weak methodologies of supporting research. The newer, better-designed research studies, critics charge, provide less support than earlier, less methodilogically sound studies.[111]

The genes-crime relationship is quite controversial since it implies that the propensity to commit crime is present at birth and cannot be altered. It raises moral dilemmas. If in utero genetic testing could detect a gene for violence, should a fetus be aborted? Should those holding a particular genetic makeup be followed and watched as a precautionary measure?

Evolutionary Views of Crime

A recent biosocial emphasis has been on evolutionary factors in criminality.[112] As human beings have evolved, certain traits and characteristics have become ingrained and instinctual. These biosocial characteristics may be responsible for some crime patterns.

Gender differences in the violence rate have been explained by the evolution of mammalian mating patterns. Hypothetically, to ensure survival of the gene pool (and the species), it is beneficial for a male of any species to mate with as many suitable females as possible, as each can bear his offspring. In contrast, because of the long period of gestation, females require a secure home and a single, stable nurturing partner to ensure their survival. Because of these differences in mating patterns, the most aggressive males mate most often and have the greatest number of offspring. Therefore, over the history of the human species, aggressive males have had the greatest impact on the gene pool. The descendants of these aggressive males now account for the disproportionate amount of male aggression and violence.[113]

There are two general evolutionary theories of crime: r/k theory and the "cheater" theory.[114]

R/K SELECTION THEORY. **R/k theory** holds that all organisms can be located along a continuum based on their reproductive drives. Those along the r end reproduce rapidly whenever they can and invest little in their offspring; those along the k end reproduce slowly and cautiously and take care in raising their offspring. Males today "lean" toward r-selection, because they can reproduce faster without the need for investment in their offspring; females are k-selected, because they can have fewer offspring but give more care and devotion to them. K-oriented people should be more cooperative and sensitive to others, while r-oriented people should be more cunning and deceptive. Males therefore should be more criminal, and they are. Persons who commit violent crimes seem to exhibit r-selection traits, such as a premature birth, early and frequent sexual activity, neglect as a child, and a short life expectancy.[115]

"CHEATER THEORY." The second evolutionary model, "cheater theory," suggests that a subpopulation of men has evolved with genes that incline them toward extremely low parental involvement. Sexually aggressive, they use their cunning to gain sexual conquests with as many females as possible. Because females would not willingly choose them as mates, they use stealth to gain sexual access, including such tactics as mimicking the behavior of more stable males. They use devious and illegal means to acquire resources they need for sexual domination. Their deceptive reproductive tactics spill over into other endeavors, where

their talent for irresponsible, opportunistic behavior supports their antisocial activities. Deception in reproductive strategies is thus linked to a deceitful lifestyle.[116]

Psychologist Byron Roth notes that cheater males may be especially attractive to those younger, less intelligent, women who begin having children at an early age. State-sponsored welfare, claims Roth, removes the need for potential mates to have the resources needed to be stable providers and family caretakers.[117] With the state meeting their financial needs, these less-intelligent women are attracted to men who are physically attractive and flamboyant. Their fleeting courtship process produces children with low IQs, aggressive personalities, and little chance of proper socialization in father-absent families. Because the criminal justice system treats them leniently, argues Roth, sexually irresponsible men are free to prey on young girls. Over time, their offspring will supply an ever-expanding supply of cheaters who are both antisocial and sexually aggressive.

Connections

The relationship between evolutionary factors and crime has just begun to be studied. Criminologists are now exploring how social organizations and institutions interact with biological traits to influence personal decision making, including criminal strategies. See the sections on latent trait theories in Chapter 10 for more on the integration of biological and environmental factors.

Evaluation of the Biological Branch of Trait Theory

Biosocial perspectives on crime raise some challenging questions for criminology. They have in turn been challenged by critics, who suggest they are racist and dysfunctional. If biology can explain the cause of street crimes, such as assault, murder, or rape, the argument goes, and if, as the official crime statistics suggest, the poor and minority-group members commit a disproportionate number of such acts, then by implication biological theory says that members of these groups are biologically different, flawed, or inferior.

Connections

Biosocial theory focuses on the violent crimes of the lower classes while ignoring the white-collar crimes of the upper and middle classes. That is, while it may seem logical to believe there is a biological basis to aggression and violence, it is more difficult to explain how insider trading and fraud are biologically related. For the causes of white-collar crime, see Chapter 13.

Biological explanations for the geographic, social, and temporal patterns in the crime rate are also problematic. Is it possible that more people are genetically predisposed to crime in the South and the West than in New England and the Midwest? Furthermore, biological theory seems to divide people into criminals and noncriminals on the basis of their physical makeup and ignores that self-reports indicate that almost everyone has engaged in some type of illegal activity during his or her lifetime.

Biosocial theorists counter that their views should not be confused with Lombrosian, deterministic biology. Rather than suggest that there are born criminals and noncriminals, they maintain that some people carry the potential to be violent or antisocial and that environmental conditions can sometimes trigger antisocial responses.[118] This would explain why some otherwise law-abiding citizens engage in a single, seemingly unexplainable antisocial act and, conversely, why some people with long criminal careers often engage in conventional behavior. It also explains why geographic and temporal patterns occur in the crime rate: People who are predisposed to crime may simply have more opportunities to commit illegal acts in the summer in Los Angeles and Atlanta than in the winter in Bedford, New Hampshire and Minot, North Dakota.

The biosocial view, then, is that behavior is a product of interacting biological and environmental events.[119] For example, Avshalom Caspi and his associates found that girls who reach physical maturity at an early age are the ones most likely to engage in delinquent acts. This finding might suggest a relationship between biological traits (hormonal activity) and crime. However, the Caspi research found that the association may also have an environmental basis. Physically mature girls are the ones most likely to have prolonged contact with a crime-prone group: older adolescent boys.[120] Here, the combination of biological change, social relationships, and routine opportunities predicts crime rates.

The most significant criticism of biosocial theory has been the lack of adequate empirical testing. In most research efforts, sample sizes are relatively small and nonrepresentative. A great deal of biosocial research is conducted with samples of adjudicated offenders who have been placed in clinical treatment settings. Methodological problems make it impossible to determine whether findings apply only to offenders who have been convicted of crimes and placed in treatment or to the population of criminals as a whole.[121] In short, more research is needed to clarify the relationships proposed by biosocial researchers and to silence critics.

Psychological Trait Theories

The second branch of trait theory focuses on the mental aspects of crime, including the association between intelligence, personality, learning, and criminal behavior.

In *The English Convict,* Charles Goring (1870–1919) used his "biometric method" to study the characteristics of

> ### Connections
>
> Chapter 1 discussed how some of the early founders of psychiatry tried to develop an understanding of the "criminal mind." Later theories suggested that mental illness and insanity were inherited and that deviants were inherently mentally damaged by reason of their inferior genetic makeup.

3,000 English convicts.[122] He found little difference in the physical characteristics of criminals and noncriminals but instead uncovered a significant relationship between crime and a condition he referred to as "defective intelligence." Goring believed that criminal behavior was inherited and could therefore best be controlled by regulating the reproduction of families exhibiting such traits as "feeblemindedness, epilepsy, insanity, and defective social instinct."[123]

Gabriel Tarde (1843–1904) used a somewhat different psychological approach in his early research: He was the forerunner of modern-day learning theorists.[124] Unlike Goring, who viewed criminals as mentally impaired, Tarde believed people learn from one another through a process of imitation. Tarde proposed three laws of imitation to describe why people engaged in crime: First, individuals in close and intimate contact with one another imitate each other's behavior. Second, imitation spreads from the top down; consequently, youngsters imitate older individuals, paupers imitate the rich, peasants imitate royalty, and so on. Crime among young, poor, or low-status people is really their effort to imitate wealthy, older, high-status people (for example, through gambling, drunkenness, accumulation of wealth).

Tarde's third law is the law of insertion: New acts and behaviors are superimposed on old ones and subsequently either reinforce or discourage previous customs. For example, drug taking may be a popular fad among college students who previously used alcohol. However, students may find that a combination of both substances provides even greater stimulation, causing the use of both drugs and alcohol to increase. Or a new criminal custom can develop that eliminates an older one—for example, train robbing has been replaced by truck hijacking. Tarde's ideas are quite similar to those of modern social learning theorists, who believe that both interpersonal and observed behavior, such as watching a movie or television, can influence criminality.

Since the pioneering work of people like Pinel, Maudsley, Tarde, and Goring, psychologists, psychiatrists, and other mental health professionals have long played an active role in formulating criminological theory. In their quest to understand and treat all varieties of abnormal mental conditions, psychologists have encountered clients whose behavior falls within categories society has labeled as criminal, deviant, violent, and antisocial.

This section is organized along the lines of the predominant psychological views most closely associated with the cause of criminal behavior; these perspectives are out-

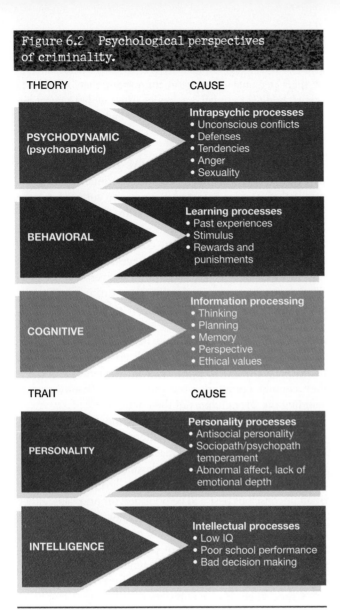

Figure 6.2 Psychological perspectives of criminality.

THEORY	CAUSE
PSYCHODYNAMIC (psychoanalytic)	**Intrapsychic processes** • Unconscious conflicts • Defenses • Tendencies • Anger • Sexuality
BEHAVIORAL	**Learning processes** • Past experiences • Stimulus • Rewards and punishments
COGNITIVE	**Information processing** • Thinking • Planning • Memory • Perspective • Ethical values

TRAIT	CAUSE
PERSONALITY	**Personality processes** • Antisocial personality • Sociopath/psychopath temperament • Abnormal affect, lack of emotional depth
INTELLIGENCE	**Intellectual processes** • Low IQ • Poor school performance • Bad decision making

lined in Figure 6.2. Some psychologists view antisocial behavior from a psychoanalytic perspective: Their focus is on early childhood experience and its effect on personality. In contrast, behaviorists stress social learning and behavior modeling as the keys to criminality. Cognitive theorists analyze human thought and perception and how they affect behavior. Other psychologists are concerned about the influence of personality or intelligence on behavior.

Psychodynamic Perspective

Psychodynamic or psychoanalytic psychology was originated by Viennese doctor Sigmund Freud (1856–1939) and has since remained a prominent segment of psychological theory.[125]

According to **psychodynamic theory,** the human mind performs three separate functions. The *conscious* mind is the aspect of the mind that people are most aware of—everyday thoughts. The *preconscious* mind contains elements of experiences that are out of awareness but can be brought back to consciousness at any time—memories, experiences. The *unconscious* part of the mind contains biological desires and urges that cannot readily be experienced as thoughts. Part of the unconscious contains feelings about sex and hostility, which people keep below the surface of consciousness by a process called **repression.**

Psychodynamic theory also holds that the human personality contains a three-part structure. The *id,* the primitive part of people's mental makeup, is present at birth; it represents unconscious biological drives for sex, food, and other life-sustaining necessities. The id follows the *pleasure principle:* It requires instant gratification without concern for the rights of others. The *ego* develops early in life, when a child begins to learn that its wishes cannot be instantly gratified. The ego is that part of the personality that compensates for the demands of the id by helping the individual guide his or her actions to remain within the boundaries of social convention. The ego is guided by the *reality principle:* It takes into account what is practical and conventional by societal standards. The *superego* develops as a result of incorporating within the personality the moral standards and values of parents, community, and significant others. It is the moral aspect of people's personalities; it passes judgments on their behavior.

HUMAN DEVELOPMENT. The most basic human drive present at birth is *eros,* the instinct to preserve and create life. Eros is expressed sexually. Consequently, early in their development humans experience sexuality, which is expressed in the seeking of pleasure through various parts of the body. During the first year of life, a child attains pleasure by sucking and biting; Freud called this the *oral stage.* During the second and third years of life, the focus of sexual attention is on the elimination of bodily wastes—the *anal stage.* The *phallic stage* occurs during ages 4 and 5; children now focus their attention on their genitals. Males begin to have sexual feelings for their mother (the Oedipus complex) and girls for their father (the Electra complex). The *latency stage* begins at age 6; during this period, feelings of sexuality are repressed until the *genital stage* begins at puberty; this marks the beginning of adult sexuality.

If conflicts are encountered during any of these *psychosexual stages* of development, a person can become fixated at that point. The person will as an adult exhibit behavior traits characteristic of those encountered during infantile sexual development. For example, an infant who does not receive enough oral gratification during the first year of life is likely as an adult to engage in such oral behavior as smoking, drinking, or drug abuse or to be clinging and dependent in personal relationships. Thus, the root of adult behavior problems can be traced to problems developed in the earliest years of life.

PSYCHODYNAMICS OF ABNORMAL BEHAVIOR. According to the psychodynamic perspective, people who experience feelings of mental anguish and are afraid they are losing control of their personalities are said to be suffering from a form of **neurosis** and are referred to as *neurotics*. Those people who have lost total control and who are dominated by their primitive id are said to suffer from **psychosis** and are referred to as *psychotics*. Their behavior may be marked by bizarre episodes, hallucinations, and inappropriate responses. According to the psychodynamic view, the most serious types of antisocial behavior, such as murder, might be motivated by psychosis, while neurotic feelings would be responsible for less serious delinquent acts and status offenses, such as petty theft and truancy.

Psychosis takes many forms, the most common being **schizophrenia.** Schizophrenics exhibit illogical and incoherent thought processes and a lack of insight into their behavior. They may experience delusions and hallucinate. For example, they may see themselves as agents of the devil, avenging angels, or the recipients of messages from animals and plants. David Berkowitz, the "Son of Sam" or "44-calibre killer," exhibited these traits when he claimed that his killing spree began when he received messages from a neighbor's dog. Paranoid schizophrenics suffer complex behavior delusions involving wrongdoing or persecution—they think everyone is out to get them.

PSYCHOSIS AND CRIME. Freud did not spend much time theorizing about crime. He did link criminality to the unconscious sense of guilt a person retains because of his Oedipus complex or her Electra complex. He believed that in many criminals, especially youthful ones, it is possible to detect a powerful sense of guilt that existed before the crime and is therefore not its result but its motive. It is as if the person is relieved to be able to fasten the unconscious sense of guilt onto something real and immediate.[126]

Other psychologists have used psychoanalytic concepts to link criminality to abnormal mental states produced by early childhood trauma. For example, Alfred Adler (1870–1937), the founder of individual psychology, coined the term **inferiority complex** to describe people who compensate for feelings of inferiority with a drive for superiority; controlling others may help reduce personal inadequacies. Erik Erikson (1902–1984) identified the **identity crisis**—a period of serious personal questioning young people undertake in an effort to determine their own values and sense of direction. Adolescents undergoing an identity crisis might exhibit out-of-control behavior and experiment with drugs and other forms of deviance.

The psychoanalyst whose work is most closely associated with criminality is August Aichorn.[127] After examining many delinquent youths, Aichorn concluded that societal stress, though damaging, could not alone result in a life of crime unless a predisposition existed that prepared youths psychologically for antisocial acts. This mental state,

which he labeled **latent delinquency,** is found in youngsters whose personality requires them (1) to seek immediate gratification (to act impulsively), (2) to consider satisfaction of their personal needs more important than relating to others, and (3) to satisfy instinctive urges without consideration of right and wrong (that is, they lack guilt).

PSYCHODYNAMICS OF CRIMINAL BEHAVIOR. Since this early work, psychoanalysts have continued to view the criminal as an id-dominated person who suffers from the inability to control impulsive, pleasure-seeking drives.[128] Perhaps because they suffered unhappy experiences in childhood or had families that could not provide proper love and care, criminals suffer from weak or damaged egos that make them unable to cope with conventional society. Weak egos are associated with immaturity, poor social skills, and excessive dependence on others; people with weak egos may be easily led by antisocial peers into crime and drug abuse. Some offenders have undeveloped superegos and consequently lack internalized representations of those behaviors that are punished in conventional society; they commit crimes because they have difficulty understanding the wrongfulness of their actions.[129]

Personality conflict or underdevelopment may result in neurotic or psychotic behavior patterns; there seems to be a significant link between abnormal personality and mental distress and disorder.[130] Offenders classified as neurotics (more commonly referred to today as conduct disorders) are driven by an unconscious desire to be punished for prior sins, either real or imaginary; they may violate the law to gain attention or punish their parents. In its most extreme form, criminality may be viewed as a form of psychosis that prevents offenders from appreciating the feelings of their victims or controlling their own impulsive needs for gratification.

Crime, then, is a manifestation of feelings of oppression and the inability of people to develop the proper defense mechanisms to keep these feelings under control. Criminality actually allows troubled people to survive by producing positive psychic results: It helps them feel free and independent, gives them the possibility of excitement and the chance to use their skills and imagination, provides them with the promise of positive gain, allows them to blame others for their predicament (for example, the police), and gives them a chance to rationalize their sense of failure ("If I hadn't gotten into trouble, I could have been a success").[131]

The psychodynamic model of the criminal offender depicts an aggressive, frustrated person dominated by events that occurred early in childhood.

Behavioral Theories

Behavior theory maintains that human actions are developed through learning experiences. Rather than focus on unconscious personality traits or biological predispositions, behavior theorists are concerned with the actual behaviors people engage in during the course of their daily lives. The major premise of behavior theory is that people alter their behavior according to the reactions they receive from others. Behavior is supported by rewards and extinguished by punishments. Behavior is constantly being shaped by life experiences.

Behavior theory is quite complex, with many different subareas. With respect to criminal activity, the behavioral view is that crimes, especially violent acts, are learned responses to life situations that do not necessarily represent abnormal or morally immature responses.

Social learning is the branch of behavior theory most relevant to criminology.[132] Social learning theorists, most notably Albert Bandura, argue that people are not actually born with the ability to act violently but that they learn to be aggressive through their life experiences. These experiences include personally observing others acting aggressively to achieve some goal or watching people being rewarded for violent acts on television or in movies. People learn to act aggressively when, as children, they model their behavior after the violent acts of adults. Later in life, these violent behavior patterns persist in social relationships. The boy who sees his father repeatedly strike his mother with impunity is the one most likely to grow up to become a battering parent and husband.

Although social learning theorists agree that mental or physical traits may predispose a person toward violence, they believe that the activation of a person's violent tendencies is achieved by factors in the environment. The specific forms that aggressive behavior takes, the frequency with which it is expressed, the situations in which it is displayed, and the specific targets selected for attack are largely determined by social learning. However, people are self-aware and engage in purposeful learning. Their interpretations of behavior outcomes and situations influence the way they learn from experiences. One adolescent who spends a weekend in jail for drunk driving may find it the most awful experience of her life, one that teaches her to never drink and drive; another may find it an exciting experience about which he can brag to his friends.

Social learning theorists view violence as something learned through a process called **behavior modeling.** In modern society, aggressive acts are usually modeled after three principal sources. The most prominent models are family members. Bandura reports that studies of family life show that children who use aggressive tactics have parents who use similar behaviors when dealing with others.

A second influence on the social learning of violence is provided by environmental experiences. People who reside in areas in which violence is a daily occurrence are more likely to act violently than those who dwell in low-crime areas where norms stress conventional behavior.

A third source of behavior modeling is provided by the mass media. Films and television shows commonly depict violence graphically. Moreover, violence is often portrayed

Does watching violent TV and movies cause kids to act in an aggressive fashion? While laboratory observations suggest a media-violence link, there is less evidence that such an association occurs in the "real world." Millions of kids watch violence every day, yet few become violent criminals. It is possible, however, that watching violent TV shows can reinforce a preexisting predisposition to commit aggressive behavior, thereby increasing the incidence of violent crime.

Net Bookmark

How much violence is really on television? The UCLA Center for Communication Policy Television Violence Monitoring Project is undertaking a study of violent incidents on TV. The results can be accessed on their home page:

http://www.ucla.edu/current/hotline/violence/toc.html

as an acceptable behavior, especially for heroes who never have to face legal consequences for their actions. For example, David Phillips found that the homicide rate increases significantly immediately after a heavyweight championship prizefight.[133] For more on this topic, see the Close-Up on "The Media and Violence."

What triggers violent acts? Various sources have been investigated by social learning theorists. One position is that a direct, pain-producing physical assault will usually trigger a violent response. Yet the relationship between painful attacks and aggressive responses has been found to be inconsistent; whether people counterattack in the face of physical attack depends in part on their skill in fighting and their perception of the strength of their attackers. Verbal taunts and insults have also been linked to aggressive responses.

close-up: *The Media and Violence*

On November 27, 1995 thieves ignited flammable liquid in a New York City subway token booth, seriously injuring the clerk. Their behavior was virtually identical to a robbery scene in the film *Money Train* (with Wesley Snipes and Woody Harrelson), which had been released a few days before.

Do the media influence behavior? Does broadcast violence cause aggressive behavior in viewers? This has become a hot topic because of the persistent theme of violence on television and in films. Critics have called for drastic measures, ranging from banning TV violence to putting warning labels on heavy metal albums out of the fear that listening to hard-rock lyrics produces delinquency.

If there is in fact a TV-violence link, the problem is indeed alarming. Systematic viewing of TV begins at age 2½ and continues at a high level during the preschool and early school years. It has been estimated that children ages 2 to 5 watch TV for 27.8 hours per week; children ages 6 to 11, 24.3 hours per week; and teens, 23 hours per week. Marketing research indicates that adolescents ages 11 to 14 rent violent horror movies at a higher rate than any other age group; kids this age use older peers and siblings and apathetic parents to gain access to R-rated films. More than 40% of U.S. households now have cable TV, which features violent films and shows. Even children's programming is saturated with violence.

The fact that kids watch so much violent TV is not surprising, considering the findings of a well-publicized study conducted in 1995 by researchers at UCLA. They found that at least 10 network shows made heavy use of violence. Of the 161 television movies monitored (every one that aired that season), 23 raised concerns about their use of violence, a violent theme, a violent title, or the inappropriate graphicness of a scene. Of the 118 theatrical films monitored (all that aired that season), 50 raised concerns about their use of violence. On-air promotions also reflect a continuing, if not worsening, problem. Some series may contain several scenes of violence, each of which is appropriate within its context. An advertisement for that show, however, will only feature those violent scenes, without any of the other context.

Even some children's television shows feature "sinister combat" as the theme. The characters are usually happy to fight and frequently do so with little provocation. A University of Pennsylvania study also found that children's programming contained an average of 32 violent acts per hour, that 56% had violent characters, and that 74% had characters who became the victims of violence (although "only 3.3% had characters who were actually killed"). The average child views 8,000 TV murders before finishing elementary school.

There have been numerous anecdotal cases of violence linked to TV and films. In 1974 a 9-year-old California girl was raped with a bottle by four other girls who said they had watched a similar act in the television movie *Born Innocent,* which depicted life in a reformatory for girls. Her parents' lawsuit against NBC, the network that broadcast the film, was dismissed in court. In 1977 Ronald Zamora killed an elderly woman and then pled guilty by reason of insanity. His attorney claimed Zamora was addicted to TV violence and could no longer differentiate between reality and fantasy; the jury did not buy the defense, and Zamora was found guilty as charged. At least 43 deaths have been linked to the movie *The Deer Hunter,* which featured a scene in which a main character kills himself while playing Russian roulette for money.

In a famous incident, John Hinckley, Jr., shot President Ronald Reagan as a result of his obsession with actress Jodie Foster, which developed after he watched her play a prostitute in the film *Taxi Driver.* Hinckley viewed the film at least 15 times. In October 1993, a 5-year-old Ohio boy set a fire that caused the death of his 2-year-old sister. The boy's mother charged that the youth had been influenced by the MTV show *Beavis and Butt-Head,* whose cartoon heroes started fires and chanted "Fire is good." MTV responded to the public outcry over the incident by moving the show's broadcast time from 7 P.M. to 10:30 P.M. A national survey conducted in the wake of the controversy found that almost 80% of the general public believes that violence on TV can cause violence "in real life."

LINKING THE MEDIA AND VIOLENCE

Psychologists believe that media violence does not in itself *cause* violent behavior, because if it did, there would be millions of daily incidents in which viewers imitated the aggression they saw on TV or in movies. But most psychologists agree that media violence *contributes* to aggression. There are several explanations for the effects of television and film violence on behavior:

- Media violence can provide aggressive "scripts" that children store in memory. Repeated exposure to these scripts can increase their retention and lead to changes in attitudes. Exposure to violent displays of any type could provide cues leading to the retrieval of these and other scripts and to the emission of aggressive behavior.
- Observational learning occurs when the violence seen on television is copied by the child viewer. Children learn to be violent from television in the same way that they learn cognitive and social skills from their parents and friends.
- Television violence increases the arousal levels of viewers and makes them more prone to act aggressively. Studies measuring the galvanic skin response of subjects—a physical indication of arousal based on the amount of electricity conducted across the palm of the hand—show that viewing violent TV shows led to increased arousal levels in young children.
- Television violence promotes attitude changes, which can then result in behavior changes. Watching television violence promotes such negative attitudes as suspiciousness and the expectation that the viewer will become involved in violence. Attitudes of frequent television viewers toward aggression become positive when they

see violence as a common and socially acceptable behavior.

- Television violence helps already aggressive youths justify their behavior. It is possible that, instead of causing violence, television helps violent youths rationalize their behavior as a socially acceptable and common activity.
- Television violence may disinhibit aggressive behavior, which is normally controlled by other learning processes. Disinhibition takes place when adults are viewed as being rewarded for violence and when violence is seen as socially acceptable. This contradicts previous learning experiences in which violent behavior was seen as wrong.

Such distinguished bodies as the American Psychological Association, the National Institute of Mental Health, and the National Research Council support the TV-violence link. They base their conclusion on research efforts indicating that watching violence on TV leads to increased levels of violence in the laboratory as well as in natural settings.

A number of experimental approaches have been tried. Groups of subjects have been exposed to violent TV shows in a laboratory setting and their behavior afterward compared to control groups who viewed nonviolent programming; observations have also been made in playgrounds, on athletic fields, and in residences. Other experiments require subjects to answer attitude surveys after watching violent TV shows. Still another approach is to use aggregate measures of TV viewing; for example, the number of violent TV shows on the air during a given time period is compared to crime rates during the same period.

Most evaluations of experimental data indicate that watching violence on TV is correlated with aggressive behaviors or at least has a short-term impact on behavior. Subjects who view violent TV shows are likely to begin aggressive behavior almost immediately.

Although this evidence is persuasive, the relationship between media and violence is still unproven. A number of critics argue that the evidence simply does not support the claim that watching TV or movies and listening to heavy metal music is related to antisocial behavior. Simon Singer found that teenage heavy metal fans were no more delinquent than nonlisteners. Candace Kruttschnitt and her associates found that an individual's exposure to violent TV shows is only weakly related to subsequent violent behavior. There is also little evidence that areas that experience the highest levels of violent TV viewing also have rates of violent crime that are above the norm.

Millions of children watch violence every night yet fail to become violent criminals. If violent TV shows caused interpersonal violence, there should be few ecological and regional patterns in the crime rate, of which there are many. Put another way, how can regional differences in the violence rate be explained considering the fact that people all across the nation watch the same TV shows and films?

Critics also assert that experimental results are inconclusive and short-lived. People may have an immediate reaction to viewing violence on TV, but aggression is quickly extinguished once the viewing ends. Experiments that show a correlation between aggression and TV fail to link the association with actual criminal behaviors, such as rape or assault. The weight of the experimental results does indicate that violent media have an immediate impact on people with a preexisting tendency toward crime and violence. But do kids who act more aggressively after watching violent TV later grow up to become rapists and killers?

SHOULD MEDIA VIOLENCE BE CURTAILED?

Considering the evidence, should the viewing of violent TV shows be curtailed or controlled? One answer would be to have government regulators limit the content of programs or restrict times that violent shows may be aired (presumably, as in the *Beavis and Butt-Head* case, after children's bedtimes). As a consequence of the UCLA survey, the TV industry has joined with the film industry to place advisory warnings on shows that have objectionable content. Critics charge that such policies run afoul of First Amendment guarantees of free speech—who is to say when a TV show is too violent?

While such practices may help guide some parents, they do little to restrict TV watching when children are home alone (although it may soon be possible to equip television sets with computer chips that prevent the reception of shows designated as having violent themes). And what about the local news or football game? For example, Garland White, Janet Katz, and Kathryn Scarborough found that when the local football team *wins*, violent assaults on women increase; sports dominance may trigger feelings of power and control, which results in sexual aggression in males. This research received nationwide attention and prompted antibattering public service announcements during the 1997 Super Bowl. If such findings are valid, it is unlikely that those concerned with media violence can engineer a ban of pro football games on television.

CRITICAL THINKING QUESTIONS

1. Should the government control the content of TV shows and limit the amount of weekly violence?
2. How can we explain the fact that millions of kids watch violent TV shows and remain nonviolent?

Sources: UCLA Center for Communication Policy, Television Violence Monitoring Project (Los Angeles, Calif., 1995); Associated Press, "Hollywood Is Blamed in Token Booth Attack," *Boston Globe,* 28 November 1995, p. 30; Garland White, Janet Katz, and Kathryn Scarborough, "The Impact of Professional Football Games upon Violent Assaults on Women," *Violence and Victims* 7 (1992): 157–171; Simon Singer, "Rethinking Subcultural Theories of Delinquency and the Cultural Resources of Youth," paper presented at the annual meeting of the American Society of Criminology, Phoenix, Arizona, November 1993; Albert Reiss and Jeffrey Roth, eds., *Understanding and Preventing Violence* (Washington, D.C.: National Academy Press, 1993); Reuters, "Seventy-Nine Percent in Survey Link Violence on TV and Crime," *Boston Globe,* 19 December 1993, p. 17; Scott Snyder, "Movies and Juvenile Delinquency: An Overview," *Adolescence* 26 (1991): 121–131; Steven Messner, "Television Violence and Violent Crime: An Aggregate Analysis," *Social Problems* 33 (1986): 218–235; Candace Kruttschnitt, Linda Heath, and David Ward, "Family Violence, Television Viewing Habits, and Other Adolescent Experiences Related to Violent Criminal Behavior," *Criminology* 243 (1986): 235–267; Jonathan Freedman, "Television Violence and Aggression: A Rejoinder," *Psychological Bulletin* 100 (1986): 372–378; Wendy Wood, Frank Wong, and J. Gregory Chachere, "Effects of Media Violence on Viewers' Aggression in Unconstrained Social Interaction," *Psychological Bulletin* 109 (1991): 371–383.

People who are predisposed to aggression by their learning experiences are likely to view insults from others as a challenge to their social status and to react with violence. Still another violence-triggering mechanism is a perceived reduction in one's life conditions. Prime examples of this phenomenon are riots and demonstrations in poverty-stricken ghetto areas. Studies have shown that discontent also produces aggression in the more successful members of lower-class groups who have been led to believe they can succeed but have been thwarted in their aspirations. While it is still uncertain how this relationship is constructed, it is apparently complex. No matter how deprived some individuals are, they will not resort to violence. It seems evident that people's perceptions of their relative deprivation have differing effects on their aggressive responses.

In summary, social learning theorists have said that the following four factors help produce violence and aggression:

1. An event that heightens arousal—such as being frustrated or provoked through physical assault or verbal abuse.

2. Aggressive skills—learned aggressive responses picked up from observing others, either personally or through the media.

3. Expected outcomes—the belief that aggression will somehow be rewarded. Rewards can come in the form of reduced tension or anger, some financial reward, enhanced self-esteem, or the praise of others.

4. Consistency of behavior with values—the belief, gained from observing others, that aggression is justified and appropriate, given the circumstances of the current situation.

Cognitive Theory

One area of psychology that has received increasing recognition in recent years has been the **cognitive school.** Psychologists with a cognitive perspective focus on mental processes and how people perceive and mentally represent the world around them and solve problems. The pioneers of this school were Wilhelm Wundt (1832–1920), Edward Titchener (1867–1927), and William James (1842–1920). Today, there are several subdisciplines within the cognitive area. The moral development branch is concerned about the way people morally represent and reason about the world. Humanistic psychology stresses self-awareness and "getting in touch with feelings." The information-processing branch focuses on the way people process, store, encode, retrieve, and manipulate information to make decisions and solve problems.

MORAL AND INTELLECTUAL DEVELOPMENT THEORY. The moral and intellectual development branch of cognitive psychology is perhaps the most important for criminological theory. Jean Piaget (1896–1980), the founder of this approach, hypothesized that people's reasoning processes develop in an orderly fashion, beginning at birth and continuing until adolescence and older.[134] At first, during the sensorimotor stage, children respond to the environment in a simple manner, seeking interesting objects and developing their reflexes. By the fourth and final stage, the formal operations stage, they have developed into mature adults who can use logic and abstract thought.

Lawrence Kohlberg applied the concept of moral development to issues in criminology.[135] He found that people travel through stages of moral development, during which their decisions and judgments on issues of right and wrong are based on different reasoning. It is possible that serious offenders have a moral orientation that differs from that of law-abiding citizens. Kohlberg's stages of development are

Stage 1: Right is obedience to power and avoidance of punishment.

Stage 2: Right is taking responsibility for oneself, meeting one's own needs, and leaving to others the responsibility for themselves.

Stage 3: Right is being good in the sense of having good motives, having concern for others, and "putting yourself in the other person's shoes."

Stage 4: Right is maintaining the rules of a society and serving the welfare of the group or society.

Stage 5: Right is based on recognized individual rights within a society with agreed-upon rules—a social contract.

Stage 6: Right is an assumed obligation to principles applying to all humankind—principles of justice, equality, and respect for human life.

Kohlberg classified people according to the stage on this continuum at which their moral development ceased to grow.

In studies conducted by Kohlberg and his associates, criminals were found to be significantly lower in their moral judgment development than noncriminals of the same social background.[136] Since his pioneering efforts, researchers have continued to show that criminal offenders are more likely to be classified in the lowest levels of moral reasoning (stages 1 and 2), while noncriminals have reached a higher stage of moral development.[137]

Recent research indicates that the decision not to commit crimes may be influenced by one's stage of moral development. People at the lowest levels report that they are deterred from crime because of their fear of sanctions; those in the middle consider the reactions of family and friends; those at the highest stages refrain from crime because they believe in duty to others and universal rights.[138]

Moral development theory suggests that people who obey the law simply to avoid punishment or who have outlooks mainly characterized by self-interest are more likely to commit crimes than those who view the law as something that benefits all of society and who sympathize with the rights of others. Higher stages of moral reasoning are associated with conventional behaviors, such as honesty, generosity, and nonviolence.

INFORMATION PROCESSING. When cognitive theorists who study information processing try to explain antisocial behavior, they do so in terms of perception and analysis of data. When people make decisions, they engage in a sequence of thought processes. They first encode information so that it can be interpreted. They then search for a proper response and decide on the most appropriate action; finally, they act on their decision.[139]

According to this cognitive approach, violence-prone people may be using information incorrectly when they make decisions. One reason is that they may be relying on mental "scripts" learned in childhood that tell them how to interpret events, what to expect, how they should react, and what the outcome of the interaction should be.[140] Hostile children may have learned improper scripts by observing how others react to events; their own parents' aggressive and inappropriate behavior would have considerable impact. Violence becomes a stable behavior because the scripts that emphasize aggressive responses are repeatedly rehearsed as the child matures.

Violence-prone kids see people as more aggressive than they actually are and as intending them ill when there is no reason for alarm. As these children mature, they use fewer cues than most people to process information. Some use violence in a calculating fashion as a means of getting what they want; others react in an overly volatile fashion to the slightest provocation. Aggressors are more likely to be vigilant, on edge, or suspicious. When they attack victims, they may believe they are defending themselves, even though they are misreading the situation.[141]

Information-processing theory has been used to explain date rape. Sexually violent males believe that when their dates say no to sexual advances, the women are really "playing games" and actually want to be taken forcefully.[142]

Treatment based on information processing acknowledges that people are more likely to respond aggressively to a provocation when thoughts intensify the insult or otherwise stir feelings of anger. Cognitive therapists attempt to teach explosive people to control aggressive impulses by viewing social provocations as problems demanding a solution rather than as insults requiring retaliation. Programs are aimed at teaching problem-solving skills that may include listening, following instructions, joining in, and using self-control. Treatment interventions based on learning social skills are relatively new, but there are some indications that this approach can have long-term benefits for reducing criminal behavior.[143]

Mental Illness and Crime

Each of the schools of psychology has a unique approach to the concept of mental abnormality. Psychoanalysts view mental illness as a retreat from unbearable stress and conflict; cognitive psychologists link it to thought disorders and overstimulation; behavior theorists might look to environmental influences, such as early family experiences and social rejection. Regardless of the cause of mental illness, is there a link between it and crime?

A great deal of early research efforts found that many offenders who engage in serious, violent crimes suffer from some sort of mental disturbance. James Sorrells's well-known study of juvenile murderers, "Kids Who Kill," found that many homicidal youths could be described in such terms as "overtly hostile," "explosive or volatile," "anxious," and "depressed."[144] Likewise, in a study of 45 males accused of murder, Richard Rosner and his associates found that 75% could be classified as having some mental illness, including schizophrenia.[145] Abusive mothers have been found to have mood and personality disorders and a history of psychiatric diagnoses.[146]

There is also a significant body of literature indicating that those who are diagnosed as mentally ill are more likely to violate the law than the mentally sound are. The reported substance abuse among the mentally ill is significantly higher than that among the general population.[147] Two recent research reports, one by Bruce Link and his associates and another by Ellen Steury, found that the diagnosed mentally ill appear in arrest and court statistics at a rate disproportionate to their presence in the population.[148]

Despite this evidence, some question remains as to whether, as a group, the mentally ill are any more criminal than the mentally sound. The mentally ill may be more likely to withdraw or harm themselves than to act aggressively toward others.[149] Research conducted in New York shows that on release, prisoners who had prior histories of hospitalization for mental disorders were less likely to be rearrested than those who had never been hospitalized.[150] And both the Link and the Steury research, which did find a mental illness–crime association, reported that the great majority of known criminals are not mentally ill and that the relationship is at best "modest."

While these research efforts give only tentative support to the proposition that mental disturbance or illness can be an underlying cause of violent crime, it is still possible that some link exists. The existing data suggest that certain *symptoms* of mental illness are connected to violence, including the feelings that others were wishing the person harm, that their mind was dominated by forces beyond their control, and that thoughts were being put into their head by others.[151] It is also likely that people suffering from other psychological disorders such as substance abuse, psychopathy, and neuroticism are the ones most at risk for chronic criminal behavior.[152] Right now major assessments and research studies are ongoing, and results should be available soon that will determine the true link between mental illness and crime.[153]

Personality and Crime

Personality can be defined as the reasonably stable patterns of behavior, including thoughts and emotions, that distinguish one person from another.[154] One's personality reflects a characteristic way of adapting to life's demands and problems. The way people behave is a function of how their personality enables them to interpret life events and make appropriate behavioral choices. Can the cause of crime be linked to personality? This issue has always caused significant debate.[155] In their early work, Sheldon Glueck and Eleanor Glueck identified a number of personality traits they believed characterized antisocial youth:[156]

self-assertiveness	sadism
defiance	lack of concern for others
extraversion	feeling unappreciated
ambivalence	distrust of authority
impulsiveness	poor personal skills
narcissism	mental instability
suspicion	hostility
destructiveness	resentment

Connections

The Glueck research is representative of the view that antisocial people maintain a distinct set of personal traits that makes them particularly sensitive to environmental stimuli. Once dismissed by mainstream criminologists, Chapter 10's section on life-course theories shows how the Gluecks' views still influence contemporary criminological theory.

Several other research efforts have attempted to identify criminal personality traits.[157] For example, Hans Eysenck identified two personality traits that he associated with antisocial behavior: extraversion-introversion and stability-instability. Extreme introverts are overaroused and avoid sources of stimulation, while extreme extraverts are unaroused and seek sensation. Introverts are slow to learn and be conditioned; extraverts are impulsive individuals who lack the ability to examine their own motives and behaviors. Those who are unstable, a condition that Eysenck calls *neuroticism,* are anxious, tense, and emotionally unstable.[158] People who are both neurotic and extraverted lack self-insight and are impulsive and emotionally unstable; they are unlikely to have reasoned judgments of life events. While extravert neurotics may act self-destructively—for example, by abusing drugs—more stable people will be able to reason that such behavior is ultimately harmful and life-threatening. Eysenck believes that the direction of the personality is controlled by genetic factors and is heritable.

A number of other personality deficits have been identified in the criminal population. A common theme is that criminals are hyperactive, impulsive individuals with short attention spans (attention deficit disorder), conduct disorders, anxiety disorders, and depression.[159] These traits make them prone to problems ranging from psychopathology to drug abuse, sexual promiscuity, and violence.[160] As a group, people who share these traits are believed to have a character defect referred to as the antisocial, sociopathic, or psychopathic personality. Although these terms are often used interchangeably, some psychologists do distinguish between sociopaths and psychopaths by suggesting that the former are a product of a destructive home environment, while the latter are a product of a defect or aberration within themselves.[161] This condition is discussed in the Close-Up "The Antisocial Personality."

RESEARCH ON PERSONALITY. Since maintaining a deviant personality has been related to crime and delinquency, numerous attempts have been made to devise accurate measures of personality and determine whether they can predict antisocial behavior. Two types of standardized personality tests have been constructed. The first are *projective techniques* that require a subject to react to an ambiguous picture or shape by describing what it represents or by telling a story about it. The Rorschach inkblot test and the Thematic Apperception Test are examples of two widely used projective tests. Such tests are given by clinicians trained to interpret responses and categorize them according to established behavioral patterns. While these tests were not used extensively, some early research found that delinquents and nondelinquents could be separated on the basis of their personality profiles.[162]

The second frequently used method of psychological testing is the *personality inventory.* This type of test requires subjects to agree or disagree with groups of questions in a self-administered survey. One of the most widely used psychological tests is the Minnesota Multiphasic Personality Inventory (MMPI). Developed by R. Starke Hathaway and J. Charnley McKinley, the MMPI has subscales that purport to measure many different personality traits, including psychopathic deviation (Pd scale), schizophrenia (Sc), and hypomania (Ma).[163]

Elio Monachesi and Hathaway pioneered the use of the MMPI to predict criminal behavior. They concluded that scores on some of the MMPI scales, especially the Pd scale, predicted delinquency. In one major effort, they administered the MMPI to a sample of ninth-grade boys and girls in Minneapolis and found that Pd scores had a significant relationship to later delinquent involvement. Other studies have detected an association between scores on the Pd scale and criminal involvement.[164] Another frequently administered personality test, the California Personality Inventory (CPI), has also been used to distinguish deviants from nondeviant groups.[165]

Despite the time and energy put into using the MMPI and other scales to predict crime and delinquency, the results have proved inconclusive. Three surveys of the literature of personality testing—one by Karl Schuessler and Donald Cressey (covering the pre-1950 period), another by Gordon Waldo and Simon Dinitz (covering the period 1950–1965), and another, more recent survey by David Tennenbaum—found inconclusive evidence that personality traits could consistently predict criminal involvement.[166] While some law violators may suffer from an abnormal personality structure, there are also many more whose personalities are indistinguishable from the norm. Efforts to improve the MMPI have resulted in the MMPI-2, a new scale with, it is hoped, improved validity; current research efforts should determine whether this version can successfully identify the potential for crime and violence.[167]

ARE SOME PEOPLE CRIME-PRONE? Interest in the personality characteristics of criminals has been increasing. Because the most commonly used scales, such as the CPI and MMPI, have not been uniformly successful in predicting criminality, psychologists have turned to other measures, including the Multidimensional Personality Questionnaire (MPQ), to assess such personality traits as control, aggression, alienation, and well-being. Research by Avshalom Caspi and his associates has found that scales of the MPQ can produce "robust personality correlates of delinquency" and that these measures are valid across genders, races, and cultures.[168] The Caspi research indicates that adolescent offenders who are "crime-prone" respond to frustrating events with strong negative emotions, feel stressed and harassed, and are adversarial in their interpersonal relationships. Crime-prone people maintain "negative emotionality"—a tendency to experience aversive affective states, such as anger, anxiety, and irritability. They are also predisposed to weak personal contraints; they have difficulty controlling impulsive behavior urges. Because they are both impulsive and aggressive, crime-prone people are quick to take action against perceived threats.

Evidence that personality traits predict crime and violence is important because it suggests that the root cause of crime can be found in the forces that influence human development at an early stage in the life course. If these results are valid, rather than focus on job creation and neighborhood improvement crime control efforts might be better focused on helping families raise children who are reasoned and reflective and enjoy a safe environment.

Intelligence and Crime

A number of the early criminologists maintained that many delinquents and criminals have below-average intelligence and that low IQ is a cause of their criminality. They believed criminals to be inherently substandard in intelligence and thus naturally inclined to commit more crimes than more-intelligent persons. Furthermore, it was thought that if authorities could determine which individuals had low IQs, they might identify potential criminals before they could commit socially harmful acts.

Because social scientists had a captive group of subjects in juvenile training schools and penal institutions, they began to measure the correlation between IQ and crime by testing adjudicated offenders. Thus, inmates of penal institutions were used as a test group around which numerous theories about intelligence were built, leading ultimately to the nature versus nurture controversy that is still going on today.

NATURE THEORY. Nature theory argues that intelligence is largely determined genetically and that low intelligence as demonstrated by a low IQ score is linked to behavior, including criminal behavior. When the newly developed IQ tests were administered to inmates of prisons and juvenile training schools in the first decades of the 20th century, the nature position gained support because a large proportion of the inmates scored low on the tests. Henry Goddard found during his studies in 1920 that many institutionalized persons were what he considered "feeble-minded"; he concluded that at least half of all juvenile delinquents were mental defectives.[169] In 1926, William Healy and Augusta Bronner tested groups of delinquent boys in Chicago and Boston and found that 37% were subnormal in intelligence. They concluded that delinquents were five to ten times more likely to be mentally deficient than normal boys.[170] These and other early studies were embraced as proof that low IQ scores indicated potentially delinquent children and that a correlation existed between innate low intelligence and deviant behavior. Intelligence tests were believed to measure the inborn genetic makeup of individuals, and many criminologists accepted the idea that individuals with substandard IQs were predisposed toward delinquency and adult criminality.

NURTURE THEORY. The rise of culturally sensitive explanations of human behavior in the 1930s led to the nurture school of intelligence. According to this theory, intelligence must be viewed as partly biological but primarily

Some but not all serious violent offenders may have a disturbed character structure commonly called **psychopathy, sociopathy,** or **antisocial personality.**

Psychopaths have a low level of guilt and anxiety and persistently violate the rights of others. Although they may exhibit superficial charm and above-average intelligence, this surface often masks a disturbed personality that makes them incapable of forming enduring relationships with others and continually involves them in such deviant behaviors as violence, risk taking, substance abuse, and impulsivity.

From an early age, the psychopath's home life was filled with frustrations, bitterness, and quarreling. Consequently, throughout life, he or she is unreliable, unstable, demanding, and egocentric. Psychopaths are risk-taking sensation seekers who are constantly involved in a variety of antisocial behaviors. They have been described as grandiose, egocentric, manipulative, forceful, and coldhearted, with shallow emotions and the inability to feel empathy with others, remorse, or anxiety over their misdeeds.

Hervey Cleckley, a leading authority on psychopathy, described psychopaths as

chronically antisocial individuals who are always in trouble, profiting neither from experience nor punishment, and maintaining no real loyalties to any person, group, or code. They are frequently callous and hedonistic, showing marked emotional immaturity, with lack of responsibility, lack of judgment, and an ability to rationalize their behavior so that it appears warranted, reasonable, and justified.

Considering these personality traits, it is not surprising that studies show that people evaluated as psychopaths are significantly more criminal- and violence-prone when compared to nonpsychopathic control groups and that psychopaths continue their criminal careers long after other offenders burn out or age out of crime. Psychopaths are continually in trouble with the law and therefore are likely to wind up in penal institutions. It has been estimated that up to 30% of all inmates can be classified as psychopaths or sociopaths, but a more realistic figure is probably 10%; not all psychopaths become criminals, and, conversely, most criminals are not psychopaths.

WHAT CAUSES PSYCHOPATHY?

Although psychologists are still not certain of the causes of psychopathy, a number of factors are believed to contribute to the development of a psychopathic or sociopathic personality. Some experts focus on family experiences, suggesting that the influence of an unstable parent, parental rejection, lack of love during childhood, and inconsistent discipline may be related to psychopathy. Early childhood experiences seem quite important. Children who lack the opportunity to form an attachment to a mother figure in the first three years of life, who suffer sudden separation from the mother figure, or who see changes in the mother figure are most likely to develop sociopathic personalities.

Psychopathy may also be related to personal traits. Donald Lynam finds that AD/HD (Attention Deficit/Hyperactive Disorder) kids are more likely to suffer from conduct problems in childhood and as they mature to fall prey to a serious form of conduct disorder he labels "fledgling psychopathy." This condition is in turn highly associated with chronic offending.

Psychopaths may also suffer from lower than normal levels of arousal. In addition, studies have found that psychopaths have lower skin conductance levels and fewer spontaneous responses than normal subjects. This view links psychopathy to autonomic nervous system (ANS) dysfunction. The ANS mediates physiological activities associated with emotions and controls heart rate, blood pressure, respiration, muscle tension,

---

sociological. Nurture theorists discredited the notion that persons commit crimes because they have low IQs. Instead, they postulated that environmental stimulation from parents, relatives, social contacts, schools, peer groups, and innumerable others create a child's IQ level and that low IQs result from an environment that also encourages delinquent and criminal behavior. Thus, if low IQ scores are recorded among criminals, these scores may reflect the criminals' cultural background, not their mental ability.

Studies challenging the assumption that people automatically committed criminal acts because they had below-average IQs began to appear as early as the 1920s. In 1926 John Slawson studied 1,543 delinquent boys in New York institutions and compared them with a control group of New York City boys.[171] Slawson found that although 80% of the delinquents achieved lower scores in abstract verbal intelligence, they were about normal in mechanical aptitude and nonverbal intelligence. These results indicated the possibility of cultural bias in portions of the IQ tests. He also found no relationship among the number of arrests, the types of offenses, and IQ.

In 1931, Edwin Sutherland evaluated IQ studies of criminals and delinquents and noted significant variation in the findings, which disproved Goddard's notion that criminals were "feebleminded."[172] The discrepancies found by Goddard were believed to reflect testing methods and scoring rather than differences in the mental ability of criminals. Sutherland's research all but put an end to the belief that crime is caused by feeblemindedness; the IQ-crime link was almost all but forgotten in the criminological literature.

REDISCOVERING IQ AND CRIMINALITY. Although the alleged IQ-crime link had been dismissed by mainstream criminologists, it became an important area of study once again when respected criminologists Travis Hirschi

papillary size, and electrical activity of the skin (or galvanic skin resistance).

Another view is that psychopathy is caused by a dysfunction of the limbic system in the brain, manifested through damage to the frontal and temporal lobes. Consequently, psychopaths may need greater-than-average stimulation to bring them up to comfortable levels (similar to the arousal theory discussed earlier in this chapter). Research shows that antisocial individuals are often sensation seekers who desire a hedonistic pursuit of pleasure, an extraverted lifestyle, partying, drinking, and a variety of sexual partners. The desire for this stimulation may originate in their physical differences.

David Lykken suggests that psychopaths have inherited a "low fear quotient" that inhibits their fear of punishment. All people have a natural or innate fear of certain stimuli—spiders, snakes, fires, strangers. Psychopaths fall on the low end of the fearfulness continuum. The normal socialization process depends on the current punishment of antisocial behavior inhibiting future transgressions. Someone who does not fear punishment is simply harder to socialize.

Psychologists have also found that psychopaths may have ineffective coping mechanisms for dealing with aversive or negative stimuli. Psychopaths may be less capable of regulating their activities than other people. While nonpsychopaths may become anxious and afraid when facing the prospect of committing a criminal act, psychopaths in the same circumstances feel no such fear. Ogloff and Wong conclude that these reduced anxiety levels result in impulsive and inappropriate behaviors and in deviant behavior, apprehension, and incarceration. Psychologists have attempted to treat patients diagnosed as psychopaths by giving them adrenaline, which increases their arousal levels.

ANTISOCIAL PERSONALITY AND CHRONIC OFFENDING

The antisocial personality concept seems to jibe with what is known about chronic offending. In a recent paper, Lawrence Cohen and Bryan Vila argue that chronic offending should be conceived as a continuum of behavior at whose apex lies the most extremely dangerous and predatory criminals. As many as 80% of these high-end chronics exhibit sociopathic behavior patterns. Though making up about 4% of the male population and less than 1% of the female population, they are responsible for half of all the serious felony offenses committed annually. Not all high-rate chronics are sociopaths, but enough are to support a strong link between personality dysfunction and long-term criminal careers.

Sources: David Lykken, "Psychopathy, Sociopathy, and Crime," *Society* 34 (1996): 30–38; Lawrence Cohen and Bryan Vila, "Self-Control and Social Control: An Exposition of the Gottfredson-Hirschi/Sampson-Laub Debate," *Studies on Crime and Crime Prevention* 5 (1996): 1–21; Donald Lynam, "Early Identification of Chronic Offenders: Who Is the Fledgling Psychopath?" *Psychological Bulletin* 120 (1996): 209–234; James Ogloff and Stephen Wong, "Electrodermal and Cardiovascular Evidence of a Coping Response in Psychopaths," *Criminal Justice and Behavior* 17 (1990): 231–245; Laurie Frost, Terrie Moffitt, and Rob McGee, "Neuropsychological Correlates of Psychopathology in an Unselected Cohort of Young Adolescents," *Journal of Abnormal Psychology* 98 (1989): 307–313; Hervey Cleckley, "Psychopathic States," in *American Handbook of Psychiatry*, ed. S. Aneti (New York: Basic Books, 1959), pp. 567–569; Spencer Rathus and Jeffrey Nevid, *Abnormal Psychology* (Englewood Cliffs, N.J.: Prentice-Hall, 1991), pp. 310–316; Helene Raskin White, Erich Labouvie, and Marsha Bates, "The Relationship between Sensation Seeking and Delinquency: A Longitudinal Analysis," *Journal of Research in Crime and Delinquency* 22 (1985): 197–211.

and Michael Hindelang published a widely read 1977 paper linking the two variables.[173] After reexamining existing research data, Hirschi and Hindelang concluded that "the weight of evidence is that IQ is more important than race and social class" for predicting criminal and delinquent involvement. Rejecting the notion that IQ tests are race- and class-biased, they concluded that major differences exist between criminals and noncriminals within similar racial and socioeconomic class categories. Their position is that low IQ increases the likelihood of criminal behavior through its effect on school performance. That is, youths with low IQs do poorly in school, and school failure and academic incompetence are highly related to delinquency and later to adult criminality.

Hirschi and Hindelang's inferences have been supported by research conducted by both U.S. and international scholars.[174] For example, Donald Lynam, Terrie Moffitt, and Magda Stouthamer-Loeber found a direct IQ-delinquency link among a sample of adolescent boys while controlling for race, class, and motivation. School performance helped explain the relationship between race and IQ only among African American youth (that is, low IQ led to school failure and delinquency); among white youth, the IQ-delinquency association was constant regardless of school performance.[175] In their influential book *Crime and Human Nature,* James Q. Wilson and Richard Herrnstein also agreed that the IQ-crime link is an indirect one: Low intelligence leads to poor school performance, which enhances the chances of criminality.[176] They concluded, "A child who chronically loses standing in the competition of the classroom may feel justified in settling the score outside, by violence, theft, and other forms of defiant illegality."[177]

The IQ-crime relationship has also been found in cross-national studies. A significant relationship between low IQ and delinquency has been found among samples of youth in Denmark;[178] Danish children with a low IQ

Is it nature or nurture? Even if some aspects of intelligence are inherited, there seems little question that those children who are raised in an environment lacking in economic resources and parental support will fail to maximize their intellectual potential. The mother here is going to college while on welfare in order to better support herself and child. Is it the responsibility of society to provide resources sufficient to enable all American youth to achieve their rightful share of intellectual development?

engage in delinquent behavior because their poor verbal ability is a handicap in the school environment.[179] Research by Canadian neuropsychologist Lorne Yeudall and his associates found samples of delinquents had IQs about 20 points lower than nondelinquent control groups on the Wechsler Adult Intelligence Scale.[180] An IQ-crime link was found by Hakan Stattin and Ingrid Klackenberg-Larsson in a longitudinal study of Swedish youth. This research is important because it shows that low IQ measures taken at age 3 were significant predictors of later criminality over the life course.[181]

IQ AND CRIME RECONSIDERED. While the Hirschi-Hindelang research increased interest and research on the association between IQ and crime, the issue is far from settled and still a matter of significant debate. A number of recent studies have found that IQ level has negligible influence on criminal behavior.[182] And a recent evaluation of existing knowledge on intelligence conducted by the American Psychological Association concluded that the strength of an IQ-crime link is "very low."[183]

In contrast, *The Bell Curve,* Richard Herrnstein and Charles Murray's influential albeit controversial book on intelligence, comes down firmly on the side of an IQ-crime link. Their extensive summary of the available literature shows that people with low IQs are more likely to commit crime, get caught, and be sent to prison. Conversely, at-risk kids with higher IQs seem to be protected from becoming criminals. Taking the scientific literature as a whole, Herrn-

stein and Murray conclude that criminal offenders have an average IQ of 92, about 8 points below the mean; chronic offenders score even lower than the "average" criminal. And to those skeptics who suggest that only low-IQ criminals get caught, they counter with data showing little difference in IQ scores between self-reported and official criminals.[184]

It is unlikely that the IQ-criminality debate will be settled in the near future. Measurement is beset by many methodological problems. The well-documented criticisms suggesting that IQ tests are race- and class-biased would certainly influence the testing of the criminal population, who are beset with a multitude of social and economic problems. Even if it can be shown that known offenders have lower IQs than the general population, it is difficult to explain many patterns in the crime rate: Why are males more criminal than females (are females three time smarter than males)? Why do crime rates vary by region, time of year and even weather patterns? Why does aging out occur? IQ does not increase with age—why should crime rates fall?

Social Policy Implications

For most of the 20th century, biological and psychological views of criminality have had an important influence on crime control and prevention policy. These views can be seen in front-end or *primary prevention* programs that seek to treat personal problems before they manifest themselves as crime. Thousands of family therapy organizations, substance abuse clinics, mental health associations, and so on are operating around the United States. Referrals to these resources are made by teachers, employers, courts, welfare agencies, and others. It is assumed that if a person's problems can be treated before they become overwhelming, some future crimes will be prevented. *Secondary prevention* programs provide such treatment as psychological counseling to youths and adults after they have violated the law. Attendance in such programs may be a mandatory requirement of a probation order, part of a diversionary sentence, or aftercare at the end of a prison sentence.

Biologically oriented therapy is also being used in the criminal justice system. Programs have altered diet, changed lighting, compensated for learning disabilities, treated allergies, and so on.[185] What is more controversial has been the use of mood-altering chemicals, such as lithium, pemoline, imipramine, phenytoin, and benzodiazepines, to control the behavior of antisocial individuals. Another practice that has elicited outcries of concern is the use of psychosurgery (brain surgery) to control antisocial behavior; surgical procedures have been used to alter the brain structure of convicted sex offenders in an effort to eliminate or control their sex drives. Results are still in the preliminary stage, but some critics have argued these procedures are without scientific merit.[186]

Some criminologists view biologically oriented treatments as a key to solving the problem of the chronic offender. Sarnoff Mednick and his associates have suggested that the biological analysis of criminal traits could pave the way for the development of preventive measures, regardless of whether the trait is inherited or acquired. They argue that a number of inherited physical traits that cause disease have been successfully treated with medication after their genetic code has been broken; why not, then, a genetic solution to crime?[187]

Whereas such biological treatment is a relatively new phenomenon, it has become commonplace since the 1920s to offer psychological treatment to offenders before, during, and after a criminal conviction. For example, since the 1970s pretrial programs have sought to divert offenders into nonpunitive rehabilitative programs designed to treat rather than punish them. Based on some type of counseling regime, diversion programs are commonly used with first offenders, nonviolent offenders, and so on. At the trial stage, judges often order psychological profiles of convicted offenders for planning a treatment program. Should they be kept in the community? Do they need a more secure confinement to deal with their problems? If correctional confinement is called for, inmates are commonly evaluated at a correctional center to measure their personality traits or disorders. Correctional facilities almost universally require inmates to participate in some form of psychological therapy: group therapy, individual analysis, transactional analysis, and so on. Parole decisions may be influenced by the prison psychologist's evaluation of the offender's adjustment.

Connections

Beyond these efforts, the law recognizes the psychological aspects of crime when it permits the insanity plea as an excuse for criminal liability or when it allows trial delay because of mental incompetency. See Chapter 2 for more on the insanity defense.

Summary

The earliest positivist criminologists were biologists. Led by Cesare Lombroso, these early researchers believed that some people manifested primitive traits that made them born criminals. Today, that research is debunked because of poor methodology, testing, and logic. Biological views fell out of favor in the early 20th century. In the 1970s, spurred by the publication of Edmund O. Wilson's *Sociobiology,* several criminologists again turned to study of the biological basis of criminality. For the most part, the effort has focused on the causes of violent crime. Interest has centered on several areas: (1) biochemical factors, such as diet, allergies, hormonal imbalances, and environmental contaminants (such as lead); (2) neurophysiological factors, such as brain disorders, EEG abnormalities, tumors, and head injuries; and (3) genetic factors, such as the XYY syndrome and inherited traits. There is also an evolutionary branch, which holds that changes in the human condition that have taken thousands of years to evolve may help explain crime rate differences.

Psychological attempts to explain criminal behavior have their historical roots in the concept that all criminals are insane or mentally damaged. This position is no longer accepted. Today, there are three main psychological perspectives. According to the psychodynamic view, originated by Sigmund Freud, aggressive behavior is linked to personality conflicts developed in childhood. In the view of some psychoanalysts, psychotics are aggressive, unstable people who can easily become involved in crime. According to behavioral and social learning theorists, criminality is a learned behavior: Children who are exposed to violence and see it rewarded may become violent as adults. In contrast, cognitive psychologists are concerned with human development and how people perceive the world. They see criminality as a function of improper information processing or moral development.

Psychological traits, such as personality and intelligence, have been linked to criminality. One important subject of study has been the psychopath, a person who lacks emotion and concern for others. The controversial issue of the relationship of IQ to criminality has been resurrected once again with the publication of studies purporting to show that criminals have lower IQs than noncriminals. Psychologists have developed standardized tests with which to measure personality traits. One avenue of research has been

Table 6.2 Biological and Psychological Theories

THEORY	MAJOR PREMISE	STRENGTHS
Biosocial		
Biochemical	Crime, especially violence, is a function of diet, vitamin intake, hormonal imbalance, or food allergies.	Explains irrational violence. Shows how the environment interacts with personal traits to influence behavior.
Neurological	Criminals and delinquents often suffer brain impairment, as measured by the EEG. Attention deficit disorder and minimum brain dysfunction are related to antisocial behavior.	Explains irrational violence. Shows how the environment interacts with personal traits to influence behavior.
Genetic	Criminal traits and predispositions are inherited. The criminality of parents can predict the delinquency of children.	Explains why only a small percentage of youth in a high-crime area become chronic offenders.
Evolutionary	As the human race evolved, traits and characteristics have become ingrained. Some of these traits make people aggressive and predisposed to commit crime.	Explains high violence rates and aggregate gender differences in the crime rate.
Psychological		
Psychodynamic	The development of the unconscious personality early in childhood influences behavior for the rest of a person's life. Criminals have weak egos and damaged personalities.	Explains the onset of crime and why crime and drug abuse cut across class lines.
Behavioral	People commit crime when they model their behavior after others they see being rewarded for the same acts. Behavior is reinforced by rewards and extinguished by punishment.	Explains the role of significant others in the crime process. Shows how family life and media can influence crime and violence.
Cognitive	Individual reasoning processes influence behavior. Reasoning is influenced by the way people perceive their environment and by their moral and intellectual development.	Shows why criminal behavior patterns change over time as people mature and develop their moral reasoning. May explain aging-out process.

to determine whether criminals and noncriminals manifest any differences in their responses to test items.

Table 6.2 reviews the biological and psychological theories of criminal behavior.

Key Terms

trait theories
somatotype
biophobia
sociobiology
equipotentiality
instincts
hypoglycemia
androgens
testosterone
premenstrual syndrome (PMS)
neurophysiology
electroencephalograph (EEG)
minimal brain dysfunction (MDB)
attention deficit/ hyperactivity disorder (AD/HD)
arousal theory
r/k theory
psychodynamic theory
repression
neurosis
psychosis
schizophrenia
inferiority complex
identity crisis
latent delinquency
behavior theory
social learning
behavior modeling
cognitive school
personality
psychopathy
sociopathy
antisocial personality

Notes

1. Israel Nachshon, "Neurological Bases of Crime, Psychopathy and Aggression," in *Crime in Biological, Social and Moral Contexts,* ed. Lee Ellis and Harry Hoffman (New York: Praeger, 1990), p. 199. Herein cited as *Crime in Biological Contexts.*

2. Raffaele Garofalo, *Criminology,* trans. Robert Miller (Boston: Little, Brown, 1914), p. 92.

3. Enrico Ferri, *Criminal Sociology* (New York: D. Appleton, 1909).

4. Richard Dugdale, *The Jukes: A Study in Crime, Pauperism, Disease, and Heredity* (New York: Putnam, 1910); Arthur Estabrook, *The Jukes in 1915* (Washington, D.C.: Carnegie Institute of Washington, 1916).

5. William Sheldon, *Varieties of Delinquent Youth* (New York: Harper Bros., 1949).

6. Lee Ellis, "A Discipline in Peril: Sociology's Future Hinges on Curing Biophobia," *American Sociologist* 27 (1996): 21–41.

7. Pierre van den Bergle, "Bringing The Beast Back In: Toward a Biosocial Theory of Aggression," *American Sociological Review* 39 (1974): 779.

8. Edmund O. Wilson, *Sociobiology* (Cambridge: Harvard University Press, 1975).

9. See, generally, Lee Ellis, "Introduction: The Nature of the Biosocial Perspective," *Crime in Biological Contexts,* pp. 3–18.

10. See, for example, Tracy Bennett Herbert and Sheldon Cohen, "Depression and Immunity: A Meta-Analytic Review," *Psychological Bulletin* 113 (1993): 472–486.

11. See, generally, Lee Ellis, *Theories of Rape* (New York: Hemisphere Publications, 1989).

12. Leonard Hippchen, "Some Possible Biochemical Aspects of Criminal Behavior," *Journal of Behavioral Ecology* 2 (1981): 1–6; Sarnoff Mednick and Jan Volavka, "Biology and Crime," in *Crime and Justice,* ed. Norval Morris and Michael Tonry (Chicago: University of Chicago Press, 1980), pp. 85–159; Saleem Shah and Loren Roth, "Biological and Psychophysiological Factors in Criminality," in *Handbook of Criminology,* ed. Daniel Glazer (Chicago: Rand McNally, 1974), pp. 125–140.

13. *Time,* 28 May 1979, p. 57.

14. Ulric Neisser et al., "Intelligence: Knowns and Unknowns," *American Psychologist* 51 (1996): 77–101.

15. Leonard Hippchen, ed., *Ecologic-Biochemical Approaches to Treatment of Delinquents and Criminals* (New York: Von Nostrand Reinhold, 1978), p. 14.

16. Michael Krassner, "Diet and Brain Function," *Nutrition Reviews* 44 (1986): 12–15.

17. Hippchen, *Ecologic-Biochemical Approaches.*

18. J. Kershner and W. Hawke, "Megavitamins and Learning Disorders: A Controlled Double-Blind Experiment," *Journal of Nutrition* 109 (1979): 819–826.

19. Richard Knox, "Test Shows Smart People's Brains Use Nutrients Better," *Boston Globe,* 16 February 1988, p. 9.

20. Ronald Prinz and David Riddle, "Associations Between Nutrition and Behavior in 5-Year-Old Children," *Nutrition Reviews Supplement* 44 (1986): 151–158.

21. Stephen Schoenthaler and Walter Doraz, "Types of Offenses Which Can Be Reduced in an Institutional Setting Using Nutritional Intervention," *International Journal of Biosocial Research* 4 (1983): 74–84; idem, "Diet and Crime," *International Journal of Biosocial Research* 4 (1983): 85–94. See also A. G. Schauss, "Differential Outcomes Among Probationers Comparing Orthomolecular Approaches to Conventional Casework Counseling," paper presented at the annual meeting of the American Society of Criminology, Dallas, 9 November 1978; A. Schauss and C. Simonsen, "A Critical Analysis of the Diets of Chronic Juvenile Offenders, Part I," *Journal of Orthomolecular Psychiatry* 8 (1979): 222–226; A. Hoffer, "Children with Learning and Behavioral Disorders," *Journal of Orthomolecular Psychiatry* 5 (1976): 229.

22. Prinz and Riddle, "Associations Between Nutrition and Behavior in 5-Year-Old Children."

23. H. Bruce Ferguson, Clare Stoddart, and Jovan Simeon, "Double-Blind Challenge Studies of Behavioral and Cognitive Effects of Sucrose-Aspartame Ingestion in Normal Children," *Nutrition Reviews Supplement* 44 (1986): 144–158; Gregory Gray, "Diet, Crime and Delinquency: A Critique," *Nutrition Reviews Supplement* 44 (1986): 89–94.

24. Mark Wolraich, Scott Lindgren, Phyllis Stumbo, Lewis Stegink, Mark Appelbaum, and Mary Kiritsy, "Effects of Diets High in Sucrose or Aspartame on the Behavior and Cognitive Performance of Children," *The New England Journal of Medicine* 330 (1994): 303–306.

25. Dian Gans, "Sucrose and Unusual Childhood Behavior," *Nutrition Today* 26 (1991): 8–14.

26. D. Hill and W. Sargent, "A Case of Matricide," *Lancet* 244 (1943): 526–527.

27. E. Podolsky, "The Chemistry of Murder," *Pakistan Medical Journal* 15 (1964): 9–14.

28. J. A. Yaryura-Tobias and F. Neziroglu, "Violent Behavior, Brain Dysrhythmia and Glucose Dysfunction: A New Syndrome," *Journal of Orthopsychiatry* 4 (1975): 182–188.

29. Matti Virkkunen, "Reactive Hypoglycemic Tendency Among Habitually Violent Offenders," *Nutrition Reviews Supplement* 44 (1986): 94–103.

30. James Q. Wilson, *The Moral Sense* (New York: Free Press, 1993).

31. Walter Gove, "The Effect of Age and Gender on Deviant Behavior: A Biopsychosocial Perspective," in *Gender and the Life Course,* ed. A. S. Rossi (New York: Aldine, 1985), pp. 115–144.

32. Alan Booth and D. Wayne Osgood, "The Influence of Testosterone on Deviance in Adulthood: Assessing and Explaining the Relationship," *Criminology* 31 (1993): 93–118.

33. Christy Miller Buchanan, Jacquelynne Eccles, and Jill Becker, "Are Adolescents the Victims of Raging Hormones? Evidence for Activational Effects of Hormones on Moods and Behavior at Adolescence," *Psychological Bulletin* 111 (1992): 62–107.

34. Booth and Osgood, "The Influence of Testosterone on Deviance in Adulthood."

35. Albert Reiss and Jeffrey Roth, eds., *Understanding and Preventing Violence* (Washington, D.C.: National Academy Press, 1993), p. 118. This report by the National Research Council Panel on the Understanding and Control of Violent Behavior is hereafter cited as *Understanding Violence.*

36. L. E. Kreuz and R. M. Rose, "Assessment of Aggressive Behavior and Plasma Testosterone in a Young Criminal Population," *Psychosomatic Medicine* 34 (1972): 321–332.

37. Lee Ellis, "Evolutionary and Neurochemical Causes of Sex Differences in Victimizing Behavior: Toward a Unified Theory of Criminal Behavior and Social Stratification," *Social Science Information* 28 (1989): 605–636.

38. For a general review, see Lee Ellis and Phyllis Coontz, "Androgens, Brain Functioning, and Criminality: The Neurohormonal Foundations of Antisociality," in *Crime in Biological Contexts,* pp. 162–193.

39. Ibid., p. 181.

40. Robert Rubin, "The Neuroendocrinology and Neurochemistry of Antisocial Behavior," in *The Causes of Crime, New Biological Approaches,* ed. Sarnoff Mednick, Terrie Moffitt, and Susan Stack (Cambridge: Cambridge University Press, 1987), pp. 239–262.

41. J. Money, "Influence of Hormones on Psychosexual Differentiation," *Medical Aspects of Nutrition* 30 (1976): 165.

42. Mednick and Volavka, "Biology and Crime."

43. For a review of this concept see, Anne E. Figert, "The Three Faces of PMS: The Professional, Gendered, and Scientific Structuring of a Psychiatric Disorder," *Social Problems* 42 (1995): 56–72.

44. Katharina Dalton, *The Premenstrual Syndrome* (Springfield, Ill.: Charles C Thomas, 1971).

45. Julie Horney, "Menstrual Cycles and Criminal Responsibility," *Law and Human Nature* 2 (1978): 25–36.

46. Diana Fishbein, "Selected Studies on the Biology of Antisocial Behavior," in *New Perspectives in Criminology,* ed. John Conklin (Needham Heights, Mass.: Allyn & Bacon, 1996), pp. 26–38.

47. Fishbein, "Selected Studies on the Biology of Antisocial Behavior"; Karen Paige, "Effects of Oral Contraceptives on Affective Fluctuations Associated with the Menstrual Cycle," *Psychosomatic Medicine* 33 (1971): 515–537.

48. H. E. Amos and J. J. P. Drake, "Problems Posed by Food Additives," *Journal of Human Nutrition* 30 (1976): 165.

49. Ray Wunderlich, "Neuroallergy as a Contributing Factor to Social Misfits: Diagnosis and Treatment," in *Ecologic-Biochemical Approaches,* pp. 229–253.

50. See, for example, Paul Marshall, "Allergy and Depression: A Neurochemical Threshold Model of the Relation Between the Illnesses," *Psychological Bulletin* 113 (1993): 23–39.

51. A. R. Mawson and K. J. Jacobs, "Corn Consumption, Tryptophan, and Cross-National Homicide Rates," *Journal of Orthomolecular Psychiatry* 7 (1978): 227–230.

52. Alexander Schauss, *Diet, Crime and Delinquency* (Berkeley, Calif.: Parker House, 1980).

53. C. Hawley and R. E. Buckley, "Food Dyes and Hyperkinetic Children," *Academy Therapy* 10 (1974): 27–32.

54. John Ott, "The Effects of Light and Radiation on Human Health and Behavior," in *Ecologic-Biochemical Approaches,* pp. 105–183. See also A. Kreuger and S. Sigel, "Ions in the Air," *Human Nature* (July 1978): 46–47; Harry Wohlfarth, "The Effect of Color Psychodynamic Environmental Modification on Discipline Incidents in Elementary Schools over One School Year: A Controlled Study," *International Journal of Biosocial Research* 6 (1984): 44–53.

55. Oliver David, Stanley Hoffman, Jeffrey Sverd, Julian Clark, and Kytja Voeller, "Lead and Hyperactivity, Behavior Response to Chelation: A Pilot Study," *American Journal of Psychiatry* 133 (1976): 1155–1158.

56. Deborah Denno, "Considering Lead Poisoning as a Criminal Defense," *Fordham Urban Law Journal* 20 (1993): 377–400.

57. Herbert Needleman, Julie Riess, Michael Tobin, Gretchen Biesecker, and Joel Greenohouse, "Bone Lead Levels and Delinquent Behavior," *Journal of the American Medical Association* 275 (1996): 363–369.

58. Ulric Neisser et al., "Intelligence: Knowns and Unknowns," *American Psychologist* 51 (1996): 77–101.

59. Terrie Moffitt, "The Neuropsychology of Juvenile Delinquency: A Critical Review," in *Crime and Justice, An Annual Review,* vol. 12, ed. Norval Morris and Michael Tonry (Chicago: University of Chicago Press, 1990), pp. 99–169.

60. Terrie Moffitt, Donald Lyman, and Phil Silva, "Neuropsychological Tests Predicting Persistent Male Delinquency," *Criminology* 32 (1994): 277–300; Elizabeth Kandel and Sarnoff Mednick, "Perinatal Complications Predict Violent Offending," *Criminology* 29 (1991): 519–529; Sarnoff Mednick, Ricardo Machon, Matti Virkkunen, and Douglas Bonett, "Adult Schizophrenia Following Prenatal Exposure to an Influenza Epidemic," *Archives of General Psychiatry* 44 (1987): 35–46; C. A. Fogel, S. A. Mednick, and N. Michelson, "Hyperactive Behavior and Minor Physical Anomalies," *Acta Psychiatrica Scandinavia* 72 (1985): 551–556.

61. R. Johnson, *Aggression in Man and Animals* (Philadelphia: Saunders, 1972), p. 79.

62. Jean Seguin, Robert Pihl, Philip Harden, Richard Tremblay, and Bernard Boulerice, "Cognitive and Neuropsychological Characteristics of Physically Aggressive Boys," *Journal of Abnormal Psychology* 104 (1995): 614–624; Deborah Denno, "Gender, Crime and the Criminal Law Defenses," *Journal of Criminal Law and Criminology* 85 (1994): 80–180.

63. Deborah Denno, *Biology, Crime and Violence: New Evidence* (Cambridge: Cambridge University Press, 1989).

64. Diana Fishbein and Robert Thatcher, "New Diagnostic Methods in Criminology: Assessing Organic Sources of Behavioral Disorders," *Journal of Research in Crime and Delinquency* 23 (1986): 240–267.

65. Lorne Yeudall, "A Neuropsychosocial Perspective of Persistent Juvenile Delinquency and Criminal Behavior." Paper presented at the New York Academy of Sciences, 26 September 1979.

66. R. W. Aind and T. Yamamoto, "Behavior Disorders of Childhood," *Electroencephalography and Clinical Neurophysiology* 21 (1966): 148–156.

67. See, generally, Jan Volavka, "Electroencephalogram Among Criminals," in *The Causes of Crime, New Biological Approaches,* ed. Sarnoff Mednick, Terrie Moffitt, and Susan Stack (Cambridge: Cambridge University Press, 1987), pp. 137–145.

68. Z. A. Zayed, S. A. Lewis, and R. P. Britain, "An Encephalographic and Psychiatric Study of 32 Insane Murderers," *British Journal of Psychiatry* 115 (1969): 1115–1124.

69. Fishbein and Thatcher, "New Diagnostic Methods in Criminology."

70. D. R. Robin, R. M. Starles, T. J. Kenney, B. J. Reynolds, and F. P. Heald, "Adolescents Who Attempt Suicide," *Journal of Pediatrics* 90 (1977): 636–638.

71. R. R. Monroe, *Brain Dysfunction in Aggressive Criminals* (Lexington, Mass.: D.C. Heath, 1978).

72. L. T. Yeudall, *Childhood Experiences as Causes of Criminal Behavior* (Senate of Canada, Issue no. 1, Thirteenth Parliament, Ottawa, 1977).

73. Stephen Faraone et al., "Intellectual Performance and School Failure in Children with Attention Deficit Hyperactivity Disorder and in Their Siblings," *Journal of Abnormal Psychology* 102 (1993): 616–623.

74. Ibid.

75. Terrie Moffitt and Phil Silva, "Self-Reported Delinquency, Neuropsychological Deficit, and History of Attention Deficit Disorder," *Journal of Abnormal Child Psychology* 16 (1988): 553–569.

76. Eugene Maguin, Rolf Loeber, and Paul LeMahieu, "Does the Relationshp Between Poor Reading and Delinquency Hold for Males of Different Ages and Ethnic Groups?" *Journal of Emotional and Behavioral Disorders* 1 (1993): 88–100.

77. Elizabeth Hart et al., "Developmental Change in Attention-Deficit Hyperactivity Disorder in Boys: A Four-Year Longitudinal Study," *Journal of Consulting and Clinical Psychology* 62 (1994): 472–491.

78. Yeudall, "A Neuropsychosocial Perspective of Persistent Juvenile Delinquency and Criminal Behavior," p. 4; F. A. Elliott, "Neurological Aspects of Antisocial Behavior," in *The Psychopath: A Comprehensive Study of Antisocial Disorders and Behaviors,* ed. W. H. Reid (New York: Brunner/Mazel, 1978), pp. 146–189.

79. Lorne Yeudall, Orestes Fedora, and Delee Fromm, "A Neuropsychosocial Theory of Persistent Criminality: Implications for Assessment and Treatment," in *Advances in Forensic Psychology and Psychiatry,* ed. Robert Rieber (Norwood, N.J.: Ablex Publishing, 1987), pp. 119–191.

80. Ibid., p. 177.

81. Ibid., pp. 24–25.

82. H. K. Kletschka, "Violent Behavior Associated with Brain Tumor," *Minnesota Medicine* 49 (1966): 1853–1855.

83. V. E. Krynicki, "Cerebral Dysfunction in Repetitively Assaultive Adolescents," *Journal of Nervous and Mental Disease* 166 (1978): 59–67.

84. C. E. Lyght, ed., *The Merck Manual of Diagnosis and Therapy* (West Point, Fla.: Merck, 1966).

85. *Understanding Violence,* p. 119.

86. M. Virkkunen, M. J. DeJong, J. Bartko, and M. Linnoila, "Psychobiological Concomitants of History of Suicide Attempts Among Violent Offenders and Impulsive Fire Starters," *Archives of General Psychiatry* 46 (1989): 604–606.

87. Matti Virkkunen, David Goldman, and Markku Linnoila, "Serotonin in Alcoholic Violent Offenders," The Ciba Foundation Symposium, *Genetics of Criminal and Antisocial Behavior* (Chichester, England: Wiley), 1995.

88. Lee Ellis, "Left- and Mixed-Handedness and Criminality: Explanations for a Probable Relationship," in *Left-Handedness: Behavioral Implications and Anomalies,* ed. S. Coren (Amsterdam: Elsevier, 1990): 485–507.

89. Lee Ellis, "Monoamine Oxidase and Criminality: Identifying an Apparent Biological Marker for Antisocial Behavior," *Journal of Research in Crime and Delinquency* 28 (1991): 227–251.

90. Walter Gove and Charles Wilmoth, "Risk, Crime and Neurophysiologic Highs: A Consideration of Brain Processes That May Reinforce Delinquent and Criminal Behavior," in *Crime in Biological Contexts,* pp. 261–293.

91. Jack Katz, *Seduction of Crime: Moral and Sensual Attractions of Doing Evil* (New York: Basic Books, 1988), pp. 12–15.

92. Lee Ellis, "Arousal Theory and the Religiosity-Criminality Relationship," in *Contemporary Criminological Theory,* ed. Peter Cordella and Larry Siegel (Boston, Mass.: Northeastern University, 1996), pp. 65–84.

93. For a general view, see Richard Lerner and Terryl Foch, *Biological-Psychosocial Interactions in Early Adolescence* (Hilldale, N.J.: Lawrence Erlbaum Associates, 1987).

94. Kerry Jang, W. John Livesley, and Philip Vernon, "Heritability of the Big Five Personality Dimensions and Their Facets: A Twin Study," *Journal of Personality* 64 (1996): 577–589.

95. David Rowe, "As the Twig Is Bent: The Myth of Child-Rearing Influences on Personality Development," *Journal of Counseling and Development* 68 (1990): 606–611; David Rowe, Joseph Rogers, and Sylvia Meseck-Bushey, "Sibling Delinquency and the Family Environment: Shared and Unshared Influences," *Child Development* 63 (1992): 59–67.

96. Patricia Brennan, Sarnoff Mednick, and Bjorn Jacobsen, "Assessing the Role of Genetics in Crime Using Adoption Cohorts," *Genetics of Criminal and Antisocial Behavior,* pp. 115–128; Gregory Carey and David DiLalla, "Personality and Psychopathology: Genetic Perspectives," *Journal of Abnormal Psychology* 103 (1994): 32–43.

97. T. R. Sarbin and L. E. Miller, "Demonism Revisited: The XYY Chromosome Anomaly," *Issues in Criminology* 5 (1970): 195–207.

98. Mednick and Volavka, "Biology and Crime," p. 93.

99. Ibid., p. 94.

100. Ibid., p. 95.

101. See Sarnoff A. Mednick and Karl O. Christiansen, eds., *Biosocial Bases in Criminal Behavior* (New York: Gardner Press, 1977).

102. David Rowe, "Genetic and Environmental Components of Antisocial Behavior: A Study of 265 Twin Pairs," *Criminology* 24 (1986): 513–532; David Rowe and D. Wayne Osgood, "Heredity and Sociological Theories of Delinquency: A Reconsideration," *American Sociological Review* 49 (1984): 526–540.

103. Edwin J. C. G. van den Oord, Frank Verhulst, and Dorret Boomsma, "A Genetic Study of Maternal and Paternal Ratings of Problem Behaviors in 3-Year-Old Twins," *Journal of Abnormal Psychology* 105 (1996): 349–357.

104. Michael Lyons, "A Twin Study of Self-Reported Criminal Behavior," Judy Silberg, Joanne Meyer, Andrew Pickles, Emily Simonoff, Lindon Eaves, John Hewitt, Hermine Maes, and Michael Rutter, "Heterogeneity Among Juvenile Antisocial Behaviors: Findings from the Virginia Twin Study of Adolescent Behavioral Development," in The Ciba Foundation Symposium, *Genetics of Criminal and Antisocial Behavior* (Chichester, England: Wiley), 1995.

105. Gregory Carey, "Twin Imitation for Antisocial Behavior: Implications for Genetic and Family Environment Research," *Journal of Abnormal Psychology* 101 (1992): 18–25; David Rowe and Joseph Rodgers, "The Ohio Twin Project and ADSEX Studies: Behavior Genetic Approaches to Understanding Antisocial Behavior," paper presented at the American Society of Criminology Meeting, Montreal, Canada, November 1987.

106. David Rowe, *The Limits of Family Influence: Genes, Experiences and Behavior* (New York: Guilford Press, 1995), p. 64.

107. R. J. Cadoret, C. Cain, and R. R. Crowe, "Evidence for a Gene-Environment Interaction in the Development of Adolescent Antisocial Behavior," *Behavior Genetics* 13 (1983): 301–310.

108. Barry Hutchings and Sarnoff A. Mednick, "Criminality in Adoptees and Their Adoptive and Biological Parents: A Pilot Study," in *Biological Bases in Criminal Behavior,* ed. S. A. Mednick and K. O. Christiansen (New York: Gardner Press, 1977).

109. For similar results, see Sarnoff Mednick, Terrie Moffitt, William Gabrielli, and Barry Hutchings, "Genetic Factors in Criminal Behavior: A Review," *Development of Antisocial and Prosocial Behavior* (New York: Academic Press, 1986), pp. 3–50; Sarnoff Mednick, William Gabrielli, and Barry Hutchings, "Genetic Influences in Criminal Behavior: Evidence from an Adoption Cohort," in *Perspective Studies of Crime and Delinquency,* ed. Katherine Teilmann Van Dusen and Sarnoff Mednick (Boston: Kluver-Nijhoff, 1983), pp. 39–57.

110. Michael Bohman, "Predisposition to Criminality: Swedish Adoption Studies in Retrospect," in *Genetics of Criminal and Antisocial Behavior,* pp. 99–114.

111. Glenn Walters, "A Meta-Analysis of the Gene-Crime Relationship," *Criminology* 30 (1992): 595–613.

112. Lawrence Cohen and Richard Machalek, "A General Theory of Expropriative Crime: An Evolutionary Ecological Approach," *American Journal of Sociology* 94 (1988): 465–501.

113. Lee Ellis, "The Evolution of Violent Criminal Behavior and Its Nonlegal Equivalent," *Crime in Biological Contexts,* pp. 63–65.

114. Lee Ellis and Anthony Walsh, "Gene-Based Evolutionary Theories of Criminology," *Criminology* (1997, in press).

115. Lee Ellis, "Sex Differences in Criminality: An Explanation Based on the Concept of r/k Selection," *Mankind Quarterly* 30 (1990): 17–37.

116. Ellis and Walsh, "Gene-Based Evolutionary Theories of Criminology."

117. Byron Roth, "Crime and Child Rearing," *Society* 34 (1996): 39–45.

118. Deborah Denno, "Sociological and Human Developmental Explanations of Crime: Conflict or Consensus," *Criminology* 23 (1985): 711–741.

119. Israel Nachshon and Deborah Denno, "Violence and Cerebral Function," in *The Causes of Crime, New Biological Approaches,* ed. Sarnoff Mednick, Terrie Moffitt, and Susan Stack (Cambridge: Cambridge University Press, 1987), pp. 185–217.

120. Avshalom Caspi, Donald Lyman, Terrie Moffitt, and Phil Silva, "Unraveling Girls' Delinquency: Biological, Dispositional, and Contextual Contributions to Adolescent Misbehavior," *Developmental Psychology* 29 (1993): 283–289.

121. Glenn Walters and Thomas White, "Heredity and Crime: Bad Genes or Bad Research," *Criminology* 27 (1989): 455–486.

122. Charles Goring, *The English Convict: A Statistical Study, 1913* (Montclair, N.J.: Patterson Smith, 1972).

123. Edwin Driver, "Charles Buckman Goring," in *Pioneers in Criminology,* ed. Hermann Mannheim (Montclair, N.J.: Patterson Smith, 1970), p. 440.

124. Gabriel Tarde, *Penal Philosophy,* trans. R. Howell (Boston: Little, Brown, 1912).

125. See, generally, Donn Byrne and Kathryn Kelly, *An Introduction to Personality* (Englewood Cliffs, N.J.: Prentice-Hall, 1981).

126. Sigmund Freud, "The Ego and the Id," in *Complete Psychological Works of Sigmund Freud,* vol. 19 (London: Hogarth, 1948), p. 52.

127. August Aichorn, *Wayward Youth* (New York: Viking Press, 1935).

128. David Abrahamsen, *Crime and the Human Mind* (New York: Columbia University Press, 1944), p. 137; see, generally, Fritz Redl and Hans Toch, "The Psychoanalytic Perspective," in *Psychology of Crime and Criminal Justice,* ed. Hans Toch (New York: Holt, Rinehart and Winston, 1979), pp. 193–195.

129. See, generally, D. A. Andrews and James Bonta, *The Psychology of Criminal Conduct* (Cincinnati: Anderson, 1994), pp. 72–75.

130. Robert Krueger, Avshalom Caspi, Phil Silva, and Rob McGee, "Personality Traits Are Differentially Linked to Mental Disorders: A Multitrait-Multidiagnosis Study of an Adolescent Birth Cohort," *Journal of Abnormal Psychology* 105 (1996): 299–312.

131. Seymour Halleck, *Psychiatry and the Dilemmas of Crime* (Berkeley: University of California Press, 1971).

132. This discussion is based on three works by Albert Bandura: *Aggression: A Social Learning Analysis* (Englewood Cliffs, N.J.: Prentice-Hall, 1973), *Social Learning Theory* (Englewood Cliffs, N.J.: Prentice-Hall, 1977), and "The Social Learning Perspective: Mechanisms of Aggression," in *Psychology of Crime and Criminal Justice,* pp. 198–236.

133. David Phillips, "The Impact of Mass Media Violence on U.S. Homicides," *American Sociological Review* 48 (1983): 560–568.

134. See, generally, Jean Piaget, *The Moral Judgment of the Child* (London: Kegan Paul, 1932).

135. Lawrence Kohlberg, *Stages in the Development of Moral Thought and Action* (New York: Holt, Rinehart and Winston, 1969).

136. Lawrence Kohlberg, K. Kauffman, P. Scharf, and J. Hickey, *The Just Community Approach in Corrections: A Manual* (Niantic: Connecticut Department of Corrections, 1973).

137. Scott Henggeler, *Delinquency in Adolescence* (Newbury Park, Calif.: Sage, 1989), p. 26.

138. Carol Veneziano and Louis Veneziano, "The Relationship Between Deterrence and Moral Reasoning," *Criminal Justice Review* 17 (1992): 209–216.

139. K. A. Dodge, "A Social Information Processing Model of Social Competence in Children," in *Minnesota Symposium in Child Psychology,* vol. 18, ed. M. Perlmutter (Hillsdale, N.J.: Lawrence Erlbaum, 1986), pp. 77–125.

140. L. Huesman and L. Eron, "Individual Differences and the Trait of Aggression," *European Journal of Personality* 3 (1989): 95–106.

141. J. E. Lochman, "Self and Peer Perceptions and Attributional Biases of Aggressive and Nonaggressive Boys in Dyadic Interactions," *Journal of Consulting and Clinical Psychology* 55 (1987): 404–410.

142. D. Lipton, E. C. McDonel, and R. McFall, "Heterosocial Perception in Rapists," *Journal of Consulting and Clinical Psychology* 55 (1987): 17–21.

143. *Understanding Violence,* p. 389.

144. James Sorrells, "Kids Who Kill," *Crime and Delinquency* 23 (1977): 312–320.

145. Richard Rosner, "Adolescents Accused of Murder and Manslaughter: A Five-Year Descriptive Study," *Bulletin of the American Academy of Psychiatry and the Law* 7 (1979): 342–351.

146. Richard Famularo, Robert Kinscherff, and Terence Fenton, "Psychiatric Diagnoses of Abusive Mothers, A Preliminary Report," *Journal of Nervous and Mental Disease* 180 (1992): 658–660.

147. Richard Wagner, Dawn Taylor, Joy Wright, Alison Sloat, Gwynneth Springett, Sandy Arnold, and Heather Weinberg, "Substance Abuse Among the Mentally Ill," *American Journal of Orthopsychiatry* 64 (1994): 30–38.

148. Bruce Link, Howard Andrews, and Francis Cullen, "The Violent and Illegal Behavior of Mental Patients Reconsidered," *American Sociological Review* 57 (1992): 275–292; Ellen Hochstedler Steury, "Criminal Defendants with Psychiatric Impairment: Prevalence, Probabilities and Rates," *Journal of Criminal Law and Criminology* 84 (1993): 354–374.

149. Marc Hillbrand, John Krystal, Kimberly Sharpe, and Hilliard Foster, "Clinical Predictors of Self-Mutilation in Hospitalized Patients," *Journal of Nervous and Mental Disease* 182 (1994): 9–13.

150. Carmen Cirincione, Henry Steadman, Pamela Clark Robbins, and John Monahan, *Mental Illness as a Factor in Criminality: A Study of Prisoners and Mental Patients* (Delmar, N.Y.: Policy Research Associates, 1991). See also idem, *Schizophrenia as a Contingent Risk Factor for Criminal Violence* (Delmar, N.Y.: Policy Research Associates, 1991).

151. John Monahan, *Mental Illness and Violent Crime* (Washington, D.C.: National Institute of Justice, 1996).

152. Howard Berenbaum and Frank Fujita, "Schizophrenia and Personality: Exploring the Boundaries and Connections Between Vulnerability and Outcome," *Journal of Abnormal Psychology* 103 (1994): 148–158.

153. See Monahan, *Mental Illness and Violent Crime.*

154. See, generally, Walter Mischel, *Introduction to Personality,* 4th ed. (New York: Holt, Rinehart and Winston, 1986).

155. D. A. Andrews and J. Stephen Wormith, "Personality and Crime: Knowledge and Construction in Criminology," *Justice Quarterly* 6 (1989): 289–310; Donald Gibbons, "Comment—Personality and Crime: Non-Issues, Real Issues, and a Theory and Research Agenda," *Justice Quarterly* (1989): 311–324.

156. Sheldon Glueck and Eleanor Glueck, *Unraveling Juvenile Delinquency* (Cambridge: Harvard University Press, 1950).

157. See, generally, Hans Eysenck, *Personality and Crime* (London: Routledge & Kegan Paul, 1977).

158. Hans Eysenck and M. W. Eysenck, *Personality and Individual Differences* (New York: Plenum, 1985).

159. David Farrington, "Psychobiological Factors in the Explanation and Reduction of Delinquency," *Today's Delinquent* (1988): 37–51.

160. Laurie Frost, Terrie Moffitt, and Rob McGee, "Neuropsychological Correlates of Psychopathology in an Unselected Cohort of Young Adolescents," *Journal of Abnormal Psychology* 98 (1989): 307–313.

161. David Lykken, "Psychopathy, Sociopathy, and Crime," *Society* 34 (1996): 30–38.

162. Sheldon Glueck and Eleanor Glueck, *Delinquents and Nondelinquents in Perspective* (Cambridge, Mass.: Harvard University Press, 1968).

163. See, generally, R. Starke Hathaway and Elio Monachesi, *Analyzing and Predicting Juvenile Delinquency with the MMPI* (Minneapolis: University of Minnesota Press, 1953).

164. R. Starke Hathaway, Elio Monachesi, and Lawrence Young, "Delinquency Rates and Personality," *Journal of Criminal Law, Criminology, and Police Science* 51 (1960): 443–460; Michael Hindelang and Joseph Weis, "Personality and Self-Reported Delinquency: An Application of Cluster Analysis," *Criminology* 10 (1972): 268; Spencer Rathus and Larry Siegel, "Crime and Personality Revisited," *Criminology* 18 (1980): 245–251.

165. See, generally, Edward Megargee, *The California Psychological Inventory Handbook* (San Francisco: Jossey-Bass, 1972).

166. Karl Schuessler and Donald Cressey, "Personality Characteristics of Criminals," *American Journal of Sociology* 55 (1950): 476–484; Gordon Waldo and Simon Dinitz, "Personality Attributes of the Criminal: An Analysis of Research Studies 1950–1965," *Journal of Research in Crime and Delinquency* 4 (1967): 185–201; David Tennenbaum, "Research Studies of Personality and Criminality," *Journal of Criminal Justice* 5 (1977): 1–19.

167. Edward Helmes and John Reddon, "A Perspective on Developments in Assessing Psychopathology: A Critical Review of the MMPI and MMPI-2," *Psychological Bulletin* 113 (1993): 453–471.

168. Avshalom Caspi, Terrie Moffitt, Phil Silva, Magda Stouthamer-Loeber, Robert Krueger, and Pamela Schmutte, "Are Some People Crime-Prone? Replications of the Personality-Crime Relationship Across Countries, Genders, Races and Methods," *Criminology* 32 (1994): 163–195.

169. Henry Goddard, *Efficiency and Levels of Intelligence* (Princeton, N.J.: Princeton University Press, 1920); Edwin Sutherland, "Mental Deficiency and Crime," in *Social Attitudes,* ed. Kimball Young (New York: Henry Holt, 1931), chap. 15.

170. William Healy and Augusta Bronner, *Delinquency and Criminals: Their Making and Unmaking* (New York: Macmillan, 1926).

171. John Slawson, *The Delinquent Boys* (Boston: Budget Press, 1926).

172. Sutherland, "Mental Deficiency and Crime."

173. Travis Hirschi and Michael Hindelang, "Intelligence and Delinquency: A Revisionist Review," *American Sociological Review* 42 (1977): 471–586.

174. Deborah Denno, "Sociological and Human Developmental Explanations of Crime: Conflict or Consensus," *Criminology* 23 (1985): 711–741; Christine Ward and Richard McFall, "Further Validation of the Problem Inventory for Adolescent Girls: Comparing Caucasian and Black Delinquents and Nondelinquents," *Journal of Consulting and Clinical Psychology* 54 (1986): 732–733; L. Hubble and M. Groff, "Magnitude and Direction of WISC-R Verbal Performance IQ Discrepancies Among Adjudicated Male Delinquents," *Journal of Youth and Adolescence* 10 (1981): 179–183; Robert Gordon, "IQ Commensurability of Black-White Differences in Crime and Delinquency," paper presented at the annual meeting of the American Psychological Association, Washington, D.C., August 1986; idem, "Two Illustrations of the IQ-Surrogate Hypothesis: IQ Versus Parental Education and Occupational Status in the Race-IQ-Delinquency Model," paper presented at the annual meeting of the American Society of Criminology, Montreal, Canada, November 1987.

175. Donald Lynam, Terrie Moffitt, and Magda Stouthamer-Loeber, "Explaining the Relation Between IQ and Delinquency: Class, Race, Test Motivation, School Failure or Self-Control," *Journal of Abnormal Psychology* 102 (1993): 187–196.

176. James Q. Wilson and Richard Herrnstein, *Crime and Human Nature* (New York: Simon & Schuster, 1985), p. 148.

177. Ibid., p. 171.

178. Terrie Moffitt, William Gabrielli, Sarnoff Mednick, and Fini Schulsinger, "Socioeconomic Status, IQ, and Delinquency," *Journal of Abnormal Psychology* 90 (1981): 152–156.

179. Ibid., p. 155. For a similar finding, see Hubble and Groff, "Magnitude and Direction of WISC-R Verbal Performance IQ Discrepancies."

180. Lorne Yeudall, Delee Fromm-Auch, and Priscilla Davies, "Neuropsychological Impairment of Persistent Delinquency," *Journal of Nervous and Mental Diseases* 170 (1982): 257–265.

181. Hakan Stattin and Ingrid Klackenberg-Larsson, "Early Language and Intelligence Development and Their Relationship to Future Criminal Behavior," *Journal of Abnormal Psychology* 102 (1993): 369–378.

182. Scott Menard and Barbara Morse, "A Structuralist Critique of the IQ-Delinquency Hypothesis: Theory and Evidence," *American Journal of Sociology* 89 (1984): 1347–1378; Denno, "Sociological and Human Developmental Explanations of Crime."

183. Ulric Neisser et al., "Intelligence: Knowns and Unknowns," *American Psychologist* 51 (1996): 77–101.

184. Richard Herrnstein and Charles Murray, *The Bell Curve: Intelligence and Class Structure in American Life* (New York, Free Press, 1994).

185. Susan Pease and Craig T. Love, "Optimal Methods and Issues in Nutrition Research in the Correctional Setting," *Nutrition Reviews Supplement* 44 (1986): 122–131.

186. Mark O'Callaghan and Douglas Carroll, "The Role of Psychosurgical Studies in the Control of Antisocial Behavior," in *The Causes of Crime, New Biological Approaches,* ed. Sarnoff Mednick, Terrie Moffitt, and Susan Stack (Cambridge: Cambridge University Press, 1987), pp. 312–328.

187. Mednick, Moffitt, Gabrielli, and Hutchings, "Genetic Factors in Criminal Behavior: A Review," pp. 47–48.

Chapter 7
Social Structure Theories

motivations for crime do not result simply from the flaws, failures, or free choices of individuals. A complete explanation of crime ultimately must consider the sociocultural environments in which people are located.[1]

Sociology has been the primary focus of criminology since early in the 20th century. In the United States, the primacy of sociological criminology was secured by research begun in the early 20th century by Robert Ezra Park (1864–1944), Ernest W. Burgess (1886–1966), Louis Wirth (1897–1952), and their colleagues in the Sociology Department at the University of Chicago. Known as the **Chicago School,** these sociologists pioneered research work on the social ecology of the city and inspired a generation of scholars to conclude that social forces operating in urban areas create criminal interactions; some neighborhoods become "natural areas" for crime.

Connections

As you may recall from Chapter 1, sociological positivism can be traced to the works of Quetelet, Comte, and Durkheim. The work of Durkheim will be reviewed again in this chapter in the sections on anomie theory.

In 1915, Robert Ezra Park called for anthropological methods of description and observation to be applied to urban life.[2] He was concerned about how neighborhood structure develops, how isolated pockets of poverty form, and what social policies could be used to alleviate urban problems. Later, Park, with Ernest Burgess, studied the social ecology of the city and found that some neighborhoods form **natural areas** of wealth and affluence, while others suffer poverty and disintegration.[3] Regardless of their race, religion, or ethnicity, the everyday behavior of people living in these areas is controlled by the social and ecological climate.

Over the next 20 years, Chicago School sociologists carried out an ambitious program of research and scholarship on urban topics, including criminal behavior patterns. Such works as Harvey Zorbaugh's *The Gold Coast and the Slum,*[4] Frederick Thrasher's *The Gang,*[5] and Louis Wirth's *The Ghetto*[6] are classic examples of objective, highly descriptive accounts of urban life. Their influence was such that most criminologists have been trained in sociology, and criminology courses are routinely taught in departments of sociology.

Sociological Criminology

There are many reasons why sociology has remained the predominant approach of U.S. criminologists during this century. First, it has long been evident that varying patterns of criminal behavior exist within the social structure. Some geographic areas are more prone to violence and serious theft-related crimes than others. Criminologists have attempted to discover why such patterns exist and how they can be eliminated. Explanations of crime as an individual-level phenomenon fail to account for these consistent patterns in the crime rate. If violence, as some criminologists suggest, is related to chemical or chromosome abnormality, how can ecological differences in the crime rate be explained? It is unlikely that all people with physical anomalies live in one section of town or in one area of the country. There has been a heated national debate over the effects of violent TV shows on adolescent aggression. Yet adolescents in cities and towns with widely disparate crime rates, ranging from Los Angeles, California to Franconia, New Hampshire, all watch the same shows and movies; how can crime rate differences in these areas be explained? If violence has a biological or psychological origin, should it not be distributed more evenly throughout the social structure?

Sociology is concerned with social change and the dynamic aspects of human behavior. It follows transformations in cultural norms and institutions and the subsequent effect they have on individual and group behavior. These concepts are useful today because the changing structure of postmodern society continues to have a tremendous effect on intergroup and interpersonal relationships.[7] A reduction in the influence of the family has been accompanied by an increased emphasis on individuality, independence, and isolation. Weakened family ties have been linked to crime and delinquency.[8]

Another important social change has been rapid advances in technology and its influence on the social system. People who lack the requisite social and educational training have found that the road to success through upward occupational mobility has become almost impossible. Lack of upward mobility may make drug dealing and other crimes an attractive solution to socially deprived but economically enterprising people. Recent evidence shows that adults who are only marginally employed are the ones most likely to commit crime; thus, the quality of employment and not merely unemployment influences criminality.[9]

Connections

The association between crime and economic class has been muddied by the ambiguous relationship between unemployment and crime. Crime rates sometimes go up during periods of full employment and drop during periods of relatively high unemployment. The Close-Up on Crime and Unemployment later in this chapter explores this issue.

Sociology's stress on intergroup and interpersonal transactions also promotes it as a source for criminological study. Criminologists believe that understanding the dynamics of interactions between individuals and important social institutions, such as their families, their peers, their schools, their jobs, criminal justice agencies, and the like, is important for understanding the cause of crime.[10] The relationship of one social class or group to another or to the existing power structure that controls the nation's legal and economic system may also be involved in criminality. Sociology is concerned with the benefits of positive human interactions and the costs of negative ones. Crime is itself an interaction and therefore should not be studied without considering the interactions of all participants in a criminal act: the law violator, the victim, the law enforcers, the lawmakers, and social institutions.

To summarize, concern about the ecological distribution of crime, the effect of social change, and the interactive nature of crime itself has made sociology the foundation of modern criminology. This chapter reviews sociological theories that emphasize the relationship between social status and criminal behavior. In Chapter 8, the focus will shift to theories that emphasize socialization and its influence on crime and deviance; Chapter 9 covers theories based on the concept of social conflict.

Economic Structure and Crime

The United States is characterized by social **stratification.** Social strata are created by the unequal distribution of wealth, power, and prestige. Social classes are segments of the population whose members have a relatively similar portion of desirable things and who share attitudes, values, norms, and an identifiable lifestyle. In American society, it is common to identify people as upper-, middle-, and lower-class citizens, with a broad range of economic variations existing within each group. The upper-upper class is reserved for a small number of exceptionally well-to-do families who maintain enormous financial and social resources. The lower class consists of an estimated 36–50 million people who live in poverty (defined officially as a family of three earning under $12,158); almost 14% of the total U.S. population now live in poverty.[11] The number of Americans living in poverty and the percentage of the population living below the **poverty line** are actually greater today than they were 20 years ago (although somewhat less than in 1960, before the War on Poverty of the Johnson administration). The government's definition of the poverty line seems quite low. A more realistic figure of an annual income of less than $18,000 per family of three would mean that more than 50 million U.S. citizens live in poverty.[12]

A new shift is occurring in the distribution of poverty. For the first time, the elderly are better off than working-class people. Federal programs such as Medicare and social security coupled with private pensions have improved the lifestyle of retirees. At the same time, the young have been hit hard: 25% of children under six now live in poverty, a frightening number considering America's self-image as the "richest country on earth." A recent report by Columbia University's Center for Children in Poverty indicates that despite stereotypes, child poverty is rising at a faster rate among white families in suburbia than among African

American families in urban areas. Nonetheless, 6% of white children can be described as extremely poor as compared to 50% of young black children.[13] Another ominous sign is the polarization of the American economy: Since 1975 the wealthy have amassed an ever greater share of total income, while the middle class and poor have seen their economic health decline. The wealthiest fifth of the population now earn 11 times more income than the poorest fifth.[14]

Net Bookmark

A number of groups are dedicated to helping the poor. The Coalition for the Homeless is the nation's oldest and most progressive organization helping homeless men, women, and children. Since 1981 they have used litigation, lobbying, grassroots organizing, public education, and direct services in the battle against this crisis. Visit their homepage:

http://www.homeless.24x7.com/who.html

Lower-Class Culture

Lower-class slum areas are scenes of inadequate housing and health care, disrupted family lives, underemployment, and despair. Members of the lower class also suffer in other ways. They are more prone to depression, less likely to have achievement motivation, and less likely to put off immediate gratification for future gain. Some are driven to desperate measures to cope with their economic plight: About 22,000 newborn babies are abandoned each year in hospitals by mothers who are poverty stricken, drug-addicted, or homeless.[15]

Members of the lower class are constantly bombarded with a flood of advertisements linking material possessions to self-worth, but they are often unable to attain desired goods and services through conventional means. Although they are members of a society that extols material success above any other, they are unable to satisfactorily compete for such success with members of the upper classes.

The social problems found in lower-class slum areas have been described as an "epidemic" that spreads like a contagious disease, destroying the inner workings that enable neighborhoods to survive; they become "hollowed out."[16] As neighborhood quality decreases, the probability that residents will develop problems sharply increases. Adolescents in the worst neighborhoods have the greatest risk of dropping out of school and becoming teenage parents.

Racial Disparity

The disabilities suffered by the lower-class citizen are particularly acute for racial minorities. African Americans have a mean income level significantly lower than that of whites and an unemployment rate markedly higher. Although two-

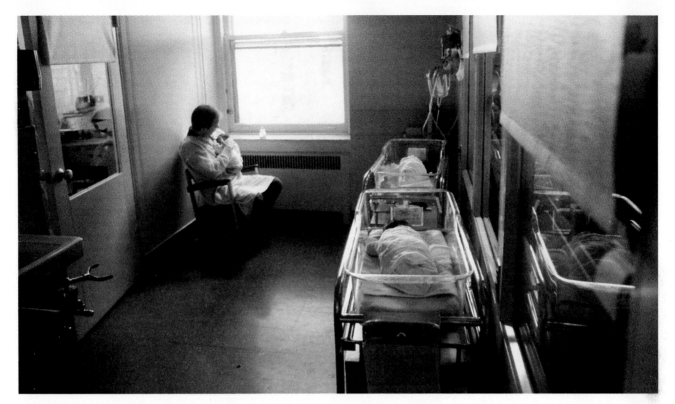

About 25% of children under age six now live in poverty, a frightening statistic considering America's self-image as the "richest country on earth." An estimated 22,000 newborn babies are abandoned each year in hospitals by mothers who are poverty stricken, drug addicted, or homeless. Here a volunteer comforts a crack-addicted baby in an urban hospital ward.

thirds to three-fourths of the urban poor are white, minorities are overrepresented within the poverty classes. The poverty rate for African American families is *three times* that of the white population. About 43% of African American children live in poverty, as compared to about 17% of white children; Latino children are also much more likely than white children to grow up in poverty (42%).[17]

Research conducted for the Joint Center for Political and Economic Studies found that more than 85% of African American children under three years of age living in families headed by women who had never married were today living in poverty. Even more disturbing is the fact that the number and percentage of African American children living in poverty in urban areas outside the South has increased substantially since 1970 (African American poverty has actually declined in the South).[18]

Economic problems are not the only ones faced by racial minorities. African American men in the United States have a much shorter life span than white men, who can expect to live an average of 6 years longer (69.4 years versus 75.4 years).[19] In fact, lifestyles among the urban African American underclass are so disturbed that their life span is considerably shorter than that of people in the poorest Third World countries. One study by doctors in New York found that while only 40% of the male residents

of Harlem live to age 65, 55% of the males in Bangladesh, one of the world's poorest countries, reach that age.[20]

The problems faced by minority-group members may soon increase, because racial segregation and isolation of poor African Americans and Hispanics in urban areas is similarly increasing.[21] A report by the Harvard University Project of School Desegregation shows that the percentage of minority students attending schools with more than a 50% minority student population has risen since 1970, reversing gains made during the civil rights movement in the 1960s. About one-third of all African American children attend schools in which more than 90% of the students are minorities; these schools often face insufficient funding and a high level of poverty.[22] Clearly, the problems of racial segregation continue and may even be growing.

The Underclass

In 1966, sociologist Oscar Lewis argued that the crushing lifestyle of slum areas produces a "culture of poverty" passed from one generation to the next.[23] The **culture of poverty** is marked by apathy, cynicism, helplessness, and mistrust of social institutions, such as schools, government agencies, and the police. This mistrust prevents slum dwellers from taking advantage of the meager opportunities

close-up: *When Work Disappears*

In 1987 William Julius Wilson provided a description of the plight of the lowest levels of the underclass, which he labeled the **truly disadvantaged.** Wilson portrayed members of this group as socially isolated people who dwell in urban inner cities, occupy the bottom rung of the social ladder, and are the victims of discrimination. They live in areas in which the basic institutions of society—family, school, housing—have long since declined. Their decline triggers similar breakdowns in the strengths of inner-city areas, including the loss of community cohesion and the application of informal sanctions against illicit behavior. These effects magnify the isolation of the underclass from mainstream society and promote a ghetto culture and behavior.

Since the "truly disadvantaged" rarely come into contact with the actual source of their oppression, they direct their anger and aggression at those with whom they are in close and intimate contact. Members of this group, plagued by underemployment or unemployment, begin to lose self-confidence, a feeling supported by the plight of kin and friendship groups who also experience extreme economic marginality. Self-doubt is a neighborhood norm, overwhelming those forced to live in areas of concentrated poverty.

In a more recent work called *When Work Disappears*, Wilson assesses the effect of joblessness and underemployment on residents in poor neighborhoods on Chicago's South Side. He argues that for the first time in the 20th century, most adults in inner-city ghetto neighborhoods are not working during a typical week. He finds that inner-city life is only marginally affected by the surge in the nation's economy brought about by new industrial growth connected with technological development. Poverty in these inner-city areas

is eternal and unchanging and if anything worsening as residents are further shut out of the economic mainstream. Difficult as life was in the 1940s and 1950s for African Americans, they at least had a reasonable hope of steady work. Now, because of the globalization of the economy, those opportunities have evaporated.

Wilson focuses on the plight of the African American community, which had enjoyed periods of relative prosperity in the 1950s and 1960s. Although racial segregation limited opportunity, growth in the manufacturing sector fueled upward mobility and provided the foundation of today's African American middle class. Those opportunities are gone, as manufacturing plants have moved to nonaccessible rural and overseas locations where the cost of doing business is lower. As manufacturing has left, service and retail establishments that depended on blue-collar spending have similarly disappeared, leaving behind an economy based on welfare and government supports. In less than 20 years, formerly active African American communities have become crime-infested slums.

The hardships faced by residents in Chicago's South Side are not unique to that community. Beyond sustaining inner-city poverty, the absence of employment opportunities has torn at the social fabric of the nation's inner-city neighborhoods. Work helps socialize young people into the wider society, instilling in them such desirable values as hard work, caring, and respect for others. When work becomes scarce, the discipline and structure it provides are absent. Communitywide underemployment destroys social cohesion, increasing the presence of neighborhood social problems ranging from drug use to educational failure. Schools in these

areas are unable to teach basic skills, and because desirable employment is lacking, there are few adults to serve as role models. In contrast to more affluent suburban households where daily life is organized around job and career demands, children in inner-city areas are unsocialized in the workings of the mainstream economy.

Wilson is not optimistic about the job prospects of lower-class African American males; neither white nor black employers seem particularly inclined to hire poor black men. He is skeptical that private employers will hire the poor as childcare providers or in other service tasks, even if given tax incentives to do so. Instead, Wilson believes that only a nationwide effort to improve schools, provide daycare, and enhance public transportation can turn the inner city around. A public works program modeled after the Depression Era efforts of the Works Project Administration (WPA) may be needed to reverse the damage of inner-city unemployment. People want to work; they must be given the opportunity for legitimate and sustaining employment.

CRITICAL THINKING QUESTIONS

1. Is it unrealistic to assume that a government-sponsored public works program can provide needed jobs in this era of budget cutbacks?
2. What are some of the hidden costs of unemployment in a community setting?
3. How would a biocriminologist explain Wilson's findings?

Sources: William Julius Wilson, *The Truly Disadvantaged* (Chicago: University of Chicago Press, 1987); *When Work Disappears, The World of the Urban Poor* (New York: Knopf, 1996).

---

available to them. Lewis's work was the first of a group that described the plight of **at-risk** children and adults. In 1970 Gunnar Myrdal described a worldwide **underclass** cut off from society, its members lacking the education and skills needed to be effectively in demand in modern society.[24] In 1983, Ken Auletta described a U.S. underclass in much the same terms.[25] Perhaps the most important recent analysis of the underclass is provided by sociologist William Julius Wilson; his work is detailed in the Close-Up, "When Work Disappears."

Sociologist William Julius Wilson is the author of *The Truly Disadvantaged* and *When Work Disappears*. According to Wilson, social breakdown in inner-city areas magnifies the isolation of the underclass from mainstream society and promotes a ghetto culture and behavior.

Are the Poor "Undeserving"?

Despite all our technological success, the fact that a significant percentage of U.S. citizens are either homeless or living in areas of concentrated poverty is an important social problem. The media frequently focus on the distress suffered by homeless and poverty-stricken families. Yet some observers view impoverished people as somehow responsible for their own fate, the so-called *undeserving poor;* if they tried, the argument goes, they could "improve themselves."[26]

This conclusion is baseless. It is a sad fact that poverty is becoming evermore concentrated among minority groups forced to live in physically deteriorated, inner-city neighborhoods that have high crime, poor schools, and excessive mortality.[27] A study by the National Research Council on inner-city poverty in the United States concluded that poor people living in areas of extreme poverty are more likely to suffer social ills than poor people living in more affluent communities.[28] People living in urban ghettos suffer higher rates of unemployment, are more dependent on welfare, and are more likely to live in single-parent households than *equally indigent people who reside in more affluent areas.* The burden of living in these high-poverty areas, then, goes beyond merely "being poor"; under these conditions, self-help and upward mobility are highly problematic.

Community effects may be particularly damaging on children. Adolescents residing in areas of concentrated poverty are more likely to suffer in their cognitive development, sexual and family formation practices, school attendance habits, and transition to employment.[29] Lack of ed-ucation and family stability make them poor candidates for employment.

These findings suggest that the poor of inner-city ghettos confront obstacles far greater than the mere lack of financial resources. The National Research Council's review indicates that the social problems faced by many ghetto residents render them unprepared to take advantage of employment opportunities even in favorable labor markets.[30] The fact that many of the underclass are African American children who can expect to spend all their life in poverty is probably the single most important problem facing the nation today.[31]

Branches of Social Structure Theory

Considering the deprivations suffered by the lower class, it is not surprising that a disadvantaged economic class position has been viewed by many criminologists as a primary cause of crime. This view is referred to here as **social structure theory.** As a group, social structure theories suggest that forces operating in deteriorated lower-class areas push many of their residents into criminal behavior patterns. These theories consider the existence of unsupervised teenage gangs, high crime rates, and social disorder in slum areas as major social problems.

Lower-class crime is often the violent, destructive product of youth gangs and marginally employed young adults. Although members of the middle and upper classes also engage in crime, social structure theorists view middle-class crime or white-collar crime as being of relatively lower frequency, seriousness, and danger to the general public. The "real crime problem" is essentially a lower-class phenomenon, beginning in youth and continuing into young adulthood.

Most social structure theories focus on the law-violating behavior of youth. They suggest that the social forces that cause crime begin to affect people while they are relatively young and continue to influence them throughout their life. Although not all youthful offenders become adult criminals, many begin their training and learn criminal values as members of youth gangs and groups.

Social structure theorists challenge those who would suggest that crime is an expression of psychological imbalance, biological traits, insensitivity to social controls, personal choice, or any other individual-level factor. They argue that people living in equivalent social environments seem to behave in a similar, predictable fashion. If the environment did not influence human behavior, crime rates would be distributed equally across the social structure, which they are not.[32] Because crime rates are higher in lower-class urban centers than in middle-class suburbs, social forces must be operating in urban slums that influence or control behavior.[33]

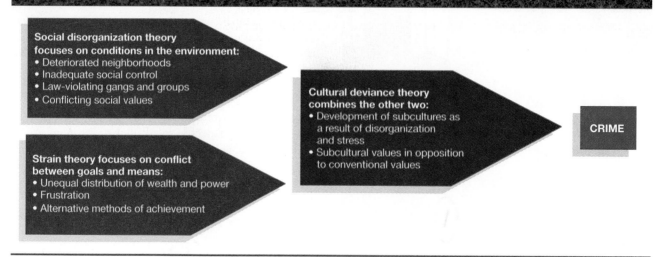

Figure 7.1 The three branches of social structure theory.

Social disorganization theory
focuses on conditions in the environment:
• Deteriorated neighborhoods
• Inadequate social control
• Law-violating gangs and groups
• Conflicting social values

Strain theory focuses on conflict
between goals and means:
• Unequal distribution of wealth and power
• Frustration
• Alternative methods of achievement

Cultural deviance theory
combines the other two:
• Development of subcultures as
  a result of disorganization
  and stress
• Subcultural values in opposition
  to conventional values

CRIME

There are three independent yet overlapping branches within the social structure perspective: social disorganization theory, strain theory, and cultural deviance theory, as outlined in Figure 7.1.

Social disorganization theory focuses on the conditions within the urban environment that affect crime rates. A disorganized area is one in which institutions of social control, such as the family, commercial establishments, and schools, have broken down and can no longer carry out their expected or stated functions. Indicators of social disorganization include high unemployment and school dropout rates, deteriorated housing, low income levels, and large numbers of single-parent households. Residents in these areas experience conflict and despair, and antisocial behavior flourishes.

Strain theory, the second branch of social structure theory, holds that crime is a function of the conflict between the goals people have and the means they can use to legally obtain them. Strain theorists argue that while social and economic goals are common to people in all economic strata, the ability to obtain these goals is class-dependent. Most people in the United States desire wealth, material possessions, power, prestige, and other life comforts. Members of the lower class are unable to achieve these symbols of success through conventional means. Consequently, they feel anger, frustration, and resentment, which is referred to as *strain.* Lower-class citizens can either accept their condition and live out their days as socially responsible, if unrewarded, citizens, or they can choose an alternative means of achieving success, such as theft, violence, or drug trafficking.

Cultural deviance theory, the third variation of structural theory, combines elements of both strain and social disorganization. According to this view, because of strain and social isolation, unique lower-class cultures develop in disorganized neighborhoods. These independent **subcultures** maintain a unique set of values and beliefs that are in conflict with conventional social norms. Criminal behavior

is an expression of conformity to lower-class subcultural values and traditions and not a rebellion against conventional society. Subcultural values are handed down from one generation to the next in a process called **cultural transmission.**

While distinct in critical aspects, each of these three approaches has at its core the view that socially isolated people, living in disorganized neighborhoods, are the ones most likely to experience crime-producing social forces. We will now examine each branch of social structure theory in some detail.

Social Disorganization Theory

Social disorganization theory links crime rates to neighborhood ecological characteristics. Crime rates are elevated in highly transient, "mixed-use" (residential and commercial property exist side by side) or "changing neighborhoods" in which the fabric of social life has become frayed. These localities are unable to provide essential services, such as education, health care, and proper housing, and experience significant levels of unemployment, single-parent families, and families on welfare and aid to dependent children (see Figure 7.2).

Social disorganization theory views crime-ridden neighborhoods as ones in which residents are trying to leave at the earliest opportunity. Since residents are uninterested in community matters, the common sources of control—the family, school, business community, social service agencies—are weak and disorganized. Personal relationships are strained because neighbors are constantly moving. Constant resident turnover weakens communications and blocks attempts at solving neighborhood problems or establishing common goals.[34]

Figure 7.2 Social disorganization theory.

Poverty
- Development of isolated slums
- Lack of conventional social opportunities
- Racial and ethnic discrimination

Social disorganization
- Breakdown of social institutions and organizations such as school and family
- Lack of informal social control

Breakdown of social control
- Development of gangs, groups
- Peer group replaces family and social institutions

Criminal areas
- Neighborhood becomes crime-prone
- Stable pockets of delinquency develop
- Lack of external support and investment

Cultural transmission
Older youths pass norms (focal concerns) to younger generation, creating stable slum culture

Criminal careers
Most youths "age out" of delinquency, marry, and raise families but some remain in life of crime

Concentric Zone Theory

Social disorganization theory was popularized by the work of two Chicago sociologists, Clifford R. Shaw and Henry McKay, who linked life in transitional slum areas to the inclination to commit crime. Shaw and McKay began their pioneering research in Chicago during the early 1920s while working for a state-supported social service agency.[35] They were heavily influenced by the thoughts of the Chicago School sociologists Ernest Burgess and Robert Park, who had pioneered the ecological analysis of urban life.

Shaw and McKay began their analysis during a period in the city's history that was not atypical of the transition taking place in many other urban areas. Chicago had experienced a mid-19th-century population expansion, fueled by a dramatic influx of foreign-born immigrants and, later, migrating southern families. Congregating in the central city, the newcomers occupied the oldest housing and therefore faced numerous health and environmental hazards.

Physically deteriorating sections of the city soon developed. This condition prompted the city's wealthy, established citizens to become concerned about the moral fabric of Chicago society. The belief was widespread that immigrants from Europe and the rural South were crime-prone and morally dissolute. In fact, local groups were created with the very purpose of "saving" the children of poor families from moral decadence.[36] It was popular to view crime as the province of inferior racial and ethnic groups.

TRANSITIONAL NEIGHBORHOODS. Shaw and McKay explained crime and delinquency within the context of the changing urban environment and ecological development of the city. They saw that Chicago had developed into distinct neighborhoods (*natural areas*), some affluent and others wracked by extreme poverty. These **transitional neighborhoods** suffered high rates of population turnover and were incapable of inducing residents to remain and defend the neighborhood against criminal groups.

Low rents in these areas attracted groups with different racial and ethnic backgrounds. Newly arrived immigrants from Europe and the South congregated in these transitional neighborhoods. Their children were torn between assimilation into a new culture and abiding by the traditional values of their parents. Informal social control mechanisms that had restrained behavior in the "old country" or rural areas were disrupted. These slum areas were believed to be the spawning grounds of young criminals.

In transitional slum areas, successive changes in the composition of population, the disintegration of the alien cultures, the diffusion of divergent cultural standards, and the gradual industrialization of the area resulted in dissolution of neighborhood culture and organization. The continuity of conventional neighborhood traditions and institutions was broken. The effectiveness of the neighborhood as a unit of control and as a medium for the transmission of the moral standards of society was greatly diminished. High population turnover impeded the establishment of common values and norms. Children growing up in these areas had little access to the cultural heritages of conventional society. For the most part, the organization of their behavior took place through participation in the spontaneous play groups and organized gangs that developed in these areas. The values they developed were then passed down through succeeding generations through cultural transmission.

CONCENTRIC ZONES. Shaw and McKay identified the areas in Chicago that had excessive crime rates. Using a model of analysis pioneered by Ernest Burgess, they noted that distinct ecological areas had developed in the city, comprising a series of five concentric circles, or zones, and that there were stable and significant differences in interzone crime rates (see Figure 7.3). The areas of heaviest concentration of crime appeared to be the transitional inner-city zones, where large numbers of foreign-born citizens had recently settled.[37] The zones farthest from the city's center had correspondingly lower crime rates. Analysis of these data indicated a surprisingly stable pattern of criminal activity in the five ecological zones over a 65-year period.

Shaw and McKay concluded that in transitional neighborhoods, multiple cultures and diverse values, both conventional and deviant, coexist. Kids growing up in the street culture often find that adults who have adopted a deviant lifestyle—the gambler, pimp, the drug dealer—are the most financially successful people in the neighborhood. Required to choose between conventional and deviant lifestyles, many slum kids opt for the latter. They join with like-minded youths and form law-violating gangs and cliques. The development of teenage law-violating groups is an essential element of youthful misbehavior in slum areas. Because of their deviant values, slum youths often come into conflict with existing middle-class norms, which demand strict obedience to the legal code. Consequently, a **value conflict** occurs that sets the delinquent youth and his or her peer group even farther apart from conventional society. The result is a fuller acceptance of deviant goals and behavior. Shut out of conventional society, neighborhood street gangs become fixed institutions, recruiting new members and passing on delinquent traditions from one generation to the next.

Shaw and McKay's statistical analysis confirmed their theoretical suspicions. They found that even though crime rates changed, the highest rates were always in zones I and II (central city and transitional area). The areas with the highest crime rates retained high rates even when their ethnic composition changed (in this case, from German and Irish to Italian and Polish).[38]

THE LEGACY OF SHAW AND MCKAY. Social disorganization concepts originally articulated by Shaw and McKay have remained prominent within criminology for more than 75 years. The most important of their findings was that crime rates corresponded to neighborhood structure. Crime was a creature of the destructive ecological conditions in urban slums. Criminals were not, as some criminologists of the time believed, biologically inferior, intellectually impaired, or psychologically damaged. Crime was a constant fixture in a slum area regardless of the racial or ethnic identity of its residents.

Since the basis of their theory was that neighborhood disintegration and slum conditions are the primary causes of

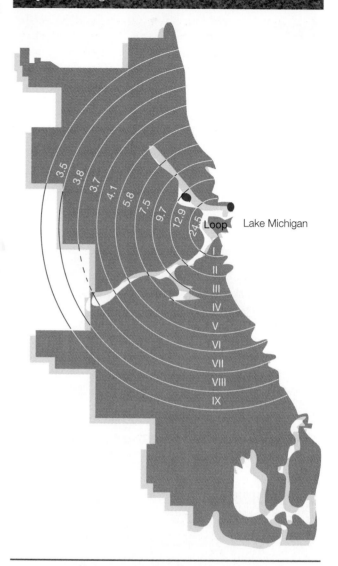

Figure 7.3 Shaw and McKay's concentric zones map of Chicago.

Note: Arabic numerals represent the rate of male delinquency.
Source: Clifford R. Shaw et al., *Delinquency Areas* (Chicago: University of Chicago Press, 1929), p. 99. Reprinted with permission. Copyright 1929 by the University of Chicago. All rights reserved.

criminal behavior, Shaw and McKay paved the way for the many community action and treatment programs developed in the last half-century. Shaw was the founder of one very influential community-based treatment program, the Chicago Area Project, which will be discussed later in this chapter.

Another important feature of Shaw and McKay's work is that it depicted both adult criminality and delinquent gang memberships as a normal response to the adverse social conditions in urban slum areas. Their findings mirror Durkheim's concept that crime can be normal and useful.

Despite these noteworthy achievements, the validity of Shaw and McKay's findings has been subject to challenge.

Some have faulted their assumption that neighborhoods are essentially stable, while others have found their definition of social disorganization confusing.[39] The most important criticism, however, concerns their use of police records to calculate neighborhood crime rates. A zone's high crime rate may be a function of the level of local police surveillance and may therefore obscure interzone crime rate differences. Numerous studies indicate that police use extensive discretion when arresting people and that social status is one factor that influences their decisions.[40] It is likely that people in middle-class neighborhoods commit many criminal acts that never show up in official statistics, while people in lower-class areas face a far greater chance of arrest and court adjudication.[41] Thus, the relationship between environment and crime rates may be a reflection of police behavior and not criminal behavior.

These criticisms aside, the Shaw-McKay theory provides a valuable contribution to our understanding of the causes of criminal behavior. By introducing a new variable—the ecology of the city—into the study of crime, the authors paved the way for a whole generation of criminologists to focus on the social influences on criminal and delinquent behavior.

The Social Ecology School

During the 1970s, criminologists were influenced by several critical analyses of social disorganization theory that presented well-thought-out challenges to its validity.[42] During this period, theories with a social psychological orientation, stressing offender socialization within the family, school, and peer group, dominated the criminological literature.

> ### Connections
>
> If social disorganization causes crime, why are the majority of low-income people law abiding? To explain this anomaly, some sociologists have devised theoretical models suggesting that individual socialization experiences mediate the effect of environmental influences. These theories will be discussed in Chapter 9.

Despite its "fall from grace," the social disorganization tradition was kept alive by "area studies" conducted by Bernard Lander in Baltimore, David Bordua in Detroit, and Roland Chilton in Indianapolis. They showed that such ecological conditions as substandard housing, low income, and unrelated people living together predicted a high incidence of delinquency.[43]

Then in the 1980s, a group of criminologists began to revive concern about the effects of social disorganization.[44] These modern-day **social ecologists** have developed a "purer" form of structural theory that stresses the relation of community deterioration and economic decline to crim-

inality while placing less emphasis on value conflict. In the following sections, some of the more recent social ecological research is discussed in some detail.

COMMUNITY DETERIORATION. A growing body of literature indicates that crime rates are associated with community-level indicators of social disorganization, including disorder, poverty, alienation, disassociation, and fear of crime.[45] Neighborhoods that are deteriorated and have a high percentage of deserted houses and apartments experience high crime rates; abandoned buildings serve as a "magnet for crime."[46] Areas in which houses are in poor repair, boarded up, and burned out and whose owners are best described as "slumlords" are also sites of the highest violence rates and gun crime.[47] The percentage of people living in poverty and the percentage of broken homes are strongly related to neighborhood crime rates.[48] Gangs flourish in deteriorated neighborhoods, adding to the crime rate. In one Chicago area study, G. David Curry and Irving Spergel found that gang homicide rates were associated with such variables as the percentage of the neighborhood living below the poverty line, the lack of mortgage investment in a neighborhood, the unemployment rate, and the influx of new immigrant groups; these factors are usually found in disorganized areas.[49]

The relationship between community deterioration and crime is not unique to the United States. Cross-national research conducted in Scandinavia found a clear link between crime and measures of social disorganization.[50] Socially disorganized neighborhoods in Great Britain experience the highest amounts of crime and victimization. Communities characterized by sparse friendship networks, unsupervised teenage peer groups, and low organizational participation also had the greatest amounts of criminality. The social disorganization model, then, is robust and has the power to explain crime rates outside the United States.[51]

EMPLOYMENT OPPORTUNITIES. The relationship between unemployment and crime is unsettled: aggregate crime rates and aggregate unemployment rates seem weakly related. Yet high unemployment may have crime-producing effects in particular neighborhoods or areas. Shaw and McKay found that areas wracked by poverty also experience social disorganization.[52]

Research indicates that neighborhoods that provide few employment opportunities for youths and adults are the most vulnerable to predatory crime.[53] Unemployment helps destabilize households, and unstable families are the ones most likely to contain children who put a premium on violence and aggression as a means of dealing with limited opportunity. Crime rates increase when large groups or cohorts of people of the same age compete for relatively scant resources.[54]

Limited employment opportunities also reduce the stabilizing influence of parents and other adults, who once

When the Post Office in Detroit announced job openings, more than 20,000 people applied for a few hundred positions. The lack of legitimate work opportunities for undereducated, untrained youths may be one reason they join gangs, sell drugs, and enter into criminal careers.

counteracted the allure of youth gangs. Elijah Anderson's analysis of Philadelphia neighborhood life found that "old heads" (respected neighborhood residents) who had at one time played an important role in socializing youth, have been displaced by younger street hustlers and drug dealers. While the "old heads" complain that these newcomers may not have "earned" or "worked for" their fortune in the "old-fashioned way," the old heads admire and envy these kids whose gold chains and luxury cars advertise their wealth amid poverty.[55]

Even the most deteriorated neighborhoods have a surprising degree of familial and kinship strength. Yet the consistent pattern of crime and neighborhood disorganization that follows periods of high unemployment can neutralize their social control capability.

COMMUNITY FEAR. Disorganized neighborhoods suffer social and physical *incivilities*—rowdy youth, trash and litter, graffiti, abandoned storefronts, burned-out buildings, littered lots, strangers, drunks, vagabonds, loiterers, prostitutes, noise, congestion, angry words, dirt, and stench. The presence of such incivilities helps convince residents of disorganized areas that their neighborhood is dangerous and that they face a considerable chance of becoming crime victims. Not surprisingly, when crime rates are actually high in these disorganized areas, fear levels undergo a dramatic increase.[56] Perceptions of crime and victimization produce neighborhood fear.[57]

Fear becomes most pronounced in areas undergoing rapid and unexpected racial and age-composition changes, especially when they are out of proportion to the rest of the city.[58] Fear can become contagious. People tell others of their personal involvement with victimization, spreading the word that the neighborhood is getting dangerous and that the chance of future victimization is high.[59] People dread leaving their homes at night and withdraw from community life. Not surprisingly, people who have already been victimized are more fearful of the future than those who have escaped crime.[60]

When fear grips a neighborhood, business conditions begin to deteriorate, population mobility increases, and a "criminal element" begins to drift into the area.[61] Fear helps produce more crime, increasing the chances of victimization, producing even more fear, in a never-ending loop.[62]

SIEGE MENTALITY. One unique aspect of community fear is the development of a **siege mentality,** in which the outside world is considered the enemy out to destroy the neighborhood. Elijah Anderson found that residents in the African American neighborhoods he studied believed in the existence of a secret plan to eradicate the population by such strategies as permanent unemployment, police brutality, imprisonment, drug distribution, and AIDS.[63] Evidence of this conspiracy hatched by white officials and political leaders could be clearly viewed in the lax law enforcement efforts in poor areas. Police cared little about black-on-black crime because it helped reduce the population. This kind of perception is only fueled by rumors that federal agencies such as the CIA control the drug trade and use profits to fund illegal overseas operations.

The siege mentality results in mistrust of critical social institutions, including business, government, and schools. Government officials seem arrogant and haughty. Residents become self-conscious, worried about respect, and sensitive to anyone who disrespects or "disses" them. When police ignore crime in poor areas, or when they are violent and corrupt, anger flares and people take to the streets and react in violent ways.

POPULATION TURNOVER. In our postmodern society, urban areas undergoing rapid structural changes in racial and economic composition also seem to experience the greatest change in crime rates. Recent studies recognize that change and not stability is the hallmark of inner-city areas. A neighborhood's residents, wealth, density, and purpose are constantly evolving. Even disorganized neighborhoods acquire new identifying features. Some may become multiracial, while others become racially homogeneous; some areas become stable and family-oriented, while in others, mobile, never-married people predominate.[64]

As areas decline, residents flee to safer, more stable localities. Those who can't leave because they cannot afford to live in more affluent communities face an even greater risk of victimization. Because of racial differences in economic well being, those "left behind" are all too often members of minority groups.[65] Those who can't move find themselves surrounded by a constant influx of new residents. High population turnover can have a devastating effect on community culture because it interrupts communication and information flow.[66] A culture may develop that dictates standards of dress, language, and behavior to neighborhood youth that are in opposition to those of conventional society. All these factors are likely to produce increasing crime rates.

COMMUNITY CHANGE. Social ecologists have attempted to chart the change that undermines urban areas. Robert Bursik and Harold Grasmick found that urban areas may have life cycles, which begin with the building of residential dwellings, followed by a period of decline with marked decreases in socioeconomic status and increases in population density.[67] Later stages in this life cycle include changing racial or ethnic makeup, population thinning, and finally a renewal stage in which obsolete housing is replaced and upgraded (*gentrification*). There are indications that areas undergoing such change experience increases in their crime rates.[68]

Sociologists Leo Scheurman and Solomon Kobrin also find that communities go through cycles in which neighborhood deterioration precedes increasing rates of crime and delinquency.[69] Those communities most likely to experience a rapid increase in antisocial behavior contain large numbers of single-parent families and unrelated people living together, have gone from having owner-occupied to renter-occupied units, and have an economic base that has lost semiskilled and unskilled jobs (indicating a growing residue of discouraged workers who are no longer seeking employment).[70] These ecological disruptions strain existing social control mechanisms and inhibit their ability to control crime and delinquency.

A large body of research developed by Robert Bursik and his associates shows that changing lifestyles in Chicago neighborhoods, including declining economic status, increasing population, and racial shifts, are associated with increased neighborhood crime rates.[71] Writing with Janet Heitgerd, Bursik found that areas adjoining neighborhoods undergoing racial change will experience corresponding increases in their own crime rates.[72] This phenomenon may reflect community reaction to perceived racial conflict. In changing neighborhoods, adults support the law-violating behavior of youths and encourage them to protect their property and way of life by violently resisting newcomers.

POVERTY CONCENTRATION. One aspect of community change may be the concentration of poverty in deteriorated neighborhoods. While poverty rates or unemployment may not be direct causes of crime, the most deteriorated areas even within the context of the slum seem to have much higher crime rates than more stable lower-class environments. William Julius Wilson describes how working and middle-class families flee inner-city poverty areas, resulting in a **concentration effect** in which elements of the most disadvantaged population are consolidated in urban ghettos. As the working and middle classes move out, they take with them their financial and institutional resources and support. Businesses are disinclined to locate in poverty areas; banks become reluctant to lend money for new housing or businesses.[73]

Areas marked by concentrated poverty become isolated and insulated from the social mainstream and more prone to criminal activity. Gangs also concentrate in these areas, bringing with them a significant increase in criminal activity. Carolyn Block and Richard Block studied the ecology of gang activity in Chicago and found that the two most dangerous areas (Garfield Park and Humboldt Park) had 76 times more gang-related street crime than the two least dangerous areas (Mount Greenwood and Edison Park).[74]

The concentration effect contradicts, in some measure, Shaw and McKay's assumption that crime rates increase in transitional neighborhoods. Today the areas that may be the most crime-prone may be stable, homogenous areas whose residents are "trapped" in public housing and urban ghettos. Ethnically and racially isolated areas maintain the highest crime rates.[75]

WEAK SOCIAL CONTROLS. Most neighborhood residents share the common goal of living in a crime-free area. Some communities have the power to regulate the behavior of their residents through the influence of community institutions, such as the family and school. Other neighborhoods, experiencing social disorganization, find that efforts at social control are weak and attenuated. When community social control efforts are blunted, crime rates increase, further weakening neighborhood cohesiveness in a never-ending cycle.

Neighborhoods maintain a variety of agencies and institutions of social control. Some operate on the primary or private level and involve peers, families, and relatives. These sources exert informal control by either awarding or withholding approval, respect, and admiration. Informal control mechanisms include direct criticism, ridicule, ostracism, desertion, and physical punishment.[76]

Communities also use internal networks and local institutions to control crime. Sources of institutional social control include businesses, stores, schools, churches, and social service and volunteer organizations.[77]

Stable neighborhoods are also able to arrange for external sources of social control. For example, community organizations and local leaders may have sufficient political clout to get funding for additional law enforcement personnel. The presence of police sends a message that the area will not tolerate deviant behavior. Criminals and drug dealers avoid such areas and relocate to easier and more appealing targets.[78]

Neighborhoods that are disorganized cannot mount an effective social control effort: As neighborhood disadvantage increases, its level of informal social control decreases.[79] In areas where social control remains high, children are less likely to become involved with deviant peers and to engage in problem behaviors.[80] Since the population is transient in disorganized areas, interpersonal relationships remain superficial; social institutions such as schools and churches cannot work effectively in a climate of alienation and mistrust. In these areas, the absence of political power brokers limits access to external funding and police protection. Without money from the outside, the neighborhood lacks the ability to "get back on its feet."[81]

Social control is also weakened because unsupervised peer groups and gangs, which flourish in disorganized areas, disrupt the influence of neighborhood control agents.[82] Children who live in disorganized neighborhoods find that involvement with conventional social institutions, such as schools and afternoon programs, is blocked; they are instead at risk for recruitment into gangs and law-violating groups.[83]

SOCIAL ALTRUISM. The inverse of communities that provide weak social controls are those that provide strong social supports for their members. Residents teach one another that they have moral and social obligations to their fellow citizens; children learn to be sensitive to the rights of others and respect differences. In contrast, less altruistic communities stress individualism and self-interest.

Areas that place a greater stress on caring for fellow citizens seem, not surprisingly, less crime-prone than those that emphasize self-reliance. In an important survey, Mitchell Chamlin and John Cochran found that social altruism (which they define as the ratio of contributions given to the United Way charity by area income levels) is inversely related to crime rates.[84] More generous and caring areas are also relatively crime free. Their findings can be interpreted in two ways: (1) crime rates are lower in altruistic areas; (2) well-funded charities help lower crime rates by providing a secure safety net for "at risk" families.

Taken in sum, the writings of the social ecology school show that (1) social disorganization produces criminality and (2) the quality of community life, including levels of change, fear, incivility, poverty, and deterioration, has a direct influence on an area's crime rate. It is not some individual property or trait that causes some people to commit crime but the quality and ambience of the community in which they reside.

Strain Theory

Inhabitants of a disorganized inner-city area feel isolated, frustrated, left out of the economic mainstream, hopeless, and eventually angry and enraged. What effect do these feelings have on criminal activities?

Criminologists who view crime as a direct result of lower-class frustration and anger are referred to as *strain theorists*. They believe that while most people share similar values and goals, the ability to achieve personal goals is stratified by socioeconomic class. Strain is limited in affluent areas because educational and vocational opportunities are available. In disorganized slum areas, however, strain occurs because legitimate avenues for success are all but closed. To relieve strain, indigent people may be *forced* to either use deviant methods to achieve their goals, such as theft or drug trafficking, or reject socially accepted goals outright and substitute other, more deviant goals, such as being tough and aggressive (see Figure 7.4).

Anomie Theory

The roots of strain theories can be traced to Emile Durkheim's notion of *anomie* (from the Greek *a nomos*, "without norms"). According to Durkheim, an anomic society is one in which rules of behavior—norms—have broken down or become inoperative during periods of rapid social change. Anomie is most likely to occur in societies that are moving from *mechanical* to *organic solidarity*. Mechanical solidarity is a characteristic of a preindustrial society that is held together by traditions, shared values, and unquestioned beliefs. In postindustrial social systems, which are highly developed and dependent on the division of labor, people are connected by their interdependent needs for each other's services and production (organic sol-

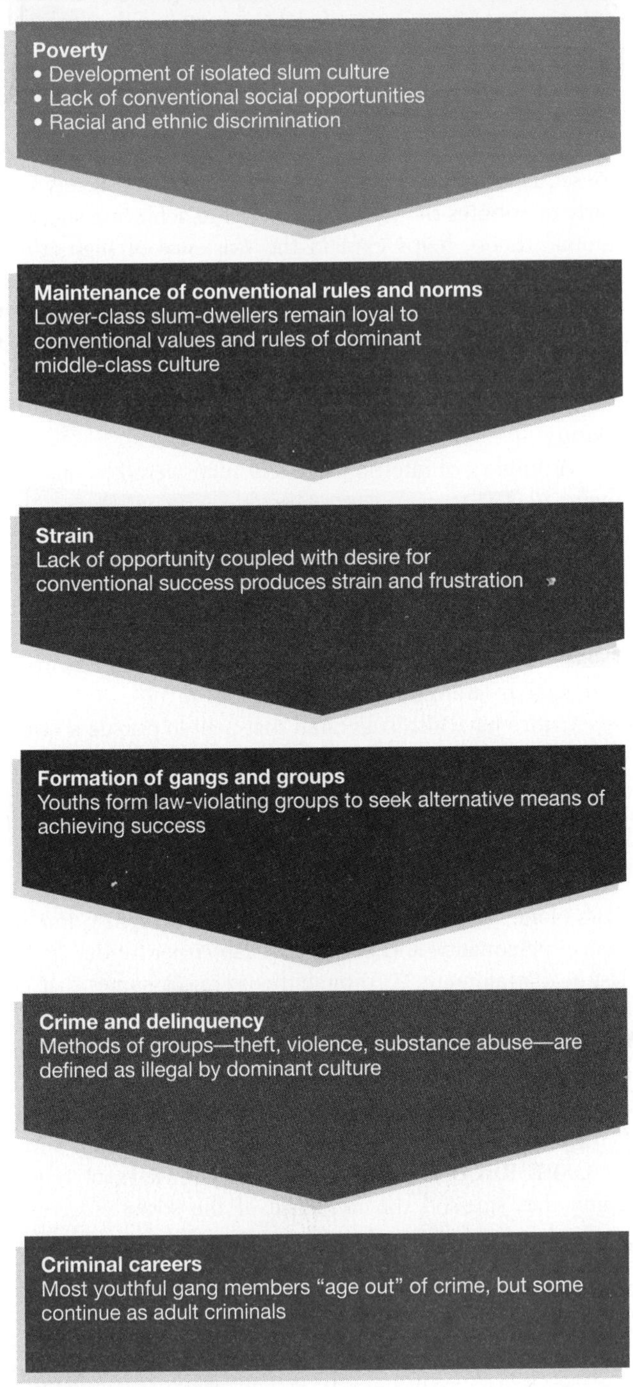

Figure 7.4 The basic components of strain theory.

Poverty
- Development of isolated slum culture
- Lack of conventional social opportunities
- Racial and ethnic discrimination

Maintenance of conventional rules and norms
Lower-class slum-dwellers remain loyal to conventional values and rules of dominant middle-class culture

Strain
Lack of opportunity coupled with desire for conventional success produces strain and frustration

Formation of gangs and groups
Youths form law-violating groups to seek alternative means of achieving success

Crime and delinquency
Methods of groups—theft, violence, substance abuse—are defined as illegal by dominant culture

Criminal careers
Most youthful gang members "age out" of crime, but some continue as adult criminals

idarity). This shift in traditions and values creates social turmoil. Established norms begin to erode and lose meaning. If a division occurs between what the population expects and what the economic and productive forces of society can realistically deliver, a crisis situation develops that can manifest itself in *normlessness,* or anomie.

Anomie undermines society's social control function. Every society works to limit people's goals and desires. If a society becomes anomic, it can no longer establish and maintain control over its population's wants and desires. Since people find it difficult to control their appetites, their demands become unlimited. Under these circumstances, obedience to legal codes may be strained, making alternative behavior choices, such as crimes, inevitable.

Durkheim's ideas were applied to criminology by sociologist Robert Merton in his **theory of anomie.**[85] Merton used a modified version of the concept of anomie to fit social, economic, and cultural conditions found in modern U.S. society.[86] He found that two elements of culture interact to produce potentially anomic conditions: culturally defined goals and socially approved means for obtaining them. For example, U.S. society stresses the goals of acquiring wealth, success, and power. Socially permissible means include hard work, education, and thrift.

Merton argued that in the United States legitimate means to acquire wealth are stratified across class and status lines. Those with little formal education and few economic resources soon find that they are denied the ability to legally acquire wealth, the preeminent success symbol.

When socially mandated goals are uniform throughout society and access to legitimate means is bound by class and status, the resulting strain produces an anomic condition among those who are locked out of the legitimate opportunity structure. Consequently, they may develop criminal or delinquent solutions to the problem of attaining goals.

SOCIAL ADAPTATIONS. Merton argued that each person has his or her own concept of the goals of society and the means at his or her disposal to attain them. Whereas some people have inadequate means of attaining success, others who do have the means reject societal goals as being unsuited to them. Table 7.1 shows Merton's diagram of the hypothetical relationship between social goals, the means for getting them, and the individual actor.

Conformity occurs when individuals both embrace conventional social goals and have the means at their disposal to attain them. In a balanced, stable society, this is the most common social adaptation. If a majority of its people did not practice conformity, the society would cease to exist.

Innovation occurs when an individual accepts the goals of society but rejects legitimate means or is incapable of attaining them through such means. Many people desire material goods and luxuries but lack the financial ability to attain them. The resulting conflict forces them to adopt innovative solutions to their dilemma: They steal, sell drugs, or extort money. Of the five adaptations, innovation is most closely associated with criminal behavior.

If successful, innovation can have serious, long-term social consequences. Criminal success helps convince otherwise law-abiding people that innovative means work better and faster than conventional ones. The prosperous drug

Table 7.1 Typology of Individual Modes of Adaptation

MODES OF ADAPTATION	CULTURAL GOALS	INSTITUTIONALIZED MEANS
I. Conformity	+	+
I. Innovation	+	−
II. Ritualism	−	+
V. Retreatism	−	−
V. Rebellion	±	±

Source: Robert Merton, "Social Structure and Anomie," in *Social Theory and Social Structure* (Glencoe, Ill.: Free Press, 1957).

dealer's expensive car and flashy clothes give out the message that crime pays. "The process thus enlarges the extent of anomie within the system," claims Merton, "so that others, who did not respond in the form of deviant behavior to the relatively slight anomie which they first obtained, come to do so as anomie is spread and is intensified."[87] This explains why crime is created and sustained in certain low-income ecological areas.

Ritualism occurs when social goals are lowered in importance and means are elevated. Ritualists gain pleasure from the practice of traditional ceremonies that have neither a real purpose nor a goal. The strict set of manners and customs in religious orders, feudal societies, clubs, and college fraternities encourage and appeal to ritualists. Ritualists should have the lowest level of criminal behavior because they have abandoned the success goal that is at the root of criminal activity.

Retreatists reject *both* the goals and the means of society. Merton suggested that people who adjust in this fashion are "in the society but not of it." Included in this category are "psychotics, psychoneurotics, chronic autists, pariahs, outcasts, vagrants, vagabonds, tramps, chronic drunkards, and drug addicts." Because such people are morally or otherwise incapable of using *both* legitimate and illegitimate means, they attempt to escape their lack of success by withdrawing—either mentally or physically.

Rebellion involves substituting an alternative set of goals and means for conventional ones. Revolutionaries who wish to promote radical change in the existing social structure and who call for alternative lifestyles, goals, and beliefs are engaging in rebellion. Rebellion may be a reaction against a corrupt and hated government or an effort to create alternate opportunities and lifestyles within the existing system.

EVALUATION OF ANOMIE THEORY. According to anomie theory, social inequality leads to perceptions of anomie. To resolve the goals-means conflict and relieve their sense of strain, some people innovate by stealing or extorting money, others retreat into drugs and alcohol, others rebel by joining revolutionary groups, while still others get involved into ritualistic behavior by joining a religious cult.

Merton's view of anomie has been one of the most enduring and influential sociological theories of criminality. By linking deviant behavior to the success goals that control social behavior, anomie theory attempts to pinpoint the cause of the conflict that produces personal frustration and consequent criminality. By acknowledging that society unfairly distributes the legitimate means to achieving success, anomie theory helps explain the existence of high-crime areas and the apparent predominance of delinquent and criminal behavior among the lower class. By suggesting that social conditions, not individual personalities, produce crime, Merton greatly influenced the directions taken to reduce and control criminality during the last half of the 20th century.

A number of questions are left unanswered by anomie theory.[88] Merton did not explain why people differ in their choice of criminal behavior. Why does one anomic person become a mugger, while another deals drugs? Anomie may be used to explain differences in crime rates, but it cannot explain why most young criminals desist from crime as adults. Does this mean that perceptions of anomie dwindle with age? Is anomie short-lived?

Critics have also suggested that people pursue a number of different goals, including educational, athletic, and social success. Juveniles may be more interested in immediate goals, such as having an active social life or being a good athlete, than long-term "ideal" achievements, such as monetary success. Achieving these goals is not a matter of social class alone; other factors, including athletic ability, intelligence, personality, and family life, can either hinder or assist goal attainment.[89] Anomie theory also assumes that all people share the same goals and values, which is false.[90] Because of these and other criticisms, the theory of anomie, along with other structural theories, fell into a period of decline for almost 20 years.

ANOMIE RECONSIDERED. Like other views of criminality that stressed the influence of the social structure, strain theories fell out of favor when criminologists turned their attention to social psychological views of criminality. However, in the 1990s there has been a resurgence of interest in strain and anomie. Many Americans may be feeling anomic because of the economic displacement brought on by a shifting economy. The "truly disadavantaged" in society seem at grave risk to both normlessness and high crime rates. In addition, some researchers have begun to reexamine original concepts and have found that with more precise and valid measurements, perceptions of anomie are in fact associated with participation in criminal activity; some of the early criticism of Merton may have been based on inadequate research results.[91] Cross-cultural research efforts have also linked anomic conditions to criminality, indicating that anomie is not unique to U.S. culture.[92]

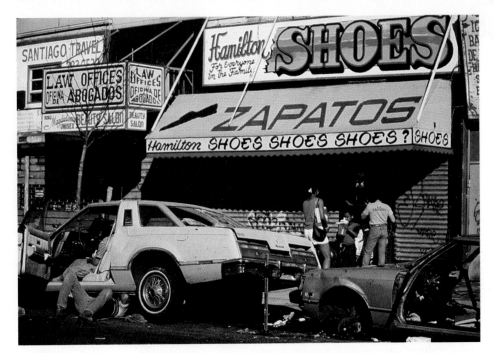

According to Messner and Rosenfeld, the relatively high American crime rates can be explained by the interrelationship between culture and institutions. The poor want to be part of the economic mainstream but lack the means to achieve their goals. Some may attempt to use legal methods, such as this curbside auto repair shop being operated in the Hamilton Heights section of New York City. Others become frustrated and angry and choose crime and drug dealing to get ahead.

What makes rich vs poor different to win at all cost

Criminologists are now producing newer versions of Merton's visionary concepts. Some of these work on the general, or macro, level; they hold that the success goal integrated within American society influences the nature and extent of the aggregate crime rate. There are also individual, or micro-level, versions of the theory; these suggest that individuals who experience anomie are more likely to commit crime than those who are immune to feelings of strain or goal conflict. Examples of both of these views are discussed next.

Institutional Anomie Theory

A recent addition to the strain literature has been the publication of *Crime and the American Dream* by Steven Messner and Richard Rosenfeld.[93] Their macro-level version of anomie theory views antisocial behavior as a function of *cultural* and *institutional* influences in American society.

Messner and Rosenfeld agree with Merton's view that the success goal is pervasive in American culture. They refer to this as the **American Dream,** a term that they use as both a goal and a process. As a goal, the American Dream involves the accumulation of material goods and wealth under conditions of open individual competition. As a process, it involves both socialization to the pursuit of material success and the belief that prosperity is an achievable goal in the American culture. Anomic conditions occur because the desire to succeed at any cost drives people apart, weakens the collective sense of community, fosters ambition, and restricts the desirability of other kinds of achievement, such as a "good name" and respected reputation.

That Americans are conditioned to succeed "at all costs" should come as no surprise, because our capitalist system encourages innovation in the pursuit of monetary rewards. Businesspeople such as Bill Gates, Warren Buffet, Ross Perot, and Donald Trump are considered national heroes and leaders. What is distinct about American society, according to Messner and Rosenfeld, and what most likely determines the exceedingly high national crime rate, is that anomic conditions have been allowed to "develop to such an extraordinary degree."[94]

Why does anomie pervade American culture? According to Messner and Rosenfeld, it is because institutions that might otherwise control the exaggerated emphasis on financial success have been rendered powerless or obsolete. There are three reasons social institutions have been undermined:

- Noneconomic functions and roles have been *devalued.* Performance in other institutional settings—the family, school, or community—is assigned a lower priority than the goal of financial success.
- When conflicts emerge, noneconomic roles become subordinate to and must *accommodate* economic roles.

The schedules, routines, and demands of the workplace take priority over those of the home, the school, the community, and other aspects of social life.

- Economic language, standards, and norms *penetrate* into noneconomic realms. Economic terms become part of the common vernacular: people want to get to the "bottom line"; spouses view themselves as "partners" who "manage" the household. Retired people say they want to "downsize" their household. Rather than paint the kitchen ourselves, I ask my wife whether we should "outsource" the job. Corporate leaders run for public office promising to "run the country like a business."

According to Messner and Rosenfeld, the relatively high American crime rates can be explained by the interrelationship between culture and institutions. At the cultural level, the dominance of the American Dream mythology ensures that many people will develop wishes and desires for material goods that cannot be satisfied by legitimate means; anomie becomes a norm, and extralegal means (crime) become a strategy for attaining material wealth. At the institutional level, the dominance of economic concerns weakens the informal social control exerted by the family, church, and school. These institutions have lost their ability to regulate behavior and have instead become a conduit for promoting material success. For example, schools are not evaluated for conveying knowledge but for their ability to train students to get high-paying jobs.

Social conditions reinforce each other in a never-ending loop: Culture determines institutions and institutional change influences culture. Thus, crime rates may rise in a healthy economy because national prosperity heightens the attractiveness of monetary rewards, encouraging people to gain financial success by any means possible, including illegal ones, while reducing the importance of social institutions to exert social control.

A recent research effort by Mitchell Chamlin and John Cochran supports the idea of institutional anomie. Chamlin and Cochran first use state-level data to show that poverty rates are associated with crime rates. However, this relationship depends on the strength of institutional controls: Areas with high levels of church membership, lower levels of divorce, and high voter turnouts also enjoy lower crime rates. Strong institutional controls (family, church, and polity), they find, may counteract the influence of economic deprivation, a finding in sync with institutional-anomie theory.[95]

The Messner-Rosenfeld version of anomie builds on Merton's macro-level views by trying to explain why the success goal has reached such a place of prominence in American culture. The message "to succeed by any means necessary" has become a national icon.

Relative Deprivation Theory

Criminologists have long assumed that **income inequality** increases both perceptions of strain and crime rates. Sharp divisions between the rich and poor create an atmosphere of envy and mistrust. According to John Braithwaite, those societies in which income inequality flourishes, *inegalitarian societies,* are especially demeaning to the poor. Criminal motivation is fueled by both perceived humiliation and the *right* to humiliate a victim in return.[96]

If income inequality causes strain, it stands to reason that crime rates will be highest in areas where the affluent and indigent live in close proximity. This is referred to as **relative deprivation.** This view is most closely associated with sociologists Judith Blau and Peter Blau.[97] Their relative deprivation theory combines concepts specified in anomie with those also found in social disorganization models.

According to the Blaus' research, lower-class people who feel deprived because of their race or class and who reside in urban areas that also house the affluent eventually develop a sense of injustice and discontent. The poor learn to distrust a society that has nurtured social inequality and blocked any chance of their legitimate advancement. Constant frustration produces pent-up aggression, hostility, and, eventually, violence and crime.[98] The Blaus maintain that a collective sense of **social injustice,** directly related to income inequality, develops in communities in which the poor and wealthy live in close proximity. This perception leads to a state of disorganization and anger. The relatively deprived justifiably feel enraged and vent their hostility in criminal behavior.

Adolescents raised in inner-city poverty areas, such as those in Boston, New York, Chicago, and Los Angeles, will experience this crime-producing frustration, since their neighborhoods are usually located in the same metropolitan area as some of the most affluent neighborhoods in the United States: Beacon Hill in Boston, Park Avenue in New York City, Lake Shore Drive in Chicago, and the Bel Air section of Los Angeles.

Relative deprivation is felt most acutely by African American youths because they consistently suffer racial and economic deprivations that place them in a lower status than other urban residents.[99] Wage inequality may motivate young males to enter the drug trade, an endeavor that increases the likelihood they will become involved in violent crimes.[100]

TESTING RELATIVE DEPRIVATION. Research shows that crime rates do in fact increase under conditions of relative deprivation, as when contiguous neighborhoods become polarized along class lines.[101] A number of research efforts have found that income inequality predicts violent and general area crime rates.[102] For example, research shows that as racial differences in income levels expanded during the 1960s and 1970s, African American arrest rates spiraled upward. Ironically, the increase occurred during a time when African Americans were enjoying a rapid improvement in income level and educational attainment.[103] This finding is important because it shows that crime rates can increase during times of relative affluence and declining unemployment rates: Groups whose standard of living may be improving might find that they are still losing ground in comparison to other groups. It is the perception of "relative deprivation" and not absolute poverty level that ushers in higher crime rates.

While some research efforts have failed to find a crime-inequality effect, the weight of the evidence supports relative deprivation, and it remains an important concept for understanding area crime rates.

IS RELATIVE DEPRIVATION "RELATIVE"? The theory of relative deprivation holds that people living in deteriorated urban areas who lack proper health care, decent clothing, and adequate shelter (resource deprivation) and who reside in close proximity to those who enjoy the benefits of higher social position will inevitably resort to such crimes as homicide, robbery, and aggravated assault.[104] Is this view restricted to the lower classes, or can it also be responsible for crimes of the affluent? In other words, is relative deprivation "relative"?

It is possible that even the most affluent Americans will feel strain when they fail to achieve "unlimited goals."[105] That is, no matter what their level of affluence, people may perceive strain because the goals they set for themselves are so lofty that they can never be achieved. The affluent may suffer when their expected standard of living or economic security declines. Research indicates that residing in an economically integrated neighborhood harms the children of the more *affluent families,* producing greater dropout rates and more out-of-wedlock births among the prosperous than the indigent.[106]

Some affluent people may feel relatively deprived when they compare themselves to the accomplishments of their even more socially successful peers. The relatively affluent may then use illegal means to satisfy their own "unrealistic" success goals. Nikos Passas has described this phenomenon:

> Upper-class individuals . . . are by no means shielded against frustrations, relative deprivation and anomia created by a discrepancy between cultural ends and available means, especially in the context of industrial societies, where the ends are renewed as soon as they are reached.[107]

Perhaps some of the individuals involved in the savings and loan scandals or Wall Street insider-trading cases felt "relatively deprived" and socially frustrated when they compared the paltry few millions they had already accumulated with the hundreds of millions held by the "truly wealthy," whom they envied.

Roy Austin and Chris Hebert's research also indicates that relative deprivation is "relative." They found that as economic inequality between blacks and whites *decreased,* white crime rates *increased.*[108] Austin and Hebert speculate that although whites maintained a distinct advantage in power and resources, they perceived the economic progress made by African Americans as a step backward for

Sociologist Robert Agnew's general strain theory (GST) shows how both positive and negative stimuli can cause strain, which can lead to anger and aggression.

themselves. Feelings of relative deprivation resulted in the rise of white power groups, antibusing movements, and higher crime rates. Crime rates rose when lower-class whites began to feel relatively less privileged than lower-class African Americans. These research efforts support the relative deprivation model and indicate it may be more complex than originally thought.

General Strain Theory

Sociologist Robert Agnew's **general strain theory** (GST) differs from the previously discussed theoretical models because of its focus on the micro-level, or individual, effects of strain and not the macro-level (social) effects. While Merton tried to explain social class differences in the crime rate, Agnew tries to explain why *individuals* who feel stress and strain are more likely to commit crimes. Agnew also attempts to offer a more general explanation of criminal activity among all elements of society rather than restrict his views to lower-class crime.[109]

MULTIPLE SOURCES OF STRESS. Agnew suggests that criminality is the direct result of **negative affective states**—anger, frustration, and adverse emotions—that come in the wake of negative and destructive social relationships. He finds that negative affective states are produced by a variety of sources of strain:

1. *Strain caused by the failure to achieve positively valued goals.* This category of strain, similar to what Merton referred to in his theory of anomie, is a result of the disjunction between aspirations and expectations. This type of strain occurs when a youth aspires for wealth

Figure 7.5   Elements of general strain theory (GST).

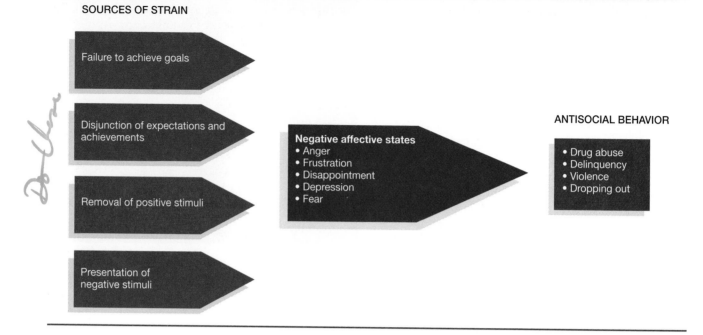

and fame but, lacking financial and educational resources, assumes that such goals are impossible to achieve.

2. *Strain caused by the disjunction of expectations and achievements.* Strain can also be produced when a disjunction exists between *expectations* and achievements. When people compare themselves to peers who seem to be doing a lot better financially or socially (such as making more money or getting better grades), even those doing relatively well feel strain. For example, they may get into college but not into a prestige school, like some of their friends. Perhaps they are not being treated fairly because the "playing field" is tilted against them. "Other kids have connections," they say. Perceptions of inequity may result in many adverse reactions, ranging from running away from its source to lowering the benefits of others through physical attacks or vandalism of their property.

3. *Strain as the removal of positively valued stimuli from the individual.* Strain may be the result of the actual or anticipated removal or loss of a positively valued stimulus from the individual.[110] For example, the loss of a girlfriend or boyfriend can produce strain, as can the death of a loved one, moving to a new neighborhood or school, and the divorce or separation of parents. The loss of positive stimuli may lead to delinquency as the adolescent tries to prevent the loss, retrieve what has been lost, obtain substitutes, or seek revenge against those responsible for the loss.

4. *Strain as the presentation of negative stimuli.* Strain may also be caused by the presence of negative or noxious stimuli. Included within this category are such pain-inducing social interactions as child abuse and neglect, crime victimization, physical punishment, family and peer conflict, school failure, and stressful life events ranging from verbal threats to air pollution.

While these sources of strain are independent of one another, they may overlap and be cumulative in practice. For example, insults from a teacher may be viewed as an unfair application of negative stimuli, which interferes with academic aspirations. The greater the intensity and frequency of strain experiences, the greater their impact and the more likely they are to cause delinquency.

According to Agnew, each type of strain will increase the likelihood of experiencing such negative emotions as disappointment, depression, fear, and, most important, anger. Anger increases perceptions of injury and of being wronged. It produces a desire for revenge, energizes individuals to take action, and lowers inhibitions; violence and aggression seem justified if one has been wronged and is righteously angry.

Because it produces these emotions, strain can be considered a predisposing factor for crime when it is chronic and repetitive and creates a hostile, suspicious, and aggressive attitude. Individual strain episodes may serve as a situational event or trigger that produces criminality, such as when a particularly stressful event ignites a violent reaction (see Figure 7.5).

COPING WITH STRAIN. Agnew recognizes that not all people who experience strain eventually become criminals. Some are able to marshal their emotional, mental, and behavioral resources to cope with the anger and frustration produced by strain. Some defenses are cognitive; individuals may be able to rationalize frustrating circumstances. Not getting the career they desire is "just not that important"; they may be poor, but the "next guy is worse off," and if things didn't work out, they "got what they deserved." Others seek behavioral solutions: They run away from adverse conditions or seek revenge against those who caused the strain. Others will try to regain emotional equilibrium with techniques ranging from physical exercise to drug abuse.

The general strain theory acknowledges that the ability to cope with strain varies with personal experiences over the life course. Kids who lack economic means are less likely to cope than those who have sufficient financial resources at their command. Personal temperament, prior learning of criminal attitudes and behaviors, and association with criminal peers who reinforce anger are among other factors affecting the ability to cope with strain. Coping with strain may also be influenced by the *source* of strain. Paul Mazerolle and Alex Piquero suggest that when individuals identify a *target* to blame for their problems, they are more likely to respond with retaliatory action ("Joe stole my girl by lying about me, so I beat him up!"). When individuals internalize blame, they are less likely to engage in criminal behavior ("I lost my girlfriend because I was unfaithful; it's all my fault"). Sometimes the source of strain is difficult to pinpoint ("I feel depressed because my parents got divorced"); Mazerolle and Piquero find that this type of ambiguous strain is unlikely to produce an aggressive response.[111]

STRAIN AND CRIMINAL CAREERS. How does GST explain both chronic offending and the stability of crime over the life course? GST recognizes that certain people have traits that may make them particularly sensitive to strain. These include having a difficult temperament, being overly sensitive or emotional, having a low tolerance for adversity, and having poor problem-solving skills. These traits, linked to aggressive and antisocial behavior, seem to be stable over a person's life cycle.[112]

> ### Connections
> As you may recall, cohort studies show that criminal behavior begins early in life, then remains stable over the life course. Considering that strain-producing interactions are not constant, explaining the stability of chronic offending is an important task for general strain theory. Chronic offending is discussed in Chapter 3.

Aggressive people who have these traits are likely to have poor interpersonal skills and are more likely to be treated negatively by others; their combative personalities make them feared and disliked. They are likely to live in families whose caretakers share similar personality traits. They are also more likely to reject conventional peers and join deviant groups. Such individuals are more likely to be subject to a high degree of strain over the course of their lives.

Crime peaks during late adolescence because this is a period of social stress caused by the weakening of parental supervision and the development of relationships with a diverse peer group. Many kids going through the trauma of family breakup and frequent changes in family structure find themselves under stress and react with involvement in precocious sexuality and substance abuse. For example, research shows that young girls of any social class are more likely to bear out-of-wedlock children if they themselves experienced an unstable family life.[113]

As they mature, their expectations may increase, and some kids are unable to meet academic and social demands. Adolescents are concerned about their standing with peers. Those deficient in these areas may become social outcasts, another source of strain. In adulthood, crime rates drop because these sources of strain are reduced. New sources of self-esteem emerge, and adults seem more likely to bring their goals in line with reality.

EVALUATING GST. Agnew's work is quite important because it both clarifies the concept of strain and directs future research agendas. It also adds to the body of literature describing how social and life history events influence offending patterns. Because sources of strain vary over the life course, so, too, should crime rates, and they do.

> ### Connections
> Explaining continuity and change in offending rates over the life course has become an important goal of criminologists. Chapter 10's analysis of latent-trait and life-course theories outlines the recent thinking on this topic.

There is also empirical support for GST. In a recent empirical analysis of his theory using longitudinal survey data, Agnew, with Helene Raskin White, found that adolescents who score high on scales measuring perceptions of strain labeled "life hassles" (for example, "My classmates do not like me," adults and friends "don't respect my opinions") and "negative life events" (being a victim of crime, the death of a close friend, serious illness) are also the ones most likely to engage in crime.[114]

Independent research efforts have concurred with Agnew's vision of strain. Some show that indicators of strain—family breakup, unemployment, moving, feelings of dissatisfaction with friends and school—are positively related to criminality.[115] G. Roger Jarjoura has found that middle-class youth who drop out of school are more likely to engage in criminal behavior than lower-class dropouts. It is possible that removing this "positive stimulus" has a greater strain effect on those who are expected to succeed because of their class position than those who already perceive more limited economic opportunities.[116]

Adolescents who report feelings of stress and anger are more likely to interact with delinquent peers and engage in criminal behaviors.[117] Research shows that persistent drug abusers report feeling a great deal of "life stress" and also associate with peers who are themselves substance users.[118] In some cases, this interaction may actually help them reduce strain and anxiety; criminality may serve as an effective "coping" mechanism that helps relieve feelings of anger and resentment. For example, they may reduce feelings of strain by lashing out at others, by stealing, or by vandalizing property.[119]

GST AND GENDER. One problem with GST is that it fails to adequately explain gender differences in the crime rate. Females experience as much as or more strain, frustration, and anger as males, yet their crime rate is much lower. Is it possible that gender differences exist in either the relationship between strain and criminality or the ability to cope with the effects of strain? In an important study, John Hoffman and S. Susan Su show that stress influences both males and females equally: stressful life events have a similar impact on delinquency and drug abuse among both males and females.[120]

If stress is experienced equally by both males and females and produces criminal behavior in both males and females, how can the much greater male crime rate be explained? It is possible that females use different coping mechanisms to deal with strain. Psychologist Lisa Broidy suggests that even when presented with similar types of strain, males and females respond with a different constellation of negative emotions.[121] Females may be socialized to be "overcontrolled" to internalize stress, blaming themselves for their problems; males can relieve strain by striking out at others and deflecting criticism with aggression. Only those females who face overwhelming stress, then, may succumb to criminality. In a recent paper, Robbin Ogle and her associates suggest that when women experience peaks of stress, their traditional coping mechanisms may be overwhelmed; they then lash out with anger amounting to rage. Women experiencing peaks of stress may be even more likely than men to explode with episodes of extreme uncontrolled violence.[122]

Cultural Deviance Theory

The third branch of social structure theory combines the effects of social disorganization and strain to explain how people living in deteriorated neighborhoods react to social isolation and economic deprivation. Because their lifestyle is draining, frustrating, and dispiriting, members of the lower class create an independent *subculture* with its own set of rules and values. While middle-class culture stresses hard work, delayed gratification, formal education, and being cautious, the lower-class subculture stresses excitement, toughness, risk taking, fearlessness, immediate gratification, and "street smarts." The lower-class subculture is an attractive alternative because the urban poor find it impossible to meet the behavioral demands of middle-class society. Unfortunately, subcultural norms often clash with conventional values. Slum dwellers are forced to violate the law because they obey the rules of the deviant culture with which they are in close and immediate contact (see Figure 7.6).

Conduct Norms

The concept that the lower class develops a unique culture in response to strain can be traced to Thorsten Sellin's classic 1938 work, *Culture Conflict and Crime,* a theoretical attempt to link cultural adaptation to criminality.[123] Sellin's main premise was that criminal law is an expression of the rules of the dominant culture. The content of the law, therefore, may create a clash between conventional, middle-class rules and splinter groups, such as ethnic and racial minorities who are excluded from the social mainstream. These groups maintain their own set of *conduct norms*—rules governing the day-to-day living conditions within these subcultures.[124] Complicating matters is the fact that most people belong to several social groups. In a complex society, the number of groups people belong to—family, peer, occupational, and religious—is quite large. "A conflict of norms is said to exist when more or less divergent rules of conduct govern the specific life situation in which a person may find himself."[125]

According to Sellin, **culture conflict** occurs when the rules expressed in the criminal law clash with the demands of group **conduct norms.** To make his point, Sellin cited the case of a Sicilian father in New Jersey who killed the 16-year-old seducer of his daughter and then expressed surprise at being arrested; he had "merely defended his family honor in a traditional way."[126] Conduct norms are universal; they are not the product of one group, culture, or political structure.

Focal Concerns

In his classic 1958 paper, "Lower-Class Culture as a Generating Milieu of Gang Delinquency," Walter Miller identified the unique value system that defines lower-class culture.[127] Obedience to these **focal concerns** dominates life among the lower class. Focal concerns do not necessarily represent a rebellion against middle-class values; rather, these values have evolved specifically to fit conditions in slum areas. The major lower-class focal concerns include:[128]

1. *Trouble.* Getting into trouble includes such behavior as fighting, drinking, and sexual misconduct. In lower-class communities, people are evaluated by their actual

Figure 7.6 Elements of cultural deviance theory.

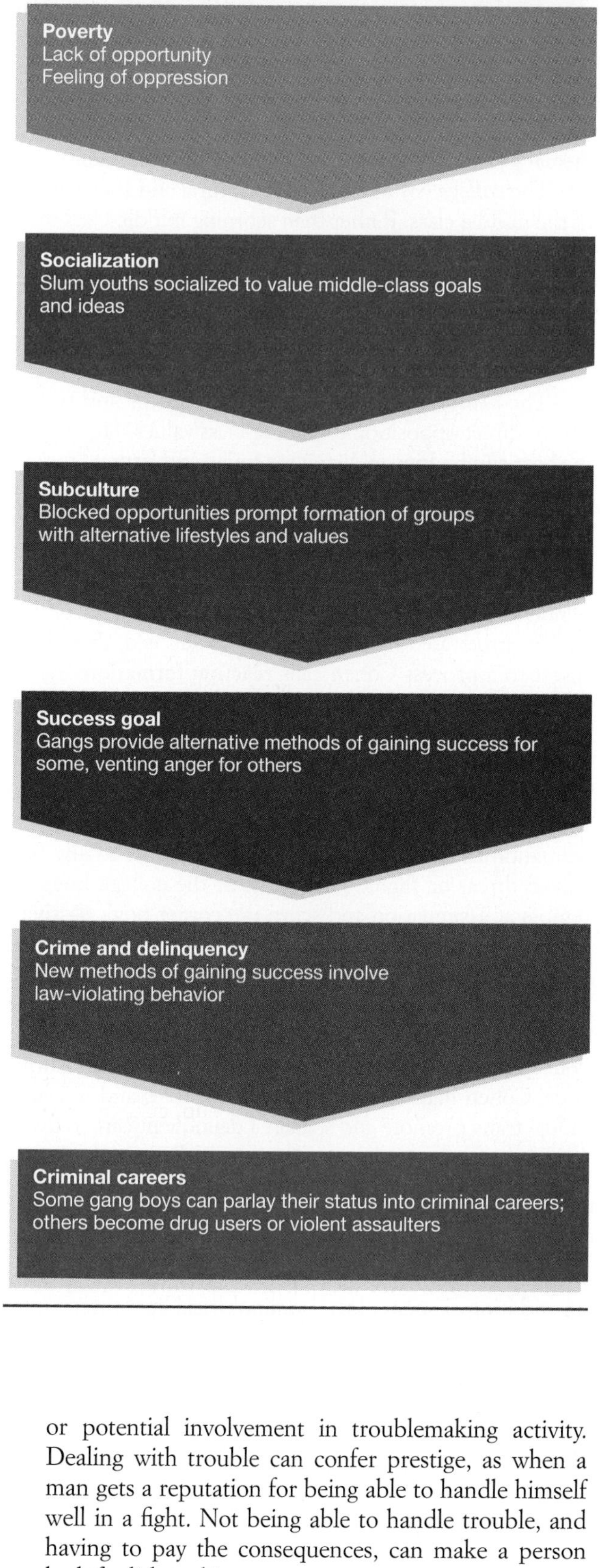

Poverty
Lack of opportunity
Feeling of oppression

Socialization
Slum youths socialized to value middle-class goals and ideas

Subculture
Blocked opportunities prompt formation of groups with alternative lifestyles and values

Success goal
Gangs provide alternative methods of gaining success for some, venting anger for others

Crime and delinquency
New methods of gaining success involve law-violating behavior

Criminal careers
Some gang boys can parlay their status into criminal careers; others become drug users or violent assaulters

or potential involvement in troublemaking activity. Dealing with trouble can confer prestige, as when a man gets a reputation for being able to handle himself well in a fight. Not being able to handle trouble, and having to pay the consequences, can make a person look foolish and incompetent.

2. *Toughness.* Lower-class males want local recognition of their physical and spiritual toughness. They refuse to be sentimental or soft and instead value physical strength, fighting ability, and athletic skill. Those who cannot meet these standards risk getting a reputation for being weak, inept, and effeminate.

3. *Smartness.* Members of the lower-class culture want to maintain an image of being "street-wise" and savvy, using their "street smarts," and having the ability to outfox and "out-con" the opponent. Although formal education is not admired, knowing essential survival techniques, such as gambling, conning, and outsmarting the law, is a requirement.

4. *Excitement.* Another important feature of the lower-class lifestyle is the search for fun and excitement to enliven an otherwise drab existence. The search for excitement may lead to gambling, fighting, getting drunk, and sexual adventures. In between, the lower-class citizen may simply "hang out" and "be cool."

5. *Fate.* Lower-class citizens believe their lives are in the hands of strong spiritual forces that guide their destinies. Getting lucky, finding good fortune, and hitting the jackpot are all slum dwellers' daily dreams.

6. *Autonomy.* A general concern exists in lower-class cultures about personal freedom and autonomy. Being independent of authority figures, such as the police, teachers, and parents, is required; losing control is an unacceptable weakness, incompatible with toughness.

According to Miller, clinging to lower-class focal concerns promotes behavior that often runs afoul of the law. Toughness may mean displaying fighting prowess; street smarts lead to drug deals; excitement may result in drinking, gambling, or drug abuse. It is this obedience to the prevailing cultural demands of lower-class society, and not alienation from conventional society, that causes urban crime.

These views of a lower-class subculture formed by strain inspired a number of formal theories that predicted the onset of gang delinquency in lower-class areas. The two best known are the theory of delinquent subcultures and the theory of differential opportunity.

Theory of Delinquent Subcultures

Albert Cohen first articulated the theory of delinquent subculture in his classic 1955 book, *Delinquent Boys.*[129] Cohen's central position was that the delinquent behavior of lower-class youths is actually a protest against the norms and values of the middle-class U.S. culture. Because social conditions make them incapable of achieving success legitimately, lower-class youths experience a form of culture conflict that Cohen labels **status frustration.**[130] As a result, many of them join in gangs and engage in behavior that is "nonutilitarian, malicious, and negativistic."[131]

Cohen viewed the delinquent gang as a separate subculture, possessing a value system directly opposed to that of the larger society. He described the subculture as one that takes "its norms from the larger culture but turns them upside down. The delinquent's conduct is right by the standards of his subculture precisely because it is wrong by the norms of the larger cultures."[132]

According to Cohen, the development of the delinquent subculture is a consequence of socialization practices found in the ghetto or slum environment. Deficient socialization renders lower-class kids unable to achieve conventional success. Cohen suggests that lower-class parents are incapable of teaching children the necessary techniques for entering the dominant middle-class culture. Developmental handicaps suffered by lower-class kids include lack of education, poor speech and communication skills, and inability to delay gratification. These children lack the basic skills necessary to achieve social and economic success in the demanding U.S. society.

MIDDLE-CLASS MEASURING RODS. One significant handicap that lower-class children face is the inability to positively impress authority figures, such as teachers, employers, or supervisors. In U.S. society, these positions tend to be held by members of the middle class who have difficulty relating to the lower-class youngster. Cohen calls the standards set by these authority figures **middle-class measuring rods.** The conflict and frustration lower-class youths experience when they fail to meet these standards is a primary cause of delinquency.

Lower-class youths who have difficulty adjusting to the middle-class measuring rods of one institution may find themselves prejudged by others. The ratings are reviewed and magnified by the periodic updating of records and the informal exchanges of information that commonly occur among the leaders of institutions, who frequently are also the pillars and decision makers of the community. A school record may be reviewed by juvenile court authorities, a juvenile court record may be opened by the military, and a military record can influence the securing of a job. A person's status and esteem in the community is largely determined by the judgments that most often reflect the traditional values of American society.[133] Negative evaluations become part of a permanent file that follows an individual for the rest of his or her life. When he or she wants to improve, evidence of prior failures is used to discourage advancement.

THE FORMATION OF DEVIANT SUBCULTURES. Cohen believes lower-class boys who suffer rejection by middle-class decision makers usually elect to join one of three existing subcultures: the corner boy, the college boy, or the delinquent boy.

The *corner boy* role is the most common response to middle-class rejection. The corner boy is not a chronic delinquent but may be a truant who engages in petty or status offenses, such as precocious sex and recreational drug abuse. His main loyalty is to his peer group, on which he depends for support, motivation, and interest. His values, therefore, are those of the group with which he is in close personal contact. The corner boy, well aware of his failure to achieve the standards of the American dream, retreats into the comforting world of his lower-class peers and eventually becomes a stable member of his neighborhood, holding a menial job, marrying, and remaining in the community.

The *college boy* embraces the cultural and social values of the middle class. Rather than scorning middle-class measuring rods, he actively strives to be successful by those standards. Cohen views this type of youth as one who is embarking on an almost hopeless path, since he is ill-equipped academically, socially, and linguistically to achieve the rewards of middle-class life.

The *delinquent boy* adopts a set of norms and principles in direct opposition to middle-class values. He engages in **short-run hedonism,** living for today and letting "tomorrow take care of itself."[134] Delinquent boys strive for **group autonomy.** They resist efforts by family, school, or other sources of authority to control their behavior. They may join a gang because it is perceived as autonomous, independent, and the focus of "attraction, loyalty, and solidarity."[135] Frustrated by their inability to succeed, these boys resort to a process Cohen calls **reaction formation.** Symptoms of reaction formation include overly intense responses that seem disproportionate to the stimuli that trigger them. For the delinquent boy, this takes the form of irrational, malicious, and unaccountable hostility to the enemy, "the norms of respectable middle-class society."[136] Reaction formation causes delinquent boys to overreact to any perceived threat or slight. They sneer at the college boy's attempts at assimilation and scorn the corner boy's passivity. The delinquent boy is willing to take risks, violate the law, and flaunt middle-class conventions.

Cohen's work helps explain the factors that promote and sustain a delinquent subculture. By introducing the concepts of status frustration and middle-class measuring rods, Cohen makes it clear that social forces and not individual traits promote and sustain a delinquent career. By introducing the corner boy–college boy–delinquent boy triad, he helps explain why many lower-class youths fail to become chronic offenders: There is more than one social path open to indigent youth.[137] His work is a skillful integration of strain and social disorganization theories and has become an enduring element of the criminological literature.

Theory of Differential Opportunity

In their well-known work *Delinquency and Opportunity*, Richard Cloward and Lloyd Ohlin also combine strain and social disorganization principles into a portrayal of a gang-sustaining criminal subculture.[138]

Cloward and Ohlin, agreeing with Cohen, found that independent delinquent subcultures exist within society: "A

According to Cloward and Ohlin's theory of differential opportunity, those who perceive themselves as failures within conventional society or who conclude that there is little hope for advancement by legitimate means may join with like-minded peers to form a gang. Therefore, gang prevention workers, such as the ones shown here, try to help troubled youth find legitimate alternatives to ganging, such as a well-paying job or educational opportunities.

delinquent subculture is one in which certain forms of delinquent activity are essential requirements for the performance of the dominant roles supported by the subculture."[139]

Youth gangs are an important part of the delinquent subculture. While not all illegal acts are committed by gang youths, they are the source of the most serious, sustained, and costly criminal behaviors. Delinquent gangs spring up in disorganized areas where youths lack the opportunity to gain success through conventional means. True to strain theory principles, Cloward and Ohlin portray slum kids as individuals who want to conform to middle-class values but lack the means to do so: "Reaching out for socially approved goals under conditions that preclude their legitimate achievement may become a prelude to deviance."[140]

DIFFERENTIAL OPPORTUNITIES. The centerpiece of the Cloward and Ohlin theory is the concept of **differential opportunity.** According to this concept, people in all strata of society share the same success goals; however, those in the lower class have limited means of achieving those goals. People who perceive themselves as failures within conventional society will seek alternative or innovative ways to gain success. People who conclude that there is little hope for advancement by legitimate means may join with like-minded peers to form a gang. Gang members provide the emotional support to handle the shame, fear, or guilt they may develop while engaging in illegal acts. Delinquent sub-

cultures reward them in a way that conventional society cannot hope to duplicate. The youth who is considered a failure at school and is only qualified for a menial job at a minimum wage can earn thousands of dollars plus the respect of his or her peers by joining a gang and engaging in drug deals or armed robberies.

Cloward and Ohlin recognize that the opportunity for success in either conventional or criminal careers is limited. In stable areas, adolescents may be recruited by professional criminals, drug traffickers, or organized crime groups. Unstable areas cannot support flourishing criminal opportunities. In these socially disorganized neighborhoods, adult role models are absent and young criminals have few opportunities to join established gangs or learn the fine points of professional crime. Cloward and Ohlin's most important finding, then, is that all opportunities for success, *both illegal and conventional,* are closed for the most "truly disadvantaged" youth.

Because of differential opportunity, kids are likely to join one of three types of gangs:

1. *Criminal gangs.* Criminal gangs exist in stable slum areas in which close connections among adolescent, young adult, and adult offenders create an environment for successful criminal enterprise.[141] Youths are recruited into established criminal gangs that provide a training ground for a successful criminal career. Gang membership provides a learning experience in which

the knowledge and skills needed for success in crime are acquired. During this "apprenticeship stage," older, more experienced members of the criminal subculture hold youthful "trainees" on tight reins, limiting activities that might jeopardize the gang's profits (for example, engaging in nonfunctional, irrational violence). Over time, new recruits learn the techniques and attitudes of the criminal world and how to "cooperate successfully with others in criminal enterprises."[142] To become a fully accepted member of the criminal gang, novices must prove themselves reliable and dependable in their contacts with their criminal associates and be "right guys." They are introduced to the middlemen of the crime business—drug importers, fences, pawn shop operators—and also to legal connections—crooked police officers and shady lawyers—who can help them gain their freedom in the rare instances when they are apprehended.

2. *Conflict gangs.* Conflict gangs develop in communities unable to provide either legitimate or illegitimate opportunities. These highly disorganized areas are marked by transient residents and physical deterioration. Crime in this area is "individualistic, unorganized, petty, poorly paid, and unprotected."[143] There are no successful adult criminal role models from whom youths can learn criminal skills. When such severe limitations on both criminal and conventional opportunity intensify frustrations of the young, violence is used as a means of gaining status. The stereotype of the conflict gang member is the swaggering gang tough who fights with weapons to win respect from rivals and engages in unpredictable and destructive assaults on people and property. Conflict gang members must be ready to fight to protect their own and their gang's integrity and honor. By doing so, they acquire a "rep," which provides them with a means for gaining admiration from their peers and consequently helps them develop their own self-image. Conflict gangs "represent a way of securing access to the scarce resources for adolescent pleasure and opportunity in underprivileged areas."[144]

3. *Retreatist gangs.* Retreatists are double failures, unable to gain success through legitimate means and unwilling to do so through illegal ones. Some retreatists have tried crime or violence but are too clumsy, too weak, or too scared to be accepted in criminal or violent gangs. They then "retreat" into a role on the fringe of society. Members of the retreatist subculture constantly search for ways of getting high—alcohol, pot, heroin, unusual sexual experiences, music. They are always "cool," detached from relationships with the conventional world. To feed their habits, retreatists develop a "hustle"—pimping, conning, selling drugs, and committing petty crimes. Personal status in the retreatist subculture is derived from peer approval.

ANALYSIS OF DIFFERENTIAL OPPORTUNITY THEORY. Cloward and Ohlin's theory is important both because of its integration of cultural deviance and social disorganization variables and its recognition of different modes of criminal adaptation. The fact that criminal cultures can be supportive, rational, and profitable seems to be a more realistic reflection of the actual world of the criminal gang than Cohen's original view of purely negativistic, destructive criminal youths who oppose all social values. Cloward and Ohlin's tripartite model of urban delinquency also relates directly to the treatment and rehabilitation of delinquents. While other social structure theorists portray delinquent youths as having values and attitudes in opposition to middle-class culture, Cloward and Ohlin suggest that many delinquents share the goals and values of the general society but lack the means to obtain success. This position suggests that delinquency prevention can be achieved by providing youths with the means for obtaining the success they truly desire without the need to change their basic attitudes and beliefs.

The validity of opportunity theory is underscored by the gang activity recorded in the nation's cities. As opportunity theory predicts, gang activity today flourishes in the inner-city ghetto areas of Detroit, New York, Los Angeles, and Chicago. In addition, smaller cities, such as Cleveland and Columbus, Ohio, and Milwaukee, Wisconsin, are now experiencing serious gang problems with the development of local gangs and the migration of gang members from larger communities. A national survey of gang migration by Cheryl Maxson, Kristi Woods, and Malcolm Klein describes the levels of movement from one city to another as "astounding." A decade ago, about 200 of the 1,100 cities they studied had gangs; today, the number is 700. Of the 150 cities in the United States with populations of more than 100,000, 82 percent had experienced gang migration from larger cities.[145]

In 1992 the National Assessment of Gang Activity, a comprehensive investigation of the nation's gang problem, surveyed police departments in the nation's 79 largest cities and found that 91% (72 cities) reported the presence of youth gangs involved in criminal activity; three other areas report the presence of drug dealing "posses" and "crews."[146] Data from these cities along with data collected from 29 smaller cities and 11 county jurisdictions showed a total of 4,881 gangs with 249,324 members. A 1994 extension and replication of the National Assessment indicated that there are 8,625 to 16,643 gangs containing between 378,807 and 555,181 members (the lower-range figures are conservative estimates, while the upper range is a statistical estimate derived by using more liberal techniques).[147] The 1994 survey also estimated that gang members commit between 437,066 and 580,331 crimes each year. The 1994 survey thus shows that gang activity is significantly higher today than ever before and that gang membership is, if anything, accelerating in the 1990s.[148]

Another survey of "gang cities" conducted throughout the 1990s by Malcolm Klein found that 94% of the 189

U.S. cities with populations of 100,000 or more and 800–900 of smaller cities with populations of 10,000–100,000 have gang problems. Combining these would create a total of more than 1,000 gang locations. While smaller cities have relatively few gang members, averaging slightly more than 100, almost half of the larger cities report having 500 or more members, including 14 cities with more than 4,000 gang members. Los Angeles alone has more than 1,000 gangs![149] Klein's estimate of 500,000 gang members coincides with the National Assessment's.[150]

Net Bookmark

Membership in Los Angeles gangs is among the highest in the nation. To learn more about their culture and history, visit the L.A. gang homepage:

http://www-bcf.usc.edu/~aalonso/Gangs/index.html

Why has gang activity increased? One compelling reason may be the involvement of youth gangs in the distribution and sales of illegal drugs. Some but certainly not all gangs are actively involved in the drug trade, replacing traditional organized crime families as the dominant supplier of illegal substances. The introduction of the relatively cheap cocaine derivative crack, which provides a powerful, albeit short-term high, helped open new markets in the drug trade.[151]

Gang formation may be the natural consequence of the evolution of the American industrial base from a manufacturing economy with a surplus of relatively high-paying jobs to a low-wage service economy.[152] The American city, which traditionally required a large population base for its manufacturing plants, now faces incredible economic stress as these plants shut down. In this uneasy economic climate, gangs form and flourish in areas where the moderating influence of successful adult role models and stable families declines and where adolescents face constrained choices and weak social controls.[153] Gang activity provides members with a stable income stream in an otherwise unproductive urban marketplace. From this perspective, youth gangs are a response to the glooming of the American economy.

The rise of gang memberships in a declining industrial market and the development of drug profits as an alternative or innovative method of financial success are social conditions predicted by opportunity theory. The prevalence of gang activity in urban America provides staunch support for the social structure approach.

Evaluation of Social Structure Theories

The social structure approach has significantly influenced both criminological theory and crime-prevention strategies. Its core concepts seem to be valid in view of the high crime and delinquency rates and gang activity occurring in the deteriorated inner-city slum areas of the nation's largest cities. The public's image of the slum includes roaming bands of violent teenage gangs, drug users, prostitutes, muggers, and similar frightening examples of criminality. All of these are present today in urban ghetto areas.

Each branch of the general structural model seems to support and amplify others. Some theorists, such as Robert Sampson and William Julius Wilson, suggest that these concepts are actually interdependent.[154] Factors that cause strain, such as lack of access to legitimate economic opportunities and economic inequality, also produce social disorganization. Stress leads to alcohol abuse and unprotected sex outside of marriage, causing an increase in impaired households, dysfunctional families, urban hostility, and the deterioration of informal social controls. Sampson and Wilson argue that government assistance in the form of welfare is needed to reduce stress in urban ghettos, thereby lowering crime rates.

Critics of the approach charge that we cannot be sure that it is lower-class culture itself that promotes crime and not some other force operating in society. Critics of this approach deny that residence in urban areas is alone sufficient to cause people to violate the law.[155] They counter with the charge that lower-class crime rates may be an artifact of bias in the criminal justice system. Lower-class areas seem to have higher crime rates because residents are arrested and prosecuted by agents of the justice system who, as members of the middle class, exhibit class bias.[156] Class bias is often coupled with discrimination against minority-group members, who have long suffered at the hands of the justice system.

Even if the higher crime rates recorded in lower-class areas are valid, it is still true that most members of the lower class are not criminals. The discovery of the chronic offender indicates that a significant majority of people living in lower-class environments are not criminals and that a relatively small proportion of the population commit most crimes. If social forces alone could be used to explain crime, how can we account for the vast number of urban poor who remain honest and law-abiding? Given these circumstances, law violators must be motivated by some individual mental, physical, or social process or trait.[157]

It is also questionable whether a distinct lower-class culture actually exists. Several researchers have found that gang members and other delinquent youths seem to value middle-class concepts, such as sharing, earning money, and respecting the law, as highly as middle-class youths. Criminologists contend that lower-class youths value education as highly as middle-class students do.[158] Opinion polls can also be used as evidence that a majority of lower-class citizens maintain middle-class values. National surveys find that people in the lowest income brackets want tougher drug laws, more police protection, and greater control over criminal offenders.[159] These opinions seem similar to conventional middle-class values rather than representative of an independent, deviant subculture.

While this evidence contradicts some of the central ideas of social structure theory, the discovery of stable patterns of lower-class crime, the high crime rates found in disorganized inner-city areas, and the rise of teenage gangs and groups support a close association between crime rates and social class position.

Social Structure Theory and Social Policy

Social structure theory has had a significant influence on social policy. If the cause of criminality is viewed as a separation between lower-class individuals and conventional goals, norms, and rules, it seems logical that alternatives to criminal behavior can be provided by giving slum dwellers opportunities to share in the rewards of conventional society.

One approach is to give indigent people direct financial aid through welfare and aid to dependent children. Although welfare has been curtailed through the Federal Welfare Reform Act of 1996, research shows that crime rates are reduced when families receive supplemental income through public assistance payments.[160]

Efforts have also been made to reduce crime rates by directly applying concepts suggested by social structure theories to social policy. Crime prevention efforts based on social structure precepts can be traced back to the **Chicago Area Project,** supervised by Clifford R. Shaw. This program attempted to organize existing community structures to develop social stability in otherwise disorganized slums. The project sponsored recreation programs for children in the neighborhoods, including summer camping. It campaigned for community improvements in such areas as education, sanitation, traffic safety, physical conservation, and law enforcement. Project members also worked with police and court agencies to supervise and treat gang youth and adult offenders. In a 25-year assessment of the project, Solomon Kobrin found that it was successful in demonstrating the feasibility of creating youth welfare organizations in high-delinquency areas.[161] Kobrin also discovered that the project made a distinct contribution to ending the isolation of urban males from the mainstream of society.

Social structure concepts, especially the views of Cloward and Ohlin, were a critical ingredient in the Kennedy and Johnson administrations' War on Poverty, begun in the early 1960s. Rather than organizing existing community structures, as Shaw's Chicago Area Project had done, this later effort called for an all-out attack on the crime-producing structures of slum areas. The cornerstone of the War on Poverty's crime-prevention effort was called Mobilization for Youth (MFY). This New York City–based program was funded with over $12 million. It was designed to serve multiple purposes: provide teacher training and education to help educators deal with the problem youth,

create work opportunities through a youth job center, organize neighborhood councils and associations, provide street workers to deal with teen gangs, and set up counseling services and assistance to neighborhood families. Subsequent War on Poverty programs included the Job Corps; VISTA (the urban Peace Corps); Head Start and Upward Bound (educational enrichment programs); Neighborhood Legal Services; and the largest community organizing effort, the Community Action Program.

War on Poverty programs, such as MFY, were sweeping efforts to change the social structure of the slum area. They sought to reduce crime by developing a sense of community pride and solidarity in poverty areas and providing educational and job opportunities for crime-prone youths. As history tells us, the programs failed. Federal and state funding often fell into the hands of middle-class managers and community developers and not the people it was designed to help. Managers were accused of graft and corruption. Some community organizers engineered rent strikes, lawsuits, protests, and the like, which angered government officials and convinced them that financial backing of such programs should be ended. Rather than appeal to the political power structure, program administrators alienated it.

Still later, the mood of the country began to change. The more conservative political climate under the Nixon, Ford, Reagan, and Bush administrations did not favor federal sponsorship of radical change in U.S. cities. Instead of a total community approach to solving the crime problem, a more selective crime-prevention policy was adopted. Some War on Poverty programs—Head Start, Neighborhood Legal Services, and the Community Action Program—have continued to help people; nonetheless, this attempt to change the very structure of society must be judged a noble failure (Head Start is discussed further in Chapter 8).

A cornerstone of all these programs has been providing job opportunities for at-risk youth on the assumption that there is an inverse association between employment and crime. The Close-Up on "Unemployment and Crime" explores this issue in depth.

Summary

Sociology has been the main orientation of criminologists because they know that crime rates vary among elements of the social structure, that society goes through changes that affect crime, and that social interaction relates to criminality. Social structure theories suggest that people's places in the socioeconomic structure of society influence their chances of becoming a criminal. Poor people are more likely to commit crimes because they are unable to achieve monetary or social success in any other way. Social structure theory has three schools of thought: social disorganization, strain, and cultural deviance theory (summarized in Table 7.2).

close-up: *Unemployment and Crime*

The social structure approach links crime to the economic deprivation experienced in ghetto areas. It follows that if people do not hold jobs, they will be more likely to turn to crime as a means of support. If jobs are available, crime rates should go down. People who hold jobs should be less criminal than the unemployed. Is this assumption valid? Is there a relationship between crime and unemployment?

Despite the logic of this proposition, little clear-cut evidence exists linking unemployment and crime rates. The crime rate has risen dramatically during times of relative economic prosperity, such as the 1960s. Thus, crime and unemployment are only weakly related. Although criminals have poorer work records than noncriminals, there is little indication that changing market conditions cause them to renounce crime and choose legitimate earning opportunities. Crime rates in cities and states are slightly linked to labor market conditions, but the relationship between them is tenuous.

A routine activities theorist (Chapter 5) might suggest that the weaker-than-expected relationship between crime and unemployment rates can be explained by the fact that while joblessness increases the motivation to commit crime, it simultaneously decreases the opportunity to gain from criminal enterprise. During periods of economic hardship, potential victims have fewer valuable items in their possession and guard those valuables more closely. Parents who are unemployed can be at home to supervise their children, reducing the opportunity for the kids to commit crime; teenagers have higher crime rates than any other age group.

These results should not be unexpected. It seems unlikely that hardworking people will turn to crime because they lost their job. Crime rates are highest among adolescents who are not yet part of the work force and are unlikely to be directly affected by employment rates.

When individual offenders are the unit of analysis, an unemployment-crime link is more readily observed. Unemployed individuals are more likely to commit crime than the employed. Surveys of adult inmates show that many were unemployed and underemployed before their incarceration; median income of both male and female inmates was below the poverty level. It is possible that on an individual level, *unemployment* increases crime because it reduces people's stake in conformity. By severing attachments to co-workers and reducing parents' ability to be breadwinners, unemployment reduces the attachment people have to conventional institutions and their ability to exert authority over their children. While this view is persuasive, it is also possible that unemployed offenders stand a greater chance of being detected, convicted, and incarcerated than the employed. Nonetheless, the fact that known offenders are often underemployed or unemployed is generally supportive of a crime-unemployment relationship.

There are a number of possible explanations for the rather weak crime-unemployment association. It may be that only extremely high unemployment rates are associated with crime. As you may recall, crime rates peaked in the 1930s during the Great Depression. It is possible that only such a long and sustained period of economic chaos can affect crime rates. Recent short-term fluctuations in the economy may be of too short a duration to have a measurable effect.

The unemployment-crime relationship may also be offense-specific, helping in part to explain the weaker than expected association. Unemployment seems to have the greatest influence on opportunistic property crimes, such as burglary, and the least on violent assaultive crimes, which may be motivated by noneconomic factors, such as rage, jealousy, or substance abuse.

It is also possible that the crime-unemployment relationship travels a different path than expected: Rather than joblessness motivating people to commit crime, it is possible that criminal behavior excludes offenders from the workplace. Put another way, an early experience with delinquent behavior and drug abuse may later result in protracted unemployment as an adult. John Hagan explains this relationship as a function of *social embeddedness:* the process by which early behavior patterns become stable, lifelong habits and tendencies. Hagan found that kids with early criminal experiences, whose friends are delinquent, and whose parents are convicted criminals become *embedded* in behaviors that result in later adult unemployment. The chain of events runs from having criminal friends and parents, engaging in delinquency, and gaining police and court contacts to losing the opportunity for meaningful employment as adults. Embeddedness in a deviant lifestyle is contrasted with the establishment of roots in a conventional one: Youths who get early work experience, who make contacts, and who learn the ropes of the job market establish the groundwork for a successful career. Hagan concludes: "Criminal youths are embedded in contexts that isolate them from the likelihood of legitimate adult employment."

So, is there an association between crime and unemployment? The data suggest that these two variables are interrelated, but it may be that crime *causes* unemployment and not that the unemployed become criminals.

CRITICAL THINKING QUESTIONS

1. To prevent crime, should all people be guaranteed the right to work?
2. Would a job at the minimum wage be a realistic crime-reducing alternative to unemployment?

Sources: Mark Collins and Don Weatherburn, "Unemployment and the Dynamics of Offender Populations," *Journal of Quantitative Criminology* 11 (1995): 231–245; John Hagan, "The Social Embeddedness of Crime and Unemployment," *Criminology* 31 (1993): 465–492; Theodore Chiricos, "Rates of Crime and Unemployment: An Analysis of Aggregate Research Evidence," *Social Problems* 34 (1987): 187–212; David Cantor and Kenneth Land, "Unemployment and Crime Rates in the Post–World War II United States: A Theoretical and Empirical Analysis," *American Sociological Review* 50 (1985): 317–332; Richard Freeman, "Crime and Unemployment," in *Crime and Public Policy,* ed. James Q. Wilson (San Francisco: Institute for Contemporary Studies, 1983), pp. 89–106.

Table 7.2   Social Structure Theories

THEORY	MAJOR PREMISE	STRENGTHS
Social Disorganization Theory		
Shaw and McKay's concentric zone theory	Crime is a product of transitional neighborhoods that manifest social disorganization and value conflict.	Identifies why crime rates are highest in slum areas. Points out the factors that produce crime. Suggests programs to help reduce crime.
Social ecology theory	The conflicts and problems of urban social life and communities, including fear, unemployment, deterioration and siege mentality, influence crime rates.	Accounts for urban crime rates and trends.
Strain Theory		
Anomie theory	People who adopt the goals of society but lack the means to attain them seek alternatives, such as crime.	Points out how competition for success creates conflict and crime. Suggests that social conditions and not personality can account for crime. Can explain middle- and upper-class crime.
General strain theory	Strain has a variety of sources. Strain causes crime in the absence of adequate coping mechanisms.	Identifies the complexities of strain in modern society. Expands on anomie theory. Shows the influences of social events on behavior over the life course.
Institutional anomie theory	Material goals pervade all aspects of American life.	Explains why crime rates are so high in American culture.
Relative deprivation theory	Crime occurs when the wealthy and poor live in close proximity to one another.	Explains high crime rates in deteriorated inner-city areas located near more affluent neighborhoods.
Cultural Deviance Theory		
Sellin's culture conflict theory	Obedience to the norms of their lower-class culture puts people in conflict with the norms of the dominant culture.	Identifies the aspects of lower-class life that produce street crime. Adds to Shaw and McKay's analysis. Creates the concept of culture conflict.
Miller's focal concern theory	Citizens who obey the street rules of lower-class life (focal concerns) find themselves in conflict with the dominant culture.	Identifies the core values of lower-class culture and shows their association to crime.
Cohen's theory of delinquent gangs	Status frustration of lower-class boys, created by their failure to achieve middle-class success, causes them to join gangs.	Shows how the conditions of lower-class life produce crime. Explains violence and destructive acts. Identifies conflict of lower class with middle class.
Cloward and Ohlin's theory of opportunity	Blockage of conventional opportunities causes lower-class youths to join criminal, conflict, or retreatist gangs.	Shows that even illegal opportunities are structured in society. Indicates why people become involved in a particular type of criminal activity. Presents a way of preventing crime.

Social disorganization theory suggests that slum dwellers violate the law because they live in areas in which social control has broken down. The origin of social disorganization theory can be traced to the work of Clifford R. Shaw and Henry D. McKay. Shaw and McKay concluded that disorganized areas marked by divergent values and transitional populations produce criminality. Modern social ecology theory looks at such neighborhood issues as community fear, unemployment, siege mentality, and deterioration.

Strain theories comprise the second branch of the social structure approach. They view crime as a result of the anger people experience over their inability to achieve legitimate social and economic success. Strain theories hold that most people share common values and beliefs, but the ability to achieve them is differentiated throughout the social structure. The best-known strain theory is Robert Merton's theory of anomie, which describes what happens when the means people have at their disposal are not adequate to satisfy their goals. Steven Messner, Richard Rosenfeld, and Robert Agnew have extended this theory by showing that strain has multiple sources.

Cultural deviance theories hold that a unique value system develops in lower-class areas. Lower-class values approve of such behaviors as being tough, never showing fear, and defying authority. People perceiving strain will bond together in their own groups or subcultures for support and recognition. Albert Cohen links the formation of subcultures to the failure of lower-class citizens to achieve recognition from middle-class decision makers, such as teachers, employers, and police officers. Richard Cloward and Lloyd Ohlin have argued that crime results from lower-class people's perception that their opportunity for success is limited. Consequently, youths in low-income areas may join criminal, conflict, or retreatist gangs.

Key Terms

Chicago School
natural areas
stratification
poverty line
culture of poverty
at-risk
underclass
truly disadvantaged
social structure theory
social disorganization
  theory
strain theory
cultural deviance theory
subcultures
cultural transmission
transitional neighborhoods
value conflict
social ecologists
siege mentality

concentration effect
theory of anomie
American Dream
income inequality
relative deprivation
social injustice
general strain theory (GST)
negative affective states
culture conflict
conduct norms
focal concerns
status frustration
middle-class measuring
  rods
short-run hedonism
group autonomy
reaction formation
differential opportunity
Chicago Area Project

Notes

1. Steven Messner and Richard Rosenfeld, *Crime and the American Dream* (Belmont, Calif.: Wadsworth, 1994), p. 11.

2. Robert Park, "The City: Suggestions for the Investigation of Behavior in the City Environment," *American Journal of Sociology* 20 (1915): 579–583.

3. Robert Park, Ernest Burgess, and Roderic McKenzie, *The City* (Chicago: University of Chicago Press, 1925).

4. Harvey Zorbaugh, *The Gold Coast and the Slum* (Chicago: University of Chicago Press, 1929).

5. Frederick Thrasher, *The Gang* (Chicago: University of Chicago Press, 1927).

6. Louis Wirth, *The Ghetto* (Chicago: University of Chicago Press, 1928).

7. Daniel Bell, *The Coming of Post-Industrial Society* (New York: Basic Books, 1973).

8. See, generally, Stephen Cernkovich and Peggy Giordano, "Family Relationships and Delinquency," *Criminology* 25 (1987): 295–321; Paul Howes and Howard Markman, "Marital Quality and Child Functioning: A Longitudinal Investigation," *Child Development* 60 (1989): 1044–1051.

9. Emilie Andersen Allan and Darrell Steffensmeier, "Youth, Underemployment, and Property Crime: Differential Effects of Job Availability and Job Quality on Juvenile and Young Adult Arrest Rates," *American Sociological Review* 54 (1989): 107–123.

10. Edwin Lemert, *Human Deviance, Social Problems and Social Control* (Englewood Cliffs, N.J.: Prentice-Hall, 1967).

11. U.S. Department of Commerce, Bureau of the Census, Census Data 1995 (Washington, D.C.: U.S. Government Printing Office, 1996).

12. Based on William Julius Wilson, "Studying Inner-City Social Dislocations: The Challenge of Public Agenda Research," *American Sociological Review* 56 (1991): 1–14.

13. National Center for Children in Poverty, News Release, 11 December 1996.

14 Children's Defense Fund, *The State of America's Children, 1996* (Washington, D.C.: Children's Defense Fund, 1996), p. 3.

15. Jennifer Dixon, "Thousands of Infants Left in Hospitals in '91," *Boston Globe,* 9 November 1993, p. 5.

16. Jonathan Crane, "The Epidemic Theory of Ghettos and Neighborhood Effects on Dropping Out and Teenage Childbearing," *American Journal of Sociology* 96 (1991): 1226–1259; see also Rodrick Wallace, "Expanding Coupled Shock Fronts of Urban Decay and Criminal Behavior: How U.S. Cities Are Becoming 'Hollowed Out,'" *Journal of Quantitative Criminology* 7 (1991): 333–355.

17. Children's Defense Fund, *The State of America's Children, 1996,* p. 2.

18. Ibid.

19. Dolores Kong, "Social, Economic Factors Seen in Black Death Rates," *Boston Globe,* 8 December 1989, p. 1.

20. Associated Press, "Harlem More Deadly Than Bangladesh," *Boston Globe,* 18 January 1990, p. 18.

21. Douglas Massey and Mitchell Eggers, "The Ecology of Inequality: Minorities and the Concentration of Poverty, 1970–1980," *American Journal of Sociology* 95 (1990): 1153–1188; Melvin Thomas, "Race, Class and Personal Income: An Empirical Test of the Declining Significance of Race Thesis, 1968–1988," *Social Problems* 40 (1993): 328–339.

22. Personal communication, Harvard Project on School Desegregation, Harvard University, Cambridge, 15 December 1993.

23. Oscar Lewis, "The Culture of Poverty," *Scientific American* 215 (1966): 19–25.

24. Gunnar Myrdal, *The Challenge of World Poverty* (New York: Vintage Books, 1970).

25. Ken Auletta, *The Under Class* (New York: Random House, 1982).

26. Herbert Gans, "Deconstructing the Underclass: The Term's Danger as a Planning Concept," *Journal of the American Planning Association* 56 (1990): 271–277.

27. Massey and Eggers, "The Ecology of Inequality."

28. Laurence Lynn and Michael G. H. McGeary, eds., *Inner-City Poverty in the United States* (Washington, D.C.: National Academy Press, 1990), p. 3.

29. Ibid.

30. Wilson, *The Truly Disadvantaged.*

31. Cynthia Rexroat, *Declining Economic Status of Black Children: Examining the Change* (Washington, D.C.: Joint Center for Political and Economic Studies, 1990), p. 1.

32. David Brownfield, "Social Class and Violent Behavior," *Criminology* 24 (1986): 421–438.

33. Charles Tittle and Robert Meier, "Specifying the SES/Delinquency Relationship," *Criminology* 28 (1990): 271–295.

34. Ruth Kornhauser, *Social Sources of Delinquency* (Chicago: University of Chicago Press, 1978), p. 75.

35. Clifford R. Shaw and Henry D. McKay, *Juvenile Delinquency and Urban Areas,* rev. ed. (Chicago: University of Chicago Press, 1972).

36. Anthony Platt, *The Child Savers: The Invention of Delinquency* (Chicago: University of Chicago Press, 1968).

37. Shaw and McKay, *Juvenile Delinquency and Urban Areas,* p. 52.

38. Ibid., p. 171.

39. For a discussion of these issues, see Robert Bursik, "Social Disorganization and Theories of Crime and Delinquency: Problems and Prospects," *Criminology* 26 (1988): 521–539.

40. Robert Sampson, "Effects of Socioeconomic Context of Official Reaction to Juvenile Delinquency," *American Sociological Review* 51 (1986): 876–885.

41. Jeffrey Fagan, Ellen Slaughter, and Eliot Hartstone, "Blind Justice? The Impact of Race on the Juvenile Justice Process," *Crime and Delinquency* 33 (1987): 224–258; Merry Morash, "Establishment of a Juvenile Police Record," *Criminology* 22 (1984): 97–113.

42. The most well-known of these critiques is Kornhauser, *Social Sources of Delinquency.*

43. Bernard Lander, *Towards an Understanding of Juvenile Delinquency* (New York: Columbia University Press, 1954); David Bordua, "Juvenile Delinquency and 'Anomie': An Attempt at Replication," *Social Problems* 6 (1958): 230–238; Roland Chilton, "Continuities in Delinquency Area Research: A Comparison of Studies in Baltimore, Detroit, and Indianapolis," *American Sociological Review* 29 (1964): 71–73.

44. For a general review, see James Byrne and Robert Sampson, eds., *The Social Ecology of Crime* (New York: Springer Verlag, 1985).

45. See, generally, Bursik, "Social Disorganization and Theories of Crime and Delinquency," pp. 519–551.

46. William Spelman, "Abandoned Buildings: Magnets for Crime?" *Journal of Criminal Justice* 21 (1993): 481–493.

47. Keith Harries and Andrea Powell, "Juvenile Gun Crime and Social Stress: Baltimore, 1980–1990," *Urban Geography* 15 (1994): 45–63.

48. Steven Messner and Kenneth Tardiff, "Economic Inequality and Levels of Homicide: An Analysis of Urban Neighborhoods," *Criminology* 24 (1986): 297–317.

49. G. David Curry and Irving Spergel, "Gang Homicide, Delinquency, and Community," *Criminology* 26 (1988): 381–407.

50. Per-Olof Wikstrom and Lars Dolmen, "Crime and Crime Trends in Different Urban Environments," *Journal of Quantitative Criminology* 6 (1990): 7–28.

51. Robert Sampson and W. Byron Groves, "Community Structure and Crime: Testing Social Disorganization Theory," *American Journal of Sociology* 94 (1989): 774–802.

52. Bursik, "Social Disorganization and Theories of Crime and Delinquency," p. 520.

53. Richard McGahey, "Economic Conditions, Organization, and Urban Crime," in *Communities and Crime,* ed. Albert Reiss and Michael Tonry (Chicago: University of Chicago Press, 1986), pp. 231–270.

54. Scott Menard and Delbert Elliott, "Self-Reported Offending, Maturational Reform, and the Easterlin Hypothesis," *Journal of Quantitative Criminology* 6 (1990): 237–268.

55. Elijah Anderson, *Streetwise: Race, Class and Change in an Urban Community* (Chicago: University of Chicago Press, 1990), pp. 243–244.

56. Pamela Wilcox Rountree and Kenneth Land, "Burglary Victimization, Perceptions of Crime Risk, and Routine Activities: A Multilevel Analysis Across Seattle Neighborhoods and Census Tracts," *Journal of Research in Crime and Delinquency* 33 (1996): 147–180.

57. Randy LaGrange, Kenneth Ferraro, and Michael Supancic, "Perceived Risk and Fear of Crime: Role of Social and Physical Incivilities," *Journal of Research in Crime and Delinquency* 29 (1992): 311–334.

58. Ralph Taylor and Jeanette Covington, "Community Structural Change and Fear of Crime," *Social Problems* 40 (1993): 374–392.

59. Wesley Skogan, "Fear of Crime and Neighborhood Change," in *Communities and Crime,* ed. Reiss and Tonry, pp. 191–232.

60. Stephanie Greenberg, "Fear and Its Relationship to Crime, Neighborhood Deterioration and Informal Social Control," in *The Social Ecology of Crime,* ed. James Byrne and Robert Sampson (New York: Springer Verlag, 1985), pp. 47–62.

61. Skogan, "Fear of Crime and Neighborhood Change."

62. Ibid.

63. Anderson, *Streetwise: Race, Class and Change in an Urban Community,* p. 245.

64. Finn Aage-Esbensen and David Huizinga, "Community Structure and Drug Use: From a Social Disorganization Perspective," *Justice Quarterly* 7 (1990): 691–709.

65. Allen Liska and Paul Bellair, "Violent-Crime Rates and Racial Composition: Convergence over Time," *American Journal of Sociology* 101 (1995): 578–610.

66. Wesley Skogan, *Disorder and Decline: Crime and the Spiral of Decay in American Neighborhoods* (New York: Free Press, 1990), pp. 15–35.

67. Robert Bursik and Harold Grasmick, "Decomposing Trends in Community Careers in Crime," paper presented at the annual meeting of the American Society of Criminology, Baltimore, November 1990.

68. Ralph Taylor and Jeanette Covington, "Neighborhood Changes in Ecology and Violence," *Criminology* 26 (1988): 553–589.

69. Leo Scheurman and Solomon Kobrin, "Community Careers in Crime," in *Communities and Crime,* ed. Reiss and Tonry, pp. 67–100.

70. Ibid.

71. See, generally, Robert Bursik, "Delinquency Rates as Sources of Ecological Change," in *The Social Ecology of Crime,* ed. Byrne and Sampson, pp. 63–77.

72. Janet Heitgerd and Robert Bursik, "Extracommunity Dynamics and the Ecology of Delinquency," *American Journal of Sociology* 92 (1987): 775–787.

73. Wilson, *The Truly Disadvantaged.*

74. Carolyn Rebecca Block and Richard Block, *Street Gang Crime in Chicago* (Washington, D.C.: National Institute of Justice, 1993), p. 7.

75. Barbara Warner and Glenn Pierce, "Reexamining Social Disorganization Theory Using Calls to the Police as a Measure of Crime," *Criminology* 31 (1993): 493–519.

76. Donald Black, "Social Control as a Dependent Variable," in *Toward a General Theory of Social Control,* ed. D. Black (Orlando, Fla.: Academic Press, 1990).

77. Bursik and Grasmick, "The Multiple Layers of Social Disorganization," paper presented at the annual meeting of the American Society of Criminology, New Orleans, November 1992.

78. Rodney Stark, "Deviant Places: A Theory of the Ecology of Crime," *Criminology* 25 (1987): 893–911.

79. Delbert Elliott, William Julius Wilson, David Huizinga, Robert Sampson, Amanda Elliott, Bruce Rankin, "The Effects of Neighborhood Disadvantage on Adolescent Development," *Journal of Research in Crime and Delinquency* 33 (1996): 389–426.

80. Ibid., p. 414.

81. Robert Bursik and Harold Grasmick, "Economic Deprivation and Neighborhood Crime Rates, 1960–1980," *Law and Society Review* 27 (1993): 263–278.

82. Skogan, *Disorder and Decline.*

83. Robert Sampson and W. Byron Groves, "Community Structure and Crime: Testing Social Disorganization Theory," *American Journal of Sociology* 94 (1989): 774–802; Denise Gottfredson, Richard McNeill, and Gary Gottfredson, "Social Area Influences on Delinquency: A Multilevel Analysis," *Journal of Research in Crime and Delinquency* 28 (1991): 197–206.

84. Mitchell Chamlin and John Cochran, "Social Altruism and Crime," *Criminology* (in press 1997).

85. Robert Merton, *Social Theory and Social Structure,* enlarged ed. (New York: Free Press, 1968).

86. For an analysis, see Richard Hilbert, "Durkheim and Merton on Anomie: An Unexplored Contrast in Its Derivatives," *Social Problems* 36 (1989): 242–256.

87. Ibid., p. 243.

88. Albert Cohen, "The Sociology of the Deviant Act: Anomie Theory and Beyond," *American Sociological Review* 30 (1965): 5–14.

89. See Robert Agnew, "The Contribution of Social Psychological Strain Theory to the Explanation of Crime and Delinquency," in *Advances in Criminological Theory* 6 (1995): 113–122.

90. These criticisms are articulated in Steven Messner and Richard Rosenfeld, *Crime and the American Dream,* p. 60.

91. Scott Menard, "A Developmental Test of Mertonian Anomie Theory," *Journal of Research in Crime and Delinquency* 32 (1995): 136–174.

92. John Hagan, Hans Merkens, and Klaus Boehnke, "Delinquency and Disdain: Social Capital and Control of Right-Wing Extremism Among East and West Berlin Youth," *American Journal of Sociology* 100 (1995): 1028–1052.

93. Messner and Rosenfeld, *The American Dream.*

94. Steven Messner and Richard Rosenfeld, "An Institutional-Anomie Theory of the Social Distribution of Crime," paper presented at the annual meeting of the American Society of Criminology, Phoenix, Arizona, November 1993.

95. Mitchell Chamlin and John Cochran, "Assessing Messner and Rosenfeld's Institutional Anomie Theory: A Partial Test," *Criminology* 33 (1995): 411–429.

96. John Braithwaite, "Poverty Power, White-Collar Crime and the Paradoxes of Criminological Theory," *Australian and New Zealand Journal of Criminology* 24 (1991): 40–58.

97. Judith Blau and Peter Blau, "The Cost of Inequality: Metropolitan Structure and Violent Crime," *American Sociological Review* 147 (1982): 114–129.

98. Peter Blau and Joseph Schwartz, *Crosscutting Social Circles* (New York: Academic Press, 1984).

99. Scott South and Steven Messner, "Structural Determinants of Intergroup Association," *American Journal of Sociology* 91 (1986): 1409–1430; Steven Messner and Scott South, "Economic Deprivation, Opportunity Structure and Robbery Victimization," *Social Forces* 64 (1986): 975–991.

100. Richard Fowles and Mary Merva, "Wage Inequality and Criminal Activity: An Extreme Bounds Analysis for the United States, 1975–1990," *Criminology* 34 (1996): 163–182.

101. Taylor and Covington, "Neighborhood Changes in Ecology and Violence," p. 582; Richard Block, "Community Environment and Violent Crime," *Criminology* 17 (1979): 46–57; Robert Sampson, "Structural Sources of Variation in Race-Age-Specific Rates of Offending Across Major U.S. Cities," *Criminology* 23 (1985): 647–673; Richard Rosenfeld, "Urban Crime Rates: Effects of Inequality, Welfare Dependency, Region and Race," in *The Social Ecology of Crime,* ed. James Byrne and Robert Sampson (New York: Springer Verlag, 1985), pp. 116–130.

102. Fowles and Merva, "Wage Inequality and Criminal Activity"; Ruth Peterson and William Bailey, "Rape and Dimensions of Gender Socioeconomic Inequality in U.S. Metropolitan Areas," *Journal of Research in Crime and Delinquency* 29 (1992): 162–177.

103. Gary LaFree, Kriss Drass, and Patrick O'Day, "Race and Crime in Postwar America: Determinants of African-American and White Rates, 1957–1988," *Criminology* 30 (1992): 157–188.

104. Kenneth Land, Patricia McCall, and Lawrence Cohen, "Structural Covariates of Homicide Rates: Are There Any Invariances Across Time and Social Space?" *American Journal of Sociology* 95 (1990): 922–963; Robert Bursik and James Webb, "Community Change and Patterns of Delinquency," *American Journal of Sociology* 88 (1982): 24–42.

105. Robert Agnew, "A Durkheimian Strain Theory of Delinquency," paper presented at the annual meeting of the American Society of Criminology, Baltimore, November 1990.

106. Jeanne Brooks-Gunn, Greg Duncan, Pamela Klato Klebanov, and Naomi Sealand, "Do Neighborhoods Influence Child and Adolescent Development?" *American Journal of Sociology* 99 (1993): 353–395.

107. Nikos Passas, "Anomie and Relative Deprivation," paper presented at the annual meeting of the Eastern Sociological Society, Boston, 1987.

108. Roy Austin and Chris Hebert, "Black Powerlessness and Crime," paper presented at the annual meeting of the American Society of Criminology, Phoenix, November 1993.

109. Robert Agnew, "Foundation for a General Strain Theory of Crime and Delinquency," *Criminology* 30 (1992): 47–87.

110. Ibid., p. 57.

111. Paul Mazerolle and Alex Piquero, "Linking General Strain with Anger: Investigating the Instrumental, Escapist, and Violent Adaptations to Strain," paper presented at the American Society of Criminology meeting, Boston, November 1995.

112. Robert Agnew, "Stability and Change in Crime over the Life Course: A Strain Theory Explanation," in *Advances in Criminological Theory,* vol. 7, *Developmental Theories of Crime and Delinquency,* ed. Terence Thornberry (New Brunswick, N.J.: Transaction Books, 1995), pp. 113–137.

113. Lawrence Wu, "Effects of Family Instability, Income and Income Instability on the Risk of Premarital Birth," *American Sociological Review* 61 (1996): 386–406.

114. Robert Agnew and Helene Raskin White, "An Empirical Test of General Strain Theory," *Criminology* 30 (1992): 475–499.

115. John Hoffman and Alan Miller, "A Latent Variable Analysis of General Strain Theory," *Journal of Quantitative Criminology* (in press, 1997); Raymond Paternoster and Paul Mazerolle, "General Strain Theory and Delinquency: A Replication and Extension," *Journal of Research in Crime and Delinquency* 31 (1994): 235–263.

116. G. Roger Jarjoura, "The Conditional Effect of Social Class on the Dropout-Delinquency Relationship," *Journal of Research in Crime and Delinquency* 33 (1996): 232–255.

117. Teresa Lagrange and Robert Silverman, "Perceived Strain and Delinquency Motivation: An Empirical Evaluation of General Strain Theory," paper presented at the American Society of Criminology meeting, Boston, November 1995.

118. Thomas Ashby Wills, Donato Vaccaro, Grace McNamara, and A. Elizabeth Hirky, "Escalated Substance Use: A Longitudinal Grouping Analysis from Early to Middle Adolescence," *Journal of Abnormal Psychology* 105 (1996); 166–180.

119. Timothy Brezina, "Adapting to Strain: An Examination of Delinquent Coping Responses," *Criminology* 34 (1996): 39–61.

120. John Hoffman and S. Susan Su, "The Conditional Effects of Stress on Delinquency and Drug Use: A Strain Theory in Assessment of Sex Differences," *Journal of Research in Crime and Delinquency* 34 (1997): 46–78.

121. Lisa Broidy, "The Role of Gender in General Strain Theory," paper presented at the American Society of Criminology meeting, Boston, November 1995.

122. Robbin Ogle, Daniel Maier-Katkin and Thomas Bernard, "A Theory of Homicidal Behavior Among Women," *Criminology* 33 (1995): 173–193.

123. Thorsten Sellin, *Culture Conflict and Crime,* bulletin no. 41 (New York: Social Science Research Council, 1938).

124. Ibid., p. 22.

125. Ibid., p. 29.

126. Ibid., p. 68.

127. Walter Miller, "Lower-Class Culture as a Generating Milieu of Gang Delinquency," *Journal of Social Issues* 14 (1958): 5–19.

128. Ibid., pp. 14–17.

129. Albert Cohen, *Delinquent Boys* (New York: Free Press, 1955).

130. Ibid., p. 25.

131. Ibid., p. 28.

132. Ibid.

133. Clarence Schrag, *Crime and Justice American Style* (Washington, D.C.: U.S. Government Printing Office, 1971), p. 74.

134. Cohen, *Delinquent Boys,* p. 30.

135. Ibid., p. 31.

136. Ibid., p. 133.

137. J. Johnstone, "Social Class, Social Areas, and Delinquency," *Sociology and Social Research* 63 (1978): 49–72; Joseph Harry, "Social Class and Delinquency: One More Time," *Sociological Quarterly* 15 (1974): 294–301.

138. Richard Cloward and Lloyd Ohlin, *Delinquency and Opportunity* (New York: Free Press, 1960).

139. Ibid., p. 7.

140. Ibid., p. 85.

141. Ibid., p. 171.

142. Ibid., p. 23.

143. Ibid., p. 73.

144. Ibid., p. 24.

145. Cheryl Maxson, Kristi Woods, and Malcolm Klein, *Street Gang Migration in the United States: Executive Summary* (Los Angeles: Center for the Study of Crime and Social Control, University of Southern California, 1995).

146. G. David Curry, Robert Fox, Richard Ball, and Daryl Stone, *National Assessment and Law Enforcement Anti-Gang Information Resources, Final Report* (Morgantown, W.V.: National Assessment Survey, 1992).

147. G. David Curry, *Gang Crime and Law Enforcement Record Keeping* (Washington, D.C.: National Institute of Justice, 1994).

148. G. David Curry, Richard Ball, and Scott Decker, "Estimating the National Scope of Gang Crime from Law Enforcement Data," in *Gangs in America,* 2nd ed, ed. C. Ronald Huff (Newbury Park, Calif.: Sage, 1996 in press).

149. Malcolm Klein, *The American Street Gang, Its Nature, Prevalence and Control* (New York: Oxford University Press, 1995), pp. 31–35.

150. Ibid., p. 217.

151. Finn-Aage Esbensen and David Huizinga, "Gangs, Drugs, and Delinquency in a Survey of Urban Youth," *Criminology* 31 (1993): 565–591; Malcom Klein, Cheryl Maxson, and Lea Cunningham, "Crack, Street Gangs, and Violence," *Criminology* 29 (1991): 623–650; see also Irving Spergel, "Youth Gangs: Continuity and Change," in *Crime and Justice,* vol. 12, ed. Michael Tonry and Norval Morris (Chicago: University of Chicago Press, 1990), pp. 171–277.

152. Felix Padilla, *The Gang as an American Enterprise* (New Brunswick, N.J.: Rutgers University Press, 1992); see also Jeffery Fagan, "The Political Economy of Drug Dealing Among Urban Gangs," in *Drugs and the Community,* ed. Robert Davis, Arthur Lurigio, and Dennis Rosenbaum (Springfield, Ill.: Charles C Thomas, 1993), pp. 19–54.

153. Pamela Irving Jackson, "Crime, Youth Gangs, and Urban Transition: The Social Dislocations of Postindustrial Economic Development," *Justice Quarterly* 8 (1991): 379–397.

154. Robert Sampson and William Julius Wilson, "Toward a Theory of Race, Crime and Urban Inequality," in *Crime and Inequality,* ed. John Hagan and Ruth Peterson (Stanford, Calif.: Stanford University Press, 1995), pp. 37–54.

155. For a general criticism, see Kornhauser, *Social Sources of Delinquency.*

156. Charles Tittle, "Social Class and Criminal Behavior: A Critique of the Theoretical Foundations," *Social Forces* 62 (1983): 334–358.

157. James Q. Wilson and Richard Herrnstein, *Crime and Human Nature* (New York: Simon & Schuster, 1985).

158. Kenneth Polk and F. Lynn Richmond, "Those Who Fail," in *Schools and Delinquency,* ed. Kenneth Polk and Walter Schafer (Englewood Cliffs, N.J.: Prentice-Hall, 1974), p. 67.

159. Kathleen Maguire and Ann Pastore, *Sourcebook of Criminal Justice Statistics, 1996* (Washington, D.C.: U.S. Government Printing Office, 1996), pp. 150–166.

160. James DeFronzo, "Welfare and Burglary," *Crime and Delinquency* 42 (1996): 223–230.

161. Solomon Kobrin, "The Chicago Area Project—25-Year Assessment," *Annals of the American Academy of Political and Social Science* 322 (1959): 20–29.

Chapter 8
Social Process Theories

many criminologists question whether a person's place in the social structure can alone control the onset of criminality. After all, the majority of people residing in the nation's most deteriorated urban areas are law-abiding citizens who hold conventional values and compensate for their lack of social standing and financial problems by hard work, frugal living, and keeping an eye to the future. Conversely, self-report studies tell us that many members of the privileged classes engage in theft, drug use, and other crimes.

The NCVS estimates that about 40 million crimes occur annually. If the average active criminal commits one crime every two weeks or so, less than 2 million people could account for almost all serious crime.[1] More than 30 million Americans now live in poverty. Even if it is assumed that all criminals come from the lower classes (which they don't), it is evident that the great majority of the most indigent Americans do not commit criminal acts even though they may have a great economic incentive to do so.

Neighborhood deterioration and disorganization alone cannot explain why one individual embarks on a criminal career while another, living in the same environment, obeys the law, gets an education, and seeks legitimate employment.[2] Relatively few delinquent offenders living in the most deteriorated areas remain persistent, chronic offenders; most desist despite the continuing pressure of social decay. Some other social forces, then, must be at work to explain why the majority of at-risk individuals do not become persistent criminal offenders.

To explain these contradictory findings, attention has focused on **social-psychological processes** and interactions common to people in *all segments of the social structure*. **Social process theories** hold that criminality is a function of individual socialization. They draw attention to the interactions people have with the various organizations, institutions, and processes of society. As they pass through the life cycle, most people are influenced by the direction of their familial relationships, peer group associations, educational experiences, and interactions with authority figures, including teachers, employers, and agents of the justice system. If these relationships are positive and supportive, they will be able to succeed within the rules of society; if these relationships are dysfunctional and destructive, conventional success may be impossible and criminal solutions may become a feasible alternative.

Social process theories share one basic concept: All people, regardless of their race, class, or gender, have the potential to become delinquents or criminals. Although members of the lower class may have the added burdens of poverty, racism, poor schools, and disrupted family lives, these social forces may be counteracted by positive peer relations, a supportive family, and educational success. In contrast, even the most affluent members of society may turn to antisocial behavior if their life experiences are intolerable or destructive.

Social process theorists thus focus their attention on the **socialization** of youths and attempt to identify the developmental factors—family relationships, peer influences, educational attainment, self-image development—that if supportive can lead to a successful life but if destructive or dysfunctional can result in antisocial behaviors and a career in crime.

The influence of social process theories has endured because the relationship between social class and crime is still uncertain. Most residents of inner-city areas refrain from criminal activity, and few of those who do commit crimes remain persistent, chronic offenders in their adulthood. If poverty were the sole cause of crime, indigent adults would be as criminal as indigent teenagers. Following a thorough review of the most recent research, Charles Tittle and Robert Meier still found the association between economic status and crime "problematic"; class position alone cannot explain crime rates.[3]

> ## Connections
>
> Chapter 3's analysis of the class-crime relationship showed why this is still a hotly debated topic. While serious criminals may be disproportionately found in lower-class areas, self-report studies show that criminality cuts across class lines. The discussion of drug use in Chapter 14 also shows that many members of the middle class engage in recreational substance abuse, an indication that many law violators are not economically motivated.

A number of research studies show that even in the most deteriorated areas, it is the quality of interpersonal interactions with parents, peers, and schools that controls criminality; income and environment alone cannot determine behavior.[4] If this research is valid, socialization and not structure may be the key to understanding crime.

Social Processes and Crime

Criminologists have long studied the critical elements of socialization to determine how they contribute to the development of a criminal career. Prominent among these elements are the family, the peer group, and school.

Family Relations

Evidence that parenting factors may play a critical role in determining whether individuals misbehave as children and even later as adults is one of the most replicated findings in the deviance literature.[5]

Family relationships have for some time been considered a major determinant of behavior.[6] Youths who grow up in a household characterized by conflict and tension, where parents are absent or separated, or where familial love and support are lacking will be susceptible to the crime-promoting forces in the environment.[7] Even those children living in so-called high-crime areas will be better able to resist the temptations of the streets if they receive fair discipline, care, and support from parents who provide them with strong, positive role models.[8] Nonetheless, living in a disadvantaged neighborhood places a terrific strain on family functioning, especially in single-parent families experiencing social isolation from relatives, friends, and neighbors. Kids who are raised within such distressed families are at risk to delinquency.[9]

The relationship between family structure and crime is critical when the high rates of divorce and single parenthood are considered. In 1960 there were 35 divorced people for every 1,000 in an intact marriage; today, there are more than 130 per 1,000.[10] Similarly, the U.S. Census Bureau reports that in 1990 28% of the 35 million families with children were headed by a single parent; in 1970, only 13% of families with children were headed by a single parent.[11] The number of never-married women with at least one child has increased 60% in the past decade.[12]

At one time, growing up in a broken home was considered a primary cause of criminal behavior. However, many criminologists today discount the association between family structure and the onset of criminality, claiming that family conflict and discord is a more important determinant of behavior than family structure.[13] Not all experts, though, discount the effects of family structure on crime. James Q. Wilson and Richard Herrnstein claim that even if single mothers (or fathers) can make up for the loss of a second parent, it is simply more difficult to do so and the chances of failure increase.[14] Single parents may find it difficult to provide adequate supervision. There is evidence that children who live with single parents receive less encouragement and less help with schoolwork. They may be more prone to rebellious acts, such as running away and truancy.[15] Children in two-parent households are more likely to want to go on to college than kids in single-parent homes; poor school achievement and limited educational aspirations have been associated with delinquent behavior.[16]

Because their incomes are reduced in the aftermath of marital breakup, many divorced mothers are forced to move to residences in deteriorated neighborhoods; disorganized neighborhoods place children at risk to crime and drug abuse.[17] Nor does remarriage seem to mitigate the effects of divorce on youth: Children living with a stepparent exhibit as many problems as youths in divorce situations and considerably more problems than those who are living with both biological parents.[18] There is also little evidence that children of divorce improve over time; family disruption has unmistakable long-term effects.

Other family factors considered to have predictive value for criminal behavior include inconsistent discipline, poor supervision, and the lack of a warm, loving, supportive parent-child relationship.[19] Children who have warm and affectionate ties to their parents report greater levels of self-esteem beginning in adolescence and extending into their adulthood; high self-esteem is inversely related to criminal behavior.[20] Parental deviance has also been linked to a child's criminal behavior. Children growing up in homes where parents suffer from mental impairment are at risk to delinquency.[21] Even at age 2, the children of drug abusers exhibit personality defects such as excessive anger and negativity.[22] Kids whose parents abuse drugs are more likely to become persistent substance abusers than the children of nonabusers.[23] John Laub and Robert Sampson have found evidence that the children of parents who engage in criminality and substance abuse are more likely to engage in law-violating behavior than the offspring of conventional parents.[24]

> ## Connections
>
> The age-graded theory of Sampson and Laub is discussed more fully in Chapter 10. While deviant parents may encourage offending, Sampson and Laub believe that life experiences can either encourage crime-prone people to offend or conversely aid them in their return to a conventional lifestyle.

There is also a suspected link between child abuse, neglect, sexual abuse, and crime.[25] A number of studies show a significant association between child maltreatment and serious self-reported and official delinquency, even when controlling for gender, race, and class.[26] Victims of child abuse are more likely to mature into abusing and violent adults than nonvictims are.[27] Child abuse is most prevalent among families living in socially disorganized neighborhoods, explaining in part the association between poverty and violence.[28]

The effect of the family on delinquency has also been observed in other cultures. For example, research on Chinese families shows that those that provide firm support inhibit delinquency, whereas families that experience parental deviance are more likely to contain youth involved in antisocial behaviors.[29]

Net Bookmark

Poor parenting has been linked to the onset of delinquency. Many groups and individuals attempt to teach positive parenting skills. Learn more about some of these techniques at the following site:

http://www.empoweringpeople.com/

Educational Experience

Adolescent achievement in the school and educational process has also been linked to criminality. Studies show that children who do poorly in school, lack educational motivation, and feel alienated are the most likely to engage in criminal acts.[30] A recent analysis of the findings of 118 studies of educational achievement found academic performance to be a significant predictor of crime and delinquency. Although white children and males seem more deeply influenced by school failure, all children who fail in school offend more frequently, commit more serious and violent offenses, and persist in their offending into adulthood.[31]

Schools help contribute to criminality when they label problem youths, setting them apart from conventional society. One method of stigmatization is the "track system" that identifies some students as college-bound and others as academic underachievers or potential dropouts.[32] Recent research indicates that many school dropouts, especially those who have been expelled, face a significant chance of entering a criminal career.[33] In contrast, doing well in school and developing feelings of attachment to teachers have been linked to resistance to crime.[34]

It is not surprising that the U.S. school system has been the subject of criticism concerning its methods, goals, and objectives.[35] The nation's educational system is underfunded, understaffed, and in crisis; reading and math ability levels have been in decline. These trends do not bode well for the crime rate. Most important, surveys indicate that an extraordinary amount of serious criminal behavior occurs within the schools themselves.[36]

Peer Relations

Psychologists have long recognized that the peer group has a powerful effect on human conduct and can have a dramatic influence on decision making and behavior choices.[37] Peer influence on behavior has been recorded in many cultures and may be a universal norm.[38]

Early in children's lives, parents are the primary source of influence and attention. Between the ages of 8 and 14, children begin to seek out a stable peer group; both the number and variety of friendships increase as children go through adolescence. Soon, friends begin to have a greater influence over decision making than parents.[39] By their early teens, children report that their friends give them emotional support when they are feeling bad and that they can confide intimate feelings to peers without worrying about their confidences being betrayed. As they go through adolescence, children form **cliques,** small groups of friends who share activities and confidences. They also belong to **crowds,** loosely organized groups of children who share interests and activities. While clique members share intimate knowledge, crowds are brought together by mutually shared activities, such as sports, religion, or hobbies. Although bonds in this "wider circle of friends" may not be intimate, kids learn a lot about themselves and their world while navigating through these relationships.[40] Popular youths can be members of a variety of cliques and crowds. In later adolescence, peer approval has a major impact on socialization.

The most popular youths do well in school and are socially astute. In contrast, children who are rejected by their peers are more likely to display aggressive behavior and disrupt group activities through bickering or other antisocial behavior.[41] Peer relations, then, are a significant aspect of maturation.

Peers exert a powerful influence on youth and pressure them to conform to group values. Peers guide children and help them learn to share and cooperate, cope with aggressive impulses, and discuss feelings they would not dare bring up at home. With peers, youths can compare their own experiences and learn that others have similar concerns and problems; they realize they are not alone. It should come as no surprise, then, that much adolescent criminal activity begins as a group process.[42]

Delinquent peers can exert tremendous influence on behavior, attitudes, and beliefs.[43] In every level of the social structure, youths who fall in with a "bad crowd" become more susceptible to criminal behavior patterns.[44] Deviant peers help provide friendship networks that support delinquency and drug use.[45] Riding around, staying out late, and partying with deviant peers provide youth with the opportunity to commit deviant acts.[46] And because delinquent friends tend to be "sticky" (once acquired, they are not easily lost), peer influence may continue through the life span.[47] Some kids join more than one group, playing a leadership role in one, being a follower in another. And even though many groups are short lived and transitory, being exposed to so many deviant influences in multiple groups may help explain why deviant group membership is highly correlated with personal offending rates.[48]

Institutional Involvement and Belief

People who hold high moral values and beliefs, who have learned to distinguish right from wrong, and who regularly attend religious services should also eschew crime and other antisocial behaviors. Religion binds people together and forces them to confront the effect their behavior has on others; committing crimes would violate the principles of all organized religions.

An oft-cited study by Travis Hirschi and Rodney Stark found that, contrary to expectations, the association between religious attendance or belief and delinquent behavior patterns was negligible and insignificant.[49] However, some more recent research by T. David Evans and his associates reached an opposing conclusion: Attendance at religious services has a significant negative impact on crime. Interestingly, the Evans research shows that participation is a more significant inhibitor of crime than the mere holding of religious beliefs and values.[50] And cross-national research shows that countries with high rates of church membership and attendance have lower crime rates than less "devout" nations.[51]

Connections

Arousal theory would also predict that church attendance is inversely correlated with crime rates, because criminals are people who need large amounts of stimulation and would not be able to sit through religious services. See Chapter 6 for more on arousal theory.

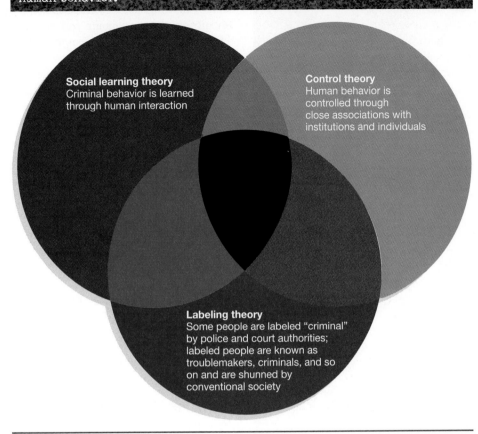

Figure 8.1 The complex web of social processes that control human behavior.

Social learning theory
Criminal behavior is learned through human interaction

Control theory
Human behavior is controlled through close associations with institutions and individuals

Labeling theory
Some people are labeled "criminal" by police and court authorities; labeled people are known as troublemakers, criminals, and so on and are shunned by conventional society

Branches of Social Process Theory

To many criminologists, the elements of socialization just described are the chief determinants of criminal behavior. According to this view, people living in even the most deteriorated urban areas can successfully resist inducements to crime if they have a good self-image, have learned moral values, and have the support of their parents, peers, teachers, and neighbors. The girl with a positive self-image who is chosen for a college scholarship, has the warm, loving support of her parents, and is viewed as someone "going places" by friends and neighbors is less likely to adopt a criminal way of life than another adolescent who is abused at home, who lives with criminal parents, and whose bond to the school and peer group is shattered because she is labeled a "troublemaker."[52]

Like social structure theory, the social process approach has several independent branches (see Figure 8.1). The first branch, **social learning theory,** suggests that people learn the techniques and attitudes of crime from close and intimate relationships with criminal peers; crime is a learned behavior. The second branch, **control theory,** maintains that everyone has the potential to become a criminal

but that most people are controlled by their bond to society; crime occurs when the forces that bind people to society are weakened or broken. The third branch, **labeling theory,** says people become criminals when significant members of society label them as such and they accept those labels as a personal identity.

Put another way, social learning theory assumes that people are born "good" and learn to be "bad"; control theory assumes that people are born "bad" and must be controlled in order to be "good"; labeling theory assumes that whether "good" or "bad," people are controlled by the reactions of others. Each of these independent branches will be discussed separately.

Social Learning Theory

Social learning theorists find that crime is a product of learning the norms, values, and behaviors associated with criminal activity. Social learning can involve the actual techniques of crime—how to hot-wire a car or roll a joint—as well as the psychological aspects of criminality—how to deal with the guilt or shame associated with illegal activities.

Social learning theorists see crime as a product of learning the norms, values, and behaviors associated with criminal activity. Social learning can involve the actual techniques of crime as well as the psychological aspects of criminality. Parental deviance may thus have a significant influence on children's behavior.

Connections

In the late 19th century, Gabriel Tarde's theory of imitation held that criminals imitate "superiors" they admire and respect. Learning theory also focuses on the influence of significant others. Tarde's work, discussed in Chapter 6, is thus a precursor to modern learning theories.

This section briefly reviews the three most prominent forms of social learning theory: differential association theory, differential reinforcement theory, and neutralization theory.

Differential Association Theory

Edwin H. Sutherland (1883–1950), often considered the preeminent U.S. criminologist, first put forth the **differential association (DA) theory** in 1939 in his text *Principles of Criminology*.[53] The final form of the theory appeared in 1947. When Sutherland died in 1950, his work was continued by his longtime associate Donald Cressey. Cressey was so successful in explaining and popularizing his mentor's efforts that DA remains one of the most enduring explanations of criminal behavior.

Sutherland's research on white-collar crime, professional theft, and intelligence led him to dispute the notion that crime is a function of the inadequacy of people in the lower classes.[54] To Sutherland, criminality stemmed neither from individual traits nor socioeconomic position; instead, he believed it to be a function of a learning process that could affect any individual in any culture.

A few ideas are basic to the theory of differential association.[55] Crime is a politically defined construct. It is defined by government authorities who are in political control of a particular jurisdiction. In societies wracked by culture conflict, the definition of crime may be inconsistent and consequently rejected by some groups of people. Put another way, people may vary in their relative attachments to criminal and noncriminal definitions. The acquisition of behavior is a social learning process, not a political or legal process. Skills and motives conducive to crime are learned as a result of contacts with pro-crime values, attitudes, and definitions and with other patterns of criminal behavior.

PRINCIPLES OF DIFFERENTIAL ASSOCIATION. The basic principles of differential association are as follows:[56]

1. Criminal behavior is learned. This statement differentiates Sutherland's theory from prior attempts to classify criminal behavior as an inherent characteristic of criminals. By suggesting that delinquent and criminal behavior is actually learned, Sutherland implied that it can be classified in the same manner as any other learned behavior, such as writing, painting, or reading.

2. Criminal behavior is learned in interaction with other persons in a process of communication. Sutherland believed that illegal behavior is learned actively. An individual does not become a law violator simply by living in a criminogenic environment or by manifesting personal characteristics, such as low IQ or family problems, associated with criminality. Instead, criminal and other deviant behavior patterns are learned. People actively participate in the process with other individuals who serve as teachers and guides to crime. Thus, criminality cannot occur without the aid of others.

3. The principal part of the learning of criminal behavior occurs within intimate personal groups. People's contacts with their most intimate social companions—family, friends, peers—have the greatest influence on their learning of deviant behavior and attitudes. Relationships with these individuals color and control the interpretation of everyday events. For example, research shows that children who grow up in homes where par-

ents abuse alcohol are more likely to view drinking as being socially and physically beneficial.[57] Social support for deviance helps people overcome social controls so that they can embrace criminal values and behaviors. The intimacy of these associations far outweighs the importance of any other form of communication—for example, movies or television. Even on those rare occasions when violent motion pictures seem to provoke mass criminal episodes, these outbreaks can be more readily explained as a reaction to peer group pressure than as a reaction to the films themselves.

4. Learning criminal behavior includes learning the techniques of committing the crime, which are sometimes complicated and sometimes simple, and learning the specific direction of motives, drives, rationalizations, and attitudes. Because criminal behavior is similar to other learned behavior, it follows that the actual techniques of criminality must be acquired and learned. Young delinquents learn from their associates the proper way to pick a lock, shoplift, and obtain and use narcotics. In addition, novice criminals must learn to use the proper terminology for their acts and then acquire "proper" reactions to law violations. For example, getting high on marijuana and learning the proper way to smoke a joint are behavior patterns usually acquired from more experienced companions. Moreover, criminals must learn how to react properly to their illegal acts—when to defend them, rationalize them, show remorse for them.

5. The specific direction of motives and drives is learned from perceptions of various aspects of the legal code as being favorable or unfavorable. Since the reaction to social rules and laws is not uniform across society, people constantly come into contact with others who maintain different views on the utility of obeying the legal code. When definitions of right and wrong are extremely varied, people experience what Sutherland calls *culture conflict*. The attitudes toward criminal behavior of the important people in an individual's life influence the attitudes that he or she develops. The conflict of social attitudes is the basis for the concept of differential association.

6. A person becomes a criminal when he or she perceives more favorable than unfavorable consequences to violating the law (see Figure 8.2). According to Sutherland's theory, individuals become law violators when they are in contact with persons, groups, or events that produce an excess of definitions favorable toward criminality and are isolated from counteracting forces. A definition favorable toward criminality occurs, for example, when a person is exposed to friends sneaking into a theater to avoid paying for a ticket or talking about the virtues of getting high on drugs. A definition unfavorable toward crime occurs when friends or parents demonstrate their disapproval of crime. Of course,

neutral behavior, such as reading a book, exists. It is neither positive nor negative with respect to law violation. Cressey argues that this behavior is important, "especially as an occupier of the time of a child so that he is not in contact with criminal behaviors during the time he is so engaged in the neutral behavior."[58]

7. Differential associations may vary in frequency, duration, priority, and intensity. Whether a person learns to obey the law or to disregard it is influenced by the quality of social interactions. Those interactions of lasting duration have greater influence than those that are more brief. Similarly, frequent contacts have greater effect than rare and haphazard contacts. Sutherland did not specify what he meant by priority, but Cressey and others have interpreted the term to mean the age of children when they first encounter definitions of criminality. Contacts made early in life probably have a greater and more far-reaching influence than those developed later on. Finally, intensity is generally interpreted to mean the importance and prestige attributed to the individual or groups from whom the definitions are learned. For example, the influence of a father, mother, or trusted friend far outweighs the effect of more socially distant figures.

8. The process of learning criminal behavior by association with criminal and anticriminal patterns involves all of the mechanisms that are involved in any other learning. This statement suggests that learning criminal behavior patterns is similar to learning nearly all other patterns and is not a matter of mere imitation.

9. While criminal behavior is an expression of general needs and values, it is not excused by those general needs and values, since noncriminal behavior is also an expression of the same needs and values. This principle suggests that the motives for criminal behavior cannot logically be the same as those for conventional behavior. Sutherland rules out such motives as desire to accumulate money or social status, personal frustration, or low self-concept as causes of crime, since they are just as likely to produce noncriminal behavior, such as getting a better education or working harder on a job. It is only the learning of deviant norms through contact with an excess of definitions favorable toward criminality that produces illegal behavior.

In sum, DA theory holds that people learn criminal attitudes and behavior while in their adolescence from close and trusted relatives and companions. A criminal career develops if learned antisocial values and behaviors are not at least matched or exceeded by conventional attitudes and behaviors. Criminal behavior is learned in a process similar to learning any other human behavior.

TESTING DIFFERENTIAL ASSOCIATION. Despite the importance of DA theory, research devoted to testing its

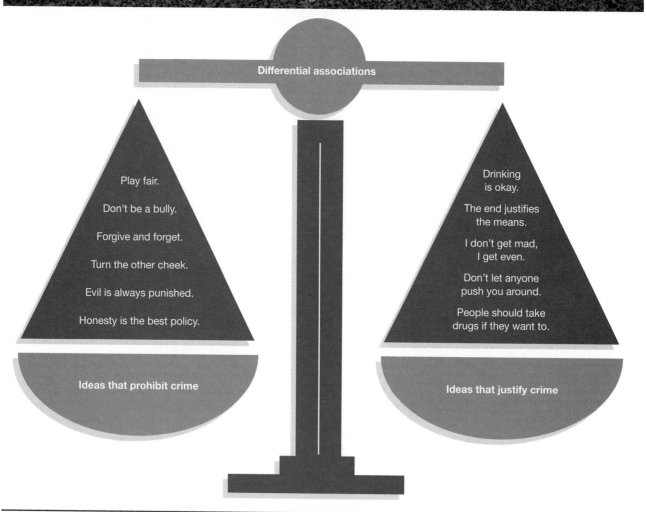

Figure 8.2 Differential association theory assumes that criminal behavior will occur when the definitions for crime outweigh the definitions against crime.

Differential associations

Play fair.

Don't be a bully.

Forgive and forget.

Turn the other cheek.

Evil is always punished.

Honesty is the best policy.

Ideas that prohibit crime

Drinking is okay.

The end justifies the means.

I don't get mad, I get even.

Don't let anyone push you around.

People should take drugs if they want to.

Ideas that justify crime

assumptions has been relatively sparse. It has proven difficult to conceptualize the principles of the theory so that they can be empirically tested. For example, social scientists find it difficult to evaluate such vague concepts as "definition toward criminality." It is also difficult to follow people over time, establish precisely when definitions toward criminality begin to outweigh prosocial definitions, and determine whether this imbalance produces criminal behavior.

Despite these limitations, several notable research efforts have been aimed at testing hypotheses derived from DA theory. One important area of research is the friendship patterns of delinquent youths. Differential association implies that criminals maintain close and intimate relations with deviant peers.[59] In a classic work, James Short surveyed institutionalized youths and found that they had maintained close associations with delinquent youths prior to their law-violating acts.[60] Similarly, Albert Reiss and A. Lewis Rhodes found an association between delinquent

friendship patterns and the probability that a youth would commit a criminal act.[61]

More recent studies have also found that law violators maintain close relationships with deviant peers in a fashion predicted by DA.[62] For example, Mark Warr found that antisocial kids who maintain delinquent friends over a long duration are much more likely to persist in their delinquent behavior than those without such peer support.[63] While his research is generally supportive of DA, Warr discovered that recently cultivated friendships had a greater influence on criminality than friends acquired earlier in life, a finding that contradicts DA's emphasis on the "priority" of criminal influences.

DA principles seem especially relevant as an explanation of the onset of substance abuse and a career in the drug trade; learning proper techniques and attitudes from an experienced user or dealer appears to be a requirement.[64] In his interview study of low-level drug dealers,

Kenneth Tunnell found that many novices were tutored by a more experienced dealer who helped them make connections with buyers and sellers. One told him:

> I had a friend of mine who was an older guy and he introduced me to selling marijuana to make a few dollars. I started selling a little and made a few dollars. For a young guy to be making a hundred dollars or so, it was a lot of money. So I got kind of tied up in that aspect of selling drugs.[65]

Tunnell found that making connections is an important part of the dealer's world. It does not seem surprising that research shows that adolescent drug users are likely to have intimate relationships with a peer friendship network that supports their substance abuse.[66]

Another approach to assessing DA theory tests the assumption that people who have assimilated procrime attitudes are also the ones most likely to engage in criminal activity.[67] These findings have been observed in cross-cultural research. In one study conducted in Hong Kong, Yuet-Wah Cheung and Agnes M. C. Ng found that DA items were the most significant predictor of delinquent behavior in a sample of 1,139 secondary school students. Cheung and Ng conclude that in Hong Kong, deviant youths may be imitating friends' behavior or attempting to "keep up appearances" by yielding to group pressure.[68]

While these findings are persuasive, self-report research in support of DA must be interpreted with caution. Since subjects are usually asked about their peer relations, learning experiences, perceptions of differential associations, and criminal behaviors simultaneously, it is impossible to determine whether differential associations were the cause or the result of criminal behavior. While it is possible that youths learn about crime and then commit criminal acts, it is also possible that experienced delinquents and criminals seek out like-minded peers after they engage in antisocial acts and that the internalization of deviant attitudes follows, rather than precedes, criminality.[69]

To answer critics, researchers must develop more valid measures of differential associations.[70] One possibility is that longitudinal analysis might be used to measure subjects repeatedly over time to determine whether those exposed to excess definitions toward deviance eventually become deviant themselves. Even then, it is difficult to show whether people who continually break the law develop a group of like-minded peers who support their behavior, rather than a process in which "innocent" people are "seduced" into crime by exposure to the deviant attitudes of more criminal peers.[71]

To remedy this problem, future research may be directed at creating more accurate means with which to test the theory's basic principles.[72] A more valid approach may be to follow a cohort over time to assess the impact of criminal friends and associations: Does repeated exposure to excess definitions toward deviance escalate deviance through the life course? Some recent research by Mark Warr illustrates the utility of this approach. Warr found that adolescents who acquire criminal friends are also the ones most likely to eventually engage in criminal behavior—a finding that supports DA. Warr notes that criminal friends are "sticky"; once gotten, they are hard to shake. They help lock people into antisocial behavior patterns through the life course. In fact, people who maintain deviant friendships and close relationships with deviant peers are the ones most likely to persist in their offending careers.[73] Deviant friends help counteract the crime-reducing effects of the aging-out process.[74]

ANALYSIS OF DIFFERENTIAL ASSOCIATION THEORY. Misconceptions about DA theory have tended to produce unwarranted criticism of its principles and meaning.[75] For example, some criminologists claim that the theory is concerned solely with the number of personal contacts and associations a delinquent has with other criminal or delinquent offenders.[76] If this assumption were true, those most likely to become criminals would be police, judges, and correctional authorities, since they are constantly associating with criminals. Sutherland stressed "excess definitions toward criminality," not mere association with criminals. Personnel of the juvenile justice system do have extensive associations with criminals, but these are more than counterbalanced by their associations with law-abiding citizens.

Another misconception is that definitions toward delinquency are acquired from learning the values of a deviant subculture.[77] According to what is known as the "cultural deviance critique," DA is erroneous because it suggests that criminals are people properly socialized into a deviant subculture. This argument has been forcefully refuted by Ronald Akers, who argues that while it is true that some people become criminals because they have been "properly" socialized into a deviant culture, DA also recognizes that individuals can embrace criminality because they have been improperly socialized into the normative culture.[78]

Although DA stresses an excess of definitions toward delinquency, it does not specify that they must come solely from lower-class criminal sources. This distinguishes Sutherland's work from social structure theories. Outwardly law-abiding middle-class parents can encourage delinquent behavior by their own drinking, drug use, or family violence. And both middle- and lower-class youth are exposed to media images that express open admiration for violent heroes, such as those played by Arnold Schwarzenegger or Jean-Claude Van Damme, who take the law into their own hands. Research by Craig Reinerman and Jeffrey Fagan indicates that the influence of differential associations is not affected by social class, supporting Sutherland's belief that deviant learning can affect middle-class as well as lower-class youth.[79]

There are, however, a number of valid criticisms of Sutherland's work. It fails to explain why one youth who is exposed to delinquent definitions eventually succumbs to them while another, living under the same conditions, avoids them.[80] It also fails to account for the origin of delinquent definitions. How did the first "teacher" learn delinquent attitudes and definitions in order to pass them on? Another apparently valid criticism of DA is that it assumes criminal and delinquent acts to be rational and systematic. This ignores spontaneous and wanton acts of violence and damage that appear to have little utility or purpose, such as the isolated psychopathic killing, which is virtually unsolvable because of the killer's anonymity and lack of criminal associations.

The most serious criticism of DA theory concerns the vagueness of its terms, which makes its assumptions difficult to test. For example, what constitutes an "excess of definition toward criminality"? How can we determine whether an individual actually has a procriminal imbalance of these definitions? It is simplistic to assume that, by definition, all criminals have experienced a majority of definitions toward criminality and all noncriminals, a minority of them. Unless the terms used in the theory can be defined more precisely, its validity remains a matter of guesswork.

Despite these criticisms, DA theory maintains an important place in the study of criminal behavior. For one thing, it provides a consistent explanation of all types of delinquent and criminal behavior. Unlike the social structure theories discussed previously, it is not limited to the explanation of a single facet of antisocial activity, such as lower-class gang activity. The theory can also account for the extensive criminal behavior found even in middle- and upper-class areas, where youths may be exposed to a variety of procriminal definitions from such sources as overly opportunistic parents and friends. And the Warr research, which suggests that criminal friends are "sticky," indicates that differential associations might be one of the keys to explaining deviance through the life course.

Differential Reinforcement Theory

Differential reinforcement (DR) theory (also called social learning theory) is another attempt to explain crime as a type of learned behavior. First proposed by Ronald Akers in collaboration with Robert Burgess, it is a version of the social learning view that combines differential association concepts with elements of psychological learning theory.[81]

According to Akers, the same process is involved in learning both deviant and conventional behavior. People neither learn to be "all deviant" or "all conforming" but rather strike a balance between the two opposing poles of behavior. The balance is usually stable but can undergo revision over time.[82]

A number of learning processes shape behavior. Direct conditioning or *differential reinforcement* occurs when behavior is either rewarded or punished during interaction with others. Differential *association* involves learning from direct or indirect interaction with others. *Imitation* occurs from observational learning experiences, such as from watching TV and films. People also learn *cognitive definitions*, which are attitudes that are favorable or unfavorable toward a behavior and can either stimulate or extinguish that behavior.

Behavior is reinforced when positive rewards are gained or when punishment is avoided (negative reinforcement). It is weakened by negative stimuli (punishment) and loss of reward (negative punishment). Whether deviant or criminal behavior is begun or persists depends on the degree to which it has been rewarded or punished and the rewards or punishments attached to its alternatives.

According to Akers, people learn to evaluate their own behavior through interaction with significant others and groups in their lives. These groups control sources and patterns of reinforcement, define behavior as right or wrong, and provide behaviors for observational learning. The more individuals learn to define their behavior as good or at least as justified, rather than as undesirable, the more likely they are to engage in it. For example, kids who hook up with a drug-abusing peer group, whose members value drugs and alcohol, encourage their use, and provide opportunities to observe people abusing substances, will be encouraged through this social learning experience to use drugs themselves.

Akers's theory posits that the principal influence on behavior is from "those groups which control individuals' major sources of reinforcement and punishment and expose them to behavioral models and normative definitions."[83] The important groups are the ones with which a person is in differential association—peer and friendship groups, schools, churches, and similar institutions. Within the contest of these critical groups, "deviant behavior can be expected to the extent that it has been differentially reinforced over alternative behavior . . . and is defined as desirable or justified."[84] Once people are initiated into crime, their behavior can be reinforced by exposure to deviant behavior models, association with deviant peers, and lack of negative sanctions from parents or peers. The deviant behavior, originated by imitation, is sustained by social support. It is possible that differential reinforcements help establish criminal careers and are a key factor in explaining persistent criminality.

The principles of differential reinforcement have been subject to empirical review by Akers and other criminologists.[85] In an important test of his theory, Akers and his associates surveyed 3,065 male and female adolescents on drug- and alcohol-related activities and their perception of variables related to social learning and DR. Items on the scale included the respondents' perception of esteemed peers' attitudes toward drug and alcohol abuse, the number of people they admired who actually used controlled substances, and whether people they admired would reward or punish them for substance abuse. Akers found a strong association between drug and alcohol abuse and social learning variables: Kids who believed they would be rewarded for deviance by those they respect were the ones most likely to engage in deviant behavior.[86]

Akers has also found that the learning-deviant behavior link is not static. The learning experience continues within a deviant group as behavior is *both* influenced by and exerts influence over group process. For example, kids may learn to smoke because of social reinforcement by peers; over time, one's smoking influences friendships and peer group memberships.[87]

Differential reinforcement theory is an important view of the cause of criminal activity. It considers how both the effectiveness and content of socialization condition crime. Because not all socialization is positive, it accounts for the fact that negative reinforcements can produce criminal results. This jibes with research showing that parental deviance is related to adolescent antisocial behavior.[88] Akers's work also fits well with rational choice theory because they both suggest that people learn the techniques and attitudes necessary to commit crime. Criminal knowledge is gained through experience. After considering the outcome of their past experiences, potential offenders decide which criminal acts will be profitable and which are dangerous and should be avoided.[89] Why do people make rational choices about crime? Because they have learned to balance risks against the potential for criminal gain.

Neutralization Theory

Neutralization theory is identified with the writings of David Matza and his associate Gresham Sykes.[90] Sykes and Matza view the process of becoming a criminal as a learning experience. However, while other learning theorists, such as Sutherland and Akers, dwell on the learning of techniques, values, and attitudes necessary for performing criminal acts, Sykes and Matza maintain that most delinquents and criminals hold conventional values and attitudes but master techniques that enable them to neutralize these values and drift back and forth between illegitimate and conventional behavior. One reason is the subterranean value structure of American society. **Subterranean values** are the morally tinged influences that have become entrenched in the culture but are publicly condemned by "right thinking" members of society. They exist side by side with conventional values and while condemned in public may be admired or practiced in private, such as viewing pornographic videos. In American culture it is common to hold both subterranean and conventional values; few people are "all good" or "all bad."

Matza argues that even the most committed criminals and delinquents are not involved in criminality all the time; they also attend schools, family functions, and religious services. Their behavior can be conceived as falling along a continuum between total freedom and total restraint. This process, which he calls **drift,** refers to the movement from one extreme of behavior to another, resulting in behavior that is sometimes unconventional, free, or deviant and at other times constrained and sober.[91] Learning techniques of neutralization allows a person to temporarily "drift away" from conventional behavior and get involved in more subterranean values and behaviors, including crime and drug abuse.[92]

TECHNIQUES OF NEUTRALIZATION. Sykes and Matza suggest that offenders develop a distinct set of justifications for their law-violating behavior. These neutralization techniques allow them to temporarily drift away from the rules of the normative society and participate in subterranean behaviors.

Sykes and Matza base their theoretical model on several observations.[93] First, criminals sometimes voice a sense of guilt over their illegal acts. If a stable criminal value system existed in opposition to generally held values and rules, criminals would be unlikely to exhibit any remorse for their acts, other than regret at being apprehended. Second, offenders frequently respect and admire honest, law-abiding persons. Really honest persons are often revered; if for some reason such persons are accused of misbehavior, the criminal is quick to defend their integrity. Those admired may include sports figures, priests and other clergy, parents, teachers, and neighbors. Third, criminals draw a line between those whom they can victimize and those whom they cannot. Members of similar ethnic groups, churches, or neighborhoods are often off limits. This practice implies that criminals are aware of the wrongfulness of their acts. Why else limit them? Finally, criminals are not immune to the demands of conformity. Most criminals frequently participate in many of the same social functions as law-abiding people, such as school, church, and family activities.

Because of these factors, Sykes and Matza conclude that criminality is the result of the neutralization of accepted social values through the learning of a standard set of techniques that allow people to counteract the moral dilemmas posed by illegal behavior.[94] Their research helped Sykes and Matza identify the following **techniques of neutralization:**

1. *Denial of responsibility.* Young offenders sometimes claim their unlawful acts were simply not their fault. The acts resulted from forces beyond their control or were accidents.

2. *Denial of injury.* By denying the wrongfulness of an act, criminals are able to neutralize illegal behavior. For example, stealing is viewed as borrowing; vandalism is considered mischief that has gotten out of hand. Society often agrees with the criminals' point of view, labeling their illegal behavior as pranks and thereby affirming the criminal's view that crime can be socially acceptable.

3. *Denial of victim.* Criminals sometimes neutralize wrongdoing by maintaining that the victim of crime "had it coming." Vandalism may be directed against a disliked teacher or neighbor; homosexuals may be beaten up

Figure 8.3   Techniques of neutralization.

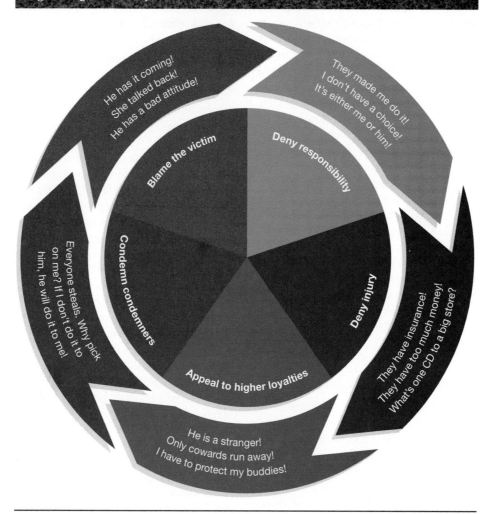

by a gang because their behavior is considered offensive. Denying the victim may also take the form of ignoring the rights of an absent or unknown victim—for example, the unseen owner of a department store. It becomes morally acceptable for the criminal to commit such crimes as vandalism when the victims, because of their absence, cannot be sympathized with or respected.

4. *Condemnation of the condemners.* An offender views the world as a corrupt place with a dog-eat-dog code. Since police and judges are on the take, teachers show favoritism, and parents take out their frustrations on their kids, it is ironic and unfair for these authorities to condemn his misconduct. By shifting the blame to others, criminals are able to repress the feeling that their own acts are wrong.

5. *Appeal to higher loyalties.* Novice criminals often argue that they are caught in the dilemma of being loyal to their own peer group while at the same time attempting to abide by the rules of the larger society. The needs of the group take precedence over the rules of society because the demands of the former are immediate and localized.

In sum, the theory of neutralization presupposes a condition in which such slogans as "I didn't mean to do it," "I didn't really hurt anybody," "They had it coming to them," "Everybody's picking on me," and "I didn't do it for myself" are used by people to neutralize unconventional norms and values so they can drift into criminal modes of behavior (see Figure 8.3).

TESTING NEUTRALIZATION THEORY.   A valid test of neutralization theory would have to be able to show that a person first neutralized his or her moral beliefs and then drifted into criminality. Otherwise, any data that showed an association between crime and neutralization could be interpreted as suggesting that people who commit crime later make an attempt at rationalizing their behavior. It is also possible that, as Michael Hindelang suggests, criminals and noncriminals have different moral values and that neutralizing them is therefore unnecessary.[95] The validity of the Sykes-Matza model depends on showing that all people share similar moral values and must neutralize them first to engage in criminal behavior.

Despite this limitation, several attempts have been made to empirically verify the assumptions of neutralization theory.[96] Recent survey research by Robert Agnew indicates that delinquents do not value or condone violent behavior and that they use neutralizations such as "It is all right to physically beat up people who call you names" to justify their aggressive activities.[97] Research also shows that institutionalized youths excuse deviant behaviors to a significantly greater degree than the general population does.[98] These findings indicate that people who commit criminal acts also have learned to rationalize their guilt. A study by Mark Pogrebin and his associates found that psychotherapists accused of sexually exploiting their clients express neutralizations for their behavior reminiscent of those identified by Sykes and Matza. Some blame the victim for "seducing them"; others claim there was little injury caused by the sexual encounter; still others seek scapegoats to blame for their actions.[99]

Are Social Learning Theories Valid?

Social learning theories make a significant contribution to our understanding of the onset of criminal behavior. Nonetheless, the general learning model has been subject to some criticism. One complaint is that learning theorists fail to account for the origin of criminal definitions. How did the first "teacher" learn criminal techniques and definitions? Who came up with the original neutralization technique?

Learning theories also imply that people systematically learn techniques that allow them to be active and successful criminals, but they fail to adequately explain spontaneous and wanton acts of violence and damage and other expressive crimes that appear to have little utility or purpose. While principles of DA can easily explain shoplifting, is it possible that a random shooting is caused by an excess of deviant definitions? It is estimated that about 70% of all arrestees were under the influence of drugs and alcohol when they committed their crime: Do "crack heads" pause to neutralize their moral inhibitions before mugging a victim? Do drug-involved kids stop to consider what they have "learned" about moral values?[100]

Little evidence exists that people learn the techniques that enable them to become criminals before they actually commit criminal acts. It is equally plausible that people who are already deviant seek out others with similar lifestyles. Early onset of deviant behavior is now considered a key determinant of criminal careers. It is difficult to see how extremely young adolescents had the opportunity to learn criminal behavior and attitudes within a peer group setting.

Despite these criticisms, learning theories maintain an important place in the study of delinquent and criminal behavior. Unlike social structure theories, they are not limited to explaining a single facet of antisocial activity—for example, lower-class gang activity; they may be used to explain criminality across class structures. Even corporate executives may be exposed to a variety of procriminal definitions and learn to neutralize moral constraints. Social learning theories can be applied to a wide assortment of criminal activity.

Social Control Theories

Social control theories maintain that all people have the potential to violate the law and that modern society presents many opportunities for illegal activity. Criminal activities, such as drug abuse and car theft, are often exciting pastimes that hold the promise of immediate reward and gratification. Considering the attractions of crime, the question control theorists pose is, "Why do people obey the rules of society?" To a choice theorist, the answer is fear of punishment; to a structural theorist, obedience is a function of having access to legitimate opportunities; to a learning theorist, obedience is acquired through contact with law-abiding parents and peers. In contrast, control theorists argue that people obey the law because behavior and passions are being controlled by internal and external forces. Some have **self-control** manifested in a strong moral sense that renders them incapable of hurting others and violating social norms. Some maintain self-control because they have a **commitment to conformity**—a real, present, and logical reason to obey the rules of society.[101] Perhaps they believe that getting caught in a criminal activity will hurt a dearly loved parent or jeopardize their chance at a college scholarship, or perhaps they feel that their job will be forfeited if they get in trouble with the law. In other words, people's behavior, including their criminal activity, is controlled by their attachment and commitment to conventional institutions, individuals, and processes. If that commitment is absent, they are free to violate the law and engage in deviant behavior; the "uncommitted" are not deterred by the threat of legal punishments.[102]

Self-Concept and Crime

Early versions of control theory speculated that low self-control is a product of weak self-concept and poor self-esteem. Youths who feel good about themselves and maintain a positive attitude are able to resist the temptations of the streets; a positive self-esteem helps kids control temptations toward delinquency. As early as 1951, Albert Reiss described how delinquents had weak "ego ideals" and lacked the "personal controls" to produce conforming behavior.[103] Scott Briar and Irving Piliavin noted that youths who believe criminal activity will damage their self-image and their relationships with others will be most likely to conform to social rules; they have a commitment to conformity. In contrast, those less concerned about their social standing are free to violate the law.[104]

Empirical research indicates that an important association between self-image and delinquency may in fact exist.[105] Howard Kaplan found that youths with poor self-concepts are the ones most likely to engage in delinquent behavior and that successful participation in criminality actually helped raise their self-esteem.[106] Youths who perceive self-rejection ("I feel I do not have much to be proud of"; "I certainly feel useless at times") are the ones most likely to engage in deviant behaviors.[107] Youths who maintain both the lowest self-image and the greatest need for approval are the ones most likely to seek self-enhancement from delinquency.[108]

Why does low self-esteem lead to criminality? It is possible that to improve self-image people will make decisions that ultimately prove harmful. Kids who are having problems in school realize that they will feel much better if they can escape teachers' critical judgments by dropping out and joining a gang whose members value their cunning and their fighting ability.

Containment Theory

In an early effort to describe how self-image controls criminal tendencies, Walter Reckless and his associates argued that youths growing up in even the most criminogenic areas can insulate themselves from crime if they have sufficiently positive self-esteem. Reckless called an individual's ability to resist criminal inducements **containments,** the most important of which are a positive self-image and "ego strength."[109] Kids with these traits can resist crime-producing "pushes and pulls." Here are some of the crime-producing forces that a strong self-image counteracts:

1. *Internal pushes.* Internal pushes include such personal factors as restlessness, discontent, hostility, rebellion, mental conflict, anxieties, and need for immediate gratification.

2. *External pressures.* External pressures are adverse living conditions that influence deviant behavior. They include relative deprivation, poverty, unemployment, insecurity, minority status, limited opportunities, and inequalities.

3. *External pulls.* External pulls are represented by deviant companions, membership in criminal subcultures or other deviant groups, and such influences as mass media and pornography.

Reckless and his associates made an extensive effort to validate the principles of containment theory. In a series of studies analyzing containment principles within the school setting, Reckless and his colleagues concluded that the ability of nondelinquents to resist crime depends on their maintaining a positive self-image in the face of environmental pressures toward delinquency. Despite the success Reckless and his associates had in verifying their containment approach, their efforts have been criticized for lack of methodological rigor, and the validity of containment theory has been disputed.

Reckless's version of control theory was a pioneering effort that set the stage for subsequent theoretical developments. These, too, follow his central premise that people are "controlled" by their feelings about themselves and others with whom they are in contact. In general then, control theory maintains that while all people perceive inducements to crime, some are better able to resist them than others.

Social Control Theory

Social control theory, originally articulated by Travis Hirschi in his influential 1969 book *Causes of Delinquency,* replaced containment theory as the dominant version of control theory.[110]

Hirschi linked the onset of criminality to the weakening of the ties that bind people to society. Hirschi assumed that all individuals are potential law violators but are kept under control because they fear that illegal behavior will damage their relationships with friends, parents, neighbors, teachers, and employers. Without these social ties or bonds, and in the absence of sensitivity to and interest in others, a person is free to commit criminal acts. Hirschi did not portray society as containing competing subcultures with unique value systems. Most people are aware of the prevailing moral and legal code. He suggested, however, that in all elements of society, people vary in their responses to conventional social rules and values. Among all ethnic, religious, racial, and social groups, people whose

According to Hirschi, potential law violators are normally kept under control because they fear that illegal behavior will damage their social relationships. Without such social ties, a person may feel free to commit criminal acts. Kids who commit crimes with their friends may appear attached, but they actually have few emotional commitments to their deviant peers.

Figure 8.4   Elements of the social bond.

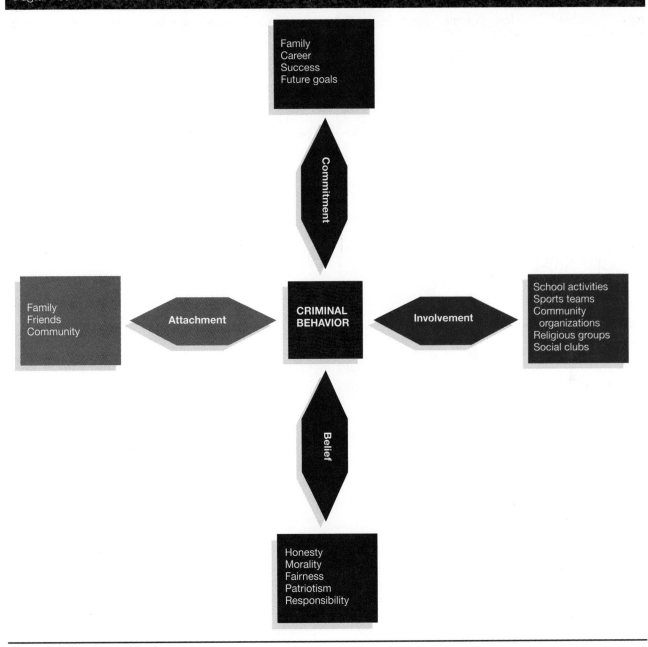

Family
Career
Success
Future goals

Commitment

Family
Friends
Community

Attachment

CRIMINAL
BEHAVIOR

Involvement

School activities
Sports teams
Community
  organizations
Religious groups
Social clubs

Belief

Honesty
Morality
Fairness
Patriotism
Responsibility

bond to society is weak may fall prey to criminogenic behavior patterns.

ELEMENTS OF THE SOCIAL BOND. Hirschi argued that the social bond a person maintains with society is divided into four main elements: attachment, commitment, involvement, and belief (see Figure 8.4).

Attachment refers to a person's sensitivity to and interest in others.[111] Psychologists believe that without a sense of attachment, a person becomes a psychopath and loses the ability to relate coherently to the world. The acceptance of social norms and the development of a social conscience depend on attachment to and caring for other human beings. Hirschi saw parents, peers, and schools as the important social institutions with which a person should maintain ties. Attachment to parents is the most important. Even if a family is shattered by divorce and separation, a child must retain a strong attachment to one or both parents. Without attachment to family, feelings of respect for others in authority are unlikely to develop.

Commitment involves the time, energy, and effort expended in conventional lines of action. It embraces such activities as getting an education and saving money for the future. Social control theory holds that if people build up a

In Hirschi's view, youths who are strongly attached to their parents are less likely to commit criminal acts. This family, which is celebrating the holiday Kwanza together, provides an environment that inhibits criminality.

strong involvement in life, property, and reputation, they will be less likely to engage in acts that will jeopardize their positions. Conversely, lack of commitment to conventional values may foreshadow a condition in which risk-taking behavior, such as crime, becomes a reasonable behavior alternative.

Heavy *involvement* in conventional activities leaves little time for illegal behavior. Hirschi believes that involvement—in school, recreation, and family—insulates a person from the potential lure of criminal behavior, while idleness enhances it.

People who live in the same social setting often share common moral *beliefs;* they may adhere to such values as sharing, sensitivity to the rights of others, and admiration for the legal code. If these beliefs are absent or weakened, individuals are more likely to participate in antisocial acts. Hirschi further suggested that the interrelationship of elements of the social bond controls subsequent behavior. For example, people who feel kinship and sensitivity to parents and friends should be more likely to adopt and work toward legitimate goals. On the other hand, a person who re-

jects social relationships probably lacks commitment to conventional goals. Similarly, people who are highly committed to conventional acts and beliefs are more likely to be involved in conventional activities.

TESTING SOCIAL CONTROL THEORY. One of Hirschi's most significant contributions was his attempt to test the principal hypotheses of social control theory. He administered a detailed self-report survey to a sample of over 4,000 junior and senior high school students in Contra Costa County, California.[112] In a detailed analysis of the data, Hirschi found considerable evidence to support the control theory model. Among Hirschi's more important findings are the following:

- Youths who were strongly attached to their parents were less likely to commit criminal acts.
- Commitment to conventional values, such as striving to get a good education and refusing to drink and "cruise around," was also related to conventional behavior.
- Youths involved in conventional activity, such as homework, were less likely to engage in criminal behavior. Youths involved in unconventional behavior, such as smoking and drinking, were more delinquency-prone.
- Delinquent youths maintained weak and distant relationships with people. Nondelinquents were attached to their peers.
- Delinquents and nondelinquents shared similar beliefs about society.

Hirschi's data lent important support to the validity of social control theory. Even when the statistical significance of his findings was less than he expected, the direction of his research data was extremely consistent. Only in rare instances did his findings contradict the theory's most critical assumptions.

SUPPORTING RESEARCH. Because of its importance and influence on criminology, social control theory has been the focus of numerous efforts to corroborate Hirschi's original findings. Associations between indicators of attachment, belief, commitment, and involvement with measures of delinquency have tended to be positive and significant.[113] Research indicates that evidence of family detachment, including intrafamily conflict, abuse of children, and lack of affection, supervision, and family pride, are predictive of delinquent conduct.[114] Youths who are detached from the educational experience are at risk to criminality.[115] Lack of attachment to family, peers, and school has been found to predict delinquency in cross-cultural samples of youth.[116]

Other research efforts have shown that positive beliefs are related to criminality. That is, children who are involved in religious activities and hold conventional religious beliefs are less likely to become involved in substance abuse.[117]

Similarly, youths who are involved in conventional leisure activities, such as supervised social activities and noncompetitive sports, are less likely to engage in delinquency than those who are involved in unconventional leisure activities and unsupervised, peer-oriented social pursuits.[118]

Cross-national surveys have also supported the general finding of social control theory.[119] In one study of Canadian youth in Edmonton, Alberta, Teresa LaGrange and Robert Silverman found that perception of parental attachment was the strongest predictor of delinquent or law-abiding behavior. They found that teens who are attached to their parents may develop the social skills that equip them both to maintain harmonious social ties and to escape life stresses such as school failure.[120]

OPPOSING VIEWS. More than 70 published attempts have been made to corroborate social control theory by replicating Hirschi's original survey techniques.[121] While there has been significant empirical support for Hirschi's work, there are also those who question some or all of its elements.

One significant criticism concerns Hirschi's contention that delinquents are detached loners whose bond to their family and friends has been broken. Some critics have questioned whether delinquents (1) do in fact have strained relations with family and peers and (2) may in fact be influenced by close relationships with *deviant* peers and family members. A number of research efforts do show that delinquents maintain relationships with deviant peers and are influenced by members of their deviant peer group.[122] However, delinquents may not be "lone wolves" whose only personal relationships are exploitive; their friendship patterns seem quite close to those of conventional youth.[123] For example, Denise Kandel and Mark Davies found that young male drug abusers maintained even more intimate relations with their peers than nonabusers did; illicit drug abuse can be used to predict strong social ties and high levels of intimacy.[124]

Hirschi made little distinction in the importance of the elements of the social bond. Yet the research evidence suggests that there may be differences. Velmer Burton and his associates found that high levels of involvement, which Hirschi suggested should reduce delinquency, may actually increase delinquent behavior. Burton speculates that the more kids are involved in behaviors outside the home, the less contact they have with parental supervision and the greater the opportunity they have to commit crime.[125] Kimberly Kempf-Leonard and Scott Decker's research with younger children found that the concepts of "involvement" and "belief" had relatively little influence over behavior patterns.[126]

Hirschi's conclusion that any form of social attachment is beneficial, even to deviant peers and parents, has also been disputed by a number of research studies. Although his classic study supported the basic principles of social control theory, Michael Hindelang did find that attachment to delinquent peers escalated rather than restricted criminality.[127] Gary Jensen and David Brownfield found that youths attached to drug-abusing parents are more likely to become drug users themselves.[128] And in a study of dropouts in the Canadian city of Edmonton, Alberta, Leslie Samuelson, Timothy Hartnagel, and Harvey Krahn found that attachment to deviant peers helped motivate dropouts to commit crime and helped facilitate their delinquent acts.[129] Finally, Mark Warr's research indicates that attachment to delinquent friends is a powerful predictor of delinquency, strong enough to overcome the controlling effect of positive family relationships.[130]

There is some question as to whether social control theory can explain all modes of criminality (as Hirschi maintained) or is restricted to particular groups or forms of criminality. When Marvin Krohn and James Massey surveyed 3,065 junior and senior high school students, they found that control variables were better able to explain female delinquency than male delinquency and minor delinquency (such as alcohol and marijuana abuse) than more serious criminal acts.[131] Similar gender differences were uncovered in school-based research by Jill Leslie Rosenbaum and James Lasley; they also found social control variables to be more predictive of female than male behavior.[132] Perhaps girls are more deeply influenced by the quality of their bond to society than are boys.

Social bonds seem to change over time, a phenomenon ignored by Hirschi. For example, using samples of 12-, 15-, and 18-year-old boys, Randy LaGrange and Helene Raskin White did indeed find age differences in the perceptions of the social bond: Mid-teens are surprisingly likely to be influenced by their parents and teachers; boys in the other two age groups are more deeply influenced by their deviant peers.[133] LaGrange and White attribute this finding to the problems of mid-adolescence, in which there is a great need to develop "psychological anchors" to conformity. It is possible, then, that at one age level, weak bonds (to parents) lead to delinquency, while at another, strong bonds (to peers) lead to delinquency.

The most severe criticism of social control theory has been leveled by sociologist Robert Agnew, who claims that Hirschi miscalculated the direction of the relationship between criminality and a weakened social bond.[134] While Hirschi's theory projects that a weakened bond leads to delinquency, Agnew suggests that the chain of events may flow in the opposite direction: Kids who break the law find that their bond to parents, schools, and society eventually becomes weak and attenuated. Other studies have also found that criminal behavior weakens social bonds and not vice versa.[135]

These criticisms aside, the weight of the existing empirical evidence is supportive of control theory, and it has emerged as one of the preeminent theories in criminology.[136] For many criminologists, it is perhaps the most important way of understanding the onset of criminal misbehavior.[137]

Labeling Theory

Labeling theory explains criminal career formation in terms of destructive social interactions and encounters. Its roots are in the symbolic interaction theory of sociologists Charles Horton Cooley and George Herbert Mead and later Herbert Blumer.[138] **Symbolic interaction theory** holds that people communicate via symbols—gestures, signs, words, or images that stand for or represent something else. People interpret symbolic gestures from others and incorporate them into their self-image. Symbols are used by others to let people know how well they are doing and whether they are liked or appreciated. How people view reality, then, depends on the content of the messages and situations they encounter, the subjective interpretation of these interactions, and how they shape future behavior. In this view, there is no objective reality. People interpret the actions of others, and this interpretation defines meaning. Because interpretation changes over time, so does the meaning of concepts and symbols.

Labeling theory picks up on these concepts of interaction and interpretation.[139] Throughout their lives, people are given a variety of symbolic labels in their interactions with others. These labels imply a variety of behaviors and attitudes; labels thus help define not just one trait but the the whole person. For example, people labeled "insane" are also assumed to be dangerous, dishonest, unstable, violent, strange, and otherwise unsound. Valued labels, including "smart," "honest," and "hard worker," which suggest overall competence, can improve self-image and social standing. Research shows that people who are labeled with one positive trait, such as being physically attractive, are assumed to maintain others, such as intelligence and competence.[140] In contrast, negative labels, including "troublemaker," "mentally ill," and "stupid," help **stigmatize** their targets and reduce their self-image.

Both positive and negative labels entail subjective interpretation of behavior: A "troublemaker" is merely someone whom people label as "troublesome"; there need not be any objective proof or measure indicating that the person is actually a troublemaker. Although a label may be a function of rumor, innuendo, or unfounded suspicion, its adverse impact can be immense.

If a devalued status is conferred by a significant other— a teacher, police officer, elder, parent, or valued peer— the negative label may cause permanent harm to the target. The degree to which a person is perceived as a **social deviant** may affect his or her treatment at home, at work, at school, and in other social situations. Kids may find that their parents consider them a "bad influence" on younger brothers and sisters. School officials may limit them to classes for people with behavior problems. Adults labeled "criminal," "ex-con," or "drug addict" may find their eligibility for employment severely restricted. And, of course, if the label is bestowed as the result of conviction for a criminal offense, the labeled person may be subject to official sanctions ranging from a mild reprimand to incarceration.

Beyond these immediate results, labeling advocates maintain that, depending on the visibility of the label and the manner and severity with which it is applied, a person will have an increasing commitment to a deviant career. "Thereafter he may be watched; he may be suspect . . . he may be excluded more and more from legitimate opportunities."[141] Labeled persons may find themselves turning to others similarly stigmatized for support and companionship. Isolated from conventional society, they may identify themselves as members of an outcast group and become locked into a deviant career.

Because stigmatization is essentially an interactive process, labeling theorists blame criminal career formation on the social agencies originally designed for its control. Often mistrustful of institutions, such as police, courts, and correctional agencies, labeling advocates find it logical that these institutions produce the stigmas that are so harmful to the very people they are trying to help, treat, or correct. Rather than reduce deviant behavior, for which they were designed, such label-bestowing institutions actually help maintain and amplify criminal behavior (see Figure 8.5).

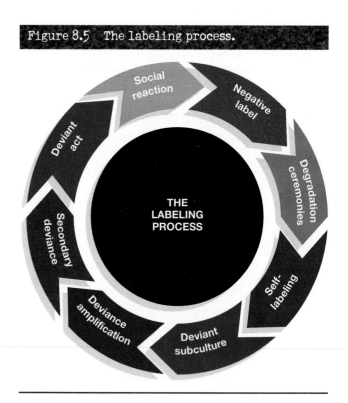

Figure 8.5 The labeling process.

Social reaction
Negative label
Deviant act
Degradation ceremonies
THE LABELING PROCESS
Secondary deviance
Self-labeling
Deviance amplification
Deviant subculture

Connections

Fear of stigma has prompted efforts to reduce the impact of criminal labels through such programs as pretrial diversion and community treatment programs. In addition, some criminologists have called for noncoercive "peacemaking" solutions to interpersonal conflict. This peacemaking or restorative justice movement is reviewed in Chapter 9.

Crime and Labeling Theory

Labeling theorists use an interactionist definition of crime. In an important statement, sociologist Kai Erickson argued, "Deviance is not a property inherent in certain forms of behavior, it is a property conferred upon those forms by the audience which directly or indirectly witnesses them."[142] This definition was amplified by Edwin Schur, who stated:

> Human behavior is deviant to the extent that it comes to be viewed as involving a personally discreditable departure from a group's normative expectation, and it elicits interpersonal and collective reactions that serve to "isolate," "treat," "correct" or "punish" individuals engaged in such behavior.[143]

Crime and deviance, therefore, are defined by the social audience's reaction to people and their behavior and the subsequent effects of that reaction; they are not defined by the moral content of the illegal act itself. In its purest form, labeling theory argues that such crimes as murder, rape, and assault are only bad or evil because people label them as such. After all, the difference between an excusable act and a criminal one is often a matter of legal definition, which changes from place to place and from year to year. Labeling theorists would argue that such acts as abortion, marijuana use, possession of a handgun, and gambling have been legal at some points and places in history and illegal at others. Howard Becker refers to people who create rules as **moral entrepreneurs.** In a famous statement, he summed up their effect as follows:

> Social groups create deviance by making rules whose infractions constitute deviance, and by applying those rules to particular people and labeling them as outsiders. From this point of view, deviance is not a quality of the act a person commits, but rather a consequence of the application by others of rules and sanctions to an "offender." The deviant is one to whom the label has successfully been applied; deviant behavior is behavior that people so label.[144]

Differential Enforcement

An important principle of labeling theory is that the law is differentially applied, benefitting those who hold economic and social power and penalizing the powerless. Labeling theorists argue that the probability of being brought under the control of legal authority is a function of a person's race, wealth, gender, and social standing. They point to studies indicating that police officers are more likely to formally arrest males, minority-group members, and those in the lower class and to use their discretionary powers to give beneficial treatment to more favored groups.[145] Similarly, labeling advocates cite evidence that minorities and the poor are more likely to be prosecuted for criminal offenses and receive harsher punishments when convicted.[146] This evidence is used to support the labeling concept that personal characteristics and social interactions are actually more important variables in the criminal career formation process than the mere violation of the criminal law.

Labeling theorists also argue that the content of the law reflects power relationships in society. They point to the evidence that white-collar crimes are most often punished by a relatively small fine and rarely result in prison sentences, and they contrast this treatment with the long prison sentences given to those convicted of "street crimes," such as burglary or car theft.[147] In sum, a major premise of labeling theory is that the law is differentially constructed and applied. It favors the powerful members of society who direct its content and penalizes people whose actions represent a threat to those in control.[148]

Becoming Labeled

Labeling theorists are not especially concerned with explaining why people originally engage in acts that result in their being labeled.[149] Labeling theorists would not dispute any of the previously discussed theories of the onset of criminality: Crime may be a result of greed, personality, social structure, learning, or control. Labeling theorists' concern is with criminal career formation and not the origin of criminal acts.

It is, however, consistent with the labeling approach to suggest that the less personal power and fewer resources a person has, the greater the chance he or she will become labeled. In the labeling view, a person is labeled deviant primarily as a consequence of the **social distance** between the labeler and the person labeled. Race, class, and ethnic differences between those in power and those without influence the likelihood of labeling. For example, a poor or minority-group teenager may run a greater chance of being officially processed for criminal acts by police, courts, and correctional agencies than a wealthy white youth would.

Of course, not all labeled people have chosen to engage in label-producing activities, such as crime. Some labels are bestowed on people for behaviors over which they have little control. Negative labels of this sort include "homosexual," "mentally ill," and "mentally deficient." In these categories, too, the probability of being labeled may depend on the visibility of the person in the community, the tolerance of the community for unusual behavior, and the person's own power to combat labels.

Consequences of Labeling

Criminologists are most concerned with two effects of labeling: the creation of stigma and the effect on self-image. Labels are believed to produce stigma. The labeled deviant becomes a social outcast who may be prevented from enjoying higher education, well-paying jobs, and other social benefits. Labeling theorists consider public condemnation an important part of the label-producing process. It may be accomplished in such "ceremonies" as a hearing in which a person is found to be mentally ill or a trial in which an individual is convicted of crime. A public record of the deviant acts causes the denounced person to be ritually separated from a place in the legitimate order and placed outside the world occupied by citizens of good standing. Harold Garfinkle has called transactions that produce irreversible, permanent labels "successful degradation ceremonies."[150]

Beyond these immediate results, the label tends to redefine the whole person. For example, the label "ex-con" may create in people's imaginations a whole series of behavior descriptions—tough, mean, dangerous, aggressive, dishonest, sneaky—that a person who has been in prison may or may not possess. People begin to react to the content of the label and what the label signifies and not to the actual behavior of the person who bears it. This is referred to as *retrospective reading,* a process in which the past of the labeled person is reviewed and reevaluated to fit his or her current outcast status. For example, boyhood friends of an assassin or killer are interviewed by the media and report that the suspect was withdrawn, suspicious, and negativistic as a youth. Now we can understand what prompted his current behavior; the label must certainly be accurate.[151]

Labels become the basis of personal identity. As the negative feedback of law enforcement agencies, parents, friends, teachers, and other figures amplifies the force of the original label, stigmatized offenders may begin to reevaluate their own identities. If they are not really evil or bad, they may ask themselves, why is everyone making such a fuss about them? Frank Tannenbaum, a labeling theory pioneer, referred to this process as the **dramatization of evil.** With respect to the consequences of labeling delinquent behavior, Tannenbaum stated:

> The process of making the criminal, therefore, is a process of tagging, defining, identifying, making conscious and self-conscious; it becomes a way of stimulating, suggesting and evoking the very traits that are complained of. If the theory of relation of response to stimulus has any meaning, the entire process of dealing with the young delinquent is mischievous insofar as it identifies him to himself or to the environment as a delinquent person. The person becomes the thing he is described as being.[152]

Primary and Secondary Deviance

One of the more well-known views of the labeling process is Edwin Lemert's concept of primary and secondary deviance.[153]

According to Lemert, **primary deviance** involves norm violations or crimes that have little influence on the actor and can be quickly forgotten. For example, a college student takes a "five-finger discount" at the campus bookstore. He successfully steals a textbook, uses it to get an A grade in a course, goes on to graduate, is admitted into law school, and later becomes a famous judge. Because his shoplifting goes unnoticed, it is a relatively unimportant event that has little bearing on his future life.

In contrast, **secondary deviance** occurs when a deviant event comes to the attention of significant others or social control agents who apply a negative label. The newly labeled offender then reorganizes his or her behavior and personality around the consequences of the deviant act. The shoplifting student is caught by a security guard and expelled from college. With his law school dreams dashed and future cloudy, his options are limited; people who know him say he "lacks character," and he begins to share their opinion. He eventually becomes a drug dealer and winds up in prison.

Secondary deviance involves resocialization into a deviant role. The labeled person is transformed into one who "employs his behavior or a role based upon it as a means of defense, attack, or adjustment to the overt and covert problems created by the consequent social reaction to him."[154] Secondary deviance produces a deviance amplification effect. Offenders feel isolated from the mainstream of society and become firmly locked into their deviant role. They may seek out others similarly labeled to form deviant subcultures or groups. Ever more firmly enmeshed in their deviant role, they are locked into an escalating cycle of deviance, apprehension, more powerful labels, and identity transformation. Lemert's concept of secondary deviance expresses the core of labeling theory: Deviance is a process in which one's identity is transformed. Efforts to control the offenders, whether by treatment or punishment, simply help solidify them in their deviant role.

A number of attempts have been made to formulate theories of deviant career formation using a labeling perspective. Following are discussions of two such efforts.

General Theory of Deviance

One theoretical model that draws on labeling theory concepts is Howard Kaplan's *general theory of deviance.* A concise analysis of Kaplan's work begins with the assumption that people who cannot conform to social group standards face negative sanctions. Sanctions are brought against those who are considered failures either because they lack desirable physical, social, or psychological traits or because they fail to behave according to group expectations.

Those exposed to negative social sanctions experience **self-rejection** and a lower self-image. The experience of self-rejecting attitudes ("At times, I think I am no good at all") results in both a weakened commitment to conventional values and behaviors and the acquisition of motives to deviate from social norms. Facilitating this attitude and value transformation is the bond social outcasts form with similarly labeled peers.[155] Membership in a deviant subculture often involves conforming to group norms that conflict

According to Lemert's theory, if these kids are caught and labeled as "druggies," they may become secondary deviants, taking on an identity associated with their negative label, and enter a life of crime. If their actions go undetected, their behavior remains primary and their drug use remains nothing more than an easily forgotten youthful indiscretion.

with those of conventional society. Deviant group membership then encourages criminality and drug abuse.

Deviant behaviors that defy conventional values can serve a number of purposes. Some acts are defiant, designed to show contempt for the source of the negative labels, while others are planned to distance the target from further contact with the source of criticism (for example, an adolescent runs away from critical parents).[156]

Kaplan has tested his theoretical model using surveys of adolescents. His findings support a model in which social sanctions lead to self-rejection, deviant peer associations, and eventual deviance amplification.[157] This model is important because it accounts for the creation of labels, their impact on self-image, and the long-term effect they have on criminal careers. Kaplan's research also shows that negative sanctions have a labeling effect if they help undermine conventional relationships and encourage deviant peer group memberships.

Differential Social Control

Karen Heimer and Ross Matsueda propose a version of labeling theory that also leans on control theory concepts; they call this the *theory of differential social control.*[158]

Agreeing with the labeling perspective, Heimer and Matsueda find that self-evaluations reflect actual or perceived appraisals made by others. Kids who view themselves as delinquents are giving an inner voice to their perceptions of how parents, teachers, peers, and neighbors feel about them. Kids who believe that others view them as antisocial or troublemakers take on attitudes and roles that reflect this assumption; they expect to be suspected and then rejected. Labeled youth may then join with similarly outcast delinquent peers who facilitate their behavior. Eventually, antisocial behavior becomes habitual and automatic.

Tempering or enhancing the effect of this **reflective role-taking** are informal and institutional social control processes. Families, schools, peers, and the social system can either help control kids and dissuade them from crime or encourage and sustain their deviance. When these groups are dysfunctional, such as when parents use drugs, they encourage, rather than control, antisocial behavior.

Heimer and Matsueda have conducted empirical research that supports the core of their model. They found that **reflected appraisal** as a rule violator has a significant effect on delinquency: Kids who believe that their parents and friends consider them deviants and troublemakers are the ones most likely to engage in delinquency. In another analysis, Heimer found that kids with "damaged" self-images are the ones most likely to engage in risk-taking behaviors, such as delinquency; self-image, influenced and directed by social interaction and approval, controls the content of behavior.[159]

This work by Heimer and Matsueda is important because it is an alternative to "traditional" labeling theory that incorporates concepts of social control and symbolic interaction. Further research on this model may revive interest in the labeling perspective.

Research on Labeling Theory

Research on labeling theory can be classified into two distinct categories. The first focuses on the characteristics of offenders who are chosen for labels. Labeling theory maintains that these offenders should be relatively powerless people who are unable to defend themselves against the negative labeling. The second type of research attempts to discover the effects of being labeled. Labeling theorists predict that people who are labeled should view themselves as deviant and commit increasing amounts of criminal behavior.

WHO GETS LABELED? It is widely believed that poor and powerless people are victimized by the law and justice system and that labels are not equally distributed across class and racial lines. For example, a report of the National Minority Advisory Council on Criminal Justice argues that although substantive and procedural laws govern almost every aspect of the American criminal justice system, discretionary decision making controls its operation at every level. From the police officer's decision on whom to arrest, to the prosecutor's decisions on whom to charge and for how many and what kind of charges, to the court's decision on whom to release or on whom to permit bail, to the grand jury's decision on indictment, to the judge's decision on the length of the sentence, discretion works to the detriment of minorities, including African Americans, Hispanics, Asian Americans, and Native Americans.[160] This allegation is supported by data accumulated by Carl Pope and William Feyerherm, who reviewed more than 30 years of research on minorities in the juvenile justice system and found that race bias adversely influences decision making.[161]

There is also evidence that those in power try to streamline the labeling process by discounting or ignoring the "protestations of innocence" made by suspects accused of socially undesirable acts, such as child abuse. Leslie Margolin found that people accused of child abuse were routinely defined as "noncredible" when they denied accusations of abuse and were only believed when they confessed their guilt. In contrast, victims were believed when they made accusations but were considered "noncredible" when they claimed the suspect was innocent.[162]

While these arguments are persuasive, little definitive evidence exists that the justice system is inherently unfair and biased. Procedures such as arrest, prosecution, and sentencing seem to be more often based on legal factors, such as prior record and crime seriousness, than personal characteristics, such as class and race.[163] These findings do little to support labeling theory.

THE EFFECTS OF LABELING. There is empirical evidence that negative labels actually have a dramatic influ-

ence on the self-image of offenders. Considerable empirical evidence indicates that social sanctions lead to self-labeling and deviance amplification.[164]

Parents do in fact negatively label their children who suffer a variety of problems, including antisocial behavior and school failure.[165] This process is important because once labeled as troublemakers, adolescents begin to reassess their self-image. Ross Matsueda found that parents who label their kids as troublemakers promote deviance amplification: Labeling causes parents to become alienated from their child; negative labels reduce a child's self-image and increase delinquency.[166]

There is also evidence that repeat and intensive official labeling does in fact produce self-labeling and damaged identities.[167] Kids labeled troublemakers in school are the ones most likely to drop out; dropping out has been linked to delinquent behavior.[168] Another study found that male drug users labeled as addicts by social control agencies eventually became self-labeled and increased their drug use.[169] And Lawrence Sherman and his associates found a limited labeling effect for people arrested in domestic violence cases: People with a low "stake in conformity"—that is, who were jobless and unmarried—increased offending after being given official labels.[170]

LABELING AND CRIMINAL CAREERS. Until recently, scant attention has been paid to the fact that stigmatization and negative labels may sustain chronic offending and criminal careers.[171] In fact, the very definition of a chronic offender is a person who has been arrested and therefore labeled multiple times in his or her offending career.

There is some empirical evidence that labeling plays an important role in persistent offending. In an important research paper, Douglas Smith and Robert Brame found that while labels may not cause adolescents to initiate criminal behaviors, experienced delinquents are *significantly more likely to continue offending if they believe that their parents and peers view them in a negative light.*[172] Labeling thus may help sustain criminality over time.

In sum, there is considerable evidence that people who are labeled by parents, schools, and the criminal justice system stand a good chance of getting involved in deviance. It is still unclear, however, whether this outcome is actually a labeling effect or the product of some other personal and social factors that also caused the labeling to occur.

Is Labeling Theory Valid?

Labeling theory has been the subject of significant academic debate. Those who criticize it point to its inability to specify the conditions that must exist before an act or individual is labeled deviant—that is, why some people are labeled while others remain "secret deviants."[173] Critics also charge that labeling theory fails to explain differences in crime rates; if crime is a function of stigma and labels, why are crime rates higher in some parts of the country at particular times of the year?[174] Labeling theory also ignores the onset of deviant behavior (that is, it fails to ask why people commit the initial deviant act) and does not deal with the reasons delinquents and criminals decide to forgo a deviant career.[175]

In probably the most devastating critique of the theory, Charles Wellford questioned the validity of several premises essential to the labeling approach.[176] His criticisms include the following points:

- Labeling theory claims that deviance is relative—that virtually no act is universally considered criminal behavior. Yet some crimes, such as rape and homicide, are universally sanctioned.
- The labeling theory proposition that almost all law enforcement is biased against the poor and minorities is spurious. Law enforcement officials most often base their arrest decisions on such factors as the seriousness of the offense and pay less attention to such issues as the race, class, and demeanor of the offender.
- Self-labeling is an invalid concept. Although labeling may indeed affect offenders' attitudes about themselves, there is little evidence that attitude changes are related to actual behavior changes.
- Crime is situationally motivated and depends more on ecological and personal conditions than labels and stigma.[177]

Because of these criticisms, a number of criminologists who once valued its premise now reject labeling theory. Some charge that it all too often focuses on "nuts, sluts, and perverts" and ignores the root causes of crime.[178]

With the "discovery" of the chronic offender, it was believed that labeling theory would receive renewed interest as an explanation of chronic offending. It seems logical that negative labeling is connected to the onset of persistent offending; after all, the chronic offender is defined as someone who has been repeatedly labeled by the justice system.[179] While this idea is intriguing, it, too, has met with criticism.[180] In an in-depth analysis of research on the crime-producing effects of labels, Charles Tittle found little evidence that stigma produces crime.[181] Tittle claims that many criminal careers occur without labeling, that labeling often comes after, rather than before, chronic offending, and that criminal careers may not follow even when labeling takes place. There is growing evidence that the onset of criminal careers occurs early in life and that those who go on to a "life of crime" are burdened with so many social, physical, and psychological problems that negative labeling may be a relatively insignificant event.[182]

While criticisms of labeling theory have reduced its importance in the criminological literature, its utility as an explanation of crime and deviance should not be dismissed Raymond Paternoster and Leeann Iovanni have identified some other features of the labeling perspective that are important contributions to the study of criminality:[183]

1. The labeling perspective identifies the role played by social control agents in the process of crime causation. Criminal behavior cannot be fully understood if the agencies and individuals empowered to control and treat it are neglected.

2. Labeling theory recognizes that criminality is not a disease or pathological behavior. It focuses attention on the social interactions and reactions that shape individuals and their behavior.

3. Labeling theory distinguishes between criminal acts (primary deviance) and criminal careers (secondary deviance) and shows that these concepts must be interpreted and treated differently.

Labeling theory is also important because of its focus on interaction and the situation of crime. Rather than view the criminal as a robotlike creature whose actions are predetermined, it recognizes that crime is often the result of complex interactions and processes. The decision to commit crime involves the actions of a variety of people, including peers, the victim, the police, and other key characters. Labels may expedite crime because they guide the actions of all parties in criminal interactions. Actions deemed innocent when performed by one person are considered provocative when engaged in by another labeled as a deviant. Similarly, labeled people may be quick to judge, take offense, or misinterpret behavior because of past experience. They experienced conflict in the past, so why not now?

An Evaluation of Social Process Theory

The branches of social process theory—social learning, social control, and labeling—are compatible because they suggest that criminal behavior is part of the socialization process. Criminals are people whose interactions with critically important social institutions and processes—the family, schools, the justice system, peer groups, employers, and neighbors—are troubled and disturbed. Although there is some disagreement about the relative importance of those influences and the form they take, there seems to be little question that social interactions shape the behavior, beliefs, values, and self-image of the offender. People who have learned deviant social values, find themselves detached from conventional social relationships, or are the subject of stigma and labels from significant others will be the most likely to fall prey to the attractions of criminal behavior. These negative influences can affect people in all walks of life, beginning in their youth and continuing into adulthood. The major strength of the social process view is the vast body of empirical data showing that delinquents and criminals are indeed people who grew up in dysfunctional families, who had troubled childhoods, and who failed at school, at work, and in marriage. Prison data show that these characteristics are typical of inmates.

While persuasive, these theories have trouble accounting for some of the patterns and fluctuations in the crime rate. If social process theories are valid, for example, people in the West and South must be socialized differently than those in the Midwest and New England, since these latter regions have much lower crime rates. How can the fact that crime rates are lower in October than in July be explained if crime is a function of learning or control? How can social processes explain why criminals escalate their activity or why they desist from crime? Once a social bond is broken, how can it be "reattached"? Once crime is "learned," how can it be "unlearned"?

Social Process Theory and Social Policy

Social process theories have had a major influence on social policymaking since the 1950s. Learning theories have greatly influenced concepts of treatment of the criminal offender. Their effect has been felt mainly by young offenders, who are viewed as being more salvageable than "hardened" criminals. Advocates of the social learning approach argue that if people become criminal by learning definitions and attitudes toward criminality, they can "unlearn" them by being exposed to definitions toward conventional behavior. This philosophy was used in numerous treatment facilities throughout the United States, the most famous being the Highfields Project in New Jersey and the Silverlake Program in Los Angeles. These residential treatment programs for young male offenders used group interaction sessions to attack the criminal behavior orientations held by residents (being tough, using alcohol and drugs, believing that school is for "sissies"), while promoting conventional lines of behavior (going straight, saving money, giving up drugs). It is common today for residential and nonresidential programs to offer similar treatment programs. They teach kids to say no to drugs, to forgo delinquent behavior, or to stay in school. It is even common for celebrities to return to their old neighborhood to tell kids to stay in school or off of drugs. If learning did not affect behavior, such exercises would be futile.

Control theories have also influenced criminal justice and other social policymaking. Programs have been developed to improve people's commitments to conventional lines of action. Some work at creating and strengthening bonds early in life before the onset of criminality. The educational system has been the scene of numerous programs designed to improve basic skills and create an atmosphere in which youths will develop a bond to their schools. The Close-Up on the Head Start program discusses perhaps the largest and most successful attempt to solidify social bonds.

Control theories' focus on the family has been put into operation in programs designed to strengthen the bond be-

Net Bookmark

The Head Start program is a major government effort to socialize youth who may otherwise have a difficult time when they start school. It also provides education for parents of young children, ranging from parenting skills to nutrition. The national program is described at the Head Start homepage: http://www.interport.net/~rmeier/jasa/nycan/hdstart.html

tween parent and child. Other programs attempt to "repair" bonds that have been broken and frayed. Examples of this approach are the career, work furlough, and educational opportunity programs being developed in the nation's prisons. These programs are designed to help inmates maintain a stake in society so they will be less willing to resort to criminal activity on their release.

Labeling theorists caution against too much intervention. Rather than ask social agencies to attempt to rehabilitate people having problems with the law, they argue that "less is better." Put another way, the more institutions try to "help" people, the more these people will be stigmatized and labeled. For example, a special education program designed to help problem readers may cause them to be labeled by themselves and others as slow or stupid; a mental health rehabilitation program created with the best intentions may cause clients to be labeled as crazy or dangerous.

The influence of labeling theory can be viewed in the development of diversion and restitution programs. Diversion programs are designed to remove both juvenile and adult offenders from the normal channels of the criminal justice process by placing them in programs designed for rehabilitation. For example, a college student whose drunk driving causes injury to a pedestrian may, before a trial occurs, be placed for six months in an alcohol treatment program. If he successfully completes the program, charges against him will be dismissed. Thus, he avoids the stigma of a criminal label. Such programs are common throughout the nation. Often, they offer counseling; vocational, educational, and family services; and medical advice. Another label-avoiding innovation that has gained popularity is restitution. Rather than face the stigma of a formal trial, an offender is asked to either pay back the victim of the crime for any loss incurred or do some useful work in the community in lieu of receiving a court-ordered sentence.

Despite their good intentions, stigma-reducing programs have not met with great success. Critics charge that they substitute one kind of stigma for another—for instance, attending a mental health program in lieu of a criminal trial. In addition, diversion and restitution programs usually screen out violent offenders and repeat offenders. Finally, there is little hard evidence that the recidivism rate of people who have attended alternative programs represents an improvement over the rate of people who have been involved in the traditional criminal justice process.

close-up: *Head Start*

Head Start is probably the best-known effort to help lower-class youths achieve proper socialization and, in so doing, reduce their potential for future criminality.

Head Start programs were instituted in the 1960s as part of the Johnson administration's War on Poverty. In the beginning, Head Start was a two-month summer program for children about to enter school, aimed at embracing the "whole child." Comprehensive programming helped promote physical health, enhance mental processes, and improve social and emotional development, self-image, and interpersonal relationships. Preschoolers were provided with an enriched educational environment to develop their learning and cognitive skills. They were given the opportunity to use pegs and pegboards, puzzles, toy animals, dolls, letters and numbers, and other materials that middle-class children take for granted and that give them a leg up in the educational process.

Today, services have been expanded beyond the two-month summer program. There are over 1,300 centers around the nation containing 36,000 classrooms servicing 740,000 children and their families, on a budget of more than $3.3 billion annually; more than 13 million children have been served by Head Start since it began. Head Start programs receive 80% of their funding from the federal government. The other 20% comes from the local community.

Head Start teachers hope to provide a variety of learning experiences appropriate to the child's age and development. These experiences allow the child to read books, understand cultural diversity, express feelings, and play with and relate to their peers in an appropriate fashion. Students are guided in developing gross and fine motor skills and self-confidence. Health care is also an issue, and most children enrolled in the program receive comprehensive health screening, physical and dental examinations, and appropriate follow-up. Many programs provide meals and in so doing help children receive proper nourishment.

Head Start programs now serve parents in addition to their preschoolers. Some programs allow parents to enroll in classes that cover parenting, literacy, nutrition/weight loss, domestic violence prevention, and other social issues. Social services, health, nutrition, and education services are also available.

Considerable controversy has surrounded the success of the Head Start program. In 1970, the Westinghouse Learning Corporation issued a definitive evaluation of the Head Start effort that found no evidence of lasting cognitive gains on the part of the participating children. Initial gains seemed to evaporate during the elementary school years, and by the third grade the performance of the Head Start children was no different than that of their peers.

While disappointing, this evaluation focused on IQ levels and gave short shrift to improvement in social competence and other survival skills. More recent research has produced dramatically different results. One report found that by age five, children who experienced the enriched daycare offered by Head Start averaged more than ten points higher on their IQ scores than their peers who did not participate in the program. Other research that carefully compared Head Start children to similar youths who did not attend the program found that the former made significant intellectual gains: Head Start children were less likely to have been retained in a grade or placed in classes for slow learners; they outperformed peers on achievement tests; and they were more likely to graduate from high school. Head Start kids also make strides in nonacademic areas: They had better health, immunization rates, nutrition, and enhanced emotional characteristics after leaving the program.

Research also shows that the Head Start program can have important psychological benefits for the mothers of participants, such as decreasing depression and anxiety and increasing feelings of life satisfaction. While findings in some areas may be tentative, they are all in the same direction: Head Start enhances school readiness and has enduring effects on social competence.

If, as many experts believe, there is a close link between school performance, family life, and crime, programs such as Head Start can help some potentially criminal youths avoid problems with the law. By implication, their success indicates that programs that help socialize youngsters can be used to combat urban criminality. While some problems have been identified in individual centers, the government has shown its faith in Head Start as a socialization agent by planning to expand services in the coming years; by 1998, total funding could be $8 billion.

CRITICAL THINKING QUESTIONS
1. Does a program like Head Start substitute one type of negative label (special-needs kid) for another (slow starter)?
2. If Head Start works, shouldn't every child have the benefit of the program?

Sources: Edward Zigler and Sally Styfco, "Head Start: Criticisms in a Constructive Context," *American Psychologist* 49 (1994): 127–132; Nancy Kassebaum, "Head Start, Only the Best for America's Children," *American Psychologist* 49 (1994): 123–126; Faith Lamb Parker, Chaya Piorkowski, and Lenore Peay, "Head Start as Social Support for Mothers: The Psychological Benefits of Involvement," *American Journal of Orthopsychiatry* 57 (1987): 220–233.

Table 8.1 Social Process Theories

THEORY	MAJOR PREMISE	STRENGTHS
Social Learning Theories		
Differential association theory	People learn to commit crime from exposure to antisocial definitions.	Explains onset of criminality. Explains the presence of crime in all elements of social structure. Explains why some people in high-crime areas refrain from criminality. Can apply to adults and juveniles.
Differential reinforcement theory	Criminal behavior depends on the person's experiences with rewards for conventional behaviors and punishment for deviant ones. Being rewarded for deviance leads to crime.	Adds learning theory principles to differential association. Links sociological and psychological principles.
Neutralization theory	Youths learn ways of neutralizing moral restraints and periodically drift in and out of criminal behavior patterns.	Explains why many delinquents do not become adult criminals. Explains why youthful law violators can participate in conventional behavior.
Control Theories		
Containment theory	Society produces pushes and pulls toward crime. In some people, they are counteracted by internal and external containments, such as a good self-concept and group cohesiveness.	Brings together psychological and sociological principles. Can explain why some people are able to resist the strongest social pressure to commit crime.
Control theory	A person's bond to society prevents him or her from violating social rules. If the bond weakens, the person if free to commit crime.	Explains the onset of crime; can apply to both middle- and lower-class crime. Explains its theoretical constructs adequately so they can be measured. Has been empirically tested.
Labeling Theory		
Labeling theory	People enter into law-violating careers when they are labeled for their acts and organize their personalities around the labels.	Explains the role of society in creating deviance. Explains why some juvenile offenders do not become adult criminals. Develops concepts of criminal careers.
General theory of deviance	People exposed to negative labels experience self-rejection, which causes them to bond with social outcasts.	Considers the relationship between negative labels, self-image, and personal relations.
Differential social control	Social rejection leads to self-fulfilling prophecy. Weak social controls encourage deviance.	Considers the role of social control in the labeling process.

Summary

Social process theories view criminality as a function of people's interaction with various organizations, institutions, and processes in society. People in all walks of life have the potential to become criminals if they maintain destructive social relationships. Social process theory has three main branches: Social learning theory stresses that people learn how to commit crimes; control theory analyzes the failure of society to control criminal tendencies; and labeling theory maintains that negative labels produce criminal careers. These theories are summarized in Table 8.1.

The social learning branch of social process theory suggests that people learn criminal behaviors much as they learn conventional behavior. Differential association theory, formulated by Edwin Sutherland, holds that criminality is a result of a person's perceiving an excess of procrime definitions over definitions that uphold conventional values. Ronald Akers has reformulated Sutherland's work using psychological learning theory. He calls his approach differential reinforcement theory. Sykes and Matza's theory of neutralization stresses youths' learning of behavior rationalizations that enable them to overcome societal values and norms and engage in illegal behavior.

Control theories maintain that all people have the potential to become criminals but that their bonds to conventional society prevent them from violating the law. Walter Reckless's containment theory suggests that a person's self-concept aids his or her commitment to conventional action. Travis Hirschi describes the social bond as containing elements of belief, commitment, attachment, and involvement. Weakened bonds allow youths to become active in antisocial behavior.

Labeling theory holds that criminality is promoted by becoming negatively labeled by significant others. Such labels as "criminal," "ex-con," and "junkie" serve to isolate people from society and lock them into lives of crime. Labels create expectations that the labeled person will act in a certain way; so-labeled people are always watched and suspected. Eventually, these people begin to accept their labels as personal identities, locking them further into lives of crime and deviance. Edwin Lemert has said that people who accept labels are involved in secondary deviance. Unfortunately, research on labeling has not supported the major premises of labeling theory. Consequently, critics have charged that it lacks credibility as a description of crime causation.

Social process theories have had a great influence on social policy. They have controlled treatment orientations as well as community action policies.

Key Terms

social-psychological processes	techniques of neutralization
social process theories	self-control
socialization	commitment to conformity
cliques	containments
crowds	social control theory
social learning theory	symbolic interaction theory
control theory	stigmatize
labeling theory	social deviant
differential association (DA) theory	moral entrepreneurs
	social distance
differential reinforcement (DR) theory	dramatization of evil
	primary deviance
neutralization theory	secondary deviance
subterranean values	self-rejection
drift	reflective role-taking
	reflected appraisal

Notes

1. See for example, James Q. Wilson and Allan Abrahamse, "Does Crime Pay?" *Justice Quarterly* 9 (1992): 359–378.

2. Alan Lizotte, Terence Thornberry, Marvin Krohn, Deborah Chard-Wierschem, and David McDowall, "Neighborhood Context and Delinquency: A Longitudinal Analysis," in *Cross-National Longitudinal Research on Human Development and Criminal Behavior,* ed. E. M. Weitekamp and H. J. Kerner (Netherlands: Kluwer, 1994), pp. 217–227.

3. Charles Tittle and Robert Meier, "Specifying the SES/Delinquency Relationship," *Criminology* 28 (1990): 271–299.

4. Lizotte, Thornberry, Krohn, Chard-Wierschem, and McDowall, "Neighborhood Context and Delinquency."

5. Denise Kandel, "The Parental and Peer Contexts of Adolescent Deviance: An Algebra of Interpersonal Influences," *Journal of Drug Issues* 26 (1996): 289–315; Ann Goetting, "The Parenting Crime Connection," *Journal of Primary Prevention* 14 (1994): 167–184.

6. Sheldon Glueck and Eleanor Glueck, *Unraveling Juvenile Delinquency* (Cambridge, Mass: Harvard University Press, 1950); Ashley Weeks, "Predicting Juvenile Delinquency," *American Sociological Review* 8 (1943): 40–46.

7. For general reviews of the relationship between families and delinquency, see Alan Jay Lincoln and Murray Straus, *Crime and the Family* (Springfield, Ill.: Charles C Thomas, 1985); Rolf Loeber and Magda Stouthamer-Loeber, "Family Factors as Correlates and Predictors of Juvenile Conduct Problems and Delinquency," in *Crime and Justice, An Annual Review of Research,* vol. 7, ed. Michael Tonry and Norval Morris (Chicago: University of Chicago Press, 1986), pp. 29–151; Goetting, "The Parenting Crime Connection."

8. Joseph Weis, Katherine Worsley, and Carol Zeiss, "The Family and Delinquency: Organizing the Conceptual Chaos" (Center for Law and Justice, University of Washington, 1982, Monograph).

9. Susan Stern and Carolyn Smith, "Family Processes and Delinquency in an Ecological Context," *Social Service Review* 37 (1995): 707–731.

10. United Press International, "U.S. One in Four Children Had Single Parent," *Boston Globe,* 21 January 1988, p. 11.

11. "Two-Parent Households with Children Declining," *Wall Street Journal,* 30 January 1991, p. A2.

12. U.S. Department of the Census, *Fertility of American Women, June 1992* (Washington, D.C.: U.S. Government Printing Office, 1993), p. 34.

13. Lawrence Rosen and Kathleen Neilson, "Broken Homes," in *Contemporary Criminology,* ed. Leonard Savitz and Norman Johnston (New York: Wiley, 1982), pp. 126–135.

14. James Q. Wilson and Richard Herrnstein, *Crime and Human Nature* (New York: Simon & Schuster, 1985), p. 249.

15. L. Edward Wells and Joseph Rankin, "Families and Delinquency: A Meta-Analysis of the Impact of Broken Homes," *Social Problems* 38 (1991): 71–90.

16. Nan Marie Astone and Sara McLanahan, "Family Structure, Parental Practices and High School Completion," *American Sociological Review* 56 (1991): 309–320.

17. Mary Pat Traxler, "The Influence of the Father and Alternative Male Role Models on African-American Boys' Involvement in Antisocial Behavior," paper presented at the annual meeting of the American Society of Criminology, New Orleans, November 1992.

18. Paul Amato and Bruce Keith, "Parental Divorce and the Well-Being of Children: A Meta-Analysis," *Psychological Bulletin* 110 (1991): 26–46.

19. Joseph Rankin and L. Edward Wells, "The Effect of Parental Attachments and Direct Controls on Delinquency," *Journal of Research in Crime and Delinquency* 27 (1990): 140–165.

20. Robert Roberts and Vern Bengston, "Affective Ties to Parents in Early Adulthood and Self-Esteem Across 20 Years," *Social Psychology Quarterly* 59 (1996): 96–106.

21. Robert Johnson, S. Susan Su, Dean Gerstein, Hee-Choon Shin, and John Hoffman, "Parental Influences on Deviant Behavior in Early Adolescence: A Logistic Response Analysis of Age- and Gender-Differentiated Effects," *Journal of Quantitative Criminology* 11 (1995): 167–192.

22. Judith Brook and Li-Jng Tseng, "Influences of Parental Drug Use, Personality, and Child Rearing on the Toddler's Anger and Negativity," *Genetic, Social and General Psychology Monographs* 122 (1996): 107–128.

23. Thomas Ashby Wills, Donato Vaccaro, Grace McNamara, and A. Elizabeth Hirky, "Escalated Substance Use: A Longitudinal Grouping Analysis from Early to Middle Adolescence," *Journal of Abnormal Psychology* 105 (1996): 166–180.

24. John Laub and Robert Sampson, "Unraveling Families and Delinquency: A Reanalysis of the Gluecks' Data," *Criminology* 26 (1988): 355–380.

25. Richard Famularo, Karen Stone, Richard Barnum, and Robert Wharton, "Alcoholism and Severe Child Maltreatment," *American Journal of Orthopsychiatry* 56 (1987): 481–485; Richard Gelles, "Child Abuse and Violence in Single-Parent Families: Parent Absence and Economic Deprivation," *American Journal of Orthopsychiatry* 59 (1989): 492–501; Cecil Willis and Richard Wells, "The Police and Child Abuse: An Analysis of Police Decisions to Report Illegal Behavior," *Criminology* 26 (1988): 695–716; Carolyn Webster-Stratton, "Comparison of Abusive and Nonabusive Families with Conduct-Disordered Children," *American Journal of Orthopsychiatry* 55 (1985): 59–69.

26. Carolyn Smith and Terence Thornberry, "The Relationship Between Childhood Maltreatment and Adolescent Involvement in Delinquency," *Criminology* 33 (1995): 451–479.

27. Herman Daldin, "The Fate of the Sexually Abused Child," *Clinical Social Work Journal* 16 (1988): 20–26; Gerald Ellenson, "Horror, Rage and Defenses in the Symptoms of Female Sexual Abuse Survivors," *Social Casework: The Journal of Contemporary Social Work* 70 (1989): 589–596.

28. Susan Zuravin, "The Ecology of Child Abuse and Neglect: Review of the Literature and Presentation of Data," *Violence and Victims* 4 (1989): 101–120.

29. Lening Zhang and Steven Messner, "Family Deviance and Delinquency in China," *Criminology* 33 (1995): 359–387.

30. *The Forgotten Half: Pathways to Success for America's Youth and Young Families* (Washington, D.C.: William T. Grant Foundation, 1988); Lee Jussim, "Teacher Expectations: Self-Fulfilling Prophecies, Perceptual Biases, and Accuracy," *Journal of Personality and Social Psychology* 57 (1989): 469–480.

31. Eugene Maguin and Rolf Loeber, "Academic Performance and Delinquency," in *Crime and Justice: A Review of Research,* vol. 20, ed. Michael Tonry (Chicago: University of Chicago Press, 1996), pp. 145–264.

32. Jeannie Oakes, *Keeping Track, How Schools Structure Inequality* (New Haven, Conn.: Yale University Press, 1985); Marc LeBlanc, Evelyne Valliere, and Pierre McDuff, "Adolescent's School Experience and Self-Reported Offending: A Longitudinal Test of Social Control Theory," paper presented at the annual meeting of the American Society of Criminology, Baltimore, November 1990.

33. G. Roger Jarjoura, "Does Dropping Out of School Enhance Delinquent Involvement? Results from a Large-Scale National Probability Sample," *Criminology* 31 (1993): 149–172; Terence Thornberry, Melaine Moore, and R. L. Christenson, "The Effect of Dropping Out of High School on Subsequent Criminal Behavior," *Criminology* 23 (1985): 3–18.

34. Carolyn Smith, Alan Lizotte, Terence Thornberry, and Marvin Krohn, *Resilient Youth: Identifying Factors That Prevent High-Risk Youth from Engaging in Delinquency and Drug Use* (Albany, N.Y: Rochester Youth Development Study, 1994), pp. 19–21.

35. National Commission on Excellence in Education, *A Nation at Risk* (Washington, D.C.: U.S. Government Printing Office, 1982).

36. *Weapons in Schools* (Washington, D.C.: Office of Juvenile Justice and Delinquency Prevention, 1989); U.S. Department of Justice, *Disorder in Our Public Schools* (Washington, D.C.: U.S. Government Printing Office, 1984).

37. Irving Janis, *Groupthink: Psychological Studies of Policy Decisions and Fiascoes* (Boston: Houghton Mifflin, 1982).

38. Lening Zhang and Steven Messner, "Family Deviance and Delinquency in China," *Criminology* 33 (1995): 359–387.

39. Thomas Berndt, "The Features and Effects of Friendships in Early Adolescence," *Child Development* 53 (1982): 1447–1469; Thomas Berndt and T. B. Perry, "Children's Perceptions of Friendships as Supportive Relationships," *Developmental Psychology* 22 (1986): 640–648; Spencer Rathus, *Understanding Child Development* (New York: Holt, Rinehart and Winston, 1988), p. 462.

40. Peggy Giordano, "The Wider Circle of Friends in Adolescence," *American Journal of Sociology* 101 (1995): 661–697.

41. Delbert Elliott, David Huizinga, and Suzanne Ageton, *Explaining Delinquency and Drug Use* (Beverly Hills, Calif.: Sage, 1985); Helene Raskin White, Robert Padina, and Randy LaGrange, "Longitudinal Predictors of Serious Substance Use and Delinquency," *Criminology* 6 (1987): 715–740.

42. See, generally, John Hagedorn, *People and Folks: Gangs, Crime and the Underclass in a Rustbelt City* (Chicago: Lakeview Press, 1988).

43. Scott Menard, "Demographic and Theoretical Variables in the Age-Period Cohort Analysis of Illegal Behavior," *Journal of Research in Crime and Delinquency* 29 (1992): 178–199.

44. Patrick Jackson, "Theories and Findings About Youth Gangs," *Criminal Justice Abstracts,* June 1989, pp. 313–327.

45. Marvin Krohn and Terence Thornberry, "Network Theory: A Model for Understanding Drug Abuse Among African-American and Hispanic Youth," in *Drug Abuse Among Minority Youth: Advances in Research and Methodology,* ed. Mario De La Rosa and Juan-Luis Recio Adrados (Washington, D.C.: U.S. Department of Health and Human Services, 1993).

46. D. Wayne Osgood, Janet Wilson, Patrick O'Malley, Jerald Bachman, and Lloyd Johnston, "Routine Activities and Individual Deviant Behavior," *American Sociological Review* 61 (1996): 635–655.

47. Mark Warr, "Age, Peers, and Delinquency," *Criminology* 31 (1993): 17–40.

48. Mark Warr, "Organization and Instigation in Delinquent Groups," *Criminology* 34 (1996): 11–35.

49. Travis Hirschi and Rodney Stark, "Hellfire and Delinquency," *Social Problems* 17 (1969): 202–213.

50. T. David Evans, Francis Cullen, R. Gregory Dunaway, and Velmer Burton, Jr., "Religion and Crime Reexamined: The Impact of Religion, Secular Controls, and Social Ecology on Adult Criminality," *Criminology* 33 (1995): 195–224.

51. Lee Ellis and James Patterson, "Crime and Religion: An International Comparison Among Thirteen Industrial Nations," *Personal Individual Differences* 20 (1996): 761–768.

52. Walter Miller, *Violence by Youth Gangs and Youth Groups as a Crime Problem in Major American Cities* (Washington, D.C.: U.S. Government Printing Office, 1975).

53. Edwin Sutherland, *Principles of Criminology* (Philadelphia: Lippincott, 1939).

54. See, for example, Edwin Sutherland, "White-Collar Criminality," *American Sociological Review* 5 (1940): 2–10.

55. This section is adapted from Clarence Schrag, *Crime and Justice: American Style* (Washington, D.C.: U.S. Government Printing Office, 1971), p. 46.

56. See Edwin Sutherland and Donald Cressey, *Criminology,* 8th ed. (Philadelphia: Lippincott, 1970), pp. 77–79.

57. Sandra Brown, Vicki Creamer, and Barbara Stetson, "Adolescent Alcohol Expectancies in Relation to Personal and Parental Drinking Patterns," *Journal of Abnormal Psychology* 96 (1987): 117–121.

58. Ibid.

59. Ross Matsueda and Karen Heimer, "Race, Family Structure and Delinquency: A Test of Differential Association and Social Control Theories," *American Sociological Review* 52 (1987): 826–840.

60. James Short, "Differential Association as a Hypothesis: Problems of Empirical Testing," *Social Problems* 8 (1960): 14–25.

61. Albert Reiss and A. Lewis Rhodes, "The Distribution of Delinquency in the Social Class Structure," *American Sociological Review* 26 (1961): 732.

62. Douglas Smith, Christy Visher, and G. Roger Jarjoura, "Dimensions of Delinquency: Exploring the Correlates of Participation, Frequency, and Persistence of Delinquent Behavior," *Journal of Research in Crime and Delinquency* 28 (1991): 6–32.

63. Mark Warr, "Age, Peers, and Delinquency."

64. Denise Kandel and Mark Davies, "Friendship Networks, Intimacy, and Illicit Drug Use in Young Adulthood: A Comparison of Two Competing Theories," *Criminology* 29 (1991): 441–467.

65. Kenneth Tunnell, "Inside the Drug Trade: Trafficking from the Dealer's Perspective," *Qualitative Sociology* 16 (1993): 361–381.

66. Krohn and Thornberry, "Network Theory," pp. 123–124.

67. Charles Tittle, *Sanctions and Social Deviance* (New York: Praeger, 1980).

68. Yuet-Wah Cheung and Agnes M. C. Ng, "Social Factors in Adolescent Deviant Behavior in Hong Kong: An Integrated Theoretical Approach," *International Journal of Comparative and Applied Criminal Justice* 12 (1988): 27–44.

69. Robert Burgess and Ronald Akers, "A Differential Association–Reinforcement Theory of Criminal Behavior," *Social Problems* 14 (1966): 128–147.

70. Ross Matsueda, "The Current State of Differential Association Theory," *Crime and Delinquency* 34 (1988): 277–306.

71. Burgess and Akers, "A Differential Association–Reinforcement Theory of Criminal Behavior."

72. Ross Matsueda, "The Current State of Differential Association Theory."

73. Graham Ousey and David Aday, Jr., "The Interaction Hypothesis: A Test Using Social Control Theory and Social Learning Theory," paper presented at the American Society of Criminology meeting, Boston, Mass., November 1995.

74. Mark Warr, "Age, Peers and Delinquency."

75. The most influential critique of differential association is contained in Ruth Kornhauser, *Social Sources of Delinquency* (Chicago: University of Chicago Press, 1978).

76. These misconceptions are derived from Donald Cressey, "Epidemiologies and Individual Conduct: A Case from Criminology," *Pacific Sociological Review* 3 (1960): 47–58.

77. Kornhauser, *Social Sources of Delinquency;* in contrast, see Matsueda, "The Current State of Differential Association Theory."

78. Ronald Akers, "Is Differential Association/Social Learning Cultural Deviance Theory?" *Criminology* 34 (1996): 229–247; for an opposing view, see Travis Hirschi, "Theory Without Ideas: Reply to Akers," *Criminology* 34 (1996): 249–256.

79. Craig Reinerman and Jeffrey Fagan, "Social Organization and Differential Association: A Research Note from a Longitudinal Study of Violent Juvenile Offenders," *Crime and Delinquency* 34 (1988): 307–327.

80. Sue Titus Reed, *Crime and Criminology,* 2nd ed. (New York: Holt, Rinehart and Winston, 1979), p. 234.

81. See, for example, Albert Bandura, *Social Learning and Personality Development* (New York: Holt, Rinehart and Winston, 1963).

82. Ronald Akers, *Deviant Behavior: A Social Learning Approach,* 2nd ed. (Belmont, Calif.: Wadsworth, 1977).

83. Ronald Akers, Marvin Krohn, Lonn Lonza-Kaduce, and Marcia Radosevich, "Social Learning and Deviant Behavior: A Specific Test of a General Theory," *American Sociological Review* 44 (1979): 638.

84. Ibid.

85. Marvin Krohn, William Skinner, James Massey, and Ronald Akers, "Social Learning Theory and Adolescent Cigarette Smoking: A Longitudinal Study," *Social Problems* 32 (1985): 455–471.

86. Ibid., pp. 636–655.

87. Ronald Akers and Gang Lee, "A Longitudinal Test of Social Learning Theory: Adolescent Smoking," *Journal of Drug Issues* 26 (1996): 317–343.

88. Gary Jensen and David Brownfield, "Parents and Drugs," *Criminology* 21 (1983): 543–554.

89. Ronald Akers, "Rational Choice, Deterrence and Social Learning Theory in Criminology: The Path Not Taken," *Journal of Criminal Law and Criminology* 81 (1990): 653–676.

90. Gresham Sykes and David Matza, "Techniques of Neutralization: A Theory of Delinquency," *American Sociological Review* 22 (1957): 664–670; David Matza, *Delinquency and Drift* (New York: Wiley, 1964).

91. Matza, *Delinquency and Drift,* p. 51.

92. Sykes and Matza, "Techniques of Neutralization," pp. 664–670; see also David Matza, "Subterranean Traditions of Youths," *Annals of the American Academy of Political and Social Science* 378 (1961): 116.

93. Sykes and Matza, "Techniques of Neutralization."

94. Ibid.

95. Michael Hindelang, "The Commitment of Delinquents to Their Misdeeds: Do Delinquents Drift?" *Social Problems* 17 (1970): 509.

96. Robert Regoli and Eric Poole, "The Commitment of Delinquents to Their Misdeeds: A Reexamination," *Journal of Criminal Justice* 6 (1978): 261–269.

97. Robert Agnew, "The Techniques of Neutralization and Violence," *Criminology* 32 (1994): 555–579.

98. Robert Ball, "An Empirical Exploration of Neutralization Theory," *Criminologica* 4 (1966): 22–32. For a similar view, see M. William Minor, "The Neutralization of Criminal Offense," *Criminology* 18 (1980): 103–120.

99. Mark Pogrebin, Eric Poole, and Amos Martinez, "Accounts of Professional Misdeeds: The Sexual Exploitation of Clients by Psychotherapists," *Deviant Behavior* 13 (1992): 229–252.

100. Eric Wish, *Drug Use Forecasting 1990* (Washington, D.C.: National Institute of Justice, 1991).

101. Scott Briar and Irvin Piliavin, "Delinquency: Situational Inducements and Commitment to Conformity," *Social Problems* 13 (1965–1966): 35–45.

102. Lawrence Sherman and Douglas Smith, with Janell Schmidt and Dennis Rogan, "Crime, Punishment, and Stake in Conformity: Legal and Informal Control of Domestic Violence," *American Sociological Review* 57 (1992): 680–690.

103. Albert Reiss, "Delinquency as the Failure of Personal and Social Controls," *American Sociological Review* 16 (1951): 196–207.

104. Briar and Piliavin, "Delinquency: Situational Inducements and Commitment to Conformity."

105. John McCarthy and Dean Hoge, "The Dynamics of Self-Esteem and Delinquency," *American Journal of Sociology* 90 (1984): 396–410; Edward Wells and Joseph Rankin, "Self-Concept as a Mediating Concept in Delinquency," *Social Psychology Quarterly* 46 (1983): 11–22.

106. Howard Kaplan, *Deviant Behavior in Defense of Self* (New York: Academic Press, 1980); idem, "Self-Attitudes and Deviant Response," *Social Forces* 54 (1978): 788–801.

107. Howard Kaplan, Robert Johnson, and Carol Bailey, "Self-Rejection and the Explanation of Deviance: Refinement and Elaboration of a Latent Structure," *Social Psychology Quarterly* 49 (1986): 110–128.

108. L. Edward Wells, "Self-Enhancement Through Delinquency: A Conditional Test of Self-Derogation Theory," *Journal of Research in Crime and Delinquency* 26 (1989): 226–252.

109. See, generally, Walter Reckless, *The Crime Problem* (New York: Appleton-Century-Crofts, 1967). Among the many research reports by Walter Reckless and his colleagues are: Walter Reckless, Simon Dinitz, and Ellen Murray, "Self-Concept as an Insulator Against Delinquency," *American Sociological Review* 21 (1956): 744–746; Reckless, Dinitz, and Murray, "The Good Boy in a High Delinquency Area," *Journal of Criminal Law, Criminology, and Police Science* 48 (1957): 1826; Walter Reckless, Simon Dinitz, and Barbara Kay, "The Self-Component in Potential Delinquency and Potential Nondelinquency," *American Sociological Review* 22 (1957): 566–570; Reckless and Dinitz, "Pioneering with Self-Concept as a Vulnerability Factor in Delinquency," *Journal of Criminal Law, Criminology, and Police Science* 58 (1967): 515–523.

110. Travis Hirschi, *Causes of Delinquency* (Berkeley: University of California Press, 1969).

111. Ibid., p. 231.

112. Ibid., pp. 66–74.

113. Marc LeBlanc, "Family Dynamics, Adolescent Delinquency, and Adult Criminality," paper presented at the Society for Life History Research Conference, Keystone, Colorado, October 1990, p. 6.

114. Patricia Van Voorhis, Francis Cullen, Richard Mathers, and Connie Chenoweth Garner, "The Impact of Family Structure and Quality on Delinquency: A Comparative Assessment of Structural and Functional Factors," *Criminology* 26 (1988): 235–261.

115. Marc LeBlanc, Evelyne Valliere, and Pierre McDuff, "Adolescent's School Experience and Self-Reported Offending: A Longitudinal

Test of Social Control Theory," paper presented at the annual meeting of the American Society of Criminology, Baltimore, November 1990.

116. Marianne Junger and Wim Polder, "Some Explanations of Crime Among Four Ethnic Groups in the Netherlands," *Journal of Quantitative Criminology* 8 (1992): 51–78.

117. John Cochran and Ronald Akers, "An Exploration of the Variable Effects of Religiosity on Adolescent Marijuana and Alcohol Use," *Journal of Research in Crime and Delinquency* 26 (1989): 198–225.

118. Robert Agnew and David Peterson, "Leisure and Delinquency," *Social Problems* 36 (1989): 332–348.

119. Josine Junger-Tas, "An Empirical Test of Social Control Theory," *Journal of Quantitative Criminology* 8 (1992): 18–29.

120. Teresa Lagrange and Robert Silverman, "Perceived Strain and Delinquency Motivation: An Empirical Evaluation of General Strain Theory," paper presented at the American Society of Criminology meeting, Boston, November 1995.

121. For a review of exciting research, see Kimberly Kempf, "The Empirical Status of Hirschi's Control Theory," in *Advances in Criminological Theory,* ed. Bill Laufer and Freda Adler (New Brunswick, N.J.: Transaction Publishers, 1992).

122. Richard Lawrence, "Parents, Peers, School—and Delinquency," paper presented at the American Society of Criminology meeting, Boston, November 1995.

123. Peggy Giordano, Stephen Cernkovich, and M. D. Pugh, "Friendships and Delinquency," *American Journal of Sociology* 91 (1986): 1170–1202.

124. Denise Kandel and Mark Davies, "Friendship Networks, Intimacy, and Illicit Drug Use in Young Adulthood: A Comparison of Two Competing Theories," *Criminology* 29 (1991): 441–467.

125. Velmer Burton, Francis Cullen, T. David Evans, R. Gregory Dunaway, Sesha Kethineni, and Gary Payne, "The Impact of Parental Controls on Delinquency," *Journal of Criminal Justice* 23 (1995): 111–126.

126. Kimberly Kempf Leonard and Scott Decker, "The Theory of Social Control: Does It Apply to the Very Young?" *Journal of Criminal Justice* 22 (1994): 89–105.

127. Michael Hindelang, "Causes of Delinquency: A Partial Replication and Extension," *Social Problems* 21 (1973): 471–487.

128. Gary Jensen and David Brownfield, "Parents and Drugs," *Criminology* 21 (1983): 543–554. See also M. Wiatrowski, D. Griswold, and M. Roberts, "Social Control Theory and Delinquency," *American Sociological Review* 46 (1981): 525–541.

129. Leslie Samuelson, Timothy Hartnagel, and Harvey Krahn, "Crime and Social Control Among High School Dropouts," *Journal of Crime and Justice* 18 (1990): 129–161.

130. Mark Warr, "Parents, Peers, and Delinquency," *Social Forces* 72 (1993): 247–264.

131. Marvin Krohn and James Massey, "Social Control and Delinquent Behavior: An Examination of the Elements of the Social Bond," *Sociological Quarterly* 21 (1980): 529–543.

132. Jill Leslie Rosenbaum and James Lasley, "School, Community Context, and Delinquency: Rethinking the Gender Gap," *Justice Quarterly* 7 (1990): 493–513.

133. Randy LaGrange and Helene Raskin White, "Age Differences in Delinquency: A Test of Theory," *Criminology* 23 (1985): 19–45.

134. Robert Agnew, "Social Control Theory and Delinquency: A Longitudinal Test," *Criminology* 23 (1985): 47–61.

135. Alan E. Liska and M. D. Reed, "Ties to Conventional Institutions and Delinquency: Estimating Reciprocal Effects," *American Sociological Review* 50 (1985): 547–560.

136. Michael Wiatrowski, David Griswold, and Mary K. Roberts, "Social Control Theory and Delinquency," *American Sociological Review* 46 (1981): 525–541.

137. Ibid.

138. George Herbert Mead, *Mind, Self and Society* (Chicago: University of Chicago Press, 1934); idem, *The Philosophy of the Act* (Chicago:

University of Chicago Press, 1938); Charles Horton Cooley, *Human Nature and the Social Order* (New York: Schocken, 1964, originally published 1902); Herbert Blumer, *Symbolic Interactionism: Perspective and Method* (Englewood Cliffs, N.J.: Prentice-Hall, 1969).

139. Bruce Link, Elmer Streuning, Francis Cullen, Patrick Shrout, and Bruce Dohrenwend, "A Modified Labeling Theory Approach to Mental Disorders: An Empirical Assessment," *American Sociological Review* 54 (1989): 400–423.

140. Linda Jackson, John Hunter, and Carole Hodge, "Physical Attractiveness and Intellectual Competence: A Meta-Analytic Review," *Social Psychology Quarterly* 58 (1995): 108–122.

141. President's Commission on Law Enforcement and the Administration of Youth Crime, *Task Force Report: Juvenile Delinquency and Youth* (Washington, D.C.: U.S. Government Printing Office, 1967), p. 43.

142. Kai Erickson, "Notes on the Sociology of Deviance," *Social Problems* 9 (1962): 397–414.

143. Edwin Schur, *Labeling Deviant Behavior* (New York: Harper & Row, 1972), p. 21.

144. Howard Becker, *Outsiders: Studies in the Sociology of Deviance* (New York: Macmillan, 1963), p. 9.

145. Christy Visher, "Gender, Police Arrest Decision, and Notions of Chivalry," *Criminology* 21 (1983): 5–28.

146. Marjorie Zatz, "Race, Ethnicity and Determinate Sentencing," *Criminology* 22 (1984): 147–171.

147. Roland Chilton and Jim Galvin, "Race, Crime and Criminal Justice," *Crime and Delinquency* 31 (1985): 3–14.

148. Joan Petersilia, "Racial Disparities in the Criminal Justice System: A Summary," *Crime and Delinquency* 31 (1985): 15–34.

149. Walter Gove, *The Labeling of Deviance: Evaluating a Perspective* (New York: Wiley, 1975), p. 5.

150. Harold Garfinkle, "Conditions of Successful Degradation Ceremonies," *American Journal of Sociology* 61 (1956): 420–424.

151. John Lofland, *Deviance and Identity* (Englewood Cliffs, N.J.: Prentice-Hall, 1969).

152. Frank Tannenbaum, *Crime and the Community* (New York: Columbia University Press, 1938), pp. 19–20.

153. Edwin Lemert, *Social Pathology* (New York: McGraw-Hill, 1951).

154. Ibid., p. 75.

155. See, for example, Howard Kaplan and Hiroshi Fukurai, "Negative Social Sanctions, Self-Rejection, and Drug Use," *Youth and Society* 23 (1992): 275–298.

156. Howard Kaplan, *Toward a General Theory of Deviance: Contributions from Perspectives on Deviance and Criminality* (College Station: Texas A&M University, n.d.).

157. Howard Kaplan and Robert Johnson, "Negative Social Sanctions and Juvenile Delinquency: Effects of Labeling in a Model of Deviant Behavior," *Social Science Quarterly* 72 (1991): 98–122; Howard Kaplan, Robert Johnson, and Carol Bailey, "Deviant Peers and Deviant Behavior: Further Elaboration of a Model," *Social Psychology Quarterly* 30 (1987): 277–284.

158. Karen Heimer and Ross Matsueda, "Role-Taking, Role-Commitment and Delinquency: A Theory of Differential Social Control," *American Sociological Review* 59 (1994): 400–437.

159. Karen Heimer, "Gender, Race, and the Pathways to Delinquency: An Interactionist Explanation," in *Crime and Inequality,* ed. John Hagan and Ruth Peterson (Stanford, Calif.: Stanford University Press, 1995).

160. National Minority Council on Criminal Justice, *The Inequality of Justice* (Washington, D.C.: National Minority Advisory Council on Criminal Justice, 1981), p. 200.

161. Carl Pope and William Feyerherm, "Minority Status and Juvenile Justice Processing," *Criminal Justice Abstracts* 22 (1990): 327–336; see also Carl Pope, "Race and Crime Revisited," *Crime and Delinquency* 25 (1979): 347–357.

162. Leslie Margolin, "Deviance on Record: Techniques for Labeling Child Abusers in Official Documents," *Social Problems* 39 (1992): 58–68.

163. Charles Corley, Stephen Cernkovich, and Peggy Giordano, "Sex and the Likelihood of Sanction," *Journal of Criminal Law and Criminology* 80 (1989): 540–553.

164. Howard Kaplan and Robert Johnson, "Negative Social Sanctions and Juvenile Delinquency: Effects of Labeling in a Model of Deviant Behavior."

165. Ruth Triplett, "The Conflict Perspective, Symbolic Interactionism, and the Status Characteristics Hypothesis," *Justice Quarterly* 10 (1993): 540–558.

166. Ross Matsueda, "Reflected Appraisals, Parental Labeling, and Delinquency: Specifying a Symbolic Interactionist Theory," *American Journal of Sociology* 97 (1992): 1577–1611.

167. Suzanne Ageton and Delbert Elliott, *The Effect of Legal Processing on Self-Concept* (Boulder, Colo.: Institute of Behavioral Science, 1973).

168. Christine Bowditch, "Getting Rid of Troublemakers: High School Disciplinary Procedures and the Production of Dropouts," *Social Problems* 40 (1993): 493–507.

169. Melvin Ray and William Downs, "An Empirical Test of Labeling Theory Using Longitudinal Data," *Journal of Research in Crime and Delinquency* 23 (1986): 169–194.

170. Sherman and Smith, with Schmidt and Rogan, "Crime, Punishment, and Stake in Conformity."

171. Charles Tittle, "Two Empirical Regularities (Maybe) in Search of an Explanation: Commentary on the Age/Crime Debate," *Criminology* 26 (1988): 75–85.

172. Douglas Smith and Robert Brame, "On the Initiation and Continuation of Delinquency," *Criminology* 4 (1994): 607–630.

173. Jack Gibbs, "Conceptions of Deviant Behavior: The Old and the New," *Pacific Sociological Review* 9 (1966): 11–13.

174. Schur, *Labeling Deviant Behavior,* p. 14.

175. Ronald Akers, "Problems in the Sociology of Deviance," *Social Problems* 46 (1968): 463.

176. Charles Wellford, "Labeling Theory and Criminology: An Assessment," *Social Problems* 22 (1975): 335–347.

177. Ibid., p. 337.

178. Alexander Liazos, "The Poverty of the Sociology of Deviance: Nuts, Sluts, and Perverts," *Social Problems* 20 (1971): 103–120.

179. Tittle, "Two Empirical Regularities (Maybe) in Search of an Explanation."

180. Paul Lipsett, "The Juvenile Offender's Perception," *Crime and Delinquency* 14 (1968): 49; Jack Foster, Simon Dinitz, and Walter Reckless, "Perception of Stigma Following Public Intervention for Delinquent Behavior," *Social Problems* 20 (1972): 202.

181. Charles Tittle, "Labeling and Crime: An Empirical Evaluation," in *The Labeling of Deviance: Evaluating a Perspective,* ed. Walter Gove (New York: Wiley, 1975), pp. 157–179.

182. David Farrington, "Early Predictors of Adolescent Aggression and Adult Violence," *Violence and Victims* 4 (1989): 79–100.

183. Raymond Paternoster and Leeann Iovanni, "The Labeling Perspective and Delinquency: An Elaboration of the Theory and an Assessment of the Evidence," *Justice Quarterly* 6 (1989): 358–394.

Chapter 9
Social Conflict Theory

I t would be unusual to pick up the morning paper and not see headlines loudly proclaiming renewed strife between the United States and its overseas adversaries, between union negotiators and management attorneys, between citizens and police authorities, or between outspoken feminists and reactionary males protecting their turf. The world is filled with conflict. Conflict can be destructive when it leads to war, violence, and death; it can be functional when it results in positive social change. Criminologists who view crime as a function of social conflict and economic rivalry are aligned with a number of schools of thought, referred to as the conflict, critical, Marxist, or radical schools of criminology, or one of their affiliated branches, including but not limited to peacemaking, left realism, radical feminism, and deconstructionism (see Figure 9.1).

The goal of social conflict theorists is to explain crime within economic and social contexts and to express the connections among social class, crime, and social control.[1] Social conflict theorists are concerned with such issues as the role government plays in creating a criminogenic environment; the relationship of personal or group power in controlling and shaping the criminal law; the role of bias in the operations of the justice system; and the relationship between a capitalist free-enterprise economy and crime rates.

Conflict theorists view crime as the outcome of class struggle. Conflict works to promote crime by creating a

Figure 9.1 The branches of social conflict theory.

social atmosphere in which the law is a mechanism for controlling dissatisfied, have-not members of society while maintaining the position of the powerful. That is why crimes that are the province of the wealthy, such as illegal corporate activities, are sanctioned much more leniently than those, such as burglary, that are considered lower-class activities.

> ## Connections
> As you may recall from Chapter 1, the philosophical and economic analysis of Karl Marx forms the historical roots of the conflict perspective of criminology.

Karl Marx identified the economic structures in society that he felt controlled all human relations. Theorists who use Marxian analysis reject the notion that law is designed to maintain a tranquil and fair society and that criminals are malevolent people who wish to trample the rights of others. Conflict theorists consider such acts as racism, sexism, imperialism, unsafe working conditions, inadequate child care, substandard housing, pollution of the environment, and war making as "true crimes." The crimes of the helpless—burglary, robbery, and assault—are more expressions of rage over unjust conditions than being actual crimes.[2] By focusing on the state's role in producing crime, Marxist thought serves as the basis for all social conflict theory.

This chapter reviews criminological theories that allege that criminal behavior is a function of conflict, a reaction to the unfair distribution of wealth and power in society. The social conflict perspective has several independent branches. One, generally referred to as **conflict theory,** assumes that crime is caused by the intergroup conflict and rivalry that exist in every society. A second branch focuses more directly on the crime-producing traits of capitalist society; the various schools of thought in this area of scholarship include critical, radical, and Marxist criminology.[3] Other sections are devoted to feminist, new realist, peacemaking, and deconstructionist thought. Hereafter, the terms radical and Marxist criminology will be used interchangeably, and, where appropriate, distinctions will be made between the various schools of thought they contain.

Marxist Thought

Karl Marx lived in an era of unrestrained capitalist expansion.[4] The tools of the Industrial Revolution had become regular features of society by 1850. Mechanized factories, the use of coal to drive steam engines, and modern transportation all inspired economic development. Production had shifted from cottage industries to large factories. Industrialists could hire workers on their own terms, and conditions in their factories were atrocious. Trade unions that promised workers salvation from these atrocities were ruthlessly suppressed by owners and government agents.

Marx had found his early career as a journalist interrupted by government suppression of the newspaper where he worked because of its liberal editorial policy. He then moved to Paris, where he met Friedrich Engels (1820–1895), who would become his friend and economic patron. By 1847 Marx and Engels had joined with a group of primarily German socialist revolutionaries known as the Communist League.

Productive Forces and Productive Relations

In 1848 Marx issued his famous manifesto—a statement of his ideas. Marx focused his attention on the economic conditions of the capitalist system. He believed its development had turned workers into a dehumanized mass who lived an existence that was at the mercy of their capitalist employers. Young children were sent to work in mines and factories from dawn to dusk. People were being beaten down by a system that demanded obedience and cooperation and offered little in return. These oppressive conditions led Marx to conclude that the character of every civilization is determined by its mode of production—the way its people develop and produce material goods (materialism).

Net Bookmark

Want to learn just about everything there is to know about Marxist theory? The Marxism-Leninism Project sets out the theories of Marxism in the words of the founders of Marxism and of their best-known followers. It is therefore a collection of their writings, selected to give the most comprehensive account of Marxism possible within the limits of a single web site.

http://www.idbsu.edu/surveyrc/Staff/jaynes/marxism/intro.html

Production has two components: (1) productive forces, which include such things as technology, energy sources, and material resources; and (2) productive relations, which are the relationships that exist among the people producing goods and services. The most important relationship in industrial culture is between the owners of the means of production, the *capitalist bourgeoisie,* and the people who do the actual labor, the *proletariat.* Throughout history, society has been organized this way—master-slave, lord-serf, and now capitalist-proletarian. According to Marx and Engels, capitalist society is subject to the development of a rigid class structure. At the top is the capitalist bourgeoisie. Next come the working proletariat who actually produce goods and services. At the bottom of society are the fringe members who produce nothing and live, parasitically, off the work of others—the lumpen proletariat.

In Marxist theory, the term *class* does not refer to an attribute or characteristic of a person or a group; rather, it denotes position in relation to others. Thus, it is not necessary to have a particular amount of wealth or prestige to be a member of the capitalist class; it is more important to have the power to exploit others economically, legally, and socially. The political and economic philosophy of the dominant class influences all aspects of life. Consciously or unconsciously, artists, writers, and teachers bend their work to the whims of the capitalist system. Thus, the economic system controls all facets of human life; consequently, people's lives revolve around the means of production. As Marx wrote:

> In all forms of society, there is one specific kind of production which predominates over the rest, whose relations thus assign rank and influence to the others. It is a general illumination which bathes all the other colours and modifies their particularity. It is a particular ether which determines the specific gravity of every being which has materialized within it.[5]

Marx believed that societies and their structures are not stable but can change through slow evolution or sudden violence. Historically, such change occurs because of contradictions present in a society. These contradictions are antagonisms or conflicts between elements in the existing social arrangement that in the long run are incompatible with one another. If these social conflicts are not resolved, they tend to destabilize society, leading to social change.

Surplus Value

How could social change occur in capitalist society? Marx held that the laboring class produces goods that exceed wages in value (the theory of **surplus value**). The excess value goes into the hands of the capitalists as profit; they then use most of it to acquire an ever-expanding capitalist base that relies on advanced technology for efficiency. Since capitalists are in constant competition with each other, they must find ways of producing goods more efficiently and cheaply. One way is to pay workers the lowest possible wages or to replace them with labor-saving machinery (see Figure 9.2). Soon the supply of efficiently made goods outstrips the ability of the laboring classes to purchase them, a condition that precipitates an economic crisis. During this period, weaker enterprises go under and are consequently incorporated into ever-expanding, monopolistic megacorporations strong enough to further exploit the workers. Marx believed that in the ebb and flow of the business cycle, the capitalist system contains the seeds of its own destruction and that from its ashes will grow a socialist state in which the workers themselves will own the means of production.

In his analysis, Marx used the **dialectic method,** based on the analysis developed by the philosopher Georg Hegel (1770–1831). Hegel argued that for every idea, or *thesis,* there exists an opposing argument, or *antithesis.* Since neither position can ever be truly accepted, the result is a merger of the two ideas, a *synthesis.* Marx adapted this analytic method for his study of class struggle. History, argued Marx, is replete with examples of two opposing forces whose conflict promotes social change. When conditions

Figure 9.2 The theory of surplus value: As surplus value increases, working people suffer.

- Labor produces goods that exceed wages in value
- Surplus value (profit) goes to capitalists
- To increase surplus value:
  Lower pay
  Automation

are bad enough, the oppressed will rise up to fight the owners and eventually replace them. Thus, in the end, the capitalist system will destroy itself.

Marx on Crime

Marx did not write a great deal on the subject of crime, but he mentioned it in a variety of passages scattered throughout his writing. He viewed crime as the product of law enforcement policies akin to a labeling process theory.[6] He also saw a connection between criminality and the inequities found in the capitalist system. He stated: "There must be something rotten in the very core of a social system which increases in wealth without diminishing its misery, and increases in crime even more rapidly than in numbers."[7]

However, Marx's collaborator, Friedrich Engels, did spend some time on the subject in his work *The Condition of the Working Class in England in 1844.*[8] Engels portrayed crime as a function of *social demoralization*—a collapse of people's humanity reflecting a decline in society. Workers, demoralized by capitalist society, are caught up in a process that leads to crime and violence. Workers were social outcasts, ignored by the structure of capitalist society and treated as brutes.[9] Left to their own devices, working people commit crime because their choice is a slow death of starvation or a speedy one at the hands of the law. The brutality of the capitalist system turns workers into animal-like creatures without a will of their own.

Developing a Social Conflict Theory of Crime

The writings of Karl Marx and Friedrich Engels greatly influenced the development of social conflict thinking. Although Marx himself did not write much on the topic of crime, his views on the relationship between the economic structure and social behavior deeply influenced other thinkers. Conflict theory was first applied to criminology by three distinguished scholars, Willem Bonger, Ralf Dahrendorf, and George Vold. In some instances, their works share the Marxist view that industrial society is wracked by conflict between the proletariat and the bourgeoisie; in other instances, their writings diverge from Marxist dogma. Here we will briefly discuss the writings of each of these pioneers.

The Contribution of Willem Bonger

Willem Bonger was born in 1876 in Holland and committed suicide in 1940, rather than submit to Nazi rule. He is famous for his Marxist/socialist concepts of crime causation, which were first published in 1916.[10]

Bonger believed that crime is of social and not biological origin and that, with the exception of a few special cases, crime lies within the boundaries of normal human behavior. The response to crime is punishment—the application of penalties considered more severe than spontaneous moral condemnation. It is administered by those in political control—that is, by the state. No act is naturally immoral or criminal. Crimes are antisocial acts that reflect current morality. Since the social structure is changing continually, ideas of what is moral and what is not change continually. The tension between rapidly changing morality, which is common in modern society, and a comparatively static, predominantly bourgeois criminal law can become very great.

Bonger believed that society is divided into have and have-not groups, not on the basis of people's innate ability but because of the system of production that is in force. In every society that is divided into a ruling class and an inferior class, penal law serves the will of the former. Even though criminal laws may appear to protect members of both classes, hardly any act is punished that does not injure the interests of the dominant class. Crimes are thus considered to be antisocial acts because they are harmful to those who have the power at their command to control society.

Bonger argued that attempts to control law violations through force are a sign of a weak society. The capitalist system, characterized by extreme competition, is held together by force rather than consensus. The social order is maintained for the benefit of the capitalists at the expense of the population as a whole. Bonger argued that all people desire wealth and happiness. Unfortunately, in a capitalist society people can enjoy luxuries and advantages only if they possess large amounts of capital. People are encouraged by capitalist society to be *egoistic,* caring only for their own lives and pleasures and ignoring the plight of the disadvantaged. As a consequence of this environment, Bonger claimed, people have become more egoistic and more capable of crime than if the system had developed under a socialist philosophy.

Although the capitalist system makes both the proletariat and the bourgeoisie crime-prone, only the former are likely to become officially recognized criminals. The key to this problem is that the legal system discriminates against the poor by legalizing the egoistic actions of the wealthy. Upper-class individuals (the bourgeoisie), will commit crime if (a) they have an opportunity to gain an illegal advantage and (b) their lack of moral sense enables them to violate social rules. It is the drive toward success at any price that pushes wealthier individuals toward criminality. Recognized, official crimes are a function of poverty. The relationship can be direct, as when a person steals to survive, or indirect, as when poverty kills the social sentiments in each person and between people.

It is not the absolute amount of wealth that affects crime but its distribution. If wealth is distributed unequally through the social structure and people are taught to equate economic advantage with superiority, those who are poor and therefore inferior will be crime-prone. The economic system will intensify any personal disadvantage people have—for example, psychological problems—and increase their propensity to commit crime.

Bonger concluded that almost all crime will disappear if society progresses from competitive capitalism, to monopoly capitalism, to having the means of production held in common, to the ultimate state of society—the redistribution of property according to the communist maxim of "to each according to his needs." If this stage of society cannot be reached, a residue of crime will always remain. If socialism can be achieved, then remaining crimes will be of the irrational psychopathic type caused by individual mental problems. Bonger's writing continues to be one of the most often-cited sources of Marxist thought.

The Contribution of Ralf Dahrendorf

In formulating their views, today's conflict theorists also rely heavily on the writings of pioneering social thinker Ralf Dahrendorf.[11] Dahrendorf believed that modern society is organized into what he called *imperatively coordinated associations.* These associations comprise two groups: those who possess authority and use it for social domination and those who lack authority and are dominated. Since the domination of one segment of society (for example, industry) does not mean dominating another (such as government), society is a plurality of competing interest groups.

In his classic work, *Class and Class Conflict in Industrial Society,* Dahrendorf attempted to show how society has changed since Marx formulated his concepts of class, state, and conflict. Dahrendorf argued that Marx did not foresee the changes that have occurred in the laboring classes. "The working class of today," Dahrendorf stated, "far from being a homogeneous group of equally unskilled and impoverished people, is in fact a stratum differentiated by numerous subtle and not so subtle distinctions."[12] Workers are divided into the unskilled, semiskilled, and skilled; the interests of one group may not match the needs of the others; Marx's concept of a cohesive proletarian class has proved inaccurate. Consequently, Dahrendorf embraced a non-Marxist conflict orientation. Dahrendorf proposed a unified conflict theory of human behavior, which can be summarized in the following four statements:

- Every society is at every point subject to processes of change; social change is everywhere.
- Every society displays at every point dissent and conflict; social conflict is everywhere.
- Every element in a society renders a contribution to its disintegration and change.
- Every society is based on the coercion of some of its members by others.

Dahrendorf did not speak directly to the issue of crime, but his model of conflict serves as a pillar of modern conflict criminology.

The Contribution of George Vold

Although Dahrendorf contributed its theoretical underpinnings, social conflict theory was actually adapted to criminology by George Vold.[13] Vold argued that crime can also be explained by social conflict. Laws are created by politically oriented groups who seek the assistance of the government to help them defend their rights and protect their interests. If a group can marshal enough support, a law will be created to hamper and curb the interests of some opposing group. As Vold wrote, "The whole political process of law making, law breaking and law enforcement becomes a direct reflection of deep-seated and fundamental conflicts between interest groups and their more general struggles for the control of the police power of the state." Every stage of the process—from the passage of the law, to the prosecution of the case, to the relationships between inmate and guard, parole agent and parolee—is marked by conflict.

Vold found that criminal acts are a consequence of direct contact between forces struggling to control society. Although their criminal content may mask their political meaning, closer examination of even the most basic violent acts often reveals political undertones.

Vold's model cannot be used to explain all types of crime. It is limited to situations in which rival group loyalties collide. It cannot explain impulsive, irrational acts unrelated to any group's interest. Despite this limitation, Vold found that a great deal of criminal activity results from intergroup clashes.

Modern Conflict Theory

Conflict theory came into criminological prominence during the 1960s. Vold and Dahrendorf had published their influential works in the late 1950s. At the same time, self-report studies were yielding data suggesting that crime and delinquency were much more evenly distributed through the social structure than had been indicated by the official statistics.[14] If this was true, then middle-class participation in crime was going unrecorded, while the lower class was the subject of discriminatory law enforcement practices.

Criminologists began to view the justice system as a mechanism to control the lower class and maintain the status quo, rather than as the means of dispensing fair and evenhanded justice.[15] The publication of important labeling perspective works, such as Lemert's *Social Pathology* and Becker's *Outsiders,* also contributed to the development of the conflict model.[16] Labeling theorists rejected the notion that crime is morally wrong and called for the analysis of the interaction among crime, criminal, victim, and social control agencies. Some criminologists charged that labeling theory did not go far enough in analyzing the important relationships in society, charging that labeling theorists were content with studying "nuts, sluts and perverts."[17]

Because they felt the labeling perspective was apolitical, a group of criminologists began to produce scholarship and research directed at (1) identifying "real" crimes in U.S. society, such as profiteering, sexism, and racism; (2) evaluating how the criminal law is used as a mechanism of social control; and (3) turning the attention of citizens to the inequities in U.S. society.[18] One of these sociologists, David Greenberg, comments on the scholarship that was produced:

> The theme that dominated much of the work in this area was the contention that criminal legislation was determined not by moral consensus or the common interests of the entire society, but by relative power of groups determined to use the criminal law to advance their own special interests or to impose their moral preferences on others.[19]

This movement was aided by the general and widespread social and political upheaval of the late 1960s and early '70s. These forces included anti–Vietnam war demonstrations, counterculture movements, and various forms of political protest. Conflict theory flourished within this framework, since it provided a systematic basis for challenging the legitimacy of the government's creation and application of law. The crackdown on political dissidents by agents of the federal government, the prosecution of draft resisters, and the like all seemed designed to maintain control in the hands of political powerbrokers.

Conflict Criminology

In the early 1970s, conflict theory began to have a significant influence on criminological study. Several influential scholars, inspired by the writings of Dahrendorf and Vold,

According to conflict theory, power is the means by which people shape public opinion to meet their personal interests. Here the family of Castine Deveroux, missing in the Oklahoma City bombing, display their grief in the aftermath of a destructive show of power. Political terrorism and violence may be the product of social conflict.

abandoned the criminological mainstream and adopted a conflict orientation. William Chambliss and Robert Seidman wrote the well-respected treatise *Law, Order and Power,* which documented how the justice system operates to protect the rich and powerful. After closely observing the system's operations, Chambliss and Seidman drew this conclusion:

> In America it is frequently argued that to have "freedom" is to have a system which allows one group to make a profit over another. To maintain the existing legal system requires a choice. That choice is between maintaining a legal system that serves to support the existing economic system with its power structure and developing an equitable legal system accompanied by the loss of "personal freedom." But the old question comes back to plague us: Freedom for whom? Is the black man who provides such a ready source of cases for the welfare workers, the mental hospitals, and the prisons "free"? Are the slum dwellers who are arrested night after night for "loitering," "drunkenness," or being "suspicious" free? The freedom protected by the system of law is the freedom of those who can afford it. The law serves their interests, but they are not "society"; they are one element of society. They may in some complex societies even be a majority (though this is very rare), but the myth that the law serves the interests of "society" misrepresents the facts.[20]

We can observe in Chambliss and Seidman's writing some of the common objectives of conflict criminology: to describe how the control of the political and economic system affects the administration of criminal justice; to show how the definitions of crime favor those who control the justice system; and to analyze the role of conflict in contemporary society. Their scholarship also reflects another major objective of conflict theory: to show how justice in U.S. society is skewed so that those who deserve to be punished the most (wealthy white-collar criminals whose crimes cost society millions of dollars) are actually punished the least, while those whose crimes are relatively minor and committed out of economic necessity (petty, underclass thieves) receive the stricter sanctions.[21]

POWER RELATIONS. Another motive of conflict theory is to describe the criminogenic influence of social and economic **power**—the ability of persons and groups to determine and control the behavior of others. The unequal distribution of power produces conflict; conflict is rooted in the competition for power. Power is the means by which people shape public opinion to meet their personal interests. According to the conflict view, crime is defined by those in power; laws are culturally relative and not bound by any absolute standard of right and wrong.[22] The ability of the powerful to control people is exemplified by the relationship between the justice system and African Americans.

The subtle and not-so-subtle ways the justice system victimizes African Americans has been well documented.[23] Poor ghetto youths are driven to commit crimes that get them processed by the system. Discretionary decisions by law enforcement officers brand them felons and not misdemeanants; they are shunted into the criminal courts and not diversion programs. Busy public defenders too often short-shrift their clients into plea bargains that assure early criminal records. Health care workers and teachers are quick to report suspected violent acts to the police, resulting in frequent and early arrests of minority adults and youths. Police departments routinely use policies of searching, questioning, and detaining all African American males in an area if a violent criminal has been described as looking or sounding black. By creating the image of pervasive black criminality and coupling it with unfair treatment, those in power further alienate poor blacks from the mainstream, perpetuating a class- and race-divided society. It is not surprising, then, that surveys show that African Americans are much more likely to perceive "criminal injustice" than white Americans.[24]

THE SOCIAL REALITY OF CRIME. Richard Quinney is one of the most influential conflict theorists. He integrated his beliefs about power, society, and criminality into a theory he referred to as the **social reality of crime.** The theory's six propositions are contained in Table 9.1.[25] According to Quinney, criminal definitions (law) represent the interests of those who hold power in society. Where conflict exists between social groups—for example, the wealthy and the poor—those who hold power will create laws to benefit themselves and hold rivals in check. So the rather harsh punishments for property crime in the United States are designed to help those who already have wealth keep it in their possession; in contrast, the lenient sanctions attached to corporate crimes are designed to give the already powerful a free hand at economic exploitation.

Quinney wrote that the formulation of criminal definitions is based on such factors as (1) changing social conditions; (2) emerging interests; (3) increasing demands that political, economic, and religious interests be protected; and (4) changing conceptions of public interest. In his sixth statement on the social reality of crime, Quinney pulled together the ideas he developed in the preceding five: Concepts of crime are controlled by the powerful, and the criminal justice system works to secure the needs of the powerful. When people develop behavior patterns that conflict with these needs, the agents of the rich—the justice system—define them as criminals. Because of their reliance on power relations, criminal definitions are a constantly changing set of concepts that mirror the political organization of society. Law is not an abstract body of rules that represents an absolute moral code. Law is an integral part of society, a force that represents a way of life and a method of doing things. Crime is a function of power relations and an inevitable result of social conflict. Criminals are not simply social misfits but people who have come up short in the struggle for success and are seeking alternative means of achieving wealth, status, or even survival.[26] Consequently,

Table 9.1 Propositions of the Social Reality of Crime

1. *Definition of crime:* Crime is a definition of human conduct that is created by authorized agents in a politically organized society.
2. *Formulation of criminal definition:* Criminal definitions describe behaviors that conflict with the interests of the segments of society that have the power to shape public policy.
3. *Application of criminal definitions:* Criminal definitions are applied by the segments of society that have the power to shape the enforcement and administration of criminal law.
4. *Development of behavior patterns in relation to criminal definitions:* Behavior patterns are structured in segmentally organized society in relation to criminal definitions, and within this context, persons engage in actions that have relative probabilities of being defined as criminal.
5. *Construction of criminal conceptions:* Conceptions of crime are constructed and diffused in the segments of society by various means of communication.
6. *The social reality of crime:* The social reality of crime is constructed by the formulation and applications of criminal definitions, the development of behavior patterns to criminal definitions, and the construction of criminal conceptions.

Source: Richard Quinney, *The Social Reality of Crime* (Boston: Little, Brown, 1970), pp. 15–23.

law violations can be viewed as political or even quasi-revolutionary acts.[27]

Connections

Quinney has changed his theoretical outlook over his long and distinguished career. He is now a leader of the Zen-inspired peacemaking movement, which seeks to remove violence and coercion from the criminal justice system and promotes healing or "restorative justice." See the section on peacemaking later in this chapter.

NORM RESISTANCE. Other writers have made influential contributions to the formation of a general conflict criminology. Austin Turk wrote that authority relationships are inevitable and that they produce social conflict. Those in society who dominate (the "authorities") are in conflict with those who are controlled by, but have little ability to control, the law (the "subjects"). Conflict is inherent in this superior-subordinate relationship because both groups have their own sets of *cultural norms* (those that express ideals and values) and *social norms* (actual group behaviors). Interaction between authorities and subjects eventually produces **norm resistance,** or open conflict between the two groups, which can take on a number of different forms. The probability of norm resistance is highest under certain conditions:

1. Authorities and subjects are both strongly committed to their cultural norms, which are in opposition to each other.

2. Subjects receive social support from their peers. People with group support will be resistant to authority or change.

3. Subjects lack sophistication. People who are sophisticated, who can accurately assess the strengths and weaknesses of their opponents, will be better able to avoid conflict with authorities.[28]

Research on Conflict Theory

Research efforts designed to test conflict theory seem quite different from those that evaluate consensus models. Similar methodologies are often used, but conflict-centered research places less emphasis on testing the hypotheses of a particular theory and instead attempts to show that conflict principles hold up under empirical scrutiny. Areas of interest include comparing the crime rates of members of powerless groups with those of members of the elite classes, examining the operation of the justice system to uncover bias and discrimination, and attempting to chart the historical development of criminal law and identify laws created with the intent of preserving the power of the elite classes at the expense of the poor.

Conflict theorists maintain that social inequality creates the need for people to commit some crimes, such as burglary and larceny, as a means of social and economic survival, and to commit others, such as assault, homicide, and drug use, as a means of expressing rage, frustration, and anger. Conflict theorists point to data showing that crime rates vary according to indicators of poverty and need. For example, David McDowall compared homicide rates in Detroit, Baltimore, Cleveland, and Memphis with infant mortality rates over a 50-year period (since the latter variable is an efficient measure of poverty) and found that the two rates were significantly interrelated.[29] Other data collected by ecologists show that crime is strongly related to measures of social inequality, such as income level, deteriorated living conditions, and relative economic deprivation.[30]

Another area of conflict-oriented research focuses on the operations of the criminal justice system: Does it operate as an instrument of class oppression or as a fair and even-handed social control agency? Some conflict researchers have found evidence of class bias. For example, criminologists David Jacobs and David Britt found that state jurisdictions with significant levels of economic disparity were also the most likely to have the largest number of police shooting fatalities. Their data suggest that police act more forcefully in areas where class conflicts create the percep-

tion that extreme forms of social control are needed to maintain order.[31] Similarly, Alan Lizotte examined criminal cases processed by the Chicago criminal courts and found that members of powerless, disenfranchised groups are the most likely to receive prejudicial sentences in criminal courts.[32] Other research efforts have shown that both white and black offenders are more likely to receive stricter sentences in criminal courts if their personal characteristics (single, young, urban, male) give them the appearance of being a member of the **dangerous classes.**[33]

Conflict theorists also point to studies showing that the criminal justice system is quick to take action when the victim of crime is wealthy, white, and male but uninterested when the victim is poor, black, and female, indicating how power positions affect justice.[34] It is not surprising, then, that Thomas Arvanites's analysis of national population trends and imprisonment rates shows that as the percentage of minority-group members increases, the imprisonment rate does likewise.[35] This outcome, suggests Arvanites, may be a function of society becoming "less tolerant of nonwhite populations and/or feeling more threatened by them." Data showing racial and class discrimination by the justice systems support conflict theory.[36]

One reason for such displays of discrimination may be the attitudes of decision makers. For example, Michael Leiber and his associates have shown that justice professionals who express racist values (that is, who consider racial differences to exist) are also more punitive and believe that courts should be stricter and that the death penalty is an effective deterrent. These researchers feel that it would not be surprising if these decision makers let race affect their judgments.[37] In another study, Leiber and Katherine Jamieson found that race has varying and subtle effects on decision making in the juvenile justice system.[38] Critical thinkers would argue that there must be a thorough rethinking of the role and purpose of the criminal justice system, giving the powerless a greater voice to express their needs and concerns, if these inequities are to be addressed.[39]

Net Bookmark

Conflict theorists suggest that governments oppress dissidents and minority-group members all over the world. Conflict is certainly not unique to the United States. Amnesty International is a nonprofit group that fights for the rights of the oppressed internationally. To learn more about what this group is doing, visit their information page:

http://www.amnesty.org/

There is still need to directly test the hypotheses of specific conflict theories. One of the few direct tests of Turk's norm resistance model, conducted by Richard Greenleaf and Lonn Lanza-Kaduce, found empirical support for the theory's core hypothesis. Using data on police-encounters in domestic disputes, Greenleaf and Lanza-Kaduce found that measures of sophistication and organization, key components of Turk's theory, predicted police officer–citizen conflict. Similar research efforts are needed to test the basic premises of specific conflict theories.[40]

Analysis of Conflict Theory

Conflict theorists attempt to identify the power relations in society and draw attention to their role in promoting criminal behavior. The aim is to describe how class differentials produce an ecology of human behavior that favors the wealthy and powerful over the poor and weak. To believe their view, we must reject the consensus view of crime, which states that law represents the values of the majority, that legal codes are designed to create a just society, and that by breaking the law criminals are predators who violate the rights of others. To a conflict theorist, the criminal law is a weapon used by the affluent to maintain their dominance in the class struggle. This view certainly has its critics. Some criminologists consider the conflict view "naive," suggesting instead that crime is a matter of rational choice made by offenders motivated more by greed and selfishness than poverty and hopelessness.[41]

Critics also point to data indicating only a weak relationship between indicators of economic factors and crime rates; such data indicate that crime is less likely to be a function of poverty and class conflict than a product of personal needs, socialization, or some other related factor.[42] For example, while Arvanites's research found that race influenced imprisonment, he found little clear-cut evidence that economic factors, such as unemployment rates or poverty levels, influenced crime rates.[43]

Similarly, studies of the criminal justice process, including police discretion, criminal court sentencing, and correctional policy, have not all found indicators of class or race bias, an outcome predicted by conflict theory.[44] Theodore Chiricos and Gordon Waldo examined the prison sentences of 10,488 inmates in three southeastern states and concluded that socioeconomic status was unrelated to the length of prison terms assigned by the courts.[45] Stephen Klein, Joan Petersilia, and Susan Turner evaluated sentencing decisions in California and found little evidence of race bias; African Americans were neither more likely to be sent to prison than white offenders nor to receive longer prison terms.[46] Evidence that the justice system is not class- and race biased refutes conflict theory and supports consensus, traditional criminology.

There is also cross-cultural research indicating that crime rates are not reduced when a free-market system is replaced by a less-competitive economic model. One analysis of crime in the African country of Tanzania found that when the free enterprise system was replaced by a socialist system, the crime rate actually increased. New crimes, such as theft by public servants and corruption, appear to increase in response to government policies establishing socialism.[47]

Despite these critiques, conflict theory has had an important niche in the criminological literature. However, more radical versions of the general conflict model have become predominant, and attention is now turned to these more critical versions of social conflict theory.

Marxist Criminology

Above all, Marxism is a critique of capitalism.[48]

Marxist criminologists view crime as a function of the capitalist mode of production: Capitalism produces haves and have-nots, each engaging in a particular branch of criminality.[49] In a capitalist society, those in political power also control the definition of crime and the emphasis of the criminal justice system.[50] Consequently, the only crimes available to the poor, or proletariat, are the severely sanctioned "street crimes": rape, murder, theft, and mugging. Members of the middle class, or petit bourgeoisie, cheat on their taxes and engage in petty corporate crime (employee theft), acts that generate social disapproval but are rarely punished severely. The wealthy bourgeoisie are involved in acts that should be described as crimes but are not—racism, sexism, and profiteering. Though there are regulatory laws to control business activities, these are rarely enforced, and violations are lightly punished. Laws regulating corporate crime are really window dressing designed to impress the working class with how fair the justice system really is. In reality, the justice system is the equivalent of an army that defends the owners of property in their ongoing struggle against the workers.[51]

The Development of a Radical Criminology

The development of radical theory can be traced to the National Deviancy Conference (NDC), formed in 1968 by a group of British sociologists. With about 300 members, this organization sponsored several national symposiums and dialogues. Members came from all walks of life, but at its core was a group of academics who were critical of the positivist criminology being taught in English and U.S. universities. More specifically, they rejected the conservative stance of criminologists and their close financial relationship with government funding agencies. Originally, the NDC was not a Marxist-oriented group but rather investigated the concept of deviance from a labeling perspective. It called attention to ways in which social control might actually be a cause of deviance rather than a response to antisocial behavior.

Many conference members became concerned about the political nature of social control. A schism developed within the NDC, with one group clinging to the now-conservative interactionist/labeling perspective and the second embracing Marxist thought. Then, in 1973, radical theory was given a powerful academic boost when British scholars Ian Taylor, Paul Walton, and Jock Young published *The New Criminology*.[52] This brilliant work was a thorough and well-constructed critique of existing concepts in criminology and a call for development of new criminological methods. *The New Criminology* became the standard resource for scholars critical of both the field of criminology and the existing legal process.

While these events were transpiring in Britain, a small group of scholars in the United States began to follow a new radical approach to criminology. The locus of the radical school was the criminology program at the University of California at Berkeley. The most noted Marxist scholars at that institution were Anthony Platt, Paul Takagi, Herman Schwendinger, and Julia Schwendinger. Marxist scholars at other U.S. academic institutions included Richard Quinney (originally a conflict theorist), William Chambliss, Steven Spitzer, and Barry Krisberg. The U.S. radicals were influenced by the widespread social ferment during the late 1960s and early 1970s. The war in Vietnam, prison struggles, and the civil rights and feminist movements produced a climate in which criticism of the ruling class seemed a natural by-product. Mainstream, positivist criminology was criticized as being overtly conservative, progovernment, and antihuman. Critical criminologists scoffed when their fellow scholars used statistical analysis of computerized data to describe criminal and delinquent behavior. As Barry Krisberg has written:

> Many of our scientific heroes of the past, upon rereading, turned out to be racists or, more generally, apologists for social injustice. In response to the widespread protests on campuses and throughout society, many of the contemporary giants of social science emerged as defenders of the status quo and vocally dismissed the claims of the oppressed for social justice.[53]

Many of the new Marxist criminologists had enjoyed distinguished careers as positivist criminologists. Some, such as Chambliss and Quinney, were moved by career interests from positivism to social conflict theory to a radical-Marxist approach to crime.

Marxists did not meet with widespread approval at major universities. Rumors of purges were common during the 1970s, and the criminology school at Berkeley was eventually closed for what many believe were political reasons. Even today, conflict exists between critical thinkers and mainstream academics. Prestigious Harvard Law School and other law centers have been the scenes of conflict and charges of purges and tenure denials because some professors held critical views of law and society. While some isolated radicals are tolerated if "they could not cause much trouble," the majority have been heavily victimized by what David Friedrichs refers to as "academic McCarthyism."[54]

In the ensuing years, new branches of a radical criminology were developing in the United States and abroad. In the early 1980s, the left realism school was started by scholars affiliated with the Middlesex Polytechnic and the University of Edinburgh in Great Britain. In the United States,

scholars influenced in part by the pioneering work of Dennis Sullivan and Larry Tifft created the peacemaking movement.[55] At the same time, feminist scholars began to apply critical analysis to the relationship between gender, power, and criminality. These movements (discussed later in this chapter) have coalesced into a rich and complex criminological tradition.

Fundamentals of Marxist Criminology

As a general rule, Marxist criminologists ignore formal theory construction, with its heavy emphasis on empirical testing. They scoff at the objective "value-free" stance of mainstream criminologists and instead argue that there should be a political, ideological basis for criminological scholarship.[56] Crime and criminal justice must be viewed in a historical, social, and economic context. Leftist criminologists use the conflict definition of crime as a political concept designed to protect the power and position of the upper classes at the expense of the poor. As you may recall, some but not all radicals would include in a list of "real" crimes such acts as violations of human rights due to racism, sexism, and imperialism and other violations of human dignity and physical needs and necessities. Part of the radical agenda then, argues criminologist Robert Bohm, is to make the public aware that these behaviors "are crimes just as much as burglary and robbery."[57]

The nature of a society controls the direction of its criminality; criminals are not social misfits but rather a product of the society and its economic system in which they reside. "Capitalism," claims Bohm, "as a mode of production, has always produced a relatively high level of crime and violence."[58] According to Michael Lynch and W. Byron Groves, three implications follow from this view:

1. Each society will produce its own types and amounts of crime.

2. Each society will have its own distinctive ways of dealing with criminal behavior.

3. Each society gets the amount and type of crime that it deserves.[59]

This analysis tells us that criminals are not a group of outsiders who can be controlled by an increased law enforcement presence. Criminality is a function of the social and economic organization of society. To control crime and reduce criminality is to end the social conditions that promote crime.

Economic Structure and Surplus Value

While no single view or theory defines Marxist criminology today, its general theme is the relationship between crime and the ownership and control of private property in a capitalist society.[60] That ownership and control, according to sociologist Gregg Barak, is the principal basis of power in

U.S. society.[61] Social conflict is fundamentally related to the historical and social distribution of productive private property. Destructive social conflicts inherent within the capitalist system cannot be resolved unless that system is destroyed or ended.

One important aspect of the capitalist economic system is the effect of surplus value. As you may recall, Marx used this term to refer to the value resulting from production when the cost of labor is less than the cost of the goods it produces. The excess value or profit can either be reinvested or used to enrich the owners. To increase the rate of surplus value, workers can be made to work harder for less pay, be made more efficient, or be replaced by "labor-saving" machines or technology. Therefore, economic growth does not have the same benefits for all elements of the population and in the long run may produce the same effect as a depression or recession!

As the rate of surplus value increases, more people are displaced from productive relationships, and the size of the "marginal" population swells. As corporations "downsize" to increase profits, high-paying labor and managerial jobs are lost to computer-driven machinery. Displaced workers are forced into service jobs at minimum wage. Many become temporary employees without benefits or a secure position.

As more people are thrust outside the economic mainstream (marginalization), a larger portion of the population is forced to live in areas (structural locations) conducive to crime. Once people are marginalized, commitment to the system declines, producing another criminogenic force: a weakened bond to society.[62]

The effect of surplus value is not unique to the United States. Crime and violence have escalated in former socialist republics that have converted to free-market economies. As you may recall, some scholars have criticized conflict theory with the argument that crime rates increase as countries change from capitalism to socialism. Yet there is evidence that an opposite change, from socialism to capitalism, drives crime rates even higher. Both China and the former Soviet Union have experienced an upsurge in gang activity as they embrace market economies; Russia may now have a murder rate higher than that of the United States.[63]

While some form of these themes can be found throughout Marxist writing, there are actually a number of schools of thought within the radical literature. Some of these different approaches are discussed in further details in the following sections.

Instrumental Marxism

One group of Marxists are referred to as **instrumentalists.** They view the criminal law and criminal justice system solely as an instrument for controlling the poor, have-not members of society; the state is the "tool" of the capitalists.

According to the instrumental view, capitalist justice serves the powerful and rich and enables them to impose their morality and standards of behavior on the entire society. Under capitalism, economic power enables its holders to extend their self-serving definition of illegal or criminal behavior to encompass those who might threaten the status quo or interfere with their quest for ever-increasing profits.[64] For example, David Jacobs's research shows how the concentration of monetary assets in the nation's largest firms is translated into the political power needed to control the tax laws and limit the firms' tax liabilities.[65]

The poor, according to this branch of Marxist theory, may or may not commit more crimes than the rich, but they certainly are arrested and punished more often. Under the capitalist system, the poor are driven to crime because a natural frustration exists in a society in which affluence is well publicized but unattainable. When class conflict becomes unbearable, frustration can spill out in riots, such as the one that occurred in Los Angeles on April 29, 1992 and was described as a "class rebellion of the underprivileged against the privileged."[66]

Because of class conflict, a deep-rooted hostility is generated among members of the lower class toward a social order they are not allowed to shape or participate in.[67] Instrumental Marxists consider it essential to *demystify* law and justice—that is, to unmask its true purpose. They charge that conventional criminology is devoted to identifying the social conditions that cause crime. Those criminological theories that focus on family structure, intelligence, peer relations, and school performance serve to keep the lower classes servile by showing why they are more criminal, less intelligent, and more prone to school failure and family problems than the middle class. **Demystification** involves the identification of the destructive intent of capitalist-inspired and -funded criminology. The goal of criminology should be to explicate the rule of law in capitalist society and show how it works to preserve ruling-class power. The essence of instrumental Marxist theory can be summarized in the following statements:

- U.S. society is based on an advanced capitalist economy.
- The state is organized to serve the interests of the dominant economic class, the capitalist ruling class.
- Criminal law is an instrument of the state and ruling class to maintain and perpetuate the existing social and economic order.
- Crime control in capitalist society is accomplished through a variety of institutions and agencies established and administered by a governmental elite, representing ruling-class interests for the purpose of establishing domestic order.
- The contradictions of advanced capitalism—the disjunction between existence and essence—require that the subordinate classes remain oppressed by whatever means necessary, especially through the coercion and violence of the legal system.
- Only with the collapse of capitalist society and the creation of a new society, based on socialist principles, will there be a solution to the crime problem.[68]

CONCEPTS OF INSTRUMENTAL MARXISM. The writings of a number of other influential instrumental Marxist theorists have helped shape this field of inquiry. According to Herman Schwendinger and Julia Siegel Schwendinger, legal relations in the United States secure an economic infrastructure that centers on a capitalist mode of production. The legal system is designed to guard the position of the owners (bourgeoisie) at the expense of the workers (proletariat). Legal relations maintain the family and school structure so as to secure the labor force. Even common-law crimes, such as murder and rape, are implemented to protect capitalism. According to the Schwendingers, the basic laws of the land (such as constitutional laws) are based on the conditions that reproduce the class system as a whole. Laws are aimed at securing the domination of the capitalist system. Although the system may at times secure the interests of the working class, for example, when laws are created that protect collective bargaining, due to the inherent antagonisms built into the capitalist system, all laws generally contradict their stated purpose of producing justice. Legal relations maintain patterns of individualism and selfishness and, in so doing, perpetuate a class system characterized by anarchy, oppression, and crime.[69]

PRIVILEGE. Barry Krisberg has linked crime to the differentials in privilege that exist in capitalist society. According to Krisberg, crime is a function of privilege. Crimes are created by the powerful to further their domination. Crimes deflect attention from the violence and social injustice the rich inflict on the masses to keep them subordinate and oppressed. Krisberg is concerned with how privilege influences criminality. He defines **privilege** as the possession of that which is valued by a particular social group in a given historical period. Privilege includes such rights as life, liberty, and happiness; such traits as intelligence, sensitivity, and humanity; and such material goods as monetary wealth, luxuries, land, and the like. The privilege system is also concerned with the distribution and preservation of privilege. Krisberg argues that force—the effective use of violence and coercion—is the major factor in determining which social group ascends to the position of defining and holding privilege.[70]

Other Marxist scholars have called for a review of the role of the professional criminologist. For example, Anthony Platt has charged that criminologists have helped support state repression with their focus on poor and minority-group criminals:

> We are just beginning to realize that criminology has serviced domestic repression in the same way that economics, political science, and anthropology have greased the wheels and even manufactured some of the important parts of modern imperialism. Given the ways in which this system has been used to repress and maintain the powerlessness of poor people, people of color, and young people, it is not too far-fetched to characterize many criminologists as domestic war criminals.[71]

Conflict scholars believe that crimes are created by the powerful to deflect attention from the violence and social injustice they inflict on the masses to keep them subordinate and oppressed. Here protesters are demonstrating against a California initiative designed to reduce the number of immigrants. Efforts to control immigration are seen as an attempt to maintain the power of the privileged classes.

Platt goes on to suggest that criminology must redefine its goals and definitions:

> In the past, we have been constrained by a legal definition of crime which restricts us to studying and ultimately helping to control only legally defined "criminals." We need a more humanistic definition of crime, one which reflects the reality of a legal system based on power and privilege. To accept the legal definition of crime is to accept the fiction of neutral law. A human rights definition of crime frees us to examine imperialism, racism, sexism, capitalism, exploitation, and other political or economic systems which contribute to human misery and deprive people of their potentialities.[72]

Michael Lynch observes that instrumental Marxist theory may be limited because it is based on assumptions that are incorrect: that law and justice always operate in the interests of the ruling class; that members of the ruling class "conspire" to control society; that what benefits one member of the ruling class benefits them all. In reality, charges

Lynch, some laws benefit the lower classes, and capitalists compete with one another rather than conspire.[73] Because of these deficiencies, some radicals have turned from instrumental theory and embraced structural Marxism.

Structural Marxism

Structural Marxists disagree with the view that the relationship between law and capitalism is unidimensional, always working for the rich and against the poor.[74] Law is not the exclusive domain of the rich, but it is used to maintain the long-term interests of the capitalist system and control members of any class who pose a threat to its existence. If law and justice were purely instruments of the capitalist class, why would laws controlling corporate crimes, such as price fixing, false advertising, and illegal restraint of trade, have been created and enforced? To a structuralist, the law is designed to keep the capitalist system operating in an efficient manner, and anyone, capitalist or proletarian, who "rocks the boat" is targeted to be sanctioned. For example, antitrust legislation is designed to prevent any single capitalist from dominating the system and preventing others from "playing the game." One person cannot get too powerful at the expense of the economic system as a whole.

One of the most highly regarded structural Marxist approaches is Stephen Spitzer's Marxian theory of deviance.[75] He finds that law in the capitalist system defines as deviant (or criminal) any person who disturbs, hinders, or calls into question any of the following:

- Capitalist modes of appropriating the product of human labor (for example, when the poor steal from the rich)
- The social conditions under which capitalist production takes place (for example, when some people refuse or are unable to perform wage labor)
- Patterns of distribution and consumption in capitalist society (for example, when people use drugs for escape and transcendence, rather than sociability and adjustment)
- The process of socialization for productive and nonproductive roles (for example, when youths refuse to be schooled or deny the validity of family life)
- The ideology that supports the functioning of capitalist society (for example, when people become proponents of alternative forms of social organization)

Among the many important points Spitzer makes is that capitalist societies have special ways of dealing with those who oppose its operation. One mechanism is to normalize formerly deviant or illegal acts by *absorbing* them into the mainstream of society—for example, through legalizing abortions. *Conversion* involves coopting deviants by making them part of the system—for example, a gang leader may be recruited to work with younger delinquents. *Containment* involves segregating deviants into isolated geographic areas so that they can easily be controlled—for example, by creating a ghetto. Finally, Spitzer believes that capitalist society actively supports some criminal enterprises, such as organized crime, so that they can provide a means of support for groups who might otherwise become a burden on the state.

Research on Marxist Criminology

Marxist criminologists rarely use standard social science methodologies to test their views, because many believe the traditional approach of measuring research subjects is antihuman and insensitive.[76] Marxists believe that the research conducted by mainstream liberal/positivist criminologists is designed to unmask the weak and powerless members of society so they can be better dealt with by the legal system—a process called *correctionalism.* They are particularly offended by purely empirical studies, such as those showing that minority-group members have lower IQs than the white majority or that the inner city is the site of the most serious crime while middle-class areas are relatively crime-free.

While uncommon, empirical research is not considered totally incompatible with Marxist criminology, and there have been some important efforts to quantitatively test its fundamental assumptions.[77] For example, Alan Lizotte and his associates have shown that the property crime rate reflects a change in the level of surplus value; the capitalist system's emphasis on excessive profits accounts for the need of the working class to commit property crime.[78]

Despite these few exceptions, Marxist research tends to be historical and analytical and not quantitative and empirical. Social trends are interpreted to understand how capitalism has affected human interaction. Marxists investigate both macro-level issues, such as how the accumulation of wealth affects crime rates, and micro-level issues, such as the effect of criminal interactions on the lives of individuals living in a capitalist society. Of particular importance to Marxist critical thinkers is the analysis of the historical development of capitalist social control institutions, such as criminal law, police agencies, courts, and prison systems.

CRIME, THE INDIVIDUAL, AND THE STATE. Marxists devote considerable attention to the study of the relationships among crime, victims, the criminal, and the state. Two common themes emerge: (1) crime and its control are a function of capitalism, and (2) the justice system is biased against the working class and favors upper-class interests. Marxian analysis of the criminal justice system is designed to identify the often-hidden processes that exert control over people's lives. It seeks an understanding of how conditions, processes, and structures became as they are today. For example, William Chambliss analyzed the process by which deviant behavior is defined as criminal or delinquent in U.S. society.[79] In a similar vein, Timothy Carter and Donald Clelland used a Marxist approach to show that dispositions in a juvenile court were a function of social class.[80] David Greenberg also studied the association between social class

Herman and Julia Schwendinger's classic study of rape provides an excellent example of Marxian critical analysis. The Schwendingers' goal has been to find out why women who are raped often feel guilty about their role in the rape experience. The Schwendingers believe that a rape victim frequently experiences guilt because she has been raised in a sexist society and has internalized discriminatory norms. Women have traditionally been viewed as the weaker sex, dependent on persons in authority, such as parents or husbands.

The Schwendingers postulate that dependency originates historically in socioeconomic conditions that are often directly related to family life in capitalist society. During the early stages of capitalism, families underwent strain when industry demanded a labor force of men, only infrequently supplemented by single women. The role of father was strained as men were separated from their households. The woman's role became more narrowly defined as childbearer and child raiser. The limited economic role of women helped define them as dependents. Married women, especially, were viewed as nonproductive, since they did not participate in commodity markets, where people earn money.

In reality, women's household productivity must be viewed as an essential contribution to working-class life; yet theirs is an unpaid contribution that often goes unappreciated by husbands and the rest of society. Since the housewife produces only for family use, her labor is necessarily unpayable; and while her needs are partly supported by the husband's wage, she is totally dependent on that wage for access to the commodities necessary for the family's existence. Because she has been socialized into dependency by the capitalist system, a woman's sense of self-worth may be more responsive to the evaluations of other persons. Furthermore, negative evaluations, such as those created by a rape experience, are likely to be turned inward by the woman, creating unwarranted self-recrimination and remorse.

The family is not the only culprit in this transaction. Schools and the mass media further reinforce dependency by teaching boys and girls in school to "look down on women." Textbooks stereotype the woman's role; girls are depicted as helpless and frightened. Vocational tests provide fewer opportunities for girls. In media presentations, women are usually depicted as housewives and mothers. When women are portrayed on television commercials, they seem "concerned mainly with clean floors and clean hair—housework and their personal appearance."

Although women have made strides in the job market, their labor is often in low-paid, low-mobility occupations, such as secretary or piece worker. Consequently, their appearance in the labor force often does little to improve their economic dependency. It is for these reasons that women often blame themselves for being raped. The Schwendingers imply that women feel they have "let down" the people they depend on when they are trapped in a rape encounter. A woman's own sense of inadequacy leads to self-blame for the attack and prevents her from focusing on the true culprits: the rapist and the capitalist system whose economic structure results in a rape-producing climate. The Schwendingers' research approach illustrates the Marxian stress on analysis and interpretation of social process and their disdain for quantitative statistical evidence.

CRITICAL THINKING QUESTIONS
1. What can society do to help women who are the victims of rape?
2. Does the Schwendingers' portrayal of rape victims seem accurate?

Sources: Herman Schwendinger and Julia Schwendinger, *Rape and Inequality* (Newbury Park, Calif.: Sage, 1983); idem., "Rape Victims and the False Sense of Guilt," *Crime and Social Justice* 13 (1980): 4–17.

and sentencing and later, with Drew Humphries, evaluated how power relationships help undermine any benefit the lower class gets from sentencing reforms.[81] In general, Marxist research efforts have yielded evidence linking operations of the justice system to class bias.[82]

In addition to conducting studies showing the relationship between crime and the state, some critical researchers have attempted to show how capitalism intervenes throughout the entire spectrum of crime-related phenomena. Research by Herman Schwendinger and Julia Schwendinger has attempted to show how capitalist social expectations affect women in the aftermath of a rape experience; their work is described in the accompanying Close-Up.

The Schwendingers' effort is a good example of Marxist analytical research.[83] Critical research of this sort is designed to reinterpret commonly held beliefs about society within the framework of Marxist social and economic ideas.[84] The goal is not to prove statistically that capitalism causes crime but rather to show that it creates an environment in which crime is inevitable. Marxist research is humanistic, situational, descriptive, and analytical rather than statistical, rigid, and methodological.

HISTORICAL ANALYSIS. A second type of Marxist research focuses on the historical background of commonly held institutional beliefs and practices. One aim is to show how changes in the criminal law corresponded to the development of capitalist economy. For example, Michael Rustigan analyzed historical records to show that law reform in 19th-century England was largely a response to pressure from the business community to make the punishment for property law violations more acceptable.[85] In a similar vein, Rosalind Petchesky has explained how the relationship between prison industries and capitalism evolved during the 19th century, while Paul Takagi has described the rise of state prisons as an element of centralized state control over deviants.[86]

Another topic of importance to Marxist critical thinkers is the development of modern police agencies. Since police often play an active role in putting down labor disputes and controlling the activities of political dissidents, their interrelationships with capitalist economics is of particular importance to Marxists. Prominent examples of research in this area include Stephen Spitzer and A. T. Scull's discussion of the history of private police and Dennis Hoffman's historical analysis of police excesses in the repression of an early union, the International Workers of the World (popularly known as the Wobblies).[87] Sidney Harring has provided one of the more important analyses of the development of modern policing, showing how police developed as an antilabor force that provided muscle for industrialists at the turn of the century.[88]

Critique of Marxist Criminology

Marxist criminology has met with a great deal of criticism from some members of the criminological mainstream who charge that its contribution has been "hot air, heat, but no real light."[89] In turn, radicals have accused mainstream criminologists of being culprits in the development of state control over individual lives and "selling out" their ideals for the chance to receive government funding. In making these charges, these theorists have caused disturbances in the halls of academia. Rumors of purges of Marxist theorists have cropped up; lawsuits involving the denial of academic tenure to Marxists have not been uncommon.

Mainstream criminologists have also attacked the substance of Marxist thought. For example, Jackson Toby argues that Marxist theory is a simple rehash of the old tradition of helping the underdog. He likens the ideas behind Marxist criminology to the ideas in such traditional and literary works as *Robin Hood* and Victor Hugo's *Les Miserables,* in which the poor steal from the rich to survive.[90] In reality, Toby claims, most theft is for luxury, not survival. Moreover, he disputes the idea that the crimes of the rich are more reprehensible and less understandable than those who live in poverty. Criminality and immoral behavior occur at every social level, but Toby believes that the relatively disadvantaged contribute disproportionately to crime and delinquency rates.[91]

Another critic, Carl Klockars, charges that Marxists ignore all the varied prestige and interest groups that exist in a pluralistic society and focus almost unilaterally on class differentials.[92] Klockars scoffs, for example, at critical thinkers who charge that efforts by the government to create social reforms are disguised attempts to control the underclass. Is it logical to believe that giving people more rights is a trick to allow greater control to be exerted over them? "People are more powerful with the right to a jury than without it. . . . The rights of free speech, free press, free association, public trial, habeas corpus, and governmental petition extended substantial power to colonials . . . who had previously been denied them."[93] Klockars's views of the problems of Marxist theory are summarized in the following statements:

- Marxist criminology as a social movement is untrustworthy. Marxists refuse to confront the problems and conflicts of socialist countries, such as the gulags and purges of the Soviet Union under Stalin.
- Marxist criminology is predictable. Capitalism is blamed for every human vice. "After class explains everything, after the whole legal order is critiqued, after all predatory and personal crime is attributed to the conditions and reproduction of capitalism, there is nothing more to say—except more of the same."[94]
- Marxist criminology does little to explain the criminality existing in states that have abolished private ownership of the means of production, such as Cuba.
- Marxists ignore objective reality. For example, they overlook empirical evidence of distinctions that exist between people in different classes. Such tactics will eventually destroy the foundation for a new postrevolutionary social science, should one be needed.
- Marxists attempt to explicate issues that, for most people, need no explanation. The revelation that politicians are corrupt and businesspeople greedy comes as a shock to no one.
- The evil that Marxists consistently discover and dramatize is seen from a moral ground set so high that it loses meaning and perspective. Every aspect of capitalist society is suspect, including practices and freedoms that most people cherish as the cornerstones of democracy (right to trial, free press, religious freedom, and so on).
- By presenting itself as a mystical, religionlike entity, Marxist criminology is relieved of the responsibility for the exploitation, corruption, crime, and human abuse that have been and continues to be perpetrated in socialist countries.

In response, Marxist scholars charge that critics rely on "traditional" variables, such as "class" and "poverty," in their analysis of radical thought. While important, these concepts do not reflect the key issues in the structural and economic process. In fact, like crime, they, too, may be the outcome of the capitalist system.[95]

Although radical criminologists dispute criticisms, they have also reponded by creating new theoretical models that incorporate Marxist ideas in an innovative manner. In the following section, we discuss some recent forms of radical theory in some detail.

Left Realism

Some radical scholars are now addressing the need for the left to respond to the increasing power of right-wing conservatives. They are troubled by the emergence of a strict "law and order" philosophy, which has at its centerpiece a policy of waiving juveniles to adult court where they may be punished severely. At the same time, they find the focus of most left-wing scholarship—the abuse of power by the ruling elite—too narrow. It is wrong, they argue, to ignore the problem of inner-city gang crime and violence, which all too often targets indigent people.[96] Those who share these concerns are referred to as left realists.[97]

Left realism is most often connected to the writings of British scholars John Lea and Jock Young. In their well-respected 1984 work *What Is to Be Done About Law and Order?* they rejected the utopian views of "idealistic" Marxists who portray street criminals as revolutionaries.[98] They took the "realistic" approach that street criminals prey on the poor and disenfranchised, thus making them doubly abused, first by the capitalist system and then by members of their own class.

Lea and Young's view of crime causation borrows from conventional sociological theory and closely resembles the *relative deprivation* approach: Experiencing poverty in the midst of plenty creates discontent; discontent without legitimate opportunity breeds crime. As they put it, "The equation is simple: relative deprivation equals discontent; discontent plus lack of political solution equals crime."[99]

Left realists argue that crime victims in all classes need and deserve protection; crime control reflects community needs. They do not view police and the courts as inherently evil tools of capitalism whose tough tactics alienate the lower classes. These institutions would in fact offer life-saving public services if their use of force could be reduced and their sensitivity to the public increased.[100] Another approach is **preemptive deterrence,** in which community organization efforts eliminate or reduce crime before it becomes necessary to use police forces. If the number of **marginalized** youth (those who feel they are not part of society and have nothing to lose by committing crime) could be reduced, delinquency rates would decline.[101]

To left realists Martin Schwartz and Walter DeKeseredy, street crime is "real"; the fear of violence among the lower classes has allowed the right wing to seize "law and order" as a political issue.[102] Gangs are not made up of "Robin Hoods," revolutionaries who steal from the rich. Most gang kids prey on members of their own race and class and are happy to keep the proceeds for themselves. According to Schwartz and DeKeseredy, gang kids may be the "ultimate capitalists," hustling their way to obtain the coveted symbols of success.[103]

Although the implementation of a socialist economy would help eliminate the crime problem, left realists recognize that something must be done in the meantime to control crime under the existing capitalist system. To create crime control policy, left realists welcome not only radical ideas but build on the work of strain theorists, social ecologists, and other "mainstream" views. Community-based efforts seem to hold the most promise as crime control techniques.

Left realism has been critiqued by radical thinkers as legitimizing the existing power structure: by supporting the existing definitions of law and justice, it suggests that the "deviant" and not the capitalist system is the cause of society's problems. Is it not advocating the very institutions that "currently imprison us and our patterns of thought and action?"[104] In rebuttal, a left realist would charge that it is unrealistic to speak of a socialist state lacking a police force or system of laws and justice; the criminal code does in fact represent public opinion.

Radical Feminist Theory

Like so many theories in criminology, most of the efforts of radical theorists have been devoted to explaining male criminality.[105] To remedy this theoretical lapse, a number of feminist writers have attempted to explain the cause of crime, gender differences in the crime rate, and the exploitation of female victims from a radical feminist perspective. Scholars in this area can usually be described as holding one of two related philosophical orientations: Marxist feminism or radical feminism.

Marxist Feminism

The first group of writers can be described as **Marxist feminists,** who view gender inequality as stemming from the unequal power of men and women in a capitalist society. They view gender inequality as a function of the exploitation of females by fathers and husbands; women are considered a "commodity" worth possessing, like land or money.[106] The origin of gender differences can be traced to the development of private property and male domination over the laws of inheritance.[107]

Marxist feminists link criminal behavior patterns to the gender conflict created by the economic and social struggles common in postindustrial societies. James Messerschmidt has made important contributions to understanding the roots of gender conflict. In *Capitalism, Patriarchy, and Crime* Messerschmidt argues that capitalist society is marked by both patriarchy and class conflict. Capitalists control the labor of workers, while men control women both economically and biologically.[108] This "double marginality" explains why females in a capitalist society commit fewer crimes than males: They are isolated in the family and have fewer opportunities to engage in elite deviance (white-collar and economic crimes), and they are also denied access to male-dominated street crimes. For example, powerful males will commit white-collar crimes, as will powerful females. How-

Marxist feminists view gender inequality as a function of the exploitation of females by fathers and husbands; women are considered a "commodity" worth possessing, like land or money. The origin of gender differences can be traced to the development of private property and male domination over the laws of inheritance. The abuse of young girls leads them into a life of petty crime, prostitution, and drug abuse.

ever, the female crime rate is restricted because of the patriarchial nature of the capitalist system.[109] Since capitalism renders women powerless, they are forced to commit less serious, nonviolent, self-destructive crimes, such as abusing drugs.

Powerlessness also increases the likelihood that women will become the target of violent acts.[110] Lower-class males are shut out of the economic opportunity structure. One way to improve their self-image is through acts of machismo that may involve violence or abuse of women. It is not surprising to find that a significant percentage of female victims are attacked by a spouse or intimate partner.

In his book *Masculinities and Crime,* Messerschmidt expands on these themes.[111] He suggests that in every culture males try to emulate what is considered "ideal" masculine behaviors. In Western culture this means being authoritative, in charge, combative and controlling. Failure to adapt these roles leaves men feeling effeminate and un-

manly. Their struggle to dominate women to prove their manliness is called **doing gender.**

Crime is a good way for men to "do gender" because it separates them from the weak and allows them to demonstrate physical bravery. Violence directed toward women is an especially economical way to demonstrate manhood. Would a weak and effeminate male ever attack a woman?

Radical Feminism

In contrast, **radical feminists** view the cause of female crime as originating with the onset of male supremacy (patriarchy), the subsequent subordination of women, male aggression, and the efforts of men to control females sexually.[112] They focus on the social forces that shape women's lives and experiences to explain female criminality.[113] For example, radical feminists attempt to show how the sexual victimization of girls is a function of male socialization because so many young males learn to be aggressive and exploitive of women. Males seek out same-sex peer groups for social support and find within them encouragement for the exploitation and sexual abuse of women. On college campuses, peers encourage sexual violence against women defined as "teasers," "pickups," or "sluts"; a code of secrecy then protects the aggressors from retribution.[114] Sexual and physical exploitation triggers a reaction among young girls. They may run away or abuse substances, which is labeled deviant or delinquent behavior.[115] In a sense, the female criminal is a victim herself.

The radical perspective is supported by a national survey conducted by the Center for Research on Women at Wellesley College, which found that 90% of adolescent girls are sexually harassed in school, almost 30% report having been pressured to "do something sexual," and 10% said they were forced to do something sexual.[116]

According to the radical feminist view, exploitation acts as a trigger for the onset of delinquent and deviant behavior. When female victims run away and abuse substances, they may be reacting to abuse at home and at school. Their attempts at survival are then labeled deviant or delinquent; victim blaming is not uncommon. Research by Jane Siegel and Linda Meyer Williams shows that a significant number (86%) of girls who had been sent to the emergency room to be treated for sexual abuse later reported engaging in physical fighting as a teen or as an adult; many of these abused girls later formed a romantic attachment with an abusive partner. Clearly many girls involved in delinquency, crime, and violence have themselves been the victims of violence in their youth and later as adults.[117]

The Wellesley survey of sexual harassment found that teachers and school officials ignore about 45% of complaints made by female students. They found that some school officials responded to reports of sexual harassment by asking the young victim, "Do you like it?" and saying, "They must be doing it for a reason." Because agents of social control often choose to ignore reports of abuse and harassment, young girls may feel trapped and desperate.

Even within the radical feminist movement there are important differences. For example, some feminist scholars charge that the movement focuses on the problems and viewpoints of of white, middle-class, heterosexual women without taking into account the special interests of lesbians and women of color.[118]

HOW THE JUSTICE SYSTEM PENALIZES WOMEN.
Radical feminists have also indicted the justice system and its patriarchal hierarchy as contributing to the onset of female delinquency.

From its inception, the juvenile justice system has viewed the great majority of female delinquents as sexually precocious girls who have to be brought under control. Writing on the "girl problem," Ruth Alexander has described how working-class young women desiring autonomy and freedom in the 1920s were considered delinquents and placed in reformatories. Lacking the ability to protect themselves from the authorities, these young girls were considered outlaws in a male-dominated society because they flouted the very narrow rules of appropriate behavior that were applied to females in this Victorian society. Girls who rebelled against parental authority or who engaged in sexual behavior deemed inappropriate were incarcerated to protect them from a career in prostitution.[119]

In a similar vein, a study of the early Los Angeles Juvenile Court by Mary Odem and Steven Schlossman found that in 1920 so-called delinquency experts identified young female "sex delinquents" as a major social problem that required a forceful public response. Civic leaders who were concerned about immorality mounted a eugenics and social hygiene campaign that identified the "sex delinquent" as a moral and sexual threat to American society and advocated a policy of eugenics or sterilization to prevent these inferior individuals from having children. Los Angeles responded by hiring the first female police officers in the nation to deal with girls under arrest and female judges to hear girls' cases in juvenile court; it also established a female detention center and a girls' reformatory.

When Odem and Schlossman evaluated the juvenile court records of delinquent girls who entered the Los Angeles Juvenile Court in 1920, they found that the majority were petitioned for either suspected sexual activity or behavior that placed them at risk of sexual relations. Despite the limited seriousness of these charges, the majority of girls were detained before their trials, and while in Juvenile Hall, all were given a compulsory pelvic exam. Girls adjudged sexually delinquent on the basis of the exam were segregated from the merely incorrigible girls to prevent moral corruption. Those testing positive for venereal disease were confined in the Juvenile Hall hospital for usually from one to three months. More than 29% of these female adolescents were eventually committed to custodial institutions.[120]

The judicial victimization of female delinquents has continued. A well-known feminist writer, Meda Chesney-Lind, has written extensively on the victimization of female delinquents by agents of the juvenile justice system.[121] She found that police in Honolulu, Hawaii, were likely to arrest female adolescents for sexual activity and to ignore the same behavior among male delinquents. Some 74% of the females in her sample were charged with sexual activity or incorrigibility, but only 27% of the boys faced the same charges. Moreover, the court ordered physical examinations in over 70% of the female cases, but only about 15% of the males were forced to undergo this embarrassing procedure. Girls were also more likely to be sent to a detention facility before trial, and the length of their detention averaged three times that of the boys. Finally, a higher percentage of females than males were institutionalized for similar delinquent acts. Chesney-Lind explains her data by suggesting that because female adolescents have a much narrower range of acceptable behavior than male adolescents, any sign of misbehavior in girls is seen as a substantial challenge to authority and to the viability of the double standard of sexual inequality. Female delinquency is viewed as relatively more serious than male delinquency and therefore is more likely to be severely sanctioned.

POWER-CONTROL THEORY.
John Hagan and his associates have created a radical-feminist model that uses gender differences to explain the onset of criminality. The most significant statements of these views are contained in a series of scholarly articles and are expanded in Hagan's 1989 book, *Structural Criminology*.[122] Hagan's view is that crime and delinquency rates are a function of two factors: (1) class position (power) and (2) family functions (control).[123] The link between these two variables is that within the family, parents reproduce the power relationships they hold in the workplace. The class position and work experiences of parents influence the criminality of children. A position of dominance at work is equated with control in the household.

In families that are **paternalistic,** fathers assume the traditional role of breadwinners, while mothers have menial jobs or remain at home to supervise domestic matters. Within the paternalistic home, mothers are expected to control the behavior of their daughters while granting greater freedom to sons. In such a home, the parent-daughter relationship can be viewed as a preparation for the "cult of domesticity," which makes girls' involvement in delinquency unlikely, while boys are freer to deviate because they are not subject to maternal control. Consequently, male siblings exhibit a higher degree of delinquent behavior than their sisters.

On the other hand, in **egalitarian** families—those in which the husband and the wife share similar positions of power at home and in the workplace—daughters gain a kind of freedom that reflects reduced parental control. These families produce daughters whose law-violating behavior mirrors their brothers'. Ironically, these kinds of relationships also occur in female-headed households with absent fathers. Similarly, Hagan and his associates found that when both fathers and mothers hold equally valued managerial positions, the similarity between the rates of their daughters' and sons' delinquency is greatest.

By implication, middle-class girls are the most likely to violate the law because they are less closely controlled than their lower-class counterparts. And in homes in which both parents hold positions of power, girls are more likely to have the same expectations of career success as their brothers. Consequently, siblings of both sexes will be socialized to take risks and engage in other behavior related to delinquency. Power-control theory, then, implies that middle-class youth of both sexes will have higher overall crime rates than their lower-class peers (although lower-class males may commit the more serious crimes).

Power-control theory has received a great deal of attention in the criminological community because it encourages a new approach to the study of criminality, one that includes gender differences, class position, and the structure of the family. While its basic premises have not yet been thoroughly tested, some critics have questioned its core assumption that power and control variables can explain crime.[124] More specifically, critics fail to replicate the finding that upper-class kids are more likely to deviate than their lower-class peers or that class and power interact to produce delinquency.[125] In response, Hagan and his colleagues suggest that these views are incorrect and that power-control theory retains its power to significantly add to our knowledge of the causes of crime.[126] Despite their assurances, empirical testing may produce further refinement of the theory. For example, Kevin Thompson found few gender-based supervision and behavior differences in worker-, manager,- or owner-dominated households.[127] However, parental supervision practices were quite different in families headed by the chronically unemployed, and these findings conformed to the power-control model. The Thompson research indicates that the concept of class used by Hagan may have to be reconsidered: Power-control theory may actually explain criminality among the truly disadvantaged and not the working class.

Deconstructionism

A number of radical thinkers have embraced semiotics and **deconstructionism.** While difficult to articulate concisely, these perspectives focus on the critical analysis of communication and language in legal codes.[128] Rules and regulations are analyzed to determine whether they contain language and content that forces racism or sexism to become institutionalized.

Deconstructionists rely on **semiotics** to conduct their research efforts. This means using language as signs that

Peacemakers view the efforts of the state to punish and control as crime encouraging rather than crime discouraging. They would agree with research showing that capital punishment has a "brutalization effect" that increases violent crime rates. Efforts to protest against the use of the death penalty, such as the one depicted here, are designed to promote less violent and more humane forms of social control.

Restorative justice is based on a social rather than a legal view of crime. A restorative system of justice views crime as an injury to personal and community relations rather than as an abstract legal violation against society. For example, when an offender attacks a victim, it is the target who is injured and with whom justice should be concerned.

Restorative justice can be contrasted with a legalistic view of criminal punishments. According to the legal view, "society" consists of (a) formal institutions and (b) individuals. Society is defined as an aggregation of people over which the state has jurisdiction. Legally, this aggregation is assumed to possess the social qualities of a group: common meanings and values, sustained interaction, and symbolic bonds. In the restorative view, in contrast, society, because of its bureaucratic nature, is not capable of manifesting such social qualities. It is only in smaller, less formal and more cohesive social groups (such as families, congregations, residential communities, and so on) that such qualities are found. Therefore, the potential for restoring social relations

damaged by crime is to be found not in the state but in social groups.

Restorative justice is in opposition to the adversary system. Without the capacity to restore damaged social relations, society's response to crime has been almost exclusively punitive. The potential of punitive state sanctions, whether they are intended to simply punish, deter, or induce treatment, necessitates an adversarial system of justice as an insurance against the infliction of undeserved punishment. In attempting to insure equal protection under the law, the procedural design of the adversarial system purposely limits consideration of the unique personal and social qualities of particular crimes. As a result of its preoccupation with the protection of individual rights, the adversarial system encourages the accused to deny, justify or excuse their actions, thereby, precluding the acceptance of responsibility. In addition, the central role of trained professionals in the adversarial process (prosecution and defense attorneys) severely limits the possibility of direct exchanges between the victim and offender. Because the adver-

saries are narrowly defined as the "accused" and the "state" (representing both society and the victim), little or no consideration can be given to community concerns and participation. Restorative justice is a direct response to the inadequacies of the adversarial process.

Restorative justice is guided by three essential principles: (1) community ownership of conflict (including crime), (2) material and symbolic reparation for victims and community, and (3) social reintegration of the offender. The restorative process begins by redefining crime in terms of a conflict among the offender, the victim, and affected constituencies (families, schools, workplaces, and so on). Therefore, it is vitally important that the resolution take place within the context in which the conflict originally occurred rather than be transferred to a specialized institution that has no social connection to the community or group from which the conflict originated. By maintaining "ownership" or jurisdiction over the conflict, the community is able to express its shared outrage about the offense. The less procedural and more sub-

indicate more than the mere meaning of words. There are many signs or language groupings in operation today. For example, sports relies very heavily on the use of signs, and to become a sports "expert" means becoming familiar with terminology such as "blitzing the quarterback" and a "hat trick." These terms convey meaning that is far greater than the words themselves and provide images to sports fans familiar with the signs that would be lost on others.

Deconstructionists believe that language is value-laden and contains the same sorts of inequities present in the rest of the social structure. Concerns with materialism and social inequality appear in the content of the law and control its direction. Capitalism puts a price tag on all merchandise. Law, legal skill, and justice are "commodities" that can be bought and sold like any other.[129]

Peacemaking Criminology

Suffering has risen out of disunity and separation from the embracing totality, and it can be ended only with the return of all sentient beings to a condition of wholeness.[130]

One of the newer movements in radical theory is **peacemaking** criminology. To members of the peacemaking movement, the main purpose of criminology is to promote a peaceful and just society. Rather than standing on empirical analysis of data sets, peacemaking draws its inspiration from religious and philosophical teachings ranging from Quakerism to Zen.

Peacemakers view the efforts of the state to punish and control as crime-encouraging rather than crime-discouraging.

These views were first articulated in a series of books with an anarchist theme written by Larry Tifft and Dennis Sullivan more than 15 years ago.[131] In his foreword to Sullivan's *The Mask of Love*, Larry Tifft writes:

> The violent punishing acts of the state and its controlling professions are of the same genre as the violent acts of individuals. In each instance these acts reflect an attempt to monopolize human interaction.[132]

Sullivan recognizes the futility of correcting and punishing criminals in the context of our conflict-ridden society:

> The reality we must grasp is that we live in a culture of severed relationships, where every available institution provides

stantive approach of restorative justice allows for shared community outrage to be directly communicated to the offender. The victim is also given a chance to voice his or her story, and the offender can directly communicate his or her need for social reintegration and treatment.

The restoration process depends on a communicative conception of law in which law is conceived as a discussion that is cohesive rather than punitive and disruptive. Communicative law encourages people to discuss the main problems in their social life (which are typically manifested in terms of interpersonal conflict). By regularly engaging in such discourse, members of a group keep alive the sense that law unites them rather than separates them. The restoration process involves an informal communicative exchange among the victim, the offender, and the community. Although restorative processes differ in structure and style, their discourse generally includes a recognition of the injury to personal and social relations, a determination and acceptance of responsibility (ideally accompanied by a statement of remorse), a commitment to both material and symbolic (e.g., an apology) reparation, and a determination of community

support and assistance for both victim and offender. The intended result of the restorative process is to repair injuries suffered by the victim and the community while assuring reintegration of the offender.

Although there is widespread agreement among proponents of restorative justice as to what constitutes restoration, a clear division exists among those who believe that restorative justice can be achieved within the context of the existing social structure and those who contend that significant social structural change must occur for the true potential of restorative justice to be realized. The former argue that the social qualities of the group can be recreated within such processes as family group conferencing, victim-offender reconciliation, and sentencing circles. The latter suggest that such social qualities cannot be effectively recreated; rather, they must exist prior to the restorative process.

The effectiveness of restorative justice ultimately depends on the stake a person has in the community (or a particular social group). Persons who do not value their membership in the group will be unlikely to accept responsibility, show remorse, or re-

pair the injuries caused by their actions. Existing restorative justice programs, such as mediation programs, will be unable to effectively reach those persons who are disengaged from all community institutions. Therefore, the relative effectiveness of existing restorative justice programs provides us with a measurement of the need for structural change.

CRITICAL THINKING QUESTIONS

1. Can you name some restorative justice initiatives in the criminal justice system? Hint: Arbitration and conflict resolution are considered restorative justice.

2. Is is possible to have a justice system based on peace and humanism, or is justice inherently punitive and coercive?

Sources: Peter Cordella, *Restorative Justice* (unpublished paper, Manchester, N.H.: St. Anselm College, 1997); see also Herbert Bianchi, *Justice as Sanctuary* (Bloomington: Indiana University Press, 1994); Nils Christie, "Conflicts as Property," *The British Journal of Criminology* 17 (1977): 1–15; L. Hulsman, "Critical Criminology and the Concept of Crime," *Contemporary Crises* 10 (1986): 63–80.

a form of banishment but no place or means for people to become connected, to be responsible to and for each other.[133]

The writings imply that mutual aid rather than coercive punishment is the key to a harmonious society. Today, advocates of the peacemaking movement, such as Harold Pepinsky and Richard Quinney (who has shifted from conflict theorist to Marxist and now to peacemaker), try to find humanist solutions to crime and other social problems.[134] Rather than punishment and prison, they advocate such policies as mediation and conflict resolution. This is generally referred to as restorative justice.

In the accomanying Close-Up, Peter Cordella, a sociologist and expert on the restorative justice movement, describes its basic principles.

Summary

Social conflict theorists view crime as a function of the conflict that exists in society. Social conflict has its theoretical basis in the works of Karl Marx, as interpreted by Willem Bonger, Ralf Dahrendorf, and George Vold. Conflict theorists suggest that crime in any society is caused by class conflict. Laws are created by those in power to protect their rights and interests. All criminal acts have political undertones. Richard Quinney has called this concept the social reality of crime. Unfortunately, research efforts to validate the conflict approach have not produced significant findings. One of conflict theory's most important premises is that the justice system is biased and designed to protect the wealthy. Research has not been unanimous in supporting this point.

Marxist criminology views the competitive nature of the capitalist system as a major cause of crime. The poor commit crimes because of their frustration, anger, and need. The wealthy engage in illegal acts because they are used to competition and because they must do so to keep their positions in society. Marxist scholars, such as Quinney, Platt, and Krisberg, have attempted to show that the law is designed to protect the wealthy and powerful and to control the poor, have-not members of society. Branches of radical theory include instrumental Marxism and structural Marxism (see Table 9.2 for a summary of these theories). Research on Marxist theory

Table 9.2 Social Conflict Theories

THEORY	MAJOR PREMISE	STRENGTHS
Conflict theory	Crime is a function of class conflict. The definition of the law is controlled by people who hold social and political power.	Accounts for class differentials in the crime rate. Shows how class conflict influences behavior.
Marxist theory	The capitalist means of production creates class conflict. Crime is a rebellion of the lower class. The criminal justice system is an agent of class warfare.	Accounts for the associations between economic structure and crime rates.
Instrumental Marxist theory	Criminals are revolutionaries. The real crime is sexism, racism, and profiteering.	Broadens the definition of crime and demystifies or explains the historical development of law.
Structural Marxist theory	The law is designed to sustain the capitalist economic system.	Explains the existence of white-collar crime and business control laws.
Radical feminist theory	The capital system creates patriarchy, which oppresses women.	Explains gender bias, violence against women, and repression.
Left realism	Crime is a function of relative deprivation; criminals prey on the poor.	Represents a compromise between conflict and traditional criminology.
Deconstructionism	Language controls the meaning and use of the law.	Provides a critical analysis of meaning.
Peacemaking	Peace and humanism can reduce crime; conflict resolution strategies can work.	Offers a new approach to crime control through mediation.

focuses on how the system of justice was designed and how it operates to further class interests. Quite often, this research uses historical analysis to show how the capitalist classes have exerted their control over the police, courts, and correctional agencies. Both Marxist and conflict criminology have been heavily criticized by consensus criminologists. Jackson Toby sees Marxists as being sentimental and unwilling to face reality. Carl Klockars's criticism suggests Marxists make fundamental errors in their concepts of ownership and class interest.

During the 1990s, new forms of conflict theory are emerging. Feminist writers draw attention to the influence of patriarchal society on crime; left realism takes a centrist position on crime by showing its rational and destructive nature; peacemaking criminology brings a call for humanism to criminology; deconstructionism looks at the symbolic meaning of law and culture.

Key Terms

conflict theory
surplus value
dialectic method
power
social reality of crime
norm resistance
dangerous classes

instrumentalists
demystification
privilege
structural Marxists
left realism
preemptive deterrence
marginalization

Marxist feminists
doing gender
radical feminists
paternalistic
egalitarian

deconstructionism
semiotics
peacemaking
restorative justice

Notes

1. Michael Lynch, "Rediscovering Criminology: Lessons from the Marxist Tradition," in Marxist Sociology: Surveys of Contemporary Theory and Research, ed. Donald McQuarie and Patrick McGuire (New York: General Hall Press, 1994).

2. Michael Lynch and W. Byron Groves, A Primer in Radical Criminology, 2nd ed. (Albany, N.Y.: Harrow and Heston, 1989), pp. 32–33.

3. Ibid., p. 4.

4. See, generally, Karl Marx and Friedrich Engels, Capital: A Critique of Political Economy, trans. E. Aveling (Chicago: Charles Kern, 1906); Karl Marx, Selected Writings in Sociology and Social Philosophy, trans. P. B. Bottomore (New York: McGraw-Hill, 1956). For a general discussion of Marxist thought, see Lynch and Groves, A Primer in Radical Criminology, pp. 6–26.

5. Karl Marx, Grundrisse: Introduction to the Critique of Political Economy, trans. Martin Nicolaus (New York: Vintage, 1973), pp. 106–107.

6. Lynch, "Rediscovering Criminology."

7. Karl Marx, "Population, Crime and Pauperism," in Karl Marx and Friedrich Engels, Ireland and the Irish Question (Moscow: Progress, 1859, reprinted 1971), p. 92.

8. Friedrich Engels, The Condition of the Working Class in England in 1844 (London: Allen & Unwin, 1950).

9. Lynch, "Rediscovering Criminology," p. 5.

10. Willem Bonger, *Criminality and Economic Conditions* (1916, abridged ed., Bloomington: Indiana University Press, 1969).

11. Ralf Dahrendorf, *Class and Class Conflict in Industrial Society* (Palo Alto, Calif.: Stanford University Press, 1959).

12. Ibid., p. 48.

13. George Vold, *Theoretical Criminology* (New York: Oxford University Press, 1958).

14. James Short and F. Ivan Nye, "Extent of Undetected Delinquency: Tentative Conclusions," *Journal of Criminal Law, Criminology, and Police Science* 49 (1958): 296–302.

15. For a general view, see David Friedrichs, "Crime, Deviance and Criminal Justice: In Search of a Radical Humanistic Perspective," *Humanity and Society* 6 (1982): 200–226.

16. Edwin Lemert, *Social Pathology* (New York: McGraw-Hill, 1951); Howard Becker, *Outsiders: Studies in the Sociology of Deviance* (New York: Macmillan, 1963).

17. Alexander Liazos, "The Poverty of the Sociology of Deviance: Nuts, Sluts and Perverts," *Social Problems* 20 (1972): 103–120.

18. See, generally, Robert Meier, "The New Criminology: Continuity in Criminological Theory," *Journal of Criminal Law and Criminology* 67 (1977): 461–469.

19. David Greenberg, ed., *Crime and Capitalism* (Palo Alto, Calif.: Mayfield Publishing, 1981), p. 3.

20. William Chambliss and Robert Seidman, *Law, Order and Power* (Reading, Mass.: Addison-Wesley, 1971), p. 503.

21. John Braithwaite, "Retributivism, Punishment and Privilege," in *Punishment and Privilege,* ed. W. Byron Groves and Graeme Newman (Albany, N.Y.: Harrow and Heston, 1986), pp. 55–66.

22. Austin Turk, "Class, Conflict and Criminology," *Sociological Focus* 10 (1977): 209–220.

23. Daniel Georges-Abeyie, "Race, Ethnicity, and the Spatial Dynamic: Toward a Realistic Study of Black Crime, Crime Victimization, and Criminal Justice Processing of Blacks," *Social Justice* 16 (1989): 35–54.

24. John Hagan and Celesta Albonetti, "Race, Class and the Perception of Criminal Injustice in America," *American Journal of Sociology* 88 (1982): 329–355.

25. Richard Quinney, *The Social Reality of Crime* (Boston: Little, Brown, 1970), pp. 15–23.

26. Austin Turk, *Criminality and Legal Order* (Chicago: Rand McNally, 1969), p. 58.

27. Lynch and Groves, *A Primer in Radical Criminology,* 2nd ed., p. 38.

28. Austin Turk, *Criminality and Legal Order* (Chicago: Rand McNally, 1969).

29. David McDowall, "Poverty and Homicide in Detroit, 1926–1978," *Victims and Violence* 1 (1986): 23–34; David McDowall and Sandra Norris, "Poverty and Homicide in Baltimore, Cleveland, and Memphis, 1937–1980," paper presented at the annual meeting of the American Society of Criminology, Montreal, November 1987.

30. Judith Blau and Peter Blau, "The Cost of Inequality: Metropolitan Structure and Violent Crime," *American Sociological Review* 147 (1982): 114–129; Richard Block, "Community Environment and Violent Crime," *Criminology* 17 (1979): 46–57; Robert Sampson, "Structural Sources of Variation in Race-Age-Specific Rates of Offending Across Major U.S. Cities," *Criminology* 23 (1985): 647–673.

31. David Jacobs and David Britt, "Inequality and Police Use of Deadly Force: An Empirical Assessment of a Conflict Hypothesis," *Social Problems* 26 (1979): 403–412.

32. Alan Lizotte, "Extra-Legal Factors in Chicago's Criminal Courts: Testing the Conflict Model of Criminal Justice," *Social Problems* 25 (1978): 564–580.

33. Terance Miethe and Charles Moore, "Racial Differences in Criminal Processing: The Consequences of Model Selection on Conclusions About Differential Treatment," *Sociological Quarterly* 27 (1987): 217–237.

34. Douglas Smith, Christy Visher, and Laura Davidson, "Equity and Discretionary Justice: The Influence of Race on Police Arrest Decisions," *Journal of Criminal Law and Criminology* 75 (1984): 234–249.

35. Thomas Arvanites, "Increasing Imprisonment: A Function of Crime or Socioeconomic Factors?" *American Journal of Criminal Justice* 17 (1992): 19–38.

36. Nancy Wonders, "Determinate Sentencing: A Feminist and Postmodern Story," *Justice Quarterly* 13 (1996): 610–648.

37. Michael Leiber, Anne Woodrick, and E. Michele Roudebush, "Religion, Discriminatory Attitudes and the Orienations of Juvenile Justice Personnel: A Research Note," *Criminology* 33 (1995): 431–447.

38. Michael Leiber and Katherine Jamieson, "Race and Decision Making Within Juvenile Justice: The Importance of Context," *Journal of Quantitative Criminology* 11 (1995): 363–388.

39. Dragan Milovanovic, "Postmodern Criminology: Mapping the Terrain," *Justice Quarterly* 13 (1996): 567–610.

40. Richard Greenleaf and Lonn Lanza-Kaduce, "Sophistication, Organization and Authority-Subject Conflict: Rediscovering and Uraveling Turk's Theory of Norm Resistance," *Criminology* 33 (1995): 565–585.

41. Jackson Toby, "The New Criminology Is the Old Sentimentality," *Criminology* 16 (1979): 513–526.

42. Kenneth Land and Marcus Felson, "A General Framework for Building Dynamic Macro Social Indicator Models: An Analysis of Changes in Crime Rates and Police Expenditures," *American Journal of Sociology* 82 (1976): 565–604.

43. Arvanites, "Increasing Imprisonment," p. 34.

44. See, generally, William Wilbanks, *The Myth of a Racist Criminal Justice System* (Monterey, Calif.: Brooks/Cole, 1987).

45. Theodore Chiricos and Gordon Waldo, "Socioeconomic Status and Criminal Sentencing: An Empirical Assessment of a Conflict Proposition," *American Sociological Review* 40 (1975): 753–772.

46. Stephen Klein, Joan Petersilia, and Susan Turner, "Race and Imprisonment Decisions in California," *Science* 247 (1990): 812–816.

47. Basil Owomero, "Crime in Tanzania: Contradictions of a Socialist Experiment," *International Journal of Comparative and Applied Criminal Justice* 12 (1988): 177–189.

48. Lynch and Groves, *A Primer in Radical Criminology,* 2nd ed., p. 6.

49. This section borrows heavily from Richard Sparks, "A Critique of Marxist Criminology," in *Crime and Justice,* vol. 2, ed. Norval Morris and Michael Tonry (Chicago: University of Chicago Press, 1980), pp. 159–208.

50. Jeffery Reiman, *The Rich Get Richer and the Poor Get Prison* (New York: Wiley, 1984), pp. 43–44.

51. For a general review of Marxist criminology, see Lynch and Groves, *A Primer in Radical Criminology,* 2nd ed.

52. Ian Taylor, Paul Walton, and Jock Young, *The New Criminology: For a Social Theory of Deviance* (London: Routledge & Kegan Paul, 1973).

53. Barry Krisberg, *Crime and Privilege: Toward a New Criminology* (Englewood Cliffs, N.J.: Prentice-Hall, 1975), p. 167.

54. David Friedrichs, "Critical Criminology and Critical Legal Studies," *Critical Criminologist* 1 (1989): 7.

55. See, for example, Larry Tifft and Dennis Sullivan, *The Struggle to Be Human: Crime, Criminology and Anarchism* (Orkney Islands, Over-the Water-Sanday: Cienfuegos Press, 1979); Dennis Sullivan, *The Mask of Love* (Port Washington, N.Y.: Kennikat Press, 1980).

56. R. M. Bohm, "Radical Criminology: An Explication," *Criminology* 19 (1982): 565–589.

57. Robert Bohm, "Radical Criminology: Back to the Basics," paper presented at the annual meeting of the American Society of Criminology, Phoenix, Arizona, November 1993, p. 2.

58. Ibid., p. 4.

59. Lynch and Groves, *A Primer in Radical Criminology,* 2nd ed., p. 7.

60. W. Byron Groves and Robert Sampson, "Critical Theory and Criminology," *Social Problems* 33 (1986): 58–80.

61. Gregg Barak, "'Crimes of the Homeless' or the 'Crime of Homelessness': A Self-Reflexive, New-Marxist Analysis of Crime and Social Control," paper presented at the annual meeting of the American Society of Criminology, Montreal, November 1987.

62. Michael Lynch, "Assessing the State of Radical Criminology: Toward the Year 2000," paper presented at the annual meeting of the American Society of Criminology, Phoenix, Arizona, November 1993.

63. Bohm, "Radical Criminology," p. 5.

64. Gresham Sykes, "The Rise of Critical Criminology," *Journal of Criminal Law and Criminology* 65 (1974): 211.

65. David Jacobs, "Corporate Economic Power and the State: A Longitudinal Assessment of Two Explanations," *American Journal of Sociology* 93 (1988): 852–881.

66. Deanna Alexander, "Victims of the L.A. Riots: A Theoretical Consideration," paper presented at the annual meeting of the American Society of Criminology, Phoenix, Arizona, November 1993.

67. Ibid., p. 2.

68. Richard Quinney, "Crime Control in Capitalist Society," in *Critical Criminology,* ed. Ian Taylor, Paul Walton, and Jock Young (London: Routledge and Kegan Paul, 1975), p. 199.

69. Herman Schwendinger and Julia Schwendinger, "Delinquency and Social Reform: A Radical Perspective," in *Juvenile Justice,* ed. Lamar Empey (Charlottesville: University of Virginia Press, 1979), pp. 246–290.

70. Krisberg, *Crime and Privilege.*

71. Elliott Currie, "A Dialogue with Anthony M. Platt," *Issues in Criminology* 8 (1973): 28.

72. Ibid., p. 29.

73. Lynch, "Rediscovering Criminology," p. 14.

74. John Hagan, *Structural Criminology* (New Brunswick, N.J.: Rutgers University Press, 1989), pp. 110–119.

75. Stephen Spitzer, "Toward a Marxian Theory of Deviance," *Social Problems* 22 (1975): 638–651.

76. Roy Bhaskar, "Empiricism," in *A Dictionary of Marxist Thought,* ed. T. Bottomore (Cambridge: Harvard University Press, 1983), pp. 149–150.

77. Byron Groves, "Marxism and Positivism," *Crime and Social Justice* 23 (1985): 129–150; Michael Lynch, "Quantitative Analysis and Marxist Criminology: Some Old Answers to a Dilemma in Marxist Criminology," *Crime and Social Justice* 29 (1987): 110–117.

78. Alan Lizotte, James Mercy, and Eric Monkkonen, "Crime and Police Strength in an Urban Setting: Chicago, 1947–1970," in *Quantitative Criminology,* ed. John Hagan (Beverly Hills, Calif.: Sage, 1982), pp. 129–148.

79. William Chambliss, "The State, the Law and the Definition of Behavior as Criminal or Delinquent," in *Handbook of Criminology,* ed. D. Glazer (Chicago: Rand McNally, 1974), pp. 7–44.

80. Timothy Carter and Donald Clelland, "A Neo-Marxian Critique, Formulation and Test of Juvenile Dispositions as a Function of Social Class," *Social Problems* 27 (1979): 96–108.

81. David Greenberg, "Socio-Economic Status and Criminal Sentences: Is There an Association?" *American Sociological Review* 42 (1977): 174–175; David Greenberg and Drew Humphries, "The Cooptation of Fixed Sentencing Reform," *Crime and Delinquency* 26 (1980): 206–225.

82. Steven Box, *Power, Crime and Mystification* (London: Tavistock, 1984); Gregg Barak, *In Defense of Whom? A Critique of Criminal Justice Reform* (Cincinnati: Anderson Publishing, 1980); for an opposing view, see Franklin Williams, "Conflict Theory and Differential Processing: An Analysis of the Research Literature," in *Radical Criminology: The Coming Crisis,* ed. J. Inciardi (Beverly Hills, Calif.: Sage, 1980), pp. 213–231.

83. Herman Schwendinger and Julia Schwendinger, "Rape Victims and the False Sense of Guilt," *Crime and Social Justice* 13 (1980): 4–17.

84. For more of their work, see Herman Schwendinger and Julia Schwendinger, *Adolescent Subcultures and Delinquency* (New York: Praeger, 1985); idem, "The Paradigmatic Crisis in Delinquency Theory," *Crime and Social Justice* 18 (1982): 70–78; idem, "The Collective Varieties of Youth," *Crime and Social Justice* 5 (1976): 7–25; idem, "Marginal Youth and Social Policy," *Social Problems* 24 (1976): 184–191.

85. Michael Rustigan, "A Reinterpretation of Criminal Law Reform in Nineteenth-Century England," in *Crime and Capitalism,* ed. D. Greenberg (Palo Alto, Calif.: Mayfield Publishing, 1981), pp. 255–278.

86. Rosalind Petchesky, "At Hard Labor: Penal Confinement and Production in Nineteenth-Century America," in *Crime and Capitalism,* ed. D. Greenberg, pp. 341–357; Paul Takagi, "The Walnut Street Jail: A Penal Reform to Centralize the Powers of the State," *Federal Probation* 49 (1975): 18–26.

87. Steven Spitzer and Andrew Scull, "Privatization and Capitalist Development: The Case of the Private Police," *Social Problems* 25 (1977): 18–29; Dennis Hoffman, "Cops and Wobblies" (Ph.D. diss., Portland State University, 1977).

88. Sidney Harring, "Policing a Class Society: The Expansion of the Urban Police in the Late Nineteenth and Early Twentieth Centuries," in *Crime and Capitalism,* ed. D. Greenberg, pp. 292–313.

89. Jack Gibbs, "An Incorrigible Positivist," *Criminologist* 12 (1987): 2–3.

90. Toby, "The New Criminology Is the Old Sentimentality."

91. Sparks, "A Critique of Marxist Criminology," pp. 198–199.

92. Carl Klockars, "The Contemporary Crises of Marxist Criminology," in *Radical Criminology: The Coming Crisis,* ed. J. Inciardi (Beverly Hills, Calif.: Sage, 1980), pp. 92–123.

93. Ibid., pp. 112–114.

94. Ibid.

95. Michael Lynch, W. Byron Groves, and Alan Lizotte, "The Rate of Surplus Value and Crime: A Theoretical and Empirical Examination of Marxian Economic Theory and Criminology," *Crime, Law and Social Change* 1 (1994): 1–11.

96. Anthony Platt, "Criminology in the 1980s: Progressive Alternatives to 'Law and Order,'" *Crime and Social Justice* 21–22 (1985): 191–199.

97. See, generally, Roger Matthews and Jock Young, eds. *Confronting Crime* (London: Sage, 1986); for a thorough review of left realism, see Martin Schwartz and Walter DeKeseredy, "Left Realist Criminology: Strengths, Weaknesses and the Feminist Critique," *Crime, Law and Social Change* 15 (1991): 51–72.

98. John Lea and Jock Young, *What Is to Be Done About Law and Order?* (Harmondsworth, England: Penguin, 1984).

99. Ibid., p. 88.

100. Richard Kinsey, John Lea, and Jock Young, *Losing the Fight Against Crime* (London: Blackwell, 1986).

101. Martin Schwartz and Walter DeKeseredy, *Contemporary Criminology* (Belmont, Calif.: Wadsworth, 1996), p. 249.

102. Schwartz and DeKeseredy, "Left Realist Criminology."

103. Ibid., p. 54.

104. Ibid., p. 58.

105. For a general review of this issue, see Kathleen Daly and Meda Chesney-Lind, "Feminism and Criminology," *Justice Quarterly* 5 (1988): 497–538; Douglas Smith and Raymond Paternoster, "The Gender Gap in Theories of Deviance: Issues and Evidence," *Journal of Research in Crime and Delinquency* 24 (1987): 140–172; Pat Carlen, "Women, Crime, Feminism, and Realism," *Social Justice* 17 (1990): 106–123.

106. Julia Schwendinger and Herman Schwendinger, *Rape and Inequality* (Beverly Hills: Sage, 1983).

107. Daly and Chesney-Lind, "Feminism and Criminology," p. 536.

108. James Messerschmidt, *Capitalism, Patriarchy and Crime* (Totowa, N.J.: Rowman and Littlefield, 1986); for a critique of this work, see Herman Schwendinger and Julia Schwendinger, "The World According to James Messerschmidt," *Social Justice* 15 (1988): 123–145.

109. Kathleen Daly, "Gender and Varieties of White-Collar Crime," *Criminology* 27 (1989): 769–793.

110. Jane Roberts Chapman, "Violence Against Women as a Violation of Human Rights," *Social Justice* 17 (1990): 54–71.

111. James Messerschmidt, *Masculinities and Crime: Critique and Reconceptualization of Theory* (Lanham, Md.: Rowman and Littlefield, 1993).

112. For a review of feminist theory, see Sally Simpson, "Feminist Theory, Crime and Justice," *Criminology* 27 (1989): 605–632.

113. Suzie Dod Thomas and Nancy Stein, "Criminality, Imprisonment, and Women's Rights in the 1990s," *Social Justice* 17 (1990): 1–5.

114. Walter DeKeseredy and Martin Schwartz, "Male Peer Support and Woman Abuse: An Expansion of DeKeseredy's Model," *Sociological Spectrum* 13 (1993): 393–413.

115. Daly and Chesney-Lind, "Feminism and Criminology." See also Drew Humphries and Susan Caringella-MacDonald, "Murdered Mothers, Missing Wives: Reconsidering Female Victimization," *Social Justice* 17 (1990): 71–78.

116. Center for Research on Women, *Secrets in Public: Sexual Harassment in Our Schools* (Wellesley, Mass.: Wellesley College, 1993).

117. Jane Siegel and Linda Meyer Williams, "Aggressive Behavior Among Women Sexually Abused as Children," paper presented at the American Society of Criminology meeting, Phoenix, Arizona, 1993, rev. version.

118. Susan Ehrlich Martin and Nancy Jurik, *Doing Justice, Doing Gender* (Thousand Oaks, Calif.: Sage, 1996), p. 27.

119. Ruth Alexander, *The "Girl Problem": Female Sexual Delinquency in New York, 1900–1930* (Ithaca, N.Y.: Cornell University Press, 1995).

120. Mary Odem and Steven Schlossman, "Guardians of Virtue: The Juvenile Court and Female Delinquency in Early 20th-Century Los Angeles," *Crime and Delinquency* 37 (1991): 186–203.

121. Meda Chesney-Lind, "Judicial Enforcement of the Female Sex Role: The Family Court and the Female Delinquent," *Issues in Criminology* 8 (1973): 51–69; see also idem, "Women and Crime: The Female Offender," *Signs: Journal of Women in Culture and Society* 12 (1986): 78–96; idem, "Female Offenders: Paternalism Reexamined," in *Women, the Courts, and Equality,* ed. Laura L. Crites and Winifred L. Hepperle (Newbury Park, Calif.: Sage, 1987): 114–139; idem, "Girls' Crime and a Woman's Place: Toward a Feminist Model of Female Delinquency," paper presented at a meeting of the American Society of Criminology, Montreal, 1987.

122. Hagan, *Structural Criminology.*

123. John Hagan, A. R. Gillis, and John Simpson, "The Class Structure and Delinquency: Toward a Power-Control Theory of Common Delinquent Behavior," *American Journal of Sociology* 90 (1985): 1151–1178; John Hagan, John Simpson, and A. R. Gillis, "Class in the Household: A Power-Control Theory of Gender and Delinquency," *American Journal of Sociology* 92 (1987): 788–816.

124. Gary Jensen, "Power-Control versus Social-Control Theory: Identifying Crucial Differences for Future Research," paper presented at the annual meeting of the American Society of Criminology, Baltimore, November 1990.

125. Gary Jensen and Kevin Thompson, "What's Class Got to Do with It? A Further Examination of Power-Control Theory," *American Journal of Sociology* 95 (1990): 1009–1023. For some critical research, see Simon Singer and Murray Levine, "Power Control Theory, Gender and Delinquency: A Partial Replication with Additional Evidence on the Effects of Peers," *Criminology* 26 (1988): 627–648.

126. For a lengthy review, see Hagan, *Structural Criminology.*

127. Kevin Thompson, "Gender and Adolescent Drinking Problems: The Effects of Occupational Structure," *Social Problems* 36 (1989): 30–38.

128. See, generally, Lynch, "Rediscovering Criminology," pp. 27–28.

129. Dragan Milovanovic, *A Primer in the Sociology of Law* (New York: Harrow and Heston, 1988) pp. 127–128.

130. Richard Quinney, "The Way of Peace: On Crime, Suffering and Service," in *Criminology as Peacemaking,* ed. Harold Pepinsky and Richard Quinney (Bloomington: Indiana Univerity Press, 1991), pp. 8–9.

131. See, for example, Tifft and Sullivan, *The Struggle to Be Human;* and Sullivan, *The Mask of Love.*

132. Larry Tifft, Foreword, to Sullivan, *The Mask of Love,* p. 6.

133. Ibid., p. 141.

134. Pepinsky and Quinney, *Criminology as Peacemaking.*

Chapter 10
Integrated Theories

hereas early criminologists readily embraced the theoretical work of their colleagues, modern criminologists have tended to be specialized; they classify themselves as choice, conflict, labeling, control, or some other kind of theorist.[1] As a result, criminological theory ranges from the most radical (Marxist, conflict, and deconstructionist theory) to the most conservative (rational choice and trait theory) views. The ideological differences among these positions create a gulf that sometimes seems impossible to bridge, especially when advocates are dismissive of competing viewpoints. Recently, however, to derive more powerful and robust explanations of crime, some criminologists have begun integrating these individual factors into complex, multifactor theories that attempt to blend seemingly independent concepts into coherent explanations of criminality.

A number of reasons account for the current popularity of integrated theory. One is practical: The development of large, computerized databases and software that facilitate statistical analysis now makes theory integration practical. Criminologists of an earlier era simply did not have the tools to conduct the sophisticated computations necessary for theory integration.

The other reason is substantive. Single-factor theories focus on the onset of crime; they tend to divide the world simply into criminals and noncriminals, those who have a crime-producing condition and those who do not. For example, people who feel anomie become deviant, while those who do not remain law-abiding; people with high testosterone levels are violent, while people with low levels are not.

The view that people can be classified as either criminals or noncriminals and that this status is stable over the course of a person's life is now being challenged. Criminologists today are concerned not only with the onset of criminality but with its termination: Why do people age out or desist from crime? If, for example, criminality is a function of intelligence, as some criminologists claim, why do most delinquents fail to become adult criminals? It seems unlikely that intelligence level increases as young offenders mature. If the onset of criminality can be explained by intelligence level, then some other factor must explain its termination.

Connections

The issue of age and crime and the "desistance" phenomenon was discussed in Chapter 3. As you may recall, crime rates peak in the teenage years and then decline over the life course. Explaining this decline has become an important focus of criminology.

It has also become important to chart the natural history of a criminal career. Why do some offenders escalate their criminal activities, while others decrease or limit their law violations? Why do some offenders specialize in a particular crime, while others become generalists? Why do some criminals reduce criminal activity and then resume it once again? Research now shows that some offenders begin their criminal career at a very early age while others begin at a later point in their lives. How can early- and late-onset criminality be explained?[2] This approach is sometimes referred to as **developmental criminology.**

Integrated theories have also helped focus on the chronic or persistent offender. Single-factor theories have trouble explaining why only a relatively few of the many individuals exposed to criminogenic influences in the environment actually become chronic offenders.

Connections

As you may recall from Chapter 3, the Philadelphia cohort studies conducted by Wolfgang and his associates identified the existence of a relatively small group of chronic offenders who committed a significant amount of all serious crimes and persisted in criminal careers into their adulthood.

For example, structural theories make a convincing case for a link between crime and social variables such as neighborhood disorganization and cultural deviance. It is more difficult for these theories to explain why only a few adolescents in the most disorganized areas mature into chronic offenders. Why do so many underprivileged youths resist crime despite their exposure to social disorganization and cultural deviance? There may be more than a single reason that one person engages in criminal behavior and another, living under similar circumstances, can avoid a criminal career.

By integrating a variety of ecological, socialization, psychological, biological, and economic factors into a coherent structure, criminologists are attempting to answer these complex questions. This chapter summarizes these integrated theories.

Overview of Integrated Theories

Integrated theories can be divided into three groups on the basis of their view of human development and change: multifactor theories, latent trait theories, and life-course theories.

The earliest integrated theories are referred to as **multifactor theories.** These theories suggest that social, personal, and economic factors each exert influence on criminal behavior. *Multifactor theories combine the influences of variables that have been used in structural, socialization, conflict, choice, and trait theories.*

The multifactor approach helps criminologists explain both criminal career formation and desistence from crime: Although many youths are at risk to crime, relatively few face the complete set of hazards that result in a criminal career, including an impulsive personality, a dysfunctional family, a disorganized neighborhood, deviant friends, and school failure.

In a critical article, David Rowe, D. Wayne Osgood, and W. Alan Nicewander proposed the concept of **latent traits** to explain the flow of crime over the life cycle. Their model assumes that a number of people in the population have a personal attribute or characteristic that controls their inclination or propensity to commit crimes.[3] This disposition or latent trait may be present at birth or established early in life and remains stable over time. Suspected latent traits include defective intelligence, impulsive personality, and genetic abnormalities. Those who carry these latent traits are in danger of becoming career criminals; those who lack them assume a much lower risk. Latent traits should affect the behavior choices of all people equally, regardless of their gender or personal characteristics.[4]

The positive association between past and future criminality detected in the cohort studies of career criminals may reflect the presence of underlying criminogenic traits. That is, if low IQ causes delinquency in childhood, it should also cause the same people to offend as adults, since intelligence is usually stable over the life span. Similarly, people who are antisocial during their adolescence are the ones most likely to be persistent criminals throughout their life span.

Because latent traits are stable, fluctuations in offending over time reflect criminal opportunities and not the propensity to commit crime. For example, assume that a stable latent trait such as low IQ causes some people to commit crime. Teenagers have more opportunity to commit crime than adults of equal intelligence; therefore, adolescent crime rates are higher. As they mature, low-IQ teens will commit less crime because they have fewer criminal opportunities. While the propensity to commit crime is stable, the opportunity to commit crime fluctuates. Latent trait theories thus integrate concepts usually associated with trait theories (personality and temperament) with rational choice theories (criminal opportunity and suitable targets).

Another approach that has emerged is **life-course theory.** In contrast to the latent trait view, life course theories hold that the propensity to commit crimes is not stable and does change over time; it is a developmental process.

According to life-course theory, some career criminals may desist from crime for a while, only to resume their activities at a later date. Some commit offenses at a steady pace, while others escalate their rate of criminal involvement. Offenders may specialize in one type of crime or become generalists who commit a variety of illegal acts. Criminals may be influenced by family matters, financial needs, and changes in lifestyle and interests. While latent traits may be important, they alone neither control the direction of criminal careers nor insure that criminal acts are predetermined at birth or soon afterward.

Life-course theories also recognize that as people mature, the factors that influence their behavior change.[5] At first, family relations may be most influential; in later adolescence, school and peer relations predominate; in adulthood, vocational achievement and marital relations may be the most critical. For example, some antisocial kids who are "in trouble" throughout their adolescence may manage to find stable work and maintain intact marriages as adults; these life events help them desist from crime. In contrast, the less fortunate who develop arrest records and get involved with the "wrong crowd" can only find menial jobs and are at risk for criminal careers. Social forces that are critical at one stage of life may have little meaning or influence at another.

> ## Connections
> Social process theories lay the foundation for assuming that peer, family, educational, and other interactions that vary over the life course influence behaviors. See the first few sections of Chapter 8 for a review of these issues.

While these three views seem irreconcilable, they in fact share some common ground.[6] They indicate that a criminal career must be understood as a passage along which people travel, that it has a beginning and an end, and that events and life circumstances influence the journey. The factors that affect a criminal career may include structural factors, such as income and status; socialization factors, such as family and peer relations; biological factors, such as size and strength; psychological factors, including intelligence and personality; and opportunity factors, such as free time, inadequate police protection, and a supply of easily stolen merchandise. Life-course and multifactor theories tend to stress the influence of changing interpersonal and structural factors (that is, people change along with the world they live in); latent trait theories assume that it is not people but criminal opportunities that change (that is, people do not change, but the opportunity to commit crime does).

These perspectives differ in their view of human development: Do people change, as life-course theories suggest, or are they stable, constant, and changeless, as the latent trait view indicates? Is there a dominant key that controls human destiny, or are there multiple influences on human behavior? Are the social and personal factors that influence people stable, or do they change as a person matures?

In the remainder of the chapter, we discuss some of the most important integrated theories that address the development and sustenance of a criminal career in some detail.

Multifactor Theories

Multifactor theories integrate a variety of variables into a cohesive explanation of criminality. Unlike the latent trait view, these theories recognize that factors that appear later in life, such as peer relations, exert an important influence on people.

Efforts to create multifactor theories are not new. Over a decade ago, Daniel Glazer combined elements of differential association with choice and control theory in his differential anticipation theory.[7] Glazer's version asserts: "A person's crime or restraint from crime is determined by the consequences he anticipates from it."[8] According to Glazer, people commit crimes whenever and wherever the expectations of gain from them exceed the expectations of losses (rational choice). This decision is tempered by the quality of their social bonds and their relationships with others (control theory), as well as their prior learning experiences (learning theory).

Since Glazer's pioneering efforts, significant attempts have been made to integrate such social process concepts as learning, labeling, and control with structural and other variables. A few prominent examples of integrated theory are discussed next.

The Social Development Model (SDM)

In their social development model (SDM), Joseph Weis, Richard Catalano, J. David Hawkins, and their associates have attempted to integrate social control, social learning, and structural models (see Figure 10.1).[9]

According to the **social development model (SDM),** a number of community-level "risk factors" make some people susceptible to the development of antisocial behaviors. For example, the quality of community organization influences the child's risk of developing antisocial behavior—social control is less effective when the frontline socializing institutions are weak in disorganized areas. In a low-income, disorganized community, families are under great stress, educational facilities are inadequate, fewer material goods are available, and respect for the law is weak. Because crime rates are high, there are greater opportunities for law violation, putting even more strain on the agencies of social control.

Net Bookmark

The social development model has its own homepage on the net. To view their publications and learn about what they are doing, go to:

http://weber.u.washington.edu/~sdrg/sdm.html

As a child matures within his or her environment, elements of socialization control the developmental process. Preexisting risk factors are either reinforced or neutralized through socialization. Children are socialized and develop bonds to their family through four processes:

1. Perceived opportunities for involvement in activities and interactions with others

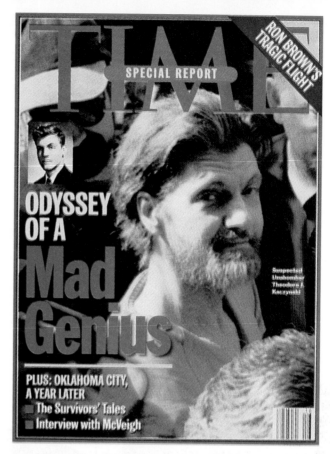

According to the social development model, as children mature, elements of socialization control their developmental process. Pre-existing risk factors are either reinforced or neutralized through socialization. Can irrational behavior such as the actions of political terrorist Theodore Kaczynski, the so-called "Unabomber," be explained in terms of environment and socialization?

2. The degree of involvement and interaction

3. The skills to participate in these interactions

4. The reinforcement (feedback) they perceive for their participation

To control the risk of antisocial behavior, a child must maintain **prosocial bonds.** These bonds are developed within the context of a family life, which not only provides prosocial opportunities but reinforces them by offering consistent positive feedback. Parental attachment, then, has the power to affect a child's behavior throughout the life course, determining both school experiences and personal beliefs and values. For those with strong family relationships, school will be a meaningful experience marked by academic success and commitment to education. Youths in this category are more likely to develop conventional beliefs and values, become committed to conventional activities, and form attachments to conventional others.

Children's antisocial behavior also depends on the quality of their attachments to others. If they remain unattached or develop attachments to deviant others, their own

Figure 10.1   The social development model of antisocial behavior.

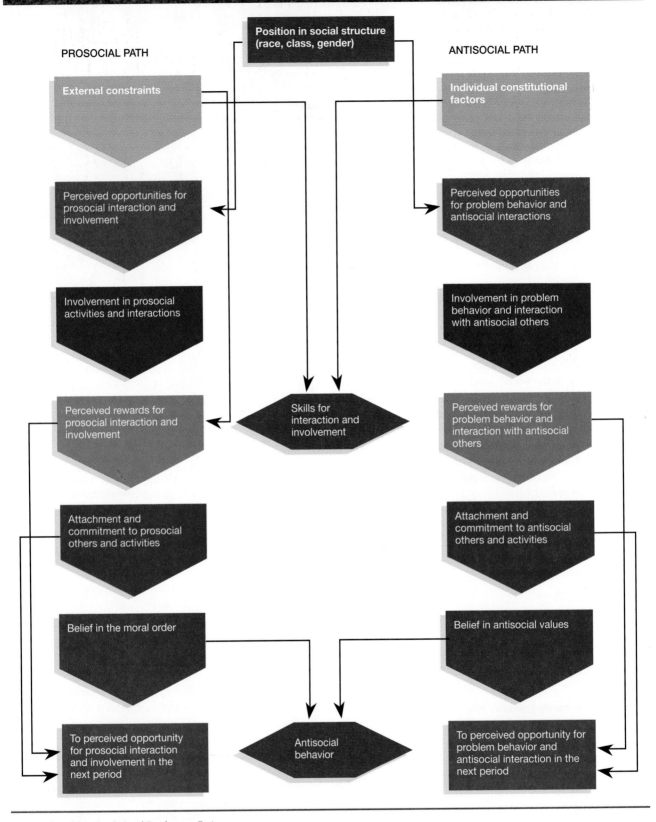

Source: Adapted from Seattle Social Development Project.

behavior may become antisocial. Unlike Hirschi's control theory, which assumes that all attachments are beneficial, SDM suggests that interaction with antisocial peers and adults promotes participation in delinquency and substance abuse over the life course.[10]

As Figure 10.1 shows, SDM also differs from Hirschi's vision of how the social bond develops. Whereas Hirschi maintains that early family attachments are the key determinants of future behavior, SDM suggests that later involvement in prosocial or antisocial behavior determines the quality of attachments. Those adolescents who perceive opportunities and rewards for antisocial behavior will form deep attachments to deviant peers, will become committed to a delinquent way of life, and will develop antisocial values and behavior. In contrast, those who perceive opportunities and rewards for prosocial behavior will take a different path, getting involved in conventional activities, forming attachments to prosocial others, and developing beliefs in the moral order.

The SDM thus holds that commitment and attachment to conventional institutions, activities, and beliefs work to insulate youths from the criminogenic influences of their environment; the prosocial path inhibits deviance by strengthening bonds to prosocial others and activities. Without the proper level of bonding, adolescents can succumb to the influence of deviant others.

Many of the core assumptions of SDM have been tested empirically, and their validity has been verified.[11] The path predicted by SDM seems an accurate picture of the onset and continuation of delinquency and drug abuse. For example, research indicates that both social learning and control-bonding factors play an important role in predicting gang membership.[12] The SDM has also guided treatment interventions that promote the development of strong bonds to family and school and help kids use these bonds to resist any opportunity or motivation to take drugs and engage in delinquent behaviors. Preliminary evaluations of one program, the Seattle Social Development Project, indicates that SDM-based interventions can help reduce delinquency and drug abuse.[13]

Elliott's Integrated Theory

Another attempt at theory integration has been proposed by Delbert Elliott and his colleagues David Huizinga and Suzanne Ageton of the Behavioral Research Institute in Boulder, Colorado.[14] Their view combines the features of strain, social learning, and control theories into a single theoretical model.

According to the Elliott view (illustrated in Figure 10.2), adolescents who live in socially disorganized areas (A) and who are improperly socialized at home (B) face a significant risk of perceiving strain (C); perceptions of strain then lead to weaked bonds with conventional groups, activities, and norms (D). Weak conventional bonds and

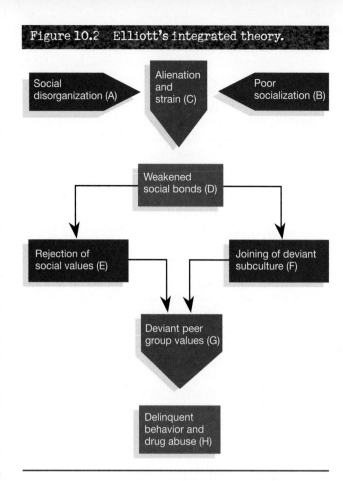

Figure 10.2 Elliott's integrated theory.

high levels of perceived strain lead some youths to reject conventional social values (E) and seek out and become bonded to deviant peer groups (F). From these delinquent associations come positive reinforcements for delinquent behaviors; delinquent peers help provide role models for antisocial behavior (G). Attachment to delinquent groups, when combined with weak bonding to conventional groups and norms, leads to a high level of delinquent behavior and drug abuse (H).

SOCIAL FACTORS. The picture Elliott and his colleagues draw of the teenage delinquent is not dissimilar to the one drawn by the SDM, with the addition of the concept of strain. Living in a disorganized neighborhood, feeling hopeless and unable to get ahead, and becoming involved in petty crimes eventually lead to a condition in which conventional social values are weakened. Concern for education, family relations, and respect for the social order are weakened. A deviant peer group becomes an acceptable substitute; consequently, the attitudes and skills that support delinquent tendencies are amplified. The result is early experimentation with drugs, and delinquency becomes a way of life. Note how both the SDM and the Elliott integrated theory assume that involvement with delinquent friends increases the risk of criminal involvement, a view disputed by Hirschi's control model.

TESTING INTEGRATED THEORY. Elliott and his colleagues tested their theoretical model with data taken from a national survey of approximately 1,800 youths interviewed annually over a three-year period. With only a few minor exceptions, the results supported their integrated theory. One difference was that some subjects reported developing strong bonds to delinquent peers even if they did not reject the values of conventional society. Elliott and his colleagues interpret this finding as suggesting that youths living in disorganized areas may have little choice but to join with law-violating youth groups, since conventional groups simply do not exist. Elliott also found that initial experimentation with drugs and delinquency predicted both joining a teenage law-violating peer group and becoming involved with additional delinquency.

In a more recent survey, Elliott and his colleagues tested their theoretical model with data taken from a national survey of more than 1,000 youths who had been interviewed annually over a three-year period.[15] The results of this newer survey generally supported their integrated theory: Bonding to a delinquent peer group escalates involvement in criminal activity.[16]

Integrated Structural Marxist Theory

Not all multifactor views of crime rely solely on mainstream concepts. In one important work, conflict theorists Mark Colvin and John Pauly have created a theory that integrates conflict concepts with structural and process factors in a theory of crime they label **integrated structural Marxist theory,** illustrated in Figure 10.3.[17]

According to Colvin and Pauly, crime is a result of socialization within the family. Coercive family relationships marked by conflict and despair are the forerunner of criminal careers. Family relations and therefore criminality are actually controlled by the marketplace.

In this viewpoint, the quality of one's work experience is shaped by the historical interaction between competition among capitalists and the level of class struggle.[18] Wage earners who occupy an inferior position in the economic hierarchy will experience coercive relationships with their supervisors and employers. Negative experiences in the workplace create strain and alienation within the family setting, which in turn relates to inconsistent and overly punitive discipline at home. Juveniles who live in such an environment will become alienated from their parents and experience adjustment problems in social institutions, especially school. For example, youths growing up in a family headed by parents who are at the bottom of workplace control structures are also the ones most likely to go to underfunded schools, do poorly on standardized tests, and be

Figure 10.3 Integrated structural Marxist theory.

Figure 10.3 Integrated structural Marxist theory.

Capitalist economic system
- Workplace environment
- Competition

Family relations
- Strain
- Alienation

Adolescent conflict
- Poor schools
- Social maladjustment
- Strain

Deviant peers
- Violence
- Theft

placed in slow learning tracks; each of these factors has been correlated with delinquent behavior.

Negative social relations at home and at school result in feelings of alienation and strain. These are reinforced by associations with groups of similarly alienated peers. In some cases, the peer groups will be oriented toward patterns of violent behavior, while in other instances the groups will enable their members to benefit economically from criminal behavior.

According to integrated structural theory, it is naive to believe that a crime control policy can be formulated without regard for its root causes. Coercive punishments or misguided treatments cannot be effective unless the core relationships with regard to material production are changed. Those who produce goods must be given a greater opportunity to control the forms of production and, in so doing, be given the power to shape their lives and the lives of their families. While integrated structural Marxist theory has not yet been subject to numerous empirical tests, recent research by Steven Messner and Marvin Krohn was generally supportive of its core principles.[19]

The Latent Trait Approach

Latent trait theories assume that some latent trait or condition, in most cases present at birth or soon after, can account for the onset of criminality. Thereafter, the propensity for crime remains stable throughout the person's life, when social forces and opportunity can influence the likelihood of crime. People age out of crime because as they mature there are simply fewer opportunities to commit crime and greater inducements to remain "straight."

What are some of the suspected traits linked to crime? As you may recall, offending patterns have been linked to such biosocial factors as attention deficit disorders and such psychological traits as impulsivity. Yet almost all biosocial and psychological advocates recognize the multidimensionality of crime. For example, as biosocial theorist Lee Ellis maintains, (1) the physical-chemical functioning of the brain is responsible for all human behavior, (2) brain function is controlled by genetic and environmental factors, and (3) environmental influences on brain function encompass both physical (drugs, chemicals, and injuries) and experiential (social) factors. Ellis finds that all three components of modern biocriminology (biochemistry, genetics, and neurology) work in concert with social and experiential factors to control crime.[20]

> ## Connections
> Individual-level factors seem ideally suited for a role in theory integration because, as noted in Chapter 6, it is evident that alone they cannot explain crime rate patterns and changes.

Here we discuss in some detail two integrated theories that assume that crime is a function of a latent trait.

Crime and Human Nature

One of the most widely read and analyzed works in the criminological literature is James Q. Wilson and Richard Herrnstein's book *Crime and Human Nature*.[21] These two prominent social scientists make a convincing argument that personal traits, such as genetic makeup, intelligence, and body build, may outweigh the importance of social variables as predictors of criminal behavior. Wilson and Herrnstein therefore propose an integrated theory of criminality that includes elements of biosocial makeup, personality, rational choice, and structure and social process.

According to Wilson and Herrnstein, all human behavior, including criminality, is determined by its perceived consequences. A criminal incident occurs when an individual chooses criminal over conventional behavior (referred to as "noncrime") after weighing the potential gains and losses of each; crime, then, is a function of *rational choice*. According to Wilson and Herrnstein, "the larger the ratio of net rewards of crime to the net rewards of noncrime, the greater the tendency to commit the crime."[22]

The rewards for crime can include material gain, sexual gratification, revenge, and peer approval. The consequences can include pangs of conscience, victim reprisals, social disapproval, and the threat of legal punishment. Although crime's negative consequences may deter some would-be criminals, their impact may be neutralized by the fact that these consequences are typically distant threats, whereas the rewards of crime are immediate and current. The rewards for choosing noncrime are also gained in the future: If you "stay clean," someday people will learn to respect you, your self-image and reputation will improve, and you may achieve happiness and freedom.

Of course, one can never be quite sure of the rewards of either crime or noncrime. The burglar hoping for the "big score" may instead experience arrest, conviction, and incarceration; people who "play it straight" may find that their sacrifice does not get them to the place in society they desire.

CHOOSING CRIME OR NONCRIME. The choice between crime and noncrime is quite often a difficult one. Criminal choices are reinforced by the desire to obtain basic rewards—food, clothing, shelter, sex—or learned goals—wealth, power, status—without having to work and save for them. Even if an individual has been socialized to choose noncrime, crime can be an attractive alternative, especially if any potential negative consequences are uncertain and delayed far into the future. By analogy, cigarette smoking is common because its potentially fatal consequences are distant and uncertain; taking cyanide or arsenic is rare because the effects are immediate and certain (although in some other ways, not too different from those of smoking).

INTEGRATING SOCIAL AND INDIVIDUAL TRAITS. Wilson and Herrnstein's model is integrative because it assumes that biological and psychological traits influence the crime-noncrime choice. They find a close link between a person's decision to choose crime and such biosocial factors as low intelligence, body type, genetic influences (parental criminality), and possessing an autonomic nervous system that responds too quickly to stimuli. Psychological traits, including an impulsive or extraverted personality and low intelligence, also determine the potential to commit crime; one of their more controversial assertions is that the relationship between crime and intelligence is "robust and significant."[23] Having these traits will not by itself guarantee that a person will become a criminal; however, all things being equal, those who have them will be more likely to choose crime over noncrime.

Wilson and Herrnstein do not ignore the influence of social factors on criminality. They believe that a turbulent family life, school failure, and membership in a deviant teenage subculture also have a powerful influence on criminality. According to Wilson and Herrnstein, biosocial, psychological, and social conditions, working in concert, can influence thought patterns and, eventually, individual behavior patterns. For example, intelligence level is considered to be an important determinant of criminal behavior choice. Its influence is mediated by a social variable, school performance: A child who chronically loses standing in the competition of the classroom may feel justified in settling the score outside by violence, theft, and other forms of defiant illegality. School failure enhances the rewards for crime by engendering feelings of unfairness. In addition, failure in school predicts, to a substantial degree, failure in the marketplace. For someone who stands to gain little from legitimate work, the rewards of noncrime are relatively weak. Failure in school, therefore, not only enhances the rewards for crime, but it predicts weak rewards for noncrime.[24]

Somewhat surprisingly, Wilson and Herrnstein do not view harsh punishment as the answer to the crime problem. They argue that the solution can be achieved by strengthening the besieged U.S. family and helping it orient children toward noncrime solutions to their problems. The family, regardless of its composition, can help a child cultivate character, conscience, and respect for the moral order. Similarly, schools can help by teaching the benefits of accepting personal responsibility and, within limits, helping students understand what constitutes "right conduct."

Wilson and Herrnstein have assembled an impressive array of supportive research in *Crime and Human Nature.* Critics of their work have focused on the fact that much of the evidence they use to support their view suffers from sampling inadequacy, questionable measurement techniques, observer bias, and neglect of sociological dimensions.[25] These criticisms aside, their work presents a dramatic attempt to integrate two of the most prominent theoretical movements in the study of criminality.

General Theory of Crime

In an important work, *A General Theory of Crime,* Michael Gottfredson and Travis Hirschi have modified and redefined some of the principles articulated in Hirschi's social control theory by integrating the concepts of control with those of biosocial, psychological, routine activities, and rational choice theories.[26]

THE ACT AND THE OFFENDER. In their **general theory of crime (GTC)**, Gottfredson and Hirschi consider the criminal offender and the criminal act as separate concepts (see Figure 10.4). On the one hand, criminal acts, such as

According to Michael Gottfredson and Travis Hirschi, the explanation for individual differences in the tendency to commit criminal acts can be found in a person's level of self-control. People with limited self-control tend to be impulsive; they are insensitive, physical (rather than mental), risk taking, short-sighted, and nonverbal, they have a "here and now" orientation, and they refuse to work for distant goals. They might become involved in the distribution of drugs because their impulsive personalities render them incapable of fearing the sanctioning power of the law.

Connections

In his original version of control theory discussed in Chapter 8, Hirschi focused on the social controls that attach people to conventional society; in this new work, he concentrates on self-control as a stabilizing force. The two views are connected, however, because both social control (or social bonds) and self-control are acquired through early experiences with effective parenting.

robberies or burglaries, are illegal events or deeds that people engage in when they perceive them to be advantageous. For example, burglaries are typically committed by young males looking for cash, liquor, and entertainment; the crime provides "easy, short-term gratification."[27] Even if the number of offenders remains constant, crime rates may fluctuate because of the presence or absence of criminal opportunities. This aspect of the theory relies on concepts similar to rational choice and routine activities theories: People commit crime when it promises rewards with minimum threat of pain or punishment. If targets are well protected by effective guardians, crime rates will diminish. Only the truly irrational offender would dare to strike out under those circumstances.

On the other hand, criminal offenders are people predisposed to commit crimes. They are not robots who commit crime without restraint; their days are also filled with conventional behaviors, such as going to school, parties, concerts, and church. But given the same set of criminal

Figure 10.4   The general theory of crime.

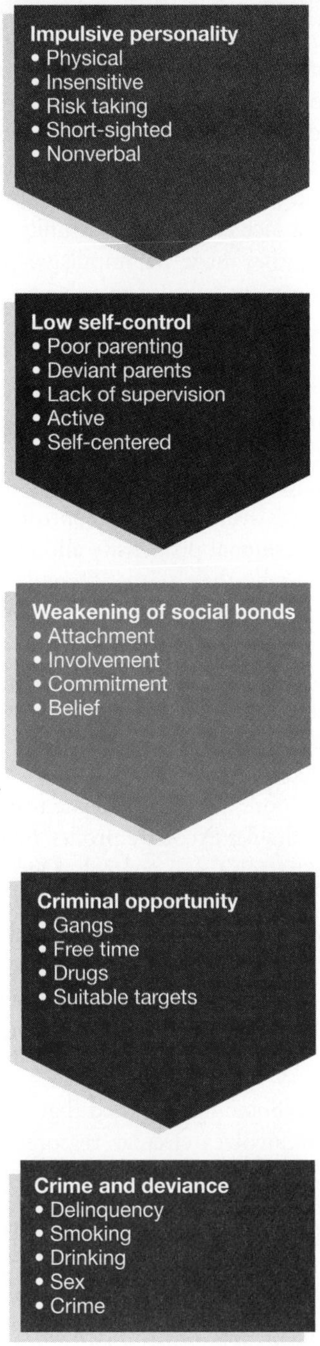

Impulsive personality
- Physical
- Insensitive
- Risk taking
- Short-sighted
- Nonverbal

Low self-control
- Poor parenting
- Deviant parents
- Lack of supervision
- Active
- Self-centered

Weakening of social bonds
- Attachment
- Involvement
- Commitment
- Belief

Criminal opportunity
- Gangs
- Free time
- Drugs
- Suitable targets

Crime and deviance
- Delinquency
- Smoking
- Drinking
- Sex
- Crime

WHAT MAKES PEOPLE CRIME-PRONE?   What, then, causes people to become excessively crime-prone? To Gottfredson and Hirschi, the explanation for individual differences in the tendency to commit criminal acts can be found in a person's level of **self-control.** People with limited self-control tend to be *impulsive.* According to Gottfredson and Hirschi, impulsive people are insensitive, physical (rather than mental), risk taking, short-sighted, and nonverbal.[28] They have a "here and now" orientation and refuse to work for distant goals; they lack diligence, tenacity, and persistence in a course of action. People who are impulsive tend to lack self-control. They are adventuresome, active, physical, and self-centered. As they mature, they have unstable marriages, jobs, and friendships.[29] People lacking self-control are less likely to feel shame if they engage in deviant acts and more likely to find these acts pleasurable.[30]

Criminal acts are attractive to these people because they provide easy and immediate gratification or, as Gottfredson and Hirschi put it, "money without work, sex without courtship, revenge without court delays."[31] Because those with low self-control enjoy risky, exciting, or thrilling behaviors with immediate benefits, they are more likely to enjoy criminal acts that require stealth, danger, agility, speed, and power than conventional acts, which demand long-term study and cognitive and verbal skills.

Considering their desire for easy pleasures, it should come as no surprise that people lacking in self-control will also engage in noncriminal behaviors that provide them with immediate and short-term gratification, such as smoking, drinking, gambling, and illicit sexuality.[32]

What causes people to lack self-control? Gottfredson and Hirschi trace the origins of poor self-control to inadequate child-rearing practices. Parents who refuse or are unable to monitor a child's behavior, to recognize deviant behavior when it occurs, and to punish that behavior will produce children who lack self-control. Kids who are not attached to their parents, who are poorly supervised, and whose parents are criminal or deviant themselves are the most likely to develop poor self-control. In a sense, lack of self-control is a "natural occurrence" that will happen in the absence of steps taken to stop its development.[33]

Low self-control develops early in life and remains stable into and through adulthood.[34] Considering the continuity of criminal motivation, Hirschi and Gottfredson have questioned the utility of the juvenile justice system and of giving special, and presumably more lenient, treatment to delinquent offenders: Why separate youthful and adult offenders legally, when the source of their criminality is essentially the same?[35]

SELF-CONTROL AND CRIME   Gottfredson and Hirschi claim that the principles of self-control theory can be used to explain all varieties of criminal behavior and all the social and behavioral correlates of crime. That is, such widely disparate crimes as burglary, robbery, embezzlement, drug dealing, murder, rape, and insider trading all stem from a

opportunities, criminogenic people have a much higher probability of violating the law than noncriminals do.

By recognizing that there are stable differences in people's propensity to commit crime, the general theory adds a biosocial element to the concept of social control: Individual differences are stable over the life course and so is the propensity to commit crime; it is only opportunity that changes.

deficiency of self-control. Likewise, gender, racial, and ecological differences in the crime rate can be explained by discrepancies in self-control. Put another way, if the male crime rate is higher than the female crime rate (which it is), the discrepancy can be explained by the fact that males have lower levels of self-control.

Unlike other theoretical models that are limited to explaining narrow segments of criminal behavior (such as theories of teenage gang formation), Gottfredson and Hirschi argue that self-control applies equally to all crimes, ranging from murder to corporate theft. For example, Gottfredson and Hirschi maintain that rates of white-collar crime remain quite low because people lacking in self-control rarely attain the position necessary to commit those crimes. However, the relatively few white-collar criminals lack self-control in the manner rapists and burglars lack self-control. Gottfredson and Hirschi recognize that all people become less crime-prone as they age. While the criminal activity of low-self-control individuals also declines, they maintain an offense rate that remains consistently higher than those with strong self-control.

SUPPORTING EVIDENCE FOR THE GTC.

Following the publication of the general theory of crime, several research efforts have been conducted that support the theoretical views of Gottfredson and Hirschi. One approach is to identify indicators of impulsiveness and self-control and determine whether scales measuring these factors correlate with measures of criminal activity; a number of studies have had success in showing this type of association.[36] For example, both male and female drunk drivers were found to be impulsive individuals who manifest low self-control.[37] Research on violent recidivists indicates that they can be distinguished from other offenders on the basis of their impulsive personality structure.[38] Studies of incarcerated youths show that they enjoy risk-taking behavior and hold values and attitudes that suggest impulsivity.[39] Kids who take drugs and commit crime have been shown to be impulsive and enjoy engaging in risky behaviors.[40] In one recent study, John Gibbs and Dennis Giever found that measures of self-control were able to predict deviant behavior (cutting class and drinking) among a sample of college students.[41] And a similar analysis of self-report data by Giever found that one of the core assumptions of GTC has validity: The quality of parental supervision influences both self-control and subsequent deviant behavior.[42]

Cross-national data have also supported the core concepts of GTC. One study of Canadian youth by Marc LeBlanc and his associates found that kids with an "egocentric personality" develop weak social ties and are more likely to engage in delinquency and nonconventional behaviors.[43]

A number of recent studies have noted that as predicted by Gottfredson and Hirschi, low self-control may interact with criminal opportunity in the decision to commit crimes.[44] It is possible that the causal chain flows from an (1) impulsive personality to (2) lack of self-control to (3) the withering of social bonds to (4) the opportunity to commit crime and delinquency to (5) deviant behavior.[45]

ANALYZING THE GENERAL THEORY OF CRIME.

Gottfredson and Hirschi's general theory provides answers to many of the questions left unresolved by Hirschi's original single-factor control model. By integrating the concepts of criminality and crime, Gottfredson and Hirschi help explain why some people who lack self-control can escape criminality: They lack criminal opportunity. People who are at risk because they have an impulsive personality may forgo criminal careers because they have noncriminal opportunities that satisfy their impulsive needs: They enroll in tennis lessons; they go to church; they join the Boy Scouts; they enter the military; they have great athletic ability and make the team. In contrast, if the opportunity is strong enough, even those people with relatively strong self-control may be tempted to violate the law; the incentives to commit crime may overwhelm self-control.

Integrating criminal propensity and criminal opportunity can explain why the so-called "good kid," who has a strong school record and positive parental relationships, gets involved in drugs or vandalism or why the corporate executive with a spotless record gets caught up in business fraud. Even a successful executive may find his or her self-control inadequate if the potential for illegal gain runs into the tens of millions. It is also possible, as Michael Benson and Elizabeth Moore contend, that the fear of failure, and not the mere desire for excessive profits, overwhelms an affluent businessperson's self-control. During tough economic times, the impulsive manager who fears dismissal may be tempted to circumvent the law to improve the bottom line.[46]

Although the general theory seems persuasive, several questions and criticisms remain unanswered, including the following.[47]

1. *Tautological.* Some have argued that the theory is tautological or involves circular reasoning: How do we know when people are impulsive? When they commit crimes! Are all criminals impulsive? Of course, or else they would have not broken the law![48] Gottfredson and Hirschi counter by saying that impulsivity is not in itself a propensity to commit crime but a condition that inhibits people from appreciating the long-term consequences of their behavior; consequently, if given the opportunity, they are more likely to indulge in criminal acts than the nonimpulsive.[49] According to Gottfredson and Hirschi, then, impulsivity and criminality are neither identical nor equivalent concepts. Some impulsive people may channel their reckless energies into noncrime activity, such as trading on the commodities markets or real estate speculation, and make a legitimate fortune for their efforts.

2. *Personality disorder.* Saying someone lacks self-control implies that he or she suffers from a personality defect

that makes him or her impulsive and rash. The view that criminals have a deviant personality is not new; psychologists have long sought evidence of a "criminal personality."[50] Yet the search for the criminal personality has proven elusive, and there is still no conclusive proof that criminals can be distinguished from noncriminals on the basis of personality alone.

3. *Ecological/individual differences.* GTC also fails to address individual and ecological patterns in the crime rate. For example, if crime rates are higher in Los Angeles than Albany, New York, can it be assumed that Angelinos are more impulsive than Albanians? There is little evidence of regional differences in impulsivity or self-control. Can these differences be explained solely by variation in criminal opportunity? Little effort has been made in GTC to account for the influence of culture, ecology, economy, and so on in criminality. Gottfredson and Hirschi might counter that crime rate differences may reflect criminal opportunity: One area might have more effective law enforcement, more draconian laws, and higher levels of guardianship. Opportunity is controlled by economy and culture.

   Although distinct gender differences in the crime rate exist, there is little evidence that males are more impulsive than females (even though females and males do in fact differ in many other personality traits).[51] Similarly, Gottfredson and Hirschi explain racial differences in crime as a failure of child-rearing practices in the African American community.[52] In so doing, they overlook issues of institutional racism, poverty, and relative deprivation, which have been shown to have a significant impact on crime rate differentials.

4. *Moral beliefs.* The general theory also ignores the moral concept of right and wrong, or "belief," which Hirschi considered a cornerstone in his earlier writings on the social bond.[53] Does this mean that learning and assimilation of moral values has little effect on criminality? Because it omits the concept of belief, the general theory of crime can be distinguished from control theories that assume that people are controlled by their sense of right and wrong.

5. *Do people change?* The general theory assumes that people do not change; it is opportunity that changes. Is it possible that human personality and behavior patterns remain little altered over the life course? Research by Scott Menard, Delbert Elliott, and Sharon Wofford indicates that factors that help control criminal behavior, such as peer relations and school performance, vary over time. Factors that have a controlling effect in early adolescence may fade and be replaced by others.[54] For example, Elliott and Menard found that having delinquent peers encourages future criminality and that the propensity to commit crimes is influenced by peer rela-

tions that develop in adolescence.[55] Graham Ousey and David Aday, Jr. found that as children mature, peer influence over delinquent behavior choices continues to grow; in contrast, the GTC suggests that the influence of friends should be stable and unchanging.[56]

   Julie Horney and her associates have shown that changing life circumstances, such as starting and leaving school, abusing substances and getting "straight," and starting or ending personal relationships, all have an influence on the frequency of offending.[57] For example, people are more likely to commit crimes when using illegal drugs and less likely when they are living with a wife. These findings contradict self-control theory, which assumes that criminality is both a constant and independent of personal relationships. However, it is uncertain whether life changes affect the *propensity* to commit crime or merely the *opportunity,* as Gottfredson and Hirschi would suggest.

6. *Cross-cultural differences.* There is evidence that criminals in other countries do not lack self-control, indicating that GTC may be culturally limited.[58] Behavior that may be considered imprudent and risky in one culture may be socially acceptable in another and therefore cannot be explained by a "lack of self-control."[59]

While these questions remain, the strength of the general theory lies in its scope and breadth; it attempts to explain all forms of crime and deviance, from lower-class gang delinquency to sexual harassment in the business community.[60] By integrating concepts of criminal choice, criminal opportunity, socialization, and personality, Gottfredson and Hirschi make a plausible argument that all deviant behaviors may originate at the same source. Continued efforts are needed to test the GTC and establish the validity of its core concepts. It remains one of the key developments of modern criminological theory.

Life-Course Theories

What causes the onset of criminality? What sustains a criminal career over a person's life course? A number of themes are now emerging. One is that the seeds of a criminal career are planted early in life: Early onset of deviance is a strong predictor of later criminality. Research now shows that kids who will later become delinquents begin their deviant careers at a very early (preschool) age.[61] Studies of narcotics addicts show that the earlier the onset of substance abuse, the more frequent, varied, and sustained the addict's criminal career.[62]

Another theme is the **continuity of crime:** The best predictor of future criminality is past criminality. Kids who are repeatedly in trouble during adolescence are the ones who will still be antisocial as adults. Criminal activity beginning early in the life course is likely to be sustained, because these offenders seem to lack the "social survival skills" necessary

Connections

As you may recall from Chapter 4, a great deal of research has been conducted on the relationship of age and crime and the activities of chronic offenders. This body of scholarship has prompted interest in the life cycle of crime.

to find work or develop the interpersonal relationships needed to allow them to "drop out" of crime.[63]

Life-course theories are inherently multidimensional, suggesting that criminality has multiple roots, including maladaptive personality traits, educational failure, and dysfunctional family relations. Criminality, according to this view, cannot be attributed to a single cause, nor does it represent a single underlying tendency.[64]

Life-course theorists conclude that multiple social, personal, and economic factors can influence criminality and that as these factors change over time, so, too, does criminal involvement.[65] As people make important transitions in their life—from child to adolescent, from adolescent to adult, from unwed to married—the nature of their social interactions changes and so, too, does their behavior. In their **social interactional theory,** Gerald Patterson and his colleagues argue that children whose socialization is ineffective because of improper, maladaptive parenting later build on this improper interactional style and engage in behavior that leads them to be rejected by their peers and to experience academic failure.[66] They then turn to deviant peers from whom they learn new forms of antisocial behavior. Patterson and his colleagues have found that early childhood family conflicts and lack of a strong bond with parents open the door for social conflict in later adolescence.[67]

The Glueck Research

One of the cornerstones of the recent life-course research lies in renewed interest in the research efforts of Sheldon and Eleanor Glueck. While at Harvard University in the 1930s, the Gluecks popularized research on the **life cycle** of delinquent careers. In a series of longitudinal research studies, they followed the careers of known delinquents to determine the factors that predicted persistent offending.[68] The Gluecks made extensive use of interviews and records in their elaborate comparisons of delinquents and nondelinquents.[69]

The Gluecks' research was a precursor of the life-course school. They focused on **early onset** of delinquency as a harbinger of a criminal career: "The deeper the roots of childhood maladjustment, the smaller the chance of adult adjustment." They also noted the stability of offending careers: Children who are antisocial early in life are the ones most likely to continue their offending careers into adulthood.

The Gluecks identified a number of personal and social factors related to persistent offending, the most important of which—family relations—included the quality of discipline and emotional ties with parents. The adolescent raised in a large, single-parent family of limited economic means and educational achievement was the one most vulnerable to delinquency.

The Gluecks did not restrict their analysis to social variables. When they measured such biological and psychological traits as body type, intelligence, and personality, they found that physical and mental factors also played a role in determining behavior. Children with low intelligence, with a background of mental disease, and with a powerful physique (mesomorphs) were the ones most likely to become persistent offenders.

The Gluecks' research was virtually ignored for nearly 30 years as the study of crime and delinquency shifted almost exclusively to the social and social-psychological factors (poverty, neighborhood deterioration, socialization) that formed the nucleus of structural and process theories. The Gluecks' methodology and their integration of biological, psychological, and social factors were heavily criticized by the mainstream sociologists who dominated the field. For many years, their work was ignored in criminology texts and overlooked in the academic curriculum.

Life Course Emerges

During the past decade, the Glueck "legacy" was "rediscovered" in a series of papers by criminologists John Laub and Robert Sampson. These scholars argued that the careful empirical measurements made by the Gluecks, which had been cast aside by the criminological community, were actually an ideal platform for studying criminal careers.[70] Laub and Sampson have reanalyzed the Glueck data and used it in a series of articles that have gained wide readership. Their work will be discussed in greater detail later in the chapter.

A 1990 review paper by Rolf Loeber and Marc LeBlanc was another important event in the development of life-course theory.[71] In this critical work, Loeber and LeBlanc proposed that criminologists devote time and effort to understanding some basic questions about the evolution of criminal careers:

1. Why do people begin committing antisocial acts?

2. Why do some stop or desist, while others continue or persist?

3. Why do some escalate the severity of their criminality—that is, go from shoplifting to drug dealing to armed robbery—while others deescalate and commit less serious crime as they mature?

4. If some terminate their criminal activity, what, if anything, causes them to begin again?

5. Why do some criminals specialize in certain types of crime, while others are generalists engaging in a garden variety of antisocial behavior?

According to Loeber and LeBlanc's developmental view, criminologists must devote their attention to the way a criminal career unfolds over a person's life cycle.

A number of key research efforts have also found that criminogenic influences change and develop over time. In their studies on delinquency prevention, Gerald Patterson and his colleagues at the Oregon Social Learning Center found that poor parental discipline and monitoring was a key to the onset of criminality in early childhood. Then, in middle childhood, social rejection by conventional peers and academic failure sustained antisocial behavior. In later adolescence, commitment to a deviant peer group created a "training ground" for crime. Kids who are improperly socialized by unskilled parents are the ones most likely to rebel by wandering the streets with their deviant peers.[72] While the onset of a criminal career is a function of poor parenting skills, its maintenance and support is connected to social relations that emerge later in life.[73]

Similar results have been obtained from the Pittsburgh Youth Study, a longitudinal analysis of elementary school–age boys that indicates that early onset is correlated with social withdrawal, depression, deviant peers, and family problems, while later onset (at ages 13 or 14) is related to low educational motivation.[74]

From these and similar efforts has emerged a view of crime that incorporates personal change and growth. The factors that produce crime and delinquency at one point in the life cycle may not be relevant at another; as people mature, the social, physical, and environmental influences on their behavior are transformed.

In the following sections, we review some of the more important concepts associated with the life-course perspective and discuss three prominent life-course theories.

Is There a Problem Behavior Syndrome?

Most criminological theories portray crime as the *result* of social problems rather than their *cause*. For example, learning theorists view a troubled home life and deviant friends as precursors of criminality; structural theorists maintain that acquiring deviant cultural values leads to criminality. In contrast, the life-course view is that criminality may best be understood as one of many social problems faced by at-risk youth. Criminality may be part of a **problem behavior syndrome (PBS),** a group of antisocial behaviors that cluster together and typically involve family dysfunction, substance abuse, smoking, precocious sexuality and early pregnancy, educational underachievement, suicide attempts, sensation seeking, and unemployment.[75] People who suffer from one of these conditions typically exhibit symptoms of the rest.[76] All varieties of criminal behavior, including violence, theft and public order crimes, may be part of a generalized PBS, indicating that all forms of antisocial behavior have similar developmental patterns.[77]

Those who suffer PBS are prone to have a range of social problems, from abusing drugs to being accident-prone to requiring more health care and hospitalization than the general population.[78] PBS has been linked to personality (for example, rebelliousness and low ego), family problems (interfamily conflict, parental mental disorder), and educational failure (school rejection).[79] Multisite research has shown that PBS is not unique to any single area of the country and that kids who suffer PBS, including drug use, delinquency, and precocious sexuality, display symptoms at a very early age.[80]

Many examples support the existence of PBS. A survey of Minnesota students in grades 6, 9, and 12 showed that children who experienced physical and sexual abuse at the hands of parents or other adults were also likely to have eating disorders (binge eating, purging, anorexia) and increased levels of cigarette smoking, alcohol consumption, stress, anxiety, hard-drug use, and suicidal thoughts; they were likely to have families with histories of alcohol abuse and drug addiction.[81] Other research links family violence to a variety of family and environmental problems that seem to cluster together: low income, single parent, residence in an isolated ghetto area, lack of family support or resources, racism, and prolonged exposure to poverty.[82]

In one important study showing the nature of PBS, Helene Raskin White studied a sample of 400 youths measured repeatedly over a six-year cycle. She found that behaviors that clustered together included delinquency, substance abuse, school misconduct and underachievement, precocious sexual behavior, violence, suicide, and mental health problems.[83] White found problem behaviors to be stable: Subjects who experienced multiple problems at age 15 continued to experience them at age 21. In a subsequent analysis of adolescent misbehavior conducted with Erich Labouvie, White found that PBS might involve one of several clusters of behavior, including drug "specialists," crime specialists, and "generalists" who engage in both delinquency and drug abuse. Generalists are the most likely to suffer PBS, displaying higher levels of psychological problems, a lack of control, and lower emotional stability.[84]

So problem behaviors—including violence, drug abuse, and theft—may cluster in a number of ways, affecting people as they mature from adolescence into adulthood.[85] The interconnection of problem behaviors should increase the risk of teenage pregnancy, AIDS, and other sources of social distress that require a combination of behaviors (sex, drug use, violence).

The Course of Criminal Careers

Life-course theorists recognize that there may be more than a single road traveled by career criminals: Some may specialize in violence and extortion; some may be involved in theft and fraud; others may engage in a variety of criminal acts. Some offenders may begin their career early in life, while others are "late bloomers" who begin committing crime at the age when most people desist.

PATHWAYS TO CRIME. Are there different pathways to crime? Using data taken from a longitudinal cohort study conducted in Pittsburgh, Rolf Loeber and his associates are now mapping the various pathways to crime traveled by at-risk youth.[86] Loeber and his associates have so far identified three distinct paths to a criminal career (see Figure 10.5):

1. The **authority conflict pathway** begins at an early age with stubborn behavior and defiance of parents. This leads to defiance (doing things one's own way, refusing to do things, disobedience) and then to authority avoidance (staying out late, truancy, running away).

2. The **covert pathway** begins with minor underhanded behavior (lying, shoplifting) that leads to property damage (setting fires, vandalism) and eventually escalates to more serious forms of criminality, ranging from joyriding, pocket picking, larceny, and fencing to passing bad checks, using bad credit cards, stealing cars, dealing drugs, and breaking and entering.

3. The **overt pathway** consists of an escalation of aggressive acts beginning with aggression (annoying others, bullying) leading to physical (and gang) fighting and on to violence (attacking someone, strongarming, forced theft).

The Loeber research indicates that each of these paths may lead to a sustained deviant career. Some youths enter two and even three paths simultaneously: They are stubborn, lie to teachers and parents, are bullies, and commit petty thefts. These are the adolescents most likely to become persistent offenders as they mature. While some persistent offenders may specialize in one type of behavior, others engage in a variety of criminal acts and antisocial behaviors. For example, they may start out cheating on tests and bullying kids in the schoolyard, then move on to take drugs, commit a burglary, steal a car, and then shoplift from a store. In the Close-Up on violent female criminals, the life course of one such offender group is discussed in detail.

ADOLESCENT-LIMITED OFFENDERS AND LIFE-COURSE PERSISTERS. In addition to taking different paths to criminality, people may begin their journey at different times in their life. Some are precocious, beginning their criminal careers at an early age; others are late bloomers who stay out of trouble until their teenage years. Some offenders may peak at an early age, while others persist into their adulthood. Research now shows that there are a number of types or "classes" of criminal careers that seem to reflect changes in the life course.[87]

According to psychologist Terrie Moffitt, whereas the prevalence and frequency of antisocial behavior peaks in adolescence and then diminishes for most offenders (she la-

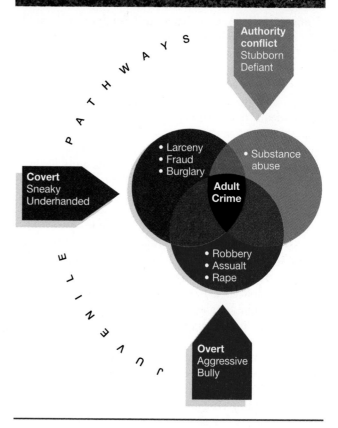

Figure 10.5 Pathways to crime: There may be more than one path to crime, although some people may take two or three simultaneously.

PATHWAYS

JUVENILE

Authority conflict
Stubborn
Defiant

Covert
Sneaky
Underhanded

• Larceny
• Fraud
• Burglary

• Substance abuse

Adult Crime

• Robbery
• Assualt
• Rape

Overt
Aggressive
Bully

bels these offenders **adolescent-limited**), a small group of **life-course persistent** deviants offend well into their adulthood.[88] Life-course persistents combine family dysfunction with severe neurological problems that predispose them to antisocial behavior patterns. These afflictions can be the result of maternal drug abuse, poor perinatal nutrition, or exposure to toxic agents such as lead. Those afflicted may have lower verbal ability, which inhibits reasoning skills, learning ability, and school achievement. During their youth, adolescent-limited delinquents mimic the behavior of these more troubled teens but reduce the frequency of their offending as they mature at around age 18.[89]

Research also shows that kids who mature faster (**pseudomaturity**) have a greater chance of becoming life-course persisters. The earlier an adolescent engages in substance abuse and sexuality or suffers emotional distress, the more likely he or she will be involved in adult deviance.[90]

EARLY VERSUS LATE ONSET. While most life-course persisters are "early starters," some begin their offending career in late adolescence, after age 14. These "late starters" are also at high risk for adult criminality regardless of what age they began their offending careers.[91]

close-up: *Violent Female Criminals*

Why do some people become persistent offenders while others desist from crime? Are the paths taken by males and females similar? While considerable research is now being devoted to gender differences in the crime rate, little has been done to chart the life course of one subset of this group: violent female street criminals. To correct this oversight, research by Deborah Baskin and Ira Sommers and by Henry Brownstein and his associates used interviews with samples of violent female felons in New York. Their data provide considerable insight into the formation and maintenance of a criminal career.

Baskin and Sommers found that about 60% of violent female offenders begin their criminal career at a very early age; about half reported regular fighting as early as 10 years old, and about 40% reported that they regularly left home carrying a weapon. In contrast, the other 40% reported that they did not engage in fighting until much later, not until they had left school. Because of the clear time differential in when these females began their criminal careers, Baskin and Sommers conducted an independent analysis of the early- and late-onset offenders.

The women in both groups suffered from severe social and emotional problems. All were likely to have been raised in single-parent families and to have received little parental supervision. Both groups experienced physical and sexual abuse at the hand of a parent or guardian and were likely to have witnessed abuse between their guardians. Almost half were raised in households that relied on public welfare. More than half had a parent who was either a substance abuser or who had been incarcerated sometime during his or her childhood.

Women in the early onset group could be distinguished by the severity of their

childhood problems. They were the ones most likely to reside in areas with high concentrations of poverty and to have family histories of psychiatric problems requiring hospitalization. They were more likely to be truant, leave school early, and associate with delinquent peers while in school. They also were more likely to be placed in a juvenile detention center.

The major distinction between the groups, however, could be found in the scale and direction of their offending careers. While both groups were drug users, early-onset women began abusing substances two years ahead of the late-onset group. The early-onset group were involved in a variety of crimes, including serious robberies, assaults, and burglaries, even before they became involved with drug use. In contrast, the later-onset group were involved mostly in nonviolent crimes, such as shoplifting and prostitution, *up until* they began taking drugs. The violent offending of the latter group was thus clearly part of a drug-crime connection. In contrast, the violent behavior of the early-onset women was part of a generalized PBS.

A number of research studies support the Baskin-Sommers findings. Helene Raskin White and Stephen Hansell found that girls who begin using alcohol early in life are the ones most likely to be aggressive and violent in their later years. Although women are less likely to be aggressive than men, early alcohol abuse was a much stronger predictor of female than male violence. Henry Brownstein and his associates conducted interviews with 215 women convicted of murder. Most of these women told a familiar story: the most violent had histories of juvenile violence, drug abuse, and personal victimization. The researchers found that 65% had participated in some violent activity and

64% claimed to have seriously harmed someone when they were growing up; 58% had been the victim of serious physical harm and 49% had been sexually abused. These women had a long-term commitment to crime, beginning in early childhood and continuing through their use of deadly violence in their adulthood. Brownstein also focused on the behavior of 19 women who had killed in the context of drug dealing. Some of these acts were motivated by economic interests, while others were motivated out of their relationship to a man—killing on behalf of a man or out of fear of a man.

These research efforts are supportive of the life-course view: Events in these women's adult lives shaped the direction of their offending careers. The researchers found that there are in fact different pathways to a crime and that both environmental and serendipitous life circumstances (such as meeting the wrong man) influences offending. These conclusions support a life-course view and repudiate the latent trait approach.

CRITICAL DISCUSSION QUESTIONS

1. What are some of the pathways to chronic offending among violent females?
2. Do you believe that some conditions present at birth can control future criminal behavior?

Sources: Deborah Baskin and Ira Sommers, "Females' Initiation into Violent Street Crime," *Justice Quarterly* 10 (1993): 559–581; Helene Raskin White and Stephen Hansell, "The Moderating Effects of Gender and Hostility on the Alcohol-Aggression Relationship," *Journal of Research in Crime and Delinquency* 33 (1996): 450–470; Henry Brownstein, Barry Spunt, Susan Crimmins, and Sandra Langley, "Women Who Kill in Drug Market Situations," *Justice Quarterly* 12 (1995): 473–498.

Why do some people enter a path to crime later rather than sooner? According to research by Ronald Simons, early-starter adolescents (those who begin their offending career before age 14) experience (a) poor parenting, which leads them into (b) deviant behaviors and then (c) involve-

ment with delinquent groups. In contrast, late starters follow a somewhat different path: (a) poor parenting leads to (b) identification with a delinquent group and then into (c) deviant involvement. By implication, adolescents who suffer poor parenting and are at risk for deviant careers can avoid criminality if they can bypass involvement with delinquent peers.[92]

Additional research efforts have found that early- and late-onset offenders take different paths into crime and are influenced by different life factors. Paul Mazzerole has found that criminal peers exert a greater influence on the late bloomers than their more precocious peers. Late starters thus seem to be influenced by their peer group interaction, a factor that develops and expands as an adolescent travels the life course.[93] In a study of incarcerated criminals, Charles Dean and his associates also found that early starters were more likely to be the victim of child abuse than later starters were. In addition, criminal punishments seemed to have a greater deterrent effect on early starters. It is possible, Dean and his associates speculate, that early starters learn from their early experiences and become more cunning criminals, increasing their offending rates while avoiding detection.[94]

The discovery that people begin their criminal careers at different ages and follow different paths and trajectories of offending gives important support for the life-course view. If all criminals have a singular latent trait that makes them crime-prone, it would be unlikely that these variations in criminal careers would be observed. It is difficult to explain such concepts as "late onset" and "adolescent-limited behavior" from the perspective of latent trait theory.

An ongoing effort has been made to track persistent offenders over their life course.[95] The early data seems to support what is already known about delinquent-criminal career patterns: Early onset predicts later offending, there is continuity in crime (juvenile offenders are the ones most likely to become adult criminals), and chronic offenders commit a significant portion of all crimes.[96]

Based on these findings, a number of systematic theories that account for the onset, continuance, and desistance from crime have been formulated. In the following sections, we discuss three life-course theories in some detail.

Farrington's Theory of Delinquent Development

One of the most important of the longitudinal studies tracking persistent offenders is the Cambridge Study in Delinquent Development. This effort has followed the offending careers of 411 London boys born in 1953.[97] This cohort study, directed since 1982 by David Farrington, is one of the most serious attempts to isolate the factors that predict the continuity of criminal behavior throughout the life course. The study uses self-report data as well as in-depth interviews and psychological testing. The boys were interviewed 8 times over a period of 24 years, beginning at age eight and continuing to age 32.[98]

The results of the Cambridge study have been quite important because they show that many of the same patterns found in the United States are repeated in a cross-national sample: the existence of chronic offenders, the continuity of offending, and early onset leading to persistent criminality.

Farrington found that the traits present in persistent offenders can be observed as early as age 8. The chronic criminal, typically a male, has been born into a low-income, large family headed by parents who have criminal records and with delinquent older siblings. The future criminal receives poor parental supervision, including the use of harsh or erratic punishment and child-rearing techniques; his parents are likely to divorce or separate.

The chronic offender tends to associate with friends who are also future criminals. By age 8, he is already exhibiting antisocial behavior, including dishonesty and aggressiveness. At school, he tends to have low educational achievement and is restless, troublesome, hyperactive, impulsive, and often truant.

After leaving school at age 18, the persistent criminal tends to maintain a relatively well paid but low-status job and is likely to have an erratic work history and periods of unemployment. Deviant behavior tends to be versatile rather than specialized. That is, the typical offender not only commits property offenses, such as theft and burglary, but also engages in violence, vandalism, drug use, excessive drinking, drunk driving, smoking, reckless driving, and sexual promiscuity—evidence of a generalized problem behavior syndrome. Chronic offenders are more likely to live away from home and have conflict with their parents. They wear tattoos, go out most evenings, and enjoy hanging out with groups of their friends. They are much more likely than nonoffenders to get involved in fights, to carry weapons, and to use them in violent encounters. The frequency of offending reaches a peak in the teenage years (about 17 or 18) and then declines in the 20s, when the offender marries or lives with a woman.

By the time he reaches his 30s, the former delinquent is likely to be separated or divorced from his wife and be an absent parent. His employment record remains spotty, and he moves often to rental units rather than owner-occupied housing. His life is still characterized by evenings out, heavy drinking and substance abuse, and more violent behavior than his contemporaries'. Because the typical offender provides the same kind of deprived and disrupted family life for his own children that he experienced, the social experiences and conditions that produce delinquency are carried on from one generation to the next.

NONOFFENDERS AND DESISTERS. Farrington has also identified factors that predict the discontinuity of criminal offenses: People who exhibit these factors have a background that puts them at risk to crime, but they either are able to remain nonoffenders or begin a criminal career but later desist. The factors that "protect" high-risk youth from even beginning a criminal career include having a personality that renders them somewhat shy, having few friends (at age 8), having a nondeviant family, and being highly re-

David Farrington's longitudinal research found that the persistent offender was typically a male who began his criminal career as a property offender. Such offenders were born into low-income, large families headed by parents who had criminal records and with delinquent older siblings. The future criminal received poor parental supervision, including the use of harsh or erratic punishment and child-rearing techniques; the parents were likely to have divorced or separated.

garded by their mother. Shy kids with few friends avoid damaging relationships with other adolescent boys—members of a high-risk group—and are therefore able to avoid criminality.

What caused offenders to desist? Holding a relatively good job helps reduce criminal activity. Unemployment seems to be related to the escalation of theft offenses; violence and substance abuse are unaffected by unemployment. In a similar vein, getting married also helps diminish criminal activity. However, finding a spouse who is also involved in criminal activity and has a criminal record increases criminal involvement.

Physical relocation also helps some offenders desist. Leaving the city and going to a more rural or suburban area was linked to reductions in criminal activity. Relocation forces offenders to sever ties with co-offenders.

Although employment, marriage, and relocation helped offenders desist, not all desisters found the key to success. At-risk youth who managed to avoid criminal convictions were unlikely to avoid other social problems. Rather than becoming prosperous homeowners with flourishing careers, they tended to live in unkempt homes and have large debts and low-paying jobs. Desisters were more likely to remain single and live alone: Youths who experience social isolation at age 8 also experience it at age 32.

THEORETICAL MODELING. Farrington has summarized these observations by proposing a theory of criminality based on his long-term data collections. Farrington's theoretical model is as follows:

1. Childhood factors predict teenage antisocial behavior and adult dysfunction. There is continuity in criminal behavior.

2. Personal and social factors are associated with criminal propensity. Kids who suffer economic deprivation, poor parenting, and an antisocial family and have personalities marked by impulsivity, hyperactivity, and attention deficit disorder are the most likely to become delinquent.

3. Adolescents who have criminogenic tendencies are motivated or "energized" to offend by their desire for material goods, excitement, and status with peers. Boys from less affluent families are unable to achieve these goals through legitimate means so they tend to commit offenses.

4. Life events influence behavior. For example, family life is critical to a deviant career. Adolescents exposed to effective child rearing, including consistent discipline and close supervision, tend to build up internal inhibitions against offending in a social learning process. In

contrast, this same learning process causes kids raised in antisocial families to model their beliefs and behaviors in a dysfunctional manner.

5. The chance of offending in any particular situation depends on the perception of the costs and benefits of crime and noncrime alternatives. More impulsive boys are more likely to offend because they are less likely to consider possible future consequences (as opposed to immediate benefits).

6. Factors that encourage criminality at one period during the life course may inhibit it in another. Being nervous and withdrawn and having few friends is negatively related to adolescent and teenage offending but positively related to adult social dysfunction.

7. Adult criminal behavior is predicted by external and internal behaviors. External behaviors include engaging in violence and getting arrested and convicted for crimes. Internalizing behaviors include psychiatric disorders, substance abuse, nervousness, and social isolation.

Farrington's theory suggests that experiences over the life course shape the direction and flow of behavior choices; people are not controlled by a single, unalterable latent trait. His work is included here as a life-course theory because it is age-graded: Although there may be continuity in offending, the factors that predict criminality at one point in the life course may not be the ones that predict criminality at another. While most adult criminals began their career in childhood, life events may help some children forgo criminality as they mature.

Interactional Theory

In an important work, Terence Thornberry has also proposed an age-graded view of crime that he calls **interactional theory** (see Figure 10.6).[99]

Thornberry agrees (with both Weis and Elliott) that the onset of crime can be traced to a deterioration of the social bond during adolescence, marked by a weakened attachment to parents, low commitment to school, and lack of belief in conventional values. Thornberry's view similarly recognizes the influence of social class position and other structural variables: Youths growing up in socially disorganized areas will also stand the greatest risk of a weakened social bond and subsequent delinquency. The onset of a criminal career is supported by residence in a social setting in which deviant values and attitudes can be learned and reinforced by delinquent peers.

Interactional theory also holds that serious delinquent youths form belief systems that are consistent with their deviant lifestyle. They seek out the company of other kids who share their interests and who are likely to reinforce their beliefs about the world and support their delinquent behavior. According to interactional theory then, delin-

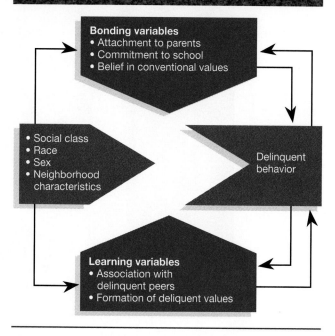

Figure 10.6 Overview of the interactional theory of delinquency.

Source: Terence Thornberry, Margaret Farnsworth, Alan Lizotte, and Susan Stern, "A Longitudinal Examination of the Causes and Correlates of Delinquency," working paper No. 1, Rochester Youth Development Study (Albany, N.Y.: Hindelang Criminal Justice Research Center, 1987), p. 11.

quents seek out a criminal peer group in the same fashion that chess buffs look for others who share their passion for the game—hanging out with other chess players helps improve their game. Similarly, deviant peers do not turn an otherwise "innocent" boy into a delinquent. They support and amplify the behavior of kids who have already accepted a delinquent way of life; they support and amplify offending patterns.

The key idea here is that causal influences are bidirectional. Weak bonds lead kids to develop relationships with deviant peers and get involved in high-rate delinquency. Frequent delinquency involvement further weakens bonds and makes it difficult to reestablish conventional ones. Delinquency-promoting factors tend to reinforce one another and sustain a chronic criminal career.

Interactional theory is considered age-graded because it incorporates an element of the **cognitive perspective** in psychology: As people mature, they pass through different stages of reasoning and sophistication.[100] Thornberry applies this concept when he suggests that criminality is a developmental process that takes on different meaning and form as a person matures. As he puts it, "The causal process is a dynamic one that develops over a person's life."[101] During early adolescence, attachment to the family is the single most important determinant of whether a youth will adjust to conventional society and be shielded from delinquency. By midadolescence, the influence of the family is replaced by the "world of friends, school and youth culture." In adulthood, a person's behavioral choices are shaped by his or her place in conventional society and his or her own nuclear family.

Thornberry's model is in its early stages of development and is being tested with a panel of Rochester, New York, youth who will be followed through their offending careers.[102] Preliminary results support interactional theory hypotheses, including the deviance amplifying powers of associating with a delinquent peer group.[103] In one analysis, Thornberry and his associates found that associating with delinquent peers does in fact increase delinquent involvement because the peer group reinforces antisocial behavior.[104] As delinquent behavior escalates, kids are more likely to seek out deviant friends. These friends reinforce delinquent beliefs (thinking it is okay to commit crimes). In contrast, conventional youths seek out friends equally conforming who then reinforce their prosocial lifestyle. As this process unfolds over the life course, antisocial kids will become part of a deviant peer network that will reinforce their behavior; conventional youths will, in turn, be reinforced by their conventional friends.[105]

Thornberry and his colleagues have found similar patterns for family and school relations: Delinquency is related to weakened attachments to family and the educational process; delinquent behavior further weakens the strength of the bonds to family and school.[106] Other researchers have supported an interactional relationship between criminal behavior and moral values (antisocial behavior weakens moral beliefs and weakened beliefs encourage criminality).[107]

The Rochester data also show that life events can make even high-risk youths resilient to delinquency. Kids who grow up in indigent households with unemployment, high mobility, and parental criminality and who are placed in the care of social service agencies can resist delinquent involvements if they have prosocial life experiences. Among those encounters developed in later adolescence that enable kids to resist delinquency are forming a commitment to school, developing an attachment to teachers, and establishing the goal of a college education; scoring high on reading and math tests is also associated with prosocial behaviors.[108]

In sum, interactional theory suggests that criminality is "part and parcel of a dynamic social process" and not simply an outcome of that process. Although crime is influenced by social forces, it also influences these processes and associations to create behavioral trajectories toward increasing law violations for some people.[109] In so doing, the interactional theory integrates elements of social disorganization, social control, social learning, and cognitive theory into a powerful model of the development of a criminal career.

Sampson and Laub's Age-Graded Theory

If there are various pathways to crime and delinquency, are there trails back to conformity? In an important work,

Crime in the Making, Robert Sampson and John Laub identify the **turning points** in a criminal career.[110] As devotees of the life-course perspective, Sampson and Laub find that the stability of delinquent behavior can be affected by events that occur later in life, even after a chronic delinquent career has been undertaken. They agree with Gottfredson and Hirschi that formal and informal social controls restrict criminality and that the onset of crime begins early in life and continues over the life course; they disagree that once this course is set, nothing can impede its progress.

Laub and Sampson reanalyzed the data originally collected by the Gluecks more than 40 years ago. Using modern statistical analysis made possible by computers (a tool unavailable to the Gluecks), Laub and Sampson found evidence supportive of the life-course view. They have found that children who enter delinquent careers are those who have trouble at home and at school and maintain deviant friends—findings not dissimilar from earlier research on delinquent careers.

TURNING POINTS IN CRIME. Laub and Sampson's most important contribution has been identifying the life events that enable adult offenders to desist from crime (see Figure 10.7). Two critical turning points are marriage and career. For example, adolescents who are at risk to crime are able to live "normal" or conventional lives if they can find good jobs or achieve successful careers. Their success may hinge on a "lucky break": They may encounter employers who are willing to give them a chance despite their record.

When they achieve adulthood, even adolescents who had significant problems with the law are able to desist from crime if they can become attached to a spouse who supports and sustains them even when the spouse knows they had gotten into trouble when they were kids. Happy marriages are life sustaining, and marital quality improves over time (as people work less and have fewer parental responsibilities); people who are married even tend to live longer.[111] Research also shows that children who grow up in two-parent families are more likely to later have happier marriages than children who are the product of divorced or never-married parents.[112] This finding suggests the marriage-crime association may be intergenerational: If people with marital problems are more crime-prone, their children will also suffer a greater long-term risk of marital failure and antisocial activity. People who cannot sustain secure marital relations or who are failures in the labor market are less likely to desist from crime.

SOCIAL CAPITAL. Social scientists recognize that people build **social capital**—positive relations with individuals and institutions that are life sustaining. In the same manner that building financial capital improves the chances for personal success, building social capital supports conventional behavior and inhibits deviant behavior. For example, a successful

Figure 10.7   Sampson and Laub's age-graded theory.

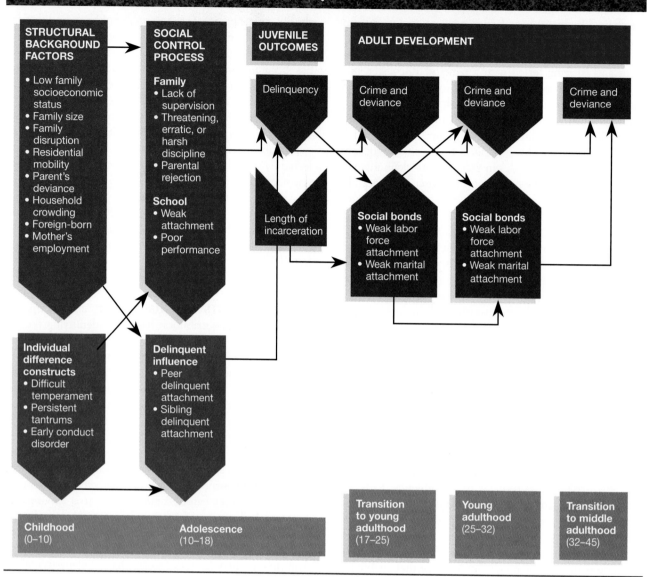

Source: Robert Sampson and John Laub, *Crime in the Making* (Cambridge, Mass.: Harvard University Press, 1993), pp. 244–245.

marriage creates social capital when it improves a person's stature, creates feelings of self-worth, and encourages people to take a chance on the individual. A successful career inhibits crime by creating a stake in conformity; why commit crime when you are doing well at your job? The relationship is reciprocal: If a person is chosen as an employee, he or she will return the "favor" by doing the best job possible; if the person is chosen as a spouse, he or she blossoms into a devoted partner. In contrast, moving to a new city reduces social capital by closing people off from long-term relationships.[113]

Sampson and Laub's research indicates that building social capital and strong social bonds reduces the likelihood of long-term deviance. This finding suggests that, in contrast to latent trait theories, events that occur in later adolescence and adulthood do in fact influence the direction of delinquent and criminal careers. Life events can either help terminate or sustain deviant careers. For example, getting arrested and punished may have little direct effect on future criminality, but it can help sustain a criminal career because it reduces the chances of employment and job stability, two factors that are directly related to crime.[114]

TESTING AGE-GRADED THEORY.   There are several indicators that age-graded is a valid criminological theory. At-risk youth with a history of delinquent behaviors have been found to desist if they later improve their peer relations, do better in school, and make effective use of their leisure time. Once begun, a delinquent career can be reversed if life conditions improve, an outcome predicted by age-

According to Sampson and Laub, building social capital helps inhibit the onset of criminality. Some treatment programs put these views into action. At the La Casita House in New York's South Bronx area, addicted homeless mothers work to get drug clean and develop marketable skills. They are allowed to keep their children with them, which adds to the mother's incentive to get well and prevents family disintegration.

graded theory.[115] Evidence shows that men who are unemployed or underemployed report higher criminal participation rates than employed men; men released from prison on parole who obtain jobs are less likely to recidivate than those who lack or lose employment.[116] There is also evidence that substance abusers who maintain a successful marriage in their 20s and become parents are the ones most likely to mature out of crime.[117] Employment and marriage are two cornerstones of age-graded theory.

Sampson and Laub have also undertaken a number of direct tests of their theoretical model. In one recent study, they found that delinquents who enter the military, serve overseas, and receive GI Bill benefits between ages 17 and 25 also enhance their occupational status and economic well-being; clearly, military service is a turning point in the life course.[118]

Other social scientists have attempted to directly test the principles of age-graded theory. In one survey effort, Daniel Nagin and Raymond Paternoster found that people who are self-centered and present oriented are less likely to accumulate social capital and more prone to commit criminal acts. In contrast, people who have accumulated social capital are unwilling to risk damage to that investment and therefore less likely to commit crime. Because they find that behavior is influenced by considerations of future punishment and that as social capital increases the risk of crime decreases, Nagin and Paternoster support the life-course model (Laub and Sampson) while contradicting one of the key assumptions of the latent trait approach of Gottfredson and Hirschi.[119]

Having established that change is possible, some important questions still need answering:

1. Why do some kids change while others resist?

2. Why do some people enter strong marriages while others fail?

3. What is it about a military career that helps reduce future criminality?

4. Does the connection between military service and desistance suggest universal military service as a crime-prevention alternative?

5. Why are some troubled youths able to conform to the requirements of a job or career while others cannot?

Some recent research by Eloise Dunlop and Bruce Johnson suggests a further avenue for study. Their in-depth case study of a female crack dealer named "Rachel" shows that social capital—family, friends, education, marriage, and employment—aided her in a "successful" career as a crack dealer. Her own crack consumption was kept under control, and she remained competent as a "manager," keeping her family life and drug dealing separate.[120]

Table 10.1 Integrated Theories

THEORY	MAJOR PREMISE	STRENGTHS
Multifactor Theories		
Social development model (SDM)	Weak social controls produce crime. A person's place in the structure influences his or her bond to society.	Combines elements of social structural and social process theories. Accounts for variations in the crime rate.
Elliott's integrated theory	Strained and weak social bonds lead youths to associate with and learn from deviant peers.	Combines elements of learning, strain, and control theories.
Integrated structural theory	Delinquency is a function of family life, which is in turn controlled by the family's place in the economic system.	Explains the relationship between family problems and delinquency in terms of social and economic conditions.
Latent Trait Theories		
General theory	Crime and criminality are separate concepts. People choose to commit crime when they lack self-control. People lacking in self-control will seize criminal opportunities.	Integrates choice and social control concepts. Identifies the difference between *crime* and *criminality*.
Human nature theory	People choose to commit crime when they are biologically and psychologically impaired.	Shows how physical traits interact with social conditions to produce crime. Can account for noncriminal behavior in high-crime areas. Integrates choice and developmental theories.
Life-Course Theories		
Farrington's theory of delinquent development	Personal and social factors control the onset and stability of criminal careers.	Makes use of data collected over a 20-year period to substantiate hypothesis.
Interactional theory	Criminals go through lifestyle changes during their offending career.	Combines sociological and psychological theories.
Age-graded theory	As people mature, the factors that influence their propensity to commit crime change. In childhood, family factors are critical; in adulthood, marital and job factors are key.	Shows how crime is a developmental process that shifts in direction over the life course.

Summary

Recently, criminologists have been combining elements from a number of different theoretical models into integrated theories of crime, outlined in Table 10.1. One approach is to use multiple factors derived from a number of structural and process theories. Examples of this approach include the social development model and Elliott's integrated theory, both of which hold that social position controls life events. The social development model suggests that living in a disorganized area helps weaken social bonds; Elliott's theory holds that strain leads to weakened bonds. Both theories find that weakened bonds lead to the development of deviant peer group associations. In another variation, integrated structural theory, Colvin and Pauly add conflict variables to structural and process factors.

Latent trait theories hold that some underlying condition present at birth or soon after controls behavior. Suspect traits include low IQ, impulsivity, and personality structure. This underlying trait explains the continuity of offending because once present, it remains with a person throughout his or her life. The latent trait theories developed by Gottfredson and Hirschi and by Wilson and Herrnstein both integrate choice theory concepts: People with latent traits choose crime over noncrime. The opportunity for crime mediates their choice.

Life-course theories argue that events that take place over the life course influence criminal choices. The cause of crime is constantly changing as people mature. At first, the nuclear family influences behavior; during adolescence, the peer group dominates; in adulthood, marriage and career are critical. There are a variety of pathways to crime: Some kids are sneaky; others are hostile; and still others, defiant. Crime may be part of a garden variety of social problems, including health, physical, and interpersonal troubles. Important life-course theories have been formulated by Terence Thornberry, David Farrington, and John Laub and Robert Sampson.

Key Terms

developmental criminology
multifactor theories
latent traits
life-course theory
social development model (SDM)
prosocial bonds
integrated structural Marxist theory
general theory of crime (GTC)
self-control
continuity of crime
social interactional theory

life cycle
early onset
problem behavior syndrome (PBS)
authority conflict pathway
covert pathway
overt pathway
adolescent-limited
life-course persistent
pseudomaturity
interactional theory
cognitive perspective
turning points
social capital

Notes

1. Emilie Andersen Allan, "Theory Is Not a Zero-Sum Game: The Quest for an Integrated Theory," paper presented at the annual meeting of the American Society of Criminology, Phoenix, Arizona, November 1993.

2. Gerald Patterson and Karen Yoerger, "Developmental Models for Delinquent Behavior," in *Mental Disorder and Crime,* ed. Sheilagh Higdins (Newbury Park, Calif.: Sage, 1993), pp. 150–159.

3. David Rowe, D. Wayne Osgood, and W. Alan Nicewander, "A Latent Trait Approach to Unifying Criminal Careers," *Criminology* 28 (1990): 237–270.

4. David Rowe, Alexander, Vazsonyi, and Daniel Flannery, "Sex Differences in Crime: Do Means and Within-Sex Variaton Have Similar Causes?" *Journal of Research in Crime and Delinquency* 32 (1995): 84–100.

5. G. R. Patterson, Barbara DeBaryshe, and Elizabeth Ramsey, "A Developmental Perspective on Antisocial Behavior," *American Psychologist* 44 (1989): 329–335.

6. Kenneth Land and Daniel Nagin, "Micro-Models of Criminal Careers: A Synthesis of the Criminal Careers and Life-Course Approaches via Semiparametric Mixed Poisson Regression Models with Empirical Applications," *Journal of Quantitative Criminology* 12 (1996): 163–190.

7. Daniel Glazer, *Crime in Our Changing Society* (New York: Holt, Rinehart and Winston, 1978).

8. Ibid., p. 125.

9. Joseph Weis and J. David Hawkins, *Reports of the National Juvenile Assessment Centers, Preventing Delinquency* (Washington, D.C.: U.S. Department of Justice, 1981); Joseph Weis and John Sederstrom, *Reports of the National Juvenile Justice Assessment Centers, The Prevention of Serious Delinquency: What to Do* (Washington, D.C.: U.S. Department of Justice, 1981).

10. Julie O'Donnell, J. David Hawkins, and Robert Abbott, "Predicting Serious Delinquency and Substance Use Among Aggressive Boys," *Journal of Consulting and Clinical Psychology* 63 (1995): 529–537.

11. Ibid., pp. 534–536; Richard Catalano, Rick Kosterman, J. David Hawkins, Michael Newcomb, and Robert Abbott, "Modeling the Etiology of Adolescent Substance Use: A Test of the Social Development Model," *Journal of Drug Issues* 26 (1996): 429–455.

12. David Brownfield, Kevin Thompson, and Ann Marie Sorenson, "Correlates of Gang Membership: A Test of Strain, Social Learning, and Control-Bonding Theories," paper presented at the annual meeting of the American Society of Criminology, Chicago, November 1996.

13. J. David Hawkins, Richard Catalano, Diane Morrison, Julie O'Donnell, Robert Abbott, and L. Edward Day, "The Seattle Social Development Project," *The Prevention of Antisocial Behavior in Children,* ed. Joan McCord and Richard Tremblay (New York: Guilford, 1992), pp. 139–160.

14. Delbert Elliott, David Huizinga, and Suzanne Ageton, *Explaining Delinquency and Drug Use* (Beverly Hills, Calif.: Sage, 1985).

15. Scott Menard and Delbert Elliott, "Delinquent Bonding, Moral Beliefs, and Illegal Behavior: A Three Wave–Panel Model," *Justice Quarterly* 11 (1994): 173–188.

16. Ibid., p. 184.

17. Mark Colvin and John Pauly, "A Critique of Criminology: Toward an Integrated Structural-Marxist Theory of Delinquency Production," *American Journal of Sociology* 89 (1983): 513–551.

18. Ibid., p. 542.

19. Steven Messner and Marvin Krohn, "Class, Compliance Structures, and Delinquency: Assessing Integrated Structural-Marxist Theory," *American Journal of Sociology* 96 (1990): 300–328.

20. Lee Ellis, "Neurohormonal Bases of Varying Tendencies to Learn Delinquent and Criminal Behavior," in *Behavioral Approaches to Crime and Delinquency,* ed. E. Morris and C. Braukmann (New York: Plenum, 1988), pp. 499–518.

21. James Q. Wilson and Richard Herrnstein, *Crime and Human Nature* (New York: Simon & Schuster, 1985).

22. Ibid., p. 44.

23. Ibid., p. 171.

24. Ibid.

25. Ibid., p. 528.

26. Michael Gottfredson and Travis Hirschi, *A General Theory of Crime* (Stanford, Calif.: Stanford University Press, 1990).

27. Ibid., p. 27.

28. Ibid., p. 90.

29. Ibid., p. 89.

30. Alex Piquero and Stephen Tibbetts, "Specifying the Direct and Indirect Effects of Low Self-Control and Situational Factors in Offenders' Decision Making: Toward a More Complete Model of Rational Offending," *Justice Quarterly* 13 (1996): 481–508.

31. Ibid.

32. Ibid.

33. Dennis Giever, "An Empirical Assessment of the Core Elements of Gottfredson and Hirschi's General Theory of Crime," paper presented at the American Society of Criminology meeting, Boston, November 1995.

34. Robert Agnew, "The Contribution of Social-Psychological Strain Theory to the Explanation of Crime and Delinquency," *Advances in Criminological Theory* 6 (1994).

35. Travis Hirschi and Michael Gottfredson, "Rethinking the Juvenile Justice System," *Crime and Delinquency* 39 (1993): 262–271.

36. David Brownfield and Ann Marie Sorenson, "Self-Control and Juvenile Delinquency: Theoretical Issues and an Empirical Assessment of Selected Elements of a General Theory of Crime," *Deviant Behavior* 14 (1993): 243–264; Harold Grasmick, Charles Tittle, Robert Bursik, and Bruce Arneklev, "Testing the Core Empirical Implications of Gottfredson and Hirschi's General Theory of Crime," *Journal of Research in Crime and Delinquency* 30 (1993): 5–29; John Cochran, Peter Wood, and Bruce Arneklev, "Is the Religiosity-Delinquency Relationship Spurious? A Test of Arousal and Social Control Theories," *Journal of Research in Crime and Delinquency* 31 (1994): 92–123.

37. Carl Keane, Paul Maxim, and James Teevan, "Drinking and Driving, Self-Control, and Gender: Testing a General Theory of Crime," *Journal of Research in Crime and Delinquency* 30 (1993): 30–46.

38. Judith DeJong, Matti Virkkunen, and Marku Linnoila, "Factors Associated with Recidivism in a Criminal Population," *The Journal of Nervous and Mental Disease* 180 (1992): 543–550.

39. David Cantor, "Drug Involvement and Offending Among Incarcerated Juveniles," paper presented at the American Society of Criminology meeting, Boston, November 1995.

40. Brownfield and Sorenson, "Self-Control and Juvenile Delinquency."

41. Jon Gibbs and Dennis Giever, "Self-Control and Its Manifestations Among University Students: An Empirical Test of Gottfredson and Hirschi's General Theory," *Justice Quarterly* 12 (1995): 231–255.

42. Dennis Giever, "An Empirical Assessment of the Core Elements of Gottfredson and Hirschi's General Theory of Crime," paper presented at the American Society of Criminology meeting, Boston, November 1995.

43. Marc LeBlanc, Marc Ouimet, and Richard Tremblay, "An Integrative Control Theory of Delinquent Behavior: A Validation, 1976–1985," *Psychiatry* 51 (1988): 164–176.

44. See, for example, Douglas Longshore, Susan Turner, and Judith Stein, "Self-Control in a Criminal Sample: An Examination of Construct Validity," *Criminology* 34 (1996): 209–228; Grasmick et al., "Testing the Core Empirical Implications of Gottfredson and Hirschi's General Theory of Crime"; Daniel Nagin and Raymond Paternoster, "Enduring Individual Differences and Rational Choice Theories of Crime," *Law and Society Review* 27 (1993): 467–489.

45. Bruce Link, Elmer Streuning, Francis Cullen, Patrick Shrout, and Bruce Dohrenwend, "A Modified Labeling Theory Approach to Mental Disorders: An Empirical Assessment," *American Sociological Review* 54 (1989): 400–423.

46. Michael Benson and Elizabeth Moore, "Are White-Collar and Common Offenders the Same? An Empirical and Theoretical Critique of a Recently Proposed General Theory of Crime," *Journal of Research in Crime and Delinquency* 29 (1992): 251–272.

47. For a general review and critique, see Kenneth Polk's book review in *Crime and Delinquency* 37 (1991): 575–581.

48. Ronald Akers, "Self-Control as a General Theory of Crime," *Journal of Quantitative Criminology* 7 (1991): 201–211.

49. Gottfredson and Hirschi, *General Theory of Crime*, p. 88.

50. Samuel Yochelson and Clifford Samenow, *The Criminal Personality* (New York: Jason Aronson, 1977).

51. Alan Feingold, "Gender Differences in Personality: A Meta Analysis," *Psychological Bulletin* 116 (1994): 429–456.

52. Gottfredson and Hirschi, *A General Theory of Crime*, p. 153.

53. Ann Marie Sorenson and David Brownfield, "Normative Concepts in Social Control," paper presented at the annual meeting of the American Society of Criminology, Phoenix, Arizona, November 1993.

54. Scott Menard, Delbert Elliott, and Sharon Wofford, "Social Control Theories in Developmental Perspective," *Studies on Crime and Crime Prevention* 2 (1993): 69–87.

55. Delbert Elliott and Scott Menard, "Delinquent Friends and Delinquent Behavior: Temporal and Developmental Patterns," in *Current Theories of Crime and Deviance*, ed. J. David Hawkins (Cambridge: Cambridge University Press, in press).

56. Graham Ousey and David Aday, Jr., "The Interaction Hypothesis: A Test Using Social Control Theory and Social Learning Theory," paper presented at the American Society of Criminology meeting, Boston, November 1995.

57. Julie Horney, D. Wayne Osgood, and Ineke Haen Marshall, "Criminal Careers in the Short-Term: Intra-Individual Variability in Crime and Its Relations to Local Life Circumstances," *American Sociological Review* 60 (1995): 655–673.

58. Otwin Marenin and Michael Resig, "A General Theory of Crime and Patterns of Crime in Nigeria: An Exploration of Methodological Assumptions," *Journal of Criminal Justice* 23 (1995): 501–518.

59. Bruce Arneklev, Harold Grasmick, Charles Tittle, and Robert Bursik, "Low Self-Control and Imprudent Behavior," *Journal of Quantitative Criminology* 9 (1993): 225–246.

60. Kevin Thompson, "Sexual Harassment and Low Self-Control: An Application of Gottfredson and Hirschi's General Theory of Crime," paper presented at the annual meeting of the American Society of Criminology, Phoenix, Arizona, November 1993.

61. R. E. Tremblay and L. C. Masse, "Cognitive Deficits, School Achievement, Disruptive Behavior and Juvenile Delinquency: A Longitudinal Look at Their Developmental Sequence," paper presented at the annual meeting of the American Society of Criminology, Phoenix, Arizona, November 1993.

62. David Nurco, Timothy Kinlock, and Mitchell Balter, "The Severity of Preaddiction Criminal Behavior Among Urban, Male Narcotic Addicts and Two Nonaddicted Control Groups," *Journal of Research in Crime and Delinquency* 30 (1993): 293–316.

63. G. R. Patterson and Karen Yoerger, "Differentiating Outcomes and Histories for Early and Late Onset Arrests," paper presented at the annual meeting of the American Society of Criminology, Phoenix, Arizona, November 1993.

64. Joan McCord, "Family Relationships, Juvenile Delinquency, and Adult Criminality," *Criminology* 29 (1991): 397–417.

65. Robert Sampson and John Laub, "Crime and Deviance in the Life Course," *American Review of Sociology* 18 (1992): 63–84.

66. Gerald Patterson, J. B. Reid, and Thomas Dishion, *A Social Interactional Approach: Antisocial Boys* (Eugene, Ore.: Castalia Press, 1992).

67. Francois Poulin, Thomas Dishion, Mike Stoolmiller, and Gerald Patterson, "Modeling Growth in Adolescent Delinquency: The Combined Effect and Developmental Specificity of Parent Bonding and Deviant Peers," paper presented at the annual meeting of the American Society of Criminology, Chicago, November 1996.

68. See, generally, Sheldon Glueck and Eleanor Glueck, *500 Criminal Careers* (New York: Knopf, 1930); idem, *One Thousand Juvenile Delinquents* (Cambridge, Mass: Harvard University Press, 1934); idem, *Predicting Delinquency and Crime* (Cambridge, Mass: Harvard University Press, 1967), pp. 82–83.

69. Sheldon Glueck and Eleanor Glueck, *Unraveling Juvenile Delinquency* (Cambridge, Mass.: Harvard University Press, 1950).

70. See, generally, John Laub and Robert Sampson, "The Sutherland-Glueck Debate: On the Sociology of Criminological Knowledge," *American Journal of Sociology* 96 (1991): 1402–1440; idem, "Unraveling Families and Delinquency: A Reanalysis of the Gluecks' Data," *Criminology* 26 (1988): 355–380.

71. Rolf Loeber and Marc LeBlanc, "Toward a Developmental Criminology," in *Crime and Justice*, vol. 12, ed. Norval Morris and Michael Tonry (Chicago: University of Chicago Press, 1990), pp. 375–473.

72. G. R. Patterson, L. Crosby, and S. Vuchinich, "Predicting Risk for Early Police Arrest," *Journal of Quantitative Criminology* 8 (1992): 335–355.

73. Patterson, DeBaryshe, and Ramsey, "A Developmental Perspective on Antisocial Behavior," pp. 331–333.

74. Rolf Loeber, Magda Southamer-Loeber, Welmoet Van Kammen, and David Farrington, "Initiation, Escalation and Desistance in Juvenile Offending and Their Correlates," *Journal of Criminal Law and Criminology* 82 (1991): 36–82.

75. Richard Jessor, John Donovan, and Francis Costa, *Beyond Adolescence: Problem Behavior and Young Adult Development* (New York: Cambridge University Press, 1991).

76. Richard Jessor, "Risk Behavior in Adolescence: A Psychosocial Framework for Understanding and Action," in *Adolescents at Risk: Medical and Social Perspectives*, ed. D. E. Rogers and E. Ginzburg (Boulder, Colo.: Westview, 1992).

77. Deborah Capaldi and Gerald Patterson, "Can Violent Offenders Be Distinguished from Frequent Offenders: Prediction from Childhood to Adolescence," *Journal of Research in Crime and Delinquency* 33 (1996): 206–231; D. Wayne Osgood, "The Covariation Among Adolescent Problem Behaviors," paper presented at the annual meeting of the American Society of Criminology, Baltimore, November 1990.

78. Todd Miller, Timothy Smith, Charles Turner, Margarita Guijarro, and Amanda Hallet, "A Meta-Analytic Review of Research on Hostility and Physical Health," *Psychological Bulletin* 119 (1996): 322–348; Marianne Junger, "Accidents and Crime," in *The Generality of Deviance*, ed. T. Hirschi and M. Gottfredson (New Brunswick, N.J.: Transaction Press, 1993).

79. Robert Johnson, S. Susan Su, Dean Gerstein, Hee-Choon Shin, and John Hoffman, "Parental Influences on Deviant Behavior in Early Adolescence: A Logistic Response Analysis of Age- and Gender-Differentiated Effects," *Journal of Quantitative Criminology* 11 (1995): 167–192; Judith Brooks, Martin Whiteman and Patricia Cohen, "Stage of Drug Use, Aggression, and Theft/Vandalism," in *Drugs, Crime and Other Deviant Adaptations: Longitudinal Studies,* ed. Howard Kaplan (New York: Plenum Press, 1995), pp. 83–96; Robert Hoge, D. A. Andrews, and Alan Leschied, "Tests of Three Hypotheses Regarding the Predictors of Delinquency," *Journal of Abnormal Child Psychology* 22 (1994): 547–559.

80. David Huizinga, Rolf Loeber, and Terence Thornberry, "Longitudinal Study of Delinquency, Drug Use, Sexual Activity, and Pregnancy Among Children and Youth in Three Cities," *Public Health Reports* 108 (1993): 90–96.

81. Jeanne Hernandez, "The Concurrence of Eating Disorders with Histories of Child Abuse Among Adolescents,"paper presented at the annual meeting of the American Society of Criminology, Phoenix, Arizona, November 1993.

82. Candace Kruttschnitt, Jane McLeod, and Maude Dornfeld, "The Economic Environment of Child Abuse," *Social Problems* 41 (1994): 299–312.

83. Helene Raskin White, "Early Problem Behavior and Later Drug Problems," *Journal of Research in Crime and Delinquency* 29 (1992): 412–429.

84. Helene Raskin White and Erich Labouvie, "Generality Versus Specificity of Problem Behavior: Psychological and Functional Differences," *Journal of Drug Issues* 24 (1994): 55–74.

85. See, generally, Richard Dembo, Linda Williams, Werner Wothke, James Schmeidler, Alan Getreu, Estrellita Berry, and Eric Wish, "The Generality of Deviance: Replication of a Structural Model Among High-Risk Youths," *Journal of Research in Crime and Delinquency* 29 (1992): 200–216.

86. Rolf Loeber, Phen Wung, Kate Keenan, Bruce Giroux, Magda Stouthamer-Loeber, Wemoet Van Kammen, and Barbara Maughan, "Developmental Pathways in Disruptive Behavior," *Development and Psychopathology* (1993): 12–48.

87. Amy D'Unger, Kenneth Land, Patricia McCall, and Daniel Nagin, "How Many Latent Classes of Delinquent/Criminal Careers? Results from Mixed Poisson Regression Analyses of the London, Philadelphia, and Racine Cohort Studies," paper presented at the annual meeting of the American Society of Criminology, Chicago, November 1996.

88. Terrie Moffitt, "Natural Histories of Delinquency," in *Cross-National Longitudinal Research on Human Development and Criminal Behavior,* ed. Elmar Weitekamp and Hans-Jurgen Kerner (Dordrecht, Netherlands: Kluwer, 1994), pp. 3–65.

89. Terrie Moffitt, "Adolescence-Limited and Life-Course Persistent Antisocial Behavior: A Developmental Taxonomy," *Psychological Review* 100 (1993): 674–701.

90. Michael Newcomb, "Pseudomaturity Among Adolescents: Construct Validation, Sex Differences, and Associations in Adulthood," *Journal of Drug Issues* 26 (1996): 477–504.

91. Paul Tracy and Kimberly Kempf-Leonard, *Continuity and Discontinuity in Criminal Careers* (New York: Plenum Press, 1996), p. 208.

92. Ronald Simons, Chyi-In Wu, Rand Conger, and Frederick Lorenz, "Two Routes to Delinquency: Differences Between Early and Later Starters in the Impact of Parenting and Deviant Careers," *Criminology* 32 (1994): 247–275.

93. Paul Mazerolle, "Understanding the Theoretical and Empirical Dimensions of Late Onset to Delinquent Behavior," paper presented at the annual meeting of the American Society of Criminology, Boston, November 1995.

94. Charles Dean, Robert Brame, and Alex Piquero, "Criminal Propensities, Discrete Groups of Offenders, and Persistence of Crime," *Criminology* 34 (1966): 547–573.

95. See, for example, the Rochester Youth Development Study, Hindelang Criminal Justice Research Center, 135 Western Avenue, Albany, New York 12222.

96. David Farrington, "The Development of Offending and Antisocial Behavior from Childhood to Adulthood," paper presented at the Congress on Rethinking Delinquency, University of Minho, Braga, Portugal, July 1992.

97. See, generally, D. J. West and David P. Farrington, *The Delinquent Way of Life* (London: Hienemann, 1977).

98. The material in the following sections is summarized from Farrington, "The Development of Offending and Antisocial Behavior from Childhood to Adulthood"; idem, "Psychobiological Factors in the Explanation and Reduction of Delinquency," *Today's Delinquent* 7 (1988): 44–46; idem, "Childhood Origins of Teenage Antisocial Behaviour and Adult Social Dysfunction," *Journal of the Royal Society of Medicine* 86 (1993): 13–17; idem, "Psychosocial Influences on the Development of Antisocial Personality," paper presented at the annual meeting of the American Society of Criminology, Phoenix, Arizona, November 1993.

99. Terence Thornberry, "Toward an Interactional Theory of Delinquency," *Criminology* 25 (1987): 863–891.

100. See, for example, Jean Piaget, *The Grasp of Consciousness* (Cambridge, Mass: Harvard University Press, 1976).

101. Ibid., p. 386.

102. This research is known as the Rochester Youth Development Study. Thornberry's colleagues on the project include Alan Lizotte, Margaret Farnworth, Marvin Krohn, and Susan Stern.

103. Terence Thornberry, Alan Lizotte, Marvin Krohn, and Margaret Farnworth, "The Role of Delinquent Peers in the Initiation of Delinquent Behavior," working paper no. 6, rev., Rochester Youth Development Study (Albany, N.Y.:, Hindelang Criminal Justice Research Center, 1993).

104. Terence Thornberry, Alan Lizotte, Marvin Krohn, Margaret Farnworth, and Sung Joon Jang, "Delinquent Peers, Beliefs, and Delinquent Behavior: A Longitudinal Test of Interactional Theory," *Criminology* 32 (1994): 601–637.

105. Terence Thornberry, Alan Lizotte, Marvin Krohn, Margaret Farnworth, and Sung Joon Jang, *Delinquent Peers, Beliefs, and Delinquent Behavior: A Longitudinal Test of Interactional Theory,* working paper no. 6, rev., Rochester Youth Development Study (Albany, N.Y.: Hindelang Criminal Justice Research Center, 1992).

106. Terence Thornberry, Alan Lizotte, Marvin Krohn, Margaret Farnworth, and Sung Joon Jang, "Testing Interactional Theory: An Examination of Reciprocal Causal Relationships Among Family, School and Delinquency," *Journal of Criminal Law and Criminology* 82 (1991): 3–35.

107. Scott Menard and Delbert Elliott, "Delinquent Bonding, Moral Beliefs, and Illegal Behavior: A Three Wave-Panel Model," *Justice Quarterly* 11 (1994): 173–188.

108. Carolyn Smith, Alan Lizotte, Terence Thornberry, and Marvin Krohn, *Resilient Youth: Identifying Factors That Prevent High-Risk Youth from Engaging in Delinquency and Drug Use* (Albany, N.Y: Rochester Youth Development Study, 1994).

109. Thornberry et al., "Delinquent Peers, Beliefs, and Delinquent Behavior," pp. 628–629.

110. Robert Sampson and John Laub, *Crime in the Making: Pathways and Turning Points Through Life* (Cambridge, Mass.: Harvard University Press, 1993); John Laub and Robert Sampson, "Turning Points in the Life Course: Why Change Matters to the Study of Crime," paper presented at the annual meeting of the American Society of Criminology, New Orleans, November 1992.

111. Terri Orbuch, James House, Richard Mero, and Pamela Webster, "Marital Quality over the Life Course," *Social Psychology Quarterly* 59 (1996): 162–171; Lee Lillard and Linda Waite, "'Til Death Do Us Part: Marital Disruption and Mortality,"*American Journal of Sociology* 100 (1995): 1131–1156.

112. Pamela Webster, Terri Orbuch, and James House, "Effects of Childhood Family Background on Adult Marital Quality and Perceived Stability," *American Journal of Sociology* 101 (1995): 404–432.

113. John Hagan, Ross MacMillan, and Blair Wheaton, "New Kid in Town: Social Capital and the Life Course Effects of Family Migration on Children," *American Sociological Review* 61 (1996): 368–385.

114. Sampson and Laub, *Crime in the Making*, p. 249.

115. Robert Hoge, D. A. Andrews, and Alan Leschied, "An Investigation of Risk and Protective Factors in a Sample of Youthful Offenders," *Journal of Child Psychology and Psychiatry* 37 (1996): 419–424.

116. For a discussion see Mark Collins and Don Weatherburn, "Unemployment and the Dynamics of Offender Populations," *Journal of Quantitative Criminology* 11 (1995): 231–245.

117. Erich Labouvie, "Maturing Out of Substance Use: Selection and Self-Correction," *Journal of Drug Issues* 26 (1996): 457–474.

118. Robert Sampson and John Laub, "Socioeconomic Achievement in the Life Course of Disadvantaged Men: Military Service as a Turning Point, circa 1940–1965," *American Sociological Review* 61 (1996): 347–367.

119. Daniel Nagin and Raymond Paternoster, "Personal Capital and Social Control: The Deterrence Implications of a Theory of Criminal Offending," *Criminology* 32 (1994): 581–606.

120. Eloise Dunlop and Bruce Johnson, "Family and Human Resources in the Development of a Female Crack-Seller Career: Case Study of a Hidden Population," *Journal of Drug Issues* 26 (1996): 175–198.

Regardless of why people commit crime in the first place, their actions are defined by law as falling into particular crime categories, or *typologies*. Criminologists often seek to group individual criminal offenders or behaviors so they may be more easily studied and understood. These are referred to as offender typologies.

In this section, crime patterns are clustered into four typologies: violent crime (Chapter 11); economic crimes involving common theft offenses (Chapter 12); economic crimes involving white-collar criminals or criminal organizations (Chapter 13); and public order crimes, such as prostitution and drug abuse (Chapter 14). This format groups criminal behaviors by their focuses and consequences: bringing physical harm to others; misappropriating other people's property; and violating laws designed to protect public morals.

Crime Typologies

Typologies can be useful in classifying large numbers of criminal offenses or offenders into easily understood categories. This text has grouped offenses and offenders on the basis of their (1) legal definitions and (2) collective goals, objectives, and consequences.

THE ROOTS OF VIOLENCE

Chapter 11
Violent Crime

> Violence is the primal problem of American history, the dark reverse of its coin of freedom and abundance.[1]

All across America, people are afraid of becoming crime victims, and they are altering their lifestyle in an effort to remain safe. They are bombarded with TV news stories and newspaper articles featuring grisly accounts of mass murder, child abuse, and serial rape. These accounts may be an unfortunate reflection of the harsh realities of American life: Despite recent declines, violence rates in the United States far exceed those in any other industrialized nation.[2]

Many people have personally experienced violence or have a friend who has been victimized; almost everyone has heard about someone being robbed, beaten, or killed; riots and mass disturbances have ravaged urban areas; racial attacks plague schools and college campuses; assassination has claimed the lives of political, religious, and social leaders all over the world.[3]

The general public also believes that the government should take a "get tough" approach to violent crime. Public opinion polls indicate that more than 75% of U.S. citizens favor the use of capital punishment for persons convicted of murder.[4] The U.S. Supreme Court has responded by making teenage criminals over the age of 16 eligible for the death penalty.[5] Many people believe that America is becoming ever more violent and that "things are just not like the good old days." Longing for the serenity of the pioneer days may be misplaced when we consider that violence has been a long-term feature of American life. The accompanying Close-Up discusses some of the reasons that American society has been stained with violent crime.

Despite all this attention and concern, we are still not sure of the causes of violence. Some experts suggest that the problem is created by a relatively small number of inherently violence-prone individuals who may themselves have been the victims of physical violence or of physical or psychological abnormalities. Other social scientists consider violence and aggression inherently human traits that can affect any person at any time. Still another view is that there are violence-prone subcultures within society whose members value force, routinely carry weapons, and consider violence to have an acceptable place in social interaction.[6]

This chapter surveys the nature and extent of violent crime. First, we briefly review some hypothetical causes of violence. Then, we turn our attention to specific types of interpersonal violence: rape, homicide, assault, robbery, and hate crimes. Finally, it will briefly examine political violence, state-sponsored violence, and terrorism.

The Roots of Violence

What causes people to behave violently? There are a number of competing explanations for violent behavior. A few of the most prominent are discussed below and illustrated in Figure 11.1.

Personal Traits

On March 13, 1995 an ex-Boy Scout leader named Thomas Hamilton took four high-powered rifles into the primary school of the peaceful Scottish town of Dunblane and slaughtered 16 children and their teacher. This horrific crime shocked the British Isles into passing strict controls on all guns.[7]

Bizarre outbursts such as Hamilton's support a link between violence and personal traits. More than 35 years ago, Laura Bender examined convicted juveniles who had killed their victims and concluded that they suffered from abnormal electroencephalogram readings, learning disabilities, and psychosis.[8]

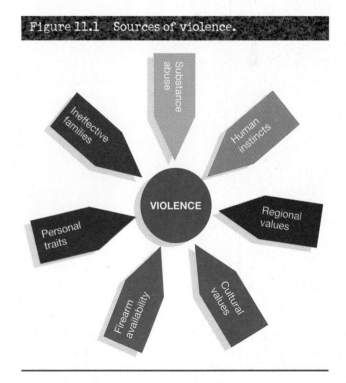

Figure 11.1 Sources of violence.

David Courtwright, an authority on the sociocultural roots of violence, describes a 19th-century American society much more violent than today's. According to Courtwright, societies with high rates of violent crime have populations with an overabundance of young males who are "awash with testosterone" and unrestrained by social controls such as marriage and family, and up until the mid-20th century, the U.S. population was disproportionately young and male.

The gender ratio of those who came to the United States involuntarily—indentured servants and slaves—was more than 2 to 1 male. Poor laborers who paid for their passage with work were almost entirely males; the gender ratio among Chinese laborers was an astounding 27 to 1. Aside from Ireland, which furnished slightly more female than male immigrants, Europeans who arrived voluntarily were also predominantly male. Because these young men outnumbered women, many could not marry, and their aggressive natures remained unrestrained by any calming influence of family life and parental responsibility.

Cultural factors worsened these population trends. Southern and western frontier culture was characterized by racism and sensitivity about personal honor. Members of some ethnic groups drank heavily and frequented saloons and gambling halls, places where petty arguments could become lethal because most patrons carried guns and knives. Violent acts often went unpunished because law enforcement agencies were unable or unwilling to take action.

Nowhere were these cultural and population effects felt more acutely than on the western frontier. Here the population was predominantly young bachelors, sensitive about honor, hostile to members of other racial or ethnic groups, heavy drinkers, morally indifferent, heavily armed, and unchecked by adequate law enforcement. It is not surprising, considering this explosive mix, that 20% of the 89,000 miners who arrived in California during the gold rush of 1849 were dead within six months. While many died from disease, others succumbed to drink and violence. Smoking, gambling, and heavy drinking became a cultural imperative, and those who were disinclined to indulge were considered social outcasts.

Over time, gender ratios equalized as more men brought families to the frontier and children of both sexes were born. The excess males in the population died, returned home, or drifted elsewhere. By mid-20th century, America's overall male surplus was disappearing and a balanced population helped bring down the crime rate.

According to Courtwright, rising violence rates in the 1960s and 1970s could be attributed to the fact that men were avoiding, delaying, or terminating marriage: In 1960 Americans spent an average of 62% of their lives with spouses and children, an all-time high; in 1980, they spent 43% with families, an all-time low. Both the illegitimacy and divorce rates began to spiral upward, guaranteeing that the number of poorly socialized and supervised children would increase dramatically. The inner-city urban ghetto became the "frontier" community of today. Gangs such as the Crips and Bloods in Los Angeles replaced the James and Dalton gangs of the old west. And although

the male-to-female ratio there is more compatible than on the western frontier, the presence of unsupervised and poorly socialized males, who have easy access to guns, drugs, and vice, has produced a crime rate of similar proportions. Although violence rates have stabilized of late, they may rise again if the decline in the family remains unchecked.

Courtwright's analysis is important because it shows that violence is not a recent development and that demographic and cultural forces are a key determinant of violent crime rates. It disputes the contention that some artifact of modern life, such as violent films and TV, is the cause of American violence. The factors that predispose societies to violence can be found in demographic and cultural factors that are unique neither to our society nor to our times.

CRITICAL THINKING QUESTIONS

1. According to Courtwright, violence rates were exceedingly high in the 19th century. How does that fact affect the charge that violent media, including TV, films, and music, is a significant cause of violent behavior?

2. How do Courtwright's views jibe with the life-course model of Sampson and Laub discussed in Chapter 10? What life-course factors produce or prevent violence?

Sources: David Courtwright, "Violence in America," *American Heritage* 47 (1996): 36–52; idem., *Violent Land: Single Men and Social Disorder from the Frontier to the Inner City* (Cambridge, Mass.: Harvard University Press, 1996).

More recent research by Dorothy Otnow Lewis and her associates found that murderous youths suffered signs of major neurological impairment (such as abnormal EEGs, multiple psychomotor impairment, and severe seizures), low intelligence as measured on standard IQ tests, a psychotic close relative, and psychotic symptoms such as paranoia, illogical thinking, and hallucinations.[9] Similarly, studies of male batterers indicate that abnormal personality structure, including depression, borderline personality syndrome, and psychopathology, are associated with various forms of spousal and family abuse.[10] While this evidence indicates that violent offenders are more prone to psychosis than other people, there is no single clinical diagnosis that can characterize their behavior.[11]

Ineffective Families

In August 1990, residents of Gainesville, Florida, were shocked when five young students were brutally murdered. Newspaper accounts told how the victims, four female University of Florida students and one male Santa Fe Community College student, had been stabbed dozens of times and raped and their mutilated bodies posed in sexually suggestive positions; one had been beheaded.[12] A 35-year-old drifter named Danny Harold Rolling was arrested and convicted for committing these horrible crimes. On March 24, 1994, after 13 days of testimony, a jury recommended Rolling be sentenced to death.[13] During the sentencing phase, Rolling had pleaded for mercy and claimed that his behavior was a result of the emotional and physical abuse he had suffered at the hands of his father. His mother, a native of Shreveport, Louisiana, submitted a videotape backing his claim of abuse and ended it by stating, "Take me, I'm the one that had to have failed him somewhere."

There is a great deal of research linking violence to either ineffective or abusive parenting. For example, Deborah Capaldi and Gerald Patterson suggest that violence is part of a broad category of multiple offending caused by inadequate parenting that inadvertently reinforces a child's coercive behavior by failing to set adequate limits or use proper and consistent discipline.[14] Absent or deviant parents, inconsistent discipline, and lack of supervision have all been linked to persistent violent offending.[15]

ABUSED KIDS. A number of research studies have found that individuals who were clinically diagnosed as abused in childhood later engaged in delinquent behaviors, including violence, at a rate significantly greater than that of unabused children.[16] Samples of convicted murderers contain a high percentage of seriously abused youth.[17] The abuse-violence association has been involved in a significant number of cases in which parents have been killed by their children; sexual abuse is also a constant factor in father (patricide) and mother (matricide) killings.[18]

One of the most outspoken critics of physical punishment of children is Murray Straus of the Family Research Laboratory at the University of New Hampshire. Straus has used survey and record data to show that children who are physically punished are the ones most likely to physically abuse a sibling and later engage in spouse abuse and other forms of criminal violence.[19]

THE BRUTALIZATION PROCESS. Using actual case studies of violent criminals, Lonnie Athens found that antisocial careers are often created in a series of stages that begin with brutal episodes during early adolescence. The first stage is the **brutalization process,** during which abusive parents or caretakers cause the young victim to develop a belligerent, angry demeanor. When confronted at home, at school, or on the street, these belligerent youths respond with **violent performance** of angry, hostile behavior. The success of their violent confrontations provides them with a sense of power and achievement. In the **virulency** stage, the emerging criminals develop a violent identity that makes them feared; they enjoy intimidating others. To Athens, this process takes now-violent youths full circle, from being the victim of aggression to being its initiator; they are now the same person they grew up despising, ready to begin the process with their own children.[20]

While a significant amount of evidence has shown the association between abuse and violent crime, it is also true that many offenders have not suffered abuse and that many abused youths do not grow up to become persistent adult offenders.[21]

Evolutionary Factors/Human Instinct

It is also possible that violent responses and emotions are actually inherent in all humans, needing only the right spark to trigger them. Sigmund Freud believed that human aggression and violence were produced by instinctual drives.[22] Freud maintained that humans have two opposing instinctual drives that interact to control behavior: **eros,** the life instinct, which drives people to self-fulfillment and enjoyment, and **thanatos,** the death instinct, which produces self-destruction. Thanatos can be expressed externally (as violence and sadism) or internally (as suicide, alcoholism, or other self-destructive habits). Because he viewed aggression as instinctual, Freud saw little hope for its treatment.

A number of biologists and anthropologists have also speculated that instinctual violence-promoting traits may be common to the human species as a whole. One view is that aggression and violence are the results of instincts inborn in all animals, including human beings. A leading proponent of this view, Konrad Lorenz, developed this theory in his famous book *On Aggression*.[23] Lorenz argued that aggressive energy is produced by inbred instincts that are independent of environmental forces. In the animal kingdom, aggression usually serves a productive purpose—for example, it leads members of grazing species to spread out over available territory to ensure an ample food supply and the survival of the fittest.

Lorenz found that humans have some of the same aggressive instincts as animals but without the inhibitions

Are these armed militiamen a product of aggressive male breeding? Or is aggression related to life experiences such as destructive families and hostile living environments?

against fatal violence that members of lower species usually maintain. That is, among lower species, aggression is rarely fatal; when a conflict occurs, the winner is determined through a test of skill or endurance. This inhibition against killing members of their own species protects animals from self-extinction. Humans, lacking this inhibition against fatal violence, are thoroughly capable of killing their own kind, and as technology develops and more lethal weapons are produced, the extinction of the human species becomes a significant possibility.

Evolutionary theories in criminology suggest that violent behavior may have become instinctual because of the long-term influences of reproductive behavior: Males who are sexually aggressive are the ones most likely to produce children; their offspring will carry genes that support aggression. Over time male aggression has become predominant. Some males carry aggression to the point of force when less violent tactics fail to yield results.[24]

Cultural Values

Explanations of the cause of violent behavior that focus on the individual offender fail to account for the patterns of violence in the United States. The various sources of crime statistics tell us that interpersonal violence is more common in large, urban, inner-city areas than in other kinds of communities.[25] It is unlikely that violent crime rates would be so high in these socially disorganized areas unless other *social forces* were in operation that encouraged violent crime.[26]

SUBCULTURE OF VIOLENCE. To explain the existence of areas and groups with disproportionately high violence rates, Marvin Wolfgang and Franco Ferracuti have suggested that a **subculture of violence** exists.[27] The subculture's norms are separate from society's central, dominant value system. In this subculture, a potent theme of violence influences lifestyles, the socialization process, and interpersonal relationships. Even though the subculture's members share some of the values of the dominant culture, they expect that violence will be used to solve social conflicts and dilemmas. In some cultural subgroups, then, violence has become legitimized by custom and norms. It is considered appropriate behavior within culturally defined conflict situations in which an individual has been offended by a negative outcome in a dispute and seeks reparations through violent means (**disputatiousness**).[28]

GANGING. Empirical evidence shows that violence rates are highest in urban areas where subcultural values support teenage gangs whose members typically embrace the use of violence.[29] Gang members are more likely to own guns and other weapons than nongang members; they are also more likely to have peers who are gun owners and more likely to carry guns outside the home.[30]

In a recent interview study of St. Louis gang boys, criminologist Scott Decker found that violence is a core value of gang membership; it helped boys define what a gang really was:

> Int: Why do you call the group you belong to a gang?
> Ans: Violence, I guess. There is more violence than a family. With a gang, it's like fighting all the time, killing, shooting.

Decker found that gang violence may be initiated for a variety of reasons: It enables new members to show toughness during initiation ceremonies; it can be used to retaliate against rivals for actual or perceived grievances; it is a response when graffiti is defaced by rivals; and it is used to protect turf from incursions by outsiders.[31]

Net Bookmark

Want to learn more about gangs in the United States? A comprehensive review of the gang literature, prepared for the federal government's Office of Juvenile Justice and Delinquency Prevention, can be accessed at its web site. The site contains information on the definition and extent of gangs, gang migration, drug use, and many other similar topics.

http://aspensys.aspensys.com:209/R0-9127-range/ncjrs/data/gangsfs.txt

Research conducted in Chicago by Carolyn Block indicates that the number of gang-related killings has increased significantly in recent years, a finding that implies that the proportion of urban violence that is a product of subcultural clashes has been growing.[32]

Regional Values

Some criminologists have suggested that *regional* values promote violence.[33] In well-known research from the 1970s, Raymond Gastil found that a significant relationship existed between murder rates and residence in the South, that these differences predated the Civil War, and that outside the South regional homicide rates are related to an influx of southern migration.[34] Gastil attributed high homicide rates to a southern culture that stresses a frontier mentality, mob violence, night riders, personal vengeance, and easily available firearms. Southerners are also thought to place greater emphasis on personal honor, own more firearms, and use different child-rearing practices than citizens in other parts of the country.[35]

Not all criminologists have agreed with Gastil's conclusions.[36] For example, when Colin Loftin and Robert Hill controlled for the effect of social class and economic variables on southern homicide rates, they concluded that any argument pointing to a southern culture of lethal violence and murder is fallacious.[37] Gastil later replied to his critics by stating that they missed his real view—that southern culture promotes violence, not just the approval of violence.[38]

While the Southern subculture view is still being debated, UCR data have been used to show that although the South has relatively high crime rates, western states today have a higher overall violence rate than southern states.[39] Despite the fact that recent evidence refutes the "southern subculture of violence" theory, the violent Southerner remains, unfortunately, an enduring myth.[40]

Substance Abuse

It has also become common to link violence to substance abuse. Drug abuse influences violence in three ways: through the actual effects of the drugs, out of the need to obtain drugs, and in relation to drug trafficking.[41]

The relationship may be **psychopharmacological** when it is the direct consequence of ingesting mood-altering substances. Experimental evidence shows that acute doses of such drugs as PCP and amphetamines may produce violent and aggressive behaviors.[42] Alcohol abuse has long been associated with all forms of violence. A direct alcohol-violence link may be formed because drinking reduces cognitive ability, making miscommunication more likely while limiting the capacity for rational dialogue and compromise.[43]

Drug ingestion may result in **economic compulsive behavior** when drug users resort to violence to gain funds to support their habit. The federally sponsored Drug Use Forecasting (DUF) survey, which involves drug testing of all arrestees in major U.S. cities, consistently shows that those people who make up the criminal population are also heavily involved in drug abuse; up to 80% of all people arrested for violent crimes test positively for drugs.[44] Surveys of prison inmates also show that a significant majority report being under the influence of drugs and alcohol at the time they committed their last criminal offense.[45]

A bond between violent crime and substance abuse is also forged by the activities of drug trafficking gangs whose members both sell and use drugs; this is referred to as a **systemic link.** Studies of gangs that engage in drug trafficking show that their violent activities may result in a significant proportion of all homicides in urban areas.[46]

In a series of studies, Paul Goldstein and his associates found that *more than half* of all homicides in New York City may be drug-related, and 84% of these incidents involve cocaine (including crack) use and sales.[47] Most of the drug-related deaths are motivated by drug trafficking and interpersonal conflict brought on by drug abuse; relatively few people are killed by drug users trying to get drug money.[48] With the waning of the crack epidemic, the violence-drug link may undergo change.

Firearm Availability

While firearm availability is not a per se cause of violence, it is certainly a facilitating factor: A petty argument can

- Of the victims of nonfatal violent crime who faced an assailant armed with a firearm, 3% suffered gunshot wounds.
- Over half of all nonfatal firearm-related injuries treated in emergency departments were known to have resulted from an assault.
- An estimated 57,500 nonfatal gunshot wounds from assaults were treated in hospital emergency departments from June 1992 through May 1993.
- Of those victims who received nonfatal gunshot wounds from crime and were treated in an emergency room, 65% arrived by emergency medical service, rescue squad, or ambulance.
- Almost half the victims of nonfatal gunshot wounds from crime were shot in an arm, hand, leg, or foot.
- About 60% of the victims of nonfatal firearm injury from crime who went to an emergency room were subsequently hospitalized.
- Over half the victims of nonfatal gunshot wounds from crime who were treated in emergency departments were black males; a quarter were black males age 15–24.
- While the majority of victims of intentional gunshot wounds were black, most victims of unintentional firearm injury and suicide attempts with firearms were white.
- For 12% of the victims of nonfatal gunshot wounds from crime, the term "drive-by" was used to describe the assault.
- The firearm injury rate for police officers declined in the early 1980s and began climbing again after 1987, but it has not exceeded the peak reached in 1980–1981.

Source: Marianne Zawitz, *Firearm Injury from Crime* (Washington, D.C.: Bureau of Justice Statistics, 1996), p. 1.

escalate into a fatal encounter if one party or the other has a handgun. It may not be coincidence that the United States, which has a huge surplus of guns and in which most firearms (80%) used in crimes are stolen or obtained through illegal or unregulated transactions, also has one of the world's highest violence rates.[49] Disturbing new evidence indicates that more than 80% of inmates in juvenile correctional facilities owned a gun just prior to their confinement, and 55% said they carried one almost all the time.[50] The Uniform Crime Reports indicate that more than half of all murders and 40% of all robberies involve a firearm.[51] Handguns are the cause of death for two-thirds of all police killed in the line of duty. The presence of firearms in the home has been found to significantly increase the risk of suicide among adolescents, regardless of how carefully the guns were secured or stored.[52] Assaults and violence among family members and other intimates are *12 times more likely to result in death* if a handgun is used than if the attacks do not involve firearms.[53] Figure 11.2 describes the association between firearms and personal injuries.

So far, we have reviewed a few of the various factors suspected to be causes of violent crime. In the remainder of the chapter, we turn our attention to the individual acts that make up violent crime in our society. When violence is directed toward strangers, it is said to be **instrumental**—designed to improve the financial or social position of the criminal, such as through an armed robbery. In contrast,

Connections

It seems logical that a ban on the sale and ownership of handguns might help reduce the violence rate. However, as you may recall from the Close-Up on Gun Control in Chapter 3, some experts believe that taking the guns out of the hands of citizens might endanger them against armed criminals.

expressive violence is designed to vent rage, anger, or frustration, as when a romantic triangle results in a murder.

Among the common-law violent crimes are rape, murder, assault, and robbery. There are also newly recognized forms of violence directed at specific goals. Included within this category are hate crimes and workplace crimes. In addition, there are violent politically motivated crimes, commonly referred to as terrorism.

Connections

Some criminologists have also focused on "violent" business or corporate crimes, such as the release of toxic and fatal pollutants into the environment. Because these latter acts are linked to business organizations, they will be covered in the sections on corporate crime in Chapter 13.

Forcible Rape

Rape (from the Latin *rapere,* to take by force) is defined by the common law as "the carnal knowledge of a female forcibly and against her will."[54] It is one of the most loathed, misunderstood, and frightening of crimes. Under traditional common-law definitions, rape involved nonconsensual sexual intercourse performed by a male against a female he is neither married to nor cohabiting with. Excluded from the crime of rape are sexual acts that are usually included in other crime categories, such as:

- Forced participation in fellatio, cunnilingus, and, in many states, anal intercourse; these are usually covered by sodomy statutes.
- Coerced participation of a male in intercourse or other sexual activity by a female or by another male or of a female by another female.
- Coerced sexual intercourse induced by the threat of social, economic, or vocational harm, rather than of physical injury.[55]

Because of its content, rape was often viewed as a sexual offense in the traditional criminological literature; overcome by lust, a man forced his attentions on a woman. Even today, some men view rape as a sexual act, including one Tennessee judge who in 1994 released an accused rapist after stating that all he needed was a girlfriend and telling the public defender's office to arrange for a dating service; public outcry led to the release being rescinded.[56]

Criminologists now consider rape to be a violent, coercive act of aggression against women and not a forceful expression of sexuality. There has been a national campaign to alert the public to the seriousness of rape, to initiate help for victims, and to change legal definitions to facilitate the prosecution of rape offenders. Such efforts have been only marginally effective in reducing rape rates, but significant change has been seen in the overhauling of rape laws and development of a vast social service network to aid victims.

History of Rape

Rape has been known throughout history. It has been the subject of art, literature, film, and theater. Paintings such as "The Rape of the Sabine Women," novels such as *Clarissa* by Samuel Richardson, poems such as "The Rape of Lucrece" by William Shakespeare, and films such as *The Accused* have sexual violence as their central theme.

In early civilization, rape was a common occurrence. Men staked a claim of ownership on women by forcibly abducting and raping them. This practice led to males' solidification of power and their historical domination of women. In fact, in her often-cited book *Against Our Will*, Susan Brownmiller charges that the criminalization of rape occurred only after the development of a monetary economy.[57] Thereafter, the violation of a virgin caused an economic hardship on her family, who expected a significant dowry for her hand in marriage. According to Brownmiller, further proof of the sexist basis of rape law can be seen in Babylonian and Hebraic law. These ancient peoples considered the rape of a virgin to be a crime punishable by death. However, if the victim was a married woman, both she and her attacker were considered equally to blame. Unless her husband chose to intervene, the victim and her attacker were put to death.

During the Middle Ages, it was a common practice for ambitious men to abduct and rape wealthy women in an effort to force them into marriage. The practice of "heiress stealing" illustrates how feudal law gave little thought or protection to women and equated them with property.[58] It was only in the late 15th century that forcible sex was outlawed, and then only if the victim was of the nobility; peasant women and married women were not considered rape victims until well into the 16th century. The Christian condemnation of sex during this period was also a denunciation of women as evil, having lust in their hearts and redeemable only by motherhood. A woman who was raped was almost automatically suspected of contributing to her attack.

Rape and the Military

In 1996 the nation was shocked when the national media revealed the presence of a "rape ring" at the Aberdeen Proving Grounds in Maryland. Nearly 20 noncommissioned officers were accused of raping or sexually harassing 19 women trainees. The investigation prompted more than 5,000 female soldiers to call military hotlines to report similar behaviors at army bases around the country. The army scandal was especially disturbing because it involved drill instructors, who are given almost total control over the lives of young female recruits who depend on them for support and nurturing.[59] A number of army officers were convicted and sent to prison.

The link between the military and rape is inescapable. Throughout recorded history, rape has been associated with armies and warfare. Soldiers of conquering armies have considered sexual possession of their enemies' women one of the spoils of war. Among the ancient Greeks, rape was socially acceptable and well within the rules of warfare. During the Crusades, even knights and pilgrims, ostensibly bound by vows of chivalry and Christian piety, took time off to rape as they marched toward Constantinople.

The belief that women are part of the spoils of war has continued through the ages, from the Crusades to the war in Vietnam. The systematic rape of Bosnian women by Serbian army officers during the civil war in the former Yugoslavia horrified the world. These crimes seemed even more atrocious because they seemed part of an official policy of genocide: Rape was used as a means of impregnating Bosnian women with Serbian children. Reports out of Haiti also indicate that rape of politically involved women became a norm in the wake of the 1991 military coup that ousted President Jean Bertrand-Aristede. Soldiers there have attacked women in their homes and raped political prisoners.[60]

Incidence of Rape

How many rapes occur each year, and what is known about rape patterns? According to the most recent UCR data, about 95,000 rapes or attempted rapes were reported to police in 1996, a rate of 70 per 100,000 females. Rape rates, which had been trending upward throughout the 1980s, began a decline in the 1990s, decreasing more than 15% between 1991 and 1996.

Population density influences the rape rate: Metropolitan areas had a rape rate significantly higher than rural areas. Nonetheless, urban areas have experienced a much higher drop in rape reports than rural areas. The police clear slightly over half of all reported rape offenses by arrest. Of the offenders arrested, about 40% are under 25 years of age, 55% are white, and 42% are black. The racial pattern of rape arrests has been fairly consistent for some time. Finally, rape is a warm-weather crime—most rapes occur during July and August, with the lowest rates occurring during December, January, and February.

These data must be interpreted with caution, because according to NCVS findings, rape is frequently underreported by victims. For example, the NCVS estimates 260,000 rape incidents took place in 1995, suggesting that only about one-third of the incidents were reported to the police.[61] Many people fail to report rapes because they are embarrassed, they believe nothing could be done, or they somehow blame themselves.

Official data may reflect reporting practices rather than crime trends: The UCR uses a common-law definition of rape (the carnal knowledge of a female forcibly and against her will) that may not jibe with current state definitions; the UCR includes in its computations assaults or attempts to commit rape, whose interpretation may differ widely from state to state; and the acts committed by serial rapists make the relationship between the number of crimes and the number of offenders problematic.[62]

Because other victim surveys indicate that at least 20% of adult women, 15% of college-aged women, and 12% of adolescent girls have experienced sexual abuse or assault sometime during their lifetime, it is evident that both the official and victimization statistics significantly undercount rape.[63]

Types of Rapists

Some rapes are planned, others are spontaneous; some focus on a particular victim, while others occur almost as an afterthought during the commission of another crime, such as a burglary.[64] Some rapists are one-time offenders, while others engage in multiple or serial rapes. Some attack their victims without warning ("blitz rapes"), others try to "capture" their victims by striking up a conversation or by offering them a ride, and still others use a personal relationship to gain access to their target.[65]

One of the best-known attempts to classify the personality of rapists was made by psychologist A. Nicholas Groth, an expert on the classification and treatment of sex offenders. According to Groth, every rape encounter contains three elements: anger, power, and sexuality.[66] Consequently, rapists can be classified according to one of these dimensions:

- The *anger rape* occurs when sexuality becomes a means of expressing and discharging pent-up anger and rage. The rapist uses far more brutality than would have been necessary if his real objective had been simply to have sexual relations with his victim. His aim is to hurt his victim as much as possible; the sexual aspect of rape may have been an afterthought. Often the anger rapist acts on the spur of the moment after an upsetting incident has caused him conflict, irritation, or aggravation. Surprisingly, anger rapes are less psychologically traumatic for the victim than might be expected. Since a woman is usually physically beaten, she is more likely to receive sympathy from her peers, relatives, and the justice system and consequently to be immune from any suggestion that she complied with the attack.

- The *power rape* involves an attacker who does not want to harm his victim as much as he wants to possess her sexually. His goal is sexual conquest, and he uses only the amount of force necessary to achieve his objective.

The power rapist wants to be in control, to be able to dominate women and have them at his mercy. Yet it is not sexual gratification that drives the power rapist; in fact, he often has consenting relationships with his wife or girlfriend. Rape is instead a way of putting personal insecurities to rest, asserting heterosexuality, and preserving a sense of manhood. The power rapist's victim usually is a woman equal in age to or younger than the rapist. The lack of physical violence may reduce the support given the victim by family and friends. Therefore, the victim's personal guilt over her rape experience is increased—perhaps, she thinks, she could have done something to get away.

- The *sadistic rape* involves both sexuality and aggression. The sadistic rapist is bound up in ritual—he may torment his victim, bind her, torture her. Victims are usually related in the rapist's view to a personal characteristic that he wants to harm or destroy. The rape experience is intensely exciting to the sadist; he gets satisfaction from abusing, degrading, or humiliating his captive. This type of rape is particularly traumatic for the victim; Groth found that victims of such crimes need psychiatric care long after their physical wounds have healed.

In his treatment of rape offenders, Groth found that about 55% were of the power type; about 40%, the anger type; and about 5%, the sadistic type. Groth's major contribution has been his recognition that rape is generally a crime of violence and not a sexual act. In all of these circumstances, rape involves a violent criminal offense in which a predatory criminal chooses to attack a victim.

Groth is not alone in attempting to classify rapists. Psychologist Raymond Knight divides rapists into four categories:

- *Opportunist*—This is an antisocial person who rapes by chance while commiting another crime or act. For example, while burglarizing a house, he rapes the occupant.
- *Perversely angry*—This person has anger toward both men and women, and rape is just another form of undifferentiated violence or expression of that anger.
- *Sexual*—The person's motives may be distorted; he has aggressive and sadistic views toward sex and fuses these feelings together into a violent sexual act.
- *Vindictive*—This offender directs his considerable anger exclusively toward women. His behavior is intended to harm and humiliate women and has no sexual motivation.[67]

Types of Rape

In their studies, criminologists usually divide rapes into two broad categories: stranger-to-stranger rapes and acquaintance rapes. Whereas the former involve people who had never met before the rape, the latter involve someone known to the victim, even family members and friends. Included within acquaintance rapes are the subcategories of *date rape,* which involves a sexual attack during a courting relationship, and *marital rape,* which is forcible sex between people who are legally married to each other.

It is difficult to estimate the ratio of rapes involving strangers to those in which victim and assailant were in some way acquainted, as women may be more reluctant to report acts involving acquaintances. By some estimates, about 50% of rapes involve acquaintances.[68]

Stranger rapes are typically more violent than acquaintance rapes; attackers are more likely to carry a weapon, threaten the victim, and harm her physically. Stranger rapes are overrepresented in official statistics because victims who are more viciously harmed are the ones most likely to contact police.

DATE RAPE. Although official crime data indicate that most rapists and victims were strangers to each other, it is likely that acquaintance rapes constitute the bulk of sexual assaults. One disturbing trend of rape involves people who are in some form of courting relationship; this is referred to as **date rape.**

There is no single form of date rape. Some incidents occur on first dates, others after a relationship has been developing, and still others after the couple have been involved for some time. In long-term or close relationships, the male partner may feel he has invested so much time and money in his partner that he is owed sexual relations or that sexual intimacy is an expression that the involvement is progressing. He may make comparisons to other couples who have dated for as long a time and are sexually active.[69]

Date rape is not unique to the United States. A survey of Canadian college women found that while the overall crime rate of Canada is lower than that of the United States, the incidence of date rape is still extremely high. About one-third of the young women surveyed had experienced an episode of physical, verbal, or psychological sexual coercion; 25% said they had had sexual relations when they did not want to during the past year.[70]

Another disturbing phenomenon is campus gang rape, in which a group of men will attack a defenseless or inebriated victim. Well-publicized gang rapes have occurred at the University of New Hampshire, Duke University, Florida State University, Pennsylvania State University, and Bentley College in Massachusetts.[71]

Date rape is believed to occur frequently on college campuses. It has been estimated that 15%–20% of all college women are victims of rape or attempted rape; one self-report survey conducted on a Midwestern campus found that all of the rapists had known their victim beforehand.[72] The actual incidence of date rape may be even higher than surveys indicate because many victims blame themselves and do not recognize the incident as a rape, saying, for example, "I should have fought back harder," "I should not have gotten drunk."[73]

Despite their seriousness and prevalence, less than one in ten date rapes may be reported to police. Some victims do not report because they do not view their experiences as a "real rape," which they believe involves a strange man "jumping out of the bushes"; others are embarrassed and frightened. Coercive sexual encounters have become disturbingly common in our culture, prompting one commentator to state:

> The conclusion is inescapable that a very substantial minority of women on American college campuses have experienced an event which would fit most states' definitions of felony rape or sexual assault.[74]

To fight back, some campus women's groups have taken to writing on bathroom walls the names of men accused of date rape and sexual assault. Administration officials labeled it "libel and harassment" when a wall-writing campaign listed the names of 15 suspected rapists at Brown University. Brown women countered that this was the only way to alert potential victims to the danger they faced from men whom they might have considered trustworthy friends.[75]

MARITAL RAPE. In 1978, Greta Rideout filed rape charges against her husband, John. This Oregon case grabbed headlines because it was the first in which a husband was prosecuted for rape while domiciled with his wife. John was acquitted, and the couple briefly reconciled; later, continued violent episodes culminated in divorce and a jail term for John.[76]

Traditionally, a legally married husband could not be charged with raping his wife; this was referred to as the **marital exemption.** The origin of this legal doctrine can be traced to the 16th-century pronouncement of Matthew Hale, England's chief justice, who wrote:

> But the husband cannot be guilty of rape committed by himself upon his lawful wife, for by their mutual matrimonial consent and contract the wife hath given up herself in this kind unto the husband which she cannot retract.[77]

However, research indicates that many women are raped each year by their husbands as part of an overall pattern of spousal abuse, and they deserve the protection of the law. While there is a popular myth that marital rapes are the result of "healthy male sexuality" (as illustrated by Rhett Butler overcoming the objections of his proper and reluctant bride Scarlett O'Hara in the classic film *Gone With the Wind*), the reality is quite the opposite. Research shows that many spousal rapes are accompanied by brutal and sadistic beatings and have little to do with normal sexual interests.[78] Not surprisingly, the marital exemption has undergone significant revision: In 1980 only three states had laws against marital rape; today almost every state recognizes marital rape as a crime.[79] Piercing the marital exemption is not unique to U.S. courts; it has been abolished in Canada, Israel, Scotland, and New Zealand.[80]

The Cause of Rape

What factors predispose some men to commit rape? The answers formulated by criminologists are almost as varied as the varieties of the crime of rape itself. However, most explanations can be grouped into a few consistent categories.

EVOLUTIONARY/BIOLOGICAL FACTORS. One explanation for rape focuses on the evolutionary/biological aspects of the male sexual drive. It is suggested that rape may be instinctual, developed over the ages as a means of perpetuating the species. In more primitive times, forcible sexual contact may have served the purpose of spreading genes and maximizing offspring. Some believe that these prehistoric drives remain in modern man. Males still have a natural sexual drive that encourages them to have intimate relations with as many women as possible.[81] The evolutionary view is that the sexual urge is correlated with the unconscious need to preserve the species by spreading the gene pool as widely as possible. Men who are "pushy" or sexually aggressive will have the reproductive edge over their more passive peers, helping spread aggressive genes through the population. In contrast, women are more cautious and want to choose stable partners who seem willing to make a long-term commitment to child rearing. This difference produces sexual tension that causes men to use forceful copulatory tactics, especially when the chances of punishment are quite low.[82] Rape is bound up with sexuality as well as violence because, according to Lee Ellis, the act involves the "drive to possess and control others to whom one is sexually attracted."[83]

MALE SOCIALIZATION. In contrast to the evolutionary biological view, some researchers argue that rape is a function of male socialization in modern society. In her book *The Politics of Rape,* Diana Russell suggests that rape is actually not a deviant act but one conforming to the qualities regarded as masculine in U.S. society.[84] From an early age, boys are taught to be aggressive, forceful, tough, and dominating. Males are taught to dominate at the same time that they are led to believe that females want to be dominated. Russell describes the *virility mystique*—the belief that males learn to separate their sexual feelings from needs for love, respect, and affection. She believes that men are socialized to be the aggressors and expect to be sexually active with many women; male virginity and sexual inexperience are marks of shame. Similarly, sexually aggressive women frighten some men and cause them to doubt their own masculinity. Sexual insecurity may lead some men to commit rape to bolster their self-image and masculine identity. Rape, argues Russell, helps keep women in their place.

If rape is an expression of male anger and devaluation of women and not an act motivated by sexual desire, it follows that men who hold so-called macho attitudes will be more likely to engage in sexual violence than men who scorn hypermasculinity. The more strongly some men are socialized into traditional sex-role stereotypes, the more likely they are to be sexually aggressive. In fact, the sexually aggressive male may view the female as a legitimate victim of sexual violence.

Connections

Recall that in Chapter 9 Messerschmidt described how the need to prove one's masculinity helped men to justify their abuse of women. Men who are sexually violent, the argument goes, do not need to prove that they are not effeminate.

PSYCHOLOGICAL VIEWS. Another view is that rapists are suffering from some type of personality disorder or mental illness. Research shows that a significant percentage of incarcerated rapists exhibit psychotic tendencies, while many others have hostile and sadistic feelings toward women.[85]

SOCIAL LEARNING. Another viewpoint is that men learn to commit rapes much as they learn any other behavior. Groth found that 40% of the rapists he studied were sexually victimized as adolescents.[86] A growing body of literature links personal sexual trauma with the desire to inflict sexual trauma on others. Evidence is mounting that some men are influenced by observing films and books with both violent and sexual content.[87] Watching violent or pornographic films featuring women who are beaten, raped, or tortured has been linked to sexually aggressive behavior in men.[88] In one startling case, a 12-year-old Providence, Rhode Island, boy sexually assaulted a 10-year-old girl on a pool table after watching TV coverage of a case in which a woman was similarly raped (the incident was made into a film, *The Accused,* starring actress Jodie Foster).[89]

Connections

This view is explored further in Chapter 14, when the issue of pornography and violence is analyzed in greater detail. Most research does not show that watching "porno films" is linked to sexual violence, but there may be a link between sexual aggression and viewing movies with sexual violence as their theme.

SEXUAL MOTIVATION. Most current views of rape hold that it is actually a violent act and not sexually motivated. Yet, as Richard Felson and Marvin Krohn point out, it might be premature to dismiss the sexual motive from all rapes.[90] They used NCVS data to show that rape victims tend to be young and that rapists prefer younger and presumably more attractive victims. Felson and Krohn also found an association between the age of rapists and their victims, indicating that men choose rape targets of approximately the same age as consensual sex partners. And, despite the fact that younger criminals are usually the most violent, older rapists tend to harm their victims more often than younger rapists do. Felson and Krohn maintain that while older criminals may be raping for motives of power and control, younger offenders are seeking sexual gratification and are therefore less likely to harm their victims.

In sum, while criminologists are still at odds over the precise cause of rape, there is evidence that it is the product of a number of social, cultural, and psychological forces.[91] Although some experts view rape as a normal response to an abnormal environment, others view it as the product of a disturbed mind and deviant life experiences.

Rape and the Law

Of all violent crimes, none has created such conflict in the legal system as rape. Women who are sexually assaulted are reluctant to report the crime to the police because of the discriminatory provisions built into rape laws; because of the sexist fashion in which rape victims are often treated by police, prosecutors, and court personnel; and because of the legal technicalities that authorize invasion of women's privacy when a rape case is tried in court. In the past police were reluctant to make arrests and courts to convict in cases where a woman was not beaten seriously (thus showing she had strenuously resisted the attack) or if she had previously known or dated her attacker. Some state laws made rape so difficult to prove that women believe the slim chance their attacker will be convicted is not sufficient to warrant their participation in the prosecutorial process.

However, recent research indicates that police and courts may have become more sensitive to the plight of rape victims and are now just as likely to investigate "acquaintance" rapes as they were "aggravated" rapes involving multiple offenders, weapons, and victim injuries. In some jurisdictions, the justice system is willing to take all rape cases seriously and not ignore those in which the victim and their attacker had a prior relationship or those that did not involve serious injury.[92]

PROVING RAPE. Proving guilt in a rape case is extremely challenging for prosecutors. First, some male psychiatrists and therapists still maintain that women fantasize rape and therefore may falsely accuse their alleged attackers. Some judges also fear that women may charge men with rape because of jealousy, false proposals of marriage, or pregnancy. While those concerned with protecting the rights of rape victims have campaigned for legal reforms, some well-publicized false accusations of rape have hindered change. In one famous incident, Gary Dotson, convicted of raping a woman in Illinois, served more than six years in prison before his alleged victim recanted her story on national television.[93] In 1996, as the Dallas Cowboys were preparing for the playoffs, a young woman accused star players Erik Williams and Michael Irvin of forcible rape, only to later admit she had lied about the incident.[94] Afterward, Irvin's lawyer, Royce West, forcefully argued that the accused men's names should have been withheld before they were formally charged. If victims' names are not released to the press, he reasoned, why shouldn't the accused be entitled to a similar right of privacy?[95] Inci-

dents like these make it more difficult for prosecutors to gain convictions in rape cases.

The sexism in U.S. society has resulted in a cultural suspicion of women, who are often seen as provocateurs in any sexual encounter with men. Consequently, the burden is shifted to the woman to prove she has not provoked or condoned the rape. Although the law does not recognize it, jurors are sometimes swayed by the insinuation that the rape was victim-precipitated; thus, the blame is shifted from rapist to victim. To get a conviction, it becomes essential for prosecutors to establish that the act was forced and violent and that no question of voluntary compliance exists. The legal consequences of rape often reflect archaic legal traditions along with inherent male prejudices and suspicions.

Rape represents a major legal challenge to the criminal justice system for a number of reasons.[96] One issue is the concept of **consent.** It is essential to prove that the attack was forced and that the victim did not give voluntary consent to her attacker. In a sense, the burden is on the victim to prove that her character is beyond question and that she in no way encouraged, enticed, or misled the accused rapist. Proving victim dissent is not a requirement in any other violent crime (robbery victims do not have to prove they did not entice their attacker by flaunting expensive jewelry), yet it can still be introduced by the defense counsel in rape cases to create a reasonable doubt about the woman's credibility. It is a common defense tactic to introduce suspicion in the minds of the jury that the woman may have consented to the sexual act and later regretted her decision. Conversely, it is difficult for a prosecuting attorney to establish that a woman's character is so impeccable that the absence of consent is a certainty. Such distinctions are important in rape cases, because male jurors may be sympathetic to the accused if the victim is portrayed as unchaste. Simply referring to the woman as sexually liberated may be enough to result in exoneration of the accused, even if violence and brutality were used in the attack.[97]

REFORM. Because of the difficulty victims have in receiving justice in rape cases, the law of rape has been changing around the country. Efforts for reform include changing the language of statutes, dropping the condition that the victim resisted, and changing the requirement that the perpetrator actually used force to add "the threat of force or injury."[98] Most states and the federal government have developed **shield laws,** which protect women from being questioned about their sexual history unless it is judged to have a direct bearing on the case. In some instances, these laws are quite restrictive, while in others, they grant the trial judge considerable discretion to admit prior sexual conduct in evidence if it is deemed relevant for the defense. In an important 1991 case, *Michigan v. Lucas,* the U.S. Supreme Court upheld the validity of shield laws and ruled that excluding evidence of a prior sexual relationship between the parties did not violate the defendant's right to a fair trial.[99]

In addition to requiring evidence that consent was not given, the common law of rape required **corroboration** that the crime of rape actually took place. This has involved the need for independent or third-party evidence from police officers, physicians, and witnesses that the accused is actually the person who committed the crime, that sexual penetration took place, and that force was present and consent absent. In the past this requirement shielded rapists from prosecution in cases where the victim delayed reporting the crime or in which physical evidence had been compromised or lost. Corroboration is no longer required except under extraordinary circumstances, such as when the victim is too young to understand the crime, had a previous sexual relationship with the defendant, or gives a version of events that is improbable and self-contradictory.[100]

Despite this reform effort, it is still essential that the victim establish her intimate and detailed knowledge of the act for her testimony to be believed in court. This testimony may include answering searching questions about her assailant's appearance, the location in which the crime took place, and the nature of the physical assault.

A number of states and the federal government have replaced rape laws with the more sexually neutral crime of *sexual assault*.[101] Sexual assault laws outlaw any type of forcible sex, including homosexual rape.[102] Research shows that the credibility of sexual assault victims is still more likely to be challenged in court than the testimony of assault victims for whom no sexual contact was involved.[103] Clearly, more efforts are needed to improve prosecutions in sexual assault cases.

George Franklin was convicted of murder on January 29, 1991. Franklin's daughter, Eileen Franklin-Lipsker (shown here testifying at the trial), remembered during psychotherapy sessions with her analyst that her father had sexually assaulted and killed her eight-year-old friend. The murder had taken place in 1969, more than 20 years earlier. Released in July 1997, after six and one-half years in prison, Franklin filed a lawsuit charging his daughter with false prosecution.

Murder and Homicide

Murder is defined in the common law as "the unlawful killing of a human being with malice aforethought."[104] It is the most serious of all common-law crimes and the only one that can still be punished by death. The fact that Western society abhors murderers is illustrated by the fact that there is no statute of limitations in murder cases. While state laws usually limit prosecution of other crimes to a fixed period, usually seven to ten years, accused killers can be brought to justice years after their crime was committed. An example of the law's reach in murder cases was the murder conviction of George Franklin on January 29, 1991. Franklin's daughter, Eileen Franklin-Lipsker, had told legal authorities that while in recent psychotherapy sessions with her analyst, she had remembered how her father had sexually assaulted and killed her 8-year-old friend. The murder had taken place in 1969, more than 20 years earlier.[105]

To prove that a murder has taken place, most state jurisdictions require prosecutors to prove that the accused intentionally and with malice desired the death of the victim. *Express* or actual malice is the state of mind assumed to exist when someone kills another person in the absence of any apparent provocation. *Implied* or constructive malice is considered to exist when a death results from negligent or unthinking behavior; even though the perpetrator did not wish to kill the victim, the killing was the result of an inherently dangerous act and therefore is considered murder. An unusual example of this concept is the attempted murder conviction of Ignacio Perea, an AIDS-infected Miami man who kidnapped and raped an 11-year-old boy. Perea was sentenced to up to 25 years in prison when the jury agreed with the prosecutor's contention that the AIDS virus could be considered a deadly weapon.[106]

"Born and Alive"

One issue that has received national attention is whether a fetus that has not yet been delivered can be a murder victim, an act referred to as **feticide.** In some instances fetal harm comes from a mother whose behavior endangers an unborn child; in others, feticide is the result of the harmful action of a third party.

Some states have prosecuted women for endangering or taking the life of their unborn fetus because of their drug or alcohol abuse; in some instances convictions have been overturned because the law only applies to a "human being who has been born and is alive."[107] At least 200 women in 30 states have been arrested and charged in connection with harming (though not necessarily causing the death of) a fetus; appellate courts have almost universally overturned convictions on the basis that they were without legal merit or unconstitutional.[108] However, in an important case, *Whitner v. State of South Carolina,* the Supreme Court ruled that a woman could be held liable for actions during pregnancy that could affect her viable fetus.[109] In holding that a fetus is a "viable person," the Court opened the door for a potential homicide prosecution if a mother's action resulted in the fetal death.

It is more common for state law to allow prosecutions for murder when a third party's actions cause the death of a fetus. Four states (Illinois, Missouri, South Dakota, and West Virginia) extend wrongful death action to the death of any fetus, while the remaining states require that the fetus be "viable"—that is, able to live outside the mother's body, or that it be "born alive" and then die afterward due to the injuries sustained in utero.[110] In a recent Texas case, a man was convicted of manslaughter in the death of a baby who was delivered prematurely after an auto accident he caused while intoxicated. It was one of the first Texas cases to hold that a person can be held criminally liable for harming a yet unborn child.[111]

Degrees of Murder

There are different levels or degrees of homicide.[112] *Murder in the first degree* occurs when a person kills another after premeditation and deliberation. **Premeditation** means that the killing was considered beforehand and suggests that it was motivated by more than a simple desire to engage in an act of violence. **Deliberation** means the killing was planned and decided on after careful thought, rather than carried out on impulse. "To constitute a deliberate and premeditated killing, the slayer must weigh and consider the question of killing and the reasons for and against such a choice; having in mind the consequences, he decides to and does kill."[113] The planning implied by this definition need not be a long, drawn-out process but may be an almost instantaneous decision to take another's life. Also, a killing accompanying a felony, such as robbery or rape, usually constitutes first-degree murder (felony murder).

Second-degree murder requires the actor to have malice aforethought but not premeditation or deliberation. A second-degree murder occurs when a person's wanton disregard for the victim's life and his or her desire to inflict serious bodily harm on the victim results in the loss of human life.

An unlawful homicide without malice is called *manslaughter* and is usually punished by from 1 to 15 years in prison. *Voluntary* or *nonnegligent manslaughter* refers to a killing committed in the heat of passion or during a sudden quarrel considered to have provided sufficient provocation to produce violence; while intent may be present, malice is not. *Involuntary* or *negligent manslaughter* refers to a killing that occurs when a person's acts are negligent and without regard for the harm they may cause others. Most involuntary manslaughter cases involve motor vehicle deaths, as when a drunk driver causes the death of a pedestrian. However, people can be held criminally liable for the death of another in any instance where their disregard of safety causes the death. For example, on February 16, 1990 Michael Patrick Berry, a man whose pit bull terrier killed a child who had wandered into his yard, was sentenced to three years and eight months in prison; it was the nation's first case in which a person was convicted for manslaughter for the actions of a pet.[114]

The Nature and Extent of Murder

It is possible to track murder rate trends from 1900 to the present with the aid of coroner's reports and UCR data. The murder rate reached a peak in 1933, a time of high unemployment and lawlessness, and then fell until 1958, when it began another upswing to a 1980 peak of 10.2 murders per 100,000 persons (a total of 23,000). Murder rates have declined in the 1990s, to about 9 per 100,000 inhabitants; murders declined by about 20% between 1992 and 1996.

What else do the official crime statistics tell us about murder today? Murder victims tend to be males over 18 years of age. There is a disturbing trend for African Americans to be murder victims; about half of all murder victims are African American. Murder, like rape, tends to be an intraracial crime; about 90% of victims are slain by members of their own race. People arrested for murder are generally young (under 35) and male (90%), a pattern that has proven consistent over time.[115]

The UCR also collects information on the circumstances of murder. A number of important patterns stand out:

- Historically, most murder victims knew or were acquainted with their attackers. During the 1990s this relationship seems to be changing. Today less than half of all victims are related to or acquainted with their assailants.
- Most murders involve firearms (70%), a majority being handguns; about 13% involve knives or cutting instruments. Some well-known weapons, such as poison, narcotics, and strangulation, are actually rarely used; there were only 12 known poisonings in 1995.
- Females are much more likely to be killed (26%) by a husband or boyfriend than males are to be killed by a wife or girlfriend (3%).
- The environmental pattern of murder is similar to that of rape. Murder rates are highest in large cities, in the South and West, and during the summer months and holiday seasons. In contrast, rural counties and northeastern states have relatively low murder rates. Some cities are extremely murder-prone. Nearly 25% of all murders in the United States occur in eight cities: New Orleans, New York, Los Angeles, Chicago, Houston, Detroit, Philadelphia, and Washington, D.C.

Today, few would deny that some relationship exists between social and ecological factors and murder. This section explores some of the more important issues related to these factors.

Murderous Relations

One factor that has received a great deal of attention from criminologists is the relationship between the murderer and the victim.[116] Most criminologists generally agree that murders can be separated into those involving strangers—typically stemming from a felony attempt, such as a robbery or drug deal—and acquaintance homicides involving disputes between family, friends, and acquaintances.[117] It is believed that the quality of relationships and interpersonal interactions may thus influence murder.

> **Connections**
>
> Recall from Chapter 4 the discussion of victim precipitation: The argument made by some criminologists is that murder victims helped create the "transaction" that led to their death.

SPOUSAL RELATIONS. Women are much more likely to be killed by their mates than men are. To address this question, Angela Browne and Kirk Williams looked at homicide data over a 12-year period and found a major shift in murder trends among people who shared an intimate relationship. The rate of homicide among married couples declined significantly, a finding they attribute to the shift away from marriage in modern society. However, Browne and Williams found significant gender differences in homicide trends among the unmarried: Whereas the number of unmarried men killed by their partners *declined,* the rate of women killed by the men they lived with *increased* dramatically. They speculate that men kill their spouses either as a means of maintaining control or because they fear losing control and power. Because people who live together without marriage have a legally and socially more "open" relationship, it is possible that males in such relationships are more likely to feel loss of control and exert their power with the use of violence.[118]

In contrast, research indicates that females who kill their mates do so after suffering repeated violent attacks.[119] It is possible that the number of males killed by their partners has declined because alternatives to abusive relationships, such as battered woman's shelters, are becoming more prevalent around the United States. Browne and Williams have shown that regions in which greater social support is provided for battered women and legislation has been passed to protect abuse victims also have lower rates of female-perpetrated homicide.[120]

STRANGER RELATIONS. The number of stranger homicides seems to be on the increase. Under what circumstances do stranger homicides occur? In an oft-cited study of homicide in nine U.S. cities, Margaret Zahn and Philip Sagi found that stranger homicides were most often "felony murders," which occur during rapes, robberies, burglaries, and the rest were random acts of urban violence that fuel public fear: A homeowner tells a motorist to move his car because it is blocking the driveway, an argument ensues, and the owner gets a pistol and kills the motorist; a young boy kills a store manager because, he says, "Something came into my head to hurt the lady."[121]

How do such murderous relations develop between two people who had never before met? In a well-known study, David Luckenbill studied murder transactions to determine whether particular patterns of behavior are common to the transaction between killer and victim.[122] He found that many homicides take a sequential form: The victim made what the offender considered an offensive move; the offender typically retaliated in a verbal or physical manner; an agreement to end things violently was forged with the victim's response; the battle ensued, leaving the victim dead or dying; the offender's escape was shaped by his or her relationship to the victim or the reaction of the audience, if any.

Homicide Networks

Some murders may thus be the result of wanton violence by a stranger, while others involve a social interaction between two or more people who know each other and whose destructive social interaction leads to the death of one party.[123] Scott Decker has found that while on the surface these deaths seem senseless, they often mask a deeper underlying cause: revenge, dispute resolution, jealousy, bad drug deals, racial bias, threats to identity or status (for example, someone who is a "badass" has his authority challenged).[124] Perpetrators and victims may be joined in what Decker calls a "homicide network" that links victims, suspects, and witnesses together.

It is often the case, he found in a study of St. Louis killings, that a prior act of violence, motivated by profit or greed, generates revenge killings. The instigator of one criminal act becomes the victim in another. Those individuals most isolated from conventional society and with the least confidence in the criminal justice system are those most likely to seek "street justice." They take the victimization of family and friends quite seriously, setting up a murderous exchange with the people they feel responsible. And if the perpetrator's identity is unknown, a "suitable representative" from their racial or ethnic group can be substituted, setting off a new round of revenge-type killings; violent exchanges become "contagious." Decker has found that people are much less likely to victimize those they consider close friends than those who are mere acquaintances or strangers.[125]

Types of Murderers

Other forms of stranger homicides take a toll on society. Thrill killing involves impulsive violence motivated by the killer's decision to kill a stranger as an act of daring or recklessness. For example, children who throw a boulder from a highway overpass onto an oncoming car may be out for thrills or kicks.[126] While some thrill killings involve relatively stable youths who exhibit few prior symptoms of violence, others are committed by youngsters with longstanding mental or emotional problems.[127]

Gang killings involve members of teenage gangs who make violence part of their group activity. Some of these gangs engage in warfare over territory or control of the drug trade; in drive-by shootings, enemies are killed and strangers are caught in the crossfire. The FBI records about 1,000 gang killings each year. Recent research on street gangs in Chicago by Carolyn Block and Richard Block shows that between 1987 and 1990 street gangs committed more than 9,000 violent acts, including 288 homicides in Chicago alone.[128]

Cult killings occur when members of religious cults, some of which are devoted to devil worship, satanism, and the "black mass," are ordered to kill by their leaders. On some occasions, the cult members are ordered to kill peers who are suspected of deviating from the leaders' teachings. Other crimes involve random violence against strangers either as a show of loyalty or because of the misguided belief that the strangers are a threat to the cult's existence. Charles Ewing cites the case of three Missouri teenagers, all members of a self-styled satanic cult, who beat another boy to death with baseball bats and then stuffed his body down a well. For months before the killing, the boys planned the crime as a human sacrifice for Satan.[129] In another incident police in Matamoros, Mexico, uncovered the grave of a 21-year-old U.S. college student, Mark Kilroy, who had served as a human sacrifice for members of a Mexican drug ring that practiced *palo mayombe,* a form of black magic; killing the youth was believed to bring immunity from bullets and criminal prosecution.[130]

Some murders blamed on the influence of Satan are not carried out by members of an organized group but rather are perpetrated by individuals who have visions of the Devil telling them to kill. In 1993 a 15-year-old Houston boy, Andrew Merritt, killed his mother after hearing the Devil tell him to "kill all the Christians"; law enforcement officials linked Andrew's passion for heavy metal music to the crime.[131]

While it is difficult to assess the numbers of stranger homicides that result from gang, cult, and thrill killings, it seems evident that they are becoming a disturbing element of U.S. violence.

Serial Murder

Donald Harvey is described as being neat, pleasant, outgoing, and remarkably normal by those who know him best. However, his co-workers in a Cincinnati-area hospital where he worked as a nurse's aide referred to Harvey as the "angel of death" because so many patients died in his ward. Their fears convinced a local TV station to conduct an investigation that resulted in Harvey's arrest and conviction on multiple murder charges. Harvey pleaded guilty to killing at least 21 patients and 3 other people, and he claims to have killed 28 others, although he cannot remember details of their deaths. Harvey claims that he was a mercy killer who "gained relief for the patients"; prosecutors described him as a thrill seeker whose behavior was triggered by his sexual ambivalence.[132] He was sentenced to life in prison with possibility of parole in 95 years. Harvey may be the most prolific serial killer in U.S. history, although it is unlikely that the true extent of his activities will ever be known.

Donald Harvey's murderous actions fall within a frightening pattern referred to as **serial murder.** Some serial murderers, such as Theodore Bundy and the Australian race-car driver and photographer Christopher Wilder, roam the country killing at random.[133] Others terrorize a city, such as the Los Angeles–based Night Stalker; the Green River Killer, who is believed to have slain more than four dozen young women in Seattle; and the Hillside Stranglers, Kenneth Bianchi and Angelo Buono, who tortured and killed 10 women in the Los Angeles area.[134] A third type of serial murderer, such as Donald Harvey and Milwaukee cannibal Jeffrey Dahmer, kill so cunningly that many victims are dispatched before the authorities even realize the deaths can be attributed to a single perpetrator.[135]

Serial killers operate over a long period of time and can be distinguished from the **mass murderer** who kills many victims in a single, violent outburst, such as Thomas Hamilton's outburst in Dunblane, Scotland, or James Huberty's murder of 21 people in a McDonald's in San Ysidro, California. The Close-Up on "Mass Murder and Serial Killing" further discusses serial and multiple killers.

TYPES OF SERIAL MURDERERS. Research shows that serial killers have long histories of violence, beginning in childhood with the targeting of other children, siblings, and small animals.[136] They maintain superficial relationships with others, have trouble relating to the opposite sex, and have guilt feelings about their interest in sex. Despite these commonalities, there is no single distinct type of serial killer. Some seem to be monsters—such as Edmund Kemper, who, in addition to killing six young female hitchhikers, killed his mother, cut off her head, and used it as a dart board. Others—such as Bianchi, Wilder, and Bundy—were suave ladies' men whose murderous actions surprised even close friends.

Consequently, the cause of serial murder eludes criminologists. Such widely disparate factors as mental illness, sexual frustration, neurological damage, child abuse and neglect, smothering relationships with mothers (David Berkowitz, the Son of Sam, slept in his parents' bed until he was ten), and childhood anxiety have been suggested as possible causes. However, most experts view serial killers as sociopaths who from early childhood demonstrated bizarre behavior, such as torturing animals; who enjoy killing; who are immune to their victims' suffering; and who, when caught, bask in the media limelight. For example, Wayne Henley, Jr., who along with Dean Corill killed 27 boys in Houston,

Criminologists James Alan Fox and Jack Levin have written extensively on two of the most frightening aspects of modern violence: mass murder and serial killing.

According to Levin and Fox, while it is difficult to estimate the number and extent of serial killings, a reasoned estimate is that up to 20 serial killers are active in a given year, accounting for up to 240 killings, or about 1% of the total number of homicides.

There are different types of serial killers. Some wander the countryside killing at random; others stay in their hometown and lure victims to their death. Theodore Bundy, convicted killer of three young women and suspected killer of many others, roamed the country killing as he went, while John Wayne Gacy killed over 30 boys and young men without leaving Chicago.

Although they share many characteristics with the general population, one "special" trait stands out: Serial killers are exceptionally skillful in their presentation of self so that they appear beyond suspicion. They kill for the fun of it. They enjoy the thrill, the sexual gratification, and the dominance they achieve over the lives of their victims. The serial killer rarely uses a gun to kill, because this method is too quick and would deprive him of his greatest pleasure, "exalting in his victim's suffering." Serial killers are not "sick" or insane, but rather "more cruel than crazy."

Fox and Levin have their own typology of serial killers:

1. *Thrill killers* strive for either sexual sadism or dominance. This is the most common form of serial murderer.

2. *Mission killers* want to reform the world or have a vision that drives them to kill.

3. *Expedience killers* are out for profit or want to protect themselves from a perceived threat.

In contrast to serial killers, mass murderers engage in a single, uncontrollable outburst called simultaneous killing. Examples of simultaneous mass murderers include Charles Whitman, who killed 14 people and wounded 30 others from atop the 307-foot tower on the University of Texas campus on August 1, 1966; James Huberty, who killed 21 people in a McDonald's in San Ysidro, California, on July 18, 1984; and George Hennard, a deranged Texas man who, on October 16, 1991, smashed his truck through a plate glass window in a cafeteria in Killeen, Texas, got out, and systematically killed 22 people before committing suicide as police closed in.

Fox and Levin find four types of mass murderers:

1. *Revenge killers* seek to get even with individuals or society at large. Their typical target is an estranged wife and "her" children or an employer and "his" employees.

2. *Love killers* are motivated by a warped sense of devotion. They are often despondent people who commit suicide and take others, such as a wife and children, with them.

3. *Profit killers* are usually trying to cover up a crime, eliminate witnesses, and carry out a criminal conspiracy.

---

offered to help prosecutors find the bodies of additional victims so he could break Chicago killer John Wayne Gacy's record of 33 murders.[137] However, Philip Jenkins's study of serial murder in England identified one group of offenders who had no apparent personality problems until late in their lives, were married and respectable, and even had careers in the armed services and police.[138]

Ronald Holmes and James DeBurger have studied serial killers and found that they can be divided into at least four types:

1. *Visionary killers.* Their murders are committed in response to some inner voice or vision that demands that some person or category of persons be killed. This type of serial killer is almost always out of touch with reality and is usually considered psychotic.

2. *Mission-oriented killers.* Their murders are motivated to rid the world of a particular type of undesirable person, such as prostitutes. They are well aware of what they are doing and are in touch with reality. Joseph Paul Franklin, for example, killed as many as 12 young black males who were with white female companions.

3. *Hedonistic killers.* These are thrill-seeking murderers who get excitement and sometimes sexual pleasure from their acts.

4. *Power/control-oriented killers.* These murderers enjoy having complete control over their victims. If they rape or mutilate their victims, the violence is motivated not by sex but by the pleasure of having power over another human being.[139]

Other types of serial killers include the *mysoped,* or sadistic child killer, who gains sexual satisfaction from torturing and killing children;[140] the *psychopathic killer,* who is motivated by a character disorder that results in his or her being unable to experience feelings of shame, guilt, sorrow, or other "normal" human emotions; and *professional hit* killers, who assassinate complete strangers for economic, political, or ideological reasons (terrorists and organized crime figures fall within this category).[141]

WHEN THE SERIAL KILLER IS A WOMAN. An estimated 10%–15% of serial killers are women. A recent study by Belea Keeney and Kathleen Heide investigated the

James Alan Fox and Jack Levin, authors of *Overkill: Mass Murder and Serial Killing Exposed*, suggest that serial killers suffer from personality disorders rather than mental illness.

4. *Terrorist killers* are trying to send a message. Gang killings tell rivals to watch out; cult killers may actually leave a message behind to warn society about impending doom.

Levin and Fox dispute the notion that all mass murderers and serial killers have biological or psychological problems, such as genetic anomalies or schizophrenia. Even the most sadistic serial murderers are not mentally ill or driven by delusions or hallucinations. Instead, they typically exhibit a sociopathic personality that deprives them of feelings of conscience or guilt to guide their behavior. Mass murderers are actually ordinary citizens driven to extreme acts. They experience long-term frustration, blame others for their problems, and then get set off by some catastrophic loss they are unable to get help to deal with.

So far, police have been successful in capturing simultaneous killers whose outburst is directed at family members or friends. The serial killer has proven a more elusive target. Today, the U.S. Justice Department is coordinating efforts to gather information on unsolved murders in different jurisdictions to find patterns linking the crimes. Unfortunately, when a serial murderer is caught, it is often the result of luck—or a snitch—and not investigative skill.

CRITICAL THINKING QUESTIONS

1. Can a mass murderer be legally sane?
2. Should there be a mandatory death sentence for all serial killers?

Sources: James Alan Fox and Jack Levin, *Overkill: Mass Murder and Serial Killing Exposed* (New York: Plenum, 1994); idem, "A Psycho-Social Analysis of Mass Murder," in *Serial and Mass Murder: Theory, Policy, and Research*, ed. Thomas O'Reilly-Fleming and Steven Egger (Toronto: University of Toronto Press, 1993); idem, "Serial Murder: A Survey," in *Serial and Mass Murder*, ed. O'Reilly-Fleming and Egger; idem, *Mass Murder* (New York: Plenum Press, 1985).

characteristics of a sample of 14 female serial killers and found a pattern of distinct gender differences.[142]

For instance, Keeney and Heide found some striking differences between the way male and female killers carried out their crimes. Males were much more likely than females to use extreme violence and torture. While males used a "hands-on" approach, including beating, bludgeoning, and strangling their victims, females were more likely to poison or smother their victims. Men tracked or stalked their victims, while women were more likely to lure victims to their death.

The researchers also found gender-based personality and behavior characteristics among serial killers. Female killers, somewhat older than their male counterparts, were abusers of both alcohol and drugs; males were not likely to be substance abusers. Women were diagnosed as having histrionic, manic-depressive, borderline, dissociative, and antisocial personality disorders; men were more often diagnosed as having antisocial personalities.

The profile of the female serial killer that emerges is a person who smothers or poisons someone she knows. During childhood, she suffered from an abusive relationship in a disrupted family. Female killers' education levels are below average, and if they work, it is in a low-status position.

CONTROLLING SERIAL KILLERS. Serial killers come from diverse backgrounds. So far, law enforcement officials have been at a loss to control random killers who leave few clues, constantly change their whereabouts, and have little connection to their victims. Catching serial killers is often a matter of luck. To help local law enforcement officials, the FBI has developed a profiling system to identify potential suspects. In addition, the Justice Department's Violent Criminal Apprehension Program (VICAP), a computerized information service, gathers information and matches offense characteristics on violent crimes around the country.[143] This way, crimes can be compared to determine whether they are the product of a single culprit.

Efforts to control serial killers take on greater importance when the rate of increase of this crime is considered. Philip Jenkins has studied serial killing over the past 50 years and reports an upsurge since the 1960s. In addition, the number of victims per criminal and the ferocity and savagery of the killings also seem to be increasing. Jenkins attributes this increase to a variety of influences, ranging from a permissive, drug-abusing culture to a mental health system so overcrowded that potentially dangerous people are released without supervision into an unsuspecting world.[144]

Assault and Battery

Although many people mistakenly believe that "assault and battery" refers to a single act, they are actually two separate crimes. Battery requires an offensive touching, such as slapping, hitting, or punching a victim. Assault requires no actual touching but involves either attempted battery or intentionally frightening the victim by word or deed. While the common law originally intended these twin crimes to be misdemeanors, most jurisdictions now upgrade them to felonies when either a weapon is used or they occurred during the commission of a felony (for example, a person is assaulted during the course of a robbery). In the UCR, the FBI defines serious assault, or aggravated assault, as "an unlawful attack by one person upon another for the purpose of inflicting severe or aggravated bodily injury"; this definition is similar to the one used in most state jurisdictions.[145]

Under common law, battery required "bodily injury," such as broken limbs or wounds. However, under modern law, an assault and battery occurs if the victim suffers a temporarily painful blow, even if no injury results. A battery can also involve "offensive touching," as when a man kisses a woman against her will or puts his hands on her body.

Nature of Assault

The pattern of criminal assault is quite similar to that of homicide—one could say that the only difference between the two is that the victim survives.[146] In 1996 the FBI recorded about 1 million assaults, a rate of about 415 per 100,000 inhabitants. Although the number and rate of assaults has increased over the past ten years, as with other crimes the rate of assault has been in a recent decline (down 8% between 1992 and 1996).

The pattern of assault is quite similar to that of murder. People arrested for assault and those identified by victims seem to be young, male, and white, although the arrest data contain a disproportionate number of minority-group members (38%). While assault victims tend to be male, as Figure 11.3 shows, women also face a significant danger.

Similarly, assault rates were highest in urban areas, during the summer months, and in southern and western regions. The most common weapons used in assaults were blunt instruments (33%), hands and feet (26%), firearms (23%), and knives (18%).

Assault in the Home

One of the most frightening aspects of assaultive behavior today is the incidence of violent attacks in the home. Crim-

- Women age 12 or older annually sustained almost 5 million violent victimizations in 1992 and 1993. About 75% of all lone-offender violence against women and 45% of violence involving multiple offenders was perpetrated by offenders whom the victim knew. In 29% of all violence against women by a lone offender, the perpetrator was an intimate (husband, ex-husband, boyfriend, or ex-boyfriend).
- Women were about 6 times more likely than men to experience violence committed by an intimate.
- Women annually reported about 500,000 rapes and sexual assaults to interviewers. Friends or acquaintances of the victims committed over half these rapes or sexual assaults. Strangers were responsible for about 1 in 5.
- Women of all races and Hispanic and non-Hispanic women were about equally vulnerable to violence by an intimate.
- Women ages 19 to 29 and women in families with incomes below $10,000 were more likely than other women to be victims of violence by an intimate.
- Among victims of violence committed by an intimate, the victimization rate of women separated from their husbands was about 3 times higher than that of divorced women and about 25 times higher than that of married women. Because the NCVS reflects a respondent's marital status at the time of the interview, which is up to 6 months after the incident, it is possible that separation or divorce followed the violence.
- Female victims of violence by an intimate were more often injured by the violence than females victimized by a stranger.

Source: Ronet Bachman and Linda Saltzman, *Violence Against Women: Estimates from the Redesigned Survey* (Washington, D.C.: Bureau of Justice Statistics, 1995), p. 1.

inologists are now aware that intrafamily violence is an enduring social problem in the United States. One area of intrafamily violence that has received a great deal of media attention is child abuse.[147] This term describes any physical or emotional trauma to a child for which no reasonable explanation, such as an accident or ordinary disciplinary practices, can be found.[148]

Child abuse can result from actual physical beatings administered to a child by hands, feet, weapons, belts, sticks, burning, and so on. Another form of abuse results from neglect—not providing a child with the care and shelter to which he or she is entitled. It is difficult to estimate the actual number of child abuse cases, since so many incidents are never reported to the police. Nonetheless, child abuse and neglect appears to be a serious social problem.

National surveys conducted by Richard Gelles and Murray Straus found that in a given year over 1 million children in the United States are subject to physical abuse from their parents.[149] Physical abuse was found to rarely be a one-time event. The average number of assaults per year was 10.5; the median, 4.5. Children of all ages suffer abuse. In general, boys are more frequently abused than girls until age 12. Among teenagers, girls are more fre-

Intrafamily violence is an enduring social problem in the United States. Children who are abused are more likely to be violent and abusive as adults, a process called the "cycle of violence." Here a San Diego, California–based childcare worker on a home visit examines a child of one of his clients. Social service agencies are often overburdened and understaffed, making it difficult for them to effectively deal with abuse cases.

quently the object of abuse. The American Humane Society, which collects data on reported child abuse, also estimates that 3 million cases are reported to authorities each year.[150]

Another aspect of the abuse syndrome is **sexual abuse**—the exploitation of children through rape, incest, and molestation by parents or other adults. Although it is difficult to estimate the incidence of sexual abuse, numerous anecdotal incidents illustrate the seriousness of the problem. Many allegations of sexual impropriety have been made against religious figures such as priests. The Boy Scouts admitted having dismissed 1,800 scoutmasters suspected of molesting children between 1971 and 1991; some of those dismissed may have moved to other troops and continued their abuse.[151]

A number of attempts have been made to gauge the extent of the sexual abuse problem. One frequently cited study, Diana Russell's survey of women in the San Francisco area, found that 38% had experienced intrafamilial or extrafamilial sexual abuse by the time they reached 18.[152] Jeanne Hernandez's more recent survey of Minnesota students in grades 6, 9, and 12 found that about 2% of the males and 7% of the females had experienced incest, while 4% of the males and 13% of the females had suffered extrafamilial sexual abuse. Although the percentage of abused females was smaller than that found by Russell, research by Glenn Wolfner and Richard Gelles indicates that up to one in five girls suffers sexual abuse.[153]

While these results are disturbing, they most likely underestimate the incidence of sexual abuse. It is difficult to get people to answer questions about youthful sexual abuse, and many victims either were too young to understand their abuse or have repressed their memory of the incidents. Children, the most common target, may be inhibited because parents are reluctant to admit abuse occurred. One study found that 57% of children referred to a clinic because they had sexually transmitted diseases claimed *not* to have been molested despite this irrefutable physical evidence. Parental response significantly influences reporting abuse: Kids whose caretakers admitted the possibility of abuse were 3.5 times more likely to report abuse than those whose parents denied any possibility that their child was a victim.[154]

The growing incidence of sexual abuse is of particular concern when its long-term impact is considered. Abused kids experience a long list of symptoms, including fear, posttraumatic stress disorder, behavior problems, sexualized behavior, and poor self-esteem. The amount of force used, its duration, and its frequency are all related to the extent of the long-term effects and the length of time needed for recovery.[155]

Causes of Child Abuse

Why do parents physically assault their children? Such maltreatment is a highly complex problem with neither a single cause nor a readily available solution. It cuts across ethnic, religious, and socioeconomic lines. Abusive parents cannot be categorized by sex, age, or educational level; they

One factor that has been associated with systematic child abuse is familial stress. Abusive parents are unable to cope with life crises—divorce, financial problems, alcohol and drug abuse, poor housing conditions. This inability leads them to maltreat their children. Statistics also show that a high rate of assault on children occurs among the lower economic classes. This has led to the misconception that lower-class parents are more abusive than those in the upper classes. However, two conditions may account for this discrepancy. First, low-income people are often subject to greater levels of environmental stress and have fewer resources to deal with it. Second, cases of abuse among poor families are more likely to be dealt with by public agencies and therefore are more frequently counted in official statistics.[157]

Two other factors have a direct correlation with abuse and neglect. First, parents who themselves suffered abuse as children tend to abuse their own children; second, isolated and alienated families tend to become abusive. A cyclical pattern of family violence seems to be perpetuated from one generation to another within families. Evidence indicates that a large number of abused and neglected children grow into adolescence and adulthood with a tendency to engage in violent behavior. The behavior of abusive parents can often be traced to negative experiences in their own childhood—physical abuse, lack of love, emotional neglect, incest, and so on. These parents become unable to separate their own childhood traumas from their relationships with their children. They also often have unrealistic perceptions of the appropriate stages of childhood development. Thus, when their children are unable to act "appropriately"—when they cry, throw food, or strike their parents—the parents may react in an abusive manner. For parents such as these, says Ruth Inglis, "the axiom about not being able to love when you have not known love yourself is painfully borne out in their case histories. . . . They spend their days going around the house, ticking away like unexploded bombs. A fussy baby can be the lighted match."[158]

Parents also become abusive if they are isolated from friends, neighbors, or relatives who can provide a lifeline in times of crisis. Potentially or actually abusing parents live in states of alienation from society; they have carried the concept of the shrinking nuclear family to its most extreme form and are cut off from ties of kinship and contact with other people in the neighborhood.[159] Many abusive and neglectful parents describe themselves as highly alienated from their families and lacking close relationships with persons who could provide help and support in stressful situations.

Public concern about child abuse has led to the development of programs designed to prevent and deter it. The reporting of child abuse by doctors, social workers, and other such persons is mandated by law. Some states have created laws that bar abusive parents from the home even before guilt has been determined at trial. Courts have begun to recognize the rights of abused children to collect damages from parents even years after the abuse took place. In one 1990 case, a Colorado court awarded two sisters $2.4 million in damages from a sexually abusive parent more than 20 years after the abuse occurred.[160]

Spouse Abuse

On the evening of June 23, 1993, John Wayne Bobbitt came home and, according to his wife, Lorena, committed a marital rape. Afterward, while he slept, Lorena used a 12-inch kitchen knife to slice off two-thirds of his penis. In a panic, she drove off and tossed the severed organ into a field. Police officers were able to recover it, and it was reattached in a 9½-hour operation. The case drew reporters from around the United States; observers at the scene described representatives of the media as a "herd of buffaloes," backing into cars and falling in ditches.[161]

John was later tried and acquitted on charges of sexual assault stemming from the alleged rape. Claiming that her actions were a result of the rape and earlier abuse, Lorena was found not guilty on a charge of malicious wounding, by reason of insanity, on January 21, 1994. No longer considered a threat, she was released from Virginia's Central State Hospital on February 28, 1994.[162]

Although one of the most highly publicized cases of the decade, the Bobbitt case is misleading: Spouse abuse overwhelmingly involves a physical assault in which a wife is injured by a husband.[163] There are indeed some cases of *husband battering*, but they typically involve a defensive measure taken by a previously abused spouse. According to criminologists Martin Schwartz and Walter DeKeseredy, the presentation of women as violent helps maintain the dominance of men in marital relations.[164]

Spouse abuse has occurred throughout recorded history. During the Roman era, men had the legal right to beat their wives for minor acts, such as attending public games without permission, drinking wine, or walking outdoors with their faces uncovered.[165] More serious transgressions, such as adultery, were punishable by death. During the later stages of the Roman Empire, the practice of wife beating abated, and by the 4th century A.D., excessive violence on the part of husband or wife could be used as sufficient grounds for divorce.[166] Later, during the early Middle Ages, love and marriage became separated.[167] The ideal woman was protected and cherished. The wife, with whom marriage had been arranged by family ties, was guarded jealously and could be punished severely for violations of duty. A husband was expected to beat his wife for "misbehaviors" and might himself be punished by neighbors if he failed to do so.[168]

Through the later Middle Ages and into modern times—that is, from 1400 to 1900—there was little objection within the community to a man using force against his wife as long as the assaults did not exceed certain limits, usually construed as death or disfigurement. By the mid-

19th century, severe wife beating had fallen into disfavor, and accused wife beaters were subject to public ridicule. Nonetheless, limited chastisement was still the rule. By the close of the 19th century, laws had been passed in England and the United States outlawing wife beating. Yet the long history of husbands' domination of their wives' lives made physical coercion difficult to control. Until recent times, the subordinate position of women in the family was believed to give husbands the legal and moral obligation to manage their wives' behavior. Even after World War II, there is evidence of English courts finding domestic assault to be a reasonable punishment for a wife who had disobeyed her husband.[169] These ideas form the foundation of men's traditional physical control of women and have led to severe cases of spousal assault.

THE NATURE AND EXTENT OF SPOUSE ABUSE. It is difficult to estimate how widespread spouse abuse is today; however, some statistics give indications of the extent of the problem. In their national survey of family violence, Gelles and Straus found that 16% of surveyed families had experienced husband-wife assaults. In police departments around the country, 60%–70% of evening calls involve domestic disputes. Nor is violence restricted to the postmarital stage of domestic relations. In a national survey of college students, James Makepeace found that more than 20% of the females had experienced violence during their dating and courtship relationships.[170]

What are the characteristics of the wife assaulter? The traits commonly found include:[171]

- *Presence of alcohol.* Excessive alcohol use may turn otherwise docile husbands into wife assaulters.
- *Hostility dependency.* Some husbands who appear docile and passive may resent their dependency on their wives and react with rage and violence; this factor has been linked to sexual inadequacy.
- *Excessive brooding.* Obsession with a wife's behavior, however trivial, can result in violent assaults.
- *Social approval.* Some husbands believe that society approves of wife assault and use this belief to justify their violent behavior.
- *Socioeconomic factors.* Men who fail as providers and are under economic stress may take their frustrations out on their wives.
- *Flash of anger.* Research shows that a significant amount of family violence resulted from a sudden burst of anger after a verbal dispute.
- *Military service.* Spouse abuse among men who have seen military service is extremely high. Similarly, those serving in the military are more likely to assault their wives than civilian husbands are. The reasons for this phenomenon may be (a) the violence promoted by military training and (b) the close proximity of military families to one another.

- *Having been battered children.* Husbands who assault their wives tend to have been battered as children.

IS SPOUSE ABUSE INTERGENERATIONAL? While it is generally agreed that child abuse is intergenerational, do the same patterns apply to spouse abuse? While there is little conclusive evidence that spouse abusers grew up in homes where spouses were abused, there is research that abused children later act abusively toward their own children and their spouses.[172]

There are a number of views on why this phenomenon occurs.[173] One is that children learn the role of parent/spouse through observation, and those who grow up in abusive households believe that harsh parenting and violent behavior are "normal" in the typical family. A second view is that harsh parenting teaches kids that it is often necessary to hit those you love, spouses as well as children. A third view is that harsh and incompetent parenting produces children with many behavioral problems, including child, spouse, and substance abuse. This variation on problem behavior syndrome suggests that people who have experienced abusive, incompetent parenting are also more likely to use drugs, commit crimes, and engage in a garden variety of antisocial behaviors, including persistent child and spouse abuse.[174] The relationship between deviant behavior and physical punishment is a constant across race, ethnic origin, and socioeconomic status.[175]

A growing amount of support is being given to battered women. Shelters for assaulted wives are springing up around the country, and laws are being passed to protect a wife's interests. Police departments have made enforcement of domestic abuse laws a top priority. It is essential that this problem be brought to public light and controlled.

Robbery

The common-law definition of **robbery**, and the one used by the FBI, is "the taking or attempting to take anything of value from the care, custody, or control of a person or persons by force or threat of force or violence and/or by putting the victim in fear."[176] A robbery is a crime of violence because it involves the use of force to obtain money or goods. Robbery is punished severely because the victim's life is put in jeopardy; the amount of force used and not the value of the items taken determines the level of punishment.

In 1996 about 540,000 robberies were reported to police, a rate of 220 per 100,000 population, a decrease of 8% in one year. As with other violent crimes, there has been a significant reduction in the robbery rate during the 1990s (down about 22% between 1992 and 1996).

NCVS data indicate that robbery is more of a problem than the FBI data show; according to the NCVS, about 1.1 million robberies were committed or attempted in 1995.

The two data sources agree, however, on the age, race, and sexual makeup of the offenders: They are disproportionately young, male, and minority-group members.

The Ecology of Robbery

The ecological pattern for robbery is similar to that of other violent crimes, with one significant exception: Northeastern states have by far the highest robbery rate (260 per 100,000).

Robbery is most often a street crime—that is, fewer robberies occur in the home than in public places, such as parks, streets, and alleys. The Bureau of Justice Statistics analyzed over 14 million robbery victimizations to provide a more complete picture of the nature and extent of robbery. It found that about two-thirds of victims had property stolen, one-third were injured, and one-fourth suffered both personal injury and property loss.[177] The public nature of robbery has greatly influenced people's behavior. Most people believe that large cities suffer the most serious instances of violent crimes, such as robbery, and, not surprisingly, many people have moved out of inner-city areas into suburban communities for this reason.

Robber Typologies

Attempts have been made to classify and explain the nature and dynamics of robbery.[178] Among the patterns identified are:

1. Robbery of persons who, as part of their employment, are in charge of money or goods. This category includes robberies in jewelry stores, banks, offices, and other places in which money changes hands.

2. Robbery in an open area. These robberies include street offenses, muggings, purse snatchings, and other attacks. Street robberies are the most common type, especially in urban areas, where this type of robbery constitutes about 60% of reported totals. Street robbery is most closely associated with mugging or "yoking"—grabbing victims from behind and threatening them with a weapon.

3. Robbery on private premises. This type of robbery involves robbing people after breaking into homes. FBI records indicate that this type of robbery accounts for about 10% of all offenses.

4. Robbery after preliminary association of short duration. This type of robbery comes in the aftermath of a chance meeting—in a bar, at a party, or after a sexual encounter.

5. Robbery after previous association of some duration between the victim and offender.

Incidents in patterns 4 and 5 are substantially less common than stranger-to-stranger robberies, which account for more than 75% of the total.

Another well-known robber typology has been created by John Conklin. Instead of focusing on the nature of robbery incidents, Conklin categorizes robber types into the following specialties:[179]

1. *Professional robber.* Professionals are those who "manifest a long-term commitment to crime as a source of livelihood, who plan and organize their crimes prior to committing them, and who seek money to support a particular lifestyle that may be called hedonistic." Some professionals are exclusively robbers, while others may engage in other types of crimes. Professionals are committed to robbing because it is direct, fast, and very profitable. They hold no other steady job and plan three or four "big scores" a year to support themselves. Planning and skill are the trademarks of the professional robber. Operating in groups in which assigned roles are the rule, professionals usually steal large amounts from commercial establishments. After a score, they may take a few weeks off until "things cool off."

2. *Opportunist robber.* Opportunists steal to obtain small amounts of money when an accessible and vulnerable target presents itself. They are not committed to robbery but will steal from cab drivers, drunks, the elderly, and other such persons if they need some extra spending money for clothes or other elements of their lifestyle. Opportunists are usually young minority-group members who do not plan their crimes. Although they operate within the milieu of the juvenile gang, they are seldom organized and spend little time discussing weapon use, getaway plans, or other strategies.

3. *Addict robber.* Addict robbers steal to support their drug habits. They have a low commitment to robbery because of its danger but a high commitment to theft because it supplies needed funds. The addict is less likely to plan crime or use weapons than the professional robber but is more cautious than the opportunist. Addicts choose targets that present a minimum of risk; however, when desperate for funds, they are sometimes careless in selecting the victim and executing the crime. They rarely think in terms of the big score; they only want enough money to get their next fix.

4. *Alcoholic robber.* Many robbers steal for reasons related to their excessive consumption of alcohol. Alcoholic robbers steal (1) when, in a disoriented state, they attempt to get some money to buy liquor or (2) when their condition makes them unemployable and they need funds. Alcoholic robbers have no real commitment to robbery as a way of life. They plan their crimes randomly and give little thought to victim, circumstance, or escape; for that reason, they are the most likely to be caught.

As these typologies indicate, the typical armed robber is unlikely to be a professional who carefully studies targets while planning a crime. People walking along the street, convenience stores, and gas stations are much more likely to be the target of robberies than banks or other highly secure environments. Robbers, therefore, seem to be diverted by modest defensive measures, such as having more than one clerk in a store or locating stores in strip malls rather than stand-alone isolation.[180]

Evolving Forms of Violence

Assault, rape, robbery, and murder are traditional forms of interpersonal violence. However, as data become available, criminologists have recognized new categories within these crime types, such as serial murder and date rape. There are also new categories of interpersonal violence now receiving attention in the criminological literature, and in the following sections we describe two of these new forms of violent crime: hate crimes and workplace violence.

Hate Crimes

Hate crimes, or **bias crimes,** are now recognized as a new category of violent personal crimes.[181] These are violent acts directed toward a particular person or members of a group merely because the targets share a discernible racial, ethnic, religious, or gender characteristic or sexual orientation. Hate crimes can include the desecration of a house of worship or cemetery, harassment of a minority-group family that has moved into a previously all-white neighborhood, or a racially motivated murder of an individual. For example, on August 23, 1989, Yusuf Hawkins, a black youth, was killed in the Bensonhurst section of Brooklyn, New York, because he had wandered into a racially charged white neighborhood.[182]

Hate crimes usually involve convenient and vulnerable targets who are incapable of fighting back. For example, there have been numerous reported incidences of teenagers attacking vagrants and the homeless in an effort to rid their town or neighborhood of people they consider undesirable.[183] Another group targeted for hate crimes is gay men and women. Gay bashing has become an all too common occurrence in U.S. cities. Racial and ethnic minorities have also been the targets of attack. Well-publicized hate crimes directed against racial minorities include incidents like the Bensonhurst one, in which gangs of white youths chased and killed black youths who wandered into their neighborhoods. In California, Mexican laborers have been attacked and killed, while in New Jersey, Indian immigrants have been the targets of racial hatred.[184]

While hate crimes are often mindless attacks directed toward "traditional" minority victims, political and economic trends may cause violent attacks to be redirected. For exam-

Hate crimes are certainly not a recent development. Here Byron De La Beckwith is shown entering a Mississippi courthouse. De La Beckwith killed civil rights leader Medgar Evers on June 12, 1963. Two trials before all-white juries resulted in hung juries, even though De La Beckwith's fingerprints were found on the murder weapon and he was heard bragging about the murder at a Ku Klux Klan rally. De La Beckwith was finally convicted of the crime in 1994, more than 30 years after the killing. This trial was the subject of the film *Ghosts of Mississippi.*

ple, Asians have been the target of hate attacks from groups who resent the growing economic power of Japan and Korea as well as the economic success of Asian Americans.[185]

THE ROOTS OF HATE. Why do people commit bias crimes? Research by sociologist Jack McDevitt finds that hate crimes are generally spontaneous incidents motivated by the victims' walking, driving, shopping, or socializing in an area in which their attacker believes they do not belong.[186] Other reasons found for bias attacks were that the victim had moved into an ethnically distinct neighborhood or had dated a member of a different race or ethnic group. Although hate crimes are often unplanned, McDevitt found that a majority of these crimes were serious incidents involving assaults and robberies.[187]

In their book *Hate Crimes,* McDevitt and Jack Levin note that hate crimes involve at least some planning, and they can be categorized into three types reflecting different motives:

1. *Thrill-seeking hate crimes.* In the same way some kids like to get together to "shoot hoops," hatemongers join forces to have fun by bashing minorities or destroying property. Inflicting pain on others gives them a sadistic thrill.

2. *Reactive hate crimes.* Perpetrators of these crimes rationalize their behavior as a defensive stand taken against "outsiders" who are threatening their community or way of life. A gang of teens who attack a new

family in the neighborhood because they are the "wrong" race are committing a reactive hate crime.

3. *Mission hate crimes.* Some disturbed individuals see it as their duty to rid the world of evil. Those on a "mission"—skinheads, the KKK, white supremacist groups—may seek to eliminate people who threaten their religious beliefs because they are members of a different faith or are a threat to racial purity because they are of a different race.[188]

In one study of Boston Police Department records, Levin and McDevitt found that thrill crimes were the most common (58%), and most of these (70%) involved assaultive behavior. Reactive crimes (42%) also involved an assault on a stranger who happened to be in the "wrong place at the wrong time." Although there was only one mission-type crime, it was the most violent incident and involved the beating of two supposedly gay males with baseball bats.[189]

THE EXTENT OF HATE CRIME. Information on the extent of hate crimes is just becoming available. There is evidence that the neo-Nazi skinhead movement now contains 70,000 members worldwide in 33 countries. Germany houses about 5,000 skins, and Hungary and the Czech Republic, 4,000 each.[190]

In the United States the FBI now collects data on hate crimes as part of the Hate Crime Statistics Act of 1990. The most current data available (1995) indicate that about 8,000 hate crimes now occur each year. If anything, this number does not represent the full extent of hate crime activity because only 9,500 law enforcement agencies serving 75% of the population are part of the reporting program.[191]

The FBI reports that race was the motivating factor in slightly more than 60% of all incidents. Of these, African Americans were the target of 62% of the incidents and whites, 25% (see Figure 11.4). Other primary motives for hate crimes were religion (16%), ethnicity (10%), and sexual orientation (13%).

Because of the extent and seriousness of the problem, a number of legal jurisdictions have made a special effort to control the spread of hate crimes. Boston maintains the Community Disorders Unit, while the New York City Police Department formed the Bias Incident Investigating Unit in 1980. When a crime anywhere in the city is suspected of being motivated by bias, the unit is notified and enters into the investigation. The unit also provides victim assistance and works with concerned organizations, such as the Commission on Human Rights and the Gay and Lesbian Task Force. These agencies deal with noncriminal bias incidents through mediation, education, and other forms of prevention.[192]

Workplace Violence

Paul Calden, a former insurance company employee, walked into a Tampa cafeteria and opened fire on a table at

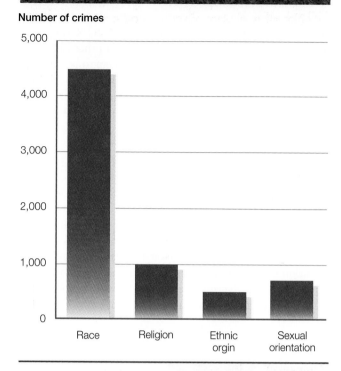

Figure 11.4 Targets of hate crimes.

Number of crimes

Source: FBI, *1995 Preliminary Hate Crime Report,* November 4, 1996.

which his former supervisors were dining. Calden shouted, "This is what you all get for firing me!" and began shooting. When he was finished, three were dead and two others wounded.[193]

It has become commonplace to read of irate employees or former employees attacking co-workers or sabotaging machinery and production lines. Workplace violence is now considered the third leading cause of occupational injury or death.[194]

Who engages in workplace violence? According to James A. Fox and Jack Levin, the typical offender is a middle-aged white male who faces termination in a worsening economy. The fear of economic ruin is especially strong in agencies such as the U.S. Postal Service, where long-term employees fear job loss because of automation and reorganization. In contrast, when younger workers kill, it is usually while committing a robbery or other felony.

A number of factors precipitate workplace violence. According to sociologist John King, one factor may simply be the conflict caused by economic restructuring. As corporations cut their staffs, long-term employees who had never thought of themselves as the type who could lose a job are suddenly unemployed. There is often a connection between sudden and undeserved layoffs and violent reactions.[195]

Another trigger may be leadership styles. Some companies, including the U.S. Postal Service, have authoritarian management styles that demand performance above all else from employees. Managers who are unsympathetic and unsupportive may help trigger workplace violence.

Not all workplace violence is caused by an injustice triggered by management. There have been incidents in which co-workers have been killed because they refused a romantic relationship with the assailant or had reported him for sexual harassment; others have been killed because they got a job the assailant coveted. There have also been cases of irate clients and customers who kill because of poor service or perceived slights. In one Los Angeles incident, a former patient opened fire and critically wounded three doctors because his demands for painkillers had gone unheeded.[196]

There are also a variety of responses to workplace "provocations." Some former employees attack supervisors to punish the company that dismissed them—a form of murder by proxy.[197] Disgruntled employees may attack family members or friends, ignoring the actual cause of their rage and frustration. Others are content with sabotaging company equipment; computer data banks are particularly vulnerable to tampering. It is also possible that the aggrieved party does nothing to rectify the situation; this inaction is referred to as "sufferance." Over time, the unresolved conflict may be compounded by some other events that eventually cause an eruption.

Can workplace violence be controlled? King suggests the intervention of third parties in a dispute resolution capacity may help provide the control necessary to stave off the rising tide of workplace violence. Fox and Levin argue for a human resources approach, with aggressive job retraining and continued medical coverage in case of layoffs and due process guarantees to thwart unfair terminations.[198]

Political Violence and Terrorism

In addition to interpersonal violence and street crime, violent behavior also involves acts that have a political motivation, including terrorism. Political crime has been with us throughout history. It is virtually impossible to find a history book of any society that does not record the existence of political criminals, "those craftsmen of dreams who possess a gigantic reservoir of creative energy as well as destructive force."[199]

It is often difficult to separate political from interpersonal crimes of violence. For example, if a group robs a bank to obtain funds for its revolutionary struggles, should the act be treated as a political crime or as a common bank robbery? In this instance, the definition of a crime as political depends on the kind of legal response the act evokes from those in power.

To be a political crime, an act must carry with it the intent to disrupt and change the government and must not merely be a simple common-law crime committed for reasons of greed or egotism. Stephen Schafer refers to those who violate the law because they believe their actions will ultimately benefit society as **convictional criminals.** They are constantly caught in the dilemma of knowing their actions may be wrong and harmful but believing these actions are necessary to create the changes they fervently desire. "A member of the Second World War Resistance," Schafer argues, "may have condemned violence, yet his own conviction overshadowed any sense of repugnance and induced him to engage in violent crimes in an effort to expel the invader from his Fatherland."[200]

One aspect of political violence that is of great concern to criminologists is terrorism.[201] Because of its complexity, an all-encompassing definition of **terrorism** is difficult to formulate, although most experts agree that it generally involves the illegal use of force against innocent people to achieve a political objective.[202] For example, according to one national commission, terrorism is "a tactic or technique by means of which a violent act or the threat thereof is used for the prime purpose of creating overwhelming fear for coercive purposes."[203]

Terrorism, then, is usually defined as a type of political crime that emphasizes violence as a mechanism to promote change. Whereas other political criminals may engage in such acts as demonstrating, counterfeiting, selling secrets, spying, and the like, terrorists make systematic use of murder and destruction or the threat of such violence to terrorize individuals, groups, communities, or governments into conceding to the terrorists' political demands.[204] However, it may be erroneous to equate terrorism with political goals, because not all terrorist actions are aimed at political change; some terrorists may desire economic or social reform, for example, by attacking women wearing fur coats or sabotaging property during a labor dispute. Terrorism must also be distinguished from conventional warfare because it requires secrecy and clandestine operations to exert social control over large populations.[205]

The term *terrorist* is often used interchangeably with *guerrilla.* The latter term, meaning "little war," developed out of the Spanish rebellion against French troops after Napoleon's invasion of the Iberian peninsula in 1808.[206] Daniel Georges-Abeyie distinguishes between the two terms by suggesting that terrorists have an urban focus, that the objects of their attacks include the property and persons of civilians, and that they operate in small bands, or cadres, of three to five members.[207] Guerrillas are located in rural areas; the objects of their attacks include the military, the police, and government officials; and their organization can grow quite large and eventually take the form of a conventional military force. However, guerrillas can infiltrate urban areas in small bands, while terrorists can make forays into the countryside; consequently, the terms have come to be used interchangeably.[208]

Historical Perspective on Terrorism

Acts of terrorism have been known throughout history. The assassination of Julius Caesar on March 15, 44 B.C., can be considered an act of terrorism. Terrorism became widespread at the end of the Middle Ages, when political leaders were subject to assassination by their enemies. The word *assassin* was derived from an Arabic term meaning "hashish eater"; it referred to members of a drug-using Moslem terrorist organization that carried out plots against prominent Christians and other religious enemies.[209] At a time when rulers were absolute despots, terrorist acts were viewed as one of the only means of gaining political rights.

At times, European states encouraged terrorist acts against their enemies. For example, Queen Elizabeth I empowered her "sea dogs," John Hawkins and Francis Drake, to carry out attacks against the Spanish fleet. These privateers would have been considered pirates had they not operated with government approval. American privateers operated against the British during the Revolutionary War and the War of 1812. As you can see, history can turn terrorists into heroes, depending on which side wins.

The term *terrorist* became popular during the French Revolution. From the fall of the Bastille on July 14, 1789 until July 1794, thousands suspected of counterrevolutionary activity went to their deaths on the guillotine. Here again, the relative nature of political crime is documented: While most victims of the French Reign of Terror were revolutionaries who had been denounced by rival factions, thousands of members of the hated nobility lived in relative tranquillity. The end of the terror was signaled by the death of its prime mover, Maximilien Robespierre, on July 28, 1794, as the result of a successful plot to end his rule; he was executed on the same guillotine to which he had sent almost 20,000 people to their deaths.

In the hundred years after the French Revolution, terrorism continued around the world. The Hur Brotherhood in India was made up of religious fanatics who carried out terrorist acts.[210] In Eastern Europe, the Internal Macedonian Revolutionary Organization campaigned against the Turkish government, which controlled its homeland (Macedonia became part of the former Yugoslavia). Similarly, the protest of the Union of Death Society, or Black Hand, against the Austro-Hungarian Empire's control of Serbia led to the group's assassination of Archduke Franz Ferdinand, an act that triggered the beginning of World War I. The Irish Republican Army developed around 1916 and kept up a steady battle with British forces from 1919 to 1923, culminating in the southern part of Ireland's gaining independence.

Between the world wars, right-wing terrorism existed in Germany, Spain, and Italy. Russia was the scene of left-wing revolutionary activity leading to the death of the czar in 1917 and the rise of the Marxist state. During World War II, resistance to the Germans was common throughout Europe; these terrorists are now, of course, considered heroes. In Palestine, Jewish terrorist groups—the Haganah, Irgun, and Stern Gang, whose leaders included Menachim Begin, who later became prime minister—waged war against the British to force them to allow Jewish survivors of the Holocaust to settle in their traditional homeland. Today, of course, many of these alleged "terrorists" are considered "freedom fighters" who laid down their lives for a just cause.

Forms of Terrorism

Today, the term *terrorism* is used to describe many behaviors and goals. We will briefly describe some of the more common forms.[211]

REVOLUTIONARY TERRORISM. Revolutionary terrorists use violence as a tool to invoke fear in those in power and their supporters. The ultimate goal is to replace the existing government with a regime that holds acceptable political views. Terrorist actions—kidnapping, assassination, bombing—are designed to draw repressive responses from governments trying to defend themselves. These responses help revolutionaries expose, through the skilled use of media coverage, the government's inhumane nature. The original reason for the government's harsh response may be lost as the effect of counterterrorist activities is felt by uninvolved people.

In Europe, socialist- and Marxist-oriented groups have been pitted against capitalist governments for the past 30 years. During the 1980s, the Marxist Baader-Meinhoff group in Germany conducted a series of robberies, bombings, and kidnappings. With the reunification of Germany, terrorist actions were believed over. Yet on April 1, 1991, the Red Army Faction, the successor to Baader-Meinhoff, claimed "credit" for assassinating Detlev Rohwedder, the head of the government agency charged with rebuilding the East German economy.[212] In Italy, the Red Brigade kidnapped and executed a former Italian president, Albert Moro, and abducted James Dozier, a U.S. general, who was later rescued by security forces.[213]

In the Middle East, terrorist activities have been linked to the Palestinians' desire to wrest a homeland from Israel. The leading group, the Palestinian Liberation Organization (PLO), had been active in directing terrorist activities against Israel. While the PLO has reached accommodation with Israel in preparation for Palestinian political control of

A law enforcement officer carries a young victim from the Murrah Building after the Oklahoma City bombing. Political terrorism is often directed at groups of government agencies who oppose the terrorist's political ideology. All too often, however, innocent people suffer the most in the attack.

the West Bank and the Gaza Strip, splinter groups have broken from the PLO, including the Abu Nidal group, the Popular Front for the Liberation of Palestine, Hamas, and the Iranian-backed Hizballah group, to continue the conflict. Although the target of Arab terrorism is presumably Israel and its Western allies, attacks are often directed at members of rival groups and factions. When the World Trade Center in New York City was bombed in 1993, the group responsible was demonstrating its hatred of U.S. policies in the Middle East.

There have been numerous tragic incidents, but two stand out because of the large loss of life: Agents of the pro-Iranian Islamic Jihad used a truck bomb to blow up the U.S. Marine compound in Beirut, Lebanon on April 18, 1983, killing 241; and on Christmas Day, 1988, Pan Am Flight 103 was blown up over Lockerbie, Scotland, and 258 U.S. citizens died.[214]

POLITICAL TERRORISM. In April of 1996, after an 11-month federal investigation had resulted in their indictment on fraud charges, members of the Freemen movement held federal officers at bay in a month-long standoff before surrendering in Jordan, Montana. Heavily armed, the Freemen are one of many right-wing groups who have conducted or plan to conduct antigovernment activities. Their peaceful surrender prevented another in a long line of bloody engagements between federal agents and right-wing militants,

such as the 1992 siege at Ruby Ridge, Idaho in which the wife of Randy Weaver, a suspected arms dealer, was gunned down by an FBI sharpshooter, and the infamous standoff in Waco, Texas that resulted in the fiery deaths of followers of Branch Davidian leader David Koresh.[215]

Political terrorism is directed at people or groups who oppose the terrorists' political ideology or whom the terrorists define as "outsiders" who must be destroyed. Political terrorists in the United States tend to be heavily armed groups organized around such themes as white supremacy, Nazism, militant tax resistance, and religious revisionism. Identified groups include or have included the Aryan Republican Army, Aryan Nation, and Posse Comitatus, as well as the traditional Ku Klux Klan organizations. Some of these groups have formed their own churches; for example, the Church of Jesus Christ Christian claims that Jesus was born an Aryan rather than a Jew and that white Anglo-Saxons are the true "chosen" people. Some groups have conducted common-law crimes such as bank robberies to fund their activities, which might include bombings and other terror tactics.[216] The Oklahoma City bombing may have been the most tragic example of such activities.

NATIONALISTIC TERRORISM. Nationalistic terrorism is designed to promote the interests of minority ethnic or religious groups that have been persecuted under majority rule. In India, Sikh radicals use violence for the purpose of recovering what they believe to be lost homelands. Sikh militants were responsible for assassinating Indian Prime Minister Indira Gandhi on November 6, 1984, in retaliation for the government's storming of their Golden Temple religious shrine (and revolutionary base) in June 1984.[217] In Egypt, fundamentalist Moslems have attacked foreign tourists in an effort to wreck the tourist industry, topple the secular government, and turn Egypt into an Islamic state.[218] In Algeria, fundamentalist Muslim groups have waged a decade-long battle against the government. On February 2, 1997, 50 militants armed with axes decapitated 31 people in the city of Medea.[219] The most well-known nationalistic terrorist group operating today is the Provisional Irish Republican Army (IRA), which is dedicated to unifying Northern Ireland with the Republic of Ireland under home rule.

NONPOLITICAL TERRORISM. Terrorist activity also involves groups that espouse a particular social or religious cause and use violence to address their grievances and not to topple governments. For example, antiabortion groups have sponsored demonstrations at abortion clinics, and some members have gone so far as to attack clients, bomb offices, and kill doctors who perform abortions.

Animal rights organization members have harassed and thrown blood at people wearing fur coats. It has also become common for environmental groups to resort to terror tactics to sabotage their enemies' ability to harm the environment. One of the biggest targets is the livestock and research animal–producing industry. Members of such groups as the Animal Liberation Front (ALF) and Earth First! acknowledge making attacks against ranches and packing plants. At least four meat-packing plants have been destroyed by arson, numerous ranches have been attacked, and livestock-processing machinery has been destroyed. ALF members free animals, such as by raiding turkey farms before Thanksgiving and rabbit farms before Easter.[220]

STATE-SPONSORED TERRORISM. State-sponsored terrorism occurs when a repressive governmental regime forces its citizens into obedience, oppresses minorities, and stifles political dissent.[221] **Death squads** and the use of government troops to destroy political opposition parties are often associated with Latin American political terrorism.[222]

Some governments have been accused of using terrorist-type actions to control political dissidents. For example, in the first 18 months of its deployment, members of the Haitian National Police allegedly executed 15 political opponents of the regime.[223]

Much of what we know about state-sponsored terrorism comes from the efforts of human rights groups. London-based Amnesty International maintains that tens of thousands of people continue to become victims of security operations that result in disappearances and extrajudicial executions.[224] Political prisoners are now being tortured in about 100 countries, people have disappeared or are being held in secret detention in about 20 countries,

and government-sponsored death squads operate in more than 35. Countries known for encouraging violent control of dissidents include Brazil, Colombia, Guatemala, Honduras, Peru, Iraq, and the Sudan. When Tupac Amaru rebels seized and held hostages at the Japanese ambassador's villa in Peru on December 17, 1996, Amnesty International charged that the action came in response to a decade-long campaign of human rights violations by national security forces and extensive abuses against opposition groups. Between January 1983 and December 1992 Amnesty International documented at least 4,200 cases of people who had "disappeared" in Peru following detention by the security forces. Thousands more were killed by government forces in extrajudicial executions, including some 500 people in 19 separate massacres.[225]

Another group, the Human Rights Watch, has reported on various state-sponsored terrorism around the world. For example, it has charged that serious human rights violations, including disappearances, torture, and extrajudicial executions, persist at alarming levels in Guatemala one year after a human rights advocate rose to the presidency.[226]

Another form of state-sponsored terrorism, notes criminologist Ronald Kramer, is **structural violence,** which involves the physical harm caused by the unequal distribution of wealth. Structural violence involves a set of social conditions from which flows poverty, disease, hunger, malnutrition, poor sanitation, premature death, and high infant mortality.[227]

It is also possible for state-sponsored terrorism to be directed at people and governments outside the state's borders. Particularly disturbing is the possibility that some "outlaw" state such as Libya or North Korea will carry out a nuclear-based attack against a nation viewed as the enemy.[228] While special expertise is needed to build such a bomb, there are enough disaffected scientists available to provide the know-how to build an effective device. Raw material such as plutonium-239 is difficult to manufacture, but there are so many existing nuclear bombs in the hands of unstable Eastern European states that nuclear terrorists might be able to purchase what they need to build a bomb. Since 1990 there have been a half-dozen cases involving the theft and transportation of nuclear material and other cases involving people who made offers to agents to sell material not yet in their possession. While these are the known cases, it is impossible to know whether client states have already purchased enriched uranium or plutonium.

In the event that a nuclear device is planted on U.S. soil, the responsibility of disabling it goes to the Department of Energy's Nuclear Emergency Search Team. This group of scientists and technicians are extensively trained in ways to neutralize devices using robots, video cameras, and other technology. Their job is critical, considering the fact that if the New York Trade Center had been attacked with a low-yield nuclear device rather than chemical explosives, both towers would have collapsed and as many as 50,000 people killed.

The most extreme form of state-sponsored terrorism occurs when a government seeks to wipe out a minority group within the jurisdiction it controls, referred to as **genocide.** The Holocaust during World War II is the most notorious example of genocide, but more recent atrocities have taken place in Cambodia, Rwanda, and Bosnia. The accompanying Close-Up discusses this issue in detail.

The Extent of Terrorism

According to the United States Department of State (April 30, 1997 news release), despite its widespread toll there have actually been fewer incidents of terrorism in recent years than ever before (296 in 1996). Unfortunately, in 1996 terrorist attacks claimed 311 lives, about double the 1995 total. Most of the casualties were the result of the work of the Tamil Tigers, a separatist group operating in Sri Lanka. About 24 Americans were killed in terrorist attacks in 1996, including 19 who were killed when a truck bomb blew up in Dhahran, Saudi Arabia. Among the deadlier attacks in 1996 were the bombing by the Tamils of a commuter train in Sri Lanka that killed 70 and a suicide bombing in Israel by the Hamas group that claimed 26 lives.

According to the U.S. State Department, Iran, Iraq, Libya, North Korea, and Cuba continue their policy of giving material, logistic, and financial support to the groups that are committing terrorism.

Who Is the Terrorist?

Terrorists engage in criminal activities, such as bombings, shootings, and kidnappings. What motivates these individuals to risk their lives and those of innocent people? One view is that terrorists hold ideological beliefs that prompt their behavior. At first, they have heightened perceptions of oppressive conditions—they feel relative deprivation.[229] Then they begin to recognize that these conditions can be changed by an active government reform effort that is not forthcoming. The terrorists conclude that they must resort to violence to encourage change.

The violence need not be aimed at a specific goal. Rather, terror tactics must contribute to setting in motion a series of events that enlist others in the cause and lead to long-term change. "Successful" terrorists must accept the fact that their "self-sacrifice" outweighs the guilt created by committing a violent act that harms innocent people. Terrorism, therefore, requires violence without guilt. The cause justifies the need for violence.[230]

According to Austin Turk, terrorists tend to come from upper- rather than lower-class backgrounds.[231] This may be because the upper classes can produce people who are more politically sensitive, articulate, and focused in their resentments. Since their position in the class structure gives them the feeling that they can influence or change society, upper-class citizens are more likely to seek confrontations with au-

thorities. Class differences are also manifested in different approaches to political violence. The violence of the lower class is more often associated with spontaneous expressions of dissatisfaction, manifested in collective riots and rampages and politically inconsequential acts. Higher-class violence tends to be more calculated and organized and uses elaborate strategies of resistance. Revolutionary cells, campaigns of terror and assassination, logistically complex and expensive assaults, and writing and disseminating formal critiques, manifestos, and theories are typically acts of the socially elite.

Upper-class political terrorism has been manifested in the death squads operating in Latin America and Asia. These vigilantes use violence to intimidate those opposing the ruling party's. One graphic example of these terrorist activities occurred in Sri Lanka on October 5, 1989 when a death squad made up of members of the ruling party's security forces beheaded 18 suspected members of the antigovernment People's Liberation Front and placed the heads around a pond at a university campus.[232]

Responses to Terrorism

Governments have tried various responses to terrorism. Law enforcement agencies have infiltrated terrorist groups and turned members over to police.[233] Rewards have been given for information leading to the arrest of terrorists. "Democratic" elections have been held to discredit terrorists' complaints that the state is oppressive. Counterterrorism laws have been passed to increase penalties and decrease political rights. In the United States, antiterrorist legislation includes acts providing jurisdiction over terrorist acts committed abroad against U.S. citizens and punishing the killing of foreign officials and politically protected persons.[234] On April 24th, 1996 President Clinton signed S.735, the Antiterrorism and Effective Death Penalty Act of 1996 into law. Among its provisions, the legislation bans fund raising in the United States that supports terrorist organizations. It also allows U.S. officials to deport terrorists from American soil without being compelled by the terrorists to divulge classified information, and to bar terrorists from entering the United States in the first place.[235] Its other provisions include:

- Requiring plastic explosives to contain chemical markers so that criminals who use them can be tracked down and prosecuted
- Enabling the government to issue regulations requiring that chemical taggants be added to some other types of explosives so that police can better trace bombs to the criminals who make them
- Increasing controls over biological and chemical weapons
- Toughening penalties over a range of terrorist crimes
- Banning the sale of defense goods and services to countries that are not "cooperating fully" with U.S. antiterrorism efforts

The most extreme form of political violence is *genocide*—the attempt to eliminate a whole group of people defined by their race, religion, ethnicity, or political beliefs. Genocidal episodes have included the destruction of European Jews by the Nazis during the Holocaust, the killing of the Armenians in Turkey at the beginning of the 20th century, the annihilation of native tribes during the Spanish conquest of Latin America, and the "ethnic cleansing" that occurred during the recent wars in the former Yugoslavia.

Psychologist Ervin Staub, an expert on genocide, has attempted to provide a framework for understanding how these unimaginable outbreaks of political mass murder can occur in a civilized society. Staub has described conditions that have preceded the onset of genocide in Western society:

- *Difficult life conditions.* The basic needs of society are not being met. Physical and material security are absent, and social groups lack a sense of positive identity, including a sense of effectiveness and control.

- *Scapegoating.* A group is identified as the cause of life's problems. Scapegoating helps replenish group identity by diminishing individual and group responsibility for life problems. Scapegoating provides a solution to problems and helps restores group solidarity: "If we all band together and deal with these people, things will be much better."

- *New ideology.* Ideologies emerge that offer the hope of a better life. People are given hope that if they join together and fulfill the ideology, success and riches will be at hand. Charges are made that the scapegoated group opposes the ideology and is a roadblock to its fulfillment.

- *Devaluation.* Members of a scapegoated group are devalued, considered lesser humans who can be harmed at will. Harmful behavior changes the perpetrators, making them increasingly prone to act aggressively.

- *"Just world" thinking.* As members of the scapegoated group are harmed, both the perpetrators and bystanders begin to believe that the people who

suffer deserve their fate. If not, why isn't someone doing something to stop the abuse?

- *Commitment.* As harm increases, so does commitment to group process and ideology. The more harm they cause their targets, the less likely perpetrators will be willing to change the course of their actions.

- *Passive bystanders.* Only bystanders, both within and outside the society, can exert pressure to stop the evolution toward group violence. For some reason, both groups remain passive, a stance that affirms the perpetrators' belief that they are right to victimize the outcast group.

- *Authority orientation.* Groups that have a strong and unquestioning respect for authority are more prone to group violence. They are less likely to oppose destructive group policies suggested by leaders. Security depends on obedience or the submission of the self to state authorities.

- *Monolithic culture.* A limited set of cultural values inhibit intergroup relations. Monolithic groups may exclude non-

Some legislative efforts have been directed at punishing specific countries identified with sponsoring or conducting terrorism. For example, the Iran and Libya Sanctions Act of 1996 imposes new sanctions on foreign companies that engage in specified economic transactions with Iran or Libya. It is intended to

- Help deny Iran and Libya revenues that could be used to finance international terrorism
- Limit the flow of resources necessary to obtain weapons of mass destruction
- Put pressure on Libya to comply with U.N. resolutions that, among other things, call for Libya to extradite for trial the accused perpetrators of the Pan Am 103 bombing

The bill provides sanctions against foreign companies that provide new investments over $40 million for the development of petroleum resources in Iran or Libya. The bill also sanctions foreign companies that violate existing U.N. prohibitions against trade with Libya in certain goods and

services, such as arms, certain oil equipment, and civil aviation services. If a violation occurs, the federal government can impose two out of seven possible sanctions against the violating company. These sanctions include:

- Denial of Export-Import Bank assistance
- Denial of export licenses to the violating company
- Prohibition on loans or credits from U.S. financial institutions of over $10 million in any 12-month period
- Prohibition on designation as a primary dealer for U.S. government debt instruments
- Prohibition on serving as an agent of the United States or as a repository for U.S. government funds
- Denial of U.S. government procurement opportunities
- A ban on all or some imports of the violating company[236]

Despite the existence of these and other antiterrorism statutes, most politically motivated acts are prosecuted as common-law crimes. Brent Smith and Gregory Orvis suggest that this approach underscores the government's effort to

members from important cultural and professional offices and from the legal process they could use to speak out against or halt destructive practices.

- *Group self-concept.* A shared belief that one's group is either superior or inferior (weak and vulnerable) is a precursor for genocidal impulses. Life's difficulties become more frustrating when they conflict with a group's feelings of superiority. Frustrated feelings of superiority combined with feelings of weakness and vulnerability lead to the embrace of destructive ideologies and scapegoating.

- *History of aggression.* Some cultures have a long history of violence and aggression. Using aggressive tactics to solve problems thus may seem normal, appropriate, and even desirable.

How does this model fit 20th-century genocides such as the Holocaust? The Germans had a long history of violence and aggression. Their culture was monolithic and featured such values as loyalty, obedience, and order. Staub points out that life conditions in Germany were difficult after World War I. The Jews were scapegoated as being responsible for the

loss of the war and the economic catastrophe that followed. The Nazi ideology promised a better tomorrow that would elevate the Germans as the "purest" race and suggested that conditions could be improved by eliminating lesser races. The Nazi ideology was appealing with its emphasis of the superiority of the German people, nationalism, and unquestioning obedience to a leader.

Because the Jews were relatively successful, it was easy to portray them as dishonest and manipulative, enhancing their devalued status. Although there was a progression of anti-Semitic actions after Hitler came to power, nonaligned Germans distanced themselves from Jews, and the rest of the world stood idly by, attending the Berlin Olympics in 1936. American corporations conducted business in Germany throughout the 1930s. These conditions provoked an escalating round of violence that eventually led to genocide and mass destruction.

By setting out the factors that support genocide, Staub provides some insight into how the risk of political mass murder can be avoided. For example, societies must stress inclusion rather than exclusion, such as by including education

about other cultures in school curriculums in order to lay a groundwork for understanding and acceptance.

CRITICAL THINKING QUESTIONS
1. Should an international peacekeeping force such as the United Nations be required to step in to prevent attacks on a group based on race or religion, or are such actions an internal matter for each nation to deal with itself?
2. Should the settling of the American West at the expense of the native American inhabitants be considered "genocide"?

Source: Ervin Staub, "Cultural-Societal Roots of Violence," *American Psychologist* 51 (1996): 117–132; idem, *The Roots of Evil: The Origins of Genocide and Other Group Violence* (New York: Cambridge University Press, 1989).

highlight the real motivation of domestic terrorism: personal profit.[237] Smith and Orvis found that politically motivated crimes are taken seriously by U.S. prosecutors, and defendants are usually charged with multiple criminal violations.

Although the United States has stated a policy prohibiting violence or assassination attempts against suspected terrorists, both federal law enforcement agencies and the U.S. military have specially trained antiterrorist squads. The military, for example, has created the renowned Delta Force, made up of members from the four service areas. Delta Force activities are generally secret, but it is known that the force saw action in Iran (1980), Honduras (1982), and Sudan (1983) and during the Grenada invasion (1983), and it was prepared to take action against the hijacking of the ship *Achille Lauro* in 1985.

Despite the U.S. government's efforts to control terrorism, any attempts to meet force with force are fraught with danger. If the government's response is retaliation in kind, it could provoke increased terrorist activity—for revenge or to gain the release of captured comrades. Of course, a weak re-

sponse may be interpreted as a license for terrorists to operate with impunity. The most impressive U.S. antiterrorist action was the bombing of Libya on April 15, 1986 in an attempt to convince its leader, Colonel Muammar Quaddafi, to desist from sponsoring terrorist organizations. While the raid made a dramatic statement, preventing terrorism is a task that so far has stymied the governments of most nations.

Summary

People in the United States live in an extremely violent society. Among the various explanations for violent crimes are personal traits, ineffective families, the presence of a subculture of violence that stresses violent solutions to interpersonal problems, regional values condoning violence, substance abuse, and the availability of firearms.

There are many types of interpersonal violent crime. Rape is defined as the carnal knowledge of a female forcibly and against her will. Rape has been known throughout history; at one time it was believed that a woman was as guilty as her attacker for her rape. At present, it is estimated that close to 100,000 rapes are reported to police each year; the true number is probably much higher. Rape is an extremely difficult charge to prove in court. The victim's lack of consent must be proven; therefore, it often seems that the victim is on trial. Consequently, changes are being made in rape law and procedure.

Murder is the unlawful killing of a human being with malice aforethought. There are different degrees of murder, and punishments vary accordingly. One important characteristic of murder is that the victim and criminal often know each other. This has caused some criminologists to believe that murder is a victim-precipitated crime. Murder victims and offenders tend to be young, black, and male.

Assault is another serious interpersonal violent crime. One important type of assault is that which occurs in the home, including child abuse and spouse abuse. It has been estimated that almost 1 million children are abused by their parents each year, and 16% of families report husband-wife violence. There also appears to be a trend toward violence between dating couples on college campuses.

Robbery involves theft by force, usually in a public place. Types of offenders include professional, opportunist, addict, and alcoholic robbers.

Political violence is another serious problem. Many terrorist groups exist, at both the national and international levels. Hundreds of terrorist acts are reported each year in the United States alone. There are political terrorists, nationalists, and state-sponsored terrorists.

Key Terms

brutalization process	premeditation
violent performance	deliberation
virulency	thrill killing
eros	gang killings
thanatos	cult killings
subculture of violence	serial murder
disputatiousness	mass murderer
psychopharmacological	battery
economic compulsive	assault
behavior	child abuse
systemic link	neglect
instrumental violence	sexual abuse
expressive violence	robbery
rape	hate crimes
date rape	bias crimes
marital exemption	convictional criminals
consent	terrorism
shield laws	death squads
corroboration	structural violence
murder	genocide
feticide	

Notes

1. David Courtwright, "Violence in America," *American Heritage* 47 (1996): 36.

2. Albert Reiss and Jeffrey Roth, *Understanding and Preventing Violence* (Washington, D.C.: National Academy Press, 1993), p. 3, Herein cited as *Understanding Violence.*

3. Hans Toch, *Violent Men* (Chicago: Aldine, 1969), p. 1.

4. Kathleen Maguire and Ann Pastore, *Sourcebook of Criminal Justice Statistics, 1995* (Washington, D.C.: U.S. Government Printing Office, 1996), p. 183.

5. *Stanford v. Kentucky,* 109 Supreme Court, 2969 (1989).

6. Robert Nash Parker and Catherine Colony, "Relationships, Homicides, and Weapons: A Detailed Analysis," paper presented at the annual meeting of the American Society of Criminology, Montreal, November 1987.

7. Stryker McGuire, "The Dunblane Effect," *Newsweek,* 28 October 1996, p. 46.

8. Laura Bender, "Children and Adolescents Who Have Killed," *American Journal of Psychiatry* 116 (1959): 510–516.

9. Dorothy Otnow Lewis, Ernest Moy, Lori Jackson, Robert Aaronson, Nicholas Restifo, Susan Serra, and Alexander Simos, "Biopsychosocial Characteristics of Children Who Later Murder," *American Journal of Psychiatry* 142 (1985): 1161–1167.

10. Amy Holtzworth-Munroe and Gregory Stuart, "Typologies of Male Batterers: Three Subtypes and the Differences Among Them," *Psychological Bulletin* 116 (1994): 476–497.

11. *Understanding Violence,* pp. 112–113.

12. "Jury Recommends Death for Florida Killer of Five," *New York Times,* 25 March 1994, p. A14.

13. Ibid.

14. Deborah Capaldi and Gerald Patterson, "Can Violent Offenders Be Distinguished from Frequent Offenders: Prediction from Childhood to Adolescence," *Journal of Research in Crime and Delinquency* 33 (1996): 206–231.

15. Pamela Lattimore, Christy Visher, and Richard Linster, "Predicting Rearrest for Violence Among Serious Youthful Offenders," *Journal of Research in Crime and Delinquency* 32 (1995): 54–83.

16. Robert Scudder, William Blount, Kathleen Heide, and Ira Silverman, "Important Links Between Child Abuse, Neglect, and Delinquency," *International Journal of Offender Therapy* 37 (1993): 315–323.

17. Dorothy Lewis et al., "Neuropsychiatric, Psychoeducational, and Family Characteristics of 14 Juveniles Condemned to Death in the United States," *American Journal of Psychiatry* 145 (1988): 584–588.

18. Charles Patrick Ewing, *When Children Kill* (Lexington, Mass.: Lexington Books, 1990), p. 22.

19. Murray Straus, "Discipline and Deviance: Physical Punishment of Children and Violence and Other Crime in Adulthood," *Social Problems* 38 (1991): 133–154.

20. Lonnie Athens, *The Creation of Dangerous Violent Criminals* (Urbana: University of Illinois Press, 1992), pp. 27–80.

21. Cathy Spatz Widom, "Child Abuse, Neglect, and Violent Criminal Behavior," *Criminology* 27 (1989): 251–271; Beverly Rivera and Cathy Spatz Widom, "Childhood Victimization and Violent Offending," *Violence and Victims* 5 (1990): 19–34.

22. Sigmund Freud, *Beyond the Pleasure Principle* (London: Inter-Psychoanalytic Press, 1922).

23. Konrad Lorenz, *On Aggression* (New York: Harcourt Brace Jovanovich, 1966).

24. See, generally, Lee Ellis and Anthony Walsh, "Gene-Based Evolutionary Theories in Criminology," *Criminology* (1997, in press).

25. Paul Joubert and Craig Forsyth, "A Macro View of Two Decades of Violence in America," *American Journal of Criminal Justice* 13 (1988): 10–25.

26. M. Dwayne Smith and Victoria Brewer, "A Sex-Specific Analysis of Correlates of Homicide Victimization in United States Cities," *Violence and Victims* 7 (1992): 279–285.

27. Marvin Wolfgang and Franco Ferracuti, *The Subculture of Violence* (London: Tavistock, 1967).

28. David Luckenbill and Daniel Doyle, "Structural Position and Violence: Developing a Cultural Explanation," *Criminology* 27 (1989): 419–436.

29. Steven Messner, "Regional and Racial Effects on the Urban Homicide Rate: The Subculture of Violence Revisited," *American Journal of Sociology* 88 (1983): 997–1007; Steven Messner and Kenneth Tardiff, "Economic Inequality and Levels of Homicide: An Analysis of Urban Neighborhoods," *Criminology* 24 (1986): 297–317.

30. Beth Bjerregaard and Alan Lizotte, "Gun Ownership and Gang Membership," *Journal of Criminal Law and Criminology* 86 (1995): 37–58.

31. Scott Decker, "Gangs and Violence: The Expressive Character of Collective Involvement," unpublished manuscript, University of Missouri–St. Louis, 1994.

32. Carolyn Rebecca Block, "Chicago Homicide from the Sixties to the Nineties: Have Patterns of Lethal Violence Changed?" paper presented at the annual meeting of the American Society of Criminology, Baltimore, November 1990.

33. See, generally, Kirk Williams and Robert Flewelling, "The Social Production of Criminal Homicide: A Comparative Study of Disaggregated Rates in American Cities," *American Sociological Review* 53 (1988): 421–431.

34. Raymond Gastil, "Homicide and the Regional Culture of Violence," *American Sociological Review* 36 (1971): 12–27.

35. Keith Harries, *Serious Violence: Patterns of Homicide and Assault in America* (Springfield, Ill.: Charles C Thomas, 1990).

36. Howard Erlanger, "Is There a Subculture of Violence in the South?" *Journal of Criminal Law and Criminology* 66 (1976): 483–490.

37. Colin Loftin and Robert Hill, "Regional Subculture of Violence: An Examination of the Gastil-Hackney Thesis," *American Sociological Review* 39 (1974): 714–724.

38. Raymond Gastil, "Comments," *Criminology* 16 (1975): 60–64.

39. Keith Harries, "Crime and Region: Is the South Still Different?" paper presented at the annual meeting of the American Society of Criminology, Chicago, November 1996; Gregory Kowalski and Thomas Petee, "Sunbelt Effects on Homicide Rates," *Sociology and Social Research* 76 (1991): 73–79.

40. F. Frederick Hawley and Steven Messner, "The Southern Violence Construct: A Review of Arguments, Evidence, and the Normative Context," *Justice Quarterly* 6 (1989): 481–511.

41. Paul Goldstein, Henry Brownstein, and Patrick Ryan, "Drug-Related Homicide in New York: 1984–1988," *Crime and Delinquency* 38 (1992): 459–476.

42. *Understanding Violence,* pp. 193–194.

43. James Collins and Pamela Messerschmidt, "Epidemiology of Alcohol-Related Violence," *Alcohol Health and Research World* 17 (1993): 93–100.

44. Thomas Feucht, *Drug Use Forecasting 1995* (Washington, D.C.: National Institute of Justice, 1996).

45. Christopher Innes, *Profile of State Prison Inmates 1986* (Washington, D.C.: Bureau of Justice Statistics, 1988).

46. Paul Goldstein, Patricia Bellucci, Barry Spunt, and Thomas Miller, "Volume of Cocaine Use and Violence: A Comparison between Men and Women," *Journal of Drug Issues* 21 (1991): 345–367.

47. Paul Goldstein, Henry Brownstein, Patrick Ryan, and Patricia Bellucci, "Crack and Homicide in New York City, 1988: A Conceptually Based Event Analysis," unpublished paper, Narcotic and Drug Research, New York, 1989.

48. Goldstein, Brownstein, and Ryan, "Drug-Related Homicide in New York: 1984–1988," p. 473.

49. *Understanding Violence,* p. 19.

50. Joseph Sheley and James Wright, *Gun Acquisition and Possession in Selected Juvenile Samples* (Washington, D.C.: National Institute of Justice, 1993).

51. Federal Bureau of Investigation, *Crime in the United States, 1995* (Washington, D.C.: U.S. Government Printing Office, 1996).

52. David Brent, Joshua Perper, Christopher Allman, Grace Moritz, Mary Wartella, and Janice Zelenak, "The Presence and Accessibility of Firearms in the Home and Adolescent Suicides," *Journal of the American Medical Association* 266 (1991): 2989–2995.

53. Linda Saltzman, James Mercy, Patrick O'Carroll, Mark Rosenberg, and Philip Rhodes, "Weapon Involvement and Injury Outcomes in Family and Intimate Assaults," *Journal of the American Medical Association* 267 (1992): 3043–3047.

54. William Green, *Rape* (Lexington, Mass.: Lexington Books, 1988), p. 5.

55. Susan Randall and Vicki McNickle Rose, "Forcible Rape," in *Major Forms of Crime,* ed. Robert Meyer (Beverly Hills, Calif.: Sage, 1984), p. 47.

56. Associated Press, "Judge Who Told Rape Suspect to Get a Girlfriend Orders Him into Custody," *Manchester Union Leader,* 19 February 1994, p. 2.

57. Susan Brownmiller, *Against Our Will: Men, Women and Rape* (New York: Simon & Schuster, 1975).

58. Green, *Rape,* p. 6.

59. Gregory Vistica, "Rape in the Ranks," *Newsweek,* 25 November 1996, pp. 29–31.

60. Diego Ribadeneira, "In Haiti's Poorest Areas, Women Tell of Rape by Armed Men," *Boston Globe,* 29 August 1993, p. 6.

61. NCVS News Release, "Victims Report 9 Percent Fewer Violent Crimes Last Year," 17 September 1996.

62. James LeBeau, "Some Problems with Measuring and Describing Rape Presented by the Serial Offender," *Justice Quarterly* 2 (1985): 385–398.

63. Angela Browne, "Violence Against Women, Relevance for Medical Practitioners," *Journal of the American Medical Association* 267 (1992): 3184–3189.

64. Mark Warr, "Rape, Burglary and Opportunity," *Journal of Quantitative Criminology* 4 (1988): 275–288.

65. James LeBeau, "Patterns of Stranger and Serial Rape Offending Factors Distinguishing Apprehended and At-Large Offenders," *Journal of Criminal Law and Delinquency* 78 (1987): 309–326.

66. A. Nicholas Groth and Jean Birnbaum, *Men Who Rape* (New York: Plenum Press, 1979).

67. Raymond Knight, "Validation of a Typology of Rapists," in *Sex Offender Research and Treatment: State-of-the-Art in North America and Europe,* ed. W. L. Marshall and J. Frenken (Beverly Hills, Calif.: Sage, 1997).

68. Julie Allison and Lawrence Wrightsman, *Rape: The Misunderstood Crime* (Newbury Park, Calif.: Sage, 1993), p. 51.

69. R. Lance Shotland, "A Model of the Causes of Date Rape in Developing and Close Relationships," in *Close Relationships,* ed. C. Hendrick (Newbury Park, Calif.: Sage, 1989), pp. 247–270.

70. Walter DeKeseredy, Martin Schwartz, and Karen Tait, "Sexual Assault and Stranger Aggression on a Canadian Campus," *Sex Roles* 28 (1993): 263–277.

71. Ibid.

72. Thomas Meyer, "Date Rape: A Serious Campus Problem That Few Talk About," *Chronicle of Higher Education* 29 (5 December 1984): 15.

73. Allison and Wrightsman, *Rape,* p. 64.

74. Martin Schwartz, "Humanist Sociology and Date Rape on the College Campus," *Humanity and Society* 15 (1991): 304–316.

75. Mark Starr, "The Writing on the Wall," *Newsweek,* 26 November 1990, p. 64.

76. Allison and Wrightsman, *Rape,* pp. 85–87.

77. Cited in Diana Russell, "Wife Rape," in *Acquaintance Rape: The Hidden Crime,* ed. A. Parrot and L. Bechhofer (New York: Wiley, 1991), pp. 129–139.

78. David Finkelhor and K. Yllo, *License to Rape: Sexual Abuse of Wives* (New York: Holt, Rinehart and Winston, 1985).

79. Allison and Wrightsman, *Rape,* p. 89.

80. Associated Press, "British Court Rejects Precedent, Finds a Man Guilty of Raping Wife," *Boston Globe,* 15 March 1991, p. 68.

81. Donald Symons, *The Evolution of Human Sexuality* (Oxford: Oxford University Press, 1979).

82. Ellis and Walsh, "Gene-Based Evolutionary Theories in Criminology."

83. Lee Ellis, "A Synthesized (Biosocial) Theory of Rape," *Journal of Consulting and Clinical Psychology* 39 (1991): 631–642.

84. Diana Russell, *The Politics of Rape* (New York: Stein & Day, 1975).

85. Paul Gebhard, John Gagnon, Wardell Pomeroy, and Cornelia Christenson, *Sex Offenders: An Analysis of Types* (New York: Harper & Row, 1965), pp. 198–205; Richard Rada, ed., *Clinical Aspects of the Rapist* (New York: Grune & Stratton, 1978), pp. 122–130.

86. Groth and Birnbaum, *Men Who Rape,* p. 101.

87. See, generally, Edward Donnerstein, Daniel Linz, and Steven Penrod, *The Question of Pornography* (New York: Free Press, 1987); Diana Russell, *Sexual Exploitation* (Beverly Hills, Calif.: Sage, 1985), pp. 115–116.

88. Neil Malamuth and John Briere, "Sexual Violence in the Media: Indirect Effects on Aggression Against Women," *Journal of Social Issues* 42 (1986): 75–92.

89. Associated Press, "Trial on TV May Have Influenced Boy Facing Sexual-Assault Count," *Omaha World Herald,* 18 April 1984, p. 50.

90. Richard Felson and Marvin Krohn, "Motives for Rape," *Journal of Research in Crime and Delinquency* 27 (1990): 222–242.

91. Larry Baron and Murray Straus, "Four Theories of Rape: A Macrosociological Analysis," *Social Problems* 34 (1987): 467–489.

92. Julie Horney and Cassia Spohn, "The Influence of Blame and Believability Factors on the Processing of Simple Versus Aggravated Rape Cases," *Criminology* 34 (1996): 135–163.

93. "Woman Urges Dotson's Release," *Omaha World Herald,* 25 April 1985, p. 3.

94. Associated Press, "Apology Is Aired for Lie About Rape," *Boston Globe,* 6 September 1990, p. 12.

95. Associated Press, "Protection Urged for Rape Suspects," *Boston Globe,* 13 January 1997, p. A5.

96. Gerald Robin, "Forcible Rape: Institutionalized Sexism in the Criminal Justice System," *Crime and Delinquency* 23 (1977): 136–153.

97. Associated Press, "Jury Stirs Furor by Citing Dress in Rape Acquittal," *Boston Globe,* 6 October 1989, p. 12.

98. Susan Estrich, *Real Rape* (Cambridge, Mass.: Harvard University Press, 1987), pp. 58–59.

99. *Michigan v. Lucas* 90–149 (1991); Comment, "The Rape Shield Paradox: Complainant Protection Amidst Oscillating Trends of State Judicial Interpretation," *Journal of Criminal Law and Criminology* 78 (1987): 644–698.

100. Andrew Karmen, *Crime Victims* (Pacific Grove, Calif.: Brooks/Cole, 1990), p. 252.

101. See, for example, Mich. Comp. Laws Ann. 750.5200-(1); Florida Statutes Annotated, Sec. 794.011. See, generally, Gary LaFree, "Official Reactions to Rape," *American Sociological Review* 45 (1980): 842–854.

102. Martin Schwartz and Todd Clear, "Toward a New Law on Rape," *Crime and Delinquency* 26 (1980): 129–151.

103. Susan Caringella-MacDonald, "The Comparability in Sexual and Nonsexual Assault Case Treatment: Did Statute Change Meet the Objective?" *Crime and Delinquency* 31 (1985): 206–223.

104. Donald Lunde, *Murder and Madness* (San Francisco: San Francisco Book, 1977), p. 3.

105. Amy Dockser Marcus, "Mists of Memory Cloud Some Legal Proceedings," *Wall Street Journal,* 3 December 1990, p. B1.

106. Lisa Baertlein, "HIV Ruled Deadly Weapon in Rape Case," *Boston Globe,* 2 March 1994, p. 3.

107. Pauline Arrillaga, "Jurors Give Drunk Driver 16 Years in Fetus' Death," *Manchester Union Leader* 22 October 1996, p. B20.

108. Center for Reproductive Law and Policy, *Punishing Women for Their Behavior During Pregnancy* (New York: Center for Reproductive Law and Policy, 1996), pp. 1–2.

109. *Whitner v. State of South Carolina,* Supreme Court of South Carolina, Opinion Number 24468, July 15, 1996.

110. Janet Kreps, *Feticide and Wrongful Death Laws* (New York: Center for Reproductive Law and Policy, 1996), pp. 1–2.

111. Arrillaga, "Jurors Give Drunk Driver 16 Years in Fetus' Death."

112. The legal principles here come from Wayne LaFave and Austin Scott, *Criminal Law* (St. Paul: West Publishing, 1986; updated, 1993). The definitions and discussion of legal principles used in this chapter lean heavily on this work.

113. Ibid.

114. Reuters, "California Man Gets 3 Years for Pit Bull's Attack on Toddler," *Boston Globe,* 17 February 1990, p. 3.

115. Marc Reidel and Margaret Zahn, *The Nature and Pattern of American Homicide* (Washington, D.C.: U.S. Government Printing Office, 1985).

116. See, generally, Reidel and Zahn, *The Nature and Pattern of American Homicide.*

117. James L. Williams, "A Discriminant Analysis of Urban Homicide Patterns," paper presented at the annual meeting of the American Society of Criminology, Baltimore, November 1990.

118. Angela Browne and Kirk Williams, "Gender, Intimacy, and Lethal Violence: Trends from 1976 Through 1987," *Gender and Society* 7 (1993): 78–98.

119. Linda Saltzman and James Mercy, "Assaults Between Intimates: The Range of Relationships Involved," in *Homicide, The Victim/Offender Connection,* ed. Anna Victoria Wilson (Cincinnati: Anderson Publishing, 1993), pp. 65–74.

120. Angela Browne and Kirk Williams, "Exploring the Effect of Resource Availability and the Likelihood of Female-Perpetrated Homicides," *Law and Society Review* 23 (1989): 75–94.

121. Margaret Zahn and Philip Sagi, "Stranger Homicides in Nine American Cities," *Journal of Criminal Law and Criminology* 78 (1987): 377–397.

122. David Luckenbill, "Criminal Homicide as a Situational Transaction," *Social Problems* 25 (1977): 176–186.

123. Michael Hazlett and Thomas Tomlinson, "Females Involved in Homicides: Victims and Offenders in Two Southern States," paper presented at the annual meeting of the American Society of Criminology, Montreal, November 1987; rev. 1988.

124. Scott Decker, "Deviant Homicide: A New Look at the Role of Motives and Victim-Offender Relationships," *Journal of Research in Crime and Delinquency* 33 (1996): 427–449.

125. Scott Decker, "Exploring Victim-Offender Relationships in Homicide: The Role of Individual and Event Characteristics," *Justice Quarterly* 10 (1993): 585–613.

126. Associated Press, "Parents Forgive Teenager Convicted of Toddler's Death," *Boston Globe,* 22 January 1987.

127. Ewing, *When Children Kill,* p. 64.

128. Carolyn Rebecca Block and Richard Block, *Street Gang Crime in Chicago* (Washington, D.C.: National Institute of Justice, 1993), p. 2.

129. Cited in Ewing, *When Children Kill,* p. 71.

130. From Foreword/Update to James A. Fox and Jack Levin, *Mass Murder,* 2nd ed. (New York: Plenum Press, 1991).

131. Cindy Horswell, "Teen Held in Mom's Shooting Death: 'The Devil Made Me Do It,'" *Houston Chronicle,* 19 May 1993, p. 1.

132. Thomas Palmer, "A Doctor Smelled Arsenic, Leading to Arrest of Serial Killer," *Boston Globe,* 20 August 1987, p. 3.

133. "Police Suspect 'Something Snapped' to Ignite Wilder's Crime Spree," *Omaha World Herald,* 15 April 1984, p. 21A.

134. Mark Starr, "The Random Killers," *Newsweek,* 26 November 1984, pp. 100–106.

135. Thomas Palmer, "Ex-Hospital Aide Admits Killing 24 in Cincinnati," *Boston Globe,* 19 August 1987, p. 3.

136. Ronald Holmes and Stephen Homes, *Murder in America* (Thousand Oaks, Calif.: Sage, 1994), p. 6.

137. Ibid., p. 106.

138. Jenkins, "Serial Murder in England, 1940–1985," p. 9.

139. Ronald Holmes and James DeBurger, *Serial Murder* (Newbury Park, Calif.: Sage, 1988), pp. 58–59.

140. Holmes and Homes, *Murder in America,* pp. 13–14.

141. Ibid., p. 17.

142. Belea Keeney and Kathleen Heide, "Gender Differences in Serial Murderers: A Preliminary Analysis," *Journal of Interpersonal Violence* 9 (1994), 37–56.

143. Jennifer Browdy, "VI-CAP System to Be Operational This Summer," *Law Enforcement News,* 21 May 1984, p. 1.

144. Philip Jenkins, "A Murder 'Wave'? Trends in American Serial Homicide 1940–1990," *Criminal Justice Review* 17 (1992): 1–18.

145. FBI, *Crime in the United States, 1992,* p. 21.

146. Keith Harries, "Homicide and Assault: A Comparative Analysis of Attributes in Dallas Neighborhoods, 1981–1985," *Professional Geographer* 41 (1989): 29–38.

147. See, generally, Joel Milner, ed., "Special Issue: Physical Child Abuse," *Criminal Justice and Behavior* 18 (1991).

148. See, generally, Ruth S. Kempe and C. Henry Kempe, *Child Abuse* (Cambridge, Mass.: Harvard University Press, 1978).

149. Richard Gelles and Murray Straus, "Violence in the American Family," *Journal of Social Issues* 35 (1979): 15–39.

150. David Wiese and Deborah Daro, *Current Trends in Child Abuse Reporting and Fatalities: The Results of the 1994 Annual Fifty-State Survey* (Chicago: National Committee to Prevent Child Abuse, 1995).

151. Steve Geissinger, "Boy Scouts Dismissed 1,800 Suspected Molesters from 1971–91," *Boston Globe,* 15 October 1993, p. 3.

152. Diana Russell, "The Incidence and Prevalence of Intrafamilial and Extrafamilial Sexual Abuse of Female Children," *Child Abuse and Neglect* 7 (1983): 133–146; see also David Finkelhor, *Sexually Victimized Children* (New York: Free Press, 1979), p. 88.

153. Jeanne Hernandez, "Eating Disorders and Sexual Abuse in Adolescents," paper presented at the annual meeting of the American Psychosomatic Society, Charleston, S.C., March, 1993; Glenn Wolfner and Richard Gelles, "A Profile of Violence Toward Children: A National Study," *Child Abuse and Neglect* 17 (1993): 197–212.

154. Louanne Lawson and Mark Chaffin, "False Negatives in Sexual Abuse Disclosure Interviews," *Journal of Interpersonal Violence* 7 (1992): 532–542.

155. For a thorough review, see Kathleen Kendall-Tackett, Linda Meyer Williams, and David Finkelhor, "Impact of Sexual Abuse on Children: A Review and Synthesis of Recent Empirical Studies," *Psychological Bulletin* 133 (1993): 164–180.

156. Wolfner and Gelles, "A Profile of Violence Toward Children."

157. Brandt Steele, "Violence Within the Family," in *Child Abuse and Neglect: The Family and the Community,* ed. R. Helfer and C. H. Kempe (Cambridge, Mass.: Ballinger Publishing, 1976), p. 12.

158. Ruth Inglis, *Sins of the Fathers: A Study of the Physical and Emotional Abuse of Children* (New York: St. Martin's Press, 1978), p. 68.

159. Ibid., p. 53.

160. Alison Bass, "Daughter Wins Sex-Abuse Case Against Father," *Boston Globe,* 18 May 1990, p. 17.

161. David Kaplan, "The Unkindest Cut," *Newsweek,* 16 August 1993, p. 56.

162. Associated Press, "Lorena Freed," *Manchester Union Leader,* 1 March 1994, p. 44.

163. Russell Dobash, R. Emerson Dobash, Margo Wilson, and Martin Daly, "The Myth of Sexual Symmetry in Marital Violence," *Social Problems* 39 (1992): 71–86; Martin Schwartz and Walter DeKeseredy, "The Return of the 'Battered Husband Syndrome': Typification of Women as Violent," *Crime, Law and Social Change* 8 (1993): 11–27.

164. Schwartz and DeKeseredy, "The Return of the 'Battered Husband Syndrome.'"

165. R. Emerson Dobash and Russell Dobash, *Violence Against Wives* (New York: Free Press, 1979).

166. Julia O'Faolain and Laura Martines, eds., *Not in God's Image: Women in History* (Glasgow: Fontana/Collins, 1974).

167. Laurence Stone, "The Rise of the Nuclear Family in Modern England: The Patriarchal Stage," in *The Family in History,* ed. Charles Rosenberg (Philadelphia: University of Pennsylvania Press, 1975), p. 53.

168. Dobash and Dobash, *Violence Against Wives,* p. 46.

169. John Braithwaite, "Inequality and Republican Criminology," paper presented at the annual meeting of the American Society of Criminology, San Francisco, November 1991, p. 20.

170. James Makepeace, "Social Factor and Victim-Offender Differences in Courtship Violence," *Family Relations* 33 (1987): 87–91.

171. Graeme Newman, *Understanding Violence* (New York: Lippincott, 1979), pp. 145–146.

172. Gerald Hotaling and David Sugarman, "An Analysis of Risk Markers in Husband to Wife Violence," *Violence and Victims* 1 (1986): 101–124.

173. Ronald Simons, Chyi-In Wu, Christine Johnson, and Rand Conger, "A Test of Various Perspectives on the Intergenerational Transmission of Domestic Violence," *Criminology* 33 (1995): 141–171.

174. Ibid., pp. 162–163.

175. Murray Straus and Sean Lauer, "Corporal Punishment of Children, Substance Abuse, and Crime in Relation to Race, Culture, and Deterrence," paper presented at the annual meeting of the American Society of Criminology, New Orleans, November 1992.

176. FBI, *Crime in the United States, 1989,* p. 16.

177. Caroline Wolf Harlow, *Robbery Victims* (Washington, D.C.: Bureau of Justice Statistics, 1989), pp. 1–5.

178. F. H. McClintock and Evelyn Gibson, *Robbery in London* (London: Macmillan, 1961), p. 15.

179. John Conklin, *Robbery and the Criminal Justice System* (New York: Lippincott, 1972), pp. 1–80.

180. James Calder and John Bauer, "Convenience Store Robberies: Security Measures and Store Robbery Incidents," *Journal of Criminal Justice* 20 (1992): 553–566.

181. James Garofalo, "Bias and Non-Bias Crimes in New York City: Preliminary Findings," paper presented at the annual meeting of the American Society of Criminology, Baltimore, November 1990.

182. Ronald Powers, "Bensonhurst Man Guilty," *Boston Globe,* 18 May 1990, p. 3.

183. "Boy Gets 18 Years in Fatal Park Beating of Transient," *Los Angeles Times,* 24 December 1987, p. 9B.

184. Ewing, *When Children Kill,* pp. 65–66.

185. Mike McPhee, "In Denver, Attacks Stir Fears of Racism," *Boston Globe,* 10 December 1990, p. 3.

186. Jack McDevitt, "The Study of the Character of Civil Rights Crimes in Massachusetts (1983–1987)," paper presented at the annual meeting of the American Society of Criminology, Reno, Nevada, November 1989.

187. Ibid., p. 8.

188. Jack Levin and Jack McDevitt, *Hate Crimes: The Rising Tide of Bigotry and Bloodshed* (New York: Plenum, 1993).

189. Jack Levin and Jack McDevitt, *Hate Crimes, A Study of Offenders' Motivations* (Boston, Mass.: Northeastern University, 1993).

190. "ADL Survey Analyzes Neo-Nazi Skinhead Menace and International Connections," *CJ International* 12 (1996): 7.

191. FBI, News Release, November 4, 1996.

192. Garofalo, "Bias and Non-Bias Crimes in New York City," p. 3.

193. Carl Weiser, "This Is What You Get for Firing Me," *USA Today,* 28 January 1993, p. 3A.

194. James Alan Fox and Jack Levin, "Firing Back: The Growing Threat of Workplace Homicide," *Annals* 536 (1994): 16–30.

195. John King, "Workplace Violence: A Conceptual Framework," paper presented at the annual meeting of the American Society of Criminology, Phoenix, Arizona, November 1993.

196. Associated Press, "Gunman Wounds 3 Doctors in L.A. Hospital," *Cleveland Plain Dealer,* 9 February 1993, p. 1B.

197. Fox and Levin, "Firing Back," p. 5.

198. Ibid., p. 20.

199. Stephen Schafer, *The Political Criminal* (New York: Free Press, 1974), p. 1.

200. Schafer, *The Political Criminal,* p. 150.

201. Robert Friedlander, *Terrorism* (Dobbs Ferry, N.Y.: Oceana Publishers, 1979).

202. Walter Laquer, *The Age of Terrorism* (Boston: Little, Brown, 1987), p. 72.

203. National Advisory Commission on Criminal Justice Standards and Goals, *Report of the Task Force on Disorders and Terrorism* (Washington, D.C.: U.S. Government Printing Office, 1976), p. 3.

204. Paul Wilkinson, *Terrorism and the Liberal State* (New York: Wiley, 1977), p. 49.

205. Jack Gibbs, "Conceptualization of Terrorism," *American Sociological Review* 54 (1989): 329–340.

206. Friedlander, *Terrorism,* p. 14.

207. Daniel Georges-Abeyie, "Political Crime and Terrorism," in *Crime and Deviance: A Comparative Perspective,* ed. Graeme Newman (Beverly Hills, Calif.: Sage, 1980), pp. 313–333.

208. Ibid., p. 319.

209. This section relies heavily on Friedlander, *Terrorism,* pp. 8–20.

210. See Friedlander, *Terrorism,* p. 16.

211. For a general view, see Jonathan White, *Terrorism* (Pacific Grove, Calif.: Brooks/Cole, 1991).

212. Jonathan Kaufman, "Trauma of a German Slaying," *Boston Globe,* 3 April 1991, p. 2.

213. Claire Sterling, "Gen. Dozier and the International Terror Network," *Wall Street Journal,* 29 December 1981, p. 12.

214. Russell Watson, "An Explosion in the Sky," *Newsweek,* 2 January 1989, pp. 16–19.

215. Peter Annin and Mark Hosenball, "A Showdown in Montana," *Newsweek,* 8 April 1996, p. 39.

216. Reuters, " Five White Separatists Indicted in Robberies," *Boston Globe* 31 January 1997, p. A8.

217. William Smith, "Libya's Ministry of Fear," *Time,* 30 April 1984, pp. 36–38.

218. Reuters, "Nile Tour Boat Is Attacked; Blast Hits Egyptian Resort," *Boston Globe,* 10 April 1993, p. 5.

219. Associated Press, "31 Decapitated South of Algiers," *Boston Globe,* 3 February 1997, p. A5.

220. Charles Hillsinger and Mark Stein, "Militant Vegetarians Tied to Attacks on Livestock Industry," *Boston Globe,* 23 November 1989, p. A34.

221. Ted Robert Gurr, "Political Terrorism in the United States: Historical Antecedents and Contemporary Trends," in *The Politics of Terrorism,* ed. Michael Stohl (New York: Dekker, 1988).

222. Martha Crenshaw, ed., *Terrorism, Legitimacy, and Power* (Middletown, Conn.: Wesleyan University Press, 1983), pp. 1–10.

223. Reuters, "New Haiti Police Have Executed 15, Rights Group Asserts," *Boston Globe,* 24 January 1997, p. A10.

224. Amnesty International, *Annual Report, 1992* (Washington, D.C.), released July 1993.

225. This report on state action in Peru can be obtained on the Amnesty International web site at http://www.amnesty.org/ailib/aipub/1996/AMR/2460396.html.

226. "Human Rights Watch/Americas Faults Ombudsman's First Year As President of Guatemala," Human Rights Watch news release, June 14, 1994.

227. Ronald Kramer, "Structural Violence and State Terrorism: Neglected Forms of Criminal Violence," paper presented at the annual meeting of the American Society of Criminology, Phoenix, Arizona, November 1993.

228. Dick Ward, "The Nuclear Terror Threat," *CJ International* 12 (1996): 1–4.

229. Theodore Gurr, *Why Men Rebel* (Princeton, N.J.: Princeton University Press, 1970).

230. M. Cherif Bassiouni, "Terrorism, Law Enforcement, and Mass Media: Perspectives, Problems and Proposals," *Journal of Criminal Law and Criminology* 72 (1981): 1–51.

231. Austin Turk, "Political Crime," in *Major Forms of Crime,* ed. R. Meier (Beverly Hills, Calif.: Sage, 1984), pp. 119–135.

232. Reuters, "18 Beheaded in Sri Lanka; Revenge for Slaying Seen," *Boston Globe,* 6 October 1989, p. 13.

233. Kaplan, "The Unkindest Cut," p. 56.

234. 18 USC 113a; 18 USC 51, 1166.

235. United States State Department news release, 25 April 1996.

236. Fact Sheet: Iran-Libya Sanctions Act of 1996, fact sheet released by the Office of the Press Secretary, The White House, Washington, D.C., August 5, 1996.

237. Brent Smith and Gregory Orvis, "America's Response to Terrorism: An Empirical Analysis of Federal Intervention Strategies during the 1980s," *Justice Quarterly* 10 (1993): 660–681.

Chapter 12
Property Crimes

as a group, **economic crimes** can be defined as acts in violation of the criminal law designed to bring financial reward to an offender. In U.S. society, the range and scope of criminal activity motivated by financial gain is tremendous: Self-report studies show that property crime among the young of every social class is widespread; national surveys of criminal behavior indicate that almost 30 million personal and household thefts occur annually; corporate and other white-collar crimes are accepted as commonplace; and political scandals ranging from Watergate to Whitewater indicate that even high government officials can be suspected of criminal acts. Whereas average citizens may be puzzled and enraged by violent crimes, believing them to be both senseless and cruel, they often view economic crimes with a great deal more ambivalence. While it is true that society generally disapproves of crimes involving theft and corruption, the public seems quite tolerant of "gentlemen bandits," even to the point of admiring such figures. They pop up as characters in popular myths and legends—Robin Hood, Jesse James, Bonnie and Clyde, D. B. Cooper. They are the semiheroic subjects of books and films, such as *48 Hours, Pulp Fiction,* and *Heat.*

How can such ambivalence toward criminality be explained? For one thing, national tolerance toward economic criminals may be prompted by the fact that, if self-report surveys are accurate, almost every U.S. citizen has at some time been involved in economic crime. Even people who would never consider themselves criminals may have at one time engaged in petty theft, cheated on their income tax, stolen a textbook from a college bookstore, or pilfered from their place of employment. Consequently, it may be difficult for society to condemn economic criminals without feeling hypocritical.

People may also be somewhat more tolerant of economic crimes because they never seem to seriously hurt anyone—banks are insured, large businesses pass along losses to consumers, stolen cars can be easily replaced. The true pain of economic crime often goes unappreciated. Convicted offenders, especially businesspeople who commit white-collar crimes involving millions of dollars, are often punished rather lightly.

This chapter is the first of two that review the nature and extent of economic crime in the United States. It is divided into two principal sections. The first deals with the concept of professional crime and focuses on different types of professional criminals, including the **fence,** a buyer and seller of stolen merchandise. Then the chapter turns to a discussion of common theft-related offenses, often referred to by criminologists as **street crimes.** These crimes include the major forms of common theft: larceny, theft by false pretenses, and embezzlement. Included within these general offense categories are such common crimes as auto theft, shoplifting, and credit card fraud. Then the chapter discusses a more serious form of theft—**burglary**—that involves forcible entry into a person's home or place of work for the purpose of theft. Finally, the crime of arson is discussed briefly. In Chapter 13, attention will be given to white-collar crimes and economic crimes that involve organizations devoted to criminal enterprise.

A Brief History of Theft

Theft offenses are common. Millions of auto thefts, shoplifting incidents, embezzlements, burglaries, and larcenies are recorded each year. National surveys indicate that 10%–15% of the U.S. population are victims of theft offenses each year. Theft is not a phenomenon unique to modern times; the theft of personal property has been known throughout recorded history. The Crusades of the 11th century inspired peasants and downtrodden noblemen to leave the shelter of their estates to prey on passing pilgrims.[1] Not surprisingly, Crusaders felt it within their rights to appropriate the possessions of any infidels— Greeks, Jews, or Moslems—they happened to encounter during their travels. By the 13th century, returning pilgrims, not content to live as serfs on feudal estates, gathered in the forests of England and the Continent to poach on game that was the rightful property of their lord or king and, when possible, to steal from passing strangers. By the 14th century, many of such highwaymen and poachers were full-time livestock thieves, stealing great numbers of cattle and sheep.[2]

The 15th and 16th centuries brought hostilities between England and France in what has come to be known as the Hundred Years' War. Foreign mercenary troops fighting for both sides roamed the countryside; loot and pillage were viewed as a rightful part of their pay. Theft became more professional with the rise of the city and the establishment of a permanent class of propertyless urban poor.[3] By the 18th century, three separate groups of property criminals were active. In the larger cities, such as London and Paris, groups of skilled thieves, pickpockets, forgers, and counterfeiters operated freely. They congregated in **flash houses**—public meeting places, often taverns, that served as headquarters for gangs. Here, deals were made, crimes plotted, and the sale of stolen goods negotiated.[4] The second group of thieves were the smugglers, who moved freely in sparsely populated areas and transported goods without bothering to pay tax or duty. The third group were the poachers, who lived in the country and supplemented their diet and income with game that belonged to a landlord. By the 18th century, professional thieves in the larger cities had banded together into gangs to protect themselves, increase the scope of their activities, and help dispose of stolen goods. Jack Wild, perhaps London's most famous thief, perfected the process of buying and selling stolen goods and gave himself the title of "Thief-Taker General of Great Britain and Ireland." Before he was hanged, Wild controlled numerous gangs and dealt harshly with any thief who violated his strict code of conduct.[5] During this period, individual theft-related crimes began to be defined by the common law. The most important of these categories are still used today.

Modern Thieves

Of the millions of property and theft-related crimes that occur each year, most are committed by **occasional criminals** who do not define themselves by a criminal role or view themselves as committed career criminals; other theft-offenders are in fact skilled, professional criminals. The following sections review these two orientations toward property crime.

Occasional Criminals

Although criminologists are not certain, they suspect that the great majority of economic crimes are the work of amateur criminals whose decision to steal is spontaneous and whose acts are unskilled, unplanned, and haphazard. Millions of theft-related crimes occur each year, and most are not reported to police agencies. Many of these theft offenses are committed by school-age youths who are unlikely to enter into a criminal career and whose behavior has been described as drifting between conventional and criminal behavior. Added to the pool of amateur thieves are the millions of adults whose behavior may occasionally violate the criminal law—shoplifters, pilferers, tax cheats—but whose main source of income comes from conventional means and whose self-identity is noncriminal. Added together, their behaviors form the bulk of theft crimes.

According to John Hepburn, occasional property crime occurs when there is an opportunity or **situational inducement** to commit crime.[6] Opportunities are available to members of all classes, but members of the upper class have the opportunity to engage in the more lucrative business-related crimes of price fixing, bribery, embezzlement, and so on, which are closed to the lower classes. Hence, lower-class individuals are overrepresented in street crime. Situational inducements are short-run influences on a person's behavior that increase risk taking. These include psychological factors, such as financial problems, and social factors, such as peer pressure. According to Hepburn, opportunity and situational inducements are not the cause of crime; rather, they are the occasion for crime; hence, the term *occasional criminal.*

It seems evident that opportunity and inducements are not randomly situated. Consequently, the frequency of occasional property crime varies according to age, class, sex, and so on. Occasional offenders are not professional criminals, nor do they make crime their occupation. They do not rely on skills or knowledge to commit their crimes, they do not organize their daily activities around crime, and they are not committed to crime as a way of life. Occasional criminals have little group support for their acts. Unlike professionals, they do not receive informal, peer group support for their crimes. In fact, they will deny any connection to a criminal lifestyle and instead view their transgressions as being "out of character." They may see their crimes as being motivated by necessity. For example, they were only

Millions of theft-related crimes occur each year, and most are not reported to police agencies. Some thieves are involved in fraudulent schemes and scams, such as "con artists" who make their living luring passersby into a rigged "game of chance." The "marks" are reassured that an observant person such as themselves surely cannot lose, but in reality they cannot win.

"borrowing" the car the police caught them with; they were going to pay back the store they stole merchandise from. Because of the lack of commitment, occasional offenders may be the most likely to respond to the general deterrent effect of the law.

Professional Criminals

In contrast, **professional criminals** make a significant portion of their income from crime. Professionals do not delude themselves with the belief that their acts are impulsive, one-time efforts, nor do they use elaborate rationalizations to excuse the harmfulness of their action ("Shoplifting doesn't really hurt anyone"). Consequently, professionals pursue their craft with vigor, attempting to learn from older, experienced criminals the techniques that will earn them the most money with the least risk. Although their numbers are relatively few, professionals engage in crimes that produce the greater losses to society and perhaps cause the more significant social harm.

Professional theft traditionally refers to nonviolent forms of criminal behavior that are undertaken with a high degree of skill for monetary gain and that exploit interests tending to maximize financial opportunities and minimize the possibilities of apprehension. The most typical forms include pocket picking, burglary, shoplifting, forgery and counterfeiting, extortion, sneak theft, and confidence swindling.[7]

Relatively little is known about the career patterns of professional thieves and criminals. From the literature on crime and delinquency, three patterns emerge: youths come under the influence of older, experienced criminals who teach them the trade; juvenile gang members continue their illegal activities at a time when most of their peers have "dropped out" to marry, raise families, and take conventional jobs; youths sent to prison for minor offenses learn the techniques of crime from more experienced thieves. For example, Harry King, a professional thief, relates this story of his entry into crime after being placed in a shelter-care home by his recently divorced mother:

> It was while I was at this parental school that I learned that some of the kids had been committed there by the court for stealing bikes. They taught me how to steal and where to steal them and where to sell them. Incidentally, some of the "nicer people" were the ones who bought bikes from the kids. They would dismantle the bike and use the parts: the wheels, chains, handlebars, and so forth.[8]

There is some debate in the criminological literature over who may be defined as a *professional* criminal. In his classic works, Edwin Sutherland used the term to refer only to thieves who do not use force or physical violence in their crimes and live solely by their wits and skill.[9] However, some criminologists use the term to refer to any criminal who identifies with a criminal subculture, who makes the bulk of his or her living from crime, and who possesses a degree of skill in his or her chosen trade.[10] Thus, one can become a professional safecracker, burglar, car thief, or fence. Some criminologists would not consider drug addicts who steal to support their habit as professionals; they lack skill and therefore are amateur opportunists, rather than professional technicians. However, professional criminals who take drugs might still be considered under the general pattern of professional crime. If the sole criteria for being judged a professional criminal is using crime as one's primary source of income, then many drug users would have to be placed in the professional category.

SUTHERLAND'S PROFESSIONAL CRIMINAL. What we know about the lives of professional criminals has come to us through their journals, diaries, autobiographies, and first-person accounts given to criminologists. The best-known account of professional theft is Edwin Sutherland's recording of the life of a professional thief or con man, Chic Conwell, in Sutherland's classic book, *The Professional Thief*.[11] Conwell and Sutherland's concept of profes-

Figure 12.1 Sutherland's typology of professional thieves.

Pickpocket ("cannon")

Sneak thief from stores, banks, and offices ("heel")

Shoplifter ("booster")

Jewel thief who substitutes fake gems for real ones ("pennyweighter")

Thief who steals from hotel rooms ("hotel prowl")

Confidence game artist

Thief in rackets related to confidence games

Forger

Extortionist from those engaging in illegal acts ("shakedown artist")

Source: Edwin Sutherland and Chic Conwell, *The Professional Thief* (Chicago: University of Chicago Press, 1937).

sional theft has two critical dimensions. First, professional thieves engage in limited types of crime, which are described in Figure 12.1.[12]

The second requirement to establish professionalism as a thief is the exclusive use of wits, front (a believable demeanor), and talking ability. Manual dexterity and physical force are of little importance. Thieves who use force or who commit crimes that require little expertise are not considered worthy of the title "professional." Professional areas of activity include such "heavy rackets" as bank robbery, car theft, burglary, and safecracking. Sutherland and Conwell's criteria for professionalism are thus weighted heavily toward con games and trickery and give little attention to common street crimes.

Professional thieves must acquire status in their profession. Status is based on their technical skill, financial standing, connections, power, dress, manners, and wide knowledge. In their world, "thief" is a title worn with pride. Conwell and Sutherland also argue that professional thieves share feelings, sentiments, and behaviors. Of these, none is more important than the code of honor of the underworld; even under threat of the most severe punishment, a professional thief must never inform (squeal) on his or her fellows.

Sutherland and Conwell view professional theft as an occupation with much the same internal organization as that characterizing such legitimate professions as advertising, teaching, or police work. They conclude:

> A person can be a professional thief only if he is recognized and received as such by other professional thieves. Professional theft is a group way of life. One can get into the group and remain in it only by the consent of those previously in

the group. Recognition as a professional thief by other professional thieves is the absolutely necessary, universal and definitive characteristic of the professional thief.[13]

PROFESSIONAL CRIMINALS: THE FENCE. Some experts have argued that Sutherland's view of the professional thief may be outdated because modern thieves often work alone, are not part of a criminal subculture, and were not tutored early in their careers by other criminals.[14] However, some recent research efforts show that the principles set down by Sutherland still have value for understanding the behavior of one contemporary criminal: the professional fence, a person who earns his or her living solely by buying and reselling stolen merchandise.

The fence's critical role in criminal transactions has been recognized since the 18th century.[15] Fences act as intermediaries who purchase stolen merchandise—ranging from diamonds to auto hubcaps—and then resell it to merchants who market the goods to legitimate customers. Much of what is known about fencing comes from three in-depth studies of individual fences by Carl Klockars, Darrell Steffensmeier, and Marilyn Walsh.[16]

Klockars examined the life and times of one successful fence who used the alias "Vincent Swaggi." Through 400 hours of listening to and observing Vincent, Klockars found that this highly professional criminal had developed techniques that made him almost immune to prosecution. During the course of a long and profitable career in crime, Vincent spent only four months in prison. He stayed in business in part because of his sophisticated knowledge of the law of stolen property: To convict someone of receiving stolen goods, the prosecution must prove that the accused was in possession of the goods and knew that the goods had been stolen. Vincent had the skills to make sure that these elements could never be proven. Also helping Vincent stay out of the law's grasp were the close working associations he maintained with society's upper classes, including influential members of the justice system. Vincent helped them purchase items at below-cost, bargain prices. He also helped authorities recover stolen goods and therefore remained in their good graces. Klockars's work strongly suggests that fences customarily cheat their thief-clients and at the same time cooperate with the law.

Sam Goodman, the fence studied by Darrell Steffensmeier, lived in a world similar to Vincent Swaggi's. He also purchased stolen goods from a wide variety of thieves and suppliers, including burglars, drug addicts, shoplifters, dockworkers, and truck drivers. According to Sam, to be successful, a fence must meet the following conditions:

1. *Upfront cash.* All deals are cash transactions, so one must always have an adequate supply of ready cash on hand.

2. *Knowledge of dealing: learning the ropes.* The fence must be schooled in knowledge of the trade, including developing a "larceny sense"; learning to "buy right" at acceptable prices; being able to "cover one's back" and

not get caught; finding out how to make the right contacts; and knowing how to "wheel and deal" and create opportunities for profit.

3. *Connections with suppliers of stolen goods.* The successful fence is able to engage in long-term relationships with suppliers of high-value stolen goods who are relatively free of police interference. The warehouse worker who pilfers is a better supplier than the narcotics addict who is more likely to be apprehended and talk to the police.

4. *Connections with buyers.* The successful fence must have continuing access to buyers of stolen merchandise who are inaccessible to the common thief.

5. *Complicity with law enforcers.* The fence must work out a relationship with law enforcement officials who invariably find out about the fence's operations. Steffensmeier found that to stay in business, the fence must either bribe officials with good deals on merchandise and cash payments or act as an informer who helps police recover particularly important merchandise and arrest thieves. This latter role of informer differentiates Steffensmeier's description of the fence's role from that of Klockars.

Marilyn Walsh found that fences handle a tremendous number of products—televisions, cigarettes, stereo equipment, watches, autos, and cameras.[17] In dealing their merchandise, fences operate through many legitimate fronts, including art dealers, antique stores, furniture and appliance retailers, remodeling companies, salvage companies, trucking companies, and jewelry stores. When deciding what to pay the thief for goods, the fence uses a complex pricing policy. Professional thieves who steal high-priced items are usually given the highest amounts—about 30%–50% of the wholesale price. For example, furs valued at $5,000 may be bought for $1,200. However, the amateur thief or drug addict who is not in a good bargaining position may receive only ten cents on the dollar.

Fencing seems to contain many of the elements of professional theft as described by Sutherland: fences live by their wits, never engage in violence, depend on their skill in negotiating, maintain community standing based on connections and power, and share the sentiments and behaviors of their fellows. The only divergence between Sutherland's thief and the fence is the code of honor; it seems likely that the fence is much more willing to cooperate with authorities than most other professional criminals.

The Nonprofessional Fence

Professional fences are the ones who have attracted the attention of criminologists. Yet like other forms of theft, fencing is not dominated by professional criminals alone; a significant portion of all fencing is performed by amateur or occasional criminals.

Using data collected in interviews with convicted thieves, fences, and people who bought stolen property, Paul Cromwell, James Olson, and D'Aunn Avary discovered that novice burglars, such as juveniles and drug addicts, often find it so difficult to establish relationships with professional fences they turn instead to nonprofessionals to unload their stolen goods.[18]

One type of occasional fence is the part-timer who, unlike professional fences, has other sources of income. Part-timers are often "legitimate" businesspeople who integrate the stolen merchandise into their regular stock. For example, the manager of a local video store buys stolen VCRs and tapes and rents them along with his legitimate merchandise. An added benefit is that profit on these items is not reported for tax purposes.

Some merchants become actively involved in theft either by specifying the merchandise they want the burglars to steal or by "fingering" victims. Some businessmen sell merchandise to people and then describe the customers' homes and vacation plans to known burglars so they can steal it back!

Some amateur fences barter stolen goods for services rendered. These "associational fences" typically have legitimate professional dealings with known criminals and include bail bonds agents, police officers, and attorneys. One lawyer bragged of getting a $12,000 Rolex watch from one client in exchange for legal services. Bartering for stolen merchandise avoids taxes and becomes a transaction in the "underground economy."

"Neighborhood hustlers" buy and sell stolen property as one of many ways they make a living; they keep some of the booty for themselves and sell the rest in the neighborhood. These deal makers are familiar figures to neighborhood burglars looking to get some quick cash.

"Amateur receivers" can be complete strangers approached in a public place by someone offering a great deal on valuable commodities. It is unlikely that anyone buying a $500 stereo for $200 cash would not suspect that it may have been stolen. Some amateur receivers make a habit of buying merchandise at reasonable prices from a "trusted friend."

The Cromwell, Olson, and Avary research indicates that the nonprofessional fence may account for a great deal of criminal receiving. It shows that both professional and amateur thieves have their own niche in the crime universe.

Criminologists and legal scholars recognize that common theft offenses fall into several categories linked together because they involve the intentional misappropriation of property for personal gain. In some cases, as in fencing, the property is bought from another who is in illegal possession of the goods. In the case of embezzlement, burglary, and larceny, the property is taken through stealth, while in others, such as bad checks, fraud, and false pretenses, it is obtained through deception. Some of the major categories of common theft offenses are discussed in the rest of this chapter in some detail.

Larceny/Theft

Larceny/theft was one of the earliest common-law crimes created by English judges to define acts in which one person took for his or her own use the property of another.[19] At common law, **larceny** was defined as "the trespassory taking and carrying away of the personal property of another with intent to steal."[20] Most state jurisdictions have incorporated the common-law crime of larceny in their legal codes. Today, definitions of larceny often include such familiar acts as shoplifting, passing bad checks, and other theft offenses that do not involve using force or threats on the victim or forcibly breaking into a person's home or place of work. (The former is robbery; the latter, burglary.)

As originally construed, larceny involved only taking property that was in the possession of the rightful owners. For example, it would have been considered larceny for someone to go secretly into a farmer's field and steal a cow. Thus, the original common-law definition required a "trespass in the taking"; this meant that for an act to be considered larceny, goods must have been taken from the physical possession of the owner. In creating this definition of larceny, English judges were more concerned with disturbance of the peace than they were with thefts. They reasoned that if someone tried to steal property from another's possession, the act could eventually lead to a physical confrontation and possibly the death of one party or the other. Consequently, the original definition of larceny did not include crimes in which the thief had come into the possession of the stolen property by trickery or deceit. For example, if someone entrusted with another person's property decided to keep it, it was not considered larceny. The growth of manufacturing and the development of the free enterprise system required greater protection for private property. The pursuit of commercial enterprise often required that one person's legal property be entrusted to a second party; therefore, larceny evolved to include the theft of goods that had come into the thief's possession through legitimate means.

To get around the element of "trespass in the taking," English judges created the concept of **constructive possession.** This legal fiction applied to situations in which persons voluntarily and temporarily gave up custody of their property but still believed that the property was legally theirs. For example, if a person gave a jeweler her watch for repair, she would still believe she owned the watch, although she had handed it over to the jeweler. Similarly, when a person misplaces his wallet and someone else finds it and keeps it—although identification of the owner can be plainly seen—the concept of constructive possession makes the person who has kept the wallet guilty of larceny.

Larceny Today

Most state jurisdictions have, as mentioned, incorporated larceny in their criminal codes. Larceny is usually sepa-

Every year about a million cases of larceny are reported to the FBI. Security forces have been assigned to commercial and residential areas to reduce the incidence of theft. Can such measures be effective, or do they simply displace crimes to other areas of the city?

rated by state statute into *petit* (or petty) *larceny* and *grand larceny*. The former involves small amounts of money or property; it is punished as a misdemeanor. Grand larceny, involving merchandise of greater value, is considered a felony and is punished by a sentence in the state prison. Each state sets its own boundary between grand larceny and petty larceny, but $50 to $100 is not unusual. This distinction often presents a serious problem for the justice system. Car thefts and other larcenies involving high-priced merchandise are easily classified, but it is often difficult to decide whether a particular theft should be considered petty or grand larceny. For example, if a ten-year-old watch that originally cost $500 is stolen, should its value be based on its original cost, on its current worth—say, $50—or on its replacement cost—say, $1,000? As most statutes are worded, the current market value of the property governs its worth. Thus, the theft of the watch would be considered petty larceny, since its worth today is only $50. However, if a painting originally bought for $25 has a current market value of $500, its theft would be considered grand larceny.

Larceny/theft is probably the most common criminal offense. Self-report studies indicate that a significant number of youths have engaged in theft-related activities. The FBI recorded about 7.4 million acts of larceny in 1996, a rate of about 3,100 per 100,000 persons; larceny rates have remained rather stable for the past five years.[21]

Shoplifting

Shoplifting is a common form of theft that involves the taking of goods from retail stores. Usually, shoplifters try to snatch goods—jewelry, clothes, records, appliances—when store personnel are otherwise occupied and hide the goods on their person. The "five-finger discount" is an extremely common form of crime; losses from shoplifting are measured in the billions of dollars each year.[22] Retail security measures add to the already high cost of this crime, which is passed on to the consumer. Shoplifting incidents have increased dramatically in the past 20 years, and retailers now expect an annual increase of 10%–15%. Some studies estimate that about one in every nine shoppers steals from department stores. Moreover, the increasingly popular discount stores, such as Kmart, Wal-Mart, and Target, have a minimum of sales help and depend on highly visible merchandise displays to attract purchasers, all of which makes them particularly vulnerable to shoplifters.

THE SHOPLIFTER. The classic study of shoplifting was conducted by Mary Owen Cameron.[23] In her pioneering effort, Cameron found that about 10% of all shoplifters were professionals who derived the majority of their income from shoplifting. Sometimes called **boosters** or **heels,** professional shoplifters intend to resell stolen merchandise to pawnshops or fences, usually at half the original price.[24]

Cameron found that the majority of shoplifters are actually amateur pilferers, called snitches in thieves' argot. Snitches are usually respectable persons who do not conceive of themselves as thieves but are systematic shoplifters who steal merchandise for their own use. They are not simply seized by an uncontrollable urge to take something that attracts them; they come equipped to steal. Usually, snitches who are arrested have never been apprehended before. For the most part, they are people who lack the kind of criminal experience that suggests extensive association with a criminal subculture.

Criminologists view shoplifters as people who are likely to reform if apprehended. Mary Owen Cameron reasoned that because snitches are not part of a criminal subculture and do not think of themselves as criminals, they are deterred by an initial contact with the law. Getting arrested has a traumatic effect on them, and they will not risk a second offense.[25] While this argument seems plausible, some criminologists argue that apprehension may have a labeling effect that inhibits deterrence and results in repeated offending. Youths who had been previously apprehended for shoplifting have been deterred by official processing.[26]

Shoplifting continues to be a serious problem. FBI data indicate that shoplifting makes up about 16% of all larceny cases; reported shoplifting has increased 30% since 1985. Many stores have installed elaborate security devices to combat shoplifting, but the growth of this type of larceny has continued.

CONTROLLING SHOPLIFTING.
One major problem associated with combating shoplifting is that many customers who observe pilferage are reluctant to report it to security agents. Store employees themselves often hesitate to get involved in apprehending a shoplifter. For example, in a controlled experiment, Donald Hartmann and his associates found that customers observed only 28% of staged shoplifting incidents that had been designed to get their attention.[27] Furthermore, only 28% of people who said they had observed an incident reported it to store employees.

In another controlled experiment using staged shoplifting incidents, Erhard Blankenburg found that less than 10% of shoplifting was detected by store employees and that customers appeared unwilling to report even serious cases.[28] Even in stores with an announced policy of full reporting and prosecution, only 70% of the shoplifting detected by employees was actually reported to managers, and only 5% was prosecuted. According to Blankenburg, foreigners, adults, and blue-collar workers were disproportionately represented among those officially punished. It is also likely that a store owner's decision to prosecute shoplifters will be based on the value of the goods stolen, the nature of the goods stolen, and the manner in which the theft was realized. For example, shoplifters who planned their crime by using a concealed apparatus, such as a bag pinned to the inside of their clothing, were more apt to be prosecuted than those who had impulsively put merchandise into their pockets.[29]

To aid in the arrest of shoplifters, a number of states have passed merchant privilege laws that are designed to protect retailers and their employers from litigation stemming from improper or false arrests of suspected shoplifters.[30] These laws protect but do not immunize merchants from lawsuits. They require that arrests be made on reasonable grounds or probable cause, detention be of short duration, and store employees or security guards conduct themselves in a reasonable fashion.

PREVENTION STRATEGIES.
Retail stores are now initiating a number of strategies designed to reduce or eliminate shoplifting. *Target removal strategies* involve using dummy or disabled goods on display while having the "real" merchandise kept under lock and key. For example, audio equipment with missing parts is displayed, and only after purchase are the necessary components installed. Some stores sell from a catalogue while keeping merchandise in stockrooms.

Net Bookmark

Shoplifting has become big business. It costs retailers in this country billions of dollars each year. These costs are passed along to consumers, who pay 5%–10% more for the things they buy. To learn more about shoplifting and what can be done about it, go to:

http://www.selectron.com/~gig/todaycov.html

Target hardening strategies involve locking goods into place or having them monitored by electronic systems. Clothing stores may use racks designed to prevent large quantities of garments from being slipped off easily.

Situational measures place the most valuable goods in the least vulnerable places, use warning signs to deter potential thieves, and have closed-circuit cameras. Goods may be tagged with devices that give off an alarm if they are taken out of the shop.

Figure 12.2 describes some of the steps retail insurers recommend to reduce the incidence of shoplifting.

PRIVATE JUSTICE.
Efforts to control the spread of shoplifting have prompted some commercial enterprises to establish highly sophisticated loss prevention units to combat would-be criminals. Melissa Davis, Richard Lundman, and Ramiro Martinez, Jr. investigated the loss prevention unit in a branch store of a large national retail chain.[31] They uncovered a private justice system that works parallel to but independent from the public justice system. Private security officers have many law enforcement powers also granted to municipal police officers, including arrest of sus-

- Train employees to watch for suspicious behavior, such as a shopper loitering over a trivial item. Have them keep an eye out for shoppers wearing baggy clothes, carrying their own bag, or using some other method to conceal products taken from the shelf.
- Develop a call code. When employees suspect that a customer is shoplifting, they can use the call to bring store management or security to the area.
- Products on lower floors face the greatest risk. Relocate the most tempting targets to upper floors.
- Use smaller exits and avoid placing the most expensive merchandise near these exits.
- Design routes within stores to make theft less tempting and funnel customers toward cashiers.
- Place service departments (credit and packaging) near areas where shoplifters are likely to stash goods. Extra supervision reduces the problem.
- Avoid creating corners where there are no supervision sight lines in areas of stores favored by young males. Restrict and supervise areas where electronic tags can be removed.

Sources: Marcus Felson, "Preventing Retail Theft: An Application of Environmental Criminology," *Security Journal* 7 (1996): 71–75; Marc Brandeberry, "$15 Billion Lost to Shoplifting," *Today's Coverage,* A Newsletter of the Grocers Insurance Group, Portland, Oregon, 1997.

pects and search and seizure. A merchant's privilege statute immunized the store police from any criminal or civil liability charges stemming from false arrest.

Private police decision making seemed to be influenced by state law allowing stores to recover civil damages from shoplifters. In the 28 states that have implemented this type of legislation, shoplifters may be required to compensate store owners for the value of the goods they attempted to steal, costs incurred because of their illegal acts, and punitive damages. Davis, Lundman, and Martinez found that store detectives use the civil damage route to defray the costs of their operation. The researchers found that the availability of civil damages had important effects on decision making. Store owners go after the more affluent shoplifters for civil recovery and ship the poor to the public criminal justice system for prosecution.[32]

Bad Checks

Another form of theft is the cashing of a bank check, to obtain money or property, that is knowingly and intentionally drawn on a nonexistent or underfunded bank account. In general, for a person to be guilty of passing a bad check, the bank the check is drawn on must refuse payment, and the check casher must fail to make the check good within ten days after finding out the check was not honored.

The best-known study of check forgers was conducted by Edwin Lemert.[33] Lemert found that the majority of check forgers—he calls them **naive check forgers**—are am-

ateurs who do not believe their actions will hurt anyone. Most naive check forgers come from middle-class backgrounds and have little identification with a criminal subculture. They cash bad checks because of a financial crisis that demands an immediate resolution—perhaps they have lost money at the racetrack and have some pressing bills to pay. Lemert refers to this condition as **closure.** Naive check forgers are often socially isolated people who have been unsuccessful in their personal relationships. They are risk-prone when faced with a situation that is unusually stressful for them. The willingness of stores and other commercial establishments to cash checks with a minimum of fuss to promote business encourages the check forger to risk committing a criminal act.

Not all check forgers are amateurs. Lemert found that a few professionals—whom he calls **systematic forgers**—make a substantial living by passing bad checks. However, professionals constitute a relatively small segment of the total population of check forgers. It is difficult to estimate the number of check forgeries committed each year or the amounts involved. Stores and banks may choose not to press charges, since the effort to collect the money due them is often not worth their while. It is also difficult to separate the true check forger from the neglectful shopper.

Credit Card Theft

The use of stolen credit cards has become a major problem in U.S. society. It has been estimated that credit card companies sustain a billion-dollar loss each year through fraud. In New York City alone, police officials estimate that 5,000 credit cards are stolen each month.[34]

Most credit card abuse is the work of amateurs who acquire stolen cards through theft or mugging and then use them for two or three days. However, professional credit card rings may be getting into the act. For example, in Los Angeles members of a credit card gang got jobs as clerks in several stores, where they collected the names and credit card numbers of customers. Gang members bought plain plastic cards and had the names and numbers of the customers embossed on them. The gang created a fictitious wholesale jewelry company and applied for and received authorization to accept credit cards from the customers. The thieves then used the phony cards to charge nonexistent jewelry purchases on the accounts of the people whose names and card numbers they had collected. The banks that issued the original cards honored over $200,000 in payments before the thieves withdrew the money from their business account and left town.[35]

To combat losses from credit card theft, Congress passed a law in 1971 limiting a person's liability to $50 per stolen card. Similarly, some states, such as California, have passed specific statutes making it a misdemeanor to obtain property or services by means of cards that have been stolen, forged, canceled, or revoked or whose use is for any reason unauthorized.[36]

Auto Theft

Motor vehicle theft is another common larceny offense. Yet because of its frequency and seriousness, it is treated as a separate category in the UCR. The FBI recorded almost 1.5 million auto thefts in 1995, accounting for a total loss of almost $8 billion.

UCR projections on auto theft are actually quite similar to the projections of the National Crime Victim Survey (1.2 million thefts in 1995). The similarity of data between these sources occurs because, since almost every state jurisdiction requires owners to insure their vehicles, auto theft is one of the most highly reported of all major crimes (75% of all auto thefts are reported to police).

A number of attempts have been made to categorize the various forms of auto theft. Typically, distinctions are made among theft for temporary personal use, for resale, and for chopping or stripping cars for parts. One of the most detailed of these typologies was developed by Charles McCaghy and his associates after examining data from police and court files in several state jurisdictions.[37] The researchers uncovered five categories of auto theft transactions:

1. *Joyriding.* Many car thefts are motivated by teenagers' desire to acquire the power, prestige, sexual potency, and recognition associated with an automobile. Joyriders do not steal cars for profit or gain but to experience, even briefly, the benefits associated with owning an automobile.

2. *Short-term transportation.* Auto theft for short-term trnsportation is similar to joyriding. It involves the theft of a car simply to go from one place to another. In more serious cases, the thief may drive to another city or state and then steal another car to continue the journey.

3. *Long-term transportation.* Thieves who steal cars for long-term transportation intend to keep the cars for their personal use. Usually older than joyriders and from a lower-class background, these auto thieves may repaint and otherwise disguise cars to avoid detection.

4. *Profit.* Auto theft for profit is, of course, motivated by hope for monetary gain. At one extreme are highly organized professionals who resell expensive cars after altering their identification numbers and falsifying their registration papers. At the other end of the scale are amateur auto strippers who steal batteries, tires, and wheel covers to sell them or reequip their own cars.

5. *Commission of another crime.* A small portion of auto thieves steal cars to use in other crimes, such as robberies and thefts. This type of auto thief desires both mobility and anonymity.

At one time, joyriding was the predominant motive for auto theft, and most cars were taken by relatively affluent, white, middle-class teenagers looking for excitement.[38]

There appears to be a change in this pattern: Fewer cars are being taking today while, concomitantly, fewer stolen cars are being recovered. Part of the reason is the increase in the number of professional car thieves who are linked to "chop shops," export rings, or both. Export of stolen vehicles has become a global problem, and the emergence of capitalism in Eastern Europe has increased the demand for U.S.-made cars.[39]

WHICH CARS ARE TAKEN MOST? Car thieves show signs of rational choice when they make their target selections. Today luxury cars and utility vehicles are in greatest demand. The Toyota Land Cruiser is 23 times more likely to be taken than the average vehicle. Many of the highly desired cars are never recovered because they are immediately shipped abroad, where they command prices three times higher than their U.S. sticker price.[40]

Car models that have been in production for a few years without many design changes stand the greatest risk of theft. These models are the ones most often taken because their parts are most valued in the secondary market; luxury cars typically experience a sharp decline in their theft rate soon after a design change. Enduring models are also in demand because older cars are more likely to be uninsured, and demand for stolen used parts is higher for these vehicles.

> ### Connections
>
> Chapter 4 discusses the rational choice view of car theft. As you may recall, cars with expensive radios and parts are more often the target of rational thieves.

CARJACKING. You may have read about gunmen approaching a car and forcing the owner to give up the keys; in some cases, people have been killed when they reacted too slowly. This type of auto theft has become so common that it has its own name, **carjacking.**[41] Carjacking is legally a type of robbery because it involves force to steal. It accounts for about 2% of all car thefts, or 35,000 per year.

Both the victims and offenders in carjackings tend to be young black men; about half of carjackings are committed by gangs or groups. These crimes are most likely to occur in the evening, in the central city, in an open area or parking garage.

Because of carjacking's violent nature, about 24% of the victims sustain injuries, about 4% of which are considered serious (gun shots, knifings, internal injuries, broken bones and teeth); about 60% of the offenders in carjackings carry handguns.

COMBATING AUTO THEFT. Because of its commonality and high loss potential, auto theft has been a target of situational crime-prevention efforts. In a thorough analysis, Ronald Clarke and Patricia Harris have outlined some of the methods being tried to combat auto theft.[42] One approach has been to increase the risks of apprehension. Information hotlines offer rewards for information leading to the arrest of car thieves. A Michigan-based program, Operation HEAT (Help Eliminate Auto Theft), is credited with recovering over 900 vehicles with a value of $11 million and resulting in the arrest of 647 people. Another approach has been to place fluorescent decals on windows that indicate that the car is never used between 1 and 5 A.M.; if police spot a car with the decal being operated during this period, they know it is stolen. Cars have also been equipped with radio transmitters. The LOJACK system involves a tracking device installed in the car that gives off a signal enabling the police to pinpoint its location.

Other prevention efforts involve making it more difficult to steal cars. Publicity campaigns have been directed at encouraging people to lock their cars. Parking lots have been equipped with theft-deterring closed-circuit TV cameras and barriers. Manufacturers have installed more sophisticated steering-column locking devices and other security systems that make theft harder.

A study by the Highway Loss Data Institute (HLDI) found that most car theft prevention methods, especially alarms, have little effect on theft rates. The most effective methods appear to be devices that immobilize a vehicle by cutting off the electrical power needed to start the engine.[43]

False Pretenses/Fraud

The crime of **false pretenses,** or **fraud,** involves a wrongdoer's misrepresenting a fact to cause a victim to willingly give his or her property to the wrongdoer, who keeps it.[44] The definition of false pretenses was created by the English Parliament in 1757 to cover an area of law left untouched by larceny statutes. The first false pretenses law punished people who "knowingly and designedly by false pretense or pretenses, [obtained] from any person or persons, money, goods, wares or merchandise with intent to cheat or defraud any person or persons of the same."[45] False pretenses differs from traditional larceny because the victims willingly give their possessions to the offender, and the crime does not, as does larceny, involve a "trespass in the taking." An example of false pretenses would be an unscrupulous merchant selling someone a chair by claiming it to be an antique but knowing all the while that it is a cheap copy. Another example would be a phony healer selling a victim a bottle of colored sugar water as an "elixir" that would cure a disease. There are many types of fraud, including confidence games.

Confidence games are run by swindlers whose goal is to separate a victim (or sucker) from his or her hard-earned money. These "con games" usually involve getting a "mark" interested in some get-rich-quick scheme, which may have illegal overtones. The criminal's hope is that when victims lose their money, they will either be too embarrassed or too afraid to call the police. There are hundreds of varieties of con games. The most common is called the **pigeon drop.**[46] A package or wallet containing money is "found" by a con man or woman. A passing victim is stopped and asked for advice about what to do, since the wallet contains no identification. Another "stranger," who is part of the con, approaches and enters the discussion. The three decide to split the money. But first, to make sure everything is legal, one of the swindlers goes off to consult a lawyer. On returning, he or she says that the lawyer claims the money can be split up, but each party must prove he or she has the means to reimburse the original owner, should one show up. The victim is then asked to give some good-faith money for the lawyer to hold. When the victim goes to the lawyer's office to pick up a share of the loot, he or she finds the address bogus and the money gone.

In the 1990s con games have been appropriated by corrupt telemarketers, who contact people, typically elderly, over the phone to bilk them out of their savings. The FBI estimates that illicit telephone pitches cost Americans some $40 billion a year.[47] In one scam, a salesman tried to get $500 out of a 78-year-old woman by telling her the money was needed as a deposit to make sure she would get $50,000 cash she had supposedly won in a contest. In another scheme a Las Vegas–based telephone con game used the name Feed America Inc. to defraud people out of more than $1.3 million by soliciting donations for various causes, including families of those killed in the Oklahoma City bombing.

With the growth of direct-mail marketing and 900 telephone numbers that charge callers over $2.50 per minute for conversations with what are promised to be beautiful and willing sex partners, a flood of new confidence games may be about to descend on the U.S. public. In all, about 436,000 people were arrested for fraud in 1995—most likely a small percentage of all swindlers, scam artists, and frauds.

Embezzlement

The crime of embezzlement was observed in early Greek culture when, in his writings, Aristotle alluded to theft by road commissioners and other government officials.[48] It was first codified into the law by the English Parliament during the 16th century to fill a gap in the larceny law.[49] Until then, to be guilty of theft a person had to take goods from the physical possession of another (trespass in the taking). However, as explained earlier, this definition did not cover instances in which one person trusted another and willfully gave that person temporary custody of his or her property. For example, in everyday commerce, store clerks, bank tellers, brokers, and merchants gain lawful possession but not legal ownership of other people's money. **Embezzlement** occurs when someone who is so trusted with property fraudulently converts it—that is, keeps it for his or her own use or the use of others. Embezzlement can be distinguished from fraud on the basis of when the criminal intent was formed. Most U.S. courts require that a serious breach of trust must have occurred before a person can be convicted of embezzlement. The mere act of moving property without the owner's consent, or damaging it or using it, is not considered embezzlement. However, using it up, selling it, pledging it, giving it away, or holding it against the owner's will is held to be embezzlement.[50]

Although it is impossible to know how many embezzlement incidents occur annually, the FBI found that only 15,200 people were arrested for embezzlement in 1995—probably an extremely small percentage of all embezzlers. However, the number of people arrested for embezzlement has increased 22% since 1986, indicating that (1) more employees are willing to steal from their employers, (2) more employers are willing to report instances of embezzlement, or (3) law enforcement officials are more willing to prosecute embezzlers.

Burglary

At common law, the crime of *burglary* is defined as "the breaking and entering of a dwelling house of another in the nighttime with the intent to commit a felony within."[51] Burglary is considered a much more serious crime than larceny/theft, since it often involves entering another's home, a situation in which the threat of harm to occupants is great. Even though the home may be unoccupied at the time of the burglary, the potential for harm to the occupants is so significant that most state jurisdictions punish burglary as a felony.

The legal definition of burglary has undergone considerable change since its common-law origins. When first created by English judges during the late Middle Ages, laws against burglary were designed to protect people whose home might be set upon by wandering criminals. Including the phrase "breaking and entering" in the definition protected people from unwarranted intrusions; if an invited guest stole something, it would not be considered a burglary. Similarly, the requirement that the crime be committed at nighttime was added because evening was considered the time when honest people might fall prey to criminals.[52]

In more recent times, state jurisdictions have changed the legal requirements of burglary, and most have discarded the necessity of forced entry. Many now protect all structures and not just dwelling houses. A majority of states have removed the nighttime element from burglary definitions as well. It is quite common for states to enact laws creating different degrees of burglary. In this instance, the more serious and heavily punished crimes involve a nighttime forced entry into the home; the least serious involve a daytime entry into a nonresidential structure by an unarmed offender. Several gradations of the offense may be found between these extremes.

The Extent of Burglary

The FBI's definition of burglary is not restricted to burglary from a person's home; it includes any unlawful entry of a structure to commit theft or felony. Burglary is further categorized into three subclasses: forcible entry, unlawful entry where no force is used, and attempted forcible entry. According to the UCR, almost 2.5 million burglaries occurred in 1995. The number of burglaries had dropped by almost 18% since 1991. Most burglaries (66%) were of residences; the remainder were business related. Burglary victims suffer losses of over $3 billion annually.

The NCVS reports that about 4.8 million residential burglaries occurred in 1995. The difference between the UCR and NCVS is explained by the fact that little more than half of all burglary victims reported the incident to police. However, similar to the UCR, the NCVS indicates that the number of burglaries has been in decline, dropping from 5.8 million in 1992 to about 4.5 million in 1995.

According to the NCVS, those most likely to be burglarized are relatively poor Hispanic and African American families (annual income under $7,500). Owner-occupied and single-family residences have lower burglary rates than renter-occupied and multiple dwellings.

Careers in Burglary

Great variety exists within the ranks of burglars. Many are crude thieves who, with little finesse, will smash a window and enter a vacant home or structure with minimal preparation. However, because it involves planning, risk, and skill, burglary has been a crime long associated with professional thieves. To become a skilled practitioner of burglary, the would-be burglar must learn the craft at the side of an experienced burglar. For example, Francis Hoheimer, an experienced professional burglar, has described his education in the craft of burglary by Oklahoma Smith when the two were serving time in the Illinois State Penitentiary. Among Smith's recommendations are

> Never wear deodorant or shaving lotion; the strange scent might wake someone up. The more people there are in a house, the safer you are. If someone hears you moving around, they will think it's someone else. . . . If they call, answer in a muffled sleepy voice. . . . Never be afraid of dogs, they can sense fear. Most dogs are friendly; snap your finger, they come right to you . . .[53]

Despite his elaborate preparations, Hoheimer spent many years in confinement.

Burglars on the Job

Burglars must "master" the skills of their "trade," learning to spot environmental cues that "nonprofessionals" fail to notice.[54] In an important book, *Burglars on the Job*, Richard Wright and Scott Decker describe the working

Figure 12.3   How burglars approach their "job."

- Targets are often acquaintances.
- Drug dealers are a favored target because they have lots of cash and drugs, and victims aren't going to call police.
- Tipsters help the burglars select attractive targets.
- Some stake out residences to learn the occupants' routine.
- Many burglars approach a target masquerading as workmen, such as carpenters or housepainters.
- Most avoid occupied residences, considering them high-risk targets.
- Alarms and elaborate locks do not deter burglars but tell them there is something inside worth stealing.
- Some call the occupants from a pay phone; if the phone is still ringing when they arrive, they know no one is home.
- After entering a residence, their anxiety turns to calm as they first turn to the master bedroom for money and drugs. They also search kitchens, believing that some people keep money in the mayonnaise jar!
- Most work in groups, one serving as a lookout while the other(s) ransack the place.
- Some dispose of goods through a professional fence; others try to pawn the goods, exchange the goods for drugs, or sell them to friends and relatives. A few keep the stolen items for themselves, especially guns and jewelry.

Source: Richard Wright and Scott Decker, *Burglars on the Job: Streetlife and Residential Break-Ins* (Boston, Mass.: Northeastern University Press, 1994).

conditions of active burglars.[55] Most are motivated by the need for cash in order to get high; they want to enjoy the good life, "keeping the party going," without the need for working. While, as Figure 12.3 shows, they approach their "job" in a rational workmanlike fashion, their lives are controlled by their culture and environment. Unskilled and uneducated, urban burglars make the choices they do because they have had few conventional opportunities for success.

Connections

According to the rational choice approach discussed in Chapter 5, burglars make rational and calculated decisions before committing crimes. If circumstances and culture dictate their activities, can their decisions be considered a matter of choice?

THE GOOD BURGLAR.   Neal Shover has studied the careers of professional burglars and uncovered the existence of a particularly successful type—the **good burglar**.[56] This is a characterization applied by professional burglars to colleagues who have distinguished themselves as burglars. Characteristics of the good burglar include (1) technical competence, (2) maintenance of personal integrity, (3) specialization in burglary, (4) financial success at crime, and (5) ability to avoid prison sentences.

Shover found that to receive recognition as good burglars, novices must develop four key requirements of the trade. First, they must learn the many skills needed to commit lucrative burglaries. This process may include learning such techniques as how to gain entry into homes and apartment houses, select targets with high potential payoffs, choose items with a high resale value, properly open safes without damaging their contents, and use the proper equipment, including cutting torches, electric saws, explosives, and metal bars. Second, the good burglar must be able to team up to form a criminal gang. Choosing trustworthy companions is essential if the obstacles to completing a successful job—police, alarms, secure safes—are to be overcome. Third, the good burglar must have inside information. Without knowledge of what awaits them inside, burglars can spend a tremendous amount of time and effort on empty safes and jewelry boxes. Finally, the good burglar must cultivate fences or buyers for stolen wares. Once the burglar gains access to people who buy and sell stolen goods, he or she must also learn how to successfully sell these goods for a reasonable profit.

Shover has found that the process of becoming a professional burglar is similar to the process Sutherland described in his theory of differential association. According to Shover, a person becomes a good burglar through learning the techniques of the trade from older, more experienced burglars. During this process, the older burglar teaches the novice how to handle such requirements of the trade as dealing with defense attorneys, bail bond agents, and other agents of the justice system. Consequently, the opportunity to become a good burglar is not open to everyone. Apprentices must be known to have the appropriate character before they are taken under the wing of the "old pro." Usually, the opportunity to learn burglary comes as a reward for being a highly respected juvenile gang member, from knowing someone in the neighborhood who has made a living at burglary, or, more often, from having built a reputation for being solid while serving time in prison.

THE BURGLARY "CAREER LADDER."   Paul Cromwell, James Olson, and D'Aunn Wester Avary, who interviewed 30 active burglars in Texas, also found that burglars go through stages of career development.[57] They begin as young novices who learn the trade from older more experienced burglars, often siblings or relatives. Novices will continue to get this tutoring as long as they can develop

Despite the interest shown in both the careers of residential burglars and the female offender in general, relatively little is known about *female burglars.* Although most burglars apprehended by the police are male, about 9%, or 33,000, are females.

To address this issue, Scott Decker, Richard Wright, Allison Redfern Rooney, and Dietrich Smith interviewed 18 females, ranging in age from 15 to 51, who were actively engaged in residential burglary. For comparison, 87 male burglars were also interviewed.

Decker and his associates found that female burglars had offending patterns quite similar to those of males. In addition to burglary, both groups engaged in other thefts, such as shoplifting and assault. The major difference was that male burglars also engaged in auto theft, while females shunned this form of larceny.

Another difference was that while females always worked with a partner, about 39% of the males said they seldom worked with others. Males also began their offending careers at an earlier age than females. About half of all females had been involved in fewer than 20 burglaries, while only 28% of males reported as few as 20 lifetime burglaries. Considering they start earlier and commit more crimes, it is not surprising that males had a much greater chance of doing time (26%) than females (6%).

There were also many similarities between the two groups. A majority of both male and female burglars reported substance abuse problems, including cocaine, heroin, and marijuana use. About 47% of the females considered themselves addicts, and 72% said they drank alcohol before they committed crimes; males reported less addiction, drug use, and alcohol abuse than females.

Decker and his associated found that the female burglars could be divided into two groups, "accomplices" and "partners." Accomplices committed burglaries because they were caught up in circumstances beyond their control. They felt compelled or pressured to commit crimes because of a relationship with another, more dominant person, typically a boyfriend or husband. Accomplices got into crime because they lacked legitimate employment, were drug dependent, or had alcohol problems. Accomplices exercised little control over their crimes and relied on others for any planning and tactics. They commonly acted as a lookout or driver.

In contrast, partners, who made up two-thirds of the sample, were involved in planning and carrying out the crimes because they enjoyed both the reward and the excitement of burglary. In planning their crimes, partners displayed many of the characteristics of the rational criminal: They helped spot targets and planned entries. As one female burglar stated:

That's one reason why we got so many youngsters in jail today. I see this, so let's go make a hit. No, no, no. If they see this and it looks good, then it's going to be there for a while. So the point is, you have to case it and make sure you know everything. I want to know what time you go to work, the time the children go to school. I know there's no one coming home for lunch. So plan it with somebody else. We'll take the new dishwasher, washing machine, and this other stuff. We just put it in the truck. Do you know when people rent a truck, nobody ever pays that any attention? They think you're moving [but] only if you rent a truck. Now if you bring it out of there and put it in the car, that's a horse of another color.

Once the burglary began, partners carried out all forms of crime-related tasks, including gaining entry, searching the house, carrying loot outside, and disposing of the stolen merchandise.

In conclusion, most female burglars maintain roles and identities quite similar

---

their own markets (fences) for stolen goods. After their education is over, novices enter the journeyman stage, characterized by forays in search of lucrative targets and by careful planning; they develop reputations as experienced, reliable criminals. Finally, they become professional burglars when they have developed advanced skills and organizational abilities that give them the highest esteem among their peers; they plan and execute their crimes after careful deliberation.

The Texas burglars also displayed evidence of rational decision making. Most seemed to carefully evaluate potential costs and benefits before deciding to commit crime. There is evidence that burglars follow this pattern in their choice of burglary sites. Burglars show preference for corner houses because they are easily observed and offer the maximum number of escape routes. They look for houses that show evidence of long-term care and wealth. Although people may erect fences and other barriers to deter burglars, these devices may actually attract crime because they are viewed as protecting something worth stealing: If there were nothing valuable inside, why go through so much trouble to secure the premises?[58]

Cromwell, Olson, and Avary also found that many burglars had serious drug habits and that their criminal activity was in part aimed at supporting their substance abuse. The accompanying Close-Up describes the activities of "professional" and "occasional" female burglars.

REPEAT BURGLARY. To what extent do burglars strike the same victim more than once? Research suggests that burglars may in fact return to the "scene of the crime" in order to repeat their offenses. One reason is that many burgled items are deemed indispensable (such as televi-

to those of their male colleagues. While some gender-based differences are evident (males more often work alone; women almost always work with others), both male and female burglars actively plan crimes for many of the same reasons.

The Decker research is important because it shows that for the majority of both male and female burglars, criminal careers may be a function of economic need and role equality, a finding that supports a feminist view of crime. It also illustrates that repeat criminals use rational choice in planning their activities.

CRITICAL THINKING QUESTIONS
1. Does the fact that so many burglars, both male and female, drink and abuse drugs conflict with a rational choice approach to crime?
2. Why are male burglars more likely to be car thieves than females are? Decker and his associates speculate that one reason may be a "strong cultural tradition linking masculinity to driving and car ownership." Can this be so?

Source: Scott Decker, Richard Wright, Allison Redfern, and Dietrich Smith, "A Woman's Place Is in the Home: Females and Residential Burglary," *Justice Quarterly* 10 (1993): 143–163.

Dietrich Smith (seated), Scott Decker, Allison Redfern Rooney, and Richard Wright.

sions and VCRs), so it is safe to assume they will be quickly replaced.[59]

Graham Farrell, Coretta Phillips, and Ken Pease have articulated why burglars would most likely try to hit the same target more than once:

- It takes less effort to burgle a home or apartment known to be a suitable target than an unknown or unsuitable one.
- The burglar is already aware of the target's layout.
- The ease of entry of the target has probably not changed, and escape routes are known.
- The lack of protective measures and the absence of nosy and intrusive neighbors, which made the first burglary a success, have probably not changed.
- Goods were observed that could not be taken out the first time.[60]

Connections

Chapter 4 discussed repeat victimization. As you may recall, it is common for particular people and places to be the target of numerous predatory crimes.

Arson

Arson is the willful and malicious burning of a home, public building, vehicle, or commercial building. Arson is a young man's crime. FBI statistics for 1995 show that juveniles accounted for 52% of arson arrests; juveniles are arrested for a greater share of this crime than any other. This was a slight decline from the previous year when, for the first time, a majority of all arson arrests (55%) in the United States had been of juveniles. One-third of those

Throughout the 1990s there have been hundreds of mysterious burnings of African American churches in the South. It is as yet undetermined whether the fires are part of a coordinated plot or are individual acts of arson.

arrested for arson were under 15, and nearly 7% were younger than 10.

Net Bookmark

The fire and arson investigations web site provides information on: fire investigation information and services, fire causes, fire-related failure analysis, fraud investigations related to loss analysis, and site analysis and review. It also provides links to consumer and professional information regarding arson and other fire-related investigation services and methods.
http://www.mhv.net/~dfriedman/arson/welcome.html
#contactus

There are several motives for arson. Juveniles may get involved in starting fires for various reasons as they mature. Juvenile firesetters fall into three general groups.[61] The first is made up of children under 7 years of age. Generally, fires started by these children are the result of accidents or curiosity. In the second group are children ranging in age from 8 to 12. Although the firesetting of some of these children is motivated by curiosity or experimentation, a greater proportion of their firesetting represents underlying psychosocial conflicts. The third group comprises adolescents between the ages of 13 and 18. These youths tend to have a long history of undetected fire play and fire-starting behav-ior. Their current firesetting episodes are usually either the result of psychosocial conflict and turmoil or intentional criminal behavior.

Wayne Wooden studied juvenile arsonists and found that they can be classified in one of four categories:

1. *The "playing with matches" firesetter.* This is the youngest fire starter, usually between the ages of 4 and 9, who set fires because parents are careless with matches and lighters. Proper instruction on fire safety can help prevent fires set by these young children.

2. *The "crying for help" firesetter.* This type of firesetter is a 7- to 13-year-old who turns to fire to reduce stress caused by family conflict, divorce, death, or abuse. These youngsters have difficulty expressing their feelings of sorrow, rage, or anger and turn to fire as a means of relieving stress or getting back at their antagonists.

3. *The "delinquent" firesetter.* Some youths set fire to school property or surrounding areas to retaliate for some slight experienced at school. These kids may break into the school to vandalize property with friends and later set a fire to cover up their activities.

4. *The "severely disturbed" firesetter.* This youngster is obsessed with fires and often dreams about them in "vibrant colors." This is the most disturbed type of juvenile firesetter and the one most likely to set numerous fires with the potential for death and damage.[62]

Adult arson may also be a function of severe emotional turmoil. Some psychologists view fire starting as a function of a disturbed personality; arson should therefore be viewed as a mental health problem and not a criminal act.[63]

It is alleged that arsonists often experience sexual pleasure from starting fires and then observing their destructive effects. While some arsonists may be sexually aroused by their activities, there is little evidence that most arsonists are psychosexually motivated.[64] It is equally likely that fires are started by angry people looking for revenge against property owners or by teenagers out to vandalize property.

Other arsons are set by "professional" arsonists who engage in **arson for profit.** Another form is **arson fraud,** which involves a business owner burning his or her property, or hiring someone to do it, to escape financial problems.[65] Over the years, investigators have found that businesspeople are willing to become involved in arson to collect fire insurance or for various other reasons, including but not limited to

- Obtaining money during a period of financial crisis
- Getting rid of outdated or slow-moving inventory
- Destroying outmoded machines and technology
- Paying off legal and illegal debt
- Relocating or remodeling a business, as when a theme restaurant has not been accepted by customers
- Taking advantage of government funds available for redevelopment
- Applying for government building money, pocketing it without making repairs, and then claiming that fire destroyed the "rehabilitated" building
- Planning bankruptcies to eliminate debts, after the merchandise supposedly destroyed was secretly sold before the fire
- Eliminating business competition by burning out rivals
- Using extortion schemes that demand that victims pay up or the rest of their holdings will be burned
- Solving labor-management problems; arson may be committed by a disgruntled employee
- Concealing another crime, such as embezzlement

Some recent technological advances may help prove that many alleged arsons were actually accidental fires. There is now evidence of an effect called **flashover** in which during the course of an ordinary fire, heat and gas at the ceiling of a room can reach 2,000 degrees. This causes clothes and furniture to burst into flame, duplicating the effects of arsonists' gasoline or explosives. It is possible that many suspected arsons are actually the result of flashover.[66]

During the past decade, hundreds of jurisdictions across the nation have established programs to address the growing concern about juvenile firesetting. Housed primarily within the fire service, these programs are designed to identify, evaluate, and treat the juvenile firesetter to prevent the recurrence of firesetting.

Summary

Economic crimes are designed to bring financial reward to the offender. The majority of economic crimes are committed by opportunistic amateurs. However, economic crime has also attracted professional criminals. Professionals earn the bulk of their income from crime, view themselves as criminals, and have skills that aid them in their lawbreaking. Edwin Sutherland's classic book *The Professional Thief* is perhaps the most famous portrayal of professional crime. According to Sutherland and his informant, Chic Conwell, professionals live by their wits and never resort to violence. A good example of the professional criminal is the fence who buys and sells stolen merchandise. There are also occasional thieves whose skill level and commitment fall below the professional level.

Common theft offenses include larceny, fraud, embezzlement, and burglary. These are common-law crimes, created by English judges to meet social needs. Larceny involves taking the legal possessions of another. Petty larceny is theft of amounts typically under $100; grand larceny, of amounts usually over $100. The crime of false pretenses, or fraud, is similar to larceny because it involves the theft of goods or money, but it differs because the criminal tricks victims into voluntarily giving up their possessions. Embezzlement is another larceny crime. It involves people taking something that was temporarily entrusted to them, such as bank tellers taking money out of the cash drawer and keeping it for themselves. Most states have codified these common-law crimes in their legal codes. Newer larceny crimes have also been defined to keep abreast of changing social conditions: passing bad checks, stealing or illegally using credit cards, shoplifting, and stealing autos.

Burglary, a more serious theft offense, was defined in the common law as the "breaking and entering of a dwelling house of another in the nighttime with the intent to commit a felony within." Today, most states have modified their definitions of burglary to include theft from any structure at any time of day. Because burglary involves planning and risk, it attracts professional thieves. The most competent are known as good burglars. Good burglars have technical competence and personal integrity, specialize in burglary, are financially successful, and avoid prison sentences.

Arson is another serious property crime. Although most arsonists are teenage vandals, there are professional arsonists who specialize in burning commercial buildings for profit.

Key Terms

economic crimes	occasional criminals
fence	situational inducement
street crimes	professional criminals
burglary	larceny
flash houses	constructive possession

boosters	confidence games
heels	pigeon drop
snitches	embezzlement
naive check forgers	good burglar
closure	arson
systematic forgers	arson for profit
carjacking	arson fraud
false pretenses	flashover
fraud	

Notes

1. Andrew McCall, *The Medieval Underworld* (London: Hamish Hamilton, 1979), p. 86.

2. Ibid., p. 104.

3. J. J. Tobias, *Crime and Police in England, 1700–1900* (London: Gill and Macmillan, 1979).

4. Ibid., p. 9.

5. Marilyn Walsh, *The Fence* (Westport, Conn.: Greenwood Press, 1977), pp. 18–25.

6. John Hepburn, "Occasional Criminals," in *Major Forms of Crime,* ed. Robert Meier (Beverly Hills, Calif.: Sage, 1984), pp. 73–94.

7. James Inciardi, "Professional Crime," in *Major Forms of Crime,* p. 223.

8. Harry King and William Chambliss, *Box Man: A Professional Thief's Journal* (New York: Harper & Row, 1972), p. 24.

9. Edwin Sutherland, "White-Collar Criminality," *American Sociological Review* 5 (1940): 2–10.

10. Gilbert Geis, "Avocational Crime," in *Handbook of Criminology,* ed. D. Glazer (Chicago: Rand McNally, 1974), p. 284.

11. Edwin Sutherland and Chic Conwell, *The Professional Thief* (Chicago: University of Chicago Press, 1937).

12. Ibid., pp. 197–198.

13. Ibid., p. 212.

14. See, for example, Edwin Lemert, "The Behavior of the Systematic Check Forger," *Social Problems* 6 (1958): 141–148.

15. Cited in Walsh, *The Fence,* p. 1.

16. Carl Klockars, *The Professional Fence* (New York: Free Press, 1976); Darrell Steffensmeier, *The Fence: In the Shadow of Two Worlds* (Totowa, N.J.: Rowman and Littlefield, 1986); Walsh, *The Fence,* pp. 25–28.

17. Walsh, *The Fence,* p. 34.

18. Paul Cromwell, James Olson, and D'Aunn Avary, "Who Buys Stolen Property? A New Look at Criminal Receiving," *Journal of Crime and Justice* 16 (1993): 75–95.

19. This section depends heavily on a classic book: Wayne LaFave and Austin Scott, *Handbook on Criminal Law* (St. Paul: West Publishing, 1972).

20. Ibid., p. 622.

21. FBI, *Crime in the United States, 1995* (Washington, D.C.: U.S. Government Printing Office, 1996), p. 45.

22. D. Hartmann, D. Gelfand, B. Page, and P. Walder, "Rates of Bystander Observation and Reporting of Contrived Shoplifting Incidents," *Criminology* 10 (1972): 248.

23. Mary Owen Cameron, *The Booster and the Snitch* (New York: Free Press, 1964).

24. Ibid., p. 57.

25. Lawrence Cohen and Rodney Stark, "Discriminatory Labeling and the Five-Finger Discount: An Empirical Analysis of Differential Shoplifting Dispositions," *Journal of Research on Crime and Delinquency* 11 (1974): 25–35.

26. Lloyd Klemke, "Does Apprehension for Shoplifting Amplify or Terminate Shoplifting Activity?" *Law and Society Review* 12 (1978): 390–403.

27. Hartmann et al., "Rates of Bystander Observation and Reporting," p. 267.

28. Erhard Blankenburg, "The Selectivity of Legal Sanctions: An Empirical Investigation of Shoplifting," *Law and Society Review* 11 (1976): 109–129.

29. Michael Hindelang, "Decisions of Shoplifting Victims to Invoke the Criminal Justice Process," *Social Problems* 21 (1974): 580–595.

30. George Keckeisen, *Retail Security versus the Shoplifter* (Springfield, Ill.: Charles C Thomas, 1993), pp. 31–32.

31. Melissa Davis, Richard Lundman, and Ramiro Martinez, Jr., "Private Corporate Justice: Store Police, Shoplifters, and Civil Recovery," *Social Problems* 38 (1991): 395–408.

32. Ibid., pp. 405–406.

33. Edwin Lemert, "An Isolation and Closure Theory of Naive Check Forgery," *Journal of Criminal Law, Criminology and Police Science* 44 (1953): 297–298.

34. "Credit Card Fraud Toll 1 Billion," *Omaha World Herald,* 16 March 1982, p. 1.

35. Ibid.

36. La Fave and Scott, *Handbook on Criminal Law,* p. 672.

37. Charles McCaghy, Peggy Giordano, and Trudy Knicely Henson, "Auto Theft," *Criminology* 15 (1977): 367–381.

38. Donald Gibbons, *Society, Crime and Criminal Careers* (Englewood Cliffs, N.J.: Prentice-Hall, 1977), p. 310.

39. Kim Hazelbaker, "Insurance Industry Analyses and the Prevention of Motor Vehicle Theft," *Business and Crime Prevention,* ed. Marcus Felson and Ronald Clarke (Monsey, N.Y.: Criminal Justice Press, 1997), pp. 283–293.

40. Ibid., p. 287.

41. Michael Rand, *Carjacking* (Washington, D.C.: Bureau of Justice Statistics, 1994), p. 1.

42. Ronald Clarke and Patricia Harris, "Auto Theft and Its Prevention," in *Crime and Justice, An Annual Review,* ed. N. Morris and M. Tonry (Chicago: Chicago University Press, 1992).

43. Hazelbaker, "Insurance Industry Analyses and the Prevention of Motor Vehicle Theft," p. 289.

44. La Fave and Scott, *Handbook on Criminal Law,* p. 655.

45. 30 Geo. III, C.24 (1975).

46. As described in Charles McCaghy, *Deviant Behavior* (New York: Macmillan, 1976), pp. 230–231.

47. Susan Gembrowski and and Tim Dahlberg, "Over 100 Here Indicted After Telemarketing Fraud Probe Around the U.S.," *San Diego Daily Transcript* Online, 8 Dec. 1995, http://www.sddt.com/files/library/95headlines/DN95_12_08/DN95_12_08_02.html

48. Jerome Hall, *Theft, Law and Society* (Indianapolis: Bobbs-Merrill, 1952), p. 36.

49. La Fave and Scott, *Handbook on Criminal Law,* p. 644.

50. Ibid., p. 649.

51. La Fave and Scott, *Handbook on Criminal Law,* p. 708.

52. E. Blackstone, *Commentaries on the Laws of England* (London: 1769), p. 224.

53. Frank Hoheimer, *The Home Invaders: Confessions of a Cat Burglar* (Chicago: Chicago Review, 1975).

54. Richard Wright, Robert Logie, and Scott Decker, "Criminal Expertise and Offender Decision Making: An Experimental Study of the Target Selection Process in Residential Burglary," *Journal of Research in Crime and Delinquency* 32 (1995): 39–53.

55. Richard Wright and Scott Decker, *Burglars on the Job: Streetlife and Residential Break-Ins* (Boston, Mass.: Northeastern University Press, 1994).

56. See, generally, Neal Shover, "Structures and Careers in Burglary," *Journal of Criminal Law, Criminology and Police Science* 63 (1972): 540–549.

57. Paul Cromwell, James Olson, and D'Aunn Wester Avary, *Breaking and Entering: An Ethnographic Analysis of Burglary* (Newbury Park, Calif.: Sage, 1991), pp. 48–51.

58. See M. Taylor and C. Nee, "The Role of Cues in Simulated Residential Burglary: A Preliminary Investigation," *British Journal of Criminology* 28 (1988): 398–401; Julia MacDonald and Robert Gifford, "Territorial Cues and Defensible Space Theory: The Burglar's Point of View," *Journal of Environmental Psychology* 9 (1989): 193–205.

59. Roger Litton, "Crime Prevention and the Insurance Industry," in *Business and Crime Prevention,* ed. Marcus Felson and Ronald Clarke (Monsey, N.Y.: Criminal Justice Press, 1997), p. 162.

60. Graham Farrell, Coretta Phillips, and Ken Pease, "Like Taking Candy, Why Does Repeat Victimization Occur?" *British Journal of Criminology* 35 (1995): 384–399.

61. Eileen M. Garry, *Juvenile Firesetting and Arson* (Washington, D.C.: Office of Juvenile Justice and Delinquency Prevention 1997).

62. Wayne Wooden, "Juvenile Firesetters in Cross-Cultural Perspective: How Should Society Respond," in *Official Responses to Problem Juveniles: Some International Reflections,* ed. James Hackler (Onati, Spain: Onati Publications, 1991), pp. 339–348.

63. Nancy Webb, George Sakheim, Luz Towns-Miranda, and Charles Wagner, "Collaborative Treatment of Juvenile Firestarters: Assessment and Outreach," *American Journal of Orthopsychiatry* 60 (1990): 305–310.

64. Vernon Quinsey, Terry Chaplin, and Douglas Unfold, "Arsonists and Sexual Arousal to Fire Setting: Correlations Unsupported," *Journal of Behavior Therapy and Experimental Psychiatry* 20 (1989): 203–209.

65. Leigh Edward Somers, *Economic Crimes* (New York: Clark Boardman, 1984), pp. 158–168.

66. Michael Rogers, "The Fire Next Time," *Newsweek,* 26 November 1990, p. 63.

Chapter 13
White-Collar and Organized Crime

he second component of economic crime involves illegal business activity. In this chapter, we divide these crimes of illicit entrepreneurship into two distinct categories: **white-collar crime** and **organized crime.** The former involves *illegal* activities of people and institutions whose acknowledged purpose is profit and gain through *legitimate* business transactions. The second category, organized crime, involves *illegal* activities of people and organizations whose acknowledged purpose is profit and gain through *illegitimate* business enterprise. Organized crime and white-collar crime are linked here because, as criminologist Dwight Smith argues, **enterprise** and not crime is the governing characteristic of both phenomena:

> White-collar crime is not simply a dysfunctional aberration. Organized crime is not something ominously alien to the American economic system. Both are made criminal by laws declaring that certain ways of doing business, or certain products of business, are illegal. In other words, criminality is not an inherent characteristic either of certain persons or of certain business activities but rather, an externally imposed evaluation of alternative modes of behavior and action.[1]

According to Smith, business enterprise can be viewed as flowing through a spectrum of acts ranging from the most "saintly" to the most "sinful."[2] Although "sinful" organizational practices may be desirable to many consumers (for example, the sale of narcotics) or an efficient way of doing business (such as the dumping of hazardous wastes), society has seen fit to regulate or outlaw these behaviors. Organized crime and the crimes of business are the results of a process by which "political, value-based constraints are based on economic activity."[3]

White-collar and organized crime share some striking similarities. Mark Haller has coined the phrase *illegal enterprise crimes* to signify the sale of illegal goods and services to customers who know they are illegal. Haller's analysis also shows the overlap between criminal and business enterprise. For example, he compares the Mafia crime family to a chamber of commerce: It is an association of "businesspeople" who join to further their business careers. Joining a crime syndicate allows one to cultivate contacts and be in a position to take advantage of "good deals" offered by more experienced players. The criminal group settles disputes between members, who, after all, cannot take their problems to court.[4]

Both these organizational crimes taint and corrupt the free market system; they involve all phases of illegal entrepreneurial activity. Organized crime involves individuals or groups whose marketing techniques (threat, extortion, smuggling) and product lines (drugs, sex, gambling, loan-sharking) have been outlawed. White-collar crimes include the use of illegal business practices (embezzlement, price fixing, bribery, and so on) to merchandise what are ordinarily legitimate commercial products.

Surprising to some, both forms of crime can involve violence. While the use of force and coercion by organized crime members has been popularized in the media and therefore comes as no shock, that white-collar crimes may result in the infliction of pain and suffering seems more astonishing. Yet experts claim that 200,000 or more occupational deaths occur each year and that "corporate violence" annually kills and injures more people than all street crimes combined.[5]

It is also possible to link organized and white-collar crime because some criminal enterprises involve both forms of activity. Organized criminals may seek out legitimate enterprises to launder money, diversify their sources of income, increase their power and influence, and gain and enhance respectability.[6] Otherwise "legitimate" businesspeople may turn to organized criminals to help them with problems of an economic nature (such as breaking up a strike or dumping hazardous waste products), stifle or threaten competition, and increase their influence. The distinction between organized crime and white-collar criminals may often become blurred.[7]

Some forms of white-collar crime may be more like organized crime than others.[8] While some corporate executives "cheat" to improve their company's position in the business world, others are motivated purely for personal gain. It is this latter group, people who engage in ongoing criminal conspiracies for their own profit, that most resembles organized crime.[9]

White-Collar Crime

In the late 1930s, the distinguished criminologist Edwin Sutherland first used the phrase *white-collar crime* to describe the criminal activities of the rich and powerful. He defined white-collar crime as "a crime committed by a person of respectability and high social status in the course of his occupation."[10]

As Sutherland saw it, white-collar crime involved conspiracies by members of the wealthy classes to use their position in commerce and industry for personal gain without regard to the law. All too often, these actions were handled by civil courts, since injured parties were more concerned with recovering their losses than seeing the offenders punished criminally. Consequently, Sutherland believed, the great majority of white-collar criminals did not become the subject of criminological study. Yet their crimes were costly: The financial cost of white-collar crime is probably several times as great as that of all the crimes that are customarily regarded as the "crime problem." The financial loss from white-collar crime, great as it is, seems less important than the damage to social relations. White-collar crimes violate trust and therefore create distrust, thereby lowering social morale and producing disorganization on a large scale. Other crimes produce relatively little effect on social institutions or social organization.[11]

Redefining White-Collar Crime

Although Sutherland's work is considered a milestone in criminological history, his focus was on corporate criminality.

Since then there has been constant disagreement over the precise definition of white-collar crime. Sutherland's major concern was the crimes of the rich and powerful. Modern criminologists have broadened their definition of white-collar crime to include a wider variety of situations.[12] More than 20 years ago Herbert Edelhertz provided a widely cited reformulation of white-collar crime, describing it as "an illegal act or series of illegal acts committed by nonphysical means and by concealment or guile to obtain money or property or to avoid the payment or loss of money or property or to obtain business or personal advantage."[13] This definition is so broad that it encompasses almost any type of nonviolent property crime, even crimes with little connection to business enterprise.[14] In contrast, a recent symposium of experts on white collar-crime formulated the following definition:

> White-collar crime consists of the illegal or unethical acts that violate fiduciary responsibility or public trust, committed by an individual of organization, usually during the course of legitimate occupational activity by persons of high or respectable social status for personal or organizational gain.[15]

While also expanding Sutherland's original concepts, this definition recognizes his focus on crimes of the upper class by limiting white-collar crimes to people with "respectable social status."

Today's definition of white-collar crime usually includes all individuals who use the marketplace for their criminal activity. This definition encompasses middle-income Americans as well as corporate titans.[16] As criminologist Gilbert Geis put it, "White-collar crimes can be committed by persons in all social classes."[17]

Included within recent views of white-collar crime are such "middle-class" acts as income tax evasion, credit card fraud, and bankruptcy fraud. Other white-collar criminals use their positions of trust in business or government to commit crimes. Their activities might include pilfering, soliciting bribes or kickbacks, and embezzlement. Some white-collar criminals set up businesses for the sole purpose of victimizing the general public. They engage in land swindles (for example, representing swamps as choice building sites), securities thefts, medical or health frauds, and so on. In addition to acting as individuals, some white-collar criminals become involved in criminal conspiracies designed to improve the market share or profitability of their corporations. This type of white-collar crime, which includes antitrust violations, price fixing and false advertising, is also known as **corporate crime.**

Ronald Kramer and Raymond Michalowski have also identified the concept of *state-corporate crime:* illegal or socially injurious actions resulting from cooperation between governmental and corporate institutions.[18] Kramer and Michalowski charge that the explosion of the *Challenger* space shuttle on January 28, 1986 was the result of a state-corporate crime involving the cooperative and criminally negligent actions of the National Aeronautics and Space Administration and Morton Thiokol, Inc., the shuttle builder.

Illegal dumping of pollutants into the water supply is a particularly noxious form of white-collar crime. Here, environmental activist Robert Kennedy, Jr., traces the source of a pollutant at a hospital waste dump site spill.

The White-Collar Crime Problem

It is difficult to estimate the extent and influence of white-collar crime on victims, because all too often those who suffer the consequences of white-collar crime are ignored by victimologists.[19] Some experts place its total monetary value in the hundreds of billions of dollars, far outstripping the expense of any other type of crime. For example, the loss due to employee theft from businesses alone amounts to $90 billion per year.[20] Beyond their monetary costs, white-collar crimes often involve damage to property and loss of human life. Violations of safety standards, pollution of the environment, and industrial accidents due to negligence can be classified as corporate violence. Laura Schrager and James Short suggest that corporate crime annually results in 20 million serious injuries, including 110,000 people who become permanently disabled, and 30,000 deaths.[21] They say that "the potential impact ranges from acute environmental catastrophes such as the collapse of a dam to the chronic effects of diseases resulting from industrial pollution."[22]

In a similar vein, sociologist Gilbert Geis charges that white-collar crime is actually likely to be much more serious than street crime:

> It destroys confidence, saps the integrity of commercial life and has the potential for devastating destruction. Think of the possible results if nuclear regulatory rules are flouted or if toxic wastes are dumped into a community's drinking water supply.[23]

The public has begun to recognize the seriousness of white-collar crimes and demand that they be controlled. A national survey of crime seriousness found that people saw white-collar crimes—such as a county judge taking a bribe to give a light sentence, a doctor cheating on Medicare claims, and a factory owner knowingly disposing of waste in a way that pollutes the water supply—as being more serious than a person stabbing another with a knife or stealing property worth $10,000 from outside a building.[24] While their acts are serious, white-collar criminals generally face monetary fines and relatively short sentences; judges and prosecutors are sometimes reluctant to incarcerate offenders who do not fit the image of "common criminals."

International White-Collar Crime

White-collar crime is not a uniquely American phenomenon. It occurs in other countries as well, as in the form of corruption of office by government agents. In China, cases of corruption account for a high percentage of all cases of economic crime. Despite the fact that the penalty for corruption is death, most of the people involved in corruption and bribery are state personnel, including some high-ranking officials.[25] In the late 1980s there were no more than 10,000 corruption cases each year; by 1996 there were six times as many. One reason may be the increase in government-sponsored businesses, which now number more than 500,000 and are growing exponentially.[26]

China is not alone in experiencing organizational crimes. In Thailand crime and corruption is skyrocketing; top executives of the Bangkok Bank of Commerce are believed to have absconded with billions in depositors' money.[27] American companies are also the targets of white-collar criminals. Agents have been inserted into U.S. companies abroad to steal trade secrets, confidential procedures, and "intellectual property" such as computer programs and technology. The cost is somewhere between a conservative $50 billion and an astounding $240 billion a year.[28]

Nikos Passas and David Nelken have studied offenses perpetrated against the European Community (EC), an organization set up to bring regularity to the economic activities of its member states, which include England, France, Germany, and most other Western European nations.[29] Passas and Nelken group the crimes into four categories:

1. *Corporate crime,* whereby legitimate companies or organizations, in the course of their usual business, occasionally cheat the EC. A strongly competitive environment may indirectly foster corporate irregularities. This environment may also be created by the illegal activities of competitors, thus putting pressure on those engaging in legal operations to consider resorting to similar illegalities.

2. *Government crime,* which includes illegal acts committed by government officials or with their knowledge and support, as well as those that lead to cover-ups of other persons' crimes. This type is somewhere between corporate crime and occupational crime: it is not perpetrated for one's (direct) personal benefit or monetary gain but for one's government and political party, the country, or the national interest.

3. *Occupational crime,* which involves people making extra money by bending or breaking the rules. While they may occasionally commit a fraud, their activities are mainly legal. Conditions under which they might be more likely to engage in such activities include financial straits or other business-related problems, which they try to solve by deviating from the rules.

4. *Organized/professional crime,* which involves people or groups of people whose primary source of income is illegal. They set out to commit frauds; they systematically look for possibilities of making money and profit illicitly. Since EC legislation provides such opportunities and loopholes, and since control systems are less than uniform and efficient throughout the EC, there is no reason that criminal enterprises would not enter this market.[30]

Crimes within these categories amount to billions in losses each year. For example, fraud in the agricultural sector, which ranges from evasion of taxes and deceitful claims to phantom operations and false or forged documentation, may amount to $8 billion per year.[31]

Components of White-Collar Crime

As noted, white-collar crimes today represent a range of behaviors involving individuals acting alone and within the context of a business structure. The victims of white-collar crime can be the general public, the organization that employs the offender, or a competing organization. Numerous attempts have been made to create subcategories or typologies of white-collar criminality. One of the best known was presented by Marshall Clinard and Richard Quinney, who divide white-collar crime into occupational and corporate categories. Occupational categories include offenses committed by individuals in the course of their occupation and by employees against their employers. The second category, corporate crime, is "the offenses committed by corporate officials for the corporation and the offenses of the corporation itself."[32] While this definition recognizes the dual nature of white-collar crime, it fails to take into account all facets; for example, it doesn't cover a public official selling undeserved privileges to the public.

Several more recent efforts have attempted to account for this diversity. For example, Herbert Edelhertz divides white-collar criminality into four distinct categories:

1. *Ad-hoc violations.* Committed episodically for personal profit; for example, welfare fraud or tax cheating.

2. *Abuses of trust.* Committed by a person in a place of trust in an organization against the organization; for example, embezzlement, bribery, or taking kickbacks.

3. *Collateral business crimes.* Committed by organizations to further their business interests; for example, antitrust violations, the use of false weights and measures, or the concealment of environmental crimes.

4. *Con games.* Committed for the sole purpose of cheating clients; for example, fraudulent land sales, sales of bogus securities, or sales of questionable tax shelters.[33]

Types of White-Collar Crime

Edelhertz's typology captures the diverse nature of white-collar criminality and illustrates how both individuals and institutions can be the victims and offenders of a white-collar crime. This text adapts a typology created by criminologist Mark Moore to organize the analysis of white-collar crime.[34] Moore's typology comprises seven elements, ranging from an individual using a business enterprise to commit theft-related crimes, to an individual using his or her place within a business enterprise for illegal gain, to business enterprises collectively engaging in illegitimate activity. While no single typology may be sufficient to encompass the complex array of acts that the term usually denotes, the analysis of white-collar crime here is meant to be so broad and inclusive that it contains the areas commonly considered important for criminological study.[35]

Moore's seven categories of white-collar crime are (1) stings and swindles, (2) chiseling, (3) individual exploitation of institutional position, (4) influence peddling and bribery, (5) embezzlement and employee fraud, (6) client frauds, and (7) corporate crime.

Stings and Swindles

The first category of white-collar crime is **swindling,** or stealing through deception by individuals who have no continuing institutional or business position and whose entire purpose is to bilk people out of their money. Offenses in this category range from door-to-door sale of faulty merchandise to the passing of millions of dollars in counterfeit stock certificates to established brokerage firms. If caught, white-collar swindlers are usually charged with common-law crimes, such as embezzlement or fraud.

> **Connections**
>
> In Chapter 12 the crime of fraud was discussed in the context of individual-level crimes that involve con games. Although similar, swindles here involve organizations that are devoted to fleecing the public.

FINANCIAL SWINDLES. Although swindlers are often considered petty thieves, swindles can run into millions of dollars. One of the largest to date involved the Equity Funding Corporation of America, whose officers bilked the public out of an estimated $2 billion in 1973. The directors of this firm, a life insurance company, claimed to have 90,000 policyholders. However, more than 60,000 of them existed as fictitious entries in the company's computer banks. Equity sold ownership and management of these bogus policies to reinsurance companies, and corporate officers pocketed the profit.[36]

The collapse of the Bank of Credit and Commerce International (BCCI) is another swindle that has cost depositors billions of dollars. BCCI was the world's seventh largest private bank, with assets of about $23 billion. Investigators believe that bank officials made billions in loans to confederates who had no intention of repaying them; BCCI officers also used false accounting methods to defraud depositors. Its officers helped clients, such as Colombian drug cartel leaders and dictators Saddam Hussein and Ferdinand Marcos, launder money, finance terrorist organizations, and smuggle illegal arms. U.S. Drug Enforcement Administration officials were able to compile a list of 379 cases in which BCCI laundered money for narcotics traffickers.[37] After the bank was shut down, hundreds of millions of dollars were spent to pay auditors to liquidate the banks holdings. For example, English liquidators alone were paid $360 million in fees between 1991 and 1994.[38]

Despite the notoriety of the Equity Funding and BCCI cases, investors continue to bite at bogus investment schemes promising quick riches.

RELIGIOUS SWINDLES. One of the most cold-blooded swindles is an investment scam that uses religious affiliations to steal from trusting investors. In the best-known case, TV evangelist Jim Bakker was convicted of defrauding followers of $3.7 million when he oversold lodging guarantees, called "lifetime partnerships," at his Heritage USA religious retreat. The jury found that Bakker had diverted ministry funds for personal use while knowing that his PTL ministry was in financial trouble. He bought vacation homes in California and Florida, a houseboat, expensive cars (including a Rolls-Royce), and unusual luxuries, such as an air-conditioned dog house. Bakker had sold hotel rooms to 153,000 people yet built only 258 rooms to accommodate them.[39] Bakker was sentenced to 45 years in prison, a harsh punishment that was later reduced on appeal (Bakker was released from prison in 1996).

In the best-known case involving a religious swindle, TV evangelist Jim Bakker was convicted of defrauding followers of $3.7 million when he oversold lodging guarantees, called "lifetime partnerships," at his Heritage USA religious retreat.

The Bakker case is not unique. The North American Securities Administrators Association estimates that swindlers using fake religious identities bilk thousands of people out of $100 million per year.[40] Swindlers take in worshippers of all persuasions: Jews, Baptists, Lutherans, Catholics, Mormons, and Greek Orthodox have all fallen prey to religious swindles. How do religious swindlers operate? Many join close-knit churches and establish a position of trust that enables them to operate without the normal investor skepticism. Some use religious television and radio shows to sell their product. Others place verses from the scriptures on their promotional literature to comfort hesitant investors. Religious swindles are tough to guard against because they are promoted in the same manner as legitimate religious fund-raising efforts and rely on the faithfuls' trust in those who devote themselves to doing charitable work.

Chiseling

Chiseling, the second category of white-collar crime, refers to cheating an organization, its consumers, or both on a regular basis. Chiselers may be individuals looking to make quick profits in their own businesses or employees of large organizations who decide to cheat on obligations to customers or clients by doing something contrary to either the law or company policy. Chiseling may involve charging for bogus auto repairs, cheating customers on home repairs, *short-weighting* (intentionally tampering with the accuracy of scales used to weigh products) in supermarkets or dairies, or fraudulently selling securities at inflated prices. It may even involve illegal use of information about company policies that have not been disclosed to the public. The secret information can be sold to speculators or used to make money in the stock market. Use of the information is in violation of the obligation to keep company policy secret.

Corporations can engage in large-scale chiseling when they misrepresent products or alter their content. The Beech-Nut Nutrition Corporation paid a $2 million fine for illegally selling a product labeled "apple juice" that was nothing more than sweetened water. Despite enforcement efforts, it is estimated that 10% of all fruit juices sold in the United States use illegal additives.[41]

PROFESSIONAL CHISELING. It is not uncommon for professionals to use their positions to chisel clients. Pharmacists have been known to alter prescriptions or substitute low-cost generic drugs for more expensive name brands. One study found that pharmacists who were business oriented—and therefore stressed merchandising, inventory turnover, and the pursuit of profit at the expense of professional ethics—were the ones most inclined to chisel customers.[42]

The legal profession has also come under fire because of the unscrupulous behavior of some of its members. In the 1970s the Watergate hearings, which revealed the unethical behavior of high-ranking government attorneys, prompted the American Bar Association to require that all law students take a course in legal ethics. This action is needed, since lawyers chisel clients out of millions of dollars each year in such schemes as forging signatures on clients' compensation checks and tapping escrow accounts and other funds for personal investments. One New York lawyer went so far as to slip the name of an imaginary heiress into a client's will and then impersonate the heiress to collect the inheritance.[43] Special funds have been set up by state governments and bar associations to reimburse chiseled clients.[44]

SECURITIES FRAUD. Chiseling can also take place in the commodity and stock markets. On an individual level, the **churning** of a client's account by an unscrupulous stockbroker involves repeated, excessive, and unnecessary buying and selling of stock with either the intent to defraud the client or in willful disregard of the client's investment interest.[45] In 1989 the federal government's long-term probe of commodity futures trading on the Chicago Board of Trade resulted in many prominent brokers being indicted under racketeering and other statutes.[46] The brokers were alleged to have engaged in such practices as prearranged trading in which two or more brokers agree to buy and sell commodity futures among themselves without offering the orders to other brokers for competitive bidding; "front running," in which brokers place personal orders ahead of a large customer's order to profit from the market effects of the trade; and "bucketing," or skimming customer trading profits.[47]

Another form of securities fraud involves using one's position of trust to profit from inside business information. The information can then be used to buy and sell securities, giving the trader an unfair advantage over the general public, which lacks this inside information. Another twist on the exploitation of a business position involves using deceptive practices to buy and sell shares in publicly traded companies.

The federal securities laws that control trading in public companies can be found in a number of different statutes, but the two primary sources are the Securities Act of 1933 and the Securities Exchange Act of 1934. These acts prohibit the use of manipulative or deceptive devices, such as mail and wire fraud, making false statements in order to increase market share, conspiracy, and similar acts of unfair market practices. The federal watchdog agency, the Securities and Exchange Commission (SEC), has within its code Rule 10b-5, which articulates general antifraud provisions for securities trading:

> It shall be unlawful for any person directly or indirectly, by the use of any means or instrumentality of interstate commerce, or of the mails or of any facility of any national securities exchange,
>   (a) To employ any device, scheme, or artifice to defraud,
>   (b) To make any untrue statement of a material fact or to omit to state a material fact necessary in order to make the statements made, in light of the circumstances under which they were made, not misleading, or
>   (c) To engage in any act, practice, or course of business which operates or would operate as a fraud or deceit upon any person, in connection with the purchase of sale of any security.[48]

Securities fraud can occur in a variety of situations. For example, as originally conceived, it was illegal for a corporate employee with direct knowledge of market-sensitive information to use that information for his or her own benefit—for example, buying stock in a company they have learned will be taken over by the larger concern for whom they are employed. In recent years, the definition of **insider trading** has been expanded by federal courts to include employees of financial institutions, such as law or banking firms, who misappropriate confidential information on pending corporate actions to purchase stock or give the information to a third party so that party may buy shares in the company. Courts have ruled that such actions are deceptive and in violation of security trading codes.

In one celebrated case, R. Foster Winans, the writer of the *Wall Street Journal*'s influential "Heard on the Street" column, was convicted on misappropriation of information charges after he wrote favorably about stocks purchased previously by a co-conspirator and then sold for profits in which the writer shared. The U.S. Supreme Court upheld the conviction of Winans and his co-conspirators on the grounds that their actions fraudulently deprived Winans's employer (the *Wall Street Journal*) of its "property," the information contained in his column; their actions also amounted to a "scheme to defraud" under the Securities and Exchange Act.[49] Winans's case is important because it signifies that insider trading can occur even if the offender neither is an employee of nor has a fiduciary interest (such as a company's outside accountants would have) in a company whose stock is traded; the Court also found that there need not be a "victim" who loses tangible property for the crime to take place.

Interpretations of what constitutes insider trading vary widely. To many, the "hot tip" is the bread and butter of stock market speculators, and the point when a tip becomes a criminal act is often fuzzy. In the most celebrated insider trading cases, billionaires Ivan Boesky and Michael Milken, two of Wall Street's most prominent **arbitrage** experts, were convicted and sentenced to prison. Arbitragers speculate on the stock of companies that are rumored to be takeover targets by other firms and hope to make profit on the difference between current stock prices and the price the acquiring company is willing to pay. Boesky used inside information on such deals as the merger negotiations between International Telephone and Telegraph and Sperry Corporation, Coastal Corporation's takeover of American Natural Resources, and the leveraged buyout of McGraw Edison. Possession of this information allowed Boesky to profit in the millions; he received a three-year prison sentence. Milken was indicted (with the help of information provided by Ivan Boesky) on 98 counts of security fraud, pled guilty to six relatively minor counts, and received a harsh ten-year prison sentence and a billion-dollar fine; his sentence was later reduced because of his cooperation with authorities in other cases.[50]

Individual Exploitation of Institutional Position

Another type of white-collar crime involves individuals' exploiting their power or position in organizations to take advantage of other individuals who have an interest in how that power is used. For example, a fire inspector who demands that the owner of a restaurant pay him to be granted an operating license is abusing his institutional position. In most cases, this type of offense occurs when the victim has a clear right to expect a service and the offender threatens to withhold the service unless an additional payment or bribe is forthcoming.

EXPLOITATION IN GOVERNMENT. Throughout U.S. history, various political and government figures have been accused of using their positions to profit from bribes and kickbacks.[51] As early as the 1830s, New York's political leaders used their position to control and profit from the city's police force. In the early 19th century, New York City's police chief, George Matsell, was the subject of numerous charges of bribe taking and profiteering. Although his wrongdoing was never proven in court, it was revealed five years after he retired in 1851 that he had "saved" enough on his modest salary to build a 20-room mansion on a 3,000-acre estate. During the Civil War, corruption increased proportionately with the amount of money being spent on the war effort. After the war, the nation's largest cities were controlled by political machines that used their offices to buy and sell political favors. The most notorious of the corrupt politicians was William Marcy "Boss" Tweed, who ruled New York City's Democratic Party (Tammany Hall) from 1857 to 1871.[52] Time and anticorruption campaigns eventually caught up with Tweed, and he died in jail.[53]

The use of political office for economic gain has not subsided. On the local and state level, it is common for scandals to emerge in which liquor license board members, food inspectors, and fire inspectors are named as exploiters. One survey of New York City workers who had contact with the building and construction trade found that all who responded to the survey had either been personally involved with corruption or had heard of its existence.[54] Even the most powerful politicians in Washington have been implicated in corrupt practices. On April 9, 1996 Former Representative Dan Rostenkowski pled guilty to two federal corruption charges in return for a 17-month prison sentence and a $100,000 fine.[55] Rostenkowski, once the chairman on the powerful House Ways and Means Committee, was accused of a pattern of corrupt activities, including converting government funds for his personal use, that spanned three decades.

EXPLOITATION IN INDUSTRY. Exploitation can also occur in private industry. It is common for purchasing agents in large companies to demand a piece of the action for awarding contracts to suppliers and distributors. In one such case, a J. C. Penney employee received $1.4 million from a contractor who eventually did $23 million of business with the company.[56] In another case, a purchasing agent for the American Chiclets division of Warner-Lambert (maker of Dentyne, Chiclets, Trident, and Dynamints) received a $300,000 kickback from the makers of the wire racks on which the gum products are displayed in supermarkets. Recently, NYNEX fired or disciplined several managers for demanding kickbacks from contractors in return for granting building maintenance contracts.[57]

In some foreign countries, soliciting bribes to do business is a common, if not expected, practice. Not surpris-
ingly, U.S. businesses have complained that stiff penalties for bribery give foreign competitors the edge over them. In European countries, such as Italy and France, giving bribes to secure contracts is perfectly legal, and in Germany corporate bribes are actually tax-deductible.[58] Some government officials will solicit bribes to allow American firms to do business in their countries. In one incident, the medical supply firm Baxter International is alleged to have bribed Arab officials to do business in Arab nations after it had been placed on a blacklist for owning a plant in Israel.[59]

Influence Peddling and Bribery

Sometimes individuals holding an important institutional position sell power, influence, and information to outsiders who have an interest in influencing or predicting the activities of the institution. Offenses within this category include government employees' taking of kickbacks from contractors in return for awarding them contracts they could not have won on merit, or outsiders' bribing of government officials, such as those in the Securities and Exchange Commission, who might sell information about future government activities. Influence peddling may not be directed solely at personal enrichment and can also involve securing a favored position for one's political party or interest group. Political leaders have been convicted of securing bribes to obtain funds to rig elections and allow their party to control state politics.[60]

One major difference distinguishes influence peddling from exploitation of an institutional position. Whereas exploitation involves forcing victims to pay for services to which they have a clear right, influence peddlers and bribe takers use their institutional positions to grant favors and sell information to which their co-conspirators are not entitled. In sum, in crimes of institutional exploitation, the victim is the person forced to pay, whereas the victim of influence peddling is the organization compromised by its own employees for their own interests.

INFLUENCE PEDDLING IN GOVERNMENT. The most widely publicized incident of government bribery was the ABSCAM case. In 1981 FBI agents, working with a convicted swindler, Melvin Weinberg, posed as wealthy Arabs looking for favorable treatment from high-ranking politicians. The pseudo-Arabs said they wished to obtain U.S. citizenship and receive favorable treatment in business ventures. As a result of this "sting," several office holders were indicted, including a U.S. senator from New Jersey, Harrison Williams.[61] Williams was convicted of accepting an interest in an Arab-backed mining venture in return for promising to use his influence to obtain government contracts. He also promised to use his influence to help the "Arab sheik" enter and stay in the United States. At Williams's trial, the prosecution played videotapes showing Williams meeting with federal undercover agents, boasting of his influence in the government, and saying he could "with great pleasure talk to the president of the United States" about the business venture; a later tape showed the senator promising to seek immigration help for the bogus sheik and agreeing to take part in the mining operation.

The ABSCAM case is certainly not unique. Senior officials at the Pentagon were found to have received hundreds of thousands of dollars in bribes for ensuring the granting of contracts for military clothing to certain manufacturers. The corruption was so pervasive that the military found it difficult to locate sufficient replacement manufacturers who were not involved in the scandal. In another Pentagon scandal, senior officials were accused of accepting bribes from defense consultants and manufacturers in return for classified information, such as competitors' bids and designs, that would give the consultants and manufacturers an edge in securing government contracts. More than $1 billion worth of contracts were suspended. The scandal touched some of the largest defense contractors in the United States, including Raytheon, Litton Industries, and Lockheed.[62]

In the mid-1980s officials at the Department of Housing and Urban Development (HUD) were involved in a scheme to use their position to defraud the government of $4–$8 billion dollars. Officials used their power to dispense huge grants to well-connected political figures. Several officials who left the department received huge consulting fees from former associates who still worked for the department. A number of officials were later convicted of taking bribes and defrauding the government, including one woman who siphoned off $5 million from the sale of repossessed homes, the largest individual theft of U.S. government funds in history. Her feat earned her the name "Robin Hud" after she claimed that she gave much of the money to charity; the judge gave her four years in prison.[63]

Federal officials are not the only ones to be accused of influence peddling. It has become all too common for legislators and other state officials to be forced to resign or even jailed for accepting bribes to use their influence. In West Virginia, two governors have been jailed on bribery charges since 1960. In Louisiana, the state insurance commissioner was convicted in 1991 on money laundering, conspiracy, and fraud charges connected to the collapse of the Champion Insurance Company, which cost policyholders $185 million; the commissioner took $2 million in bribes in return for regulatory favors.[64] And overseas, foreign businessmen and officials have been implicated in corruption. For example, in Italy, the former chairperson of the Montedison agricultural chemical firm admitted making illegal payments to political leaders to secure contracts.[65]

CORRUPTION IN THE CRIMINAL JUSTICE SYSTEM. Agents of the criminal justice system have also gotten caught up in official corruption, a circumstance that is particularly disturbing because society expects a higher standard of moral integrity from people empowered to uphold the law and judge their fellow citizens. When federal pros-ecutors mounted Operation Greylord to expose corruption in the Cook County, Illinois, court system, they uncovered examples of judges selling favors to corrupt attorneys for up to $50,000 in under-the-table payments; one culprit received a 15-year prison sentence. The credibility of the justice process is critically weakened when officials who hold power over other people's reputation, not to speak of their freedom and liberty, engage in criminal behavior.

Police officers have been particularly vulnerable to charges of corruption. More than 20 years ago, New York Mayor John Lindsay appointed a commission under the direction of Judge Whitman Knapp to investigate allegations of police corruption. The **Knapp Commission** found that police corruption was pervasive and widespread, ranging from patrol officers' accepting small gratuities from local businesspeople to senior officers receiving payoffs in the thousands of dollars from gamblers and narcotics violators.[66] The commission found that construction firms made payoffs to have police ignore violations of city ordinances, such as double parking, obstruction of sidewalks, and noise pollution. Bar owners paid police to allow them to operate after hours or to give free reign to the prostitutes, drug pushers, and gamblers operating on their premises. Drug dealers allowed police to keep money and narcotics confiscated during raids in return for their freedom.

In 1993 New York City empowered the **Mollen Commission** to investigate corruption among city police. The commission found that a relatively small number (compared to the pervasive corruption found earlier by the Knapp Commission) of rogue cops were immersed in a pattern of violence, coercion, theft, and drug dealing. Testifying before the commission to gain a reduced sentence on a narcotics charge, one officer told of "shaking down" drug dealers, brutalizing innocent citizens, and intimidating fellow officers to force their silence. Protected by the "blue curtain"—the police officer code of secrecy—rogue cops were able to purchase luxury homes and cars with the profits from their illegal thefts, extortion, and drug sales.[67]

Even the high visibility given the Mollen Commission has failed to completely eliminate corruption. Figure 13.1 illustrates some recent examples of cases involving corruption in New York City.

One approach to controlling corruption is to strengthen the internal administrative review process within police departments. Some departments have adopted an *accountability system* that holds supervisors at each level directly responsible for the illegal behaviors of the officers under them; a commander can be forced to resign or be demoted if one of his or her command is found guilty of corruption. Outside review boards or special prosecutors have been formed to investigate reported incidents of corruption; outsiders, though, may face the problem of the blue curtain, which is quickly raised when police officers feel their department is under scrutiny.

Anticorruption training and education programs have been instituted for new recruits in the training academy. In

48th Precinct, the Bronx

The 48th Precinct is the latest focus of corruption inquiries, with two dozen officers under investigation, police officials say. After sting operations involving undercover officers posing as drug dealers, eight officers from the 48th have been indicted. One of the officers has also been charged by the Rockland County District Attorney with participating in a suburban cocaine ring. Officers from the 48th are believed to have robbed drug dealers, sold narcotics, and beat up suspects.

73rd Precinct, Brooklyn

During the summer of 1993, a former police officer told investigators about officers who broke down the doors of drug dealers and divided the booty in an abandoned coffin factory. Jurors acquitted three officers of extortion charges but deadlocked on civil rights charges stemming from what prosecutors said were illegal searches and arrests based on false evidence.

109th Precinct, Queens

In 1994 the Police Department received a series of complaints from residents in and around Flushing that several officers were using drugs on the job. Four officers were ordered to take drug tests: One resigned and the other three failed their tests and were dismissed. The department also set up a series of corruption stings, resulting in the arrests of two officers and one former officer, who are accused of stealing $1,400 while responding to a false report of a kidnapping. Police officials say more officers are under investigation.

30th Precinct, Harlem

In August 1993, several Harlem police officers were videotaped breaking into an apartment that had been set up by the undercover officers as a phony drug den. The sting operation, which followed reports that officers had been shaking down drug dealers and stealing property on their beats, opened up one of the city's biggest police corruption scandals in decades. In the days and months that followed, more than two dozen other officers and supervisors were arrested. The most recent arrests came in May 1995, when two officers and a sergeant were accused of falsifying arrest records and lying in court to win convictions.

Source: "Pockets of Corruption," *New York Times*, 9 April 1995, p. 43.

1996 the city of Philadelphia agreed to implement a set of reforms to combat corruption in order to settle a lawsuit brought by civil rights organizations. Among the measures taken to reduce corruption were

- A policy mandating that all citizens' complaints be forwarded for investigation by the internal affairs division
- Development of computer files containing all types of complaints and suits against individual officers, which could be easily accessed during investigations
- A policy requiring that internal affairs give a high priority to any police officer's claim that another officer is corrupt or has used excessive force
- Reporting and recording of all incidents in which an officer used more than incidental force

- Training officers to treat citizens without racial bias; a deputy commissioner will be assigned to monitor charges of race discrimination
- A review of all policies and practices to insure they do not involve or have the potential for race bias[68]

While such efforts are important, it will be difficult to eradicate police corruption without changing the social context of policing. Police operations must be made more visible, and the public must be given freer access to police operations. It is also possible that some of the vice-related crimes the police now deal with might be decriminalized or referred to other agencies. Although decriminalization of vice cannot in itself end the problem, it could lower the pressure placed on individual police officers and help relieve their moral dilemmas, such as whether it is really wrong to take money from drug dealers or gamblers.

INFLUENCE PEDDLING IN BUSINESS. Politicians and government officials are not the only ones accused of bribery; business has had its share of scandals. In the 1970s, revelations were made that multinational corporations regularly made payoffs to foreign officials and businesspeople to secure business contracts. Gulf Oil executives admitted paying $4 million to the South Korean ruling party; Burroughs Corporation admitted paying $1.5 million to foreign officials; Lockheed Aircraft admitted paying $202 million. McDonnell-Douglas Aircraft Corporation was indicted for paying $1 million in bribes to officials of Pakistani International Airlines to secure orders.[69]

In response to these revelations, Congress in 1977 passed the Foreign Corrupt Practices Act (FCPA), which makes it a criminal offense to pay bribes to foreign officials or to make other questionable overseas payments. Violations of the FCPA draw strict penalties for both the defendant company and its officers.[70] Moreover, all fines imposed on corporate officers are paid by them and not absorbed by the company. For example, for violation of the antibribery provisions of the FCPA, a domestic corporation can be fined up to $1 million. Company officers, employees, or stockholders who are convicted of bribery may have to serve a prison sentence of up to five years and pay a $10,000 fine.

Congressional dissatisfaction with the harshness and ambiguity of the bill has caused numerous revisions to be proposed. Despite the penalties imposed by the FCPA, corporations that deal in foreign trade have continued to give bribes to secure favorable trade agreements.[71] In 1995, for example, several former executives of the Lockheed Aircraft Corporation pled guilty to bribery in the sale of transport aircraft to the Egyptian government.[72]

Embezzlement and Employee Fraud

The fifth type of white-collar crime involves individuals' use of their positions to embezzle company funds or appropriate company property for themselves. Here, the company or organization that employs the criminal, rather than an outsider, is the victim of the white-collar crime.

BLUE-COLLAR FRAUD.   Employee theft can reach all levels of the organizational structure. Blue-collar employees have been involved in systematic theft of company property, commonly called **pilferage.** The techniques of employee theft are quite varied:

- Piece workers zip up completed garments into their clothing and take them home.
- Cashiers ring up lower prices on single-item purchases and pocket the difference. Some will work with an accomplice and ring up [the lower] prices as [the accomplice goes] through the line.
- Clerks do not tag sale merchandise and then [they] sell it at its original cost, pocketing the difference.
- Receiving clerks obtain duplicate keys to storage facilities and then return after hours to steal.
- Truck drivers make fictitious purchases of fuel and repairs and then split the gains with truckstop owners. Truckers have been known to cooperate with the receiving staff of department stores to cheat employers. In one instance, truckers would keep 20 cases of goods out of every 100 delivered. The store receiving staff would sign a bill of lading for all 100, and the two groups split the profits after the stolen goods were sold to a fence.
- Some employees simply hide items in garbage pails [or] incinerators or under trash heaps until they can be retrieved later.[73]

John Clark and Richard Hollinger found that about 35% of employees they surveyed reported involvement in pilferage.[74] Clark and Hollinger's data indicate that employee theft is most accurately explained by factors relevant to the work setting, such as job dissatisfaction and the workers' belief they were being exploited by employers or supervisors. Economic problems played a relatively small role in the decision to pilfer. So while employers attributed employee fraud to economic conditions and declining personal values, workers themselves say they steal because of strain and conflict. It is difficult to determine the value of goods taken by employees, but it has been estimated that pilferage accounts for 30% to 75% of all shrinkage and amounts to losses of billions of dollars annually.[75]

MANAGEMENT FRAUD.   Blue-collar workers are not the only employees who commit corporate theft. Management-level fraud is also quite common. Such acts include (1) converting company assets for personal benefit; (2) fraudulently receiving increases in compensation (such as raises or bonuses); (3) fraudulently increasing personal holdings of company stock; (4) retaining one's present position within the company by manipulating accounts; and (5) concealing

unacceptable performance from stockholders.[76] There have been a number of well-publicized examples of management fraud. In one recent case, high-ranking employees of the Leslie Fay clothing company were implicated in a fraudulent scheme to overstate company profits. In its accounting reports, inventories were overstated while the cost of making garments was understated to enhance profits; profits and revenues were also inflated. The false entries resulted in millions being paid to executives because their bonuses were tied to company profits.[77]

Employee fraud seems widespread. A survey of 300 companies by the national accountant firm of KPMG Peat Marwick found that 75% reported having fallen prey to employee fraud during the previous 12 months; the estimated total loss was $250 million.[78]

The most significant cases of management fraud in the nation's history occurred in the savings and loan industry. The Close-Up on pages 348–349 discusses this scandal.

Client Frauds

A sixth component of white-collar crime is theft by a client from an organization that advances credit to its clients. Included in this category are insurance fraud, credit card fraud, fraud related to welfare and Medicare programs, and tax evasion. For example, some critics suggest that welfare recipients cheat the federal government on a regular basis. A government report released in 1994 claims that about $1 billion is lost through error and fraudulent claims.[79] These offenses are grouped together because they involve theft from organizations that have many individual clients who may take advantage of their positions of trust to steal from the organizations.

HEALTH CARE FRAUD.   Client frauds may be common even among upper-income people.[80] Some physicians have been caught cheating the federal government out of Medicare or Medicaid payments. Abusive practices include such techniques as "ping-ponging" (referring patients to other physicians in the same office), "gang visits" (billing for multiple services), and "steering" (directing patients to particular pharmacies). Doctors who abuse their Medicaid or Medicare patients in this way are liable to civil suit.

Of a more serious nature are fraudulent acts designed to cheat both the government and the consumer. Such medical frauds generally involve billing for services not actually rendered, billing in excessive amounts, setting up kickback schemes, and providing false identification on reimbursement forms. For example, Operation Backbone, a 1997 undercover operation in New York State, netted 12 chiropractors and 8 other professionals who were fraudulently overbilling insurance companies. One doctor saw a patient 11 times and billed for 150 office visits; another treated a patient once and sent in 90 claims. One of the chiropractors was secretly videotaped coaching a patient

Check kiting is a scheme whereby a client with accounts in two or more banks takes advantage of the time required for checks to clear to obtain unauthorized use of bank funds. For example, a person has $5,000 on account in a bank and cashes a check for $3,000 from an account in another bank in which he has no funds. The bank cashes the check because he is already a customer. He then closes his account before the check clears or writes checks on his account that total $5,000 and are cleared because he has funds in his account. In some instances, the kiter expects the bank to cover a withdrawal before a check is presented to another bank for collection; he simply wants a short-term interest-free loan. Others have no intention of ever covering the transaction but instead want to take cash out of the system after building accounts to artificially high amounts. Kiting can be a multimillion-dollar offense involving checks written and deposited in banks in two or more states and sometimes among banks in multiple countries.

Net Bookmark

The Financial Crimes Enforcement Network (FinCEN) is one of the primary agencies that establishes, oversees, and implements the U.S. Treasury's policies to prevent and detect money laundering. It provides analytical case support, through the use of state-of-the-art technology and intelligence analyses, to many federal agencies as well as to state and local law enforcement organizations. FinCEN also administers the Bank Secrecy Act, which is a key component of Treasury's efforts to combat money laundering. In addition, FinCEN is becoming a leader in international efforts to build effective counter–money laundering policies and cooperation throughout the world.

http://www.ustreas.gov/treasury/bureaus/fincen/

on how to fake injuries when examined by physicians evaluating his insurance claim.[81] In another case a psychiatrist was convicted of submitting false claims by turning in bills that described an individual counseling session as a "family" session that entitled him to higher fees.[82] Doctors involved in these schemes are liable to criminal prosecution under federal and state law.[83] In 1993 Congress passed what is known as the "Stark Amendments."[84] These prohibit physicians from making a referral to a health care provider that accepts Medicare patients if that physician or a family member holds a financial interest. The Stark laws (named after its sponsor, Congressman Pete Stark of California) would, for example, prohibit a surgeon from investing in an X-ray lab and then sending all her patients to that lab for X-rays.

It has been estimated that $100 billion spent annually on federal health care is lost to fraudulent practices.[85] Despite the magnitude of this abuse, state and federal governments have been reluctant to prosecute Medicaid fraud.[86]

BANK FRAUD. Bank fraud can encompass such diverse schemes as "check kiting" (see Figure 13.2), check forgery, false statements on loan applications, money laundering, sale of stolen checks, bank credit card fraud, unauthorized use of automatic teller machines (ATMs), auto title frauds, and illegal transactions with offshore banks.[87] To be found guilty of bank fraud, one must knowingly execute or attempt to execute a scheme to fraudulently obtain money or property from a financial institution. For example, a car dealership would violate the bank fraud statute by securing loans on titles to cars it no longer owns. Or a real estate owner would be guilty of bank fraud if he obtained a false appraisal on a piece of property with the intention of obtaining a bank loan in excess of the property's real worth. Penalties for bank fraud amount to a maximum fine of $1 million and up to 30 years in prison.

TAX EVASION. Another important aspect of client fraud is tax evasion. This is a particularly challenging area for

criminological study, since (1) so many U.S. citizens regularly underreport their income, and (2) it is often difficult to separate honest error from deliberate tax evasion. The basic law on tax evasion is contained in the U.S. Internal Revenue Code, section 7201, which states:

> Any person who willfully attempts in any manner to evade or defeat any tax imposed by this title or the payment thereof shall, in addition to other penalties provided by law, be guilty of a felony and, upon conviction thereof, shall be fined not more than $100,000 or imprisoned not more than 5 years, or both, together with the costs of prosecution.

To prove tax fraud, the government must find that the taxpayer either underreported his or her income or did not report taxable income. No minimum dollar amount is stated before fraud exists, but the government can take legal action when there is a "substantial underpayment of tax." A second element of tax fraud is "willfulness" on the part of the tax evader. In the major case on this issue, willfulness was defined as a "voluntary, intentional violation of a known legal duty and not the careless disregard for the truth."[88] Finally, to prove tax fraud, the government must show that the taxpayer has purposely attempted to evade or defeat a tax payment. If the offender is guilty of passive neglect, the offense is a misdemeanor. Passive neglect simply means not paying taxes, not reporting income, or not paying taxes when due. On the other hand, affirmative tax evasion, such as keeping double books, making false entries, destroying books or records, concealing assets, or covering up sources of income, constitutes a felony.

Tax evasion is a difficult crime to prosecute. Because legal tax avoidance is a favorite U.S. pastime, it is often hard to prove the difference between the careless, unintentional nonreporting of income and willful fraud. The line between legal and fraudulent behavior is so fine that many people are willing to step over it. In fact, it has been estimated that the "underground economy" may amount to about 33% of the nation's production; workers who provide services under the table and off the books range from

close-up: *The Savings and Loan Scandal*

For ten or more years, the owners and managers of some of the nation's largest savings and loan (S&L) institutions swindled investors, depositors, and the general public out of billions of dollars. It has been conservatively estimated that over the next 40 years, the cost of rectifying these S&L fraud cases could total $500 billion, a number almost too staggering to imagine. It is possible that 1,700 S&Ls—about half the industry—may eventually collapse. Government reports indicated that criminal activity was a central factor in 70%–80% of these cases.

How could crimes of this magnitude have been committed? In a number of important analyses, Kitty Calavita, Henry Pontell, and Robert Tillman have looked at the events that created the S&L crisis. At first, problems were created by the industry's efforts to remove federal regulations that had restricted its activities and way of doing business. In 1980, to help the industry recover from money-losing years, the federal government allowed the formerly conservative S&Ls to expand their business operations beyond residential housing loans. Savings banks could now get involved in high-risk commercial real estate lending and corporate or business loans. They were allowed to compete for deposits with commercial banks by offering high interest rates. The S&Ls made deals with brokerage firms to sell high-interest certificates of deposit, encouraging investors around the nation to pour billions of dollars into banks they had never seen. Even more damaging, ownership rules were relaxed so that almost anyone could own or operate an S&L. Yet the government insured all deposits. Even if crooked owners offered

outlandish interest rates to attract deposits and then lent them to shady businesspeople, the federal government guaranteed that depositors could not lose money. Why ask questions about to whom you were giving your money and what it was being used for if the government *guaranteed* the principal?

Given this green light, the S&Ls made irresponsible and outright fraudulent loans. Losses began to mushroom. In the first six months of 1988, the industry lost an estimated $7.5 billion.

S&L violations fell into a number of categories. The first was making high-risk investments (unlawful risk taking) in violation of law and regulation, including risky loans to commercial real estate developers. Sometimes kickbacks were made to encourage the loans.

A second criminal activity was collective embezzlement (looting). This involved robbing one's own bank by siphoning off funds for personal gain. For example, Erwin Hansen took over Centennial Savings and Loan of California in 1980 and threw a Christmas party that cost $148,000 for 500 friends and guests and included a ten-course, sit-down dinner, roving minstrels, court jesters, and pantomimes. Hansen and his companion, Beverly Haines, traveled extensively around the world in the bank's private airplanes, purchased antique furniture at the S&L's expense, refurbished their home at a cost of over $1 million, and equipped it with a chef. Before it went bankrupt, the bank bought a fleet of luxury cars and an extensive art collection. As the Commissioner of the California Department of Savings and Loans stated in 1987, "The best way to rob a bank is to own one."

Other practices involved outright fraud. Land was sold or "flipped" between conspirators, driving up the assessed evaluation. The overpriced land could then be sold to or mortgaged by a friendly bank owned by a co-conspirator for far more than it was worth. One loan broker bought a piece of property in 1979 for $874,000, flipped it, and then sold it two years later to a S&L he had bought for $55 million. Another method was *reciprocal lending* in which bank insiders would lend each other money that was never paid back and then trade the bad loans back and forth to delay discovery of the fraud. Linked financing involved loans based on receipts of deposits in an equivalent amount; the loans were never repaid. Insiders received a "finder's fee" for attracting deposits, and bank operators got bonuses for increasing business. "S&L," some suggested, stood for squander and liquidate.

When the banks became shaky, some owners engaged in *desperation dealing* to increase profits and salvage the bank. This involved lending money with inadequate underwriting or making loans to one borrower exceeding the limits set by law.

In the aftermath of these white-collar crimes, owners committed their final betrayal—covering up their crimes. Sometimes the cover-up was accomplished by shady accounting practices or fabricated income statements. The S&L crisis was allowed to develop because the conspirators were "respected" businesspeople who had lavish lifestyles and political connections. For example, the collapse of Denver-based Silverado Banking Savings and Loan cost taxpayers $1 billion. While the sum was not extraordinary, the case

---

moonlighting construction workers to "gypsy" cabdrivers (there are an estimated 21,000 gypsy cabs in New York City alone, twice the number of legal ones).[89] The IRS estimates that more than $120 billion in taxes go uncollected each year because individuals fail to report all their income; nearly a third of that amount is from self-employed workers, including professionals, laborers, and door-to-door salespeople.[90]

The IRS may be losing its battle against tax cheats. The number of audits it conducts is actually declining. In 1980 it audited about 8% of all people whose incomes exceeded $50,000; today, the number of audits has declined to 1.8%.[91] And despite some well-publicized cases involving the wealthy, such as a $16 million judgment against singer Willie Nelson and the prosecution and conviction of multi-millionaire Leona Helmsley, the IRS has been accused of

One notorious savings and loan case involved Susan and Jim McDougal, who were Bill Clinton's partners in the so-called "Whitewater" deal. In June 1996 the McDougals were convicted of fraud and conspiracy for dipping into funds at their Arkansas-based savings and loan to bankroll their risky business schemes.

Keating of the Lincoln Saving and Loan by-pass federal regulators; they are now known as the "Keating Five."

The S&L crisis was a result of the unregulated finance capitalism that dominated the U.S. economy in the 1980s. Because nothing is produced or sold, financial institutions are ripe for fraud. After all, their business is the manipulation of money; the line between smart business practices and white-collar crime is often thin. While white-collar criminals are all too often treated leniently, the savings and loan case will result in criminal prosecutions for many years. Between 1988 and 1992, more than 3,200 defendants had been charged, 2,600 convicted, and 1,700 sent to prison.

CRITICAL THINKING QUESTIONS
1. Should S&L criminals have their personal incomes and homes confiscated by the government?
2. What motivates already wealthy businesspeople to steal?
3. Are white-collar crime and organized crime really the same thing?

Sources: Henry Pontell, Kitty Calavita, and Robert Tillman, Fraud in the Savings and Loan Industry: White-Collar Crime and Government Response (Report to the National Institute of Justice, Washington, D.C., 1994); Robert Tillman and Henry Pontell, "Organizations and Fraud in the Savings and Loan Industry," Social Forces 73 (1995): 1439–1463; Kitty Calavita and Henry Pontell, "Savings and Loan Fraud as Organized Crime: Toward a Conceptual Typology of Corporate Illegality," Criminology 31 (1993): 519–548; idem, "'Heads I Win, Tails You Lose': Deregulation, Crime, and Crisis in the Savings and Loan Industry," Crime and Delinquency 36 (1990): 309–341; Rich Thomas, "Sit Down Taxpayers," Newsweek, 4 June 1990, p. 60; John Gallagher, "Good Old Bad Boy," Time, 25 June 1990, pp. 42–43; L. Gordon Crovitz, "Milken's Tragedy: Oh, How the Mighty Fall before RICO," Wall Street Journal, 2 May 1990, p. A17.

was notable because President George Bush's son Neil was on Silverado's board of directors. The president was embarrassed when Neil Bush was called to testify before the House Banking Committee on his relationships with two developers who owed the bank considerable sums. One had given Bush $100,000 to invest with the condition that they share in the profits but not the losses. Even Neil Bush admitted, "I know it sounds a little fishy."

The crimes were also difficult to detect because they involved acts of business out of the public view. Bankers secretively dipped into depositors' money to fund parties, yachts, and tours of Europe, all ostensibly for business purposes. Much of the fraud revolved around seemingly innocent loans and mortgages made to associates for investment purposes. Of course, the investments later turned out to be worthless, and the bank and its stockholders were left accountable. Because the government guarantees deposits, it was forced to take over the banks and reorganize their assets. Bank examiners were taken in because the S&L managers had made numerous cash contributions to politicians and used these connections to establish their legitimacy.

Another reason the S&L fraud went undetected for so long was the involvement of high-ranking government officials and Wall Street brokerage firms with first-class credentials. Drexel Burnham Lambert induced banks to purchase "junk bonds" (bonds issued in leveraged buyouts of corporations without sound backing). When these were devalued, the banks lost billions. Five U.S. senators, including Alan Cranston of California and John Glenn of Ohio, are alleged to have helped Charles

targeting middle-income taxpayers and ignoring the upper classes and large corporations.

Corporate Crime

The final component of white-collar crime involves situations in which powerful institutions or their representatives willfully violate the laws that restrain these institutions from doing social harm or that require them to do social good. This is also known as *corporate* or *organizational crime.*

Interest in corporate crime first emerged in the early 1900s, when a group of writers, known as the *muckrakers,* targeted the unscrupulous business practices of John D. Rockefeller, Andrew Carnegie, J. P. Morgan, and other corporate business leaders.[92] In a 1907 article, sociologist E. A. Ross described the "criminaloid," a business leader

During the 19th century, business trusts controlled commerce in the United States. This political cartoon from 1889 suggests that the United States Senate was in the grasp of these powerful cartels. The power of the trusts was curtailed by passage of the Sherman Anti-Trust Act, which made it illegal to conspire to limit open trade.

who while enjoying immunity from the law victimized an unsuspecting public.[93] It was Edwin Sutherland who focused theoretical attention on corporate crime when he began his research on the subject in the 1940s; corporate crime was probably what he had in mind when he coined the phrase "white-collar crime."[94]

Corporate crimes are socially injurious acts committed by companies to further their business interests. The target of their crimes can be the general public, the environment, or even their company's workers. What makes these crimes unique is that the perpetrator is a legal fiction—a corporation—and not an individual. In reality, it is company employees or owners who commit corporate crimes and who ultimately benefit through career advancement or greater profits. Some of the acts included in the category of corporate crime are price fixing and illegal restraint of trade, false advertising, and the use of company practices that violate environmental protection statutes. The variety of crimes contained within this category is great, and the damage they cause vast. The following subsections will examine some of the most important offenses.

ILLEGAL RESTRAINT OF TRADE AND PRICE FIXING. A restraint of trade involves a contract or conspiracy designed to stifle competition, create a monopoly, artificially maintain prices, or otherwise interfere with free market competition. The control of restraint of trade violations has its legal basis in the **Sherman Antitrust Act.** For violations of its provisions, this federal law created criminal penalties of up to three years' imprisonment and $100,000 in fines

for individuals and $1 million in fines for corporations.[95] The act outlaws conspiracies between corporations designed to control the marketplace.

In most instances, the act leaves to the presiding court's judgment the determination of whether corporations have conspired to "unreasonably restrain competition." However, four types of market conditions are considered so inherently anticompetitive that federal courts, through the Sherman Antitrust Act, have defined them as illegal per se, without regard to the facts or circumstances of the case. The first is *division of markets,* in which firms divide a region into territories and each firm agrees not to compete in the others' territories.[96] The second is the *tying arrangement,* in which a corporation requires customers of one of its services to use other services it offers. For example, in the case of *Northern Pacific Railways v. United States,* a federal court ruled that the railroad's requirement that all tenants of its land use the railroad to ship all goods produced on the land was an illegal restraint of trade.[97] A third type of absolute Sherman Act violation is *group boycotts,* in which an organization or company boycotts retail stores that do not comply with its rules or desires. Finally, *price fixing*—a conspiracy to set and control the price of a necessary commodity—is considered an absolute violation of the act.

Of all criminal violations associated with restraint of trade, none, perhaps, is as important as **price fixing.** Michael Maltz and Stephen Pollack have described the four forms this act usually takes.[98] The first is *predation,* in which large firms agree among themselves to bid below market prices to drive out weaker firms. The goal is to reduce competition and permit the remaining firms to raise their prices with relative impunity. A second scheme is *identical bidding.* Here, all competitors agree to submit identical bids for each contract, although they may vary bids from contract to contract. The price is well above what would have been expected if collusion had not occurred. Purchasing agents use their discretion to choose among bidders; however, identical bidding usually ensures all vendors of getting a share of the market without losing any profitability. *Geographical market sharing* involves dividing the potential market into territories within which only one member of the conspiring group is permitted a low bid. The remaining conspirators either refrain from bidding or give artificially high bids. *Rotational bidding* involves a conspiracy in which the opportunity to submit a winning bid for a government or business contract is rotated among the institutional bidders. The conspirators meet in advance and determine who will give the low bid. The winning bid is, of course, higher than it should be, since the losers have all submitted abnormally high bids. Close coordination among the bidders is essential; therefore, these schemes usually involve only a few large firms.

Despite enforcement efforts, restraint-of-trade conspiracies are quite common. The best-known case involved some of the largest members of the electrical equipment industry.[99] In 1961, 21 corporations, including industry leaders Westinghouse and General Electric, were successfully prosecuted; 45 executives were found guilty of criminal violations of the Sherman Antitrust Act. Company executives met secretly—they referred to their meetings as "choir practice"—and arranged the setting of prices on sales of equipment, the allocation of markets and territories, and the rigging of bids. At the sentencing, fines amounting to $1,924,500 were levied against the defendants, including $437,500 against General Electric and $372,500 against Westinghouse. Although these fines meant little to the giant corporations, subsequent civil suits cost General Electric $160 million. Even more significant was that seven defendants, all high-ranking executives, were sentenced to jail terms.

It is common for even the largest U.S. corporations to use *deceptive pricing* schemes when they respond to contract solicitations. Deceptive pricing occurs when contractors provide the government or other corporations with incomplete or misleading information on how much it will actually cost to fulfill the contract they are bidding on or use mischarges once the contracts are signed.[100] For example, defense contractors have been prosecuted for charging the government for costs incurred on work they are doing for private firms or shifting the costs on fixed-price contracts to ones in which the government reimburses the contractor for all expenses ("cost-plus" contracts). One well-known example of deceptive pricing occurred when the Lockheed Corporation withheld information that its wage costs would be lower than expected on the C-5 cargo plane. The resulting overcharges were an estimated $150 million. Although the government was able to negotiate a cheaper price for future C-5 orders, it did not demand repayment on the earlier contract. The government prosecutes approximately 100 cases of deceptive pricing in defense work each year involving 59% of the nation's largest contractors.[101]

FALSE CLAIMS AND ADVERTISING. In 1991 the Food and Drug Administration seized all the Citrus Hill orange juice stored in a Minneapolis warehouse. It seems that the nation's third largest-selling breakfast drink had billed itself as "pure squeezed," "100% pure," and "fresh," despite the fact that it was made from concentrate. The federal agency also objected to the fact that Procter & Gamble, which sells Citrus Hill, had claimed, "We pick our oranges at the peak of ripeness, then we hurry to squeeze them before they lose their freshness."[102]

Executives in even the largest corporations are sometimes caught in the position in which stockholders' expectations of ever-increasing company profits seem to demand that sales be increased at any cost. At times, executives respond to this challenge by making claims about their product that cannot be justified by its actual performance. However, the line between clever, aggressive sales techniques and fraudulent claims is a fine one. It is traditional to show a product in its best light, even if that involves resorting to fantasy. It is neither fraudulent to show a delivery service vehicle taking off into outer space nor to imply that taking one sip of iced tea will make people feel they have just jumped into a swimming pool. However, it is illegal to knowingly and purposely advertise a product as possessing qualities that the manufacturer realizes it does not have.

Charges stemming from false and misleading claims have been common in several U.S. industries. For example, the Federal Trade Commission reviewed and disallowed advertising by the three major U.S. car companies claiming that new cars got higher gas mileage than buyers actually could expect. The Warner-Lambert drug company was prohibited from claiming that Listerine mouthwash could prevent or cure colds. Sterling Drug was prohibited from claiming that Lysol disinfectant killed germs associated with colds and flu. The A&P food company was sanctioned for mispricing and for advertising unavailable products. An administrative judge ruled that the American Home Products Company falsely advertised Anacin as a tension reliever. The list seems endless.[103]

In the pharmaceutical industry, false advertising has a long history.[104] It has been common for medicines to be advertised as cure-alls for previously incurable diseases. Such medicines include alleged cures for cancer and arthritis and drugs advertised to give energy and sexual potency. How can we explain the frequency of false advertising by drug manufacturers? The problem often arises because several competing companies market similar products and the key to successful sales is believed to be convincing the public that one of these products is far superior to the rest.

Sometimes the intense drive for profits leads to falsification of data and unethical and illegal sales promotions.[105]

It has been difficult for authorities to police such violations of the public trust. Often, the most serious consequence to the corporation is an order that it refrain from using the advertising or that it withdraw the advertising claims. Criminal penalties for false claims are rarely given. Recently, "900" telephone numbers have been used to advertise products involving sex and companionship, with high fees charged for each phone call. The Federal Trade Commission filed charges against some companies for using deception in their ad campaigns by promising services they cannot deliver or for overcharging for information calls.[106]

ENVIRONMENTAL CRIMES. Much attention has been paid to the intentional or negligent environmental pollution caused by many large corporations. The numerous allegations in this area involve almost every aspect of U.S. business. There are many types of environmental crimes. Some corporations have endangered the lives of their own workers by maintaining unsafe conditions in their plants and mines. It has been estimated that 21 million workers have been exposed to hazardous materials while on the job. The National Institute of Occupational Safety and Health estimated that it would cost about $40 million just to alert these workers to the danger of their exposure to hazardous waste and $54 billion to watch them and track whether they developed occupationally related disease.[107]

Some industries have been particularly hard hit by complaints and allegations. The asbestos industry was inundated with lawsuits after environmental scientists found a close association between exposure to asbestos and the development of cancer. Over 250,000 people have filed 12,000 lawsuits against 260 asbestos manufacturers. In all, some insurance company officials estimate, asbestos-related lawsuits could amount to as much as $150 billion. Similarly, some 100,000 cotton mill workers suffer from some form of respiratory disease linked to prolonged exposure to cotton dust. About one-third of the workers are seriously disabled by brown lung disease, an illness similar to emphysema.[108]

The control of workers' safety has been the province of the Occupational Safety and Health Administration (OSHA), which sets industry standards for the proper use of such chemicals as benzene, arsenic, lead, and coke. Intentional violation of OSHA standards can result in criminal penalties.

A second type of environmental crime committed by large corporations is illegal pollution of the environment. Sometimes pollution involves individual acts caused by negligence on the part of the polluter. Two cases stand out. The first was the leaking of methyl isocynate from a Union Carbide plant in Bhopal, India, on December 3, 1984. Estimates of the death toll range from 1,400 to 10,000 people; another 60,000 were injured. Union Carbide later reported that the plant had not been operating safely and should have been closed. The firm blamed the negligence on local officials who were running the plant.[109] The second case occurred when the tanker *Exxon Valdez* ran aground on a reef off the coast of Alaska on March 24, 1989, dumping 11 million gallons of crude oil and fouling 700 miles of shoreline. On March 13, 1991, Exxon agreed to pay $1 billion in criminal and civil fines rather than face trial; this is the largest amount paid as a result of environmental pollution to date.[110]

The nature and scope of environmental crimes have prompted the federal government to pass a series of control measures designed to outlaw the worst abuses.[111] These measures include the following acts:

- The Clean Air Act provides sanctions against companies that do not comply with the air quality standards established by the EPA.[112] The act can impose penalties on any person or institution that, for example, knowingly violates EPA plan requirements or emission standards, tampers with EPA monitoring devices, or makes false statements to EPA officials. The Clean Air Act was amended in 1990 to toughen standards for emissions of many air pollutants.

- The Federal Water Pollution Control Act, more commonly called the Clean Water Act, punishes the knowing or negligent discharge of a pollutant into navigable waters.[113] According to the act, a pollutant is any "man-made or man-induced alteration of the chemical, physical, biological, and radiological integrity of the water."

- The Rivers and Harbors Act of 1899 (Refuse Act) punishes any discharge of waste materials that damages natural water quality.[114]

- The Resource Conservation and Recovery Act of 1976 provides criminal penalties for four acts involving the illegal treatment of solid wastes: (1) knowing transportation of any hazardous waste to a facility that does not have a legal permit for solid waste disposal; (2) knowing treatment, storage, or disposal of any hazardous waste without a government permit or in violation of the provision of the permit; (3) deliberately making any false statement or representation in a report filed in compliance with the act; and (4) destruction or alteration of records required to be maintained by the act.[115]

- The Toxic Substance Control Act addresses the manufacture, processing, or distributing of chemical mixtures or substances in a manner not in accordance with established testing or manufacturing requirements; commercial use of a chemical substance or mixture that the commercial user knew was manufactured, processed, or distributed in violation of the act's requirements; and noncompliance with the reporting and inspection requirements of the act.[116]

- The Federal Insecticide, Fungicide and Rodenticide Act regulates the manufacture and distribution of toxic pesticides.[117]

- The Comprehensive Environmental Response, Compensation, and Liability Act, also referred to as the "Superfund," requires the cleanup of hazardous waste at contaminated sites.[118]

Considering the uncertainties of federal budget allocations, there is some question whether these acts can be enforced well enough to effectively deter environmental crime. It is possible that the solution to the environmental problem must be found on the local level.

High-Tech Crime

The Moore typology of white-collar crime is a useful way of organizing traditional methods of entrepreneurial crime. However, a whole new breed of high-tech crimes are emerging that contain elements of fraud, theft, swindles, and false claims. These crimes are difficult to categorize because they can be committed by corporations and individuals, can be singular or ongoing, and can involve the theft of information, resources, or funds. High-tech crimes cost consumers billions of dollars each year and will most likely increase dramatically in the years to come.

What are some of these emerging forms of white-collar crime?

Internet Crimes

More than 24 million people are on the Internet in the United States and Canada alone, and the number entering cyberspace is growing rapidly. Criminal entrepreneurs view this vast pool as a target for high-tech crimes.

There have been a number of highly publicized cases in which adults have solicited teenagers in Internet "chat rooms." Others have used the net to sell and distribute obscene material, prompting some service providers to censor or control sexually explicit material.

Selling pornographic material on the net is just one type of illegal use. Bogus get-rich-quick schemes, weight-loss scams, and investment swindles have also been pitched on the net. In some cases these fraudulent acts can actually be dangerous to clients. For example, in a 1995 case a Minnesota woman advertised the health benefits of "germanium" on an Internet provider, claiming that it could cure AIDS, cancer, and other diseases. Germanium products, however, have been banned because they cause irreversible kidney damage.[119]

Enforcement of the law on the net can fall to a number of different agencies. The Securities and Exchange Commission, Federal Trade Commission, Secret Service, and state attorney generals' offices have all had personnel assigned to be "cybercops." In 1996 the federal government passed the Communications Decency Act, which proscribes the use of a computer to provide minors with "indecent material," as well as the knowing use of a computer to intentionally harass the recipient of the communication.[120] Some civil liberties groups consider this law tantamount to censorship, and suits have been filed in federal court requesting clarification of its provisions; so far the Justice Department has suspended enforcement until the case has been settled.[121] At the time of this writing, the U.S. Supreme Court is considering the merits of the case.

Computer Crimes

Computer-related thefts are a new trend in employee theft and embezzlement. The widespread use of computers to record business transactions has encouraged some people to use them for illegal purposes. Computer crimes generally fall into five categories:[122]

1. Theft of services, in which the criminal uses the computer for unauthorized purposes or an unauthorized user penetrates the computer system; included in this category is the theft of processing time and services not entitled to an employee

2. Use of data in a computer system for personal gain

3. Unauthorized use of computers employed for various types of financial processing to obtain assets

4. Theft of property by computer for personal use or conversion to profit

5. Making the computer itself the subject of a crime, such as placing a virus in it to destroy data

Net Bookmark

Want to learn more about computer crime? Log onto the U.N.'s page on computer crime. Topics include definition of computer crime, the extent of crime and losses, perpetrators of computer crime, the vulnerability of computer systems to crime, common types of computer crime, and legal issues involving the use and abuse of computers.

http://www.ifs.univie.ac.at/~pr2gq1/rev4344.html#crime

While most of these crime types involve using computers for personal gain, the last category typically encompasses activities that are motivated more by malice than profit. When computers themselves are the target, criminals are typically motivated by (a) revenge for some perceived wrong, (b) a need to exhibit their technical prowess and superiority, (c) a desire to highlight the vulnerability of computer security systems (so that they will be hired as consultants?), (d) a need to spy on other people's private financial and personal information (computer voyeurism), and (e) the desire to assert a philosophy of open access to all systems and programs.[123]

TYPES OF COMPUTER CRIME. Several common techniques are used by computer criminals. In fact, computer theft has become so common that experts have created their own jargon to describe theft styles and methods:

1. *The Trojan horse.* One computer is used to reprogram another for illicit purposes. In a recent incident, two high school–age computer users reprogrammed the computer at DePaul University, preventing that institution from using its own processing facilities. The youths were convicted of a misdemeanor.

2. *The salami slice.* An employee sets up a dummy account in the company's computerized records. A small amount—even a few pennies—is subtracted from customers' accounts and added to the account of the thief. Even if they detect the loss, the customers don't complain, since a few cents is an insignificant amount to them. The pennies picked up here and there eventually amount to thousands of dollars in the dummy account.

3. *"Super-zapping."* Most computer programs used in business have built-in antitheft safeguards. However, employees can use a repair or maintenance program to supersede the antitheft program. Some tinkering with the program is required, but the "super-zapper" is soon able to order the system to issue checks to his or her private account.

4. *The logic bomb.* A program is secretly attached to the company's computer system. The new program monitors the company's work and waits for a sign of error to appear, some illogic that was designed for the computer to follow. Illogic causes the logic bomb to kick into action and exploit the weakness. The way the thief exploits the situation depends on his or her original intent—theft of money or defense secrets, sabotage, and so on.

5. *Impersonation.* An unauthorized person uses the identity of an authorized computer user to access the computer system.

6. *Data leakage.* A person illegally obtains data from a computer system by leaking it out in small amounts.

A different type of computer crime involves the installation of a virus in a computer system. A **virus** is a program that disrupts or destroys existing programs and networks. All too often, this high-tech vandalism is the work of "hackers," who consider their efforts to be "pranks." In one well-publicized case, a 25-year-old computer whiz named Robert Morris unleashed a program that wrecked a nationwide electronic mail network. His efforts netted him three years' probation, a $10,000 fine, and 400 hours of community service; some critics felt this punishment was too lenient to deter future virus creators.[124]

An accurate accounting of computer crime will probably never be made, since so many offenses go unreported.

Sometimes company managers refuse to report the crime to police lest they display their incompetence to stockholders and competitors.[125] In other instances, computer crimes go unreported because they involve such "low visibility" acts as copying computer software in violation of copyright laws.[126]

CONTROLLING COMPUTER CRIME. As computer applications become more varied, so, too, will the use of computers for illegal purposes. The growth of computer-related crimes prompted Congress to enact the Counterfeit Active Device and Computer Fraud and Abuse Act (amended 1986).[127] This statute makes it a felony for a person to use illegal entry to a computer to make a gain of $5,000, to cause another to incur a loss of $5,000, or to access data affecting the national interest. Violation of this act can bring up to 10 years in prison and a $10,000 fine. Repeat offenders can receive a 20-year prison sentence and a $100,000 fine. In 1994 the Computer Abuse Amendments Act was passed to update federal enforcement efforts.[128] This statute addresses six areas of computer-related abuses, including obtaining information related to national defense, obtaining financial records, or using a "federal interest computer" to defraud or obtain something of value or destroy data. The 1994 Act criminalizes "reckless conduct," which means that hackers who plant viruses will now fall under federal law.

In addition to the Computer Abuse acts, people who pirate or illegally software come under the jurisdiction of the Criminal Copyright Infringement Act, which punishes copying and distribution of software for financial gain or advantage.[129] Computer crime may also be controlled by other federal statutes, including the Electronic Communications Privacy Act of 1986, which prohibits unauthorized interception of computer communications and prohibits obtaining, altering, or preventing authorized access to data through intentional unauthorized access to the stored data.[130] The act is designed to prevent hackers from intercepting computer communications and invading the privacy of computer users.[131]

The Cause of White-Collar Crime

When Ivan Boesky pled guilty to one count of security fraud, he agreed to pay a civil fine of $100 million, the largest at that time in SEC history. Boesky's fine was later superseded by Michael Milken's fine of more than $1 billion. How, people asked, can people with so much disposable wealth get involved in a risky scheme to produce even more? There probably are as many explanations for white-collar crime as there are white-collar crimes. Herbert Edelhertz, an expert on the white-collar crime phenomenon, suggests that many offenders feel free to engage in business crime because they can easily rationalize its effects. Some convince themselves that their actions are not really crimes, because the acts involved do not resemble street crimes. For example, a banker who uses his position of trust to lend his institution's assets to a company he secretly controls may see himself as a shrewd businessman, not as a criminal. Or a pharmacist who chisels customers on prescription drugs may rationalize her behavior by telling herself that it does not really hurt anyone. Further, some businesspeople feel justified in committing white-collar crimes because they believe that government regulators do not really understand the business world or the problems of competing in the free enterprise system. Even when caught, many white-collar criminals cannot see the error of their ways. For example, one offender who was convicted in the electrical industry price-fixing conspiracy discussed earlier categorically denied the illegality of his actions. "We did not fix prices," he said, "I am telling you that all we did was recover costs."[132] Some white-collar criminals believe that everyone violates business laws, so it is not so bad if they do so themselves. Rationalizing greed is a common trait of white-collar criminals.

Greedy or Needy?

Greed is not the only motivation for white-collar crime; need also plays an important role. Executives may tamper with company books because they feel the need to keep or improve their jobs, satisfy their egos, or support their children. Blue-collar workers may pilfer because they need to keep pace with inflation or buy a new car. Kathleen Daly's analysis of convictions in seven federal district courts indicated that many white-collar crimes involve relatively trivial amounts. Women convicted of white-collar crime typically work in lower-echelon positions, and their acts seem motivated more out of economic survival than greed and power.[133]

Even people in the upper echelons of the financial world, such as Ivan Boesky, may carry scars from an earlier needy period in their lives that can only be healed by accumulating ever greater amounts of money. As one of Boesky's associates put it:

> I don't know what his devils were. Maybe he's greedy beyond the wildest imaginings of mere mortals like you and me. And maybe part of what drives the guy is an inherent insecurity that was operative here even after he had arrived. Maybe he never arrived.[134]

A well-known study of embezzlers by Donald Cressey illustrates the important role need plays in white-collar crime.[135] According to Cressey, embezzlement is caused by what he calls a "nonshareable financial problem." This condition may be the result of offenders' living beyond their means, perhaps piling up gambling debts; offenders feel they cannot let anyone know about such financial problems without ruining their reputations. Cressey claims that the door to solving personal financial problems through criminal means is opened by the rationalizations society has developed for white-collar crime: "Some of our most respectable citizens got their start in life by using other people's money temporarily"; "in the real estate business, there is nothing wrong about using deposits before the deal is closed"; "all people steal when they get in a tight spot."[136] Offenders use these and other rationalizations to resolve the conflict they experience over engaging in illegal behavior. Rationalizations allow offenders' financial needs to be met without compromising their values.

There are a number of more formal theories of white-collar crime. In the following sections we examine two of the more prominent ones in detail.

Corporate Culture Theory

The corporate culture view is that some business organizations promote white-collar criminality in the same way that lower-class culture encourages the development of juvenile gangs and street crime. According to the corporate culture view, some business enterprises cause crime by placing excessive demands on employees while at the same time maintaining a business climate tolerant of employee deviance. New employees learn the attitudes and techniques needed to commit white-collar crime from their business peers in a learning process reminiscent of the way Edwin Sutherland described how gang boys learn the techniques of drug dealing and burglary from older youths through differential association.

A number of attempts have been made to use corporate culture and structure to explain white-collar crime. For example, Ronald Kramer argues that business organizations will encourage employee criminality if they encounter serious difficulties in attaining their goals, especially making profits. Some organizations will create cost-reduction policies that inspire lawbreaking and corner cutting to become norms passed on to employees. When new employees balk at violating business laws, they are told informally, "This is the way things are done here, don't worry about it." Kramer finds that a business's organizational environment, including economic, political, cultural, legal, technological, and interorganizational factors, influences the level of white-collar crime. If market conditions are weak, competition intense, law enforcement lax, and managers willing to stress success at any cost, conditions for corporate crime are maximized.[137]

Kramer's view is analogous to the cultural deviance approach suggesting that crime occurs when obedience to subculture norms and values causes people to break the rules of conventional society. However, cultural deviance theory was originally directed at lower-class slum boys, not business executives. Kramer's view is that the same crime-producing forces may be operating among both socioeconomic groups.

CORPORATE CLIMATE. Australian sociologist John Braithwaite has promoted the corporate culture view in his writings on white-collar crime.[138] According to Braithwaite's model, businesspeople in any society may find themselves in a situation where their organization's stated goals cannot be achieved through conventional business practices; they perceive "blocked opportunities." In a capitalist society, up-and-coming young executives may find that their profit ratios are below par; in a socialist society, young bureaucrats panic when their production levels fall short of the five-year plan. Under such moments of stress, entrepreneurs may find that illegitimate opportunities are the only solution to their problem; their careers must be saved at all costs. So when a government official is willing to take a bribe to overlook costly safety violations, the bribe is gratefully offered. Or when insider trading can increase profits, the investment banker leaps at the chance to engage in it. But how can traditionally law-abiding people overcome the ties of conventional law and morality?

Braithwaite believes that organizational crime is a function of the corporate climate. Organizational crime flourishes in corporations that contain an ongoing employee subculture that resists government regulation and socializes new workers in the skills and attitudes necessary to violate the law. For example, junior executives may learn from their seniors how to meet clandestinely with their competitors to fix prices and how to rationalize this as a "good, necessary and inevitable thing." The existence of law-violating subcultures is enhanced when a hostile relationship exists between the organization and the governmental bodies that regulate it. When these agencies are viewed as uncooperative, untrustworthy, and resistant to change, corporations will be more likely to develop clandestine, law-violating subcultures. A positive working relationship with their governmental overseers will reduce the need for a secret, law-violating infrastructure to develop. Illegal corporate behavior can exist only in secrecy; public scrutiny brings the "shame" of a criminal label to people whose social life and community standing rests on their good name and character.

SHAME OF DISCOVERY. The shame of discovery has an important moderating influence on corporate crime. Its source may be external: the general community, professional or industry peers, or government regulatory agencies. The source of shame and disapproval can also be internal. Many corporations have stated policies that firmly admonish employees to obey the rule of law. For example, it is common for corporations to encourage whistle-blowing by co-workers and to sanction workers who violate the law and cause embarrassment. These organizations are "full of antennas" to pick up irregularities and make it widely known that certain individuals or subunits are responsible for law violations. In a sense, corporations that maintain an excess of definitions unfavorable to violating the law will be less likely to contain deviant subcultures and concomitantly less likely to violate business regulations. In contrast, corporate crime thrives in organizations that iso-late people within spheres of responsibility, where lines of communication are blocked or stretched thin, and in which deviant subcultures are allowed to develop with impunity.

Those holding the corporate culture view, such as Braithwaite and Kramer, would view the savings and loan and insider trading scandals as prime examples of what happens when people work in organizations whose cultural values stress profit over fair play, in which government scrutiny is limited and regulators are viewed as the enemy, and in which senior members encourage newcomers to believe that "greed is good."

The Self-Control View

Not all criminologists agree with the corporate culture theory. Travis Hirschi and Michael Gottfredson take exception to the hypothesis that white-collar crime is a product of the corporate culture.[139] If that were true, there would be much more white-collar crime than actually exists, and white-collar criminals would not be embarrassed by their misdeeds, as most seem to be. Instead, Hirschi and Gottfredson maintain, the motives that produce white-collar crimes are the same as those that produce any other criminal behaviors; "the desire for relatively quick, relatively certain benefit, with minimal effort." As you may recall, Hirschi and Gottfredson's general theory of crime holds that criminals lack self-control; the motivation and pressure to commit white-collar crime is the same for any other form of crime. White-collar criminals are people with low self-control who are inclined to follow momentary impulses without consideration of the long-term costs of such behavior.[140] They find that white-collar crime is relatively rare because, as a matter of course, business executives tend to hire people with self-control, thereby limiting the number of potential white-collar criminals. Hirschi and Gottfredson have collected data showing that the demographic distribution of white-collar crime is similar to that for other crimes. For example, gender, race, and age ratios are the same for such crimes as embezzlement and fraud as they are for street crimes, such as burglary and robbery.

Business executives and corporate executives seem to be people who would have above-average, rather than below-average, self-control. Can Gottfredson and Hirschi's view of white-collar crime be correct?[141] There is some independent evidence developed by David Weisburd, Ellen Chayet, and Elin Waring that white-collar criminals are often repeat offenders. They also share many characteristics with street criminals (such as being impulsive and egocentric), although they begin their careers later in life and offend at a slower pace.[142]

Even if the Gottfredson-Hirschi view is accurate, it is possible that white-collar offenders manifest a wide range of self-control. And, as Michael Benson and Elizabeth Moore suggest, the level of offenders' self-control may determine the path they take to crime. Benson and Moore have found that some people with low self-control impulsively commit fraud and other crimes to pursue their own self-interest; these are most like common criminals. Others with high self-control pursue "ego gratification in an aggressive and calculating fashion"; they are the products of the "greed is good" philosophy. In the middle are offenders who take advantage of criminal opportunities to satisfy an immediate personal need; in them, self-control becomes overwhelmed by special problems. Benson and Moore, then, view self-control as a variable and not a constant, that interacts with need and opportunity to produce white-collar crimes.[143]

Controlling White-Collar Crime

Conflict theorists argue that, unlike lower-class street criminals, white-collar criminals are rarely prosecuted and, when convicted, receive relatively light sentences. This claim is supported by studies of white-collar criminality that show it is rare for a corporate or white-collar criminal to receive a serious criminal penalty.[144] Paul Jesilow, Henry Pontell, and Gilbert Geis found that physicians who engage in Medicaid fraud are rarely prosecuted, and when they are, judges are reluctant to severely punish them. As one official told them, "When we convicted a guy, I wanted to see him do hard time. But what the hell, seeing what's going on in prisons these days and things like that, I think to put one of these guys in prison for hard time doesn't make any sense."[145] Marshall Clinard and Peter Yeager's analysis of 477 corporations found that only one in 10 serious and one in 20 moderate violations resulted in sanctions.[146] In a subsequent analysis, Yeager found that when white-collar statutes are enforced, the tendency is to penalize small, powerless businesses while treating the market leaders more leniently.[147]

There are a number of reasons for the leniency afforded white-collar criminals. Although white-collar criminals may produce millions of dollars of losses and endanger human life, some judges believe they are not "real criminals" but businesspeople just trying to make a living.[148] As Clinard and Yeager report, businesspeople often seek legal advice and are well aware of the loopholes in the law. If caught, they can claim that they had sought legal advice and believed they were in compliance with the law.[149] White-collar criminals are often considered nondangerous offenders because they usually are respectable, older citizens who have families to support. These "pillars of the community" are not seen in the same light as a teenager who breaks into a drugstore to steal a few dollars. Their public humiliation at being caught is usually deemed punishment enough; a prison sentence seems unnecessarily cruel.

Judges and prosecutors may identify with the white-collar criminal based on shared background and world-views; they may have engaged in similar types of illegal behavior themselves.[150] Still another factor complicating white-collar crime enforcement is that many legal business and governmental acts seem as morally tinged as those made illegal by government regulation. For example, the U.S. Air Force forced a general to step down and punished two others for mismanaging the C-17 cargo plane, which accrued $1.5 billion in cost overruns. Their alleged misconduct included funneling $450 million in payments to the contractor, McDonnell Douglas, that were "premature, improper and possibly illegal."[151] Despite their questionable morality and ethics, these acts were not treated as crimes. Yet when compared to other business practices made illegal by government regulation, such as price fixing, the distinctions are hard to see. It may seem unfair to prosecutors and judges to penalize some government and business officials for actions not too dissimilar from those applauded in the *Wall Street Journal*.[152]

Finally, some corporate practices that result in death or disfigurement are treated as civil actions in which victims receive monetary damages. The best-known case involved the A. H. Robins Company's Dalkon Shield intrauterine device, which caused massive trauma to hundreds of thousands of women, including pelvic disease, infertility, and septic abortions, and a suspected 20 deaths. The outcome of the case was that the company went through bankruptcy and set up a multibillion-dollar trust for the survivors.[153] More recently, a number of drug companies, including Bristol Myers Squibb, set up a similar trust fund to compensate victims who suffered because their products used in breast implant surgery were deemed defective and dangerous. In 1997 the nation's leading tobacco companies agreed to set up a multibillion dollar trust to compensate smokers and their families for illness and death related to smoking. Although these cases involve much more serious injury than, say, insider trading, they are not considered criminal matters.

White-Collar Law Enforcement Systems

On the federal level, detection of white-collar crime is primarily in the hands of administrative departments and agencies.[154] Usually, the decision to pursue criminal rather than civil violations is based on the seriousness of the case and the perpetrator's intent, actions to conceal the violation, and prior record.

Any evidence of criminal activity is then sent to the Department of Justice or the FBI for investigation. Some other federal agencies, such as the Securities and Exchange Commission and the U.S. Postal Service, have their own investigative arms. Usually, enforcement is reactive (generated by complaints) rather than proactive (involving ongoing investigations or the monitoring of activities). Investigations are carried out by the various federal agencies and the FBI. The FBI has made enforcement of white-collar laws one of its top three priorities (along with combating foreign counterintelligence and organized crime). If criminal prosecution is called for, the case will be handled by attorneys from the criminal, tax, antitrust, and civil rights divisions of the Justice Department. If insufficient evidence is available to warrant a criminal prosecution, the case will be handled civilly or administratively by some other federal agency. For example, the Federal Trade Commission can issue a cease-and-desist order in antitrust or merchandising fraud cases.

On the state and local levels, enforcement of white-collar laws is often disorganized and inefficient. Confusion may exist over the jurisdiction of the state attorney general and local prosecutors. The technical expertise of the federal government is often lacking on the state level.

Local and state law enforcement officials have made progress in a number of areas, such as control of consumer fraud. The Environmental Crimes Strike Force in Los Angeles County is considered a model for the control of illegal dumping and pollution.[155] The number of state-funded technical assistance offices to help local prosecutors has increased significantly; more than 40 states offer such services.

There is evidence that local prosecutors will pursue white-collar criminals more vigorously if they are part of a team effort that includes a network of law enforcement agencies.[156] However, as Michael Benson, Francis Cullen, and William Maakestad found in their national survey, local prosecutors did not consider white-collar crimes particularly serious problems. They were more willing to prosecute cases if the offense caused substantial harm and other agencies failed to take action. Relatively few prosecutors participated in interagency task forces designed to investigate white-collar criminal activity.[157] Benson and his colleagues found that local prosecutors believed that the criminal law should be used against corporate offenders and that tougher criminal penalties would improve corporate compliance with the law.

The number of prosecutors who believe that upper-class criminals are not above the law is growing. While their findings were encouraging, Benson and colleagues also found that the funds and staff needed for local white-collar prosecutions are often scarce. Crimes considered more serious, such as drug trafficking, usually take precedence over corporate violations. Coordination is uncommon, and there is relatively little resource sharing. It is likely that concern over the environment may encourage local prosecutors to take action against those who violate state pollution and antidumping laws.[158]

Corporate Policing

White-collar crime law enforcement is often left to business organizations themselves. Corporations spend hundreds of millions of dollars each year on internal audits that help unearth white-collar offenses. Local chambers of commerce, the insurance industry, and other elements of the business community have mounted campaigns against white-collar crime. According to Stuart Traub, corporate enforcement strategies can take a variety of forms:

- *Security strategies* involve employing contract security personnel and private police officers who guard merchandise and conduct surveillance in sensitive areas. Passive security measures include use of badges, passes, key cards, and checkpoints to restrict access to merchandise. Closed-circuit TV and other monitoring devices are used for surveillance.
- *Screening and education strategies* involve using preemployment screening and background checks to weed out potential problems. Personality and integrity tests help screen applicants. Stores are teaching employees how to spot theft and the best ways to report problems.
- *Whistle-blowing strategies* involve creating "hotlines" in which employees can report theft anonymously without fear of repercussions. Third-party firms may be called in to maintain hotlines because employees may be reluctant to report fellow workers to their own employer.[159]

Aiding the investigation of white-collar offenses is a movement toward protecting employees who blow the whistle on their firm's violations. At least five states—Michigan, Connecticut, Maine, California, and New York—have passed laws protecting workers from being fired if they testify about violations.[160] Without such help, the hands of justice are tied.

White-Collar Control Strategies: Compliance

The prevailing wisdom, then, is that many white-collar criminals avoid prosecution and that those who are prosecuted receive lenient punishments. What efforts have been made to bring violators of the public trust to justice?

White-collar enforcement typically involves two strategies designed to control organizational deviance: compliance and deterrence.[161]

Compliance strategies aim for law conformity without the necessity of detecting, processing, or penalizing individual violators. At a minimum, they ask for cooperation and self-policing within the business community. Compliance systems attempt to create conformity by providing economic incentives to companies to obey the law. They rely on administrative efforts to prevent unwanted conditions before they occur. Compliance systems depend on the threat of economic sanctions or civil penalties (referred to as *economism*) to control corporate violators.

One method of compliance is to set up administrative agencies to oversee business activity. For example, the Securities and Exchange Commission regulates Wall Street activities, and the Food and Drug Administration regulates drugs, cosmetics, medical devices, meats, and other foods. The legislation creating these agencies usually spells out the penalties for violating regulatory standards. This approach has been used to control environmental crimes, for example, by levying heavy fines based on the quantity and quality

Compliance strategies aim for law conformity by threatening to impose economic sanctions if regulations are violated. Here a federal inspector looks over a pig carcass in a processing plant in San Antonio, Texas. Inspections are aimed at encouraging compliance with federal regulations on meat packing. Critics charge that the economic penalties imposed by compliance strategies are applied only after crimes have occurred, require careful governmental regulation, and often amount to only a slap on the wrist.

of pollution released into the environment.[162] A recent case involved a lawsuit brought against the Sherwin-Williams paint company for a longtime pattern of dumping dangerous chemicals into the sewers on Chicago's South Side.[163]

A number of states, including New Jersey, Arkansas, California, and Ohio, have passed stringent laws making firms liable for cleaning up toxic sites; some prohibit the sale of companies or their assets unless environmental safety conditions have been met.[164]

In another form of economism, the federal government has instituted a policy of barring people and businesses from receiving government contracts if they are found to have engaged in fraudulent practices, such as bribing public officials. For example, in June 1993, the Computer Sciences Company was banned from bidding on government contracts because it had made false claims in a contract; the ban was lifted one month later when the company paid $2.1 million in damages.[165]

While it is difficult to gauge the effectiveness of compliance, research indicates that strict enforcement of regulatory laws can reduce violations of illegal or dangerous business practices. For example, one study found that strict enforcement of penalties under the Occupational and Safety Health Act can significantly reduce workplace injuries.[166]

In sum, compliance strategies attempt to create a marketplace incentive to obey the law; for example, the more a

company pollutes, the more costly and unprofitable that pollution becomes. Compliance strategies limit individual blame and punishment, a practice whose deterrent effect seems problematic. They also avoid stigmatizing and "shaming" businesspeople by focusing on the act, rather than the actor, in white-collar crime.[167]

Compliance systems are not applauded by all criminologists. Some experts point out that economic sanctions have limited value in controlling white-collar crime because economic penalties are imposed only after crimes have occurred, require careful governmental regulation, and often amount to only a slap on the wrist.[168] Compliance is particularly difficult to achieve if the federal government adopts a pro-business, antiregulation fiscal policy that encourages economic growth by removing controls over business.

It is also possible for corporations hit with fines and regulatory fees to pass the costs on to consumers in the form of higher prices or reduced services. Shareholders who had little to do with the crime may see their stock dividends cut or share prices fall.[169]

The fines and penalties involved in compliance strategies may be of little import for a company doing billions in annual business. When the Baxter International pharmaceutical company was banned from bidding on new federal contracts for one year because it had deceived government purchasing agents, the punishment was a blow to its corporate reputation. Yet Baxter does $130 million in sales to federal agencies out of a total revenue of $8.5 billion annually. While humiliating, the ban affects a relatively small amount of the company's business.[170]

Because of these conditions, some criminologists maintain that the punishment of white-collar crimes should contain a retributive component similar to that used in common-law crimes. White-collar crimes, after all, are immoral activities that have harmed social values and deserve commensurate punishment.[171] Furthermore, as Raymond Michalowski and Ronald Kramer point out, corporations can get around economic sanctions by moving their rule-violating activities overseas, where legal controls over injurious corporate activities are lax or nonexistent.[172]

White-Collar Control Strategies: Deterrence

Deterrence strategies involve detecting criminal violations, determining who is responsible, and penalizing them to deter future violations.[173] Punishment serves as a warning to potential violators who might break rules if other violators had not already been penalized. Deterrence systems are oriented toward apprehending violators and punishing them rather than creating conditions that induce conformity to the law.

Deterrence strategies should—and have—worked, since white-collar crime by its nature is a rational act whose perpetrators are extremely sensitive to the threat of criminal sanctions. Gilbert Geis cites numerous instances in which prison sentences for corporate crimes have produced a significant decline in white-collar activity.[174] Similar research by Steven Klepper and Daniel Nagin suggests perceptions of detection and punishment for white-collar crimes appear to be a powerful deterrent to future law violations.[175]

PUNISHING WHITE-COLLAR CRIMINALS. There have been dramatic examples of deterrence strategies used by federal and state justice systems to prevent white-collar crime. It is not extraordinary to hear of corporate officers receiving long prison sentences in conjunction with corporate crimes. Woody Lemons received a 30-year sentence for his role as chairman of the Vernon S&L.[176] Corporate executives have even been charged with murder because of the actions of their companies, as the Close-Up "Can Corporations Commit Murder?" discusses.[177]

Are such stiff penalties the norm, or are they infrequent instances of governmental resolve? A survey conducted by the U.S. Bureau of Justice Statistics reviewed enforcement practices in nine states and found that (1) white-collar crimes account for about 6% of all arrest dispositions, (2) 88% of all those arrested for white-collar crimes were prosecuted, and (3) 74% were subsequently convicted in criminal court. The survey also showed that while 60% of white-collar criminals convicted in state courts were incarcerated (a number comparable to the punishment given most other kinds of offenders), relatively few white-collar offenders (18%) received a prison term of more than a year.[178]

There are indications that deterrence policies may be aided now that the federal government has created sentencing guidelines that control punishment for convicted criminals. Prosecutors can now control the length and type of sentence through their handling of the charging process. The guidelines also create mandatory minimum prison sentences that must be served for some crimes; judicial clemency can no longer be counted on.[179]

IS THE TIDE TURNING? This new "get tough" deterrence approach appears to be affecting all classes of white-collar criminals. While the prevailing wisdom is that the affluent corporate executive usually avoids serious punishment, research by David Weisburd and his associates indicates that high-status offenders are more likely to be punished than previously believed.[180] The Weisburd research seems to indicate that public displeasure with such highly publicized white-collar crimes as the S&L scandal, the HUD fraud, and the BCCI case may be producing a backlash that is resulting in more frequent use of prison sentences. Some commentators now argue that the government may actually be going overboard in its efforts to punish white-collar criminals, especially for crimes that are the result of negligent business practices rather than intentional criminal conspiracy.[181] Nonetheless, relatively few white-collar offenders are prosecuted, and when they are convicted many escape serious punishment.

Organized Crime

The second branch of organizational criminality is *organized crime*—ongoing criminal enterprise groups whose ultimate purpose is personal economic gain through illegitimate means. In this case, a structured enterprise system is set up to supply consumers on a continuing basis with merchandise and services banned by the criminal law but for which a ready market exists: prostitution, pornography, gambling, and narcotics. The system may resemble a legitimate business run by an ambitious chief executive officer, his or her assistants, staff attorneys, and accountants, with highly thorough and efficient accounts receivable and complaint departments.[182]

Because of its secrecy, power, and fabulous wealth, a great mystique has grown up about organized crime. Its legendary leaders—Al Capone, Meyer Lansky, Lucky Luciano—have been the subjects of books and films. The famous *Godfather* films popularized and humanized organized crime figures; the media all too often glamorizes them.[183] Most citizens believe that organized criminals are capable of taking over legitimate business enterprises

close-up: *Can Corporations Commit Murder?*

One of the most controversial issues surrounding the punishment of white-collar criminals is the prosecution of corporate executives who work for companies that manufacture products believed to have caused the death of workers or consumers. Are the executives guilty of manslaughter or even murder?

FEDERAL LAW

The Occupational Safety and Health Act makes employers criminally liable if their wilful violation of a safety rule causes the death of an employee. For example, in one case corporate officers of a Massachusetts asbestos firm were indicted when they made false statements to Occupational Safety and Health Administration (OSHA) officials about the safety of worker respirators when in reality the safety and fit of the devices had not been tested. While OSHA can bring criminal charges, critics maintain that it rarely does, preferring to punish even serious crimes with fines and economic penalties. For example, OSHA negotiated a $10 million fine with IMC Fertilizer and Angus Chemical following a 1991 plant explosion in which eight workers were killed. OSHA also fined Firestone Tire Company $7.5 million in 1994 after determining that the company had violated OSHA standards by failing to properly use locks and lockout procedures when servicing equipment, resulting in the death of a maintenance worker.

STATE ENFORCEMENT

States may also bring criminal charges for the death of an employee. More than 20 years ago, a local prosecutor failed in an attempt to convict Ford Motor Company executives on charges of homicide in crashes involving Pintos, as a result of deaths due to known dangers in the car's design. The Pinto had a gas tank that burst into flame when involved in a low-velocity, rear-end collision. Though the design defect could have been corrected for about $20 per car, the company failed to take prompt action. When three people were killed in crashes, an Indiana prosecutor brought murder charges against Ford executives. However, they were acquitted because the jury did not find sufficient evidence that they intended the deaths to occur.

The question of whether corporate executives could be successfully prosecuted for murder was answered on June 16, 1985 when an Illinois judge found three officials of the Film Recovery Systems Corporation guilty of murder in the death of a worker. The employee died after inhaling cyanide poison under "totally unsafe" work conditions. During the trial, evidence was presented showing that employees were not warned that they were working with dangerous substances, that company officials ignored complaints of illness, and that safety precautions had been deliberately ignored. The murder convictions were later overturned on appeal. Nonetheless, the Film Recovery case remains the only one in which a employer was tried and convicted of murder.

The Pinto and Film Recovery cases opened the door for prosecuting corporate executives on violent crime charges stemming from unsafe products or working conditions. There is little question that corporate liability may be increasing. As Nancy Frank points out, a number of states have adopted the concept of unintended murder in their legal codes. This means that persons can be charged and convicted of murder if their acts, although essentially unintended, are imminently dangerous to another or have a strong probability of causing death or great bodily harm. This legal theory would include corporate executives who knew about the dangers of their products but chose to do nothing because either correction would lower profits or they simply did not care about consumers or workers.

A case illustrating this legal doctrine involved the fire on September 3, 1991 at Imperial Food Products, a North Carolina chicken processing plant. The fire, which claimed 25 lives, was deadly because the plant had no sprinkler system, windows, or escape routes. Company executives had *locked* exit doors to prevent employee pilferage. Emmett Roe, the firm's owner, was convicted of involuntary manslaughter and received a 19-year prison sentence. In this case and others around the country, local prosecutors are taking the initiative to prosecute corporate executives as violent criminals.

CRITICAL THINKING QUESTIONS

1. If the Ford executives knew they had a dangerous car, should they have been found guilty of murder, even though the deaths were the result of collisions?
2. Is it fair to blame a single executive for the activities of a company that has thousands of employees?

Sources: Althea Gregory, Dennis Knoer, and Florence Kao, "Employment-Related Crimes,"*American Criminal Law Review* 33 (1995): 575–606; Occupational Safety and Health Act, 29 U.S.C. sections 651-678 (1994); John Wright, Francis Cullen, and Michael Blankenship, "The Social Construction of Corporate Violence: Media Coverage of the Imperial Food Products Fire," paper presented at the annual meeting of the American Society of Criminology, Phoenix, November 1993); Nancy Frank, "Unintended Murder and Corporate Risk Taking: Defining the Concept of Justifiability," *Journal of Criminal Justice* 16 (1988): 17–24; Francis Cullen, William Maakestad, and Gray Cavender, "The Ford Pinto Case and Beyond: Corporate Crime, Moral Boundaries and the Criminal Sanction," in *Corporations as Criminals,* ed. Ellen Hochstedler (Beverly Hills, Calif.: Sage, 1984), pp. 107–130.

if given the opportunity. Almost everyone is familiar with such synonyms as the *mob, underworld, Mafia, wiseguys, syndicate,* or *La Cosa Nostra.* Although most of us have neither met nor seen members of organized crime families, we feel sure that they exist, and most certainly, we fear them. This section briefly defines organized crime, reviews its history, and discusses its economic effect and control.

Characteristics of Organized Crime

A precise description of the characteristics of organized crime is difficult to formulate, but we can identify some of its general traits:[184]

- Organized crime is a conspiratorial activity, involving the coordination of numerous persons in the planning and execution of illegal acts or in the pursuit of a legitimate objective by unlawful means (for example, threatening a legitimate business to get a stake in it). Organized crime requires continuous commitment by primary members, although individuals with specialized skills may be brought in as needed. Crime organizations are usually structured along hierarchical lines—a chieftain supported by close advisers, lower subordinates, and so on.

- Organized crime has economic gain as its primary goal, although power and status may also be motivating factors. Economic gain is achieved through maintaining a near monopoly on illegal goods and services, including drugs, gambling, pornography, and prostitution.

- Organized crime activities are not limited to providing illicit services. They encompass such sophisticated activities as laundering illegal money through legitimate businesses, land fraud, and computer crimes.

- Organized crime employs predatory tactics, such as intimidation, violence, and corruption. It appeals to greed to accomplish its objectives and preserve its gains.

- By experience, custom, and practice, organized crime's conspiratorial groups are usually very quick and effective in controlling and disciplining their members, associates, and victims. The individuals involved know that any deviation from the rules of the organization will evoke a prompt response from the other participants. This response may range from a reduction in rank and responsibility to a death sentence.

- Organized crime is not synonymous with the "Mafia," the most experienced, most diversified, and possibly best-disciplined of these groups. The Mafia is actually a common stereotype of organized crime. Although several families in the organization called the Mafia are important components of organized crime activities, they do not hold a monopoly on underworld activities.

- Organized crime does not include terrorists dedicated to political change. Although violent acts are a major tactic of organized crime, the use of violence does not mean that a group is part of a confederacy of organized criminals.

Activities of Organized Crime

What are the main activities of organized crime? The traditional sources of income are derived from providing illicit materials and using force to enter into and maximize profits in legitimate businesses.[185] Annual gross income from criminal activity is at least $50 billion, more than 1% of the gross national product; some estimates put gross earnings as high as $90 billion, outranking most major industries in the United States.[186] Most organized crime income comes from narcotics distribution (over $30 billion annually), loan-sharking (lending money at illegal rates—$7 billion), and prostitution ($3 billion). However, additional billions come from gambling, theft rings, and other illegal enterprises. For example, the Attorney General's Commission on Pornography concluded that organized crime figures exert substantial influence and control over the pornography industry.[187]

Organized criminals have infiltrated labor unions, taking control of their pension funds and dues. Alan Block has described mob control of the New York waterfront and its influence on the use of union funds to buy insurance, health care, and so on from mob-controlled companies.[188] Hijacking of shipments and cargo theft are other sources of income. One study found that the annual losses due to theft of air cargo amount to $400 million; rail cargo, $600 million; trucking, $1.2 billion; and maritime shipments, $300 million.[189] Underworld figures engage in the fencing of high-value items and maintain international sales territories. In recent years, they have branched into computer crime and other white-collar activities.

Organized Crime and Legitimate Enterprise

Outside of criminal enterprises, additional billions are earned by organized crime figures who force or buy their way into legitimate businesses and use them both for profit and as a means of siphoning off ("laundering") otherwise unaccountable profits. Merry Morash claims that mob control of legitimate enterprise today is influenced by market conditions. Businesses most likely to be affected are low technology (such as garbage collection), have uniform products, and operate in rigid markets where increases in price will not result in reduced demand. In addition, industries most affected by labor pressure are highly susceptible to takeovers because a mob-controlled work stoppage would destroy a product or interfere with meeting deadlines. Morash lists five ways in which organized criminals today become involved in legitimate enterprise: (1) business activity that supports illegal enterprises—for example, providing a front; (2) predatory or parasitic exploitation—for example, demanding protection money; (3) organization of monopolies or cartels to limit competition; (4) unfair advantages gained by such practices as manipulation of labor unions and corruption of public officials; and (5) illegal manipulation of legal vehicles, particularly stocks and bonds.[190]

These traits show how organized crime is more like a business enterprise than a confederation of criminals seeking to merely enhance their power. Nowhere has this relationship been more visible than in the 1985 scandal that rocked the prestigious First National Bank of Boston. Federal prosecutors charged that the bank made unreported cash shipments of $1.2 million. It received $529,000 in small bills and sent $690,000 in bills of $100 or more. The bank was fined $500,000 for violating a law that requires banks to report any cash transaction of $10,000 or more. The bank's transaction came under scrutiny during an FBI investigation of the Angiulo crime family, which bought more than $41.7 million in cashier's checks from the bank.[191]

The First National scandal illustrates that organized crime today involves a cooperative relationship among big business, politicians, and racketeers. The relationship is an expensive one: It has been estimated that organized crime activities stifle competition, resulting in the loss of 400,000 jobs and $18 billion in productivity. And since organized crime's profits go unreported, the rest of the population pays an extra $6.5 billion in taxes.[192]

The Concept of Organized Crime

The term *organized crime* conjures up images of strong men in dark suits, machine-gun-toting bodyguards, rituals of allegiance to secret organizations, professional "gangland" killings, and meetings of "family" leaders who chart the course of crime much like the board members at General Motors decide on the country's transportation needs. These images have become part of what criminologists refer to as the **alien conspiracy theory** concept of organized crime. This is the belief, adhered to by the federal government and many respected criminologists, that organized crime is a direct offshoot of a criminal society—the **Mafia**—that first originated in Italy and Sicily and now controls racketeering in major U.S. cities. A major premise of the alien conspiracy theory is that the Mafia is centrally coordinated by a national committee that settles disputes, dictates policy, and assigns territory.[193] Not all criminologists believe in this narrow concept of organized crime, and many view the alien conspiracy theory as a figment of the media's imagination.[194] Instead, they characterize organized crime as a group of ethnically diverse gangs or groups who compete for profit in the sale of illegal goods and services or who use force and violence to extort money from legitimate enterprises. These groups are not bound by a central national organization but act independently on their own turf. We will now examine each of these two perspectives in some detail.

Alien Conspiracy Theory: La Cosa Nostra

According to the alien conspiracy theory, organized crime really consists of a national syndicate of 25 or so Italian-dominated crime families that call themselves **La Cosa Nostra**. The major families have a total membership of about 1,700 "made men," who have been inducted into organized crime families, and another 17,000 "associates," who are criminally involved with syndicate members.[195] The families control crime in distinct geographic areas. New York City, the most important organized crime area, alone contains five families—the Gambino, Columbo, Lucchese, Bonnano, and Genovese families—named after their founding "godfathers." In contrast, Chicago contains a single mob organization called the "outfit," which also influences racketeering in such cities as Milwaukee, Kansas City, and Phoenix. The families are believed to be ruled by a "commission" made up of the heads of the five New York families and bosses from Detroit, Buffalo, Chicago, and Philadelphia. The commission settles personal problems and jurisdictional conflicts and enforces rules that allow members to gain huge profits through the manufacture and sale of illegal goods and services (see Figure 13.2).[196]

DEVELOPMENT OF A NATIONAL SYNDICATE. How did this concept of a national crime cartel develop? The first "organized" gangs consisted of Irish immigrants who made their home in the slum districts of New York City.[197] The Forty Thieves, considered the first New York gang with a definite, acknowledged leadership, were muggers, thieves, and pickpockets on the Lower East Side of Manhattan from the 1820s to just before the Civil War. Around 1890, Italian immigrants began forming gangs modeled after the Sicilian crime organization known as the Mafia; these gangs were called the Black Hand. In 1900, Johnny Torrio, a leader of New York's Five Points gang, moved to Chicago and helped his uncle, Big Jim Colosimo, organize the dominant gang in the Chicago area. Other gangs also flourished in Chicago, including those of Hymie Weiss and "Bugs" Moran. A later leader was the infamous Al "Scarface" Capone. The turning point of organized crime was the onset of Prohibition and the Volstead Act. This created a multimillion-dollar bootlegging industry overnight. Gangs vied for a share of the business, and bloody wars for control of rackets and profits became common. However, the problems of supplying liquor to thousands of illegal drinking establishments (speakeasies) required organization and an end to open warfare.

In the late 1920s, several events helped create the structure of organized crime. First, Johnny Torrio became leader of the Unione Siciliano, an ethnic self-help group that had begun as a legitimate enterprise but had been taken over by racketeers. This helped bring together the Chicago and New York crime groups; and since Torrio was Italian, it also spurred the beginnings of détente between Italians and Sicilians, who had been at odds with one another. Also during the 1920s, more than 500 members of Sicilian gangs fled from Europe to the United States to avoid prosecution; these new arrivals included future gang leaders Carlo Gambino, Joseph Profaci, Stefano Maggadino, and Joseph Bonnano.[198]

In December 1925, gang leaders from across the nation met in Cleveland to discuss strategies for mediating their differences nonviolently and for maximizing profits. A

Figure 13.2   Traditional organization of the Mafia "family."

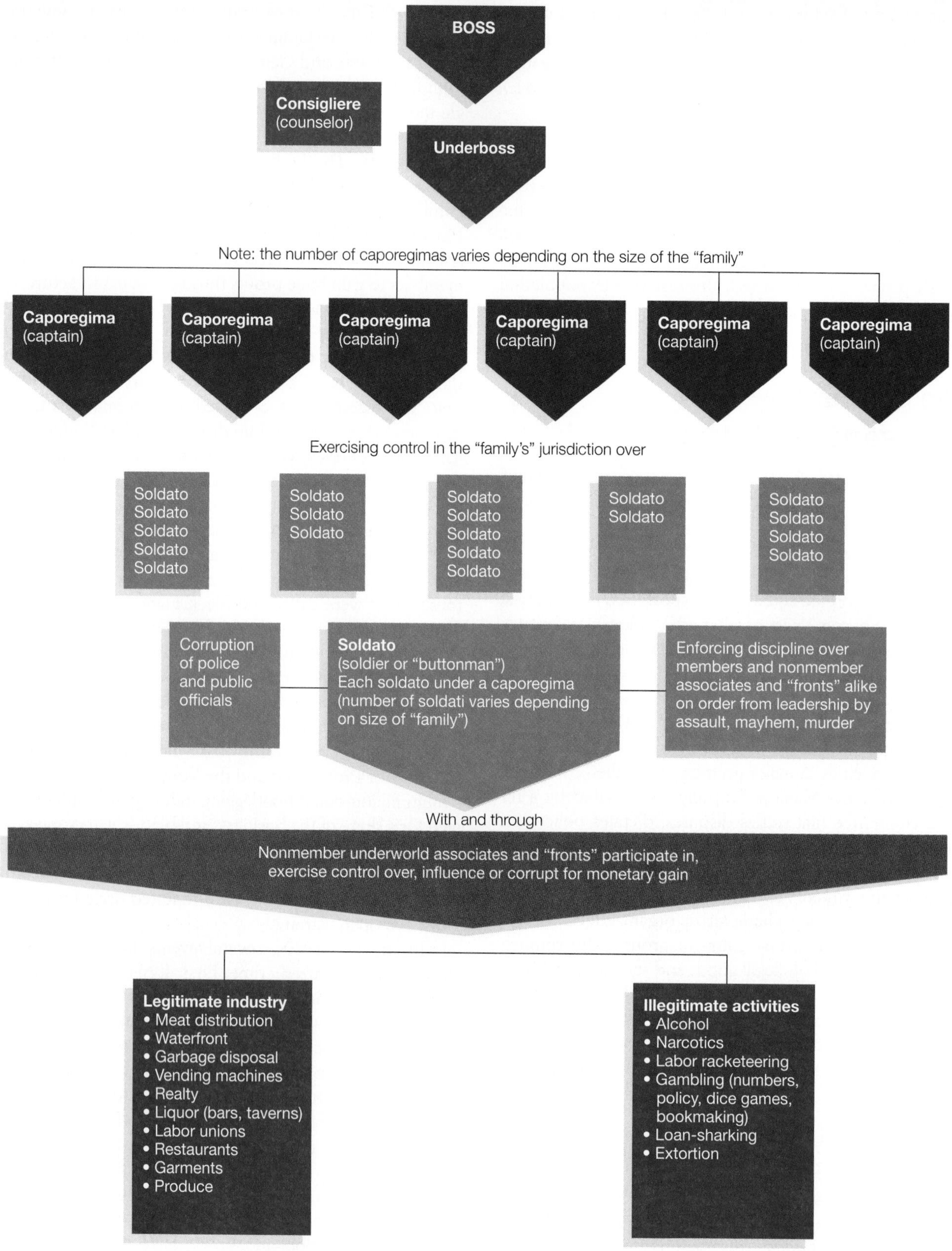

BOSS

Consigliere
(counselor)

Underboss

Note: the number of caporegimas varies depending on the size of the "family"

Caporegima
(captain)

Caporegima
(captain)

Caporegima
(captain)

Caporegima
(captain)

Caporegima
(captain)

Caporegima
(captain)

Exercising control in the "family's" jurisdiction over

Soldato
Soldato
Soldato
Soldato
Soldato

Soldato
Soldato
Soldato

Soldato
Soldato
Soldato
Soldato
Soldato

Soldato
Soldato

Soldato
Soldato
Soldato

Corruption
of police
and public
officials

Soldato
(soldier or "buttonman")
Each soldato under a caporegima
(number of soldati varies depending
on size of "family")

Enforcing discipline over
members and nonmember
associates and "fronts" alike
on order from leadership by
assault, mayhem, murder

With and through

Nonmember underworld associates and "fronts" participate in,
exercise control over, influence or corrupt for monetary gain

Legitimate industry
• Meat distribution
• Waterfront
• Garbage disposal
• Vending machines
• Realty
• Liquor (bars, taverns)
• Labor unions
• Restaurants
• Garments
• Produce

Illegitimate activities
• Alcohol
• Narcotics
• Labor racketeering
• Gambling (numbers,
  policy, dice games,
  bookmaking)
• Loan-sharking
• Extortion

Source: U.S. Senate, Permanent Subcommittee on Investigations, Committee on Governmental Affairs, *Hearings on Organized Crime and Use of Violence,* 96th Cong., 2d Sess., April 1980, p. 117.

similar meeting took place in Atlantic City in 1929 and was attended by 20 gang leaders, including Lucky Luciano, Al Capone, and "Dutch" Schultz. Despite such efforts, however, gang wars continued into the 1930s. In 1934, according to some accounts, another meeting in New York, called by Johnny Torrio and Lucky Luciano, led to the formation of a national crime commission and acknowledged the territorial claims of 24 crime families around the country. This was considered the beginning of La Cosa Nostra.

Under the leadership of the national crime commission, organized crime began to expand in a more orderly fashion. Benjamin "Bugsy" Siegel was dispatched to California to oversee West Coast operations. The end of Prohibition required a new source of profits, and narcotics sales became the mainstay of gangland business. Al Polizzi, a Cleveland crime boss, formed a news service that provided information on horse racing, thereby helping create a national network of gang-dominated bookmakers. After World War II, organized crime families began using their vast profits from liquor, gambling, and narcotics to buy into legitimate businesses, such as entertainment, legal gambling in Cuba and Las Vegas, hotel chains, jukebox concerns, restaurants, and taverns. By paying off politicians, police, and judges and by using blackmail and coercion, organized criminals became almost immune to prosecution. The machine-gun-toting gangster had given way to the businessman-racketeer. In the 1950s, cooperation among gangland figures reached its zenith. Gang control over unions became widespread, and many legitimate businesses made payoffs to promote labor peace. New gang organizations arose in Los Angeles, Kansas City, and Dallas.

POST-1950 DEVELOPMENTS. In 1950, the Senate Special Committee to Investigate Organized Crime in Interstate Commerce, better known as the Kefauver Committee (after its chairman), was formed to look into organized crime. It reported the existence of a national crime cartel whose members cooperated to make a profit and engaged in joint ventures to eliminate enemies. The Kefauver Committee also made public the syndicate's enforcement arm, Murder Inc., which, under the leadership of Albert Anastasia, disposed of enemies for a price. The committee also found that corruption and bribery of local political officials were widespread. This theme was revived by the Senate Subcommittee on Investigations, better known as the McClellan Committee, in its investigation of the role organized crime played in labor racketeering. The committee and its chief counsel, Robert Kennedy, uncovered a close relationship between gang activity and the Teamsters Union, then led by Jimmy Hoffa. Hoffa's disappearance and assumed death has been linked to his gangland connections. Later investigations by the committee produced the testimony of Joseph Valachi, former underworld "soldier," who detailed the inner workings of La Cosa Nostra. The leaders of the national crime cartel at this time were Frank Costello, Vito Genovese, Carlo Gambino, Joseph Bonnano, and Joseph Profaci, all of New York; Sam Giancana of Chicago; and Angelo Bruno of Philadelphia.

During the next 15 years, gang activity expanded further into legitimate businesses. Nonetheless, gangland jealousy, competition, and questions of succession produced an occasional flare-up of violence. The most well-publicized conflict occurred between the Gallo brothers of Brooklyn—Albert, Larry, and Crazy Joe—and the Profaci crime family. The feud continued through the 1960s, uninterrupted by the death of Joseph Profaci and the new leadership of his group by Joe Colombo. Eventually, Colombo was severely injured by a Gallo hired assassin, and in return Joey Gallo was killed in a New York restaurant, Umberto's Clam House. Gallo's death once again brought peace in the underworld. Emerging as the most powerful syndicate boss was Carlo Gambino, who held this position until his death by natural causes in 1976.

In sum, the alien conspiracy theory sees organized crime as being run by an ordered group of ethnocentric (primarily of Italian origin) criminal syndicates, maintaining unified leadership and shared values. These syndicates are in close communication with one another and obey the decisions of a national commission charged with settling disputes and creating crime policy.

The Mafia Myth

Some scholars charge that the Cosa Nostra version of organized crime is fanciful. They argue that the alien conspiracy theory is too heavily influenced by media accounts and by the testimony of a single person, mobster Joseph Valachi, before the McClellan Committee. Valachi's description of La Cosa Nostra was relied on by conspiracy theorists as an accurate portrayal of mob activities. Yet critics question its authenticity and direction. For example, criminologist Jay Albanese compared Valachi's statements to those of another mob informer, Jimmy Frantianno, and found major discrepancies with respect to the location and size of organized criminal activity.[199]

The challenges to the alien conspiracy theory have produced alternative views of organized crime. For example, Philip Jenkins and Gary Potter studied organized crime in Philadelphia and found little evidence that this supposed "Mafia stronghold" was controlled by an Italian-dominated crime family.[200] Sociologist Alan Block has argued that organized crime is both a loosely constructed social system and a social world that reflects the existing U.S. system, not a tightly organized national criminal syndicate. The system is composed of "relationships binding professional criminals, politicians, law enforcers, and various entrepreneurs."[201] In contrast, the social world of organized crime is often chaotic because of the constant power struggle between competing groups. Block rejects the idea that an all-powerful organized crime commission exists and instead views the world of professional criminals as one shaped by the political economy. Block found that independent crime organizations can be characterized as either enterprise syndicates or power syndicates. The former are involved in providing services and include madams, drug distributors, bookmakers, and so on. These are "workers in the world of illegal enterprise." They have set positions with special tasks to perform if the enterprise system is to function. In contrast, power syndicates perform no set task except to extort or terrorize. Their leaders can operate against legitimate business or against fellow criminals who operate enterprise syndicates. Through coercion, buyouts, and other similar means, power syndicates graft themselves onto enterprise systems, legal businesses, trade unions, and so on.

Block's view of organized crime is revisionist since it portrays mob activity as a quasi-economic enterprise system swayed by social forces and not a tightly knit, unified cartel dominated by ethnic minorities carrying out European traditions. His world of organized crime is dominated by business leaders, politicians, and union leaders who work hand in hand with criminals. Moreover, the violent, chaotic social world of power struggles does not lend itself to a tightly controlled syndicate.

Organized Crime Groups

Even such devoted alien conspiracy advocates as the U.S. Justice Department now view organized crime as a loose confederation of ethnic and regional crime groups, bound together by a commonality of economic and political objectives.[202] Some of these groups are located in fixed geographical areas. For example, the so-called Dixie Mafia operates in the South. Chicano crime families are found in areas with significant Hispanic populations, such as California and Arizona. White-ethnic crime organizations are found across the nation. Some Italian and Cuban groups operate internationally. Some have preserved their past identity, while others are constantly changing.

One important recent change in organized crime is the interweaving of ethnic groups into the traditional structure. African American, Hispanic, and Asian racketeers now compete with the more traditional groups, overseeing the distribution of drugs, prostitution, and gambling in a symbiotic relationship with old-line racketeers. Since 1970, Russian and Eastern groups have been operating on U.S. soil. As many as 2,500 Russian immigrants are believed to be involved in criminal activity, primarily in Russian enclaves in New York City. Beyond extortion from immigrants, Russian organized crime groups have cooperated with Mafia families in narcotics trafficking, fencing of stolen property, money laundering, and other "traditional" organized crime schemes.[203] As the traditional organized crime families drift into legitimate businesses, the distribution of contraband on the street is handled by newcomers, characterized by Francis Ianni as "urban social bandits."[204]

Have these newly emerging groups achieved the same level of control as traditional crime families? Some experts argue that minority gangs will have a tough time developing the network of organized corruption, which involves working with government officials and unions, that traditional crime families enjoyed.[205]

As law enforcement pressure has been put on traditional organized crime figures, other groups have filled the vacuum. For example, the Hell's Angels motorcycle club is now believed to be one of the leading distributors of narcotics in the United States. Similarly, Chinese criminal gangs have taken over the dominant role in New York City's heroin market from the traditional Italian-run syndicates.[206]

In sum, most experts now agree that it is simplistic to view organized crime in the United States as a national syndicate that controls all illegitimate rackets in an orderly fashion. This view seems to ignore the variety of gangs and groups, their membership, and their relationship to the outside world.[207] Mafia-type groups may play a major role in organized crime, but they are by no means the only ones that can be considered organized criminals.[208]

Organized Crime Abroad

The United States is not the only country that confronts organized criminal gangs. The Cali and Medellin drug cartels in Colombia are world famous for both their vast drug trafficking profits and their unflinching use of violence to achieve their objectives. When Pablo Escobar, the head of the Medellin cartel, was captured and killed by police and soldiers on December 2, 1993, experts predicted that drug smuggling would *increase* with the shift of the cocaine trade to the control of the smoother and more business-like Cali cartel.[209]

Drug-dealing gangs are not the only form of organized crime abroad. Japan has a long history of organized criminal activity by *Yakuza* gangs. In 1993 officials of the Kirin Brewery, Japan's largest beer maker, resigned after allegations were made that they paid over 33 million yen in *sokaiya*—extortion money—to racketeers who threatened their business.[210] In China, organized gangs use violence to enforce contracts between companies, serving as an alternative to the legal system. They also help smuggle many of the 100,000 mainland Chinese who enter the United States each year. In June 1993, a Chinese ship packed with illegal immigrants foundered off the coast of New York, and ten of them drowned.[211]

Russia has been beset by organized crime activity since the breakup of the Soviet Union. As of 1993, an estimated 3,000 criminal gangs were active in Russia. Bloody shootouts have become common as gangs attempt to stake out territory and extort businesses. In one incident, an auto dealership was attacked and two security guards killed when the owner failed to pay "protection money."[212]

Computer and communications technology has fostered international cooperation among crime cartels. East European and Russian gangs sell arms seized from the former Soviet Army to members of the Sicilian Mafia; Japanese and

Italian mob members have met in Paris; drug money from South America is laundered in Canada and England.[213]

Controlling Organized Crime

George Vold argued that the development of organized crime parallels early capitalist enterprises. Organized crime uses ruthless and monopolistic tactics to maximize profits; it is also secretive and protective of its operations and defensive against any outside intrusion.[214] Consequently, controlling its activities is extremely difficult.

The federal and state governments actually did little to combat organized crime until fairly recently. One of the first measures aimed directly at organized crime was the Interstate and Foreign Travel or Transportation in Aid of Racketeering Enterprises Act (Travel Act).[215] The Travel Act prohibits travel in interstate commerce or use of interstate facilities with the intent to promote, manage, establish, carry on, or facilitate an unlawful activity; it also prohibits the actual or attempted engagement in these activities. In 1970 Congress passed the Organized Crime Control Act (see the Close-Up on forfeiture for some of its provisions). Title IX of the act, probably its most effective measure, has been the **Racketeer Influenced and Corrupt Organization Act (RICO)**.[216]

RICO did not create new categories of crimes but rather new categories of offenses in *racketeering activity,* which it defined as involvement in two or more acts prohibited by 24 existing federal and 8 state statutes. The offenses listed in RICO include such state-defined crimes as murder, kidnapping, gambling, arson, robbery, bribery, extortion, and narcotic violations and such federally defined crimes as bribery, counterfeiting, transmission of gambling information, prostitution, and mail fraud.

RICO is designed to limit patterns of organized criminal activity by prohibiting involvement in an act intended to

- Derive income from racketeering or the unlawful collection of debts and to use or invest such income
- Acquire through racketeering an interest in or control over any enterprise engaged in interstate or foreign commerce
- Conduct business enterprises through a pattern of racketeering
- Conspire to use racketeering as a means of making income, collecting loans, or conducting business

An individual convicted under RICO is subject to 20 years in prison and a $25,000 fine. Additionally, the accused must forfeit to the U.S. government any interest in a business in violation of RICO. These penalties are much more potent than simple conviction and imprisonment. To enforce these policy initiatives, the federal government created the Strike Force Program. This program, operating in 18 cities, brings together various state and federal law enforcement officers and prosecutors to work as a team against racketeering. Several states, including New York, Illinois, New Jersey, and New Mexico, have created their own special investigative teams devoted to organized criminal activity.

These efforts began to pay off more than a decade ago when in April 1985 a New York–based strike force successfully obtained indictments against members of the Lucchese, Genovese, and Bonnano families.[217] The investigation also uncovered evidence to support the national crime cartel concept. Similar sweeps were conducted in Boston, Chicago, and Miami during the remainder of the decade. From 1985 to 1987 many major organized crime figures were indicted, convicted, and imprisoned, including Gennaro Angiulo, second in command in New England, who received a 45-year sentence; Tony Salerno, Tony Corallo, Carmine Persico, and Gennaro Langella of the New York families, who each got 100 years in prison; and Nicodemo Scarfo of Philadelphia, who got 14 years for extortion. The arrest and imprisonment of John Gotti, the so-called "Dapper Don," was a firm illustration of the decline of white-ethnic organized crime families and their replacement with emerging groups. Some of these convictions are now in question because of allegations that the FBI secretly uses mobsters as informants to gain warrants.

The Future of Organized Crime

Indications exist that the traditional organized crime syndicates are in decline. Law enforcement officials in Philadelphia, New Jersey, New England, New Orleans, Kansas City, Detroit, and Milwaukee all report that years of federal and state interventions have severely eroded the Mafia organizations in their areas.[218] What has caused this alleged erosion of Mafia power? First, a number of the reigning family heads are quite old, in their 70s and 80s, prompting some law enforcement officials to dub them "the Geritol gang."[219] A younger generation of mob leaders is stepping in to take control of the families, and there are indications they lack the skill and leadership of the older bosses. In addition, active government enforcement policies have halved what the estimated made membership was 20 years ago; a number of the highest-ranking leaders have been imprisoned. Additional pressure comes from newly emerging ethnic gangs that want to "muscle in" on traditional syndicate activities, such as drug sales and gambling. For example, Chinese Triad gangs have been active in New York and California in the drug trade, loan-sharking, and labor racketeering. Other ethnic crime groups include black and Colombian drug cartels and the Sicilian Mafia, which operates independently of U.S. groups.

The Mafia has also been hurt by changing values in U.S. society. White, ethnic inner-city neighborhoods, which were the locus of Mafia power, have been reduced in size as families move to the suburbs. Organized crime groups have consequently lost their political and social base of

Forfeiture is government seizure of property derived from or used in criminal activity. Its use as a sanction aims to strip racketeers and drug traffickers of their economic power, as the traditional sanctions of imprisonment and fines have been found inadequate to deter or punish enormously profitable crimes. Seizure of assets aims not only to reduce the profitability of illegal activity but to curtail the financial ability of criminal organizations to continue illegal operations.

Forfeiture is not a new sanction. During the Middle Ages, "forfeiture of estate" was a mandatory result of most felony convictions. The crown could seize all of a felon's real and personal property. Forfeiture derived from the common law concept of "corruption of blood" or "attaint," which prohibited a felon's family from inheriting or receiving his or her property or estate. The common law mandated that descendants could not inherit property from a relative who may have attained the property illegally: "[T]he Corruption of Blood stops the Course of Regular Descent, as to Estates, over which the Criminal could have no Power, because he never enjoyed them."*

*C. Yorke, "Some Consideration on the Law of Forfeiture for High Treason," 2nd ed. (1746), p. 26; cited in D. Fried, "Rationalizing Criminal Forfeiture," *Journal of Criminal Law and Criminology* 79 (1988): 329.

TWO TYPES OF FORFEITURE:
CIVIL AND CRIMINAL
Civil forfeiture is a proceeding against property that has been used in criminal activity. Property subject to civil forfeiture often includes vehicles used to transport contraband, equipment used to manufacture illegal drugs, cash used in illegal transactions, and property purchased with the proceeds of the crime. No finding of criminal guilt is required in such proceedings. The government is required to post notice of the proceedings so that any party who has an interest in the property may contest the forfeiture. The types of property that may be forfeited have been expanded since the 1970s to include cash, securities, negotiable instruments, property including houses or other real estate, and proceeds traceable directly or indirectly to violations of certain laws. Common provisions permit seizure of conveyances, such as airplanes, boats, or cars; raw materials, products, and equipment used in manufacturing, trafficking, or cultivation of illegal drugs; and drug paraphernalia.

Criminal forfeiture is a part of the criminal action taken against a defendant accused of racketeering or drug trafficking. Forfeiture is a sanction imposed on conviction that requires the defendant to forfeit various property rights and interests related to the violation. In 1970 Congress revived this sanction that had been dormant in U.S. law since the Revolution. Over 100 federal forfeiture statutes are in force.

It is possible for prosecutors to proceed both civilly and criminally against people involved in criminal conspiracies; this does not amount to double jeopardy. In the recent case, *United States v. Ursery* (1996), Jerome Ursery paid a fine of $13,250 to settle a civil forfeiture claim against his home after police seized 147 marijuana plants on the premises. He was later criminally prosecuted and sentenced to prison. In its opinion, the Court argued that the Constitution bars successive prosecutions for the same crime, not successive punishments.

USE OF FORFEITURE
The federal government originally provided for criminal forfeiture in the Racketeer Influenced and Corrupt Organization statute and the Comprehensive Drug Abuse Prevention and Control Act (Controlled Substances Act), both enacted in 1970. Before that time, civil forfeiture had been provided in federal laws on some narcotics, customs, and revenue infractions. More recently, language on forfeiture has been included in the Comprehensive Crime Control Act of 1984, the Money Laundering Act of 1986, and the Anti-Drug Abuse Act of 1986. Most state forfeiture

---

operations. In addition, the "code of silence," which served to protect Mafia leaders, is now being broken regularly by younger members who turn informer rather than face prison terms. For example, the reign of John Gotte, the most powerful mob boss in New York, was ended by testimony given at his murder trial by his one-time ally Sammy "The Bull" Gravano. It is also possible that success has hurt organized crime families; younger members are better educated than their forebears and equipped to seek their fortunes through legitimate enterprise.[220]

Jay Albanese, a leading expert on organized crime, predicts that pressure by the federal government will encourage organized crime figures to engage in "safer" activities, such as credit card and airline ticket counterfeiting and illicit toxic waste disposal. Instead of running illegal enterprises, established families may be content with financing younger entrepreneurs and channeling or laundering profits through their legitimate business enterprises. There may be greater effort among organized criminals in the future to infiltrate legitimate business enterprises to obtain access to money for financing and the means to launder illicitly obtained cash. Labor unions and the construction industry have been favorite targets in the past.[221]

While these actions are considered a major blow to Italian-dominated organized crime cartels, they are unlikely to stifle criminal entrepreneurship. As long as vast profits can be made from selling narcotics, producing pornography, or taking illegal bets, many groups stand ready to fill the gaps and reap the profits of providing illegal goods and services. It is likely that the New York and Chicago mobs,

procedures appear in controlled substances or RICO laws. A few states provide for forfeiture of property connected with the commission of any felony. Most state forfeiture provisions allow for civil rather than criminal forfeiture.

ZERO TOLERANCE

Although law enforcement officials at first applauded the use of forfeiture as a hard-hitting way of seizing the illegal profits of drug law violators, the practice has been criticized because the government has often been overzealous in its application. For example, million-dollar yachts have been seized because someone aboard possessed a small amount of marijuana; this confiscatory practice is referred to as **zero tolerance.** Zero tolerance has been criticized by scholars because it is often used capriciously, the penalty is sometimes disproportionate to the crime involved, and it makes the government "a . . . partner in crime." The forfeiture law, argues David Fried, was originally viewed as a way of preventing organized-crime figures from invading legitimate businesses, not as a means for the state to unfairly increase punishments and create a new class of "crime victim."

Responding to this sort of criticism, the Supreme Court restricted such confiscatory practices in two recent cases, *Austin v. United States* and *Alexander v. United States*, in which the Court held that the seizure of property must be pro-portional to the seriousness of the crime in both civil and criminal forfeitures. In the *Alexander* case, the government seized an entire chain of adult book stores and ordered the destruction of the entire inventory of 100,000 items after the owner had been convicted of selling 7 *obscene items; Austin* involved the civil seizure of the defendant's home and business after he was convicted of possessing two grams of cocaine.

WHAT HAPPENS
TO FORFEITED PROPERTY?

In 1984 the federal government established the Department of Justice Assets Forfeiture Fund to collect proceeds from forfeitures and defray the costs of forfeitures under the Comprehensive Drug Abuse Prevention and Control Act, along with the Customs Forfeiture Fund for forfeitures under customs laws. These acts also require that the property and proceeds of forfeiture be shared equitably with state and local law enforcement agencies commensurate with their participation in the investigations leading to forfeiture.

Once property is legally forfeited, its disposition is a matter of governmental discretion. It may be sold and all profits retained by the government agency, or it can be used directly by the agency or awarded to a third party, such as an informant. Attempts by the defendant to transfer the property or sell it to an "innocent" third party can be overturned by the government. In a recent (1996) case, *Bennis v. Michigan*, the Supreme Court ruled that a person's car or home can be forfeited if it is involved in a crime even if the owner was unaware that his or her property was being used for criminal purposes.

All is not lost when the government seizes personal property. Defendants can recover their possessions by repurchasing them at appraised value, by petitioning for their return from the agency that seized them, or by filing a claim in a court of law.

CRITICAL THINKING QUESTIONS

1. Should a person's home be seized if police find a small amount of narcotics on the premises?
2. Should *all* convicted criminals be stripped of their assets?

Sources: David Taube, "Civil Forfeiture," Eighth Survey of White Collar Crime, *American Criminal Law Review* 30 (1993): 1025–1047; Bureau of Justice Statistics, *Report to the Nation on Crime and Justice*, 2nd ed. (Washington, D.C.: National Institute of Justice, 1988), p. 93; David Fried, "Rationalizing Criminal Forfeiture," *Journal of Criminal Law and Criminology* 79 (1988): 328–436; *Austin v. United States* 113 S.Ct. 2801 (1993); *Alexander v. United States* (1993); *Bennis v. Michigan* 116 S.Ct. 994, 58 CrL 2060 (1996).

with a combined total of almost 1,500 made members, will continue to ply their trade.

Summary

White-collar and organized criminals are similar because they both use ongoing illegal business enterprises to make personal profits. There are several types of white-collar crime. Stings and swindles involve the use of deception to bilk people out of their money. Chiseling customers, businesses, or the government on a regular basis is a second common type of white-collar crime. Surprisingly, many professionals engage in chiseling offenses. Other white-collar criminals use their positions in business and the marketplace to commit economic crimes. Their crimes include exploitation of position in a company or the government to secure illegal payments; embezzlement and employee pilferage and fraud; client fraud; and influence peddling and bribery. Further, corporate officers sometimes violate the law to improve the position and profitability of their businesses. Their crimes include price fixing, false advertising, and environmental offenses. More recently, computers have been used to commit high-tech crimes.

So far, little has been done to combat white-collar crimes. Most offenders do not view themselves as criminals and therefore do not seem to be deterred by criminal statutes. Although thousands of white-collar criminals are prosecuted each year, their numbers are insignificant compared with the magnitude of the problem. The government has used various law enforcement strategies to combat white-collar crime. Some involve deterrence, which uses punishment to frighten potential abusers. Others involve economism or compliance strategies, which create economic incentives to obey the law.

The demand for illegal goods and services has produced a symbiotic relationship between the public and an organized criminal network. Although criminal gangs have existed since the early 19th century, their power and size were spurred by the Volstead Act and Prohibition in the 1920s. Organized crime supplies alcohol, gambling, drugs, prostitutes, and pornography to the public. It is immune from prosecution because of public apathy and because of its own strong political connections. Organized criminals used to be white ethnics—Jews, Italians, and Irish—but today African Americans, Hispanics, Asians, and other groups have become included in organized crime activities. The old-line "families" are more likely to use their criminal wealth and power to buy into legitimate businesses.

There is debate over the control of organized crime. Some experts believe there is a national crime cartel that controls all activities. Others view organized crime as a group of disorganized, competing gangs dedicated to extortion or to providing illegal goods and services. Efforts to control organized crime have been stepped up. The federal government has used antiracketeering statutes to arrest syndicate leaders. But as long as there are vast profits to be made, illegal enterprises will continue to flourish.

Key Terms

white-collar crime	price fixing
organized crime	virus
enterprise	compliance
corporate crime	deterrence
swindling	alien conspiracy theory
chiseling	Mafia
churning	La Cosa Nostra
insider trading	Racketeer Influenced and
arbitrage	Corrupt Organization
Knapp Commission	Act (RICO)
Mollen Commission	forfeiture
pilferage	zero tolerance
Sherman Antitrust Act	

Notes

1. Dwight Smith, Jr., "White-Collar Crime, Organized Crime and the Business Establishment: Resolving a Crisis in Criminological Theory," in *White Collar and Economic Crime: A Multidisciplinary and Crossnational Perspective,* ed. P. Wickman and T. Dailey (Lexington, Mass.: Lexington Books, 1982), p. 53.

2. See, generally, Dwight Smith, Jr., "Organized Crime and Entrepreneurship," *International Journal of Criminology and Penology* 6 (1978): 161–177; idem, "Paragons, Pariahs, and Pirates: A Spectrum-Based Theory of Enterprise," *Crime and Delinquency* 26 (1980): 358–386; Dwight Smith, Jr., and Richard S. Alba, "Organized Crime and American Life," *Society* 16 (1979): 32–38.

3. Smith, "White-Collar Crime, Organized Crime and the Business Establishment," p. 33.

4. Mark Haller, "Illegal Enterprise: A Theoretical and Historical Intepretation," *Criminology* 28 (1990): 207–235.

5. Nancy Frank and Michael Lynch, *Corporate Crime, Corporate Violence* (Albany, N.Y.: Harrow and Heston, 1992), p. 7.

6. Nikos Passas and David Nelken, "The Thin Line Between Legitimate and Criminal Enterprises: Subsidy Frauds in the European Community," *Crime, Law and Social Change* 19 (1993): 223–243.

7. Ibid., p. 238.

8. For a thorough review, see David Friedrichs, *Trusted Criminals* (Belmont, Calif.: Wadsworth, 1996).

9. Kitty Calavita and Henry Pontell, "Savings and Loan Fraud as Organized Crime: Toward a Conceptual Typology of Corporate Illegality," *Criminology* 31 (1993): 519–548.

10. Edwin Sutherland, *White-Collar Crime: The Uncut Version* (New Haven, Conn.: Yale University Press, 1983).

11. Edwin Sutherland, "White-Collar Criminality," *American Sociological Review* 5 (1940): 2–10.

12. See, generally, Herbert Edelhertz, *The Nature, Impact and Prosecution of White-Collar Crime* (Washington, D.C.: U.S. Government Printing Office, 1970), pp. 73–75.

13. Ibid., p. 11.

14. James Coleman, "What Is White Collar Crime? New Battles in the War of Definitions," in James Helmkamp, Richard Ball, and Kitty Townsend, *Proceedings of the Academic Workshop, "Definitional Dilemma: Can and Should There Be a Universal Definition of White Collar Crime?"* (Morgantown, W.V.: National White Collar Crime Center, 1996), pp. 77–86.

15. James Helmkamp and Richard Ball, "Progress in the Definition and Exploration of White-Collar Crime," paper presented at the annual meeting of the American Society of Criminology, Chicago, November 1996, p. 9.

16. David Weisburd and Kip Schlegel, "Returning to the Mainstream," in *White-Collar Crime Reconsidered,* ed. Kip Schlegel and David Weisburd (Boston: Northeastern University Press, 1992), pp. 352–365.

17. Gilbert Geis, "Avocational Crime," in *Handbook of Criminology,* ed. Daniel Glazer (Chicago: Rand McNally, 1974), p. 284.

18. Ronald Kramer and Raymond Michalowski, "State-Corporate Crime," paper presented at the annual meeting of the American Society of Criminology, Baltimore, November 1990.

19. Elizabeth Moore and Michael Mills, "The Neglected Victims and Unexamined Costs of White-Collar Crime," *Crime and Delinquency* 36 (1990): 408–418.

20. Stuart Traub, "Battling Employee Crime: A Review of Corporate Strategies and Programs," *Crime and Delinquency* 42 (1996): 244–256.

21. Laura Schrager and James Short, "Toward a Sociology of Organizational Crime," *Social Problems* 25 (1978): 415–425.

22. Ibid., p. 415.

23. Gilbert Geis, "White-Collar and Corporate Crime," in *Major Forms of Crime,* ed. Robert Meier (Beverly Hills: Sage, 1984), p. 145.

24. Bureau of Justice Statistics, *The Severity of Crime* (Washington, D.C.: U.S. Government Printing Office, 1984).

25. Xie Baogue, "The Function of the Chinese Procuratorial Organ in Combat Against Corruption," *Police Studies* 11 (1988): 38–43.

26. Dai Yisheng, "Expanding Economy and Growing Crime," *CJ International* 11 (1995): 916.

27. Jim Moran, "Thailand, Crime and Corruption Become Increasing Threat," *CJ International* 12 (1996): 5.

28. Sam Perry, "Economic Espionage and Corporate Responsibility," *CJ International* 11 (1995): 3–4.

29. Nikos Passas and David Nelkin, "The Fight Against Fraud in the European Community: Cacophony Rather Than Harmony," *Corruption and Reform* 6 (1991): 237–266.

30. Ibid. See also Passas and Nelkin, "The Thin Blue Line Between Legitimate and Criminal Enterprises."

31. Nikos Passas, "European Integration, Protectionism, and Criminogenesis: A Case Study on Farm Subsidy Frauds," *Mediterranean Quarterly* 5 (1994): 66–84.

32. Marshall Clinard and Richard Quinney, *Criminal Behavior Systems: A Typology* (New York: Holt, Rinehart and Winston, 1973), p. 117.

33. Edelhertz, *The Nature, Impact and Prosecution of White-Collar Crime.*

34. Mark Moore, "Notes Toward a National Strategy to Deal with White-Collar Crime," in *A National Strategy for Containing White-Collar Crime,* ed. Herbert Edelhertz and Charles Rogovin (Lexington, Mass.: Lexington Books, 1980), pp. 32–44.

35. For a general review, see John Braithwaite, "White-Collar Crime," *Annual Review of Sociology* 11 (1985): 1–25.

36. Scott Paltrow, "Goldblum Now in Consulting and on Parole," *Wall Street Journal,* 22 March 1982, p. 25.

37. Nikos Passas, "Structural Sources of International Crime: Policy Lessons from the BCCI Affair," *Crime, Law and Social Change* 19 (1994): 223–231.

38. Nikos Passas, "Accounting for Fraud: Auditors' Ethical Dilemmas in the BCCI Affair," in *The Ethics of Accounting and Finance,* ed. W. Michael Hoffman, Judith Brown Kamm, Robert Frederick, and Edward Petry (Westport, Conn.: Quorum Books, 1996), pp. 85–99.

39. Paul Nowell, "Bakker Convicted of Fraud," *Boston Globe,* 6 October 1989, p. 1.

40. Earl Gottschalk, "Churchgoers Are the Prey as Scams Rise," *Wall Street Journal,* 7 August 1989, p. C1.

41. Diana Henriques, "10 Percent of Fruit Juice Sold in U.S. Is Not All Juice, Regulators Say," *New York Times,* 31 October 1993, p. 1.

42. Richard Quinney, "Occupational Structure and Criminal Behavior: Prescription Violation of Retail Pharmacists," *Social Problems* 11 (1963): 179–185; see also John Braithwaite, *Corporate Crime in the Pharmaceutical Industry* (London: Routledge and Kegan Paul, 1984).

43. Amy Dockser Marcus, "Thievery by Lawyers Is on the Increase, with Duped Clients Losing Bigger Sums," *Wall Street Journal,* 26 November 1990, p. B1.

44. Ibid.

45. James Armstrong et al., "Securities Fraud," *American Criminal Law Review* 33 (1995): 973–1016.

46. Robert Rose and Jeff Bailey, "Traders in CBOT Soybean Pit Indicted," *Wall Street Journal,* 3 August 1989, p. A4.

47. Scott McMurray, "Futures Pit Trader Goes to Trial," *Wall Street Journal,* 8 May 1990, p. C1; idem, "Chicago Pits' Dazzling Growth Permitted a Free-for-All Mecca," *Wall Street Journal,* 3 August 1989, p. A4.

48. Securities Act of 1933, 15 U.S.C. Sec. 77a to 77aa (1982); Securities Exchange Act of 1934, 15 U.S.C. Sec. 78a to 78kk (1982); 17 C.F.R. 240.10b-5 (1987).

49. *Carpenter v. United States* 484 U.S. 19 (1987); also see John Boland, "The SEC Trims the First Amendment," *Wall Street Journal,* 4 December 1986, p. 28.

50. Tim Metz and Michael Miller, "Boesky's Rise and Fall Illustrate a Compulsion to Profit by Getting Inside Track on Market," *Wall Street Journal,* 17 November 1986, p. 28; Wade Lambert, "FDIC Receives Cooperation of Milken Aide," *Wall Street Journal,* 25 April 1991, p. A3.

51. This section depends heavily on Frank Browning and John Gerassi, *The American Way of Crime* (New York: Putnam, 1980), p. 151.

52. Ibid., p. 293.

53. Ibid.

54. Edward Ranzal, "City Report Finds Building Industry Infested by Graft," *New York Times,* 8 November 1974, p. 1.

55. Toni Locy, "Former Lawmaker Gets Plea Deal," *Washington Post,* 17 April 1996.

56. Marshall Clinard and Peter Yeager, *Corporate Crime* (New York: Free Press, 1980), pp. 166–167.

57. Fraud Update, The White Paper (1991): 3–4.

58. Ibid., p. 67.

59. Ibid.

60. United Press International, "Minority Leader in N.Y. Senate Is Charged," *Boston Globe,* 17 September 1987, p. 20.

61. "Now Williams—Last, Not Least of ABSCAM Trials," *New York Times,* 5 April 1982, p. E7.

62. Edward Pound, "Honored Employee Is a Key in Huge Fraud in Defense Purchasing," *Wall Street Journal,* 2 March 1988, p. 1.

63. Discussed in Friedrichs, *Trusted Criminals,* p. 147.

64. Larry Tye, "A Tide of State Corruption Sweeps from Coast to Coast," *Boston Globe,* 25 March 1991, p. 1.

65. Maureen Kline, "Italian Magistrates Query Montedison Former Chairman," *Wall Street Journal,* 19 July 1993, p. A6.

66. *The Knapp Commission Report on Police Corruption* (New York: George Braziller, 1973), pp. 1–3, 170–182.

67. Michael Rezendes, "N.Y. Hears of Police Corrupted," *Boston Globe,* 10 October 1993, p. 1.

68. "Philadelphia Police Corruption Brings Major Reform Initiative," *Criminal Justice Newsletter,* 1 October 1996, pp. 4–5.

69. Cited in Hugh Barlow, *Introduction to Criminology,* 2nd ed. (Boston: Little, Brown, 1984).

70. Pub. L. No. 95-213, 101-104, 91 Stat. 1494.

71. Thomas Burton, "The More Baxter Hides Its Israeli Boycott Role, the More Flak It Gets," *Wall Street Journal,* 25 April 1991, p. 1.

72. "Newsbreaks," *Aviation Week and Space Technology,* 10 July 1995, p. 19.

73. Charles McCaghy, *Deviant Behavior* (New York: Macmillan, 1976), p. 178.

74. John Clark and Richard Hollinger, *Theft by Employees in Work Organizations* (Washington, D.C.: U.S. Government Printing Office, 1983), pp. 2–3.

75. "Business Fraud Prevails, May Worsen, Study Says," *Wall Street Journal,* 17 August 1993, p. A4.

76. J. Sorenson, H. Grove, and T. Sorenson, "Detecting Management Fraud: The Role of the Independent Auditor," in *White-Collar Crime, Theory and Research,* ed. G. Geis and E. Stotland (Beverly Hills, Calif.: Sage, 1980), pp. 221–251.

77. Teri Agins, "Report Is Said to Show Pervasive Fraud at Leslie Fay," *Wall Street Journal,* 27 October 1993, p. B4.

78. "Business Fraud Prevails," p. A4.

79. Associated Press, "U.S. Reports $1 Billion in Welfare Overpayments in '91," *Boston Globe* 12 April 1994, p. 14.

80. See Kristine DeBry, Bonny Harbinger, and Susan Rotkis, "Health Care Fraud," *American Criminal Law Review* 33 (1995): 818–838.

81. Bruce Lambert, "12 Chiropractors Among 20 Arrested in Insurance Fraud Sting," *New York Times,* 22 May 1997, p. A30.

82. *United States vs. Marrero,* 904 F.2d 151 (5th cir.) 1990.

83. Medicare and Medicaid Anti-Fraud and Anti-Kickback Statute, 42 U.S.C. section 1320a-7b (1994).

84. 42 U.S.C. section 1395nn (1993).

85. Laura Johannes and Wendy Bounds, "Corning Agrees to Pay $6.8 Million to Settle Medicare Billing Charges," *Wall Street Journal,* 22 February 1996, p. B2.

86. Ibid.

87. 18 U.S.C. section 1344 (1994).

88. *United States v. Bishop,* 412 U.S. 346 (1973).

89. Carl Hartman, "Study Says Underground Economy May Represent 33 Percent of Production," *Boston Globe,* 16 February 1988, p. 38.

90. Alan Murray, "IRS in Losing Battle Against Tax Evaders Despite Its New Gear," *Wall Street Journal,* 10 April 1984, p. 1.

91. Paul Duke, "IRS Excels at Tracking the Average Earner but Not the Wealthy," *Wall Street Journal,* 15 April 1991, p. 1.

92. Nancy Frank and Michael Lynch, *Corporate Crime, Corporate Violence* (Albany, N.Y.: Harrow and Heston), pp. 12–13.

93. Ibid.

94. Sutherland, "White-Collar Criminality," pp. 2–10.

95. 15 U.S.C. 1–7 (1976).

96. See *United States v. Sealy, Inc.,* 383 U.S. 350.

97. *Northern Pacific Railways v. United States,* 356 U.S. 1 (1958).

98. Michael Maltz and Stephen Pollack, "Suspected Collusion Among Bidders," in *White-Collar Crime, Theory and Research,* ed. G. Geis and E. Stotland (Beverly Hills, Calif.: Sage, 1980), pp. 174–198.

99. Gilbert Geis, "White-Collar Crime: The Heavy Electrical Equipment Antitrust Cases of 1961," in *Corporate and Governmental Deviance,* ed. M. Ermann and R. Lundman (New York: Oxford University Press, 1978), pp. 58–79.

100. Tim Carrington, "Federal Probes of Contractors Rise for Year," *Wall Street Journal,* 23 February 1987, p. 50.

101. Ibid.

102. Bruce Ingersoll and Alecia Swasy, "FDA Puts Squeeze on P&G over Citrus Hill Labeling," *Wall Street Journal,* 25 April 1991, p. B1.

103. Clinard and Yeager, *Corporate Crime.*

104. John Conklin, *Illegal But Not Criminal* (Englewood Cliffs, N.J.: Prentice-Hall, 1972), pp. 45–46.

105. For an analysis of false claims, see Jonathan Kaye and John Patrick Sullivan, "False Claims," in Eighth Survey of White-Collar Crime, *American Criminal Law Review* 30 (1993): 643–657.

106. For an in-depth review, see Ninth Survey of White Collar Crime, *American Criminal Law Review* 31 (1994): 703–721.

107. "Econotes," *Environmental Action* 13 (October 1981): 7.

108. "Econotes," *Environmental Action* 13 (September 1981): 5.

109. "Union Carbide Says Bhopal Plant Should Have Been Closed," *Wall Street Journal,* 21 March 1985, p. 18.

110. "Judge Rejects Exxon Alaska Spill Pact," *Wall Street Journal,* 25 April 1991, p. A3.

111. See, generally, Gary Green, *Occupational Crime* (Chicago: Nelson-Hall, 1990), pp. 136–138.

112. 42 U.S.C. Sec. 7401–7642 (1988), amended 1990, 104 Stat. 2399 (1990).

113. 33 U.S.C. 1251–1387 (1988).

114. 33 U.S.C. 407 (1988).

115. 42 U.S.C. 6901–92 (k) (1988).

116. 15 U.S.C. 2601–2629 (1988).

117. 7 U.S.C. 136 (1988).

118. 42 U.S.C. 9601–9675 (1988).

119. Roger Fillion, "Cracking Down on Internet Crime," *Boston Globe,* 28 December 1995, p. 65.

120. Pub. L. No. 104-104, Title V sections 501–551 (1996).

121. Xan Raskin and Jeannie Schaldach-Paiva, "Computer Crimes," *American Criminal Law Review* 33 (1995): 541–573.

122. M. Swanson and J. Terriot, "Computer Crime: Dimensions, Types, Causes and Investigations," *Journal of Political Science and Administration* 8 (1980): 305–306; Donn Parker, "Computer-Related White-Collar Crime," in *White-Collar Crime, Theory and Research,* ed. G. Geis and E. Stotland (Beverly Hills, Calif.: Sage, 1980), pp. 199–220.

123. Anne Branscomb, "Rogue Computer Programs and Computer Rogues: Tailoring Punishment to Fit the Crime," *Rutgers Computer and Technology Law Journal* 16 (1990): 24–26.

124. David Stipp, "Computer Virus Maker Is Given Probation, Fine," *Wall Street Journal,* 7 May 1990, p. B3.

125. Erik Larson, "Computers Turn out to Be Valuable Aid in Employee Crime," *Wall Street Journal,* 14 January 1985, p. 1.

126. John Hagan and Fiona Kay, "Gender and Delinquency in White-Collar Families: A Power-Control Perspective," *Crime and Delinquency* 36 (1990): 391–407.

127. Comprehensive Crime Control Act of 1984, Pub. L. No. 98-473, 2101-03, 98 Stat. 1837, 2190 (1984) (adding 18 USC 1030 (1984). Amended by Pub. L. No. 99-474, 100 Stat. 1213 (1986) codified at 18 U.S.C. 1030 (Supp. V 1987).

128. 18 U.S.C. section 1030 (1994).

129. Copyright Infringement Act 17 U.S.C. section 506(a) 1994.

130. 18 U.S.C. 2510-2520 (1988 and Supp. II 1990).

131. Eighth Survey of White-Collar Crime, *American Criminal Law Review,* 30 (1993): 501.

132. Herbert Edelhertz and Charles Rogovin, eds., *A National Strategy for Containing White-Collar Crime* (Lexington, Mass.: Lexington Books, 1980), Appendix A, pp. 122–123.

133. Kathleen Daly, "Gender and Varieties of White-Collar Crime," *Criminology* 27 (1989): 769–793.

134. Quoted in Metz and Miller, "Boesky's Rise and Fall Illustrate a Compulsion to Profit by Getting Inside Track on Market," p. 28.

135. Donald Cressey, *Other People's Money: A Study of the Social Psychology of Embezzlement* (Glencoe, Ill.: Free Press, 1973).

136. Ibid., p. 96.

137. Ronald Kramer, "Corporate Crime: An Organizational Perspective," in *White-Collar and Economic Crime: A Multidisciplinary and Crossnational Perspective,* ed. P. Wickman and T. Dailey (Lexington, Mass.: Lexington Books, 1982), pp. 75–94.

138. John Braithwaite, "Toward a Theory of Organizational Crime," paper presented at the annual meeting of the American Society of Criminology, Montreal, November 1987.

139. Travis Hirschi and Michael Gottfredson, "Causes of White-Collar Crime," *Criminology* 25 (1987): 949–974.

140. Michael Gottfredson and Travis Hirschi, *A General Theory of Crime* (Stanford, Calif.: Stanford University Press, 1990), p. 191.

141. For an opposing view, see Darrell Steffensmeier, "On the Causes of 'White-Collar' Crime: An Assessment of Hirschi and Gottfredson's Claims," *Criminology* 27 (1989): 345–359.

142. David Weisburd, Ellen Chayet, and Elin Waring, "White-Collar and Criminal Careers: Some Preliminary Findings," *Crime and Delinquency* 36 (1990): 342–355.

143. Michael Benson and Elizabeth Moore, "Are White-Collar and Common Offenders the Same? An Empirical and Theoretical Critique of a Recently Proposed General Theory of Crime," *Journal of Research in Crime and Delinquency* 29 (1992): 251–272.

144. David Simon and D. Stanley Eitzen, *Elite Deviance* (Boston: Allyn & Bacon, 1982), p. 28.

145. Jesilow, Pontell, and Geis, "Physician Immunity from Prosecution and Punishment for Medical Program Fraud," p. 19.

146. Clinard and Yeager, *Corporate Crime,* p. 124.

147. Peter Yeager, "Structural Bias in Regulatory Law Enforcement: The Case of the U.S. Environmental Protection Agency," *Social Problems* 34 (1987): 330–344.

148. Geis, "Avocational Crime," p. 390.

149. Clinard and Yeager, *Corporate Crime,* p. 288.

150. See, generally, Stanton Wheeler, David Weisburd, Elin Waring, and Nancy Bode, "White-Collar Crimes and Criminals," *American Criminal Law Review* 25 (1988): 331–357.

151. Susanne Schafer, "One General Fired, Two Punished for Mismanaging C-17 Plane," *Boston Globe,* 1 May 1993, p. 3.

152. Paul Blustein, "Disputes Arise over Value of Laws on Insider Trading," *Wall Street Journal,* 17 November 1986, p. 28.

153. Paul Barrett, "For Many Dalkon Shield Claimants Settlement Won't End the Trauma," *Wall Street Journal,* 9 March 1988, p. 29.

154. This section relies heavily on Daniel Skoler, "White-Collar Crime and the Criminal Justice System: Problems and Challenges," in *A National Strategy for Containing White-Collar Crime,* ed. Herbert Edelhertz and Charles Rogovin (Lexington, Mass.: Lexington Books, 1980), pp. 57–76.

155. Theodore Hammett and Joel Epstein, *Prosecuting Environmental Crime: Los Angeles County* (Washington, D.C.: National Institute of Justice, 1993).

156. Michael Benson, Francis Cullen, and William Maakestad, "Local Prosecutors and Corporate Crime," *Crime and Delinquency* 36 (1990): 356–372.

157. Ibid., pp. 369–370.

158. Ibid., p. 371.

159. Traub, "Battling Employee Crime: A Review of Corporate Strategies and Programs," pp. 248–252.

160. Alan Otten, "States Begin to Protect Employees Who Blow Whistle on Their Firms," *Wall Street Journal,* 31 December 1984, p. 11.

161. This section relies heavily on Albert Reiss, Jr., "Selecting Strategies of Social Control over Organizational Life," in *Enforcing Regulation,* ed. Keith Hawkins and John M. Thomas (Boston: Klowver Publications, 1984), pp. 25–37.

162. John Braithwaite, "The Limits of Economism in Controlling Harmful Corporate Conduct," *Law and Society Review* 16 (1981–1982): 481–504.

163. "EPA Sues Sherwin-Williams: Pattern of Pollution at Paint Factory Is Alleged," *Wall Street Journal,* 19 July 1993, p. 1.

164. "Making Firms Liable for Cleaning Toxic Sites," *Wall Street Journal,* 9 March 1988, p. 29.

165. Rhonda Rundle, "Computer Sciences Will Pay $2.1 Million to Settle Charges by U.S. Government," *Wall Street Journal,* 19 July 1993, p. B8.

166. Wayne Gray and John Scholz, "Does Regulatory Enforcement Work? A Panel Analysis of OSHA Enforcement," *Law and Society Review* 27 (1993): 177–191.

167. Michael Benson, "Emotions and Adjudication: Status Degradation Among White-Collar Criminals," *Justice Quarterly* 7 (1990): 515–528; John Braithwaite, *Crime, Shame and Reintegration* (Sydney: Cambridge University Press, 1989).

168. John Braithwaite and Gilbert Geis, "On Theory and Action for Corporate Crime Control," *Crime and Delinquency* 28 (1982): 292–314.

169. Frank and Lynch, *Corporate Crime, Corporate Violence,* pp. 33–34.

170. James Miller, "U.S. Ban on Baxter International Bids Hurt Reputation More Than Business," *Wall Street Journal,* 16 August 1993, p. A3.

171. Kip Schlegel, "Desert, Retribution and Corporate Criminality," *Justice Quarterly* 5 (1988): 615–634.

172. Raymond Michalowski and Ronald Kramer, "The Space Between Laws: The Problem of Corporate Crime in a Transnational Context," *Social Problems* 34 (1987): 34–53.

173. Ibid.

174. Geis, "White-Collar and Corporate Crime," p. 154.

175. Steven Klepper and Daniel Nagin, "The Deterrent Effect of Perceived Certainty and Severity of Punishment Revisited," *Criminology* 27 (1989): 721–746.

176. "The Follies Go On," *Time,* 15 April 1991, p. 45.

177. Bill Richards and Alex Kotlowitz, "Judge Finds Three Corporate Officials Guilty of Murder in Cyanide Death of Worker," *Wall Street Journal,* 17 June 1985, p. 2.

178. Donald Manson, *Tracking Offenders: White-Collar Crime* (Washington, D.C.: Bureau of Justice Statistics, 1986); Kenneth Carlson and Jan Chaiken, *White-Collar Crime* (Washington, D.C.: Bureau of Justice Statistics, 1987).

179. Robert Bennett, "Foreword," Eighth Survey of White-Collar Crime, *American Criminal Law Review* 30 (1993).

180. David Weisburd, Elin Waring, and Stanton Wheeler, "Class, Status, and the Punishment of White-Collar Criminals," *Law and Social Inquiry* 15 (1990): 223–243.

181. Mark Cohen, "Environmental Crime and Punishment: Legal/Economic Theory and Empirical Evidence on Enforcement of Federal Environmental Statutes," *Journal of Criminal Law and Criminology* 82 (1992): 1054–1109.

182. See, generally, President's Commission on Organized Crime, Report to the President and the Attorney General, *The Impact: Organized Crime Today* (Washington, D.C.: U.S. Government Printing Office, 1986). Herein cited as *Organized Crime Today.*

183. Frederick Martens and Michele Cunningham-Niederer, "Media Magic, Mafia Mania," *Federal Probation* 49 (1985): 60–68.

184. *Organized Crime Today,* pp. 7–8.

185. Alan Block and William Chambliss, *Organizing Crime* (New York: Elsevier, 1981).

186. *Organized Crime Today,* p. 462.

187. Attorney General's Commission on Pornography, *Final Report* (Washington, D.C.: U.S. Government Printing Office, 1986), p. 1053.

188. Alan Block, *East Side/West Side* (New Brunswick, N.J.: Transaction Books, 1983), pp. VII, 10–11.

189. G. R. Blakey and M. Goldsmith, "Criminal Redistribution of Stolen Property: The Need for Law Reform," *Michigan Law Review* 81 (August 1976): 45–46.

190. Merry Morash, "Organized Crime," in *Major Forms of Crime,* ed. Robert Meier (Beverly Hills, Calif.: Sage, 1984), p. 198.

191. Stephen Koepp, "Dirty Cash and Tarnished Vaults," *Time,* 25 February 1985, p. 65.

192. Roy Rowan, "The 50 Biggest Mafia Bosses," *Fortune,* 10 November 1986, p. 24.

193. Donald Cressey, *Theft of the Nation* (New York: Harper and Row, 1969).

194. Dwight Smith, Jr., *The Mafia Mystique* (New York: Basic Books, 1975).

195. *Organized Crime Today,* p. 489.

196. Robert Rhodes, *Organized Crime: Crime Control Versus Civil Liberties* (New York: Random House, 1984).

197. This section borrows heavily from Browning and Gerassi, *The American Way of Crime,* pp. 288–472; and August Bequai, *Organized Crime* (Lexington, Mass.: Lexington Books, 1979).

198. *Organized Crime Today,* p. 52.

199. Jay Albanese, "God and the Mafia Revisited: From Valachi to Frantianno," paper presented at the annual meeting of the American Society of Criminology, Toronto, 1982.

200. Philip Jenkins and Gary Potter, "The Politics and Mythology of Organized Crime: A Philadelphia Case Study," *Journal of Criminal Justice* 15 (1987): 473–484.

201. Block, *East Side/West Side.*

202. *Organized Crime Today,* p. 11.

203. Omar Bartos, "Growth of Russian Organized Crime Poses Serious Threat," *CJ International* 11 (1995): 8–9.

204. Francis Ianni, *Black Mafia: Ethnic Succession in Organized Crime* (New York: Pocket Books, 1975).

205. Robert Kelly and Rufus Schatzberg, "Types of Minority Organized Crime: Some Considerations," paper presented at the annual meeting of the American Society of Criminology, Montreal, November 1987.

206. Peter Kerr, "Chinese Now Dominate New York Heroin Trade," *New York Times,* 9 August 1987, p. 1.

207. Jenkins and Potter, "The Politics and Mythology of Organized Crime."

208. William Chambliss, *On the Take* (Bloomington: Indiana University Press, 1978).

209. Russell Watson, "Death on the Spot," *Newsweek,* 13 December 1993, pp. 18–20.

210. Yumiko Ono, "Top Kirin Brewery Executives Resign Amid Reports of Paying Off Racketeers," *Wall Street Journal,* 19 July 1993, p. A6.

211. Michael Elliott, "Global Mafia," *Newsweek,* 13 December 1993, pp. 22–29.

212. Associated Press, "Gangland Violence Rises and Startles in Moscow," *Boston Globe,* 22 July 1993, p. 44.

213. Ibid.

214. George Vold, *Theoretical Criminology,* 2nd ed., rev. Thomas Bernard (New York: Oxford University Press, 1979).

215. 18 U.S.C. 1952 (1976).

216. Pub. L. No. 91-452, Title IX, 84 Stat. 922 (1970) (codified at 18 U.S.C. 1961–68, 1976).

217. Ed Magnuson, "Hard Days for the Mafia," *Time,* 4 March 1985.

218. Selwyn Raab, "A Battered and Ailing Mafia Is Losing Its Grip on America," *New York Times,* 22 October 1990, p. 1.

219. Ibid.

220. Ibid., p. B7.

221. Jay Albanese, *Organized Crime in America,* 2nd ed. (Cincinnati: Anderson, 1989), p. 68.

Chapter 14
Public Order Crimes:
Sex and Substance Abuse

as President Bill Clinton was preparing to address the Democratic Convention in August 1996, he was presented with some shocking news. His senior political adviser, Dick Morris, had resigned in the wake of a tabloid story about his year-long affair with $200-an-hour call girl Sherry Rowlands. What was most disturbing about the affair were allegations that, in order to impress Rowlands, Morris may have revealed government information, including the still secret discovery of what appeared to be life on Mars. He even let her listen in when he chatted with President Clinton on the phone! At first, Morris's wife, attorney Eileen McGann, seemed willing to try to work out their marriage. She told a national magazine, "While I'm trying to understand, that doesn't mean I don't feel any pain or anger. I'm not happy about what he did, and sometimes I think about dismembering him, and good friends have offered to help me dig up the backyard and bury him."[1]

The couple later announced their marriage had ended. Morris was a famous and powerful political operative; Rowlands was a mature 37-year-old well paid for her sexual favors. Their actions were voluntary and noncoercive. Should their sex-for-money agreement be considered a crime—that is, prostitution? Or was this a private matter that should be beyond the reach of governmental control?

It has long been the custom in the United States and other countries to ban or limit behaviors that are believed to run contrary to social norms, customs, and values. These behaviors are often referred to as **public order crimes** or **victimless crimes,** although the latter term can be misleading.[2] Public order crimes include acts that interfere with the operations of society and the ability of people to function efficiently. Put another way, while such common-law crimes as rape or robbery are considered *mala in se*—evil unto themselves—inherently wrong and damaging, there are also *mala prohibitum* crimes—behaviors outlawed because they conflict with social policy, prevailing moral rules, and current public opinion. Statutes designed to uphold public order usually prohibit the manufacture and distribution of morally questionable goods and services: erotic material, commercial sex, mood-altering drugs. They may also ban acts that a few people holding political power consider morally tinged, such as homosexual contact. These crimes are controversial in part because millions of otherwise law-abiding citizens—students, workers, professionals—often engage in these outlawed activities and consequently become involved in criminal activity. These statutes are also controversial because they represent the selective prohibition of desired goods, services, and behaviors; in other words, they outlaw sin and vice.

This chapter is divided into three main sections. The first briefly discusses the relationship between law and morality. The second deals with public order crimes of a sexual nature: homosexual acts, deviant sex, prostitution, and pornography. The third focuses on the abuse of drugs and alcohol.

Law and Morality

Legislation of moral issues has been a continual source of frustration for lawmakers. There is little debate that the purpose of the criminal law is to protect society and reduce social harm. When a store is robbed or a child assaulted, it is relatively easy to see, and thereafter condemn, the social harm done the victim. It is, however, more difficult to sympathize with or even identify the victim of "immoral" acts, such as pornography or prostitution, in which the parties may be willing participants; if there is no victim, can there be a crime? Should acts be made illegal merely because they violate prevailing moral standards? If so, who defines morality?

Consider the case of Heidi Fleiss, the young California woman arrested in 1993 while taking out the trash at her $1.6 million Benedict Canyon home (previously owned by film star Michael Douglas). Fleiss was charged with running the most exclusive call-girl ring in Los Angeles. Fearing that she would "tell all" to the press, a number of prominent movie executives and entertainers issued unsolicited statements denying that they were patrons of Fleiss's ring; other well-known stars admitted to being her clients. Some of her "girls" claimed that it was common to make between $10,000 and $50,000 per month.[3]

In 1993 Heidi Fleiss was charged with running the most exclusive call girl ring in Los Angeles. She was later sentenced to three years in prison, a punishment that stunned even members of the jury that had convicted her. Should a person such as Fleiss, who sells sexual favors to willing customers, be incarcerated while many people convicted of murder, rape, and robbery are placed on probation without ever having to serve time in prison or jail?

Should Fleiss be punished for her acts? Her clients were people who *wanted* to hire call girls and who *willingly* put up the money to purchase their services. It hardly seems possible that these clients could be considered crime victims. What of Fleiss's alleged employees? They *willingly* engaged in sexual activity for money, and their income was far higher than they would have earned in "legitimate jobs." Although "immoral," should Fleiss, her employees, and her clients be considered criminals for engaging in this "victimless crime"?

To answer this question, we might first consider whether there is actually a "victim" in so-called victimless crimes. Some participants may have been coerced or forced into their acts and are therefore its "victims." For example, opponents of pornography, such as Andrea Dworkin, charge that women involved in "adult films" are far from being highly paid stars; they are "dehumanized—turned into objects and commodities."[4] Research on prostitution shows that many young runaways and abandoned children are coerced into a "life on the streets," where they are cruelly treated and held as virtual captives.[5]

Even if public order crimes do not actually harm their participants, perhaps society as a whole should be considered the victim of these crimes. Is the community harmed when an adult book store opens or a brothel is established? Does this send out a message that a neighborhood is in decline? Does it help educate children that deviance is to be tolerated and profited from?

Debating Morality

Some scholars argue that acts such as pornography, prostitution, and drug use erode the moral fabric of society and therefore should be punished by law. They are crimes, according to the great legal scholar Morris Cohen, because "it is one of the functions of the criminal law to give expression to the collective feeling of revulsion toward certain acts, even when they are not very dangerous."[6] In his classic statement on the function of morality in the law, Sir Patrick Devlin stated:

> Without shared ideas on politics, morals, and ethics no society can exist. . . . If men and women try to create a society in which there is no fundamental agreement about good and evil, they will fail; if having based it on common agreement, the argument goes, the society will disintegrate. For society is not something that is kept together physically; it is held by the invisible bonds of common thought. If the bonds were too far relaxed, the members would drift apart. A common morality is part of the bondage. The bondage is part of the price of society; and mankind, which needs society, must pay its price.[7]

According to this view then, so-called victimless crimes are prohibited because one of the functions of criminal law is to express public morality.[8]

Some argue that basing criminal definitions on moral beliefs is an impossible task: Who defines morality? Are we not punishing differences rather than social harm? Are photographs of nude children by famed photographer Robert Mapplethorpe art or obscenity? As U.S. Supreme Court Justice William O. Douglas so succinctly put it, "What may be trash to me may be prized by others."[9]

In the Puritan society of Salem, Massachusetts, were not women burned at the stake as witches because their behavior seemed strange or different? In Africa today, an estimated 100 million women have had their external genitals removed. The surgery is done to ensure virginity, remove sexual sensation, and render them suitable for marriage. Critics of this practice, led by American author Alice Walker (who wrote *The Color Purple*), consider the procedure to be mutilation and torture; others argue that this ancient custom should be left to the discretion of the indigenous people who consider it part of their culture. "Torture," counters Walker, "is not culture." Can an outsider define the morality of another culture?[10]

Some influential legal scholars have questioned the propriety of legislating morals. H. L. A. Hart states:

> It is fatally easy to confuse the democratic principle that power should be in the hands of the majority with the utterly different claim that the majority, with power in their hands, need respect no limits. Certainly there is a special risk in a democracy that the majority may dictate how all should live.[11]

Joseph Gussfield argues that the purpose of outlawing acts because they are immoral is to show the moral superiority of those who condemn the acts over those who partake of them. The legislation of morality "enhances the social status of groups carrying the affirmed culture and degrades groups carrying that which is condemned as deviant."[12]

Criminal or Immoral?

It is possible that acts that most of us deem highly immoral are not criminal. There is no law against lust, gluttony, avarice, spite, or envy, although they are considered some of the "seven deadly sins." Nor is it a crime in most jurisdictions to ignore the pleas of a drowning person, even though such callous behavior is quite immoral.

Violations of conventional morality may also be tolerated because they serve a useful social function. For example, there is some evidence that watching sexually explicit films can provide excitement and release tension that might otherwise be satisfied in more harmful and violent acts.[13] Immoral behavior may be condoned because it provides ancillary benefits to legitimate enterprises: Illegal betting on football games draws people to watch TV at the neighborhood bar; people go to legitimate massage parlors or hire escort services because they believe employees will engage in sex for profit on the side.[14]

Some acts also seem both well intentioned and moral but are still considered criminal: It is a crime (euthanasia) to kill a loved one who is suffering from an incurable disease to spare the person further pain; it is larceny to steal a rich man's money to feed a poor family; marrying many women (polygamy) is considered a crime (bigamy), even though it may conform to religious beliefs.[15] As legal experts Wayne LaFave and Austin Scott, Jr., argue: "A good motive will not normally prevent what is otherwise criminal from being a crime."[16]

It might be possible to settle this argument by saying that immoral acts can be distinguished from crimes on the basis of the social harm they cause: Acts that are extremely harmful to the public usually become outlawed. Yet this perspective does not always hold sway. Some acts that cause enormous amounts of social harm are perfectly legal: All of us are well aware of the illness and death associated with the consumption of tobacco and alcohol, although they remain legal to produce and sell; manufacturers continue to sell sports cars and motorcycles that can accelerate to over 100 mph, even though the legal speed limit is at most 65. More people die each year from alcohol-, tobacco-, and auto-related deaths than from all drug-related deaths combined. Should drugs be legalized and fast cars outlawed?

Even if an act were outlawed simply because it caused social harm, the law might prove difficult or impossible to enforce unless the public was united in its disapproval. For example, assisted suicide may be against the law because many people believe it causes "social harm," but so far prosecutors have failed to gain convictions in assisted suicide cases because so many people view it as a humanitarian act and refuse to convict people such as Dr. Jack Kevorkian.

Vigilante Justice

In the early West, "vigilance committees" were set up in San Francisco and other boom towns to pursue cattle rustlers and stagecoach robbers and to dissuade undesirables from moving in. These vigilantes held to a strict standard of morality, which resulted in sure and swift justice being handed down upon capturing a culprit.

The avenging vigilante has remained part of the popular culture. Fictional "do gooders" who take it on themselves to enforce the law, battle evil, and personally deal with those who they consider immoral have become enmeshed in the public psyche. From the Lone Ranger to Batman (the "Caped Crusader"), the righteous **vigilante** is expected to go on **moral crusades** without any authorization from legal authorities. Who called on Superman to battle for "truth, justice, and the American way"? The assumption that it is okay to take matters into your own hands if the cause is right and the target is "immoral" is not lost on the younger generation. It should come as no surprise that gang boys sometimes take on the "street" identity of "Batman" or "Superman" so that they can battle their rivals with impunity.

Fictional characters are not the only ones who take it upon themselves to fight for "moral decency"; members of special interest groups are also ready to do battle. Popular targets of moral crusaders are abotion clinics, pornographers, gun dealers, and logging companies. For example, on March 21, 1993 Baylor University regents voted against allowing nude modeling in art classes after school administrators were swamped with phone calls objecting to "nudity in the classroom."[17] In 1996 Key West, Florida passed a new town ordinance prohibiting nude body painting at the town's annual "Fantasy Fest," a raucous Mardi Gras–like festival. The Monroe County Christian Coalition had launched an all-out offensive against Fantasy Fest, calling it "depravity and debauchery," and the city commission responded by curbing some of the more outrageous activities.[18]

The Baylor and Key West incidents illustrate the pressure that can be placed on governing boards by moral crusaders. Howard Becker has labeled people who go on moral crusades in order to control the definition of morality **moral entrepreneurs.** These rule creators, argues Becker, operate with an absolute certainty that their way is right and that any means are justified to get their way; "the crusader is fervent and righteous, often self-righteous."[19]

Moral crusades are often directed against people clearly defined as evil by one segment of the population even though they may be admired by others. For example, anti-"smut" campaigns may attempt to ban the books of a popular author from the school library or prevent a "controversial" figure from speaking at the local college. One way for moral crusaders to accomplish their goal is to prove to all who will listen that some unseen or hidden trait makes their targets truly evil and unworthy of a public audience. This kind of moral crusade may be aided, according to sociologist Daniel Claster, by the fact that an essential facet of the American culture is to divide people into "bad guys" and "good guys." This polarization of good and evil creates a climate in which those categorized as "good" are deified, while the "bad" are demonized.[20]

Categorizing people as all good or all bad influences the nature of social control. Crime control policies influenced by exaggerated or one-sided moral judgments may be overly punitive and ineffective. For example, the death penalty is justified if murderers are "bad guys"—unrepentant monsters who commit serial murders and mutilate their victims. If, instead, murderers were viewed as "good guys"—the disturbed victims of child abuse and neglect—it would be out of the question to consider the death penalty.

Enforcement of morally tinged statutes has become a significant problem for law enforcement agencies. If laws governing morally tinged behavior are enforced too vigorously, local authorities are branded as reactionaries who waste time on petty issues. If, on the other hand, police agencies ignore public order crimes, they are accused of being soft on immorality and social degeneracy. "Society would be a lot better off," the argument goes, "if the cops cracked down on 'those people.'" Who "those people" are and what should be done about them is a matter of great public debate.

Let us now turn to specific examples of public order crimes.

Illegal Sexuality

One type of public order crime relates to what conventional society considers to be deviant sexual practices. Among these outlawed practices are homosexual acts, paraphilias, prostitution, and pornography. Laws controlling these behaviors have been the focus of much debate.

Homosexual Behavior

Homosexuality—the word derives from the Greek *homos*, meaning "same"—refers to erotic interest in members of one's own sex. However, to engage in homosexual behavior does not necessarily mean one is a homosexual. Some people may engage in homosexuality because heterosexual partners are unavailable (as in the armed services). Some may have sex forced on them by aggressive homosexuals, a condition common in prisons. Some adolescents may experiment with partners of the same sex, even though their sexual orientation is heterosexual. Albert Reiss has described the behavior of delinquent youths who engage in homosexual behavior for money but still regard themselves as heterosexuals and who discontinue all homosexual activities as adults.[21] Finally, it is possible to be a homosexual but not to engage in sexual conduct with members of the same sex. To avoid this confusion, it might be helpful to adopt the definition of a *homosexual* as one "who is motivated in adult life by a definite preferential erotic attraction to members of the same sex and who usually (but not necessarily) engages in overt sexual relations with them."[22]

Homosexual behavior has existed in most societies. Records of it can be found in prehistoric art and hieroglyphics. In their review of the literature on 76 preliterate societies, C. S. Ford and F. A. Beach found that male homosexuality was viewed as normal in 49 of these societies and female homosexuality was normal in 17.[23] Some cultures include homosexual experiences as part of their "manhood rituals."[24] Even when homosexuality was banned or sanctioned, it still persisted.

In the United States, it is estimated that 3% to 16% of the male population and 2% to 6% of the female population are exclusively homosexual, although many more may have had homosexual experiences sometime in their lives.[25] These numbers have been the subject of fierce debate, and the percentage of the population that is exclusively gay is still not known with certainty.

ATTITUDES TOWARD HOMOSEXUALITY. Throughout much of Western history, homosexuals have been subject to discrimination, sanction, and violence. The Bible implies that God destroyed the ancient cities of Sodom and Go-

morrah because of their residents' deviant behavior, presumably homosexuality; Sodom is the source of the term **sodomy** (deviant intercourse). The Bible expressly forbids homosexuality—in Leviticus in the Old Testament and Paul's Epistles, Romans, and Corinthians in the New Testament—and this prohibition has been the basis for repressing homosexual behavior.[26] Gays were brutalized and killed by the ancient Hebrews, a practice continued by the Christians who ruled Western Europe. Laws providing the death penalty for homosexuals existed until 1791 in France, until 1861 in England, and until 1889 in Scotland. Up until the Revolution, some American colonies punished homosexuality with death. In Hitler's Germany, 50,000 homosexuals were put in concentration camps; up to 400,000 more from occupied countries were killed. Research indicates that "gay bashing" is still widespread and that 90% of gay men and lesbians report being the target of physical abuse, verbal abuse, or threats because of their sexual identity.

> ## Connections
>
> As you may recall from Chapter 11, gay men and women are still subject to thousands of incidents of violence and other hate crimes each year.

Today, many reasons are given for an extremely negative overreaction to homosexuals, referred to as *homophobia*.[27] The cause of antigay feelings is uncertain. Some religious leaders believe that the Bible condemns same-sex relations and that this behavior is therefore a sin. Some are ignorant about the lifestyle of gays and fear that homosexuality is a disease that can be caught or that homosexuals will seduce their children.[28] Others develop a deep-rooted hatred of gays because they are insecure about their own sexual identity. Research shows that males who express homophobic attitudes are also those most likely to become aroused by erotic images of homosexual behavior. Homophobia may thus be associated with homosexual arousal that the homophobe is either unaware of or denies.[29]

Surveys indicate that negative attitudes toward gays persist in our society. During the 1960s, 67% of people surveyed believed that homosexuality was obscene and vulgar. Fewer than 20% believed that laws banning homosexuality should be repealed.[30] Studies since the 1970s indicate that a majority of people still view gays as sick, sinful, or dangerous.[31] The Gallup Poll indicates that more than half the general public neither considers homosexuality an acceptable lifestyle nor believes that gays should be allowed to hold teaching jobs, become members of the clergy, or serve as president.[32]

Is it possible for antigay attitudes to change? There are some indications that antigay bias can be reversed. Harvard University now offers courses on gay life, and there is a gay studies major at the City University of New York and at San Francisco State College.[33] Books are being published that explain their new family life to the estimated 7 million children living full- or part-time with gay and lesbian parents; titles include *Daddy's Roommate* and *Heather Has Two Mommies*.[34]

HOMOSEXUALITY AND THE LAW. Homosexuality, considered a legal and moral crime throughout most of Western history, is no longer a crime in the United States. In the case of *Robinson v. California*, the U.S. Supreme Court determined that people could *not* be criminally prosecuted because of their status (for example, drug addict or homosexual).[35] Despite this protection from criminal prosecution based on status, most states and the federal government criminalize the lifestyle and activities of homosexuals. No state or locality allows same-sex marriages, and homosexuals cannot obtain a marriage license to legitimize their relationship, although lawsuits are pending to allow homosexual marriages.[36]

Oral and anal sex and all other forms of nongenital heterosexual intercourse are banned in about half the states under statutes prohibiting sodomy, deviant sexuality, or buggery. Maximum penalties range from three years to life in prison, with ten years being the most common sentence.[37] In 1986 the Supreme Court, in *Bowers v. Hardwick,* upheld a Georgia statute making it a crime to engage in consensual sodomy, even within the confines of one's own home.[38] The Court disregarded Bowers's claims that homosexuals have a "fundamental right" to engage in sexual activity and that consensual, voluntary sex between adults in the home is a private matter that should not be controlled by the law. If all sex within the home were a private matter, Justice Byron White argued for the majority, then such crimes as incest and adultery could not be prosecuted. Citing the historical legal prohibitions against homosexual sodomy, the Court distinguished between the right of gay couples to engage in the sexual behavior of their choice and the sexual privacy the law affords married heterosexual couples. Ironically, the Georgia statute, which carries a 20-year prison sentence, is not directed solely toward homosexuals but refers to a "person" in its prohibition of sodomy.[39]

Prestigious legal bodies, such as the American Law Institute (ALI), have called for the abolition of statutes prohibiting homosexual sex, unless force or coercion is used.[40] A number of states, including Illinois, Connecticut, and Nebraska, have adopted the ALI's Model Penal Code policy of legalizing any consensual sexual behavior between adults as long as it is conducted in private and is not forced; in all, about 20 states have decriminalized private, consensual sodomy between adult homosexuals.[41]

Homosexuals still suffer other legal restrictions. While 40 states have laws banning sexual discrimination, Miami repealed its gay rights ordinance in 1977; in 1985 Houston voters rejected by a four-to-one margin a proposal to eliminate sexual preference in hiring, firing, and promoting city employees.[42] In 1992 major ballot initiatives in Colorado and Oregon were designed to restrict the civil liberties of gay men and women; while the Oregon legislation failed, the Colorado initiative won a majority of votes but was later overturned by the Supreme Court.[43] As late as 1993, voters in Cincinnati repealed a city ordinance that banned discrimination in housing or employment based on sexual orientation.[44]

Although the U.S. Civil Service Commission found in 1975 that homosexuals could not be barred from federal employment, gays are still considered security risks and are not allowed to work in high-security jobs; it was not until December 1993 that the FBI lifted its ban on homosexuals.[45] The backlash over President Clinton's attempt to make good on his campaign promise to allow gays in the military produced the first crisis of his presidency. The compromise (so far) has been a "don't ask, don't tell" policy. In 1996 the Supreme Court gave tacit approval to the "don't ask" policy by declining to hear a case brought by Navy Lieutenant Paul Thomasson who had been discharged in 1994 for openly declaring himself homosexual.[46]

Homosexuals may still be evicted from private housing at the landlord's discretion. Gays are prohibited from living together in public housing projects. In most areas, private employers may also discriminate against gay men and women. For example, a federal court upheld the right of an airline to fire a pilot who underwent a sex-change operation.[47] Gays have also lost custody of their children because of their sexual orientation, although more courts are now refusing to consider a gay lifestyle alone as evidence of parental unfitness.[48]

In sum, although it is not a crime to be a homosexual, homosexual acts are still illegal in most states. However, most police agencies enforce laws banning homosexual practices only if they are forced to do so, if the acts occur in public places, or if the acts are done for financial consideration.[49]

Paraphilias

On October 21, 1996 more than 250,000 Belgians took to the streets to protest what they considered the government's inept handling of a case involving the deaths of four children, allegedly at the hands of a pedophile ring led by a convicted rapist, Marc Dutroix. Two of the victims (eight-year-old girls) had been imprisoned and molested for months in Dutroix's home. They starved to death when he was arrested and sent to jail on an unrelated charge. Other children had been kidnapped, raped, tortured, and allegedly sold into sexual slavery by the ring, which many believe to have enjoyed high-level protection from prosecution.[50]

The case of pedophile Marc Dutroix is an extreme example of sexual abnormality, or **paraphilia.** From the Greek *para* "(to the side of")" and *philos* ("loving"), paraphilias are bizarre or abnormal sexual practices involving recurrent sexual urges focused on (1) nonhuman objects (underwear, shoes, leather); (2) humiliation or the experience of receiving or giving pain (sadomasochism, bondage); or (3) children or others who cannot grant consent.[51] Some paraphilias, such as wearing clothes normally worn by the opposite sex (transvestic fetishism), can be engaged in by adults in the privacy of their homes and do not involve a third party; these are usually out of the law's reach. Others, however, present a risk of social harm and are subject to criminal penalties. This group of outlawed sexual behavior includes:

- *Asphyxiophilia or autoerotic asphyxia*—using a noose, ligature, plastic bag, mask, volatile chemicals, or chest compression to attempt partial asphyxia and oxygen deprivation to the brain to enhance sexual gratification; almost all cases involve males
- *Frotteurism*—rubbing against or touching a nonconsenting person in a crowd, elevator, or other public area
- *Voyeurism*—obtaining sexual pleasure from spying on a stranger while he or she disrobes or engages in sexual behavior with another
- *Exhibitionism*—deriving sexual pleasure from exposing the genitals to surprise or shock a stranger
- *Sadomasochism*—deriving pleasure from receiving pain or inflicting pain on another
- *Pedophilia*—attaining sexual pleasure through sexual activity with prepubescent children; research indicates that at least 20% of males report sexual attraction to one child or more, although the rate of sexual fantasies or the potential for sexual contact is much lower[52]

Paraphilias that involve unwilling or underage victims are subject to legal prosecution. Most state criminal codes carry specific laws banning indecent exposure and voyeurism. Others prosecute paraphilias under common-law assault and battery or sodomy statutes. In their extreme, paraphilias can lead to sexual assaults in which the victim suffers severe harm and the offender a prison term.

In a high percentage of cases, the victims are children. Studies of sexual offenders serving time in state prisons indicate that two-thirds had victims under the age of 18, and 58% of those—or nearly 4 in 10 imprisoned violent sex offenders—said their victims were age 12 or younger.

Although the vast majority of violent sex offending involves males assaulting female victims, females account for a small percentage of known offenders, and males account for a small percentage of victims. In a very small fraction of sexual assaults, victim and offender are of the same sex.

Victim and offender are likely to have had a prior relationship as family members, intimates, or acquaintances. Based on police-recorded incident data, in 90% of the incidents involving children younger than 12, the child knew the offender. The FBI's UCR arrest data, as well as court conviction data and prison admissions data, all point to a sex offender who is older than other violent offenders, generally in his early thirties, and more likely to be white than other violent offenders.[53]

Prostitution

Prostitution has been known for thousands of years. The term derives from the Latin *prostituere,* which means "to cause to stand in front of." By implication, the prostitute is viewed as publicly offering his or her body for sale. The earliest record of prostitution appears in ancient Mesopotamia, where priests engaged in sex to promote fertility in the community. All women were required to do temple duty, and passing strangers were expected to make donations to the temple after enjoying its services.[54]

Modern commercial sex appears to have its roots in ancient Greece, where Solon established licensed brothels in 500 B.C. The earnings of Greek prostitutes helped pay for the temple of Aphrodite. Famous men openly went to prostitutes to enjoy intellectual, aesthetic, and sexual stimulation; prostitutes, however, were prevented from marrying.[55]

Although some early Christian religious leaders, such as St. Augustine and St. Thomas Aquinas, were tolerant of prostitution as a necessary evil, this tolerance disappeared after the reformation. Martin Luther advocated the abolition of prostitution on moral grounds, and Lutheran doctrine depicted prostitutes as emissaries of the devil who were sent to destroy the faith.[56]

In more recent times, prostitution was tied to the rise of English brewery companies during the early 19th century. Saloons controlled by the companies employed prostitutes to attract patrons and encourage them to drink. This relationship was repeated in major U.S. cities, such as Chicago, until breweries were forbidden to own the outlets that distributed their product.

Today, there are many variations of prostitution, but in general, **prostitution** can be defined as the granting of nonmarital sexual access, established by mutual agreement of the prostitutes, their clients, and their employers, for remuneration. This definition is sexually neutral, since prostitutes can, of course, be straight or gay, male or female. A recent analysis has amplified the definition of prostitution by describing the conditions usually present in a commercial sexual transaction:

- *Activity that has sexual significance for the customer.* This includes the entire range of sexual behavior, from sexual intercourse to exhibitionism, sadomasochism, oral sex, and so on.
- *Economic transaction.* Something of economic value, not necessarily money, is exchanged for the activity.
- *Emotional indifference.* The sexual exchange is simply for economic consideration. Although the participants may know each other, their interaction has nothing to do with affection.[57]

INCIDENCE OF PROSTITUTION. It is difficult to assess the number of prostitutes operating in the United States.[58] Fifty years ago, about two-thirds of noncollege-educated men, but only about one-fourth of college-educated men, had visited a prostitute; about 20% of college-educated men had been sexually initiated by prostitutes.[59] It is likely that the number of men who hire prostitutes has declined sharply, a trend punctuated by a significant drop (20%) in the number of prostitutes arrested during the past decade (although it is also possible that police are less willing to make arrests in cases of prostitution).[60]

How can these changes be accounted for? Changing sexual mores, brought about by the so-called sexual revolution, have liberalized sexuality. Men are less likely to engage prostitutes because legitimate alternatives for sexuality are more open to them. In recent years, the prevalence of sexually transmitted diseases has changed sexual attitudes to the point where many men may avoid visiting prostitutes for fear of irreversible health effects. Many prostitutes are intravenous drug takers. About 47% of males and 85% of females arrested for prostitution test positively for drug abuse. Drug use increases their chances of contracting the AIDS virus and becoming carriers; a study conducted by the U.S. Centers for Disease Control of 1,305 prostitutes in eight U.S. cities found that almost 7% tested positively for the HTLV-I virus, which has been linked to leukemia and multiple sclerosis.[61]

Despite such supposed changes in sexual morality, the Uniform Crime Reports indicate that about 100,000 prostitution arrests are made annually, with the gender ratio being about 60 to 40 female.[62] More alarming is the fact that about 1,000 arrests are of minors under 18. In 1995, about 181 recorded arrests were of children age 15 and under; a few (56 arrests) were kids under 12, including 31 who were under 10 years of age. Arguing that the criminal law should not interfere with sexual transactions because no one is harmed is undermined by these disturbing statistics.

TYPES OF PROSTITUTION. Several types of prostitutes operate in the United States. Prostitutes who work the streets in plain sight of police, citizens, and customers are referred to as *hustlers, hookers,* or *streetwalkers.* Although glamorized by the Julia Roberts character in the film *Pretty Woman* (who winds up with multimillionaire Richard Gere), streetwalkers are considered the least attractive, lowest paid, most vulnerable men and women in the profession. Streetwalkers wear bright clothing, makeup, and jewelry to attract customers; they take their customers to hotels. The term *hooker,* however, is not derived from the ability of streetwalkers to hook clients with their charms. It actually stems from the popular name given women who followed Union General "Fighting Joe" Hooker's army during the Civil War.[63] Because streetwalkers must openly display their occupation, they are likely to be involved with the police. Studies indicate they are most likely to be members of ethnic or racial minorities who live in poverty. Many are young runaways who gravitate to major cities to find a new and exciting life and escape from sexual and physical abuse at home.[64] Of all prostitutes, streetwalkers have the highest incidence of drug abuse and larceny arrests, and they are the toughest.[65]

Although the incidence of prostitution may be on the decline, the Uniform Crime Reports indicate that about 100,000 prostitution arrests are made annually; about 1,000 arrests are of minors under 18. Should prostitution be decriminalized and efforts made to regulate the sex trade and protect young girls and boys rather than punish them?

Bar girls, or *B-girls,* as they are also called, spend their time in bars, drinking and waiting to be picked up by customers. Although alcoholism may be a problem, B-girls usually work out an arrangement with the bartender so they are served diluted drinks or water colored with dye or tea, for which the customer is charged an exorbitant price. In some bars, the B-girl is given a credit for each drink she gets the customer to buy. It is common to find B-girls in towns with military bases and large transient populations.[66]

Also called bordellos, cathouses, sporting houses, and houses of ill repute, **brothels** flourished in the 19th and early 20th centuries. They were large establishments, usually run by **madams,** that housed several prostitutes. A madam is a woman who employs prostitutes, supervises their behavior, and receives a fee for her services; her cut is usually 40% to 60% of the prostitutes' earnings. The madam's role may include recruiting women into prostitution and socializing them in the "trade."[67] The madam, often a retired prostitute, is the senior administrator and owner. She makes arrangements for opening the place, attracts prostitutes and customers, works out understandings with police authorities, and pacifies neighbors. The madam is part psychologist, part parent figure, and part business entrepreneur.

Some brothels and their madams have received national notoriety. Polly Adler wrote a highly publicized autobiography of her life as a madam called *A House Is Not a Home.* Sally Stanford maintained a succession of luxuriously furnished brothels in San Francisco. Stanford never made a secret of her profession; she actually listed her phone number in the city directory. In 1962 and 1970, she ran for the San Francisco City Council.

In 1984, socialite Sydney Biddle Barrows was arrested by New York police for operating a million-dollar-a-year prostitution ring out of a bordello on West Seventy-Fourth Street.[68] Descended from a socially prominent family who traced their line to the *Mayflower,* Barrows ranked her 20 women on looks and personality from A ($125 per hour) to C ($400 per hour) and kept 60% of their take. Her "black book" of clients was described by police as a mini *Who's Who.*

Brothels declined in importance following World War II. The closing of the last brothel in Texas is chronicled in the play and movie *The Best Little Whorehouse in Texas.* Today, the most well-known brothels exist in Nevada, where prostitution is legal outside large population centers. Such houses as Mustang Ranch, Miss Kitty's, and Pink Pussycat service customers who drive out from Reno and Las Vegas.

The aristocrats of prostitution are **call girls.** They charge customers up to $1,500 per night and may net over $100,000 per year. Some gain clients through employment in escort services, while others develop independent customer lists. Many call girls come from middle-class backgrounds and service upper-class customers. Attempting to dispel the notion that their service is simply sex for money, they concentrate on making their clients feel important and attractive. Working exclusively via telephone "dates," call girls get their clients by word of mouth or by making arrangements with bellhops, cab drivers, and so on. They either entertain clients in their own apartments or make "outcalls" to clients' hotels and apartments. Upon retiring from "the life," a call girl can sell her datebook listing client names and sexual preferences for thousands of dollars. Despite the lucrative nature of their business, call girls suffer considerable risk by being alone and unprotected with strangers. It is common for them to request the business cards of their clients to make sure they are dealing with "upstanding citizens."

A relatively new phenomenon, *call houses,* combines elements of the brothel and call-girl rings. In this type of operation, a madam receives a call from a prospective customer, and if she finds the client acceptable, arranges a meeting between the caller and a prostitute in her service. The madam maintains a list of prostitutes who are on call rather than living together in a house. The call house insulates the madam from arrest because she never meets the client or receives direct payment.[69]

Prostitutes known as *circuit travelers* move around in groups of two or three to lumber, labor, and agricultural camps. They will ask the foremen for permission to ply their trade, service the whole crew in an evening, and then move on.

A phenomenon in commercial sex, *rap booths* are located in the adult entertainment zones of such cities as New York and San Francisco.[70] The prostitute and her customer occupy booths that are separated by a glass wall. They talk via telephone for as long as the customer is willing to pay. The more money he spends, the more she engages in sexual banter and disrobing. There is no actual touching, and sex is through masturbation, with the prostitute serving as a masturbation aid similar in function to a pornographic magazine.

With the prevalence of drug abuse and the introduction of "crack" cocaine to the street culture in the mid-1980s, a new form of prostitution, trading sex for drugs, became common. Surveys conducted in New York and Chicago have found that a significant portion of female prostitutes have substance abuse problems, and more than half claim that prostitution is the method they use to support their drug habit; on the street, women who barter drugs for sex are called **skeezers.** Not all drug-addicted prostitutes barter sex for drugs, but those who do report more frequent drug abuse and sexual activity than other prostitutes.

There is some question about the impact that bartering sex for drugs has on prostitutes. The prevailing wisdom is that those who engage in the practice are victims who are often the target of violent attacks and rapes. However, when interviewed by Paul Goldstein and his associates, barterers viewed themselves as being engaged in economic transactions in which they are treated fairly.[71] In opposition to widely held beliefs, these prostitutes are not drug slaves or victims who have no control over their lives. Many expressed the view that bartering gave them the "benefit" of the deal—valuable drugs for a few minutes of sexual service. However, as Lisa Maher and Kathleen Daly discovered, while the crack trade had done little to improve the relative position of female offenders, trading crack for sex actually lowered wages of experienced street sex workers because it encouraged intense competition from novices; violence and victimization also increased.[72]

Some "working girls" are based in **massage parlors.** Although it is unusual for a masseuse to offer all the services of prostitution, oral sex and manual stimulation are common. Most localities have attempted to limit commercial sex in massage parlors by passing ordinances specifying that the masseuse keep certain parts of her body covered and limiting the areas of the body that can be massaged.

Photography studios and model and escort services are other possible covers for commercial sex. Some photo studios will allow customers to put body paint on models before the photo sessions start. Stag party girls will service all-male parties and groups by putting on shows and having sex with participants. In years past, many hotels had live-in prostitutes. Today's hotel prostitute makes a deal with the bell captain or manager to refer customers to her for a fee; some second-rate hotels still have resident prostitutes.

BECOMING A PROSTITUTE. Why does someone turn to prostitution? Both male and female prostitutes often come from troubled homes marked by extreme conflict and hostility and from poor urban areas or rural communities. Divorce, separation, or death splits the family; most prostitutes grew up in homes with absent fathers.[73] Many prostitutes were initiated by family members into sex as young as 10 to 12 years of age; they have long histories of sexual exploitation and abuse.[74] The early experiences with sex helped teach them that their bodies have value and that sexual encounters can be used to obtain affection, power, or money.

Lower-class girls who get into "the life" report conflict with school authorities, poor grades, and an overly regimented school experience.[75] Drug abuse, including heroin and cocaine addiction, are often factors in the prostitute's life.[76] Other personal characteristics found among samples of prostitutes include growing up in a slum neighborhood; being born out of wedlock or into a broken home; dropping out of school; fantasizing about money and success; being a member of a "loose crowd"; seeing prostitutes in the neighborhood; having unfortunate experiences with a husband or boyfriend; and having trouble keeping a job.[77] However, there is no actual evidence that people become prostitutes because of psychological problems or personality disturbances. Money, drugs, and survival seem to be greater motivations.

Research indicates that few girls were forced into the life by a pimp. Pimps may convince girls by flattery, support, promises, and affection, but relatively few kidnap or coerce kids into prostitution. There is more evidence that friends or relatives introduce kids into prostitution. Most report having entered prostitution voluntarily because they disliked the discipline of conventional work.[78] Jennifer James claims that the primary cause of women becoming prostitutes is the supply-and-demand equation operating in society.[79] She contends that male clients are socialized to view sex as a commodity that can be purchased. The quantity of sex, rather than its quality, has the higher value for U.S. males. Women who are socialized to view themselves as sex objects may easily step over the line of propriety and accept money for their favors. These women view their bodies as salable commodities, and most prostitution does in fact pay better than other occupations available for women with limited education. Helping to push women to take the final step into prostitution are the troubled personal circumstances described previously. James backs up her view with a research study that found that only 8% of prostitutes claim to have started because of dire economic necessity, while 57% were motivated by a desire for money and luxuries. This issue is discussed on pages 386–387 in the Close-Up on child prostitution in the U.S. and Japan.

PIMPS. A pimp derives part or all of his livelihood from the earnings of a prostitute. The pimp helps steer customers to the prostitute, stays on the alert for and deals with police, posts bail, and protects his prostitutes from unruly customers.[80] To the prostitute, the pimp is a surrogate father, a husband, and a lover. She may sell her body to customers, but she reserves her care and affection for her pimp. Pimps can pick up established "working girls" or they can "turn out" young girls who have never been in "the life." Occasionally, but not as often as the media would like us to believe, they pick up young runaways, buy them clothes and jewelry, and turn them into **"baby pros."**

What attracts men to the life of the pimp? One view is that many pimps originally worked on the fringes of prostitution as bellhops, elevator operators, or barmen and subsequently drifted into the profession. An opposing view is that pimps began as young men seduced by older prostitutes who taught them how to succeed in the life, how to behave, and how to control women.[81]

The role of the pimp is changing. The decline of the brothel, the development of independent prostitutes, and the control of prostitution by organized crime has decreased the number of full-time pimps.[82] Many prostitutes are drug-dependent, and in some areas drug dealers have replaced pimps as the controlling force in prostitution. Even the cost of sex is drug-dependent, rather than being controlled by a pimp, with the going rate for sexual services geared to the cost of a rock of crack.[83] Even when a prostitute has a pimp, the relationship is often short-lived and unstable. Dorothy Bracey found that pimps are reluctant to work with younger prostitutes today because they face more severe legal penalties if caught running juveniles and because they consider juveniles unstable and untrustworthy.[84]

LEGALIZE PROSTITUTION? Prostitution is illegal in all states except Nevada (except in the counties in which Las Vegas and Reno are located). Typically, prostitution is considered a misdemeanor, punishable by a fine or a short jail sentence. The federal government's **Mann Act** (passed in 1925) prohibits bringing women into the country or transporting them across state lines for the purposes of prostitution. Often called the "white slave act," it carries a $5,000 fine, five years in prison, or both.

Feminists have staked out conflicting views of prostitution. One position is that women must become emancipated from male oppression and reach sexual equality. The *sexual equality* view considers the prostitute to be a victim of male dominance. In patriarchal societies such as our own, male power is predicated on female subjugation, and

Table 14.1 Sources, Estimated Revenue, and Services of the Sex-for-Profit Industry

SOURCE	ESTIMATED ANNUAL REVENUE	SERVICES/EXAMPLES
Cable, satellite, pay-per-view television	$150 million	Playboy, Adam & Eve, Spice channels; pay-per-view movies
Magazines	$1 billion	*Penthouse, Playboy, Hustler,* thousands of selected titles
Adult videos	$3.1 billion, including $300 million in rentals	An estimated 30% of the entire video market
CD-ROM	$300 million	Sexually oriented interactive games and films, 150 new titles each year
Phone sex	$1 billion	Typical company has 25 employees, grosses $2 million per year
Internet sex	$100 million	Personals, live interaction strip shows, pictures on the net
Strip clubs	$3 billion	2,200 in the U.S. becoming more "upscale"
Private dancing	$250 million	Dancers on call serve as independent contractors
Escort services	$1 billion	Girls on call summoned by beepers; typical service employs 50 people and grosses $4 million

Source: Anthony Flint, "Selling Sex in the 90s," *Boston Globe,* 1 December 1996, p. A36.

prostitution is a clear example of this gender exploitation.[85] In contrast, for some feminists the fight for equality depends on controlling all attempts by men or women to impose their will on women. The free choice view is that prostitution is an expression of women's status as an equal; if freely chosen, it can be an expression of women's equality and not a symptom of subjugation.[86]

Advocates of both positions argue that the penalties for prostitution should be reduced (decriminalized); neither side advocates outright legalization. Decriminalization would relieve already desperate women of the additional burden of severe legal punishment. In contrast, legalization might be coupled with regulation by male-dominated justice agencies. For example, required medical examinations would mean increased male control over women's bodies. While both sides advocate change in the criminal status of prostitution, few communities, save San Francisco, have openly debated or voted on its legalization.

Pornography

The term **pornography** derives from the Greek *porne,* meaning "prostitute," and *graphein,* meaning "to write." Most cities have stores devoted to the display and sale of books, magazines, and films that depict explicit sex acts of every imaginable kind. It has also become common for suburban video stores to rent and sell sexually explicit tapes, which make up to 15% of the home rental market. The purpose of this material is to provide sexual titillation and excitement for paying customers. Although material depicting nudity and sex is typically legal and protected by the First Amendment's provision limiting the government control of speech, most criminal codes contain provisions prohibiting the production, display, and sale of *obscene* material.

Obscenity, derived from the Latin *caenum* for "filth," is defined by Webster's dictionary as "deeply offensive to morality or decency . . . designed to incite to lust or depravity."[87] The problem of controlling pornography centers on this definition of obscenity. Police and law enforcement officials can legally seize only material that is judged obscene. "But who," critics ask, "is to judge what is obscene?" At one time, such novels as *Tropic of Cancer* by Henry Miller, *Ulysses* by James Joyce, and *Lady Chatterley's Lover* by D. H. Lawrence were prohibited because they were considered obscene. Today, they are considered works of great literary value. Thus, what is obscene today may be considered a work of art, or at least socially acceptable, at a future time. After all, *Playboy* and *Penthouse* magazines, sold openly on most college campuses, display nude models in all kinds of sexually explicit poses. Allowing individual judgments on what is obscene makes the Constitution's guarantee of free speech unworkable. Could not antiobscenity statutes also be used to control political and social dissent? The uncertainty surrounding this issue is illustrated by Supreme Court Justice Potter Stewart's famous 1964 statement on how he defined obscenity: "I know it when I see it."

Because of this legal and moral ambiguity, the "sex trade" is booming around the United States. Table 14.1 lists the various components in the industry.

Child prostitution is now a worldwide problem. Girls from Latin America are being sold for sex in Europe and the Middle East. Southeast Asian girls wind up in Northern Europe and the Middle East, and Russian and Ukrainian girls are sold in Hungary, Poland, and the Baltic States. In Asia an estimated 1 million children are part of the sex trade. Thailand is the leader, but child prostitution is a growing problem in India, Bangladesh, and the Philippines. Sex tours are a common practice in these nations, and the United Nations has called for sanctions to punish operators. Child prostitution is not unique to undeveloped countries, either; it is actually common in two of the wealthiest nations on earth: the United States and Japan.

CHILD PROSTITUTION IN THE UNITED STATES

The National Center on Child Abuse and Neglect defines *juvenile prostitution* as "the use of, or participation by, children under the age of majority in sexual acts with adults or other minors where no force is present." The lack of force may make the relationship between a juvenile prostitute and the customer appear to be an equal economic exchange; however, victims' advocates acknowledge that in re-

ality, the juvenile is a victim, often of an abusive family life, low self-esteem, and a lack of economic alternatives. It is difficult to measure the number of children who are actually involved in prostitution. Estimates from law enforcement officials, social service providers, and researchers have ranged from tens of thousands to 2.4 million children annually. A reasonable estimate is that there are 100,000 to 300,000 juvenile prostitutes per year. While experts debate the extent of the problem, about 1,000 juveniles are arrested each year for prostitution, some as young as 10 and 11 years old.

Where do these children come from, and how do they get recruited into prostitution? Often, these children come from dysfunctional families; having suffered physical, sexual, or emotional abuse, they become runaways, trying to escape their home environment. About 75% of juvenile prostitutes are runaways or "throwaways," who were encouraged or forced to leave home by their families.

Research suggests that most of the children who become prostitutes seem to suffer from a negative self-image. Whether by parents, school officials, or peers, these youngsters have been convinced that they have little self-worth. Many of the children "want to be wanted," and the at-

tention of customers and pimps can foster the illusion that these people really care.

A negative self-image and a lack of marketable skills may force children into prostitution as a means of economic survival. Pimps and other prostitutes may offer food and shelter in exchange for money raised through prostitution. Once the juveniles have entered this lifestyle, they may find it difficult to get out.

Some may suffer more severe forms of mental disorders, including schizophrenia, depression, and emotional instability. Of course, these problems may be associated with the dysfunctional family life of kids who get involved in prostitution.

Juvenile prostitutes are typically under the control of a pimp. To increase his profits, a pimp may be a member of an organized ring, sending the juvenile on a circuit that could encompass numerous locations over several states. A booking agent often works as the middleman, organizing the circuit schedule and providing a facade of legitimacy between the pimp and the police. Although most kids become prostitutes by choice, once in the life they may find themselves subject to the pimp's "control, rules, orders, drugs, violence, and manipulation."

Aside from any possible emotional traumas associated with life as a juvenile

---

THE DANGERS OF PORNOGRAPHY

Dear Ann Landers,

. . . several months ago, I caught my husband making calls to a 900-sex number. After a week of denial, he admitted that for several years he had been hooked on porn magazines, porn movies, peep shows, strippers and phone sex. This addiction can start early in life. With my husband it began at age 12, with just one simple, "harmless" magazine. By the time he was 19, it had become completely out of control. . . . For years my husband hated himself and it affected his entire life.[88]

Opponents of pornography argue that it degrades both the men and women who are photographed and members of the public who are sometimes forced to see obscene material. Pornographers exploit their models, who may include underage children. The Attorney General's Commission on Pornography, set up by the Reagan administration

to review the sale and distribution of sexually explicit material, concluded that many performers and models are the victims of physical and psychological coercion.[89] The so-called kiddy porn industry is estimated to amount to over $1 billion. Each year, over a million children are believed to be used in pornography or prostitution, many of them runaways whose plight is exploited by adults.[90]

CHILD PORNOGRAPHY RINGS. How does child pornography get made and distributed? Many of the "hardcore" pictures that find their way into the hands of collectors are the work of pornographic groups or rings, adults who join together to exploit children and adolescents for sex. Ann Wolbert Burgess studied 55 child pornography rings and found that the typical one contained from 3 to 11 children, predominantly males, some of nursery-school age. The adults who controlled the ring used a position of

prostitute, numerous physical risks endanger the child. Sexually transmitted diseases, pregnancy, and AIDS are constant dangers. The biological effects of sex at such an early age are not clearly documented but include damage to the vaginal and anal areas. These juveniles rarely seek medical help, for fear they may be brought to the attention of authorities.

Along with risks of disease come the risks of violence, both from pimps and from customers. Although they claim to protect the juveniles, the pimps may allow customers to "rough up" the youths "to teach them a lesson." Some pimps may use cruel and bizarre punishments, such as forcing juveniles to sit on a hot stove, for those who don't meet their quotas or who cause problems. Prostitutes are also easy targets for muggers and other criminals. These juveniles are often out late at night with large amounts of cash and are unlikely to report a victimization to the police.

CHILD PROSTITUTION IN JAPAN

According to recent reports, child prostitution is much more common and accepted in Japan, a country known for its relatively low crime rates. It is perfectly legal to have sex with a 14-year-old in Tokyo. Lured from the suburbs for quick and easy cash, 15-year-olds walk the street in their school uniforms. In 1995 police arrested 5,481 girls under age 18 for prostitution, an increase of 38% since 1993. But this number is most likely a vast undercount, as most school-girl prostitutes in Tokyo cannot be detained on any charges because prostitution is legal unless arranged by a pimp.

In some poor Asian nations such as Thailand, most young girls are forced into prostitution because they are indigent. Not so in Japan, where kids seem to be plying the streets to satisfy their expensive tastes for fashionable clothes and accessories. Girls in junior high school have joined telephone clubs, where men can wait for calls from teenage girls. There are also dating clubs where men go pick out young girls. For example, the Melon Club, which advertises openly on busy streets, features a one-way mirror looking onto a main room where girls wait, lounging on sofas, playing videogames, and reading comic books. Customers pay $100, half of which goes to the girl. Many of the girls give out their portable phone numbers and begin freelancing. Some clubs have hundreds of girls on the payroll. Other girls bypass the clubs, posting beeper or phone numbers on bulletin boards or walking the streets in their school uniforms.

Counselors report that many of the middle-class girls they talk to see nothing wrong with prostitution. Most come from relatively affluent two-parent families, sharing none of the social problems of their American sisters. The threat of AIDS is low in Japan, with only nine or ten new cases reported each year. Moreover, civic groups, including teachers and mothers' groups, fear criminalizing prostitution because girls and their families would be shamed if they had to testify against patrons; school officials fear humiliation if a girl at their school was arrested. So while prostitution appears on the wane in the United States, it is flourishing in Japan.

CRITICAL THINKING QUESTIONS

1. It seems ironic that juvenile prostitution flourishes in Japan, a country with a very low crime rate and strict moral code. What does this tell us about the association among crime, culture, and morality?

2. If prostitution were legalized, would its rate increase, decrease, or remain the same? What would be the benefits and drawbacks?

Sources: Reuters, "UN Cites Sharp Rise in Child Labor, Prostitiution," *Boston Globe*, 12 November 1996, p. A6; Valerie Reitman, "Japan's New Growth Industry: Schoolgirl Prostitution, Prevention Efforts Are Blocked by Lax Laws—And Mothers' Groups," *Wall Street Journal*, 2 October 1996, p. A14; R. Barri Flowers, *Female Crime, Criminals and Cellmates* (Jefferson, N.C.: McFarland & Co., 1995), pp. 154, 156; Jennifer Williard, *Juvenile Prostitution* (Washington, D.C.: National Victim Resource Center, 1991).

trust to recruit the children and then continued to exploit them through a combination of material and psychological rewards.

Burgess found that different types of child pornography rings exist. *Solo sex rings* involve several children and a single adult, usually male, who uses a position of trust (counselor, teacher, Boy Scout leader) to recruit children into sexual activity. *Transition rings* are impromptu groups set up to sell and trade photos and sex. *Syndicated rings* have well-structured organizations that recruit children and create extensive networks of customers who desire sexual services.[91] The sexual exploitation by these rings can have a devastating effect on the child victim. Burgess found that children suffered from physical problems ranging from headaches and loss of appetite to genital soreness, vomiting, and urinary infections. Psychological problems include mood swings, withdrawal, edginess, and nervousness. Exploited children were prone to such acting-out behavior as setting fires and becoming sexually focused in the use of language, dress, and mannerisms. In cases of extreme and prolonged victimization, children may lock onto the sex group's behavior and become prone to further victimization or even become victimizers themselves.

DOES PORNOGRAPHY CAUSE VIOLENCE? An issue critical to the debate over pornography is whether viewing it produces sexual violence or assaultive behavior against women. This debate was given added interest when serial killer Ted Bundy claimed his murderous rampage was fueled by reading pornography.

Some evidence exists that viewing sexually explicit material actually has little effect on behavior. In 1970 the National Commission on Obscenity and Pornography reviewed all available material on the effects of pornography

Chapter Fourteen   Public Order Crimes: Sex and Substance Abuse   **387**

Net Bookmark

Does pornography exploit children? The findings of a study funded by the Office of Juvenile Justice and Delinquency Prevention on "Images of Children, Crime and Violence in *Playboy, Penthouse, and Hustler*" can be accessed at:

http://www.iglou.com/first-principles/abstract.html

and authorized independent research projects. The commission found no clear relationship between pornography and violence, and it recommended that federal, state, and local legislation not interfere with the rights of adults who wish to read, obtain, or view explicit sexual materials.[92] Almost 20 years later, the highly controversial Attorney General's Commission on Pornography, sponsored by a conservative Reagan administration, called for legal attacks on hard-core pornography and condemnation of all sexually related material but also found little evidence that obscenity is a cause per se of antisocial behavior.[93]

How might we account for this surprisingly insignificant association? Some explanation may be found in Danish sociologist Berl Kutchinsky's widely cited research showing that the rate of sex offenses actually declined shortly after pornography was decriminalized in Denmark in 1967.[94] He attributed this trend to the fact that viewing erotic material may act as a safety valve for those whose impulses might otherwise lead them to violence. In a similar vein, Michael Goldstein found that convicted rapists and sex offenders report less exposure to pornography than a control group of nonoffenders.[95]

It is possible that viewing prurient material may have the unintended side effect of satisfying erotic impulses that otherwise might result in more sexually aggressive behavior. This issue is far from settled. A number of criminologists believe that the positive relationship between pornography consumption and rape rates in various countries, including the United States, is evidence that obscenity may indeed have a powerful influence on criminality.[96] Nonetheless, the weight of the evidence shows little relationship between violence and pornography per se.

While there is little or no documentation of a correlation between pornography and violent crime, there is stronger evidence that people exposed to material that portrays violence, sadism, and women enjoying being raped and degraded are likely to be sexually aggressive toward female victims.[97] Even the Attorney General's Commission on Pornography concluded in 1986 that a causal link could be drawn between exposure to violent sexually explicit material and sexual violence. After reviewing the literature on the subject, the Commission found that while the behavioral effects of sexually nonviolent and nondegrading pornography were insignificant, exposure to sexually violent and degrading materials:

- leads to a greater acceptance of rape myths and violence against women;
- [has] more pronounced effects when the victim is shown enjoying the use of force or violence;
- is arousing for rapists and for some males in the general population; and
- has resulted in sexual aggression against women in controlled laboratory settings.[98]

Laboratory experiments conducted by a number of leading authorities have found that men exposed to violence in pornography are more likely to act aggressively toward women.[99] The evidence suggests that violence and sexual aggression are not linked to erotic or pornographic films per se but that erotic films depicting violence, rape, brutality, and aggression may evoke similar feelings in viewers. This finding is especially distressing because it is common for adult-only books and films to have sexually violent themes, such as rape, bondage, and mutilation.[100]

PORNOGRAPHY AND THE LAW. All states and the federal government prohibit the sale and production of pornographic material. Child pornography is usually a separate legal category, involving either (1) the creation or reproduction of materials depicting minors engaged in actual or simulated sexual activity ("sexual exploitation of minors") or (2) the publication or distribution of obscene, indecent, or harmful materials to minors.[101] Under existing federal law, trafficking in obscenity (18 U.S.C. Sec.1462, 1464, 1466), child pornography (18 U.S.C. Sec.2252), harassment (18 U.S.C. Sec.875[c]), illegal solicitation or luring of minors (18 U.S.C. Sec.2423[b]), and threatening to injure someone (18 U.S.C. Sec.875[c]) are all felonies punished by long prison sentences.

Despite the fact that state and federal law control the production and sale of obscene materials, the punishment of pornographers often creates moral and legal dilemmas. The problems were highlighted by two incidents that occurred in 1990. The first was a posthumous exhibition featuring the works of gay photographer Robert Mapplethorpe. The exhibition was heavily criticized by conservative politicians because it contained images of nude children and men in homoerotic poses and because it had received federal funding. When Cincinnati's Contemporary Arts Center mounted the show, obscenity charges were brought against its director; he was later found not guilty. The actions taken against the Mapplethorpe exhibit brought waves of protest from artists and performers, as well as from civil libertarians who fear governmental control over art, music, and theater. The second incident occurred on June 8, 1990 when an undercover detective walked into a record shop in Fort Lauderdale, Florida and bought a copy of "As Nasty as They Wanna Be," the hit album of the rap group 2 Live Crew. He and six of his fellow officers then arrested store owner Charles Freeman on the charge of distributing obscene material. This was the first arrest following a federal judge's decision that the group's songs (for example, "Me So Horny") contained lyrics having a sexual content that violated local community standards of decency and were therefore obscene.[102]

To many, these incidents represented an exercise of the criminal law that was a direct attack on the First Amendment's guarantee of free speech. Should free expression be controlled if it offends some people's sense of decency?

The First Amendment protects free speech and prohibits police agencies from limiting the public's right of free expression. However, the Supreme Court held in the twin cases of *Roth v. United States* and *Alberts v. California* that the First Amendment protects all "ideas with even the slightest redeeming social importance—unorthodox ideas, controversial ideas, even ideas hateful to the prevailing climate of opinion . . . but implicit in the history of the First Amendment is the rejection of obscenity as utterly without redeeming social importance."[103] In the 1966 case of *Memoirs v. Massachusetts,* the Supreme Court again required that for a work to be considered obscene, it must be shown to be "utterly without redeeming social value."[104] These decisions left unclear how obscenity is defined. If a highly erotic movie tells a "moral tale," must it be judged legal even if 95% of its content is objectionable?

A spate of movies made after the *Roth* decision alleged that they were educational or told a moral tale so they could not be said to lack redeeming social importance. Many state obscenity cases were appealed to federal courts so judges could decide whether the films totally lacked redeeming social importance. To rectify the situation, the Supreme Court redefined its concept of obscenity in the case of *Miller v. California:*

> The basic guidelines for the trier of fact must be (a) whether the average person applying contemporary community standards would find that the work taken as a whole appeals to the prurient interest; (b) whether the work depicts or describes, in a patently offensive way, sexual conduct specifically defined by the applicable state law, and (c) whether the work, taken as a whole, lacks serious literary, artistic, political or scientific value.[105]

To convict a person of obscenity under the *Miller* doctrine, the state or local jurisdiction must specifically define obscene conduct in its statute, and the pornographer must engage in that behavior. The Court gave some examples of what is considered obscene: "patently offensive representations or descriptions of masturbation, excretory functions and lewd exhibition of the genitals." In subsequent cases, the Court overruled convictions for "offensive" or "immoral" behavior; these are not considered obscene.

The *Miller* doctrine has been criticized for not spelling out how community standards are to be determined.[106] Obviously, a plebiscite cannot be held to determine the community's attitude for every trial concerning the sale of pornography. Works that are considered obscene in Omaha might be considered routine in New York, but how can we be sure? To resolve this dilemma, the Supreme Court articulated in *Pope v. Illinois* a reasonableness doctrine: A work is obscene if a reasonable person applying objective (national) standards would find the material lacking in any social value.[107] While *Pope* should help clarify the legal definition of obscenity, the issue is far from settled. Justice John Paul Stevens in his dissent offered one interesting alternative: The First Amendment protects material "if some reasonable persons could [find] serious literary[,] artistic, political or scientific value" in it.[108] Stevens believes that if anyone could find merit in a work, it should be protected by law. Do you?

Controlling Sex for Profit

Sex for profit predates Western civilization. Considering its longevity, there seems to be little evidence that it can be controlled or eliminated by legal means alone. Recent reports indicate that the business is currently booming and now amounts to $10 billion per year.[109] The Attorney General's Commission on Pornography advocated a strict law enforcement policy to control obscenity, urging that "the prosecution of obscene materials that portray sexual violence be treated as a matter of special urgency."[110] Since then, the federal government has made a concerted effort to prosecute adult movie distributors. Law enforcement has been so fervent that industry members have filed suit claiming they are the victims of a "moral crusade" by right-wing zealots.[111]

While politically appealing, law enforcement crusades may not necessarily obtain the desired effect. A "get tough" policy could make sex-related goods and services a relatively scarce commodity, driving up prices and making their sale even more desirable and profitable. And going after national distributors may help decentralize the adult movie and photo business and encourage local rings to expand their activities, such as by making and marketing videos as well as still photos or distributing them through on-line computer networks.

An alternative approach has been to control or restrict the sale of pornography within acceptable boundaries and areas. For example, municipal governments have tolerated or even established restricted adult entertainment zones in which obscene material can be openly sold. In the case of *Young v. American Mini Theaters,* the Supreme Court permitted a zoning ordinance that restricted theaters showing erotic movies to one area of the city, even though it did not find that any of the movies shown were obscene.[112] The state, therefore, has the right to regulate adult films as long as the public has the right to view them.

Restricting the sale of sexually related material to a particular area can have unforeseen consequences. Skyrocketing real estate prices in the downtown areas of such cities as Boston and New York have made the running of sex clubs and stores in those areas relatively unprofitable. Land that was used for adult movie houses has been redeveloped into high-priced condominiums and office buildings. The number of striptease clubs in Boston's Combat Zone shrank from 22 in 1977 to five within ten years as the area was redeveloped.[113]

The threat of government regulation may also convince some participants in the sex-for-profit industry to police themselves. While some forms of sexually explicit material and activities will be tolerated by local law enforcement agencies, others will bring prompt legal control. For example, child pornography usually spurs otherwise complacent governmental agencies to take swift action. Efforts to control this problem have been supported by the courts. The landmark *New York v. Ferber* case indicates the Supreme Court's willingness to allow the states to control child pornography.[114] In this case, Paul Ferber, a Manhattan bookstore owner, was sentenced to 45 days in jail for violating a New York statute banning material that portrays children engaged in sexually explicit, although not necessarily obscene, conduct. He challenged the law as a violation of free speech. By unanimously upholding Ferber's conviction, the Supreme Court found that kiddy porn is damaging to the children it exploits and therefore can be legally banned. In his opinion, Justice Byron White said, "It has been found that sexually exploited children are unable to develop healthy affectionate relationships in later life, have sexual dysfunction and have a tendency to become sexual abusers as adults." The Court also found that the films were an invasion of the child's privacy that the child could not control.

Fear of government control may have already had an influence on the content of nationally distributed adult magazines. Criminologists have uncovered a correlation between rape rates and the circulation rates of national adult magazines.[115] The federal government has consequently asked the states to toughen their laws governing the distribution of sex-related material. Some mainstream sex magazines may have altered their content rather than risk provoking public officials.

Technological change will provide the greatest challenge to those seeking to control the sex-for-profit industry. Adult movie theaters are closing all over the nation as people are able to buy or rent tapes in their local video stores and play them in the privacy of their homes.[116] Adult CD-ROMs are now a staple of the computer industry. Internet sex services include live, interactive stripping and sexual activities.[117] The government has moved to control the broadcast of obscene films via satellite and other technological innovations. On February 15, 1991, Home Dish Only Satellite Networks, Inc. was fined $150,000 for broadcasting pornographic movies to its 30,000 clients throughout the United States; it was the first case to involve prosecution for the illegal use of satellites to broadcast obscene films.[118] Since then, federal agents have stepped up their efforts to control broadcast and Internet-based pornography. In one raid, federal agents arrested at least 12 people for allegedly trafficking in child pornography and arranging for child sex through electronic mail via the America Online computer service. The investigation, called "Innocent Images," led to raids of more than 120 homes and offices.[119]

In the long run, the popularity of pornography on the Internet, on CD-Roms, and broadcast via satellite may overwhelm efforts by law enforcement officials and spur the growth of sex-related materials.

Substance Abuse

The problem of substance abuse stretches across the United States. Large urban areas are beset by drug-dealing gangs, drug users who engage in crime to support their habits, and alcohol-related violence. Rural areas are important staging centers for the transshipment of drugs across the country and are often the site of the production of synthetic drugs and marijuana farming.[120]

Another indication of the concern about drugs has been the increasing number of drug-related arrests, from less than half a million in 1977 to about 1.5 million in 1996. Similarly, the proportion of prison inmates incarcerated for drug offenses has increased by 300% since 1986.[121] Clearly, the justice system views drug abuse as a major problem and is taking what decision makers regard as decisive measures to control it.

Net Bookmark

The National Clearinghouse for Alcohol and Drug Information (NCADI) is the information service of the Center for Substance Abuse Prevention of the U.S. Department of Health and Human Services. NCADI is the world's largest resource for current information and materials concerning substance abuse prevention.

http://www.health.org/

Despite the scope of the drug problem, it is still viewed by some as another type of victimless public order crime. There is great debate over the legalization of drugs and the control of alcohol. Some consider drug use a private matter and drug control another example of government intrusion into people's private lives. Furthermore, legalization could reduce the profit of selling illegal substances and drive suppliers out of the market.[122] Others see these substances as dangerous, believing that the criminal activity of users makes the term *victimless* nonsensical. Still another position is that the possession and use of all drugs and alcohol should be legalized but that the sale and distribution of drugs should be heavily penalized. This would punish those profiting from drugs and would enable users to be helped without fear of criminal punishment.

When Did Drug Use Begin?

The use of chemical substances to change reality and provide stimulation, relief, or relaxation has gone on for thousands of years. Mesopotamian writings indicate that opium was used 4,000 years ago—it was known as the "plant of joy."[123] The ancient Greeks knew and understood the problem of drug use. At the time of the Crusades, the Arabs were using marijuana. In the Western Hemisphere, natives of Mexico and South America chewed coca leaves and used "magic mushrooms" in their religious ceremonies.[124] Drug use was also accepted in Europe well into the 20th century. Recently uncovered pharmacy records circa 1900 to 1920 showed sales of cocaine and heroin solutions to members of the British royal family; records from 1912 show that Winston Churchill, then a member of Parliament, was sold a cocaine solution while staying in Scotland.[125]

In the early years of the United States, opium and its derivatives were easily obtained. Opium-based drugs were adopted for use in various patent medicine cure-alls. Morphine was used extensively to relieve the pain of wounded soldiers in the Civil War. By the turn of the century, an estimated 1 million U.S. citizens were opiate users.[126]

Several factors precipitated the stringent drug laws that are in force in the United States today. The rural religious creeds of the 19th century—for example, those of the Methodists, Presbyterians, and Baptists—emphasized individual human toil and self-sufficiency while designating the use of intoxicating substances as an unwholesome surrender to the evils of urban morality. Religious leaders were thoroughly opposed to the use and sale of narcotics. The medical literature of the late 1800s began to designate the use of morphine and opium as a vice, a habit, an appetite, and a disease. Late 19th- and early 20th-century police literature described drug users as habitual criminals. Moral crusaders in the 19th century defined drug use as evil and directed the actions of local and national lawmakers to outlaw the sale and possession of drugs. Some well-publicized research efforts categorized drug use as highly dangerous.[127] Drug use was also associated with the foreign immigrants who were recruited to work in factories and mines and brought with them their national drug habits. Early antidrug legislation appears to be tied to prejudice against immigrating ethnic minorities.[128]

After the Spanish-American War of 1898, the United States inherited Spain's opium monopoly in the Philippines. Concern over this international situation, along with the domestic issues outlined above, led the U.S. government to participate in the First International Drug Conference, held in Shanghai in 1908, and a second one at The Hague in 1912. Participants in these two conferences were asked to strongly oppose free trade in drugs. The international pressure, coupled with a growing national concern, led to the passage of the antidrug laws discussed in this chapter.

Alcohol and Its Prohibition

The history of alcohol and the law in the United States has also been controversial and dramatic. At the turn of the century, a drive was mustered to prohibit the sale of alcohol. The **temperance movement** was fueled by the belief that the purity of the U.S. agrarian culture was being destroyed by the growth of the city. Urbanism was viewed as a threat to the lifestyle of the majority of the nation's population, then living on farms and in villages. The forces behind the temperance movement were such lobbying groups as the Anti-Saloon League led by Carrie Nation, the Women's Temperance Union, and the Protestant clergy of the Baptist, Methodist, and Congregationalist faiths.[129] They viewed the growing city, filled with newly arriving Irish, Italian, and Eastern European immigrants, as centers of degradation and wickedness. The propensity of these ethnic people to drink heavily was viewed as the main force behind their degenerate lifestyle. The eventual prohibition of the sale of alcoholic beverages brought about by ratification of the Eighteenth Amendment in 1919 was viewed as a triumph of the morality of middle- and upper-class Americans over the threat posed to their culture by the "new Americans."[130]

Prohibition turned out to be a failure. It was enforced by the Volstead Act, which defined intoxicating beverages as those containing .5% or more of alcohol.[131] What doomed Prohibition? One factor was the use of organized crime to supply illicit liquor. Also, the law made it illegal only to sell alcohol, not to purchase it; this factor cut into the law's deterrent capability. Finally, despite the work of Elliot Ness and his "Untouchables," law enforcement agencies were inadequate, and officials were more than likely to be corrupted by wealthy bootleggers.[132] Eventually, in 1933, the Twenty-First Amendment to the Constitution repealed Prohibition, signaling the end of the "noble experiment."

Commonly Abused Drugs Today

A wide variety of drugs are available to drug abusers. Some are addicting, others not. Some provide hallucinations; others cause a depressing, relaxing stupor; and a few give an immediate, exhilarating uplift. This section will discuss some of the most widely used illegal drugs.[133]

ANESTHETICS. Anesthetic drugs are used as nervous system depressants. Local anesthetics block nervous system transmissions; general anesthetics act on the brain to produce a generalized loss of sensation, stupor, or unconsciousness (called narcosis). The most widely abused anesthetic drug is phencyclidine (PCP), known on the street as "angel dust." PCP can be sprayed on marijuana or other plant leaves and smoked, or it can be drunk or injected; the last two methods are extremely hazardous. Originally developed as an animal tranquilizer, PCP causes hallucinations and a spaced-out feeling. The effects of PCP can last up to two days; the danger of overdose is extremely high.

VOLATILE LIQUIDS. Volatile liquids are liquids that are easily vaporized. Some substance abusers inhale vapors from lighter fluid, paint thinner, cleaning fluid, and model airplane glue to reach a drowsy, dizzy state sometimes accompanied by hallucinations. The psychological effect produced by inhaling these substances is a short-term sense of excitement and euphoria followed by a period of disorientation, slurred speech, and drowsiness. Amyl nitrate ("poppers") is a commonly used volatile liquid that is sold in capsules that are broken and inhaled. Poppers allegedly increase sensation and are sometimes used during sexual activity to prolong and intensify the experience.

BARBITURATES. The hypnotic-sedative drugs—barbiturates—are able to depress the central nervous system into a sleeplike condition. On the illegal market, barbiturates are called "goofballs" or "downers" or are known by the color of the capsules—"reds" (Seconal), "blue dragons" (Amytal), and "rainbows" (Tuinal). Barbiturates can be prescribed by doctors as sleeping pills. In the illegal market, they are used to create relaxed, sociable, and good-humored feelings. However, if dosages get too high, users become irritable and obnoxious and finally slump off into sleep. Barbiturates are probably the major cause of drug overdose deaths.

TRANQUILIZERS. Tranquilizers have the ability to relieve uncomfortable emotional feelings by reducing levels of anxiety. They ease tension and promote a state of relaxation. The major tranquilizers are used to control the behavior of the mentally ill who are suffering from psychoses, aggressiveness, and agitation. They are known by their brand names—Ampazine, Thorazine, Pacatal, Sparine, and so on. The minor tranquilizers are used by the average citizen to combat anxiety, tension, fast heart rate, and headaches. The most common are Valium, Librium, Miltown, and Equanil. These mild tranquilizers are easily obtained by prescription. However, increased dosages can lead to addiction, and withdrawal can be painful and hazardous.

AMPHETAMINES. Amphetamines ("uppers," "beans," "pep pills") are synthetic drugs that stimulate action in the central nervous system. They produce an intense physical reaction: elevated blood pressure, increased breathing rate, heightened bodily activity, and elevated mood. Amphetamines also produce psychological effects, such as increased confidence, euphoria, fearlessness, talkativeness, impulsive behavior, and loss of appetite. The commonly used amphetamines are Benzedrine ("bennies"), Dexedrine ("dex"), Dexamyl, Bephetamine ("whites"), and Methedrine ("meth," "speed," "crystal meth," "ice"). Methedrine is probably the most widely used and most dangerous amphetamine. Some people swallow it in pill form; heavy users inject it for a quick rush. Long-term heavy use can result in exhaustion, anxiety, prolonged depression, and hallucinations.

CANNABIS (MARIJUANA). Commonly called "pot," "grass," "ganja," "maryjane," "dope," and a variety of other names, marijuana is produced from the leaves of *Cannabis sativa,* a hemp plant grown throughout the world. Hashish (hash) is a concentrated form of cannabis made from unadulterated resin from the female plant. Smoking large amounts of pot or hash can cause drastic distortion in auditory and visual perception, even producing hallucinatory effects. Small doses produce an early excitement ("high") that gives way to a sedated effect and drowsiness. Pot use is also related to decreased physical activity, overestimation in time and space, and increased food consumption ("the munchies"). When the user is alone, marijuana produces a quiet, dreamy state. In a group, it is common for users to become giddy and lose perspective. Although marijuana is not physically addicting, its long-term effects have been the subject of much debate.

HALLUCINOGENS. Hallucinogens are drugs, either natural or synthetic, that produce vivid distortions of the senses without greatly disturbing the viewer's consciousness. Some produce hallucinations, while others cause psychotic behavior in otherwise normal people. One common hallucinogen is mescaline, named after the Mescalero Apaches, who first used it. Mescaline occurs naturally in the peyote, a small cactus that grows in Mexico and the southwestern United States. After initial discomfort, mescaline produces vivid hallucinations in all ranges of colors and geometric patterns, a feeling of depersonalization, and out-of-body sensations. A synthetic and highly dangerous form of mescaline used for a brief period in the 1960s was called STP. However, the danger of this drug made its use short-lived.

A second group of hallucinogens are alkaloid compounds. Alkaloids occur in nature or can be made in the laboratory. They include such familiar hallucinogens as DMT, morning glory seeds, and psilocybin. These compounds can be transformed into a D-lysergic acid diethylamide-25, commonly called LSD. This powerful substance (800 times more potent than mescaline) stimulates cerebral sensory centers to produce visual hallucinations in all ranges of colors, to intensify hearing, and to increase sensitivity. Users often report a scrambling of sensations; they may "hear colors" and "smell music." Users also report feeling euphoric and mentally superior, although to an observer they appear disoriented and confused. Unfortunately, anxiety and panic (a "bad trip") may occur during the LSD experience, and overdoses can produce psychotic episodes, flashbacks, and even death.

Marijuana is produced from the leaves of *Cannabis sativa,* a hemp plant grown throughout the world. Here a marijuana crop is being destroyed by drug agents. Despite such efforts, marijuana remains widely used by teens and young adults.

COCAINE. Cocaine is an alkaloid derivative of the coca leaf first isolated in 1860 by Albert Niemann of Gottingen, Germany. When originally discovered, it was considered a medicinal breakthrough that could relieve fatigue, depression, and various other symptoms. Its discovery was embraced by no less a luminary than Sigmund Freud, who used it himself and prescribed it for his friends, patients, and relatives. It quickly became a staple of popular patent medicines. When pharmacist John Styth Pemberton first brewed his new soft drink in 1886, he added cocaine to act as a "brain tonic" and called the drink Coca-Cola; this secret ingredient was taken out in 1906.[134] When its addictive qualities and dangerous side effects became apparent, cocaine's use was controlled by the Pure Food and Drug Act of 1906. Until the 1970s, cocaine remained an underground drug—the property of artists, jazz musicians, beatniks, and sometimes even jet-setters.

Cocaine, or coke, is the most powerful natural stimulant. Its use produces euphoria, laughter, restlessness, and excitement. Overdoses can cause delirium, increased reflexes, violent manic behavior, and possible respiratory failure. Cocaine can be sniffed, or "snorted," into the nostrils or injected. The immediate feeling of euophoria ("rush") is short-lived, and heavy users may snort coke as often as every ten minutes. Mixing cocaine and heroin is called "speedballing"; this practice is highly dangerous and is alleged to have killed comedian John Belushi.

COCAINE DERIVATIVES: FREEBASE AND CRACK. A great deal of public attention has been focused on cocaine use and the popularity of new, more potent forms of cocaine, such as **freebase** and **crack.** Freebase is a chemical produced from street cocaine by treating it with a liquid to remove the hydrochloric acid with which pure cocaine is bonded during manufacture. The free cocaine, or cocaine base (hence, the term *freebase*) is then dissolved in a solvent, usually ether, that crystallizes the purified cocaine. The resulting crystals are crushed and smoked in a special glass pipe; the high produced is more immediate and powerful than snorting street-strength coke. Unfortunately for the user, freebase is dangerous to make since it involves highly flammable products, such as ether (you may recall the accident that seriously injured comedian Richard Pryor), it is an expensive habit, and it is highly addictive.

Despite the publicity, crack is not a new substance and has been on the street for more than 15 years. Crack, like freebase, is processed street cocaine. Its manufacture involves using ammonia or baking soda to remove the hydrochlorides and create a crystalline form of cocaine base that can then be smoked.[135] However, unlike freebase, crack is not a pure form of cocaine and contains both remnants of hydrochloride and additional residue from the baking soda (sodium bicarbonate). In fact, crack gets its name from the fact that the sodium bicarbonate often emits a crackling sound when the substance is smoked.

Research by Thomas Mieczkowski indicates that today, smoking crack is the preferred method of cocaine ingestion among persistent users.[136] Also referred to as "rock," "gravel," and "roxanne," crack apparently was introduced and gained popularity on both coasts simultaneously. It is relatively reasonable in cost and can provide a powerful high; users rapidly become psychologically addicted to crack. An even more powerful form of the drug is "spacebase"—crack cut with LSD, heroin, or PCP.

There are indications that the use of crack and other cocaine derivatives in the general population is less pervasive than previously believed.[137] However, there also is disturbing evidence that crack use, because of its relatively low cost and easy availability, is concentrated among the poor and the lower classes, who are susceptible to this powerful and relatively inexpensive drug. One study of drug-using delinquents in Miami found that about 90% had used crack during their lifetime and about 30% reported being daily users. So while crack may not be the national epidemic among the middle class as some thought it would turn into, its use has had a powerful effect in the inner city.[138] The accompanying Close-Up details the nature of the "crack epidemic" that hit the country in the 1980s.

NARCOTICS. Narcotic drugs can produce insensibility to pain (analgesia) and free the mind of anxiety and emotion (sedation). Users experience a rush of euphoria, relief from fear and apprehension, release of tension, and elevation of spirits. After experiencing this uplifting mood for a short period, users become apathetic and drowsy and nod off. Narcotics can be injected under the skin or into a muscle. Experienced users inject the drugs directly into the bloodstream (mainlining), which provides an immediate "fix."

The most common narcotics are derivatives of opium, a drug produced from the opium poppy flower. The Chinese popularized the habit of smoking or chewing opium extract to produce euphoric feelings. *Morphine* (from Morpheus, the Greek god of dreams), a derivative of opium, is about ten times as strong and is used legally by physicians to relieve pain. It was first popularized as a pain reliever during the Civil War, but its addictive qualities soon became evident. *Heroin* was first produced as a painkilling alternative to morphine in 1875 because, although 25 times more powerful, it was considered nonaddicting by its creator Heinrich Dreser. (The drug's name derives from the fact that it was originally considered heroic because of its painkilling ability).[139]

Heroin is today the most commonly used narcotic in the United States. Because of its strength, dealers cut it with neutral substances, such as sugar (lactose); "street heroin" is often only 1%–4% pure. Users can rapidly build up a tolerance to the drug, so they constantly need larger doses to feel an effect. They may also change the method of ingestion to get the desired kick. At first, heroin is usually sniffed or snorted; as tolerance builds, it is injected beneath the skin (skin-popped) and eventually shot directly into a vein (mainlined). Through this process, the user becomes an *addict*—a person with an overpowering physical and psychological need to continue taking a particular substance or drug by any means possible. If addicts cannot get a supply of heroin sufficient to meet their habit, they will suffer withdrawal symptoms. These include irritability, depression, extreme nervousness, pain in the abdomen, and nausea. It is estimated that there are about 700,000 practicing heroin addicts and another 2 million to 3 million people who have tried heroin at least once in their lives.[140] Heroin abuse is generally considered a lower-class phenomenon, although a fair number of middle- and upper-class users exist. Even physicians are known to have serious narcotic-abuse problems.[141] The popularity of heroin in the 1990s has been linked to its relatively low cost, ready supply, and the effect of government efforts to control other substances such as crack cocaine; the drug of choice seems to be shifting from crack to heroin. While the popularity of heroin is increasing among the middle class, it is still common to associate heroin addiction with minority youths in lower-class, inner-city neighborhoods.

Other opium derivatives used by drug abusers include codeine, Dilaudid, Percodan, and Prinadol. It is also possible to create synthetic narcotics in the laboratory. Synthetics include Demerol, Methadone, Nalline, and Darvon. Although it is less likely for a user to become addicted to synthetic narcotics, it is still possible, and withdrawal symptoms are similar to those experienced by users of natural narcotics.

STEROIDS. Anabolic steroids are used to gain muscle bulk and strength for athletics and body building. Black market sales of these drugs now approach $1 billion annually. While not physically addicting, steroid use can be almost an obsession among people who desire athletic success. Long-term users may spend up to $400 a week on steroids and may support their habit by dealing the drug.

Steroids are dangerous because of the significant health problems associated with long-term use: liver ailments, tumors, hepatitis, kidney problems, sexual dysfunction, hypertension, and mental problems such as depression. Steroid use runs in cycles, and other drugs, such as Clomid, Teslac, and Halotestin, that carry their own dangerous side effects are used to curb the need for high dosages. Finally, steroid users often share needles, which puts them at high risk for contracting the AIDS virus.

DESIGNER DRUGS. **Designer drugs** are chemical substances made and distributed in relatively small batches that induce mood-altering effects. Their chemical characteristics place them somewhere within the broad families of drugs thus far described. Because they are chemically unique, they escape federal regulation until their danger is recognized and they are added to the schedule of controlled substances. Popular today are MDMA or "ecstasy," which combines an amphetamine-like rush with hallucinogenic experiences; the hallucinogens DMT and

In the 1980s thousands of people selling crack suddenly appeared on the streets of New York City. The media proclaimed that a crack epidemic was sweeping the nation: In 1986, *Time* and *Newsweek* published five cover stories on crack; more than 1,000 articles appeared in the national news media. Rumors sprung up about the drug: Women were driven to prostitution to support their habits; juveniles were being enticed into the crack trade; crack dealers were becoming wealthy; the drug was instantly addicting. While these rumors captured the public's imagination, little scientific evidence existed that could document the nature and extent of crack usage. The federal government then funded the Careers in Crack Project to contact and conduct in-depth interviews with known addicts to systematically analyze how crack affects users, those around them, and the community in which they live.

Based on more than 1,000 interviews conducted in New York City, the project investigators found that in contrast to public myth, the typical crack user was an experienced substance abuser who began crack use in his or her late twenties. Introduced to the drug socially at parties, the person's initiation into crack abuse was little different from his or her involvement with other drugs. Users found crack no more addicting than powdered cocaine or

heroin; however, their consumption of crack far exceeded their use of any other drug. Many reported having used crack four or more times per day, spending more than $1,000 per month.

By 1988 crack had become the most frequently sold and most lucrative drug in the street markets of New York. However, crack use did not appear to increase the frequency of users' nondrug crimes. For example, crack use was not associated with the initiation of violent behaviors such as assault or armed robbery. While some women increased the frequency of their prostitution to obtain drug money, few initiated careers in prostitution because of crack. Women involved with crack did, however, become more involved in hard drug use, sales, and nondrug crime than had been the case with their heroin or cocaine use. Where crack seemed to have an effect on crime was the increase in violent behavior associated with its marketing; drug suppliers often used violence as a mechanism for establishing power and collecting money owed them in drug deals.

The "crack epidemic" appears to have gone through several distinct phases, beginning in New York around 1982 when cocaine snorters sought ever more pure forms of the drug to increase their high. Freebase was too complicated and expensive to produce, and crack provided a bet-

ter "bang for the buck." Once crack caught on in 1984, it spread rapidly among the hard-drug-using population. By 1987 most of the at-risk population had started using crack, and expansion faded. Popularity began to wane in 1989 when, not coincidentally, state and local criminal justice agencies aimed their drug control strategies at crack users and dealers. It is unclear whether targeting dealers ended the crack plague or whether it simply fizzled out on its own. Nonetheless, there is still a large number of hardcore users, especially young people who reached maturity during the height of the epidemic. Crack addiction, like all substance abuse, is likely to persist in some form as long as unemployment, inequality, and lack of treatment and opportunity plague the inner cities of America.

CRITICAL THINKING QUESTIONS

1. Can increased police presence and severe sanctions reduce drug use in the inner city? That is, can a general deterrent reduce or end drug use?
2. Is it fair to punish crack smokers more heavily than cocaine snorters, considering the former are more often African American and the latter white?

Source: Bruce Johnson, Andrew Golub, and Jeffrey Fagan, "Careers in Crack: Drug Use, Drug Distribution, and Nondrug Criminality." *Crime and Delinquency* 41 (1995): 275–295.

2c-B or "Nexus"; and steroid substitute GHB, which causes drowsiness.

ALCOHOL. Although the sale and purchase of alcohol is legal today in most U.S. jurisdictions, excessive alcohol consumption is considered a major substance abuse problem. A government survey found that in 1995, 111 million Americans age 12 and older had used alcohol in the past month (52% of the population). About 32 million had engaged in binge drinking (5 or more drinks on at least one occasion in the past month), and about 11 million were heavy drinkers (drinking five or more drinks per occasion on 5 or more days in the past 30 days). About 10 million current drinkers were under age 21 in 1995. Of these, 4.4 million were binge drinkers, including 1.7 million heavy drinkers.[142]

The cost of alcohol abuse is quite high. Alcohol may be a factor in nearly half of all U.S. murders, suicides, and accidental deaths.[143] Alcohol-related deaths number 100,000 a year, far more than those from all illegal drugs combined; recent data suggest that after declining between 1979 and 1985, the number of alcohol-related deaths is on the rise.[144] The economic cost of the nation's drinking problem is equally staggering. An estimated $117 billion is lost each year, including $18 billion from premature deaths, $66 billion in reduced work effort, and $13 billion for treatment efforts.[145]

Considering these problems, why do so many people drink alcohol to excess? Drinkers report that alcohol reduces tension, diverts worries, enhances pleasure, improves social skills, and transforms experiences for the better.[146]

While these reactions may follow the limited use of alcohol, higher doses act as a sedative and depressant. Long-term use has been linked with depression and numerous physical ailments ranging from heart disease to cirrhosis of the liver (although some research has linked moderate drinking to a reduced probability of heart attack).[147] And while many people think that drinking stirs their romantic urges, the weight of the scientific evidence indicates that alcohol decreases sexual response.[148]

The Extent of Substance Abuse

Despite a continuing effort to control it, the use of mood-altering substances persists in the United States. What is the extent of the substance abuse problem today? Despite the media attention given to the incidence of drug abuse, there is actually significant controversy over the nature and extent of drug use. The media assume that drug use is a pervasive and growing menace that threatens to destroy the American way of life. This view is counterbalanced by national surveys showing that drug use is now less than it was two decades ago.

A number of important national surveys attempt to chart trends in drug abuse in the general population. Of these, the two most important are the annual self-report survey of drug abuse among students conducted by the Institute of Social Research (ISR) at the University of Michigan[149] (which is based on the self-report responses of about 17,000 12th-graders, 15,500 10th graders, and 18,800 8th graders in hundreds of schools around the United States) and the National Household Survey of Drug Abuse conducted by the Department of Health and Human Services (which involves in-home interviews with approximately 10,000 people each year).[150] What do these surveys tell us about drug abuse in America?

The ISR survey results indicate that while the use of all drugs has declined from their high point in the late 1970s and early 1980s, the proportion of students using any illicit drugs began to increase in 1991 among 8th graders and in 1992 among 10th and 12th graders. As Figure 14.1 indicates, for 8th graders, the proportion using any illicit drug during the prior year more than doubled between 1991 and 1996 (from 11% to 24%), and between 1992 and 1996 it nearly doubled among 10th graders (from 20% to 38%) and rose by about half among 12th graders (from 27% to 40%). Marijuana use accounted for much of the overall increase in illicit drug use, as it continued its strong resurgence. All measures of marijuana use showed an increase at all three grade levels in 1996.

The 1995 Household Survey (the latest one available) also shows that drug use in the general population, which had declined from a peak in the 1980s, is once again increasing. Between 1992 and 1995, the number of people who said they had used drugs during the previous month doubled; 10.9% now say they are users. The most significant increases were in marijuana use (8.2% said they

smoked pot), cocaine use (.8% had used it), and hallucinogen use (1.7%). About 1.5 million people reported being cocaine users in 1995, down from a peak of 5.7 million in 1985. Despite the substantial reduction in cocaine use since 1985, an estimated 530,000 Americans still used cocaine for the first time in 1995. Of the cocaine users, an estimated 582,000 (0.3% of the population) were frequent cocaine users in 1995. Frequent use, defined as use on 51 or more days during the past year, was not significantly different than in 1994 (734,000) or 1985 (781,000).

Why Is Drug Abuse Increasing?

The recent upward trend in drug abuse among adolescents indicates that while general usage is still lower than it was 20 years ago, the drug problem has not gone away and may be on the increase. Why has drug use remained a major social problem? When drug use declined in the 1980s, one reason may have been changing perceptions about the harmfulness of drugs, such as cocaine and marijuana; as people come to view these drugs as harmful, they tend to use them less. Considering the widespread publicity linking drug use, needle sharing, and the AIDS virus, it comes as no surprise that people began to see drug taking as dangerous and risky. In the 1990s the perceived risk of drugs has been on the decline. For example, while the ISR reports that 79% of seniors in 1991 thought they ran a "great risk" if they were regular marijuana users, today only about 60% view drug taking as "risky."

In addition, when drug use declined, youths reported greater disapproval of drug use among their friends, and peer pressure may have contributed to lower use rates. In the 1990s the number of youths disapproving of drugs has declined (although a majority still disapprove); with lower disapproval has come increased usage.

It also appears that it is easier to obtain drugs, especially for younger adolescents. For example, the ISR survey found that in 1992 about 40% of 8th graders said it was easy to obtain "pot"; today about 50% say it is easy to get that drug, an increase of 25%. Finally, parents may now be unwilling or reluctant to educate their children about the dangers of substance abuse because as "baby boomers" they were drug abusers themselves in the '60s and '70s.

It should come as no surprise that a cohort of young people who perceive little peer rejection for drug use, who consider drugs risk-free and easily available, and whose parents either ignore or condone drug use will increase the frequency of their substance abuse.

Are the Surveys Accurate?

While ISR is methodologically sophisticated, it relies on self-report evidence that is subject to error. Drug users may boastfully overinflate the extent of their substance abuse, underreport out of fear, or simply be unaware or forgetful.

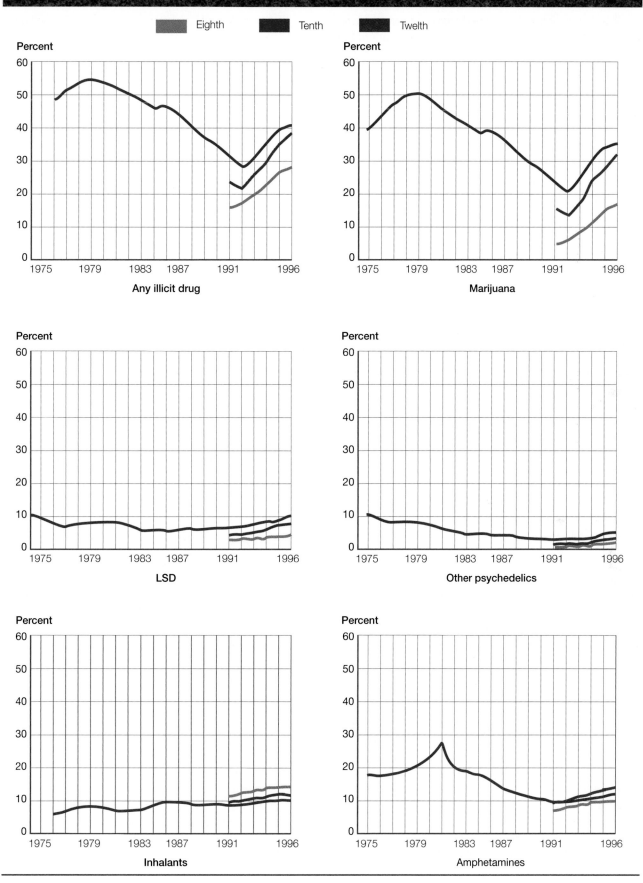

Source: The Monitoring the Future Study, University of Michigan, 1996.

About 20% of those in the ISR survey say they would not or are not sure if they provide honest answers.

Another problem is that both national surveys overlook important segments of the drug-using population. For example, the NIDA survey misses people who are homeless, in prison, in drug rehabilitation clinics, or in AIDS clinics, as well as those (about 18% of the people contacted) who refuse to participate in the interviews. The ISR survey omits kids who are institutionalized and those who have dropped out of school; research indicates that dropouts may, in fact, be the most frequent users of dangerous drugs.[151] These surveys also rely on accurate self-reporting by drug users, a group whose memory and dependability may both be questionable. As you may recall, a number of studies indicate that serious abusers underreport drug use in surveys.[152]

Both surveys also make use of statistical estimating methods to project national use trends from relatively small samples. Sometimes this practice can result in misleading conclusions. For example, in one year (1991) the Household Survey estimated that 148,000 of the total 701,000 heroin users were age 79 and that 32% of the users were over 60. This estimate was based on the responses of a single 79-year-old woman who admitted to using heroin; the 32% over age 60 figure was derived from only seven heroin-using senior citizens.[153]

While these weaknesses are troubling, both surveys are administered yearly, in a consistent fashion, so that any sources of inaccuracy are hopefully consistent over time. That is, the effects of overreporting and underreporting and of missing subjects should have a consistent effect in every survey year.

Both national surveys have attempted to improve their methodologies and become more valid. For example, the ISR survey now includes 8th and 10th graders in an attempt to survey youth before they drop out of school.

AIDS and Drug Use

Drug use is closely tied to the threat of AIDS.[154] Since monitoring of the spread of AIDS began in 1981, about one-fourth of all adult AIDS cases reported to the Centers for Disease Control in Atlanta have occurred among intravenous (IV) drug users. It is now estimated that as many as one-third of all IV drug users are AIDS carriers.[155]

One reason for the AIDS–drug use relationship is the widespread habit of needle sharing among IV users. For example, a recent study of drug "shooting galleries" in Los Angeles conducted by researcher Douglas Longshore found that about one quarter of users shoot drugs in these abandoned buildings, private apartments, or other sites where for a small entry fee injection equipment can be borrowed or rented for a fee.[156] Most users (72%) share needles, and while some try to use bleach as a disinfectant, the majority ignore this safety precaution. Asking for or bringing bleach ruins the moment because it reminds the addicts of the risk of AIDS; others are too high to be bothered. As one user told Longshore:

> After I started shooting coke, all hell broke loose, no holds barred, couldn't be bothered to get bleach. That was out of the question. Literally picking needles up that I had no idea who had used . . . I was just out of my mind insane. [HIV] wasn't a consideration. It was more like, I hope this is going to be okay. You just aren't in your right mind anymore.[157]

Because the AIDS virus is spread through blood transfer, the sharing of HIV-contaminated needles is the primary mechanism for transmitting AIDS among the drug-using population. Needle sharing has been encouraged because a number of states, in an effort to control drugs, have outlawed the over-the-counter sale of hypodermic needles. Consequently, legal jurisdictions have developed outreach programs to help these drug users; others have made an effort to teach users how to clean their needles and syringes; a few states have gone so far as to provide addicts with sterile needles.[158]

Drug users also have a significant exposure to AIDS because they tend to have multiple sex partners, some of whom may be engaging in prostitution to support a drug habit. And while research shows that women do not initiate careers in prostitution to support drug habits, prostitutes who acquire a drug habit appear to increase the frequency of their sexual activities.[159] Thus, members of the drug culture can be exposed to AIDS even if they do not inject drugs or share needles.[160]

While the threat of AIDS may be having an impact on the drug-taking behavior of recreational and middle-class users, drug use may be still increasing among the poor, high school dropouts, and other disadvantaged groups.

The Cause of Substance Abuse

What causes people to abuse drugs? Although there are many views on the causes of drug use, most can be characterized as seeing the onset of an addictive career as either an environmental or a personal matter.

SUBCULTURAL VIEW. Those who view drug abuse as having an environmental basis concentrate on lower-class addiction. Because a disproportionate number of drug abusers are poor, the onset of drug use can be tied to such factors as racial prejudice, devalued identities, low self-esteem, poor socioeconomic status, and the high level of mistrust, negativism, and defiance found in lower socioeconomic areas.

Residing in a deteriorated, inner-city slum area is often correlated with entry into a drug subculture. Youths living in these depressed areas, where feelings of alienation and hopelessness run high, often come in contact with established drug users who teach them that narcotics provide an answer to their feelings of personal inadequacy and stress.[161] Perhaps the youths will join with peers to learn the techniques of drug use and receive social support for their habit. Research shows that peer influence is a significant predictor of drug careers and that it actually grows stronger as people mature through the life cycle.[162] Shared feelings and a sense of intimacy lead the youths to become fully enmeshed in what has been described as the "drug use subculture."[163]

Those who can take advantage of educational or vocational opportunities can forgo the drug culture and "make it" in the legitimate economic structure. Upward mobility is available to only a few because of the deterioration of the manufacturing economy. The indigent, especially among minority-group members, are much more likely to abuse substances than the upwardly mobile. This phenomenon takes on even greater importance considering the recent polarization of some minority communities into distinct groups of relatively affluent abstainers and desperately poor abusers.[164]

PSYCHODYNAMIC VIEW. Yet not all drug abusers reside in lower-class slum areas; the problem of middle-class substance abuse is very real. Consequently, some experts have linked substance abuse to personality disturbance and emotional problems that can strike people in any economic class. Psychodynamic explanations of substance abuse suggest that drugs help youths control or express unconscious needs and impulses. Drinking alcohol may reflect an oral fixation, which is associated with other nonfunctional behaviors, such as dependence and depression.[165] A young teen may resort to drug abuse to remain dependent on an overprotective mother, to reduce the emotional turmoil of adolescence, or to cope with troubling impulses.[166]

Research on the psychological characteristics of drug abusers does in fact reveal the presence of a significant degree of personal pathology. Studies have found that addicts suffer personality disorders characterized by a weak ego, low frustration tolerance, anxiety, and fantasies of omnipotence. Many addicts exhibit psychopathic or sociopathic behavior characteristics, forming what is called an *addiction-prone personality*.[167] For example, alcoholism may reflect the need to reduce the emotional turmoil of adolescence or to cope with unconscious sexual impulses. Research on the psychological characteristics of narcotics abusers reveals a significant degree of personal pathology. Personality testing of known users suggests that a significant percentage suffer from psychotic disorders, including various levels of schizophrenia.

These views have been substantiated by research involving a sample of over 20,000 people in five large U.S. cities. The results of this first large-scale study on the personality characteristics of abusers indicate a significant association between mental illness and drug abuse: About 53% of drug abusers and 37% of alcohol abusers have at least one serious mental illness. Conversely, 29% of the di-

agnosed mentally ill people in the survey have substance abuse problems.[168]

GENETIC FACTORS. It is also possible that substance abuse has a genetic basis. Research has shown that the biological children of alcoholics reared by nonalcoholic adoptive parents more often develop alcohol problems than the biological children of the adoptive parents.[169] In a similar vein, a number of studies comparing alcoholism among identical twins and fraternal twins have found that the degree of concordance (both siblings behaving identically) is twice as high among the identical twin groups. These inferences are still inconclusive because identical twins are more likely to be treated similarly than fraternal twins are and therefore are more likely to be influenced by environmental conditions.

Taken as a group, studies of the genetic basis of substance abuse suggest that people whose parents were alcoholic or drug dependent have a greater chance of developing a problem than children of nonabusers do. Nonetheless, most children of abusing parents do not become drug dependent themselves, suggesting that even if drug abuse is heritable, environment and socialization must play some role in the onset of abuse.[170]

SOCIAL LEARNING. Social psychologists suggest that drug abuse patterns may also result from the observation of parental drug use. Parental drug abuse begins to have a damaging effect on children as young as two years old, especially when parents manifest drug-related personality problems such as depression or poor impulse control.[171] Children whose parents abuse drugs are more likely to have persistent abuse problems than the children of nonabusers.[172]

People who learn that drugs provide pleasurable sensations may be the most likely to experiment with illegal substances; a habit may develop if the user experiences lower anxiety, fear, and tension levels.[173] Having a history of family drug and alcohol abuse has been found to be a characteristic of violent teenage sexual abusers.[174] Heroin abusers report an unhappy childhood, which included harsh physical punishment and parental neglect and rejection.[175]

James Inciardi, Ruth Horowitz, and Anne Pottieger found a clear pattern of adult involvement in adolescent drug abuse. Kids on crack began their careers with early experimentation with alcohol at age 7, began getting drunk at age 8, had alcohol with an adult present by age 9, and became regular drinkers by the time they were 11 years old.[176] Drinking with an adult present, presumably a parent, was a significant precursor of future substance abuse and delinquency. "Adults who gave children alcohol," the researchers argue, "were also giving them a head start in a delinquent career."[177]

PROBLEM BEHAVIOR SYNDROME (PBS). For many people, substance abuse is just one of many problem behaviors. Longitudinal studies show that drug abusers are maladjusted, alienated, and emotionally distressed and that their drug use is one among many social problems.[178] Having a deviant lifestyle begins early in life and is punctuated with criminal relationships, a family history of substance abuse, educational failure, and alienation. People who abuse drugs lack commitment to religious values, disdain education, and spend most of their time in peer activities. A recent metaanalysis of PBS research conducted by John Donovan found robust support for the interconnection among problem drinking and drug abuse, delinquency, precocious sexual behavior, school failure, family conflict, and other similar social problems.[179]

RATIONAL CHOICE. Not all people who abuse drugs do so because of personal pathology. Some may choose to use drugs and alcohol because they want to enjoy their effects: get high, relax, improve creativity, escape reality, increase sexual responsiveness. Research indicates that adolescent alcohol abusers believe that getting high will make them powerful, increase their sexual performance, and facilitate their social behavior; they care little about negative future consequences.[180] Claire Sterck-Elifson's research on middle-class, drug-abusing women shows that most were introduced by friends or lovers in the context of "just having some fun":

> It all started out so wonderful; we had the best time together. On special nights he would lay out a few lines and we would snort it with a silver straw . . . we would have the best sex . . . I started wanting more and I was irritated that he made me wait for it . . .[181]

Substance abuse, then, may be a function of the rational, albeit mistaken, belief that drugs can be of benefit to the user. The decision to use drugs involves evaluating personal consequences (addiction, disease, legal punishment) and the expected benefits of drug use (peer approval, positive affective states, heightened awareness, relaxation). Adolescents may begin using drugs because they believe their peers expect them to do so and they want to comply with or please those with whom they are in close and intimate contact.[182]

In sum, there are many views of why people take drugs, and no one theory has proven to be an adequate explanation of all forms of substance abuse. Recent research efforts show that drug users suffer a variety of family and socialization difficulties, have addiction-prone personalities, and are generally at risk for many other social problems.[183] As James Inciardi points out,

> There are as many reasons people use drugs as there are individuals who use drugs. For some, it may be a function of family disorganization, or cultural learning, or maladjusted personality, or an "addiction-prone" personality. . . . For others, heroin use may be no more than a normal response to the world in which they live.[184]

Types of Criminal Drug Users

All too often, the general public groups all drug users together without recognizing there are many varieties, ranging from adolescent recreational drug users to adults who run large smuggling operations.[185]

ADOLESCENTS WHO DISTRIBUTE SMALL AMOUNTS OF DRUGS. Many adolescents begin their involvement in the drug trade with the use and distribution of small amounts of drugs; they do not commit any other serious criminal acts. Kenneth Tunnell found in his interviews with low-level drug dealers that many started out as "stash dealers" who sold drugs to maintain a consistent access to drugs for their own consumption.[186]

Most of these petty dealers occasionally sell marijuana, crack, and PCP to support their own drug use. Their customers are almost always personal acquaintances, including friends and relatives. Deals are arranged over the phone, in school, or in public hangouts and meeting places; however, the actual distribution takes place in more private areas, such as at home or in cars. Petty dealers do not consider themselves seriously involved in drugs. They are insulated from the legal system because their activities rarely result in apprehension and sanction.

ADOLESCENTS WHO FREQUENTLY SELL DRUGS. A small number of adolescents, most often multiple-drug users or heroin or cocaine users, are high-rate dealers who bridge the gap between adult drug distributors and the adolescent user. Although many are daily users, they are not "strung-out junkies" and maintain many normal adolescent roles, such as going to school and socializing with friends. These dealers often have adults who "front" for them—that is, lend them drugs to sell without up-front cash. The teenagers then distribute the drugs to friends and acquaintances, returning most of the proceeds to the supplier while keeping a "commission" for themselves. They may also keep drugs for their own personal use, and, in fact, some consider their drug dealing as a way of "getting high for free." Frequent dealers are more likely to sell drugs in public and can be seen in known drug-user hangouts in parks, schools, or other public places. Deals are irregular, so the chances of apprehension are slight.

TEENAGE DRUG DEALERS WHO COMMIT OTHER DELINQUENT ACTS. A more serious type of drug-involved youth are those who use and distribute multiple substances and also commit both property and violent crimes. Although these youngsters make up about 2% of the teenage population, they commit 40% of the robberies and assaults and about 60% of all teenage felony thefts and drug sales. There is little gender or racial difference among these youths: Girls are as likely as boys to become high-rate, persistent drug-involved offenders, white youths as

other thefts. While these youths may be part of street gangs, their drug dealing actions are often independent of gang activity; while some gangs are drug oriented, the majority are not involved in drug trafficking.[187]

ADOLESCENTS WHO CYCLE IN AND OUT OF THE JUSTICE SYSTEM. Some drug-involved youths are failures at both dealing and crime. They do not have the savvy to join gangs or groups and instead begin committing unplanned, opportunistic crimes that increase their chances of arrest. They are heavy drug users, which both increases apprehension risk and decreases their value for organized drug distribution networks. Drug-involved "losers" can earn a living steering customers to a seller in a "copping" area, touting drug availability for a dealer, or acting as a lookout. However, they are not considered trustworthy or deft enough to handle drugs or money. They may bungle other criminal acts, which solidifies their reputation as undesirable. Although these persistent offenders get involved in drugs at a very young age, they receive little attention from the justice system until they have developed an extensive arrest record. By then, they are approaching the end of their minority and will either spontaneously desist or become so deeply entrenched in the drug-crime subculture that little can be done to treat or deter their illegal activities.

DRUG-INVOLVED YOUTHS WHO CONTINUE TO COMMIT CRIMES AS ADULTS. Although about two-thirds of substance-abusing youths continue to use drugs after they reach adulthood, about half desist from other criminal activities. Those who persist in both substance abuse and crime as adults have the following characteristics:

- They come from poor families.
- They have other criminals in the family.
- They do poorly in school.
- They started using drugs and committing other delinquent acts at a relatively young age.
- They use multiple types of drugs and commit crimes frequently.
- They have few opportunities in late adolescence to participate in legitimate and rewarding adult activities.

Some evidence also exists that these drug-using persisters have low nonverbal IQs and poor physical coordination. Nonetheless, there is still little scientific evidence to indicate why some drug-abusing kids drop out of crime while others remain active into their adulthood.

OUTWARDLY RESPECTABLE ADULTS WHO ARE TOP-LEVEL DEALERS. A few outwardly respectable adult dealers sell large quantities of drugs to support themselves in high-class lifestyles. Outwardly respectable dealers often seem indistinguishable from other young professionals. However, they are rarely drawn from the highest professional

There are many views as to why people take drugs, and no one theory has proven an adequate explanation of all forms of substance abuse. Recent research efforts show that drug users suffer a variety of family and socialization difficulties, have addiction-prone personalities, and are generally at risk for many other social problems; drug use seems to be part of a "problem behavior syndrome."

likely as black youths, middle-class adolescents raised outside cities as likely as lower-class city kids.

These youths are frequently hired by older dealers to act as street-level drug runners. Each member of a "crew" of 3 to 12 boys will handle small quantities of drugs, perhaps three bags of heroin, which are received on consignment and sold on the street; the supplier receives 50%–70% of the drug's street value. The crew members also act as lookouts, recruiters, and guards. While they may be recreational drug users themselves, crew members refrain from using addictive drugs such as heroin; some major suppliers will only hire "drug-free kids" to make street deals. Between drug sales, the young dealers commit robberies, burglaries, and

circles, such as those of physicians or attorneys, nor are they likely to have worked their way up from lower-class origins. Upscale dealers seem to drift into dealing from many walks of life. Most often, they come from professions and occupations that are unstable, have irregular working hours, and accept drug abuse. Former graduate students, musicians, performing artists, and barkeepers are among those who are likely to fit the profile of the adult who begins drug dealing in his or her 20s. Some will use their business skills and drug profits to get into legitimate enterprise or illegal scams. Others will drop out of the drug trade because they are the victims of violent crime committed by competitors or disgruntled customers; a few wind up in jail or prison.

SMUGGLERS. Smugglers import drugs into the United States. What little is known about drug smugglers indicates they are generally men, middle-age or older, who have strong organizational skills, established connections, capital to invest, and a willingness to take large business risks. Smugglers are a loosely organized, competitive group of individual entrepreneurs. There is a constant flow in and out of the business as some sources become the target of law enforcement activities, new drug sources become available, older smugglers become dealers, and former dealers become smugglers.

ADULT PREDATORY DRUG USERS WHO ARE FREQUENTLY ARRESTED. Many users who begin abusing substances early in their adolescence will continue in drugs and crime in their adulthood. Getting arrested, doing time, using multiple drugs, and committing predatory crimes is a way of life for them. They have few skills, did poorly in school, and have a long criminal record. The threat of conviction and punishment has little effect on their criminal activities. These "losers" have friends and relatives involved in drugs and crime. They specialize in robberies, burglaries, thefts, and drug sales. They filter in and out of the justice system and will begin committing crimes as soon as they are released. In some populations, at least one third of adult males are involved in drug trafficking and other criminal acts well into their adulthood.[188]

ADULT PREDATORY DRUG USERS WHO ARE RARELY ARRESTED. Some drug users are "winners." They commit hundreds of crimes each year but are rarely arrested. On the streets, they are known for their calculated violence. Their crimes are carefully planned and coordinated. They often work with partners and use lookouts to carry out the parts of their crimes that have the highest risk of apprehension. These "winners" are more likely to use recreational drugs, such as coke and pot, than the more addicting heroin or opiates. Some may become high-frequency users and risk apprehension and punishment. But for the lucky few, their criminal careers can stretch for up to 15 years without interruption by the justice system.

LESS PREDATORY DRUG-INVOLVED ADULT OFFENDERS. Most adult drug users are petty criminals who avoid violent crime. They are typically high school graduates and have regular employment that supports their drug use. They usually commit petty thefts or pass bad checks. They will stay on the periphery of the drug trade by engaging in such acts as helping addicts shoot up, bagging drugs for dealers, operating shooting galleries, renting needles and syringes, and selling small amounts of drugs. These petty criminal drug users do not have the stomach for a life of hard crime and drug dealing. They will violate the law in proportion to the amount and cost of the drugs they are using. Pot smokers will have a significantly lower frequency of theft violations than daily heroin users, whose habit is considerably more costly.

WOMEN WHO ARE DRUG-INVOLVED OFFENDERS. Women who are drug-involved offenders constitute a separate type of substance abuser. Although women are far less likely than men to use addictive drugs, female offenders are just as likely to be involved in drugs as male offenders. Not usually violent criminals, female drug users are often involved in prostitution and low-level drug dealing; a few become top-level dealers. Female abusers are quite often mothers. Because they share needles, they are at high risk of contracting AIDS, and many pass the HIV virus to their newborn children. Female addicts are offered fewer services than men because treatment programs are geared toward males. Their children are often malnourished, mistreated, and exposed to a highly criminal population. Some are sold to pornographers and become involved in the sex-for-profit trade; others grow up to become criminals themselves.

The causes of female drug abuse are quite complex. For example, Karen Joe's study of female Asian Pacific American drug abusers found that from early childhood these women lived in an environment of heated conflict, economic marginality, and parental substance abuse. They were first introduced to drugs by male relatives and school peers. They drifted into using "ice" and cocaine while interacting with their intimate partners and extended kin, such as cousins.[189]

Drugs and Crime

One of the main reasons for the criminalization of particular substances is the significant association believed to exist between drug abuse and crime. Research suggests that many criminal offenders have extensive experience with drug use and that drug users do in fact commit an enormous amount of crime. Alcohol abuse has also been linked to criminality and appears to be an important precipitating factor in domestic assault and homicide cases.[190] Arrestees who test positively for drugs are also more likely to recidivate than nonusers.[191]

While the drug-crime connection is powerful, it is still uncertain whether the relationship is causal, as many users had a history of criminal activity *before* the onset of their substance abuse.[192] Nonetheless, if drug use is not a per se *cause* of crime—that is, turning otherwise law-abiding citizens into criminals—it certainly amplifies the extent of their criminal activities.[193] And as addiction levels increase, so, too, do the frequency and seriousness of criminality.[194]

Research Methods

Two approaches have been used to study the relationship between drugs and crime. One has been to survey known addicts to assess the extent of their law violations; the other has been to survey known criminals to see whether they were or are drug users.

USER SURVEYS. Numerous studies have examined the criminal activity of drug users. They show that people who take drugs have extensive involvement in crime.[195] Alcohol abuse has been linked to serious, violent offending patterns: People with long histories of drinking are also more likely to report violent offending patterns.[196] One often-cited study of this type was conducted by sociologist James Inciardi. After interviewing 356 addicts in Miami, Inciardi found that they reported 118,134 criminal offenses during a 12-month period; of these, 27,464 were index crimes.[197] If this behavior is typical, the country's estimated 500,000 heroin users could be responsible for a significant amount of all criminal behavior. In a more recent analysis, M. Douglas Anglin and George Speckart surveyed 671 known California addicts and found persuasive evidence of a link between drug use and property crime.[198] While their research also indicated that drug use is not an initiator of crime (since many users had committed crime before turning to drugs), there was strong evidence that the amount and value of crime increased proportionately with the frequency of the subjects' drug involvement. Interestingly, Anglin and Speckart found little evidence of an association between the frequency of drug use and violent crimes. The findings of these two surveys are typical of others measuring the criminality of narcotics users.[199]

SURVEYS OF KNOWN CRIMINALS. The second method used to link drugs and crime is testing known criminals to determine the extent of their substance abuse. The most recent survey of prison inmates disclosed that most (80%) have engaged in a lifetime of drug and alcohol abuse. More than one-third claim to have been under the influence of drugs when they committed their last offense, including about 14% who were under the influence of crack and 6% who were using heroin; about 62% claimed to have used a major drug, such as heroin, cocaine, PCP, or LSD, on a regular basis before their arrest.[200] These data support the view that a strong association exists between substance abuse and serious crime (unless one believes that only substance-abusing criminals are caught and sent to prison).

Another important source of data on the drug abuse–crime connection is the federally sponsored Drug Use Forecasting (DUF) program. All arrestees in 23 major cities around the country are tested for drug use.[201] The most recent DUF data show that drug use among arrestees has been stable. Nonetheless, at every site a majority of male arrestees tested positive for at least one of ten drugs, most commonly cocaine or marijuana. The rate of male arrestees testing positive for at least one drug ranged from 51% to 83%. Similarly, all but one site reported overall rates of drug use of 50% or greater among female arrestees. A majority of female arrestees at 20 sites tested positive for at least one of ten drugs; rates across sites ranged from 41% to 84%. Consistent with past years, this overall measure of drug use was driven primarily by high rates of cocaine, marijuana, and, at a few sites, opiate or methamphetamine use. The 1995 DUF found that in general cocaine use had diminished somewhat but that marijuana use was on the rise (see Figure 14.2).

It is of course possible that most criminals are not actually drug users but that police are more likely to apprehend muddled-headed substance abusers than clear-thinking abstainers. A second, and probably more plausible, interpretation is that the DUF data are so powerful because most criminals are in fact substance abusers. The

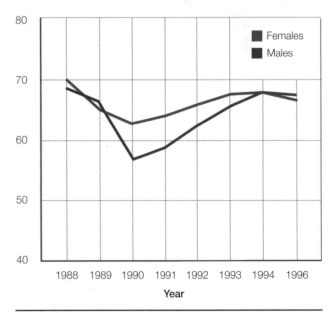

Figure 14.2 Trends in substance abuse by arrestees tested in the Drug Use Forecasting (DUF) program, 1988–1996.

Average percent positive for any drug

Source: Center for Substance Abuse Research (CESAR), Research Report (College Park: University of Maryland, December 23, 1996). Updated with data from K. Jack Riley, *Drug Use Forecasting 1996* (Washington, D.C.: National Institute of Justice, 1997).

drug–crime relationship may thus be explained in three ways: Some may commit crime to support a drug habit; others may become violent while under the influence of drugs or alcohol, which lower inhibitions and increase aggression levels; or the drug–crime connection may be a function of the violent world of drug distributors, who regularly use violence to do business.[202]

In sum, research testing both the criminality of known narcotics users and the narcotics use of known criminals produces strong association between drug use and crime. Even if the crime rate of drug users were actually half that reported in the research literature, users would be responsible for a significant portion of the total criminal activity in the United States.

The Cycle of Addiction

The drug-crime connection may also be mediated by the amount of drugs that users require and their ability to support their habit through conventional means. During their interviews with drug users, Charles Faupel and Carl Klockars found a variety of addict types.[203] *Occasional users* are people just beginning their addiction, who use small amounts of narcotics and whose habit can be supported by income from conventional jobs; narcotics have relatively little influence on their lifestyles. In contrast, *stabilized junkies* have learned the skills needed to purchase and process larger amounts of heroin. Their addiction enables them to maintain their normal lifestyles, although they may turn to drug dealing to create contacts with drug suppliers. Separately, Faupel has found that full-time working people involved in drugs actually commit more crime than those *not* in the labor force. Employment, then, does little to reduce their criminal activity, typically drug dealing, that helps finance drug habits.[204]

If stable users make a "big score," perhaps through a successful drug deal, they may significantly increase their drug use and become *free-wheelers*. Their increased narcotics consumption then destabilizes their lifestyle, destroying family and career ties. When their finances dry up, free-wheelers may return to stabilized use or become *street junkies*, whose habit cannot be satisfied through conventional means. Because their traditional lifestyle has been destroyed, street junkies turn to petty crime to maintain an adequate supply of drugs. Cut off from a stable source of quality heroin, not knowing from where his or her next fix or the money to pay for it will come, looking for any opportunity to make a buck, getting "sick" or "jonesing," being pathetically unkempt and unable to maintain even the most primitive routines of health or hygiene, the street junkie lives a difficult, hand-to-mouth (or more precisely, arm-to-arm) existence. Because they are unreliable and likely to become police informants, street junkies pay the highest prices for the poorest quality heroin; lack of availability increases their need to commit habit-supporting crimes.

Faupel and Klockars conclude that addiction is not a unidimensional process. There are various stages in the career of a hard-drug user, and criminal activity may vary according to the user's drug lifestyle. Their view is that crime is a "drug facilitator," enabling addicts to increase their heroin consumption according to the success of their criminal careers.

Drugs and the Law

The federal government first initiated legal action to curtail the use of some drugs early in the 20th century.[205] In 1906 the Pure Food and Drug Act required manufacturers to list on the labels the amounts of habit-forming drugs in products but did not restrict their use. However, the act prohibited the importation and sale of opiates except for medicinal purposes. In 1914 the Harrison Narcotics Act restricted the importation, manufacture, sale, and dispensing of narcotics. It defined narcotic as any drug that produces sleep and relieves pain, such as heroin, morphine, and opium. The act was revised in 1922 to allow the importation of opium and coca (cocaine) leaves for qualified medical practitioners. The Marijuana Tax Act of 1937 required registration and payment of a tax by all persons who imported, sold, or manufactured marijuana. Since marijuana was classified as a narcotic, those registering would also be subject to criminal penalty.

In later years, other federal laws were passed to clarify existing drug statutes and revise penalties. For example, the Boggs Act of 1951 provides mandatory sentences for violating federal drug laws. The Durham-Humphrey Act of 1951 made it illegal to dispense barbiturates and amphetamines without a prescription. The Narcotic Control Act of 1956 increased penalties for drug offenders. In 1965 the drug abuse control act set up stringent guidelines for the legal use and sale of mood-modifying drugs, such as barbiturates, amphetamines, LSD, and any other "dangerous drugs," except narcotics prescribed by doctors and pharmacists. Illegal possession was punished as a misdemeanor and manufacture or sale as a felony. Then, in 1970, the Comprehensive Drug Abuse Prevention and Control Act set up unified categories of illegal drugs and the penalties associated with their sale, manufacture, or possession. The law gave the U.S. attorney general discretion to decide in which category to place any new drug.

Since then, various federal laws have attempted to increase penalties imposed on drug smugglers and limit the manufacture and sale of newly developed substances. For example, the 1984 Controlled Substances Act set new, stringent penalties for drug dealers and created five categories of narcotic and nonnarcotic substances subject to federal laws.[206] The Anti-Drug Abuse Act of 1986 again set new standards for minimum and maximum sentences for drug offenders, increased penalties for most offenses, and created a new drug penalty classification for large-scale offenses (such as trafficking in more than one kilogram of heroin), for which the penalty for a first offense was ten years to life in prison.[207] With then President George Bush's endorsement, Congress passed the Anti-Drug Abuse Act of 1988, which created a coordinated national drug policy under a "drug czar," set treatment and prevention priorities, and, symbolizing the government's hard-line stance against drug dealing, imposed the death penalty for drug-related killings.[208]

For the most part, state laws mirror federal statutes. Some, such as New York's, apply extremely heavy penalties for sale or distribution of dangerous drugs, involving long prison sentences of up to 25 years.

Alcohol Abuse

While drug control laws have been enacted on both the federal and state levels, state legislatures have also acted to control alcohol-related crimes. One of the more serious problems is the alarming number of highway fatalities linked to drunk driving. In an average week, nearly 500 people die in alcohol-related accidents, and 20,000 are injured. Annually that amounts to 25,000 deaths, or about half of all auto fatalities. Spurred by such groups as Mothers Against Drunk Drivers, state legislatures are beginning to create more stringent penalties for drunk driving. For example, Florida has enacted legislation creating a minimum fine of $250, 50 hours of community service, and six months' loss of license for a first offense; a second offense brings a $500 fine and ten days in jail. In Quincy, Massachusetts, judges have agreed to put every drunk-driving offender in jail for three days.[209] In California, a drunk driver faces a maximum of six months in jail, a $500 fine, the suspension of his or her operator's license for six months, and impoundment of the vehicle. As a minimum penalty, a first offender could get four days in jail, a $375 fine, and a loss of license for six months, or three years' probation, a $375 fine, and either two days in jail or restricted driving privileges for 90 days.[210] In New York, persons arrested for drunk driving now risk having their automobiles seized by the government under the state's new Civil Forfeiture Law. Originally designed to combat drug trafficking and racketeering, the new law will allow state prosecutors to confiscate cars involved in felony drunk-driving cases, sell them at auction, and give the proceeds to the victims of the crime; Texas enacted a similar law in 1984.[211] More than 30 jurisdictions have passed laws providing severe penalties for drunk drivers, including mandatory jail sentences.

A study conducted by the federal government's National Institute of Justice in such cities as Seattle, Minneapolis, and Cincinnati found that such measures significantly reduced traffic fatalities in the target areas studied.[212] However, there is a price to pay for get-tough policies. In California, arrest rates and court workload increased dramatically, and the use of plea bargaining, which first decreased, eventually rose and reduced the impact of legal reform.[213] Similarly, corrections facilities have become overloaded, prompting the building of expensive new ones to house exclusively drunk-driving offenders.

Alcoholics are a serious problem, because treatment efforts to help chronic sufferers have not proven successful.[214] Severe punishments have little effect on their future behavior.[215] In addition, chronic alcoholics are arrested over and over again for public drunkenness and are therefore a burden on the justice system. To remedy this situation, a federal court in 1966 ruled that chronic alcoholism may be used as a defense to crime.[216] However, in a subsequent case, *Powell v. Texas,* the Supreme Court ruled that a chronic alcoholic could be convicted under state public drunkenness laws.[217] Nonetheless, the narrowness of the decision, 5 to 4, allowed those states desiring to excuse chronic alcoholics from criminal responsibility to do so. Thus, the trend has been to place arrested alcoholics in detoxification centers under a civil order rather than treat them as part of the justice system.

Drug Control Strategies

Substance abuse remains a major social problem in the United States. Politicians looking for a "safe" campaign issue can take advantage of the public's fear of drug addiction by calling for a "war on drugs." These "wars" have been declared even during periods when drug usage is stable or in decline.[218] Can these efforts pay off? Can illegal drug use be eliminated or controlled?

A number of drug control strategies have been tried with varying degrees of success. Some are aimed at deterring drug use by stopping the flow of drugs into the country, apprehending and punishing dealers, and cracking down on street-level drug deals. Others focus on preventing drug use by educating potential users to the dangers of substance abuse (convincing them to "say no to drugs") and by organizing community groups to work with the at-risk population in their area. Still another approach is to treat known users so they can control their addictions. Some of the more important of these efforts are discussed here.

Source Control

One approach to drug control is to deter the sale and importation of drugs through the systematic apprehension of large-volume drug dealers, coupled with the enforcement of strict drug laws that carry heavy penalties. This approach is designed to capture and punish known international drug dealers and deter those who are considering entering the drug trade.

A major effort has been made to cut off supplies of drugs by destroying overseas crops and arresting members of drug cartels in Central and South America, Asia, and the Middle East, where drugs are grown and manufactured (see Figure 14.3). This approach is known as source control. The federal government has been in the vanguard of

Figure 14.3 How drugs get to the United States.

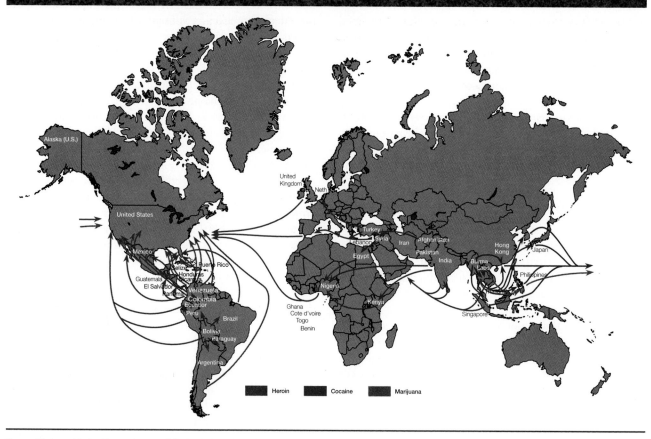

Source: Marianne Zawitz, *Drugs, Crime, and the Justice System* (Washington, D.C.: Bureau of Justice Statistics, 1994), pp. 47–51.

encouraging exporting nations to step up efforts to destroy drug crops and prosecute dealers. Three South American nations, Peru, Bolivia, and Colombia, have agreed with the United States to coordinate control efforts. Translating words into deeds is a formidable task. Drug lords are willing and able to fight back through intimidation, violence, and corruption when necessary. The United States was forced to invade Panama with 20,000 troops in 1989 to stop its leader, General Manuel Noriega, from dealing cocaine. The Colombian drug cartels do not hesitate to use violence and assassination to protect their interests.

The amount of narcotics produced each year is so vast that even if three-quarters of the opium crop were destroyed, the U.S. market would still require only 10% of the remainder to sustain the drug trade. An estimated 24,000 tons of marijuana, 337,000 tons of coca leaf, and 4,000 tons of opium are produced annually.[219] Because drug users in the United States are able and willing to pay more for drugs than anyone else in the world, if the supply were reduced, whatever drugs existed would find their way to the United States.

Adding to control problems is the fact that the drug trade is an important source of revenue for many countries, and destroying the drug trade would undermine the econ-omies of Third World nations. An estimated 1 million people in Peru, Bolivia, and Colombia depend on the drug trade to earn their living. In Burma, Thailand, and Laos, hundreds of thousands of people are engaged in cultivating and processing heroin. The federal government estimates that U.S. citizens spend over $40 billion annually on illegal drugs, and much of this money is funneled overseas. And even if the government of one nation is willing to cooperate in vigorous drug suppression efforts, suppliers in other nations, eager to cash in on the seller's market, would be encouraged to turn more acreage over to coca or poppy production.

The difficulty of source control is illustrated by the pursuit, capture, and slaying of alleged billionaire drug lord Pablo Escobar on December 2, 1993. His Medellin drug cartel at one time controlled 80% of the cocaine imported into the United States; *Forbes* magazine included him in its annual list of billionaires. While he was in hiding, his drug empire had been replaced by his competitors, the Cali cartel. When the Colombian government put pressure on the drug cartels, even more powerful Mexican organizations emerged to take over the drug trade. In 1997 Mexico's government announced that it had arrested General Jesus Guttierrez Rebello, its top antinarcotics enforcer, for his suspected links to drug traffickers.[220]

Eradication efforts in one country may also encourage crop development in another. For example, the Bolivian government's voluntary coca eradication program surpassed its annual target in 1996, kept cultivation levels from significantly expanding, and reduced potential coca leaf production by 12%. Unfortunately, this decline was more than offset by a 32% increase in both coca cultivation and potential coca leaf production in Colombia, despite an aggressive aerial eradication program by Colombian enforcement authorities. Colombian coca cultivation has nearly tripled since 1987, and source control efforts have convinced the Colombian drug cartels of the importance of controlling all facets of cocaine production at home.[221]

As of 1997, the drug trade remains a dynamic force. Even after suffering considerable losses, its wealth, power, and organization equal or even exceed the resources of many national governments. Hundreds of tons of cocaine flow not only to the United States and Western Europe but to markets in Latin America, Asia, Africa, and the countries of the former Soviet Union. The lines between cocaine and heroin-consuming countries are blurring. Cocaine and heroin trafficking, once limited to a few major routes and destinations in North America and Europe respectively, has become all but universal. The United States, once the world's primary cocaine user, is now also consuming increasing quantities of high-purity heroin. Europe, traditionally the major Western market for heroin, has acquired a voracious appetite for cocaine and amphetamines. Colombian cocaine syndicates have established distribution centers on virtually every continent.

Large Mexican drug organizations have gained control of much of the U.S.-bound cocaine traffic formerly dominated by the Colombians. Meanwhile, Colombian cocaine syndicates have turned increasingly to heroin production. A substantial amount of the heroin seized on the East Coast of the United States can now be traced to Colombian refiners. At the same time, Nigerian smuggling organizations that formerly specialized in heroin shipments have branched out into cocaine.

Synthetic drugs have been gaining popularity over the last half decade and are well on their way to becoming the drug-control nightmare of the next century. Methamphetamines (MDMA or "ecstasy," in particular) may be displacing cocaine as the stimulant of choice on the world drug market. Mexico is the principal supplier for the United States, but there are centers of methamphetamine production in countries as far apart as Poland, Japan, and the Philippines. There have even been reports of some heroin refiners in Burma adding methamphetamine to their product line.[222]

Interdiction Strategies

Law enforcement efforts have also been directed at interdicting drug supplies as they enter the country. Border patrols and military personnel using sophisticated hardware have been involved in massive interdiction efforts; many impressive multimillion-dollar seizures have been made. Yet the U.S. borders are so vast and unprotected that meaningful interdiction is impossible. And even if all importation were shut down, home-grown marijuana and laboratory-made drugs, such as "ice," LSD, and PCP, could become the drugs of choice. Even now, their easy availability and relatively low cost are increasing their popularity among the at-risk population.

Law Enforcement Strategies

Local, state, and federal law enforcement agencies have been engaged in an active fight against drugs. One approach is to direct efforts at large-scale drug rings. The long-term consequence has been to decentralize drug dealing and encourage younger independent dealers to become major suppliers. Ironically, it has proven easier for federal agents to infiltrate and prosecute traditional organized crime groups than to take on drug-dealing gangs. Consequently, some nontraditional groups have broken into the drug trade. For example, the Hell's Angels motorcycle club has become one of the primary distributors of cocaine and amphetamines in the United States.[223] Police can also target, intimidate, and arrest street-level dealers and users in an effort to make drug use so much of a hassle that consumption is cut back and the crime rate reduced. Approaches that have been tried include "reverse stings" in which undercover agents pose as dealers to arrest users who approach them for a buy. Police have attacked fortified crack houses with heavy equipment to breach their defenses. They have used racketeering laws to seize the assets of known dealers. Special task forces of local and state police have used undercover operations and drug sweeps to discourage both dealers and users.[224]

While some street-level enforcement efforts have had success, others are considered failures. Drug sweeps have clogged courts and correctional facilities with petty offenders while proving a costly drain on police resources. There are also suspicions that a displacement effect occurs: Stepped-up efforts to curb drug dealing in one area or city simply encourage dealers to seek out friendlier "business" territory.[225] Table 14.2 sets out the law enforcement agencies responsible for drug control.

Punishment Strategies

Even if law enforcement efforts cannot produce a general deterrent effect, the courts may achieve the required result by severely punishing known drug dealers and traffickers. A number of initiatives have made the prosecution and punishment of drug offenders a top priority. State prosecutors have expanded their investigations into drug importation and distribution and created special prosecutors to focus on drug dealers. The fact that such drugs as crack are considered such a serious problem may have convinced judges and prosecutors to expedite substance abuse cases.

One study of court processing in New York found that cases involving crack had a higher probability of pretrial detention, felony indictment, and incarceration sentences than other criminal cases.[226] Some states, such as New Jersey and Pennsylvania, report that these efforts have resulted in sharp increases in the number of convictions for drug-related offenses.[227] Once convicted, drug dealers can get very long sentences. Research by the federal government shows that the average sentence for drug offenders sent to federal prison is about six years.[228]

However, these efforts often have their downside. Defense attorneys consider using delay tactics to be sound legal maneuvering in drug-related cases. Courts are so backlogged that prosecutors are anxious to plea-bargain. The consequence of this legal maneuvering is that about 25% of people convicted on federal drug charges are granted probation or some other form of community release.[229] Even so, prisons have become jammed with inmates, many of whom were involved in drug-related cases. Many drug offenders sent to prison do not serve their entire sentence because they are released in an effort to relieve prison overcrowding. The average prison stay is slightly more than one year, or about one-third of the original sentence. In fact, of all criminal types, drug offenders spend the least amount of their sentence behind bars.[230] It is unlikely that the public would approve of a drug control strategy in which locking up large numbers of traffickers forces prison officials to release an equal number of violent criminals before they served out their sentence.

Community Strategies

Another type of drug control effort relies on the involvement of local community groups to lead the fight against drugs. Representatives of various local government agencies, churches, civic organizations, and similar institutions are being brought together to create drug prevention awareness programs.

Citizen-sponsored programs attempt to restore a sense of community in drug-infested areas, reduce fear, and promote conventional norms and values.[231] According to a survey by Saul Weingart, these efforts can be classified into one of four distinct categories.[232] The first involves law enforcement efforts, which may include block watches, cooperative police-community efforts, and citizen patrols. Some of these citizen groups are nonconfrontational, willing to simply observe or photograph dealers, take down their license plate number, then notify police. On occasion, telephone hotlines

Nonpunitive treatment approaches have been used to control substance abuse. One type of drug control effort relies on the involvement of local community groups to lead the fight against drugs. Representatives of various local government agencies, churches, civic organizations, and similar institutions are being brought together to create drug prevention awareness programs. Another type of effort provides treatment facilities and counseling for known users. Here a client awaits admission to a methadone clinic.

have been set up to take anonymous tips on drug activity. Other groups engage in confrontational tactics that may even include citizens' arrests. Some of these community-based efforts are home-grown, while others attract outside organizations, such as the Guardian Angels or Black Muslims. Area residents have gone so far as contracting with private security firms to conduct neighborhood patrols.

Another tactic is to use the civil justice system to harass offenders. Landlords have been sued for owning properties that house drug dealers; neighborhood groups have formed and scrutinized drug houses for building code violations. Information acquired from these various sources is turned over to local authorities, such as police and housing agencies, for more formal action.

There are also community-based treatment efforts in which citizen volunteers participate in self-help support programs, such as Narcotics Anonymous or Cocaine Anonymous, which have more than 1,000 chapters nationally. Other programs provide youth with martial arts training, dancing, and social events as an alternative to the drug life.

Weingart also found that community drug prevention efforts are designed to enhance the quality of life, improve interpersonal relationships, and upgrade the neighborhood's physical environment. Activities might include the creation of drug-free school zones (which encourage police to keep drug dealers away from the vicinity of schools). Consciousness-raising efforts include demonstrations and marches to publicize the drug problem and build solidarity among the participants. Politicians have been lobbied to get better police protection or tougher laws passed: In New York City, residents went so far as sending bags filled with crack collected from street corners to the mayor and police commissioner to protest drug dealing. Residents have cleaned up streets, fixed broken street lights, and planted gardens in empty lots to broadcast the message that they have local pride and do not want drug dealers in their neighborhood.

While community crime-prevention efforts seem appealing, there is little conclusive evidence that they are an effective drug control strategy. Some surveys indicate that most residents do not participate in programs. There is also evidence that community programs work better in stable, middle-income areas than in those that are crime-ridden and disorganized.[233] While these findings are discouraging, some studies have also found the opposite: that deteriorated areas can sustain successful antidrug programs.[234] Future evaluations of community control efforts should determine whether they can work in the most economically depressed areas.

Drug Education and Prevention Strategies

Prevention strategies are aimed at convincing youths not to get involved in drug abuse. Heavy reliance is placed on educational programs that teach kids to say no to drugs. The most widely used program is Drug Abuse Resistance Education, or DARE. This program is an elementary school course designed to give students the skills for resisting peer pressure to experiment with tobacco, drugs, and alcohol. It is unique because it employs uniformed police officers to carry the antidrug message to the students before they enter junior high school. The program has five major focus areas:

- Providing accurate information about tobacco, alcohol, and drugs
- Teaching students techniques to resist peer pressure
- Teaching students respect for the law and law enforcers
- Giving students ideas for alternatives to drug use
- Building the self-esteem of students

DARE is based on the concept that young students need specific analytical and social skills to resist peer pressure and say no to drugs. Instructors work with children to raise their self-esteem, provide them with decision-making tools, and help them identify positive alternatives to substance abuse. More than 10,000 communities in 49 countries now use the DARE program, and more than 20 million students attend its seminars. DARE is quite expensive to implement; the average cost per full-time police officer/trainer is over $90,000. Evaluations indicate, however, that the program does little to reduce drug use or convince abusers that drugs are harmful.[235] While DARE may be effective with some subsets of the population, such as female and Hispanic students, overall success appears problematic at best.[236] One problem may be that typically little distinction is made among the types of students who are enrolled in the program, so that classrooms may contain some youths who are receptive to the DARE message and others who are openly hostile.[237] A number of prominent locations, including Seattle and Spokane, in Washington, have recently dropped the DARE program because community and law enforcement officials were skeptical about its drug-reducing capability.[238]

Drug education programs still hold promise as an effective means of reducing the onset of drug abuse. And while the DARE evaluation indicates less-than-hoped-for success, evaluations of similar programs (Project Alert) indicate that prevention strategies are capable of reducing the onset of drug use and cigarette smoking among students.[239] On February 25, 1997 President Clinton announced that antidrug education initiatives will be a major segment of his administration's drug control policy.[240] Part of the strategy will be an aggressive antidrug advertising campaign broadcast on television during prime-time hours.

Drug Testing Programs

Drug testing of private employees, government workers, and criminal offenders is believed to prevent people from involvement in substance abuse.

In the workplace, employees are tested to enhance on-the-job safety and productivity. In some industries, such as mining and transportation, drug testing is considered essential because abuse can pose a threat to the public.[241] Business leaders have been enlisted in the fight against drugs. Mandatory drug-testing programs in government and industry are common. More than 40% of the country's largest companies, including IBM and AT&T, have drug-testing programs. The federal government requires employee testing in regulated industries, such as nuclear energy and defense contracting. About 4 million transportation workers are subject to testing.

Drug testing is also quite common in government and criminal justice agencies. About 30% of local police departments test applicants, and 16% routinely test field officers. However, larger jurisdictions serving populations over 250,000 are much more likely to test applicants (84%) and field officers (75%). Drug testing is also part of the federal government's Drug Free Workplace Program, whose goal is to improve productivity and safety. Employees most likely to be tested include presidential appointees, law enforcement officers, and people in positions of national security.

Criminal defendants are now routinely tested at all stages of the justice system, from arrest to parole. The goal is to reduce criminal behavior by detecting current users and curbing their abuse. Can such programs reduce criminal activity? Two recent evaluations of pretrial drug-testing programs found little evidence that monitoring defendants' drug use influenced their behavior.[242]

Treatment Strategies

A number of approaches are taken to treat known users, getting them clean of drugs and alcohol and thereby reducing the at-risk population. One approach rests on the assumption that users have low self-esteem and treatment efforts must focus on building a sense of self. Efforts have included involving users in worthwhile programs of outdoor activities and wilderness training to create self-reliance and a sense of accomplishment.[243] More intensive efforts use group therapy approaches relying on group leaders who have been substance abusers. Through group sessions, users get the skills and support to help them reject the social pressure to use drugs. These programs are based on the Alcoholics Anonymous idea that users must find within themselves the strength to stay clean and that peer support from those who understand their experiences can help them achieve a drug-free life.

There are also residential programs for the more heavily involved, and a large network of drug treatment centers has been developed. Some are detoxification units that use medical procedures to wean patients from the more addicting drugs to others, such as methadone, that can be more easily regulated. Methadone is a drug similar to heroin, and addicts can be treated at clinics where they receive methadone under controlled conditions. However, methadone programs have been undermined because some users sell their methadone in the black market, while others supplement their dosages with illegally obtained heroin.

Other therapeutic programs attempt to deal with the psychological causes of drug use. Hypnosis, aversion therapy (getting users to associate drugs with unpleasant sensations, such as nausea), counseling, biofeedback, and other techniques are often used.

Despite their good intentions, little evidence has been found that these treatment programs can efficiently terminate substance abuse. A stay in a residential program can help stigmatize people as "addicts," even though they never used hard drugs; while in treatment, they may be introduced to hard-core users whom they will associate with upon release. Users do not often enter these programs voluntarily and have little motivation to change.[244] And even those who could be helped soon learn that there are simply more users who need treatment than there are beds in treatment facilities. Many facilities are restricted to users whose health insurance will pay for short-term residential care; when their insurance coverage ends, patients are often released, even though their treatment program is incomplete.

Employment Programs

Research indicates that drug abusers who obtain or keep ongoing employment will end or reduce the incidence of their substance abuse.[245] Not surprisingly, then, a number of efforts have been made to provide vocational rehabilitation for drug abusers. One approach is the supported work program, which typically involves job-site training, ongoing assessment, and job-site intervention. Rather than teach about work skills in a classroom, support programs rely on helping drug abusers deal with real-life work settings. Other programs have provided training to overcome the barriers to employment, including help with motivation, education, experience, the job market, job-seeking skills, and personal issues. For example, female abusers may be unaware of childcare resources that would enable them to seek employment opportunities while their children are cared for. Another approach is to help addicts improve their interviewing skills so that once a job opportunity can be identified they are equipped to convince potential employers of their commitment and reliability.

A recent analysis of job programs by Jerome Platt found that relatively few programs exist, and those that do have shortcomings that either limit their implementation or raise questions about their utility and effectiveness. Platt argues that the content of employment programs must be shaped by a comprehensive approach to the employment problems of drug abusers that recognizes the effect of societal attitudes and job market forces on the success of employment programs.[246]

Legalization

Despite the massive effort to control drugs through prevention, deterrence, education, and treatment strategies, the fight against substance abuse has not proven successful. It is difficult to get people out of the drug culture because of the enormous profits involved in the drug trade: 500 kilos of coca leaves worth $4,000 to a grower yields about 8 kilos of street cocaine valued at about $300,000. A drug dealer who can move 100 pounds of coke into the United States can make $1.5 million in one shipment. An estimated 60 tons of cocaine are imported into the country each year, with a street value of $2 billion.[247] It has also proven difficult to control drugs by convincing known users to quit; few treatment efforts have proven successful.

Considering these problems, some commentators have called for the legalization or decriminalization of restricted drugs. Legalization is warranted, according to Ethan Nadelmann, because the use of mood-altering substances is customary in almost all human societies; people have always wanted, and will find ways of obtaining, psychoactive drugs.[248] Banning drugs serves to create networks of manufacturers and distributors, many of whom use violence as part of their standard operating procedures. While some may charge that drug use is immoral, Nadelmann questions whether it is really any worse than the unrestricted use of alcohol and cigarettes, both of which are addicting and unhealthful. Far more people die each year because they abuse these legal substances than are killed in drug wars or from abusing illegal substances (since an estimated 100,000 people per year die from alcohol-related causes and another 320,000 from tobacco-related causes).[249]

Nadelmann also argues that just as Prohibition failed to stop the flow of alcohol in the 1920s while at the same time increasing the power of organized crime, the policy of prohibiting drugs is similarly doomed to failure. When drugs were legal and freely available earlier in this century, the proportion of Americans using drugs was not much greater than today; most users managed to lead normal lives, probably because of the legal status of their drug use.[250]

If drugs were legalized, the argument goes, price and distribution could be controlled by the government. This would reduce addicts' cash requirements, thus crime rates would go down, as users would no longer need the same cash flow to support their habit. Drug-related deaths would decline because government control would reduce needle sharing and the spread of AIDS, and drugs would not be cut with a variety of other substances. Legalization would also destroy the drug-importing cartels and gangs. Since drugs would be bought and sold openly, the government would reap a tax windfall from both taxes on the sale of drugs and the income taxes paid by drug dealers on profits that have been part of the hidden economy. Of course,

Figure 14.4 Strategies for controlling drugs.

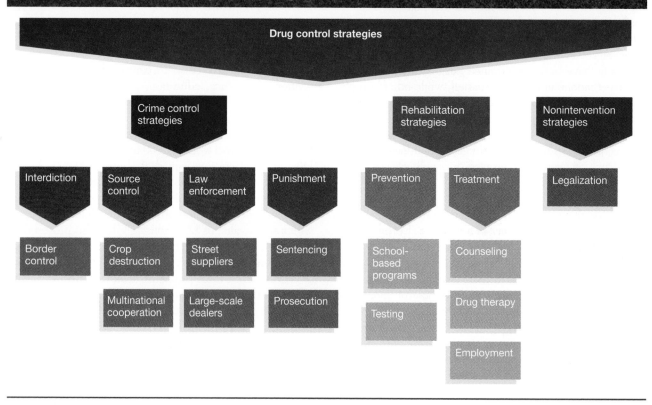

drug distribution would be regulated, like alcohol, keeping it out of the hands of adolescents, public servants such as police and airline pilots, and known felons. Those who favor legalization point to the Netherlands as a country that has legalized drugs and remains relatively crime-free.[251]

While legalization can have the short-term effect of reducing the association between drug use and crime, it may also have grave social consequences. According to David Courtwright, legalization would result in an increase in the nation's rate of drug usage, creating an even larger group of nonproductive, drug-dependent people who must be cared for by the rest of society.[252] If drugs were legalized and freely available, drug users might significantly increase their daily intake. In countries such as Iran and Thailand, where drugs are cheap and readily available, the rate of narcotics use is quite high. Historically, the availability of cheap narcotics has preceded drug use epidemics, as was the case when British and American merchants sold opium in 19th-century China.

Courtwright also suggests that efforts to control legal use would backfire. If juveniles, criminals, and members of other at-risk groups were forbidden to buy drugs, who would be the customers? Noncriminal, nonabusing middle-aged adults? And would not those prohibited from legally buying drugs create an underground market almost as vast as the current one? If the government tried to raise money by taxing legal drugs, as it now does for liquor and ciga-

rettes, might not that encourage drug smuggling to avoid tax payments? These "illegal" drugs might then fall into the hands of adolescents.

The problems of alcoholism should serve as a warning of what can happen when controlled substances are made readily available. For example, since women may be more disposed to becoming dependent on crack than men, the number of drug-dependent babies could begin to match or exceed the number delivered with fetal alcohol syndrome.[253] Drunk-driving fatalities, which today number about 25,000 per year, may be matched by deaths due to driving under the influence of pot or crack. And while distribution would be regulated, it is likely that adolescents would have the same opportunity to obtain potent drugs as they now have to obtain beer and hard liquor.

While decriminalization or legalization of controlled substances is unlikely in the near term, further study is warranted. What effect would a policy of partial decriminalization (for example, legalizing small amounts of marijuana) have on drug use rates? Would a get-tough policy help "widen the net" of the justice system and actually deepen some youths' involvement in substance abuse? Can society provide alternatives to drugs that will reduce teenage drug dependency?[254] The answers to these questions have proven elusive.

The various efforts at drug control are summarized in Figure 14.4.

Summary

Public order crimes are acts considered illegal because they conflict with social policy, accepted moral rules, and public opinion. There is usually great debate over public order crimes. Some charge that they are not really crimes at all and that it is foolish to legislate morality. Others view such morally tinged acts as prostitution, gambling, and drug abuse as harmful and therefore subject to public control.

Many public order crimes are sex-related. Although homosexuality is not a crime per se, homosexual acts are subject to legal control. Some states still follow the archaic custom of legislating long prison terms for consensual homosexual sex.

Prostitution is another sex-related public order crime. Even though prostitution has been practiced for thousands of years and is legal in some areas, most states outlaw commercial sex. There are several kinds of prostitutes, including streetwalkers, B-girls, and call girls. Studies indicate that most prostitutes come from poor, troubled families and have abusive parents. However, there is little evidence that prostitutes are emotionally disturbed, addicted to drugs, or sexually abnormal. Although prostitution is illegal, some cities have set up adult entertainment areas where commercial sex is tolerated by law enforcement agents.

Pornography involves the sale of sexually explicit material intended to sexually excite paying customers. The depiction of sex and nudity is not illegal, but it does violate the law when it is judged obscene. *Obscenity* is a legal term that today is defined as material offensive to community standards. Thus, each local jurisdiction must decide what pornographic material is obscene. A growing problem is in the exploitation of children in obscene materials—kiddy porn. The Supreme Court has ruled that local communities can pass statutes outlawing any sexually explicit material. There is no hard evidence that pornography is related to crime or aggression, but data suggest that sexual material with a violent theme is related to sexual violence by those who view it.

Substance abuse is another type of public order crime. Debate continues over the legalization of drugs, usually centering on such nonaddicting drugs as marijuana. However, most states and the federal government outlaw a wide variety of drugs they consider harmful, including narcotics, amphetamines, barbiturates, cocaine, hallucinogens, and marijuana. One of the main reasons for the continued ban on drugs is their relationship to crime. Numerous studies have found that drug addicts commit enormous amounts of property crime.

Alcohol is another commonly abused substance. Although it is legal to possess, it, too, has been linked to crime. Drunk driving and deaths caused by drunk drivers are growing national problems. Many strategies are used to control substance abuse, ranging from source control to treatment. So far, no single method seems effective. While legalization is debated, the facts that so many people already take drugs and that drug abuse is associated with crime make legalization unlikely in the near future.

Key Terms

public order crimes	call girls
victimless crimes	skeezers
vigilante	massage parlors
moral crusades	baby pros
moral entrepreneurs	Mann Act
homosexuality	pornography
sodomy	obscenity
paraphilia	temperance movement
prostitution	freebase
brothels	crack
madams	designer drugs

Notes

1. Eleanor Clift, "A Terrible, Terrible Trauma," *Newsweek,* 30 September 1996, p. 57.

2. Edwin Schur, *Crimes Without Victims* (Englewood Cliffs, N.J.: Prentice-Hall, 1965).

3. Charles Fleming and Michele Ingrassia, "The Heidi Chronicles," *Newsweek,* 16 August 1993, p. 51.

4. Andrea Dworkin, quoted in "Where Do We Stand on Pornography," *Ms,* January–February 1994, p. 34.

5. Jennifer Williard, *Juvenile Prostitution* (Washington, D.C.: National Victim Resource Center, 1991).

6. Morris Cohen, "Moral Aspects of the Criminal Law," *Yale Law Journal* 49 (1940): 1017.

7. Sir Patrick Devlin, *The Enforcement of Morals* (New York: Oxford University Press, 1959), p. 20.

8. See Joel Feinberg, *Social Philosophy* (Englewood Cliffs, N.J.: Prentice-Hall, 1973), chap. 2, 3.

9. *United States v. 12 200-ft Reels of Super 8mm Film,* 413 U.S. 123 (1973) at 137.

10. David Kaplan, "Is It Torture or Tradition?" *Newsweek,* 20 December 1993, p. 124.

11. H. L. A. Hart, "Immorality and Treason," *Listener* 62 (1959): 163.

12. Joseph Gussfield, "On Legislating Morals: The Symbolic Process of Designating Deviancy," *California Law Review* 56 (1968): 58–59.

13. E. Hatfield, S. Sprecher, and J. Traupman, "Men and Women's Reactions to Sexually Explicit Films: A Serendipitous Finding," *Archives of Sexual Behavior* 6 (1978): 583–592.

14. Henry Lesieur and Joseph Sheley, "Illegal Appended Enterprises: Selling the Lines," *Social Problems* 34 (1987): 249–260.

15. Wayne LaFave and Austin Scott, Jr., *Criminal Law* (St. Paul, Minn.: West Publishing, 1986), p. 12.

16. Ibid.

17. "Baylor U. Cancels Art Class on Nudes," *Boston Globe,* 22 March 1993, p. 21.

18. Boston Reuters, "In Key West, Body Paint No Longer Counts as Clothes," *Boston Globe,* 22 October 1996, p. A14.

19. Howard Becker, *Outsiders* (New York: Macmillan, 1963), pp. 13–14.

20. Daniel Claster, *Bad Guys and Good Guys, Moral Polarization and Crime* (Westport, Conn.: Greenwood Press, 1992), pp. 28–29.

21. Albert Reiss, "The Social Integration of Queers and Peers," *Social Problems* 9 (1961): 102–120.

22. Judd Marmor, "The Multiple Roots of Homosexual Behavior," in *Homosexual Behavior*, ed. J. Marmor (New York: Basic Books, 1980), p. 5.

23. C. S. Ford and F. A. Beach, *Patterns of Sexual Behavior* (New York: Harper & Bros., 1951).

24. J. Money, "Sin, Sickness, or Status? Homosexual Gender Identity and Psychoneuroendocrinology," *American Psychologist* 42 (1987): 384–399.

25. A. Kinsey, W. Pomeroy, and C. Martin, *Sexual Behavior in the Human Male* (Philadelphia: W. B. Saunders, 1948); A. Kinsey, W. Pomeroy, C. Martin, and P. H. Gebhard, *Sexual Behavior in the Human Female* (Philadelphia: W. B. Saunders, 1953); Morton Hunt, *Sexual Behavior in the 1970s* (New York: Dell Books, 1974), p. 317.

26. J. McNeil, *The Church and the Homosexual* (Kansas City, Mo.: Sheed, Andrews, and McNeel, 1976).

27. Marmor, "The Multiple Roots of Homosexual Behavior," pp. 18–19.

28. Ibid., p. 19.

29. Henry Adams, Lester Wright, and Bethany Lohr, "Is Homophobia Associated with Homosexual Arousal?" *Journal of Abnormal Psychology* 105 (1996): 440–445.

30. M. Weinberg and C. J. Williams, *Male Homosexuals: Problems and Adaptations* (New York: Oxford University Press, 1974).

31. Spencer Rathus, *Human Sexuality* (New York: Holt, Rinehart and Winston, 1983), p. 395.

32. "Homosexuality and Politics: A Newsweek Poll," *Newsweek*, 25 September 1989, p. 19.

33. Mark Muro, "Gay Studies Goes Mainstream," *Boston Globe*, 30 January 1991, p. 35.

34. "Daddy Is out of the Closet," *Newsweek*, 7 January 1991, p. 60.

35. 376 U.S. 660; 82 S.Ct. 1417; 8 L.Ed.2d 758 (1962).

36. Richard Keil, "Gay Couple Sues D.C. over Marriage License," *Boston Globe*, 27 November 1990, p. 5.

37. F. Inbau, J. Thompson, and J. Zagel, *Criminal Law and Its Administration* (Mineola, N.Y.: Foundation Press, 1974), p. 287.

38. *Bowers v. Hardwick*, 106 S.Ct. 2841 (1986); reh. den. 107 S.Ct. 29 (1986).

39. Georgia Code Ann. 16–6–2 (1984).

40. American Law Institute, Model Penal Code, Section 207.5.

41. Gary Caplan, "Fourteenth Amendment—The Supreme Court Limits the Right to Privacy," *Journal of Criminal Law and Criminology* 77 (1986): 894–930.

42. Associated Press, "Voters in Houston Defeat 'Sexual Orientations' Issues," *Omaha World Herald*, 20 January 1985, p. 1.

43. Christopher Boyd, "Gay Rights Coming of Age," *Boston Globe*, 7 December 1992, p. 3.

44. Andy Mead and Gail Gibson, "Private Life Stirs a Public Furor," *Boston Globe*, 9 November 1993, p. 3.

45. Carolyn Skorneck, "Reno Orders FBI to End Hiring Bias Against Gays," *Boston Globe*, 4 December 1993, p. 3.

46. John Biskupic, "Justices Let Stand 'Don't Ask, Don't Tell' Policy," *Boston Globe*, 22 October 1996, p. A6.

47. Associated Press, "Court Rules Against Transsexual Pilot," *Omaha World Herald*, 31 August 1984, p. 3.

48. Associated Press, "Court Gives Sons Back to Gay Father," *Boston Globe*, 16 October 1996, p. A5.

49. For the classic study of homosexual encounters, see Laud Humphreys, *Tearoom Trade: Impersonal Sex in Public Places* (Chicago: Aldine, 1970).

50. Reuters, "Belgians Promise to Clean Up Courts," *Boston Globe*, 22 October 1996, p. A17.

51. See, generally, Spencer Rathus and Jeffery Nevid, *Abnormal Psychology* (Englewood Cliffs, N.J.: Prentice-Hall, 1991), pp. 373–411.

52. Kathy Smiljanich and John Briere, "Self-Reported Sexual Interest in Children: Sex Differences and Psychosocial Correlates in a University Sample," *Violence and Victims* 11 (1996): 39–50.

53. Lawrence A. Greenfeld, *Sex Offenses and Offenders: An Analysis of Data on Rape and Sexual Assault* (Washington, D.C.: Bureau of Justice Statistics, 1997).

54. See, generally, V. Bullogh, *Sexual Variance in Society and History* (Chicago: University of Chicago Press, 1958), pp. 143–144.

55. Rathus, *Human Sexuality*, p. 463.

56. Annette Jolin, "On the Backs of Working Prostitutes: Feminist Theory and Prostitution Policy," *Crime and Delinquency* 40 (1994): 60–83.

57. Charles McCaghy, *Deviant Behavior* (New York: Macmillan, 1976), pp. 348–349.

58. Rathus, *Human Sexuality*, p. 463.

59. Cited in Ibid.

60. FBI, *Crime in the United States, 1995*, p. 221.

61. Michael Waldholz, "HTLV–I Virus Found in Blood of Prostitutes," *Wall Street Journal*, 5 January 1990, p. B2.

62. FBI, *Crime in the United States, 1995*, p. 172.

63. Charles Winick and Paul Kinsie, *The Lively Commerce* (Chicago: Quadrangle Books, 1971), p. 58.

64. Mark-David Janus, Barbara Scanlon, and Virginia Price, "Youth Prostitution," in *Child Pornography and Sex Rings*, ed. Ann Wolbert Burgess (Lexington, Mass.: Lexington Books, 1989), pp. 127–146.

65. Jennifer James, "Prostitutes and Prostitution," in *Deviants: Voluntary Action in a Hostile World*, ed. E. Sagarin and F. Montanino (New York: Scott, Foresman, 1977), p. 384.

66. Winick and Kinsie, *The Lively Commerce*, pp. 172–173.

67. Paul Goldstein, "Occupational Mobility in the World of Prostitution: Becoming a Madam," *Deviant Behavior* 4 (1983): 267–279.

68. Alessandra Stanley, "Case of the Classy Madam," *Time*, 29 October 1984, p. 39.

69. Goldstein, "Occupational Mobility in the World of Prostitution," (1983): 267–270.

70. Described in Rathus, *Human Sexuality*, p. 468.

71. Paul Goldstein, Lawrence Ouellet, and Michael Fendrich, "From Bag Brides to Skeezers: A Historical Perspective on Sex-for-Drugs Behavior," *Journal of Psychoactive Drugs* 24 (1992): 349–361.

72. Lisa Maher and Kathleen Daly, "Women in the Street-Level Drug Economy: Continuity or Change?" *Criminology* 34 (1996): 465–491.

73. D. Kelly Weisberg, *Children of the Night: A Study of Adolescent Prostitution* (Lexington, Mass.: Lexington Books, 1985), pp. 44–55.

74. Gerald Hotaling and David Finkelhor, *The Sexual Exploitation of Missing Children* (Washington, D.C.: U.S. Department of Justice, 1988).

75. N. Jackman, Richard O'Toole, and Gilbert Geis, "The Self-Image of the Prostitute," in *Sexual Deviance*, ed. J. Gagnon and W. Simon (New York: Harper & Row, 1967), pp. 152–153.

76. Weisberg, *Children of the Night*, p. 98.

77. Winick and Kinsie, *The Lively Commerce*, p. 51.

78. Paul Gebhard, "Misconceptions About Female Prostitutes," *Medical Aspects of Human Sexuality* 3 (July 1969): 28–30.

79. James, "Prostitutes and Prostitution," pp. 388–389.

80. Winick and Kinsie, *The Lively Commerce*, p. 109.

81. James, "Prostitutes and Prostitution," p. 419.

82. Winick and Kinsie, *The Lively Commerce*, p. 120.

83. Goldstein, Ouellet, and Fendrich, "From Bag Brides to Skeezers," p. 359.

84. Dorothy Bracey, *"Baby Pros": Preliminary Profiles of Juvenile Prostitutes* (New York: JohnJay Press, 1979).

85. Andrea Dworkin, *Pornography* (New York: Dutton, 1989).

86. Jolin, "On the Backs of Working Prostitutes," pp. 76–77.

87. *Merriam-Webster Dictionary* (New York: Pocket Books, 1974), p. 484.

88. Ann Landers, "Pornography Can Be an Addiction," *Boston Globe,* 19 July 1993, p. 36.

89. Attorney General's Commission Report on Pornography, Final Report (Washington, D.C.: U.S. Government Printing Office, 1986), pp. 837–901. Hereinafter cited as Pornography Commission.

90. John Hurst, "Children—A Big Profit Item for the Smut Peddlers," *Los Angeles Times,* 26 May 1977, cited in *Take Back the Night,* ed. Laura Lederer (New York: William Morrow, 1980), pp. 77–78.

91. Albert Belanger et al., "Typology of Sex Rings Exploiting Children," in *Child Pornography and Sex Rings,* ed. Ann Wolbert Burgess (Lexington, Mass.: Lexington Books, 1984), pp. 51–81.

92. *The Report of the Commission on Obscenity and Pornography* (Washington, D.C.: U.S. Government Printing Office, 1970).

93. Pornography Commission, pp. 837–902.

94. Berl Kutchinsky, "The Effect of Easy Availability of Pornography on the Incidence of Sex Crimes," *Journal of Social Issues* 29 (1973): 95–112.

95. Michael Goldstein, "Exposure to Erotic Stimuli and Sexual Deviance," *Journal of Social Issues* 29 (1973): 197–219.

96. John Court, "Sex and Violence: A Ripple Effect," *Pornography and Aggression,* ed. Neal Malamuth and Edward Donnerstein (Orlando, Fla.: Academic Press, 1984).

97. See Edward Donnerstein, Daniel Linz, and Steven Penrod, *The Question of Pornography* (New York: Free Press, 1987).

98. Pornography Commission, pp. 901–1037.

99. Edward Donnerstein, "Pornography and Violence Against Women," *Annals of the New York Academy of Science* 347 (1980): 277–288; E. Donnerstein and J. Hallam, "Facilitating Effects of Erotica on Aggression Against Women," *Journal of Personality and Social Psychology* 36 (1977): 1270–1277; Seymour Fishbach and Neil Malamuth, "Sex and Aggression: Proving the Link," *Psychology Today* 12 (1978): 111–122.

100. Don Smith, "Sexual Aggression in American Pornography: The Stereotype of Rape," paper presented at the annual meeting of the American Sociological Association, 1976.

101. State Laws on Obscenity, Child Pornography and Harassment: http://www.itaa.org/porn1.html.

102. Tracy Fields, "Florida Vendor Booked for Rap Record Sale," *Boston Globe,* 9 June 1990, p. 1; Richard Lacayo, "The Rap Against a Rap Group," *Time,* 25 June 1990, p. 18.

103. 354 U.S. 476; 77 S.Ct. 1304 (1957).

104. 383 U.S. 413 (1966).

105. 413 U.S. 15 (1973).

106. R. George Wright, "Defining Obscenity: The Criterion of Value," *New England Law Review* 22 (1987): 315–341.

107. *Pope v. Illinois,* 107 S.Ct. 1918 (1987).

108. Ibid. at 1927 (Stevens, J., dissenting).

109. Anthony Flint, "Skin Trade Spreading Across U.S.," *Boston Globe,* 1 December 1996, pp. 1, 36–37.

110. Pornography Commission, pp. 376–377.

111. Bob Cohn, "The Trials of Adam and Eve," *Newsweek,* 7 January 1991, p. 48.

112. 427 U.S. 50 (1976).

113. Kevin Cullen, "The Bad Old Days Are Over," *Boston Globe,* 23 December 1987, p. 33.

114. 50 L.W. 5077 (1982).

115. Joseph Scott, "Violence and Erotic Material—The Relationship Between Adult Entertainment and Rape?" paper presented at the annual meeting of the American Association for the Advancement of Science, Los Angeles, 1985.

116. Ibid.

117. Flint, "Skin Trade Spreading Across the U.S.," p. 36.

118. Associated Press, "N.Y. Firm Fined for Broadcasting Pornographic Films by Satellite," *Boston Globe,* 16 February 1991, p. 12.

119. Jared Sandberg, "U.S. Cracks Down on On-Line Child Pornography," *Wall Street Journal,* 14 September 1995, p. A3.

120. Ralph Weisheit, "Studying Drugs in Rural Areas: Notes from the Field," *Journal of Research in Crime and Delinquency* 30 (1993): 213–232.

121. See, generally, Marianne Zawitz, ed., *Drugs, Crime and the Justice System* (Washington, D.C.: U.S. Government Printing Office, 1992). Herein cited as *Drugs.*

122. Arnold Trebach, *The Heroin Solution* (New Haven, Conn.: Yale University Press, 1982).

123. James Inciardi, *The War on Drugs* (Palo Alto, Calif.: Mayfield, 1986), p. 2.

124. See, generally, David Pittman, "Drug Addiction and Crime," in *Handbook of Criminology,* ed. D. Glazer (Chicago: Rand McNally, 1974), pp. 209–232; Board of Directors, National Council on Crime and Delinquency, "Drug Addiction: A Medical, Not a Law Enforcement, Problem," *Crime and Delinquency* 20 (1974): 4–9.

125. Associated Press, "Records Detail Royals' Turn-of-Century Drug Use," *Boston Globe,* 29 August 1993, p. 13.

126. See Edwin Brecher, *Licit and Illicit Drugs* (Boston: Little, Brown, 1972).

127. James Inciardi, *Reflections on Crime* (New York: Holt, Rinehart and Winston, 1978), p. 15.

128. William Bates and Betty Crowther, "Drug Abuse," in *Deviants: Voluntary Actors in a Hostile World,* ed. E. Sagarin and F. Montanino (New York: Foresman and Co., 1977), p. 269.

129. Inciardi, *Reflections on Crime,* pp. 8–10; see also A. Greeley, William McCready, and Gary Theisen, *Ethnic Drinking Subcultures* (New York: Praeger, 1980).

130. Joseph Gusfield, *Symbolic Crusade* (Urbana: University of Illinois Press, 1963), chap. 3.

131. McCaghy, *Deviant Behavior,* p. 280.

132. Ibid.

133. This section relies heavily on the descriptions in Kenneth Jones, Louis Shainberg, and Curtin Byer, *Drugs and Alcohol* (New York: Harper & Row, 1979), pp. 57–114.

134. Rathus and Nevid, *Abnormal Psychology,* p. 344.

135. Jeffrey Fagan and Ko-Lin Chin, "Initiation into Crack and Powdered Cocaine: A Tale of Two Epidemics," *Contemporary Drug Problems* 16 (1989): 579–617.

136. Thomas Mieczkowski, "The Damage Done: Cocaine Methods in Detroit," *International Journal of Comparative and Applied Criminal Justice* 12 (1988): 261–267.

137. News release, Institute of Social Research, University of Michigan, Ann Arbor, 31 January 1997.

138. John Hagedorn, "Homeboys, Dope Fiends, Legits, and New Jacks," *Criminology* 32 (1994): 197–220.

139. Rathus and Nevid, *Abnormal Psychology,* p. 342.

140. These numbers are open to debate. See Inciardi, *The War on Drugs,* pp. 70–71; Jerome Platt and Christina Platt, *Heroin Addiction* (New York: Wiley, 1976), p. 324.

141. Charles Winick, "Physician Narcotics Addicts," *Social Problems* 9 (1961): 174–186.

142. Data in this section come from U.S. Department of Health and Human Services, *The Household Survey on Drug Abuse, 1995* (Washington, D.C.: Department of Health and Human Services, 1996).

143. Ibid.

144. Associated Press, "Alcohol Deaths Stopped Declining," *Boston Globe,* 27 January 1991, p. 8.

145. Ibid.

146. D. J. Rohsenow, "Drinking Habits and Expectancies About Alcohol's Effects for Self Versus Others," *Journal of Consulting and Clinical Psychology* 51 (1983): 752–756.

147. G. Kolata, "Study Backs Heart Benefits in Light Drinking," *New York Times,* 3 August 1988, p. A24.

148. Spencer Rathus, *Psychology,* 4th ed. (New York: Holt, Rinehart and Winston, 1990), p. 161.

149. The annual survey is conducted by Lloyd Johnston, Jerald Bachman, and Patrick O'Malley of the Institute of Social Research, University of Michigan, Ann Arbor.

150. U.S. Department of Health and Human Services, *The Household Survey on Drug Abuse, 1995.*

151. Eric Wish, *Drug Use Forecasting Program, Annual Report 1990* (Washington, D.C.: National Institute of Justice, 1990).

152. Thomas Gray and Eric Wish, *Maryland Youth at Risk: A Study of Drug Use in Juvenile Detainees* (College Park, Md.: Center for Substance Abuse Research, 1993); Eric Wish and Christina Polsenberg, "Arrestee Urine Tests and Self-Reports of Drug Use: Which Is More Related to Rearrest?" paper presented at the annual meeting of the American Society of Criminology, Phoenix, November 1993.

153. Thomas Mieczkowski, "The Prevalence of Drug Use in the United States," in *Crime and Justice, A Review of Research,* vol. 20, ed. Michael Tonry (Chicago: University of Chicago Press, 1996), pp. 349–414.

154. See, generally, Mark Blumberg, ed., *AIDS, The Impact on the Criminal Justice System* (Columbus, Ohio: Merrill Publishing, 1990).

155. Scott Decker and Richard Rosenfeld, "Intravenous Drug Use and the AIDS Epidemic: Findings for a Twenty-City Sample of Arrestees," paper presented at the annual meeting of the American Society of Criminology, Baltimore, November 1990.

156. Douglas Longshore, "Prevalence and Circumstances of Drug Injection at Los Angeles Shooting Galleries," *Crime and Delinquency* 42 (1996): 21–35.

157. Ibid., p. 30.

158. Mark Blumberg, "AIDS and the Criminal Justice System: An Overview," in *AIDS, The Impact on the Criminal Justice System,* p. 11.

159. Bruce Johnson, Andrew Golub, and Jeffrey Fagan, "Careers in Crack, Drug Use, Drug Distribution, and Nondrug Criminality," *Crime and Delinquency* 41 (1995): 275–295.

160. Ibid., pp. 2–3.

161. C. Bowden, "Determinants of Initial Use of Opioids," *Comprehensive Psychiatry* 12 (1971): 136–140.

162. Marvin Krohn, Alan Lizotte, Terence Thornberry, Carolyn Smith, and David McDowall, "Reciprocal Causal Relationships Among Drug Use, Peers, and Beliefs: A Five-Wave Panel Model," *Journal of Drug Issues* 26 (1996): 205–428.

163. R. Cloward and L. Ohlin, *Delinquency and Opportunity: A Theory of Delinquent Gangs* (Glencoe, Ill.: Free Press, 1960).

164. Kellie Barr, Michael Farrell, Grace Barnes, and John Welte, "Race, Class, and Gender Differences in Substance Abuse: Evidence of Middle-Class/Underclass Polarization Among Black Males," *Social Problems* 40 (1993): 314–326.

165. Rathus and Nevid, *Abnormal Psychology,* p. 361.

166. Rathus, *Psychology,* p. 158.

166. Platt and Platt, *Heroin Addiction,* p. 127.

167. Alison Bass, "Mental Ills, Drug Abuse Linked," *Boston Globe,* 21 November 1990, p. 3.

168. D. W. Goodwin, "Alcoholism and Genetics," *Archives of General Psychiatry* 42 (1985): 171–174.

170. For a thorough review of this issue, see John Petraitis, Brian Flay, and Todd Miller, "Reviewing Theories of Adolescent Substance Use: Organizing Pieces in the Puzzle," *Psychological Bulletin* 117 (1995): 67–86.

171. Judith Brooks and Li-Jung Tseng, "Influences of Parental Drug Use, Personality, and Child Rearing on the Toddler's Anger and Negativity," *Genetic, Social and General Psychology Monographs* 122 (1996): 107–128.

172. Thomas Ashby Wills, Donato Vaccaro, Grace McNamara, and A. Elizabeth Hirky, "Escalated Substance Use: A Longitudinal Grouping Analysis from Early to Middle Adolescence," *Journal of Abnormal Psychology* 105 (1996): 166–180.

173. Denise Kandel and Mark Davies, "Friendship Networks, Intimacy and Illicit Drug Use in Young Adulthood: A Comparison of Two Competing Theories," *Criminology* 29 (1991): 441–471.

174. J. S. Mio, G. Nanjundappa, D. E. Verlur, and M. D. DeRios, "Drug Abuse and the Adolescent Sex Offender: A Preliminary Analysis," *Journal of Psychoactive Drugs* 18 (1986): 65–72.

175. D. Baer and J. Corrado, "Heroin Addict Relationships with Parents During Childhood and Early Adolescent Years," *Journal of Genetic Psychology* 124 (1974): 99–103.

176. James Inciardi, Ruth Horowitz, and Anne Pottieger, *Street Kids, Street Drugs, Street Crime: An Examination of Drug Use and Serious Delinquency in Miami* (Belmont, Calif.: Wadsworth, 1993), p. 43.

177. Ibid.

178. John Wallace and Jerald Bachman, "Explaining Racial/Ethnic Differences in Adolescent Drug Use: The Impact of Background and Lifestyle," *Social Problems* 38 (1991): 333–357.

179. John Donovan, "Problem-Behavior Theory and the Explanation of Adolescent Marijuana Use," *Journal of Drug Issues* 26 (1996): 379–404.

180. A. Christiansen, G. T. Smith, P. V. Roehling, and M. S. Goldman, "Using Alcohol Expectancies to Predict Adolescent Drinking Behavior After One Year," *Journal of Counseling and Clinical Psychology* 57 (1989): 93–99.

181. Claire Sterck-Elifson, "Just for Fun?: Cocaine Use Among Middle-Class Women," *Journal of Drug Issues* 26 (1996): 63–76.

182. Icek Ajzen, *Attitudes, Personality and Behavior* (Homewood, Ill.: Dorsey Press, 1988).

183. Judith Brook, Martin Whiteman, Elinor Balka, and Beatrix Hamburg, "African-American and Puerto Rican Drug Use: Personality, Familial, and Other Environmental Risk Factors," *Genetic, Social, and General Psychology Monographs* 118 (1992): 419–438.

184. Inciardi, *The War on Drugs,* p. 60.

185. These lifestyles are described in Marcia Chaiken and Bruce Johnson, *Characteristics of Different Types of Drug-Involved Offenders* (Washington, D.C.: National Institute of Justice, 1988).

186. Kenneth Tunnell, "Inside the Drug Trade: Trafficking from the Dealer's Perspective," *Qualitative Sociology* 16 (1993): 361–381.

187. Carolyn Rebecca Block, Antigone Christakos, Ayad Jacob, and Roger Przybylski, *Street Gangs and Crime* (Chicago: Illinois Criminal Justice Information Authority, 1996).

188. Hilary Saner, Robert MacCoun, Peter Reuter, "On the Ubiquity of Drug Selling Among Youthful Offenders in Washington, D.C., 1985–1991: Age, Period, or Cohort Effect?" *Journal of Quantitative Criminology* 11 (1995): 362–373.

189. Karen Joe, "The Lives and Times of Asian-Pacific American Women Drug Users: An Ethnographic Study of Their Methamphetamine Use," *Journal of Drug Issues* 26 (1996): 199– 218.

190. Carolyn Rebecca Block and Antigone Christakos, "Intimate Partner Homicide in Chicago over 29 Years," *Crime and Delinquency* 41 (1995): 496–526.

191. Douglas Smith and Christina Polsenberg, "Specifying the Relationship Between Arrestee Drug Test Results and Recidivism," *Journal of Criminal Law and Criminology* 83 (1992): 364–377.

192. George Speckart and M. Douglas Anglin, "Narcotics Use and Crime: An Overview of Recent Research Advances," *Contemporary Drug Problems* 13 (1986): 741–769; Charles Faupel and Carl Klockars, "Drugs-Crime Connections: Elaborations from the Life Histories of Hard-Core Heroin Addicts," *Social Problems* 34 (1987): 54–68.

193. M. Douglas Anglin, Elizabeth Piper Deschenes, and George Speckart, "The Effect of Legal Supervision on Narcotic Addiction and Criminal Behavior," paper presented at the annual meeting of the American Society of Criminology, Montreal, November 1987, p. 2.

194. Speckart and Anglin, "Narcotics Use and Crime: An Overview of Recent Research Advances," p. 752.

195. Ibid.

196. Helene Raskin White and Stephen Hansell, "The Moderating Effects of Gender and Hostility on the Alcohol-Aggression Relationship," *Journal of Research in Crime and Delinquency* 33 (1996): 450–470; D. Wayne Osgood, "Drugs, Alcohol, and Adolescent Violence," paper presented at the annual meeting of the American Society of Criminology, Miami, 1994.

197. James Inciardi, "Heroin Use and Street Crime," *Crime and Delinquency* 25 (1979): 335–346; see also W. McGlothlin, M. Anglin, and B. Wilson, "Narcotic Addiction and Crime," *Criminology* 16 (1978): 293–311.

198. M. Douglas Anglin and George Speckart, "Narcotics Use and Crime: A Multisample, Multimethod Analysis," *Criminology* 26 (1988): 197–235.

199. David Nurco, Ira Cisin, and John Ball, "Crime as a Source of Income for Narcotics Addicts," *Journal of Substance Abuse Treatment 2* (1985): 113–115.

200. Allen Beck, Darrell Gilliard, Lawrence Greenfeld, Caroline Harlow, Thomas Hester, Lewis Jankowski, Tracy Snell, James Stephen, and Danielle Morton, *Survey of State Prison Inmates, 1991* (Washington, D.C.: Bureau of Justice Statistics, 1993). The survey of prison inmates is conducted by the Bureau of Justice Statistics every five to seven years.

201. Thomas E. Feucht, *1995 Drug Use Forecasting Annual Report on Adult and Juvenile Arrestees* (Washington, D.C.: National Institute of Justice, 1996).

202. Paul Goldstein, "The Drugs-Violence Nexus: A Tripartite Conceptual Framework," *Journal of Drug Issues* 15 (1985): 493–506.

203. Faupel and Klockars, "Drugs-Crime Connections."

204. Charles Faupel, "Heroin Use, Crime and Unemployment Status," *Journal of Drug Issues* 18 (1988): 467–479.

205. See Jones, Shainberg, and Byer, *Drugs and Alcohol,* pp. 137–146.

206. Controlled Substance Act, 21 U.S.C. 848 (1984).

207. Anti-Drug Abuse Act of 1986, Pub. L. No. 99-570, U.S.C. 841 (1986).

208. Anti-Drug Abuse Act of 1988, Pub. L. No. 100-690; 21 U.S.C. 1501; Subtitle A–Death Penalty, Sec. 7001, Amending the Controlled Substances Abuse Act, 21 U.S.C. 848.

209. Bennett Beach, "Is the Party Finally Over?" *Time,* 26 April 1982, p. 58.

210. "New Drunken Driver Law Shows Results in California," *Omaha World Herald,* 26 May 1982, p. 34.

211. Faye Silas, "Gimme the Keys," *ABA Journal* 71 (1985): 36.

212. Fred Heinzelmann, *Jailing Drunk Drivers* (Washington, D.C.: National Institute of Justice, 1984).

213. Rodney Kingsworth and Michael Jungsten, "Driving Under the Influence: The Impact of Legislative Reform on Court Sentencing Practices," *Crime and Delinquency* 34 (1988): 3–28.

214. Jones, Shainberg, and Byer, *Drugs and Alcohol,* pp. 190–193.

215. Gerald Wheeler and Rodney Hissong, "Effects of Criminal Sanctions on Drunk Drivers: Beyond Incarceration," *Crime and Delinquency* 34 (1988): 29–42.

216. *Easter v. District of Columbia,* 361 F.2d 50 (D.C. Cir. 1966).

217. 392 U.S. 514 (1968).

218. Eric Jensen, Jurg Gerber, and Ginna Babcock, "The New War on Drugs: Grass Roots Movement or Political Construction?" *Journal of Drug Issues* 21 (1991): 651–667.

219. *Drugs,* p. 36.

220. Christopher Wren, "U.S. Is Certifying Mexico as an Ally in Fighting Drugs," *New York Times,* 1 March 1997, p. 1; Diego Ribandneira, "In Escobar Death, No Curb in Drugs Seen," *Boston Globe,* 4 December 1993, p. 2.

221. Bureau for International Narcotics and Law Enforcement Affairs, *International Narcotics Control Strategy Report, 1996* (Washington, D.C.: U.S. Department of State, 1997).

222. Ibid.

223. Walter Shapiro, "Going After the Hell's Angels," *Newsweek,* 13 May 1985, p. 4l.

224. David Hayeslip, "Local-Level Drug Enforcement: New Strategies," *NIJ Reports,* March/April 1989.

225. Mark Moore, *Drug Trafficking* (Washington, D.C.: National Institute of Justice, 1988).

226. Steven Belenko, Jeffrey Fagan, and Ko-Lin Chin, "Criminal Justice Responses to Crack," *Journal of Research in Crime and Delinquency* 28 (1991): 55–74.

227. *FY 1988 Report on Drug Control* (Washington, D.C.: National Institute of Justice, 1989), p. 103.

228. Carol Kaplan, *Sentencing and Time Served* (Washington, D.C.: Bureau of Justice Statistics, 1987).

229. Ibid., p. 2.

230. *Time Served in Prison and on Parole* (Washington, D.C.: Bureau of Justice Statistics, 1988).

231. Robert Davis, Arthur Lurigio, and Dennis Rosenbaum, eds., *Drugs and the Community* (Springfield, Ill.: Charles C Thomas, 1993), pp. xii–xv.

232. Saul Weingart, "A Typology of Community Responses to Drugs," in *Drugs and the Community,* ed. Davis, Lurigio, and Rosenbaum, pp. 85–105.

233. Davis, Lurigio, and Rosenbaum, *Drugs and the Community,* pp. xii–xiii.

234. Bureau of Justice Statistics, *Drugs, Crime and the Justice System* (Washington, D.C.: Bureau of Justice Statistics, 1992), pp. 109–112.

235. Earl Wyson, Richard Aniskiewicz, and David Wright, "Truth and DARE: Tracking Drug Education to Graduation as Symbolic Politics," *Social Problems* 41 (1994): 448–471.

236. Dennis Rosenbaum, Robert Flewelling, Susan Bailey, Chris Ringwalt, and Deanna Wilkinson, "Cops in the Classroom: A Longitudinal Evaluation of Drug Abuse Resistance Education (DARE)," *Journal of Research in Crime and Delinquency* 31 (1994): 3–31.

237. Wyson, Aniskiewicz, and Wright, "Truth and DARE," p. 466.

238. Los Angeles Times, "Seattle Rethinks Drug Education," *Boston Globe,* 1 December 1996, p. A9.

239. Phyllis Ellickson and Robert Bell, "Challenges to Social Experiments: A Drug Prevention Example," *Journal of Research in Crime and Delinquency* 29 (1992): 79–101; idem, "Drug Prevention in Junior High: A Multi-Site Longitudinal Test," *Science* 247 (1990): 1299–1305.

240. Robert Jackson, "Clinton Targets Youth in New Drug Plan," *Boston Globe,* 26 February 1997, p. A3.

241. *Drugs,* pp. 115–122.

242. John Goldkamp and Peter Jones, "Pretrial Drug-Testing Experiments in Milwaukee and Prince George's County: The Context of Implementation," *Journal of Research in Crime and Delinquency* 29 (1992): 430–465; Chester Britt, Michael Gottfredson, and John Goldkamp, "Drug Testing and Pretrial Misconduct: An Experiment on the Specific Deterrent Effects of Drug Monitoring Defendants on Pretrial Release," *Journal of Research in Crime and Delinquency* 29 (1992): 62–78.

243. See, generally, Peter Greenwood and Franklin Zimring, *One More Chance* (Santa Monica, Calif.: Rand Corporation, 1985).

244. Eli Ginzberg, Howard Berliner, and Miriam Ostrow, *Young People at Risk, Is Prevention Possible?* (Boulder, Colo.: Westview Press, 1988), p. 99.

245. The following section is based on material found in Jerome Platt, "Vocational Rehabilitation of Drug Abusers," *Psychological Bulletin* 117 (1995): 416–433.

246. Ibid., p. 428.

247. Robert Taylor and Gary Cohen, "War Against Narcotics by U.S. Government Isn't Slowing Influx," *Wall Street Journal,* 27 November 1984, p. 1.

248. Ethan Nadelmann, "America's Drug Problem," *Bulletin of the American Academy of Arts and Sciences* 65 (1991): 24–40.

249. Ibid., p. 24.

250. Ethan Nadelmann, "Should We Legalize Drugs? History Answers Yes," *American Heritage* (February/March 1993): 41–56.

251. See, generally, Ralph Weisheit, *Drugs, Crime and the Criminal Justice System* (Cincinnati: Anderson, 1990).

252. David Courtwright, "Should We Legalize Drugs? History Answers No," *American Heritage* (February/March 1993): 43–56.

253. James Inciardi and Duane McBride, "Legalizing Drugs: A Gormless, Naive Idea," *Criminologist* 15 (1990): 1–4.

254. Kathryn Ann Farr, "Revitalizing the Drug Decriminalization Debate," *Crime and Delinquency* 36 (1990): 223–237.

Glossary

absolute deterrent A legal control measure designed to totally eliminate a particular criminal act.

Academy of Criminal Justice Sciences The society that serves to further the development of the criminal justice profession; its membership includes academics and practitioners involved in criminal justice.

access control A crime prevention technique that stresses target hardening through security measures, such as alarm systems, that make it more difficult for criminals to attack a target.

accountability system A way of dealing with police corruption by making superiors responsible for the behavior of their subordinates.

acquittal Release or discharge, especially by verdict of a jury.

active precipitation The view that the source of many criminal incidents is the aggressive or provocative behavior of victims.

actus reus An illegal act. The *actus reus* can be an affirmative act, such as taking money or shooting someone, or a failure to act, such as failing to take proper precautions while driving a car.

addict A person with an overpowering physical and psychological need to continue taking a particular substance or drug by any means possible.

addiction-prone personality The view that the cause of substance abuse can be traced to a personality with a compulsion for mood-altering drugs.

adjudication The determination of guilt or innocence; a judgment concerning criminal charges. Most offenders plead guilty as charged. The remainder are adjudicated by a judge and a jury or by a judge alone, and others are dismissed.

adversary system The procedure used to determine truth in the adjudication of guilt or innocence in which the defense (advocate for the accused) is pitted against the prosecution (advocate for the state), with the judge acting as arbiter of the legal rules. Under the adversary system, the burden is on the state to prove the charges beyond a reasonable doubt. This system of having the two parties publicly debate has proved to be the most effective method of achieving the truth regarding a set of circumstances. (Under the accusatory, or inquisitorial, system, which is used in continental Europe, the charge is evidence of guilt that the accused must disprove, and the judge takes an active part in the proceedings.)

affidavit A written statement of fact, signed and sworn to before a person having authority to administer an oath.

age of onset Age at which youths begin their delinquent careers. Early onset of delinquency is believed to be linked with chronic offending patterns.

aging out The process by which individuals reduce the frequency of their offending behavior as they age. It is also known as spontaneous remission, because people are believed to spontaneously reduce the rate of their criminal behavior as they mature. Aging out is thought to occur among all groups of offenders.

aggregate data Data collected on groups of people rather than individuals. A good example of aggregate data is the Uniform Crime Reports index crimes; although the number of criminal incidents that occur in a given area can be counted, little data are provided on the offenders who commit the crimes or the circumstances in which they occurred. Self-report surveys are usually considered individual-level data, since subjects' responses can be examined on a case-by-case basis.

aggressive preventive patrol A patrol technique designed to suppress crime before it occurs.

alien conspiracy theory The view that organized crime was imported to the United States by Europeans and that crime cartels have a policy of restricting their membership to people of their own ethnic background.

alienation A mental condition marked by normlessness and role confusion.

alternative sanctions The group of punishments falling between probation and prison; "probation plus." Community-based sanctions, including house arrest and intensive supervision, serve as alternatives to incarceration.

American Society of Criminology The professional society of criminology that is devoted to enhancing the status of the discipline.

androgens Male sex hormones.

anesthetics Drugs used as nervous system depressants. Local anesthetics block nervous system transmissions; general anesthetics act on the brain to produce a generalized loss of sensation, stupor, or unconsciousness.

anger rape A rape motivated by the rapist's desire to release pent-up anger and rage.

anomie A condition produced by normlessness. Because of rapidly shifting moral values, the individual has few guides to what is socially acceptable. According to Merton, anomie is a condition that occurs when personal goals cannot be achieved by available means. In Agnew's revision anomie can occur when positive or valued stimuli are removed or negative or painful ones applied.

antisocial personality Synonymous with psychopath, the antisocial personality is characterized by a lack of normal responses to life situations, the inability to learn from punishment, and violent reactions to non-threatening events.

appeal A review of lower-court proceedings by a higher court. Appellate courts do not retry the case under review. Rather, the transcript of the lower-court case is read by the appellate judges, who determine the legality of lower-court proceedings. When appellate courts reverse lower-court judgments, it is usually because of "prejudicial error" (deprivation of rights), and the case is remanded for retrial.

appellate courts Courts that reconsider a case that has already been tried to determine whether the measures used complied with accepted rules of criminal procedure and were in line with constitutional doctrines.

arbitrage The practice of buying large blocks of stock in companies that are believed to be the target of corporate buyouts or takeovers.

argot The unique language that influences the prison culture.

arousal theory A view of crime suggesting that people who have a high arousal level seek powerful stimuli in their environment to maintain an optimal level of arousal. These stimuli are often associated with violence and aggression. Sociopaths may need greater than average stimulation to bring them up to comfortable levels of living; this need explains their criminal tendencies.

arraignment The step in the criminal justice process at which the accused are read the charges against them, asked how they plead, and advised of their rights. Possible pleas are guilty, not guilty, *nolo contendere,* and not guilty by reason of insanity.

arrest The taking of a person into the custody of the law, the legal purpose of which is to restrain the accused until he or she can be held accountable for the offense at court proceedings. The legal requirement for an arrest is probable cause. Arrests for investigation, suspicion, or harassment are improper and of doubtful legality. The police have the responsibility to use only the reasonable physical force necessary to make an arrest. The summons has been used as a substitute for arrest.

arrest warrant A written court order by a magistrate authorizing and directing that an individual be taken into custody to answer criminal charges.

arson The intentional or negligent burning of a home, structure or vehicle for criminal purposes such as profit, revenge, fraud, or crime concealment.

Aryan Brotherhood A white supremacist prison gang.

assembly-line justice The view that the justice process resembles an endless production line that handles most cases in a routine and perfunctory fashion.

atavistic traits According to Lombroso, the physical characteristics that distinguish born criminals from the general population and are throwbacks to animals or primitive people.

attainder The loss of all civil rights because of a conviction for a felony offense.

attorney general The senior federal prosecutor and cabinet member who heads the Justice Department.

Auburn system The prison system developed in New York during the 19th century that stressed congregate working conditions.

authoritarian A personality type that revolves around blind obedience to authority.

authority conflict pathway The path to a criminal career that begins with early stubborn behavior and defiance of parents.

bail The monetary amount for or condition of pretrial release, normally set by a judge at the initial appearance. The purpose of bail is to ensure the return of the accused at subsequent proceedings. If the accused is unable to make bail, he or she is detained in jail. The Eighth Amendment provides that excessive bail shall not be required.

bail bonding The business of providing bail to needy offenders, usually at an exorbitant rate of interest.

Bail Reform Act of 1984 Federal legislation that provides for both greater emphasis on release on recognizance for nondangerous offenders and preventive detention for those who present a menace to the community.

base penalty The model sentence in a structured sentencing state, which can be enhanced or diminished to reflect aggravating or mitigating circumstances.

behaviorism The branch of psychology concerned with the study of observable behavior rather than unconscious motives. It focuses on the relationship between particular stimuli and people's responses to them.

beyond a reasonable doubt Degree of proof required for conviction of a defendant in criminal and juvenile delinquency proceedings. It is less than absolute certainty but more than high probability. If there is doubt based on reason, the accused is entitled to the benefit of that doubt by acquittal.

bill of indictment A document submitted to a grand jury by the prosecutor asking it to take action and indict a suspect.

Bill of Rights The first ten amendments to the U.S. Constitution.

blameworthiness The amount of culpability or guilt a person maintains for participating in a particular criminal offense.

blue curtain According to William Westly, the secretive, insulated police culture that isolates the officer from the rest of society.

booking The administrative record of an arrest listing the offender's name, address, physical description, date of birth, and employer; the time of arrest; the offense; and the name of arresting officer. Photographing and fingerprinting of the offender are also part of booking.

boot camp A short-term militaristic correctional facility in which inmates undergo intensive physical conditioning and discipline.

bot Under Anglo-Saxon law, the restitution paid for killing someone in an open fight.

bourgeoisie In Marxist theory, the owners of the means of production; the capitalist ruling class.

broken windows The term used to describe the role of the police as maintainers of community order and safety.

brothel A house of prostitution, typically run by a madam who sets prices and handles "business" arrangements.

brutalization effect The belief that capital punishment creates an atmosphere of brutality that enhances rather than deters the level of violence in society. The death penalty reinforces the view that violence is an appropriate response to provocation.

brutalization process According to Athens, the first stage in a violent career during which parents victimize children, causing them to develop a belligerent, angry demeanor.

burden of proof Duty of proving disputed facts on the trial of a case. The duty commonly lies on the person who asserts the affirmative of an issue and is sometimes said to shift when sufficient evidence is furnished to raise a presumption that what is alleged is true.

burglary Breaking into and entering a home or structure for the purposes of committing a felony.

call girls Prostitutes who make dates via the phone and then service customers in hotel rooms or apartments. Call girls typically have a steady clientele who are repeat customers.

capital punishment The use of the death penalty to punish transgressors.

career criminal A person who repeatedly violates the law and organizes his or her lifestyle around criminality.

***Carriers* case** A 15th-century case that defined the law of theft and reformulated the concept of taking the possessions of another.

certiorari Literally, "to be informed of, to be made certain in regard to." *See* writ of certiorari.

challenge for cause Removing a juror because he or she is biased, has prior knowledge about a case, or otherwise is unable to render a fair and impartial judgment in a case.

chancery court A court created in 15th-century England to oversee the lives of high-born minors who were orphaned or otherwise could not care for themselves.

charge In a criminal case, the specific crime the defendant is accused of committing.

Chicago Crime Commission A citizen action group set up in Chicago to investigate problems in the criminal justice system and explore avenues for positive change; the forerunner of many such groups around the country.

child abuse Any physical, emotional, or sexual trauma to a child for which no reasonable explanation, such as an accident, can be found. Child abuse can also be a function of neglecting to give proper care and attention to a young child.

chivalry hypothesis The idea that low female crime and delinquency rates are a reflection of the leniency with which police treat female offenders.

choice theory The school of thought holding that people will engage in delinquent and criminal behavior after weighing the consequences and benefits of their actions. Delinquent behavior is a rational choice made by a motivated offender who perceives that the chances of gain outweigh any perceived punishment or loss.

chronic offender According to Wolfgang, a delinquent offender who is arrested five or more times before he or she is 18 and who stands a good chance of becoming an adult criminal; such offenders are responsible for more than half of all serious crimes.

chronicity State of being a chronic recidivist.

Christopher Commission An investigatory group led by Warren Christopher that investigated the Los Angeles Police Department in the wake of the Rodney King beating.

churning A white-collar crime in which a stockbroker makes repeated trades to fraudulently increase his or her commissions.

civil death The custom of terminating the civil rights of convicted felons, such as forbidding them the right to vote or marry. No state uses civil death today.

civil law All law that is not criminal, including torts (personal wrongs), contract, property, maritime, and commercial law.

Civil Rights Division That part of the U.S. Justice Department that handles cases involving violations of civil rights guaranteed by the Constitution and federal law.

classical theory The theoretical perspective suggesting that (1) people have free will to choose criminal or conventional behaviors; (2) people choose to commit crime for reasons of greed or personal need; and (3) crime can be controlled only by the fear of criminal sanctions.

classification The procedure in which prisoners are categorized on the basis of their personal characteristics and criminal history and then assigned to an appropriate institution.

cocaine The most powerful natural stimulant. Its use produces euphoria, laughter, restlessness, and excitement. Overdoses can cause delirium, increased reflexes, violent manic behavior, and possible respiratory failure.

Code of Hammurabi The first written criminal code developed in Babylonia about 2000 B.C.

coeducational prison An institution that houses both male and female inmates who share work and recreational facilities.

cognitive theory The study of the perception of reality and of the mental processes required to understand the world we live in.

cohort study A study using a sample of subjects whose behavior is followed over a period of time.

common law Early English law, developed by judges, that incorporated Anglo-Saxon tribal custom, feudal rules and practices, and the everyday rules of behavior of local villages. Common law became the standardized law of the land in England and eventually formed the basis of the criminal law in the United States.

community notification laws Recent legislative efforts that require convicted sex offenders to register with local police when they move into an area or neighborhood.

community policing A police strategy that emphasizes fear reduction, community organization, and order maintenance rather than crime fighting.

community service restitution An alternative sanction that requires an offender to work in the community at such tasks as cleaning public parks or helping handicapped children in lieu of an incarceration sentence.

community treatment The actions of correctional agencies that attempt to maintain the convicted offender in the community, instead of a secure facility; includes probation, parole, and residential programs.

compensation Financial aid awarded to the victims of crime to repay them for their loss and injuries.

complaint A sworn allegation made in writing to a court or judge that an individual is guilty of some designated (complained of) offense. This is often the first legal document filed regarding a criminal offense. The complaint can be "taken out" by the victim, the police officer, the district attorney, or another interested party. Although the complaint charges an offense, an indictment or information may be the formal charging document.

compliance A white-collar enforcement strategy that encourages law-abiding behavior through both the threat of economic sanctions and the promise of rewards for conformity.

concurrent sentences Literally, running sentences together. Someone who is convicted of two or more charges must be sentenced on each charge. If the sentences are concurrent, they begin the same day and are completed after the longest term has been served.

conduct norms Behaviors expected of social group members. If group norms conflict with those of the general culture, members of the group may find themselves described as outcasts or criminals.

conflict view The view that human behavior is shaped by interpersonal conflict and that those who maintain social power will use it to further their own needs.

conjugal visit A prison program that allows inmates to receive private visits from their spouses for the purpose of maintaining normal interpersonal relationships.

consecutive sentences Prison sentences for two or more criminal acts that are served one after the other.

consensus view of crime The belief that the majority of citizens in a society share common ideals and work toward a common good and that crimes are acts that are outlawed because they conflict with the rules of the majority and are harmful to society.

consent decree Decree entered by consent of the parties. Not properly a judicial sentence but in the nature of a solemn contract or agreement of the parties that the decree is a just determination of their rights based on the real facts of the case, if such facts are proved.

constable The peacekeeper in early English towns. The constable organized citizens to protect his territory and supervised the night watch.

constructive intent The finding of criminal liability for an unintentional act that is the result of negligence or recklessness.

constructive possession In the crime of larceny, willingly giving up temporary physical possession of property but retaining legal ownership.

containments According to Reckless, internal and external factors and conditions that help insulate youths from delinquency-promoting situations. Most important of the internal containments is a strong self-concept, while external containments include positive support from parents and teachers.

continuance A judicial order to continue a case without a finding, to gather more information or allow the defendant to begin a community-based treatment program.

continuity of crime The view that crime begins early in life and continues throughout the life course. Thus, the best predictor of future criminality is past criminality.

contract system (attorney) Providing counsel to indigent offenders by having attorneys under contract to the county to handle all (or some) such cases.

contract system (convict) The system used earlier in the century in which inmates were leased out to private industry to work.

convict subculture The separate culture in the prison that has its own set of rewards and behaviors. The traditional culture is now being replaced by a violent gang culture.

conviction A judgment of guilt; a verdict by a jury, a plea by a defendant, or a judgment by a court that the accused is guilty as charged.

co-offending Committing criminal acts in groups. It is believed that a significant number of delinquent and criminal acts involve more than one offender.

corner boy According to Cohen, a role in the lower-class culture in which young men remain in their birth neighborhood, acquire families and menial jobs, and adjust to the demands of their environment.

corporal punishment The use of physical chastisement, such as whipping or electroshock, to punish criminals.

corporate crime White-collar crime involving a legal violation by a corporate entity, such as price fixing, restraint of trade, or hazardous waste dumping.

corpus delicti The body of the crime, made up of the *actus reus* and *mens rea.*

corrections The agencies of justice that take custody of offenders after their conviction and are entrusted with their treatment and control.

court administrator The individual who controls the operations of the courts system in a particular jurisdiction; he or she may be in charge of scheduling, juries, judicial assignment, and so on.

court-leet During the Middle Ages, the local hundred or manor court that dealt with most secular violations.

court of last resort A court that handles the final appeal on a matter. The U.S. Supreme Court is the official court of last resort for criminal matters.

courtroom work group The phrase used to denote that all parties in the adversary process work together to settle cases with the least amount of effort and conflict.

courts of limited jurisdiction Courts that handle misdemeanors and minor civil complaints.

covert pathway A path to a criminal career that begins with minor underhanded behavior and progresses to fire starting and theft.

crack A smokable form of purified cocaine that provides an immediate and powerful high.

crackdown The concentration of police resources on a particular problem area, such as street-level drug dealing, to eradicate or displace criminal activity.

crime A violation of societal rules of behavior as interpreted and expressed by a criminal legal code created by people holding social and political power. Individuals who violate these rules are subject to sanctions by state authority, social stigma, and loss of status.

crime control A model of criminal justice that emphasizes the control of dangerous offenders and the protection of society. Its advocates call for harsh punishments, such as the death penalty, as a deterrent to crime.

crime displacement An effect of crime prevention efforts in which efforts to control crime in one area shift illegal activities to another.

crime fighter A police style that stresses dealing with hard crimes and arresting dangerous criminals.

criminal anthropology Early efforts to discover a biological basis of crime through measurement of physical and mental processes.

Criminal Division The branch of the U.S. Justice Department that prosecutes federal criminal violations.

criminal justice process The decision-making points from the initial investigation or arrest by police to the eventual release of the offender and his or her reentry into society; the various sequential criminal justice stages through which the offender passes.

criminal law The body of rules that define crimes, set out their punishments, and mandate the procedures in carrying out the criminal justice process.

criminal sanction The right of the state to punish people if they violate the rules set down in the criminal code; the punishment connected to commission of a specific crime.

criminology The scientific study of the nature, extent, cause, and control of criminal behavior.

cross-examination The process in which the defense and the prosecution interrogate witnesses during a trial.

cross-sectional data Survey data that derive from all age, race, gender, and income segments of the population being measured simultaneously. Since people from every age group are represented, age-specific crime rates can be determined. Proponents believe that this is a sufficient substitute for the more expensive longitudinal approach that follows a group of subjects over time in order to measure crime rate changes.

cruel and unusual punishment Physical punishment that is far in excess of that given to people under similar circumstances and is therefore banned by the Eighth Amendment. The death penalty has so far not been considered cruel and unusual if it is administered in a fair and nondiscriminatory fashion.

culpable Referring to a wrongful act that does not involve malice. It connotes fault rather than guilt.

cultural transmission The concept that conduct norms are passed down from one generation to the next so that they become stable within the boundaries of a culture. Cultural transmission guarantees that group lifestyle and behavior are stable and predictable.

culture conflict According to Sellin, a condition brought about when the rules and norms of an individual's subcultural affiliation conflict with the role demands of conventional society.

culture of poverty The view that people in the lower class of society form a separate culture with its own values and norms that are in conflict with conventional society; the culture is self-maintaining and ongoing.

curtilage The fields attached to a house.

custodial convenience The principle of giving jailed inmates the minimum comforts required by law to contain the costs of incarceration.

cynicism The belief that most peoples' actions are motivated solely by personal needs and selfishness.

DARE Drug Abuse Resistance Education, a school-based antidrug program initiated by the Los Angeles police and now adopted around the United States.

day fines Fines geared to the average daily income of the convicted offender in an effort to bring equity to the sentencing process.

day reporting centers Nonresidential, community-based treatment programs.

deadly force The ability of the police to kill suspects if they resist arrest or present a danger to an officer or the community. The police cannot use deadly force against an unarmed fleeing felon.

decarceration A correctional philosophy that stresses the "least restrictive alternative possible" for removing as many people from secure detention as possible and making use of community alternatives.

decriminalization Reducing the penalty for a criminal act but not actually legalizing it.

defeminization The process by which policewomen become enculturated into the police profession at the expense of their feminine identity.

defendant The accused in criminal proceedings; he or she has the right to be present at each stage of the criminal justice process, except grand jury proceedings.

defense attorney The counsel for the defendant in a criminal trial who represents the individual from arrest to final appeal.

defensible space The principle that crime prevention can be achieved through modifying the physical environment to reduce the opportunity individuals have to commit crime.

degenerate anomalies According to Lombroso, the primitive physical characteristics that make criminals animalistic and savage.

deinstitutionalization The movement to remove as many offenders as possible from secure confinement and treat them in the community.

demeanor The way in which a person outwardly manifests his or her personality.

demystify The process by which Marxists unmask the true purpose of the capitalist system's rules and laws.

desert-based sentences Sentences in which the length is based on the seriousness of the criminal act and not the personal characteristics of the defendant or the deterrent impact of the law; punishment is based on what people have done and not on what they or others may do in the future.

desistance The process in which crime rate declines with the perpetrator's age; synonymous with the aging-out process.

detective The police personnel assigned to investigate crimes after they have been reported, to gather evidence, and to identify the perpetrator.

detention Holding an offender in secure confinement before trial.

determinate sentence A fixed term of incarceration, such as three years' imprisonment. Determinate sentences are felt by many to be too restrictive for rehabilitative purposes; the advantage is that offenders know how much time they have to serve—that is, when they will be released. *See also* indeterminate sentence

deterrence The act of preventing crime before it occurs by means of the threat of criminal sanctions. Deterrence involves the perception that the pain of apprehension and punishment outweighs any chances of criminal gain or profit.

developmental criminology A branch of criminology that examines change in a criminal career over the life course. Developmental factors include biological, social, and psychological change. Among the topics of developmental criminology are desistance, resistance, escalation, and specialization.

deviance Behavior that departs from the social norm.

differential association According to Sutherland, the principle that criminal acts are related to a person's exposure to an excess amount of antisocial attitudes and values.

diffusion of benefits An effect that occurs when an effort to control one type of crime has the unexpected benefit of reducing the incidence of another.

direct examination The questioning of one's own (prosecution or defense) witness during a trial.

directed verdict The right of a judge to direct a jury to acquit a defendant because the state has not proven the elements of the crime or otherwise has not established guilt according to law.

disaggregate Analyzing the relationship between two or more independent variables while controlling for the influence of a third dependent variable. For example, looking at the relationship between conviction for murder and the likelihood of a death sentence disaggregated by race would entail separate analysis of the sentencing outcomes of whites and African-Americans convicted of first-degree murder.

discouragement An effect that occurs when an effort made to eliminate one type of crime also controls others, because it reduces the value of criminal activity by limiting access to desirable targets.

discretion The use of personal decision making and choice in carrying out operations in the criminal justice system. For example, police discretion can involve the decision to make an arrest, while prosecutorial discretion can involve the decision to accept a plea bargain.

disposition For juvenile offenders, the equivalent of sentencing for adult offenders. The theory is that disposition is more rehabilitative than retributive. Possible dispositions may be to dismiss the case, release the youth to the custody of his or her parents, place the offender on probation, or send him or her to a correctional institution.

disputatiousness In the subculture of violence, it is considered appropriate behavior for a person who has been offended to seek satisfaction through violent means.

district attorney The county prosecutor who is charged with bringing offenders to justice and enforcing the laws of the state.

diversion An alternative to criminal trial usually featuring counseling, job training, and educational opportunities.

DNA profiling The identification of criminal suspects by matching DNA samples taken from them with specimens found at crime scenes.

double bunking The practice of holding two or more inmates in a single cell because of prison overcrowding; upheld in *Rhodes v. Chapman*.

double marginality According to Alex, the social burden African American police officers carry by being both minority group members and law enforcement officers.

drift According to Matza, the view that youths move in and out of delinquency and that their lifestyles can embrace both conventional and deviant values.

drug courier profile A way of identifying drug runners based on their personal characteristics; police may stop and question individuals based on the way they fit the characteristics contained in the profile.

Drug Enforcement Administration (DEA) The federal agency that enforces federal drug control laws.

due process The constitutional principle based on the concept of the primacy of the individual and the complementary concept of limitation on governmental power; a safeguard against arbitrary and unfair state procedures in judicial or administrative proceedings. Embodied in the due process concept are the basic rights of a defendant in criminal proceedings and the requisites for a fair trial. These rights and requirements have been expanded by appellate court decisions and include (1) timely notice of a hearing or trial that informs the accused of the charges against him or her; (2) the opportunity to confront accusers and to present evidence on the accused's own behalf before an impartial jury or judge; (3) the presumption of innocence under which guilt must be proven by legally obtained evidence and the verdict must be supported by the evidence presented; (4) the right of an accused to be warned of constitutional rights at the earliest stage of the criminal process; (5) protection against self-incrimination; (6) assistance of counsel at every critical stage of the criminal process; and (7) the guarantee that an individual will not be tried more than once for the same offense (double jeopardy).

Durham rule A definition of insanity used in New Hampshire that required that the crime be excused if it was a product of a mental illness.

early onset A term that refers to the assumption that a criminal career begins early in life and that people who are deviant at a very young age are the ones most likely to persist in crime.

economic compulsive behavior Behavior that occurs when drug users resort to violence to gain funds to support their habit.

economic crime An act in violation of the criminal law that is designed to bring financial gain to the offender.

economism The policy of controlling white-collar crime through monetary incentives and sanctions.

egalitarian family A family structure in which both parents share equal authority and power.

ego identity According to Erikson, ego identity is formed when persons develop a firm sense of who they are and what they stand for.

electroencephalogram (EEG) A device that can record the electronic impulses given off by the brain, commonly called brain waves.

embedded Becoming entrenched in a delinquent way of life, thereby reducing any chances of future success in the marketplace.

embezzlement A type of larceny that involves taking the possessions of another (fraudulent conversion) that have been placed in the thief's lawful possession for safekeeping, such as a bank teller misappropriating deposits or a stockbroker making off with a customer's account.

enterprise syndicate An organized crime group that profits from the sale of illegal goods and services, such as narcotics, pornography, and prostitution.

entrapment A criminal defense maintaining that the police originated the criminal idea or initiated the criminal action.

entrepreneur One willing to take risks for profit in the marketplace.

equipotentiality View that all individuals are equal at birth and are thereafter influenced by their environment.

equity The action or practice of awarding each his or her just due; sanctions based on equity seek to compensate individual victims and the general society for their losses due to crime.

***ex post facto* laws** Laws that make an act criminal after it was committed or that retroactively increase the penalty for a crime; for example, an *ex post facto* law could change shoplifting from a misdemeanor to a felony and penalize offenders with a prison term, even though they had been apprehended six months prior. Such laws are unconstitutional.

exceptional circumstances doctrine Under this policy, courts would hear only those cases brought by inmates in which the circumstances indicated a total disregard for human dignity, while denying hearings on less serious crimes. Cases allowed access to the courts usually involve a situation of total denial of medical care.

exclusionary rule The principle that prohibits using evidence illegally obtained in a trial. Based on the Fourth Amendment "right of the people to be secure in their persons, houses, papers, and effects, against unreasonable searches and seizures," the rule is not a bar to prosecution, as legally obtained evidence may be available that may be used in a trial.

excuse A defense to a criminal charge in which the accused maintains he or she lacked the intent to commit the crime (*mens rea*).

expressive crime A crime that has no purpose except to accomplish the behavior at hand, such as shooting someone.

expressive violence Violence that is designed not for profit or gain but to vent rage, anger, or frustration.

extinction The phenomenon in which a crime prevention effort has an immediate impact that then dissipates as criminals adjust to new conditions.

extraversion a personality trait marked by impulsivity and the inability to examine motives and behavior.

false pretenses Illegally obtaining money, goods, or merchandise from another by fraud or misrepresentation.

Federal Bureau of Investigation (FBI) The arm of the U.S. Justice Department that investigates violations of federal law, gathers crime statistics, runs a comprehensive crime laboratory, and helps train local law enforcement officers.

felony A serious offense that carries a penalty of incarceration in a state prison, usually for one year or more. Persons convicted of felony offenses lose such rights as the rights to vote, hold elective office, or maintain certain licenses.

fence A buyer and seller of stolen merchandise.

field training officer A senior police officer who trains recruits in the field.

fixed time rule A policy in which people must be tried within a stated period after their arrest; overruled in *Barker v. Wingo,* which created a balancing test.

flat or fixed sentencing A sentencing model mandating that all people who are convicted of a specific offense and who are sent to prison must receive the same length of incarceration.

focal concerns According to Miller, the value orientations of lower-class cultures; features include the needs for excitement, trouble, smartness, fate, and personal autonomy.

folkways Generally followed customs that do not have moral values attached to them, such as not interrupting people when they are speaking.

foot patrols Police patrols that take officers out of cars and put them on a walking beat to strengthen ties with the community.

forfeiture The seizure of personal property by the state as a civil or criminal penalty.

fraud Taking the possessions of another through deception or cheating, such as selling a person a desk that is represented as an antique but is known to be a copy.

free venture Privately run industries in a prison setting in which the inmates work for wages and the goods are sold for profit.

free will The idea that people are in charge of their own destinies and are free to make personal behavior choices unencumbered by environmental controls; the opposite of determinism. Choice theories are based on the concept of free will.

functionalism The sociological perspective that suggests that each part of society makes a contribution to the maintenance of the whole. Functionalism stresses social cooperation and consensus of values and beliefs among a majority of society's members.

furlough A correctional policy that allows inmates to leave the institution for vocational or educational training, for employment, or to maintain family ties.

general deterrence A crime control policy that depends on the fear of criminal penalties. General deterrence measures, such as long prison sentences for violent crimes, are aimed at convincing the potential law violator that the pains associated with crime outweigh its benefits.

general intent Actions that on their face indicate a criminal purpose, such as breaking into a locked building or trespassing on someone's property.

gentrification A process of reclaiming and reconditioning deteriorated neighborhoods by refurbishing depressed real estate and then renting or selling the properties to upper-middle-class professionals.

good faith exception The principle of law holding that evidence may be used in a criminal trial even though the search warrant used to obtain it is technically faulty, if the police acted in good faith and to the best of their ability when they sought to obtain it from a judge.

good-time credit Time taken off a prison sentence in exchange for good behavior within the institution, such as ten days per month. The device is used to limit disciplinary problems within the prison.

graffiti Inscription or drawing made on a wall or structure. Used by delinquents for gang messages and turf definition.

grand jury A group (usually consisting of 23 citizens) chosen to hear testimony in secret and to issue formal criminal accusations (indictments). It also serves an investigatory function.

grass eaters A term used for police officers who accept payoffs when their everyday duties place them in a position to be solicited by the public.

greenmail The process by which an arbitrager buys large blocks of a company's stock and threatens to take over the company and replace the management. To ward off the threat to their positions, members of management use company funds to repurchase the shares at a much higher price, creating huge profits for the corporate raiders.

guardian *ad litem* A court-appointed attorney who protects the interests of a child in cases involving the child's welfare.

habeas corpus *See* writ of habeas corpus

habitual criminal statutes Laws that require long-term or life sentences for offenders who have multiple felony convictions.

halfway house A community-based correctional facility that houses inmates before their outright release so that they can become gradually acclimated to conventional society.

Hallcrest Report A government-sponsored national survey of the private security industry conducted by the Hallcrest Corporation.

hallucinogens Drugs, either natural or synthetic, that produce vivid distortions of the senses without greatly disturbing the viewer's consciousness. Some produce hallucinations, and others cause psychotic behavior in otherwise normal people.

hands-off doctrine The judicial policy of not interfering in the administrative affairs of a prison.

hate crimes Acts of violence or intimidation designed to terrorize or frighten people considered undesirable because of their race, religion, ethnic origin, or sexual orientation.

hearsay evidence Testimony that is not firsthand but relates information told by a second party.

heroin The most dangerous commonly used drug made from the poppy plant. Users rapidly build a tolerance for it, fueling the need for increased doses in order to feel a desired effect.

hot spots of crime The locations of a significant portion of all police calls. These hot spots include taverns and housing projects.

house of correction A county correctional institution generally used for the incarceration of more serious misdemeanants, whose sentences are usually less than one year.

hue and cry In medieval England, the policy of self-help used in villages demanding that all respond if a citizen raised a hue and cry to get their aid.

hulks Mothballed ships that were used to house prisoners in 18th-century England.

hundred In medieval England, a group of 100 families who were responsible for maintaining the order and trying minor offenses.

hustle The underground prison economy.

identity crisis A psychological state, identified by Erikson, in which youth face inner turmoil and uncertainty about life roles.

importation model The view that the violent prison culture reflects the criminal culture of the outside world and is neither developed in nor unique to prisons.

impulsivity According to Gottfredson and Hirschi's general theory, the trait that produces criminal behavior; impulsive people lack self-control.

incapacitation The policy of keeping dangerous criminals in confinement to eliminate the risk of their repeating their offense in society.

inchoate crimes Incomplete or contemplated crimes such as criminal solicitation or criminal attempts.

indeterminate sentence A term of incarceration with a stated minimum and maximum length, such as a sentence to prison for a period of from three to ten years. The prisoner would be eligible for parole after the minimum sentence had been served. Based on the belief that sentences should fit the criminal, indeterminate sentences allow individualized sentences and provide for sentencing flexibility. Judges can set a high minimum to override the purpose of the indeterminate sentence. *See also* determinate sentence

index crimes The eight crimes that, because of their seriousness and frequency, the FBI reports the incidence of in the annual Uniform Crime Reports. Index crimes include murder, rape, assault, robbery, burglary, arson, larceny, and motor vehicle theft.

indictment A written accusation returned by a grand jury charging an individual with a specified crime after determination of probable cause; the prosecutor presents enough evidence (a *prima facie* case) to establish probable cause.

indigent Needy and poor or lacking the means to provide a living.

inevitable discovery A rule of law stating that evidence that almost assuredly would be independently discovered can be used in a court of law, even though it was obtained in violation of legal rules and practices.

information Like an indictment, a formal charging document. The prosecuting attorney makes out the information and files it in court. Probable cause is determined at the preliminary hearing, which, unlike grand jury proceedings, is public and attended by the accused and his or her attorney.

inhalants Vapors from lighter fluid, paint thinner, cleaning fluid, and model airplane glue sniffed to reach a drowsy, dizzy state, sometimes accompanied by hallucinations.

initial appearance The stage in the justice process during which the suspect is brought before a magistrate for consideration of bail. The suspect must be taken for initial appearance within a "reasonable time" after arrest. For petty offenses, this step often serves as the final criminal proceeding, either through adjudication by a judge or the offering of a guilty plea.

inmate social code The informal set of rules that govern inmates.

inmate subculture The loosely defined culture that pervades prisons and has its own norms, rules, and language.

insanity A legal defense maintaining that a defendant was incapable of forming criminal intent because he or she suffered from a defect of reason or mental illness.

insider trading Illegal buying of stock in a company based on information provided by someone who has a fiduciary interest in the company, such as an employee or an attorney or accountant retained by the firm. Federal laws and the rules of the Securities and Exchange Commission require that all profits from such trading be returned and provide for both fines and a prison sentence.

instrumental Marxist theory The view that capitalist institutions, such as the criminal justice system, have as their main purpose the control of the poor to maintain the hegemony of the wealthy.

instrumental violence Violence designed to improve the financial or social position of the criminal.

intensive probation supervision A type of intermediate sanction involving small probation caseloads and strict daily or weekly monitoring.

interactional theory The idea that interaction with institutions and events during the life course determines criminal behavior patterns; crimogenic influences evolve over time.

interactionist perspective The view that one's perception of reality is significantly influenced by one's interpretations of the reactions of others to similar events and stimuli.

interrogation The method of accumulating evidence in the form of information or confessions from suspects; questioning that has been restricted because of concern about the use of brutal and coercive methods and to protect against self-incrimination.

interstitial area In criminology, a space or separation in the social fabric; an interstitial area encourages the formation of gangs.

investigation An inquiry concerning suspected criminal behavior for the purpose of identifying offenders or gathering further evidence to assist the prosecution of apprehended offenders.

jail A place to detain people awaiting trial, hold drunks and disorderly individuals, and confine convicted misdemeanants serving sentences of less than one year.

jailhouse lawyer An inmate trained in law or otherwise educated who helps other inmates prepare legal briefs and appeals.

just desert The philosophy of justice that asserts that those who violate the rights of others deserve to be punished. The severity of punishment should be commensurate with the seriousness of the crime.

justice model A philosophy of corrections that stresses determinate sentences, abolition of parole, and the view that prisons are places of punishment and not rehabilitation.

justification A defense to a criminal charge in which the accused maintains that his or her actions were justified by the circumstances and therefore he or she should not be held criminally liable.

juvenile delinquency Participation in illegal behavior by a minor who falls under a statutory age limit.

juvenile justice process Court proceedings for youths within the juvenile age group. Under the paternal (*parens patriae*) philosophy, juvenile procedures are informal and nonadversary, invoked *for* the juvenile offender rather than against him or her; a petition instead of a complaint is filed; courts make findings of involvement or adjudication of delinquency instead of convictions; and juvenile offenders receive dispositions instead of sentences. Court decisions (*In re Kent* and *In re Gault*) have increased the adversarial nature of juvenile court proceedings. However, the philosophy remains one of diminishing the stigma of delinquency and providing for the youth's well-being and rehabilitation rather than seeking retribution.

Kansas City study An experimental program that evaluated the effectiveness of patrol. The Kansas City study found that the presence of patrol officers had little deterrent effect.

Knapp Commission A public body that led an investigation into police corruption in New York and uncovered a widespread network of payoffs and bribes.

labeling The process by which a person becomes fixed with a negative identity, such as "criminal" or "ex-con," and is forced to suffer the consequences of outcast status.

labeling theory Theory that views society as creating deviance through a system of social control agencies that designate certain individuals as deviants. The stigmatized individual is made to feel unwanted in the normal social order. Eventually, the individual begins to believe that the label is accurate, assumes it as a personal identity, and enters into a deviant or criminal career.

landmark decision A decision handed down by the Supreme Court that becomes the law of the land and serves as a precedent for similar legal issues.

latent trait A stable feature, characteristic, property, or condition, present at birth or soon after, that makes some people crime-prone over the life course.

learning disabilities Neurological dysfunctions that prevent people from learning up to their potential.

left realism A branch of conflict theory that holds that crime is a "real" social problem experienced by the lower classes and that lower-class concerns about crime must be addressed by radical scholars.

legalization The removal of all criminal penalties from a previously outlawed act.

life course The study of changes in criminal offending patterns over a person's entire life. Are there conditions or events that occur later in life that influence the way people behave, or is behavior predetermined by social or personal conditions at birth?

life history A research method that uses the experiences of an individual as the unit of analysis, such as using the life experience of an individual gang member to understand the natural history of gang membership.

longitudinal (cohort) research Research that tracks the development of a group of subjects over time.

lower courts A generic term referring to those courts that have jurisdiction over misdemeanors and conduct preliminary investigations of felony charges.

make-believe families Peer units, with mother and father figures, formed by women in prison to compensate for the loss of family and loved ones.

***mala in se* crimes** Acts that are outlawed because they violate basic moral values, such as rape, murder, assault, and robbery.

***mala prohibitum* crimes** Acts that are outlawed because they clash with current norms and public opinion, such as tax, traffic, and drug laws.

mandamus *See* writ of mandamus

mandatory sentence A statutory requirement that a certain penalty shall be set and carried out in all cases on conviction for a specified offense or series of offenses.

Manhattan Bail Project The innovative experiment in bail reform that introduced and successfully tested the concept of release on recognizance.

Mann Act Federal legislation that made it a crime to transport women across state lines for the purpose of prostitution.

marijuana (*Cannabis sativa*) A hemp plant grown throughout the world. Its main active ingredient is tetrahydrocannabinol (THC), a mild hallucinogen that alters sensory impressions and can cause drastic distortion in auditory and visual perception, even producing hallucinatory effects.

marital exemption The practice in some states of prohibiting the prosecution of husbands for the rape of their wives.

masculinity hypothesis The view that women who commit crimes have biological and psychological traits similar to those of men.

mass murder The killing of a large number of people in a single incident by an offender who typically does not seek concealment or escape.

matricide The murder of a mother by her son or daughter.

maxi-maxi prisons High-security prisons, based on the federal prison in Marion, Illinois, that house the most dangerous inmates in around-the-clock solitary confinement.

maximum-security prisons Correctional institutions that house dangerous felons and maintain strict security measures, high walls, and limited contact with the outside world.

meat eaters A term used to describe police officers who actively solicit bribes and vigorously engage in corrupt practices.

medical model A view of corrections holding that convicted offenders are victims of their environment who need care and treatment to be transformed into valuable members of society.

medium-security prisons Less secure institutions that house nonviolent offenders and provide more opportunities for contact with the outside world.

mens rea "Guilty mind." The mental element of a crime or the intent to commit a criminal act.

methadone A synthetic narcotic used as a substitute for heroin in drug-control efforts.

middle-class measuring rods According to Cohen, the standards by which teachers and other representatives of state authority evaluate lower-class youths. Because they cannot live up to middle-class standards, lower-class youths are bound for failure, which gives rise to frustration and anger at conventional society.

minimum-security prisons The least secure institutions that house white-collar and nonviolent offenders, maintain few security measures, and have liberal furlough and visitation policies.

***Miranda* warning** The result of two U.S. Supreme Court decisions (*Escobedo v. Illinois* [378 U.S. 478] and *Miranda v. Arizona* [384 U.S. 436]) that require police officers to inform individuals under arrest of their constitutional right to remain silent and to know that their statements can later be used against them in court, that they can have an attorney present to help them, and that the state will pay for an attorney if they cannot afford to hire one. Although aimed at protecting an individual during in-custody

interrogation, the warning must also be given when the investigation shifts from the investigatory to the accusatory stage—that is, when suspicion begins to focus on an individual.

misdemeanor A minor crime usually punished by less than one year's imprisonment in a local institution, such as a county jail.

Missouri Plan A way of picking judges through nonpartisan elections as a means of ensuring judicial performance standards.

Mollen Commission An investigative unit set up to inquire into police corruption in New York in the 1990s.

monetary restitution A sanction requiring that convicted offenders compensate crime victims by reimbursing them for out-of-pocket losses caused by the crime. Losses can include property damage, lost wages, and medical costs.

moonlighting The practice of police officers holding after-hours jobs in private security or other related professions.

moral crusades Efforts by interest-group members to stamp out behavior they find objectionable. Typically, moral crusades are directed at public order crimes, such as drug abuse or pornography.

moral entrepreneurs Interest groups that attempt to control social life and the legal order in order to promote their own personal set of moral values. People who use their influence to shape the legal process in ways they see fit.

motion An oral or written request asking the court to make a specified finding, decision, or order.

motivated offenders The potential offenders in a population. According to rational choice theory, crime rates will vary according to the number of motivated offenders.

murder transaction The concept that murder is usually a result of behavior interactions between the victim and the offender.

National Crime Survey The ongoing victimization study conducted jointly by the Justice Department and the U.S. Census Bureau that surveys victims about their experiences with law violation.

negative affective states According to Agnew, the anger, depression, disappointment, fear, and other adverse emotions that derive from strain.

neighborhood policing A style of police management that emphasizes community-level crime-fighting programs and initiatives.

neurological Pertaining to the brain and central nervous system.

neuroticism A personality trait marked by unfounded anxiety, tension, and emotional instability.

neurotics People who fear that their primitive id impulses will dominate their personality.

neutralization The ability to overcome social norms and controls. Neutralization theory holds that offenders adhere to conventional values while "drifting" into periods of illegal behavior. In order to drift, people must first neutralize legal and moral values.

niche A way of adapting to the prison community that stresses finding one's place (niche) in the system rather than fighting for one's individual rights.

no bill A decision by a grand jury not to indict a criminal suspect.

nolle prosequi The term used when a prosecutor decides to drop a case after a complaint has been formally made. Reasons for a *nolle prosequi* include insufficient evidence, reluctance of witnesses to testify, police error, and office policy.

nolo contendere No contest. An admission of guilt in a criminal case with the condition that the finding cannot be used against the defendant in any subsequent civil cases.

nonintervention A justice philosophy that emphasizes the least intrusive treatment possible. Among its central policies are decarceration, diversion, and decriminalization. Less is better.

oath-helpers During the Middle Ages, groups of 12 to 25 people who would support the accused's innocence.

obitiatry According to Jack Kevorkian, the practice of helping people take their own lives.

obscenity According to current legal theory, sexually explicit material that lacks a serious purpose and appeals solely to the prurient interest of the viewer. While nudity per se is not usually considered obscene, open sexual behavior, masturbation, and exhibition of the genitals is banned in most communities.

official crime Criminal behavior that has been recorded by the police.

opportunist robber Someone who steals small amounts when a vulnerable target presents itself.

organizational crime Crime that involves large corporations and their efforts to control the marketplace and earn huge profits through unlawful bidding, unfair advertising, monopolistic practices, or other illegal means.

paraphilias Bizarre or abnormal sexual practices that may involve recurrent sexual urges focused on objects, humiliation, or children.

parens patriae Power of the state to act in behalf of the child and provide care and protection equivalent to that of a parent.

parole The early release of a prisoner subject to conditions set by a parole board. Depending on the jurisdiction, inmates must serve a certain proportion of their sentences before becoming eligible for parole. If an inmate is granted parole, the conditions may require him or her to report regularly to a parole officer, refrain from criminal conduct, maintain and support his or her family, avoid contact with other convicted criminals, abstain from using alcohol and drugs, remain within the jurisdiction, and so on. Violations of the conditions of parole may result in revocation of parole, in which case the individual will be returned to prison. The concept behind parole is to allow the release of the offender to community supervision, where rehabilitation and readjustment will be facilitated.

parricide The killing of a close relative by a child.

Part I offenses Another term for index crimes.

Part II offenses All crimes other than index and minor traffic offenses. The FBI records annual arrest information for Part II offenses.

partial deterrent A legal measure designed to restrict or control rather than eliminate an undesirable act.

particularity The requirement that a search warrant state precisely where the search is to take place and what items are to be seized.

passive precipitation The view that some people become victims because of personal and social characteristics that make them "attractive" targets for predatory criminals.

paternalism An approach to government or organizations in which leaders are seen as father figures and others are treated as "children."

pathways The view that the path to a criminal career may have more than one route, beginning with mild misconduct and escalating to serious crimes.

patriarchy A male-dominated system. The patriarchal family is one dominated by the father.

patricide The murder of a father by his son or daughter.

peacemaking A branch of conflict theory that stresses humanism, mediation, and conflict resolution as a means to end crime.

Pennsylvania system The prison system developed in Pennsylvania during the 19th century that stressed total isolation and individual penitence as a means of reform.

peremptory challenge The dismissal of a potential juror by either the prosecution or the defense for unexplained, discretionary reasons.

persisters Those criminals who do not age out of crime; chronic delinquents who continue offending into their adulthood.

pilferage Theft by employees through stealth or deception.

plain view The doctrine that evidence that is in plain view to police officers may be seized without a search warrant.

plea An answer to formal charges by an accused. Possible pleas are guilty, not guilty, *nolo contendere,* and not guilty by reason of insanity. A guilty plea is a confession of the offense as charged. A not guilty plea is a denial of the charge and places the burden on the prosecution to prove the elements of the offense.

plea bargaining The discussion between the defense counsel and the prosecution by which the accused agrees to plead guilty for certain considerations. The advantage to the defendant may be a reduction of the charges, a lenient sentence, or (in the case of multiple charges) dropped charges. The advantage to the prosecution is that a conviction is obtained without the time and expense of lengthy trial proceedings.

pledge system An early method of law enforcement that relied on self-help and mutual aid.

police discretion The ability of police officers to enforce the law selectively. Police officers in the field have great latitude to use their discretion in deciding whether to invoke their arrest powers.

police officer style The belief that the bulk of police officers can be classified into ideal personality types. Popular style types include supercops, who desire to enforce only serious crimes, such as robbery and rape; professionals, who use a broad definition of police work; service-oriented officers, who see their job as a helping profession; and avoiders, who do as little as possible. The actual existence of ideal police officer types has been much debated.

poor laws Seventeenth-century laws that bound out vagrants and abandoned children to masters as indentured servants.

population All people who share a particular personal characteristic, such as all high school students or all police officers.

positivism The branch of social science that uses the scientific method of the natural sciences and suggests that human behavior is a product of social, biological, psychological, or economic forces.

power control According to Hagan, the power and standing each parent has in the economic structure, which determines the manner in which the parents exert control over their families and, in particular, adolescent behavior.

power groups Criminal organizations that do not provide services or illegal goods but trade exclusively in violence and extortion.

power rape A rape motivated by the need for sexual conquest.

power syndicates Organized crime groups that use force and violence to extort money from legitimate businesses and other criminal groups engaged in illegal business enterprises.

praxis The application of theory in action; in Marxist criminology, applying theory to promote revolution.

precocious sexuality Sexual experimentation in early adolescence.

preliminary hearings The step at which criminal charges initiated by an information are tested for probable cause; the prosecution presents enough evidence to establish probable cause—that is, a *prima facie* case. The hearing is public and may be attended by the accused and his or her attorney.

premenstrual syndrome The stereotype that several days prior to and during menstruation females are beset by irritability and poor judgment as a result of hormonal changes.

preponderance of the evidence The level of proof in civil cases; more than half the evidence supports the allegations of one side.

presentence report An investigation performed by a probation officer attached to a trial court after the conviction of a defendant. The report contains information about the defendant's background, education, previous employment, and family; his or her own statement concerning the offense; the person's prior criminal record; interviews with neighbors or acquaintances; and his or her mental and physical condition (that is, information that would not be made record in the case of a guilty plea or that would be inadmissible as evidence at a trial but could be influential and important at the sentencing stage). After conviction, a judge sets a date for sentencing (usually ten days to two weeks from the date of conviction), during which time the presentence report is made. The report is required in felony cases in federal courts and in many states, is optional with the judge in some states, and in others is mandatory before convicted offenders can be placed on probation. In the case of juvenile offenders, the presentence report is also known as a social history report.

presumptive sentences Sentencing structures that provide an average sentence that should be served along with the option of extending or decreasing the punishment because of aggravating or mitigating circumstances.

preventive detention The practice of holding dangerous suspects before trial without bail.

primary deviance According to Lemert, deviant acts that do not help redefine the self and public image of the offender.

primary sociopaths People with an inherited trait that predisposes them to antisocial behavior.

prison A state or federal correctional institution for incarceration of felony offenders for terms of one year or more.

pro bono The practice by private attorneys of taking the cases of indigent offenders without fee as a service to the profession and the community.

probability sample A randomly drawn sample in which each member of the population being tapped has an equal chance of being selected.

probable cause The evidentiary criterion necessary to sustain an arrest or the issuance of an arrest or search warrant; less than absolute certainty or "beyond a reasonable doubt" but greater than mere suspicion or "hunch." A set of facts, information, circumstances, or conditions that would lead a reasonable person to believe that an offense was committed and that the accused committed that offense. An arrest made without probable cause may be susceptible to prosecution as an illegal arrest under "false imprisonment" statutes.

probation A sentence entailing the conditional release of a convicted offender into the community under the supervision of the court (in the form of a probation officer), subject to certain conditions for a specified time. The conditions are usually similar to those of parole. (Probation is a sentence, an alternative to incarceration; parole is administrative release from incarceration.) Violation of the conditions of probation may result in revocation of probation.

problem-oriented policing A style of police management that stresses proactive problem solving rather than reactive crime fighting.

procedural law The rules that define the operation of criminal proceedings. Procedural law describes the methods that must be followed in obtaining warrants, investigating offenses, effecting lawful arrests, using force, conducting trials, introducing evidence, sentencing convicted offenders, and reviewing cases by appellate courts (in general, legislatures have ignored postsentencing procedures). While the substantive law defines criminal offenses, procedural law delineates how the substantive offenses are to be enforced.

progressives Early 20th-century reformers who believed that state action could relieve human ills.

proof beyond a reasonable doubt The standard of proof needed to convict in a criminal case. The evidence offered in court does not have to amount to absolute certainty, but it should leave no reasonable doubt that the defendant committed the alleged crime.

property in service The 18th-century practice of selling control of inmates to shipmasters who would then transport them to colonies for sale as indentured servants.

prosecutor Representative of the state (executive branch) in criminal proceedings; advocate for the state's case—the charge—in the adversary trial; for example, the attorney general of the United States, U.S. attorneys, attorneys general of the states, district attorneys, and police prosecutors. The prosecutor participates in investigations both before and after arrest, prepares legal documents, participates in obtaining arrest or search warrants, decides whether to charge a suspect and, if so, with which of-

fense. The prosecutor argues the state's case at trial, advises the police, participates in plea negotiations, and makes sentencing recommendations.

prosecutorial agency A federal, state, or local criminal justice agency whose principal function is the prosecution of alleged offenders.

proximity hypothesis The view that people become crime victims because they live or work in areas with large criminal populations.

psychoanalytic (psychodynamic) approach Branch of psychology holding that the human personality is controlled by unconscious mental processes developed early in childhood.

psychopath A person whose personality is characterized by a lack of warmth and feeling, inappropriate behavior responses, and an inability to learn from experience. While some psychologists view psychopathy as a result of childhood trauma, others see it as a result of biological abnormality.

psychotics In Freudian theory, people whose id has broken free and now dominates their personality. Psychotics suffer from delusions and experience hallucinations and sudden mood shifts.

Racketeer Influenced and Corrupt Organizations Act (RICO) Federal legislation that enables prosecutors to bring additional criminal or civil charges against people whose multiple criminal acts constitute a conspiracy. RICO features monetary penalties that allow the government to confiscate all profits derived from criminal activities. Originally intended to be used against organized criminals, RICO has also been used against white-collar criminals.

random sample A sample selected on the basis of chance so that each person in the population has an equal opportunity to be selected.

rational choice The view that crime is a function of a decision-making process in which the potential offender weighs the potential costs and benefits of an illegal act.

reaction formation According to Cohen, rejecting goals and standards that seem impossible to achieve. Because a boy cannot hope to get into college, for example, he considers higher education a waste of time.

reasonable competence The standard by which legal representation is judged: Did the defendant receive a reasonable level of legal aid?

reasonable doubt The possibility that a defendant did not commit the crime. A jury cannot find the defendant guilty if a reasonable doubt exists that he or she committed the crime. The level of proof needed to convict in a criminal trial is "beyond a reasonable doubt."

recidivism Repetition of criminal behavior; habitual criminality. Recidivism is measured by (1) criminal acts that result in conviction by a court when committed by individuals who are under correctional supervision or who had been released from correctional supervision within the previous three years, and (2) technical violations of probation or parole in which a sentencing or paroling authority has taken action resulting in an adverse change in the offender's legal status.

recoupment Forcing indigents to repay the state for at least part of their legal costs.

reflected appraisal According to Matsueda and Heimer, a youth's self-evaluation based on his or her perceptions of how others evaluate him or her.

reflective role-taking According to Matsueda and Heimer, the phenomenon that occurs when youths who view themselves as delinquents are giving an inner-voice to their perceptions how significant others feel about them.

reintegration The correctional philosophy that stresses reintroducing the inmate into the community.

reintegrative shaming A method of correction that encourages offenders to confront their misdeeds, experience shame because of the harm they caused, and then be reincluded in society.

relative deprivation The condition that exists when people of wealth and poverty live in close proximity to one another. Some criminologists attribute crime rate differentials to relative deprivation.

release on recognizance A nonmonetary condition for the pretrial release of an accused individual; an alternative to monetary bail that is granted after the court determines that the accused has ties in the community, has no prior record of default, and is likely to appear at subsequent proceedings.

restitution A condition of probation in which the offender repays society or the victim of crime for the trouble the offender caused. Monetary restitution involves a direct payment to the victim as a form of compensation. Community service restitution may be used in victimless crimes and involves work in the community in lieu of more severe criminal penalties.

revocation An administrative act performed by a parole authority that removes a person from parole or a judicial order by a court removing a person from parole or probation, in response to a violation on the part of the parolee or probationer.

right to counsel The right of the accused to the assistance of defense counsel in all criminal prosecutions.

right to treatment The philosophy espoused by many courts that offenders have a statutory right to treatment. A federal constitutional right to treatment has not been established.

rights of defendant Powers and privileges that are constitutionally guaranteed to every defendant in a criminal trial.

role diffusion According to Erikson, a phenomenon that occurs when youths spread themselves too thin, experience personal uncertainty, and place themselves at the mercy of leaders who promise to give them a sense of identity they cannot develop for themselves.

routine activities The view that crime is a "normal" function of the routine activities of modern living. Offenses can be expected if there is a suitable target that is not protected by capable guardians.

sadistic rape A rape motivated by the offender's desire to torment and abuse the victim.

sample A limited number of people selected for study from a population.

schizophrenia A type of psychosis often marked by bizarre behavior, hallucinations, loss of thought control, and inappropriate emotional responses. Schizophrenic types include catatonic, which characteristically involves impairment of motor activity; paranoid, which is characterized by delusions of persecution; and hebephrenic, which is characterized by immature behavior and giddiness.

search and seizure The legal term, contained in the Fourth Amendment to the U.S. Constitution, that refers to the searching for and carrying away of evidence by police during a criminal investigation.

secondary deviance According to Lemert, accepting deviant labels as a personal identity. Acts become secondary when they form a basis for self-concept, as when a drug experimenter becomes an "addict."

secondary sociopaths People who are constitutionally normal but whose life experiences influence their antisocial behavior. Suspected influences include poor parenting, racial segregation, and social conflict.

seductions of crime According to Katz, the visceral and emotional appeal that the situation of crime has for those who engage in illegal acts.

selective incapacitation The policy of creating enhanced prison sentences for the relatively small group of dangerous chronic offenders.

self-control theory According to Gottfredson and Hirschi, the view that the cause of delinquent behavior is an impulsive personality. Kids who are impulsive may find that their bond to society is weak.

self-fulfilling prophecy Deviant behavior patterns that are a response to an earlier labeling experience. People act in synch with social labels, even if the labels are falsely bestowed.

self-report study A research approach that requires subjects to reveal their own participation in delinquent or criminal acts.

sentence The criminal sanction imposed by the court on a convicted defendant, usually in the form of a fine, incarceration, or probation. Sentencing may be carried out by a judge, jury, or sentencing council (panel of judges), depending on the statutes of the jurisdiction. *See also* determinate sentence; indeterminate sentence

sequester The insulation of jurors from the outside world so that their decision making cannot be influenced or affected by extralegal events.

serial murder The killing of a large number of people over time by an offender who seeks to escape detection.

sheriff The chief law enforcement officer in a county.

shield laws Laws designed to protect rape victims by prohibiting the defense attorney from inquiring about their previous sexual relationships.

shire-gemot During the Middle Ages, an assemblage of local landholders who heard more serious and important criminal cases.

shire reeve In early England, the senior law enforcement figure in a county, the forerunner of today's sheriff.

shock incarceration A short prison sentence served in boot camp–type facilities.

shock probation A sentence in which offenders serve a short prison term to impress them with the pains of imprisonment before they begin probation.

short-run hedonism According to Cohen, the desire of lower-class gang youths to engage in behavior that will give them immediate gratification and excitement but in the long run will be dysfunctional and negative.

situational crime prevention A method of crime prevention that stresses tactics and strategies to eliminate or reduce particular crimes in narrow settings, such as reducing burglaries in a housing project by increasing lighting and installing security alarms.

skeezers Prostitutes who trade sex for drugs, usually crack.

skinhead Member of a white supremacist gang, identified by a shaved skull and Nazi or Ku Klux Klan markings.

social bond Ties a person has to the institutions and processes of society. According to Hirschi, elements of the social bond include commitment, attachment, involvement, and belief.

social capital Positive relations with individuals and institutions that are life sustaining.

social control The ability of society and its institutions to control, manage, restrain, or direct human behavior.

social disorganization A neighborhood or area marked by culture conflict, lack of cohesiveness, transient population, insufficient social organizations, and anomie.

social learning theory The view that human behavior is modeled through observation of human social interactions, either directly from observing those who are close and from intimate contact, or indirectly through the media. Interactions that are rewarded are copied, while those that are punished are avoided.

social process Operations of formal and informal social institutions. Elements of the social process include socialization within family and peer groups, the educational process, and the justice system.

social structure The various stratifications that characterize the fabric of postindustrial society. Within the social structure are the various classes, institutions, and groups of society.

socialization Process of human development and enculturation. Socialization is influenced by key social processes and institutions.

sociobiology Branch of science that views human behavior as being motivated by inborn biological urges and desires. The urge to survive and preserve the species motivates human behavior.

sociopath Person whose personality is characterized by lack of warmth and affection, inappropriate responses, and an inability to learn from experience. The term is used interchangeably with *psychopath* and *antisocial personality disorder.*

sodomy Illegal sexual intercourse. Sodomy has no single definition, and acts included within its scope are usually defined by state statute.

somatotyping A system developed for categorizing people on the basis of their body build.

special (specific) deterrence A crime control policy suggesting that punishment be severe enough to convince convicted offenders never to repeat their criminal activity.

specific intent The intent to accomplish a specific purpose as an element of crime, such as breaking into someone's house for the express purpose of stealing jewels.

spontaneous remission Another term for the aging-out process.

stalking laws Laws that make it a criminal offense to stalk or harass a victim even though no actual assault or battery has occurred.

standard of proof The level of proof needed to process a person at various stages of the justice system; the standard of proof for an arrest to be made is "probable cause." The Supreme Court has made the "beyond a reasonable doubt" standard a due process and constitutional requirement for conviction at trial.

stare decisis To stand by decided cases; the legal principle by which the decision or holding in an earlier case becomes the standard by which subsequent similar cases are judged.

statutory law Laws created by legislative bodies to meet changing social conditions, public opinion, and custom.

steroids Drugs used to gain muscle bulk and strength for athletics and body building.

stigma An enduring label that taints a person's identity and changes him or her in the eyes of others.

stimulants Synthetic drugs that stimulate action in the central nervous system. They produce an intense physical reaction: increased blood pressure, increased breathing rate, increased bodily activity, and elevated mood. One widely used set of stimulants, amphetamines, produce psychological effects such as increased confidence, euphoria, fearlessness, talkativeness, impulsive behavior, and loss of appetite.

sting An undercover police operation in which police pose as criminals to trap law violators.

stoopers Petty criminals who earn their living by retrieving winning tickets that are accidentally discarded by racetrack patrons.

stop and frisk The situation where police officers who are suspicious of an individual run their hands lightly over the suspect's outer garments to determine whether the person is carrying a concealed weapon. Also called a "patdown" or "threshold inquiry," a stop and frisk is intended to stop short of any activity that could be considered a violation of Fourth Amendment rights.

strain The emotional turmoil and conflict caused when people believe they cannot achieve their desires and goals through legitimate means. Members of the lower-class might feel strain because they are denied access to adequate educational opportunities and social support.

stratification Grouping according to social strata or levels. American society is considered stratified on the basis of economic class and wealth.

street crime Illegal acts designed to prey on the public through theft, damage, and violence.

strict-liability crimes Illegal acts whose elements do not contain the need for intent, or *mens rea;* they are usually acts that endanger the public welfare, such as illegal dumping of toxic wastes.

structural Marxist theory The view that the law and the justice system are designed to maintain the capitalist system and that members of both the owner and worker classes whose behavior threatens the stability of the system will be sanctioned.

subculture A group that is loosely part of the dominant culture but maintains a unique set of values, beliefs, and traditions.

subpoena A court order requiring the recipient to appear in court on an indicated time and date.

substantive criminal laws A body of specific rules that declare what conduct is criminal and prescribe the punishment to be imposed for such conduct.

suitable target According to routine activities theory, a target for crime that is relatively valuable, easily transportable, and not capably guarded.

summons An alternative to arrest usually used for petty or traffic offenses; a written order notifying an individual that he or she has been charged with an offense. A summons directs the person to appear in court to answer the charge. It is used primarily in instances of low risk, where the person will not be required to appear at a later date. The summons is advantageous to police officers in that they are freed from having to spend time on arrest and booking procedures; it is advantageous to the accused in that he or she is spared time in jail.

sureties During the Middle Ages, people who made themselves responsible for the behavior of offenders released in their care.

surplus value The Marxist view that the laboring classes produce wealth that far exceeds their wages and goes to the capitalist class as profits.

surrebuttal Introducing witnesses during a criminal trial to disprove damaging testimony by other witnesses.

suspended sentence A prison term that is delayed while the defendant undergoes a period of community treatment. If the treatment is successful, the prison sentence is terminated.

symbolic interaction The sociological view that people communicate through symbols. People interpret symbolic communication and incorporate it within their personality. A person's view of reality, then, depends on his or her interpretation of symbolic gestures.

systemic link Violent behavior that results from the conflict inherent in the drug trade.

team policing An experimental police technique in which groups of officers are assigned to a particular area of the city on a 24-hour basis.

technical parole violation Revocation of parole because conditions set by correctional authorities have been violated.

technique of neutralization According to neutralization theory, the ability of delinquent youth to neutralize moral constraints so they may drift into criminal acts.

temperance movement An effort to prohibit the sale of liquor in the United States that resulted in the passage of the Eighteenth Amendment to the Constitution in

1919, which prohibited the sale of alcoholic beverages.

thanatos According to Freud, the instinctual drive toward aggression and violence.

threshold inquiry A term used to describe a stop and frisk.

tithings During the Middle Ages, groups of about ten families who were responsible for maintaining order among themselves and dealing with disturbances, fires, wild animals, and so on.

tort The law of personal wrongs and damage. Tort actions include negligence, libel, slander, assault, and trespass.

totality of the circumstances A legal doctrine mandating that a decision maker consider all the issues and circumstances of a case before judging the outcome. For example, before concluding whether a suspect understood a *Miranda* warning, a judge must consider the totality of the circumstances under which the warning was given. The suspect's age, intelligence, and competency may influence his or her understanding and judgment.

transferred intent The principle that if an illegal yet unintended act results from the intent to commit a crime, that act is also considered illegal.

transitional neighborhood An area undergoing a shift in population and structure, usually from middle-class residential to lower-class mixed use.

turning points According to Laub and Sampson, the life events that alter the development of a criminal career.

venire The group called for jury duty from which jury panels are selected.

vice squad Police officers assigned to enforce morally tinged laws, such as those governing prostitution, gambling, and pornography.

victim-precipitated crime A crime in which the victim's behavior was the spark that ignited the subsequent offense, as when the victim abused the offender verbally or physically.

victimization survey A crime measurement technique that surveys citizens to measure their experiences as victims of crime.

victimology The study of the victim's role in criminal transactions.

virulency According to Athens, a stage in a violent career in which criminals develop a violent identity that makes them feared. They consequently enjoy hurting others.

voir dire The process in which a potential jury panel is questioned by the prosecution and the defense to select jurors who are unbiased and objective.

waiver The act of voluntarily relinquishing a right or advantage; often used in the context of waiving one's right to counsel (for example, the *Miranda* warning) or waiving certain steps in the criminal justice process (such as the preliminary hearing). Essential to waiver is the voluntary consent of the individual.

warrant A written court order issued by a magistrate authorizing and directing that an individual be taken into custody to answer criminal charges.

watch system In medieval England, men organized in church parishes to guard against disturbances and breaches of the peace at night; they were under the direction of the local constable.

watchman A style of policing that stresses reacting to calls for service rather than aggressively pursuing crime.

wergild Under medieval law, the money paid by the offender to compensate the victim and the state for a criminal offense.

white-collar crime Illegal acts that capitalize on a person's status in the marketplace. White-collar crimes can involve theft, embezzlement, fraud, market manipulation, restraint of trade, and false advertising.

Wickersham Commission Created in 1931 by President Herbert Hoover to investigate the state of the nation's police forces, a commission that found police training to be inadequate and the average officer incapable of effectively carrying out his duties.

widening the net The charge that programs designed to divert offenders from the justice system actually enmesh them further in the process by substituting more intrusive treatment programs for less intrusive punishment-oriented outcomes.

wite The portion of the wergild that went to the victim's family.

work furlough A prison treatment program that allows inmates to leave during the day to work in the community and return to prison at night.

writ of certiorari An order of a superior court requesting that the record of an inferior court (or administrative body) be brought forward for review or inspection.

writ of habeas corpus A judicial order requesting that a person detaining another produce the body of the prisoner and give reasons for his or her capture and detention. Habeas corpus is a legal device used to request that a judicial body review the reasons for a person's confinement and the conditions of confinement. Habeas corpus is known as "the great writ."

writ of mandamus An order of a superior court commanding that a lower court, administrative body, or executive body perform a specific function. It is commonly used to restore rights and privileges lost to a defendant through illegal means.

Subject Index

biological determinism, 10
biological trait theories, 131–142, 156
    biochemical conditions, 133–134
    evaluation of, 141–142
    evolutionary contributions, 141
    genetic contributions, 139–141
    neurophysiological conditions, 136–139
biological traits, crime and, 259–260
biological/psychological perspective, 12
biophobia, 132
biosocial view of crime, 142
blacks. *See* African Americans
blameworthy, 123
block watches, 94
blue curtain, 344
Bobbitt, Lorena, 34, 300
Boesky, Ivan, 342, 355
Boggs Act, 404
Bolivia, 407
boosters, 323
bootlegging, 363
bourgeoisie, 11, 228, 235
Brady, James, 60, 62
Brady Handgun Control Act, 42, 60
brain activity, criminality and, 137
brain dysfunctions, 138
brain functioning, criminality and, 133, 258
brain tumors, crime and, 136, 138
breaking and entering, 328
breast implants, 357
bribes, 343, 345
brothels, 382–383
Brown University, 289
brutalization effect, 116, 283
Bundy, Ted, 295, 296, 387
Buono, Angelo, 295
burden of proof, 31
burglars
    career ladder of, 329–330
    choice of targets by, 104, 105, 330
    earnings of, 103
    female, 330–331
    types of, 328–329
Burglars on the Job (Wright and Decker),
    328–329
burglary, 32, 47, 318, 328–331
    defined, 36, 328
    incidence of, 328
    repeat, 330–331
    techniques of, 329
    victims of, 81
Bush, Neil, 349
bystanders, passive, 310

C

Calden, Paul, 304
California Personality Inventory, 151
call girls, 376, 383
caller ID, 112
Cambridge Study of Delinquent Development,
    268–270
Campbell, Horret, 55
cannabis, 392
capable guardians, 87, 105
capital punishment, 116–117, 123

capitalism
    as cause of crime, 228–229, 230, 235,
        236–237, 238
    gender inequality and, 242
Capitalism, Patriarchy, and Crime
    (Messerschmidt), 242
car theft. *See* automobile theft
career criminals, 68–71, 105, 122–123
    See also chronic offenders
Careers in Crack Project, 395
carjacking, 326
Carrier's case, 35
cartographic school, 10
Centennial Savings and Loan, 348
Center for Research on Women, 243
cerebral allergies, 136
Challenger explosion, 338
Champion Insurance Company, 343
cheater theory, 141
check forgers, 325
check kiting, 347
checks, bad, 325
Chicago
    concentric zones in, 169–170
    gangs in, 55
    South Side, 166
Chicago Area Project, 188
Chicago Board of Trade, 341–342
Chicago School, 11, 163
child abuse, 78, 81, 197, 298–299
    causes of, 299–300
    criminality and, 265, 283
child pornography, 386–387, 388, 390
child prostitution, 386–387
children
    at-risk, 166
    drug education for, 410
    family relations of, 196–197
    firesetting by, 332
    peers and, 198
    poverty and, 164
    social development of, 255–257
    as victims, 78, 81, 197, 298–299
China
    corruption in, 339
    crime in, 5, 237
    gangs in, 366
chiseling, 341
chivalry hypothesis, 65
choice theory, 12, 101–123
    differential reinforcement theory and, 205
    drug use and, 400
    policy implications of, 123
    summary of, 124
Christian Coalition, 378
chronic offenders, 64, 68–71, 118, 119
    IQ of, 154
    labeling and, 216, 217
    latent traits and, 254, 259–263
    life course of, 264–268
    selective incapacitation of, 122–123
    strain and, 181
    traits of, 268–270
church fires, 332
church membership, criminality and, 198
churning, of stock, 341

circuit judges, 28, 29
circuit travelers, 383
civil law, 30
claims
    false, 351–352
    fraudulent, 346
class, social, 58–62, 164, 187
    in Marxist theory, 228–229
Class and Class Conflict in Industrial Society
    (Dahrendorf), 230
class bias, 234, 239–240
class conflict, 237, 242
class struggle, 229, 258
classical criminology, 101–102
Clean Air Act, 352
clearance, of crimes, 46
client frauds, 346–348
climate, crime and, 58
Clinton, Bill, 376
cliques, 198
closure, 325
Coalition for the Homeless, 164
Coca-Cola, 393
cocaine, 393–394, 396, 403, 411
Code of Hammurabi, 25
cognitive definitions, 204
cognitive perspective, on delinquency, 270
cognitive theory, 148–149, 156
cohort research, 19–20, 68–69, 70
college campuses, rapes on, 289
Colombia, drug traffic in, 366, 406, 407
commitment, 209–210
common law
    defined, 28–29
    history of, 26–30
    in other cultures, 30
common-law crimes, 32
Communications Decency Act, 353
communities, life cycles of, 173
community notification laws, 42
community organization, 94
community programs, 188
    to control drugs, 408–409
community protection, 93–94
compensation, for victims, 26, 91
compliance strategies, for business, 358
Comprehensive Crime Control Act, 91, 368
Comprehensive Drug Abuse Prevention and
    Control Act, 368, 404
Comprehensive Environmental Response,
    Compensation, and Liability Act, 353
Computer Abuse Amendment Act, 354
computer crimes, 353–354
Computer Sciences Company, 359
con artists, 319
concentration effect, 173
concentric zone theory, 169–171, 190
*Condition of the Working Class in England in
    1844* (Engels), 229
conduct disorders, 144
conduct norms, 182
confidence games, 328
conflict, 227
    community ownership of, 246
conflict criminology, 11
conflict gangs, 186

conflict theory, 12, 16, 17, 18, 227–228, 248
  analysis of, 235
  modern, 231–235
  research on, 234–235
conformity, 175, 198
  commitment to, 207
consensus view, 16, 18
consent, rape and, 291
conspiracy, 32
constructive intent, 37
constructive possession, 322
containment, 239
containment theory, 208
Contemporary Woman and Crime, The (Simon), 66
continuity of crime, 70, 263–264
control theory, 199, 207–211, 218, 220
Controlled Substances Act, 404
convictional criminals, 305
Corill, Dean, 295
corner boy, 184
corporal punishment, 120
corporate crime, 337, 338, 339, 349–353
corporate culture, 355–356
corporate policing, 348
correctionalism, 239
corroboration, rape and, 292
corruption, 339, 343, 344
  See also police corruption
Counsel Connect, 42
Counterfeit Active Device and Computer Fraud
    and Abuse Act, 354
court escorts, 91
court-leet, 26
crack cocaine, 393–394, 395, 407–408
  bartering sex for, 383
crackdowns, 114
credit card theft, 325
crime
  anomie theory of, 174–178, 190
  conflict theory of, 16, 17, 18, 228
  consensus view of, 16, 18
  consequences of, 259
  continuity of, 70, 263–264
  control theories of, 207–211, 220
  corporate, 337, 338, 339, 349–353
  costs of, 77
  cultural deviance theory of, 168, 182–187, 190
  cultural differences in, 57
  definition of, 18–19
  delinquent subcultures and, 183–184
  differential association and, 200–204
  differential opportunity and, 184–187
  differential reinforcement and, 204–205
  drugs and, 402–405
  earnings from, 103
  ecology of, 58
  economic, 318, 337–353
  eliminating, 110–123
  family relations and, 196–197
  general theory of, 260–263, 274
  high-tech, 353–354
  history of, 25–28
  household patterns of, 80
  how criminologists view, 16–19
  human nature and, 259–260
  inchoate, 29

integrated theories of, 253–274
intelligence and, 151–154
interactionist view of, 17–18
labeling theories of, 212–217, 220
learning techniques of, 104
learning to commit, 201
legal definition of, 36–37
Marx on, 229
mental illness and, 149–150
offense-specific/offender-specific, 103
organized, 360–369
pathways to, 266
personality and, 150–151
place of, 104
as political, 231, 233
race and, 66–67
rationality of, 107–110
relative deprivation theory of, 178–179, 190
seductions of, 109–110
self-concept and, 207–208
social class and, 58–62
social disorganization theory of, 168–174, 190
social learning theories of, 199–207, 220
social processes and, 196–198
social reality of, 233–234
strain theory of, 168, 174–182, 190
structuring, 104
substance abuse and, 84
unemployment and, 188
white-color, 337–353
  See also violent crime
Crime, Shame, and Reintegration (Braithwaite), 120
Crime and Everyday Life (Felson), 89
Crime and Human Nature (Wilson and Herrnstein), 259
Crime and the American Dream, 177
crime control, left realist view of, 242
crime discouragers, 112, 113
crime displacement, 103112
crime patterns, 58–68
crime prevention, 93–94
  drugs and, 408–409
  primary, 154–155
  secondary, 155
  situational, 110–113
  social structure and, 188
  See also deterrence
Crime Prevention Through Environmental Design (Jeffery), 110
crime-prone areas, 173
crime rate
  age and, 53–54, 62–65
  calculation of, 46
  changes in, 52–53
  drugs and, 55
  ecological differences in, 163
  economy and, 54
  effect of incarceration rates on, 122
  firearms and, 54–55, 58
  gangs and, 55
  gender and, 5, 64, 65–66, 182
  international, 4
  justice policy and, 55–56
  juvenile, 53–54, 62–63
  neighborhood structure and, 170, 171–174
  regional, 58, 59

relative deprivation and, 178–179
seasonality of, 10
social change and, 89
social environment and, 167
trends in, 87
unemployment and, 171
crime statistics, 46–51
  international, 4–5
crime trends, 51–57
crime typology, 14
Crime Victims Compensation Program, 91
crimes
  clearance of, 46
  common-law, 32
  economic, 318
  environmental, 352–353
  instrumental vs. expressive, 58
  public order, 376
  reporting of, 47–48, 53
  victimless, 376, 377
criminal anthropology, 10, 12, 132
criminal behavior systems, 14
criminal careers, evolution of, 264–268
criminal codes, 33
Criminal Copyright Infringement Act, 354
criminal gangs, 185–186, 329
criminal justice system, 6
  corruption in, 344–345
  females and, 244
  Marxian analysis of, 239
criminal law, 30–31
  changing, 42
  functions of, 33–35
  history of, 25–28
criminal syndicates, 365
Criminal Violence, Criminal Justice (Silberman), 67–68
criminality, 103
  benefits of, 109–110
  biological basis of, 131–142
  female, 243
  individual differences in, 261
  interactional theory of, 270–271
  life-course theories of, 263–273, 274
  Marxist view of, 236
  multifactor theories of, 254–259
  onset of, 263–264, 265, 266–268
  risk factors for, 255
  self-control and, 261–262
  structuring, 104
criminological enterprise, 13
criminologists, 5
  activities of, 13–16
  leftist, 236
criminology
  classical, 8–9
  conflict, 11, 231–232
  criminal justice and, 6
  defined, 5, 6
  developmental, 253
  deviance and, 6–7
  ethical issues in, 21–22
  history of, 7–10
  major perspectives on, 12
  Marxist, 235–241
  multidisciplinary nature of, 16
  peacemaking, 246–247

hundred-gemot, 26
hundreds, 26
husband battering, 300
hustlers, 382
hypoglycemia, 134

I

id, 143, 144
identity, labels as basis for, 214
identity crisis, 144
ignorance, as defense, 38
imitation, 145, 204
    crime and, 142
    See also social learning
imperatively coordinated associations, 230
Imperial Food Products, 361
impulsiveness, 261, 262
incapacitation strategies, 110, 121–122, 124
incarceration, 121
    effectiveness of, 122
incest, 299
inchoate crimes, 29, 32
incivilities, 172
income, victimization and, 81, 83
income inequality, 178–179
index crimes, 46, 47
industry, crime in, 343, 346, 350–351
inequality
    gender, 242
    income, 178–179
    social, 234
inferiority complex, 144
influence peddling, 343–346
informal sanctions, 117–118
information processing, 149
innovation, 175
Inquisition, 7
insanity defense, 38–39
insider trading, 342
instinct, 133, 283–284
    rape and, 290
Institute for Social Research (ISR), 52–53, 67, 396, 398
institutional anomie theory, 177–178, 190
institutional position, exploitation of, 342–343
instrumental crimes, 58
instrumental Marxism, 237–239, 248
instrumental violence, 286
insurance fraud, 347
integrated structural Marxist theory, 258
integrated theories, 253–254
integrated theory, Elliott's, 257–258
intelligence (IQ), crime and, 21, 151–154, 254, 259–260
intent, criminal, 37
interactional theory, 270–271, 274
interactionist view, 17–18
Internal Revenue Code, 347
International Association of Auto Theft Investigators, 46
International Association of Crime Analysts, 46
Internet, pornography on, 390
Internet crimes, 353
Interstate and Foreign Travel or Transportation in Aid of Racketeering Enterprises Act, 367
intimate violence, 3
intoxication, as defense, 40

involvement, 210, 211
IQ. *See* intelligence
Iran and Libya Sanctions Act, 310
Irish Republican Army (IRA), 308
irresistible impulse test, 38
Irvin, Michael, 291
ISR. *See* Institute for Social Research

J

Japan
    child prostitution in, 387
    crime rates in, 57
    organized crime in, 366
    shame as crime deterrent in, 121
Jones, Adrienne, 3
joyriding, 326
Judas Priest lawsuit, 30
judge-made law, 29
Jukes and Kallikaks, 132
junkies, 404
jury trial
    origins of, 28
Just and Painful (Newman), 120
just desert, 123
justice
    restorative, 246–247
justification, as defense, 37, 40–41
juvenile homicide rates, 56
juvenile justice system
    females and, 244
    racial bias in, 234
    See also delinquency
juvenile prostitution, 386–387
juveniles, firesetting by, 332

K

Kaczynski, Theodore, 255
Kanka, Megan, 42
Kansas City police department, 114
Keating, Charles, 349
Kefauver Committee, 365
Kemper, Edmund, 295
Kennedy, Robert, Jr., 338
Kevorkian, Jack, 14, 42
Key West, Florida, 378
kickbacks, 343
kiddy porn, 386, 390
Kilroy, Mark, 295
King, Harry, 320
Klaas, Polly, 33
Knapp Commission, 344
Koresh, David, 307

L

La Casita House, 273
La Cosa Nostra, 363, 365
labeling, 212
    consequences of, 213–214
    in schools, 198
labeling theory, 199, 212–217, 220, 231
    research on, 216
    validity of, 216–217
labor racketeering, 365
Landers, Ann, 386
language, semiotics and, 245–246
larceny, 32, 47, 322–328
    defined, 328

grand, 323
    petty, 323
late-onset criminality, 266–268
latency stage, 143
latent delinquency, 144
latent traits, 254, 259–263
law, 233
    civil, 30
    classification of, 30–32
    in Marxist view, 238, 239
    morality and, 376–378
    obedience to, 207
    sociology of, 14
    statutory, 29, 30
    tort, 30–31
    See also common law; criminal law
Law Journal Extra, 38
lead ingestion, criminality and, 136
learning
    biochemistry and, 133
    of criminal behavior, 200-201
    criminality and, 144–148
    of deviant behavior, 204–205
learning processes, 204
learning theory, 142
left-handers, 138
left realism, 242, 248
legal codes, early, 25
legal ethics, 341
legalization, 6, 34, 42, 239, 384–385, 390, 411–412
Leslie Fay clothing company, 346
lex talionis, 25
liberal feminist theory, 66
Libya, 310, 311
life-course persistent offenders, 266
life-course theories, 254, 263–273, 274
life span
    crime over, 64
    race and, 165
lifestyle
    criminal choices and, 104
    high-risk, 86–87, 88
    victimization and, 80–81, 86–87, 95
lighting, as influence on antisocial behavior, 136
loan-sharking, 362
Lockheed Aircraft, 345, 351
LOJACK, 327
Lombrosian theory, 9–10
longitudinal research, 19–20
Lord, Steven, 85
Los Angeles, gangs in, 187
loss, by victims, 77
lower-class subculture, 164, 167, 182, 187
LSD, 392, 397

M

madams, 382–383
Mafia, 362, 363, 364, 365–366, 367–368
Magoto, Marita, 15
mala in se crimes, 31–32
mala prohibitum crime, 32, 34–35, 376
malice, 292, 293
mandatory sentences, 60, 122
Mann Act, 384
manslaughter, 32, 293
Mapplethorpe, Robert, 388

oral stage, 143
organized crime, 337, 339, 360–361
   activities of, 362
   characteristics of, 362
   concept of, 363–366
   controlling, 367, 368–369
   ethnic groups and, 366
   future of, 367–368
   history of, 363, 365
   international, 366
   legitimate enterprise and, 362–363
   RICO and, 367, 368
Organized Crime Control Act, 367
Outsiders (Becker), 231

P

Palestinian Liberation Organization (PLO),
   306–307
Panama, 406
paraphilias, 380–381
parenting
   crime and, 196
   violence and, 283
parents
   abusive, 299–300
   murder of, 82
parricide, 82
Part I crimes, 46, 47
Part II crimes, 46
pathways to crime, 266
patriarchy, 242, 243
patricide, 82
Patterns in Criminal Homicide (Wolfgang), 14
PBS. *See* problem behavior syndrome
PCP, 391–392
peacemaking, 236, 246–247, 248
pedophilia, 42, 381
peer group
   criminality and, 198, 202–203
   delinquent, 258
   differential association with, 204
   drug use and, 399
   influence of, 268, 270, 271
pencyclidine (PCP), 391–392
Penn, William, 28
penology, 14–15
Pentagon scandal, 344
perceptual deterrence, 117
Perea, Ignacio, 292
personality
   crime-prone, 151, 152–153
   criminal choices and, 104
   criminality and, 150–151
   defined, 150
   drug use and, 399
   impulsive, 261, 262
personality disorder, 262–263
personality tests, 150–151
personality traits
   of chronic offenders, 181
   genetics and, 139
Peru, 308
phallic stage, 143
pharmaceutical industry, false advertising in,
   351–352
pharmacists, chiseling by, 341
Philadelphia, police corruption in, 345
phrenology, 9

pigeon drop, 328
pilferage, 324, 346
pimps, 384
Pinto, 361
pleasure principle, 143
PLO, 306–307
poachers, 318
police
   Marxist view of, 241
   private, 325
police corruption, 343, 344, 345
police patrols, 114
police presence, 114
political machines, 343
political power, 237
political prisoners, 308
political violence, 305–311
Politics of Rape, The (Russell), 290
pollution, 338, 352, 359
poppers, 392
population density, crime and, 58
population trends, 56
population turnover, 173
populations, research, 19
pornography, 377, 385–390
   child, 386–387, 388, 390
   controlling, 389–390
   legal aspects of, 388–389
   violence and, 387–388
positivism, 9, 102
posttraumatic stress syndrome, 90
poverty, 164–167
   concentration of, 173
   crime and, 171, 230
   war on, 188
poverty line, 164
power, 232
power-control theory, 244–245
powerlessness, 243
predatory crime, 87
preemptive deterrence, 242
premeditation, 293
premenstrual syndrome (PMS), 135–136
preponderance of evidence, 31
President's Commission on Law Enforcement
   and the Administration of Justice, 50
price fixing, 350
primary prevention, 154–155
Principles of Criminology (Sutherland), 200
private property, control of, 236–237
private security officers, 324–325
privilege, 238
problem behavior syndrome (PBS), 268, 301,
   399–400
Profaci crime family, 365
Professional Thief, The (Sutherland), 320
Prohibition, 363, 391, 411
projective tests, 150
proletariat, 11, 228, 235
property, forfeiture of, 368–369
property crime, 32, 81, 318–333
prosocial bonds, 255
prosocial experiences, 271
prostitution, 108, 376–377, 381–385
   child, 386–387
   defined, 381
   history of, 381

incidence of, 381–382
legalization of, 384–385
organized crime and, 362
turning to, 384
types of, 382–383
proximity hypothesis, 86–87, 95
pseudomaturity, 266
psychedelics. *See* hallucinogens
psychodynamic perspective, 143–144, 156
   on drug abuse, 399
psychological trait theories, 142–154, 156
   behavioral, 144–148
   cognitive, 148–149
   personality, 150–151
   psychodynamic, 143–144
psychological traits, crime and, 259–260,
   268–270
psychopathy, 152–153
psychopharmacology, 285
psychosexual stages, 143
psychosis, 144, 282
psychosurgery, 155
public order crimes, 376
public welfare offenses, 37
punishment
   certainty of, 113–114
   corporal, 120
   as deterrent, 35, 113–121
   for drug offenders, 407–408
   as general deterrent, 113–118
   history of, 25–28
   perception of, 117
   proportional to crime, 101
   severity of, 115–116, 117
   as specific deterrent, 118–121
   of white-collar crime, 360, 361
Pure Food and Drug Act, 393, 404

Q

questionnaires, self-report, 49

R

r/k selection theory, 141
race
   crime and, 66–67
   victimization and, 81, 83, 84
racial bias
   in criminal justice system, 234, 235
   in juvenile justice system, 216
racial disparity, 164–165
racism, 236, 245
Racketeer Influenced and Corrupt Organization
   Act (RICO), 367, 368
radiation, as influence on antisocial behavior,
   136
radical feminist theory, 242–245, 248
rap booths, 383
rape, 32, 47, 286–292
   capitalism and, 240
   causes of, 289–291
   crisis intervention for, 91–92
   date, 85, 149, 287–289
   defined, 48, 286
   gang, 289
   guilt of victim and, 240
   history of, 287
   incidence of, 4, 53, 287–288
   laws regarding, 291–292

Name Index

Table of Cases

Photo Credits

Contents

ix: © Rhonda Gregory/American Fast Photo/ Saba Press Photos; x: © Asahi Shimbun/Sipa Press; xi: © James Coburn/Edmond Evening Sun/Sipa Press; xii: © Eduardo Citrinblum; xiii: © Andrew Holbrooke; xiv: © Dan Lamont/ Matrix; xv: © Paul Moseley/Fort Worth Star Telegram/Sipa Press; xvi: Dennis Meyer/Norfolk Daily News—AP/Wide World Photos; xvii: © Todd Yates/Black Star.

Chapter 1

2: © Richard Hartog/The Outlook-Sipa Press; 3: © Robert Ruiz/Fort Worth Star Telegram/ Sipa Press; 8: T. H. Matteson, "The Trial of George Jacobs, August 5, 1692." Oil on canvas. 39 × 53 inches. #1,246. Peabody Essex Museum, Salem, MA; 15: Ed Bailey/AP/Wide World Photos; 17: © Hardy A. Saffold/Sipa Press.

Chapter 2

24: © Rhonda Gregory/American Fast Photo/ Saba Press Photos; 27: Musees Royaux Des Beaux-Arts, Art Resource, NY; 33 (left): © Scott Manchester-Petaluma Times/Sygma; (right): James Keyser/Time Magazine. Copyright Time, Inc. 34: J. Scott Applewhite-AP/Wide World Photos; 40: Brian Snyder, Pool-AP/Wide World Photos.

Chapter 3

45: © Asahi Shimbun/Sipa Press; 54: © Mark Peterson/Saba; 55: © Mattew Polak/Sygma; 62: AP/Wide World Photos; 63: © Karen Garber-The Corning Leader/Sipa; 71: © T. Stoddart-Katz/Saba.

Chapter 4

76: © James Coburn/Edmond Evening Sun/ Sipa Press; 78: © Claus Bergman-Conti/Sipa Press; 82: Courtesy of Kathleen Heide, Ph.D.; 84: © R. Jonathan Rehg/Gamma Liaison Network; 89: Courtesy of Marcus Felson; 90: © Steve Lehman/Saba; 93: © Jean-Marc Giboux/Gamma Liaison Network.

Chapter 5

100: © Eduardo Citrinblum; 106: © Mark Richards; 109: Justin Ide-AP/Wide World Photos; 110: Citywide Corporate Photography, Newark, courtesy of Ronald Clarke; 114: © Joe Bensen/Stock, Boston; 120: © Lannis Waters/ Palm Beach Post.

Chapter 6

130: © Mehau Kulyk/Science Photo Library-Photo Researchers, Inc.; 135: Courtesy of Diana Fishbein; 138: Dr. Alan Zametkin/Clinical Brain Imaging, courtesy of Office of Scientific Information, NIMH; 139: Courtesy of Lee Ellis; 145: © Dan Habib/Impact Visuals; 154: © Alex Quesada/Matrix.

Chapter 7

162: © Andrew Holbrooke; 165: © Stephen Shames/Matrix; 167: Ted Thai/Time Magazine. Copyright Time, Inc.; 172: © Jim West/Impact Visuals; 177: Jodi Cobb/National Geographic Society Image Collection; 179: Courtesy of Robert Agnew; 185: © Alon Reininger/Contact Press Images.

Chapter 8

195: © Andrew Holbrooke; 200: © Peter Poulides/Tony Stone Images; 208: © Todd Yates/Black Star; 210: © Richard Hutchings/ Photo Edit; 215: © Brooks Kraft/Sygma.

Chapter 9

226: © Dan Lamont/Matrix; 232: Steve Liss/ Time Magazine. Copyright Time, Inc.; 238: © Todd Bigelow/Black Star; 243: © Stephen Shames/Matrix; 245: Paul Sakuma-AP/Wide World Photos.

Chapter 10

252: © Christopher Morris/Black Star; 255: Copyright © 1996 Time, Inc. Reprinted by permission; 260: Photo by John Florence, University of Arizona News Services; 269: © Todd Yates/ Black Star; 273: © Alex Quesada/ Matrix.

Chapter 11

280: © Paul Moseley/Fort Worth Star Telegram/ Sipa Press; 284: © Kenneth Jarecke/Contact Press Images; 292: © John Green, 1990; 297 (left): Photo by Glenn Pike, Northeastern University; (right): J. D. Levine, Northeastern University; 299: © Steve Smith; 303: William Campbell/Time Magazine. Copyright Time, Inc.; 307: © Charles H. Porter/Sygma.

Chapter 12

317: Dennis Meyer/Norfolk Daily News-AP/ Wide World Photos; 319: © Claus Gugleberger/ Black Star; 323: © Ralf-Finn Hestoft/Saba; 331: Photo by Jody Miller, courtesy of Richard Wright; 332: © Bise/Gamma Liaison Network.

Chapter 13

336: © Kirk Condyles/Impact Visuals; 338: © Alex Quesada/Matrix; 341: © Sygma; 349: Washington Post photo by Robert A. Reeder. © 1996 by The Washington Post. Reprinted by permission; 350: Library of Congress; 359: © Paul S. Howell/Gamma Liaison Network.

Chapter 14

375: © Todd Yates/Black Star; 376: © Blake Little/Sygma; 382: © Chris Gierlich/Saba Press Photos; 393: © William Campbell/Sygma; 401: © Lawrence Migdale; 409: © Andrew Lichtenstein/Impact Visuals.